Twentieth-Century
Literary Criticism

Guide to Gale Literary Criticism Series

For criticism on	Consult these Gale series
Authors now living or who died after December 31, 1999	*CONTEMPORARY LITERARY CRITICISM (CLC)*
Authors who died between 1900 and 1999	*TWENTIETH-CENTURY LITERARY CRITICISM (TCLC)*
Authors who died between 1800 and 1899	*NINETEENTH-CENTURY LITERATURE CRITICISM (NCLC)*
Authors who died between 1400 and 1799	*LITERATURE CRITICISM FROM 1400 TO 1800 (LC)* *SHAKESPEAREAN CRITICISM (SC)*
Authors who died before 1400	*CLASSICAL AND MEDIEVAL LITERATURE CRITICISM (CMLC)*
Authors of books for children and young adults	*CHILDREN'S LITERATURE REVIEW (CLR)*
Dramatists	*DRAMA CRITICISM (DC)*
Poets	*POETRY CRITICISM (PC)*
Short story writers	*SHORT STORY CRITICISM (SSC)*
Black writers of the past two hundred years	*BLACK LITERATURE CRITICISM (BLC)* *BLACK LITERATURE CRITICISM SUPPLEMENT (BLCS)*
Hispanic writers of the late nineteenth and twentieth centuries	*HISPANIC LITERATURE CRITICISM (HLC)* *HISPANIC LITERATURE CRITICISM SUPPLEMENT (HLCS)*
Native North American writers and orators of the eighteenth, nineteenth, and twentieth centuries	*NATIVE NORTH AMERICAN LITERATURE (NNAL)*
Major authors from the Renaissance to the present	*WORLD LITERATURE CRITICISM, 1500 TO THE PRESENT (WLC)* *WORLD LITERATURE CRITICISM SUPPLEMENT (WLCS)*

ISSN 0276-8178

Volume 105

Twentieth-Century Literary Criticism

**Criticism of the
Works of Novelists, Poets, Playwrights,
Short Story Writers, and Other Creative Writers
Who Lived between 1900 and 1999,
from the First Published Critical
Appraisals to Current Evaluations**

Linda Pavlovski
Editor

GALE GROUP

TM

*Detroit
New York
San Francisco
London
Boston
Woodbridge, CT*

STAFF

Lynn M. Spampinato, Janet Witalec, *Managing Editors, Literature Product*
Kathy D. Darrow, Ellen McGeagh, *Product Liaisons*
Linda Pavlovski, *Editor*
Mark W. Scott, *Publisher, Literature Product*

Jennifer Baise, *Editor*
Thomas Ligotti, *Associate Editor*
Scott Darga, *Assistant Editor*
Jenny Cromie, Mary Ruby, *Technical Training Specialists*
Deborah J. Morad, Joyce Nakamura, Kathleen Lopez Nolan, *Managing Editors*
Susan M. Trosky, *Director, Literature Content*

Maria L. Franklin, *Permissions Manager*
Sarah Tomasek, *Permissions Associate*

Victoria B. Cariappa, *Research Manager*
Tracie A. Richardson, *Project Coordinator*
Sarah Genik, Ron Morelli, Tamara C. Nott, *Research Associates*
Nicodemus Ford, *Research Assistant*

Dorothy Maki, *Manufacturing Manager*
Stacy L. Melson, *Buyer*

Mary Beth Trimper, *Manager, Composition and Electronic Prepress*
Gary Leach, *Composition Specialist*

Michael Logusz, *Graphic Artist*
Randy Bassett, *Imaging Supervisor*
Robert Duncan, Dan Newell, *Imaging Specialists*
Pamela A. Reed, *Imaging Coordinator*
Kelly A. Quin, *Editor, Image and Multimedia Content*

Library of Congress Catalog Card Number 76-46132
ISBN 0-7876-4565-6
ISSN 0276-8178
Printed in the United States of America

10 9 8 7 6 5 4 3 2 1

Contents

Preface vii

Acknowledgments xi

Preface

Since its inception more than fifteen years ago, *Twentieth-Century Literary Criticism* (*TCLC*) has been purchased and used by nearly 10,000 school, public, and college or university libraries. *TCLC* has covered more than 500 authors, representing 58 nationalities and over 25,000 titles. No other reference source has surveyed the critical response to twentieth-century authors and literature as thoroughly as *TCLC*. In the words of one reviewer, "there is nothing comparable available." *TCLC* "is a gold mine of information—dates, pseudonyms, biographical information, and criticism from books and periodicals—which many librarians would have difficulty assembling on their own."

Scope of the Series

TCLC is designed to serve as an introduction to authors who died between 1900 and 1999 and to the most significant interpretations of these author's works. Volumes published from 1978 through 1999 included authors who died between 1900 and 1960. The great poets, novelists, short story writers, playwrights, and philosophers of the period are frequently studied in high school and college literature courses. In organizing and reprinting the vast amount of critical material written on these authors, *TCLC* helps students develop valuable insight into literary history, promotes a better understanding of the texts, and sparks ideas for papers and assignments. Each entry in *TCLC* presents a comprehensive survey on an author's career or an individual work of literature and provides the user with a multiplicity of interpretations and assessments. Such variety allows students to pursue their own interests; furthermore, it fosters an awareness that literature is dynamic and responsive to many different opinions.

Every fourth volume of *TCLC* is devoted to literary topics. These topics widen the focus of the series from the individual authors to such broader subjects as literary movements, prominent themes in twentieth-century literature, literary reaction to political and historical events, significant eras in literary history, prominent literary anniversaries, and the literatures of cultures that are often overlooked by English-speaking readers.

TCLC is designed as a companion series to Gale's *Contemporary Literary Criticism,* (*CLC*) which reprints commentary on authors who died after 1999. Because of the different time periods under consideration, there is no duplication of material between *CLC* and *TCLC*.

Organization of the Book

A *TCLC* entry consists of the following elements:

■ The **Author Heading** cites the name under which the author most commonly wrote, followed by birth and death dates. Also located here are any name variations under which an author wrote, including transliterated forms for authors whose native languages use nonroman alphabets. If the author wrote consistently under a pseudonym, the pseudonym will be listed in the author heading and the author's actual name given in parenthesis on the first line of the biographical and critical information. Uncertain birth or death dates are indicated by question marks. Single-work entries are preceded by a heading that consists of the most common form of the title in English translation (if applicable) and the original date of composition.

■ A **Portrait of the Author** is included when available.

■ The **Introduction** contains background information that introduces the reader to the author, work, or topic that is the subject of the entry.

■ The list of **Principal Works** is ordered chronologically by date of first publication and lists the most important works by the author. The genre and publication date of each work is given. In the case of foreign authors whose works have been translated into English, the English-language version of the title follows in brackets. Unless otherwise indicated, dramas are dated by first performance, not first publication.

- Reprinted **Criticism** is arranged chronologically in each entry to provide a useful perspective on changes in critical evaluation over time. The critic's name and the date of composition or publication of the critical work are given at the beginning of each piece of criticism. Unsigned criticism is preceded by the title of the source in which it appeared. All titles by the author featured in the text are printed in boldface type. Footnotes are reprinted at the end of each essay or excerpt. In the case of excerpted criticism, only those footnotes that pertain to the excerpted texts are included.

- A complete **Bibliographical Citation** of the original essay or book precedes each piece of criticism.

- Critical essays are prefaced by brief **Annotations** explicating each piece.

- An annotated bibliography of **Further Reading** appears at the end of each entry and suggests resources for additional study. In some cases, significant essays for which the editors could not obtain reprint rights are included here. Boxed material following the further reading list provides references to other biographical and critical sources on the author in series published by Gale.

Indexes

A **Cumulative Author Index** lists all of the authors that appear in a wide variety of reference sources published by the Gale Group, including *TCLC*. A complete list of these sources is found facing the first page of the Author Index. The index also includes birth and death dates and cross references between pseudonyms and actual names.

A **Cumulative Nationality Index** lists all authors featured in *TCLC* by nationality, followed by the number of the *TCLC* volume in which their entry appears.

A **Cumulative Topic Index** lists the literary themes and topics treated in the series as well as in *Classical and Medieval Literature Criticism, Literature Criticism from 1400 to 1800, Nineteenth-Century Literature Criticism,* and the *Contemporary Literary Criticism* Yearbook, which was discontinued in 1998.

An alphabetical **Title Index** accompanies each volume of *TCLC*. Listings of titles by authors covered in the given volume are followed by the author's name and the corresponding page numbers where the titles are discussed. English translations of foreign titles and variations of titles are cross-referenced to the title under which a work was originally published. Titles of novels, dramas, nonfiction books, and poetry, short story, or essay collections are printed in italics, while individual poems, short stories, and essays are printed in roman type within quotation marks.

In response to numerous suggestions from librarians, Gale also produces an annual paperbound edition of the *TCLC* cumulative title index. This annual cumulation, which alphabetically lists all titles reviewed in the series, is available to all customers. Additional copies of this index are available upon request. Librarians and patrons will welcome this separate index; it saves shelf space, is easy to use, and is recyclable upon receipt of the next edition.

Citing *Twentieth-Century Literary Criticism*

When writing papers, students who quote directly from any volume in the Literary Criticism Series may use the following general format to footnote reprinted criticism. The first example pertains to material drawn from periodicals, the second to material reprinted from books.

George Orwell, "Reflections on Gandhi," *Partisan Review* 6 (Winter 1949): 85-92; reprinted in *Twentieth-Century Literary Criticism,* vol. 59, ed. Jennifer Gariepy (Detroit: The Gale Group, 1995), 40-3.

William H. Slavick, "Going to School to DuBose Heyward," *The Harlem Renaissance Re-examined,* ed. Victor A. Kramer (AMS, 1987), 65- 91; reprinted in *Twentieth-Century Literary Criticism,* vol. 59, ed. Jennifer Gariepy (Detroit: The Gale Group, 1995), 94-105.

Suggestions are Welcome

Readers who wish to suggest new features, topics, or authors to appear in future volumes, or who have other suggestions or comments are cordially invited to call, write, or fax the Managing Editor:

Managing Editor, Literary Criticism Series
The Gale Group
27500 Drake Road
Farmington Hills, MI 48331-3535
1-800-347-4253 (GALE)
Fax: 248-699-8054

Acknowledgments

The editors wish to thank the copyright holders of the excerpted criticism included in this volume and the permissions managers of many book and magazine publishing companies for assisting us in securing reproduction rights. We are also grateful to the staffs of the Detroit Public Library, the Library of Congress, the University of Detroit Mercy Library, Wayne State University Purdy/Kresge Library Complex, and the University of Michigan Libraries for making their resources available to us. Following is a list of the copyright holders who have granted us permission to reproduce material in this volume of *TCLC*. Every effort has been made to trace copyright, but if omissions have been made, please let us know.

COPYRIGHTED EXCERPTS IN *TCLC*, VOLUME 105 WERE REPRODUCED FROM THE FOLLOWING PERIODICALS:

American Philosophical Quarterly, v. 3, April, 1966. Reproduced by permission.—*The American Political Science Review,* v. 74, March, 1980. Copyright, 1980, by American Political Science Association. Reproduced by permission.—*The Anglo-Welsh Review,* v. 26, Spring, 1977 for "Dylan Thomas's Image of the 'Young Dog' in the Portrait" by Richard A. Davies./1986 for "La Recherche du Temps Gallois: Dylan Thomas's Development as a Prose Writer" by John Ackerman./ 1986 for a review of "The Collected Letters of Dylan Thomas" by James A. Davies. All reproduced by permission of the authors.—*Commentary,* v. 69, May, 1980 for "Isaiah Berlin's Enlightenment" by Sidney Hook. Copyright © 1980 by the American Jewish Committee. All rights reserved. Reproduced by permission of the publisher and the author./v. 107, February, 1999. Copyright © 1999 Commonweal Publishing Co., Inc. Reproduced by permission of Commonweal Foundation.—*Commonweal,* v. CXXXV, August 14, 1998. Copyright © 1998 Commonweal Publishing Co., Inc. Reproduced by permission of Commonweal Foundation.—*Dutch Quarterly Review,* v. 11, 1981. Reproduced by permission.—*Encounter,* v. XLIII, October, 1974 for "A Glamorous Salon" by Alan Ryan. © 1974 by the author. Reprinted by permission of The Peters Fraser and Dunlop Group Limited on behalf of Alan Ryan./v. LIII, October, 1979 for "Column" by Goronury Rees. © 1979 by the author. Reproduced by permission of David Higham Associates on behalf of the author./v. LVI, May, 1981 for "The Liberal Mind" by Anthony Quinton. © 1981 by the author. Reproduced by permission of the author.—*Essays in Criticism,* v. XVIII, July, 1968 for "Imitation and Invention: The Use of Borrowed Material in Dylan Thomas's Prose" by Walford Davies. Reproduced by permission of the Editors of *Essays in Criticism* and the author.—*Journal of Modern Literature,* v. 2, September, 1971. © Temple University 1971. Reproduced by permission.—*Mind,* v. XXXVIL, October, 1928; v. XXXIX, January, 1930; v. XXXIX, April, 1930; v. XLIV, July, 1935; n.s. v. 96, January, 1987. © Oxford University Press 1928, 1930, 1935, 1987. All reproduced by permission.—*The Nation,* for "A Dedicated Man" by Mark Van Doren. Reproduced by permission of the executors of the estate of Mark Van Doren.—*The New Republic,* v. 212, February 20, 1995; v. 217, December 1, 1997. © 1995, 1997 The New Republic, Inc. Both reproduced by permission of *The New Republic.*—*The New York Review of Books,* November 11, 1976; v. XXXVI, August 17, 1989; v. XLIV, December 18, 1997. Copyright © 1976, 1989, 1997 Nyrev, Inc. All reproduced with permission from *The New York Review of Books.*—*The New York Times,* April 20, 1979. Copyright © 1979 by The New York Times Company./February 14, 1954. Copyright © 1954, renewed 1982 by The New York Times Company. Both reproduced by permission./February 9, 1981 for "Friends and Heroes" by Peter Stansky. Copyright © 1981 by The New York Times Company. Reproduced by permission of the author./July 13, 1997 for "An Idea Whose Time Won't Come" by John Gray. Copyright © 1997 by The New York Times Company. Reproduced by permission of the author./November 8, 1997 for "An Appreciation; Memories of a Captivating Conversationalist" by Alan Ryan. Copyright © Alan Ryan 1997. Reprinted by permission of The Peters Fraser and Dunlop Group Limited on behalf of Alan Ryan.—*Partisan Review,* v. LIX, Spring, 1992 for "On Isaiah Berlin" by David Sidorsky. Copyright © 1992 by Partisan Review. Reproduced by permission of the author.—*Philosophy and Literature,* v. 21, October, 1997. © The Johns Hopkins University Press. Reproduced by permission.—*Political Studies,* v. XXVIII, December, 1980; v. XXXI, September, 1983; v. XXXVII, March, 1989; v. XLI, June, 1993. All reproduced by permission of Blackwell Publishers.—*Renascence,* v. XXV, Spring, 1973. © copyright, 1973, Marquette University Press. Reproduced by permission.—*The Review of Politics,* v. 60, Summer, 1998. Copyright, 1998, by the University of Notre Dame. Reproduced by permission.—*Slovene Studies: Journal of the Society for Slovene Studies,* v. 3, 1981; v. 4, 1982. Both reproduced by permission.—*Social Research,* v. 61, Fall, 1994 for "The Singular and the Plural: On the Distinctive Liberalism of Isaiah Berlin" by Steven Lukes. Copyright 1994 by New School for Social Research. Reproduced by permission of the publisher and the author.—*Social Theory and Practice,* v. 16, Fall, 1990 for "Response to Berlin and McBride" by Timothy M. Renick./v. 16, Fall, 1990 for "'Two Concepts of Liberty' Thirty Years Later: A Sartre-Inspired Critique" by William L. McBride. Both reproduced by permission of the publisher and the authors.—*The Southern Review,* v. 3, 1967 for "Dylan Thomas: The Position in Calamity" by Paul West. Reproduced by permission of the author.—*Studies in Short Fiction,* v.

VI, Winter, 1969; v. 23, Spring, 1986. Copyright 1969, 1986 by Newberry College. Both reproduced by permission.—*The Times Literary Supplement,* December 30, 1977. © The Times Supplements Limited 1977. Reproduced from The Times Literary Supplement by permission.

COPYRIGHTED EXCERPTS IN *TCLC*, VOLUME 105, WERE REPRODUCED FROM THE FOLLOWING BOOKS:

Arms, George. From *Toward a New American Literary History: Essays in Honor of Arlin Turner.* Edited by Louis J. Budd, Edwin H. Cady, and Carl H. Anderson. Duke University Press, 1980. Copyright © 1980 by Duke University Press. Reproduced by permission.—Korg, Jacob. From *Dylan Thomas.* Twayne Publishers, Inc., 1965. Copyright © 1965 by Twayne Publishers, Inc. All rights reserved. Reproduced by permission.—Kreft, Bratko. From a preface in *The Bailiff Yerney and His Rights,* translated from the Slovene by Sidonie Yeras and H. C. Sewell Grant. Ljubljana, 1968. Reproduced by permission.—Pratt, Annis. From *Dylan Thomas' Early Prose: A Study in Creative Mythology.* University of Pittsburgh Press, 1970. Copyright © 1970, University of Pittsburgh Press. All rights reserved. Reproduced by permission.

PHOTOGRAPHS APPEARING IN *TCLC*, VOLUME 105, WERE RECEIVED FROM THE FOLLOWING SOURCES:

Berlin, Sir Isaiah, photograph. Courtesy of The Library of Congress.—Thomas, Dylan, 1953 , photograph. AP/Wide World Photos. Reproduced by permission.

Isaiah Berlin
1909-1997

Russian-born English historian, political philosopher, essayist, educator, and translator

INTRODUCTION

Berlin is best known for a long, distinguished, and influential career as a historian of ideas and a political philosopher. He was the champion of a pluralistic liberalism based on skepticism regarding human perfectibility, final solutions to human problems, and the ameliorative powers of rationalism. Berlin's theories were also based upon the conviction that the human condition demands choices between often conflicting values of equal worthiness.

BIOGRAPHICAL INFORMATION

Born to a wealthy and distinguished Jewish family in Riga, Latvia, Berlin grew up in St. Petersburg, Russia, where he enjoyed a comfortable youth, with loving parents, and an intellectually stimulating environment until the Russian Revolution. In 1921, fearful for their safety, his family emigrated to England, where his father, a timber merchant, had previously managed to deposit their fortune. After attending St. Paul's School, Berlin enrolled in Oxford in 1931, and became a lecturer in philosophy in 1932. He was associated with the university until his death. Berlin spent the Second World War working for the British Foreign Service in Washington, D.C.; his dispatches to Downing Street impressed Winston Churchill with their intelligence and vivacity. After the war he was assigned to the British embassy in Moscow. During his time in the Soviet Union, Berlin met the dissident poets Anna Akhmatova and Boris Pasternak. Their determination to bear witness in their art to the inhumanity of totalitarianism despite censorship, terror, and desolation influenced his later pro-Cold War stance. Berlin became known as a writer in the 1950s with the publication of his study of Leo Tolstoy and the place of determinism in history *The Hedgehog and the Fox* (1953). In the mid 1970s, Henry Hardy, one of his graduate students, embarked upon a project of collecting all Berlin's disparately published essays and unpublished lectures; seven volumes resulted. In the 1960s Berlin taught at Harvard and Princeton and was appointed to a chair at the City University of New York. In 1965 he was invited to create a college at Oxford dedicated to the natural and social sciences. Through his friendship with McGeorge Bundy, then head of the Ford Foundation, and his prominence in the Jewish Community in London, Berlin secured funding for building the college; he also gathered

the faculty and supervised the design of the buildings. Berlin's sociability was legendary, and he was on familiar terms with many notable figures of the twentieth century and served as an advisor to such figures as Churchill, David Ben Gurion, John F. Kennedy, and Margaret Thatcher. Berlin's fame and prestige grew in his later years. He was knighted by Queen Elizabeth in 1957, became president of the British Academy in 1974, received numerous honorary degrees from prestigious universities, and was awarded the Jerusalem prize in 1979, the Erasmus Prize in 1983, and the Agnelli Prize for contributions to the ethical understanding of advanced societies in 1988. He died in 1997.

MAJOR WORKS

The body of Berlin's work, comprising a variety of essays and lectures on related themes, reflects the ongoing engagement of a public intellectual. In essays on Niccolò Machiavelli, Giambattista Vico, J. G. Herder, Joseph de le Maistre, Benjamin Disraeli, Karl Marx, Ivan Turgenyev,

Alexander Herzen, and Tolstoy, as well as on themes including liberty, the incommensurability of equally worthy values, the Enlightenment, romanticism, and fascism, Berlin explored the tensions between monism and pluralism, negative and positive freedom, individual liberty and social justice, historical determinism and free choice, and rationalism and anti-rationalism. Informed by impeccable scholarship, Berlin's essays are well-regarded for their relevance to current problems and for his ability to give readers the impression of immediate contact with the figures about whom he wrote.

CRITICAL RECEPTION

Berlin is regarded by many as a towering figure in twentieth-century thought. His writings on negative and positive liberty have served as the starting point for numerous discussions in scholarly and political journals. His metaphor of the fox for those with wide ranging interests who can see things from varying perspectives, and the hedgehog for those who know "one big thing" has become a common designator of literary and political types. Because of his radio lectures in England, he became known to a general as well as to an academic audience. The liberalism he espoused has been challenged by ideological opponents on the left and on the right.

PRINCIPAL WORKS

Karl Marx: His Life and Environment (biography) 1939
The Hedgehog and the Fox: An Essay on Tolstoy's View of History (essays) 1953
The Age of Enlightenment (philosophy) 1956
Historical Inevitability (lecture) 1957
Four Essays on Liberty (political theory) 1969
Fathers and Children (lecture) 1972
Vico and Herder: Two Studies in the History of Ideas (history) 1976
Concepts and Categories: Philosophical Essays (philosophy) 1978
Russian Thinkers (history) 1978
Against the Current: Essays in the History of Ideas (history) 1979
Personal Impressions (essays) 1980
The Crooked Timber of Humanity: Chapters in the History of Ideas (history) 1990
The Magus of the North: J. G. Hamann and the Origins of Modern Irrationalism (history) 1993
The Sense of Reality (history) 1997

CRITICISM

Times Literary Supplement (essay date 1939)

SOURCE: "In the Name of Marx: The Philosopher and the Fight," in *The Times Literary Supplement,* No. 1966, October 7, 1939, p. 570.

[*In the following excerpt a reviewer praises Berlin's study of Karl Marx.*]

Mr. Berlin has packed a great deal into this scholarly and admirably written little volume [*Karl Marx: His Life and Environment*]. It is a biographical sketch, a vividly condensed study of the background of ideas and personalities against which Marx's labours grew to maturity, a summary of the theory and the diverse implications of historical materialism and a review of Marx's historic achievement. In all these respects the book is a model of objective clarity. One could wish that Mr. Berlin had a taste for shorter sentences, but on the other hand it must be said that his elaborate and almost neo-Augustan precision of style is not without charm.

Whatever else he might be, Marx declared towards the end of his life, he was not a Marxist. The saying should be borne in mind as an aid to distinguishing between Marx's ideas and the things that have been said and done in his name. Though the essence of his philosophy is the claim that, unlike other philosophies, it is a means of changing the world and not merely of explaining it, though also it was Marx who in fact created the International and in so doing directed the practical course of Socialism on the Continent of Europe, it is as a thinker, needless to say, and not as a man of action that he carries the astonishing weight of his influence. He was never a popular leader or agitator, though there may have been something of the thwarted *Realpolitiker,* as others have suggested, in the man who denounced yet appeared to envy Lassalle's dealings with Bismarck. The library was Marx's real field of battle; the laws governing the history of society were the weapons he fashioned for the predetermined victory of the proletariat.

Life Of Poverty

Having wisely emphasized this view of his subject at the start, Mr. Berlin goes on to describe the man. Marx is not an attractive figure. Only the affectionate simplicity of his family life and the enduring trust of his friendship with Engels soften the portrait of an overbearing and aggressive theorist, harshly intolerant, at once insensitive and thin-skinned, uncompromising and jealous, contemptuous of personal authority even while he strove for undisputed intellectual leadership. Marx was approachable to others only on his own terms. Yet the most forbidding features of the man, as Mr. Berlin justly points out, were traced either by the force of circumstance or by the indomitable logic of his convictions. In Germany there was no place for him, and in exile he lived for much the greater part of the time in desolating poverty and squalor. Three of his children died during the years in Soho through conditions directly attributable to the extreme of poverty. Marx himself, at the very time he inaugurated the International, tried to find employment as a booking clerk in a railway office and was defeated by his tattered clothes even more than by his illegible handwriting. Pride took chilling and unlovely forms in him, as it might well have done in somebody much more sentimental than Marx. Yet there were still more powerful reasons for the air of virulent assertiveness, the brutality of thought he exhibited in public. This sprang from the heart of his analysis of society. He was helping to wage, he believed, the greatest battle in human history, in which the enemy's greatest source of strength consisted of the "liberal illusions" it had itself created. For humanitarian ideals, for any sort of appeal to natural rights or conscience, he had the profoundest contempt; these formed the smoke-screen behind which the capitalist order lay entrenched. The romanticism of phrase of democratic movements, like the emotional indulgences of pseudo-revolutionaries, had to be fought tooth and nail if the fight was to be prosecuted along the entire front. The ruthlessness of Marx's methods of controversy (as of Lenin's) has its explanation here.

A NEW SOLUTION

Mr. Berlin, it would seem, is not unsympathetic to the materialist standpoint, but is scrupulously fair in presentation. He is helpful in defining the extent of Marx's originality as a thinker. Marx was at times almost generous in acknowledging his indebtedness to others, but more often he exhibited an irritable vulnerability on the subject. Perhaps that was natural enough in the circumstances, since while others looked for the elements of novelty in Marx's synthesis he himself, as Mr. Berlin says, had sought only truth. Even before Feuerbach the materialist view of history is to be discovered in Holbach; the class war is implicit in Saint-Simon; Babeuf, and Blanqui after him, formulated the dictatorship of the proletariat; the labour theory of value derives from the classical economists, and so on. Marx's achievement was to modify and combine existing views to form a new hypothesis for a problem as yet unsolved, and with it a new solution.

The decisive years were the two years he spent in Paris, from 1843 to 1845. The intellectual ferment in which the famous cluster of political exiles, poets, painters, and radical politicians of those years had their being is very well described, and there are excellent brief sketches of Bakunin, Weitling, Proudhon (whose ideas are paraphrased with conspicuous lucidity) and others. The prolonged clash with Bakunin is handled a little perfunctorily, possibly for want of space; but later on the contrast with Lassalle, in whom Mr. Berlin rightly recognizes an early sower of the seed of romantic fascism among the industrial population of Germany, gives the author an opportunity, which he takes with both hands, to demonstrate Marx's roughhewn consistency of mind and purpose. At his most unattractive the man had the imposing self-confidence and something of the dense passion of a minor Hebrew prophet.

The comprehensiveness of his theory of history and society is, for Mr. Berlin, without parallel. "Even if all its specific conclusions were proved false, its importance in cre-

ating a wholly new attitude to social and historical questions, and so opening new avenues of human knowledge, would be unimpaired." He is, in this view, the true father of modern economic history and of modern sociology, whose doctrine of movement in dialectical opposites has become part of the permanent background of civilized thought. His largest miscalculation is also the measure of his historic significance. Marx set out "to refute the proposition that ideas govern the course of history." Perhaps nothing has so weakened the force of his materialistic thesis as the extent of its own influence on human affairs.

Times Literary Supplement (essay date 1953)

SOURCE: "Fox and Hedgehog," in *The Times Literary Supplement,* No. 2703, November 20, 1953, p. 743.

[*In the following essay, the reviewer contemplates Berlin's distinction between "foxes" and "hedgehogs."*]

There are artists, historians and philosophers whose processes of thinking, feeling and creating seem to range far and wide over the infinite variety and multiplicity of experience without seeking to find a single focal point round which to organize their creation, a single all-illuminating vision. There are artists, historians and philosophers for whom this single point, this single vision, dominates and permeates everything they think and feel and create, prophets dedicated to one coherent view of life, to one consistent aim or purpose. This contrast between, so to speak, the centrifugal and centripetal types of human thinking is picturesquely portrayed by Mr. Isaiah Berlin in the symbolism of *The Fox and the Hedgehog*—the title which he has given to his revised version of a brilliant essay published in a recent number of the *Oxford Slavonic Papers.* The key to the enigma is a fragment from the Greek poet Archilochus: "The fox knows many things, the hedgehog one big thing." In this sense we are invited to regard Aristotle, Montaigne, Shakespeare, Goethe, Pushkin and Balzac as "foxes," and Plato, Pascal, Hegel, Dostoevsky, Nietzsche (and, no doubt, Marx) as "hedgehogs."

The distinction, if not pressed far enough to become, as Mr. Berlin says, artificial and scholastic, is amusing and instructive. The theme of Mr. Berlin's essay is its application to the hard case of Tolstoy, who seems pre-eminently to combine the qualities of both fox and hedgehog. No great writer, no great artist, has ever been more sensitive than Tolstoy to the immense, the bewildering, diversity of the world of phenomena, more eager to embrace and reflect life in all its innumerable facets, more determined to see human beings as human beings, and not as pawns in some transcendental game of chess played by an all-wise and all-powerful Providence, law of evolution or dialectic. Yet nobody has striven more passionately—one might say, more desperately—than Tolstoy to discover the fundamental core of reality at the heart of epiphenomenal diversity, the single, ultimate, all-reconciling truth to which the data of a conflicting and tormenting experience can be triumphantly reduced. It is a commonplace to see Tolstoy the artist at odds with Tolstoy the philosopher, to lament that at the end he sacrificed his art to the pursuit of a truth that always eluded and frustrated him. But the separation is artificial. It is Tolstoy the philosopher who is also Tolstoy the supreme artist.

The crux of the problem is to be found in Tolstoy's philosophy of history, as revealed in pronouncements scattered through his novels, diaries and letters and in the would-be systematic (though sometimes strangely elusive) exposition of the epilogue to *War and Peace.* Mr. Berlin, in a searching and profound analysis, lays bare the latent contradiction—

> the unresolved conflict between Tolstoy's belief that the attributes of personal life alone were real and his doctrine that analysis of them is insufficient to explain the course of history (*i.e.,* the behaviour of societies).

It is the first belief which leads Tolstoy so magnificently to debunk the "historic forces," the "cunning of reason," the material or moral laws in which philosophers of history have discovered the mainspring of the course of events, as well as the "heroes" and great men in whom these supposed laws and forces found their embodiment. Nowhere is Tolstoy so eloquent and so cogent as when he is sweeping away the mystical mumbojumbo of those who seek to "explain" history, to reduce the infinite diversity of individuals to a tidy, manageable and universal pattern. Yet in this process he is constantly contradicted and frustrated by his other conviction, not less profound and scarcely less explicit, of the need to explain—by his refusal to tolerate the notion of history as an accidental, frivolous and meaningless conglomeration of individual actions; and it is this eternal and eternally unreconciled contradiction which drives him into the picture of a real life lived by ordinary, simple, unreflecting people as the ultimate stuff of history. No reader of Tolstoy's wonderful prose remains unmoved by the evocation of the guiding principle of simple truth and mature wisdom as exemplified in Karataev and Pierre, in General Kutuzov, in Natasha and Nicolas. Yet few who pause to reflect can avoid the conclusion that, considered as an explanation of history, this is just another piece of mumbojumbo like all the rest—the only form of historical mystification which Tolstoy the sceptic and Tolstoy the nihilist did not debunk. Here, and here alone, what Mr. Berlin calls "the hard cutting edge" of Tolstoy's common sense failed to cut.

But is the dilemma peculiar to Tolstoy? And can one escape from it by becoming, or by being born, a fox, that is to say, by being content to reflect and portray the manifold diversity of life without striving to relate it to any central or unifying vision or principle? Is not this to forswear the function of the artist, the historian, the philosopher, to commit a new *trahison des clercs*? But there is, perhaps, another classification which lies beneath Mr. Berlin's division of thinkers and artists into foxes and hedgehogs, and to some extent cuts across it. Perhaps we may find this

other line of demarcation between those who, whether serenely and confidently or after turmoil and torment of soul, achieve to their own satisfaction this synthesis between the individual and the universal, the multiplicity and the unity, the world of phenomena and the inner vision, and those who fail to achieve it. Into the first category we must surely bring not only Montaigne, Goethe and Pushkin, who are Mr. Berlin's foxes, but Plato, Dante and Hegel, who are his hedgehogs, while the second would have to include the Shakespeare of the great tragedies and Pascal as well as Tolstoy. But this is an issue not merely of personal temperament and caprice, but surely also of time and place. Do not both Tolstoy and Dostoevsky, opposites in almost every respect, reflect the discordant realities of late nineteenth-century Russia? And does not the opposition between them consist primarily in the fact that Dostoevsky came to believe that he had, so to speak, up his sleeve a *deus ex machina* who would ultimately resolve the discords and contradictions, whereas Tolstoy, the supreme critic and sceptic, did not? But both were great artists and thinkers precisely because they refused to be "foxes," and staked their lives and their art on the quest for a guiding principle of unity in the diversity of storm and stress in which their fate had been cast.

Times Literary Supplement (essay date 1954)

SOURCE: "History and Morals," in *The Times Literary Supplement,* No. 2759, December 17, 1954, p. 821.

[*In the following essay, the reviewer discusses Berlin's ideas regarding historical determinism and human responsibility in* Historical Inevitability.]

For the past 200 years or more, historians and philosophers of history have been busily engaged in an attempt to organize the past experience of mankind, to marshal the facts of history into an orderly sequence of cause and effect, and to enlarge our understanding of the past, in the spoken or unspoken belief that such understanding would contribute to the more effective management of the present and the future. Vico and Condorcet, Kant and Hegel, Marx and Comte, Buckle and the addicts of geopolitics, the political adapters of Darwinism and the racial theorists, have all paid their tribute to this belief. Some were idealists, others materialists; some, according to later canons of judgment, were reputable, others less reputable; some were holists, others presented only fragmentary pictures of past experience. But, one and all, they took it for granted that history was a meaningful process, and that its meaning could be elucidated by those who studied it with care and insight. On the evidence of these two centuries Mr. Isaiah Berlin seems right in saying, in his last year's Comte Memorial Lecture, which has just been published under the title *Historical Inevitability,* that "one of the deepest of human desires is to find a unitary pattern in which the whole of experience, past, present, and future, actual, possible and unfulfilled, is symmetrically ordered."

The general view of history thus described seems to rest on three essential postulates. In the first place, the events of the past are related to one another as cause and effect, and it is the business of the historian to unravel and establish that relation. The annalist is content to say that one thing followed another; what distinguishes the historian is the proposition that one thing led to another. Secondly, while historical events were of course set in motion by the individual wills, whether of "great men" or of ordinary people, the historian must go behind the individual wills and inquire into the reasons which made the individuals will and act as they did, and study the "factors" or "forces" which explain individual behaviour. Thirdly, while history never repeats itself, it presents certain regularities, and permits of certain generalizations, which can serve as a useful guide to future action.

In the cold, wintry light of the middle years of the twentieth century, faith in the capacities of human reason and in the potentialities of human behaviour has been dimmed; and a view of history whose colouring was so self-confident and so optimistic could scarcely survive the eclipse. More than one contemporary writer has convicted it of overweening presumption; and Mr. Berlin's lecture, though originally delivered in honour of one of its leading champions, is in fact a frontal attack on it. Mr. Berlin has no difficulty in showing that the methods of history are not those of science, and that attempts to reduce history to a scientifically regular pattern of world order have gone very wide of the mark. But his main targets of attack are two: the "historicists," who hold that the function of the historian is simply to explain, that everything in history can be reduced to the action of "vast impersonal forces," that "to know all is to forgive all," and that there can therefore be no place in history for moral judgments; and the "moralists," who maintain that since we are all involved in the "human predicament," and are limited by our own particular conditions of time and space, we lack the right or quality to pronounce judgment on the shortcomings of others differently situated. These, for Mr. Berlin, are "the great *alibis* pleaded by those who cannot and do not face the facts of human responsibility."

Mr. Berlin does not—it need hardly be said—reject causation, or wish to go back to the kind of history which was primarily concerned to tell us that King John was a bad King. But is it really so difficult to reconcile the principle of causation in history with the principle of moral responsibility? Most people would be perfectly ready to attribute, say, a sudden increase in crime to such impersonal factors as bad housing or the incidence of a great war (and this is the kind of cause which historians normally seek to establish), without ceasing at the same time to hold the individual criminal to account. In everyday life different people react to the same occurrence not merely in different ways but, so to speak, on different planes, according to their different personal or professional standpoints and preoccupations. More can be said than Mr. Berlin seems to allow for the proposition that, whereas moral judgments on human actions are rightly and properly pronounced by the theologian or the moral philosopher, by the statesman or the common man, the specific function of the historian, *qua* historian, is not to judge but to explain. These are, however, fundamental problems; and they have received fresh illumination from Mr. Berlin's sparkling and trenchant criticism.

William Barrett (essay date 1954)

SOURCE: "Sharp Eyes for the Multiple Things," in *The New York Times*, February 14, 1954, p. 4.

[*In the following review of* The Hedgehog and the Fox, *Barrett praises Berlin's interpretation of the digressions on history which punctuate Tolstoy's* War and Peace.]

Most of us, I imagine, reading *War and Peace* tend to skim over the long disquisitions on history as rather tedious breaks in a marvelously exciting story, and nearly all critics hitherto have given official sanction to this habit by attempting to prove that these historical essays are an unnecessary blemish upon a great work of art. However, Isaiah Berlin—lecturer in philosophy at Oxford and famous as a scholar, diplomatist and conversationalist in at least two continents—has chosen to subject these historical passages to careful attention. In this brilliant essay [*The Hedgehog and the Fox*] he not only succeeds in making very good sense out of Tolstoy's historical theory but also finds in it an indispensable key to the complex and divided personality of the great Russian novelist.

The fox, said the old Greek poet, knows many things, but the hedgehog only one big thing. On this ancient bit of wisdom Mr. Berlin bases his distinction between two fundamental human types: those who have sharp eyes, like the fox, for the multiple things of the world, and those, like the hedgehog, whose defense consists of a single centripetal impulse—that is, who seek an inner unified vision. Tolstoy, in Mr. Berlin's view, was a fox who all his life sought, unsuccessfully, to be a hedgehog.

The glory of Tolstoy's novels lies precisely in their almost superhuman sensitivity to the multiplicity of things, their ability to record the individual feel and tone of persons, places and situations in their concrete objectivity; but the other half of Tolstoy, particularly during his latter years, is the agonizing search for an inner unifying vision with which his foxlike appetite for multiplicity can lie down in peace. The theory of history in *War and Peace* comes out of this deep cleft in the man himself.

The theory maintains, very simply, that the human understanding can never comprehend history, since the historic process involves an infinity of causes that lie beyond our grasp. Mr. Berlin seems to me to be altogether right in rescuing his theory from the charge of "mysticism." It is, rather, an entirely lucid and intellectually cogent theory, and a deterministic one to boot, though rather discomforting to the facile determinism of some historians. The individual, from the point of view of history, is never free, since he is caught in a web of infinite circumstances and causes.

On the other hand, *War and Peace* as a novel swarms with an extraordinary number of vivid personal lives each of which throbs with its own sense of decision and choice. This conflict between the feeling of freedom and the rational truth of determinism Tolstoy never succeeded in resolving for himself during his whole life.

Dissatisfied with the patness and artificiality of the historians' theories, Tolstoy was led in turn to distrust all theory as the falsification of the fullness of life itself. Hence, the great heroes that emerge in the novel are Kutuzov, the aged general who as the embodiment of the Russian earth triumphs over the intellectual cleverness of foreign generals, and the peasant Karataev who has a much deeper human wisdom than the Petersburg intellectual Pierre. Indeed, *War and Peace* is one of the most formidable attacks upon rationalism ever penned.

Some of Mr. Berlin's best pages occur toward the end, where he seeks to establish a connection between Tolstoy and the French Catholic thinker, Joseph de Maistre. On the surface no two people might seem more apart than the apostle of the Russian earth and the French clerical reactionary. But Tolstoy had studied Maistre carefully. Both had the same foxlike sharpness of reason to tear apart all modern forms of rationalism. Both believed that in the end man's reason was doomed to self-destruction once cut off from the earth and his past, *la terre et les morts.*

Not only does Mr. Berlin command all the materials of erudition, literary and philosophical, for his task, but he has a deep and subtle feeling for the puzzle of Tolstoy's personality, and he writes throughout, and particularly toward the last pages, with a wonderful eloquence. This essay, I am sure, will take its place amid the permanent literature about Tolstoy.

Alan Ryan (essay date 1974)

SOURCE: "A Glamorous Salon," in *Encounter*, Vol. XLIII, No. 4, October, 1974, pp. 67-72.

[In the following essay, Ryan describes the style and the substance of Berlin's work in the history of ideas.]

At the very first lecture I ever attended as an undergraduate a clever voice behind me remarked, "Lectures have been obsolete since Gutenberg; it's typical that Oxford hasn't noticed yet." Since I, if pressed, would have guessed that Gutenberg was somewhere in Sweden, I was relieved to discover that the clever voice had borrowed the joke from a previous night's speaker at the Union—John Wain, I think. I discovered almost as quickly that the Gutenberg revolution had reached Oxford. Lectures were sparsely at-

tended, and libraries were over-crowded, for undergraduates had found out that the printed word stuck in the mind more readily than did the spoken word.

None the less, some lecturers could attract large audiences; a few could hold them. A. J. P. Taylor modestly justified his habit of lecturing at nine in the morning by the need to comply with the fire regulations and avoid overcrowding his hearers. But the biggest draw at the box-office were the lectures in which Isaiah Berlin annually conducted a horde of the curious on the Grand Tour from Athens to Greenwich Village—the history of ideas from *The Republic* to *Partisan Review.*

It is, perhaps, misleading to call it a Grand Tour, for that suggests places rather than people, and the most striking thing about these lectures was the extent to which they were about distinct and individual people. Maurice Bowra remarked in his *Memories* on the way Isaiah Berlin in the '30s introduced Oxford to a galaxy of (dead and illustrious) foreigners, all but threatening to fill your living-room with the quarrelling Belinsky and Gogol, with Vico explaining the nature of anachronism to an admiring Herder and Michelet, or with an enraged Marx, denouncing the incurable romanticism and idealism of "that donkey Moses Hess." All the histrionic skills of Berlin as a lecturer were directed to the one end of bringing to life the immortal dead, in order that they and his audience could converse with each other. To the undergraduate coming across all this for the first time, it was like being allowed to sit in on a particularly glamorous *salon,* with no responsibility for its success or failure and therefore no pressure on oneself. It was, of course, enormously enjoyable—just as laughing at really good jokes somehow makes one feel terribly witty, so listening in on this sort of conversation made one feel very much cleverer than usual.

Berlin's lecturing manner was not exactly inimitable; the feeblest undergraduate parody was instantly recognisable. But by the same token it was extremely distinctive. In spite of the enormous speed of the delivery, it was the dramatic pause that worked the greatest charm. Beginning a lecture on Machiavelli with the observation that Machiavelli wrote lucidly and plainly, he would continue: "None the less [long pause] there are no fewer than [long pause] twenty [longer pause] five distinct interpretations of what his views really were" (this last at a great speed). It gave a splendid impression of Berlin rushing upon Machiavelli, then drawing back amazed as he began to count the staggering number of diverse accounts of his ideas. His description of the philosophies of Hegel and Schelling as "dark swamps, into which many men ventured and from which few ever returned" was, in the same way, delivered with such deliberation as to make it entirely credible that "few go there now: *vestigia terrent.*"

The problems of cooling this down for the printed page are obvious enough—and even ***Karl Marx*** still reads in places like the peroration of a lecture after three drastically revised editions. Reviewing ***Four Essays on Liberty,***

Anthony Kenny rightly complained that once they are deprived of the help given by inflexion and emphasis, sentences of 90 words (there is one of 110 in *Fathers and Children*) fall to pieces in the mind. The trouble is, of course, that the style is in many ways part of the argument, and a less evocative manner would betray the case which Berlin wants to make.

I've said that the point of the lecturing manner was to bring intellectual personalities to life. This is dictated as a proper goal of the history of ideas by two of Berlin's guiding beliefs. The first is what he calls the "liberal" inclination to see "tendencies, and political attitudes as functions of human beings" as opposed to the "radical" inclination to see "human beings as functions of social tendencies."[1] This is a major theme of *Historical Inevitability*; and it is one of the grounds of Berlin's dislike of Marx. Whatever virtues Marx possessed—and on the whole Berlin is not grudging about them—there is something repulsive in his attempt to reduce the moral and intellectual passions of individual men to the determined products of class conflict. The second belief is a slightly anxious allegiance to Belinsky. On Berlin's reading, the greatest impact of Belinsky on his liberal and radical friends was to alienate them permanently from any such ideal as "art for art's sake" or "ideas for ideas' sake." The question which Belinsky asked of any work of literature, philosophy or political theory was "what kind of man could think that?", or "what kind of man would I become by thinking like that?"

In *Fathers and Children,* Berlin describes Turgenev's reactions to those (both to Left and Right) who assailed him over his portrait of Bazarov in *Fathers and Sons*. The radicals were outraged because they saw Bazarov as a half-educated, nihilist buffoon, and thought Turgenev was, through him, ridiculing radicalism generally. The conservatives were outraged because Turgenev seemed quite genuinely to sympathise with this hideous creation of his. Turgenev did not reply that both criticisms were a lot of nonsense, that Bazarov was a character in a novel and ought to be judged on pure aesthetic criteria. He spent a great deal of unprofitable effort trying to persuade all sides of the goodness of his motives in drawing Bazarov as he did. For Berlin, too, criticism is in this sense a personal matter. A theory takes its life from the lives of its defenders. Of course, one mustn't exaggerate; ideas have a life of their own, too, and without such a life we could hardly use the ideas to construct a picture of their possessors. None the less, their importance lies in what it is like to believe in them.

This ties in with another of Berlin's standing obsessions—not exactly one which is peculiar to himself, since on his own account it has been the central problem of historiography since Vico. This is the question of how the *Geisteswissenschaften* differ from the *Naturwissenschaften*. The dust over "Historical Inevitability" hasn't settled more than twenty years later, but the central issue of that essay emerges as the issue of the extent to which we can, or

should, or must, see history from the participants' viewpoint. Roughly, Berlin's case is that in explaining other people's behaviour we have to employ the categories we employ in making up our own minds what to do. *We* work out what it would be *reasonable* to do, what it would be *best* to do; we assess courses of action and try to pick the best. In doing this, we assume that we are swayed by reasons, not moved by causes of which we have no knowledge. We have, therefore, to make the same assumptions in explaining what other men are up to.

The essay wavers between suggesting that the determinism of scientific history is false and suggesting only that determinism, true or false, is inconsistent with our ordinary ways of speaking about human action. Clearly, the second is the more plausible position, though it is also the weaker position in leaving it wide open whether advances in the human sciences will eventually force us to think of ourselves in very—perhaps as yet unimaginably—different ways.

Berlin sometimes suggests that what is wrong with inevitabilist views of history is that they blunt their adherents' moral sensibilities. He sides with Moses Hess in fearing men who are

> disposed to deceive themselves or others by systematically representing what would normally be recognised as acts of cruelty, exploitation, injustice and oppression as being mysteriously transformed into virtuous actions, or at least means to virtue, by the sanctifying process of historical necessity—the inexorable march of "God in history"—the historical dialectic.

From the point of view of the history of ideas, Berlin's own approach has a very different kind of drawback—not political, but visual. This is that the man of the moment, through whose eyes the world is presently viewed, becomes immensely vivid and his contemporaries correspondingly pale. This in turn can make the hero of one account look mysteriously less attractive in a different context. Thus, in *A Marvellous Decade,* and in his introduction to *From the Other Shore,* Berlin seems to present Herzen as unequivocally the most rational, self-aware and self-possessed of all his liberal contemporaries. He was, of course, quite at odds with the world in which he found himself, both in and out of Russia; but he never sought an escape in utopia. He loathed the complacent stupidity of bourgeois France and England, and he sympathised very deeply with the suffering of the serfs of his native country, whom he wished to see emancipated but not transformed into the proletarians of the West. None the less, in looking for a Russian road to socialism, he did not blink the fact that the rural masses were brutal, superstitious and often deeply reactionary. But in *Fathers and Children,* when it is Turgenev's doubts and hesitations that occupy the stage, Herzen appears as he appeared to Turgenev, something of a simple-minded populist, whose need to believe in the imminence of revolution in Russia blinded him to the frailty of its human instruments. There is, doubtless, no real contradiction here—Herzen *did* sometimes put more trust in the Russian masses than mature reflection warranted—but there is a certain awkwardness about the shifting perspective.

Although this approach to the history of ideas is so personal, part of Berlin's impact at least must be explained in terms of the large and striking antitheses which he has made famous. The best known "teams" of thinkers are probably the "Hedgehogs" and the "Foxes." But the positive and negative libertarians come close behind; and they turn out on inspection to be alliances of Monists versus Pluralists and Transcendentalists versus empiricists. As an analytical tactic, this division of thinkers into exponents of one half of an antithesis can be criticised—no thinker fits his category exactly, and on Berlin's view of the complexity of truth, he shouldn't do so either. It might also be said that categories as large as this are likely to be short of explanatory power. An early reviewer of *The Hedgehog and the Fox* doubted whether the boxes would hold their contents; more recently, Anthony Arblaster shrewdly, if unkindly, pointed out that the need to produce teams of opponents under each category brought Berlin himself perilously close to the role he deplores—that of the *terrible simplificateur,* ironing out the diversities, denying the importance of the individual awkward case.[2]

Often however the antithesis functions only to start an argument. In *The Hedgehog and the Fox,* the implausibility of the initial line-up is forgotten in the argument that the key to Tolstoy's greatness and to his failures lies in his attempt to subject his perception of the variety and diversity of history to a monistic theory of the direction in which it was moving and the forces which were impelling it—or, as Berlin says elsewhere, that his "whole life bears witness to the proposition to the denial of which his last years were dedicated: that the truth is seldom wholly simple or clear."[3]

The antithesis which has aroused the most serious argument is the distinction between positive and negative conceptions of liberty, to which Berlin's inaugural lecture was devoted. Many critics have accused Berlin of neglecting the way that poverty and ignorance can hinder a person's search for happiness just as effectively as tyranny or legal oppression. Others have argued that Berlin's distinction between *liberty* and *the conditions of liberty,* which meets this first objection, is just a liberal evasion, since poverty, at any rate in a class society, is not a merely natural consequence of nature's stinginess and man's feebleness, but a form of oppression in itself. The propertyless are, in Professor Macpherson's *Marxisant* phrase, the victims of the "extractive power" of the propertied, and an adequate conception of negative liberty would include freedom from that extractive power.[4] An even readier criticism is that it is impossibly hard to attribute a clearly positive or clearly negative conception of liberty to any actual thinker we care to name, for even Hegel, who certainly has *a* positive conception of liberty whereby I am free only when my rational, social self is in command, also stresses the importance of negative freedom—that is, of having a secure area

in which no one has the power to compel me to do or not to do anything in particular.

There has been one sustained attempt to show that the whole dichotomy collapses, made by Professor Gerald McCallum, who has argued that there is only one concept of liberty—that of an agent being free from some sort of restraint to do some sort of action—and that liberty is always this triadic relationship between agents, restraints and actions.[5] In *Four Essays on Liberty,* Berlin denies this, and says that a man who gets out of jail is properly said to be free, whether or not we have in mind any action which he is free to do. This doesn't really meet the case. It is surely true that we call a man free when he gets out of jail, just because being in jail is a much larger than usual restraint on practically any action you care to think of.

The point is, in any case, not one on which Berlin needed to insist. If he wants to think in terms of antithetical conceptions, he can surely allow "liberty" to be the name of a triadic relationship, and insist that there are two concepts of human agents closely related to two concepts of what important kinds of action human beings should perform and two concepts of what obstacles there are to their performing them. And this might as well be called "two concepts of liberty." Indeed, if this weren't so, the great variety of topics which Berlin includes in **"Two Concepts of Liberty"** would have no reason to be there. The chief point which the essay makes is a point about the diversity of goods. The reason why negative liberty—leaving people alone so far as possible—is an important political goal is that there is no *summum bonum* in terms of which to justify interference. It is not a matter of whether it is linguistically proper to call a man "free" because he lives in a democracy or a fiercely nationalistic state; rather, it is a matter of insisting that democratic government, national self-determination and extensive civil rights are different and not always compatible goods.

It is their—often unwilling—perception of this that unites the disparate subjects of several lectures.[6] **"The Originality of Machiavelli"**, for instance, argues that what was so appalling about Machiavelli was not so much his willingness to espouse brutality in politics as the brutality of his insistence that there was *no* natural harmony, that private virtue was certainly virtue but inconsistent with political *virtù,* that saving one's soul was perfectly laudable, but that men couldn't expect to save both their souls and their cities. The point of his lecture on "Montesquieu" is to show how Montesquieu's relativism led him reluctantly to the liberal's acceptance of the diversity of ultimate goods, while Mill, of course, emerges very naturally as a thinker who tries to smuggle liberty, equality, self-determination and so on under the umbrella of utility, only to abandon the attempt in favour of a celebration of diversity.

This ethical pluralism explains two other allegiances—again explicable in a rough and ready fashion as two dichotomies—which are defended in **"Two Concepts of Liberty"**, and even more explicitly in **"A Marvellous Decade."**

The first is a commitment to the empirical rather than the transcendental self. Negative freedom is a strongly empiricist concept in looking only to the prohibitions addressed to people as they now are. Men's wants, ignorant as they might be, are their wants; their frustration causes misery, and this misery really is a loss and ought to be admitted as such. In the essay on Belinsky in **"A Marvellous Decade"** there is almost a sigh of relief from Berlin at the point where Belinsky abandons his attempt to see the miseries and horrors of the empirical Russia as mere dross on the surface of the "real" and therefore benign history of Russia. Belinsky became if anything more unhappy after this change of mood; but he could no longer fall into the bad faith of devaluing the sufferings of his contemporaries. And one of Berlin's rare moments of enthusiasm for Jeremy Bentham occurs when he quotes his view that all laws are evil—restricting a man's freedom is an evil, and even if it is an evil which is justified a million times over, it is still a case of doing evil that good may follow.

This emphasis on the empirical self is paralleled by an equal stress on the importance of the present as opposed to the future. It is an interesting feature of Berlin's liberalism that it owes very little to *English* liberalism. The reason, perhaps, is that English liberals were neither tempted nor appalled by the grandiose utopian and historicist schemes of European thinkers. Mill was to some extent an exception, in falling for Comte in a genteel and modest way and then revolting against him. Still, it is not to Mill but to Herzen that Berlin has always looked for the exemplary, present-centred, strongly this-worldly thinker. The great objection to positive libertarians lies in Herzen's famous question: "Do you really wish to condemn human beings alive today to the mere sad role of caryatids supporting a floor for others one day to dance upon?"

The current style in the history of ideas is not very like Berlin's. Quentin Skinner and John Dunn have argued for a much cooler, less present-centred approach, in which the extent of the *differences* between ourselves and our predecessors, and between our problems and their problems, is emphasised. They have backed this up, not just by some persuasive essays on the nature of historical explanation, but by some exemplary work on Hobbes and Locke. Both Skinner and Dunn insist on the extent to which the problems of Hobbes or Locke were not ours. Berlin, I think, would always insist that problems of a certain scope at least endure across time, and his technique suggests that contextual cross-purposes are not a danger to be taken too seriously. *Fathers and Children,* for instance, points out that a parallel between Bazarov and the *enragés* of the student left is not exact—he was a revolutionary utilitarian who looked to science for salvation, where they are romantics who are rebelling against the triumphs of science. None the less, the assumption that what appeals to us in Turgenev owes everything to the problems he shares with us is not just made, but insisted on repeatedly.

The justification for treating the past in this way is not easy to spell out briefly—or, indeed, at all. But three things may be at any rate gestured at. The first is that we live in an historical culture, in which most activities take place against a backdrop of historical models; to make use of that culture, some access to a usable past is essential. With many of our ideas, it is only by getting some feeling for what has been done with them that they become intelligible at all. In the second place, one might borrow an analogy from the visual arts; there are, of course, art historians who are concerned with the documentation surrounding a painting, or with the technique employed in it, and so on. But the spectator also needs help in order to look at the painting in the first place, to see what's in it. The exact relationship between what we now see and what a contemporary audience might have seen is problematic, but certainly we can be taught to see something without either falsifying or ignoring what a contemporary audience might have seen.

Lastly, it is wholly compatible with an appreciation of Berlin's talent for recreation to insist on the most stringent standards of historical accuracy. To doubt this is to insist too fiercely that *what* a man achieves is the internal accusative of his intentions, and that we can only say what he did when we can also say what he was doing. No doubt his intentions and their context have a certain priority. But the question of what is important in what he did and thought can be constantly re-opened, because we constantly want to start new conversations with the past. Reluctance to exploit the history of ideas in this way is carrying a decent professionalism to puritan extremes.

Notes

1. *Fathers and Children* (Clarendon Press: Oxford University Press, 1973), pp. 49-50.

2. Anthony Arblaster, "Vision and Revision", *Political Studies* (1971), pp. 81-6.

3. "Tolstoy and Enlightenment", Encounter, February 1961, p. 40.

4. C. B. Macpherson, "Berlin's Division of Liberty", Ch. V of *Democratic Theory* (Clarendon Press: Oxford University Press, 1973).

5. Gerald McCallum Jr., "Negative and Positive Freedom," *Philosophical Review,* 1967, pp. 312-24.

6. In spite of occasional rumours in publishers' catalogues, most of Berlin's lectures and essays remain uncollected in book form. The exceptions are the four essays in *Four Essays on Liberty* (Clarendon Press, Oxford, 1969): "Political Ideas in the Twentieth Century", "Historical Inevitability", "Two Concepts of Liberty" and "John Stuart Mill and the Ends of Life." Among essays from Encounter which ought to be more readily accessible are the four instalments of "A Marvellous Decade" (June, November, December 1955 and April 1956), "Russian Populism" (July 1960), "Tolstoy and Enlightenment" (February 1961) and "J. G. Herder" (July and August 1965). "The Philosophical Ideas of Giambattista Vico" appeared in the *Proceedings* of the London Italian Institute,

1959, "Montesquieu" appeared in the *Proceedings of the British Academy,* 1955, "The Originality of Machiavelli" appeared in *Studies on Machiavelli* (G. C. Sansoni, Rome, 1972), "The Life and Opinions of Moses Hess" was published by Cambridge University Press in 1959 (the Lucien Wolff Lecture, 1957), "Does Political Theory Still Exist?" appeared in P. Laslett and W. G. Runciman (eds), *Philosophy, Politics and Society* (second series, Blackwell, Oxford, 1964), "The Concept of Scientific History" appeared in W. H. Dray (ed.), *Philosophical Analysis and History* (Harper & Row, New York, 1966). This is, of course, a very partial list, but it includes (I think) almost everything which bears directly on the issues discussed here. But if we are not to have Berlin's collected essays for some time still, it would be a useful second best if someone would produce a bibliography instead!

Arnaldo Momigliano (essay date 1976)

SOURCE: "On the Pioneer Trail," in *New York Review of Books,* November 11, 1976, pp. 33-8.

[*In the following reflection on Berlin's* Vico and Herder, *Momigliano focuses on the problem of what relation pluralism bears to relativism inside cultural and historical contexts.*]

I

There is perhaps a slight element of prejudice in the opinion, widespread among us Piedmontese, that San Gennaro and Giambattista Vico must be left to the Neapolitans. This opinion is in deed prejudiced in so far as it does not take into account that both San Gennaro and Vico have proved embarrassing to educated Neapolitans, and more especially to the descendants of those lawyers who in the eighteenth century came down from the provinces to Naples to fill high positions in the administration and who embodied the Enlightenment.

Benedetto Croce and Fausto Nicolini, the scions of two such Abruzzese families (as Nicolini was fond of recollecting), are exactly a case in point. To be the historians of Naples, and more specifically the interpreters and editors of Vico, they had to come to terms both with the saint of the plebeians and with the plebeian philosopher who had understood the fancies of the "*bestioni*" so well. As for San Gennaro, it was simple enough. Croce expressed his sympathy for a popular Catholicism which in his judgment was more meaningful than the Catholicism of the theologians and did not claim the approval of the educated: see his essays in *Uomini e cose della Vecchia Italia* II (1927) and *Varietà di storia letteraria e civile* II (1949).

Vico was of course more difficult, as one can see from the extensive work on him that Croce and Nicolini produced during a period of some forty years. Vico stuck to Catholi-

cism, kept sacred and profane history separate, and not only contemplated recurrences of barbarism but described barbarian ages (and religious peoples) with suspicious relish. Furthermore, an important factor in his historical cycles was the antagonism between patricians and plebeians which monarchies were able to control only for limited periods—before and after barbarism: "For the plebeians, once they knew themselves to be of equal nature with the nobles, naturally will not submit to remaining their inferiors in civil rights; and they achieve equality either in free commonwealths or under monarchies" (*The New Science,* prg. 1087, translated by T. G. Bergin and M. H. Fisch). A very obliging fellow in his daily transactions, Vico was not equally accommodating when he took up the pen to write the *Scienza Nuova.*

Croce never denied the existence of mystery in human life and never closed his eyes to violence and barbarism. But he invariably refused to have mystery turned into religion and perhaps only toward the end of his life faced the recurrence of barbarism as a foreseeable possibility. In his Hegelian heyday when he wrote on Vico (1911) he believed in dialectical progress, in elites, and in civilized conversation with past ages from a well-chosen vantage point. Thus his answer to Vico was to deny the existence of historical cycles and of class struggle and to turn Vico's interpretation of myth and language into a chapter of the history of aesthetics. If only Vico had realized that fantasy and logic, economic calculation and morality follow each other in circles within any human mind at any given moment!

Of course if Vico had recognized all that, he would have written the three original volumes of Croce's *Filosofia dello Spirito* rather than the *Scienza Nuova.* But one of the most endearing traits of Croce was to believe that if only somebody else had taken the trouble of sorting out the four activities of the Spirit, Croce himself would have got on earlier with the real job, which was to read poetry and to write history.

In an acute paper at the American Vico Symposium of 1969 Hayden White was one of the first to see how embarrassing Vico had proved to Croce and to his faithful friend Nicolini. One must read the whole of the historical works of Croce and Nicolini to be aware of the extent to which they found Vico uncongenial, notwithstanding their devotion to him, a devotion inseparable from their attachment to the city in which they lived. But a summary, sensitive and well informed, of their attitude to Neapolitan society is provided in the recent book by Croce's daughter Elena, *La Patria Napoletana* (Milano, Mondadori, 1974). There Vico is kept in his place—almost unheard—at the other end of the social scale. Quite a different family symbolizes the Neapolitan motherland throughout 150 years. This is the family of Gaetano Filangieri, a younger son of the Duke of Arianello who at the end of the eighteenth century was admired by the whole of enlightened Europe as a legislator and administrator.

II

But now we shall perhaps have the chance of seeing whether—and how—Vico can survive without (so at least I presume) the direct support of San Gennaro. An Institute for Vico Studies has been created in New York. Its first international conference in January 1976 collected a galaxy of Vico scholars from various countries and was supported by the National Endowment for the Humanities, the American Council of Learned Societies, and the Rockefeller Foundation. This is the culmination of the new Anglo-Saxon interest in Vico which the reliable translation of the *Scienza Nuova* by Thomas Bergin and Max Fisch (1948) both made possible and encouraged. The recent book by Leon Pompa, a lecturer in the University of Edinburgh and a contributor to the New York conference, is another sign.

Isaiah Berlin has contributed more than anybody else to this new popularity of Vico since his long essay on him appeared in the volume *Arts and Ideas in Eighteenth Century Italy* in 1960. Berlin was a consulting editor of the notable symposium on Vico published in 1969 by Giorgio Tagliacozzo, the present director of the Institute for Vico Studies, and wrote one of the best papers in it. Berlin was also a participant in and contributor to the 1976 conference.

Yet I am reluctant to associate Berlin too closely with the present Vico vogue. A distinction is perhaps indicated by the title (***Vico and Herder***) of the volume in which Berlin has republished new versions of his Vico essay of 1960 and of a shorter, but very substantial, paper on Herder originally published in 1965. Vico and Herder together are something different from Vico alone. It is one thing to see in Vico the inventor of a new way of philosophizing "which has re-emerged only in our century" (as the blurb of the 1969 *Symposium* claims); it is another thing to take him as the first in that line of thinkers on human societies in which Herder was the next (without really knowing about his predecessor). As Berlin of course recognizes, their thoughts became commonplace in many nineteenth-century intellectual circles—perhaps less so in the twentieth century.

Vico and Herder were the pioneers in the study of human imagination and myth-making. They looked at societies, not at individuals. Vico took Homer not as an individual poet, but as the expression of heroic Greece in its myth-making mood: this is what he called the "discovery of the true Homer." Herder chose Biblical poetry as his test case. He interpreted it as the voice of the national soul of the Hebrews in their worship of God and in their struggles with very earthly foes. Both attributed to poetry, and more generally to language, an essential function in shaping the life of each ethnic group. Both appreciated spontaneity and growth in societies which clung to their ancestral environments. Both practiced a new type of historical research aimed at discovering those strata of human experience which are least controlled by reason and scholastic argument. Not surprisingly they found what they wanted either in very ancient civilizations or in rustic "unspoiled" modern surroundings. Thus they came to contribute powerfully to the study of heroic ages (a term dear to Vico) or to modern folk poetry (a term made fashionable by Herder).

By the nature of their approach to history both Vico and Herder were bound to emphasize development in societies. But in their actual description of it they sharply diverged. Vico proposed a scheme of *corsi* and *ricorsi* in which civilization and barbarism alternated: too much civilization, that is too much reason, inevitably produced a reaction, a return to uncontrolled imagination and passion, which are the substance of barbarism. Vico probably never made up his mind whether Christianity would prevent further returns of barbarism. The last pages of the *Scienza Nuova* in the 1744 version, which are dedicated to this subject, are among the most obscure and difficult of the book. They show how uncertain Vico must have been about the impact of Christianity on the course of profane history. Herder, who had more time and inclination to change his mind repeatedly, presented a variety of solutions unified by a preference for the organic scheme in which each civilization corresponds to a stage of individual human life from childhood to old age. But Herder too defended the right of each civilization to be itself—that is to live as it suited it best, with its own religion, language, art, and morality.

Berlin is profoundly sympathetic to this approach to past and present civilizations. He must have found in Vico and Herder a welcome alternative to that analytical philosophy—carefully eschewing any problem about poetry and myth, indeed about history in general—with which he grew up at Oxford. More specifically he must have found in Vico and Herder confirmation and support in his own lifelong fight for cultural pluralism and respect for minorities (including his own—should I say our own—the Jewish minority). In this sense this volume on Vico and Herder is clearly connected with his study of Moses Hess and with some parts of his ***Four Essays on Liberty.***

"Pluralism," wrote Berlin in one of those essays, "with the measure of 'negative' liberty that it entails, seems to me a truer and more humane ideal than the goals of those who seek in the great, disciplined, authoritarian structures the ideal of 'positive' self-mastery by classes or peoples or the whole of mankind." Berlin is especially attracted by Vico and seems to have formed a bond of admiration and personal understanding with the man from Naples who in poverty and solitude created a new science—the science of what is most spontaneous and traditional in human societies.

But to me what berlin has to say about the various aspects of the thought of Vico and Herder is not the most interesting part of his work. However skillful and eloquent the interpreter may be, there is not much chance of saying anything very new about such well-known thinkers. It seems to me ironic that, having perceived so clearly the weakness of previous research on the sources of Vico's thought (as exemplified by Professor Nicola Badaloni's learned studies), Berlin should indulge in speculations about the influence of French Renaissance jurists on Vico. Being a trained lawyer, Vico unquestionably knew—and often quoted—his Cujas, Hotman, Brisson, and Godefroy, but he never shared their efforts to understand specific laws by referring them to specific events and was altogether unable to follow them in their exacting textual exegesis. They tried to distinguish between Roman and German Law. He rejected their claims (without much understanding them) in the memorable prg. 1075 of the 1744 *Scienza Nuova*:

> For the erudite interpreters of Roman Law resolutely deny that these two barbarian types of ownership were recognized by Roman Law, being misled by the difference in names and failing to understand the identity of the institutions themselves.[1]

Vico was not interested in the differences between national laws, but in the transition from heroic wisdom to human jurisprudence and vice versa.

What seems to me the really interesting feature of this book is Berlin's awareness that Vico and Herder introduced into European thought ambiguities and ambivalences which, being rooted in reality, are easier to recognize than to discard. The problem emerging from each page is: How are we going to avoid moral relativism if we accept with Vico and Herder that societies are at their best when they succeed in expressing themselves most individually in language, customs, institutions, and religion? Berlin formulates his problem most explicitly in the essay on Herder, which can be said to hinge on it. There are, however, several explicit indications also in his essay on Vico, for instance:

> Right and wrong, property and justice, equality and liberty, the relations of master and servant, authority and punishment—these are evolving notions between each successive phase of which there will be a kind of family resemblance, as in a row of portraits of the ancestors of modern society, from which it is senseless to attempt, by subtracting all the differences, to discover a central nucleus—the original family as it were, and declare that this featureless entity is the eternal face of mankind. [p. 87]

Neither Vico nor Herder would have admitted to relativism. But if relativism was not intended, what right had the Greeks to be Greeks rather than reasonable men as the Enlightenment conceived reasonable men to be? Berlin very patiently analyzes the arguments of Vico and Herder to discover whether they presented a pluralistic image of human behavior without turning into moral relativists. He does that with sympathy and gentleness, but also with his typical ultimate firmness. If I understand him correctly, he has to admit defeat: there is no reconciliation in Vico and Herder between cultural pluralism and absolute values. What is worse, there is no hope—at least no immediate hope—of bargaining oneself out of the dilemma. If San Gennaro has to be left to the Neapolitans (and Confucius to the Chinese) human brotherhood must depend on some-

thing less (or more) than universal rules of behavior, universal faith, and universal knowledge—to which some people used to add even universal language, either mathematics or Esperanto.

I do not think (as Berlin seems to be inclined to admit) that we can save from relativism Vico's famous principle that man is able to understand his own history in a very different way from that of understanding the physical world, because he makes history, but merely observes nature. As soon as one grants that each society has its own methods of understanding and evaluating human affairs, no generally valid knowledge of history is admissible. Even without this logical difficulty I would hardly find Vico's evaluation of historical knowledge very convincing. We are all increasingly aware that man can control the physical world more easily than his own history. Faced by the claims of the unconscious, of biological determinism, and of economic materialism, historians are inclined nowadays to envy the physicists and chemists who can manipulate nature by experiment. It is by no means obvious (as Vico would like to have it) that my understanding of my own past is clearer or more direct than my understanding of the past of the solar system.

In any event, it seems to me that, if cultural pluralism is accepted, Berlin leaves us with an open question about the inevitability of moral relativism. He could hardly have done otherwise, unless he had turned his two essays into a theoretical disquisition on the way to reconcile national traditions with universal values.

III

There is, however, a difference between his essay on Vico and his essay on Herder which may at least help to indicate where a future discussion on the *truth* of Vico and Herder could start from the very premises laid down by Berlin. He presents his essay on Herder as an analysis of three rather precise notions which the German thinker introduced into European culture—the notions of Populism, Expressionism, and Pluralism. By populism Berlin means the cultural, rather than political, interpretation Herder gave to the fact of belonging to a specific nation: populism was different from, if not opposed to, nationalism. By expressionism Berlin means the emphasis on the self-expression of groups as such. And by pluralism he means the multiplicity and incommensurability of the values of different societies.

Now it is remarkable that Berlin does not put forward a similar set of notions for Vico. Though Vico produced theories about myth, language, poetry, symbols, and stages of human evolution which have received attention and approval in many quarters, he cannot be described as a philosopher who gave an ideology (as Herder did) to later generations. Herder had a direct influence on romanticism and nationalism which not even the most extravagant admirer of Vico could claim for him. A careful comparison of what E. Quinet owed to Herder with what J. Michelet really got out of his beloved Vico would, I believe, confirm the far greater contribution by Herder to the national consciousness of the nineteenth century.

This is perhaps hardly surprising. As I had opportunity to emphasize in previous papers on Vico (most recently in a review of Pompa's book in *The Times Literary Supplement,* September 5, 1975), Vico was not even fighting his immediate contemporaries. He was trying to re-establish against Spinoza the separation between sacred and profane history, and was of course defending against Descartes the legitimacy of historical as opposed to mathematical knowledge. He was also undermining Grotius's notion of natural law. If in dividing the spheres of the natural and of the supernatural, of the profane and of the sacred, he seemed to be passably oblivious of Redemption as such, we have to remember that he lived in a city where the miracles of the local saints were more effective witnesses to the truth of Revelation than the original act of Salvation.

Though Vico was susceptible to interpretation in a populist key, one cannot say that—at least in Italy, where his thought was really effective—he encouraged research in popular poetry or myths or national differences. Where Vico's influence is clearly visible he mostly provides a vague religious and providentialistic meaning to history—a somewhat edulcorated alternative to Catholicism—or, in more recent times, a painless introduction to Marxism. One of the few exceptions has recently been illustrated by Franco Venturi in *Rivista Storica Italiana* 87, 1975, 770-784. Under the influence of the first *Scienza Nuova* of 1725 Lorenzo Boturini Benaduci worked in Mexico between 1736 and 1743 to learn local languages and to study ancient monuments and traditions. His expulsion from Mexico prevented the completion of the great historical work he had been preparing, but he managed to publish a summary of the *Nueva historia general de la America Septentrional* in Madrid in 1746. No other direct or indirect disciple of Vico, as far as I know, imitated Boturini. Vico did not persuade his followers, as Herder did, to learn difficult languages and to explore remote civilizations.

On any interpretation (I think Berlin would agree) Vico's relativism was more homely and less radical than Herder's. Vico reflected on Homer, on Roman and feudal law, and on Dante. Like many of his contemporaries he was fascinated by the yet undeciphered Egyptian hieroglyphs, but was unable to read any Oriental text. He conscientiously kept away from the Bible. Being aware that Spinoza had treated it as a purely human document, he was determined not to repeat what he considered an error. He refused to extend his notion of myth to the Biblical stories.

In short, classical and Christian Western Europe was still Vico's world. It was no longer Herder's world. Herder had discovered the poetry of the Ancient East either in the original or in translation; he was enchanted by what he believed to be the authentic bardic poetry of Ossian, and he

felt deeply about his German ancestors. With Herder one is at times on the brink of racism, as R.G. Collingwood did not fail to remark in 1936 when he delivered his lectures on the *Idea of History.* Though Vico and Herder are separated by little more than a generation (Herder was born in 1744, the year Vico died), that generation had brought about a new learning and a new patriotism, As the new patriotism is well known, I want to focus attention on the new learning, which Berlin mentions only briefly.

Between Vico and Herder there was a revolution in historical research. Oriental languages were studied as never before, and the ancient sites of Persia and India began to be known. Religious and legal texts, the existence of which had hardly been realized, were made available in translation, and scholars began to explore in earnest the secular literatures of the same territories. Even in attitudes toward Greece there was a change: more knowledge of ancient sites and of modern dialects and customs. The Bible lost its isolation. The ancient poetry of the Hebrews was compared with the poetry of other ancient nations. Their prophets were set beside other religious masters such as Zoroaster. The comparison of Biblical with other Oriental institutions became frequent. Discovery and comparison gave new glamour to Arabia, Persia, and India, not to speak of China, while the claims of the Hebrews and early Christians to uniqueness began to be doubted. This was the revolution which either induced or confirmed in Herder the persuasion that God was saying different things to different peoples.

In 1753 Robert Lowth published the lectures on Hebrew poetry which he had delivered in Oxford in the previous ten years. They were the first analysis of Biblical poetry *qua* poetry:

> Why should we heap praise on Homer, Pindar and Horace and pass over in silence Moses, David and Isaiah? . . . In them we can contemplate poetry in its earliest stage, not so much excogitated by man as fallen from heaven.

A few years later, in 1758, the great Hebrew scholar of Gottingen, David Michaelis, in republishing Lowth's lectures with notes and additions, could reproach the English author for not having compared Hebrew with Arabic poetry and not having noticed that Moses in *Numbers* 21, 27 had inserted an Amorite (Michaelis says by mistake "a Moabite") poem and therefore disproved by implication the divine origin of Hebrew poetry.

In 1754 Abraham-Hyacinthe Anquetil-Duperron—with two handkerchiefs and two shirts as luggage—enrolled in a regiment of the Compagnie des Indes in order to learn to read the sacred books of India and Persia (or rather of the Parsees). It is equally characteristic of the period that he was turned into the recipient of a stipend from the king of France even before he boarded the ship which took him to India. The result was the first translation of the Zend-Avesta in 1771.

What E. Quinet in 1841 was going to call the "Renaissance Orientale" had started. Anquetil saw the implications. In the preface to his great work he outlined the design of a new Academy, a *"corps de Missionnaires Litteraries"* who were to work in Africa, Asia, and America, learning languages, exploring and collecting texts. After twelve years in the field the Academicians were to return to Paris to publish what they had collected and to enjoy fame. Sir William Jones, who had published his treatise on Oriental poetry in French the year before (1770), put into practice some of Anquetil's ideas in 1784, when he created the Bengal Asiatic Society. He mastered Sanskrit well enough to publish Kalidasa's *Sakuntala,* which took Goethe by storm.

Hardly less influential were the travels of Carsten Niebuhr in Arabia and Persia which resulted in the classic *Beschreibung von Arabien* (1772). Niebuhr provided a background to Mohammed and, by his new description of Persepolis (which had already been visited by Jean Chardin and others), to Zoroaster. Together, Niebuhr and Anquetil posed the question, which has not been solved to everybody's satisfaction even now, of the relation between Zoroaster and Achaemenid Persia.

The Oriental Renaissance was reinforced rather than contradicted by the contemporary fashion of looking for Greek landscape and monuments in Greece instead of admiring Roman copies in Italian museums. Winckelmann himself formulated the program of the new era of exploration in Greece, though he never saw either Sicily or the Aegean. The *Antiquities of Athens* by Stuart and Revett was published in 1762 under the patronage of the London Society of Dilettanti. Each traveler to Greece and the East (or for that matter to Celtic Scotland or to medieval Spain) was a refugee from the Paris Enlightenment.

Herder, though a not very adventurous and increasingly disenchanted traveler himself, can be said to have been present in spirit whenever a new archaeological or literary discovery was made. He liked drawings of ancient places and read in the original or in translation all that came on the market from Anquetil to Niebuhr, from Ossian to the *Cid,* which he imitated in a successful pastiche. Niebuhr stimulated him to an interpretation of the friezes of Persepolis based shakily on Persian literary tradition. I am not sure how much of Firdausi's *Book of Kings* Herder knew. In the *Persepolitanische Briefe* he addressed a dozen German professors to ask for approval of his interpretation and finally turned to Zoroaster himself. ("Appear, Goldstar, legislator of Persia, philosopher, wise and glorious Zoroaster, appear." He did not appear.) Niebuhr also inspired him to make a very suggestive comparison between the most famous of Jehuda Ha-Levi's *Songs of Sion,* which he translated, and some Arab poetry about the ruins of Persepolis.

The Sacred Books, becoming available suddenly from the East in all their exotic beauty, were a pointer in the direction of pluralism and relativism. If for Vico the basic alternative had been between barbarism and civilization (each with its own attractions), Herder was presented with a variety of equally attractive civilizations: it became difficult to find barbarians to escape to.

IV

At this point it is almost irrelevant to distinguish between the different intellectual climates in which Vico and Herder lived and their different personal attitudes. Herder was much more committed to the relativity of values because he knew too many of them and was, psychologically, less prepared to choose among them. He was much more susceptible to poetical emotions and therefore much more subjective than Vico. He liked out-of-the-way pieces of evidence, to the point of being carried away by a forgery like Macpherson's Ossian. Possibly he was also drawn to relativism by his virtual abandonment of any separation between sacred and profane history. This aspect of his personality would have to be discussed in much more detail. In some of his earlier papers Herder tended to treat the Bible, like Homer or Herodotus, as a purely human document. Later—even in his fine book on. Hebrew poetry (1782-1783)—he no longer excluded Revelation altogether from his interpretation. But it was a Revelation which could hardly serve as a criterion for a choice between religious or moral codes: it was a Revelation mixed with Spinozism and therefore manifested in all the actions of mankind.

Furthermore, Herder was almost entirely devoid of that interest in the development of private property and other institutions which gave some direction and order to Vico's speculations on history. Such interest constituted Vico's first line of defense against the sort of relativism which makes it impossible to choose either in the past or in the present (and therefore in the future). N. Badaloni in one of his most recent utterances on Vico, which happens to discuss Berlin's essay in its first version, contended that according to the *Scienza Nuova* man can know his own history only when he is capable of rationality and operates according to a just social order.

Badaloni implies that there are for Vico both social and intellectual conditions for true historical knowledge, but when these conditions are satisfied, knowledge is absolute. In Badaloni's formulation (Introduction to Vico, *Opere filosofiche,* Sansoni, Florence 1971, p. XXIX) there is obviously too much of his own Marxism: Vico was thinking of a human history guided by Divine Providence. But it is correct that even in autobiographical terms Vico felt that only at a particular time and within a particular society had it been possible for him to discover the New Science. Providence linked true historical knowledge to certain conditions:

> By this work, to the glory of the Catholic religion, the principles of all gentile wisdom human and divine have been discovered in this our age and in the bosom of the true Church, and Vico has thereby procured for our Italy the advantage of not envying Protestant Holland,

England or Germany their three princes of this science. [*The Autobiography,* translated by M.H. Fisch and T.G. Bergin: the three princes are Grotius, Selden, and Pufendorf]

Our attention, however, should rather concentrate on what it would be proper to call the second line of Vico's defense against subjectivity because it may turn out to be decisive and help to save Herder too. Vico alludes repeatedly to his project of a dictionary of the mental utterances common to all the nations and underlying their different languages: Berlin refers to it in another context (p. 48). The project, first formulated in the *Scienza Nuova* of 1725, was taken up again in the 1744 version and is explained in prg. 144-145 (Bergin and Fisch translation):

> Thence issues the mental dictionary for assigning origins to all the divers articulated languages. It is by means of this dictionary that the ideal eternal history is conceived, which gives us the histories in time of all nations.

Vico claimed to have found a universally valid language underlying the individual languages. He recognized that a universal history—of whatever type—cannot be written without the conviction that different civilizations communicate with each other.

In Herder this conviction is less clearly stated. But when all has been said about language as the expression of national and tribal peculiarities, it remains true—and Herder recognizes this emphatically—that languages are translatable, that cultures borrow from each other through verbal communications, and that ultimately man is capable of universal understanding through language. Language—Herder presses on—is that "organ of understanding," is "the treasure house of human thoughts." Not by chance, it was in direct reference to Herder and his translations that Madame de Staël in *De l'Allemagne* praised the German language as uniquely suitable to render the "naïve expressions of the language of each country."

Thus Vico and Herder bring us back to the basic question of language. What I see as the next step after Berlin's essays is an attempt to assess the validity of the notions of Vico and Herder about language as a precondition for whatever validity one is inclined to attribute to their notions about history.

V

As I implied in my initial remarks, I do not see much future in the Italian Vico tradition, as it stands now. Whatever the merits of Vico's original intuition they have not helped the Italians to build up a historical method or an interpretation of the past with distinctive features. If anything, Italian "Vichismo" was and is a compromise—with Catholicism in the past, with Marxism in the present.

Whether the independent approach to Vico which is now being elaborated in Anglo-Saxon countries will lead to something of lasting value, it is too early to say. A fashion is not necessarily a method or a principle of interpretation. We shall have to read the Acts of the 1976 Vico Congress when they are published. But the recent collective volume edited by G. Tagliacozzo and D.P. Verene which presents itself as a continuation of the *International Symposium* of 1969 (*Giambattista Vico's Science of Humanity,* The Johns Hopkins University Press, 1976, 496 pp.) has a disturbing feature among its many merits. The majority of the contributors who are concerned with the vitality of Vico's ideas compare him with one other thinker (respectively Kant, Dilthey, Wundt, Husserl, Wittgenstein, Piaget, etc.) and conclude that the two thinkers can supplement each other. The invariable success of such a formula should have been a warning.

There remains, however, the question which seems to be central to Berlin's book and which I should have liked to see even more sharply pushed into prominence by him: the question whether the defense and glorification of the peculiarities of each and any civilization are intrinsically bound up with moral (perhaps even logical) relativism. If this question is given priority, Herder may seem to become more relevant than Vico, because Herder was exposed to a variety of cultural experiences which were unknown to Vico. On the other hand, by his approach to institutional problems, and especially to land ownership, and by his keen interest in a universal vocabulary of the mind, Vico offers means of resistance to a relativism which was to a large extent also his own. Before we celebrate the vitality of Vico and Herder let us be certain where they are leading us.

Note

1. Translated by T.G. Bergin and M.H. Fisch.

Aileen Kelly (essay date 1977)

SOURCE: "Isaiah Berlin and Russian Thought," in *The Times Literary Supplement,* No. 3953, December 30, 1977, pp. 1523-4.

[*In the following introduction to* Russian Thinkers, *Kelly explains Berlin's insights into the conflict between iconoclasm and the need for an overriding belief which dominated nineteenth century Russian intellectual activity.*]

> Do not look for solutions in this book—there are none; in genral modern man has no solutions.—ALEXANDER HERZEN, introduction to *From the Other Shore.*

In an attempt to explain the Russian Revolution to Lady Ottoline Morrell, Bertrand Russell once remarked that, appalling though Bolshevik despotism was, it seemed the right sort of government for Russia: "If you ask yourself how Dostoevsky's characters should be governed, you will understand."

The view that despotic socialism was no more than Russia deserved would be accepted by many Western liberals as not unjust, at least with regard to the "devils" of Dostoevsky's novel, the Russian radical intelligentsia. In the degree of their alienation from their society and of their impact on it, the Russian intelligentsia of the nineteenth century were a phenomenon almost *sui generis.* Their ideological leaders were a small group with the cohesiveness and sense of mission of a religious sect. In their fervent moral opposition to the existing order, their single-minded preoccupation with ideas, and their faith in reason and science, they paved the way for the Russian Revolution, and thereby achieved major historical significance. But they are all too often treated by English and American historians with a mixture of condescension and moral revulsion; because the theories to which they were so passionately attached were not their own, but borrowed from the West and usually imperfectly understood; and because in their fanatical passion for extreme ideologies they are held to have rushed, like Dostoevsky's devils, to blind self-destruction, dragging their country, and subsequently much of the test of the world, after them. The Russian Revolution and its aftermath have done much to strengthen the belief, deeply entrenched in the Anglo-Saxon outlook, that a passionate interest in ideas is a symptom of mental and moral disorder.

One liberal voice has strongly and consistently dissented from this view of the Russian intelligentsia—a voice of remarkable distinction. Isaiah Berlin is one of the most outstanding liberal thinkers of this century: his *Four Essays on Liberty* are contributions of the first importance to the study of the fundamental problems of political philosophy. His originality as a thinker derives from a combination of a liberalism in the English tradition with a wholly European fascination with ideas and their effects on political practice: his writings are penetrated with the conviction that liberal values are best understood and defended by those who seek to understand the part played by ideas in action, and in particular the intellectual and moral attractions of what he calls the "great despotic visions" of the right and left. His distinctive contribution to English intellectual life has been an effective opposition to the past half-century of relative indifference to intellectual movements in Europe. In essays and lectures, masterpieces of vivid and lucid exposition, he has acquainted a wide audience with great European intellectual traditions, with the ideas and personalities of some of the most original thinkers of the post-Renaissance world, and, in the essays collected together for the first time in *Russian Thinkers,* with the phenomenon of the Russian intelligentsia.

Isaiah Berlin's approach to the intelligentsia has been directed by his interest in the way in which ideas are "lived through" as solutions to moral demands. In contrast to the majority of studies on this subject, which set out to judge political solutions in the light of historical hindsight, he is above all concerned with the social and moral questions which the intelligentsia posed, the dilemmas that they sought to resolve. Though his essays on Russian subjects stand by themselves, with no need of philosophical annotation or cross-reference, they are also a substantial contribution to the central theme of all his writings on intellectual history, and their originality can best be appreciated if they are approached within this wider framework.

The central concern of Berlin's writings has been the exploration of what he sees as one of the most fundamental of the open issues on which men's moral conduct depends: are all absolute values ultimately compatible with one another, or is there no single final solution to the problem of how to live, no one objective and universal human ideal? In wide-ranging studies he has explored the psychological and historical roots and consequences of monist and pluralist visions of the world. He has argued that the great totalitarian structures built on Hegelian and Marxist foundations are not a terrible aberration, but rather a logical development of the major assumption in all the central currents of Western political thought: that there is a fundamental unity underlying all phenomena, deriving from a single universal purpose. This can be discovered, according to some, through scientific inquiry, according to others, through religious revelation, or through metaphysical speculation. When discovered, it will provide men with a final solution to the question of how to live.

Though the most extreme forms of this faith, with their dehumanizing visions of men as instruments of abstract historical forces, have led to criminal perversions of political practice, he emphasizes that the faith itself cannot be dismissed as the product of sick minds. It is the basis of all traditional morality and is rooted in "a deep and incurable metaphysical need", arising from man's sense of an inner split and his yearning for a mythical lost wholeness. This yearning for absolutes is very often the expression of an urge to shed the burden of responsibility for one's fate by transferring it to a vast impersonal monolithic whole— "nature, or history, or class or race, or the 'harsh realities of our time', or the irresistible evolution of the social structure, that will absorb and integrate us into its limitless, indifferent, neutral texture, which it is senseless to evaluate or criticise, and against which we fight to our certain doom".

Berlin believes that precisely because monistic visions of reality answer fundamental human needs, a truly consistent pluralism has been a comparatively rare historical phenomenon. Pluralism, in the sense in which he uses the word, is not to be confused with that which is commonly defined as a liberal outlook—according to which all extreme positions are distortions of true values and the key to social harmony and a moral life lies in moderation and the golden mean. True pluralism, as Berlin understands it, is much more toughminded and intellectually bold: it rejects the view that all conflicts of values can be finally resolved by synthesis and that all desirable goals may be reconciled. It recognizes that human nature is such that it generates values which, though equally sacred, equally ultimate, exclude one another, without there being any possibility of establishing an objective hierarchical relation between them. Moral conduct therefore may involve making agonizing choices, without the help of universal criteria, between incompatible but equally desirable values.

This permanent possibility of moral uncertainty is, in his view, the price that must be paid for recognition of the true nature of one's freedom: the individual's right to self-direction, as opposed to direction by state or church or party, is plainly of supreme importance if one holds that the diversity of human goals and aspirations cannot be evaluated by any universal criteria, or subordinated to some transcendent purpose. But he maintains that, although this belief is implicit in some humanist and liberal attitudes, the consequences of consistent pluralism are so painful and disturbing, and so radically undermine some of the central and uncritically accepted assumptions of the Western intellectual tradition, that they are seldom fully articulated. In seminal essays on Vico, Machiavelli and Herder, and in **"Historical Inevitability",** he has shown that those few thinkers who spelt out the consequences of pluralism have been consistently misunderstood, and their originality undervalued.

In his *Four Essays on Liberty* he suggests that pluralist visions of the world are frequently the product of historical claustrophobia, during periods of intellectual and social stagnation, when a sense of the intolerable cramping of human faculties by the demand for conformity generates a demand for "more light", an extension of the areas of individual responsibility and spontaneous action. But, as the dominance of monistic doctrines throughout history shows, men are much more prone to agoraphobia: and at moments of historical crisis, when the necessity of choice generates fears and neuroses, men are eager to trade the doubts and agonies of moral responsibility for determinist visions, conservative or radical, which give them "the peace of imprisonment, a contented security, a sense of having at last found one's proper place in the cosmos". He points out that the craving for certainties has never been stronger than at the present time; and his *Four Essays on Liberty* are a powerful warning of the need to discern, through a deepening of moral perceptions—a "complex vision" of the world—the cardinal fallacies on which such certainties rest.

Like many other liberals Berlin believes that such a deepening of perceptions can be gained through a study of the intellectual background to the Russian Revolution. But his conclusions are very different from theirs. With the subtle moral sense which led him to radically new insights into European thinkers, he refutes the common view that the Russian intelligentsia were, to a man, fanatical monists: he shows that their historical predicament strongly predisposed them to both types of vision of the world, the monist and the pluralist—that the fascination of the intelligentsia derives from the fact that the most sensitive among them suffered simultaneously, and equally acutely, from historical claustrophobia and from agoraphobia, so that at one and the same time they were both strongly attracted to messianic ideologies and morally repelled by them. The result, as he reveals, was a remarkably concentrated self-searching which in many cases produced prophetic insights into the great problems of our own time.

The causes of that extreme Russian agoraphobia which generated a succession of millenarian political doctrines are well known: in the political reaction following the failure of the revolution of 1825, which had sought to make Russia a constitutional state on the Western model, the small Westernized intellectual elite became deeply alienated from their backward society. With no practical outlet for their energies, they channelled their social idealism into a religiously dedicated search for truth. Through the historiosophical systems of Idealist philosophy, then at the height of its influence in Europe, they hoped to find a unitary truth which would make sense of the moral and social chaos around them and anchor them securely in reality.

This yearning for absolutes was one source of that notorious consistency which, as Berlin points out, was the most striking characteristic of Russian thinkers—their habit of taking ideas and concepts to their most extreme, even absurd, conclusions: to stop before the extreme consequences of one's reasoning was seen as a sign of moral cowardice, insufficient commitment to the truth. But Berlin emphasizes that there was a second, conflicting motivation behind this consistency. Among the Westernized minority, imbued through their education and reading with both Enlightenment and Romantic ideals of liberty and human dignity, the primitive and crushing despotism of Nicholas I produced a claustrophobia which had no parallel in the more advanced countries of Europe. As a result the intelligentsia's search for absolutes began with a radical denial of absolutes—of traditional and accepted faiths, dogmas and institutions, political, religious and social; since these, they believed, had distorted man's vision of himself and of his proper social relations. As Berlin shows in his essay **"Russia and 1848",** the failure of the European revolutions in 1848 had the effect in Russia of accelerating this process: it resulted among the intelligentsia in a profound distrust of Western liberal and radical ideologues and their social nostrums. For the most morally sensitive among the intelligentsia, intellectual consistency implied above all a process which they called "suffering through" the truth, the stripping off, through a painful process of inner liberation, of all the comforting illusions and half-truths which had traditionally concealed or justified forms of social and moral despotism. This led to a critique, with far-reaching implications, of the unquestioned assumptions at the base of everyday social and political conduct. This consistency, with the tensions engendered by its compound of faith and scepticism, and the insights to which it led, is the central theme of Berlin's essays on Russian thinkers.

In a number of vivid portraits of individual thinkers, he shows that the most outstanding members of the intelligentsia were continually torn between their suspicion of absolutes and their longing to discover some monolithic truth which would once and for all resolve the problems of moral conduct. Some surrendered to the latter urge: Bakunin began his political career with a famous denunciation of the tyranny of dogmas over individuals, and ended it by demanding total adherence to his own dogma of the wisdom of the simple peasant; and many of the young "nihilist" iconoclasts of the 1860s accepted without question the dogmas of a crude materialism. In other thinkers the battle was more serious and sustained. The critic Belinsky is often cited as the arch-example of the intelligentsia's inhuman fanaticism: from Hegelian principles he deduced that the despotism of Nicholas I was to be admired, contrary to all the instincts of conscience, as the expression of cosmic harmony. But Berlin points out, in an intensely moving study of Belinsky, that if the longing for faith led him briefly to defend such a grotesque proposition, his moral integrity soon drove him to reject this blinkered vision for a fervent humanism which denounced all the great and fashionable historiosophical systems as molochs, demanding the sacrifice of living individuals to ideal abstractions. Belinsky, epitomizes the paradox of Russian consistency: their desire for an ideal which would resist all attempts at demolition led the intelligentsia to apply themselves to the work of demolition with an enthusiasm and lucidity which exposed the hollowness of those assumptions about society and human nature on which the belief in absolute and universal solutions is based. In an essay on the populist tradition which dominated Russian radical thought in the nineteenth century, Berlin shows that the populists were far ahead of their time in their awareness of the dehumanizing implications of contemporary liberal and radical theories of progress, which placed such faith in quantification, centralization, and rationalization of productive processes.

Most of the intelligentsia regarded their destructive criticism as a mere preliminary, the clearing of the ground for some great ideological construction; Berlin sees it as thoroughly relevant to our own time, when only a consistent pluralism can protect human freedom from the depredations of the systematizers. Such a pluralism, he shows, was fully articulated in the ideas of a thinker whose originality has hitherto been largely overlooked—Alexander Herzen.

The founder of Russian populism, Herzen was known in the West as a Russian radical with a utopian faith in an archaic form of socialism. Isaiah Berlin, in two essays on Herzen, and in introductions to his greatest works, *From the Other Shore* and *My Past and Thoughts,* has transformed our understanding of him, firmly establishing him as "one of Russia's three moral preachers of genius", the author of some of the most profound of modern writings on the subject of liberty.

Like other members of the intelligentsia, Herzen had begun his intellectual career with a search for an ideal, which he found in socialism; he believed that the instincts of the Russian peasant would lead to a form of socialism superior to any in the West. But he refused to prescribe his ideal as a final solution to social problems, on the grounds that a search for such a solution was incompatible with respect for human liberty. At the beginning of the 1840s he was attracted, like Bakunin, to the Young Hegelians, with their belief that the way to freedom lay through negation of the outworn dogmas, traditions and institutions to which

men habitually enslaved themselves and others. He espoused this rejection of absolutes with a thoroughgoing consistency equalled only by Stirner, deriving from it a deeply radical humanism. He attributed the failure of liberating movements in the past to a fatally inconsistent tendency to idolatry on the part even of the most radical iconoclasts, who liberate men from one yoke only to enslave them to another. Rejection of specific forms of oppression never went far enough: it failed to attack their common source—the tyranny of abstractions over individuals. As Berlin shows, Herzen's attacks on all deterministic philosophies of progress demonstrate how well he understood that "the greatest of sins that any human being can perpetrate is to seek to transfer moral responsibility from his own shoulders to an unpredictable future order", to sanctify monstrous crimes by faith in some remote utopia.

Berlin emphasizes that Herzen's own predicament was a very modern one, in that he was torn between the conflicting values of equality and excellence: he recognized the injustice of elites but valued the intellectual and moral freedom, and the aesthetic distinction, of true aristocracy. But while refusing, unlike the ideologists of the left, to sacrifice excellence to equality, he understood, with J. S. Mill, something which has only become clear in our own day: that the common mean between these values, represented by "mass societies", is not the best of both worlds, but more frequently, in Mill's words, an aesthetically and ethically repellent "conglomerated mediocrity", the submergence of the individual in the mass. With great conviction and in a language as vivid and committed as Herzen's own, Berlin has perceived and conveyed to the English reader the originality of Herzen's belief that there are no general solutions to individual and specific problems, only temporary expedients which must be based on an acute sense of the uniqueness of each historical situation, and on a high degree of responsiveness to the particular needs and demands of diverse individuals and peoples.

Berlin's exploration of the self-searching of Russian thinkers includes studies of two writers—Tolstoy and Turgenev. These studies refute a widespread misconception about the relations between Russian writers and thinkers: namely, that in Russia literature and radical thought form two distinct traditions related only by mutual hostility. Tolstoy's and Dostoevsky's well-known aversion to the intelligentsia is frequently quoted to emphasize the gulf between Russia's great writers, who were concerned with exploring men's spiritual depths, and the intelligentsia, materialists concerned only with the external forms of social existence. In his essays on Tolstoy and Turgenev Berlin shows that their art can be understood only as a product of the same moral conflict as that experienced by the radical intelligentsia. The essays have a dual significance: as works of criticism they offer insights which should make a fundamental difference to our understanding of two of Russia's greatest writers; as studies of conflicts between two opposing visions of reality they are a significant contribution to the history of ideas.

In his famous study of Tolstoy's view of history, **"The Hedgehog and the Fox"**, and in the less well-known essay, **"Tolstoy and Enlightenment"**, Berlin shows that the relation between Tolstoy's artistic vision and his moral preaching may be understood as a titanic struggle between the monist and pluralist visions of reality. Tolstoy's "lethal nihilism" led him to denounce the pretensions of all theories, dogmas and systems to explain, order or predict the complex and contradictory phenomena of history and social existence, but the driving force of this nihilism was a passionate longing to discover one unitary truth encompassing all existence and impregnable to attack. He was thus constantly in contradiction with himself, perceiving reality in its multiplicity but believing only in "one vast, unitary whole". In his art he expressed an unsurpassed feeling for the irreducible variety of phenomena, but in his moral preaching he advocated simplification, reduction to one single level, that of the Russian peasant or the simple Christian ethic. In some of the most psychologically delicate and revealing passages ever written on Tolstoy, Berlin shows that his tragedy was that his sense of reality was too strong to be compatible with any of the narrow ideals he set up; the conclusions articulated in Herzen's writings were demonstrated in the tragedy of Tolstoy's life: his inability, despite the most desperate attempts, to harmonize opposing but equally valid goals and attitudes. Yet his failure, his inability to resolve his inner contradictions, gives Tolstoy a moral stature apparent even to those most mystified or repelled by the content of his preaching.

Few writers would seem to have less in common than Tolstoy, the fanatical seeker after truth, and Turgenev, a writer of lyrical prose, the poet of "the last enchantments of decaying country houses". But in his essay on Turgenev Berlin shows that though by temperament he was a liberal, repelled by dogmatic narrowness and opposed to extreme solutions, he had been deeply influenced in his youth by the moral commitment of his contemporaries and their opposition to the injustices of autocracy. He fully accepted his friend Belinsky's belief that the artist cannot remain a neutral observer in the battle between justice and injustice, but must dedicate himself, like all decent men, to the search to establish and proclaim the truth. The effect of this was to turn Turgenev's liberalism into something quite distinct from the European liberalism of that time, much less confident and optimistic, but more modern. In his novels, which chronicled the development of the intelligentsia, he examined the controversies of the middle years of the nineteenth century between Russian radicals and conservatives, moderates and extremists, exploring with great scrupulousness and moral perception the strengths and weaknesses of individuals and groups, and of the doctrines by which they were possessed. Berlin emphasizes that the originality of Turgenev's liberalism lay in the conviction which he shared with Herzen (even though he thought that Herzen's populism was his last illusion) as against Tolstoy and the revolutionaries (even though he admired their single-mindedness), that there was no final solution to the central problems of society. In an age when liberals and radicals alike were complacent in their faith in the inevitability of progress, when political choices seemed mapped out in advance by inexorable historical forces—the laws governing economic markets, or the conflict of social classes—which could be made to assume responsibility for their results, Turgenev perceived the hollowness of the certainties invoked by liberals to justify the injustices of the existing order, or by radicals to justify its merciless destruction. He thus anticipated the predicament of the radical humanist in our century, which one of the most morally sensitive political thinkers of our time, Leszek Kolakowski, has described as a continual agony of choice between the demands of *Sollen* and *Sein,* value and fact:

> The same question recurs repeatedly, in different versions: how can we prevent the alternatives of *Sollen/Sein* from becoming polarizations of utopianism/opportunism, romanticism/conservatism, purposeless madness versus collaboration with crime masquerading as sobriety? How can we avoid the fatal choice between the Scylla of duty, crying its arbitrary slogans, and the Charybdis of compliance with the existing world, which transforms itself into voluntary approval of its most dreadful products? How to avoid, this choice, given the postulate—which we consider essential—that we are never able to measure truly and accurately the limits of what we call "historical necessity"? And that we are, consequently, never able to decide with certainty which concrete fact of social life is a component of historical destiny and what potentials are concealed in existing reality.

Kolakowski's formulation of this dilemma of our time is surely valid. Yet Turgenev, a thinker of a very different type, faced it over a century ago. Before proponents of onesided visions, conservative or utopian, possessed the technological equipment for experiments on limitless human material, it was not so difficult as it is now to defend the view that one or other extreme vision, or even a middle way between them, was the whole answer. Isaiah Berlin has shown that, at a time when liberals, as well as the ideologists of the left, were still confident of the sufficiency of their systems, Turgenev had attained a more complex vision and had embodied it in his art.

There is no doubt with which of the three figures with whom he deals in most detail Berlin's greatest sympathies lie. He shows us that, for all Tolstoy's moral grandeur, his blindness at those moments when he relinquishes the humane vision of his art for a domineering dogmatism is repellent; and that Turgenev, for all the clarity of his vision, his intelligence and sense of reality, lacked the courage and moral commitment which he so much admired in the radical intelligentsia: his vacillation between alternatives was too often a state of "agreeable and sympathetic melancholy", ultimately dispassionate and detached.

It is with Herzen that Berlin has the greatest affinity (although he points out that there was substance in Turgenev's assertion that Herzen never succeeded in ridding himself of one illusion—his faith" in the "peasant sheepskin coat"); he ended his Inaugural Lecture, **"Two Concepts of Liberty"**, with a quotation from an author whom he did not identify: "To realize the relative validity of one's convictions and yet stand for them unflinchingly, is what distinguishes a civilized man from a barbarian." Herzen, who, as he shows, had the subtle vision of a Turgenev together with a self-sacrificing commitment to the truth which was the equal of Tolstoy's, was in this sense both brave and civilized. In his understanding that "one of the deepest of modern disasters is to be caught up in abstractions instead of realities", he possessed to a very high degree that consistent pluralism of outlook which for Berlin is the essence of political wisdom.

It is often said of the Russians that their national peculiarity consists in expressing in a particularly extreme fashion certain universal characteristics of the human condition; and for many the historical significance of the Russian intelligentsia derives from the fact that they embodied the human thirst for absolutes in a pathologically exaggerated form. Berlin's essays present us with a very different and much more complex interpretation of the intelligentsia's "universality", showing that for a variety of historical reasons they embodied not one, but at least two fundamental, and opposing, human urges. The urge to assert the autonomy of the self through revolt against necessity continually clashed with their demand for certainties, leading them to sharp perceptions of moral, social and aesthetic problems which in this century have come to be regarded as of central importance.

That this aspect of their thought has aroused so little attention in the West is due in some measure to the glaring intellectual defects of the writings of most members of the intelligentsia. The repetitiousness, the incoherence, the proliferation of half-digested ideas from foreign sources in the writings of men like Belinsky, together with the political disasters for which they are held responsible, have led the majority of Western scholars fervently to echo Chaadaev's famous pronouncement that if Russia has some universal lesson to give to the would, it is that its example is at all costs to be avoided. But with an acute instinct for quality, helped by a total absence of that condescension which is the frequent concomitant of historical hindsight, Isaiah Berlin has discerned behind the formal shortcomings of the intelligentsia's writings a moral passion worthy of attention and respect. His essays in this field are a vindication of the belief which he has preached to his English audience over many years: that enthusiasm for ideas is not a failing or a vice; that on the contrary, the evils of narrow and despotic visions of the world can be effectively resisted only through an unswerving moral and intellectual clarity of vision that can penetrate to and expose the hidden implications and extreme consequences of social and political ideals.

As he points out in his *Four Essays on Liberty,* no philosopher has ever succeeded in finally proving or refuting the determinist proposition that subjective ideals have no influence on historical events: but the essays in *Russian Thinkers,* with their deep perception of the moral essence of a man as the source of his humanity, of the way in which ideals are "lived through" in inner conflicts, argue more powerfully than any logical demonstration in support of the belief which penetrates all Isaiah Berlin's writings: that men are morally free and are (more often than the determinists who hold the field believe) able to influence events for good or evil through their freely held ideals and convictions.

John Leonard (essay date 1979)

SOURCE: "Books of The Times," in *The New York Times,* April 20, 1979, p. C29.

[*In the following review of* Concepts and Categories, *Leonard traces the development of Berlin's thought, interests, and literary style from the 1930s through the 1960s.*]

They must have had fun—Isaiah Berlin and Stuart Hampshire and A. J. Ayer—lolling around Oxford in the late 1930's, wrangling over positivism and symbolic logic, verification and phenomenalism, wondering about linguistics. And it must have been more of an emotional wrench than Mr. Berlin, now Sir Isaiah, is willing to concede in his brief preface to this book, when he decided at the end of the war to look in another direction:

"I asked myself whether I wished to devote the rest of my life to a study, however fascinating and important in itself, which, transforming as its achievements undoubtedly were, would not, any more than criticism or poetry, add to the store of positive human knowledge. I gradually came to the conclusion that I should prefer a field in which one could hope to know more at the end of one's life than when one had begun, and so I left philosophy for the field of the history of ideas."

As a splendid result, of course, we have his books on Marx, on Vico and Herder, on liberty and the Enlightenment, and the wonderful essays on Tolstoy and Herzen included in *Russian Thinkers. Russian Thinkers* was the first of four volumes of Sir Isaiah's essays that Viking is publishing, to Viking's credit, in this country, and *Concepts and Categories* is the second.

I must be said straight off that *Concepts and Categories* is not nearly so accessible to the general reader—me, for instance,—as *Russian Thinkers* was. For all that modern philosophy is obsessed with linguistics, modern philosophers seem to have trouble with the language. I find it hard to believe that a stylist so impeccable as Sir Isaiah could have written the following passage, although he did in 1939:

"If we look upon our concept of a given material object as a finite complex of sensible characteristics (to be referred to as m) selected more or less arbitrarily and un- self-consciously from the wider set of uniformly co-variant characteristics n, then m, which is constitutive of the object for a given observer, will differ for different individuals, times and cultures, although a certain minimum of overlapping common reference is needed for the possibility of communication in the present, and of understanding of records of the past."

To be sure, I've quoted the worst, and he may be ironic. As the essays—on, variously, the purpose of philosophy, verification, empirical propositions and hypothetical statements, logical translation, the concept of scientific history, the abiding need for political theory and whether or not the truth shall set us free—proceed from the 1930's to the 60's, the prose proceeds from a conceptual warm-up, with cramps, to the Olympic trials of clarity and elegance, of sprint and vault. It is as if he had to leave philosophy to find English.

Perhaps more to the point: He seems to have been uncomfortable among the concepts and categories, the fishy abstractions, swimming or floating in the aquarium of pure thought, unattached to people and history or memory and context. He presupposes models, paradigms and exceptions to the rule that do battle with one another. He understands that values—happiness, knowledge, justice, mercy, liberty, equality, efficiency, independence—will tend to clutter and compromise and compete and contradict. He insists on a messy pluralism to accommodate the sincerity and the nonsense: No ideologues need apply. He appears to be a socialist who nevertheless believes in original sin, and whose vexations are therefore qualms: *Everything* is more complicated outside the aquarium.

And so it is not a surprise that he is suspicious of logical positivism, of phenomenalism, of empiricism itself, of formal logic, of ideology and statistics, of running dogmas, not to mention the French. He has this peculiar capacity to remember Plato and Kant, Mill and Carnap, and to remind us that thinking *about* thinking isn't new; it is merely imperfect. His concepts are dimensional, including time. His categories are plausibility, belonging, likelihood and "sense of reality." His aquarium is history.

History is what informs these difficult essays. Sir Isaiah would just as soon be talking to Spinoza as to A. J. Ayer, because the problems are the same, and the individuals might have been interesting back then. He is the skeptic who aspires to faith and complains all the way along the road to Oz. Thought, for him, requires embodiment, a person with whom to argue. It needs the angle of the ages. Any single notion of value presides, if at all, with spurs.

He asks for elbow room for our messy values. Our adventure, he suggests, isn't so much chemistry as it is music. History, a symphony orchestra, is trying to make harmony out of discord, and the instruments are true only to themselves, and the existential saxophone may not get along with the various lyres of the Platonists, and even though we will all die, we might as well think about why.

Encounter (essay date 1979)

SOURCE: "Column," in *Encounter,* Vol. LIII, No. 4, October, 1979, pp. 23-5.

[In the following essay, a reviewer explores Berlin's challenge to western rationalism.]

Maurice Bowra once said of Isaiah Berlin that, "though like Our Lord and Socrates Berlin has not written much", his influence was immense. As in all Bowra's best jokes, this had a measure of truth in it, when it was said. Indeed, even Berlin's greatest friends and admirers once found it difficult to account for the reputation which, so it seemed, he had so effortlessly acquired.

His rooms in Oxford, in Corpus, All Souls, New College, were always the Mecca of an endless pilgrimage of those who came to sit at his feet and acquire wisdom, and also to enjoy the pleasure of his company and the dazzling effect of his personality; and no one who came was rejected. I myself first met him, when we were both undergraduates, on a beautiful summer afternoon in Christchurch Meadows. Since I was then deeply absorbed in Rilke's *Duineser Elegien* we discussed angels. I came away convinced that he knew more about angels than I ever should, that by a kind of empathy he perfectly and intuitively understood everything that Rilke had intended, but most of all that this was one of the most remarkable people I had met or was ever likely to meet.

But that was all a long time ago. The essays in *Against the Current*[1] cover a period of nearly 25 years, from 1955 to 1978. They have all been previously published but hitherto have not been easily available, unless one was an addict of academic journals, learned periodicals, and obscure publications with a limited circulation. Now, reading them together in this admirably collected edition of Berlin's writings, one is overwhelmed not only by their brilliance, weight and force, but by the striking unity of outlook and attitude that emerges from their treatment of an apparently widely disparate range of subjects.

I am not competent to judge Berlin's strictly philosophical writings *Concepts and Categories,* (published before he abandoned technical philosophy for the study of the history of ideas), which form the second volume of this collected edition. But surely this third volume, together with the first, *Russian Thinkers,* justifies a claim that Berlin is one of the most penetrating, imaginative and original thinkers of our day. I should hasten to add that reading these essays is also a profoundly enjoyable and exhilarating experience; for in addition to his other gifts, Berlin also has all those which would have made him, like Heine or Marx, a scintillating journalist.

Against the Current covers a variety of subjects which range from Machiavelli in the 15th century to George Sorel in the 20th. Between come essays on Giambattista Vico, Montesquieu, Johann Georg Hamann, Moses Hess, Alexander Herzen, Disraeli and Marx, and Verdi. Diverse as these essays are, however, they have a common theme, which may be roughly described as the reaction across the centuries, but particularly since the 18th, against an intellectual tradition which has been the mainspring of European thought and its greatest glory; that is to say, the tradition which reached its culmination in the French Enlightenment of the 18th century and still provides the intellectual foundation for the fantastic scientific and technological progress of which today we both enjoy and suffer the results.

To concentrate one's view on writers and thinkers who have tried to resist or controvert this tradition is indeed to swim against a current which has seemed to have swept everything irresistibly before it, including God, religion, established institutions and conventions and, not least, the belief in original sin. Yet in doing so Berlin has rediscovered for us certain aspects of the human mind, or spirit, which today have become increasingly powerful and are urgently and pressingly relevant to contemporary problems. It is as if beneath the surface currents of history there lay deeper waters which have not yet fully revealed to us all that is to be found in them.

Perhaps the most disconcerting of these rediscoveries is one which, in Berlin's view, underlies the immortal fame and notoriety of Machiavelli. In his essay *The Originality of Machiavelli,* he addresses himself to a fascinating historical puzzle. Perhaps more than any other political thinker, Machiavelli was fortunate in possessing a literary style which is, by universal consent, pre-eminently simple, lucid and intelligible, such, indeed, as he who runs may read. How is it then that today thinkers and scholars cannot agree on what he really meant? Berlin presents us with a list of no less than 22 distinct and well-documented interpretations of Machiavelli's views, and today men are no nearer to agreeing on which one is right than they ever were.

Moreover, beneath this puzzle lies another. How is it that, despite the meticulous analysis to which his writings and his character have been subjected, Machiavelli still has the capacity to surprise and shock us? After all, there is nothing he says which others have not said, rather more portentously, later, and, even more, nothing which statesmen and politicians have not taken almost for granted. Dr Kissinger can murder a few million Cambodians on the Machiavellian principle that the end justifies the means, and no one lifts an eyebrow. Why then should Machiavelli remain a scandal and a scoundrel?

The answer, according to Berlin, is that Machiavelli said or implied something which denies the whole tradition of European thought. He simply does not care about, or is not interested in, the question whether the political doctrines he recommends to the statesman in *The Prince* are compatible with either Christian or pagan ethics. Nor, if they are not, does he think that Christian or pagan political morality is necessarily false. All he says is that if you wish to be a Prince, that is, a statesman or a politician, you must give up morality; otherwise, give up being a Prince, because you will surely fail.

So cool, so dispassionate, so neutral a view of political action is profoundly disturbing to all those who accept the assumption that beneath all the flux of appearances the world is ultimately One. This is the common assumption underlying the long tradition of Western thought. Its thinkers and philosophers have, under a variety of forms, felt as Yeats did for a moment in "A Meditation in Time of War:

> *For one throb of the Artery . . .*
> *I knew that One is animate*
> *Mankind inanimate fantasy.*

Machiavelli's view implies that, on the contrary, the One is a figment of reason, that there are incompatible worlds, of the statesman, the saint, the moralist or the artist, only you cannot inhabit them all at the same time.

In this principle, says Berlin, lies the real originality of Machiavelli, and the secret of why he still has the power to shock us. Yet shocking or not, and in a sense tragic, as the doctrine may be, it is also a profoundly liberating one. The idea that there may be a variety of possible worlds offers a prospect of choice, and of freedom, which is not open to men confined in the strait-jacket of reason and its demand that all our instincts, passions, inclinations and affections shall be shown to conform to the ultimate unity of the All, in which all contradictions are finally resolved.

In one form or another this theme underlies all the essays collected in this book. It would be wrong, of course, to ascribe to Berlin views which are those of the thinkers whom he has chosen for examination. Yet his choice of these particular thinkers for discussion, and the depth of sympathy and understanding, the eloquence and, at moments, the passion with which he expounds their views cannot but make one feel that there is a measure of agreement between the subjects of these essays and their author. Indeed, the only direct statement of personal belief in the book, in the final essay on **"Nationalism: Past Neglect and Present Power"**, comes as a completely natural conclusion to everything that has gone before; in particular, perhaps, to the essay on **"The Life and Opinions of Moses Hess."**

Hess is today an almost entirely forgotten figure, except to scholars interested in the early history of socialism. He was, it would seem, irretrievably consigned to the rubbish-bin of history by Karl Marx's summary dismissal of him, in what Berlin describes as one of Marx's "rare moments of good humour", as "the donkey Hess."

Yet this man, who, unlike Marx, had an almost childlike simplicity and innocence of character, and was moved above all by a profound sympathy with the humble and oppressed, is credited by Berlin with a discovery which, in its direct effect upon our own times and problems, has had an importance at least as great as Marx's discovery of "scientific socialism", which after all has affected us only in weirdly distorted forms. That discovery was Zionism, at a time when the movement to which the name was later attached did not yet exist, when the Jews themselves had not yet adopted it as the only means of salvaging their own identity, and certainly no one except Hess had the slightest inkling of the immense importance it was to have in 20th-century history.

Yet perhaps the most interesting aspect of Hess's great discovery, apart from its practical consequences, was the way in which he came to make it. He was a socialist, a revolutionary, an itinerant agitator; and reason, following the ideas of the Enlightenment, assured him of the ultimate victory of the working class. But in Hess, faith in the power of reason to bring about the emancipation of the working class did not obstruct or conflict with a gift for seeing things as they really are, and his own experience told him what he, as a Jew, really was. It was introspection and intuition which told him that the values embodied in his Jewish upbringing, in his family ties and affections, in Jewish religion and tradition, in Jewish hopes of a return to Zion could never be realised in a society in which the rational and enlightened solution of the Jewish problem lay, as for Marx, in progressive assimilation into Western society and culture.

Hess, by examination of his own experience, was persuaded that he and his people could not realise their own identity except by reversing the Diaspora. In this, as in other political problems, the donkey proved a far better guide to the future than Marx.

Hess, with his innocent eye for experience, might in many ways stand as an exemplar of all those whom Berlin celebrates in these essays. Their subjects, Machiavelli, Vico, Montesquieu, Herder, Herzen and others form at first glance an ill-assorted group, and their fortunes, in their own lifetime and later, varied to an astonishing degree. Some, like Vico, lived and died in total obscurity. Montesquieu, when alive, achieved, and has retained, immortal fame, though for reasons which were largely based on misunderstanding. Herder founded a school of historical thought which has had immense influence; his compatriot Hamann, friend of Immanuel Kant and once celebrated as "the Magus of the North", is today totally forgotten and unread, not least because the intrinsic difficulty of what he had to say led him to adopt a style so obscure and contorted as to be unreadable. Herzen lived nearly all his adult life in exile and has earned immortality for his memoirs, which are a masterpiece; but he also left a permanent mark on history as one of the earliest and most influential precursors of the Russian Revolution, which in almost every way proved to be destructive of everything he believed in.

Indeed, a part of the fascination of these essays is the range of human personality and human thought which they display. Yet varied though their subjects are in their character and ideas, as in their lives and in what followed, they had certain things in common which gives the book a unity which has a compelling interest.

One of the most important and fundamental is the belief that in direct experience and intuition human beings can achieve knowledge of a reality which is not accessible to reason, and sometimes may conflict with it. Experience, in this context, includes everything which they absorb through the senses and the affections, through family and kinship, and through tradition, religion and the arts; it takes a multiplicity of forms according to the society and the culture to which men belong and for the overwhelming majority of human beings constitutes the only reality which their lives possess.

A second theme is the belief that the varieties of human experience are such that they cannot be reduced to a single and unitary pattern, such as reason, both deductive and inductive, employing the methods which have proved so brilliantly successful in the physical sciences, seeks to impose on them. The stuff out of which experience is made is as rich, dense, confused as life itself, and refuses to conform to universal laws such as reason professes to discover. Unlike inanimate matter, it obeys no observable and demonstrable principles and regularities except under particular circumstances of time and place; it resembles, not a machine, but a plant or an organism.

Lastly, and as a corollary, there is the belief in the unique reality of the individual human being as the centre of the experience which streams in on him from within and without. This belief has no logical or rational foundation; yet it is this alone which ultimately gives meaning and significance to human life.

These beliefs, in the subjects of Berlin's essays, combine to produce a view of life fundamentally opposed to the main current of Western thought which, until comparatively recently, has since the Greeks assumed that there is a basis of reality which is logical, rational and coherent, and in which, by the application of reason, all contradictions can be resolved.

It would be impossible, except in his own words, to do justice to the gifts of sympathy and imagination, and to the range and depth of knowledge with which Berlin explores this contradiction, and pursues it, through the highways and byways of history, to conclusions which are not only surprising and disturbing, but have the sharpest and most direct relevance to the problems of the contemporary world.

Against the Current certainly represents a most remarkable intellectual achievement. There are few books published in our time which more dazzlingly illuminate some of the most crucial problems of Western culture and civilisation.

Note

1. *Against the Current: Essays in the History of Ideas.* By Isaiah Berlin. Edited and with a Bibliography by Henry Hardy. With an Introduction by Roger Hausheer. The Hogarth Press, £9.50.

Robert A. Kocis (essay date 1980)

SOURCE: "Reason, Development, and the Conflicts of Human Ends: Sir Isaiah Berlin's Vision of Politics," in

The American Political Science Review, Vol. 74, No. 1, March, 1980, pp. 38-52.

[In the following essay, Kocis examines Berlin's concept of negative and positive liberty, and explores and evaluates several critiques of it.]

What makes life worth living? To this, the central question of political and all practical philosophy, Sir Isaiah Berlin returns a singularly striking answer: there is no system to the cosmos, no plan to human development, nor any pattern to human values which can provide a reason for living. Only each individual's artistic and creative capacities can provide such a reason. Nothing outside of us, be it God, Reason, History, Spirit, or the Good, provides a purpose for existence which we can discover; we are not only the discoveres, but actually the creators, of meaning and purpose in the universe. Captivated by a vision of humanity as self-creative and developing in unpredictable and conflicting directions and by a vision of the world as not infused by any cosmic pattern or purpose, Berlin denies that any of us can demonstrate that our way of life is morally superior to others; thus, we need to tolerate one another.

Berlin's defense of tolerance and freedom is fairly unique. As he depicts it, our Western tradition has rested on one basic, yet mistaken assumption: that for every real question, there is one true answer (Berlin, 1962). Berlin is convinced that accepting this belief draws a theorist inevitably to its logical implication: that there is only one true way for all people to live, and those who refuse or fail to live by the light of reason must be brought to the truth. Berlin calls this belief "rationalism" and he relentlessly seeks out and exposes it at the base of political theories. By inclination more a physician than a metaphysician, Berlin sees this assumption of a pattern to things which entails one final, right solution to all human problems as both the heart of the metaphysical doctrine of rationalism and as the source of many political difficulties of the nineteenth and twentieth centuries (Berlin, 1969, p. 167): "One belief, more than any other, is responsible for the slaughter of individuals on the altars of the great historical ideal. . . . This is the belief that somewhere, in the past or in the future, in divine revelation or in the mind of an individual thinker, in the pronouncements of history or science, or in the simple heart of an uncorrupted good man, there is a final solution."

Thus Berlin sees two competing approaches to life on which views of politics and society rest; political theorists face two logical alternatives. Either theorists can make the rationalist assumption of a pattern to things and so of one correct answer to life's questions; or they can reject this assumption and remain devoted to life's diversity and variety. Theorists of the first group are called rationalists, monists, or "hedgehogs"; the second group includes empiricists, romantics, pluralists, and "foxes" (cp. Berlin, 1953). With his commitment to an unpatterned universe, to human creativity and to the plurality of values, Berlin is clearly a member of the second group who is aware of the need to fuse these two traditions (cp. Berlin, 1969, p. 199).

THE PROBLEM WITH BERLIN'S ACCOUNT OF MORAL PLURALISM

Berlin's is an almost coherent theory; despite his concern to unveil the rationalist assumption of other thinkers, Berlin himself appears to make (and perhaps must make) this assumption. This difficulty is logical and its source lies in his theory of human nature. Although he is empiricist and romantic enough to recognize that there are a variety of ways of life and to claim further that they are each valid and equally stable, still he insists that there is an eternal truth about human beings: they are capable of living life for their own purposes. This vision of humanity becomes *a prioristic*—any individual said to be totally lacking the basic moral intuitions of normal people would be said to be inhuman. On this view, there are certain things which we *could not do or be and remain human* (Berlin, 1962, pp. 26-27). The resulting emphasis on freedom and choice requires that we all live in such a way as not to deny others the possibility of making their own choices about life. We are agents, creators of ourselves and our world; to violate this truth is to do violence to ourselves and to deny our humanity.

Where Berlin's more empiricist and romantic view of humanity as creative suggests a dramatic vision of people facing moral ultimates among which they can only choose (Berlin, 1971, p. 31), his more universalist view of our purposiveness leads to a claim that some values, like negative liberty, have a more basic validity than other values, in that they protect the human capacity for choice (Berlin, 1955, pp. 287-88). Where Berlin's romantic vision of humanity leads to a meta-ethical claim that our values cannot be rank-ordered (1955, p. 294), his more rationalistic vision of people as choosers implies a substantive ethic which values negative liberty as "a truer and more humane ideal" (Berlin, 1969, p. 171) than positive liberty. It is my contention that this conflict which first surfaces in his account of human nature later tears his theory apart, rendering his meta-ethical doctrine of pluralism incompatible with his substantive ethical endorsement of liberty. For Berlin faces a dilemma: either the rationalists are right that we can discover some order to our values which best guarantees our humanity, or he cannot insist that negative liberty is "a truer and more humane ideal" than any other.

Yet Berlin's liberalism might be rendered internally consistent if we were to treat liberty, not as the highest of values, but rather as a basal or foundation value, as Nicolai Hartmann (1932) and Charles Fried (1970) treated justice and privacy. These "lower" values constitute a base which provides the moral and psychic foundation for achieving the higher reaches of human perfection. Without this foundation, the other things we value—excellence, equality, nobility, fraternity, dignity—become elusive ideals which remain beyond the reach of human beings. In the absence of these values, we devolve into a more bestial existence (Berlin, 1955, pp. 287-88): "Liberty . . . is very hard to attain and preserve, but without it all things wither." Still, Berlin insists, in the presence of these values, we develop "in a variety of conflicting directions" (1969, p. 205). The "deep structure" of Berlin's image of politics, then, involves an image of us as developing in a variety of directions once a certain basal level has been assured by liberty.

In other words, examining Berlin's views unveils a compelling vision of liberal politics. Despite the logical flaws, Berlin's vision is clear—to deny human beings the chance to choose their life-plans for themselves is a violation of their personhood. Thus he fears the rationalists, whose commitment to some higher goal endangers human choice. However, most of Berlin's critics fail to deal with this claim which Berlin recognizes as most basic. Either they concede to him his claim that rationalism leads ineluctably to one picture of how we must live (and so leads to despotism and paternalism); or they fail to come to grips with the propensity of rationalistic views of the universe, of humanity, and of morality to lead to a conclusion that we must be coerced to live according to plan. Yet this conflict is basic to a consideration of the controversy between the proponents of "negative" and "positive" liberty; if Berlin is right that the positive doctrine rests on some patterned vision of what we must be, then it does not accord with a vision of human beings as able to choose their own ends.

My contention is that a consideration of Berlin and his critics will lead us to an insight into the nature of politics. For Berlin's vision of liberty has been attacked both for including too much politics and for excluding politics. On the one hand, Berlin's claim about the essentially political nature of human freedom has been reduced to a question of formal logic by MacCallum; and his claim that liberty rests on rationalistic grounds has been challenged by Macpherson who would like to terminate liberal politics and substitute participation in economic planning. On the other hand, his defense of negative liberty is depicted as apolitical by Crick who, together with Fromm, would use politics to achieve the full life for all. Against all of these, we can see Berlin (1962, p. 8) as maintaining that politics is an interaction between human beings aimed at resolving conflicts engendered by choosing competing ends of life: "If we ask the Kantian question, 'In what kind of world is political philosophy . . . in principle possible?' the answer must be 'Only in a world where ends collide.'" Thus, liberal politics, based on a recognition of the plurality of valid and conflicting ends of life, aims to free people to choose among the ends as they see fit. It does not provide us with the good life, but it makes pursuit of the good life possible.

THE NATURE AND FOUNDATIONS OF
NEGATIVE AND POSITIVE LIBERTY

But the liberal tradition is not monolithic; one of the many significant controversies within liberalism concerns the very nature of liberty itself. T. H. Green, from within the tradition of British Idealism, first popularized the distinction between "negative" and "positive" liberty by criticizing the legalist tradition of human rights as being too empty and formalistic—too negative—and urging that the state be more positively concerned with the material needs of its citizens. With this, welfare concerns were introduced into the liberal tradition. Berlin (1969, p. 171) fears that this trend will end by elevating material welfare over liberty, so he reminds us that negative liberty is "a truer and more humane ideal" than positive liberty because the positive conception of liberty is rooted in a rationalistic view of the world.

Berlin's point is not that the goals of positive libertarians are evil—rather, they are so compelling that, in pursuing them, we inevitably lose sight of the more basic liberties of the negative kind. Indeed, his point is that in pursuit of other goals we must never sacrifice our basic liberties, since they guarantee our human dignity. Nor does this make of Berlin an opponent of humane policies which aid the less advantaged in our societies; his claim is that it makes a difference how we justify these policies. To initiate a system of transfer payments to funnel government funds to indigent citizens because they are viewed as helpless dependents leads inexorably to paternalism and despotism (even if it is benevolent); to advocate the same policy because a certain minimum of material welfare is necessary for any person to pursue his or her own purposes is to foster human freedom and independence. As Berlin puts it (1969, p. xlvi): "The case for the . . . welfare state and socialism . . . can be constructed with as much validity from considerations of the claims of negative liberty as from its positive brother; and if, historically, it was not made so frequently, that was because the kind of evil against which the concept of negative liberty was directed as a weapon was not laissez-faire, but despotism."

Berlin's insight is that human dignity is to be found in our capacity to make our own choices—the flaw of rationalistic views is that they justify violence to, and denigration of, persons. The always-present desire for some higher good or another readily provides some people with justifications for present indignities by appeal to some future good. Berlin (1956, p. 25) fondly quotes Herzen on the logic of this perversion: "Do you really wish to condemn human beings alive today to the mere sad role of caryatids supporting a floor for others one day to dance upon?" The problem is that the goal of a future life which requires present indignities is self-destructive, leading to an abasement and mockery of human life. As Berlin sees it, any vision of liberty, like positive liberty, which (by virtue of its rationalist foundations) requires the repression of individuals and the imposition of alien purposes upon them is necessarily faulty, a form of deception rooted in a misrepresentation of human nature.

Berlin's distinction between negative and positive liberty rests on a simple and commonsense understanding of freedom, locating within it both positive and negative dimensions. Simply, any agent's desire for freedom derives from the wish that his or her actions be truly his or her own and not anybody else's. In Berlin's words (1969, p. xliii): "I wish to determine myself, and not be directed by others, no matter how wise or benevolent; my conduct derives an irreplaceable value from the sole fact that it is my own, and not imposed upon me." Thus, to be free may take either of two senses: it may mean being free from coercion or it may mean having a positive capacity to govern oneself. The first is the negative sense of liberty, and the latter is its positive counterpart. Negative liberty is concerned with moral and political rights to live for one's own purposes within a certain realm. Positive liberty is geared to providing people with the capacity to become better, more rational beings who live for higher purposes; it aims at creating a new, and better, society.

Berlin distinguishes the two by reference to the types of questions to which they respond. The first, negative sense of liberty addresses questions like "What is the area within which the subject . . . is or should be left to do or be, without interference by other persons?" (Berlin, 1969, pp. 121-22) or "How much am I governed?" (p. xliii) or "Over what area am I master?" (p. xliii). The first definition of liberty is involved in defining an area within which no one has a right to intervene, an area in which agents have a right to make their own decisions. Intrusion into this realm is a violation of the person, denying human purposiveness. This sense of liberty emphasizes protecting individuals in their choices and requires maintaining the inviolability of persons.

By contrast, positive liberty is concerned with questions of who can be a governing agency and of who is to have the power to coerce others to act. Such questions include: "What or who is the source of control or interference that can determine someone to do, or be, this rather than that?" (p. 122) or "By whom am I governed?" (p. xliii) or "Who is master?" (p. 133). It is not concerned with a defensive rampart, but with which agency is to exercise a positive capacity to get things done. It would seem, then, that positive liberty is not a freedom from coercion but the ability to do or become something. It is not protective of the person who is, but creative of new circumstances in which the person changes. A fundamentally different approach to life and politics, positive liberty emphasizes the creation of a capacity for those who are rational to realize a better life, while negative liberty is committed to the importance of restraints on that capacity so that human dignity might be respected.

In his critique of positive liberty, Berlin might be seen to be offering us an insight into political theorizing: any view of the nature of morality and society which assumes that there is one right answer to questions about how people are to live is inevitably drawn to a (perverse) kind of Platonic politics which requires government by the elite of guardians who know the right answer to life's questions. Berlin's fundamental argument is that this rationalistic positing of the existence of *the right answer* to questions of how we are to live inevitably leads proponents of posi-

tive liberty down the road to paternalism: if one right answer exists, then those who have discovered it have an obligation to bring this truth to the unenlightened. If there is one truth about how to live, then all people must be made aware of the right answer and must be made to act in accord with it. Berlin fears theorists of positive liberty because they must have some vision of a (possible?) world without scarcity and conflict, or a view of human developmental powers which will carry us into a new age, or a view of some higher good which requires of them a commitment to the expansion of human powers to require action of other people. Possessed of and by a truth of how people are to live, they are logically and reasonably compelled to require all to act in accord with this truth.

If Berlin is right, the problem with positive liberty is that this subsuming of all people under one ideal lays the foundation for violence. Any who fail to see its truth are either ignorant or irrational; pursuit of any other end is subversive of the pursuit of the one right end. Any persons who pursue other ends are classified as perverse, as not knowing what is truly good for them. If they will not choose to do what the enlightened know to be right, they have to be coerced so that the good life will not be denied to the rest of humanity.

Berlin (1969, p. 133) finds this view frightening and dehumanizing:

> Once I take this view, I am in a position to ignore the actual wishes of men or societies, to bully, oppress, torture them in the name, and on behalf, of their "real" selves, in the secure knowledge that whatever is the true goal of man (happiness, performance of duty, wisdom, a just society, self-fulfillment) must be identical with his freedom—the free choice of his "true," albeit often submerged and inarticulate, self.

Berlin locates the psychological basis for this perversion of liberty in the metaphysical division of the self into a bundle of instincts and the latent rational controller. Once this division has been assumed, only the latently rational aspect of a person is seen to have access to the one true way for people to live and those who are not governed by reason are not to be taken seriously, or even as (full) human beings. They must be irrational and reactionary—they do not desire the same things as the enlightened do. Berlin suspects that such a view holds out no hope for the unenlightened; if they do not behave properly, the hopes of all will be dashed, to the detriment of all mankind. They must not be permitted to destroy the great experiment—it is of more importance than their perverse wishes. Coercion is justified.

Berlin (1969, p. 152) notes that what begins as a doctrine of freedom is thus perverted to a doctrine of coercion and repression; step by step it leads "from an ethical doctrine of individual responsibility and individual self-perfection to an authoritarian state obedient to the directives of an *elite* of Platonic guardians." Because he sees the positive doctrine of liberty as rooted in the rationalistic tradition,

Berlin senses that it will seek to impose its vision of the good of man upon us all, smothering our capacity for creating that good for ourselves. All of the diversity, color, and variety of politics would be lost, along with our human dignity, if the positive ideal of liberty were pursued too zealously. Pursuit of this, or any, ideal as the true good for all would depoliticize our world, reducing political questions to technical questions (Berlin, 1962, p. 8).

LIBERTY DE-POLITICIZED: A FORMAL LOGICAL RELATIONSHIP?

However, it may well be that questions of liberty are not political questions after all; they may be questions of logic and meaning. Gerald MacCallum (1972) has offered a reasoned and closely argued critique of this distinction between two kinds of liberty which Berlin has employed in his arguments. MacCallum questions the need for the distinction, arguing that the two conceptions of liberty are both formally involved in any statement about human freedom. Where Berlin sees two fundamentally different approaches to life and politics, MacCallum sees one logical relationship. Liberty, properly understood, is neither positive nor negative. Rather, liberty is a single, triadic relationship (MacCallum, 1972, p. 175): an agent (X) is free from some constraint (Y) to do, be, or become something (Z). MacCallum identifies three variables which may range over agents (X), over preventing conditions like constraints, restrictions, interferences, and barriers (Y), and over actions or conditions of character or circumstances (Z).

It is not the case, MacCallum continues, that two different conceptions of liberty are at the root of the controversies over negative and positive liberty. Rather, the disputants disagree over the ranges of these variables. MacCallum contends that where the advocates of negative liberty take X to extend over common-sense persons, advocates of the positive doctrine may either restrict the range of the agent variable to only those who are rational—"the retreat to the inner citadel" (1972, p. 184; Berlin, 1969, pp. 135-40)—or expand it so that "the institutions and members, the histories and futures of the communities in which the living human body is found are considered to be inextricable parts of the 'person'" (MacCallum, p. 185). Similarly, the negative libertarian's limiting of obstacles to those actions or arrangements of others who might interfere with an agent is rejected by members of the positive tradition, since "it is quite irrelevant whether difficulties in the way of the policies are or are not *due to* arrangements made by human beings. The only question is whether the difficulties can be removed by human arrangements, and at what cost" (MacCallum, p. 186). Finally, disagreement over the range of the last variable centers around a difference between focusing on the conditions of character (by the positive faction) and emphasizing actions (by the negative faction). One may be free to do something—to perform specific actions, as the negative libertarians would have it; or one may be free to be or become something—people are free for the purpose of developing and need more than the absence of constraints, and so they must be provided the positive capacity to actualize certain potentials.

Yet MacCallum's formal logic obscures a deeper conflict about the ends of life: is a person to be freed to pursue some rationally specified purpose or is s/he to be freed to pursue his or her own purposes? In dismissing MacCallum's critique, Berlin hints at this, writing that liberty needs no further or higher purposes: "A man struggling against his chains or a people against enslavement need not consciously aim at any definite further state. A man need not know how he will use his freedom; he just wants to remove the yoke. So do classes and nations" (1969, p. xliii n.). However obliquely, Berlin appears to be contending that if liberty were to be construed as containing its own purposes, it would leave no room for the purposes of those who struggle to achieve it. However, Berlin's footnote does not constitute a refutation of MacCallum: he fails to show that there is anything wrong with MacCallum's triadic relationship as an account of liberty, opting to suggest that it flies in the face of some of our intuitions about why people seek freedom. What is wrong with MacCallum's formal analysis of liberty?

Initially, the problem is that the analysis is formal; its strength is also its weakness. This is not to say that formal logics and grammars are inherently flawed and of no use to political theory; but they are limited. Linguists have become very sensitive to the fact that linguistic forms can obscure a more profound logic; depth grammars have been developed because formalistic grammars cannot account for the underlying differences between sentences like "John is easy to please" and "John is eager to please." Formal grammars face difficulties distinguishing "easy" from "eager"-one (formal) variable could be made to cover both of these "dispositions" with respect to pleasing. However, the underlying logic of the two sentences is fundamentally different: in the one, some agent other than John is aiming to please John and finds this easy, while in the other sentence John is aiming to please someone else and seems willing to go to great lengths to do so. With some difficulty, a formalist could describe these sentences in terms of a single triadic relationship: "X (some agent) is Y (in some way disposed) to Z (to pleasing)." Yet this formal analysis obscures a deeper logical problem concerning which agent is aiming to please; formalist grammars are not always sensitive to the differences of which person is seeking an end.

MacCallum's analysis of sentences expressing relationships of human freedom is similarly flawed by an inability to identify who should be deciding about human ends. Formally, MacCallum's account is flawless—it is possible to formalize all freedoms as "X is free from Y to do or be Z." But the purpose of analysis is to lay bare the underlying logical reality; MacCallum's analysis fails to do so. To clarify the underlying logic, two points about the relationship of freedom to human ends must be made. First, it is true but trivial to claim that all liberties can be expressed formally as a triadic relationship since the sorts of things which follow "X is free from Y to . . ." are as different as "easy" and "eager" in the earlier example. It is certainly true that liberties, such as freedom of religious belief, can be so expressed: all citizens are free from governmental interference to believe what they will about a deity. But not all freedoms are liberties; some are capacities. One may be free to speak one's own mind or free to become rational or "a new socialist man." The difference between the two is that the first permits a variety of different human purposes, while the second implies that some human purposes are to take precedence over others. One may be free to pursue one's own ends (however foolish) or one may be free to pursue certain ends specified by more rational agents. This difference between freeing someone to become the sort of person he or she wishes to be and freeing a person to fit some mold is obscured by MacCallum's formalist analysis.

Second, this conflict about the ends of life is symptomatic of a larger and deeper philosophical disagreement. One side of this argument holds that freedom is the ability to pursue certain rationally specified ends, while the other concentrates on an individual's space to choose his or her ends. This political dimension of liberty must not be obscured by logical formalism. Negative freedoms, interpreted as liberties and rights, are protective of the agent's right to choose his or her ends without interference and include the freedoms to worship, to speak, to write, and to assemble. Positive freedoms, interpreted as capacities, are expansive of an individual's powers to pursue certain specified ends, including the freedoms to be rational, to be American, to be Soviet, and to be a fully integrated personality. This second group of freedoms involves a series of higher ends and is not directly related to questions of legal/civil liberties and human rights; could anyone have a right to be rational?

However, it is here that the force of Berlin's reply to MacCallum can be fully felt. For freeing human beings need not (and perhaps should not, or even, must not) involve some higher purpose; it is enough to free them to find their own purposes. Unhappily, as Berlin notes, freeing people in the negative sense entails freeing them to do even those things which we might see as mistaken; freeing them to pursue their own purposes may well mean that they will not pursue the ends we prefer. We might well free them to become better human beings, but their ends might lead them to become something totally different from, and even contrary to, our expectations. Criticizing Rousseau and the Jacobins, Berlin (1969, p. 148) writes that for them, "Freedom is not freedom to do what is irrational, or stupid, or wrong. To force empirical selves into the right pattern is not tyranny, but liberation." Positive liberty becomes the freedom to do what is rational, to do what rational agents would want to do. Berlin is right to protest that giving freedom this purpose is a transformation and perversion of liberty, making of it a means to some other end rather than a condition for our decisions about the ends of life. Actual persons are not protected by this freedom; only abstract and more rational persons are worthy of the freedom to decide for themselves. We might conclude then that if we want people to be something in particular, we need to coerce them, not to free them. To speak of freeing them to pursue our ends is a mockery; human beings can only be freed to pursue their own ends.

To ignore who is to make decisions about human ends is to remove all politics from a discussion of liberty. If all people agreed on what is the highest good, there would be no conflict over whether we should be free to pursue our own ends—our ends would all be the same and only the irrational would seek perverse ends. In passages unrelated to his comments on MacCallum, Berlin explores the dimensions of removing politics from a consideration of freedom and making the questions of freedom into questions of formal logic.

We might begin this exploration of the political dimensions of liberty by noting that any effort to include a foreign or higher end in a definition of liberty amounts to an advocacy of a paternalistic approach to liberation and government. If there is some higher end to be achieved in human liberation, then other persons are not to be counted as full moral agents capable of their own purposes but treated like children who must be taught what is best for them. With this higher end and their best interests in mind, leaders are to initiate them into the best life. Rather than agreeing with MacCallum that freedom includes this sense of (higher) purpose, Berlin (1969, p. 136) may be taken to be showing that this vision of purpose is the very root of oppression: "For if the essence of men is that they are autonomous beings—authors of values, of ends in themselves, the ultimate authority of which consists precisely in the fact that they are willed freely—then nothing is worse than to treat them as if they were not autonomous, but natural objects. . . ." To treat human beings as natural objects is to treat them as determined by outside forces and as not capable of their own purposes; the purposes we actually have must not be as good as those brought with the positive sense of liberty. The advocate of positive liberty becomes a kind of despot in Berlin's eyes (1969, p. 137): "'Nobody can compel me to be happy in his own way,' said Kant. 'Paternalism is the greatest despotism imaginable.' This is so because it is to treat men as if they were not free, but human material for me, the benevolent reformer, to mould in accordance with my own, not their, freely adopted purposes. . . ." But this capacity for ends is what is distinctively human about each person and to deny it is to deny human status to a person (1969, p. 137): "But to manipulate men, to propel them towards goals which you—the social reformer—see, but they may not, is to deny their human essence, to treat them as objects without wills of their own, and therefore to degrade them." Deception is wrong for the same reasons, writes Berlin: to deceive people or to trick them into seeking ends preferred by the deceiver, even though it may later be to their advantage, is "to treat them as sub-human, to behave as if their ends are less ultimate and sacred than" those of the deceiver (1969, p. 137).

No proper sense of liberty, as Berlin sees it, could be paternalistic; liberty for the sake of being or doing something desired by others is not truly liberty. The political dimensions of negative liberty carry with them the implication that various human values might conflict; but positive liberty assumes that human ends can be rationally specified and ranked. This is the crucial difference between the two which is obscured by MacCallum's formalist analysis: negative liberty would preserve the ground of politics on which conflicting human ends grow, so that our ability to choose is preserved, while positive liberty would harmonize human ends. Hence, we might conclude that it is certainly true that freedoms can be specified formally as a single triadic relationship; but it is more profoundly true that two divergent and opposed approaches to life can both address questions of liberty using that single form. MacCallum's critique fails because it does not get below the surface of the logical form of statements of freedom to the political question of who shall choose the ends of life for each person.

LIBERTY DE-POLITICIZED: WELFARE AND THE HARMONY OF HUMAN ENDS

However, this does not mean that Berlin's account of liberty is not open to criticism from another angle by those who oppose its political dimension: perhaps positive liberty is needed to foster human development. Berlin's refusal to see freedom as a capacity or to see any need for a higher purpose for freedom is what leads C. B. Macpherson (1973) to argue that Berlin's definition of negative liberty accords too little importance to welfare as a condition for human growth. This controversy operates at two levels, beginning with Macpherson's rejection of the distinction between liberty and its conditions and proceeding to an attempt at refuting Berlin's claim that positive liberty is inherently rationalistic.

Berlin insists that providing people with the material conditions necessary for the enjoyment of liberty is not the same thing as freeing them; "Useless freedoms should be made usable, but they are not identical with the conditions indispensable for their utility" (1969, p. liv). Berlin argues that this is "not a merely pedantic distinction" since zealots who free people in the sense of providing them with material goods would downgrade the importance of freedom of choice. "In their zeal to create social and economic conditions in which alone freedom is of genuine value, men tend to forget freedom itself; and if it is remembered, it is liable to be pushed aside to make room for these other values with which the reformers or revolutionaries have become preoccupied" (1969, p. liv).

Macpherson targets this distinction for destruction, contending that it empties liberty of some necessary content. His complaint is that Berlin's negative liberty "does not include access to the means of life and the means of labour, in spite of the fact that that lack of access does diminish negative liberty, that is, does diminish the area in which a man cannot be interfered with." Because Berlin seems to remove access to the means of life and the means of labor from his definition of liberty, Macpherson sees him as removing such "class-imposed denials from the de-

partment of liberty into the department of justice or equality." Unfortunately, as Macpherson sees it, this is some sort of a degeneration into reactionary thinking; Berlin's move "seems to me an unfortunate reversion towards the extreme liberalism of Herbert Spencer" (Macpherson, 1973, p. 102). Projecting guilt by (false) association, Macpherson appeals to our intuitions which suggest that depriving people of food seems to make their formal freedoms empty, which is true enough; but that does not establish an identity between these conditions and liberty. All that Macpherson's argument proves is that the conditions are necessary, which Berlin would not deny. Having a paper and pen is a necessary condition for writing an article; however, providing a paper and pen does not make someone a writer. Other conditions must be met for sufficiency. Neither would feeding people be equivalent to freeing them (except from hunger, which is not a form of political liberation but of liberation from natural forces).

Indeed, providing sufficient material security, health, knowledge, and certain minimums of equality, justice, and mutual confidence is necessary for the exercise of liberty. Still, Berlin argues (1969, p. lv) that providing exactly those things, especially in the name of liberty, can result in a dangerous and disastrous travesty:

> To provide for material needs, for education, for equality and security . . . is not to expand liberty. We live in a world characterized by regimes (both right- and left-wing) which have done, or are seeking to do, precisely this; and when they call it freedom, this can be as great a fraud as the freedom of a pauper who has a legal right to purchase luxuries. Indeed, one of the things that Dostoevsky's celebrated fable of the Grand Inquisitor in *The Brothers Karamazov* is designed to show is precisely that paternalism can provide the conditions of liberty, yet withhold freedom itself.

Macpherson's concern for these material conditions of liberty is laudable; but to portray them as necessary conditions for enjoying liberty, as Berlin does, is not to spurn them. Rather, Berlin is fully aware that "freedom for the wolves has often meant death for the sheep. The blood-stained history of economic individualism and unrestrained capitalist competition does not, I should have thought, today need stressing." Indeed, Berlin argues that there is available a stronger argument than the warm-hearted altruism of Macpherson to condemn these deprivations: they have resulted in "brutal violations of 'negative' liberty—of basic human rights" (1969, p. xlv). Decrying this as an "odious mockery," Berlin has no desire to throw people to the mercy of the market without the protection of rights; however, we must be careful of the reasons which move us to protect others from social injustice. It is better, Berlin would say, to provide people with protection and material goods because they are seen as purposive beings who need these things to seek their own purposes than it is to provide them with material goods because they are seen as dependents who must be taken care of and brought to the true way of living. The danger of paternalism which lurks in demands for welfare is perverse indeed: the goal of pro-

viding the material conditions of liberty may finally subvert liberty itself. Berlin writes (1969, pp. lviii-lix):

> Those who are obsessed by the truth that negative lib-
> erty is worth little without sufficient conditions for its
> active exercise, or without the satisfaction of other hu-
> man aspirations, are liable to minimize its importance,
> to deny it the very title of freedom, to transfer it to
> something that they regard as more precious, and fi-
> nally to forget that without it human life, both social
> and individual, withers away.

The conflict between Macpherson and Berlin, then, centers
around the roles that liberty and material welfare are to
have in fostering human growth. Macpherson fears that
Berlin neglects material welfare and ignores the effects of
class divisions; Macpherson would have us pursue the
goals of material security and harmony. Berlin may even
seem rather hard-hearted alongside Macpherson because
he insists that welfare is not the same as liberty and that
liberty is a more sacred ideal. But Berlin's ideal is not a
state where people are formally free yet starving. Berlin's
position might even be more sensitive to human needs and
shortcomings in that he would not permit the single-
minded pursuit of any one goal, not even Macpherson's
collective material welfare, to dictate to people what they
ought to do with their lives. Thus Macpherson's first objection to Berlin is not convincing: regarding material welfare as a necessary condition for enjoying liberty is not the
same as contending that it should be ignored. It is only a
way of reminding us that the concerns of liberty are also
important to human potential; perhaps they are more important, not in that they are concerned with a higher good
than welfare, but in that they constitute a more basic value.

The second aspect of the disagreement between these two
theorists is substantive and concerns the nature of positive
liberty: is it inherently rationalistic? Where Berlin contends that positive liberty is rooted in a rationalistic view
of the world or of humanity, Macpherson argues that not
all forms of positive liberty are rationalistic. Macpherson
(1973, p. 105) distinguishes among three senses of positive liberty: PL^1 is the basic sense of positive liberty, involving conscious self-direction; PL^2 is a debased form
which imposes rational freedom on those said to be not
fully rational; and PL^3 involves the democratic right to
participate in the sovereign authority. Macpherson begins
his argument by noting that positive liberty is indeed concerned with the individual's ability to develop into a "fully
human being" (p. 105). But, he wants to argue, this is no
concession since the degeneration of doctrines of positive
liberty into rationalistic perversions and denials of liberty
is "due not to the logic of positive liberty, nor to the assumptions of the idealist and rationalist theorists who have
pushed positive liberty, in thought, to positions which have
supported such repulsive extremes. I want to argue now
that it is due rather to a specific failure of liberal theory
. . ." (p. 107). This failure is the failure to see how class
divisions and scarcity give rise to conflict. This liberal error is responsible for the slide from PL^1 to PL^2. Macpherson seems willing to grant Berlin that PL^1 becomes PL^2 if

a series of assumptions is made and quotes Berlin's specification of those assumptions:

> first, that all men have one true purpose, and only one,
> that of rational self-direction; second, that the ends of
> all rational beings must of necessity fit into a single,
> universal, harmonious pattern, which some men may
> be able to discern more clearly than others; third, that
> all conflict, and consequently all tragedy, is due solely
> to the clash of reason with the irrational or the insuffi-
> ciently rational—the immature and underdeveloped ele-
> ments in life—whether individual or communal, and
> that such clashes are, in principle, avoidable, and for
> wholly rational beings impossible; and finally, that
> when all men have been made rational, they will obey
> the rational laws of their own natures, which are one
> and the same in them all, and so be at once wholly
> law-abiding, and wholly free (Macpherson, 1973, p.
> 111; Berlin, 1969, p. 154).

But, contends Macpherson (1973, p. 111), not all versions
of positive liberty need make all these assumptions: "My
point is that the last three assumptions are not needed in
any concept of positive liberty, and are indeed inconsistent
with PL^1." There is a difference, Macpherson writes, between believing (1) that there is some pattern to human
development and (2) that "if the chief impediments to
men's developmental powers were removed . . . there
would emerge not a pattern but a proliferation of many
ways and styles of life, which could not be prescribed and
which would not necessarily conflict" (pp. 111-12).

But Berlin would not be so critical if positive liberty assured that people could develop in a variety of ways; indeed, some de-patterned version of human change and
growth seems close to his heart. For instance, he begins
his essay on J. S. Mill (p. 173) with a quotation from Mill
suggesting the "importance, to man and society, . . . of
giving full freedom to human nature to expand itself in innumerable and conflicting directions." If this were what
positive liberty meant, then Macpherson is right that Berlin would have no reason to oppose it. But the controversy
over the nature of positive liberty is real and involves the
possibility that, as we develop in diverse directions, conflict might cease. Berlin, following Mill, believes that we
will grow in various and conflicting directions; Macpherson feels that these directions will not conflict. The error
in liberal theory to which Macpherson refers centers
around the unwillingness to see that conflict begins with
scarcity and class divisions. Where Berlin sees the conflict
between values to be a necessary truth about the human
situation, Macpherson sees this conflict as contingent upon
scarcity and the divisions between people based on exploitation.

Macpherson (p. 113) seems ready to concede that the conflicts between values which we experience are real, that
opposite views can be "maintained by men (and groups)
of equally good will. That is what makes their perpetual
presence plausible." But this concession is nothing more
than a claim that such conflicts are born in class-divided
societies based on a postulate of infinite desirousness (p.

113). "But how many of those conflicts would remain endemic in a society without class conflict and without scarcity?" Pessimistic liberals like Berlin err; Macpherson writes (p. 113), "We do not have to go to the opposite extreme of a brainwashed utopia to envisage a society where diverse, genuinely human (not artificially contrived) desires can be simultaneously fulfilled." We must conclude, then, that their disagreement is about human nature, especially about what we can be: Macpherson feels that our ultimate values can be rationally harmonized as we develop, while Berlin is convinced that human dignity would have to be sacrificed to overcome the diversity of human ends. Given his assumption of the feasibility of a harmonious society based on people made rational, Macpherson contends that the conflicts of values need not be perpetual; if the conflict of values is not perpetual, then repressive monism is not necessary to achieve positive liberty—we need only be freed to develop. This leads Macpherson to conclude (p. 113) that "the monism which is the essence of PL^2 [the rationalist perversion] is not entailed by PL^1 [rational self-direction]." In other words, in a world where values do not conflict, no rationalist monism is needed to endorse positive liberty, and there is no need to worry about the slip from PL^1 to PL^2.

Or is there? The problem with Macpherson's argument is that the rationalist assumption is not needed at this point in the argument because it had been smuggled in earlier; we must back-track a bit to detect the point of entrance. Both theorists seem to agree that ours is not a world in which all values are compatible. Berlin argues that one must make rationalist assumptions about this world or about human development to make an argument for positive liberty. But in speaking of a world or a society in which values do not conflict, Macpherson makes just such an assumption of an order to human development which renders consonant all of the things (fully developed, rational) people desire. One may not have to go to the extreme of a brainwashed utopia to make this assumption, but one does have to cross a threshhold into rationalism.

Logically, the difficulty with Macpherson's critique is that, in his belief in men's developmental powers, Macpherson links together two conjuncts which are contradictory. Clearly, he is right in asserting (pp. 111-12) that there is a difference between believing that there is a pattern into which all rational beings fit and believing that "if the chief impediments to men's developmental powers were removed, if, that is to say, they were allowed equal freedom, there would emerge not a pattern but a proliferation of ways and styles of life which could not be prescribed and which would not necessarily conflict." While this second assumption is more attractive, it is also self-contradictory: the assumption that there would be no pattern to human development so that ways of life could not be prescribed opposes the assumption that the ways of life into which we would develop need not conflict. If we assume (as both Macpherson and Berlin believe) that human values now conflict, then there are only two possibilities for human development: either we will continue to develop in the directions in which our conflicting values pull us, so that we develop in conflicting directions; or we must develop according to some pattern which will harmonize our rational desires so that human ends need not conflict in the future. To assume that the conflicts which are a necessary part of our current existence need not be a part of some more developed existence is to see a pattern at work in human development; to see an end of the conflict between our desires is to see us developing toward some more rational existence in which there could be a rational accommodation of values. Given Macpherson's diagnosis of the problem, the prescription is simple: create a new society without scarcity and class divisions and our rational desires will no longer conflict. The problem, as any opponent of rationalism would see it, is that in this end-state after scarcity and classes, any agent whose desires do conflict with some one else's rational desires cannot be rational, cannot fit the pattern. Such an agent must be less developed, a remnant of the bourgeois period, still under the control of irrational impulses. Since this person does not fit the new pattern in which we have been liberated from scarcity and social divisions, this individual with irrational and conflictual desires is also to be "liberated." The rationalist perversion of liberty remains: in the name of freeing people, we (the benevolent reformers of Macpherson) must coerce them to live as we think fit.

Finally, we must again note that the disagreement separating these theorists is substantive: the question is simply whether or not positive liberty need be rationalistic in depending upon some assumption of a pattern to the cosmos or to human development. Macpherson denies that positive liberty need be rationalistic and advocates a concern for this notion of freedom with a view to eliminating scarcity and class conflict so that we might develop to a stage where all of the various manifestations of human capacities need not conflict with one another. However, we must conclude that Macpherson's conception of positive liberty, despite his efforts to avoid the errors of rationalism, finally rests on the assumption that humanity will develop so that all rational human desires are harmonized.

We might conclude, then, that since Macpherson sees the conflict of values as ephemeral and rooted in scarcity and class divisions while Berlin views this conflict between the things which people desire as a perpetual and necessary condition of human existence, the two would disagree about the nature of politics. Berlin would have to view politics as some form of human interaction based on a recognition that we are capable of unique and conflicting ends which are legitimate. Thus negative liberty acquires its distinctly political value because of the possibility that some people, captured by their vision of the good, would attempt to impose their view of what is good upon other recalcitrant persons, denying the validity of their ends and purposes and so degrading them. Hence the conflict of values, coupled with our metaphysical compulsion to unify our world, yields the need for a liberal society where persons are protected from such impositions by others.

By contrast, from Macpherson's point of view, Berlin's liberal kind of politics exists in this vale of tears where we now live, in the midst of scarcity and divisions; but armed with a vision of human perfectibility, he believes that we will move beyond this pitiful situation, transcending (liberal) politics. While politics is necessary in the present world, ridden as it is with strife, it has meant the creation of institutions which enable some to bend the wills of others (and if not their wills, at least their energies) to their own purposes. Thus, politics is inevitably tied up with the conflict between classes and with scarcity. Macpherson's goal comes to be the removal of the conflict-generating elements in society. Once the conflicts are eliminated, Macpherson's command economy would involve the citizens in a lot of democratic participation in the development of the economic plan; but would this participation be political? Berlin would suggest that decisions to be made about the plan would not be about human ends; all ends would have been harmonized. Rather, the decisions to be made would concern means to rational ends, and so would be technical instead of political: there would be no politics in a world with no scarcity and no divisions. Politics is necessary not because we are weak and irrational; rather, politics is needed because human dignity entails that each person is capable of his or her own ends, which no authority can dictate.

FREEDOM HYPER-POLITICIZED: PARTICIPATION AS "THE GOOD OF MAN"

Curiously, where Macpherson sees Berlin as making the liberal error of viewing politics (and the value conflicts on which it is based) as a necessary and eternal part of the human condition when it is contingent upon class divisions and scarcity, Crick criticizes Berlin for not including enough politics in his conception of freedom. In his "Freedom as Politics," Crick (1967, p. 211) argues that politics, seen as the free activity of men in the *polis,* is missing in Berlin's too-negative conception of liberty. "Negative liberty is the wrong end of the right stick: it only defines what we seek to avoid harming in others while we act more positively ourselves." Enamored of the virtues of the ancient republic, Crick rejects the "liberal belief that all power is inherently evil." Returning to an ideal of "freedom as citizenship," Crick is less concerned with the individual and his or her rights against the state, and focuses instead on the need for republican virtues, "on those conditions which were necessary to operate successfully the kind of state characterized as republican" (p. 211).

Crick's critique of Berlin is respectful and friendly. He notes (p. 212) that the gap between Berlin and him is not that great: "Here is my whole difference with Berlin—perhaps in some circumstances a slight one: between being able to choose and actually choosing." He believes that Berlin confines negative liberty too narrowly, and "while he has shown a great skill in defending the nymph of liberty from abuse, he has been unnecessarily modest in denying her exercise and is at fault in letting her languish with so little to do" (p. 195). In Crick's eyes, whatever

Berlin's negative liberty is, it is *not political liberty.* Dedicated as he is to the republican ideal, he is not willing to countenance as a political liberty any liberty which does not confer upon a citizen the capacity to participate in the governance of the community. In the ancient *polis,* those who had political liberties were those who had a voice in the government. No others had liberty in the political sense. From Crick's perspective, Berlin seems to separate freedom from any republican notion of virtue: the problem is that Berlin seems to ignore "any possible social or political context" (p. 198).

Crick is worried that Berlin's "freedom" is concerned with the absence of constraint and not with the capacities for self-rule which mark a republic. For him, people must be political actors; it is not enough that they are *free to act; they must act* if they are to be free citizens. Failure to act subverts the goal of republican citizenship. In particular, they must act as responsible citizens of a republic. Crick writes that what "is missing in Berlin's analysis, odd though it may sound to say so, is any analysis of the link between freedom and political action—a typically liberal lack . . ." (p. 199). The problem, as Crick sees it, is that if people are free as Berlin would like them to be, free to choose their own responsibilities and ends, they may even be free from the responsibilities of the *polis:* "Freedom is being left alone from politics," writes Crick of Berlin's liberty, and not accepting this, asks, "Is it?" (p. 199). Because Berlin is concerned with freeing people from constraints and not with integrating them into communities where they could become citizens, Crick (p. 198) finds a negatively free person to be isolated. "I would call such a condition simply 'isolation' or more often 'loneliness'—put more sympathetically, 'splendid isolation' or 'the self-reliant individual'. . . ." Such people need not possess the proper dedication to republican virtues, and Crick sees this as a serious problem. Crick wants to free us for the purpose of becoming good, active citizens.

In his need to free persons to behave responsibly as citizens, Crick worries, as he notes that Erich Fromm and Dostoyevsky had worried, that we might abdicate our responsibilities, turning to some "expert" who assumes those responsibilities for us (p. 196). The responsibility for one's own fate becomes so large a burden that we seem ready to surrender that freedom for some security. Citing the Germans who mistakenly voted Hitler into power, Crick asks if they were still free at the moment of voting. Answering the question as he thinks Berlin must, basing it on his view of liberty as the absence of constraints, Crick depicts them as free at that moment—their votes were not coerced. Here, Crick becomes restive: "Isn't it, in fact, more *informative and explanatory* to say that such people are rejecting freedom—often very consciously—rather than exhibiting it?" (p. 198).

Is Berlin committed to viewing such voters as free? Although Berlin is often less than clear about whether he is talking about an individual's being free for making some one particular decision or about a social arrangement in which all members have the maximum freedom for making such decisions, there can be little doubt that he sees negative liberty as a social virtue and that our obligations with respect to it are to seek social arrangements in which it would be fostered. Negative liberty is the ideal of a liberal tradition which Berlin is defending; noting that democracies can cease to be free in this sense, Berlin asks what would make a society free. He responds (1969, p. 165) that "no society is free unless it is governed by at any rate two interrelated principles; first, that no power, but only rights, can be regarded as absolute, so that all men, whatever power governs them, have an absolute right to refuse to behave inhumanly; and second, that there are frontiers, not artifically drawn, within which men should be inviolable. . . ." Voting one's freedom away, like selling oneself into slavery then, even if not a coerced action, is in no way the free action of a free person in a free society. Freeing people to throw their liberties away is not what liberalism is all about.

Taking both Crick and Fromm together as advocates of the full life, Berlin declares (1969, pp. xlii-xliii) that they simply misunderstand the nature of negative liberty: "The freedom of which I speak is opportunity for action, rather than action itself. If, although I enjoy the right to walk through open doors, I prefer not to do so, but to sit still and vegetate, I am not thereby rendered less free." Freedom is not acting, but being situated where one has the possibility of acting. What separates Berlin from Crick and Fromm is their emphasis on the full life, on the realization of certain potentialities which require self-assertion. Berlin is sympathetic with their ideal, but insists that it is something other than liberty and that liberty is more important. Granting that "apathetic neglect of various avenues to a more vigorous and generous life" may be condemned on other grounds, Berlin has no objection to fostering such a vision of the full life, so long as such apathy is not "considered incompatible with the notion of being free." Berlin's misgiving is that neither Crick nor Fromm would see the issue this way: "But I fear that Dr. Fromm would consider such abdication as a symptom of lack of integration, which for him is indispensable to— perhaps identical with—freedom. . . ." Similarly, Crick, with his dedication to the republican ideal, "would look upon such apathy as too inert and timid to deserve to be called freedom" (1969, p. xliii). Berlin fears that both Crick and Fromm would be willing to coerce us to fit their ideals of assertive activity.

Berlin concludes his response to Crick and Fromm by conceding that he finds "the ideal advocated by these champions of the full life sympathetic; but to identify it with freedom seems to me conflation of two values. To say that freedom is activity as such is to make the term cover too much; it tends to obscure and dilute the central issue—the right and freedom to act—about which men have argued and fought during almost the whole of recorded history" (1969, p. xliii). This vision of the full life is one of many values which Berlin sees as ultimate and in conflict with liberty. While we must take it into account, we must not permit it to overshadow liberty.

Despite the overwhelming dissimilarities between their beliefs, Macpherson and Crick agree in criticizing Berlin for not providing enough participation. Is participation necessary for human freedom? Berlin contends that it is not, although participation is certainly conducive to freedom. From a logical point of view, there is no *necessary* connection between participation in democratic or republican politics and the liberal arrangement of society. Even kings and conquerors can provide people with an area in which they are free to choose for themselves. As a matter of fact, Berlin writes (1969, p. 130), the politics of participation does help to secure the liberty he defends, and that may provide a justification for this sort of political arrangement. However, that such politics would secure liberty is not a logical claim, but an empirical one.

There is a fundamental difference about the nature of politics, then, which leads Crick to regret the absence of (a certain kind of) politics in Berlin's account of freedom. When Crick accuses Berlin of ignoring the political contexts of freedom, of constructing a notion of liberty which lacks a political dimension, his point is that politics of a certain (republican and participatory) kind is not given proper emphasis. Crick (1967, p. 211) is thus advocating a different hierarchy of ideals, in which the participation of the citizen in the *polis* becomes of paramount importance. "I have really returned to a view of 'freedom as citizenship' which was current in the late seventeenth century and throughout the eighteenth, but which hardly survived the mid-nineteenth century. . . . This viewpoint did not center so much on individual rights against the state, but on those conditions which were necessary to operate successfully the kind of state characterized as republican." For Berlin this would entail coercing people to participate; and while this may be justified on other grounds, it is not political liberation.

A NON-RATIONALIST PERSPECTIVE ON FREEDOM AND POLITICS

But in ignoring this republican ideal of political participation, Berlin is not ignoring politics, nor is his free individual in a state of splendid isolation. Rather, Berlin has a different conception of politics which is born of the concern he shares with Oakeshott about rationalism in politics. There is a conception of politics as civil interaction, or civil conversation, common to Oakeshott and Berlin. Both are concerned with politics as public deliberation about arranging society. From their perspective, political activity becomes "a pursuit of intimations" (Oakeshott, 1962, p. 127). Political questions are not simply of the form "how should I vote?" but also of the form "how shall we live?"

On the republican version, politics becomes tied to policy and assumes that the basic structure of the society and the polity are already established and settled. On the second version, the classic liberal view of Oakeshott and Berlin, politics is as much concerned with the conditions under which a republic (or any polity) can pursue certain policies. On the first version, constitutionalism is not a political but a legal topic; on the second version, the issues of constitutionalism are paradigmatically political. It is this conception of politics which leads Berlin to view questions of negative liberty as of paramount importance. It also inspired Oakeshott's expression of the need for civility in those interactions between *cives* which he calls "civic conversation." Thus Oakeshott writes that politics "is concerned with an imagined and wished-for condition of *respublica*, a condition in some respect different from its current condition and alleged to be more desirable. It is deliberation designed to specify and find reasons for, and action designed to promote the change from the one to the other" (1975, p. 168). It is this concern with the conditions of sociality which characterizes the politics of Oakeshott (1975, p. 163): "In considering the engagement to deliberate the conditions prescribed in *respublica* in terms, not of their authority but of their desirability, to imagine them different from what they are and to undertake or to resist their alteration, we are concerned with politics properly speaking."

Common to both theorists is not only a conception of the sorts of questions which are political but also an opposition to conceiving of political questions as automatically answerable by reference to a rationalist structure of the cosmos and to some transcendent purpose deriving from that view of the universe; in short, both oppose rationalism as it may corrupt politics, conceived as deliberations about the structure of society. For Oakeshott, politics (as the pursuit of intimations in a tradition) is neither so emotive as to be based on an irrational cohesion of persons (irrationalism) nor is it the drawing of implications from axiomatic assumptions (rationalism)—it is tied neither to reason nor to its negation. Both could be dangerous; but the greater danger is posed by those who see politics as the technical exploration of the implications of some master plan because they misunderstand the nature of human existence and of politics: politics is not an endeavor infused with some set and agreed-upon *telos*, but is interaction among people with conflicting purposes. Hence, the state is not a telic or purposive entity (Oakeshott, 1975). Efforts to transform the state into an enterprise association, aimed at achieving some greater good for us, is predicated upon an assumption about politics which is contrary to fact. It should not surprise us, then, if the results are a travesty of our ideals. Politics needs no other purpose than the protection and maintenance of civility among people.

Actually, although Berlin would agree that an implication of this is that political liberty needs no other purpose than the protection of human dignity in choices, he would not go quite so far as Oakeshott on this issue. For Berlin, a government may legitimately pursue other goals, and may even have some goal like fostering the welfare of its members. But these goals are not the same as liberty and no increment in these other values offsets the loss of fundamental liberties. But the effect of both theories is the same: the pursuit of goals by any government is viewed with suspicion, since these other ends may conflict with the basic

liberties necessary for free and independent persons. Both Berlin and Oakeshott oppose teleological approaches to politics because of their opposition to the paternalist implications and the rationalist foundations of such politics.

CONCLUSION: POLITICAL OBLIGATION AND THE CONFLICTING ENDS OF LIFE

All of Berlin's critics considered here would de-politicize the issue of human liberty, choosing to ignore the questions of who is to decide on the ends for which we are to live. If asked the question of what makes life worth living, they would all entertain the possibility that there might be one substantive answer which is rationally and logically sound. MacCallum treats the issue as logical and not political, assuming that logic requires that all forms of freedom involve some vision of a higher good. Macpherson advocates the goal of harmony of ends, to be achieved by creating a society without scarcity and class divisions. And Crick would use participation to bring all people closer to his ideal of full human development. By contrast, Berlin would respond that each person must answer this question for him/herself. Yet even Berlin confuses the issue by treating negative liberty as one among many equally ultimate goods; if liberty is simply one among many ends, how can one argue that it is a truer and more humane ideal than any other?

We must conclude then that Berlin's opposition to rationalism makes him too skeptical. His contribution to a discussion of the political dimensions of liberty is that we must not give in to the metaphysical impulse to try to impose our visions of the highest good upon others. But his view is limited in that it cannot provide the grounds for an obligation to tolerate others; if there are no grounds for ranking liberty as either a higher or a more basic good than any other, then we would have no obligation to meet its requirements if we were to become obsessed with some other value. If all of the ends are equally ultimate, then why not commit ourselves to some one or another even if it should require a sacrifice of some liberty? Skepticism results in too weak a defense of liberty.

The ethical and psychological foundations of liberalism are more rationalistic than Berlin would permit, and must be so. The tradition of Natural Rights is not totally mistaken in its defense of liberty; our human nature requires that we recognize certain rights. If we are to defend liberty as a true and humane ideal, there must be truths about humanity and our values which require that liberty. It is not really the case that Berlin would see all ways of life as equally stable and viable; a liberal society would better suit his vision of human purposiveness than would a slave society. Berlin correctly directs our attention away from architectonic visions of politics. The timber of human nature is crooked since we are metaphysically compulsive creatures, driven by a need to detect a pattern to things. Once possessed of this pattern, we seek to impose it upon other people. Hence, negative liberty is a necessity if human dignity, rooted in the capacity to choose one's goals for oneself, is to be protected. Paradoxically, the very plurality of competing and equally ultimate values seems to entail that one of these values (negative liberty) is in some way more important than some others. It seems that Berlin has captured the truth of two conflicting intuitions about human moral experience: we live for a variety of conflicting purposes, yet we must structure our societies so that we are protected in the choices of these purposes. These ethical intuitions can only be rendered consonant by viewing negative liberty as a basal value.

Despite his opposition to transformational psychologies, then, Berlin's vision of human moral psychology must be developmental: people must secure the base of liberty which guarantees that their actions are truly their own before moving on to the heights. Without the security of this base, the other things we value—excellence, equality, nobility, fraternity—become elusive ideals which remain beyond the reach of human beings. These higher ideals may well be conflicting; all that is needed for social life is agreement upon the requirements of civility which constitute the base. Of course, this is not to say that it is logically impossible for human beings to develop higher values in the absence of lower values; the difficulty confronted in such an effort is not logical but psychological in nature. In other words, it certainly is possible for a given society to proceed as though it were not the case that human beings develop in a secure context, but such a society (even though it may achieve some things of value) would not remain stable because human needs would not be met. In fact, Berlin seems to recognize and concede the logical force of this claim when he writes that liberty is not simply license nor is it easily achieved, "but without it all things wither" (1955, pp. 287-88). Or somewhat differently, as J. Roland Pennock put it (1979, p. 137), this view of human nature as developing once certain basal conditions have been met, while not universally accepted, at the very least "suggests in a general way how liberty can be of primary importance, a primary value, and yet not be a major concern of men under all conditions." Certainly liberty is of special importance, yet we cannot say that it is the highest or the most important of the values. Liberty, then, is a true and humane ideal because it provides people with the psychic security that their actions are their own, and the assurance that no one else will be able to dictate their goals to them. This is the foundation upon which we erect the structure of our moral obligations, the basis on which we require things of one another.

Thus, despite Berlin's compelling vision of the dangers of rationalism, we must recognize that both the rationalists and their opponents are right in that they each detect one dimension of politics. Clearly, there are some eternal truths (say, about human purposiveness) which require that we respect other persons as beings with their own lives to live. Equally clearly, the recognition of such political and moral obligations does not necessarily entail that all people have an obligation to seek some one, rationally specified, goal. Rather, what is distinctly human about us is that we are each uniquely capable of living for our own purposes.

There is no one goal towards which all people should be moving; our political obligations are not defined by our commitment to the highest good, to be discovered by all rational agents. Rather, we require of each other a certain basic minimum of humanity and civility; beyond that base, we should be moving in a variety of directions, since to do otherwise is to deny our humanity.

References

Berlin, Sir Isaiah (1953). *The Hedgehog and the Fox.* New York: Simon & Schuster.

———. (1955). "Montesquieu." *Proceedings of the British Academy* 41: 267-96.

———. (1956). "A Marvellous Decade IV: Herzen and the Grand Inquisitors." *Encounter* 6, No. 5: 20-34.

———. (1962). "Does Political Theory Still Exist?" In Peter Laslett and W. G. Runciman (eds.), *Philosophy, Politics, and Society,* 2nd Ser., Oxford: Blackwell.

———. (1971). "The Question of Machiavelli." *New York Review of Books,* 4 November 1971, pp. 20-32.

Crick, Bernard (1967). "Freedom as Politics." In Peter Laslett and W. G. Runciman (eds.), *Philosophy, Politics, and Society,* 3rd Ser. New York: Barnes and Noble.

Fried, Charles (1970). *The Anatomy of Values: Problems of Personal and Social Choice.* Cambridge, Mass.: Harvard University Press.

Hartmann, Nicolai (1932). *Ethics.* Translated by Stanton Coit. New York: Macmillan.

MacCallum, Gerald (1972). "Negative and Positive Freedom." In Peter Laslett and W. G. Runciman (eds.), *Philosophy, Politics, and Society,* 4th Ser. Oxford: Blackwell.

Macpherson, C. B. (1973). *Democratic Theory: Essays in Retrieval.* Oxford: Clarendon Press.

Oakeshott, Michael (1962). *Rationalism in Politics and Other Essays.* New York: Basic Books.

———. (1975). *On Human Conduct.* Oxford: Clarendon Press.

Pennock, J. Roland (1979). *Democratic Political Theory.* Princeton, N.J.: Princeton University Press.

Sidney Hook (essay date 1980)

SOURCE: "Isaiah Berlin's Enlightenment," in *Commentary,* Vol. 69, No. 5, May, 1980, pp. 61-4.

[*In the following essay, Hook reflects on Berlin's observations on Enlightenment and anti-Enlightenment thought.*]

Isaiah Berlin's third volume of collected essays, ***Against the Current,*** falls within the area of historical sociology This is the last of the twelve divisions in which Arthur O.

Lovejoy, the father of the academic discipline known as the history of ideas, charted the interests and themes customarily explored under that rubric. The field is concerned, among other things, with the ruling ideas, the climates of opinion, the underlying intellectual currents and tendencies that affect historical and social development.

As these and other writings attest, Isaiah Berlin has emerged since Lovejoy's death as the most distinguished explorer of a vast area of thought in the humanities and social studies. The intellectual styles of Lovejoy and Berlin, however, are quite different and achieve their respective effects of excellence in different ways. Lovejoy was concerned with the intricate structure of argument and had an unerring eye for the weaknesses, breaks, and lacunae in the logical connecting tissues. Biographical details about the thinkers he discussed were at best peripheral: one gets little sense of the flavor and texture of their personalities. Berlin, on the other hand, relates the ideas of his protagonists more closely to their times and lives. Without neglecting the main articulation of the arguments, he presents them more dramatically. The history of thought in his quick-paced exposition unrolls as an exciting battlefield of ideas.

Berlin's special virtue lies in the skill and imaginative power with which he restates the positions of the thinkers he expounds. This sympathetic insight and persuasiveness sometimes make more credible than the original texts themselves how and why ideas that at first sight appear odd or bizarre seem plausible and valid to those who hold them. The result is that Berlin's essays possess a compelling interest; they convey a sense of the *actualité* of the past to our own times and conditions.

The title of this collection expresses the underlying theme of most of the essays. They are devoted to thinkers and movements that contest the central ideas of the Enlightenment and beyond that of the entire Western, rational, scientific tradition. Among these Enlightenment ideas are the views that "human nature was fundamentally the same in all times and places," and that "one set of universal and unalterable principles governed the world [of] inanimate and animate nature, facts and events, means and ends, private life and public, all societies, epochs, and civilizations. . . ." These dogmas of the Enlightenment were already challenged in the early 18th century by Vico in his criticism of the Cartesian presursors of scientific rationalism. Even earlier, Machiavelli, too, had rejected the foundation stone of pious rationalist moral faith.

Berlin summarizes the more frontal attack on the assumptions and presuppositions of the Enlightenment launched by German thinkers like Hamann, Herder, Fichte, and Schelling with able assists from Burke, Rousseau, and de Maistre. What they rejected in the philosophy of the Enlightenment was its emphasis on the universal, the objective, the cosmopolitan, and the rule of law. They contended that these abstractions could not do justice to the particular, the historical, the parochial, the wisdom of the idiomatic, the spontaneity of the creative mind, the ineffability and mystery of the individual as well as the national spirit. These are the concrete modes in which we encounter experience.

The counter-theses to the doctrines of the Enlightenment and the Western scientific tradition as applied to human affairs are stated by Berlin in chapters on "The Counter Enlightenment," "The Divorce Between the Sciences and the Humanities," "Nationalism," and supplemented by chapters on Vico, Machiavelli, Hume, Hess, Herzen, Sorel, Marx, and Disraeli.

In the chapters devoted to Vico, Berlin presents an eloquent case for the view that there are two radically different approaches to the world represented by the tradition of the sciences and that of the humanities. The first takes as its model the basic pattern of inquiry of the natural sciences, which it regards as applicable to all disciplines and areas of experience. The second is concerned with the values that are central to culture and history, an area in which there is no cumulative growth of knowledge but only growth of insight and understanding won by "informed imagination" and intuition.

Although the thought of the Enlightenment is a preeminent illustration of the scientific approach, Berlin attributes this mode of thought to the entire intellectual tradition of the West from Greek antiquity to contemporary positivism. He dates the first formulation of the notion that we are here confronted with two irreducibly different approaches to the world to Vico, the Neapolitan philosopher. Berlin himself firmly shares Vico's view. He is familiar with the enormous difficulties this dualistic approach to knowledge faces—for example, how can we test the truth of an insight or attribution of motives without ultimate reference to behavior?—but they are not here explored.

Another thinker who preceded the Enlightenment, the implication of whose doctrines, according to Berlin, shattered a cardinal principle not only of the Enlightenment but of the entire Western world since the fall of Rome, was Machiavelli. To him Berlin devotes a masterly essay based on a scholarship so comprehensive as almost to terrify the reader into a state of humility. In it he argues that the true originality of Machiavelli is his recognition that there exist at least two sets of ultimate virtues or moral systems that are incompatible in principle and irreconcilable in practice, and that therefore there is no answer or even sense to the question of what, morally and politically, is the best way of life. Berlin contends that it is a vague sense of this frightening truth that inspires the horror of so many of Machiavelli's readers, as much as their revulsion at what he specifically condones and prescribes in the behavior of his Prince. For on Berlin's view, Machiavelli takes for granted, as the supreme end, the existence and health of "a state conceived after the analogy of Periclean Athens, or Sparta but above all the Roman Republic," whose vital functioning requires the deceptions and murders and the other evil things that we associate with Machiavellian policy.

It is perhaps presumptuous for someone who can make no claim to scholarly competence in this field to raise a question about the validity of these views. But a minor difficulty initially presents itself. If what Machiavelli is doing is glorifying the ethos of ancient Greece and Rome by explicating the rationale of its statecraft in relation to its values, why is it that we do not experience the same horror and revulsion when we immerse ourselves in the study of the culture of antiquity as when we read Machiavelli's advice to those who would rule the state? And granting our disapproval of slavery, and the mitigating influence of Christianity, how do we account for the prolonged and systematic inculcation of the values of classical civilization in the educational systems of Western Europe, often accompanied by dispraise of Machiavelli, its troubador?

What is objectionable in Machiavelli's outlook is not the attitude expressed in the famous paragraph of *The Discourses* in which he writes: "When it is absolutely a question of the safety of one's country, there must be no consideration of just or unjust, of merciful or cruel, of praiseworthy or disgraceful; instead, setting aside every scruple, one must follow to the utmost any plan that will save her life and keep her liberty." Italicize the word "absolutely" and we have a position which many of Machiavelli's critics would share when confronting an enemy that would extinguish national existence and freedom. This position does not deny that evil things must sometimes be done—after all, injustices and cruelties are unavoidable in any war; it justifies them on the ground that they are necessary to avoid greater evils.

The impression of the reader of this passage and of *The Prince,* however, is not that this attitude was valid in Machiavelli's eyes only in exceptional circumstances or in extreme situations but, as Berlin himself insists, in normal everyday life. The result is the impression that Machiavelli is advocating terror *en permanence,* the breakdown of all norms of legality, at any real or imaginary threat to the political order. If the Prince regards the country as always in a critical, desperate condition, it is always in a state of incipient or actual civil war. No community whose rulers so conceived its condition could sustain itself except by a barbarous tyranny certain to destroy republican liberties. J. N. Figgis, whose view Berlin mentions only to dismiss it out of hand, seems to me to be perfectly correct in asserting that to adopt these procedures as a rule, as a mode of normal life, rather than when it is truly a question of the actual safety and survival of the lives and freedoms of the citizens of the community, is to suspend "the *habeas corpus* acts of the whole human race."

But the correctness of Berlin's reading of Machiavelli's intent or of the reasons for posterity's shocked rejection of his counsel has no bearing on the validity of what Berlin regards as Machiavelli's "cardinal achievement." This is to have brought home in vivid fashion the disturbing truth "that ends equally ultimate, equally sacred, may contradict each other, that entire systems of value may come into collision without possibility of rational arbitration, and

that not merely in exceptional circumstances . . . but (this was surely new) as part of the normal human situation." This truth is not as new with Machiavelli as Berlin suggests. Intimations of it are to be found in Greek thought and even in such religious thinkers as Augustine and Pascal. Every form of naturalism is committed to some variant of it.

Most human beings (except hopeless fanatics) have plural and, taken in specific contexts, conflicting ends in life. In our own moral economy we mediate these conflicts by assessing the consequences of alternative actions on the whole constellation of values that are relevant to the problem at hand and selecting what promises to have the most prosperous issue with the least costs. *But there are always costs.* The phenomenology of the moral experience reveals that our starting point is always a conflict between the good and the good (or the right and the right).

The graver and more complex problems, of course, are those that arise on an interpersonal and intercultural level. And I summarize a position that would require a volume to do justice to by saying that the possibility of developing a common morality depends upon our finding a shared interest on which we can either build or, despite basic differences, live and let live. In the absence of a shared interest, even if it is no more than the desire for peace or a tolerance for what is radically incommensurable, war may result. One may be convinced that this view is true and yet remain unpersuaded that Machiavelli implicitly held it or that it "follows from the contrasts he draws between the conduct he admires and that which he condemns." The civic virtues of Athens and Rome would never have emerged had the conduct Machiavelli admired become the norm and rule of daily life. Nor, I suspect, would the society resulting from this permanent terror have been one in which he himself would have wanted to live.

The chapters on Moses Hess and Disraeli and Marx concern themselves not so much with thinkers who are critics of the Enlightenment as with the "search for identity" occasioned by the consequences of the Enlightenment for the Jews of Western Europe. The essay on Hess is not only a sympathetic exposition of Hess's ideas but a tribute to him as a human being of singular moral purity and who, with respect to the position and future of European Jewry, was uncannily perceptive. It does something to redress the incomplete and patronizing treatment of Hess by those, including this reviewer, who in the past have evaluated Hess's contributions only in the light of their relation to Marxism and ignored his remarkable anticipations of the case for Zionism. History has vindicated Hess's insight that socialism as a movement owes its persistent renewals more to its ethical appeal than to economic interests.

Although Berlin disclaims the role of a psychologist, in his fascinating chapter on **"Disraeli, Marx, and the Search for Identity"** he offers an explanation for Disraeli's proud and inflated consciousness of himself as a Jew and as a descendant of the Jewish aristocracy of King Solomon's time, and for Marx's systematic dispraise of Judaism and anti-Semitic remarks about Jews, in terms of their respective experience as outsiders of their communities. More specifically, he attributes their divergent views and emotional judgments about Jews to a consuming desire to be different from what the conventional prejudice about Jews assumed them to be, to escape from the constraints, discriminations, and social punishments that were visited on Jews, and to the "self-hatred and self-contempt" bred among those who despite themselves secretly wish to belong to the favored groups that despise them. In Disraeli's case this led to the aristocratic elite with whom he identified; in Marx's case to the espousal of the cause of the proletariat. Berlin maintains that the psychological need to overcome the taint of their origins was largely at the root of Disraeli's hostility to the methods of scientific inquiry and of Marx's faith in his dialectical teleology.

The chapter reads with the gripping plausibility of a well-written novel. But some questions emerge to break the spell it weaves. Except for the element of absurd exaggeration both in Disraeli's apotheosis of the Jews and in Marx's denunciation of them, what evidence exists that either was motivated by a compelling desire to transcend his origins? Surely not all Jews to whom Orthodoxy was no longer credible, or who were nurtured in a secular environment, were impelled to seek a new identity? Or are we to infer the phenomenon of self-hatred as an inescapable consequence of anti-Semitism?

"What does seem clear," Berlin writes, "is that Marx was a man of strong will and decisive action, who decided once and for all to destroy within himself the source of the doubts, uneasiness, and self-questioning which tended to torment men like Börne, Heine, Lassalle, and a good many others including the founders of Reform Judaism. . . ." But in all the voluminous writings of Marx there is not a line to indicate that Marx had any doubts, uneasiness, and self-questioning about himself as a Jew. As for Disraeli, Berlin quotes him as saying: "Fancy calling a fellow an adventurer when his ancestors were on intimate terms with the Queen of Sheba. . . ." Whatever else this signifies, it is not "self-hatred."

The subtitle of Berlin's concluding chapter on nationalism is **"Past Neglect and Present Power."** In it he reveals that Marx was not alone in misconstruing the significance and enduring influence of nationalism. He maintains that no one anticipated that nationalism would exert the powerful influence it has had in the last third of our century. By nationalism he means not national sentiment, not xenophobia, not patriotism conceived in Santayana's phrase as "piety for the sources of one's being" which includes love of country and pride of ancestry. He defines it, rather, as a complex sentiment consisting of four elements: "belief in the overriding need to belong to a nation; in the organic relationships of all the elements that constitute a nation; with value of our own simply because it is ours; and, finally, faced by rival contenders for authority or loyalty, the supremacy of its claims."

I would modify this somewhat by suggesting that the first element is not the belief in the overriding need to belong to *a* nation but to *this* nation (an individual prepared to transfer his allegiance from one nation to another cannot be considered a nationalist). Further, the belief in the organic nature of culture and the loyalty to our nation because it is our own, like the love of our children and parents because they are our own, is closer to what is ordinarily regarded as patriotism than to modern nationalism. It is Berlin's fourth ingredient—the belief in the supremacy of one's nation *über Alles* when conflicts or difficulties with other nations arise—which makes the decisive difference. No one seems able to explain why and how legitimate patriotic feeling becomes transformed into chauvinism or jingoism or whatever name we give to fanatical nationalism; why the virus of nationalism sometimes gets out of hand and results in a kind of self-infection. Minority peoples in identifiable areas of large sovereign states get bitten by the nationalist bug and seek their future in a revival of the glories and myths of their past. Malaysia rather than Switzerland threatens to be the paradigm for multiracial or ethnic nations of our time.

Thomas Masaryk once asserted that the only thing that would ever unite the nations of the earth and abate the raging fever of nationalism would be a threat to their survival from denizens of outer space. And history shows that the necessity of struggling against a common enemy is a unifying force. But not always. Churchill's offer to France of a national union when Hitler was in the ascendancy was not accepted. And explain it as one will, the threat of Communism to Western Europe has so far not led to an impressive degree of cooperation and willingness to sacrifice, or to evanescence of fanatical nationalisms.

Why should it be so difficult for a good German or good Frenchman to be a good European, or for a good European to be a citizen of the world? Do not human beings have reasonable grounds for believing that what they have in common, when a conflict arises, is more important than what divides them? The crucial element that is too often missing is this desire to seek reasonable grounds.

Aside from what may be said by way of comment on Berlin's treatment of individual thinkers, there remains the larger issue of the conflict between the Enlightenment and its opponents which he takes as his main theme. Berlin is well aware of the complexity of this theme, and of how variant are the intellectual emphases in those loosely classified as Enlightenment thinkers as well as their critics and enemies. After all, if thinkers like Diderot, Rousseau, Hume, and Kant are to be considered figures of the European Enlightenment, their differences are in some respects much more important than their similarities. And if we stretch the term "irrationalism" to include all those who entered the lists *against* the Enlightenment, surely there are worlds of difference between thinkers like Herzen and Hess, on the one hand, and others like Sorel, enraptured precursors of totalitarianism, not to mention nationalist and racist extremists who believed that the Enlightenment was responsible for the Second Fall of Man, the French revolution.

It seems to me that it is necessary to draw a distinction between the critics of the Enlightenment and its enemies. Critics of the Enlightenment did not contest the validity of reason or scientific method as compared to alternative, traditional ways of reaching truth about the nature of the physical and social world or of settling conflicting claims on how best to further human welfare. They took issue either with some dominant conception of reason or the presumed scope of scientific method or with particular conclusions of a historical and political character. In this sense, Marx and Hess were not hostile to the Enlightenment; they regarded themselves as inheritors of its traditions, replacing its inadequate conceptions of man and society with historically more realistic and therefore more scientific views. Where, with respect to social reform and revolution, the thinkers of the Enlightenment taught that good will and human readiness were all, Marx and Hess stressed the ripeness of the conditions required for successful action. Bentham scoffed at the notion of natural rights central to the writings of most of the philosophers of the Enlightenment, yet sought by reliance on his calculus of pleasure and pain to diminish human suffering and improve the human estate. For all their criticisms of their predecessors, the utilitarians were really men of the Enlightenment.

The controversies between the various schools of rationalism and empiricism are family quarrels. They are of an entirely different order from the position of those who opposed the Enlightenment with reasons of the heart or gut, thinking of the blood, the authority of history, divine revelations, or self-certifying intuitions. Whatever the excesses and errors of Enlightenment thought, they could always be checked by further reflection; and whenever they influenced action, they could be judged and modified by their fruits in experience. But the ideas of the enemies of the Enlightenment, even when they were well-intentioned, allowed for no self-corrective procedures; and when they acquired power, their absurdities led periodically to mass atrocities.

Perhaps the greatest division among Enlightenment thinkers was between those who thought they could derive a way of life from the principles of the physical world, who in effect imposed an ethos upon a cosmos, and those who recognized that at best the physical order conditioned the achievement of the good society, whose nature was independent of the truths of the physical world. Berlin is well aware of this. He tells us that the entire Enlightenment believed that the nature of man was fundamentally the same in all times and climes but goes on to indicate the compatibility of such a view with differences so profound that they seem more significant than the nominal agreements:

> What the entire Enlightenment has in common is denial of the central Christian doctrine of original sin, believing instead that man is born either innocent and good, or morally neutral and malleable by education or environment, or at worst, deeply defective but capable of radical and indefinite improvement by rational education in favorable circumstances, or by a revolutionary reorganization of society. . . .

This covers quite a spectrum of readings about the nature of man as a basis for reasonable programs and expectations of social change. All we need do is to make explicit the realization that man is a finite, limited, imperfect creature and therefore always open to the solicitations of evil and the corruption of power and place—the kernel of the Christian myth of original sin—to box the compass of secular positions about the nature of human nature. This leaves, as the permanent legacy of the Enlightenment, meliorism or the belief in the *possibility* of change in human nature.

John N. Gray (essay date 1980)

SOURCE: "On Negative and Positive Liberty," in *Political Studies,* Vol. XXVIII, No. 4, December, 1980, pp. 507-26.

[In the following essay, Gray examines the components of the arguments Berlin advances, and other writers' responses to them, regarding the nature and value of negative and positive freedom.]

It is the argument of an influential school of philosophers working within a tradition of thought strongly influenced by logical positivism and by linguistic analysis that disputes about the nature of freedom may be resolved conclusively and to the satisfaction of all reasonable students of the subject. Among such exponents of what I shall henceforth call a *restrictivist*[1] approach to the subject of freedom there are wide differences as to the nature of freedom and about the means whereby discussion about its nature is to be rationally foreclosed. Some writers are prepared to treat as decisive the production of a stipulative definition of freedom backed up by weighty arguments about its operational utility. Others make their ultimate appeal to intuitions about freedom which are supposed to be embedded in ordinary thought and practice, or to allegedly standard uses of the concept in classic texts of social and political thought. Whatever their disagreements in these areas, restrictivists all hold that it must in principle be possible to elaborate a preferred view of freedom against the background of an authoritative elucidation of the concept of freedom, so that the resultant theory of freedom will commend itself to all reasonable men. What restrictivists have in common, in other words, is a rejection of the claim that freedom is what has been called an *essentially contestable concept.*[2]

Typically, though not perhaps necessarily, restrictivists also take up three secondary positions on the subject of freedom. Firstly, they are inclined to view freedom as primarily a *descriptive* concept, to which evaluative connotations have become attached in ordinary usage; they repudiate the contention that evaluative judgements and moral and political commitments must inevitably inform any judgement we make about freedom. Secondly, as well as holding that discourse about freedom is, or might in certain contexts someday become, evaluatively neutral, restrictivists characteristically affirm that rational consensus on the proper uses of the concept of freedom can be reached in the absence of any prior agreement on broader issues in social and political theory: they deny that differing uses of the concept of freedom can be shown to hinge on divergent conjectures about man and society in such a way that uses of it are always theory-loaded. Thirdly, restrictivists are disposed to reject the claim that metaphysical views about the self and its powers are germane to disputes about the nature of social freedom: like the theoretical commitments of the social sciences, such metaphysical commitments are held to be immaterial to the conduct of disputes about freedom.

Restrictivist theses about freedom demonstrably endorse naïve and superseded positions in the philosophy of mind and action and in the theory of our knowledge of the social world. At the same time, much argument in favour of the essentially contestable character of moral and political concepts seems to break down inasmuch as it turns on a central paradox. This paradox may be expressible in the question whether the notion of an essentially contestable concept may itself be incoherent. For how can it be the case that arguments and considerations are available in terms of which a contest can be carried on about the proper use of a concept, if it is also supposed that none of these considerations is capable of settling the contest? I have elsewhere argued that some notions of the essential contestability of concepts may be free of this obscurity.[3] Whether or not my own attempted rehabilitation of essential contestability theses is successful, it seems important to note that the difficulties my contribution was intended to resolve are not decisive in the evaluation of Berlin's argument about freedom. For while it is implicitly acknowledged in his *Two Concepts of Liberty* that disputes about the notion of freedom cannot be resolved by methods of conceptual analysis or stipulative redefinition which are neutral with respect to rival moral and political commitments, Berlin does there insist that there are arguments which favour one view of freedom over the others he considers. It is the burden of *Two Concepts of Liberty* that these are precisely arguments invoking substantive moral and political values, drawing on controversial positions in social theory and involving metaphysical claims.

In that lecture Berlin develops an argument of unsurpassed perspicuity which suggests that judgements about freedom cannot be insulated in restrictivist fashion from evaluative questions, from disputes in social theory or from metaphysical commitments. In this paper I want to ask what are the principal theses of Berlin's argument about liberty, and how far his account is acceptable. My conclusion is that, whereas Berlin's argument is not vulnerable to most of the objections its critics have advanced, yet the logic of his argument comples Berlin to acknowledge the relevance to questions of social freedom of considerations having to do with the conditions of rational choice and with the real will—considerations germane to positive conceptions of freedom of just the sort whose role in political thought Berlin judges to have been lamentable. Further, I consider Berlin's assumption that negative conceptions of freedom have some sort of special congruence with the mainstream of the liberal tradition. Here, I shall give reasons for thinking it is a view of freedom as consisting in the non-restriction of options that is most germane to liberalism's central concerns. It is this conception of freedom rather than any narrowly negative view which expresses the spirit of Berlin's account most adequately. I shall conclude by contending that, whereas this view may appear to contain one of the important elements of the positive conception in that it is concerned with internal as well as external conditions of free choice and action, it remains none the less recognizably a variant of the negative view. It also represents the best point of departure for further work in the theory of social freedom.

My examination of Berlin's account will be in six sections. Firstly, I will consider Berlin's conceptual analysis of freedom, concentrating on the relation between elucidations of the concept of freedom and arguments about what is the preferred view of freedom. Secondly, I will look at Berlin's account of the relations between freedom and the values which freedom may serve, and, more broadly, between judgements about freedom and evaluative judgements generally. Thirdly, I will examine Berlin's distinction between questions about freedom (on the one hand) and questions about power and ability (on the other), looking most closely at the connections, if any, between judgements about social freedom and judgements about the conditions of rational choice and about the real will. Fourthly, I will address myself to Berlin's views about the role of social theory in making judgements about freedom, and, especially, to his arguments about the place of conjectures about causality and intentionality in such judgements. Fifthly, I will consider Berlin's account of the place of negative and positive views of freedom in the thought of central exponents of the liberal intellectual tradition, arguing that, as in Bentham, severely negative conceptions of liberty tend to support authoritarian rather than liberal political orders. Sixthly, and lastly, I will consider briefly the dependency of Berlin's account of freedom on the claim, reiterated throughout his writings and in my view a contribution to social and political theory of the first importance, that some moral and political values which are fundamental in our thought about human conduct are incommensurable with one another. I will suggest that it is this break with the monist tradition in ethics and philosophy that we inherit from the classical period of Platonic and Socratic rationalism which motivates Berlin in assigning to liberty a privileged place among the political values he judges to be worthy of promotion. For, as Berlin sees it, it is an inexorable result of the truth that some basic moral and political goods are incommensurable and that the central excellences of human life are competitive and may sometimes be uncombinable that moral and political dilemmas are insusceptible of any definitively rational solution. The concept of a perfect man, like that of a perfect society, has, accordingly, no clear application and must be judged to be incoherent. The privileged status of freedom among the ends of political life derives for Berlin from the constitutive role he conceives moral conflicts to have in political life, and from the source of such conflicts in the ineradicable diversity of men's purposes. Berlin's advocacy of the priority of liberty is grounded, then, in the doctrine of value-pluralism which he has always promoted.

FREEDOM: THE CONCEPT AND ITS RIVAL CONCEPTIONS

The distinction between a concept and its rival conceptions is one which has been introduced into social philosophy by John Rawls, though similar distinctions may be found earlier in philosophy. 'It seems natural', Rawls writes, 'to think of the concept of justice as being specified by the role which these different sets of principles, these different conceptions, have in common'. Later he writes that the various conceptions of justice are 'the outgrowth of different notions of society against the background of opposing views of the natural necessities and opportunities of human life. Fully to consider a conception of justice we must make explicit the conception of social cooperation from which it derives'.[4] Now it is plain that, when Berlin speaks of two *concepts* of liberty, he intends us to understand this as a reference to what Rawls would call two *conceptions* of liberty. Indeed, Berlin acknowledges that they have a common root, when he says that '"positive" and "negative" liberty, in the sense in which I use these terms, start at no great logical distance from each other'.[5] Again, in the first paragraph of his introduction to the book in which the lecture is collected, Berlin says of it that it is concerned with 'the importance of two major *conceptions* of liberty in the history of ideas'.[6] When he later speaks of the competition between positive and negative conceptions as involving 'not two different interpretations of a single concept, but two profoundly divergent and irreconcilable attitudes to the ends of life',[7] he is not departing from his earlier claim that the concept of liberty has spawned two rival conceptions. Rather, he is asserting that *some* positive conceptions mistakenly identify distinct political values with freedom or liberty. In making this assertion, however, unlike many of his critics, Berlin does not commit the error of supposing that it is an easy and unproblematic matter to identify the distinguishing features of the *concept* of liberty. That this is so may be seen by considering briefly G. C. MacCallum's criticism of Berlin's account.

In conformity with his aim of producing a formal scheme within which all discourse about social freedom may be framed, MacCallum urges us to treat liberty as a concept always designating a triadic relation which holds between agents, constraints and acts, and which has the general form: 'This or that person (or persons) is free (or not free) from this or that constraint (or set of constraints) to do (or not to do) so and so'. As MacCallum himself puts it:

> Whenever the freedom of some agent or agents is in question, it is always freedom from some constraint or restriction, interference with, or barriers to doing, not doing, becoming or not becoming something. Such freedom is thus always *of* something, an agent or agents, *from* something, *to do*, not do, become or not become something; it is a triadic relation. Taking the format 'X is (is not) free from Y to do (not do, become, not become) Z', X ranges over agents, Y ranges over 'preventing conditions', and Z ranges over actions or conditions of character or circumstances.[8]

Several points need making at once about MacCallum's analysis. First of all, just as it can be shown that any elucidation of the *concept* of justice which (like Rawls's) incorporates strong requirements of impartiality and of equal consideration of human interests is unacceptably restrictive in that it limits the range of coherent conceptions of justice, so MacCallum's triadic analysis of the concept of liberty may well be non-neutral with respect to rival conceptions of liberty. In so far as MacCallum's analysis of the concept of freedom has substantive implications for the conduct of disputes about how freedom is to be conceived, his proposal must be judged to have a measure of inherent disputability about it—no less, indeed, than is possessed by proposals regarding the preferred conception of freedom. Filling in the blank spaces in MacCallum's analysis involves committing oneself to specific uses of other, no less disputed concepts. It is partly in virtue of the contestability of these latter concepts, which collectively constitute the criteria of correct application of the concept of freedom, that the concept of freedom is itself so contestable and may be used to promote opposed conceptions of freedom. Further, Berlin has given us a reason for thinking that MacCallum's analysis cannot possibly comprehend exhaustively all intelligible locutions having to do with freedom. For, as he has observed,[9] a man or a people struggling against impediments which they judge to be restrictive of their freedom need not aim, consciously or unconsciously, at any other state; having attained their freedom, they may behave in every respect as before. If a man may wish to be rid of his chains, without having in mind any ulterior end apart from the freedom he gains in attaining this, it seems that freedom must be regarded as basically a dyadic rather than as a triadic concept.

Finally, it seems hard, if not impossible, to accommodate within MacCallum's triadic analysis the conception of individual freedom as possessing a certain social status, which Berlin later discusses in another context.[10] As C. S. Lewis has noted, in its early uses to call a man free was simply to describe his legal rights and duties, and to contrast them with those of a slave: unlike a slave, a free man was entitled to take part in the political life of his city and to affect the workings of its legislative institutions.[11] It is true enough that the idea of freedom as the entitlement to participate in political decision-making was not the only conception of freedom current among the Greeks. As Berlin has himself characterized it, freedom was contrasted by the Stoics with the heteronomous condition of a man whose choices go against the universal rational order and are accordingly immoral; for the Stoics, as for Rousseau, who revived this understanding of freedom, it is none other than obedience to laws which one prescribes to himself. Again, we find in Plato a strongly positive, intrapersonal conception of freedom, which commits that bifurcation of self which Berlin regards as the seminal error of positive libertarianism. Now both the understanding of freedom as consisting in the entitlement to a voice in political decision-making and the understanding of freedom as rational choice in accordance with standards which are one's own and which accord with a natural moral order are present in the modern liberal tradition, but, as Berlin has emphasized, neither is distinctive of it. In its seventeenth-century exponents, for example, to demand that men be set free was to demand that their inner life, spontaneous associations and productive endeavours be protected from the encroachments of Church and State. Clearly enough, this liberal conception of freedom as non-interference within a protected sphere of life differs from both of the conceptions of freedom that were current among the Greeks, since a society of free men in both Greek senses would be compatible with the absence of typical liberal immunities. A modern conception of freedom as independence or autonomy, in which a free man is characterized as one who governs himself and is governed by no-one else, must equally be distinguished from all the views of freedom we have considered so far. For a man who is autonomous in this modern sense, which is intimated in the writings of Kant, Humboldt, Tocqueville and Mill, enjoys immunities which the Greek citizen lacked, and has capacities of rational self-determination which the Greek freeman need not have possessed. We can see now that, without indulging in paradox, Socrates could have claimed to have remained a free man throughout his imprisonment, since at no time did he exchange his status for that of a slave. If I am right in supposing that MacCallum's scheme cannot accommodate such usages, it is clearly defective.

At this point in my argument it may be worth pointing out that, while it is true that Berlin nowhere claims that his contrastive analysis of the concept of liberty is jointly exhaustive of all coherent conceptions of liberty, and, indeed, explicitly acknowledges that the boundary between the concept of liberty and other, cognate, concepts is a shifting and variable one which can never be definitively specified, it is also true that, contrary to the imputations of several of his critics, Berlin nowhere claims that negative and positive conceptions of liberty are mutually exclusive. Marshall Cohen, for example, has argued that Berlin neglects or undervalues the fact that deprivation of the 'positive' freedom to be one's own master may be judged an infringement of a man's 'negative' freedom, if his desire for self-determination has been thwarted by the interferences of others.[12] Berlin's thesis, however, is not that negative and positive liberty are antinomies or contraries, but that, while their subject matters *may* overlap, they need not do so, and as a rule do not. An example of this truth is that, while having a voice in the affairs of the community in which he lives may assist a man to attain

the status of an autonomous agent, the overall effect of a democratic regime may be to obstruct his efforts to achieve that status. This is only to say that liberal writers of the seventeenth century were not inconsistent in promoting liberal freedoms of thought, expression and association while repudiating democratic institutions. In general, Berlin's claim is not that the questions, 'Who is master?' and 'Over what area am I master?' are always entirely distinct in their significance, but that they are generally distinguishable, and that much of importance in social and political thought hangs on the difference between them. His claim is that the answers to these questions capture opposed conceptions of freedom, each of which constitutes a coherent and legitimate application of the generic concept of freedom which is their common source.

The Concept Of Freedom: Descriptive or Evaluative?

That freedom is primarily a descriptive concept has been argued persuasively, though not in the end successfully, by Felix Oppenheim in a valuable book.[13] 'Meaningful disagreement about the value of freedom depends', he argues, 'on agreement on that about which one disagrees'. Our aim must be to 'arrive at a system of definitions acceptable to everybody because they do not conflict with anybody's political ideology'. He summarizes his own position as follows:

> Thus, in the case of the concept of social, political and inter-personal freedom, the expression we must explicate is, 'With respect to B, A is free to do X'. This expression can be defined by 'B makes it neither impossible nor punishable for A to do X'. Not only does this definition remain close to ordinary usage, it is also descriptive, and in two ways: the defining expression consists exclusively of descriptive terms, and it is 'value-free' in the sense that it can be applied to determinate states of affairs by anyone independently of his political convictions.[14]

According to this view, advanced also (though in different variants) by such writers as J. P. Day and W. A. Parent,[15] the judgement that a man is free to do something neither entails nor presupposes any judgement about that being the right thing for him to do, that it is in his real interest for him to do it, or that such an action forms part of a good or praiseworthy way of life. Answering the question whether a man is free to do something, on this account, does not (or need not) involve making an evaluative judgement of any sort. The question is an empirical question, sometimes (it is true) a peculiarly difficult one, to which there is always a single right answer. As against this view, W. E. Connolly has argued, convincingly to my mind, that 'The positive normative import of "free" . . . is not attached to it accidentally but flows from its identification of factors pertinent to human wellbeing in situations where something is absent'.[16] Significantly, Connolly's position on this matter is not importantly different from Berlin's, as he expresses it in an important footnote where the evaluative character of judgements about freedom is explicitly acknowledged:

The extent of my freedom seems to depend on (a) how many possibilities are open to me (though the method of counting these can never be more than impressionistic. Possibilities of action are not discrete entities like apples, which can be exhaustively enumerated); (b) how easy or difficult each of these possibilities is to actualize; (c) how important in my plan of life, given my character and circumstances, these possibilities are when compared with each other; (d) how far they are closed and opened by deliberate human acts; (e) what value not merely the agent, but the general sentiment of the society in which he lives, puts on the various possibilities.

Berlin continues:

All these magnitudes must be 'integrated', and a conclusion, necessarily never very precise, or indisputable, drawn from this process. It may well be that there are many incommensurable kinds and degrees of freedom, and that they cannot be drawn up on any single scale of magnitude . . . Total patterns of life must be compared directly as wholes, though the method by which we make the comparison, and the truth of the conclusions, are difficult or impossible to demonstrate. But the vagueness of the concepts, and the multiplicity of the criteria involved, is an attribute of the subjectmatter itself, not of our imperfect method of measurement, or incapacity for precise thought.[17]

A similar, though more restricted, point is made by Hart, when in a forceful argument,[18] he says of Rawls that:

He admits that different opinions about the value of the conflicting liberties will affect the way in which different persons view this conflict (between them). Nonetheless, he insists that to arrive at a just resolution of the conflict we must try to find the point at which the danger to liberty from the marginal loss in control over those holding political power just balances the security of liberty gained by the greater use of constitutional devices (p. 230). I cannot myself understand, however, how such weighing or striking of a balance is conceivable if the only appeal is, as Rawls says, to 'a greater liberty'.

Three aspects of Berlin's position as to the relevance of evaluative judgements about the goodness of entire ways of life to judgements about social freedom may be noted at this point. First, Berlin's position is strengthened when it is noticed that writers in the restrictivist tradition differ deeply among themselves as to what may constitute a preventing (liberty-limiting) condition. The great majority, of whom Oppenheim may be taken as a typical but unusually fairminded and clear example, contend that being free to perform an act entails, not only that it has not been rendered physically impossible by the intervention of another, but that other agents have not rendered it ineligible by applying coercion or invoking sanctions. Being free to act, then, on this view, involves the absence, not just of force, but also of coercion (which comprehends, among other things, the threat of force). More recently, however, a number of writers[19] have sought to undermine this commonsensical view according to which being free to act implies the non-punishability of the act as well as the absence of forcible restraint with respect to it. The arguments of these writers, whose lineage extends back at least as far as Hobbes, for whom freedom to act was no more than the possibility of unimpeded motion, are worth careful attention despite their obvious counter-intuitive aspects. Their claim is that coercion cannot itself be restrictive of social freedom, which consists simply in the absence of forcible restraint of bodily movement. Those who hold that force alone can be restrictive of liberty often hold also that social freedom is not a variable magnitude. They claim that freedom, unlike utility (say), can be neither increased or diminished, but only redistributed within the universe of agents. It seems that this is, in part at least, a conceptual claim, trading on the fact that whenever we have an instance of social unfreedom, we find someone unable to perform some sort of action in virtue of his standing in a relationship with someone else whose actions or omissions bear decisively on his inability to perform the act in question. Connected with this is the claim that social freedom itself cannot be in competition with any other value so that liberalism cannot be characterized as a philosophy which stipulates that liberty is accorded priority over other values.

Arguably, if such arguments are valid, then they constitute a *reductio ad absurdum* of this species of stringent negative libertarianism. For, in leaving us no way of characterizing freedoms except in the physicalistic language of unimpeded behaviours, this approach ignores the vital truth that the subject matter of freedom is action rather than behaviour. As Berlin has intimated, if the subject matter of freedom *is* action rather than behaviour, it may be that the disputable character of judgements about freedom has its source in the fact that we possess no principle of counting for free actions which is not also a principle of evaluating their worth or significance for human well-being. Overall comparative judgements about the freedom of an individual or a society cannot then avoid being evaluative judgements about the relative value of the actions that that freedom comprehends. The ineliminable evaluative dimension of comparative judgements about on-balance freedom thus derives from two sources, which may not be wholly unrelated: from the difficulty in determining what is to count as a constraint and the impossibility of characterizing constraints on liberty in purely physical terms; and from the difficulty of aggregating particular liberties to act into the subject of an overall judgement. Again, a conservation of freedom thesis seems to have strongly counter-intuitive implications. Consider two cities, otherwise identical, in one of which there are traffic control regulations and in the other of which there are none. It seems absurd to say that in the latter city, in which chaos reduces everyone's prospects of personal mobility, there is as much freedom as in the former, but that it is differently distributed. Further, even if social freedom was a zero sum concept, comparative judgements about it would be required by any principle specifying its just distribution. Finally, if social freedom is a variable magnitude, then equalizing liberty will sometimes conflict with the objective of maximizing it, and a choice between the two policies will have to be made. (Inasmuch as differing distributions of *liberty* will have widely differing effects on other values, a competition between liberty and other values may re-emerge here.) If this is right, then Rawls's greatest equal liberty principle conceals a crippling ambiguity, even if it is true (which may well be doubted) that the expression 'the greatest liberty' stands for anything very determinate.

Secondly, and no less crucially, an argument recognizing that judgements about freedom are inescapably evaluative does not commit us to the absurd but perennially popular view that freedom cannot compete with other values. If we acknowledge that individuating options with a view to comparing different states of affairs as to the magnitude and distribution of freedom within them always involves invoking our evaluative commitments to one way of life among others, we are not thereby bound to endorse the mistaken view that all bona fide freedoms cohere to compose the good for man. This can be seen from the fact that asserting as a necessary truth the proposition that an option, and a free act, must appeal to some good or value, does not entail the Socratic paradox that an agent cannot choose what is bad. For the resultant on-balance of a free act is not precluded from being a bad state of affairs. As Berlin has always emphasized, the values and virtues of different ways of life may not ultimately be combinable, so the claim that everything that deserves to be accounted a free act must be expressive of a value in no way supports the very different claim that freedoms cannot embody values which are inescapably in conflict with one another. This must be evident from Berlin's reiterated emphasis that freedoms may have to be curtailed, either because their exercise conflicts with that of other, perhaps incommensurably valuable freedoms, or because they compete with other values that are largely distinct from those comprehended in typical judgements about freedom. An example of a conflict of the latter kind is suggested by F. A. Hayek, when he compares the situation of a conscripted soldier, well-fed and comfortably housed, with that of a wandering vagabound, dependent for his survival on his wits.[20] Recognizing, as both Berlin and Hayek do, that the vagabond's freedom may have little or no value to him, is not to deny that it is freedom that is lost when he is eventually conscripted. Such cases as this only point to the relevance of the distinction often made by writers in the liberal tradition, and clearly stated by Berlin, between a man's having a freedom and his enjoying conditions in which its exercise is on balance valuable to him. The fact that evaluative differences may exist even in this paradigm case of the freedom of little value, with some men judging the circumstances of the conscripted soldier unfavourably in comparison with that of the wandering vagabond, only reinforces the insight that there is an inherently disputable character in judgements about freedom, and that one of the sources of this is in divergent moral and political commitments.

Thirdly, Berlin's explicit recognition of the ways in which evaluative judgements about the merits of rival forms of social life inform the comparative judgements we make

about freedom in no way commits him to any reductionist thesis about the value of freedom. It simply does not follow from the claim that all judgements about freedom are inescapably normative that there is not a distinguishable domain of evaluative considerations salient to the use of the concept of freedom. How is this? It might be supposed that, if the magnitude of freedom depends on other judgements about relative values of available options, then comparative judgements about freedom tend to be collapsed into judgements about the ability of sets of social arrangements to satisfy these other values. If this is so, the claim that judgements about freedom cannot help being evaluative might seem to set in motion a reductionist thesis about the value of freedom, after all, and this thesis seems dubiously consistent with any value-pluralism such as Berlin's. Such an objection to Berlin's account is misconceived, however, inasmuch as it is no part of Berlin's arguments that comparative judgements about freedom are uniquely determined by reference to the values freedom is thought to serve. Much of the time, Berlin is concerned to stress that our judgements about freedom are underdetermined by our other evaluative commitments: he insists that each thing is what it is and not another thing. This is not incompatible with his claim that our broader moral and political commitments necessarily inform and constrain our judgements about freedom. Nor is this latter claim in conflict with Berlin's insistence that only some considerations and values are specially salient to judgements about freedom. Along with most classical liberals, Berlin contends that wealth and power, for example, are not typically to be regarded as values which should inform our assessment of the magnitudes of freedom. Disagreements arise among liberals, not primarily as to whether any other values enter the comparative judgements about freedom, but mainly as to the range and content of these values. None of the participants in such disputes need commit the error of supposing freedom to be reducible to the other values he specifies as most relevant to freedom. Thus no one who thinks as Berlin does about the evaluative aspects of judgements above liberty is committed to the view that judgements about social freedom are 'reducible without remainder' to appraisals of the excellence of rival ways of life. Some such *disappearance thesis* about the concept of liberty is plainly endorsed by Dworkin. He argues in support of his claim that there is no right to liberty that, given there is no element or ingredient common to the basic liberties, comparative judgements of different societies in respect of their sponsorship of these liberties are to be cashed out wholly in terms of their promoting equality of consideration.[21] But equality will remain as indeterminate an idea as liberty, and must equally be the subject of a disappearance thesis, unless uses of it can be shown to hinge upon some one feature, or tightly-knit family of features, characteristic of a worthwhile life. Again, it is necessary to stress that the content of our judgements about freedom is not exhausted by the other values that inform them, and not all our other values are in the same degree salient to our judgements about freedom. Alan Ryan has observed that locutions in which the word 'free' occurs outside of any moral or political context may illuminate the word's central moral and political uses, by showing that it presupposes a circumstance in which something valued is lacking.[22] Once the evaluative dimensions of discourse using the concept of freedom have been noted against descriptive accounts of the concept, we need to follow Connolly in taking up Ryan's suggestion, and go on to try to delimit areas of human interests and needs relevant to questions of social freedom from areas that are not. Only if we are successful in doing this can we avoid the wildly counterintuitive results of reductionist theses such as Dworkin's.

It is Berlin's central claim that, whereas there are two distinct and coherent conceptions of liberty, 'negative' and 'positive', positive liberty suffered a transformation as a result of which values other than liberty, such as the values of self-realization and of an integrated community, came to be misrepresented as aspects of liberty itself. While the idea of negative liberty, too, is recognized by Berlin to have been gravely abused as a licence for exploitation, there is a sense in which the perversion of the positive conception is morally and logically more culpable, since it involves the metamorphosis of a doctrine of limitation on political authority into a doctrine of the equivalence of authoritarian determination with individual self-mastery. Berlin distinguishes as 'the essence of liberty, both in the "positive" and "negative" senses' what he calls 'the holding off of something or someone . . . of others who trespass on my field or assert their authority over me, or of obsessions, fears, neuroses, irrational forces . . . intruders and despots of one kind or another.'[23] It is the mutation in the concept of liberty in its positive variants in their legitimate form as conceptions of self-determination in such writers as Spinoza and Kant into the idea of government by objective reason as expressed in the institutions of the State which we find in the later Fichte and in the English Idealists that warrants Berlin's claim that:

> It is only the confusion of desire for liberty with this profound and universal craving for status and understanding, further confounded by being identified with the notion of social self direction, that makes it possible for men, while submitting to the authority of oligarchs and dictators, to claim that this in some sense liberates them.[24]

While what Berlin says here seems to me to be both true and important, I want to draw attention to what I think is an unresolved (and perhaps insuperable) difficulty in one variant of the negative conception of liberty which he contrasts with the authentic germ of the positive notion of rational self-determination. This is that no viable conception of liberty can altogether dispense with considerations deriving from the difficult idea of the real or rational will. Speaking of the way in which the positive conception of freedom as self-mastery has supported the division of the human personality into two parts, one transcendental and rational and the other empirical and contingent, Berlin comments that this fact illustrates the obvious truth that 'conceptions of freedom directly derive from views of what constitutes a self, a person, a man.'[25] Later, in criticism of Kantian positive libertarianism, Berlin says that

'the authority of reason and the duties it lays upon man is identified with individual freedom, on the assumption that only rational ends can be the "true" objects of a "free" man's "real" nature.' He comments: 'I have never . . . understood what reason means in this context: and here wish merely to point out that the *a priori* assumptions of this philosophical psychology are not compatible with empiricism: that is to say, with any doctrine founded on knowledge derived from experience of what men are and seek.'[26] Now it is undoubtedly true that some positive conceptions of liberty depend crucially on a rationalist philosophical psychology in which a noumenal or rational self can be distinguished from a phenomenal empirical personality. This seems to be true of Rawls's theory of justice as fairness, for example, in that there the project of developing a 'moral geometry', in which questions of rightness and distributive justice are definitively answerable, appears to founder unless a conception of the rational self is invoked and given philosophical plausibility. Again, in the case of J. S. Mill, to whom Berlin[27] attributes a mainly negative conception of liberty, it is arguable that the idea of a free man which is at the centre of *On Liberty* requires for its support a philosophical psychology decisively different from, and incompatible with, that empiricist view of the self expounded (with some reservations) in Mill's 'official' philosophical writings (such as the *System of Logic* and *Hamilton*).

While it is, then, importantly true that questions about liberty cannot be insulated from controversial metaphysical commitments in the areas of the philosophy of mind and action, it remains the case that there are good reasons to doubt that any coherent conception of liberty can avoid incorporating requirements to do with the conditions of rational choice. One set of reasons why this is so is suggested by Benn and Weinstein, who in a well-known paper reject the conception of freedom as the absence of impediments or restraints and develop the most systematic argument we have so far for an account of freedom as the nonrestriction of options. Claiming that it is apposite to discuss whether a man is free to do something only if it is a possible object of reasonable choice, they declare programmatically that 'Our conception of freedom is bounded by our notions of what might be worthwhile doing . . . Incomprehension, not hostility, is the first obstacle to toleration.'[28] Now it might seem that we are here approaching a conception of freedom as rational self-determination of just the sort Berlin has always resisted. The claim we are advancing is that comparative judgements about freedom always invoke judgements about the preferences of the standard rational chooser, and the suggestion I am noting is that there is something at least problematic about counting as a freedom an opportunity to act which no reasonable man would ever take. Are we not approaching a conflation of acting freely with acting reasonably? In his important paper, **'From Hope and Fear Set Free',**[29] Berlin has criticized the belief that individual and social freedom are necessarily or always augmented by an increase of knowledge and has attacked the identification of the rational life with the life of a free man. He has emphasized, there and elsewhere, that the freedom of societies as well as of individuals must comprehend opportunities for actions which are wilful, perverse and even consciously irrational. It might seem then that Berlin is at one with those, often moral and practical sceptics, who sever freedom to act from any requirements of rationality. Such a position, it seems to me, is stronger than any Berlin explicitly embraces in his writings. In **'From Hope and Fear Set Free'** the object of his criticism is a thesis of metaphysical rationalism which applies in the area of practical reasoning that every dilemma of choice has one right answer. Certainly, Berlin is committed to repudiating any view of freedom as the nonrestriction of options which incorporates such a rationalist picture of practical deliberation. This is not the same as denying the relevance to questions of social freedom of any of the requirements of rational choice. Further, I suggest that the conception of rational choice that is appropriate there is a minimalist and meagre one, stipulating only that an agent *have a reason* for what he does. What such a requirement disqualifies as rational conduct is only the behaviour of a delirious agent, where no goal or end may be imputed to him which renders intelligible what he does. True, this minimal requirement of rational choice is liable to be extended so as to disqualify the incorrigibly delusional, the phobia-ridden and the hypnotized agent, and such an extension undoubtedly revives some notion of the rational or real will. My claims are, first, that we need to invoke this difficult notion since no viable conception of social freedom can altogether dispense with it. Second, I suggest that some useful variant of the idea of a real or rational will may survive the demise of the rationalist metaphysics and philosophical psychology in which it has traditionally been embedded. Third, whereas Berlin has nowhere endorsed this line of thought about freedom, I claim there is nothing in his writings which is strictly inconsistent with it.

One way of making these points is to say that, while the distinction between social freedom and power or ability is an important one, it is one which is difficult or impossible to make where the powers and abilities in question have to do with the subjective conditions of choice. Nor is this conclusion surprising when we recall Berlin's observation that conceptions of freedom derive directly from views of the self. Once Berlin has recognized that options are not discrete, countable entities like apples, but are individuated by reference to evaluative judgements endorsing disputable views of the nature of the self, it seems intuitively incongruous that he goes on to deny that whether a man really has an option to do something depends, in part, on whether that action is subjectively available to him. Feinberg has pointed out that much will turn on how we draw the boundaries of the self, and there are obvious difficulties in using a purely spatial criterion to do so.[30] Any view of freedom as the nonrestriction of options is bound to remain radically incomplete, however, in the absence of an account of the nature and powers of the self whose options it is that are opened and closed by human action and omission.

These questions arise clearly in the problem—as yet unresolved, in my view—of the avowedly contented slave. As Berlin recognizes in the introduction to the revised version of his lecture,[31] his original definition of negative freedom as the absence of the interferences of others in the area in which an individual wishes to act, though it identifies a paradigm case of freedom, has damagingly paradoxical implications. For it makes the measure of an agent's freedom relative to his desires. Since it can never be assumed in advance of empirical research what are a man's desires, there is an important sense in which negative freedom (as Berlin originally conceives of it) is consistent with the presence and absence of any conditions whatsoever. In other words, except in so far as they contain references to the state of mind of the agent, or presuppose the truth of some general proposition about human wants, attributions of negative freedom or its absence can (logically) tell us nothing informative about the actual alternatives available to an agent. Since, on Berlin's original account, the degree of a man's freedom is the extent to which his desires are frustrated by the interferences of others, a man may always increase his freedom by trimming his desires. And this has the consequence that we are precluded from describing as unfree the wholly contented slave—or, more, generally, from lamenting the lack of liberty in a perfectly engineered *brave new world* in which desires and opportunities always coincide. Nor does Berlin's revised account, in which possible desires are included in the judgement, satisfactorily resolve the question. For unless we have some principle of counting which is non-neutral as between the slave and the non-slave, there will be desires which the slave could satisfy, and which in the non-slave will necessarily be frustrated. Only by invoking some norm of human nature which is discriminatory as to the wants which are to be counted, and which includes evaluations of the agent's states of mind, can the intuition that the wholly contented slave remains unfree be supported. This suggests that what we might call the phenomenonological and the sociological aspects of freedom cannot, after all, be hermetically sealed off from one another. It must be pointed out, however, that since invoking a norm of human nature in the way I have suggested is bound to be a highly questionable procedure, Berlin's account of this matter is not without difficulties. They are not difficulties peculiar to his account, however, but rather obstacles in the way of any political theory which recognizes the dependency of views of freedom on conceptions of man.

FREEDOM AND SOCIAL THEORY

One of the most striking features of Berlin's argument is its explicit acknowledgement that controversial questions in social theory are decisively relevant to questions of social freedom. This emerges in the course of his attempt to render more precise the boundaries of the negative conception. Characterizing negative freedom as the area within which a man may act *unobstructed* by others, Berlin comments: 'If I am prevented by others from doing what I could otherwise do, I am to that extent unfree; and, if this area is contracted by other men beyond a certain minimum. I can be described as being concerned, or, it may be, enslaved.' Berlin goes on to point out that coercion is not a term that covers every form on inability: 'Coercion implies the deliberate interference of other human beings within the area in which I could otherwise act.'[32] That is to say that coercion is distinguishable from other, cognate concepts, such as power, force and violence, in that every instance of coercion presupposes an intention on the part of the coercer to secure the compliance of the coerced agent in a course of conduct which he would not otherwise follow (or which it would be incongruous for him to follow in so far as he is a normally constituted human being). So, in the absence of an intention on the part of another person that he should act otherwise than he desired to act (or might be expected to act in his capacity as an agent with standard human interests and motivations), a man can be prevented from acting as he might otherwise do, but he cannot be said to have been coerced. A man is not coerced, then, unless his action complies with the intention of another person (and unless several other necessary conditions are satisfied).

Berlin makes it clear that he rejects the view which identifies freedom with the absence of force and coercion: the test of unfreedom, he says, is 'the part that I believe to be played by other human beings, directly or indirectly, with or without the intention of doing so, in preventing me from doing what I might otherwise do'.[33] Here the requirement of intentionality built into the concept of coercion is being disavowed and replaced by a requirement of causality, in which the role of *preventive* causation is crucial, and in which the relevance to questions of liberty of social arrangements no-one has designed and which accord with no-one's intentions is determined by their *alterability* or *remediability*. The remediability or alterability of social arrangements, like the avoidability of any given governmental policy, can, in turn, only be determined with the assistance of a social theory. As Berlin puts it:

> It is only because I believe that my inability to get a given thing is due to the fact that other human beings have made arrangements whereby I am, whereas others are not, prevented from having enough money with which to pay for it, that I think myself a victim of coercion or slavery. In other words, this use of the term depends on a particular social and economic theory about the causes of my poverty or weakness.[34]

The aptness of Berlin's construal is seen when we apply it to debates between *laissez-faire* liberals and Marxists, for example, about whether a man's suffering the evil of unemployment in an unregulated market economy may count as a restriction of his freedom. It is clear that the disagreement between the libertarian and the Marxist turns, at least in part, on a divergence in their respective theories of unemployment. For the *laissez-faire* liberal, there is a natural rate of unemployment in every complex society, and attempts to reduce unemployment below that point can only result in inflation, underemployment and diminution of living standards. For the Marxist, on the other hand, unemployment is a feature, not of every complex society, but

only of complex societies which are pre-socialist. As Berlin's remark that the argument for socialism may be couched wholly in terms of its contribution to negative liberty suggests, the Marxist is wholly justified in judging that unemployment in capitalist societies restricts freedom, *provided* his account of its origins is accepted. It will not always be easy, of course, to apply the test of alterability or avoidability to specific social arrangements and governmental policies, since even well-formed theories may be unable to give decisive guidance in some cases. Could the mass unemployment of the 1930s, for example, be considered restrictive of negative liberty? It might be so considered, even by a *laissez-faire* liberal, if it could be shown that it resulted from misguided monetary policies whose application was in no way inevitable. These difficulties aside, the important point about Berlin's account is that it allows that even 'impersonal social forces' may be restrictive of (negative) freedom, always providing they are demonstrably avoidable and remediable. In this respect, his account differs markedly from other, superficially similar accounts (such as that of Oppenheim).[35]

THE CONCEPT OF FREEDOM AND THE LIBERAL TRADITION

One of Berlin's most controversial claims is that there is some special kinship between negative views of liberty and the intellectual traditions of classical liberalism. Much here depends on how widely we construe the negative conception. It may be true that thinkers such as Hobbes and Bentham embraced a severely negative view of liberty, but neither of these is indisputably a liberal. Equally, neither Locke's nor (as Berlin acknowledges) Kant's view of liberty was negative: each saw the loss of liberty as consisting in the submission to arbitrary will, and liberty as being preserved and enlarged by conformity to rational law. Nor can J. S. Mill finally be characterized unequivocally as a negative libertarian. For, despite the classical-liberal subject matter of *On Liberty* in the grounds and limits of political obligation, the conception of freedom at work there is one, deriving as much from Tocqueville as from Humboldt, of which it is the notion of a free or autonomous man rather than that of free act or a free society that is centrally constitutive.

Apart from such historical considerations, my argument so far has been that a freedom-promoting policy is one which expands the options open to men, and this (on Berlin's own account) must include diminishing internal and subjective restrictions on the availability of options. Against those classical liberals who insist that their intellectual tradition is partly defined by advocacy of a narrowly negative view of liberty, I would argue that the general commitment to freedom actually comprehends a commitment to an open society in which rival modes of thought and life conflict and compete. It is only via such competition and conflict, indeed, that options become available to free men, and only thus that one dimension of their freedom can be enlarged. It is a disadvantage of the position of those who attach a stringent negative libertarianism so closely to classical liberalism, that the link between en-

dorsing the priority of liberty and supporting cultural pluralism is severed. At this point a contrast between Berlin's
views and those of F. A. Hayek may be helpful. While
Hayek's conception of freedom has some strongly positive
connotations, it is akin to Berlin's in rejecting any necessary connection with wealth or power. It differs from Berlin's, however, in that Hayek sometimes writes as if the
institution of predictable and uniform laws protecting the
basic liberal freedoms is a sufficient condition of social
freedom. Hayek's view appears to be that a liberal social
order may be, and perhaps must be a society in which a
dominant moral and intellectual tradition drastically cur-
tails the options open to its members. Berlin's view is
surely more faithful to liberalism's classical concerns in
recognizing that, though the institution of predictable and
uniform laws is a necessary condition of the promotion of
liberty through the enlargement of options, it is not sufficient to render a diversity of options and life-styles subjectively accessible to men, without which they must fail to
attain the status of free men.

Berlin's claim about the necessary connection holding between classical liberalism and negative libertarianism becomes plausible once we allow that the negative view may
encompass a conception of freedom as the nonrestriction
of options. It would be an implausible claim, if Berlin
were to be interpreted as contending that the severely
negative view which some scholars find in Hobbes and
Bentham was partly constitutive of liberalism. Against the
objection that, on this interpretation of his argument, Berlin leans too far in the direction of a positive conception, I
contend that the positive conceptions to which he objects
are still excluded by the conception of freedom I ascribe
to him. This is suggested by Berlin's favourite example of
the mutation of the concept of freedom in the intellectual
development of Fichte. In the late work of Fichte, we find
a strong positive view of freedom deeply embedded in a
rationalist metaphysics, and it is this variant of positive
libertarianism that Berlin seeks to subvert. It may be true
that the version of negative freedom as the non-restriction
of options I have attributed to Berlin is not easily distinguishable from some variants of the positive view in which
the rationalist heritage has been abandoned. I do not regard this as a serious defect in my account, however, since
Berlin has never unreservedly endorsed a negative conception, or maintained that the distinction between negative
and positive conceptions can always be applied uncontro-
versially.

FREEDOM, REASON AND
THE INCOMMENSURABILITY OF VALUES

Berlin's arguments against adopting as our preferred conception of freedom the positive view are not arguments
which appeal to ordinary usage, or which profess to employ any evaluatively neutral method of conceptual analysis. It would, in any case, be surprising if such a pre-
eminently distinguished historian of ideas were to adopt
this approach, displaying as it does an insensitivity to the
sources of past and present disputes about the nature of

freedom in opposed moral and political commitments.
Berlin's arguments for the negative view are, rather, substantive moral and political arguments, appealing to values
and considerations which, it is to be hoped, he shares with
the majority of his readers. To this extent, Berlin's mode
of argument distinguishes his position clearly from that of
those in the restrictivist tradition. At the same time, it is a
central feature of his argument against adopting the positive view that it has long been supported by an immemo-
rial error—the error of supposing that values cohere in an
harmonious whole. Berlin's opposition to this view, his repudiation of monism in philosophy, undoubtedly constitutes his master idea. It is an idea which is subversive of
the dominant tradition in Western thought, and which has
the most profound import for the enterprise of social and
political theory. Berlin's thesis, which so far as I know has
no precedent in the history of ideas, is that the conflict of
values, though it may be more readily visible in societies
(such as our own) which contain a diversity of moral traditions and which possess a highly developed historical
sensibility, is an ineradicable feature of human experience.
Its implication is that we must dismiss once and for all the
reigning illusion of the Enlightenment, the chimera of a
rational morality, and its step-child, the project of a science of politics. From the incoherence of the notion of a
supreme good, of a perfect man or a perfect society, we
must deduce the incoherence of the idea of a society
which, in transcending fundamental conflicts, has abolished politics and ended history. A frictionless utopian society in which all good things coexist must be abandoned
as an object of moral and political endeavour, then, not
because its achievement would violate sociological or historical laws, or go against the grain of human nature, but
because it is strictly unintelligible. A liberal society in
which moral conflicts are openly revealed is commended
to us, not because it alone satisfies the demands of human
nature, but because in it the competition of goods which is
an unalterable feature of the human predicament is not
shirked or evaded, but actively embraced.

At this point it may be worth summing up my conclusions
about Berlin's argument, and indicating what are the outstanding problems that remain. First, I have claimed that
Berlin sees the two specific conceptions of liberty with
which he is primarily concerned as issuing from a common source in the generic concept of liberty. Each of the
two conceptions captures a legitimate interpretation of the
shared concept, but it is Berlin's thesis that genuine variants of the positive conception soon suffered a transformation in which values largely distinct from liberty came to
be misrepresented as aspects of it. Secondly, I have contended that, whereas comparative judgments about freedom are in Berlin's account inescapably evaluative, this
does not commit Berlin to a reductionist view of the value
of liberty or in any way compromise his doctrine of value-
pluralism. Thirdly, I have suggested that Berlin's own
variant of the negative conception is a view of freedom as
the non-restriction of options. Some specification of the
conditions necessary for rational choice must be comprehended in any such view, and I have submitted that such a

specification will make use of a notion of the real or rational will without endorsing the rationalist doctrines with which it has usually been associated. Fourthly, I have noted Berlin's acknowledgement of the dependency of judgements about freedom on controversial positions in social theory. Berlin's account is distinguished from other, superficially similar accounts, in that it allows that impersonal social forces may restrict liberty, providing they are humanly alterable. Fifthly, I have argued that Berlin's thesis that there is a close connection between negative libertarianism and classical liberalism is most plausible if we adopt his variant of the negative conception. For purposes of exposition, I have contrasted Berlin's view with that of F. A. Hayek. Sixthly, I have identified as the primary source of Berlin's liberalism and antiutopianism his doctrine of value-pluralism. A liberal society in which a wide diversity of ends is promoted is recommended to us as being most in accordance with this basic truth.

I do not doubt that difficulties remain for Berlin's account of the concept of freedom, and for any similar account. It might be thought, for example, that the advocacy of value-pluralism and of the priority of liberty are not mutually supportive in the way I have sketched, but rather pull in different directions. If such fundamental values as freedom, equality and welfare may compete, and if there is no common unit in terms of which the competition may be resolved, what sense can there be in attaching priority to liberty? Indeed, if (as Berlin suggests) different freedoms may have incommensurable values, how are we to make even the impressionistic judgements of on-balance freedom of which he speaks? Berlin's advocacy of value-pluralism may even raise the spectre of relativism once again. For, it men hold deeply divergent views of the ends of life, between which reason is incompetent to arbitrate, are they not likely also to hold rival views of human nature? If so, we cannot expect the emergence of any common conception of man. In this case, however, given the dependency of rival views of freedom on different pictures of man, what grounds can be given for favouring any one view over any other? Does not Berlin's value-pluralism actually tend to support a thesis of the essential contestability of the concept of freedom, after all?

These are large and complex questions, a proper treatment of which must (at best) await further work in this area. It is not self-evident that they are fatal to Berlin's account. Whether or not the problems such questions pose are really crucial for Berlin's argument, the magnitude of his achievement cannot be doubted. If, as I have argued, no viable view of liberty can fail to accommodate some of the conditions of rational choice, then some variant of the view of freedom as autonomy which abandons the rationalist heritage may turn out to be the preferred conception. But, if further progress is attained in the theory of freedom, however, it will be against the background of Berlin's work. For, in demonstrating the error of assimilating liberty to morality, and of supposing that morality forms a coherent system, he has made a permanent contribution to reflection on freedom, and to social and political thought in general.

Notes

1. I owe the term 'restrictivist', and its use in these contexts, to W. L. Weinstein, who employed it in an unpublished paper on 'The Variability of the Concept of Freedom', delivered to the Political Thought Conference in Oxford in January 1975. I have profited greatly from Weinstein's important paper, a copy of which he has been kind enough to give me. I do not claim, however, that my use of the term 'restrictivist' always corresponds with his intention in coining the term. Different versions of the restrictivist thesis may be found in F. Oppenheim, J. P. Day and W. A. Parent, referred to in footnotes 14, 15 below.

2. The notion of an essentially contestable concept owes its currency to W. B. Gallie's paper, 'Essentially Contested Concepts', *Proceedings of the Aristotelian Society,* 56 (1956), 167-98.

3. See my paper 'On Liberty, Liberalism and Essential Contestability' in *British Journal of Political Science,* 8 (1978), 385-402.

4. These quotations come from J. Rawls, *A Theory of Justice* (London, Oxford University Press, 1972), pp. 5-6, 9-10.

5. I. Berlin, *Four Essays on Liberty* (London, Oxford University Press, 1968), p. xliii.

6. Berlin, *Four Essays,* p. ix.

7. Berlin, *Four Essays,* p. 166.

8. See G. C. MacCallum, Jr., 'Negative and Positive Freedom', *Philosophical Review,* 76 (1967), 312-34.

9. See his *Four Essays,* p. xliii.

10. See *Four Essays,* p. 156 et seq. I am not sure if Berlin is ready to consider any conception of a man as having a certain individual status a coherent conception of social freedom.

11. See his *Studies in Words* (Cambridge, Cambridge University Press, 1961), p. 111.

12. See Cohen's paper, 'Berlin and the Liberal Tradition', *Philosophical Quarterly,* 10 (1960), 216-27.

13. Felix Oppenheim, *Dimensions of Freedom* (New York, St. Martin's Press, 1961).

14. Felix Oppenheim, '"Facts and Values" in Politics', *Political Theory,* 1 (1973) 54-78, p. 56.

15. For J. P. Day's account, see his 'On Liberty and the Real Will', *Philosophy,* 95 (1970), 177-92, together with his 'Threats, Offers, Law, Opinion and Liberty' in *American Philosophical Quarterly,* 14 (1977), 257-72; and for W. A. Parent's see his 'Recent Work on the Concept of Liberty', *American Philosophical Quarterly,* 11 (1974), 149-67.

16. W. E. Connolly, *The Terms of Political Discourse* (Lexington, Mass., D. C. Heath, 1974), p. 141.

17. Berlin, *Four Essays,* p. 130.

18. H. L. A. Hart, 'Rawls on Liberty and Its Priority', in N. Daniels (ed.), *Reading Rawls,* (Oxford, Basil Blackwell, 1975), p. 241.

19. See especially Hillel Steiner, 'Negative Liberty', in *Proceedings of the Aristotelian Society,* 75 (1974/5), 33-50.

20. F. A. Hayek, *The Constitution of Liberty* (London, Routledge and Kegan Paul, 1960), p. 11.

21. R. M. Dworkin, *Taking Rights Seriously* (London, Duckworth, 1978), Ch. 12.

22. See Alan Ryan, 'Freedom', *Philosophy,* 40 (1965), 93-112.

23. *Four Essays,* p. 158.

24. *Four Essays,* p. 158.

25. *Four Essays,* p. 134.

26. *Four Essays,* pp. 153-4 (footnote).

27. *Four Essays,* p. 137.

28. S. I. Benn and W. L. Weinstein, 'Being Free to Act and Being a Free Man', *Mind,* 80 (1971), 194-211.

29. From Fear and Hope Set Free', in I. Berlin, *Concepts and Categories* (London, Hogarth Press, 1978), pp. 173-98.

30. See Joel Feinberg, *Social Philosophy* (Englewood Cliffs, N.J., Prentice-Hall, 1973), Ch. 1.

31. *Four Essays,* pp. xxxvii-xl.

32. *Four Essays,* p. 122 et seq.

33. *Four Essays,* p. 123.

34. *Four Essays,* p. 123.

35. On Oppenheim's account, see Connolly, *Terms of Political Discourse,* pp. 162-4.

Peter Stansky (lecture date 1981)

SOURCE: "Friends and Heroes," in *The New York Times,* February 8, 1981, pp. 1, 26.

[*In the following review of Berlin's* Personal Impressions, *Stansky focuses attention on Berlin's accounts of meetings with Boris Pasternak and Anna Akmatohva.*]

Only the title is bland. The contents of this fourth and final volume of Isaiah Berlin's **Selected Writings** bear the distinctive stamp of one of the great thinkers and writers of our age. The general reader, unfamiliar with his work, or put off by the formidable subject matter of the earlier volumes—**Concepts and Categories: Philosophical Essays, Against the Current: Essays in the History of Ideas, Russian Thinkers**—will find **Personal Impressions** altogether welcoming and rewarding.

Berlin is something of a mythic figure, not least in the dazzling flow of his conversation. His writing reflects the diversionary excursions, unexpected self-interruptions and recommencements, of a great talker—at home equally with Russian history and literature, with political philosophy, with Marx, Herder and Vico, or with subtle ruminations on the world as he has known it. We are assured in his company of a supremely intelligent, highly civilized approach to whatever he touches upon. In the present book, he is at his most conversational. And yet, for all the brilliance of these pieces, they are, with a few quite extraordinary exceptions, perhaps a little muted—at least I am tempted to think so, comparing their relative restraint with the exhilarating experience of listening to him discourse impromptu. I can still remember an occasion, almost 20 years ago, when, in an hour of subdued fireworks, talking nonstop to William Abrahams and myself, he provided us with arresting views of the young writers of the left in England in the 1930's. Enlightening though his recollections were of those writers he knew—Auden, for example, and Stephen Spender—he was, if possible, even more incandescent on those he hadn't actually known, about whom his hypotheses, speculations and interpretations proved astonishingly on the mark—a reminder that biography is more a matter of intelligence, intuition and understanding than a mere collection of external facts.

Noel Annan, in his introduction, resorts to the French word eloge—eulogy, encomium, praise—to characterize these essays. Two of them indeed were originally delivered as eulogies at memorial services for colleagues at Oxford (where Berlin has spent a good part of his life as a Fellow of All Souls, and the first president of Wolfson College), while several others were written for memorial volumes and symposia. Despite this, they are all, even the slightest of them, free of pieties and the glossings over such occasions tend to encourage. Sir Isaiah—he was knighted in 1957—knows that to speak less than truthfully of his friends is to do them a disservice. He can distinguish astutely between a virtue and a flaw, and appreciate what a less subtle intelligence might fail to recognize: how a flaw may contribute as much to greatness as a virtue.

Greatness, in all its variety and peculiarity, shows itself in the men and women about whom he is writing, whether dominating figures in the world at large (Churchill, Roosevelt, Chaim Weizmann), or in the more special, sometimes recondite worlds of literature, science, history, classics and linguistic philosophy. How wide his acquaintance has been! Except for Einstein and Roosevelt, he has known all his subjects—whether Boris Pasternak or Anna Akhmatova, Lewis Namier or Aldous Huxley—which adds a particular authority to what he would modestly have us read as no more than personal impressions.

So much of the book was written to order, as it were, that one might assume it to be no more than a gathering of occasional pieces. But as one progresses from the earliest (on Churchill) to the most recent (his meetings with Russian poets), one becomes aware of certain recurrent concerns that provide a unity of tone and conviction and emphasize the contrast between the world into which he was born—and from which he was uprooted at the age of 10—

and the world in which he has lived ever since. This is a contrast that Berlin himself may not have consciously set out to create, but to this reader at least it is impressively and movingly there.

In his opening essays, on Churchill and Roosevelt, he pays tribute to the former as "the saviour of his country" and to the latter as "the greatest leader of democracy, the greatest champion of social progress in the twentieth century." The world the Prime Minister and the President came to symbolize and did their best to serve and preserve was the world that welcomed Berlin, a Latvian Jew, as well as such figures as Chaim Weizmann, a Russian Jew, Lewis Namier, a Polish Jew, and Felix Frankfurter, an Austrian Jew. Each was entranced by a vision of England, more ideal perhaps than real, that offered a future far richer in possibilities of self-fulfillment (and even survival, as things turned out) than the future accessible to them in Eastern Europe. Writing about Frankfurter—but the passage applies with equal relevance to the others—Berlin recalled his "touching and enjoyable Anglomania—the childlike passion for England, English institutions, Englishmen—for all that was sane, refined, not shoddy, civilised, moderate, peaceful, the opposite of brutal, decent—for the liberal and constitutional traditions that before 1914 were so dear to the hearts and imaginations especially of those brought up in eastern or central Europe, more particularly to members of the oppressed minorities, who felt the lack of it to an agonizing degree, and looked to England and sometimes to America—those great citadels of the opposite qualities—for all that ensured the dignity and liberty of human beings."

As emigrants to the democracies of the West, they would make their mark in their new countries: Namier as historian, Berlin as philosopher, Weizmann as scientist, Frankfurter as jurist. Namier and Berlin would both be knighted; Weizmann, the greatest of Zionists, won the friendship of Balfour and through him the support of England for the establishment of a Jewish homeland in Palestine, while Frankfurter, in America, became professor at the Harvard Law School, a friend and adviser of Franklin Roosevelt and in due course a Justice of the Supreme Court. Honors heaped upon honors! For Jews, prepared by temperament and ancestral memories to expect the worst, it was an ironic, marvelous fate. Marvelous, too, in that it seems to have reinforced in them a sense of their own Jewishness—there was no arriviste pretension to being other than what they were, and it was not really inconsistent that they should have been both Anglomaniacs and dedicated Zionists. Thus Weizmann, with his "passion for England," as Berlin notes, "wanted the new Jewish society—the new state—to be a political child of English—almost exclusively English—experience."

I suspect that they learned quite early to temper "Anglomania" with irony. Berlin himself, writing from the center of the English Establishment, has preserved a measure of distance from it even as he cooperates with it—he has done useful service to the state and made notable contributions to English education and philosophy. Yet his Jewishness is as essential a part of his character as his Englishness. It fortifies the detachment—not an intellectual coldness but a simple recognition and appreciation of difference—that enables him to see things around him (and about himself) with exceptional clarity.

This proved of inestimable value when he returned to Russia in the summer of 1945 for the first time since his family left in 1919—a visit that "affected me profoundly and permanently changed my outlook," and that, some 35 years later, found enduring expression in "Meetings With Russian Writers in 1945," the last, most impressive and most recent of the essays in *Personal Impressions*.

That summer Berlin, who had been working as a temporary official in the British Embassy in Washington, was told that he was being sent to the embassy in Moscow to fill "a gap until the New Year, when someone less amateur would be free to come." His assignment was to read, summarize and comment on the content of the Soviet press. The task was not arduous, in part because the periodicals he read were so predictable . . . the facts and propaganda virtually identical in them all. This meant that he had ample time for the usual sightseeing, but in addition, "unlike many foreigners, at any rate non-Communist visitors from the west," he writes, "I had the extraordinary good fortune to meet a number of Russian writers, at least two among them persons of outstanding genius." Those two were the poets Boris Pasternak and Anna Akhmatova. In his powerfully evocative and moving accounts of them both, Berlin proves himself a master of memoir.

Here is his meeting with Pasternak (in the writers' village of Peredelkino, outside Moscow): "It was a warm, sunlit afternoon in early autumn. Pasternak, his wife, and his son Leonid were seated round a rough wooden table in the tiny garden at the back of the dacha. The poet greeted us warmly. He was once described . . . as looking like an Arab and his horse: he had a dark, melancholy, expressive . . . face . . . ; he spoke slowly, in a low tenor monotone, with a continuous, even sound, something between a humming and a drone, which those who met him always remarked; each vowel was elongated as if in some plaintive, lyrical aria in an opera by Tchaikovsky, but with more concentrated force and tension."

Here is Akhmatova (in Leningrad in a sometime palace converted to a kind of tenement): "We climbed up one of the steep dark staircases to an upper floor, and were admitted to Akhmatova's room. It was very barely furnished—virtually everything in it had, I gathered, been taken away—looted or sold—during the siege; there was a small table, three or four chairs, a wooden chest, a sofa and, above the unlit stove, a drawing by Modigliani. A stately, gray-haired lady, a white shawl draped about her shoulders, slowly rose to greet us. Anna Andreevna Akhmatova was immensely dignified, with unhurried gestures, a noble head, beautiful, somewhat severe features, and an expression of immense sadness. I bowed—it seemed appropriate, as she looked and moved like a tragic queen—thanked her for receiving me, and said that people in the west would be glad to know that she was in good health, for nothing had been heard of her for so many years."

In an earlier essay, Berlin remarks, "Although I am far from taciturn myself, I was, for once, perfectly content to listen." This was obviously true in his Russian encounters. He listened and, as a corollary, answered the multitude of curious, often touching questions that were put to him. There is a memorable vignette of one of Pasternak's guests at lunch, "a woman with an indescribably innocent and sweet expression . . . a teacher who had recently returned after 15 years in a labour camp, to which she had been condemned solely for teaching English." She asked Berlin if Virginia Woolf "was still writing—she had never seen a book by her, but from an account in an old French newspaper, which in some mysterious fashion had found its way into her camp, she thought she might like her work."

"I told her (and the other guests) all I could of English, American, French writing: it was like speaking to victims of shipwreck on a desert island cut off for decades from civilization—all they heard, they received as new, exciting and delightful."

The richness of this essay, the wealth of particularities that illuminate each page and make it so fascinating—yes, and troubling—to read, by the same token make it extremely difficult to summarize. Doing so, one is conscious of the injustice being done to it: In a masterpiece of 70 pages, Berlin encompasses a society that still remains painfully remote, for all that we have been told of it.

Perhaps the single most haunting, truly terrible passage in this extraordinary memoir comes in the course of Berlin's visit with Akhmatova. "She broke off and spoke of the years 1937-8, when both her husband and her son had been arrested and were sent to prison camps (this was to happen again), of the queues of women who waited days and nights, week after week, month after month, for news of their husbands, brothers, fathers, sons, for permission to send food or letters to them—but no news ever came, no messages ever reached them—when a pall of death in life hung over the cities of the Soviet Union while the torture and slaughter of millions of innocents were going on. She spoke in a dry matter-of-fact voice, occasionally interrupting herself with 'No, I cannot, it is no good, you come from a society of human beings, whereas here we are divided into human beings and . . .' Then a long silence. 'And even now . . .'"

The contrast is inevitable between a world exemplified by two poets of genius, Russians passionately attached to the country that was preparing to silence them, and a world of "constitutional traditions that . . . ensured the dignity and liberty of human beings," to which their visitor would be returning. It is a contrast heartbreaking to contemplate, though Berlin himself is too modest and too much the artist even to allude to it. At the end he writes, "I remember

vividly the expression on their faces, their gestures and their words. When I read their writings I can, to this day, hear the sound of their voices." These **"Meetings With Russian Writers in 1945"**—like so much of this splendid book—bring the past to life. It lives for Berlin, and thanks to him, it lives for us.

Anthony Quinton (review date 1981)

SOURCE: "The Liberal Mind," in *Encounter,* Vol. LVI, No. 5, May, 1981, pp. 83-6.

[*In the following review of* Personal Impressions, *Quinton draws a picture of Berlin from an examination of Berlin's portraits of others.*]

Autobiographies are ordinarily the work of those who in certain crucial ways are unselfconscious, those who have no doubts about their own importance or interestingness, a state of mind that is the typical outcome of complete absence of a sense of humour. In the greatest autobiographies this is carried to a point of monstrosity, as in the cases of St Augustine and Rousseau, two of the most detestable human beings known to history. Cellini and Gibbon are considerably less awful, but they diffuse a chilling radiation of self-regard.

Memoirs, the record of what the subject observed rather than of what he felt and did, are the appropriate form for less self-worshipping, more self-critical spirits—for, one might say, the Isherwoods of real life, cameras preoccupied with the surrounding scene and not at all disposed to go on about their lenses, focal length, exposure speed and so forth. Being, perhaps, one degree more squeamish and humane than even the memoirists of the world, Sir Isaiah Berlin is not prepared to reveal himself through a continuous account of the interesting people he has encountered. In these *éloges*—one or two of them were, in fact, funeral orations—he and the course of his life are revealed very much *per accidens*. But a good deal is, nevertheless, communicated. His splendidly uncorseted prose is entirely reliable in its promise of pneumatic bliss, that, to be a little more specific, of being taken to its author's heart, of having his inward sentiments made clear.

He has, of course, come across some interesting and important people. But of the two men he writes of in *Personal Impressions*[1] who would have to be accounted the most important, Roosevelt and Einstein, he never met the former. And one or two of the academic people he writes about are somewhat of the village Hampden order, rescued from oblivion only by the brilliance of his account of them. But even in the grander cases the person taking the impression is as much present to the reader's mind for much of the time as the person giving it. That is in no way due to any deliberate solicitation of the reader's notice. Where he does significantly lapse into the first person singular, Berlin is usually representing himself in a gently unflattering, more or less comical light, as, for example, unable to get a word in edgeways in the presence of some equally voluminous but less companionable talker.

His intellectual vitality and range of reference, together with the copious and glittering prose in which they are so naturally expressed, are part of the reason for the very personal character of these personal impressions. But their author is interestingly distinctive in a cultural as well as an intellectual way. He was born in Latvia (then, as now once again, after two decades of independence, part of the Russian empire) a few years before the war of 1914 and left it for England in 1919 when he was ten. But he has remained, for all the successful part he has played in various rather intensely English institutions, in Oxford and out of it, both Russian and also Russian Jewish.

The Russian aspect of his personality comes out most directly here in the fine concluding essay about meetings with Anna Akhmatova and Boris Pasternak in Russia in 1945 and after. (Its most substantial product is the collection of essays on Russian thinkers which is the first of the series of four volumes of which this is the last.) He could speak their language, he was fully immersed in their literary environment, "The magnificent flowering of Russian poetry which had begun in the 1890s—the bold, creative, numerous, vastly influential experiments in the arts at the beginning of the twentieth century. . . ." But above all he could draw on a whole childhood of accumulated impressions of life in Russia at the time when his two subjects were establishing their literary careers.

At a deeper level Berlin's Russianness expresses itself in an informed concern about English political naivety and in an implied criticism of the element of priggish, pleasure-fearing respectability in English life. Neither of these themes is pursued at all explicitly. Indeed the former theme is only vestigially present, for example in the implied criticism of the kind of wet, *bien pensant* leftism represented by Herbert Read, against whom Berlin defends the prose of Winston Churchill. Churchill's prose, he argues, is the fitting expression of his particular, highly dramatic but nevertheless grownup conception of the historic strife of nations.

In general, it is not surprising that someone who knew Russia before the deluge and escaped to the shrinking remainder of the civilised world should be anxious about the threat of Asiatic despotism and concerned at the weak recognition of that threat around him among the English, happily at play in their enchanted garden. The overt form this takes is Berlin's continuing project of acquainting the English with traditions of social and political thought which go far beyond the limits set by their codes of acceptable argument and action, particularly in the essays of the third volume of this series, *Against the Current.*

The other side of his Russian background reveals itself in the qualities he singles out for praise in the friends about whom he writes. Of Maurice Bowra he says:

"All his life he liked freedom, individuality, independence, and detested everything that seemed to him to cramp and constrict the forces of human vitality. . . . He had little sympathy for those who recoiled from the forces of life—cautious, calculating conformists, or those who seemed to him prigs or prudes. . . ."

Reflecting on the influence of a more unlikely friend, Aldous Huxley, he notes particularly his role as an emancipator for young Englishmen in the 1920s and mentions an early friend whose life was in effect transformed by "the earlier, 'cynical', God-denying Huxley, the object of fear and disapproval to parents and schoolmasters." The romantic immoderation and exorbitance of Auberon Herbert is praised for its dissolvent effect on prudent narrow-mindedness. There really is a regular and systematic difference between the attitudes of the Russians and the English to the private behaviour of human beings. Russian parties are feasts in which no thought is taken for the empty larder of tomorrow; greetings and partings are occasions for operatic displays of emotion; in social life time is of no consequence. "I must have a little time on my own" is not a thought that seems naturally to occur to the Russian mind. Berlin joyfully welcomes anything in the nature of the people he has met that tends in the direction of personal abundance and fulfilment and away from the pinched mouths, drily-cleared throats and exact time-tables of English life.

Five of the fifteen people celebrated in the book are Jewish, and the essays on them are in various ways the best, particularly those on Weizmann and Namier. The latter is really the gem of the collection in many ways; it is extremely funny and yet at the same time both affectionate and respectful of Namier's power and distinction of mind. The first president of Israel and the most influential British historian of the 20th century were both Eastern Jews, one from the Russian Empire, the other from the Austrian Empire. It was in this part of the world, that of Berlin's own beginnings, that Zionism was a matter of the utmost, even deadly seriousness and not just a particular variant on the general romantic theme of 19th-century nationalism. The Jews of western Europe could see assimilation as a real possibility. They were comparatively few in number; divisions within Christianity in the countries where they lived left their dissent less exposed; their legal and social disabilities were much attenuated; they were not confined by either to particular occupations to anything like the hostility-exciting extent that the Jews of the Russian Empire were. Both Weizmann and Namier rejected the idea of assimilation.

Berlin's feeling for the world from which they came gives his accounts of Weizmann and Namier a special force. There is a particular intimacy to his understanding of their attitude toward England—a complex amalgam of love, exasperation, wonder, gratitude, disappointment, amusement. Both of them gave long and deep devotion to the idea of England. In the case of the more realistic and practically involved Weizmann, that devotion gave way in the end to a sad sense of betrayal. Namier's more fanciful notion of

England had to withstand a series of painful personal rebuffs. They were quite as much a result of his corrugations of temperament as of prejudice, which he was well designed to excite in those he met, even in its most inert and dormant forms.

One thing Berlin picks out as the specifically intellectual strand in Namier's Anglophilia is his endorsement of what he took to be a traditional English distaste for abstract theory. It took

> "a humane, civilised and, above all, sober, undramatised, empirical view of life. Englishmen seemed to him to take account, more than most men, of the real ends of human life—pleasure, justice, power, freedom, glory, the sense of human solidarity which underlay both patriotism and adherence to tradition; above all they loathed abstract principles and general theories."

That accords with his own hostility to all forms of historical determinism, with his conviction that the moving force of history is above all the free and morally assessable choices of individual human beings.

Berlin's more theoretical writings attest to his commitment to liberty as the first, even if as only *primus inter pares,* of political goods. With Namier and Weizmann he sees it as more secure, established and instinctive an element of the social arrangements of England than it is of any other country. At the same time he recognises and deplores the subjective repressions and puritanisms of English life. It could well be argued that the persistence of liberty here is not unconnected with private restraint and self-denial. Social mechanisms of control can be dispensed with where people have themselves pretty firmly in hand. Riot police are not needed for the likes of John Stuart Mill. Berlin does not explicitly make this point but it is entirely in keeping with his view that all good things cannot be enjoyed together, that there is no single all-embracing end for mankind.

Much of Berlin's sophisticated and manysided scheme of opinions and ideals emerges coherently in this book despite the extremely contingent nature of its ingredients, nearly all of which were written in response to invitations. There are three lectures, six contributions to collective volumes of one sort or another, two book reviews and only one item that appears to be self-initiated, the piece on Roosevelt, which powerfully evokes the hopeful exception he constituted, with his unflagging faith in the future, to the generally desperate atmosphere of the 1930s.

Apart from the major political figures and the distinguished Jewish subjects the main concern is with Oxford academics, four of the five being particularly identified with All Souls. Two of these, the historian Richard Pares and the political theorist John Plamenatz, are described as having "moral charm", a real human characteristic which is instantly recognisable even if one has never properly had the thought of it before, let alone adjoined the two words that so neatly indicate it. The account of Plamenatz is perhaps the most delicately perceptive of any in the book. Plamenatz, although descended from a Montenegrin family of politically explosive tradition and, it appears, with a propensity to smuggling, was a gentle, withdrawn, profoundly unemphatic person, happiest in the life of the common room at All Souls when there was an opportunity for him to converse with somebody in French. Plunged into English life at about the same time as Berlin, but when only five, he remained uninsistently foreign. Berlin likens him as "a noble exile" to Conrad, and reveres him in much the way Bertrand Russell did Conrad.

Naturally enough much of the concrete detail of personal reminiscence in these essays is set in Oxford. He is conscious of the limitations of its academic inhabitants. Of the scintillating effect of Judge Felix Frankfurter on it he writes;

> "The mixture of intellectual gaiety and general happiness generated at this and other parties was too uncommon in so artificial an establishment as the University of Oxford—where self-consciousness is the inevitable concomitant of the occupations of its inhabitants—not to stand out, as a peak of human feeling and of academic emancipation."

Of Hubert Henderson, finely described as one who "did not particularly expect or take pleasure in agreement", he says that he "suffered from neither of those two notorious occupational complexes of dons—a repressed yearning for spectacular worldly success and influence, and a resentful *odium academicum* of those who aspire to it."

Berlin's style is a well-known cultural resource. The extravagance of a Russian host is revealed in those great mounds of succulent adjectives, those glittering comparisons with interesting figures from the whole range of European culture. In his conviction of the inexhaustible individuality of each human being he cannot be content with the abstractness of a single comparison or an unqualified characterisation. The conformity between mode of expression and underlying beliefs being expressed that he discerns in Churchill is present in his own case; he practises as a writer the acknowledgment of personal uniqueness that he preaches elsewhere.

This fourth and final volume of the series in which Henry Hardy has brought together Isaiah Berlin's hitherto uncollected writings does not contain his most substantial and important works. But it is, perhaps, the most characteristic in its ready and generous admission of the gifts of others, its affectionate sensitivity, its unfailing ability to criticise without contempt and to disagree without rancour. It provides an invigorating spectacle of the liberal mind at its most assured and unobstructed, glorying in the variety of human character and achievement which it is the chief purpose of liberalism to applaud and protect.

Note

1. *Personal Impression.* By Isaiah Berlin. Chatto & Windus, £9.50.

Robert A. Kocis (essay date 1983)

SOURCE: "Toward a Coherent Theory of Human Moral Development: Beyond Sir Isaiah Berlin's Vision of Human Nature," in *Political Studies,* Vol. XXXI, No. 3, September, 1983, pp. 370-93.

[In the following excerpt, Kocis criticizes the use Berlin makes of rationalist and romantic thought in his philosophy of liberty, and Berlin responds.]

Sir Isaiah Berlin rightly contends that the 'ideas of every philosopher concerned with human affairs in the end rest on his conception of what man is and can be. To understand such thinkers, it is more important to grasp this central notion or image, which may be implicit, but which determines their picture of the world, than even the most forceful arguments with which they defend their views and refute actual and possible objections.'[1] Despite Berlin's belief that this basic vision of human life 'will, as a rule, turn out to be relatively simple and unsophisticated',[2] his own image of us is complex, subtle, and highly sophisticated. Perhaps more than any other political philosopher of his generation, Berlin has sought to articulate the complexity of human life on which our freedoms are based. Fearful of the rationalistic dangers of 'expressivism' and other theories of self-realization, Berlin sees us as self-creative, as incomplete and incapable of completion, and as capable of living in a variety of different, contradictory, yet equally valid ways. Because we cannot prove that any one way of life is 'the best', we must tolerate one another and respect others' freedom to live as they see fit.

However, this vision—which seems so compelling when first examined—turns out to be an incompatible blend of Kantian individualism and Herderian pluralism. Where the first leads Berlin to a defence of 'negative' liberty as a 'truer and more humane ideal'[3] than 'positive' liberty, the second element commits him to an ethical 'pluralism', a claim that there are no rational grounds for claiming an ethical hierarchy. Although his Kantian vision precludes any ethical relativism, Berlin's pluralism may not provide a sufficiently solid foundation for our moral and political obligations.[4] Thus we must consider the possibility that Berlin is wrong in his claims about human nature: first, that we are purposive agents, torn by an internal tension, and capable of living in a variety of ways; and second, that developmental theories ultimately culminate in paternalistic coercion (and denial of the human essence) because they seek to identify lawful regularities in human growth which imply that one way of life is superior to all others. Both claims are, I contend, false. His substantive account of us is fraught with a tension, while his criticism of developmental theories is misplaced (i.e., the danger of monism and oppression lies not in lawful regularities but in an overly-rigid teleology).

It is my contention that Berlin's almost-coherent liberalism can be reconstructed on the basis of an 'open-ended' (or non-teleological) account of human moral develop-ment. In other words, if we are to provide an account of why our obligations make sense yet still defend the human freedom to seek one's own ends, it seems that we must rely on some vision of the progression to 'higher' goods once our liberties (that is, the 'lower' or more basic goods) have been secured. Not all such theories are inherently rationalistic. Developmental theories become threats to our humanity (via oppressive, coercive, and monistic political practice) only if development is seen as culminating in 'the highest' form of life which then becomes the model for all lives, permitting no deviation from this true path. A pluralistic developmentalism could, by contrast, view a limited array of obligations as providing the necessary ground of security on which our other moral potentials can grow while still permitting—if not requiring—that there are no rational grounds for believing that some one end of human development is to take precedence over all the others. Berlin is right, then, to oppose rationalism; but he is wrong to presume that all developmental theories are inherently rationalistic and he mistakenly refuses to employ a developmental theory to defuse a tension within his vision of our nature.

RATIONALISM AND HUMAN CHANGEABILITY

At the root of much of Berlin's political and ethical philosophy—including his theory of human nature—is a conviction that the Western tradition of rationalism is fundamentally mistaken. In Berlin's eyes, our tradition has been so dominated by this monism that even the anti-rationalist movements (including romanticism, existentialism, and much of empiricism) accept as sacred the basic assumption of rationalism: every real question about human existence and actions has one and only one true answer. The consequences of acting on this mistaken assumption have been disastrous. 'One belief, more than any other, is responsible for the slaughter of individuals on the altars of the great historical ideals,' Berlin writes, and this is the 'belief that somewhere, in the past or the future, in divine revelation or in the mind of an individual thinker, in the pronouncements of history or science, or in the simple heart of an uncorrupted good man, there is a final solution.'[5] This rejection of a belief in 'the final solution' places Berlin outside the mainstream of Western political thought.

Yet his is not simply a utilitarian calculation that the result of acting on this belief—whether or not it is mistaken—has been human suffering. Rather, Berlin is convinced that the belief is itself incoherent, so that suffering is the not surprising result of acting on a mistaken belief. For if this belief is false, Berlin notes, then 'the idea of the sole true, objective, universal human ideal crumbles. The very search for it becomes not merely utopian in practice, but conceptually incoherent.'[6] Logically, the claim that a final solution can come to be known depends either on some rationalistic view of the cosmos (like Hegel's notion of Spirit) or on some rationalistic view of human nature. The psychological foundation, in turn, of a belief in 'the final solution' could be either (a) some eternal truth about our unchanging and rational human nature which makes the certainty of such an answer possible; or (b) a truly discoverable pattern to human development which enables us to foresee a time when all valid human desires will be simultaneously achievable, thereby ending the irrationality which breeds current tragedy/disaster and the apparent need for a final solution. We can see Berlin, then, as rejecting the rationalistic element of any account of human nature which would begin with seemingly unchanging drives and instincts which would require that we all live in one way (block A, Table 1) or with some account of the psychological laws which move people from one stage of development to the next until the true human end has been reached (block C, Table 1).

Berlin addresses questions of human nature, then, in the context of his opposition to rationalistic monism. What he seeks is akin to what he thinks John Stuart Mill sought: a fusion of rationalism and romanticism.[7] But, compelling as it seems, Berlin's account of human nature fails to harmonize this dissonance.

The Problem in Berlin's Account of Human Nature and a Possible Solution

Given Berlin's project—fusing romanticism and rationalism—it is no surprise that his vision of human nature is subtle and complex. For the sake of simplicity, we might see his account of human nature as proceeding along three distinct levels: the monistic, the dualistic, and the pluralistic. Alone, no one of these levels captures all of Berlin's significant claims about us; but the three together do not constitute a coherent package.

At the first level, Berlin sees human beings as single, unified agents. In this romanticized version of Kant, purposiveness replaces rationality as the central, essential, and universal characteristic of the species. Any being said to be totally lacking the basic moral intuitions of normal persons would be said to be in human.[8] We are characterized by agency and creativity. Considering cases which illustrate the universality of certain of our moral traits, Berlin writes that the truth of them lies 'at the basis of modern translations into empirical terms of the kernel of truth in the old *a priori* Natural Law doctrines'.[9] At this level, then, we may conclude that there is, for Berlin, an eternal and universal essence of humanity which extends universality to some of our moral values, but does not entail that we must all live in one way (and so is probably a static kind of non-teleological theory, block D, Table 1).

TABLE 1. A Typology of Theories of Human Nature.

	Static	Environmentalist	Developmentalist
Teleological	A	B	C
Non-teleological	D	E	F

A=human needs are static and the satisfaction of those needs requires that we all live in one way

D=human needs are static but numerous and diverse, so that we might live in any number of different ways

B=humans can be shaped and moulded and some vision of the good should guide this shaping so that we all become good

E=humans can be shaped and moulded, but there is no one mould into which we should all be cast

C=human needs and motives change and grow, culminating in the highest level of development

F=human needs and motives change and grow, but after a certain minimum is assured, people develop in diverse and conflicting directions

At the second level, Berlin's is a more romantic, and even tragic, view of us as torn from within, so that the formal unity of agency is subjected to divisive forces.[10] On the one hand, there is within us a need to attend to life in all its diversity and detail, a need simply to observe (i.e., a need to be like a 'fox'). On the other hand, there is also within us a strong drive to coherence, a drive to find a pattern into which we can fit all of life's diversity (i.e., a need to be like a 'hedgehog'). The conflict between these two drives/forces can result in compulsion, so that we feel that we must act even when we should know to stop. Not being able to bring these competing forces into some sort of rational balance is taken, by Berlin, to be a kind of pathological immaturity. Giving in to the metaphysical compulsion to bring everything into one pattern can make of us dangerous tyrants, pushing and shoving others to fit into our vision of the good life, as if they were not also persons. If, at the first level, Berlin's more formalistic vision of humanity requires that our dignity be respected, this romantic second level entails the possibility of human heroism and nobility, as well as the possibility of tragedy and depravity. (These drives/forces are either instinctual, and so a version of block D, Table 1, or they are developmental and so a version of block F.)

Finally, at the third level, the empirical diversity of human cultures suggests to Berlin that there are a number of different ways of life which seem to suit human nature.[11] No one of these ways is demonstrably superior to others. For Berlin, this entails that our values are pluralistic and that our cultures are only relatively good. In short, Berlin is convinced that any one of a number of ways of life is equally stable, equally viable, and equally good for us as human beings. (Apparently, this 'organicism'[12] is a version of block E, Table 1.)

Berlin lays these levels one over the other, creating a many-faceted view of humanity. The universalism of the first level can only be characterized as a romanticized version of Kantian personalities. But, at the second and third levels, the concerns with diversity, variety, creativity, and tragedy are natural opponents of this universalism. This tension is not inconsequential, since it leads Berlin to contradictory ethical implications from each of these visions. Berlin's vision of our purposiveness suggests to him some need for a liberal society, just as Kant's vision of our rationality suggested to him the need for liberal autonomy. For if we are naturally purposive beings, then not just any form of life will do; we need the rights of a liberal society to protect us in our purposes. Any form of life which denies us this freedom to live for ourselves is necessarily defective.

But if the path from purposiveness to liberty seems direct, the paths from the dualist and pluralist levels must seem less so; perhaps they even require a detour through purposiveness. Because (at the dualistic level) we are torn by the internal conflict between universality and diversity, it can happen that some of us are not sufficiently mature, and so too compulsive, to recognize that other persons need to choose their ends if they are to retain their dignity. This second level, then, might be seen as reinforcing the need for moral and political rights, *if* our purposiveness is to be protected (i.e., only if the first level describes us accurately). But—significantly—if human dignity were not dependent upon each person's having his/her own purposes, then we might be willing to permit those who are convinced that they have the truth to try their hand at creating a new and better society, thereby unleashing their compulsiveness.

Similarly, Berlin believes that the third (pluralistic) level of his vision of our nature entails some degree of liberty. If there are a number of ways of life which accord equally well with human nature, then there will always be some people who would prefer to opt for one alternative way of life. However, again, the liberality of society is not a necessary implication of this level without the premise drawn from the universalist account of humanity as purpose-seeking. If many different ways of life are suitable for humanity, then it would not matter if some were to impose their preferences on others unless we were convinced that purposiveness is a distinctively human characteristic whose loss entails the loss of our humanity.

Thus, Berlin's complex vision of humanity involves two contradictory strains: there is a monistic, formalistic strain (Kantian) emphasizing the universality of human purposiveness and requiring liberty; and there is a dualistic and pluralistic strain (Herderian) centring on the variety of arrangements suitable for us as humans and which need not require that a way of life have any particular characteristic. On the one hand, from the more universalist strain, Berlin concludes that liberty is of special value; this vision of humanity entails a substantive ethical defence of liberty as a value deserving a special status among the goods. On the other hand, on the basis of his more pluralistic vision of humankind, Berlin concludes that there is a variety of goods to which humans can subscribe. This doctrine, which Berlin calls pluralism, is a depiction of morality as lacking any rationally-discoverable structure, so that there are no rational grounds for preferring one value (not even liberty) over any other. Where Berlin's pluralistic meta-ethic precludes the possibility of rank-ordering the values or claiming that one is 'better' than another, his substantive ethical theory expresses his valuing of negative liberty as significantly more important than another value. If we assume that the conflicting intuitions (that we value liberty as es-

pecially important for the achievement of the other values, and also that we must not impose our ideals—not even liberty—upon others) are basically valid, then we must seek another account of human nature on which to ground them.

This alternative psychological theory must recognize the plurality of ideals for which people can live and act; yet it must also provide the ground for justifying our moral obligations to respect the rights of others. It would seem that only a developmental moral psychology could accommodate both claims. Yet this theory must exclude the possibility of any one path of growth which would be best for all people. If we were to illustrate this alternative vision of the emerging higher motivations with a device like Maslow's pyramid, we would need to invert a second pyramid and place it atop the peak of Maslow's. This would suggest that 'self-actualization' is not a single goal, but a series of (probably conflicting) goals. With this vision of human moral psychology, we can adopt Berlin's pluralism (for the higher values) without failing to show the reason behind our moral obligations (for example, it is reasonable to require that we respect each other's rights so that we might be secure enough to move on to the higher goods). This view would be most properly conceived as a form of non-teleological developmentalism (block F, Table 1). Such a view of human moral development enables us to retain the kernel of truth in Berlin's pluralism without sacrificing our moral obligations, enabling us to portray liberty as a value of fundamental importance to human growth without depicting it as the height of human moral accomplishment. Yet Berlin argues that such a theory is flawed by a propensity to rationalistic monism.

THE LOGIC OF THE PERVERSION OF DEVELOPMENTALISMS

It is Hegel's cosmic vision of the underlying logical and psychological pattern to human moral development which is the vision that Berlin sees as necessarily implying a kind of authoritarianism. Yet in rejecting historicism, Berlin is not rejecting history but opting for a more empirical conception of history. Hegel sees history as a great museum, filled with artefacts from tried and failed experiments at living, each made obsolete by the success of the 'Cunning of Reason'. Like dinosaurs, the unfree of antiquity could not survive, since the human spirit requires freedom. By contrast, Berlin sees history as a kind of zoo, where there are a number of different ways of life, each appropriate for the species living them. To try to make a nineteenth-century Londoner of a second-century Roman is as great a mistake as trying to make a gorilla of an elephant. Each is unique, each has its own needs—there is no one right way for all humans to live. There is no one trial which, by virtue of its clear superiority, will end the historical search for life's worth and meaning.

Where Berlin sees no logic informing a choice between different ways of life, so that there is a variety of competing and equally valid models for living, Hegel detected a grand pattern of logical development connecting one lower form of life with each subsequent, higher form of life. Unlike Berlin, who sees the ancient ideal of the republic as a viable alternative to modernity, Hegel would see the whole *ethos* of that life as psychologically unbearable for fully-developed moderns. The human spirit is moved by a need to be free, and one way of life will give way before another until the final goal of freedom for all people is reached. He appreciates that the ancient Greeks had a great and vibrant civilization, but he could not see it as a viable alternative or even as a stable way of life. Rather, sooner or later, a Socrates would happen along, insisting that it was not enough to accept the way of the gods and asserting that people need to be reflective and conscious of their lives. The conviction that 'the unexamined life is not worth living' expresses the human need to surpass the accepted way of life, yielding a predisposition to think and challenge which is not conducive to the preservation of an *otherwise* satisfactory way of life. And so Hegel follows the march of rational human needs for freedom through history, discovering a coherence to our development, detecting a moral progression in the succession of cultures. Hegel was convinced that people would eventually eliminate the ruined patterns of life, and settle into a way of life which would prove satisfactory. Hegel proves to be Berlin's most powerful adversary because he most adequately suggests that there are rational criteria for choosing one life (say, the free life of a modern German) over another (say, the squalor, misery, and degradation of the life of an ancient Greek or Chinese slave or peasant). Antiquity may have had beautiful ideals, reflecting a concern for nobility, but life in such a society would be unbearable for us.

Hegel thought that this implied the inevitability of human freedom. Although such a view of the developmental need for freedom requires a dedication to liberty, still Berlin insists that the conception of human existence at its core inevitably perverts this dedication: coercing the empirical person comes to be justified by appeal to the more rational being she/he might become. Examining the metaphor of 'self-mastery', Berlin detects in it the conceptual danger of the 'metaphysical division of the person'.[13] In expressing the ways in which we liberate ourselves from the slavery to our own drives, we normally begin to speak in terms of two distinct agents: the one is moved by brutish instincts, a slave to his/her nature; the other embodies the faculty of reason, and is a higher, more noble, more developed, and ideally dominant self. This self then becomes identified with the 'real' self, with our 'higher nature', and becomes the goal toward which all of us are to strive or be pushed. This 'higher self', writes Berlin, 'is then contrasted with irrational impulse, uncontrolled desires, my "lower" nature, the pursuit of immediate pleasures, my "empirical" or "heteronomous" self, swept by every gust of desire and passion, needing to be rigidly disciplined if it is ever to rise to the full height of its "real" nature. . . .'[14] Only the rational purposes of the fully developed persons lying submerged in us are then worth pursuing. If we are permitted to seek our perverse purposes, none of us will ever reach the good life. Thus, since we all would seek this good life if only our rational selves were in control of our irrational impulses, we must be coerced to be rational.

In this way, such a division of the self results in a destruction of our chances to choose our own purposes; in other words, it destroys our humanity. So Berlin objects that 'it is one thing to say that I know what is good for X while he himself does not, and a very different one to say that he has *eo ipso* chosen it, not indeed consciously, not as he seems in everyday life, but in his role as a rational self which his empirical self may not know—the "real" self which discerns the good, and cannot help choosing it once it is revealed.'[15]

Berlin's hostility to theories of 'self-realization' is thus understandable: 'This monstrous impersonation, which consists in equating what X would choose if he were something he is not, or at least not yet, with what X actually seeks and chooses, is at the heart of all political theories of self-realization.'[16] Thus, views of self-realization seem inevitably to result in a denial of each person's purposes, setting against our real and existent purposes those more rational purposes we should have if we are ever to achieve the harmoniously good life as some reformer sees it. Berlin concludes that this finally denies what is distinctively human in us: 'To threaten a man with persecution unless he submits to a life in which he exercises no choice of his goals; to block before him every door but one, no matter how noble the prospect upon which it opens, or how benevolent the motives of those who arrange this, is to sin against the truth that he is a man, a being with his own life to live.'[17]

Thus, Berlin concludes that transformational views are a new mask for paternalism—'the greatest despotism imaginable'[18] for both Berlin and Kant. Taking up a transformational view of human nature leads one to feel that 'I am in a position to ignore the actual wishes of men or societies, to bully, oppress, torture them in the name, and on behalf, of their "real" selves, in the secure knowledge that whatever is the true goal of man (happiness, performance of duty, wisdom, a just society, self-fulfilment) must be identical with his freedom—the free choice of his "true", albeit often submerged and inarticulate, self.'[19] It will not do to coerce people to be better; this retreat to 'the inner citadel' of our truly rational nature purports to provide answers to life's most pressing and puzzling questions, but it does so only by imposing the ideals of one person or group upon others. The elements of developmentalism in the doctrines of Vico, Herder, Hegel and Marx lead, Berlin fears, to one unified view of what it 'really' means to be human. All will lead, in practice, to a despotism by those who best understand the dynamics of human development. All are not only antithetical to liberty, but they are antithetical to humanity, because they deny a vision of persons as having their own purposes, as having their own lives to live, as having their own reasons for being the persons they are and not the persons that the rationalist ideal declares that they ought to be.

RATIONALISM, DEVELOPMENTALISM, AND TELEOLOGY

Berlin's opposition to rationalistic monism, coupled with his desire to fuse the traditions of rationalism and romanticism, does not lead him down the romantic path chosen by less empirical thinkers like Vico, Herder, Hegel and Marx. For, despite the romantic (anti-rationalistic) elements in their thought, they are all fatally flawed by the assumption that all questions about human existence can, in principle, be answered. The problem with such views, from Berlin's perspective, is that inevitably they group all persons into one of two classes: the enlightened (who detect the pattern of human growth and are instrumental in fostering it) and the unenlightened (who are ignorant of that pattern of growth and are an impediment to it). This chasm between the fully-developed and the undeveloped—much like the chasm between the rational and the appetitive within Plato's *Republic*—ultimately perverts the hopes of Marxism: 'But his [Lenin's] practice was strangely like that of those irrationalist reactionaries who believed that man was everywhere wild, bad, stupid, and unruly, and must be held in check and provided with objects of uncritical worship. This must be done by a clear-sighted band of organizers, whose tactics—if not ideals—rested on the truths perceived by elitists . . . men who had grasped the true nature of social development . . .'[20] This implies that those who are not yet rational (less than fully developed) must be moved along the true path.

In Berlin's eyes, the only hope for human liberation is to keep in mind that there are certain classical models of life, based on valid moralities, among which it is human to choose. Human liberty is thus the key to dignity, since it protects each person's ability to live for his/her own purposes. It is human to change; but we cannot *be changed* and retain our humanity. To the extent that developmental theories permit—or even require—that the undeveloped be developed/changed, so these theories are prone to rationalist monism and ultimately to oppressive practices.

Yet, obviously, developmental theories are not rationalistic in the same way that static views are; where, from the perspective of static views, our nature is universal and eternal so that our needs and motivations are always the same (always requiring that we live in only one way), developmental views recognize that it is human to change. But if the developmentalists are right, then there is a fairly ordered set of principles governing human development. Berlin's is a 'slippery slope' argument: once theorists take a step in the direction of expressing these laws, they begin down the slope and are unable to prevent the slide down to oppression. If there were demonstrable dynamics of human change, after all, then these laws could be discovered by the more astute, whose obligation it would then become to see that we live up to our potential. Instead of freeing people to live as they see fit, transformational views—despite the best of intentions—may result in our coercing each other in the rush to a more satisfying existence. So Berlin mistakenly argues that openended developmentalism (block F) logically culminates in teleological developmentalism (block C, Table 1). Yet, I want to argue, Berlin should be arguing for an open-ended developmentalism (block F) in his classical defence of liberty.

However, he is precluded from this move because he cast his arguments against expressivism and theories of self-realization in such general terms that all efforts to understand the regularities of human moral development are seen to be rationalistically flawed and so committed to one final end. Of course, the 'truth' to be discovered about development—and so the danger—in such accounts is that some one goal moves (or will end) this growth. All the thinkers Berlin criticizes have or imply some account of that one, true, highest goal which all rational humans seek. Berlin is aware of the role of teleology in this perversion, but he does not assign to it the centrality it deserves: 'So long as only one ideal is the true goal, it will always seem to men that no means can be too difficult, no price too high, to do whatever is required to realize the ultimate goal. Such certainty is one of the great justifications of fanaticism, compulsion, persecution.'[21] Berlin is convinced that a vision of human actualization necessarily entails the threatening conclusion that some one form of life is the most developed and thus constitutes the highest goal toward which all humans should be moving. We must then actualize this rationally specified goal, and not our own perverse goals, in our lives.

Berlin is right that there is some kind of perversion of an ideal occurring here; but he is wrong to attribute it to the detecting of lawful regularities in growth and change. The problem is rather to be found in the rigid commitment to teleology in these theories; goalers can become gaolers. Berlin has thus misunderstood the nature of developmental theories, depicting them as necessarily culminating in some single way of life which is supposed to be best for all of humanity. But not all versions of developmentalism need be monistic and teleological; they need not even be prone to monism and teleology.

TOWARD AN OPEN-ENDED DEVELOPMENTALISM

Although Hegel was not squarely within the liberal tradition, still his dedication to liberty and his defence of liberty as historically necessary remain gripping, even if mistaken. Contemporary thinking about politics and about human nature, whether Marxist or liberal, has not broken this grip, as we seek a way to account for the obvious human ability to grow and progress as well as to regress and become violent. Yet few contemporary theorists are committed to a vision of the one ideal to end all history. For example, a psychological theory like Maslow's can suggest that certain things are necessary to unleash various human potentials—starving people do not seek liberty, equality, and fraternity—without declaring that there is only one right way to live. Hence, we may recognize that some regularities govern the process of change without becoming committed to psychological teleology. As J. Roland Pennock puts it, such a view of the capacity of human nature to develop once certain basic conditions have been met, while not universally accepted, at the very least 'suggests in a general way how liberty can be of primary importance, a primary value, and yet not be a major concern of men under all conditions'.[22] Liberty is not the height of human accomplishment nor the end of human development; it is simply necessary to such development.

Similarly, the psychological security of justice might be seen as neutralizing egotism, thereby unleashing the growth of the higher moral sentiments. As our rights are secured and respected, each of us might find that our selfish instincts are neutralized, enabling our higher motivations to emerge. For instance, Rawls' theory of justice can be seen as resting on an open-ended developmentalism: 'The key to Rawls's moral psychology is his acceptance of a modernized version of Rousseau's moral psychology, that given the neutralization of their egoistic impulses, men's moral potentialities will be released.'[23] Rousseau had suggested that improper institutions could thwart this development; Rawls is more sanguine in his contention that in a well-ordered society, 'the hazards of the generalized prisoner's dilemma are removed by the match between the right and the good'.[24] The point of such a moral psychology is that it is not a matter of inculcating these higher values (despite Brian Barry's argument that Rawls is advocating such conditioning[25]—that is, that Rawls is best understood in terms of block B rather than block F in Table 1). Rather, it is a matter of creating a context in which they might be *called forth*. No Skinnerian who would condition us to be 'good', Rawls is concerned with eliciting our nobler instincts, and would view an imposition of 'virtue' as a violation of his first principle. Thus, on the basis of a developmental psychology, Rawls argues that we can rationally establish a monism of the right (which establishes our moral obligations) while permitting a pluralism of the goods (which creates space for individuals to grow in a variety of directions).

Chapman's defence of liberalism is in this respect, as in many others, similar to Rawls'. He too sees necessity at work in human development. But, unlike Hegel, Chapman does not think this necessity will bring about an end to history or to human diversity. He detects a kind of psychodynamic at work in history, due to a pressing human need for stable individuation which can be met only under conditions of liberty and justice. The existence of a 'universal human dynamic in the shape of a drive to individuality'[26] convinces Chapman that any effort to thwart such a drive creates a resistance which pushes us back toward an equilibrium point. This is an image of the human personality as a grand mobile, as an equilibrated balancing act. Of course, not all equilibria need be identical, but all of the forces within us must be in balance. There is a necessity to human moral development, then, but it is not necessary that we all develop into one specified kind of human being.

A proponent of such an open-ended theory might maintain that Berlin's criticism rests on a misunderstanding of developmentalisms; the laws of human development are not

objects out in the world, standing against the human material they direct, but are themselves internal. They do not change us; we initiate the change because of our all too human needs. Each historical change from one way of life to another can then be seen as an expression of a deeply-felt human yearning. Once people become aware that their current way of life is not satisfying their needs and that there is an alternative which promises to satisfy them, it is only human to pursue the new way of life with its promise. We desire new ways of life which offer a greater possibility of self-realization.

This claim that our internal needs are expressed in cultural changes has been called 'expressionism'[27] by Berlin and 'expressivism'[28] by Charles Taylor; Hegel remains its classic proponent. Berlin traces the idea back to Herder and uses the development of this idea as an example of the way a developmental psychology is eventually pushed to its final, rationalistic, conclusion by people seeking to act on it. Sharing Vico's concern for detecting the organic interconnections of various aspects of a culture, Herder claimed that each aspect of a culture was an 'expression' of the personality or quality of an individual or group. As each person or people strives to express its most deeply felt longings, we come to a higher level of self-realization. Herder links this notion with that of populism (a belief that individuals value belonging to a group and that persons identify with their people) to conclude that the various ways of life open to us are finally incompatible. In short, Herder concludes that nationalism (belonging to a people or *volk*) is natural.

Berlin is fascinated and appalled by the perverse logic that twists a pluralistic theory like expressivism into monistic and oppressive political practices. Herder began as 'one of the earliest opponents of uniformity as the enemy of life and freedom. . . . Herder is an early and passionate champion of variety: uniformity mains and kills.'[29] Thus, so long as expressivism remains pluralistic, it can (and did) lead to a defence of liberty and diversity in the name of the various aspects of the human soul which need to be expressed. Yet, despite its pluralistic beginnings, the very idea of expressivism is flawed by its propensity to monism, leading its adherents inevitably to the conclusion that there is one preferred way of life, which best expresses universal needs. Berlin's definition of the term reveals his deep distrust:

> 2. Expressionism: the doctrine that human activity in general, and art in particular, expresses the entire personality of the individual or group, and are intelligible only to the degree to which they do so . . . This is connected with the further notions that every form of self-expression is in some sense artistic, and that self-expression is part of the essence of human beings as such; which in turn entail such distinctions as those between integral and divided, or committed or uncommitted (that is, unfulfilled) lives; and thence lead to the concept of various hindrances, human and non-human, to the self-realization that all creatures, whether or not they are aware of it, live for.[30]

In short, although Herder is a pluralist, his expressivism is logically prone to monism and so to paternalism.

Much as Plato's distinction between truth and opinion led him (quite logically) to advocate rule by wise guardians, so this idea of expressivism has within it the roots of Hegel's view that some ways of life do not adequately express one or another aspect of human personalities and are thus not fulfilling. If this expressivist view of our nature is accurate, then the more rational among us are more aware of the needs which human beings must express and they can consequently lead all of us to a more satisfying existence. So Berlin concludes that it is not enough to see the laws of human development as internal; the very existence of laws provides some people with an apparent obligation to push and prod the rest of us toward a different life. Although Herder is enough of a relativist to avoid an absolute scale against which each cultural expression of the human spirit is to be measured, the view itself is flawed because it can be made to justify violence to real persons (who are not *fully* human yet) in the rush to a more fulfilling life.

Against the developmentalists and the expressivists, Berlin holds up (his notion of) Mill's model of human change: there is no pattern, but novelty, variety, and creativity to be found in change. There is no one end which will complete our quest; rather, we are perpetually incomplete and incapable of completion. There can be little doubt that Berlin and Mill agree fundamentally about human nature: both see humanity as purposive; both value human diversity; and both are committed to a tolerance of different, even eccentric, life styles. Both recognize that we change, rejecting the ancient notion of an eternal species; and both are convinced that there is no one ideal or end which will be suitable for all people. But Berlin has not correctly described the vision of life and humanity underlying their shared liberality. My contention here is that Mill is a kind of developmentalist and that, in misunderstanding Mill, Berlin has misunderstood his own accomplishment. For there are, I contend, elements of developmentalism in both of their accounts of human nature; if Berlin's slippery slope argument were accurate, then both he and Mill would already be on the slope toward oppression.

A DEVELOPMENTALIST ACCOUNT OF MILL AND BERLIN

A. Strains of Developmentalism in Mill. An exegesis and critical assessment of Mill is not possible here. Rather, for our purposes (which involve determining if Berlin is right that the very notion of a lawful pattern to human change necessarily leads to a repudiation of some ways of life and to an elevation of the one right way of life), it will be enough to show that there are strains of developmentalism in Mill's writings. Some of Berlin's critics have noted this; and some of Mill's writings suggest that the critics are more accurate than is Berlin in this case.

Mandelbaum, an historian concerned with the ways we changed our conception of ourselves in the nineteenth century, suggests that there were two principal types of psy-

chological theories opposed to the static ideals of personality inherited from the Enlightenment. The first group of theories about human change depict the impetus for change as originating externally, in the environment. This type of theory includes both the environmentalist (or associationist) tradition which holds that human experiences condition our characters and the organicist view which holds that great cultural templates determine human character. (These would be found in either block B or block E, Table 1.) By contrast, there was a second type of psychological theory which was a description of us as changing from within; these views Mandelbaum calls 'self-transformational'.[31] As a representative of the self-transformational theorists, Mandelbaum chose Mill (putting him, in effect, either in block C or block F, Table 1).

Of course, much of the change in us which is of concern to Mill originates in the accidents of experiential associations (that is, some elements of Mill's thinking are best classified as environmentalist, as in block E, Table 1). Yet, Mandelbaum insists, there is a notion of progress running through Mill's writings, suggesting that human changes have not been simply random but progressive. The element of teleology here leads me to think that Mandelbaum would see Mill as primarily a representative of teleological developmentalism (as in block C, Table 1).

Similarly, Cumming has taken Berlin to task for overlooking the developmentalist aspects of Mill's psychology. Cumming fears that there is 'no scope left in Berlin's analysis . . . for a process of development . . .'.[32] The insight to be discovered in Mill's account, as Cumming notes in Berlin's own choice of quotation from Mill, is 'the importance . . . of giving full freedom to human nature to expand itself in innumerable and conflicting directions'.[33] Cumming's point is that Berlin ignores Mill's developmentalism: 'But there is one phrase which Berlin does not pick up in his interpretation—"to expand itself".'[34] Cumming concludes that Mill's account is developmental and derives its power from its avoidance of the heteronomy of environmentalism and organicism. (If Cumming is right, Mill belongs in block C, Table 1.)

A considerable portion of Mill's writings indicate that there are at least elements of developmentalism in his account.[35] Only a few can be mentioned here. First, we should note that Mill's defence of the 'liberal principle', that rights must be respected as (almost) absolute and liberties can never be infringed except to prevent or redress a wrong, rests on a vision of the process of human moral maturation: 'It is perhaps, hardly necessary to say that this doctrine is meant to apply only to human beings in the maturity of their faculties,'[36] writes Mill. The principles of liberty cannot be applied to any state of society 'anterior to the time when mankind have become capable of being improved by free and equal discussion'. If a people has matured to reason, they should be free; if not, then 'there is nothing for them but implicit obedience to an Akbar or a Charlemagne. . . .'[37]

Second, Mill suggests that education fosters human development. 'Whatever invigorates the faculties in however small measure, creates an increased desire for their unim-peded exercise. . . .'[38] For Mill, we are progressive be-ings; the human spirit is such that, so long as it is not held down by exterior forces, exposure to reality (say, through education) generates pressures in demand of freedom. In short, there is no doubt in Mill's mind that some ways of life are superior to others, and that there are pressures within us which, so long as they are not deflected, would lead us to a life of freedom (that is, Mill can be thought of as in block C, Table 1).[39]

B. Strains of Developmentalism in Berlin. Berlin's theory of human nature is also a (disguised) form of developmen-talism, I contend, although his conception is less teleologi-cal than is Mill's. Two aspects of his writings support this contention: first, Berlin recognizes certain negative psy-chodynamics (or processes of degeneration) and, second, his vision of human life also involves a more positive psy-chodynamic (or process of human moral development).

Any realistic account of development must recognize that our purposes can degenerate under adverse conditions. Im-plicit in some of Berlin's writings is a claim that human potential can be thwarted. Underlying Berlin's diagnosis of the ills of the twentieth century, for instance, is a view of the regularities of human development: compelled by our own rationalism, we may seek to impose our ideals upon others. Yet, if humans are denied the psychic security of the liberty to live their own lives, then it can be pre-dicted that the quality of their lives will deteriorate as they seek to restore their dignity.[40]

A good example of such degeneration, and of the resultant internal forces which lead people to lash out in their need for change, is Berlin's metaphor of the 'bent twig' to de-scribe the virulence of nationalism. In Berlin's view, na-tionalism is not a central human tendency, somehow the outgrowth of a need for community. Rather, it is a result of the thwarting of another human tendency toward dig-nity and self-respect. Thus, the historical insults and hu-miliations inflicted on one group (say, the Germans) by another group (say, the French) deprived the first of their personal and collective dignity. The result of this disequili-bration was an outburst of nationalistic sentiment. The metaphor suggests that humiliation is a force bending the green twig of human potential, providing it with the force to snap back. Nationalism becomes some kind of destructive-yet-reconstructive force aimed at re-equilibrating the conflicting forces by seeking to end op-pression and so to re-establish dignity and self-respect. Thus, despite his criticisms of laws of human development which connect one historical event with a later one, Berlin employs them to explain phenomena like nationalism.

Similarly, Berlin's interpretation of Machiavelli rests on a perception of this dynamic of degeneration. Machiavelli's reading of Christianity suggests that some ways of life stifle the human need for a public life. Berlin's Machia-velli claims that human nature cannot tolerate this: 'the nature of man dictates a public morality that is different

from, and may come into collision with, the virtues of men who profess to believe in, and try to act by, Christian precepts . . . Men cannot long survive in such conditions.'[41] Indeed, if Machiavelli and Aristotle are right about our nature, then 'political activity is intrinsic to hu-man nature, and while individuals here and there may opt out, the mass of mankind cannot do so. . . .'[42] This almost Rousseauist analysis leaves the reader with the impression that, if bent too far, the twig no longer snaps back, but snaps off. Humanity withers and dies in the absence of certain conditions; there are predictable processes of hu-man deterioration.

Liberty, for Berlin as for Montesquieu, is a necessary con-dition for human development: without it, all higher hu-man values fail to flower. Thus, liberty occupies a special place in the constellation of values. 'Liberty is not total in-dependence, nor is it licence,' writes Berlin in this context. 'It is very hard to attain and preserve, but without it all things wither. No amount of efficiency of government, na-tional glory, prosperity, social equality, can compensate for its loss.'[43] Liberty seems to be of special value to Berlin, not only as an end, but also as a condition for achieving other ends. In its absence, the hope of achieving other ends withers. In Berlin's theory, then, the reason why we value liberty in a special way is because other values flour-ish in its presence and wither in its absence. We so value liberty because we are the sorts of beings who can nurture other ends in its context; but, without it, a negative dy-namic is unleashed—'without it all things wither'.

Further, implicit in this claim about degeneration is a view that, if liberty is secured, we will develop in positive, though probably contradictory, directions. This suggests that bringing liberty into a form of life where it was ab-sent leads to a transformation of people, unleashing their potentials to achieve other goods. It is not only the case that in its absence other potentials wither; it is also true that its presence is conducive to human growth. In other words, there is also a positive dimension to the laws of psychology, although it need not specify that one way of life is best for all people. Thus we need liberty to avoid the destructive effects of deterioration and to develop a va-riety of potentials for other goods.

If Berlin offers us a view of humanity as growing and de-generating in accord with certain regularities, then the dif-ference between Berlin and the expressivists is not one of form but of substance. Both Berlin and the expressivists see us as developing, as changing in response to deeply felt internal needs. But they differ over what those needs are. The expressivists see us as having a stronger need for community than Berlin detects; for Berlin, the dynamics of nationalism are the result of the more intense and more basic needs for dignity and self-respect. If, however, a de-velopmentalist theory elevates the need for community to the status of the highest of the human ideals, then the dan-ger does exist of forcing people to be 'free', of coercing persons into intense interrelations with one another. Then 'good government' would become paternalistic and even oppressive, insisting that one way of life is good for all people and that the substance of this life is clearly known (or knowable). But Berlin is probably right that a view of human nature which focuses on our purposiveness, rather than on our need for community, is less likely to be teleologically perverted because it requires that persons be free to pursue their own ends, one of which could be community. Here, then, is the distance which separates Berlin from the Marxists and other communitarian philosophers: liberty is an end more basic to the good life than is community. The difference between Berlin and Macpherson—not only one of the most powerful exponents of a Marxian position but also one of the most true to Marx—does not centre around the developmentalism espoused by Macpherson but around the teleological conviction, articulated by Macpherson, that we are moving ineluctably toward coherence and harmony.[44]

We must conclude, then, that both Berlin and Mill have elements of developmentalism in their theories; yet the anti-teleological nature of their thought, taken in the round, militates against perversion (although this is somewhat less true of Mill than of Berlin). Of course, the danger does exist that someone could smuggle into such a vision the assumption that there is some target toward which we are developing. Then they could attempt to justify the imposition of their single ideal upon others. But this error does not originate in developmentalism, in lawful regularities of change, nor even in the distinction between fulfilled and unfulfilled lives. This mistake originates in the teleological assumption that we are developing *toward* some rationally specifiable end rather than *out of* our pre-social (or pre-moral or pre-political) confusion of liberty with licence and out of the consequent mistaking of self-interest for the good. In other words, some developmental theorists insist that only one (or one group) of our potentials is worth realizing; yet other theorists more accurately recognize that there are many forms of self-realization.

CONCLUSION

Berlin's is an almost coherent defence of liberty and our liberal tradition. But his pluralistic vision of morality ultimately rests on a mistaken opposition to theories of human moral development. This difficulty is logical and can first be seen by detecting the contradictory ethical implications Berlin draws from the various levels of his vision of our nature: his universalistic and Kantian vision of human purposiveness leads him to defend 'negative' liberty as a 'truer and more humane ideal' than 'positive' liberty, which suggests that morality possesses a logical structure; while his Herderian doctrine of pluralism is a claim that humanity can live in a plurality of ways and that there is consequently no rational structure to morality which would enable us to rank values (and ways of life) in order of importance. The one level requires some minimal structure for morality, while the other precludes efforts to construct such a structure, since it must involve an ethical hierarchy culminating in the highest of the goods, which should then define the best life, which in turn becomes the rationally specified goal that we are all under an obligation to seek.

To remedy this difficulty without falling into the errors of rationalism as Berlin has outlined them, we need a non-teleological developmentalism. This would be a claim that because we grow as we do, we need the ground of moral obligations as a basis on which to grow; yet because we develop in diverse and conflicting directions, there is no ethical certainty that any one ideal is the highest of the goods. Ethically, this would suggest, and be compatible with, a kind of 'monism of the right and pluralism of the goods'.[45]

Most importantly, the incoherence charge levelled by Berlin against expressivism is not necessarily applicable to all kinds of developmentalism. Indeed, elements of Berlin's own account of humanity are best thought of as a kind of open-ended developmentalism. Such an account enables us to argue that liberty is needed (probably along with justice, privacy, and stable personal relations) to prevent the destructive dynamics of degeneration; but once the ground has been provided for growth, human self-realization will carry us off in a variety of conflicting directions. Berlin rightly opposes the Hegelian and Marxist historiosophers because they see human development as moving inevitably toward one, single, coherent goal; and he has become rightly convinced that humans develop in a variety of conflicting directions. Liberty comes to be of special importance, then, not because it is the highest of the goods, but because it is one of the most basic of human values. For indeed, liberty is not the end (not the *telos*) of human moral development nor the height of human accomplishment. Rather, it is simply the very basic foundation on which that accomplishment becomes humanly possible.

REPLY TO ROBERT KOCIS BY ISAIAH BERLIN

It is my impression, gained mainly from reading the last pages of Dr Kocis's article, that while he is in general agreement with what he thinks that I am trying to say, he believes my argument to be marred by serious errors and a degree of incoherence; these flaws can, however, in his view, be removed without sacrificing the heart of what he takes to be my main (and tenable) theses; and this he then proceeds to try to demonstrate. I have no doubt that he attempts his rescue operation in perfectly good faith, and that he has read my writings with much care and the most sympathetic attention. It is all the more surprising, therefore, that he should have misunderstood and therefore misinterpreted much of what I think. This may well be due to my own failure to make some of my views sufficiently clear; but Kocis misunderstands some of these so radically that I am grateful to the Editor for inviting me to comment on the points raised by my critic. For if he has been so seriously misled, so may others have been. I do not wish to try the patience of the reader too far, and shall therefore confine myself to essentials.

To take Kocis's points in his own order. He thinks that I am influenced by two incompatible doctrines—Kant's moral universalism and Herder's social and historical pluralism. I have indeed been deeply influenced by some of the doctrines of these thinkers, but I see nothing incompatible between the particular views that I have derived from them. To Herder I owe the notion that men's ultimate ends vary and that questions that have beset mankind are capable of more than one valid answer. This has led me to believe that the view that to every genuine question there is one true answer and one only, and that therefore those who possess this truth are thereby entitled to control the lives of those who do not, has, on occasion, resulted in attempts to justify moral and political despotism. Kocis says that I believe that romanticism, existentialism and 'much of empiricism' maintain the proposition that there is one and only one answer to the problems of men and societies. I do not know about 'much of empiricism', but I have done my best to show that so far as romanticism (and its heir, existentialism) are concerned, the contrary is the case; that they lead to the very opposite of monism, namely to a pluralism, sometimes of an exceedingly irrationalist kind. As for Kant, I fully accept his view that the ability to choose (what Kocis calls 'agency and creativity') belongs to men as such. Kocis speaks of my conception of 'an eternal and universal human essence'—if by this he means no more than a particular characteristic, in this case a capacity for choice, this does indeed seem to me to be a *sine qua non* of being a fully developed human being, and Kant's doctrine of the freedom of the will to be directly bound up with this conception. I have just used the term 'fully developed'; yet Kocis thinks that I confuse teleology with what he calls 'developmentalism'. Throughout his article he holds me guilty of ignoring men's capacity for development, and indeed its realization, and adds Professor Cumming's voice to his own; and also that I wish to fuse romanticism and rationalism. I do not know why he attributes these shortcomings to me. I doubt if any sane thinker ever denied the possibility of human development, either of the growth of individuals to maturity or of societies from barbarism to civilization. There is, so far as I know, nothing in my writings that remotely suggests that I do not believe this. Kocis is, of course, perfectly right in supposing that if development is interpreted as an inexorable movement towards a single, universal goal (which he correctly ascribes to Hegel), then I do indeed reject this, as did Herder, at any rate in his younger years (his later doctrines are somewhat ambivalent on this). Nor, of course, do I hold that romanticism and rationalism are combinable, nor do I know of any rationalist or romantic or anyone else who believed this. There may be some tendency towards both positions in Mill, but that is a different matter.

Still more surprisingly, I am held to believe that all men need to be both foxes and hedgehogs. The simile of hedgehogs and foxes used in my attempt to explain Tolstoy's theory of history is one that makes no pretence to being a profound psychological or metaphysical categorization of men, least of all a dichotomy. I do not retract it—it seemed helpful to me in discussing Tolstoy—but it is no more than a simile and was not intended as a serious typology. Nor, of course, do I believe that all men are either foxes or hedgehogs, and cannot be neither or both; I must confess

that all this seems to me to have been dragged in gratuitously. Still more astonishing is the charge that 'not being able to bring these competing forces into some sort of rational balance is taken, by Berlin, to be a kind of pathological immaturity'. Tolstoy is not a good example of immaturity, even without the addition of 'pathological'. Nor do I think that 'we are—presumably all of us—torn by the internal conflict between universality and diversity': where have I ever said or hinted at this? My view is very different: it is what Kocis correctly calls 'pluralism', to be carefully distinguished from relativism or subjectivism.

Kocis goes further. He says that if my pluralism is valid—if all ends are of equal value for all men—then why would it hurt anyone if some men were to impose their preferences on others? But this again is a radical misunderstanding. Many ends have been and are pursued by different men and societies, many but not an unlimited number; they may be various and changing, but their range is finite: bounded by the fact that the nature of men entails the possibility (indeed, the necessity) of communication between them. Each man or society places a higher value on certain ends of life than on those of others, the value of which must, nevertheless, be capable of being recognized even by their bitterest adversaries—that is what is meant by saying that these ends are objective human ends, that is, such that any human being can, by a sufficient effort of the imagination, see how such ends, however low in his own scale of values, can come to be pursued by men, perhaps in societies and situations and with inclinations very different from his own, yet unquestionably human—that is, creatures with whom he could in principle achieve communication, holding views which, *mutatis mutandis,* he can conceive himself as capable of holding. Perhaps all this entails no more than that men pursue recognizable human purposes. Kocis says that I believe that mankind is purpose-seeking. Yes, indeed—not, after all, much to ask for: purposeless man is an odd thought; and belief in the right to bind a purpose of my own on others who do not share my outlook is not part of my view. Pluralism is the best of all antidotes to authoritarianism and paternalism, even if one considers their purposes to be wholly rational: Kant is the strongest upholder of this universal right to self direction.

Kocis keeps returning to the alleged contradiction between Kant and Herder in my thought. I must repeat that there is in my view no conflict between Kant's view that purposiveness is a universal human characteristic and that pursuit of rational ends requires freedom of choice, and Herder's 'dualistic or pluralistic strain' that allows for a variety of arrangements (or goals) pursued by men—arrangements properly described as human, not, as Kocis says, merely ways of life that do not require 'any particular characteristic'. Such arrangements and goals, I must repeat, given the limitations of men's natures, cannot be infinite in number, but must be recognizable as human ends in all their rich but not endless variety. Of course there are certain minimum conditions required if social life is to be tolerable at all; but once this minimum is achieved there are various directions in which societies may pursue their own ways of life, ways that may well be unique to them, their times and their places.

Now I come to what Kocis rightly regards as a very fundamental charge, namely, that to me 'there are no rational grounds for preferring one value over any other'. This would entail a wild anarchism in which, I confess, I cannot recognize myself. It is true that I have argued against the idea that it must be possible, at least in principle, to conceive a state of affairs in which all human problems find their complete solution, that is, the ideal of total and universal human perfection. I believe that this notion is incoherent because it presupposes the possibility of a perfect harmony between values that are, so far as I can see, in principle incompatible, any of which (or combinations of which) may be final ends for particular individuals or societies. But it is a very far cry from this to say that 'there are no rational grounds for preferring one value over any other'. Of course one can give excellent *reasons* (that is what I regard as 'being rational')—to take Hume's famous example—for rejecting an act that would destroy the universe in order to end the pain in my little finger. These reasons would be based both on empirical knowledge and moral convictions shared with the great majority of mankind. I can give equally good reasons for refusing to take someone's life rather than adding to my own comfort, or choosing to resist those who are bent on the destruction of my family, my friends, my country, rather than seeking my own personal safety—and so on. What rationality means here is that my choices are not arbitrary, incapable of rational defence, but can be explained in terms of my scale of values—my plan or way of life, an entire outlook which cannot but be to a high degree connected with that of others who form the society, nation, party, church, class, species to which I belong. Of course in terms of an entire outlook, some values are higher than others, so that a 'lower' value will be set aside in favour of a 'higher' one; and in cases of serious conflict 'trade-offs' or compromises can constitute rational solutions. But this does not entail the belief that there can be no rational choice of ends save within a single scheme of life valid for all men. Men, because they are men, have enough in common biologically, psychologically, socially, however this comes about, to make social life and social morality possible. But this does not entail the necessity of a single universally valid hierarchy of ends, even as an ideal, with corresponding differences of status, or of rights, or duties, or privileges, or permitted ways of life, such as genuine ethical or political monists seem to me to be committed to. Of course a basic liberty of choice, by individuals or societies, of some ends as being preferable to others (with reasons ultimately grounded in one's basic conception of human nature) is presupposed in the pluralism which I defend, or, as Kocis also believes, by any doctrine that deserves to be described as ethical. But this is, *pace* Kocis, something altogether different from, nor even connected with, the concept of 'negative liberty', which in my lecture applied in any case to political life only. There are social and political liberties, of whatever kind, that may have to be sacrificed, at

any rate in a crisis, in favour of more immediately pressing needs, whether individual or collective—say, to save men from murder or starvation or injustice or degradation, or to prevent some other disastrous frustration of basic human needs. But none of this is relevant to liberty of choice by a moral agent: the exercise of free will is, as Kant taught, the basis of all morality. The confusion between these not unrelated but distinct senses of 'liberty' is fundamental. It seems to me that Kocis is far from clear on this point.

He continues to be full of surprises. He says that I see 'the ancient ideal of the Republic as a viable alternative to modernity', unlike Hegel, who did not make this mistake. I have never thought of myself as a follower of Hegel, but on this point I cannot but accept his views. Of course choices are limited by the circumstances of men and their environment—the attempt to turn to some classical ideal is impractical, indeed, absurd, for reasons excellently stated by Herder—we are what we are, and although we change and develop, mankind is not infinitely malleable: to return to the past is impossible, an ideal both utopian and false: and a policy of conditioning men is in the end impracticable as well as immoral. My critic seems to disapprove of Vico's or Herder's 'developmentalism', but why? Why does he say that in my eyes 'it is human to change; but we cannot *be changed* and retain our humanity' (Kocis's italics)? Whoever denied that men could be changed by education, by the civilizing process, by a dozen causes, beliefs, ideals? It is true that we cannot be both wholly conditioned and yet be treated as free beings; but that is very different from saying that we actually cease to be human even under the most horrible oppression—these are indeed curious words to put in my mouth, yet I have no doubt that Kocis sincerely believes that these are my sentiments—I do not for a moment question that what he wishes to do is to establish the truth about my views before he criticizes them. I feel sure that his attribution of belief in something static and changeless as part of my view of men is entirely sincere; if I did hold this odd opinion, his strictures would certainly be justified. More than this, I am held to confuse teleology, which we both believe may lead to despotism, with 'lawful regularities in growth and change'. Even the most static-minded monists in the history of thought—Plato, for example—have not been guilty of this strange delusion—why should I alone be charged with it?

Kocis cites Professors Chapman and Pennock as criticizing my views, but nothing quoted from these authors contains opinions which I should dream of disputing—again, I can only plead that I am being strangely misrepresented. One of my deepest beliefs is that one of the causes of continuous change in human history is the fact that it is precisely the fulfilment (or partial fulfilment) of some human aspiration that itself transforms the aspirant, and breeds, in time, new needs, new goals, new outlooks, that are *ex hypothesi* unpredictable; and that this is one of the main objections to the view that it is possible to discover rigorous laws of social change, and its corollary, a knowable causal determinism. Indeed, the novel situations that are created by the very fulfilment of men's original ideals (or their frustrations), and the new outlooks that spring from this, refute the doctrine of a single, final, unalterable, universal goal for mankind—and if this leads to empiricism and liberalism (to use Kocis's words), so be it; indeed, this is surely one of the strongest of all arguments for such liberalism and for reliance on a cautious assessment of day-to-day experience. For it seems to me that, in the end, all that we can know is what specific men in fact hope and fear, love and hate, ask for and reject—not what they or their successors will one day live for or seek to avoid. The belief in an open future itself rests on anticipation of change, and indeed, development, although not necessarily in a wholly predictable direction; to accuse me of ignoring this seems to me most odd. It is relatively less important, though equally mistaken, to say that I believe that what Professor Charles Taylor and I have called Herder's 'expressivism' (this is less misleading than 'expressionism' used in my earlier version) leads to monism: whatever Hegel may have thought, the passage quoted says the exact opposite of what Kocis takes it to mean—the 'self-realisation that all creatures . . . live for' is not a striving for a single universal goal: there is constant stress on the rich variety of forms of life and goals that Herder so eloquently, and in my view rightly, celebrated. So far from 'deep distrust' of Herder's pluralism and expressivism, I accept it fully; but I am truly puzzled not so much by the repetition of the statement that there is no way—according to me—'to rank the values (and ways of life) in order of importance', of which I have already spoken, as by the statement, not attributed to me, that a non-teleological developmentalism 'would be a claim that because we grow as we do, we need the ground of moral obligations as a basis on which to grow'. What can this mean? Growth is a fact, a process—how can 'an obligation' be 'a basis' of a natural process?

I should like to end by saying that I fully realize that Kocis is basically at one with me about the heart of my doctrine—mine, and Herder's too, whose 'expressivism' is perhaps the most valuable of all his insights, his very reason for denying absolute final solutions in his early essay of 1774 (*Yet Another Philosophy of History*). This is the classical exposition of the position which inspired Humboldt, and through him, of what is most generous and libertarian in J. S. Mill, and of such developments of this outlook—still a minority view among contemporary political theorists—as those to which Kocis and I both belong. If Kocis wants to call me a non-teleological developmentalist (although I am not sure what this phrase means) I am happy to accept this sobriquet if it means no more than belief that aims are necessarily related to social change or growth, and to the emergence of social rules and ways of life that are themselves largely due to the influence of environment and social change. This reads uncommonly like a truism: perhaps it is none the less true for that. To read anything I have written as incompatible with it is (I should like to assure Kocis in the friendliest possible manner) based on a serious misunderstanding, particularly surprising in a work of so intelligent, scrupulous, well read and basically sympathetic a critic. When this happens to any writer, he must ask himself whether he may not be as much responsible for it as his reader. To deny this seems to me inexcusable vanity.

Notes

1. I. Berlin, 'Georges Sorel', *Times Literary Supplement,* 31 December 1971, p. 1617.

2. Berlin, *Four Essays on Liberty* (London, Oxford University Press, 1969), pp. 200-1.

3. Berlin, *Essays on Liberty,* p. 171.

4. See, for example, Siedentop's claim that Berlin's, like other empiricist philosophies of mind, does not adequately ground our moral and political obligations; 'Two Liberal Traditions' in A. Ryan (ed.), *The Idea of Freedom: Essays in Honour of Isaiah Berlin* (London, Oxford University Press, 1979), p. 155.

5. Berlin, *Essays on Liberty,* p. 167.

6. Berlin, 'The Question of Machiavelli' (Bobbs-Merrill Reprint #68813), p. 13.

7. Berlin, *Essays on Liberty,* p. 199.

8. Berlin, 'Does Political Theory Still Exist?' in Laslett and Runciman (eds), *Philosophy, Politics, and Society* (Second Series) (Oxford, Blackwell, 1962), throughout.

9. Berlin, 'Does Political Theory Still Exist?', p. 27.

10. See Berlin's, *The Hedgehog and the Fox* (London, Weidenfeld & Nicolson, 1953; New York, Simon & Schuster, 1953; New York, New American Library, 1957), especially the 'Introduction'.

11. See, for example, Berlin's, 'The Question of Machiavelli', *The New York Review of Books,* 4 November 1971, 20-32.

12. M. Mandelbaum, *History, Man, and Reason* (Baltimore, The Johns Hopkins Press, 1971), especially Part II.

13. Berlin, *Essays on Liberty,* pp. 132-3.

14. Berlin, *Essays on Liberty,* p. 132.

15. Berlin, *Essays on Liberty,* p. 133.

16. Berlin, *Essays on Liberty,* p. 133.

17. Berlin, *Essays on Liberty,* p. 127.

18. Berlin, *Essays on Liberty,* p. 137.

19. Berlin, *Essays on Liberty,* p. 133.

20. Berlin, *Essays on Liberty,* p. 19.

21. Berlin, 'Machiavelli', *NYRB,* p. 31.

22. J. R. Pennock, *Democratic Political Theory* (Princeton, NJ, Princeton University Press, 1979), p. 137.

23. J. Chapman, 'Rawls's Theory of Justice', *American Political Science Review* 69 (June 1975), 588-93; p. 589.

24. J. Rawls, *A Theory of Justice* (Cambridge, Mass., Harvard University Press, 1971), p. 577.

25. B. Barry, *The Liberal Theory of Justice* (London, Clarendon Press, 1975).

26. J. Chapman, 'Towards a General Theory of Human Nature and Dynamics' in Pennock and Chapman (eds), *NOMOS XVII: Human Nature in Politics* (New York, Atherton, 1977), p. 306.

27. Berlin, *Vico and Herder* (London, Chatto & Windus, 1976), p. 153.

28. C. Taylor, *Hegel* (Cambridge, Cambridge University Press, 1975), p. 47.

29. Berlin, *Vico and Herder*, p. 176.

30. Berlin, *Vico and Herder*, p. 153.

31. Mandelbaum, *History, Man & Reason*, Part II.

32. R. D. Cumming, 'Is Man Still Man?', *Social Research* (Autumn 1973), p. 500.

33. Cumming, 'Still Man?', p. 497; and Berlin, *Essays on Liberty*, p. 173.

34. Cumming, 'Still Man?', p. 497.

35. As a matter of fact (rather than of logic), Mill's developmentalism strikes me as much too teleological (probably because of his nineteenth-century belief in progress and his ethnocentrism). But the point here must be one of logic: if Mill's theory of human nature is developmental, and if Berlin does not detect in it the errors of rationalism, then Berlin cannot attribute the errors of rationalism to all developmental theories.

36. J. S. Mill, *Utilitarianism, On Liberty, and Representative Government,* (edited by H. B. Acton) (New York, Dutton & Co., 1972), p. 73.

37. Mill, *Utilitarianism*, p. 73.

38. Mill, *Utilitarianism*, p. 203.

39. Of course, this is only *part* of an account of Mill's view. (For a more thorough account of Mill's theory, see Gaus, 'The Convergence of Rights and Utility in Rawls and Mill', *Ethics,* forthcoming, and his *The Modern Liberal Theory of Man* (London, Croom-Helm, forthcoming).) Other parts incline Mill in other directions. His metaphysical teleology, along with his defence of the 'clerisy', suggests a more teleological view.

40. The flip-side of the 'negative' claim is, of course, that once secured, people develop in a variety of directions.

41. Berlin, 'Machiavelli', *NYRB,* p. 11.

42. Berlin, 'Machiavelli', *NYRB,* p. 7.

43. Berlin, 'Montesquieu', *Proceedings of the British Academy,* 41 (1955), 267-96; pp. 27-8.

44. See Macpherson's critique of Berlin, Essay V of *Democratic Theory: Essays in Retrieval* (Oxford, Clarendon Press, 1973), especially pp. 104-6 and 110-12; see also my response to it in 'Reason, Development and the Conflicts of Human Ends: Sir Isaiah Berlin's Vision of Politics', *American Political Science Review,* LXXIV (March 1980), 38-52; especially pp. 44-8.

45. Rawls, *Theory of Justice,* pp. 446-52.

Beata Polanowska-Sygulska (essay date 1989)

SOURCE: "One Voice More on Berlin's Doctrine of Liberty," in *Political Studies,* Vol. XXXVII, No. 1, March, 1989, pp. 123-7.

[*In the following essay, Polanowska-Sygulska defends Berlin's wariness of positive freedom.*]

Sir Isaiah Berlin's famous essay on political freedom, **'Two Concepts of Liberty'**,[1] was described by Professor Marshall Cohen as 'academic, inflated and obscure'.[2] It is perhaps an indication of the value of the essay that it should produce such a violent reaction. However, this characterization of the essay has relevance to the problem of political liberty itself for there is no doubt that the concept is of its nature obscure. Nevertheless, though philosophically so vague, the burning issue of liberty cannot be treated as merely academic in the contemporary world. Let this serve as justification for my adding one more voice to a long and complex discussion.

I

Participants in the debate have recognized different threads of Berlin's essay as the most significant ones. Many have concentrated on his conception of negative freedom, some criticizing its narrowness and tracing its links with classical liberalism.[3] It seems to me, however, that the main value and originality of Berlin's approach lies not so much in his discussion of negative liberty but in his perceptive critique of the positive concept. The proportions of the essay devoted to the two aspects in a way confirm this impression. Berlin devotes nine pages to understanding of the negative concept, whereas his critique of the positive concept occupies 24 pages. Some commentators have discussed both threads of Berlin's essay. Nevertheless, what most of them have concentrated upon has been the distinction between the two concepts, not the critique of the positive one.[4] Several authors claim to have solved the problem by arguing away the distinction.[5] A significant exception is Charles Taylor, who questioned Berlin's whole approach to the relationship between the negative and positive concepts.[6] But in my opinion the only author to have taken up and elaborated upon the most original part of Berlin's doctrine, namely the critique of the positive concept, is C. B. Macpherson. This is the only discussion that does not evade in one way or another Berlin's central thesis that positive doctrines of liberty are particularly susceptible to distortion.[7] C. B. Macpherson attempts to refute

Berlin's main argument in the following way. He quotes Berlin's statement of the four central assumptions of the positive view of liberty:

> first, that all men have one true purpose, and one only, that of rational self-direction; second, that the ends of all rational beings must of necessity fit into a single universal, harmonious pattern, which some men may be able to discern more clearly than others; third, that all conflict and consequently all tragedy, is due solely to the clash of reason with the irrational or the insufficiently rational—the immature and undeveloped elements in life—whether individual or communal, and that such clashes are, in principle, avoidable, and for wholly rational beings impossible; finally, that when all men have been made rational, they will obey the rational laws of their own natures, which are one and the same in them all, and so to be at once wholly law-abiding and wholly free.[8]

Macpherson maintains that only the first assumption is inherent in all doctrines of the positive freedom. In other words, he questions Berlin's thesis of the necessary logical bond between the notion of 'freedom to' and rationalist monism. According to Macpherson the first assumption is even inconsistent with the last three. For what flows from the acceptance of the 'positive' idea of freedom is not 'a preordained harmonious pattern'[9] but a 'proliferation of many ways and styles of life'.[10]

A hint of the same view, that there is no logical connection between rational self-direction and rationalist metaphysics, has been expressed by John Gray: 'I suggest that some useful variant of the idea of a real or rational will may survive the demise of the rationalist metaphysics and philosophical psychology in which it has traditionally been embedded'.[11] Robert Kocis's conception of rational self-direction is also similar to that of Macpherson: '"self-actualization" is not a single goal, but a series of (probably conflicting) goals',[12] 'there are many forms of self-realization'.[13]

Sir Isaiah Berlin maintains his view and simultaneously rejects Macpherson's objection.[14] According to him, the first assumption implies that to every problem there is in principle only one objective solution. If there is no answer, in principle, to a question or if there are two answers it cannot be a real question. Thus

> my realization of myself as a rational being must rest on the perception of what the problem is. To this question there is in principle only one true answer. What is true of me is also true of you in the similar circumstances, because we are both human beings.

At this point the door is open to rationalist metaphysics. Thus the idea of rational self-realization logically entails the conviction expressed in the last three assumptions, if it is taken strictly.

II

This question has yet another dimension. The problem of human liberty is an object of concern in many intellectual fields other than general political theory—philosophy, so-

cial psychology or literature, for example. It is the role of the last to reflect the mood of contemporary culture. My impression is that one does not often nowadays come across the parallel of freedom as an experience of space in an upward flight. Naive as this remark may be, the ancient myth of Icarus can be taken as the incarnation of the idea of 'freedom from'. This very notion, though limited to the social context, seems to form the basis of the classical liberal image of freedom. The vision one encounters today has much more affinity with Kierkegaard's choice of the existential stage or Heidegger's postulate of authentic existence than with Icarus's flight. It is no longer the space devoid of obstacles but the horizon of choice that stands for human liberty. Let me back this digression up with some quotations which, though chosen at random, speak for themselves. It is how two modern writers, Thomas Merton and Alberto Moravia, see human liberty.

> . . . I cannot make the universe obey me. I cannot make other people conform to my whims and fancies. I cannot make even my body obey me. When I give it pleasure, it deceives my expectation and makes me suffer pain. When I give myself what I conceive to be freedom, I deceive myself and find that I am the prisoner of my own blindness and selfishness and insufficiency . . . we too easily assume that we are our real selves, and that our choices are really the ones we want to make, when, in fact, our acts of free choice are (though morally imputable, no doubt) largely dictated by psychological compulsions, flowing from our inordinate ideas of our own importance. Our choices are too often dictated by our false selves.[15]

> . . . a man has a beautiful life when he is free, when he lives according to his own principles, directing himself by his own internal inspiration, and not humbly sticking to universally valid norms. To live beautifully means to choose one's own way and follow it despite the price one has to pay. To me that man has lived his life beautifully, who has had an opportunity to reveal the whole fullness of his personality, not the one who has lived 'respectably'. A man does not live to be 'respectable', but to express himself as a personality. To me an opportunity of human fulfilment is a synonym of freedom.[16]

It was the contemporary reality that generated existentialism and induced this very notion of human freedom.

III

Let us now return to the social context. Reading Fromm's *Fear of Freedom* one cannot help noticing certain parallels: '. . . positive freedom consists in the spontaneous activity of the total, integrated personality'.[17] While Merton and Moravia drew their visions of liberty from the standpoint of the isolated individual, Fromm's conception undoubtedly involves a social context. And this is where the political theorist should apply all his imagination. The following excerpt strikes a reader of Fromm as especially significant.

> Positive freedom also implies the principle that there is no higher power than this unique individual self, that

man is the centre and purpose of his life: that the growth and realization of man's individuality is an end that can never be subordinated to purposes which are supposed to have greater dignity.[18]

It is worth mentioning that a similar idea was put forward by one of Berlin's critics, namely by Charles Taylor.

> . . . each person has his/her own original form of re-alisation. Some others, who know us intimately, and who surpass us in wisdom, are undoubtedly in a posi-tion to advise us, but no official body can possess a doctrine or a technique whereby they could know how to put us on the rails, because such a doctrine or tech-nique cannot in principle exist if human beings really differ in their self-realisation.[19]

Does this mean that both authors somehow want to protect their doctrines against potential distortions? Why did they take such precautions? Were they aware that their concep-tions were vulnerable to perversion? Let us now examine the origin of such an apprehension.

An explanation of this problem is provided by **'Two Con-cepts of Liberty'.** The adherents of the positive view of freedom, however, would challenge Sir Isaiah's critique and probably his line of defence. It seems valid to follow their argument and to examine the theoretical conse-quences that may be drawn from their vision of liberty. Let us concentrate upon one concrete doctrine, namely that of C. B. Macpherson. What follows from his simulta-neous acceptance of the first assumption (that is, that all men have one true purpose, and one only, that of rational self-direction) and rejection of the rationalist monism which he claims is inherent in the last three assumptions? If there is no universal pattern and liberty is understood in the positive way a countless number of collisions are bound to emerge. This is because any social doctrine aim-ing at regulating relationships among men must provide some universal principle. Classical liberalism structured society by granting every individual an independent sphere. There is no way in which liberty identified with self-realization and abstracted from any universal pattern of development could perform the same role. What is it then that can make the positive doctrine of freedom a social one, not merely an individualist, possibly existentialist, conception of personal self-fulfilment?

It is my thesis that every defence of positive liberty pre-supposes some *tacit, universal value*, that fulfils the task of structuring society. This value is seen as indispensable and fundamental. At the same time, given the great per-suasive appeal of the term 'liberty', it is hard for a theorist to abandon the concept. Thus he expands or even changes its meaning in order to protect the preferred value. Is this the case in Macpherson's discussion? Let us come back once again to his paper. The following excerpt seems to support my contention.

> . . . if the chief impediments to men's developmental powers were removed, if, that is to say, they were al-lowed *equal freedom*, there would emerge not a pattern

but a proliferation of many ways and styles of life which could not be prescribed and which would not necessarily conflict.[20]

However, the removal of the 'chief impediments', which is essential to achieving 'equal freedom', implies the emer-gence of an authority which would perform the task. By providing equal conditions for self-realization, the author-ity must simultaneously define them. Thus it will not be merely the scope of an individual's independent sphere that will be decided upon by some external authority, but also *the very content of his freedom*. This model is bound to produce a limited range of patterns (if not one), rather than a proliferation of many ways and styles of life.

In conclusion, it seems to me that Berlin's main thesis that positive conceptions of liberty are particularly susceptible to distortions remains valid. For if a doctrine of 'freedom to' is to fulfil a social function, it must provide some prin-ciple, whether explicit or implicit, by which to structure society. In both cases the term 'liberty' loses its original connotation as a sphere of independence and will mean whatever a theorist wishes.

Notes

1. I. Berlin, 'Two concepts of liberty', in *Four Essays on Liberty,* (Oxford, Oxford University Press, 1975, pp. 118-72.

2. M. Cohen, 'Berlin and the liberal tradition', *The Philosophical Quarterly,* 10 (1980), p. 216.

3. See A. S. Kaufman, 'Professor Berlin on negative freedom', *Mind,* 71 (1962), 241-3; Cohen, 'Berlin and the liberal tradition', pp. 216-27, H. Steiner, 'Individual liberty', *Proceedings of the Aristotelian Society,* 75 (1974-75), 33-6; J. N. Gray, 'On negative and positive liberty', *Political Studies,* 28 (1980), 523-4. For discussion on the disadvantages of the rigid negative approach, see also A. Ryan, 'Freedom', *Philosophy,* 40 (1965), 108-11.

4. See, Gray, 'On negative and positive liberty', pp. 510-13; J. Gray, 'Introduction', in Z. Pelczynski and J. Gray (eds), *Conceptions of Liberty in Political Philosophy* (London, Athlone Press, 1984), pp. 4-6; H. J. McCloskey, 'A critique of the ideals of liberty', *Mind,* 74 (1965), 483-6; L. J. Macfarlane, 'On two concepts of liberty', *Political Studies,* 14:1 (1966), 77-81; D. Nicholls, 'Positive liberty', *American Political Science Review,* 56 (1962), 114-15, footnote 8. For an objection on the ground of the incompleteness of the two concepts of liberty see also S. I. Benn, 'Freedom and persuasion', *The Australasian Journal of Philosophy,* 45 (1967), 260-2.

5. See G. MacCallum, Jr, 'Negative and positive freedom', *The Philosophical Review,* 76 (1967), 312-34; J. Feinberg, *Social Philosophy* (Englewood Cliffs, N.J., Prentice-Hall, 1973), pp. 9-14; W. A. Parent, 'Some recent work on the concept of

liberty', *American Philosophical Quarterly,* 11 (July 1974), 149-67 (see especially pages 152 and 166).

6. C. Taylor, 'What's wrong with negative liberty', in A. Ryan (ed.), *The Idea of Freedom* (Oxford, Oxford University Press, 1979), pp. 175-93.

7. C. B. Macpherson, 'Berlin's division of liberty', in C. B. Macpherson, *Democratic Theory: Essays in Retrieval* (Oxford, Oxford University Press, 1973), pp. 95-119. Though Cohen does actually engage in a discussion on Berlin's critique of the conceptions of positive freedom, he conducts it from a position of fundamental disagreement: see Cohen, 'Berlin and the liberal tradition', pp. 218, 221-7.

8. Berlin, *Four Essays on Liberty,* p. 154.

9. Macpherson, *Democratic Theory,* p. 112

10. Macpherson, *Democratic Theory,* p. 111.

11. Gray, 'On negative and positive liberty', p. 520.

12. R. A. Kocis, 'Toward a coherent theory of human moral development. Beyond Sir Isaiah Berlin's vision of human nature', *Political Studies,* 31:3 (1983), p. 375.

13. Kocis, 'Toward a coherent theory of human moral development', p. 386.

14. In a private conversation, July 1986.

15. T. Merton, *No Man Is an Island* (London, Hollis & Carter, 1955), pp. 20-1.

16. This is my translation from an interview with Alberto Moravia, published in a Polish periodical: 'Podróż po wyboistej drodze z Alberto Moravia', *Forum,* 48 (1977), p. 18.

17. E. Fromm, *Fear of Freedom* (London, Routledge & Kegan Paul, 1960), p. 222.

18. Fromm, *Fear of Freedom,* p. 228.

19. Taylor, 'What's wrong with negative liberty', p. 180.

20. Macpherson, *Democratic Theory,* pp. 111-12.

Joseph Brodsky (essay date 1989)

SOURCE: "Isaiah Berlin at Eighty," in *The New York Review of Books,* Vol. XXXVI, No. 13, August 17, 1989, pp. 44-5.

[In the following essay, Brodsky offers an eightieth birthday tribute to Berlin.]

It is almost a rule that the more complex a man is, the simpler his billing. A person with a retrospective ability gone rampant often would be called an historian. Similarly, one to whom reality doesn't seem to make sense gets dubbed a philosopher. Social critic or ethical thinker are standard labels for somebody who finds the ways of his society reprehensible. And so it goes, for the world al-ways tries to arrest its adolescence, to appear younger than it is. Few people have suffered this fear of grown-ups more than Sir Isaiah Berlin, now eighty, who is frequently called all these things, at times simultaneously. What follows is not an attempt to redress the terminological chaos: it is but a tribute by a simpleton to a superior mind from which the former for a number of years has been learning about mental subtlety but apparently hasn't learned enough.

A study in genealogy normally is owing to either pride in one's ancestry or uncertainty about it; our history of ideas is no exception. Given the fruit this century came to bear, however, there are additional reasons for such scrutiny, which have nothing to do with attempts to braindish or ascertain the origins of our nobility. These reasons are revulsion and fear.

The quest for universal social justice that preoccupied European thought for, roughly speaking, the last four centuries has too often in our era resulted in its exact opposite. Considering the number of lives this quest has claimed, its Holy Grail proved to be the fixture of a literal dead end, and with a total disregard for the individual in its wake. A subject for revulsion, this effect should also be perceived as a cry from the future, given the rate of population growth throughout the world. After all, the temptation of social planning has turned out to be irresistible even for relatively humble social units.

That is what instills fear. In a manner of speaking, every bullet flies from the future. A mass society is natural prey for any presumption, but above all to a socialist one, which may eventually yield only to that of a computer. For this reason, poring over the genealogical chart of European philosophical thought through the last four centuries is not all that different from scanning the horizon: in either case, though, one looks out not for the cavalry but for an Indian scout.

There are not many of these scouts, and few of them are much good. The invention of ethical and political doctrines, which blossomed into our own social sciences, is a product of times when things appeared manageable. The same goes for the criticism of those doctrines, though as a voice from the past this criticism proved prophetic. All it lacked was the appropriate volume, but then one of the main distinctions between Indian scouts and cavalry is their discretion.

They were always discreet, as well as few in number—those opponents of political certitude, doubters of social blueprints, disbelievers in universal truths, exiles from the Just City. It could not be otherwise since for them to be shrill in social discourse would have been a contradiction in terms. Even systematization often seemed to them contradictory because a system would entitle them to mental privilege over the very subjects of their ponderings.

Their actual lives and careers were diverse but not spectacular. Some of them would advance their views in magazines. Others would do so in a treatise or, even better, in a novel. Still others applied their principles to the offices they held or disciplines they were mastering. They were the first to shrink from being called philosophers; above all, they never tried to shout anyone down.

This posture had little to do with either humility or modesty. In fact it could and perhaps should be perceived as an echo of a polytheistic notion of the world, for these people firmly believed in the multiplicity of the human predicament, and the core of their social formula was, essentially, pluralism. This of course drew fire or silence from social reformers of every stripe, both democratic and autocratic, whose most high-minded common contention would even today be that pluralism is pregnant with moral relativism.

It is. But then moral absolutism is not so hot either. Its main attraction is that it is unattainable and, for a social reformer, that it provides an attractive embellishment for his designs. Yet the bottom line of every social order is not the moral superiority of its members but their safety, which, in fact, moral superiority doesn't necessarily guarantee.

Every discourse on social matters boils down, of course, to the issue of free will. This is something of a paradox, however, since regardless of whether the will is free or not, in any outcome of such discourse it will be curbed. One's curiosity regarding the nature of the will is therefore either sadistic or academic or both. ("Let's see how free is what we are curbing.")

In any case, with pluralism one would think a danger far greater than moral relativism (which is the reality of the world anyway) or shackling the will, is the implicit dismissal of the metaphysical properties of the species, the short shrift that pluralism, like nearly any other social formula, gives to the notion that man can be driven as much by his appetite for the infinite as by necessity.

The pluralist formula shares this danger with every form of social organization, including theocracy. Man's metaphysical instinct (or potential) is substantial enough to overshoot the confines of any creed, not to mention ideology. At the very least, that is what is responsible for the emergence of art, music, and, particularly, poetry. In many ways, this is both a self- and world-negating instinct and its exercise may easily make the finest social tapestry fade. Whether a society benefits from this humbling effect is another matter. One suspects that it may.

On the basis of this suspicion one perceives the equating of man's metaphysical potential with its absence as a danger. Everything that reduces man's spiritual tenor is a danger. The antihierarchical pathos of pluralism may render society's sense dull to the pitch of the human maximum, which is always a solo performance. Worse still, it may perceive this solo as a subject for applause, exacting no obligations from its audience.

But if it were only a matter of the quality of the applause, that would be fine. Regrettably, what passes for social pluralism is echoed in the life of cultures and even civiliza-

tions. For they and their values, too, are conflicting and diverse enough to make up society, especially given their current Biblical proximity (we are literally only a stone's throw from one another), especially given the world's emerging ethnic composition. From now on when we are talking about the world we are talking about a society.

The need for a common denominator, for a universal set of values, is dictated by our concern for our safety (and one wouldn't be wrong to regard Herder as a precursor of the League of Nations). Alas, the development of this common denominator is fraught with a cultural realignment so enormous that one is not keen to ponder it. We already hear, for example, about equating tolerance (this high-pitched solo of Christianity) with intolerance.

Alas, the trouble with ethics is that it always answers the question "How to live?" not, "In the name of what?" or even "What for?" It is clear that it tries to supplant those questions and their answers with its own; that moral philosophy tends to operate at the expense of metaphysics. Perhaps rightly so, given the world's population prospects; perhaps it's time to bid the Enlightenment farewell, to learn an inflected guttural tongue and step into the future.

One is almost ready to do so when in walks Isaiah Berlin, at age eighty, carrying under his arm seven not very long books: ***The Age of Enlightenment, Four Essays on Liberty, Vico and Herder, Against the Current, The Hedgehog and the Fox, Russian Thinkers,*** and ***Personal Impressions.*** He does not look like an Indian scout; his mind, however, has been to the future. The volumes under his arm are its map, where the East overlaps with the West, where the North flows South.

This is not how I first saw him, though, seventeen years ago, when he was sixty-three and I thirty-two. I had just left the country where I'd spent those thirty-two years and it was my third day in London, where I knew nobody.

I was staying in St. John's Wood, in the house of Stephen Spender, whose wife had come to the airport three days before to fetch W. H. Auden, who had flown in from Vienna to participate in the annual Poetry International Festival in Queen Elizabeth Hall. I was on the same flight, for the same reason. As I had no place to stay in London, the Spenders offered to put me up.

On the third day in that house in the city where I knew nobody the phone rang and Natasha Spender cried, "Joseph, it's for you." Naturally, I was puzzled. My puzzlement hadn't subsided when I heard in the receiver my mother tongue, spoken with the most extraordinary clarity and velocity, unparalleled in my experience. The speed of sound, one felt, was courting the speed of light. That was Isaiah Berlin, suggesting tea at his club, the Atheneum.

I accepted, although of all my foggy notions about English life, that of a club was the foggiest (the last reference I had seen to one was in Pushkin's *Eugene Onegin*). Mrs.

Spender gave me a lift to Pall Mall and before she deposited me in front of an imposing Regency edifice with a gilded Athena and Wedgewoodlike cornice, I, being unsure of my English, asked her whether she wouldn't mind accompanying me inside. She said that she wouldn't, except that women were not allowed. I found this puzzling, again, opened the door, and announced myself to the doorman.

"I'd like to see Sir Isaiah Berlin," I said, and attributed the look of controlled disbelief in his eyes to my accent rather than to my Russian clothes. Two minutes later, however, climbing the majestic staircases and glancing at the huge oil portraits of Gladstones, Spencers, Actons, Darwins, et alia, that patterned the club's walls like wallpaper, I knew that the matter with me was neither my accent nor my turtleneck but my age. At thirty-two I was as much out of sync here as if I were a woman.

Presently I was standing in the huge, mahogany-cum-leather shell of the club's library. Through high windows the afternoon sun was pouring its rays onto the parquet as though testing its resolve to refract light. In various corners two or three rather ancient members were sunk deep in their tall armchairs, in various stages of newspaper-induced reverie. From across the room, a man in a baggy three-piece suit was waving to me. Against the sunlight, the silhouette looked Chaplinesque, or penguinish.

I walked toward him and we shook hands. Apart from the Russian language, the only other thing we had in common was that we both knew that language's best poet, Anna Akhmatova, who dedicated to Sir Isaiah a magnificent cycle of poems, *Sweetbriar's Bloom.* The cycle was occasioned by a visit Isaiah Berlin, then secretary of the British embassy in Moscow, paid to Akhmatova in 1946. Aside from the poems, that encounter provoked Stalin's wrath, the dark shadow of which completely enveloped Akhmatova's life for the next decade and a half.

Since in one of the poems from that cycle—spanning in its own turn a decade—the poet assumed the persona of Dido, addressing her visitor as Aeneas, I wasn't altogether surprised by the opening remark of that bespectacled man: "What has she done to me? Aeneas! Aeneas! What sort of Aeneas am I really?" Indeed, he didn't look like one, and the mixture of embarrassment and pride in his voice was genuine.

Years later on the other hand, in his own memoirs about visiting Pasternak and Akhmatova in 1946, when "the world's strength was all spent / and only graves were fresh," Sir Isaiah himself compares his Russian hosts to victims of a shipwreck on a desert island, inquiring about the civilization which they've been cut off from for decades. For one thing, the essence of this simile echoes somewhat the circumstances of Aeneas's appearance before the queen of Carthage; for another, if not participants themselves, then the context of their meeting was epic enough to endure subsequent disclaimers.

But that was years later. Now I was staring at a face I saw for the first time. The paperback edition of *The Hedgehog and the Fox* that Akhmatova had once given to me to pass

on to Nadezhda Mandelstam lacked a picture of its author; as for a copy of *Four Essays on Liberty* it came to me from a book shark with its cover torn off—out of caution, given the book's subject. It was a wonderful face, a cross, I thought, between a wood grouse and a spaniel, with large brown eyes ready at once for flight and for hunting.

I felt comfortable with this face being old because the finality of its features alone excluded all pretension. Also, in this foreign realm where I had suddenly found myself, it was the first face that looked familiar. A traveler always clings to a recognizable object, be it a telephone or a statue. In the parts I was from that kind of face would belong to a physician, a schoolteacher, a musician, a watchmaker, a scholar—to someone from whom you vaguely expect help. It was also the face of a potential victim, and so I suddenly felt comfortable.

Besides, we spoke Russian—to the great bewilderment of the uniformed personnel. The conversation naturally ran to Akhmatova until I asked Sir Isaiah how he had found me in London. The answer made me recall the front page of that mutilated edition of *Four Essays on Liberty,* and I felt ashamed. I should have remembered that that book, which for three years served me as an antidote to all sorts of demagoguery in which my native realm was virtually awash, was dedicated to the man under whose roof I now stayed.

It turned out that Stephen Spender was Sir Isaiah's friend from their days at Oxford. It turned out that so, though a bit later, was Wystan Auden, whose "Letter to Lord Byron" had once been, like those *Four Essays,* my daily pocket companion. In a flash I realized that I owed a great deal of my sanity to men of a single generation, to the Oxford class, as it were, of circa 1930; that I was, in fact, also an unwitting product of their friendship; that they wandered through each other's books the way they did through their rooms at Corpus Christi or University College; that those rooms had, in the end, shrunk to the paperbacks in my possession.

On top of that, they were sheltering me now. Of course, I wanted to know everything about each one of them, and immediately. The two most interesting things in this world, as E.M. Cioran has remarked somewhere, are gossip and metaphysics. One could add, they have a similar structure: one can easily be taken for the other. That's what the remainder of the afternoon turned into, owing to the nature of the lives of those I was asking about, and owing to my host's tenacious memory.

The latter of course made me think again about Akhmatova, who also had this astonishing ability to retain everything: dates, details of topography, names and personal data of individuals, their family circumstances, their cousins, nephews, nieces, second and third marriages, where their husbands or wives were from, their party affiliations, when and by whom their books were published, and, had they come to a sorry end, the identities of those who had denounced them. She, too, could spin this vast, weblike, palpable fabric on a minute's notice, and even the timbre of her low monotone was similar to the voice I was listening to now in the Atheneum's library.

No, the man before me was not Aeneas, because Aeneas, I think, remembered nothing. Nor was Akhmatova a Dido to be destroyed by one tragedy, to die in flames. Had she permitted herself to do so, who could describe their tongues? On the other hand, there is indeed something Virgilian about the ability to retain lives other than your own, about the intensity of attention to others' fates, and it is not necessarily the property of a poet.

But, then again, I couldn't apply to Sir Isaiah the label "philosopher," because that mutilated copy of *Four Essays on Liberty* was more the product of a gut reaction against an atrocious century than a philosophical tract. For the same reason, I couldn't call him a historian of ideas. To me, his words always were a cry from the bowels of the monster, a call not so much for help as *of* help—a normal response of the mind singed and scarred by the present, and wishing it upon nobody as the future.

Besides, in the realm I was from, "philosophy" was by and large a foul word and entailed the notion of a system. What was good about *Four Essays on Liberty* was that it advanced none, since "liberty" and "system" are antonyms. As to the smart-alecky retort that the absence of a system in itself is a system, I was pretty confident that I could live with this syllogism, not to mention in this sort of system.

And I remember that as I was making my way through that book without a cover I'd often pause, exclaiming to myself: How Russian this is! And by that I meant not only the author's arguments, but also the way that they were presented: his piling up of subordinate clauses, his digressions and questions, the cadences of his prose which resembled the sardonic eloquence of the best of nineteenth-century Russian fiction.

Of course I knew that the man entertaining me now in the Atheneum was born in Riga—I think Akhmatova told me so. She also thought that he was a personal friend of Churchill's, whose favorite wartime reading had been Berlin's dispatches from Washington. She was also absolutely sure that it was Berlin who arranged for her to receive an honorary degree from Oxford and the Etna Taormina Prize for Poetry in Italy in 1963. (Having seen something of Oxford dons years later, I think that making these arrangements was a good deal rockier than she could have imagined.) "His great hero is Herzen," she would add with a shrug and turn her face to the window.

Yet for all that, what I was reading wasn't "Russian." Nor was it Western rationalism marrying Eastern soulfulness, or Russian syntax burdening English clarity with its inflections. It appeared to me to be the fullest articulation of a unique human psyche, aware of the limitations imposed

upon it by either language, and cognizant of those limitations' perils. Where I had cried, "Russian!" I should have said "human." The same goes for the passages where one might have sighed, "How English!"

The fusion of two cultures? Reconciliation of their conflicting values? If so, it would only reflect the human psyche's appetite for and ability to fuse and reconcile a lot more. Perhaps what could have been perceived here as faintly Eastern was the notion that reason doesn't deserve to have such a high premium put on it, the sense that reason is but an articulated emotion. That's why the defense of rational ideas turns out sometimes to be a highly emotional affair.

I remarked that the place looked positively English, very Victorian, to be precise. "Indeed so," replied my host with a smile. "This is an island within an island. This is what's left of England, an idea of it, if you will." And, as though not sure of my fully grasping the nuance, he added, "a Herzen idea of London. All it lacks is fog." And that was itself a glance at oneself from the outside, from afar, from a vantage point which was the psychological equivalent of the mid-Atlantic. It sounded like Auden's "Look, stranger, on this island now. . . ."

No, neither a philosopher nor a historian of ideas, not literary critic or social utopian, but an autonomous mind in the grip of an outward gravity, whose pull extends its perspective on this life insofar as this mind cares to send back signals. The word, perhaps, would be "*penseur,*" were it not for the muscular and crouching associations so much at odds with this civilized, alert figure comfortably reclining in the bottle-green leather armchair at the Atheneum—the West and the East of it mentally at the same time.

That is where an Indian scout normally is, that's where one would be looking for him. At least in the beleaguered fort I was from one learns not to look in one direction only. The sad irony of all this is of course that, so far as I know, not a line of Berlin's writings has been translated into the language of the country which needs that intellect the most, and which could profit from those writings enormously. If anything, that country could learn from him a lot more about its intellectual history—and by the same token about its present choices—than it seems capable of thus far. His syntax, to say the least, wouldn't be an obstacle. Nor should they be perturbed by Herzen's shadow, for while Herzen indeed was appalled by and sought to change the mental climate of Russia, Berlin seems to take on the entire world's weather.

Short of being able to alter it, he still helps one to endure it. One cloud less—if only a cloud in one's mind—is improvement enough, like removing from a brow its "tactile fever." Ah improvement far greater is the idea that it is the ability to choose that defines a being as human; that, hence, choice is the species's recognized necessity—which flies into the moronic face of the reduction of the human adventure to the exclusively moral dimensions of right and wrong.

Of course, one says all this with the benefit of hindsight, sharpened by what one could have read of Berlin since. I think, however, that seventeen years ago, with only *The Hedgehog and the Fox* and *Four Essays on Liberty* on my mind, I could not have reacted to their author differently. Before our tea at the Atheneum was over I knew that others' lives are this man's forte, for what other reason could there be for a sixty-three-year-old knight of England to talk to a thirty-two-year-old Russian poet? What could I possibly tell him that he didn't already know, one way or the other?

Still, I think I was sitting in front of him on that sunny July afternoon not only because his work is the life of the mind, the life of ideas. Ideas of course reside in people, but they can also be gleaned from clouds, water, trees; indeed, from a fallen apple. And at best I could qualify as an apple fallen from Akhmatova's tree. I believe he wanted to see me not for what I knew but for what I didn't—a role in which, I suppose, he quite frequently finds himself vis-à-vis most of the world.

To put it somewhat less stridently, if not less autobiographically, with Berlin the world gets one more choice. This choice consists not so much of following his precepts as of adopting his mental patterns. In the final analysis, Berlin's notion of pluralism is not a blueprint but rather a reflection of the omniscience of his own unique mind, which indeed appears to be both older and more generous than what it observes. This omniscience in other words is very man-like and therefore can and should be emulated, not just applauded or envied.

Later the same evening, as we sat for supper in Stephen Spender's basement, Wystan said, "Well, how did it go today with Isaiah?" And Stephen immediately asked, "Yes, is his Russian really good?" I began, in my tortured English, a long story about the nobility of old Petersburg pronunciation, about its similarity to Stephen's own Oxonian, and how Isaiah's vocabulary was free of unpalatable accretions of the Soviet period and how his idiom was so much his own, when Natasha Spender interrupted me and said, "Yes, but does he speak Russian as fast as he speaks English?" I looked at the faces of those three people who had known Isaiah Berlin for much longer than I had lived and wondered whether I should carry on with my exegesis. Then I thought better of it.

"Faster," I said.

William L. McBride (essay date 1990)

SOURCE: *"Two Concepts of Liberty* Thirty Years Later: A Sartre-Inspired Critique," in *Social Theory and Practice*, Vol. 16, No. 3, Fall, 1990, pp. 297-322.

[In the following essay, McBride challenges Berlin's concept of negative liberty by comparing it to Jean-Paul Sartre's concept of freedom.]

"Two Concepts of Liberty" was first delivered by Isaiah Berlin as an inaugural lecture, upon his installation in the Chichele Chair of Social and Political Theory at Oxford, on October 31, 1958. Oxford's influence in the world of philosophy, at least in the English-speaking world, was at that time still at a height from which it has since greatly declined. But Berlin himself was never regarded as a quintessential proponent, if indeed there ever really was such a thing, of Oxford analytic philosophy. He was always somewhat apart: an enormously engaging lecturer to audiences of scholars and undergraduates alike, endowed with a vast repertoire of cultural allusions from diverse times and places that would put to shame the ordinary philosophy don. I remember once attending a lecture that he gave at Yale just a few years after his installation in the Chichele Chair; while I cannot recall the exact title or topic, except that much of it had to do with the notion of historical determinism, two impressions of it remain fresh in my mind—first, that he unashamedly admitted having written it up on the airplane ride from England, and second, that it was an exceptionally illuminating and valuable lecture. As one watched him and listened to his intense, clipped, extremely rapid-fire delivery, it was easy to forget that Isaiah Berlin had originally come from an entirely different world from comfortable, intensely cerebral Oxford: namely, Riga, Latvia, and the cultural milieu of Mother Russia.

When I was originally invited to participate in this symposium on freedom or liberty (I, like Berlin, will use the two words interchangeably) I thought at once of the individual upon whose philosophy of freedom, as it is so often denominated, I have lavished the greater part of my scholarly attention for the last several years, Jean-Paul Sartre. But at the same time I also thought of Isaiah Berlin and his lecture, **"Two Concepts of Liberty,"** of which I had purchased an original copy when I first visited Blackwell's in Oxford in the spring of 1960, and to which I find students in social and political philosophy, usually in independence of any invitation on my part, still making frequent and usually favorable allusion. It has been, in short, a most unusually influential essay. It is probably unnecessary for me to say that I do not regard that influence as altogether positive or helpful for advancing thinking about freedom, since I have already called this lecture a "Sartre-inspired *critique.*" On this point I agree with the late, much lamented Gerald MacCallum, professor of political and legal philosophy at the University of Wisconsin, who once wrote an article "challeng[ing] the view that we may usefully distinguish between two kinds of concepts of political and social freedom—negative and positive." But MacCallum, by entitling his article "Negative and Positive Freedom,"[1] no doubt inadvertently contributed to the ongoing perception (for example, on the part of students pursuing bibliographies or books, such as Rawls's *A Theory of Justice,* in which MacCallum's piece is referenced) that Berlin's original essay and the distinction that it draws are authoritative.

My choice of this last word is quite deliberate. For if there is one theme, in dealing with the idea of liberty, on which Isaiah Berlin, Jean-Paul Sartre, and I agree—in contrast, for example, with a near-contemporary of Berlin's, the late Hannah Arendt—it is the desire, which he attributes to the lovers of negative liberty like himself, "to curb authority as such," whereas the proponents of positive liberty are said to "want [authority] placed in their own hands."[2] Of course, the authority at issue here is above all political authority, but I think it not unfair to the spirit of Berlin's philosophy to extend the questioning of authority that he favors to alleged intellectual authority as well. And that will be the ultimate purpose of this paper: to re-examine and put into question some currently authoritative conceptions of social and political freedom, beginning with Isaiah Berlin's. In seeking to achieve this purpose, I shall begin by summarizing a few of the main points of the famous lecture on **"Two Concepts of Liberty"** and trying a little harder than Berlin himself does to elucidate, with the aid of his text, some of the most salient characteristics of that concept to which he most closely adheres. I shall then quickly narrate the evolution of Sartre's perspectives on liberty, starting with one that bears a number of resemblances to Berlin's, in order to help illuminate some of the inadequacies of the latter. I shall conclude by considering three situations in which Berlin's concept of negative liberty can be seen to be insufficient to explain the complexities of freedom and unfreedom as they are experienced by the human beings involved in such situations: those of the citizens of an impoverished African or Asian nation attempting to emerge from colonial rule, of women in a sexist society, and of would-be players in a or the "free market."

1.

As is true of all philosophical texts, **"Two Concepts of Liberty"** appeared within a definite historical context, out of which its author's motives for writing it were derived. Its context was, to put the matter as simply as possible, the Cold War. As Berlin very clearly states at the end of his introductory section, our attitudes are likely to remain obscure to ourselves, "unless we understand the dominant issues of our own world. The greatest of these is the open war that is being fought between two civilizations and two systems of ideas which return different and conflicting answers to what has long been the central question of politics—the question of obedience and coercion."[3] Therefore, he says, "any aspect of this issue is worthy of examination." It is in the later context of the apparent collapse of one of those "civilizations" and "systems of ideas" and of the consequent end of the Cold War that we are now reconsidering the essay, and it is for this reason that in the title of this talk I have chosen to call attention to the fact of historical distance from the time at which **"Two Concepts of Liberty"** was first delivered.

Let me briefly explore a few of the implications of that original context for the philosophical content of Berlin's message. Berlin had left Russia many years earlier, it is true, but he continued and even to this day continues to be steeped in Russian culture, to speak the Russian language even more rapidly than English, so it is said, and of course

to remain *au courant* with the dramatic events of that country's twentieth-century history. Stalin and the Stalinist ideology strongly promoted the doctrine of the "two camps," which at one time was said to entail the view that even Marxist-Leninist mathematics and linguistics were radically, qualitatively different disciplines from their Western counterparts, until Stalin himself called a halt to this extreme of "two camps" insanity by writing a long essay on linguistics that rejected this interpretation.[4] It is difficult, when one sees oneself as locked in mortal combat with an implacable opponent in the realm of ideas, to avoid adopting and assenting to the congruent counterparts of the opponent's position. Something of this sort helps to explain the excessive polarity, well criticized by MacCallum and others, that characterizes the fundamental opposition between the two concepts of liberty of Berlin's title. Of course, he does not go so far as to claim that only would-be totalitarian intellectuals subscribe to one or another version of positive liberty; indeed he attributes one of its two main sub-divisions to Kant, the other to T.H. Green, neither of whom he would for a moment have characterized as totalitarians. And it is true that one of the few slight but significant emendations that he made in a later published edition of the essay involved a retreat from his earlier concluding endorsement of negative liberty as a truer and more "humane ideal" than positive liberty and his substitution of "pluralism, with the measure of 'negative' liberty that it entails"[5] as the name of that ideal, since it had been pointed out to him by friendly critics that the sort of clear-cut taking of sides involved in the first formulation was deeply inconsistent with his own value pluralism. Nevertheless, the spirit of the lecture remains that of two camps, and there is never a question in the reader's mind as to which one is Berlin's. I would like to remark in passing that much the same dilemma confronts some of today's advocates of postmodernism as a radically pluralistic way of thinking that above all eschews totalities and bipolarities, who nonetheless feel a compulsion sharply to distinguish "them," the modernists, from "us."

Actually, Berlin remarks early on[6] that there are over two hundred senses of the word "freedom" to be found in the history of ideas, but that he will confine himself to two of the most central ones. It is obvious from the outset that his own usage of the term, especially of negative freedom, will be simultaneously descriptive and normative: this, he will say, is what the concept of freedom precisely *means,* and this concept defines that free state of affairs for the human individual that is most desirable and is indeed one of the supreme human values. It is an end in itself and as such an absolute, although of course it is not to be taken as the sole ultimate end. However, when one yields freedom, as so understood, in favor of some other important end such as security, one ought to be clear that it is freedom that one is yielding. Likewise, when one advocates some other desirable goals that may not be in conflict with, and may even be assisted to achievement by, an atmosphere in which there is a large measure of freedom in Berlin's sense—such goals as self-fulfillment or participation in a democratic election process or knowledge or virtuousness—one should not sloppily contend that they, too, are parts or aspects of the meaning of freedom.

The highly analytic way of looking at the world that Berlin employs here has its great merits. When being practiced well, it can convey the appearance of great rigor. But its underpinnings, as critics of analytic methodologies have often pointed out, are not self-evident or self-justifying. I shall confine myself, since I do not wish to make this a lecture primarily on methodology, to just one aspect of the problem of Berlin's analytic method here, that implied in the second word of his title, "concepts." To identify distinct concepts, whether two or more and whether or not one is valorized over others, is to legislate about linguistic usage and thought. It is to say, as, for example, Berlin does, "Everything is what it is: liberty is liberty, not equality or fairness or justice or human happiness or a quiet conscience."[7] Of course, there is no way for any thinker, whether self-consciously "analytic" or not, to avoid making some such move; but it is important that it be recognized for what it is, an effort to channel readers' or listeners' ways of thinking about the subject matter at hand along precise lines that some or many of them might otherwise not have been inclined to adopt—to say, "This is the way in which you *ought* to think about what, for example, 'liberty' really means." And so, of course, it is a deliberate attempted infringement on their prior "negative" freedom to think whatever they wanted about, say, "liberty"—an infringement or legislation carried out, to be sure, for a good intellectual cause.

It is just this sort of conceptual legislation that Berlin, in his essay, attributes pre-eminently to the proponents of "positive" liberty. Probably the single most fatal move that they make, as Berlin understands it, is to begin to think of human personalities in terms of "higher" and "lower" selves. Clearly, if selves are so divided, it would be desirable for the higher parts to gain the upper hand over the lower ones. Such victory is then identified by the "positive" liberty crowd with *true* freedom. This can come either in the form of the doctrine of self-abnegation favored by Epicurus or Kant, according to which succumbing to the impulse of one's appetite is unfreedom, whereas obeying a law that one has prescribed to oneself is freedom, or in the less individualistic, more society-oriented "self-realization" doctrines advanced by such diverse thinkers as Rousseau (from whom some of Kant's own central formulas were borrowed), Hegel, Marx, T.H. Green, and many others. Further developments of this way of thinking can lead to entire political and legal systems based on the notion that it is the right and even the duty of the State to protect its citizens from the threats posed by their own lower selves to the mutual realization of their own highest and truest interests.

This, then, is the intellectual and sociopolitical nightmare of "positive" freedom against the background of which Berlin poses as the embattled defender of the ideal of simple, "negative" freedom. The extent to which this picture had, and now still has, the ring of truth has been forcefully confirmed to us of late by witnesses such as Vaclav Havel, who suffered so much at the hands of people, generally very petty yet politically powerful people, who thought in roughly this way. But is Berlin's own "negative" freedom idea really so very simple? At first, it may seem so. For example, he forthrightly admits "negative" freedom means the possibility of an individual's pursuing wishes, goals, and desires that may appear exceedingly trivial or unworthy to everyone else, just as long as he or she does not thereby impinge on others' pursuits. Thus, all the machinery involved in trying to catalogue "higher" and "lower" desires, of which we already find such a detailed version, for example, in Plato's account of imperfect-to-degenerate personality types in the *Republic,* ought to be dismantled. For another thing, Berlin expresses strong agreement with Bentham and Hobbes when, contrary no doubt to the vast majority of Western philosophers writing on this topic, they observe that all laws, however worthy and value-producing some of them may be, by definition constitute in some way or to some degree curtailments of the freedom of someone or other—a simple and not necessarily damaging truth that lovers of law are always constructing endless epicycles to avoid admitting. The concept of "negative" liberty may at this point seem to some to be a rather austere notion, perhaps realizable in human society only at a certain cost, for example, in the average level of civility which citizens might feel constrained to maintain, but nevertheless a clear and self-consistent notion.

But just how clear and self-consistent is it in reality? A first indication of difficulty is to be found in Berlin's introduction to the volume *Four Essays on Liberty,* in which **"Two Concepts of Liberty"** was republished in 1969. Here, he admits to having erred in the original version by equating liberty, at least the liberty he endorses, with "the absence of obstacles to the fulfillment of a man's desires."[8] As he has now come to see, it would then be the case that, "I could increase freedom as effectively by eliminating desires as by satisfying them." But this implication, which comes close to the Epicurean notion of self-abnegation that Berlin has identified as the first version of "positive" freedom, is of course not one that Berlin wishes to derive from his concept of "negative" liberty.

The concept is meant, as the text I just cited shows clearly, to be a quantitative one, conceivable in terms of more or less. But the question is, more or less of what? In a very important footnote, Berlin explicitly uses the language of "magnitudes" and identifies the units of these magnitudes as "possibilities." He says that "the extent of my freedom" depends on five variables with respect to these possibilities: how many, how easy to actualize, how relatively important they are in my plan of life, how much deliberate human acts close or open them, and what value is placed on them by the society in which one lives as well as by oneself. And he observes that, while the nature of the subject-matter obviously makes very precise calculation impossible in this domain, still "we can give valid reasons for saying that the average subject of the King of Sweden is, on the whole, a good deal freer today than the average citizen of the Republic of Rumania."[9]

In the revised version of 1969, while Berlin retains "the subject of the King of Sweden" as his example of someone with large quantities of "negative" freedom—an obvious but in fact not especially cogent allusion to his controversial claim that there can be more freedom in some autocracies than in some democracies, or in other words that the form of government is not the determinative factor when it comes to assessing freedom—he now replaces the Republic of Rumania with two other illustrations of less free citizenries, "Spain or Albania."[10] We could speculate at length on his motives for making this substitution, in light of changing political conditions at the time and of his wish to mitigate somewhat the impression of being a partisan Cold Warrior, but I prefer to focus for a moment on some implications of his use of this language of magnitudes. It is of interest not only because of the way in which Berlin employs it and the many potential dilemmas that it creates for his own thinking, but also because it is such a commonplace way of talking about sociopolitical freedom for both philosophers and non-philosophers of the most varied orientations. To me, it conjures up thoughts of Leibniz, thoughts of objective possibilities and combinations of possibilities in an extremely complex but in principle calculable world. But this leads us into the realm of ontology, a realm that Berlin, as he makes clear in his rejection of the claim made by some critics that he has in effect taken a definitive position on the question of historical determinism, does not wish to enter. However, has he not in fact entered it with his talk about the extent of "negative" freedom—an ontological concept if there ever was one—as determined by the magnitudes of measurable possibilities? He has even specified, by his references to the individual's life-plan and to the social judgments of the relative values of different possibilities as determined by "the general sentiment of the society in which he lives,"[11] just which kinds of possibilities count more than others. What does this entail, if not that very rank-ordering of the values of individuals' various ends, "save in so far as they may frustrate the purposes of others," that he elsewhere commends "Mill, and liberals in general" for eschewing at those moments at which they are being most consistent?[12] At the very least, we may already conclude that consistency is not Berlin's own strongest suit.

But there are still more serious problems to come. Against a number of his critics, such as C.B. MacPherson and Bernard Crick,[13] Berlin wishes to hue steadfastly to the idea that freedom itself can and should be distinguished sharply from its conditions, such as a certain level of food, material well-being, and need-satisfaction in general, without which it is unrealistic to expect human beings to be able to exercise their freedom.[14] (This Berlinian distinction between freedom and its conditions appears to be the ancestor of John Rawls's notorious distinction in *A Theory of Justice* between freedom and the worth or value of one's freedom,[15] which itself has drawn a great deal of negative criticism.) But how in the world, if freedom is supposed to be measurable in terms of quantifiable magnitudes of possibilities, can we possibly exclude consideration of an individual's "conditions" from a judgment of the degree to

which he or she is free? It is at this point in his definitional argument that Berlin, it seems to me, begins to retreat from a notion of sociopolitical freedom that is concrete and, in a very meaningful though non-Berlinian sense, "positive" enough to permit rough comparisons, such as ordinary political observers frequently attempt to make, between the freedom enjoyed by Albanians and that enjoyed by Swedes, towards a notion that is highly abstract and hence truly and in the fullest sense "negative."

Two passages, one in the original essay and one in the introduction to the later edition, seem to me to epitomize Berlin's conception of freedom as negativity. In the first passage, it will be noted, he finds this to be the core conception of both of the versions of liberty that he has been delineating:

> The essence of the notion of liberty, both in the 'positive' and the 'negative' senses, is the holding off of something or someone—of others, who trespass on my field or assert their authority over me, or of obsessions, fears, neuroses, irrational forces—intruders and despots of one kind and another.[16]

A decade later, he says: "The fundamental sense of freedom is freedom from chains, from imprisonment, from enslavement by others. The rest is extension of this sense, or else metaphor."[17] One senses here his admirable hatred of coercion and his awareness of the ubiquitous dangers of being coerced in the contemporary world. We can all, I think and hope, share something of this feeling. But one is also reminded of the picture that is painted by Berlin's nemesis, Rousseau, of life in the first stage of his imaginary state of nature in the *Discourse on the Origin of Inequality,* a work that does not, of course, pose the same ideological threat, in Berlin's mind, as does *The Social Contract.* For in that *Second Discourse* Rousseau characterizes individuals in the first stage of human history as being copiously endowed, so to speak, with negative freedom, wandering through the primitive forests without any attachments except those temporary ones necessitated by copulation and reproduction; even mothers would, presumably, have liberated themselves from the care of their offspring much earlier than in civilized society. It is of this same negative freedom that Rousseau was no doubt thinking when he began the first chapter of the first book of *The Social Contract* with the famous assertion that "Man was born free," although everywhere he is in fact in chains.

But there is an obvious problem about life in this imagined earliest Rousseauean state of nature, a problem of which Rousseau himself, that master of paradoxes of the human condition, was keenly aware: it really would have been totally uncivilized, meaning, among other things, that human creatures in that state would have had a very limited range of real possibilities for doing anything at all besides eating, sleeping, copulating, and, in the case of females, having babies. They would have been supremely innocent and also supremely ignorant. And Rousseau, despite the false, oversimplified picture of him to be found in some textbooks, not only did not believe that it would be possible to return to such a state, but did not even find it especially admirable or desirable or valuable. In fact, in the *Second Discourse,* his real nostalgia is reserved for the next stage of his imaginary human history, when humans would have begun to socialize, to get together in small groups and engage in some non-cutthroat, non-threatening competitive and other collaborative activities, but before the rise of destructive conflict brought about by competition for scarce, newly-discovered resources such as minerals. One way in which Rousseau attempts to explain how humans might have evolved from the stupid first state of nature into something more attractive before the onset of destructive conflict is to say that the race was always characterized by "perfectibility," by which I take him to mean a richness of future possibilities.[18] But none of these possibilities would have been ready-to-hand, or known, at the very first stage. Hence, to revert to Berlin's language, the "extent of freedom" of the individuals at that stage would have been extremely limited, even though "chains," "imprisonment," and "enslavement by others" would also have been entirely unthinkable at that point. If freedom really is, as Berlin has asserted in the last passage of his that I have cited, essentially just freedom from such things, then it really does make sense to treat it as fully and entirely *negative,* albeit as a rich and suggestive negativity, one that can be of considerable use as a kind of limiting-case concept. But such a notion cannot possibly be the whole story about sociopolitical freedom either as an ideal or as a reality.

2.

It is just this notion of human freedom as supreme negativity, or "nothingness" (the need to translate *"néant"* into the more substantive-sounding "nothingness" for the sake of elegant English already distorts somewhat the connotations of the original) for which Jean-Paul Sartre is no doubt still best known among students of philosophy. *Being and Nothingness,* the book in which a metaphysics of freedom beginning with this core insight is worked out in enormous detail, was written during the early years of the Second World War and published while the war was still raging. As a challenge to various alternative metaphysics of determinism, as a confrontation with some of the conceptual problems involved in maintaining an absolutist position about freedom that is very comparable to Berlin's in some of the latter's more self-consistent moments that I have identified, but with the difference that Sartre is clear-headed enough to recognize that what he is trying to assert involves ontological claims and hence ontological difficulties, this book is still unsurpassed and well worth the considerable effort required to work through it with students or by oneself. Consider, in particular, its treatment of the various elements of what Sartre calls the "facticity" of my individual situation—facts about where I live, about my past, about my environment, about my human contemporaries, and about my death as a physically (though not logically) certain and temporally imprecise future event—as "coefficients of adversity" that act as resistances to, or channelers of, the exercise of my freedom. This re-

mains, to my mind, an extremely illuminating way of retaining an hypothesis of human freedom as conceptually absolute while acknowledging the basic realities of the almost infinite constraints that surround and often seem to engulf us. By contrast with Berlin, whose principal purpose in expounding on "negative" liberty was the moralistic one of extolling its virtues over the rival, "positive" concept, Sartre's focus in *Being and Nothingness* is primarily descriptive, at an ontological level; but it is clear both from the text itself and from his other, more literary writings of the same period that Sartre wishes to uphold a similar, open-ended and indeterminate kind of freedom, rather than any "positive" conception of freedom as individual or collective self-determination, as his normative ideal. What other conviction could have lain behind his notorious assertion, for which he later appears to have felt a certain embarrassment, that, in light of the universal tendency "to sacrifice man in order to give rise to the [ideal of] self-cause, . . .

> it comes to the same thing to get drunk in solitude or to lead people. If one of these activities wins out over the other, it . . . will be . . . because of the degree of consciousness that it possesses of the ideal goal; and, in that case, it will come about that the quietism of the solitary drunkard will win out over the vain agitation of the leader of peoples?[19]

That, I submit, is the spirit of "negative" freedom taken to an extreme!

But Sartre himself was not satisfied with the philosophical position on freedom, or indeed on many other related notions, that he had taken in *Being and Nothingness.* On the one hand, he was dissatisfied with those elements of his early thinking about freedom that smack of Stoic indifference or apathy—the "stone walls do not a prison make" approach—which in fact resemble the "error" in "Two Concepts of Liberty" to which Berlin later confessed, that of equating liberty with the absence of obstacles to the fulfillment of one's desires and thus of implying that freedom could be as well realized by shrinking one's desires as by satisfying them. On the other hand, the experience of having been the subject of an occupying power during wartime had made Sartre, like so many of the French, more sensitive to the ways in which freedoms which we normally take for granted (such as the freedom to conduct day-to-day business in our community surrounded by the conventional signs and symbols and language of this community rather than by ones imposed from another tradition) can be taken away. If one sees the portion of the film "Sartre," in which pictures of wartime Paris festooned with Nazi symbols and signs in German are shown along with a voice-over reading from an immediate post-Liberation essay that Sartre began with the words, "Never were we more free than under the German Occupation," one can better understand what he meant there: while all of these coercions and deprivations of the German Occupation of course resulted in individuals' being in fact less rather than more free in the most obvious ways, their other effect was to make people more aware of the garden-variety, normally taken-for-granted freedoms that remained to them. (As he went on to say: "Since the Nazi poison infiltrated itself into our thought, every accurate thought was a conquest; since an omnipotent police sought to compel us to silence, every word became precious as a declaration of principle."[20]) While it is precisely this experience of totalitarian control by advocates of a so-called "higher" freedom—sloganizing, though no doubt in the Nazis' case more cynically than sincerely, that *"Arbeit macht frei"*—that was later to motivate Berlin to praise the merits of "negative" liberty, Sartre was coming to realize that the concept of liberty as essentially negative was inadequate for capturing the meaning of the word within this or any other sociopolitical context.

In addition to the considerations that I have advanced thus far for Sartre's growing awareness of this inadequacy, there was yet another that loomed increasingly large during the postwar years: the fact of widespread powerlessness among the people of the rest of the world, outside of Europe and North America and a few other enclaves, who made up the vast majority of the world's population. It seemed to Sartre (though not to Berlin) unproblematic to say that natives of colonies in Africa were unfree (we might nowadays forget how tenaciously and brutally France and some other European powers fought for years to cling to these colonies after World War II). What was and is perhaps more problematic, although this is a complex issue that I shall only be able to skirt here, is his belief that the existence of this condition of vast global disparities with respect to scarcity and, complementarily, to access to what Rawls calls "social primary goods" has the effect of diminishing or blocking the increase of the freedom even of those living in comparative abundance. This belief, to be sure, is directly opposed to Berlin's distinction between the conditions of freedom and freedom itself.

In the most important philosophical work of his later years, the *Critique of Dialectical Reason,* written during the same time-period as Berlin's **"Two Concepts"** essay, Sartre identifies freedom with action, or *praxis,* as performed by human beings even under conditions of extreme constraint and limitation—as, for example, in the kind of work that has to be done in order to satisfy even the most basic material needs under conditions of great scarcity. He then goes on to show, in sharp contrast to the virtually unmitigated individualism characteristic of all of *Being and Nothingness,* how under certain circumstances, usually some new external threat, it may be possible for groups of individuals to act together to overcome some of their previous constraints and limitations and forge a new social order. At first glance, this valorizing of collective action might appear to reproduce precisely the move from "negative" to "positive" liberty against which Berlin has warned us; Sartre's partial indebtedness to both Hegel and Marx in developing this new conceptual framework may seem to clinch that case. But in fact, the situation is not nearly so simple. The Sartre of the *Critique* is no self-realization theorist of the sort that Berlin so deplores: he has no conception of a "lower" and a "higher" self, or indeed of any

essential self at all, and he is very explicit in denying to groups and institutions any claim to be organisms, entities higher than the individuals who create and sustain them. Moreover, if one of the implications of his analysis is that freedom is more fully expressed and productive of more future possibilities when human beings break with habitual, routine ways of acting in order to try to take some control over their destinies, this by no means leads him to envisage the "happy-ever-after" fairytale of life in the new society that Berlin finds so abhorrent. On the contrary, the structure of the latter half of the *Critique* is such as to show how easily the attempt to advance freedom can lead to extremes of institutionalization, bureaucracy, and authoritarianism that make the new condition of human beings in society more obviously constrained and coerced than before—now actively, by the net outcomes of their own "free" actions, rather than passively by material circumstances. Most of the completed part of the unfinished second volume of the *Critique* goes on to analyze a paradigm example of just such a result, the Soviet Union under Stalin during the 1930s.

Finally, in his last and longest *magnum opus, The Family Idiot,* Sartre shows through his often agonizingly detailed study of Flaubert in the context of his society and times just how much is conditioned, determined for us by the nearly infinite mass of our "coefficients of adversity." In a certain sense, there has been no radical reversal of Sartre's philosophical positions concerning human freedom since the epoch of *Being and Nothingness,* and even that earlier language is reproduced from time to time in the late work. And yet the emphasis, the intellectual landscape, is completely changed. I am particularly enamored, in this connection, of a short passage in an interview that Sartre gave to representatives of *The New Left Review* shortly before the time of publication of *The Family Idiot;* it goes as follows:

> I believe that a man can always make something of what has been made of him. That is the definition that I would today give of liberty: that small movement which makes of a totally conditioned social being a person who does not replace the totality of what he or she has received from his or her conditioning.[21]

As can be seen even in this brief interview text, Sartre never lost interest in the ontological dimension of freedom, even while he continued throughout his life to be identified as a champion of sociopolitical freedom in the normative sense. Berlin's concern in **"Two Concepts of Liberty,"** on the other hand, was almost exclusively normative, or at least that is what he intended. One might, I suppose, question whether the "negative" freedom that Berlin champions there should be called "sociopolitical" freedom at all, given his single-minded insistence on the supreme importance of each individual's being free from external social constraints. But it is obvious that Berlin meant his essay to be seen as a statement of sociopolitical values, or more precisely of one particularly important sociopolitical value, and that is how it has been read. What Sartre came increasingly to believe, however, over roughly the second half of his life was that freedom was meaningless as a norm or value—in other words, worthless—when understood and realized only in its purely negative form. Without, as I have argued, moving to a position that could accurately be labeled "positive freedom" in Berlin's sense, Sartre increasingly recognized, like so many of Berlin's critics, the inherently relational nature of virtually all human freedom except when it is considered as a concept-limit (even though I am sure that he would have regarded MacCallum's formula of freedom as a triadic relation—of *x,* from *y,* to do or become or not to do or not become z^{22}—as too simple and schematic). To assert this is not just to say, as no doubt Berlin himself would be willing to say, that human society is a vast field of relationships; it is to maintain that the concept of human freedom considered as a value necessarily entails reference to other persons besides the ἰδιώτηζ, and hence can no longer be captured by the formula of "negative liberty" as soon as the complexity of our understanding of it advances beyond the elementary level of human beings at the first stage of Rousseau's imaginary state of nature. Let us now, finally, consider a few concrete cases in order to illustrate the inadequacy of the concept of negative liberty for understanding the experience of human freedom and unfreedom in a sociopolitical context.

3.

One of the, to my mind, less attractive passages in "Two Concepts of Liberty" is Berlin's allusion to what he regards as a fairly common experience in recently-liberated African or Asian former colonies. It is, he says, the

> desire for reciprocal recognition that leads the most authoritarian of democracies to be, at times, consciously preferred by its members to the most enlightened oligarchies, or sometimes causes a member of some newly liberated Asian or African state to complain less today, when he is rudely treated by members of his own race or nation, than when he was governed by some cautious, just, gentle, well-meaning administrator from outside.[23]

Unless we understand this phenomenon whereby, he says, people in this situation may have fewer "elementary human rights" than before and yet claim to be freer, their ideals and behavior will be unintelligible. Berlin's effort at understanding it consists in affirming that solidarity, fraternity, and equality are deeply important values that are somehow operative in these situations, but insisting that to call this congeries of values "social freedom" is to be fuzzy-minded, to make a category mistake. It is precisely at this point in his discussion that Berlin advances the definition of the essence of liberty as a "holding off" of others that I have already cited.

MacCallum comments briefly and unfavorably on this passage in a footnote to his article, suggesting that Berlin needs to analyze further the connection between self-rule and rule by one's peers as well as the root notion of freedom involved in the idea of being the "author," or autho-

rizer, of the sovereignty that holds sway over one as it is advanced in Hobbes's version of social contract theory.[24] It seems to me that MacCallum is being too "cautious, just, gentle" with Berlin here, although of course it is for MacCallum merely an incidental point. What particularly amazed me about this passage in **"Two Concepts of Liberty"** when I went back to analyze it more carefully was two aspects: the perhaps unintentional but extremely insensitive and provocative language about the almost saintly, beneficent former colonial administrator that I have just recalled, and the fact that Berlin himself, who has a considerable feeling for language most of the time, speaks of the African or Asian state in question as "newly liberated." In fact, I began writing my analysis by using this expression, "liberated," to designate such states while adding parenthetically that this was of course my own expression, not Berlin's, only to realize that it was, in fact, Berlin's as well!

It is with this example that I think my earlier point about the element of legislation, or of dictation, if one prefers stronger language, that is involved in Berlin's loose linguistic analytic methodology becomes clear: members of these newly liberated states speak of what they have obtained as liberty, he is saying, and one can understand their strong positive feelings about what they have obtained, but they should not call it "liberty," since this is not the way in which the word should be understood. If defenders of the now-suspect terminology—current-day members, for example, of one or another "National Liberation Front"—were simply to respond by insisting that what they are advocating is, indeed, freedom (or at least one very important aspect of freedom) as they understand it, then we would be at an intellectual impasse with no exit. However, there is another philosophical route open beyond conceptual analysis, a route that was popularized by Sartre, de Beauvoir, and other twentieth-century Continental European philosophers, namely, the resort to *lived experience.* While it lacks the precision of, for example, mathematical calculation, so, too, as Berlin readily admits, does his method when dealing with an abstract concept such as "liberty." Now, I myself do not have the time here to undertake a phenomenological description of the colonial experience, and in any event it has been done often enough and skillfully enough before, by Sartre among others. But a few remarks are in order.

The situation of the African or Asian subject of a European colonial power when confronting, as he or she in most cases frequently needed to, an official representing that power was by definition one of powerlessness, however well-meaning some of these officials may have been. As a class, the colonized were in effect adult children in their own lands, dependent, even in those colonies in which elaborate systems of rights and justices may have prevailed, on the good graces of another class from which they were in principle excluded for the ongoing decision to sustain those legal systems rather than, for example, to suspend them by declaring a state of emergency. What was involved, in other words, was more than and different from a mere lack of solidarity or fraternity with the Europeans, although that was also involved: it was an entire structure of sociopolitical relationships within which the colonized were condemned, without appeal, to play a subordinate role, at least as long as the colonial system itself remained in place. The powerlessness experienced by the colonial subjects in this situation must, it seems to me, be characterized as a situation of unfreedom; to insist that this is a linguistic error, that something other than one very important aspect of what is commonly understood as freedom is involved strikes me as being simply perverse.

There is another element involved in the colonial subject's predicament that Berlin refuses as it were on principle to admit as being involved with freedom: the element of the future. To the extent in which a colonizing power, whether in Asia or Africa or Eastern Europe, treats its system of domination as if it were timeless and unending, it is striving to impose an attitude of hopelessness on its colonial subjects; of course, the possibility is always present, as we have seen so dramatically this past year, for a number of them to break with this attitude and to overthrow the entire system. What is needed to free oneself from an imposed atmosphere of hopelessness is a sense of a project, as Sartrean terminology would express it, towards a future that is open, free, perhaps radically different from the present. But Berlin, for one, does not seem to regard this as a necessary part of the notion of freedom. In his one, very brief footnote comment, in his later essay, on MacCallum's claim that liberty must be a triadic relation, he replies that this seems to be an error, that this need not be so, since MacCallum's third element of an object or objective of freedom need not always be present: "A man," Berlin says, "struggling against his chains or a people against enslavement need not consciously aim at any definite further state. A man need not know how he will use his freedom; he just wants to remove the yoke. So do classes and nations."[25]

The error here, it seems to me, is Berlin's, and it is an error about human experience. It is no doubt true and even important that persons, much less peoples, struggling for liberation need not have in mind a "*definite*" future state; in fact, given the notion to which both he and I suscribe of history as somehow open-ended, it is always an illusion when they do. But they must, it seems to me, have a more or less vague or determinate goal beyond the present, enslaved state of affairs in order to motivate the first movement towards liberation at all. Berlin simply refuses to acknowledge this. On the other hand, it is of course fascinating to see that in this brief footnote, which it will be recalled is a product of a later period than **"Two Concepts of Liberty"** itself, Berlin rather un-self-consciously speaks of the freeing of enslaved classes and nations, the very terminology with which he had earlier taken issue.

My second situational example is one to which Berlin never alludes in his essay, which was written in the standard language of the period without any concern about sexist pronouns or about the relentless, repeated references to "a man" (as in the citation just given) or to "men" that yield no hint that another gender might exist. This is not meant so much as a reproach as it is an observation. However, the utility of looking at the doctrine of **"Two Concepts of Liberty"** from the perspective of women's liberation was suggested to me by a brief appreciative article, "Isaiah Berlin at Eighty," that appeared in the 17 August 1989 issue of *The New York Review of Books*. Joseph Brodsky, the author, tells of having first met Berlin in 1972, three days after having quit his native Russia on the pretext of attending a poetry festival in London, through the good offices of Stephen Spender and W. H. Auden, both mutual friends of Berlin's. Berlin telephoned him at the Spenders' and suggested that they meet at his club, the Atheneum, to which Brodsky was duly driven by Mrs. Spender. When Brodsky proposed, in view of his poor command of English, that she accompany him inside, she said that she would not mind doing so but that women were not permitted inside the club.[26] Much of the ensuing conversation inside the Club, as Brodsky reports it, has to do with his and Berlin's common acquaintance, Anna Akhmatova, who had been visited by Berlin in 1946 when he was secretary of the British embassy in Moscow, had thereby incurred Stalin's displeasure, and had dedicated one of her best books of poetry, poetry that Brodsky calls the best in the Russian language, to Berlin.

While this narrative suggests strongly that Berlin is no misogynist, the aspect of it that especially caught my attention was Mrs. Spender's systematic exclusion, simply as a woman, from this gathering-place of British men of power, the Atheneum Club. Brodsky mentions the detail, as I take it, primarily as an illustration of a foreign newcomer's initiation into the quaint and often unexpected ways of the British. Berlin, though foreign-born, was hardly a newcomer: years before his installation in the Chichele Professorship, he had already served in an important position in His Majesty's government. While I cannot be sure as to just how he would have defended his use of the Club as a place for receiving male guests at the tiem, while being aware that even the most distinguished female visitors— even Anna Akhmatova, had she traveled to London—were routinely denied access to it, I feel reasonably confident that he probably would have demurred at saying that a systematic violation of liberty, at least of "negative" liberty, was involved. (Indeed, had he felt strongly that such a violation was involved, I feel reasonably confident that he would have done the honorable thing and refused to frequent the Club on a regular basis.) What "yoke," he might well have asked rhetorically, (as many another male under similar circumstances has asked), was being placed on the necks of women by the expectation that they were never to enter this all-male sanctuary, where they would never have felt at home anyway? But as we know from more recent trends in litigation and legislation in this country, serious issues of freedom, and not simply of the "positive" freedom of self-realization, are indeed now widely seen to be involved in the exclusion of women as a class from such places that are important for the transaction of one's professional affairs—such as, if one is a writer, making contacts with other writers. The barring of access to some simply on the basis of their sex or race or religion or similar irrelevancies is surely a form of "chains, . . . imprisonment, . . . enslavement by others," to use Berlin's words, even though in this case the "prison" is, physically speaking, the world outside the building from which one is barred, rather than itself a building. Without the empowerment that comes with the elimination of these restrictions, the group in question—in this case women—simply remains unfree. But Berlin's own intellectual framework seems ill-equipped to deal satisfactorily with this truth.

Finally, let me turn from the previous two situations, about which I would anticipate finding widespread agreement with my contention that a denial of freedom of a sort not readily explicable in terms of Berlin's understanding of "negative" liberty is involved, to a final and very current one about which I anticipate little agreement: the situation of the so-called "free market," which affects virtually everyone today. Paradoxically enough, it is on this issue, though not on the other two, that I can call upon the powerful rhetoric of Isaiah Berlin for some initial reinforcement. I cite the following passage from his later Introduction to *Four Essays on Liberty*:

> . . . In view of the astonishing opinions that some of my critics have imputed to me, . . . I should have made even clearer that the evils of unrestricted *laissez-faire,* and of the social and legal systems that permitted and encouraged it, led to brutal violations of 'negative' liberty—of basic human rights . . . And I should perhaps have stressed (save that I thought this too obvious to need saying) the failure of such systems to provide the minimum conditions in which alone any degree of significant 'negative' liberty can be exercised by individuals or groups, and without which it is of little or no value to those who may theoretically possess it. For what are rights without the power to implement them?[27]

He goes on to say that "the case for social legislation or planning, for the welfare state and socialism, can be constructed with as much validity from the claims of negative liberty as from those of its positive brother," and remarks that the only reason for his laying stress on the dangers of totalitarian regimes rather than of "liberal ultra-individualism" for human freedom is that the former are at present on the rise while the latter is on the wane.

O tempora! O mores! What better evidence than this text have we for measuring the historical distance that we have traversed, not just since 1958, but even since 1969? In some of the very countries that Berlin would rightly have identified, back in those years, as sufferers of a severe deprivation of liberty in the name of a high ideal of liberty, there are now widespread and prominent movements in favor of that very "liberal ultra-individualism" that Berlin here dismisses; Poland is the most salient example at the moment, but we have only to read the daily newspapers to know that it is not alone in this respect. The slogan of these movements is, once again as of old, the "free market," or, in Berlin's words in the larger passage from which I have just quoted, "an uncontrolled 'market' economy."

The conceptual error involved in this sloganizing is patent: markets are free only in the sense, roughly, in which mechanics might speak of "free play" in a machine, whereas the implication of the slogan as it is used is that the "freeing" of market mechanisms from controls means *eo ipso* an extension of human freedom, conceived in Berlin's sense of "negative" freedom. While I have discussed this matter elsewhere in more detail than is possible here,[28] I would like simply to suggest that the ruthless implementation of "free market" reforms in societies with a previous history of economic controls is likely to result not only in a diminution for many of the "conditions of freedom"—a point that no one denies, since there is no way of avoiding widespread inflation and unemployment of at least a temporary kind when such drastic measures are undertaken—but also in a diminution of freedom itself, to the (questionable) extent to which the two notions are separable for purposes of analysis. This can best be understood by considering the lived experiences of the participants in a comparatively, though not entirely, free market economy such as our own: it is easy to show that the government's principled refusal to regulate, or in some cases its decision to deregulate, the effects of "free market" forces in such areas of public life as health care, education, and transportation has constituted a drastic curb on the freedoms of some of its citizens. Of course, as G.A. Cohen acknowledges in an interesting and highly relevant contribution, with which I find myself largely in agreement, to a *Festschrift* in Isaiah Berlin's honor, economic security and equal access to education, for example, are not themselves the same thing as freedom, and to that extent the distinction between freedom and its conditions is valid; but the lack of such security or access surely does reduce the magnitude of freedoms enjoyed by those who suffer from this lack, and the illicit reduction, by "free market" ideologists, of the notion of sociopolitical freedom to the freedom to possess private property cannot conjure away this reality.[29] In a similar vein, Sartre's *Critique of Dialectical Reason* contains an extended analysis of the phenomenon of the "free market" in its quintessential form, the classical stock market prior to the onset of regulation, which brings out the extent to which this market imposes "heteronomy" and unfreedom on all of its participants, even those comparatively few who may appear to have succeeded in determining the actual prices.[30] As it seems to me, it is an indication of the weakness and inadequacy of Berlin's key notion of "negative" liberty for grasping the complex, relational character of liberty in a sociopolitical context that this very notion is so frequently advanced by defenders of the so-called "free market" in support of their fetish, even though Berlin himself correctly saw it as the threat to human freedom that it can be and is under appropriate circumstances.

4.

My purpose in this paper has been exploratory and explanatory and not primarily accusatory. Although I have found some seemingly obvious inconsistencies in Berlin's highly influential essay and his later *apologia* for it, and could no doubt have identified several more, the refutation of Berlin's ideas merely for the sake of refuting them has not been of much interest to me, particularly since I feel a sympathy with the anti-authoritarian spirit in which he set out to elaborate them. In "criticizing" Berlin's "negative" concept, I have insisted on its inadequacy, both as a descriptive concept and as an ideal, for understanding human liberty in society, rather than on its putative incoherence. In this respect, the history of the evolution of Sartre's thinking about freedom has been of great assistance to me. In his attack on what he called "positive" liberty, Berlin was, it seems to me, correct in his insight that freedom cannot and should not be reduced to any particular form of self-realization and that, when it is, totalitarian consequences follow. But freedom is much more complex than his construction of it suggests. Moreover, as Berlin would certainly agree, freedom is a very fragile asset, its achievement always threatened. The threats are sometimes alien and external, of course, as in the case of National Socialism. But they are sometimes also to be found within practices that are so familiar to us that we do not notice the unfreedoms that they perpetuate, such as has been true of sexist practices even now and in the very recent past. And, finally, the threats sometimes lurk within political slogans that may at first appear to be especially friendly to freedom—not only the self-realization slogans that tout an alleged "higher freedom" to which we must supposedly try to attain, but also slogans that seem to support "negative" freedom, such as the slogan of "the free market" or, more generally, "free enterprise."

Notes

1. Gerald MacCallum, "Negative and Positive Freedom," *Philosophical Review* 76 (1967): 312-34.

2. Isaiah Berlin, *Two Concepts of Liberty* (Oxford: Clarendon Press, 1958), p. 51.

3. Berlin, *Two Concepts of Liberty,* p. 6.

4. Joseph Stalin, *Marxism and Linguistics* (New York: International Publishers, 1951).

5. Isaiah Berlin, *Four Essays on Liberty* (Oxford: Oxford University Press, 1969), p. 171; *Two Concepts of Liberty,* p. 56.

6. Berlin, *Two Concepts of Liberty,* p. 6.

7. Berlin, *Two Concepts of Liberty,* p. 10.

8. Berlin, *Four Essays on Liberty,* p. xxxviii.

9. Berlin, *Two Concepts of Liberty,* p. 15.

10. Berlin, *Four Essays on Liberty,* p. 130.

11. Berlin, *Two Concepts of Liberty,* p. 15.

12. Berlin, *Two Concepts of Liberty,* p. 38.

13. See the general discussion of these two critics, along with MacCallum, in R.A. Kocis, "Reason, Development, and the Conflicts of Human Ends: Sir Isaiah Berlin's Vision of Politics," in *American Political Science Review* 74 (1980): 38-52.

14. Berlin, *Four Essays on Liberty,* p. liv.

15. John Rawls, *A Theory of Justice* (Cambridge: Harvard University Press, 1971), p. 204. Two pages earlier, he mentions his indebtedness to MacCallum's article, but the distinction between freedom and its worth is not articulated in the latter.

16. Berlin, *Two Concepts of Liberty,* p. 43.

17. Berlin, *Four Essays on Liberty,* p. lvi.

18. Summarizing what he has shown in Part I of the *Second Discourse,* Rousseau speaks of "*perfectibility,* the social virtues, and the other faculties that natural man had received in potentiality [en puissance]."-*Du Contrat Social* (Paris: Editions Garnier, 1954), p. 65 (underlining his, my translation).

19. Jean-Paul Sartre, *L'être et le néant* (Paris: Librairie Gallimard, 1957), pp. 721-22 (my trans.). Standard English translation is in *Being and Nothingness,* tr. H. Barnes (New York: Philosophical Library, 1956), p. 627.

20. *Sartre*—un film réalisé par Alexandre Astruc et Michel Contat (Paris: Librairie Gallimard, 1977), p. 71 (my trans.).

21. "Sartre par Sartre" in *Situations* IX (Paris: Librarie Gallimard, 1972), pp. 101-2 (my trans.).

22. MacCallum, "Negative and Positive Freedom," p. 314.

23. Berlin, *Two Concepts of Liberty,* p. 42-43.

24. MacCallum, "Negative and Positive Freedom," p. 326.

25. Berlin, *Four Essays on Liberty,* p. xliii.

26. Joseph Brodsky, "Isaiah Berlin at Eighty," *New York Review of Books,* August 17, 1989, p. 44.

27. Berlin, *Four Essays on Liberty,* pp. xlv-xlvi.

28. In "Idea and Reality: The Case of the 'Free' Market," paper presented at a conference on "Idea and Reality" at Eotvos Loran University, Budapest, and to be published in the proceedings.

29. G.A. Cohen, "Capitalism, Freedom and the Proletariat," in A. Ryan ed., *The Idea of Freedom: Essays in Honor of Isaiah Berlin* (Oxford: Oxford University Press, 1979), esp. p. 13. Jan Narveson is the author to whom Cohen pays particular attention in this regard.

30. Sartre, *Critique of Dialectical Reason,* Vol. I, tr. A. Sheridan-Smith (London: NLB, 1976), pp. 277-92.

Timothy M. Renick (essay date 1990)

SOURCE: "Response to Berlin and McBride," in *Social Theory and Practice,* Vol. 16, No. 3, Fall, 1990, pp. 323-35.

[*In the following essay, Renick extends McBride's critique of Berlin's concept of negative liberty—see previous es-*

say—to include McBride in the criticism, and introduces the concept of political obligation.]

> An "individual" may be an individual or indivisible because he has so little in him that you cannot imagine it possible to break him into lesser parts, or because, however full and great his nature, it is so thoroughly one, so vital and true to itself, that like a work of art, the whole of his being cannot be separated into parts without ceasing to be what it essentially is. In the former case, the individual is an "atom;" in the latter, he is a "great individuality."[1]

These words mark an appropriate starting place for a discussion of William McBride's "'**Two Concepts of Liberty**' Thirty Years Later: A Sartre-Inspired Critique." First, they focus our attention directly upon the issue Isaiah Berlin asserts is prior to all others in shaping our philosophical understandings of freedom. "Conceptions of freedom," Berlin writes, "directly derive from views of what constitutes a self, a person, a man."[2]

Second, they propose a vision of the self (that is, "an individual . . . vital and true to itself, a whole which cannot be separated into parts") which might be at home in the pages of Sartre and which shares certain significant characteristics with the vision of the free individual suggested by McBride in his essay.

Third, and perhaps most interesting, these words are taken from the pages of Bernard Bosanquet, a nineteenth-century British Idealist, and a student and follower of Thomas Hill Green. The careful reader of Berlin and McBride will recognize at least the second of these names; Green, and the school of thought he founded, is for Berlin (and I suspect for McBride as well) the very embodiment of the dangers of so-called "positive freedom." As McBride puts it, to Berlin, Green is a notorious representative of the "less individualistic, more society-oriented self-realization doctrines" which give the state the right and even the duty to paternalistically protect the individual's higher self from his or her lower self. Amid such a system, Berlin argues, the state has the power to force the individual to be "free," to coerce one into realizing one's own highest self.[3] Berlin calls this Idealist vision "a monstrous impersonation" of true liberty.[4] McBride suggests that Berlin's assessment "rings true" and sees recent history as "forcefully confirming" the profound dangers of "self-realization doctrines" like Green's.[5]

I disagree. I would like to argue that British Idealism in general, and the arguments of T. H. Green in particular, have philosophical resources with which to respond to such criticisms. More than this, I would like to suggest that there are considerable benefits to be gained from mining such resources. In particular, some of the very inadequacies that McBride maps out concerning Berlin's concept of freedom may be more cogently addressed by Green's Idealist account than by McBride's own Sartre-inspired alternative. If my suspicions here are correct—if Green's account can indeed offer a concept of freedom

which is able both to overcome the inadequacies of Berlin's and McBride's versions of freedom and to do so without the negative consequences both men so fear—then we will have reintroduced into the debate an important and too-often-dismissed alternative to prevailing philosophical renderings of political freedom.

1.

Before I begin to construct this argument, let me set out its foundation by a discussion of some of the points at which McBride's views and my own converge, for it is in his perceptive criticisms of Berlin's concept of negative liberty that McBride begins to direct our attention to some of the qualities needed for a philosophically rich and intellectually cogent conception of political freedom.

First I share with McBride (and Gerald MacCallum) strong doubts concerning our ability to even consistently distinguish two kinds of political freedom, negative and positive.[6] In practice, the lines between the two supposedly distinct realms blur dramatically. John Stuart Mill's heuristic struggle in *On Liberty* to maintain a realm of freedom demarcated by the harm principle is important historical testament to this fact; after all, is any act truly "self regarding," affecting no person but oneself?[7]

But one need not go beyond the pages of Berlin's **"Two Concepts of Liberty"** for evidence of the problems which come from trying to consistently maintain a realm of negative freedom. If, as McBride holds, even Berlin allows that "all laws . . . in some way or to some degree" constitute curtailments of freedom, it is difficult to understand how we are both to work toward a state with "just laws" and defend the frontiers of "negative liberty" as sacred.[8] The two would seem to be in perpetual conflict.

And yet, both courses are exactly what Berlin advocates. In fact, his strong advocacy of the sacredness of the boundaries of negative freedom represents a second point about which McBride and I agree. If in the years since writing **"Two Concepts of Liberty"** Berlin has (as he claims) qualified his original support for the conception of "negative liberty," the qualifications are slight and not particularly consistent. Thus, while in his 1969 reintroduction to the 1958 essay, Berlin does say that no concept of freedom "is either inviolable, or sufficient, in some absolute sense," he goes on to add: "for the great majority of men, at most times, in most places, the frontiers [of negative freedom] are sacred, that is to say to overstep them leads to inhumanity."[9] Thus, the boundaries of negative freedom come to define what human action is—in many ways, they come to define what humanity, in essence, is. These boundaries can be overstepped, but, according to Berlin, only in extremely exceptional circumstances in order to avert a "sufficiently terrible alternative."[10]

What Berlin offers here is in many ways a variation on the category of "supreme emergency" introduced by political-philosopher Michael Walzer. In times of war, Walzer argues, we have an "absolute" obligation never to intentionally take the life of an innocent. Yet he also holds that there may be certain rare historical moments—the plight of Britain in the war years 1939-40 is the only example he can cite—when the consequences which would result from holding to that absolute standard are so grave that we must temporarily and regretfully violate it; in order to avert the possibility of a world dominated by Nazism, Walzer argues, Britain was justified in intentionally bombing German population centers.[11]

Berlin says here something quite similar about the frontiers of negative liberty. They are sacred, and they must consistently be regarded as such. The rare exception to this standard, he writes, merely "proves the rule: precisely because we regard such situations as being wholly abnormal, and such measures as abhorrent, to be condoned only in emergencies so critical that the choice is between great evils. . . ."[12] In all other instances, in all other scenarios, regardless of consequences, one must maintain the frontiers of negative freedom.

This leads us to a third crucial point of agreement between Mcbride and myself. McBride correctly sees that consistently maintaining a conception of negative freedom (if such a concept is even coherent) results in a host of troubling implications. Berlin's concept of freedom is neither rich nor nuanced enough to adequately reflect our deep moral intuitions about freedom, justice, and the world around us.

The final part of McBride's essay is largely dedicated to arguing for this thesis. For example, Berlin suggests that a benevolent colonial ruler in Asia or Africa may provide "greater freedom" for his subjects than does an ineffectual government of democratic self-rule. This claim is understandable given Berlin's vision of freedom; a dictator who sets out to protect and preserve the boundaries of privacy which transcribe each individual, no matter how autocratic his or her means, would indeed be a great champion of freedom by Berlin's account. McBride argues that true freedom is more than this; self-rule is itself "one very important aspect of what is commonly understood as freedom."[13] The power of McBride's critique rests in his showing us that Berlin's conception of freedom cannot appreciate this important human truth.

McBride's examples of the freedoms denied to women by an all-male social club and to various individuals by the so-called free-market system play a similar illustrative role in his essay. Both cases offer scenarios in which the very protection of Berlin's negative freedom—allowing men to meet "freely" where and with whom they choose and all persons to buy and sell products in a "free" market—serves to create unfreedom by the standard of McBride's richer (though largely unspecified) concept of freedom. Important moral intuitions, McBride suggest, are simply not accounted for by Berlin's account.

I concur with McBride's various criticisms here, yet I would go further. Perhaps the most damning practical implication of Berlin's concept of negative freedom is passed over by McBride: its implication for the issue of political obligation. It is the inability to deal with political obligation which calls into gravest question not merely Berlin's concept of negative liberty but McBride's Sartre-inspired rendering as well.

McBride actually approaches this issue in the first part of his essay. He speculates that Rousseau had something very similar to Berlin's negative freedom in mind when he wrote in *The Social Contract,* "Man was born free, though everywhere he is in chains." McBride then observes: "But there is an obvious problem about life in this imagined earliest Rousseauean state of nature, a problem of which Rousseau himself . . . was aware: it really would have been totally uncivilized, meaning . . . that human creatures in that state would have had a very limited range of *possibilities* for doing anything at all" beyond acts of basic human survival.[14] According to McBride's reading of Rousseau, the state of nature—even one replete with an abundance of negative freedom—is not something to long for wistfully but instead something to overcome and move beyond.

Robert Nozick confronts, I believe, a similar realization in *Anarchy, State and Utopia.* This is a point to which I want to devote some attention. (After all, how often do any of us get the opportunity to claim that Rousseau and Nozick agree on a substantive point of philosophy?) In fact, an examination of Nozick is particularly appropriate to our discussion, for among contemporary political philosophers, he is the most consistent and committed supporter of a Berlin-like concept of negative freedom.

Nozick holds that the most fundamental and sacred right each of us possesses is the right "not to be forced to do certain things." Even in the state of nature, he writes, men and women have the "freedom to order their actions and dispose of their possessions and persons as they see fit . . . without asking leave or dependency upon the will of any other man."[15] In language almost identical to Berlin's, Nozick writes that natural rights "circumscribe a line . . . in moral space around the individual," creating an inviolable boundary which "limits the actions of others" and within which "each person may exercise his rights as he chooses."[16] Here, in many ways, is the "atom-like" vision of the individual lamented by Bosanquet. And as Nozick readily concedes, there is cause for lamentation.

Nozick's reasoning here is crucial to our discussion. As is the case of the individual possessing negative freedom in Rousseau's state of nature, Nozick's individual soon finds that she is free to do very little with her negative freedom. She lives in a world in which, Nozick writes, "private and personal enforcement of one's rights (including those rights that are violated when one is excessively punished by others) leads to feuds, to an endless series of acts of retaliation and exactions of compensation." There is "no way to settle such disputes," no authority to adjudicate conflicts, and no "way to punish or exact compensation from a stronger adversary" who has violated one's rights. Might, in practice, comes to make right. Anarchy ensues.[17]

The interesting question for Nozick—and a question, I would argue, that Berlin, too, needs to confront—is: accepting negative freedom as a sacred starting point, is there any philosophically consistent way to overcome this anarchism? Can individuals transcribed by the boundary of negative freedom ever rightly be obligated to yield to the punishments or penalties? In other words, can such individuals ever be obligated to a "state," no matter how just that state is?

Nozick's *Anarchy, State and Utopia* is an extended attempt to answer these questions in the affirmative (though, as Nozick admits, the resulting state can be, at best, nothing more than a protection agency with limited policing powers). Most philosophical commentators believe that, given his starting premises, Nozick's attempt to establish even such a "minimal state" fails. I agree. I have argued this point in detail elsewhere and will not rehash my arguments here.[18]

There are troubling and extreme implications which follow from Nozick's consistent defense of negative freedom. He struggles in the pages of *Anarchy, State and Utopia,* for example, to justify preventing epileptic drivers from traveling on the roads of his "minimal state." After all, they have the inviolable right to act as they see fit until they interfere with the rights of others. Does a society have to stand back and wait until an innocent third party is killed before action can be taken? Apparently, yes. And even then, the only justifiable act would seem to be exacting compensation from the epileptic driver for the damage done; a law which restrains her from driving again in the future transgresses the boundaries of her negative freedom. This is indeed troubling, but the example could be made much stronger. What of blind drivers? Can a society ever have the power to prevent them from driving? Perhaps here is where Berlin could make the claim that a "supreme emergency" is present, and negative freedom must yield to prevent a rare and grave evil. But how rare is this and a host of like evils? Plus, the more consistent defender of negative freedom, Nozick, for example, does not have the option of declaring a supreme emergency.[19]

Elsewhere, Nozick grapples with the troubling "possibility of surrounding an individual." He means this quite literally: what if someone, exercising her negative liberty, chooses to buy up all the land surrounding you at a given moment? You would appear to have no right to move from the spot on which you stand; any such movement would be a transgression of the property buyer's negative freedom. Nozick's suggestion (one which he ultimately rejects) of employing "helicopters able to lift straight up above the height of the private airspace in order to transport you away without trespass" is testament to the absurd and, ultimately, unacceptable implications of negative freedom.

Again, Berlin might argue that a "supreme emergency" exists. But the implications of Nozick's account cut far deeper than this. No law, no matter how just, would seem to bind any persons at any time without violating their negative freedom. No political obligations can exist.

Of course these cases are silly. That is precisely my point. Holding consistently to a concept of negative freedom seems inevitably to lead to silly implications. And importantly, offering a sensible response to these scenarios—telling the blind driver that her freedom is not being denied when we prevent her from taking to the roads, that the "freedom" to drive is not a right but a privilege—are responses unavailable to the consistent advocate of negative freedom.

In order to break this impasse, we appear to require an entirely different understanding of both the individual and the freedom he or she possesses. Can such an understanding be constructed without exposing the individual to the oppressive societal paternalism so feared by Berlin and McBride? It is toward an answer to this question—and a closer look at the arguments of T. H. Green—that I turn my attention in the final part of this essay.

2.

"To submit is the first step to true freedom," Green writes. "Freedom in all forms of doing what one will with one's own is valuable only as a means to an end."[20]

With these words, Berlin's worst nightmares are apparently realized. Gone is the idea of freedom as a natural birthright. Gone, too, is the idea of freedom as an object, a thing, at all. Freedom, Green tells us, is not a possession but a process. "It is the power on the part of the citizens as a body to make the most and best of themselves, . . . the power of all men equally for contributions to the common good."[21] By Green's account, freedom is not the ability to do what one likes as much as it is the ability to do what one *is* like. And we, as fundamentally social individuals, are most like ourselves when we serve not individualistic ends, but societal ones. We are most fully human when we serve the common good.

In Green's day, this concept of freedom morally grounded his fight to institute mandatory education for grade-schoolers in England. "Parents are not to be allowed to do as they will with their children, either to set them to work or to let them run wild without elementary education," he writes.[22] Such respect for the negative freedom of the parents is not freedom at all. Child and parent alike could be truly free, Green argues, only by advancing the good of society, and that good depends on an educated youth.

In our present discussion, Green's concept of freedom satisfies many of our intuitions about the specific cases discussed by McBride and myself. If denying women access to a social club quashes the flourishing of women, prevents (to use McBride's example) a woman writer from making the acquaintances she needs to get her valuable work published and read, then this denial subverts the good of society and hence is a denial of freedom itself. The blind driver who threatens the common good when she gets behind the wheel of a car is not having her freedom limited when she is banned from the roads; true freedom is served only by such a ban (though it also would be served only by providing other—and safer—means of mobility for that same person). Indeed, the very tension between freedom and the obligation to obey just laws dissipates amid Green's account. The free act becomes the just act. Political obligations become viable.

As we have seen, this is certainly not the case for Berlin and his conception of negative freedom. What is particularly interesting for our purposes is that it also may not be the case for McBride and his Sartre-inspired conception of freedom. McBride holds that, in his *Critique of Dialectical Reason,* Sartre moves away from the "virtually unmitigated individualism" of his *Being and Nothingness;* Sartre distances himself from his claim, for example, that "it comes down to the same thing to get drunk in solitude or to lead people." In the *Critique,* he allows that "under certain circumstances, usually some new external threat, it may be possible for groups of individuals to act together" to a certain extent. But the Sartre of the Critique, McBride quickly adds, "is no self-realization theorist of the sort that Berlin so deplores." In an important passage, McBride explains: "Sartre has no conception of a lower and higher self, or indeed of any essential *self* at all, and he is very explicit in denying to groups and institutions any claim to be organisms, entities higher than the individuals who create and sustain them."[23]

Yet it is precisely Green's belief that there *is* an entity higher than the self (that is, the common good) which allows Green to resolve the tension between freedom and the obligation to obey just laws. Sartre's individual may be more inclined to perform the socially supportive act than is Berlin's defender of negative freedom, but it is not clear why. Indeed, in the absence of a value or values which are "higher than the individuals who create them," the post-*Critique* Sartrean individual seems just as unable to justify the belief that "leading people is superior to getting drunk in solitude" as her pre-*Critique* counterpart. Each person's priorities remain, by definition, unsurpassed and unsurpass*able.*

This admission leads to unsettling, but by now familiar, implications. Can McBride's Sartre-inspired individual both preserve her freedom and be obligated to even the most just state? Certainly this is a question to be addressed before one accepts McBride's concept of freedom.

Of course, there are also questions to be addressed before one accepts Green's concept of freedom. We may applaud Green's efforts to require parents to send their grade-school-age children to school and to prevent blind persons from driving. But has not he provided license for the most extreme and abhorrent interference by society and the state in individual lives? If we are free only to the extent that we serve the common good, cannot society force us into the voting booth on election day, demand we stop smoking, indeed legislate what consenting adults may do in the privacy of their own bedroom (. . . whoops, sorry, I drifted for a moment from the realm of imaginary ex-

cesses to actual Georgia State law)? Might not the state do all of this under the guise of making us more free? Is not obligation traded for oppression?

This is the fear of Berlin and McBride. Indeed, McBride writes at the close of his essay: ". . . Berlin was, it seems to me, correct in his insight that freedom cannot and should not be reduced at any particular form of self-realization and that, when it is, totalitarian consequences follow."[24]

Berlin and McBride appear to be correct. This appearance, I believe, is deceptive.

A closer look at Green's arguments shows us why. At one point in his *Lectures on the Principles of Political Obligation,* Green poses a revealing question: "Only outward acts *can* be a matter of legal obligation; but what sort of outward acts *should* be matter of legal obligation?" Green does not respond, as Berlin and McBride seem to fear, that all just acts must be legally required. To the contrary, he writes, "The enforcement of an outward act, the moral character of which depends on a certain motive and disposition, may often contribute to render that motive and disposition impossible: and from that fact arises a limitation to the proper province of law. . . ."[25] Georgia legislators take note: the mere fact that a moral obligation exists does not mean that this obligation is or should be enforced by law.

Green presents a similar argument in his discussion of rights:

> The capacity for rights, then, being a capacity for spontaneous action regulated by a conception of a common good . . . is a capacity which cannot be generated—which on the contrary is neutralized—by any influences that interfere with the spontaneous actions of social interests. Now, any direct enforcement of the outward conduct, which ought to flow from social interests, by means of threatened penalties—and a law requiring such conduct necessarily implies such penalties for disobedience to it—does interfere with the spontaneous action of those interests, and consequently checks the growth of the condition of the beneficial exercise of rights.[26]

Thus, restraint in the use of force and coercion is not merely justifiable according to the common good, it is demanded. The common good, Green writes, is served only by "the life of a free citizen. And the qualification for such a life is a spontaneous habit of acting with reference to the common good."[27]

There is a powerful irony here. What Green, the embodiment of self-realization doctrine, has done is to philosophically secure a realm of *negative freedom* (though he does not, of course, call it such). Morally, the individual choice of each citizen must be protected, though not because such choice is an end in and of itself (as it is, at times, for Berlin, Nozick, and perhaps McBride), but rather because the free flourishing of individuality serves the common good, benefits all. As such, the negative freedom provided for by Green is not an absolute, nor should it be if our discussion of McBride and Nozick has taught us anything. The interests of the whole, the common good, demand that we force the blind person to stay off the road; it may demand that we legally force the all-male social club to amend its sexist practices. But by Green's account, in neither case is a person's rights or freedom violated by the resulting law. We need not declare a "supreme emergency;" we do not have to admit, rather sheepishly, that our absolute values are not as absolute as we had claimed. And we are not left, as Berlin is, with a need to make use of a supposedly secondary value, the good of society, to determine our enforcement of a supposed primary one, the boundaries of negative freedom. Green's account can provide for both freedom and obligation.

Indeed, in the hands of Green, the common good is a double-edged sword which not only fashions obligations to society but also carves out a revered place for individual choice. By giving the common good this important dual role, Green offers philosophical substance to his claim that human beings are both social and individual in nature. The true freedom of individuals continues to be determined by a social end, the common good; but individuals retain the power to alienate that freedom—they retain their claim to individual choice—in all but the most socially significant of situations.

Importantly, Green's support for individual choice is not merely a concession on his part that society cannot control all. It is a positive affirmation of the undeniable, indeed essential, good that comes from allowing for the individual's self-determination. It is, in many ways, a rich understanding of freedom, and a cogent portrayal of individuality.

And it should cause us to stop at least long enough to ask, whose account, Green's or Berlin's, is in fact a "monstrous impersonation" of true liberty?

Notes

1. Bernard Bosanquet, *Philosophical Theory of the State* (London: MacMillan, 1930), p. 79.

2. Isaiah Berlin, *Four Essays on Liberty* (New York: Oxford University Press, 1970), p. 134.

3. William McBride, "'Two Concepts of Liberty' Thirty Years Later: A Sartreinspired Critique," paper presented at Georgia State University, April 6, 1990, p. 302.

4. Isaiah Berlin, *Two Concepts of Liberty* (Oxford: Oxford University Press, 1958), p. 18.

5. McBride, p. 302.

6. McBride, p. 298; see G. MacCallum, "Negative and Positive Freedom," *Philosophical Review* 76 (1967): 312-34.

7. John Stuart Mill, *On Liberty* (Indianapolis: Bobbs-Merrill, 1968).

8. McBride, p. 303.

9. Berlin, *Four Essays on Liberty,* pp. lx and lxi.

10. Berlin, *Four Essays on Liberty,* p. lx.

11. Michael Walzer, *Just and Unjust Wars* (New York: Basic Books, 1977), Chapter 16. Walzer takes the dictate never to intentionally take the life of the innocent so seriously that, although he argues that Churchill morally *had* to bomb German cities, Walzer also believes that Churchill nonetheless "must accept the burdens of criminality" for the act (p. 260).

12. Berlin, *Four Essays on Liberty,* pp. lx-lxi.

13. McBride, p. 315.

14. McBride, p. 306.

15. Robert Nozick, *Anarchy, State, and Utopia* (New York: Basic Books, 1974), pp. 51 and 10. These arguments are obviously based upon John Lockes concept of rights in the *Second Treatise.*

16. Nozick, *Anarchy, State, and Utopia,* pp. 57 and 166.

17. Nozick, *Anarchy, State, and Utopia,* pp. 11-12.

18. Timothy Renick, *Political Obligation and the Common Good: A Study in Theological and Philosophical Ethics* (University Microfilms: 1986); see especially Chapter 1.

19. Nozick, *Anarchy, State, and Utopia,* p. 79.

20. T. H. Green, "Liberal Legislation and Freedom of Contract," in *The Political Theory of T. H. Green: Selected Writings,* John Rodman, ed. (New York: Appleton Century Crofts, 1964), pp. 51-52; see Bosanquet, *Philosophical Theory of the State,* pp. 100 and 138.

21. Green, *The Political Theory of T. H. Green,* p. 126.

22. Green, *The Political Theory of T. H. Green,* p. 50. It is interesting to note that the piece of legislation that was at the center of this battle, the Education Act of 1870, was so controversial at the time that its proponents (including Green) did not even try to get compulsory school attendance adopted as a national measure. The achievement was in being allowed, as an individual school board, to require attendance of one's own students. Green, an important political as well as philosophical figure in late-nineteenth-century England, was also a vocal advocate of workers' rights, minimum-wage laws and public health reforms.

23. McBride, p. 308 for the first quote, pp. 310-311 for the others.

24. McBride, p. 311.

25. Thomas Hill Green, *Lectures on the Principles of Political Obligation* (London: Longmans, Green, Inc., 1906), p. 34.

26. Green, *Lectures,* p. 208.

27. Green, *Lectures,* p. 208.

David Sidorsky (essay date 1992)

SOURCE: "On Isaiah Berlin," in *Partisan Review,* Vol. LIX, No. 2, Spring, 1992, pp. 309-15.

[*In the following review, Sidorsky examines Berlin's concept of pluralism.*]

There is an old dogma which can be traced back before Aristotle's argument with the Platonists to the conflict between followers of Parmenides and of Heracleitus that all philosophers can be divided into two camps: monists who are the champions of the One and pluralists who are the champions of the Many. This doctrine rises to the stature of an aphorism only with its topping and undercutting conclusion that all historians of philosophy can be divided into two groups: those who believe that all philosophers are either monists or pluralists, and those who do not. The recurrent theme of Isaiah Berlin's new collection of essays, *The Crooked Timber of Humanity,* sketching the career of ideas that have shaped modern politics, particularly some of its most destructive and catastrophic tendencies, is that monism, particularly in its utopian varieties has been the central, harmful illusion of the twentieth century. (Berlin writes of our century in an essay on European unity, "It is by now a melancholy commonplace that no century has seen such remorseless and continued slaughter of human beings by one another as our own.") The recognition of pluralism, traced to the thought of romanticism and of the counter-Enlightenment, appropriately mixed with an openness to reality derived from empiricism and a moderating of ambition generated by skepticism, provides the intellectual antidote.

The most attractive formulation of the argument is in the opening autobiographical essay, **"The Pursuit of the Ideal."** In it, Berlin examines what might be termed, to adapt Keynes's title for his account of Cambridge, "Oxford's early beliefs," the ideal of historical progress which he shared. It was a viewpoint derived from the historicism of Marx and Hegel that was built upon the Enlightenment faith in the application of the methods of the natural sciences to social problems. This faith is seen as a continuation of the philosophical rationalistic tradition, exemplified by the confidence of Socrates in the power of argument. In Berlin's special case it also represented the moral to be drawn from the great Russian writers that there was a way to transform the human condition through the properly educated heart, even when a proper education may require in a Rousseauist Tolstoy or a Slavophile Dostoevsky some unlearning of the false sophistication of the West.

Alongside the autobiographical memoir Berlin provides an analytical formulation of this belief in "the Platonic ideal" that "all genuine questions" have one true answer, that there must be a "dependable path toward" those true answers, and there can be no incompatability among them. The force of this formulation, it seems to me, sets up an effective and ironic contrast between the severity of the expectation for truth in moral and political thought with the proliferation of the concepts of undecidable propositions, incompleteness theorems in mathematics, and of indeterminacy and statistical probability in physics.

Although Berlin often presents the philosophical issue in direct and incisive manner, throughout this volume he does not, as a rule, join the issue in philosophical terms but focuses upon the intellectual history of the relevant concepts. So the confrontation with this Platonic *cum* enlightenment monism comes through his reading and interpretation of Machiavelli. This is not the Machiavelli who analyzed the strategies of political realism but the Machiavelli who affirmed the tragic dilemma which Berlin had earlier explored in his celebrated essay, **"The Originality of Machiavelli."** For, in terms of the public domain with its values of international peace, domestic order and civic virtue, the ideal society can be identified with the more stable periods of the Roman empire. In terms of the realization of human spirituality, individual piety or the expression of moral good will, an alternative historical period, perhaps within medieval Christianity, would provide the ideal society. The differences between these two ideals cannot be synthesized or adjudicated and there is no neutral point of view from which they can be ranked and evaluated. Each of these ideals embodies objective values that develop from different features of an historically changing human nature.

This point is generalized for Berlin in the Vichian representation of history, particularly "cultural history." The values of the society portrayed by Homer and the literary accomplishment of that portrait are not commensurable with the values demonstrated in the writings of Dante or, in turn, with its poetic virtues. Thus, any attempt to compare the two on a single hierarchical scale would be incoherent. The conclusion is that historical societies demonstrate an incompatible plurality of values which are not reducible to a single inclusive ideal.

One philosophical issue which must then be confronted is whether pluralism leads to value relativism, and Berlin's argument is that it does not. Value pluralism involves the recognition that it is difficult for a person of one culture to enter into the frame of reference of any other culture and understand the people and their expression from the agent's point of view. Yet this recognition has led to many strategies to achieve a more authentic and empathetic understanding of the products of another culture, rather than to interpret them as abnormal or variant extensions of the native culture or of a fixed human nature. These efforts, pioneered on Berlin's account by such founding fathers of pluralism as Herder and Vico, belie the thesis of the cultural relativist. An understanding of the differences to be found in the "worlds" presented in the writings of Homer, Dante or Sidney Sheldon, and an insight into the disparate styles of these authors, while excluding a single straightline measure would also demonstrate that the values ascribed to each are held for objective grounds and are not simply in the eyes of the beholder.

One important point of confirmation, which Berlin points to without pressing the argument, is the importance and unavoidability of assertions of a factual character within cultural or religious points of view. As a harbinger of pluralism, Berlin takes note of Montesquieu's support for Montezuma's remark that the Aztec religion might be best for Aztecs and the Christian religion best for Spaniards. Yet if the Aztec religion did assert that human sacrifice is a necessary condition for the sun to keep moving across the sky, that claim is false. The pluralist's recognition that different religions may represent responses to legitimate differences of human beings in different societies need not lead to a relativistic thesis that all practices are equally good and that there can be no basis for crosscultural criticism or judgment.

From the encounter with pluralism, freed from the illusory specter of relativism, Berlin sketches an important political moral which stands in sharp contrast to the totalitarian implications that had been derived from monism in the past century. It is the lesson of minimalism, of the transcendent value of maintaining a modicum of stability and equilibrium in confronting a potential escalation of conflict and of stressing the minimization of suffering and the inevitability of limits in human historical action when weighing the benefits that can be achieved through resort to force.

Berlin has placed this political approach in the tradition of liberalism alongside John Stuart Mill's development of the concept of liberty which is required for a defense against the oncoming threat of "uniformitarian despotism" and Alexander Herzen's realization of the cruel deception of the sacrifice of life on the altars of historical progress. It is interesting to note its degree of convergence with the other traditions shaped by the realities of the failure of the promises of National Socialism and of internationalist Marxism. Karl Popper in his early postwar and post-positivistic writings argued the theoretical indeterminateness and unpredictability of history and the practical turn to piecemeal social reform against large-scale "social engineering." Even more closely, Michael Oakeshott has identified the sources of political morality within the conservation of pluralistic institutional traditions, a morality which is saved from relativism by the possibility of criticism and convergence via the "intimations of that tradition." (One particularly noteworthy parallel is Oakeshott's exegesis of the Tower of Babylon story as demonstrating that Utopian ideals cannot be constructed in the historical world because of the diversity of human languages with their incommensurate conceptual frames.) Berlin's focus in this volume is not upon the comparative adequacy of the liberal tradition but upon the significance for contemporary history of the recurrent debate, in diverse ways, between monism and pluralism in modern political thought.

Thus in the essay, **"The Decline of Utopian Ideas in the West,"** that debate which had been dramatically developed in his intellectual autobiography emerges with significant variations. For Berlin shows how the Platonic monistic ideal became embodied in the ideas of a universal natural law, related in Europe, to the status of a universal Roman law and a single Roman Catholic faith. The pluralist challenge to this universalism was ever present in the irrepressible local traditions. These traditions influenced the Protestant Reformation and found expression in it. The Protestant location of religious salvation in individual faith rather than in a universal code of practice was a catalyst for the emergence of the pluralist idea. Yet Berlin, as a chronicler of the paradoxes of cultural history, proceeds to demonstrate that the forces that gave birth to the Protestant Reformation also gave rise to modern physics with its powerful reinforcement of the idea of universal truths that are discoverable and verifiable by men and women of all cultures, historical periods or social inheritance. With the extension by the Enlightenment of this vision of scientific truth from modern physics to the domain of economic and political events, the basis had been laid for modern utopianism, particularly as expressesd in many Marxist, socialist, and anarchist political movements.

The decisive counter for pluralism was developed in the thought of critics of the Enlightenment, especially among the Romantics like Herder. Political or moral ideals for the Romantics were not universal Platonic archetypes found by rational inquiry but creations of the Self, whether an individual or a collective self. In another work, Berlin had cited Herder's outcry against the classical ideal in Germany that "we are not Greeks, we are not Romans," and it is a corollary of the quest for self-expression that the ideal society for a German must be different than it would be for a Frenchman of the Enlightenment. Although Berlin comments and clarifies the dark role that this romantic idea of self expression has played in the will to power of modern nationalism, he demonstrates its potential for pluralism in its rejection of any universal and uniform social model that is to be imposed upon another person. Since every moral ideal is the creation of one group ego or cultural self, there cannot be any Platonic republic, utopian ideal or perfect society produced for another society. The political corollary of this principle of the necessary imperfection of fixed ideals is that each society must be left to do its own thing, rather than to be guided into conformity with the laws which best suit universal human nature.

This principle can be clearly differentiated from the realistic or pragmatic argument that a perfect society can be projected as a theoretically coherent idea but is unattainable in practice. For the notion of a single perfect society is conceptually incoherent if it must include an incompatible set of expressive values. This distinction can be seen in the parallel criticism of anarchistic utopianism. Again, the argument is not that a society in which the use of force or the threat of force would be replaced by the persuasive power of love and reason is an ideal possibility which cannot be realized. Since every society necessarily requires that its members will be bound by some set of rules, norms or laws, and the idea of a rule or law presupposes a sanction for its violation, the assumption that there could be an anarchic society in which sanctions would be inadmissable is conceptually contradictory. On this analysis, it would follow that one reason for the escalation of coercion by utopians lies in the fact that while seeming to goad persons along the path to a harmonious even if asymptotic ideal, they are asserting moral authority in the name of a self-contradictory idea. It is this theorem of the impossibility of a perfect society which is the logical analogue for Berlin of the expressive Kantian aphorism that from the crooked timber of humanity, nothing straight can be made. It reinforces the political moral of the limited scope that should be given to politics in social transformation.

Berlin ascribes to the romantic thought of the nineteenth century a critical place in refuting the idea of a single universal society that can progress toward perfection, primarily because of its view that ideals are the creation, rather than the discovery, of plural groups. Yet even while delineating this he indicates his refusal to "condone the extravagances of romantic irrationalism." For the romantic view that ideals are the creation of the self also meant that these ideals were not checked by such Enlightenment icons as "Reason" and "Nature." An ideal could be pursued even though it violated the moral criterion, singularly stressed by Kant but implicit to some degree in any moral behavior, of not asserting moral imperatives which were in conflict with those of other communities of rational beings. Similarly, contrary to naturalism, a political course could be followed even though the evidence available by inquiry into the relevant facts of the situation weighed in for its abandonment. Berlin tellingly quotes Fichte: "I do not accept what nature offers because I must . . . I believe it because I will."

Such an attitude, as the French existentialists showed in the Second World War, can inspire resistance in the face of incredible odds, for in being prepared to defy both logic and fact, it can be defiant of alien power. Yet, it has also blazed a trail which Berlin partly tracks in his essay **"On the Apotheosis of the Romantic Will"** to "romantic self-assertion, nationalism, the worship of heroes and leaders, and in the end to Fascism and brutal irrationalism and the oppression of minorities."

In the longest single essay in this volume, Berlin does not focus on the roots of Fascism within romanticism or nationalism, however, but on its sources in the thought of Joseph de Maistre. In one sense this is not surprising, since Maistre's writings provide a paradigm for monism, and he was the model for Berlin's earlier portrait of the hedgehog who "knows one big thing," in contrast to the pluralist fox. On the other hand it is puzzling (a mark of the originality of Berlin's interpretation), since Maistre is familiarly classified as a champion of the restoration of throne and altar after the French Revolution, while Fascism is not identified with the cause of an hereditary monarch or with support of the Catholic Church.

The resolution of this puzzle depends in part upon the meaning ascribed to Fascism, especially whether it involved an essential reference to a reorganization of the economy. In the propaganda of Fascist and Nazi movements—the programs of the corporate state in Italy or Spain with its governmental control of industry and labor, or, for the nationalization and socialization of business and finance in Germany, the promise expressed in its name, National Socialist Workers party—the economic factor seemed to be central to the definition. In the historical memory of Fascism, this appears as a secondary aspect of the development of totalitarian states in continuous pursuit of military expansion.

Apart from the economic issue, Berlin's thesis requires the distinction between the conservative critics of the French Revolution like Burke and the proto-Fascism of Maistre. Both share an opposition to any effort to impose the "abstract" revolutionary ideals of liberty, equality, and fraternity against the historical and institutional wisdom concretized in the traditional order, hierarchy and patriarchy. Despite Maistre's claims for restoration of the traditional institutions, however, Berlin sustains the distinction by sketching the totality of Maistre's ideological counter-revolutionary passion, which would subvert any effort to conserve a balance between liberty and order or equality and hierarchy. Most significantly, the conservative recognition of the inevitability of force in political arrangements emerges in Maistre as the celebration of the ubiquitousness and the utility of terror.

(Perhaps, particularly from the American perspective, there is some significance in Burke or Toqueville's supporting American independence or the American revolution, and at the same time condemning the French, while Maistre could see in both the bitter fruit of rational ideas applied to politics. Thus, Maistre suggests that since the city of Washington is the projected product of rational planning, rather than of historical growth, he is prepared to wager "a thousand to one" that it will never be built.)

Berlin refers to this prediction as comically false, and it contrasts with his insight about future Russian developments when he wrote that "If the Russians . . . play with this serpent (of modern doctrines) no people will be more cruelly bitten." These predictions provide a foil to his comprehensive view of Maistre as the "terrifying prophet" who, while arguing for restoration of an irretrievable past, projected a vision of the new order. That "order which Maistre had outlined as the only remedy against the dissolution of the social fabric came into being," Berlin writes "in our own time, in its most hideous form." Thus, Berlin concludes that the "totalitarian society, which Maistre, in the guise of historical analysis, visualized, became actual." Its actualization has shown the power of Maistre's insight, not as a conservative thinker but as the prophet of the Fascist reality "of our day."

In the course of developing this intellectual portrait, Berlin reviews and analyzes many of Maistre's criticisms of the Enlightenment and the Revolution. Among these is his original critique of the theory of language as a constructed artifact advanced by reductionist philosophers and his biting analysis of Rousseau's praise of the primitive. There is a degree of ambivalence about his temperament which appears to combine an objective quality of realism with an extremist tendency to fanaticism. Berlin cites a letter of Maistre's ally, Lammenais: "He was endowed with a generous and noble soul, and his books are all as if written on the scaffold."

This recognition of the difference between Maistre's temperament and his beliefs points to another factor in assessing the role that ideas and beliefs play in political activity. There is a direct line, for example, that can be traced in the career of Charles Maurras between his actions for the restoration of throne and altar and his subsequent support for the government of Petain. T. S. Eliot shared the convictions of Maurras on both the monarchy and the church, and Eliot's teacher at Harvard, Irving Babbitt, was as ardent a critic of the French revolutionary heritage during the same period. Yet it is impossible to envisage Eliot or Babbitt being involved in Maurras's activities like having his bodyguard of Camelots du Roi violently break up a lecture on Racine and chase the speaker from the hall.

The general point is the distance between the intellectual constructions of nineteenth century thought that he surveys and the political movements of the twentieth century which were built on these foundations. For in the political actions of Lenin, Stalin, or Hitler the history that seems to emerge is not so much one of persons guided by utopian ideas toward terrible deeds as it seems to be one in which they manipulated these ideas as instruments to express their need to coerce and oppress others, or their desire to expand power.

The parallel point is that monistic ideals, when advanced by persons of skeptical or ironic temperament bear within them safeguards on the use of force in their realization. Plato, whose idea of the perfect state is the primary source of monism, also provides us with the cautionary ironic drama in which the republic ruled by the philosopher king devolves into an absolutist tyranny. A source of Kant's metaphor in Isaiah XL, 4 that "the crooked shall be made straight," is usually read as a form of eschatological utopian prophecy, appropriate to the Kantian denial. Yet the religious skeptics also muted the utopian prospect by interpreting the equivocal text as a much more limited messianism, reading the phrase in its literal sense to mean that the rugged terrain of the abandoned land can be made level again, with the restoration of political sovereignty. Religious ironists through the ages, from Chaucer to Kafka and Agnon (in his novella *That Which is Crooked Shall be Made Straight*) have shown how the prophetic reading can be sustained while the tangled skein of things remains irremediable in this life. Agon's narrative for example tells a tragic story of a separation between a loving husband and wife which is brought about by a series of cruel twists of fate. The rectification which proves the monistic faith that "the crooked shall be made straight" takes place when the digger of their graves, knowing of the lifelong love and separation, decides to bury them beside each other. Texts which may assert monistic truths and project absolute ideals can be rendered either more ambiguously and skeptic-

cally or in a more dogmatic and totalitarian way, depending on the temperament of their interpreters.

In this volume, however, Berlin has respected the constraints of the history of ideas, and he avoids detailed comments on the connections between these ideas and their exploitation in institutional history by persons of extraordinary temperament, even when he has himself been a participant or witness of that history. The sense of great excitement generated by his works, then, is not derived from the impress of its relevance to contemporary history, although that is implicit throughout these essays. Rather, it has its source in the fusion of the prose style with the intellectual substance, the power and rhythm of the movement of the sentences as they lead to the shape and clarity of the intellectual portrait. This achievement is an intrinsic confirmation of Berlin's central theme of objective pluralism. For the romantic critic could correctly point out that the style reflects the unique qualities of the individual, without contradicting the classical thesis that its objectification can provide all men with an ideal form to be pursued.

David West (essay date 1993)

SOURCE: "Spinoza on Positive Freedom," in *Political Studies*, Vol. XLI, No. 2, June, 1993, pp. 284-98.

[*In the following excerpt, West summarizes Spinoza's concept of positive freedom in order to refute Berlin's assertion that it is likely to produce coercive systems of government; Berlin's response to West follows.*]

Isaiah Berlin's influential attack on the *positive* concept of liberty has set much of the tone for political thought within the liberal tradition. Liberal theorists have echoed the warnings about any account which sees freedom as the expression of the 'rational' or 'true' self, as the fulfilment of the 'real' or 'authentic' interests rather than the actual preferences of the agent. By and large these theorists have shared Berlin's fear that by a 'monstrous impersonation' a positive notion of freedom would encourage that particularly insidious form of paternalism which views coercion as the essential means to true freedom. Paternalistic coercion forces me to act according to my true self, according to the dictates of my real will, and thereby allegedly frees me from the tyranny of the misguided and irrational promptings of my actual will. Coercion can make me truly free. Berlin attributes what he diagnoses as the 'rationalist theory of politics' underlying positive accounts of freedom to such diverse figures as Plato, Spinoza, Rousseau, Kant, Hegel, Fichte, Comte and even Locke.[1] Bentham and Constant figure as lonely representatives of that tradition of liberalism satisfied with the more modest but less dangerous ideal of *negative* liberty. Bentham is celebrated for recognising that freedom also involves the freedom to do wrong, to behave in ways which other people, especially people in authority, may regard as irrational or even evil for, in Bentham's words, 'Is not liberty to do evil, liberty? If not, what is it?'[2] Only the tradition of negative liberty recognises that virtue is not equivalent to knowledge, that the 'ends of all rational beings' may not 'fit into a single universal, harmonious pattern', that there is an irreducible plurality of ultimate values and ways of life and that, therefore, people must be allowed to pursue whatever goals and preferences they may happen to have, however much we might disapprove of them.[3]

Against Berlin's attack on positive freedom and against the substance, though perhaps not the spirit, of the tradition of negative liberty, I shall argue that Berlin's account is only partly justified. It is largely justified in the case of both Hegel and Marx who can with some justice be interpreted as philosophers of 'objective reason'. Their basic principles may indeed lead to unpalatable conclusions. By contrast, Spinoza's account of human freedom differs in two crucial respects from the syndrome identified by Berlin. In the first place, Spinoza's metaphysical monism and his account of individual *conatus* render implausible the rationalist assumption of a single, correct way of life. Secondly, the account of positive freedom which Spinoza builds on this metaphysical foundation does not encourage the despotic impersonation which so worries Berlin.[4] On the contrary, this central feature of Spinoza's philosophy explains, at least in part, his ability to reconcile a defence of liberal toleration with the explicitly Hobbesian premisses of his political philosophy.

HEGEL, MARX AND THE REIFICATION OF POSITIVE FREEDOM

In common with much twentieth-century political thought it is the double trauma of fascism and Stalinist communism which forms the implicit backdrop for Berlin's strictures on positive freedom. He observes that 'socialized forms' of this doctrine of freedom are 'at the heart of many of the nationalist, Marxist, authoritarian, and totalitarian creeds of our day'.[5] He presumably refers to the same ideologies when he remarks that the tendency to 'preserve our absolute categories or ideals at the expense of human lives' is 'an attitude found in equal measure on the right and left wings in our days'.[6] Indeed, Berlin's diagnosis of the dangers of positive freedom can be applied with reasonable success to these creeds. In what follows, I shall confine my remarks to Hegel and the problematic relationship of Marxism and liberty.

Berlin describes a series of stages in the evolution of a fully-fledged and insidious concept of positive freedom. As he admits, his initial definition of positive freedom is not too distant from the notion of negative freedom: 'The "positive" sense of the word "liberty" derives from the wish on the part of the individual to be his own master'.[7] The relevant notion of positive freedom is the result of the transition, by what Berlin describes as an 'independent momentum', to a much stronger notion. From the 'experience of liberating myself from spiritual slavery, or slavery to nature' I become aware of a 'higher nature', a self which 'calculates and aims at what will satisfy it in the long run',

a 'real', or 'ideal', or 'autonomous' self which is contrasted with 'irrational impulse, uncontrolled desires, my "lower" nature, the pursuit of immediate pleasures, my "empirical" or "heteronomous" self, swept by every gust of desire and passion'.[8] This catalogue of terms serves to identify a distinctively positive notion of freedom. Negative freedom exists when we are able to act according to our will. Positive freedom requires beyond this that the will itself is formed autonomously. If what I want is the product either of external interference or subjective incapacity then I cease to be truly 'my own master'.[9] However, Berlin goes on to describe a further and more sinister transition. Paternalistic actions may, Berlin admits, sometimes be justified. However, the paternalist is likely to take excessive liberties, if he can plausibly claim that his actions are not only really in my interests but actually willed by me, because they correspond to the *real* wishes of my *true* self. In other words 'if it is my good, then I am not being coerced, for I have willed it, whether I know this or not, and am free—or "truly" free'.[10] This transition is particularly insidious when the real self is understood as a collective entity 'identified as being the "true" self which, by imposing its collective, or "organic", single will upon its recalcitrant "members", achieves its own, and, therefore, their, "higher" freedom'.[11] This collective entity may take a variety of forms—'a tribe, a race, a church, a state'.[12] It is this 'monstrous impersonation', Berlin claims, which is 'at the heart of all political theories of self-realization' and which is implicated in the tyrannical regimes of fascism and Stalinism.[13]

Indeed, something like this absorption of the individual into an organic collective is perpetrated by the main targets of Berlin's criticism, the Hegelians. At the heart of what has been called the Hegelian turn in philosophy is an account of the social constitution of the individual which underlies Hegel's notion of positive freedom. The individual's impulses and inclinations are understood not as given prior to society but rather as formed or constituted within it. This fact allows the theoretical reconciliation of universal and particular, individual and society, inclination and morality. The moral or rational will can be conceived as something not necessarily opposed to and imposed upon a pre- or asocial individual nature, but rather as a rationalization of inclinations which itself produces the individual. The will, in Hegel's words, is 'particularity reflected into itself and so brought back to universality, i.e. it is individuality'.[14] In acting according to the dictates of this rational will, the individual both conforms to the ethical demands of the community and fulfils her true self, achieving the *positive* freedom of concrete self-realisation rather than the abstract and, in Hegel's terms, merely *negative* freedom of Kantian autonomy.

However the Hegelian solution is flawed. Against Kant's transcendentalism, Hegel maintains that there can be no critical vantage point outside of society, no abstractly rational and universal 'morality' (*Moralität*) in terms of which a society might be criticised. Rather the individual must rely on 'ethical life' (*Sittlichkeit*) or the concrete values of a particular community. However Hegel is calm about the absence of transcendental values, only because existing society is identified as an episode within a predetermined dialectic of 'spirit', a stage in the unfolding history of human self-development. As this dialectic is unique—all societies are found a place in the series as either higher or lower forms—the only position from which existing society can be criticised is a later stage. The debate between 'left' and 'right' Hegelians arises from the obvious question which remains. Should existing society be understood as essentially the *last* or as only the *latest* stage of the dialectic? With the right Hegelian solution the individual is effectively absorbed into an organic community conceived as the culmination of history. Far from society being judged in terms of its usefulness for its members, individuals find their true fulfilment, their positive freedom, only by playing their part within society. Because the developmental logic of cultural forms is also an ideal or intellectual one, individuals only have significance as representatives of ideas or of the conflicts between ideas. The refractory material of the particular human individual, the material basis for difference, is left behind. The suppression of individuality which Berlin attributes to Hegelian worshippers of the state is at hand.[15]

The absorption of the individual into the history of an idealized community is, in a different way, also at the heart of the sacrifice of negative freedom perpetrated by Marxism, though this time on the left Hegelian assumption that present society will inevitably be replaced by a higher one, a later stage in the dialectic. Marx provides an at least partially convincing critique of Hegel's philosophy of right. The apparently noble but abstract ideals of 'bourgeois' justice or 'right' only serve to mask the exploitative realities of civil society. Bourgeois principles of justice simply regulate and legitimise the antagonistic relations of capitalist civil society, diverting attention from the necessary transition to a higher form of society where these relations would no longer prevail. A just society is inferior to a society where the scarcity and selfishness which render justice necessary (Hume's 'circumstances' of justice) have been abolished.[16] However the initially attractive utopian vision implicit in Marx's critique of capitalist alienation is soon overwhelmed in the subsequent development of historical materialism. The consequentialism of most of its later exponents, their hard-headed view that the end justifies the means, is fatally reinforced by absolute confidence in the imminence of communism. The dangers are only too apparent in some of the declarations of central figures in the Marxist tradition. Trotsky, for example, asserts that 'that is permissible . . . which *really* leads to the liberation of mankind'[17] and that 'no proletarian revolution, however mature, could avoid ruthlessness and violence'.[18] With a favourable outcome guaranteed, there is little danger that the revolution might be corrupted nor any real need for the movement to engage in the battle for intellectual and moral leadership.[19] The absorption of the individual into the organic community is exacerbated by historical prophecy.

In fact, however, the syndrome which Berlin attributes to the positive conception of freedom can more usefully be analysed as three distinct claims. What I shall call the *thesis of positive freedom* refers to the claim that the freedom to do one's will does not guarantee the freedom of that will or the authenticity of one's wants. Negative freedom may not amount to real or genuine freedom but this claim must be distinguished from what might be called the *thesis of the reified self*. The self is reified to the extent that it is regarded as an object of knowledge which can be known, in principle, as well or better by a person other than that self. This thesis is implied by any view which abolishes the privileged status of subjective preferences. There are several possible versions of the reification thesis. The *thesis of the social self* identifies the true or authentic self with a social or collective entity ('a tribe, a race, a church, a state'). Once this identification has been made it becomes plausible to suppose that the true interests of the members of the organically conceived society are more reliably ascertained by the philosophical observer, the leader or the priest, by the revolutionary hero or the party intellectual. It is this version of the reification thesis which can most appropriately be attributed to Hegel and Marx. Of course, other versions are possible, for example, religious theories of the soul, the Kantian postulate of a noumenal rationality or the naturalistic appeal to a biologically defined normality.

Arguably, what is significant in each case is that the 'true' self is identified in such a way that the views of someone other than that self become authoritative. The rational self can be understood more adequately by the moralist or the legislator, the soul by the theologian or priest, biological normality by the natural scientist. The member of the organic collectivity can only be truly free with the help of a strictly imposed discipline or sense of duty, or in a state of subjection to the dictates of a charismatic leader. Against Berlin, I would suggest that the chief danger derives from this pretension to a knowledge of someone's interests or self or will more adequate than that person's self-knowledge. Berlin's 'monstrous impersonation' arises from the *reification* of the real self and its interests, not from the thesis of positive freedom alone. In fact, as we shall see, considered by itself the thesis of positive freedom might equally well be taken to discourage rather than to imply a totalitarian outcome. This outcome is not a necessary consequence of the thesis of positive freedom as such.

SPINOZA: THE BASIS FOR AN
ALTERNATIVE ACCOUNT OF POSITIVE FREEDOM

What seems inadequate, then, about Berlin's presentation is the implication that any positive conception of freedom involves a potentially tyrannical reification of the self. Positive freedom may, on the contrary, be defined so as to enrich rather than to undermine the negative freedoms prized by the liberal tradition. It may be possible to provide an account of positive freedom which does not rely on a reified view of the self. Spinoza, in particular, should be rescued from Berlin's global condemnation of all rationalist theories of politics. He is especially interesting because he provides an early defence of toleration but on premisses which are very close to those of Hobbes. I shall suggest that it is Spinoza's particular conception of positive freedom which allows him to avoid the authoritarian conclusions to which these premisses have often been taken to lead.

Spinoza's characterization of government, or the 'right of supreme authorities', is evidently influenced by Hobbes. The natural right of 'every individual thing extends as far as its power'.[20] There is no moral restraint on the power or right of the individual prior to the contract which founds the state, for 'wrong-doing cannot be conceived of, but under dominion'.[21] For Spinoza:

> the law and ordinance of nature, under which all men are born, and for the most part live, forbids nothing but what no one wishes or is able to do, and is not opposed to strifes, hatred, anger, treachery, or, in general, anything that appetites suggest.[22]

Spinoza's 'realist' account is close to Hobbes' description of 'the right of nature' as 'the Liberty each man hath, to use his own power, as he will himselfe, for the preservation of his own Nature; that is to say, of his own Life; and consequently, of doing any thing, which in his own Judgement, and Reason, hee shall conceive to be the aptest means thereunto'.[23]

Spinoza also understands the origin of 'dominion' in terms of a founding contract. The fear and anxiety which would infect life in the state of nature, the impossibility of an individual's maintaining self-defence when 'he is overcome daily by sleep, often by disease or mental infirmity, and in the end by old age'[24] explain the origin of the 'commonwealth'. The natural right of the isolated individual could never be made good in the state of nature and exists, therefore, 'in opinion rather than fact'. It finds its natural expression in a form of social contract:

> And so our conclusion is, that that natural right, which is special to the human race, can hardly be conceived, except where men have general rights, and combine to defend the possession of the lands they inhabit and cultivate, to protect themselves, to repel all violence, and to live according to the general judgment of all. For . . . the more there are that combine together, the more right they collectively possess.[25]

Furthermore, the upshot of this very Hobbesian derivation of the state shares other features with Hobbes' account. The subject's duty to obey the dictates of the sovereign appears equally absolute, for 'however inquitious the subject may think the commonwealth's decisions, he is none the less bound to execute them'.[26] Also, although democracy is favoured as the 'perfectly absolute dominion', the identification of power and right has other unpalatable consequences. Spinoza excludes from citizenship 'women and slaves' who are 'under the authority of men and masters' as well as 'children and wards' who are 'under the authority of parents and guardians'.[27] The subordinate

position of women is justified by their natural subjection to the authority of men as a result of 'their weakness'. The equation of right with power has the seemingly familiar implication that power is always right.

However, Spinoza undoubtedly has a much more liberal outcome in mind. The individual 'justly cedes the right of free action, though not of free reason and judgment':

> No, the object of government is not to change men from rational beings into beasts or puppets, but to enable them to develop their minds and bodies in security, and to employ their reason unshackled . . . In fact the true aim of government is liberty.[28]

Spinoza also excludes something like Mill's 'private sphere' from the legitimate scope of the rule of law. The law should not seek to interfere with those areas of life where the harm caused by the interference of law would be likely to outweigh the benefits. For '(H)e who seeks to regulate everything by law, is more likely to arouse vices than to reform them.'[29] By contrast, according to Hobbes' account the sovereign has the absolute right of life or death over his subjects, though 'by allowing him to *kill me*, I am not bound to kill my selfe when he commands me'.[30] Apart from this and a few other not very reassuring concessions (the right to refuse to serve in the army 'without Injustice' 'though his Soveraign have Right enough to punish his refusall with death') other liberties, for Hobbes, 'depend on the Silence of the Law'.[31] We are only at liberty to do those things which the law does not expressly forbid. The law is not constrained by any system of natural rights.[32]

What enables Spinoza to avoid the authoritarian conclusions to which Hobbes' similar premisses so swiftly and surely seem to lead? The crucial difference derives from Spinoza's positive conception of freedom and the related metaphysical account of the individual. In Spinoza's system, human beings are unequivocally part of nature, a realm governed exclusively by cause and effect. Nature is also conceived monistically. Mind and body are equally basic and fundamental attributes or aspects of the one substance. This 'dual aspect theory' of mind and body is referred to by Deleuze as a form of 'parallelism'. The theory 'does not consist merely in denying any real causality between the mind and the body, it disallows any primacy of the one over the other'. This implies, in an anticipation of theories of the unconscious, that 'the body surpasses the knowledge that we have of it, *and that thought likewise surpasses the consciousness that we have of it.*'.[33] In this metaphysical system there is no room for traditional notions of free will. Our conviction that our wills are free is based on an illusion. For Spinoza, what we perceive as decisions of the mind are, like all other mental phenomena, simply material processes viewed 'under the attribute of thought'. The illusion of freedom is a simple consequence of consciousness, or more precisely, the inevitable *partiality* of consciousness: 'men believe themselves to be free, simply because they are conscious of their actions, and unconscious of the causes whereby those actions are determined'.[34]

There is, of course, a long philosophical tradition of 'compatibilists' who maintain that free will can be reconciled with determinism. Hobbes himself is responsible for a classic statement of this position but crucially for Hobbes, firmly within the traditions of empiricism and negative liberty, freedom is compatible with determinism because it applies only to the 'man' and not to the will. In making this point Hobbes provides a classic statement of a negative concept of freedom:

> from the use of the word Free-Will, no Liberty can be inferred of the will, desire, or inclination, but the Liberty of the man; which consisteth in this, that he find no stop in doing what he has the will, desire, or inclination to doe.[35]

We are only unfree, on this interpretation, if we are prevented from doing what we are causally determined to will. The fact that our decisions are themselves caused, lies beyond the scope of negative freedom in this sense.

Spinoza's approach is very different, although it is built on a moral ontology he largely shares with Hobbes. The basic unit of Spinozist ethics is the individual but this is not the individual of the mainstream of liberal theory. Rather, as Deleuze succinctly remarks, '(A)n individual is first of all a singular essence, which is to say, a degree of power'.[36] Two famous propositions of the ethics express this claim:

> Everything, in so far as it is in itself, endeavours to persist in its own being . . . The endeavour, wherewith everything endeavours to persist in its own being, is nothing else but the actual essence of the thing in question.[37]

This *conatus*, the endeavour of every individual 'to persist in its own being', is the basic 'unit of force' in Spinoza's ethics. As for Spinoza there is no creator independent of existence—God is simply nature under another attribute—he rejects any idea of human essence as implying some purpose of life common to all human beings. Hampshire's comparison of Spinoza with Aristotle is enlightening on this point. Like Aristotle, Spinoza values a thing in terms of the degree to which it realizes its nature or essence. For Aristotle, however, this essence is common to all the individuals of a particular kind. Spinoza, on the other hand,

> identifies the essential nature of any individual thing with its individuality, with that which makes it a distinct individual: and this is its power of self-maintenance in relation to other things. Its virtue is its power as an individual.[38]

The difference is very significant. Aristotle's account of human essence serves to distinguish human beings from other species (and is explicitly humanist in this sense): it is in the exercise of that capacity namely rationality, that the *summum bonum* for human beings consists. Rationality in this disembodied sense leads swiftly to the reified conception of the self at the heart of the tyrannical degeneration of positive freedom described by Berlin. The good

life is essentially the same for all human beings. However, no such universal standard of behaviour can be derived from Spinoza's definition of *individual* essence. This much he has in common with Hobbes. For both of them the individual is no more and no less than 'its power of self-maintenance in relation to other things'.[39]

Where Spinoza clearly differs from Hobbes is in the role which *rationality* plays in the self-maintenance of the individual. Although Spinoza does not see the exercise of rationality as the goal of human life, he differs from Hobbes in seeing rationality as an essential *means* of achieving the good life. Rationality is not just useful instrumentally as a way of better ensuring the satisfaction of our impulses and inclinations. Rather it is essential for the full development of our individuality or, in other words, essential for our positive freedom.[40] The central arguments of the *Ethics* explore this relationship between rationality and individuality which, as we have seen, is also central to Hegel's account of positive freedom.[41] Spinoza's overriding intention is to identify the means whereby individuals more effectively 'persist in their own being'. Although all our actions are causally determined, Spinoza wishes to distinguish between different ways in which our decisions may be caused. In particular he distinguishes between mental events and states (including decisions of the will, emotions and inclinations) whose causes are 'internal' and those whose causes are 'external' to the individual. The former are classed as 'actions' or affections in regard to which we are active and the latter as 'passions' or occasions where we are passive in relation to our affections. This distinction is the basis for his account of positive freedom. We are active or free when the causes of our actions are internal and unfree when these causes are external to us.

However 'internality' might seem at first sight to bear no obvious resemblance to a criterion of positive freedom. An individual could, presumably, be enslaved by his or her *inner* drives or passions but even those emotions or affections which do not obviously come 'from outside' the individual, which apparently arise quite spontaneously within us, may be external in Spinoza's sense. This is because the criterion of internality is at the same time a criterion of rationality. Stuart Hampshire's restatement of the distinction between active and passive emotions is succinct and worth quoting at some length:

> I experience an active emotion, if and only if the idea which is the psychological accompaniment of the 'affection' is logically deducible from the previous idea constituting my mind; only if it is so deducible, can I be said to have an adequate idea of the cause of my emotion. If the idea annexed to the emotion is not deducible from a previous idea in my mind, it follows that the emotion or 'affection' must be the effect of an external cause, and that I am in this sense passive in respect of it. As the ideas constituting my mind are the psychical equivalents of the modifications of my body, I can only have adequate knowledge of the causes of those of my 'affections' which are not the effects of external causes.[42]

Because for Spinoza ideas are modifications of my body 'under the attribute of thought', the conclusion that 'I can only have adequate knowledge of the causes of those of my "affections" which are not the effects of external causes' would seem to follow.[43] So the realm of activity understood as internally caused and understood as adequately conceived fall together. Adequate understanding of the causes of mental states or events is a test or criterion of internality. Passive affections resist the understanding, they cannot be adequately conceived because their causes are external to the individual. The self, if it is ruled by passive affections, acts from reasons which are not its own and therefore acts less than rationally and less than freely.

Significantly, Spinoza is not committed to the view that freedom consists simply in the outright *mastery* of the passions by reason. Only the one eternal substance 'God or Nature' could be completely determined by internal causes and, in that sense, completely free. By definition, the one substance includes everything and so cannot be determined by anything external to itself. The individual human being, on the other hand, is only a small part of nature and can never be completely independent of external influences. However, the extent of the individual's independence from external causes is subject to the exertions of the understanding. In Spinoza's system rationality or understanding is not merely a symptom of freedom, but also a means of attaining it. The improvement of the understanding is a form of emancipation. Everyone has 'the power of clearly and distinctly understanding himself and his [passive] emotions, if not absolutely, at any rate in part, and consequently of bringing it about that he should become less subject to them'.[44] In the process of understanding my affections I achieve at least partial freedom, because through the exercise of my understanding I free myself from subjection to those influences which are transient and variable.

As natural beings we can never hope to be free of all passions or to be totally active beings but we are subject both to 'sad' and to 'joyful' passions. Sad passions correspond to a diminution in the power of the individual, joyful passions to an increase of this power. As Deleuze puts it:

> when we encounter an external body that does not agree with our own . . . it is as if the power of that body opposed our power, bringing about a subtraction or a fixation; when this occurs, it may be said that our power of acting is diminished or blocked, and that the corresponding passions are those of *sadness* . . . when we encounter a body that agrees with our nature, one whose relation compounds with ours, we may say that its power is added to ours; the passions that affect us are those of *joy,* and our power of acting is increased or enhanced.[45]

The *Ethics* looks in detail at the ways in which through understanding we can achieve the maximum degree of freedom in relation to our passions and, insofar as we are subject to passions, how understanding can liberate us from the 'sad' passions. Spinoza's detailed moral and psychological insights and observations are thus contributions to the *moralistes* tradition of Montaigne, Pascal, la Rochefoucauld, Nietzsche and Freud. This is a tradition of *positive* freedom because it concentrates on freeing the individual from the delusions and obsessions which are destructive of it.

How, then, is Spinoza able to avoid the authoritarian conclusions usually attributed to Hobbes? The toleration of religious and ideological diversity is essential because the true freedom of the individual is inconceivable without the unhindered exercise of the understanding. Religious and intellectual freedom is therefore a prime goal of political organization beyond mere stability. Further, understanding cannot be established once for all or by one for all. The particular affections of every individual, reflecting their unique situation in the natural order, are peculiar to them (or at least cannot be known not to be so). The transformation of these affections into active emotions or joyful passions must be performed by each and all for themselves. Spinoza's *Ethics* is designed to aid in the practice of that self-understanding. Although people can certainly be forced to *act* in a certain way, they cannot be forced to *believe,* let alone *understand* anything. However unlimited the power of the sovereign, 'it can never prevent men from forming judgments according to their intellect, or being influenced by any given emotion'.[46]

Spinoza was inevitably unaware of the many modern techniques of psychological manipulation and subliminal persuasion, sophisticated forms of advertising and so on. Still the strength of his position remains. Such forms of manipulation could only serve to increase the passivity of the individual. They might bring about behaviour which we take to be symptomatic of virtue but they could never bring about genuine understanding or true virtue, because the only *effective* understanding is one inextricably linked to individual will or *conatus*. In fact Spinoza's *Ethics* is a major work within the tradition which emphasises the identification of virtue and happiness. Virtue, like freedom, is understood as the optimal realisation of the individual's 'endeavour to persist in its own being'. Ethical behaviour is in the enlightened interest of individuals. Deleuze distinguishes ethics in this sense from *morality,* which 'always refers existence to transcendent values' and for which 'moral law is an imperative' that 'has no other effect, no other finality than obedience'. In general:

> Law is always the transcendent instance that determines the opposition of values (Good-Evil), but knowledge is always the immanent power that determines the qualitative difference of modes of existence (good-bad).[47]

Morality, as distinct from ethics, is a command imposed upon the individual that must simply be obeyed. Even the Kantian imperative is based on the requirements of a being of 'pure practical reason' which coincides with contingent individuals only by metaphysical fiat. Ethics, on the other hand, is a form of knowledge which is potentially effective. Our understanding of ethics is inseparable from the process in which we become more active in relation to our 'affections', the process in which we become more genuinely free.

Thus, a positive notion of freedom in Spinoza's sense seems, if anything, *more* resistant to the paternalistic impersonation which Berlin is so concerned to prevent. For the tradition of negative liberty, the *causes* of the will are unimportant, so long as we are free to do whatever our will decides. It follows that causing someone to believe or want something is not necessarily incompatible with her liberty. Such interference could be condemned only as the violation of a presumed interest in autonomy or the desire to remain free of such interference but the force of such a wish for autonomy is weak, as long as it is just one wish amongst many. The paternalist could still argue that he knows best how to maximise the overall preference satisfaction of someone. By contrast, it is the strength of Spinoza's account that he is in a better position to identify such interference as incompatible with the subject's freedom, however benign the intention. There can be no paternalistic justification for attempting to *impose* understanding on the individual, because such an imposition can only increase the passivity of the one subjected to it and must inevitably fail to encourage the practice of her self-understanding. Freedom in Spinoza's sense is inseparable from the individual's overall self-fulfilment. Individual preferences are only authenticated as truly personal preferences in that practice of freedom and understanding.

At the same time, freedom in Spinoza's sense does not require the complete isolation of the individual from external influence or social context. In fact the exercise of understanding is something the individual is unable to achieve alone. In his political treatises Spinoza argues, as we have seen, that in the state of nature our powers are neutralised by fear. The improvement of human understanding is inconceivable without the security guaranteed by the commonwealth but the forces of the individual are further enhanced by membership in the commonwealth, for 'to man there is nothing more useful than man' and 'our intellect would be more imperfect, if mind were alone, and could understand nothing besides itself'.[48] Society is necessary for the full development of individuality. It is not simply a necessary evil, a constraint which inevitably limits the negative freedom of individuals. Understanding is impossible without language and culture, without the insights of a moral tradition, even if that tradition cannot be taken as the source of a list of moral rules which the individual has only to obey in order to be virtuous.

CONCLUSION

Spinoza's ethics and in particular his conception of positive freedom have considerable attractions. They recognize no absolute division or opposition between body and mind, rationality and feeling. We are inevitably subject to both active and passive emotions but the exercise of reason can make us less susceptible to the 'bondage' of the passive emotions, less at the mercy of whim and circumstance. Unlike Kant, Spinoza has no problem about the interest we take in morality because it is in our interest to be moral. Virtue is tantamount to the fuller development of our individuality. Virtue is the expression of individual *conatus* or power, rationalized by the understanding. However the outcome of a rationalized *conatus* is potentially different for every individual and understanding must be exercised by everyone for themselves, so no one can justifiably impose their interpretation of virtue or the good life on another. Spinoza's conception of positive freedom allows us to condemn forms of interference which, despite their apparent compatibility with negative freedom, it would be implausible not to see as intrusions on liberty. On the other hand, his notion of positive freedom, far from inviting tyranny, makes paramount the autonomous practice of self-understanding. The self, as Spinoza describes it, is sociable but resists being absorbed into the social. Society is a necessary catalyst but never a substitute for the practice of freedom.

Obviously considerable problems are faced in the attempt to develop further something like Spinoza's account of positive freedom. I have simply tried to provide support for two broad conclusions. First, Berlin's global assault on positive freedom and rationalist political thought misses the mark as far as at least one significant philosophical tradition is concerned. Spinoza's metaphysics and ethics do not support the rationalist assumption that we can identify a single form of life or set of values, defining the 'good life' or the 'rational' or 'real' self and then impose it on an unwilling humanity. Individual *conatus* is the ultimate and intrinsically plural ethical foundation for his account of positive freedom. It follows, secondly, that much of the liberal tradition may have been led astray in its almost automatic rejection of positive freedom.[49] This is particularly worrying to the extent that, as a result, the dangers of a negative conception of freedom have also been neglected. A negative account of freedom can offer only weak resistance to forms of manipulation which are cultural, ideological or psychological. A more resilient resistance to these forms of manipulation would require the further development of a positive conception of liberty.

A REPLY TO DAVID WEST

Isaiah Berlin

I should like to begin by a rebuttal of Mr. West's allegation that I imply that any conception of positive freedom must involve a potentially tyrannical 'reification' of the self. This is not so. I did not say that the concept of positive freedom itself, only that perverted interpretations of it can lead, and indeed have led, to such consequences. Positive freedom or liberty is an unimpeachable human value.

That said, I fully accept Mr. West's lucid and plausible account of Spinoza's conception of individual freedom, and of conduct founded on the degree of understanding of the unity of what there is (including oneself). He argues that my view of the political effects of some perversions of positive freedom do not apply to Spinoza's conception of it, which he assumes to be correct. On this, I should like to make two comments:

(a) It is true that the ideologies of the tyrannies of which I was thinking were principally those inspired by the teaching of Hegel and Marx, not of the doctrines of Spinoza, who seems to me to be an intellectual descendant of the Greek Stoics, Zeno and his followers, and later Epictetus, for whom fully rational men, and only they, are truly free. Self-direction by reason (or the rational order of Nature), and, best of all, the suppression of emotion, impulse, and other 'heteronomous' influences, generate the freedom usually called 'inner' or spiritual, which cannot be touched by the coercion exercised by, *ex hypothesi,* irrational agents or agencies. In my writings I did my best to distinguish this 'inner' or moral freedom, which is proof against all mental or physical pressures (Epictetus's rational slave who was freer than his less rational master) from political freedom, with which alone I was concerned. To speak of 'inner', 'real' freedom seemed to me a metaphor; but I did not emphasise this point. Political freedom seems to me an altogether different matter, and directly concerned with coercion, whatever its relation to the impregnable life of reason. Political freedom must be measured by the number and character of the doors open to an agent (understood in empirical terms), whether he chooses to enter them or not. What Mr West rightly calls Spinoza's Hobbesian ideas do not deal with this at all. His liberalism seems confined to the freedom needed for the rational pursuit of the truth.

(b) Hence Spinoza's conception of positive freedom seems to me no less open to distortion than that of any other metaphysical account of self direction, however valid in itself. Spinoza seems to me to hold, in common with other rationalist thinkers, that to any genuine question there can only be one true answer, supplied by the methods of rational reflection, all other answers being false. Truth, for such philosophers, is one and identical for everyone, everywhere, at all times. *Quod semper, quod ubique, quod ab omnibus.* Those who attain it, know how human beings should live and act. Failure to do so is caused by the confusing influence of irrational factors—emotions, impulses, 'drives', 'complexes', and the like, which cloud reason. For 'true'—that is, rational—freedom to be achieved, human beings must be shown the way to the correct, that is, rational ways of thought and conduct; in so far as they are endowed with reason, unobstructed by emotion, they cannot but follow these ways (does Spinoza say anything at all about the will? I cannot think of one instance). Mr West refers to Spinoza's view of the will. The obstacles to rational thought must be removed, if possible, by the persuasive power of argument. However, if this fails, should such beings be abandoned to their irrational 'drives'? The obvious case is that of children, who may resist education. In such situations it is thought that some coercion may be applied in the children's own interest, to make rational beings of them. By a parity of reasoning, all irrationality, heteronomy, passion, which resist or darken reason, must

be removed, or at the very least controlled, by rational self understanding, education and also legislation—that is, if necessary, the sanction of force, of coercive action. This is the doctrine of the best known thinkers of the French Enlightenment in the eighteenth century, some of whom claimed to be inspired by Spinoza. From this to thought control—and other forms of coercive rule—(remote though this may have been from the ideas of the liberal *philosophes*), allegedly in the interests of those sunk in error, to enable them to see the universally valid truth, is no very great step. This kind of (at best) paternalism, so hotly attacked by Kant, applied to Hegel, Marx, and, I believe, Plato. Spinoza's views can, I believe, be as easily twisted (misinterpreted) in this direction as that of any other champion of the rule of positive liberty (in itself, a basic human value with which I have, of course, no quarrel). Bismarck, who is reported to have greatly admired Spinoza, could easily have defended his *Kulturkampf* against the (irrational) clericals in this way. Something needs to be added to, or modified in, Spinoza's rational ethics if we are to be saved from this.

I do not hope to convince Mr West of this: I only wish to make clear where I think his criticism is misdirected.

Notes

1. Isaiah Berlin, 'Two Concepts of Liberty' in *Four Essays on Liberty* (Oxford, Oxford University Press, 1969), p. 151.

2. Cited by Berlin, 'Two Concepts of Liberty', p. 148, (footnote).

3. Berlin, 'Two Concepts of Liberty', p. 154.

4. In this respect Spinoza differs from Kant. According to Kant also we cannot be *coerced* to be good, because for people to act in the right way involves them 'knowing why they ought to do so, which nobody could do for, or on behalf of anyone else' (Berlin, 'Two Concepts of Liberty', p. 152). Nevertheless, according to Berlin, the Kantian legislator will almost inevitably assume that anyone who opposes what is evidently a rational law is *pro tanto* irrational and must be disciplined for his or her own sake. I shall not discuss the force of this claim against Kant. My concern here is to argue that Spinoza's philosophy and, in particular, his ethics and his philosophy of mind, do not allow the same assumption.

5. Berlin, 'Two Concepts of Liberty', p. 144.

6. Berlin, 'Two Concepts of Liberty', p. 171.

7. Berlin, 'Two Concepts of Liberty', p. 131.

8. Berlin, 'Two Concepts of Liberty', p. 132.

9. As Berlin describes it the distinction between negative and positive *freedom* does not, of course, correspond to the distinction between negative and positive *rights*. Positive rights are generally held to support claims to material resources, whereas negative rights simply require the non-intervention

of others. Thus a *negative* right to life implies a duty on the part of others not to murder, whereas a *positive* right to life implies a claim to resources in the form of food, shelter and so on. The distinction between negative and positive rights is at issue in the well-worn argument between libertarians and 'social' liberals. Libertarians are satisfied with the strictly negative liberty secured by negative rights, for example the liberty defended by Nozick's minimal state. On the other hand, 'social liberals' and liberal socialists think that genuine rights (to free speech, access to the law, equal opportunity and so on) must be positive rights. They involve resources and therefore imply measures of welfare and redistribution. In other words, they argue that even negative liberties can only be secured by means of positive rights. The significant point here is that both positive and negative rights may be involved in the protection of negative freedoms.

10. Berlin, 'Two Concepts of Liberty', p. 134.

11. Berlin, 'Two Concepts of Liberty', p. 132.

12. Berlin, 'Two Concepts of Liberty', p. 132.

13. Berlin, 'Two Concepts of Liberty', pp. 133-4.

14. G. W. F. Hegel, *The Philosophy of Right* (Oxford, Clarendon Press, 1952), p. 23.

15. The unpalatable conservatism of Roger Scruton is a contemporary manifestation of an analogous tendency. See his *The Meaning of Conservatism* (London & New York, Penguin Books, 1980).

16. For a clear discussion of Marx's critique of bourgeois right, see S. Lukes, *Marxism and Morality* (Oxford, Oxford University Press, 1987). On the 'circumstances of justice' see Hume, *A Treatise of Human Nature,* (ed.) L. A. Selby-Bigge (Oxford, Clarendon Press, 1888), pp. 486ff. Compare Michael Sandel's parallel critique of Rawls in *Liberalism and the Limits of Justice* (Cambridge, Cambridge University Press, 1982), esp. ch. 1.

17. In *Their Morals and Ours,* cited by Lukes, *Marxism and Morality,* p. 119.

18. Cited in Lukes, *Marxism and Morality,* p. 114.

19. The Marxism of Antonio Gramsci obviously has very different implications.

20. Benedict de Spinoza, 'A Political Treatise' in *A Theologico-Political Treatise and A Political Treatise,* translated with an Introduction by R. H. M. Elwes (New York, Dover Publications, 1951), II 4, p. 292.

21. Spinoza, 'Political Treatise', II 19, p. 298.

22. Spinoza, 'Political Treatise', II 8, p. 294.

23. Thomas Hobbes, *Leviathan* (London, Dent, 1973), p. 66.

24. Spinoza, 'Political Treatise', III 11, p. 306.

25. Spinoza, 'Political Treatise', II 15, pp. 296-7.

26. Spinoza, 'Political Treatise', III 5, pp. 302-3.

27. Spinoza, 'Political Treatise', XI 3, p. 386. However, it is worth recalling that even J. S. Mill excludes 'barbarians' from the protection of a liberal civilization. See 'On Liberty', in *Utilitarianism, On Liberty and Considerations on Representative Government,* (ed.) H. B. Acton (London, Dent, 1972), p. 73.

28. Spinoza, 'A Theologico-Political Treatise' in *A Theologico-Political Treatise and A Political Treatise,* XX, p. 259.

29. Spinoza, 'Theologico-Political Treatise', XX, p. 261.

30. Hobbes, *Leviathan,* II 21, p. 114.

31. Hobbes, *Leviathan,* II 21, p. 115.

32. Compare Roger Scruton's less than libertarian account of individual rights in *The Meaning of Conservatism,* ch. 4.

33. G. Deleuze, *Spinoza: Practical Philosophy* (San Francisco, City Light Books, 1988), p. 18.

34. Spinoza, 'The Ethics' in *The Chief Works of Benedict de Spinoza,* Vol. 2, translated with an Introduction by R. H. M. Elwes (New York, Dover Publications, 1955), III 2, footnote p. 134.

35. Hobbes, *Leviathan,* p. 110. In fact, as Michael Oakeshott has pointed out, Hobbes develops something much more like a positive concept of freedom in his discussion of what Oakeshott calls the 'moralization of pride'. Oakeshott claims that Hobbes 'was unmistakably a philosopher of the morality of individuality'. See 'The moral life and the writings of Thomas Hobbes' in his *Rationalism in Politics* (London, Methuen, 1962), pp. 289 and 294. In an interesting way Hobbes and Spinoza seem to have complementary strengths and weaknesses: a more developed political philosophy with Hobbes, a more developed moral theory with Spinoza.

36. Deleuze, *Spinoza: Practical Philosophy,* p. 27.

37. Spinoza, 'Ethics', III 6 and 7, p. 136. This view of *conatus* is not very different from Hobbes' description of the 'generall inclination of all mankind, a perpetuall and restlesse desire of Power after power, that ceaseth only in death', *Leviathan,* p. 49.

38. Stuart Hampshire, 'Spinoza and the idea of freedom' in P. F. Strawson (ed.), *Studies in the Philosophy of Thought and Action* (Oxford, Oxford University Press, 1968), pp. 55-6.

39. Hampshire, 'Spinoza and the idea of freedom', p. 56.

40. It is at least arguable whether regarding *individuality* as what we are essentially can be condemned as a form of essentialism. Individuality can be understood as an essence which denies essence, individuality as the potential for difference. In

Sartre's terms, for human beings 'existence comes before essence'. See Jean-Paul Sartre, *Existentialism and Humanism* (New York, Haskell, 1977). On Hobbes, see also footnote 35 above.

41. See above, Section II.

42. S. Hampshire, *Spinoza* (Harmondsworth, Penguin Books, 1951), pp. 136-7.

43. Hampshire, *Spinoza,* p. 137.

44. Spinoza, 'Ethics', p. 249.

45. Deleuze, *Spinoza: Practical Philosophy,* pp. 27-8.

46. Spinoza, 'Theologico-Political Treatise', XX, p. 258. Compare Hobbes' remark on torture that 'what is in that case confessed, tendeth to the ease of him that is Tortured; not to the informing of the Torturers', *Leviathan,* p. 73.

47. Deleuze, *Spinoza: Practical Philosophy,* pp. 23-5.

48. Spinoza, 'Ethics', IV18, footnote, p. 201.

49. Of course, a notable defence of positive liberty is advanced by Charles Taylor in his 'What's wrong with negative liberty?', *Philosophical Papers* Vol. 2 (Cambridge, Cambridge University Press, 1985).

Steven Lukes (essay date 1994)

SOURCE: "The Singular and the Plural: On the Distinctive Liberalism of Isaiah Berlin," in *Social Research,* Vol. 61, No. 3, Fall, 1994, pp. 687-717.

[*In the following essay, Lukes defines Berlin's Liberalism in the context of his counter-Enlightenment scholarship.*]

John Gray's attack [in his "Against the New Liberalism," *Times Literary Supplement,* July 3, 1992] has several objects in view: among them a "tradition of liberal theorizing" that "does little more than articulate the prejudices of an Anglo-American academic class that lacks any understanding of political life in our age," as exhibited by its "alienated counter culture, hostile to its own society and enamored of various exotic regimes," and a continuing commitment to egalitarian communism despite the Soviet collapse. Yet the attack seems oddly out of focus, for these targets hardly constitute a united front. For one thing, none of the liberal philosophers Gray attacks (Rawls, Dworkin, Nozick, Ackerman, and Nagel) is either an alienated fellow-traveller or an undisillusioned post- or neo-marxist.

Even if we confine our attention to Gray's case against the "new liberalism," his scatter-gun misfires and, when it hits, scarcely wounds. Thus, Rawls is criticized for lacking a "theory of human nature" (such as those found in Aristotle or Mill) but also for failing to see human beings as "constituted by their histories and their communities, with all their conflicting demands"; and Sir Isaiah Berlin is commended for seeing that "incommensurabilities among

ultimate values set a limit to the ambitions of theory in both ethics and politics"—yet these underly what Rawls calls the "fact of pluralism" and Nagel the "fragmentation of value" and constitute the starting point of their recent liberal writings.

The basic trouble with Gray's argument is that he has set his sights on what he claims to be a "central feature" of "recent political philosophy," namely, "the continued hegemony within it of an Enlightenment project that history has passed by." He supposes this hegemony to hold sway over all the thinkers he attacks—liberals, communitarians, and marxists—and to be the deep cause of their several errors.

What is this "Enlightenment project" that it has become so fashionable to declare *passé?* According to Gray, it is "the hope that human beings will shed their traditional allegiances and local identities and unite in a universal civilisation grounded in generic humanity and a rational morality." Animated by such a hope, Gray maintains the thinkers he criticizes cannot "grapple with the political dilemmas of an age in which political life is dominated by renascent particularism, militant religions and resurgent ethnicities."

What is a liberal (or indeed any reasonable person) supposed to do in the face of such dilemmas? Abandon the belief that there is a human nature unchanging across human diversity and the quest for a theory of it? Give up the idea of a "rational morality"—that is, the idea that moral and political judgements and actions should be grounded in reason? Of course, Kant and Condorcet and others had cosmopolitan (albeit Eurocentric) visions of the future which no reasonable person (and none of the liberals attacked by Gray) could now seriously entertain. And they had little feeling for or understanding of the cultural diversity and value pluralism that constitute the background against which contemporary Anglo-American liberals have sought to pursue *their* distinctively modern enlightenment project. That project can be summed up as the attempt to find principles for regulating the politics of a widely pluralistic society that can secure reasonable agreement. Liberals, as Jeremy Waldron has put it, "demand that the social order should in principle be capable of explaining itself at the tribunal of each person's understanding" (Waldron, 1987).

Gray, by contrast, seems to say that *that* project too is doomed. Why? Because "renascent particularisms, militant religions and resurgent ethnicities" render it hopeless? Because in the "real world" human beings are "constituted by their histories and their communities, with all their conflicting demands" and cannot step back from or outside them? Because the attempt to eliminate "practices of exclusion and subordination" is bound to be fruitless? Many contemporary voices make such assertions, which have become a kind of orthodoxy in certain quarters. Liberalism, born of the Enlightenment, is bound to reject them.

The thought of the Enlightenment had many sharp and profound critics, who ruthlessly exposed its weaknesses and above all its insensitivity to the pluralism of values.

No one has written about such critics to greater effect and better purpose than Sir Isaiah Berlin. The argument of the essay that follows is that his work, far from showing the Enlightenment project to be anachronistic and doomed, has helped to set the agenda for the enlightenment project of contemporary liberalism.

Sir Isaiah Berlin is a challenging thinker. The challenge of his thought—and, more particularly, as I shall argue, of his *way* of thinking—has not, I believe, diminished over the last half-century but, on the contrary, only grown in force and relevance. In this article, I shall try to identify to what, in my view, that challenge amounts.

It is not, in the first place, a question of *difficulty*, either of thought or of expression. To the contrary, Berlin's writings are exceptionally accessible to an exceptionally wide audience. As a writer and as a lecturer, he has always displayed a rare gift for communicating at several levels to a wide range of different publics: from specialist scholars, historians, and philosophers to the general reader or listener or lover of literature with a taste for ideas. His prose is never abstruse or even abstract: ideas are always attributed to persons in identifiable times and places. As Joseph Brodsky has remarked, "'others' lives are this man's forte" (the "two most interesting things in this world," Brodsky adds, being "gossip and metaphysics") (Brodsky, 1991, pp. 214, 211). The ideas and arguments about which Berlin writes are, as Bernard Williams has observed, always *someone's,* developed in response to some specific, and specified, situation (Williams, 1978, p. xii).

Consider, for example, his account of the origins of nationalism, in reaction to the French Enlightenment, as "a vision in the heads of a small group of German poets and critics":

> writers who felt most acutely displaced by the social transformation through which Germany, and in particular Prussia, was passing under the westernising reforms of Frederick the Great. Barred from all real power, unable to fit themselves into the bureaucratic organisation which was imposed on traditional ways of life, acutely sensitive to the incompatibility of their basically Christian, Protestant, moralistic outlook with the scientific temper of the French Enlightenment, harried by the petty despotism of two hundred princes, the most gifted and independent among them responded to the undermining of their world, which had begun with the humiliation inflicted upon their grandfathers by the armies of Louis XIV, by a growing revolt. They contrasted the depth and poetry of the German tradition, with its capacity for fitful but authentic insights into the inexhaustible, inexpressible variety of the life of the spirit, with the shallow materialism, the utilitarianism, and the thin, dehumanised shadow play of the worlds of the French thinkers. This is the root of the romantic movement, which in Germany, at any rate, celebrated the collective will, untrammelled by rules which men could discover by rational methods, the spiritual life of the people in whose activity—or impersonal will—creative individuals could participate, but which they could not observe or describe. The conception of the political life

of the nation as the expression of this collective will is the essence of political romanticism—that is, nationalism (Berlin, 1980a, pp. 348-49).

This passage illustrates well several aspects of Berlin's prose that help explain its accessibility: clarity, precision of historical reference, the characterising of complex ideas while looking for their "root" and their "essence," the real effort to convey the "world from within" (how did these particular Germans see the French Enlightenment?) in a way that makes the acceptance of the ideas in question seem as plausible as possible (why did it appear like *that* to *them*?). It also illustrates its literary qualities, which Brodsky found to be "typically Russian": "his piling up of subordinate clauses, his digressions and questions, the cadences of his prose which resembled the sardonic eloquence of the best of nineteenth-century Russian fiction" (Brodsky, 1991, p. 212). Berlin himself records that Tolstoy and "other Russian writers, both novelists and social thinkers, of the mid-nineteenth century . . . did much to shape my outlook" (Berlin, 1990a, pp. 2-3).

The accessibility of Berlin's writing is not, however, bought at the price of vulgarisation or simplification. He invites the reader or listener to consider ideas or arguments or world-views, the scholarly debates over which he has pondered and mastered but rarely displays. He quotes sparsely, and he does not analyse texts in detail, preferring to present overall interpretations of thinkers, in part as faithful and sympathetic reporter, in part as their contemporary interlocutor, in part as advocate, to the reader, of his own position, drawn from the consideration of their world-views. Almost always Berlin's essays (and all his writings are essays, save the life of Marx [Berlin, 1978] and the recently-published study of Hamann [Berlin, 1993]) are reflections on some large perennial question, the sort of question on which most of us reflect at some time or other. Is there an overall pattern to history and can it be known, as Saint-Simon and Comte, Hegel and Marx maintained? Is there, as the thinkers of the Enlightenment were convinced, "a movement, however tortuous, from ignorance to knowledge, from mythical thought and childish fantasies to perception of reality face to face, to knowledge of true goals, true values as well as truths of fact?" (Berlin, 1990, p. 7). Are "the positive values in which men have believed" ultimately compatible or are conflicts of values "an intrinsic, irremovable element in human life" (Berlin, 1969a, p. 167)? Is human nature much the same in all times and places, as Hume believed and Vico denied? Are the methods of the natural sciences applicable with equal success to the fields of ethics, politics, and human relationships in general, as positivists maintain and Vico, once more, denied? If not, why not? His essays draw the reader into the discussion of such questions by making the ways in which certain thinkers of particular interest to him addressed and sought to answer them come alive.

That they come alive in his pages, and that they used to do so in the lecture hall, is indisputable. Why is this? In what does his peculiar gift for making ideas vivid consist?

I think part of the answer, at least, is given by the very mixing of perspectives delineated above: Berlin as interpreter, interlocutor, and thinker. As interpreter, he possesses to a remarkable degree that faculty that Vico called *fantasia*—the ability to *enter* into other world-views, to "hear men's voices, to conjecture (on the basis of such evidence as we can gather) what may have been their experience, their forms of expression, their values, outlook, aims, ways of living" (Berlin, 1990b, pp. 64-5). His interpretations usually focus on the central animating vision of the thinker in question, rather than on the logic of his arguments, and on thinkers for whom this is the most revealing approach—for arguments are often (but, of course, not always) "only the outworks—the defensive weapons against real and possible objections on the part of actual and potential critics and opponents" (Berlin, 1990c, p. 161). As interlocutor, he extends his *fantasia* to picturing how contemporaries understood and responded to the thinkers under discussion. In this way, his approach to some extent incorporates the context of intelligibility on which Professor Quentin Skinner lays such stress: but an exclusive focus on this makes the transcontextual relevance and continuing power of ideas unintelligible. Berlin as thinker in his own right is concerned to marshal the ideas he discusses into the service of a larger argument, or set of arguments, that is presently alive. Often, as in his essays on John Stuart Mill (Berlin, 1969b) and Georges Sorel (Berlin, 1980b), his interpretation conveys where the thinker under discussion would stand on the issues of our own day or, as in the essay on Joseph de Maistre, how his thought strikes a disturbing contemporary note. For Berlin, the history of ideas is never merely historical but at the same time an exploration of their strengths and weaknesses and, as he writes in his essay on Sorel, of "the relevance of these ideas to our time" (Berlin, 1980b, p. 296).

Yet the challenge his thought presents is not, in the second place, that of an ambitious, all-embracing *system* of thought. He is not a systematic thinker. He is not interested in linking metaphysics and morals (though he holds that morals are generally based on metaphysics in the sense that moral and political judgements are grounded in views of the nature of man and the universe), or philosophy, politics, and economics, or the biological and social sciences in some overall conception of evolution. He does not seek to elaborate a set of principles with wide application across different intellectual disciplines or spheres of social life. He is not what is these days called a "foundationalist." He is not after firmly based principles or axioms from which moral and political conclusions can be derived, or which can provide a criterion for ranking values or a metric by means of which they can be compared. He does not even present a "theory" of liberty or of equality (the two values about which he has written explicitly), or of the relations between them, for our times.

Joseph Brodsky, who had read Berlin in the Soviet Union and first met him in the early 1970s, saw this absence of system as intrinsic to the very idea of liberty. "In the realm I was from," he has written, "'philosophy' was by and large a foul word and entailed the notion of a system. What was good about *Four Essays on Liberty* was that it advanced none, since 'liberty' and 'system' are antonyms" (Brodsky, 1991, p. 212). But this goes too far and misses what is distinctive of Berlin's liberalism. Many of the great liberal thinkers have exhibited, in varying degrees, the *esprit de système* that Berlin so notably lacks—Kant, Adam Smith, John Stuart Mill, and, in our own day, Friedrich von Hayek, Sir Karl Popper, and, in a different way, John Rawls.

Berlin's positive views, to which we will come in due course, are, it is true, inimical to such system-building and his favorite liberal heroes—Benjamin Constant, Alexis de Tocqueville, Alexander Herzen—are none of them builders of systems. As for Kant, Berlin is fond of quoting his phrase, "Out of the crooked timber of humanity no straight thing was ever made,"[1] preferring its message to the overall message of the work from which it comes, *The Idea for a Universal History in a Cosmopolitan Perspective,* in which Kant writes of "the hidden plan of nature" being "to bring into existence an internally and externally perfected political constitution," and civil unification is characterised by means of an exactly opposite image: "as trees in a wood which seek to deprive each other of air and sunlight are forced to strive upwards and so achieve a beautiful straight growth; while those that spread their branches at will in isolated freedom grow stunted, tilted and crooked."[2]

Moreover, the John Stuart Mill he admires is not the inheritor, transmitter, and modifier of one of the most intellectually powerful of such systems, still potent in our own day, namely, utilitarianism. Mill's thought, he writes, "runs directly counter to traditional—that is, eighteenth-century—utilitarianism, which rested on the view that there exists an unalterable nature of things, and answers to social, as to other, problems, can, at least in principle, be scientifically discovered once and for all" (Berlin, 1969b, p. 182). Mill, he writes,

> broke with the pseudo-scientific model, inherited from the classical world and the age of reason, of a determined human nature, endowed at all times, everywhere, with the same unaltering needs, emotions, motives, responding differently only to differences of situation and stimulus, or evolving according to some unaltering pattern. For these he substituted (not altogether consciously) the image of man as creative, incapable of self-completion, and therefore never wholly predictable: fallible, a complex combination of opposites, some reconcilable, others incapable of being resolved or harmonised, unable to cease from his search for truth, happiness, novelty, freedom, but with no guarantee, theological or logical or scientific, of being able to attain them: a free, imperfect being, capable of determining his own destiny in circumstances favourable to his reason and gifts (Berlin, 1969b, p. 205).

Berlin's Mill, in short, is a failed utilitarian, driven by a

> passionate belief that men are made human by their capacity for choice—choice of evil and good equally.

Fallibility, the right to err, as a corollary of the capacity for self-improvement, distrust of symmetry and finality as enemies of freedom—these are the principles which Mill never abandons. He is acutely aware of the many-sidedness of the truth and of the irreducible complexity of life, which rules out the very possibility of any simple solution, or the idea of a final answer to any concrete problem (Berlin, 1969b, p. 192).

But it was certainly Alexander Herzen—who by the middle of the last century had become "the acknowledged leader of all that was generous, enlightened, civilised, humane in Russia" (Berlin, 1980c, p. 202)—whose liberalism most closely foreshadows and, as he acknowledges, influenced his own, with its distrust and scepticism of closed, general intellectual systems and its fear of the consequences of their being believed in. Thus, Berlin writes of Herzen's

> deep distrust (something that most of his allies did not share) of all general formulas as such, of the pro-grammes and battle-cries of all the political parties, of the great, official historical goals—progress, liberty, equality, national unity, historic rights, human solidar-ity—principles and slogans in the name of which men have been, and doubtless would soon again be, violated and slaughtered, and their forms of life condemned and destroyed (Berlin, 1980c, p. 196).

Herzen, he writes, was sceptical about "the meaning and value of abstract ideals as such, in contrast with the con-crete, short-term, immediate goals of identifiable living in-dividuals," of "the degree to which human beings can be transformed' and, more deeply still, about 'whether such changes, even if they were achieved by fearless and intel-ligent and revolutionaries or reformers, ideal images of whom floated before the eyes of his Westernising friends in Russia, would in fact lead to a juster and freer order, or on the contrary to the rule of new masters over new slaves" (Berlin, 1980c, pp. 196, 197). Herzen came to fear that "the ideals and watchwords of politics turn out, on exami-nation, to be empty formulas in the name of which devout fanatics happily slaughter hecatombs of their fellows" (Berlin, 1980c, p. 208). Herzen believed that "remote ends were a dream, that faith in them was a fatal illusion; that to sacrifice the present or the immediate and foreseeable future to these distant ends must always lead to cruel and futile forms of human sacrifice." Though Herzen believed in "reason, scientific methods, individual action, empiri-cally discovered truths," he tended to suspect that "faith in general formulas, laws, prescription in human affairs was an attempt, sometimes catastrophic, always irrational, to escape from the uncertainty and unpredictable variety of life to the false security of our own symmetrical fantasies" (Berlin, 1980c, p. 211).

In such passages as these, Berlin was speaking through the mouths of his subjects against what was the dominant in-tellectual and political system of our time, to which many of his students, readers, and critics were, in different ways and to different degrees, attracted, namely, marxism. Many of the notes struck were familiar. They were sounded by many other contemporary liberals—notably, Sir Karl Pop-

per, Sidney Hook, Jacob Talmon, Raymond Aron, Norb-erto Bobbio. Yet Berlin's voice was always distinctive. It was never stridently and aggressively polemical, or com-placently celebratory of the "end of ideology," in the man-ner of the anticommunist liberals in the United States (often ex-marxists themselves). It spoke for the most part about and through thinkers of the past but never crudely or manipulatively, blaming this or that thinker for the totali-tarian horrors that were to come. Berlin was always a more nuanced and subtle interpreter than Popper or Tal-mon. Moreover, readers and listeners were left free to see parallels and analogies in patterns of thought where they would. Finally, unlike Aron but like Bobbio (and Mill and Herzen), Berlin was always unmistakably, if watchfully and cautiously, a man of the left, an enthusiast for the New Deal, and a supporter of the postwar Welfare State, warning his friends and allies and students just where cer-tain ways and patterns of thought could lead. He raised his voice against raised voices: against intolerance, strident simplifications, overarching schemes that promise cogni-tive and moral certainties, purporting both to interpret and to change the world—or, indeed, to preserve it. He agreed with Herzen that we "have marvelled enough at the deep, abstract wisdom of nature and history; it is time to realise that nature and history are full of the accidental and sense-less, of muddle and bungling" (Berlin, 1980c, p. 206).

The challenge of Berlin's thought is not, therefore, in the third place, that it defends any particular set of political principles or project or program. It is not a defense of the "market order" à la Hayek, or of "piecemeal social engi-neering" à la Popper, or of the "minimal state" à la Nozick, or of a "well-ordered society," more or less social-democratic and liberal, governed by the Difference Prin-ciple à la Rawls, or of "complex equality" with demar-cated spheres of justice à la Walzer. It offers no particular view of constitutionalism or representative democracy or political economy. It provides neither an explanatory theory of nor a normative model for a well-functioning liberal order. Nor is it an argument against "rationalism in politics," the deployment of rational principles in political life as such, an invocation to pursue the "intimations of traditions" à la Oakeshott. Nor does it conclude from the alleged failure of the Enlightenment project of justifying morality that we are in for "coming ages of barbarism and darkness" à la MacIntyre. Nor, as I shall argue, does it lend support to John Gray's attack on "the continued he-gemony within [recent political philosophy] of an Enlight-enment project that history has passed by" (Gray, 1992). Nor, finally, despite its distrust, scepticism, and fear of overarching cognitive and moral claims, is it a forerunner of fashionable postmodernist, relativist positions that pur-port to deconstruct and undermine the very appeal to rea-son and reasonableness in the discussion of the central questions of political theory.

Berlin's challenge consists, rather, in his lifelong effort to defend and advocate a certain *way of thinking* about moral and political questions, rather than a particular explanatory or normative theory, a set of what Collingwood called "ab-

solute presuppositions" that govern how we are to understand the world, rather than a distinctive set of propositions about it.[3] Such presuppositions are, as Collingwood
insisted, not true or right or based on evidence or demonstrable as propositions are, but rather form part of the
framework within which we judge which propositions are
true or right or convincing. They are, so to speak, the master assumptions that, for a given culture and period, guide
expectations, determining which sorts of propositions and
theories we are prepared to count as "true" or "right." The
"absolute presuppositions of any given society, at any
given phase of its history, form a structure which is subject to "strains" and if "the strains are too great, the structure collapses and is replaced by another" (Collingwood,
1972, p. 48). Most of Berlin's writings have been devoted
to furthering the task of undermining one such framework
or structure with a view to replacing it by another.

The framework under attack he variously calls "monism,"
the "*philosophia perennis*" (Berlin, 1990a, p. 8, the "old
perennial belief in the possibility of realising ultimate harmony" (Berlin, 1990a, p. 17), the "platonic ideal" that

> as in the sciences, all genuine questions must have one
> true answer and one only, all the rest being necessarily
> errors, . . . that there must be a dependable path to-
> wards the discovery of these truths, . . . [and] that the
> true answers, when found, must necessarily be compat-
> ible with one another and form a single whole, for one
> truth cannot be incompatible with another—that we
> know *a priori* (Berlin, 1990a, pp. 5-6).

Applied to morals and politics, according to Berlin, this
amounts to a utopian belief in "the discoverability and
harmony of objectively true ends, true for all men, at all
times and places (Berlin, 1990d, p. 211). The *locus classi-
cus* in Berlin's *oeuvre* where this doctrine is most eloquently described and attacked is the last section of his
lecture **"Two Concepts of Liberty."** It is, he claims there,
responsible more than any other belief, for "the slaughter
of individuals on the altars of the great historical ideals,"
including "liberty itself, which demands the sacrifice of individuals for the freedom of society." It is the belief that
"somewhere in the past or in the future, in divine revelation or in the mind of an individual thinker, in the pronouncements of history or science, or in the simple heart
of an uncorrupted good man, there is a final solution."
This ancient faith, he writes, rests on "the conviction that
all positive values in which men have believed must, in
the end, be compatible, and perhaps even entail one another." And, to illustrate the Enlightenment's commitment
to this belief, he cites Condorcet, "one of the best me who
ever lived," who wrote that "Nature binds truth, happiness
and virtue together as by an indissoluble chain," and spoke
similarly of liberty, equality, and justice (Berlin, 1969a, p.
167).

Against monism, thus understood, he defends and advocates "pluralism"—not in the political scientist's or soci-
ologist's senses but a "pluralism of values"—the belief
that in the world of ordinary experience we are "faced

with choices between ends equally ultimate, and claims
equally absolute, the realisation of some of which must inevitably involve the sacrifice of others"; that "the ends of
men are many, and not all of them are in principle compatible with each other," so that "the possibility of conflict—and of tragedy—can never wholly be eliminated
from human life, either personal or social" and "the necessity of choosing between absolute claims is then an inescapable characteristic of the human condition"; and that
human goals are "not all of them commensurable, and in
perpetual rivalry with one another." For, "In the end, men
choose between ultimate values; they choose as they do,
because their life and thought are determined by fundamental categories and concepts that are, at any rate over
long stretches of time and space, a part of their being and
thought and sense of their own identity; part of what makes
them human" (Berlin, 1969a, pp. 168, 169, 171-72).

Berlin derives this conception of pluralism from a number
of sources. Indeed, much of his very best writing consists
in his interpretations of thinkers whom he sees as its precursors and articulators. It was, he tells us, the reading of
Machiavelli that planted in his mind "the realisation, which
came as something of a shock, that not all the supreme
values pursued by mankind now and in the past were necessarily compatible with one another" (Berlin, 1990a, p.
8). The "originality" of Machiavelli, according to Berlin,
was to have juxtaposed two "moral outlooks," "systems of
value," and "sets of virtues"—the Christian and the pagan—and seen that they were "not merely in practice, but
in principle incompatible" (Berlin, 1980d, p. 69), thereby
planting "a permanent question mark in the path of posterity" stemming from his "recognition that ends equally ultimate, equally sacred, may contradict each other, that entire
systems of value may come into collision without possibility of rational arbitration . . . as part of the normal human
situation" (Berlin, 1980d, p. 74).

From Vico's *La scienza nuova* (which Collingwood urged
him to read) and other unsystematic works he derived a
similar message. What he valued in Vico was:

> his insistence on the plurality of cultures and the con-
> sequently fallacious character of the idea that there is
> one and only one structure of reality which the enlight-
> ened philosopher can see as it truly is . . . men ask
> different questions of the universe, and their answers
> are shaped accordingly; such questions, and the sym-
> bols or acts that express them, alter or become obsolete
> in the course of cultural development; to understand
> the answers one must understand the questions that
> preoccupy an age or a culture; they are not constant
> nor necessarily more profound because they resemble
> our own more than others that are less familiar to us.
> Vico's relativity went further than Montesquieu's. If
> his view was correct, it was subversive of the very no-
> tion of absolute truths and of a perfect society founded
> on them, nor merely in practice but in principle (Berlin,
> 1980e, p. 6).

In Herder, the great inspirer of cultural nationalism and
eventually of political nationalism, this view was deepened and radicalized—more particularly the earlier Herder,

fired by "a relativistic passion for the individual essence and flavour of each culture." For Herder, who rejected the absolute criteria of progress then fashionable among the *philosophes* in Paris,

> no culture is a mere means towards another; every human achievement, every human society is to be judged by its own internal standards . . . there is a plurality of incommensurable cultures. To belong to a given community, to be connected with its members by indissoluble and impalpable ties of common language, historical memory, habit, tradition and feeling, is a basic human need no less natural than that for food and drink or security or procreation. One nation can understand and sympathise with the institutions of another only because it knows how much its own mean to itself. Cosmopolitanism is the shedding of all that makes one most human, most oneself (Berlin, 1980e, p. 12).

Indeed, it is striking how this central, lifelong theme is central to his readings of virtually all the thinkers about whom he has written. Thus, he notes the "continuous dialectic" in Montesquieu's thought between absolute values based in permanent human interests and a sense of their relativity to time and place in a concrete situation, and he commends his "very clear perception of the fact that no degree of knowledge, or of skill or of logical power, can produce automatic solutions of social problems, of a final and universal kind" (Berlin, 1980f, p. 159). He is interested in David Hume chiefly because of his "peculiar relationship" with the German opponents of the Enlightenment, notably Hamann and Jacobi, for whom Hume's scepticism had removed "the *a priori* bonds needed to guarantee the indestructible validity of the rationalist edifice" (Berlin, 1980g, p. 186). His abiding and intense interest in these founding fathers of Romanticism and in the Counter-Enlightenment as a whole is motivated by the same set of concerns.

What drives all these studies is the urge to pinpoint the weaknesses of the monism of the Enlightenment by consulting the thoughts of its most dangerous and implacable enemies, to discover the sources of pluralism in all their exuberant variety, sometimes in surprising places, and to trace the extreme and sometimes bizarre lengths to which it has been taken and the consequences to which it has led.

Thus, he sees Joseph de Maistre not just as an extreme Catholic reactionary but as "an unyielding adversary of all that the *lumières* of the eighteenth century had stood for—rationalism, individualism, liberal compromise and secular enlightenment" (Berlin, 1990c, p. 106), who sounded "what is perhaps the earliest note of the militant antirational Fascism of modern times" (Berlin, 1990c, p. 150), but whose world is "much more realistic and more ferocious than that of the romantics (Berlin, 1990c, p. 158), and whose genius consisted in "the depth and the accuracy of his insight into the darker, less regarded, but decisive factors in social and political behaviour" (Berlin, 1990c, p. 166). For Maistre, Nature was a "scene of brutality, pain and chaos" governed by an unfathomable divine purpose

and Reason but a "flickering" light (Berlin, 1990c, pp. 132, 122). His originality was to point out "the persistence and extent of irrational instinct, the power of faith, the force of blind tradition, the wilful ignorance about their human material of the progressives—the idealistic social scientists, the bold political and economic planners, the passionate believers in technocracy"; with "much exaggeration and perverse delight" he underlined "that the desire to immolate oneself, to suffer, to prostrate oneself before authority, indeed before superior power, no matter whence it comes, and the desire to dominate, to exert authority, to pursue power for its own sake—that these were forces historically at least as strong as the desire for peace, prosperity, liberty, justice, happiness, equality" (Berlin, 1990c, pp. 166-67).

His study of Sorel, similarly, focuses on a penetrating critic of "shallow optimism, characteristic of the shallow eighteenth century," a thinker in revolt against "the rationalist ideal of frictionless contentment in a harmonious social system in which all ultimate questions are reduced to technical problems, soluble by appropriate techniques" (Berlin, 1980b, pp. 302, 331-32). He believed that myths could direct energies and inspire action, enabling "free moral agents . . . collectively to resist and create and mould the world to their will,"—a doctrine that led him to emphasize "the power of the irrational in human thought and action" (Berlin, 1980b, pp. 320, 323). Erratic and inconstant in his politics, ending up an admirer of both Lenin and Mussolini, Sorel, like Maistre, rejected the assumption that "reality was a harmonious whole" (Berlin, 1980b, p. 302), but unlike him believed that "to impose form on the chaos that we find in the world of nature and the world of thought—that is the end of both art and science and belongs to the essence of man as such" (Berlin, 1980b, p. 299). An "eccentric visionary, a penetrating and cruel critic of the vices of parliamentary democracy and bourgeois humanitarianism," Sorel believed, throughout all the twists and turns of his career, in "absolute moral ends that are independent of any dialectical or other historical pattern, and in the possibility, in conditions which men can themselves create, of realising these ends by the concerted power of the free and deliberate collective will" (Berlin, 1980b, pp. 327, 329-30), thereby feeding the "anti-intellectual and anti-Enlightenment stream in the European radical tradition," with his "hatred of democracy, the bourgeois republic, and above all the rational outlook and liberal values of the intelligentsia" (Berlin, 1980b, p. 316).

It is, however, to Romanticism, above all German Romanticism, that Berlin attributes the major role in the formulation and propagation of value pluralism, notably in the studies of Herder, in the small volume about Hamann, and in his various essays on romanticism. To Herder, as we have seen, he assigns the discovery of "a plurality of incommensurable cultures." But it was Johann Georg Hamann, according to Berlin, who lit the "fuse" which "set off the great romantic revolt, the denial that there was an objective order, a *rerum natura,* whether factual or normative, from which all knowledge and all values stemmed, and by which all action could be tested" (Berlin, 1993, pp. 122-23). Hamann's "profoundly irrationalist spiritual vision," his "obscurantist particularism and denigration of systematic thought" were accompanied, however, by "inspired insights," defending "the inarticulate, the mystical, the demonic, the dark reaches and mysterious depths" (Berlin, 1993, pp. 119, 122, 115). His view of the world was of "an unorderable succession of episodes, each carrying its value in itself, intelligible only by direct experience, a 'living through' this experience, unintelligible—dead—when it is reported by others" (Berlin, 1993, p. 114). Hamann remained "blind to the worst abuses of the regime in which he lived," seeing only "the vices of the 'great simplifiers' who were seeking to destroy living men and women in the name of hollow abstractions—ideals like reason, progress, liberty or equality" (Berlin, 1993, p. 125). His "hatred and blind irrationalism," Berlin acknowledges,

> have fed the stream that has led to social and political irrationalism, particularly in Germany, in our own century, and has made for obscurantism, a revelling in darkness, the discrediting of that appeal to rational discussion in terms of principles intelligible to most men which alone can lead to an increase in knowledge, the creation of conditions for free co-operative action based on conscious acceptance of common ideals, and the promotion of the only type of progress that has ever deserved this name (Berlin, 1993, pp. 121-22).

As this last passage makes very clear, Berlin's challenge amounts to an extraordinarily paradoxical argument. For it would seem that it was the Enlightenment—the major modern source of "the only type of progress that has ever deserved this name" and the origin of the very idea of the "left"—that espoused monism—the "one belief, more than any other, . . . responsible for the slaughter of individuals on the altars of the great historical ideals." And, apparently, it was the Counter-Enlightenment—whose principal figures variously foreshadowed "the militant anti-rational Fascism of modern times" and fed the streams of anti-intellectual radicalism and "social and political irrationalism, particularly in Germany"—that gave birth to value pluralism that was part of the "great mutation in western thought and feeling that took place in the eighteenth century" which made toleration into an "intrinsic value" and shaped "the concepts of liberty and human rights as they are discussed today" (Berlin, 1980a, p. 333). It was the rationalist *philosophes,* committed to optimism and cosmopolitanism, whose belief in the reconcilability of all human values in a single, harmonious unity would ultimately lead to the dangerous illusion of the "possibility of a final solution"—the prospect that mankind could be made "just and happy and creative and harmonious for ever" for which no price could be too high to pay (Berlin, 1990a, p. 15). And it was theocratic reactionaries and particularist, often irrationalist romantic thinkers, contemptuous of shallow optimism and cosmopolitan ideals, whose "deep and radical revolt against the central tradition of western thought" and acute sensitivity to the "virtues of diversity" in life and thought would turn out to lay the foundations of "modern liberal culture" (Berlin, 1990d, p. 208).

This is a very striking argument, whose audacity is only reinforced by the repeated (if unconscious or forgetful) use of the Nazi phrase "final solution" in relation to Enlightenment rationalism. But how convincing is it? To answer this, we need, I believe, to look more closely at its various component claims and at the strength of the links between them. What exactly, according to Berlin, does value pluralism assert that monism denies? And how exactly does the latter pose dangers from which the former offers protection?

There are several distinct elements that go to make up pluralism of values, as Berlin repeatedly describes it. In the first place, there are several features of values that are worth distinguishing. They are *plural,* not forms or derivatives of a single value or fixed set of values. Thus, freedom must not be identified with "equality, justice, happiness, knowledge, love, creation, and other ends that men seek for their own sakes" (Berlin, 1969a, p. lviii). They can be *incompatible,* that is, not jointly realizable in a single life or a single society: there are "logical, psychological and sociological limits on what range of values an individual can seriously respect in one life, or one society respect in the lives of various of its citizens" (Williams, 1978, p. xvii). They can be *incomparable:* there may be no relevant respect in which one value can be judged in relation to another, even if *de facto* an individual or a culture must choose between them. And they can be *incommensurable:* there may be no scale or metric, whether cardinal or ordinal, by reference to which one may be judged higher or lower or equal to the other, no "common standard in terms of which to grade them" (Berlin, 1976, p. 212).

In the second place, Berlin's value pluralism stresses the place of values within social or cultural wholes. They are *integrated* in such wholes. Ideals, he writes, "belong to the form of life which generates them . . . values—ends—live and die with the social wholes of which they form an intrinsic part" (Berlin, 1976, p. 212).

In the third place, and closely related to this, he sometimes has suggested that this integration has a *relativistic* implication: that values are not only culture-specific in fact, but that their validity is also culture-bound. Thus,

> Each 'collective individuality' is unique and has its own aims and standards, which will themselves inevitably be superseded by other goals and values—ethical, social and aesthetic. Each of these systems is objectively valid in its own day, in the course of 'Nature's long year' which brings all things to pass. All cultures are equal in the sight of God, each in its time and place (Berlin, 1976, p. 212).

Finally, Berlin holds that the foregoing ideas together entail the *rejection of perfection:* the "possibility, at least in principle, of universal, timeless solutions of problems of value." A believer in pluralism will find "the notion of the perfect civilisation in which the ideal human being realises his full potentialities" to be "patently absurd: not merely difficult to formulate, or impossible to realise in practice, but incoherent and unintelligible" (Berlin, 1976, p. 212).

Conversely, monists hold that the diverse goods human beings seek are forms of or derive from a single overarching good,[4] and that when they are not jointly realizable, they can be subject to a complete and consistent ordering—or, if they are "moral utopians," monists may believe, as Marx and Engels did, that the incompatibility can be overcome by overcoming the conditions that generated it. (It is not clear whether monists must altogether deny the *plurality* and the frequent *incompatibility* of values, but they will insist that they can be ranked along some comprehensive scale that will guide choices between them, and, thus, they will deny their *incomparability* and certainly their *incommensurability*). They attach little or no significance to the place of values within social or cultural wholes, believing rather that since human nature is unaltering, human beings respond with the same needs, emotions, and motives to different situations and circumstances. They are, therefore, absolutists, probably (though not necessarily) taking their own culture's standards to be of universal validity. And, thus, they are led to believe in the possiblity, at least in principle, of achieving perfection—of "universal, timeless solutions of problems of value." Armed with these beliefs, monists are likely to become "single-minded"—"ruthless fanatics, men possessed by an all-embracing coherent vision" who "do not know the doubts and agonies of those who cannot wholly blind themselves to reality." They are committed to the notion that

> there must exist final objective answers to normative questions, truths that can be directly demonstrated or directly intuited, that it is in principle possible to discover a harmonious pattern in which all values are reconciled, and that it is towards this unique goal that we must make; that we can uncover some single central principle that shapes this vision, a principle which, once found, will govern our lives (Berlin, 1969a, p. lv).

There are several problems with this argument stated in this, its most extreme form. The different components of pluralism seem to be separable and not to entail one another. One can believe in the plurality and incompatibility of values without holding that some, or even any, are incomparable or incommensurable. And even if you believe that values are plural and can be incompatible, incomparable, and incommensurable, you may not take cultural differences, let alone incommensurable ones, seriously.

There is, moreover, a difficulty about this last idea, as Berlin derives it from Vico and Herder. If one takes the idea that values inhere in cultural wholes too literally, one will all too easily misperceive the extent to which cultures are conglomerations—clusters or assemblages of heterogeneous elements with varying origins. Where do the boundaries between them lie? One should always recall that the simplifying perception of the internal coherence and distinctness of cultures one from one another is invariably perpetrated by interested parties—including populist and nationalist intellectuals and, one may add, social anthropologists in search of unified and uncontaminated objects of study. On this point it is worth citing Mary Midgley's comment that of course cultures differ, but "they differ in a way which is much more like that of climactic regions or ecosystems than it is like the frontiers drawn between nation states" (Midgley, 1991, p. 84).

More deeply, a very important question is: *how* do they differ? If they really do differ in "aims and standards" that cover "ethical, social and aesthetic" spheres of life in such a way that what is "objectively valid in its own day" is always superseded, then we have come extremely close to the kind of cultural relativism that would render mutual intelligiblity across cultures itself unintelligible—a conclusion Berlin explicitly rejects and which his whole doctrine of pluralism is intended to preclude. For how could we even perceive, let alone make sense of, the cultural differences in beliefs and practices on which Berlin lays such stress except against the shared background of criteria of truth and falsity and standards of reasoning but also of common concepts and dispositions, beliefs and practices? How, to take a famous example, could we make sense of Herodotus's story of Darius, King of Persia, who discovered that the Greeks at his court were horrified at the thought of eating their fathers' dead bodies, and that the tribe of the Callatiae were no less horrified at the idea of burning them (while Darius knew that the *right* thing was to put them on high towers for the vultures to eat)? Only by presupposing the common notion of "honouring the dead" that can take these different forms in different cultures.[5]

Furthermore, if value pluralism were to take a relativist turn, then this would break any link with liberal tolerance. For if what is "objectively valid," and "reasonable," and "rationally justifiable" were always internal to given cultural "wholes," then no culture could ever be criticized for mistreating another or indeed its own members. Moreover, far from *exhibiting* liberal tolerance, such relativism is, in effect, a concealed form of ethnocentrism, denying "them" access to "our" standards of objectivity, reasonableness, and justification.

Finally, there is the difficulty of the alleged dangers of monism from which pluralism, according to Berlin, can render us immune. One problem with this part of the argument is that it does lay exclusive stress on the role of ideas in accounting for the "slaughter of individuals on the altars of the great historical ideals." On the other hand, his *métier* is the analysis and history of ideas, and his hypothesis that monism encourages or facilitates at least one kind of ruthless fanaticism certainly merits investigation. Obviously enough, he had Stalinist communism in mind. Yet it is not hard to think of resolute monists who have been very far from drawing the perfectionist conclusions he so abhors. Utilitarianism is, if anything is, a monist system of thought, and yet if Professor Sheldon Wolin is right, the early Utilitarians were preoccupied with pain and scarcity and sought the minimization of suffering and anxiety (Wolin, 1961, pp. 314-331). And, indeed, monism is, on Berlin's own account, so broadly defined and so omnipresent ("this ancient and almost universal belief, on which so much traditional thought and action and philosophical doctrine rests") that it can hardly be surprising that it has led "at times" to "absurdities in theory and barbarous consequences in practice" (Berlin, 1969a, p. lvi).

Nor is it clear that the pluralism he so eloquently defends leads naturally to liberal conclusions. Why should it not lead to fanatical one-sidedness on the ground that a comprehensive or neutral or objective view of all sides is in any case unavailable? Berlin has cited Max Weber's *Politics as a Vocation* as a classic statement of it (Berlin, 1969, p. lvi), yet Weber's liberalism is far from unambiguous. Perhaps the most dramatic example of thoroughly value-pluralist or "decisionist" anti-liberalism is the case of Carl Schmitt, the Nazi-sympathizing legal theorist, for whom politics reduces to the opposition between friend and foe and whose hostility to liberal democracy is probably unequalled by any other major modern thinker.

Berlin is, of course, alive to some of these problems and has gone some way to meeting them in his writings and most recent interview (Berlin, 1994a). One reason, I believe, why his central master-argument against monism and for pluralism seems vulnerable to them lies precisely in the interpretive method to which I alluded above that renders his writings so vivid: the mixing of perspectives that leaves the reader sometimes unsure just *whose* voice he is hearing. Is he being addressed by, say, Hamann or Herder or Vico (as interpeted by Berlin or as Berlin understands his contemporaries to have interpreted him) or by Berlin *in persona propria*? The very fact that the thinkers Berlin discusses were, for the most part, unaware of the difficulties I have outlined and that they would, indeed, in some instances have embraced them as virtues rather than counting them as objections, makes it all the more important to develop the case for pluralism and show its links with liberalism in terms that are free of the peculiar obsessions of the Counter-Enlightenment, of which Berlin has painted such a graphic picture. The case for liberal pluralism needs to be made independently of preliberal and anti-liberal thinkers, however important may have been their contribution to making it possible.

As I have suggested, the elements of such a case are present in Berlin's writings. Consider, first, the priority of liberty as an absolute and universal precondition for valuable lives being valuable. In his lecture **"Two Concepts of Liberty,"** Berlin already made it clear that the preservation of some minimum area of liberty is a value that is, in comparison with others, overriding. Moreover, it is not merely objectively compelling to "us" because internal to "our" culture. He writes there that "some portion of human existence must remain independent of the sphere of social control." Citing Constant, Jefferson, Burke, Paine, and Mill, he argues that "we must preserve a minimum area of personal freedom if we are not to 'degrade or deny our nature'"—the minimum being that "which a man cannot give up without offending against the essence of his human nature." What, Berlin asks, is this essence, and what are the standards which it entails? This, he answers,

"has been, and perhaps always will be, a matter of infinite debate" (Berlin, 1969a, pp. 126-27).[6] The point is that he did not reject the question as absurd. As he remarks in the introduction to **Four Essays on Liberty,** "to contract the area of human choice is to do harm to men in an intrinsic, Kantian, not merely utilitarian sense" (Berlin, 1969a, p. lii). And as he writes, with reference to Herzen, ". . . liberty—of actual individuals, in specific times and places—is an absolute value" (Berlin, 1979, p. 87).

Berlin is, therefore, prepared to contemplate the existence of an unchanging human nature. Indeed, he does so explicitly, seeing it as a presupposition of mutual intelligibility, and its limits, across the variety of human groups, classes, churches, races, or cultures. "Incompatible [their] ends may be," he writes, "but their variety cannot be unlimited, for the nature of men, however various and subject to change, must possess some generic character if it is to be called human at all" (Berlin, 1990e, p. 80). Where the possibility of communication breaks down, we speak of "derangement, of incomplete humanity." He makes a similar observation in a recent interview: "in the end there is something called human nature. It's modifiable, it takes different forms in different cultures but unless there were a human nature, the very notion of human beings would become unintelligible" (Berlin, 1994a, p. 73). In this sense, at least, mankind is, indeed, "much the same in all times and places."

Moreover, Berlin explicitly disavows relativism and, indeed, in a paper published in 1980, has criticized himself for having previously characterised Vico and Herder as relativists: both of them, he then made clear, "insist on our need and ability to transcend the values of our own culture or nation or class, or those of whatever other windowless boxes some cultural relativists wish to confine us to" (Berlin, 1990e, p. 85). He takes relativism to be the view that "men's outlooks are unavoidably determined by forces of which they are often unaware" (Berlin, 1990e, p. 78), and that these outlooks are "subjective," only to be understood and judged from within. Pluralism, by contrast, he takes to be the view that life affords "a plurality of values, equally genuine, equally ultimate, above all equally objective; incapable, therefore, of being ordered in a timeless hierarchy, or judged in terms of some one absolute standard." There is, he writes,

> a finite variety of values and attitudes, some of which one society, some another, have made their own, attitudes and values which members of other societies may admire or condemn, (in the light of their own value-systems) but can always, if they are sufficiently imaginative and try hard enough, contrive to understand—that is, see to be intelligible ends of life for human beings situated as these men were (Berlin, 1990e, p. 79).

Yet none of this prevents criticism within and across cultures: "Vico experiences no intellectual discomfort—nor need he do so—when he damns in absolute terms the social injustice and brutality of Homeric society. Herder is not being inconsistent when he denounces the great conquerors and destroyers of local cultures—Alexander, Caeser, Charlemagne . . ." (Berlin, 1990e, pp. 86-7). The criticism in question may take the form of attempts at what he has called "empirical enlightenment" (Berlin, 1994a, p. 81)—or one can "reject a culture because one finds it morally or aesthetically repellent" (Berlin, 1990e, p. 87).

Furthermore, he has gone some way to limiting the scope and range of such value pluralism. Thus, in the first place, he ventures the thought that "more people in more countries at more times accept more common values that is often believed" (Berlin, 1994a, p. 85). Second, he has suggested in his Agnelli lecture (Berlin, 1990a) the thought that many conflicts between incompatible values, even where incommensurable, are capable of resolution through "trade-offs," especially in the field of public policy where the principle of resolution appealed to is utilitarian in a very broad sense (minimizing suffering or not frustrating too many people's ultimate ends). The hard cases are dilemmas where both choices are morally binding, where there is no way of not doing wrong.

I suggest that all this can be read as a counter-argument or sub-text that qualifies and limits the master-argument against monism and for pluralism delineated above. Its upshot is to begin to refine the value pluralism to which he remains committed in a way that is consonant with the liberalism he has always defended and, more generally, with the values of the left. It is a pluralism intended to be compatible with the absolute, overriding, and universal value of liberty, the existence of a common human nature, rational criticism, and the tractability of many but not all value conflicts in public and private life. He certainly does not return an unambiguously affirmative answer to the questions whether we truly believe that "value judgments are not judgments at all, but arbitrary acts of self commitment," that "the sciences of man are irrelevant to political purposes, that anthropology, psychology, sociology can instruct us only about means, about techniques," that "since values collide, there are no reasons for choosing one rather than another, so that if men, or groups of men, are possessed by different outlooks, that is the end of the matter, so that war between them is a more honourable proceeding (for those who believe in honour) than attempts to find an intermdiate solution that fully satisfied the beliefs of neither side" (Berlin, 1994b, pp. 120-21).

Like Herzen, he believes in "reason, scientific methods, individual action, empirically discovered truths." Unlike Hamann, he believes in "that appeal to rational discussion in terms of principles intelligible to most men which alone can lead to an increase in knowledge, the creation of conditions for free cooperative action based on conscious acceptance of common ideals, and the promotion of the only type of progress that has ever deserved this name." The ultimate challenge of Berlin's thought is, in short, to develop and defend a pluralism of values that preserves the central message of the Enlightenment while firmly rejecting the nihilism and relativism of its past and present detractors.[7]

Notes

1. See, for example, Berlin, 1990a, p. 19.

2. Quoted and translated in Anderson, 1992, p. 234.

3. See Collingwood, 1972, Chapter V.

4. Compare what Aristotle said against the Platonists: that "of honour, wisdom and pleasure, the accounts are distinct and diverse. The good, therefore, is not some common element answering to one idea" (Aristotle, 1954, 1, 6, 1069b, pp. 9-10).

5. For an excellent discussion of the implications of this story, see Midgley, 1991.

6. See also Mack, 1993.

7. The present article is a slightly modified version of the introduction to Berlin, 1994a.

Bibliography

Anderson, Perry, "The Pluralism of Isaiah Berlin," in *A Zone of Engagement* (London: Verso, 1992).

Aristotle, *The Nicomachean Ethics,* Ross, Sir David, ed. (London: Oxford University Press, 1954).

Berlin, Isaiah, "Two Concepts of Liberty," in *Four Essays on Liberty* (London: Oxford University Press, 1969a).

Berlin, Isaiah, "John Stuart Mill and the Ends of Life," in *Four Essays on Liberty* (London: Oxford University Press, 1969b).

Berlin, Isaiah, "Herder and the Enlightenment," in *Vico and Herder. Two Studies in the History of Ideas* (London: Hogarth, 1976).

Berlin, Isaiah, *Karl Marx: His Life and Environment, 4/E* (Oxford: Oxford University Press, 1978). First published London, 1939.

Berlin, Isaiah, "Herzen and Bakuin on Individual Liberty," in Hardy, Henry and Kelly, Aileen, eds., *Russian Thinkers* (New York: Viking Press, 1979).

Berlin, Isaiah, "Nationalism. Past Neglect and Present Power," in Hardy, Henry, ed., *Against the Current. Essays in the History of Ideas* (London: Hogarth, 1980a).

Berlin, Isaiah, "Georges Sorel," in Hardy, Henry, ed., *Against the Current. Essays in the History of Ideas* (London: Hogarth, 1980b).

Berlin, Isaiah, "Herzen and His Memoirs," in Hardy, Henry, ed., *Against the Current. Essays in the History of Ideas* (London: Hogarth, 1980c).

Berlin, Isaiah, "The Originality of Machiavelli," in Hardy, Henry, ed., *Against the Current. Essays in the History of Ideas* (London: Hogarth, 1980d).

Berlin, Isaiah, "The Counter-Enlightenment," in Hardy, Henry, ed., *Against the Current. Essays in the History of Ideas* (London: Hogarth, 1980e).

Berlin, Isaiah, "The Pursuit of the Ideal," in Hardy, Henry, ed., *The Crooked Timber of Humanity. Chapters in the History of Ideas* (London: John Murray, 1990a).

Berlin, Isaiah, "Giambattista Vico and Cultural History," in Hardy, Henry, ed., *The Crooked Timber of Humanity. Chapters in the History of Ideas* (London: John Murray, 1990b).

Berlin, Isaiah, "Joseph de Maistre and the Origins of Fascism," in Hardy, Henry, ed., *The Crooked Timber of Humanity. Chapters in the History of Ideas* (London: John Murray, 1990c).

Berlin, Isaiah, "The Apotheosis of the Romantic Will. The Revolt Against the Myth of an Ideal World," in Hardy, Henry, ed., *The Crooked Timber of Humanity. Chapters in the History of Ideas* (London: John Murray, 1990d).

Berlin, Isaiah, "Alleged Relativism in Eighteenth-Century European Thought," in Hardy, Henry, ed., *The Crooked Timber of Humanity. Chapters in the History of Ideas* (London: John Murray, 1990e).

Berlin, Isaiah, in Hardy, Henry, ed., *The Magus of the North. J.G. Hamann and the Origins of Modern Irrationalism* (London: John Murray, 1993).

Berlin, Isaiah, *Tra Filosofia e Storia delle Idee: La societa pluralistica e i suoi nemici,* Intervista autobiografica e filosofica a cura di Steven Lukes, Florence, Ponte alle Grazie, 1994a.

Berlin, Isaiah, "The Romantic Revolution. A Crisis in the History of Modern Thought" (unpublished), translated in Italian in *Tra Filosofia e Storia delle Idee: La societa pluralistica e i suoi nemici,* 1994b.

Brodsky, Joseph, "Isaiah Berlin: A Tribute," in Margalit, Edna and Margalit, Avishai, eds., *Isaiah Berlin: A Celebration* (London: Hogarth, 1991).

Collingwood, R.G., *An Essay on Metaphysics* (Lanham: University Press of America, 1972).

Gray, John, "Against the New Liberalism," *Times Literary Supplement* (July 3, 1992):13-15.

Mack, Eric, "Isaiah Berlin and the Quest for Liberal Pluralism," Public Affairs Quarterly 7 No. 3 (July 1993): 215-30.

Midgley, Mary, *Can't We Make Moral Judgements?* (Bristol: The Bristol Press, 1991).

Waldron, Jeremy, "Theoretical Foundation of Liberalism," *Philosophical Quarterly,* 37 (1987): 127-150.

Williams, Bernard, Introduction to Isaiah Berlin, in Hardy, Henry, ed., *Concepts and Categories. Philosophical Essays* (London: Hogarth, 1978).

Wolin, S.S., *Politics and Vision* (London: Allen and Unwin, 1961).

Avishai Margalit (essay date 1995)

SOURCE: "The Philosopher of Sympathy: The Daring Humanism of Isaiah Berlin," in *The New Republic,* Vol. 212, No. 8, February 20, 1995, pp. 31-6.

[*In the following encomium, Margalit outlines Berlin's life and work.*]

People who talk with Isaiah Berlin are often struck by a feeling of regret that he does not write his autobiography. Many have annoyed him with their excited pleas that he should devote himself to this task. The demand is understandable. After all, Berlin was at several "observation posts" from which he could follow closely the unfolding of some of the central events in this century.

In 1915, when Berlin was 6, his family moved from Riga and eventually ended up in Petrograd. From a window above a Petrograd shop in Wassily Ostrov, the child Shaya, as he was affectionately called by his parents (it is a diminutive of the original Hebrew for "Isaiah"), watched the Russian Revolution. In 1920, when he was almost 11, the family emigrated to England. They landed in March, the young Isaiah wearing a coat with a fur collar and knowing very little English. In July of that same year, he won the Surbiton's Arundel House School's first prize for an English essay.

Later Berlin was posted at still another central event of the century. At the British Embassy in Washington, the young don from Oxford served as a first secretary during World War II, in order to report to the British government on American public opinion during the war. The folklore about Berlin in Washington is vast, and it includes the true story of Churchill being impressed by the reports from Washington and asking to meet "this man Berlin," shortly after which the British prime minister found himself entertaining Irving Berlin. The mix-up between Isaiah and Irving was not new. Already in 1932, when Berlin was elected first Jewish Fellow of All Souls College in Oxford, there was much excitement in the Jewish community in England, and the Chief Rabbi is on record in the Jewish Chronicle congratulating Irving Berlin for his election.

Another extraordinary perch came Berlin's way in the Soviet Union, during the period between the end of World War II and the return of Stalin to his reign of terror. He was an attache in the British Embassy in Moscow and met the great, embattled figures of Russian literature. Looking at Berlin's life, indeed, one feels that he has met everyone worth meeting: Freud and Virginia Woolf, Stravinsky, Akhmatova and Pasternak, Nehru, Eliot, Toscanini, Churchill, Auden, Malraux, Edmund Wilson and Bertrand Russell (Russell: "These characters in the Bible are dreadful people." Berlin: "What have you against Jonathan?" Russell: "Come to think of it, I rather like Jezebel. She reminds me of many modern young women of today"), not to mention the major and minor deities of politics and society.

And so, given his prodigious memory and his narrative gift, the demand for an autobiography is eminently justified. But Berlin rebuffs such pleas. He claims in his defense that he has already written lengthy personal impressions, now collected in a book, and that everything he had to tell is there. But it is precisely the existence of *Personal Impressions* that leaves one with a taste for more. One wishes to know more, surely, about the "old Menshevik" Rachmilewitch, of whom Berlin says that he was the purest intellectual he ever met, and influenced him more than anyone else. He met him in London when he was 16, and it was Rachmilewitch who did much to open before him the great panorama of music (Berlin's first published article was about Verdi), Kant, Marx, the radical thought of Russia during the nineteenth century, and philosophies of science: the life of the mind in all its aspects.

Berlin also claims—it is his last line of defense—that he is not sufficiently interested in himself to write his own biography. This is not an affectation; it is sincere, and it cuts deep. But it puts me in mind of Nietzsche's comment that the basic feature of a great psychologist is a lack of curiosity in himself. This, of course, was long before our psychological age. The philosopher was thinking of a person, usually a writer, who has the power of imagination to enter into the minds of other people; and this, too, is one of Berlin's great skills.

Indeed, the problem of empathy has been one of the lasting preoccupations of Berlin's work. For him, there is an essential difference between scientific understanding and the understanding of human affairs. To understand history, religion, culture and literature, one needs to understand people. Berlin traces these types of understanding to the writings of the thinkers he has done so much to rescue from oblivion, Vico, Herder and Hamann. Berlin is himself one of the great Versteheren, or "understanders." He is a psychologist of ideas as much as a historian of ideas. He is addicted to the observation of people, and paints their portraits in the subtlest and most vivid hues.

Perhaps the most famous of Berlin's discriminations of human character is the one that he borrowed from the Greek poet Archilochus, between the hedgehog and the fox. "The fox knows many little things, the hedgehog knows one big thing." Thus Tolstoy is a fox (who vainly tried in old age to become a hedgehog) and Dostoyevsky is a hedgehog. Berlin proceeds usefully to classify other thinkers and writers into foxes and hedgehogs. (The philosopher Nelson Goodman once whimsically asked him what would be the proper animal metaphor for one who spends his life knowing one little thing.)

The Berlin memory bank is capable of cashing in any character description for its gold equivalent, namely, an illustrative story or an unforgettable quotation. In what sense was Chaim Weizmann, the leader of the Zionist movement and Berlin's close friend, an ironic man? Well, Berlin will tell Weizmann's last words. When, on his deathbed, he coughed badly and felt choked, Weizmann's

doctor told him to spit. "But there is no one to spit at," he replied in Yiddish, and died. It was also Weizmann who said that it is not necessary to be mad in order to be a Zionist, but it helps. Berlin is fond of that latter dictum, but the beautiful profile that he draws of Weizmann emphasizes his hero's normality. He presents him as the perfect non-neurotic Jew, and a great man.

"The great man" is a central category in Berlin's view of history. He is, Berlin believes, someone who is capable of changing our notions of what people can do; someone who, in the public sphere, aims at, and causes, a significant historical change of direction, which would have been regarded as improbable before he acted. Genius, by contrast, is not like greatness. Asked how he managed to leap so high, Nijinsky replied that most people, when they jump, come down at once, "but why not linger in the air a little before coming down?" That is genius, and it shows itself in art, in mathematics, in music, in philosophy, in literature. The action is simple and clear, but the rest of us do not know how to begin to do it. But great men (and women) are doers in the social sphere, and we may follow where they lead. Even monsters such as Stalin or Hitler are, for Berlin, great men; but not Gorbachev, for example, since Gorbachev did not intend the consequences of his actions.

For good or for ill, admirably or contemptibly, a great man may single-handedly affect the shape of major historical events. In Berlin's hands, however, the idea of the great man is not an expression of elitism. He intends with it, rather, to celebrate the role of the individual in history. Also the role of freedom: Berlin is a famous foe of the idea of historical inevitability. Berlin does not believe in laws of history that determine every historical event. A historian is not a scientist. In contrast with the scientist, who endeavors to discover underlying similarities between apparently disparate phenomena, the historian strives to highlight what is unique about an age or an event.

Unlike other philosophers, Berlin is concerned not only with the sense of a great idea, but also with its sensibility. He studies the systematic connection between an idea and the feelings that are attached to it, such as the connection between the idea of nationalism and the sentiment of belonging. For this reason, Berlin's heroes are not only those who have enriched our thought, but also those who have contributed to our culture. His deep interest in the Romantic movement, and especially in the conceptions of will and of genius that are central to it, springs partly from the recognition of their crucial impact on our shared sensibility. To make sense of an idea, one turns to logic and philology. To understand the sensibility of an idea, one turns to empathy, and hence to Berlin.

An intriguing case in point is provided by Berlin's new book, *The Magus of the North* (Farrar, Straus and Giroux), which is devoted to the thought of Georg Hamann, "a God-intoxicated" thinker. Hamann was a contemporary of Kant, and a fellow citizen of Konigsberg. Spiritually, there can be no doubt that Hamann is very distant from Berlin. Hamann's "sleepwalker's certainty," the mysterious, intuitive method of knowledge that is undisturbed by reality, is the complete opposite of Berlin's skepticism, which prizes a robust sense of reality. And yet Berlin understands Hamann so well that he seems to approve of him implicitly, almost.

In the New Testament, the Magi came from the East, led by the bright star of Bethlehem. Hamann, the self-appointed Magus, was led mostly by a pessimistic Paulinian shadow cast on human nature and human reason. According to Hamann, we do not believe for reasons any more than we taste for reasons or smell for reasons. Our heart beats, he says, before our head thinks. And Hamann is attentive to the beats of the heart, especially in religion and poetry. When the head thinks "enlightened" thoughts, such as the immanent, naturalistic idea that one and the same type of explanation holds good for men and minerals, Hamann believes that this head is sick.

The city of Berlin, the Enlightenment city of Lessing and Mendelssohn, was, for Hamann, Babylon. The key to understanding him as a thinker, he declared, was his hatred of Babylon; and the key used by Berlin (the man, not the city) to crack Hamann's enigmatic personality is his penetrating hatred of the Enlightenment. For Berlin, any person who, like Hamann, is nurtured equally by the Bible and by the non-believer Hume, deserves cracking. Hamann believed that language is an incarnation of God. I don't know about that; but a reader of *The Magus of the North* will see how ably Berlin has succeeded in fleshing out the life and the thought of Hamann from Hamann's own language, which is notoriously suggestive and obscure. Here are Berlin's conclusions about his subject, and they nicely capture his own voice as well:

Kant has rightly won the day, but Hamann and his followers express a continual revolt against taking so much blandly for granted, against leaving out so much, perhaps necessarily, but with too little regret, with no qualms, as if what the theory cannot embrace is mere expendable rubbish: psychological idiosyncrasy, oddities and quirks, which theory cannot notice and which in a rational universe will themselves be ironed out, so that the facts will only be such as the infallible theory fits. . . . His cry came from an outraged sensibility: he spoke as a man of feeling offended by a passion for a cerebral approach; as a moralist who understood that ethics is concerned with relations between real persons (under God as the ultimate ruler whose will they try to obey as his servants); as a man who was offended by the enunciation of principles that claimed a pseudo-scientific objectivity not derived from individual or social experience; as a German humiliated by an arrogant and, it seemed to him, spiritually blind West; as a humble member of a dying social order, trampled by the inhuman tempo of centralization in the political and cultural sphere. . . . He struck the first blow against the quantified world; his attack was often ill-judged, but he raised some of the greatest issues of our times by refusing to accept their advent.

The reader of this extraordinary book will come to feel that it is finally impossible to understand someone so different from oneself without to some extent identifying with him. And this suspicion about the negative capability of Isaiah Berlin increases when one recalls his affecting account of the dark figure of Joseph de Maistre, one of the founding fathers of fascism. This, at first, is troublesome. How is such empathy possible without some sympathy?

Berlin is liberal through and through, one of the most important liberal thinkers of our time, but he is a particular kind of liberal. He believes in the morality of liberalism, not in its psychology. The psychology of liberalism, which was inherited from the Enlightenment, strikes him as shallow. It is the Counter-Enlightenment (a term that Berlin coined), as it was represented by Hamann and de Maistre, that does more justice to the complexity of the human psyche. It was a shallow but influential assumption of the Enlightenment that all human beings are, in their nature, seekers of happiness, knowledge and justice, and that they are capable of objectively recognizing these ends. But Berlin is no worshiper of human nature. God may have created the animals, but man creates himself.

It is not only for a more compelling psychology that Berlin turns to the Counter-Enlightenment. He also finds in the darker thinkers an important warning about the limits of science. While he does not share Hamann's hostility toward science, he does share Hamann's aversion to scientism, that is, to the pretense that everything can be explained in accordance with the scientific model. Berlin has respect for science, and even for scientists; as the founder and first president of Wolfson College in Oxford, he recruited more scientists, proportionately, than had any of the ancient, illustrious Oxford colleges. But there is a great gulf between respecting science and accepting the ideology of scientism. Scientism hides from us the deep Kantian truth, that "out of timber as crooked as that from which man is made nothing entirely straight can be carved." Within the human sciences, people cannot be expected to be arranged into classifications and patterns governed by natural laws; and certainly they cannot be aligned within a social order built according to a master plan.

I have no doubt that if anyone were to approach Berlin in the ancient rabbinic way, with the request that he should teach all there is to know while standing on one foot, he would receive in reply Kant's adage about the crooked timber. The fact that it is impossible to "straighten" people is, for Berlin, a source of joy, not a source of gloom. He is happy about human diversity. And so he is skeptical about progress as the march of humanity toward a well-defined goal, and prefers what his contemporary Karl Popper described as piecemeal engineering, that is, mending and improving upon those areas of human activity in which we may be able to predict the outcome of our deeds. Such areas may include health, or education, or the Tennessee Valley project. Berlin was acquainted with, and impressed by, the New Deal and the New Dealers, and counted some of them, notably Felix Frankfurter, among his friends. For

Berlin, the America of the New Deal was America at its best; and he never shared the Oxonian suspicion of things American as vulgar.

Berlin's special sort of liberalism emerged from his recognition that not all values are commensurable. Not even in utopia can harmony reign among all values. Equality and freedom, for example, are bound to clash. Since no single form of life can give expression to all the values that we respect, it is important that forms of life different from our own flourish. Without diverse forms of life, we will all be poorer. Only a liberal society among all societies can do justice to diversity. In Herder's simile, later perverted by Mao, this is the garden in which the greatest number of flowers will bloom.

Among Berlin's many famous essays, his inaugural lecture at Oxford in 1958 on **"Two Concepts of Liberty"** is the most famous. In that remarkable discussion, he draws a contrast between negative liberty, which is your liberty from my interference in your actions, and positive liberty, which is your liberty to realize your "real interests." Positive liberty may become positively dangerous when negative liberty is denied in the name of "real interests," which are usually defined by others. This is not to say that Berlin is a libertarian. For libertarians, liberalism is based solely on negative liberty. For Berlin, negative liberty is only one justification for liberalism. Pluralism is the other. And liberty is a necessary condition of pluralism.

Two good things have happened to Berlin in recent years that saved him from becoming a figure of the past, a member merely of the generation that Noel Annan described in *Our Age*. The first was the collapse of the Soviet Union. This was bad news for the Sovietologists, who lost their subject, but for Berlin the fall of the Soviet Union has returned to center-stage the subjects that have always preoccupied him: nationalism, pluralism, liberalism, Russia.

Berlin likes to remark upon a curious historical fact. The "prophetic" thinkers of the nineteenth century predicted some important developments of our century: revolutions in the Third World (Bakunin), conformism in democratic societies (Tocqueville), the central role of the military- industrial complex (Burckhardt), the concentration of capital and the effect of technological innovations (Marx). Yet all of them believed that nationalism was on the wane. But Berlin, who shuns prophecy, has always assigned supreme importance to nationalism, and to the hold of nationalist feelings over people. He prefers to think of nationalism in Herder's terms, as cultural nationalism, which is based on the idea that one's humanity finds its best expression in one's particular culture.

In Berlin's world, there is room for different cultures, and there is no need for rivalry among them. Herderian nationalism is the embodiment of pluralism among nations. At the same time Berlin does not deny the realities of political nationalism, and the "bad" versions of it that are based on theories of superiority and hatred toward the other. Yet he insists that a worldview that does not heed the intensity of nationalist feelings, good or bad, is bound to be irrelevant. How to deal with nationalism is, for Berlin, the central question that liberals should be asking themselves these days.

The second good thing that happened to Berlin in recent years was the publication of his collected writings, some of which originally appeared in esoteric and inaccessible publications. The appearance of his writings in many volumes (edited by the industrious Henry Hardy) refuted the myth that he will leave just an oral legacy. Much of the written material was owed to invitations to write and to lecture ("I'm like a taxi driver: I go where I am summoned"), and yet it exhibits an impressive unity of style and purpose. Wittgenstein once said of the genius that "he has a particular kind of lens to concentrate light into a burning point"; and the collected Berlin changes his image from that of a concave lens, which spreads rays of light in all directions, to a convex one. The burning point, in Berlin's case, is the impossibility of harmonizing all human values.

Berlin has been a Zionist all his life. His father once explained the son's attraction to Zionism as an extension of the Hebrew lessons he received as a child, even after the family moved to England. Zionism is the national liberation movement of the Jewish people; and Berlin maintains that it was Zionism that in fact created the Jewish nation. In their two millennia of exile, the Jews lost the crucial features of a nation. They had neither a territory of their own nor a common spoken language, and—since the French Revolution—they even ceased to be a religious community in the traditional way. And yet, although there is no simple definition for the Jewish people, Berlin sees no difficulty in defining the Jews and in recognizing their right to a homeland and their need for freedom from the domination of others.

One drizzly day in Oxford I was walking with Berlin, when suddenly he stopped, waved his umbrella in the air, and asked: "What do you think is common to all Jews?" He continued to specify, in his customary way: "I mean, to the Jew from San'a, from Marrakech, from Riga, from Glasgow?" And right away he answered his own question: "A sense of social unease. Nowhere do almost all Jews feel entirely at home." Unlike Herder, Berlin tends to identify the need of belonging to a group with the urge to feel at home; and the absence of such a need results in the life of the stranger. "But you yourself are a counter-example," I said. "Surely you feel at home in England." "Yes and no," was his reply. "I am a devoted Anglophile, not an Englishman."

In one important sense, Zionism has been, for Berlin, a success story. It succeeded in giving the Jewish inhabitants of Israel a home, and a sense of home. For Berlin, the Jewish people are an extended family, not a spiritual community dedicated to Judaism. His feeling of solidarity with his fellow Jews is basic, spontaneous and unapologetic. It is a family tie. As in a family, there are black sheep, whom Berlin is good at spotting, and there are always embarrassing and irritating relatives. The concern for the family, however, is first and foremost a concern for the welfare of its members, for preventing the suffering and the persecution that have been their lot for so long just because of their Jewishness. Berlin believes that there is truth in the historian Lewis Namier's dubious remark that "there is no modern Jewish history, only a Jewish martyrology." But Berlin is no romantic of suffering, and he sees no glory in martyrdom.

Berlin is not a religious man, and he shows no trace especially of the religious feeling that the Jews are the chosen people. More interesting, he betrays no secular version of this sentiment. But he does feel strongly that the Jews are an old, interesting and somewhat neurotic family, and he has no patience for Jews who are estranged from their people. In private conversations he is quite fond of unmasking Jews who deny their identity. For him, even Lenin's maternal grandfather falls under faint suspicion.

Berlin's own family is old and intriguing. He is a direct descendant of Shneor Zalman of Liadi, the founder of the Hasidic dynasty of Lubavitch at the time of the Napoleonic wars. He is the second cousin of the late Lubavitcher Rebbe Menachem Schneerson, the one whose followers in Brooklyn and elsewhere declared him to be the Messiah. (Yehudi Menuhin belongs to another branch of the same family tree.) His wife Aline, too, has an old and no less fascinating pedigree. She was born into the family of the Barons de Ginsbourg, who distinguished themselves for three generations, up until the Russian Revolution, as grand bankers in Russia and in Paris, and were prominent in Jewish diplomacy during the pogroms against the Jews in the days of the Czars; they were also among the most pre-eminent philanthropic families in the modern history of the Jews.

One of Berlin's earliest childhood memories is the wedding of his aunt to Isaac Landoberg. Isaac Landoberg later became Yitzhak Sadeh, who is a legend in Israel. Like Garibaldi, who founded the Red Shirts, Sadeh founded the Palmach, the striking forces of the Haganah, the main Jewish underground organization in Palestine and the forerunner of the Israeli Defense Forces. These units eventually played a decisive role in Israel's War of Independence in 1948. Sadeh was not only a general, but also a writer and an essayist. In his early days in Russia, however, he was a boxer, a wrestler and an avid footballer, as well as a painters' model and an art dealer: a pagan, in sum. During the Russian Revolution he came to Petrograd, as a Social Revolutionary officer, to visit the Berlins. Berlin's mother was so terrified of his huge Mauser pistol that she took it from him and put it away in a bowl of cold water, lest it explode. Eventually Sadeh managed to switch sides in the revolution, and served with the White Army; but he ended his life, in Israel as a pro-Soviet romantic socialist. In Berlin's eyes, he remained an enchanting adventurer.

On one of Berlin's visits to Palestine, in late 1947, he met Sadeh again. Those were the last days of the British Man-

date rule in Palestine, days of rampant terror. Sadeh, who was on the British authorities' wanted list, met Berlin at the back of a Tel Aviv cafe. That visit in Palestine, just like the early memories from the streets of Petrograd, bred in Berlin a profound aversion to terror. Berlin is not a pacifist (he was opposed to the Munich agreement, which was popular in Britain at the time), but he detested the methods of Begin's and Shamir's underground, and his attitude did not change when they became prime ministers of Israel.

But it was also that visit to Palestine which strengthened his emotional ties to Sadeh. A strong family feeling is, for Berlin, one of the "primary colors" of human emotion. And Berlin has a deep interest in human emotion, despite the fact that by far the greatest part of his adult life was spent at Oxford, where the the most popular emotion seems to be embarrassment, or the need to avoid it. I do not mean to exaggerate Berlin's "Russian soul." He is a calm and subtle and rational man, who is nourished by much more than the primary colors. And yet the intensity of his intellectual interest in human feeling is remarkable. And so it is no wonder that he has translated Turgenev's *First Love,* which he believes contains the most perfect description of falling in love for the first time, and also Turgenev's play *A Month in the Country,* which deals with the same theme. (The play was produced in Berlin's translation in London in 1981.)

But it is to opera, above all, that Berlin turns for the strongest and purest of the human emotions; and he finds them in Verdi, not in Wagner. One glance at him, returning from the beach to his home atop the hill above Paraggi, near Portofino, walking the steep climb like a teenager with the Walkman adorning his head, and accompanying the music with a conductor's wave of the finger or an occasional humming of a tune, will convince anyone that this is an opera junkie who requires his shot in the ears in ever-increasing daily doses. In a revealing remark, he once confessed that it was his friendship with the pianist Alfred Brendel that opened his eyes to the dimension of tragedy in the music of the Romantics. Berlin is not blind to the tragic, but it does not come naturally to him.

"All my life I have been greatly overestimated," I have often heard him say. And then, "I am all for it. Long may it last." I am convinced, however, that as a philosopher Berlin has been underestimated. True, his contributions to political philosophy and to the history of ideas have won much admiration, but not so his contribution to general philosophy, and especially to the important current in twentieth-century thought known as analytic philosophy.

Analytic philosophy is based on the notion that many traditional philosophical problems can be solved, or rather dissolved, by means of linguistic analysis, which will expose the illusory nature of the problems themselves. There were two main directions in analytical philosophy. One was that of the logical positivists of Vienna, who dealt with constructed or artificial languages, that is, with mathematics, logic and the language of science. The other maintained that philosophy should turn its attention to natural languages, the languages that are used by ordinary people, since it is within those languages that philosophical problems arise. The center of "ordinary language philosophy" in the postwar years was Oxford, and the person whose name is most identified with this trend in Oxford was the charismatic J. L. Austin, Berlin's colleague and friend at All Souls College.

What goes generally unacknowledged is Berlin's own contribution to the formation of this influential current in twentieth-century philosophy. It was in his rooms at All Souls during the '30s that the group of "founding fathers" would meet. The business on the table there, as well as in similar rooms in Vienna and Cambridge (where Wittgenstein and his disciples toiled) was the discovery of a criterion that can distinguish among significant sentences, such as scientific ones, and meaningless sentences, such as metaphysical and theological ones. And the proposal under examination was known as the "verification principle," or the idea that a sentence is meaningful only if it can, in principle, be verified.

Does it make sense to say that my toothache is more painful than yours? And, if it does make sense, are we to infer that I ascribe a mind to you, the states of which I can directly verify? With this question at the center of his paper, Berlin entered the lion's—that is, Wittgenstein's—den in Cambridge. By the time it was over, Wittgenstein had subjected him to an hour and a half of fierce cross-examination, with all the others mute and dumb. He then strode toward Berlin, shook his hand, thanked him for the lecture and pronounced that they had a good discussion. Like Daniel, Berlin left the lair unscathed. The master had approved.

But Berlin was soon disenchanted with the linguistic turn in philosophy. In one of his essays he refers to Tolstoy's pedagogical tour in Germany, to his report of one incident in particular, in which the teacher showed his pupils a progressive textbook with pictures of fish and asked them what they see. "A fish," responded the brightest boy. "No," said the teacher, and proceeded relentlessly to torture the class until finally he extracted the intended answer, which was that they saw not a fish but a picture that represents a fish. For Tolstoy, this was a farcical sort of pedantry, and it is not hard to sense Berlin's identification with Tolstoy's disapprobation. The linguistic turn in philosophy was based precisely on the distinction that the teacher tried so to extract from his pupils, the distinction between an object and its representation. To Berlin, this has always seemed a little fishy.

I suspect that Berlin, so happily attached to the real world, was always ambivalent toward the concerns of philosophy proper. I can see him writing what Hamann wrote to Kant (he quotes this in **The Magus of the North**): "I look on the best demonstration in philosophy as the sensible girl looks on a love letter," that is, with both pleasure and sus-

picion. It was perhaps this ambivalence that masked Berlin's significant role in the analytical philosophy of his time. But finally he abandoned it, for the views and the personalities of the great Russian intellectuals—Herzen, Turgenev, Bakunin, Belinsky, Nekrasov. They had an enormous impact on him. His study of them has dominated his life even more, perhaps, than music.

Berlin has, curiously, very few enemies. For many years he has held powerful academic positions, yet people love to love him. When the Frankfurter Allgemeine Zeitung sent him its well-known questionnaire, his answer to the question "What are your faults?" was "I am too anxious to please." (His answer to the question "Who would you like to have been?" was "Alexander Herzen.") In an essay on slavery and the emancipation of the Jews, Berlin ascribes the tendency toward ingratiation to Jews newly out of the ghetto. Being eager to please, however, does not make one universally liked; and so the explanation for the universal admiration of Berlin must be sought elsewhere.

It is not far to seek. Berlin is so beloved because he is slow to judge, and so forgiving of faults and foibles, so utterly lacking in malice. Many who have met him, even briefly, have felt an instant familiarity. Once, at a dinner in Paris, Berlin was seated next to Lauren Bacall. She asked him where he lived. "Oxford," he said. "Then perhaps," she asked, "you know my Oxford friend Isaiah Berlin?" "I am he," he replied. She was not the only one who, upon meeting this unforgettable man, felt instinctively and immediately close.

P. N. Furbank (essay date 1997)

SOURCE: "On Pluralism," in *Raritan: A Quarterly Review,* Vol. 17, No. 1, Summer, 1997, pp. 83-95.

[*In the following critique, Furbank argues that Berlin's concept of pluralism is politically invalid.*]

We have heard a great deal about "pluralism" in the last decade or two, and it would be easy to gain the impression that pluralism was not only an ethical concept but a political one—that, politically speaking, it has something of value to add to democracy and is, indeed, a rival to it. I want to argue that this is a fallacy.

Of course, it is not instantly clear what people mean by *pluralism.* Isaiah Berlin, who claims Herder to have been in a sense the inventor of pluralism as a doctrine, defines it as

> the belief not merely in the multiplicity, but in the incommensurability, of the values of different cultures and societies and, in addition, in the incompatibility of equally valid ideals, together with the implied revolutionary corollary that the classical notions of an ideal man and of an ideal society are intrinsically incoherent and meaningless.

Let us begin with a very general question. What are we to think of that phrase, "the incompatibility of equally valid ideals"? Here Berlin is speaking not so much of different cultures or societies as of humankind in general, and it is of course true that some human ideals may very well be incompatible. Chastity and free love, or honor-seeking and Christian humility are, as ideals, not compatible with each other. But this is not what he has in mind, for chastity and free love, and honor-seeking and Christian humility, are directly related to each other as opposites. What he is envisaging, rather, is *unrelated* ideals or values; and one asks oneself in what sense can ideals be unrelated (have no intrinsic relevance to one another) yet at the same time be incompatible?

At all events what is being ignored here is an altogether familiar part of our experience—the occasions when ideals or values, *our own* ideals or values, come into conflict. Suppose that somebody regards truthfulness as an ideal, and also loving-kindness. It is not difficult to imagine a situation in which he or she finds the claims of truthfulness (or brutal candor) at war with those of personal kindness. It is the sort of painful dilemma we are finding ourselves in all the time. I have selected a conflict from everyday life, though of course there are rarer and more tragic ones, like those that faced Huckleberry Finn and Antigone.

Faced with such a problem, what does one do? Knowing that one must make a choice, we refer the choice to instinct—or rather, to spontaneous feeling. That is to say, we present the issue, and all the likely consequences of choosing one way or the other, to our imagination, with all the honesty that we possibly can (this is where the discipline of ethics comes in); and having done this, we wait and see what our heart tells us to do. There is nothing in the least irrational in this process (i.e., in asking oneself "What do I really feel?" "Which set of values means most to me here?" and acting in accordance with the answer). Nor is there any dereliction of moral principle, for morality comes in, in the manner in which one considers alternatives and chooses. When Huck Finn faced his famous choice, he will have told himself, in thoroughly Kantian fashion, to face it *honestly*—not to let any selfish motive blur the way he presented it to himself.

The thing to get hold is that conflicts between values of this kind are not some sort of freakish anomaly, but are the main stuff of our moral life. It is easy to regard oneself as subscribing, in principle, to this and to that moral value; the hard thinking and serious heart-searching come precisely when we find two of these values in conflict. But the fact that these values of ours—"equally valid" values, to use Berlin's words—sometimes come into conflict does not mean that they are incompatible. For most of the time they live peacefully side by side with one another, and that is all that can be asked of them; that is all that *compatibility* in this case can be supposed to mean.

This is indeed the conclusion some philosophers come to. Bernard Williams, for instance, broadly takes this standpoint, and so does Thomas Nagel. "It is my view," writes Williams in *Moral Luck,* "that value-conflict is not necessarily pathological at all, but something necessarily involved in human values, and to be taken as central by an adequate understanding of them." Nagel comes to much the same conclusion in *Mortal Questions.* He holds, very sensibly, that it is an illusion to suppose that all values represent, or can be reduced to, some single ultimate "good." Human beings, as he says, "are complex creatures who can view the world from many perspectives—individual, relational, impersonal, ideal, etc.—and each perspective presents a different sort of claim."

All the same—and this is what is puzzling—both Williams and Nagel treat the matter as philosophically disturbing. Williams goes along with Isaiah Berlin's epithet "incommensurable." He holds that, despite various qualifications, there is still "something true and important" in the view that the gains and losses in values entailed in social progress are incommensurable, there being no "common currency" in which they can be computed; that "values, or at least the most basic values, are not only plural but in a real sense incommensurable." But this is odd, for as he himself makes clear, if you spell out the possible senses in which values could be said to be commensurable, you see at once how fallacious, indeed absurd, they all are. The truth of the matter is plain, according to Williams:

1. There is no one currency in terms of which each conflict of values can be resolved.

2. It is not true that for each conflict of values, there is some value, independent of any of the conflicting values, which can be appealed to in order to resolve that conflict.

3. It is not true that for each conflict of values, there is some value which can be appealed to (independent or not) in order rationally to resolve that conflict.

From which it might be simpler to conclude that what we have here is no deep philosophical impasse, but rather that the idea of values being commensurable or incommensurable simply makes no sense.

That there is some kind of muddle here comes out even more vividly in Alasdair MacIntyre's *After Virtue* of 1981. MacIntyre, as is well known, puts forward a sort of "World We Have Lost" theory of ethics and politics, turning on the notion that "we" have more or less completely lost any understanding of morality. As, after some gigantic natural catastrophe, people might try to reassemble the disordered fragments of earlier scientific knowledge, uncomprehendingly lumping together phlogiston theory with Einsteinian relativity, so in the twentieth century (according to MacIntyre) we continue to use ethical terms but have lost all grasp of the conceptual scheme that gave them their significance. This scheme he identifies, loosely, with Aristotle's theory of the Virtues—one according to which, says MacIntyre, the concept of "the good life for man" comes before the concept of a virtue. The "good life" is essentially social, it is a "practice with goods internal to itself," involving a notion of the "narrative unity" of a human being's life, and the virtues are those "dispositions" which sustain this practice and the quest for the good. By contrast with this coherently ordered system, he says, in the present age incoherence reigns and "pluralism threatens to submerge us all." Moral debate in the present day is characteristically interminable, and it could scarcely be otherwise, since the arguments used in it suffer from "conceptual incommensurability." Indeed the process of moral debate today is only a masquerade, for underlying it is the view that there are, and can be, no "unassailable criteria" for resolving moral issues. "Emotivism"—that is to say the doctrine that all evaluative judgments are merely expressions of personal preference—has won the day.

There is a lot to be said about MacIntyre's theory (mostly against it), but one point comes out very neatly from what he says about Aristotle. For, following in the steps of Plato, Aristotle holds that the virtues are unified and inseparable, flourishing side by side harmoniously and without conflict in the character of the good man. Now, as MacIntyre himself points out, Aristotle is pitching things rather strongly here; for he had only to think of the *Antigone* and the *Philoctetes* of Sophocles to remember that there might be tragic, and in a sense irresolvable, conflicts of values. But of course these tragic conflicts are by no means the only ones needing mention. The virtues on which Aristotle perhaps lays most emphasis of all are Justice and Friendship; and what could be more obvious— more familiar to everyone's experience in whatever society, including ancient Greek citystates—than that the claims of justice are sometimes going to clash painfully with the claims of friendship? According to Plutarch's Life of Aristides, a difference over this with his rival Themistocles was a dominating factor in the early part of Aristides' career.

> Themistocles, joining an association of partisans, fortified himself with considerable strength; insomuch that when some one told him that were he impartial he would make a good magistrate; "I wish," replied he, "I may never sit on that tribunal where my friends shall not plead a greater privilege than strangers." But Aristides walked, so to say, alone on his own path in politics, being unwilling, in the first place, to go along with his associates in illdoing, or to cause them vexation by not gratifying their wishes; and, secondly, observing that many were encouraged by the support they had in their friends to act injuriously, he was cautious; being of opinion that the integrity of his words and actions was the only right security for a good citizen.

Reading Plutarch after MacIntyre gives one the feeling of rejoining the real world; and it brings home to us that what we are learning here from Aristotle is not something about ethics and the nature of the good life but about the folly of taking political philosophers literally. (For the fact that Justice and Friendship are sometimes going to come into conflict can hardly have escaped Aristotle.) The function of political philosophy, it serves to remind us, is essentially devious, amounting in many cases—for instance Hobbes, not to mention Leo Strauss and Michael Oake-

shott—to what you might call licensed farce. (It would be a naive reader who supposed Hobbes actually believed, or expected anyone else literally to believe, that nothing a sovereign or a master may do can ever be called injustice. This is a notion belonging to the realm of *fantastic* logic, which is where it gets its force.) Meanwhile, it would seem as if this business of the "conflict of values" might be a false problem—a false problem *philosophically,* though an intensely serious one humanly.

But let us now consider Isaiah Berlin's definition of pluralism, not in relation to ethics in general, but as a political concept, and in regard to what it says about diversity of cultures. Here too one or two things seem not to be good logic. For one thing, what does it mean to speak of the values of different cultures as being "incommensurable"? That is to say, what else could they be? What would it mean, even in theory, for a value to be measured? It must mean, if anything, measuring it against some other value, and this would lead to an infinite regression. (Perhaps, like Nietzsche, one might aspire to "transvalue all values," but that is a different matter.)

The problem comes out more clearly in another passage in the same book of Berlin's, **Vico and Herder**:

> What he [Herder] rejects is the single overarching standard of values, in terms of which all cultures, characters, and acts can be evaluated. Each phenomenon to be investigated presents its own measuring rod, its own internal constellation of values in the light of which alone "the facts" can be truly understood.

Berlin is touching here on a favorite theme of his, that Western thought, up to a very late era, has been dominated by the theory (on the part of thinkers of all brands) that there is single ideal way of life, dedicated to a single supreme value, in which all other values are subsumed. Herder, according to Berlin, was perhaps the first clearly to realize that values might be irredeemably diverse and the quest for the one right way of life or ideal society was intrinsically absurd.

There is, one feels, something not quite right in this account. Perry Anderson put it very well in a review of Berlin's **The Crooked Timber of Humanity.**

> Can Ancient, or Medieval, or Early Modern society really have been so ideologically monolithic that the possibility of alternative conceptions of a good life was never seriously entertained? At the very outset of his story, Berlin seems to have mislaid Mount Olympus. What was Classical polytheism but the personification of many and contrary values?

What Berlin is actually saying, one feels, is rather less than it claims. As regards cultures, all it really amounts to is that each culture or society has to be understood in its own terms and in the light of its own values. That is to say, it is a statement about *understanding,* not about evaluation. No meaning can be attached to the idea of measuring (i.e., evaluating) a culture by its own standard of measurement; for a measuring rod, it needs hardly be said, cannot be measured by itself. Measurement, and hence incommensurability, do not come into the matter, and the doctrine being attributed to Herder is simple cultural relativism—the view that, though one may try to understand and empathize with a culture not one's own, one must not presume to judge it.

This is, moreover, not an absurd doctrine and is one sometimes proclaimed by anthropologists. But, after reading Lévi-Strauss's great chapter "Un Petit Verre du rhum" in *Tristes Tropiques,* one is likely to regard it as a pious fiction, and an unnecessary one. Lévi-Strauss's answer to the "relativist" is very helpful to us, and it deserves to be set out at some length.

He asks: is not the ethnographer in a hopeless dilemma? He has his own society to observe. So why does he devote to *other* societies the patience and devotion he owes to this one? The answer is that very few ethnographers have a neutral attitude towards their subject. If they are empire builders or missionaries, they are committed to propagating a colonial system. If they are scientists or academics, then the odds are that (for whatever reason) they are misfits in their own society. Thus the value they attach to exotic cultures rests on false foundations, being merely a function of their dislike for their own culture. Subversive among his own people, the ethnographer grows intensely protective and conservative towards an alien culture, simply because it *is* alien. Thus his critics would seem to have an unanswerable case: in finding reasons for preferring an alien culture, is he not in fact appealing to the values of his own culture, and thus indirectly affirming its superiority over all others? It seems as though, to have any claim to be a scientist, he needs to renounce value-judgments of any kind and admit that, among the possibilities open to humankind, each society makes its own choice, and these choices are simply not to be compared one with another.

But then, does this mean that the ethnographer must pass no criticism on cruelty, injustice, and deprivation, just because they occur in another society, and even though members of that society protest against them themselves? How can this square with fighting such things in his own country? The problem looks insurmountable; and if it were so, the ethnographer's choice would be clear.

> He is an ethnographer, he has chosen to be one; he must accept the mutilation that this entails. He has chosen in favor of "others" and must suffer the consequences. His role will be merely to understand these others—being precluded from acting in their name, since the very fact that they *are* others prevents him from thinking or desiring in their place and thereby identifying with them. Further, he must renounce action even as regards his own society, for fear of adopting prejudices in regards to values that he may also meet with other societies.

But fortunately, says Lévi-Strauss, the dilemma is not really so complete, and there is a way out, by means of a two-stage process of reasoning. First, it is to be remem-

bered that no society is perfect, even in its own eyes: every society contains by its nature an "impurity" in regard to its own proclaimed norms, an injustice, insensibility, or cruelty according to those norms. Now this is where the ethnographer has something valuable to offer. For when only a few societies are compared together they appear extremely different, but on comparing a large number, as an ethnographer does, one finds that no society is without certain advantages for its members, and also that the dose of "impurity" or "iniquity" in societies tends to be fairly constant. (Perhaps it represents a "specific inertia" resisting all efforts at social organization.)

Extended comparison between societies can thus teach moderation and good faith. It is a school for correcting, for instance, a prejudice such as Western societies nurse against cannibalism. To an observer from a different society the opposite practice, of "vomiting" enemies of society into prisons and the like, might seem equally strange and horrific.

There are indeed those, says Lévi-Strauss, who count it the great glory of Western civilization that it, and it alone, has produced ethnographers, but this is a flattering delusion. The truth, more probably, is that it has done so because of the weight of its own guilt (in particular for its treatment of the New World). It produces ethnographers out of a compulsion to reassure itself that other cultures share some of the same ills, and in the hope of finding some explanation for its own. The ethnographer is a symbol of expiation. On the other hand we should not, out of self-condemnation, allow ourselves to glorify some other culture, whether past or present. That would be the worst dishonesty; for it would be to forget that, if we belonged to that culture, we would find it as intolerable as our own and critize it for much the same reasons.

Men, says Lévi-Strauss, are born social (the "natural man" being an unnecessary fiction); and all humankind has the same task, to find the formula of a livable society. Other societies are not better than ours, and even if we thought they were we would have no way of proving it; but getting to know other societies is a way of detaching ourselves mentally from our own, thus putting ourselves in a position to take the "second step." This consists of using other societies to help in identifying the principles of social existence, in order to apply them to reforming our own. For it is only our own society we can change without risking its destruction, the changes that we are introducing coming, in this case, from within it.

As will be seen, far from affirming the incomparability of cultures, à la Herder or Isaiah Berlin, Levi-Strauss attaches the highest importance to comparing them and to discerning in them various likenesses across a difference. His analysis of the ethnographer's dilemma is, moreover, a magnificent example of what I have called one of the rules of humanism: that one should always be asking about what—given one's particular situation vis-a-vis other humans—one has the right, or does not have the right, to say.

Isaiah Berlin represents Herder as holding that human beings only flourish "when the individual is happily integrated into the 'natural community,' which grows spontaneously, like a plant, and is not held together by artificial
clamps, or soldered together by sheer force, or regulated
by laws and regulations invented, whether benevolently or
not, by the despot or his bureaucrats." Each of these "natural societies," in the words of Herder's *Yet Another Philosophy of History,* contains within itself the "ideal of its
own perfection, wholly independent of all comparison
with those of others."

Here there seems to be involved a further and quite different fallacy: a false idea of the relation of political theory
to actual societies. For it is not the case, historically, that
societies have organized themselves according to (in Herder's phrase) the "ideal of their own perfection," or as Aristotle would put it, "for some good purpose." "Societies,"
in the large sense of the word (as opposed, I mean, to
things like the Kipling Society, or what Michael Oakeshott
liked to call "enterprise associations") are not created for a
purpose at all. They come into being through a variety of
possible causes, both short-term and long-term—migra-
tion, plague, famine, religious rivalry, military defeat, or
the disintegration of empires. It is not as though someone
one day thought up feudalism as the blueprint for an ideal
society. It would only be otherwise, and societies would
be purpose-built affairs, dedicated to some supreme value,
if the founders and first members of new societies had not
been living in society up to that moment. But on the contrary, the founder-members of even the most abstractly
conceived societies—shall we say the United States, or
Soviet Russia—were burdened with a huge baggage of
memories, customs, and ancient habits of thought. They
arrived on the scene, like Aeneas, with their household
gods in their arms. There are, and can be, no truly fresh
beginnings in human history. From which it follows that in
any society a great many different values or ideals, expressive of ancient experience, will be active. (Things are different, of course, with a utopia. For a utopia is a blueprint
designed for human beings who are assumed to have no
past.) That certain of these values may be taken up and
glorified by the powers-that-be, and others hounded down
with persecuting ferocity, or that some societies are infinitely less tolerant than others, is an all-important matter,
but a different one.

Herder's view, moreover, makes us ask ourselves what
sense, if any, it makes to speak of a "plural," or "pluralist"
society? The phrase would presumably denote a society in
which diverse religions, adherences, languages, or sets of
customs (perhaps even diverse romantic national
aspirations) were able to flourish side by side in amity;
and one thing is clear, the last place you would look for
such a thing is one of Herder's "natural societies," the
kind that grow "spontaneously like a plant" and are dedicated to "the ideal of their own perfection." They are, by
definition, just the sort of society that will bitterly resent
such disagreement within its midst. To have a plural society you will require "artificial clamps" and very tough

rules, no doubt drawn up by bureaucrats—the very things
that Herder is represented as abhorring. Indeed one might
go further. One tends to associate the concept of pluralism
with liberal thinkers, but it could be argued that it is only
likely to flourish under despotism. For it may be supposed
that, under a regime like that of the Ottoman Turks, so
long as a subject kept the peace and paid his taxes, it
would be a matter of perfect indifference to his rulers what
he believed, or how he worshipped, or what language he
spoke. Moreover the subject would pay his rulers the same
compliment. Ernest Gellner has a nice fantasy of a "typical burgher" in an agrarian society, hearing that the local
Pasha had been overthrown and wondering anxiously
whether his successor will be more, or less, grasping and
corrupt, more, or less, just and merciful: "If, at that point,
his wife dared ask the burgher what language the new Pasha spoke in the intimacy of his home life—was it Arabic,
Turkish, Persian, French or English?—the hapless burgher
would give her a sharp look, and wonder how he would
cope with all his difficulties when, at the same time, his
wife had gone quite mad." A culturally plural society presents little difficulty, assuming that its members do not expect to play any part in politics; and even in the epoch of
industrialization and nationalism the point to some degree
still holds. Some would say that the Austro-Hungarian empire found a very successful way of handling cultural diversity. The anthropologist Malinowski once wrote: "I
should like to put it on record that no honest and sincere
Pole would ever have given anything but praise to the political regime of the old Dual Monarchy. Prewar Austria in
its federal constitution presented, in my opinion, a sound
solution to all minority problems. It was a model of a miniature League of Nations."

Finally, Berlin's essay on Herder raises a further and even
more general puzzle. According to him, Herder holds that,
though cultures are incommensurable, each culture "is
what it is, of literally inestimable value in its own society,
and consequently to humanity as a whole"; and further,
Herder preaches ("no less than his opponent Kant") that
"only persons and societies, and almost all of these, are
good in themselves—indeed they are all that is good,
wholly good, in the world that we know." But why, one
asks, are we to think that almost all societies are good in
themselves? For whom, apart from God, can a society be
said to be good? Whom is it imagined as pleasing or ben-
efiting: presumably not another society? Perhaps "Humanity as a whole?" But what is this fabulous Leviathan, "Humanity as a whole"? What do we know about it or what it
feels? What organs does it possess for receiving pleasure
or benefit?

The truth seems to be that this is looking for "Humanity"
in the wrong place. Its real home is in the individual and
the single exemplar of the human species: the human being whose passion, to use D. H. Lawrence's words, is "to
be within himself the whole of mankind." Here it does
make sense to speak of "good" and "goodness"; for goodness concerns individuals only.

From which it follows that pluralism is not really a political concept at all, nor is a "plural society" a meaningful phrase. "Pluralism" is simply the name for the thing that Herder and Isaiah Berlin so admirably do as individuals: that is to say, projecting themselves into alien ways of thought and feeling and holding conflicting values in tension in their mind.

Of course, I suppose it could be argued that a society was good exactly to the extent that it encouraged its citizens to emulate Berlin and Herder and perform such acts of pluralistic imagining. But then, by this criterion, there would be nothing much to choose from between a liberal democracy, such as that within which Berlin has flourished, and a benevolent despotism of the kind that produced Herder. As a *political* concept, pluralism seems to lead to some awkward conclusions, and it had better be given up.

Simon Upton (essay date 1997)

SOURCE: "Isaiah Berlin as Anti-Rationalist," in *Philosophy and Literature*, Vol. 21, No. 2, October, 1997, pp. 126-32.

[*In the following essay, Upton examines John Gray's challenges to Berlin's liberalism.*]

For over half a century Sir Isaiah Berlin has been a towering figure in the literature of political philosophy and the history of ideas. He has repeatedly distilled the essence of key subjects of political discourse. Through his exploration of intellectual currents that run, frequently, beyond the insularity of the English speaking world, he has provided new insights into debates that go to the heart of how Western civilization understands the relationship between its citizens and its institutions. For readers of this journal, his identification of the cultural roots of political and social identity will be familiar.

Yet he stands somehow to one side of the debates that have consumed academia for over half of the twentieth century. I went through the index pages, references and bibliographies in a range of tomes that have accumulated on my shelves over the last ten years. Some celebrated essays are, justly, touchstones. But overwhelmingly, references to Berlin are scarce and, when they are present, tangential. The preoccupations of academic political philosophers have been elsewhere. The heat of debate has focused on all sorts of rationalistic enterprises that seek uniquely foundational premises for our political arrangements. Hence the ubiquitousness of a theorist like Rawls. Theories of justice, community and rights abound. Berlin's limpid prose seems somehow detached from this cerebral frenzy. John Gray's thesis is that beneath this detachment from the fray lies a subversiveness that is truly yawning; that while the pyrotechnics of neo-Lockean or Hobbesian scholars may seem to set up clamorous disputes, they are all of a piece when set against the conclusions Gray seeks

to draw from the totality of Berlin's writings. Gray's particular quarry is Berlin's ethical thinking. Here lies a value pluralism that is subversive of reason's ameliorating and harmonizing powers—of perfectionism, in short. Ethical reasoning takes place within a sphere of incommensurable and radical choices. There *is* no alchemy of rational choice that can dispel irresolvable moral conflict. As Gray puts it, "We have no reason to abandon the richness and depth of moral life, with all its undecidable dilemmas, for the empty vistas of moral theory."

This approach, Gray insists, is ultimately subversive of philosophy itself since the richness and depth of moral life will be encountered not in the quietude of academic reflection but in the world at large. While admitting to unresolved tensions in Berlin's writing, Gray is pleased to discern in his subject a conception of philosophical inquiry that is a meditation on empirical, cultural and historical anthropology rather than an abstract Kantian enterprise that starts from a conception of human agency that can be described prior to an investigation of its cultural or historical context.

This naturalism, this determination to stay in touch with lived experience, is a vein that Gray mines in many of Berlin's studies of the Counter-Enlightenment—in particular his writings on Hamann and Herder. The human condition is not described by radically situated individuals or the products of saturated communitarianism. Rather, reasoning beings are embedded within shared forms of cultural life. History, the business of describing the course of human agency, thus becomes a process of imaginative empathy and reconstruction; human society is conceived in organic rather than constructivist terms. And in language, custom, mores, and institutions, we encounter irrefutable evidence of the plurality—and particularity—of human affections.

The lens through which Gray then approaches Berlin's political philosophy is one that keeps in view the tension between seeking to render the world of human agency and social interaction rationally intelligible while accepting as unavoidable the particularistic allegiances that are grounded in a plurality of cultural and historical settings. On the one hand, there is the weight of the Enlightenment seeking political institutions that reflect a rational and moral unity of mankind; on the other, the romantic assertion that political commitment is ultimately a (groundless) act of will by agents whose radical choices are taken within local and particular institutions shaped in turn by organic, cultural forms. Depending on how you weigh these competing elements in his writing, Berlin can be read as providing more, or perhaps less, comfort for the familiar foundational claims for liberal political philosophy.

Gray's assessment is firmly on the pessimistic side of this argument. Berlin's value pluralism, he maintains, is not just subversive of an authoritarian imposition of the Good, but any account of the Right as well. A liberalism that is founded in a conception of rational choice will founder as surely as utilitarianism must in the face of value pluralism. This applies even to freedom itself: the incommensurable and conflicting nature of liberty at stake in the real world means that radical choices between them must be made and these choices will appeal to controversial conceptions of the Good. Faced with the hard question of whether the fact of value pluralism must support the primacy of freedom of choice (and hence liberal institutions), Gray concludes that Berlin's answer, though not unequivocal, is to be construed in the negative. And even if Berlin is equivocal, Gray certainly is not. He addresses three arguments, each a counter-argument to the notion that pluralism supports liberalism.

First there is the claim that a denial of freedom involves a denial of the objective reality of value pluralism in this world. In other words, liberal institutions best express the unavoidably pluralistic nature of values. Gray's counter is that illiberal regimes only deny value pluralism if they assert the *universal* worth of the way of life they promote: provided their advocacy is particularist and local, they actually endorse the plurality of worthwhile forms of life.

The second argument replies to the claim that if the rational incomparability of goods and evils is true, there can never be good reasons to impose any particular ranking of values. This, Gray claims, is to ascribe to freedom of choice a pre-eminence that is inconsistent with value pluralism to the point, even, of creating a philosophy of Right. There may be valuable forms of life that would be undone by the exercise of free choice. To insist on it is to deny people an illiberal form of life that may be otherwise valuable.

Finally, Gray tackles the claim that negative liberty (secured through liberal institutions) has value because it facilitates a crucial human function: the making of choices among goods (and evils) that are rationally incomparable. Liberalism, on this argument, is supportive of something that is constitutive of what it is to be human. Gray's answer to this claim is similar to the preceding justification: there may be good reason to impose a particular ranking on the competing values people are faced with, he says, if the result is to preserve a worthwhile way of life that would otherwise be undermined by leaving choices in the hands of citizens. As long as an illiberal regime eschews the hubris of claiming that its ranking is uniquely rational or even better than any other known ranking, it "may coherently justify to its subjects the restraints on negative freedom it imposes on them, not by reasoning—illicitly, from a value-pluralist standpoint—from the unique rationality of the pattern of incommensurable goods it thereby secures, but instead from the worth of the particular way of life that is thereby protected."

To which I find myself protesting (to the first two arguments in turn), what about the individual? What comfort is it to the individual to learn that the illiberal regime which constrained him is only particularist in its claims? Isn't it for the individual to decide whether or not a form of life

that must limit political freedom for its survival is worthwhile? And to the third argument, what about the human condition? Is it coherent to advance a form of life that cuts radically across what it means to be human?

Gray is careful not to deny that there can be good reasons to support a liberal order. Conflicting values demand reasonable trade-offs and those may prefer liberal conclusions. Rather, it is the argument that value pluralism *entails* liberalism that is found wanting—"liberal values can have no claim on reason that cannot be contested, or overturned, by the claims of goods that are embedded in nonliberal ways of life." Which leaves us adrift without definitive ethical foundations for our political institutions. What sort of a liberal regime would be justifiable? What curtailment of freedoms would be justifiable—and on what sort of franchise—to support a "worthwhile" illiberal state? Is Singapore comfortably within the pale of reasonable trade-offs? One is tempted to speculate that it all depends on whether or not you are an agonistic liberal viewing Singaporean democracy from afar or an opposition politician seeking a slightly more "liberal" form of life. Is Iran definitely beyond the pale? Does the possibility of exile or exit from a suffocating form of life cure the objection of an individual or minority for whom the absence of certain liberties renders life miserable?

These are all questions that cannot be avoided once pluralism as an ethical foundation for liberalism is rejected. Gray would no doubt counsel that the sense of helplessness this conclusion is likely to spark in the heart of philosophical liberals should be regarded as the authentic experience of humanity whose fate is "agonistic pluralism." Faced with the ultimate validity of conflicting claims, we should, in Berlin's words, "maintain a precarious equilibrium that prevents the occurrence of desperate situations, of intolerable choices" as the first requirement of a decent society.

How precarious that equilibrium is depends, at least in part, on the extent to which we can claim that human beings hold anything in common. The greater the sphere of shared values, the more likely it is that societies will throw up political institutions that are recognizable and justifiable to one another. Conversely, a minimal description of the human condition will entail a greater diversity (and incompatibility) of prevailing value systems and institutions. Gray places Berlin at the minimal end of the spectrum. He points to a common capacity for making choices but insists that this will radically underdetermine any particular form of life. Indeed, the sheer diversity of forms of life, cultures, languages, and institutions is evidence of a human disposition to develop "a specific and particularist identity."

This, it seems to me, lies at the heart of the matter. To what extent does that disposition belie a common capacity for understanding the human condition; and to what extent does a recognition of the capacity for both choice-making and self-creation have consequences for how we treat one another? Gray locates a minimal universalism in Berlin's thought that describes a "common human horizon" which encompasses a minimum content of morality without which there is simply unintelligibility. This tantalizing minimum (Gray nods in the direction of fairness and consideration for others' interests) will itself be shaped by specific cultural inheritances. But its content is so slender (in Gray's account at least) that it cannot ground a fully fledged political philosophy. Which leads Gray to the conclusion that if value pluralism is true "all the way down" then "the identity of practitioners of a liberal form of life is a contingent matter, not a privileged expression of universal human nature."

The weight of Gray's reading of Berlin is that we can say little outside of our local cultural rabbit burrows about how the world should be organized. One can swiftly agree with Gray's rejection of the rationalistic excesses of a generation of theorists who have claimed that particular decision rules are uniquely persuasive in settling the conflicts that lie at the heart of liberal societies let alone others. And one can share the implicit unease Gray holds in the face of triumphalist claims for the inevitability of globalization. Whatever the civilizing power of commerce, the potential for cultural dislocation and conflict in the face of all-pervasive consumerism is real and foolishly ignored by those who would rationalize the world as a seamless marketplace devoid of political or cultural particularity.

But are liberal conclusions thus reduced to mere rhetoric just because we cannot summons a philosophical theory to ground liberalism in logically irrefutable terms? That is by no means the conclusion Berlin has reached. In a brief but closely argued reply with Bernard Williams to the charge that liberalism cannot be grounded in pluralism, Berlin insists that a plurality of values does not render reason impotent. The fact that reason may not be able to generate some lexical priority rule does not negate the *reasonable* discussion of choosing between values. As Berlin and Williams note, it is from concrete discussion about social and historical realities that the weaknesses and strengths of liberalism will be illuminated and, they add, "the brutal and fraudulent simplifications which, *as a matter of fact,* are the usual offerings of its actual enemies."[1] Whatever Gray's doubts about the ethical arguments that may be mustered to support liberal institutions, one is left in little doubt about the empirical reasons that Berlin would advance as being persuasive in liberalism's defense.

Why should we concern ourselves with such a concentrated dose of closely argued political philosophy? An intellectually parochial answer would center on Gray's treatment of Berlin's understanding of romanticism and the tension between individual and collective self-creation and transformation as evidenced in art and language. The extent to which particularist cultural attachments can or should shape our political arrangements has been at the heart of some of the most horrendous conflicts humanity has faced in recent times. While Gray's warnings against hubristic universalism are timely, respect for diversity of

cultural forms does not of itself recommend against some key liberal premises. It would be an extraordinary irony if we were to throw into doubt the historical and practical success of liberalism at the very moment that it has won the affections of more people than ever before and in doing so discredited the claims of some particularly vicious secular theodicies.

Any truly impassioned piece of political philosophy will reflect the real mental and philosophical anguish of its author. Otherwise, it is just so much arid theorizing. Gray's study of Berlin is the unmistakable product of his own odyssey through the tricky waters of contemporary liberal theorizing. Gray's diagnosis of Berlin's radical brand of value pluralism is fatal for utilitarianism, fundamental rights, contractarianism, the more fantastic versions of rational choice theory. But in reaching the verdict, Gray cites the very subject matter of his own distinguished contribution over two decades to our understanding of J. S. Mill, F. A. Hayek, James Buchanan, John Rawls, and a host of lesser Hobbesian, Lockean, and Kantian theorists.

Berlin's oeuvre consistently exposes the worm that has gnawed at the core of Gray's philosophical pilgrimage. Some academics stop thinking and move on to ever more arcane defenses of established positions. If *Isaiah Berlin* is anything to go by, Gray's scholarship shows every sign of continuing in a restless and self-critical vein. This is 189 pages of intense, engaged writing but it is as much about its author's despair for the intellectual game-playing of so much contemporary philosophy as it is a skilled distillation of the wide ranging output of one of the most distinguished men of letters of our time. This is agonistic scholarship. Who knows where its author will end up?

Note

1. Isaiah Berlin and Bernard Williams, "Pluralism and Liberalism: a Reply," *Political Studies* 62 (1994): 306-09.

Leon Wieseltier (essay date 1997)

SOURCE: "When A Sage Dies, All Are His Kin," in *The New Republic,* Vol. 217, No. 217, December 1, 1997, pp. 27-31.

[*In the following eulogy, Wieseltier enumerates the qualities which, he asserts, made Berlin a sage.*]

I.

"When a sage dies," says the Talmud, "all are his kin."

The rabbis were speaking practically, not philosophically. They were ruling that, when a sage dies, everyone must observe some of the practices of mourning. When a sage dies, for example, all must rend their garments. "But do you really think that all are his kin?" the text asks itself, incredulously. For all are obviously not his kin. It is a big world. The injunction seems sentimental, onerous. "So say, rather, that all are like his kin." A distinction! But it is not enough of a distinction to release anybody from the duty to mourn.

And if you never knew the man, if you never sat in the dust at his feet, if you never heard him teach? Still he is not a stranger. The Talmud proceeds to the story of the death of Rabbi Safra, a scholar and a merchant of the fourth century. "When Rabbi Safra died, the rabbis did not rend their garments, because they said: 'We did not study with him ourselves.' But Abbaye said to them: 'Does it say "when your master dies"? No, it says "when a sage dies"! Besides, every day in the house of study we consider his views.'" If you know the teaching, you know the teacher. You are required to rend.

In Oxford, last week, a sage died. And every day in the house of study we consider his views. Who are Isaiah Berlin's kin, who must mourn?

II.

The pluralists are his kin, and they must mourn. Isaiah Berlin was the most original, the most lucid, the most erudite, and the most relentless enemy of the idea of totality in his age, which was an age of totality. More precisely, an age of failed totality; and it owed that failure, which was the late and saving glory of an inglorious modernity, not least to the notions of this professor and his crowded, benevolent mind. "It seems to me," he wrote, "that the belief that some single formula can in principle be found whereby all the diverse ends of men can be harmoniously realized is demonstrably false." The geniality of the statement should not obscure the scale of the claim. It is the language of a don, but it is the conception of a world-historical thinker. What made him a world-historical thinker was his assault on the idea of the world-historical.

From Parmenides to Marx, philosophers dreamed of the single principle, the single method, the single being, metaphysical or anti-metaphysical, sacred or profane, that would account for everything that exists, and bring everything that exists under a single description. Berlin set out to awaken Western thought from that dream. His lifelong analysis of the ideal of wholeness exposed it as a dangerous illusion. But he did not repudiate it only on moral and political grounds. He carried the criticism of totality beyond the criticism of totalitarianism, back to the elementary consideration of its philosophical sense. He showed that it had no philosophical sense.

"In the house of history," he wrote, "there are many mansions." But the force of Berlin's attack on holism in all its forms was owed to the fact that it was not only a historical attack, it was also a logical attack. It is commonly assumed that his defense of pluralism was the work of his years as a political thinker and a historian of ideas, but in fact Berlin's quarrel with totality originated in his early papers, in the Oxford-style exercises in analytical philoso-

phy that he later liked to disavow. "I could not bring myself to re-read them," he said about these writings; but it was in his animadversions against logical positivism that he began to suggest what is preposterous about "the infallible knowledge of incorrigible propositions," and "the Ionian fallacy of asking what everything is made of," and "the privileged class of basic propositions . . . and the desire to translate all other propositions into them or combinations of them. . . ." It was logic that made Berlin a liberal.

For Berlin, pluralism was not a conclusion drawn prudently from experience, a kind and expedient concession to the obstacles that life puts in the way of the right and the good. Rather, pluralism was a conclusion drawn from a proper analysis of concepts, from a strict reflection about the nature of human values and human goods, which are essentially incompatible, not just empirically incompatible, with one another. "The notion of a total human fulfillment is a formal contradiction." A formal contradiction: Is there a greater curse upon an idea? But this was the curse that Berlin cast upon the idea of totality, and may the idea never escape the curse. It was Berlin who demonstrated that the illiberal view of the world was not only an evil, it was also an error; that the liberal view of the world is not only a practical necessity, it is also a theoretical necessity. If society must be pluralist, it is because reality is plural; because pluralism is what there is.

Berlin was one of liberalism's great foundationalists, and his writings will stand as a permanent embarrassment to those who believe that justice can dispense with philosophy. The pluralism that the preached was not a gospel of relaxation. "If, as I believe, the ends of men are many, and not all of them are in principle compatible with each other, then the possibility of conflict—and of tragedy—can never be wholly eliminated from human life, either personal or social." The strife and the sorrow of which Berlin warned might wrack the same society, the same culture, the same individual. Pluralism promises peace, not serenity. But Berlin kindled to the friction. He prized the shadows of the Many over the darkness of the One; for it is darkness, and not light, that the One generally vouchsafes. He had an almost aesthetic relationship to the heterogeneity that he championed. In his work and in his person, he demonstrated that the world of the Many is a more enchanted world, not a less enchanted world, than the world of the One. In this way, Berlin made a fruitful contribution to the idea of happiness.

III.

The rationalists are his kin, and they must mourn.

The rationalists? Surely not the rationalists. For it was Berlin, was it not, who shook the confidence of reason, and denied that reason was immune to time and to place, and denounced the rationalism of the Enlightenment as an indefensible absolutism? Yes, it was Berlin. But something has gone a little awry in the appreciation of his work in recent years. Some people think that they have detected in "value-pluralism" and the "incommensurability thesis" endorsements of the miserable flight from reason that characterizes so much of contemporary intellectual life. Thus, one reads that "there is in Berlin's idea of radical choice arising from conflicts among incommensurables a decisionist, voluntarist, or existentialist element." Berlin's attack on absolutes has been taken to imply relativism, or subjectivism, or perspectivism, or even a quaint postmodernism.

This is all exaggerated and imprecise. There is not a whiff of fumisme in Berlin, not a touch of Fichte or Sartre. "We seek to adjust the unadjustable, we do the best we can," but we do not do so gratuitously, or helplessly, or in the service only of our interests. The hero of Berlin's epic of the collision of ends is a deliberative hero, whose choices are rational, or at least reasonable, and merit praise or blame. He does not despair of coherence or truth. Berlin's point is not that reason has been retired by irony or by will; it is that reason dictates many things, and comes with costs. It was not against reason that Berlin inveighed, it was against the church of rationalism (or the temple of Sarastro, as he liked to call it); and it was reason, not unreason, that he pitted against rationalism's dogmas. When **"Herder and the Enlightenment,"** his extraordinary essay of 1964, was reprinted last year in a new collection of his writings, Berlin added a note in which he described Herder's standpoint, which was also his own standpoint, as "objective pluralism." It was not one of his magical formulations, but it suffices to establish that he offers no comfort to the cheerful obscurers.

What is "objective pluralism"? It is the view that a pluralist world is a porous world, that societies and cultures and minds are not so shut up within themselves that meaningful communication among them, or meaningful comparison between them, is impossible ("it is idle to tell men to learn to see other worlds through the eyes of those whom they seek to understand, if they are prevented by the walls of their own culture from doing so"); and also the view that each of these societies and cultures and minds may be evaluated by logical and moral categories that apply across them all. About relativism, Berlin wrote that "I take it to mean a doctrine according to which the judgment of a man or a group, since it is the expression of a taste, or emotional attitude or outlook, is simply what it is, with no objective correlate that determines its truth or falsehood." And this he rejected. He would not countenance the ideal of an islanded existence. It made the study of different forms of life and ancient forms of life and primitive forms of life impossible. Is "objectivity," then, another term for universalism? Berlin did not speak keenly of universalism, and in his writings he often identified it with what a historian once called "uniformitarianism." But really he abhorred only a coercive universalism (and its incarnation on earth, communism). He was a universalist of the multiformitarian kind.

What bothered Berlin about rationalism was its insulation. This was especially true of rationalism in Oxford, as he

recalled it in an elegiac but devastating memoir of J.L. Austin. For nothing was more vivid to Berlin than the reality of an idea; the external reality as well as the internal reality. A particular idea occurred in a particular time and a particular place. This did not mean that the idea was contingent, or nothing more than an expression of the individual who thought it. It might be a necessary idea; but even necessary ideas do not think themselves. An abstract conception is voluptuously actual. A thought is an experience. Berlin did not become a historian of ideas because he believed that ideas are nothing but history. His historicism was a way of making reason worldly; or of acting on the rude and marvelous discovery that reason already was worldly, even when it pretended otherwise.

It was not only for its more various picture of the human that Berlin kept returning to what he called the counter-Enlightenment. He was on a mission. He was a spy for reason in the house of unreason. (His studies in the history of romanticism and reaction were the most important cables that he ever wrote.) He needed all the dank and complicating information, if he was to get on with the unapologetically progressive task of understanding the conditions for the development of personality and decency. He belongs in the small and valorous company of rationalists who did not flinch before the facticity of unreason, who knew that reason cripples itself when it regards only itself, who taught reason sympathy.

IV.

The democrats are his kin, and they must mourn.

Berlin criticized classical rationalism as much for some of its effects as for some of its assumptions. He showed that, even in its nobler versions, it often culminated in a sanctimonious and sometimes murderous authoritarianism. "One belief, more than any other, is responsible for the slaughter of individuals on the altars of the great historical ideals—justice or progress or the happiness of future generations, or the sacred mission or emancipation of a nation or race or class, or even liberty itself, which demands the sacrifice of individuals for the freedom of society. This is the belief that somewhere, in the past or in the future, in divine revelation or in the mind of an individual thinker, in the pronouncements of history or science, or in the simple heart of an uncorrupted good man, there is a final solution." A final solution: the phrase recurs often in Berlin's studies of Western thought, and he saw no need to remark upon its chill.

Was it really a surfeit of reason from which this century suffered? Of course not. But this was not Berlin's claim. He was warning, rather, of the perversion of reason. He admired the power of the mind to understand, but he feared the power of the mind to unify; and he was adamant that unifying was not the same as understanding. It was plain to him that the crimes of his century were the crimes of monism, and he toiled to make this plain to others. In political theory, monism took the form of what he called "positive liberty." He was against it; it was a fancy invitation to compulsion, a theory of authority disguised as a theory of freedom. Freedom for, freedom to: this kind of freedom was a demand for a prescription for a way to live, and it defined freedom as conformity to such a prescription, as obedience. Berlin maintained, against Lenin but also against Kant, that freedom was not obedience, that it was the obstreperous antithesis of conformity.

Freedom was not general, it was individual. In his appraisal of political ideas and political systems, Berlin never took his eyes off "the empirical spatio-temporal existence of the finite individual." For this reason, he became the unvatic prophet of "negative liberty." This he defined as "a maximum degree of non-interference compatible with the minimum demands of social life." In Berlin's hands, the homely ideal of non-interference was homely no more. It was transformed into philosophy's powerful weapon against despotism. Berlin gave it grandeur: "It seems unlikely that this extreme demand for liberty has ever been made by any but a small company of highly civilized and self-conscious human beings." Or, a little morbidly, it may be that the objective of the struggle for freedom, of the longest and bloodiest struggle in human history, was nothing more magnificent than the right to be left alone.

Berlin was himself one of those highly civilized and self-conscious human beings. He, too, imagined the reign of respect, the paradise of no paradise. He was the heir in his time of Mill and Constant. He simply and truly detested determinisms. He did not deny that power was legitimate (though he discussed anarchism with glee, and took a wicked pleasure in contrasting Marx unfavorably to Bakunin); but he demanded that power be legitimate, and he propounded an exceedingly stringent criterion for its legitimacy. He was not a libertarian, and he criticized "the evils of unrestricted laissezfaire, and of the social and legal systems that permitted and encouraged it, [that] led to brutal violations of 'negative' liberty"; but he criticized collectivism more. (In 1917, as a boy in Petrograd, he watched the Russian Revolution.) "Genuine belief in the inviolability of a minimum extent of individual liberty," he wrote, "entails [an] absolute stand." This, from the master anti-absolutist! But there was nothing paradoxical about this stand. It was the corollary of his consecration.

Berlin's writings display in abundance the natural democracy of the contrapuntal mind. He was not a party man or a fisher of souls. With his friend Lionel Trilling, he believed that "a criticism which has at heart the interests of liberalism might find it s most useful work not in confirming liberalism in its sense of general rightness but rather in putting under some degree of pressure the liberal ideas and assumptions of the present time." Berlin did not exempt liberals and democrats from the fairness and the candor of his judgment. The conflation of freedom with power by modern revolutionaries, he observed, "has, perhaps, blinded some contemporary liberals to the world in which they live. Their plea is clear, their cause is just. But they do not allow for the variety of human needs. Nor yet for

the ingenuity with which men can prove to their satisfaction that the road to one ideal also leads to its contrary." He was wise in part because he was not ingenious.

V.

The nationalists are his kin, and they must mourn.

Not all the nationalists, no. Berlin was withering about the low side of belonging, about "the pathological developments of nationalism in our own time," about "modern national narcissism: the self-adoration of peoples, of their conviction of their own immeasurable superiority to others and consequent right to dominate them." He carefully delineated the debt that fascism and other outrages of collective will owed to romanticism. He was alienated by the celebration of the organic and the mythological that characterizes, and inflames, nationalist thinking and nationalist feeling. And yet he was not prepared to follow his faith in individualism all the way to an internationalist conclusion. He was sharply critical of liberals and socialists for having scanted the reality, and the validity, and the durability, of group feeling.

Berlin had two reasons for lingering over nationalism. The first was his indignation at injustice. In his view, nationalism almost always originated as an effort at redress, as an attempt to right a wrong. "It usually seems to be caused by wounds." In response to oppression and exploitation, a people desires recognition and independence. Not to understand such desires, and the solidarity out of which they arise, is to be morally obtuse, or worse. "The consciousness that although all oppression is hateful, yet to be ordered about by a man of my own community or nation, or class or culture or religion, humiliates me less than if it is done by strangers . . . that sentiment is surely intelligible enough." Nationalism, in Berlin's wonderful phrase, is "the straightening of bent backs."

But this is a purely reactive account of nationalism, and a purely political one; and for Berlin it did not suffice. The second reason for his interest in nationalism was his interest in the world as it is. For there are nations, formed or forming, stateless or in states, with languages, traditions, customs, institutions, and beliefs of their own. Regardless of what theory has to say about it, the human world is already so constituted and so diversified. Berlin's nationalism was an expression of his humanism. As a matter of principle, he dignified human needs and human aspirations. And the past was philosophically significant for him. The sphere of freedom that Berlin described was not a stripped and empty shell, and he did not seek to secure it for the purpose of Nietzschean melodrama. He did not require people to create themselves and their meanings. Identities are not only invented, they are also inherited; and they are invented out of what is inherited. Berlin never recoiled from the involuntary dimensions of life. This supremely unmystical man warmly invoked "the nation as a society of the living, the dead, and those yet unborn (sinister as this could prove to be when driven to a point of pathological exacerbation)."

He was the great teacher of liberal nationalism, which is surely one of the urgent teachings of our time. Berlin revered Mazzini. "True internationalism must be based on mutual regard and respect between nations. To have internationalism you must have nations." And those nations must be held to common standards of right and wrong. Is this universalism? It is. "No culture that we know lacks the notions of good and bad. There are universal values." The ethical trumps the ethnic. But Berlin's liberal nationalism was not only a brake upon the thralldom of the group to the nation. It was also a brake upon the thralldom of the individual to the nation. Berlin did not agree that nationalism required the immersion of the individual in the group. "Total harmony with others is incompatible with self-identity." There is dignity in membership; but in partial membership. Partial membership is still profound. The part is precious, but it must not be mistaken for the whole. The participation in shared traditions is an important element in the cultivation of personality, until it becomes its only element, and then it leads to the degradation of personality. Berlin prized authenticity, except ideologically.

The most deeply felt essay in the history of ideas that he wrote, I think, was his essay on Moses Hess, and these are the most deeply felt words in the essay:

> Through his most extreme and radical beliefs there persists a conviction that there is never any duty to maim or impoverish oneself for the sake of an abstract ideal; that nobody can, or should, be required to vivisect himself, to throw away that which affords him the deepest spiritual satisfaction known to human beings—the right to self-expression, to personal relationships, to the love of familiar places or forms of life, of beautiful things, or the roots and symbols of one's own, or one's family, or one's nation's past. He believed that nobody should be made to sacrifice his own individual pattern of the unanalyzable relationships—the central emotional or intellectual experiences—of which human lives are compounded, to offer them up, even as a temporary expedient, for the sake of some tidy solution, deduced from abstract and impersonal premises, some form of life derived from an alien source, imposed upon men by artificial means, and felt to be the mechanical application of some general rule to a concrete situation for which it was not made. All that Hess, toward the end of his life, wrote or said, rests on the assumption that to deny what inwardly one knows to be true, to do violence to the facts for whatever tactical or doctrinal motive, is at once degrading and doomed to futility.

Berlin was a creature of loyalties, and he expounded a critical philosophy of loyalty. He lived a dutiful, polycentric, generous, and unidolatrous life. "I remain totally loyal to Britain, to Oxford, to liberalism, to Israel," he remarked. He was, you might say, a rootful Jewish cosmopolitan, and so the most blessed of men.

VI.

The Jews were his kin, and they must mourn. He was a happy Zionist. "The origins of Zionism were very civilized and Herderian," he observed, meaning that his own nationalism had the same philosophical ground as the nationalism of others. It was owed also to his understanding of history, to his awareness of an emergency, to "the realization (it seems destined to come, late or soon, to almost every Jewish social thinker, whatever his views), that the Jewish problem is something sui generis, and seems to need a specific solution of its own, since it resists the solvent of even the most powerful universal panaceas." But Berlin's Zionism was not just an intellectual's Zionism. It was a bias of his heart. The sensation of peoplehood never deserted him. He vibrated to his patrimony.

Not to all of it, though. He was rather indifferent to Judaism as a religion, and rather ignorant about it, even if he liked to remind you that he was a cousin of the Lubavitcher rebbe. (The messiah would have profited from his cousin's thoughts about messianism in history.) He never quite overcame the Zionist condescension toward Yiddish. And in Jewish politics there was much that he would not accept. He condemned the chauvinists and the jingoists in the Zionist movement and in the Jewish State. (When asked about the Arabs who oppose Israel, he replied that "understanding people who oppose us is what Herder taught us." Consider that first "us," and then that second "us," and you will have the whole man.) And yet, as a Jew, Berlin was free, glad, open, busy, grateful, and utterly without anxiety. His past made him feel princely, as it should have. There was our exilarch, in Oxford; and there he is buried.

And those for whom he was not only a sage but also a master, those who sat in the dust at his feet—they, too, must mourn, for they are the mourners who will remember the teacher and not just the teaching. They will remember him in his all gentleness and all his gaiety, in his uncanny ability to see through them, and with sweetness and severity to explain them to themselves. They will remember him at the big white door, how delighted he was to see them, and how delighted they were that he was delighted to see them. They will remember him slouched in his chair by the fire, telling tales of what he had seen and what he had heard, singing "Rachel, quand du Seigneur" or "A un dottor della mia sorte," imparting to them all that he had satisfied himself was true, until they were emboldened to think that they, too, might become a link in the chain. (He was indeed an unforgettable talker; but it was what he said that was unforgettable.) They will remember him

> . . . unvexed, unwarped By partial bondage. In his steady course, No piteous revolutions had he felt, No wild varieties of joy and grief. Unoccupied by sorrow of its own, His heart lay open; and, by nature tuned And constant disposition of his thoughts To sympathy with man, he was alive To all that was enjoyed where'er he went, And all that was endured; for, in himself Happy, and quiet in his cheerfulness, He had no painful pressure from within That made him turn aside from wretchedness With coward fears. He could afford to suffer With those whom he saw suffer. Hence it came That in our best experience he was rich, And in the wisdom of our daily life. They will remember him, and their mourning will rend them.

"When a sage dies, all are his kin." A dispute is recorded between the last great rabbis of Germany in the Middle Ages, Meir ben Baruch of Rothenberg and his student Asher ben Jehiel. Meir leniently ruled that you mourn for a sage "if you know the ideas that he introduced, but if you know none of the ideas that he introduced, and he was not your master, then you are not required to rend when you hear the news after the funeral, since you do not [as Abbaye said] consider his views in the house of study every day." Asher stringently demurred, likewise in the name of Abbaye: "Does it say 'when your master dies'? No, it says 'when a sage dies'!" And so there is no reprieve from mourning. In 1286, when the Hapsburg emperor acted on the official view of the Jews as "serfs of Our Chamber," and promulgated capricious and punitive policies of taxation, Meir and his family attempted to leave Germany, but he was informed upon and imprisoned, and he died in the dungeon seven years later. In 1303, to avoid the fate of his teacher, Asher left Germany for Spain. About the mourning for a sage, they disagreed; but they agreed, certainly, that unreason was impending and wisdom was escaping.

Alfred Brendel (essay date 1997)

SOURCE: "On Isaiah Berlin," in *The New York Review of Books,* Vol. XLIV, No. 20, December 18, 1997, p. 12.

[*In the following reminiscence, the world-renowned pianist discusses Berlin's love of music.*]

No one ever wrote obituaries like Isaiah. Unlike some of those printed in British papers, they appraised mainly by praising. Isaiah knew a vast amount about an amazing number of people. Never full of himself, he was full of others. His curiosity was insatiable, his criticism playful rather than malicious. The first person to be critical about was himself. Always keen to take in new information, his memory seized on it, and retained it precisely. A lot of gossip was sifted through and put to higher use. I have never met anyone with a more remarkable memory. Isaiah could sum up books he had read a long time ago with exemplary clarity, and quote from them with astonishing accuracy. He could also hum musical themes, while tapping with the right hand on his knee, from the obscurest operas. To talk to people of all backgrounds, professions, and persuasions—or better, to communicate with them—was what he liked best.

Isaiah was convinced of the power of individuality and the force of genius. He had his heroes. In music, they were Verdi and Rossini, whom he also admired as human beings. He deemed both of them "naive" (in Schiller's sense), yet the "sentimentalists" Beethoven and Schubert also found their way to his heart. The somewhat labored distinction between *naiv* and *sentimentalisch* seemed to become increasingly blurred to him, Schubert being an important later acquaintance while Beethoven moved up to be the favorite of his last years. In a radio program, he mentioned the andantino from Schubert's late A major Sonata as the piece he wished to be played in his memory.

Stravinsky was a friend. One of the stories Isaiah delighted in telling was this: as Stravinsky stood weeping at Rimsky-Korsakov's funeral, Rimsky's widow admonished him by saying, "Pull yourself together, young man, we've still got Glazunov." Among contemporary composers, Harrison Birtwistle and George Benjamin stirred his interest. Opera, Russian as well as Italian, was familiar ground: for many years Isaiah was on the board of London's Covent Garden. But to please him, it needed opera producers who served the composer, not themselves. Among performers, Toscanini and Schnabel had been his guiding lights. To another performer, it was moving to see this dearest and most enlightened of friends looking for solace in music, a solace which helped him to face a century that, at its close, he deeply deplored.

Stuart Hampshire (essay date 1997)

SOURCE: "On Isaiah Berlin," in *The New York Review of Books,* Vol. XLIV, No. 20, December 18, 1997, p. 11.

[*In the following recollection, Hampshire portrays the unity of Berlin's intellect and personality.*]

By the superabundance of his curiosities and the range of his interests, Isaiah Berlin burst through all the usual restraints and cautions of academic thinking. He was in fact a peculiar kind of genius in academia. True scholarship has behind it a desire, even a compulsion, to dominate and to monopolize a field of study: a totalitarian wish to be first and everywhere in the field, in the spirit of A.E. Housman. Berlin never in his life thought of himself as a scholar and had no desire for mastery or monopoly. When in the summer of 1936 I traveled with him to Ireland on holiday, I remarked, censoriously, that he seemed to study texts only when conversation with his friends lapsed and he needed a substitute.

In one of my still-vivid pictures of him that summer he is standing in an Irish country bus, holding a copy of *Bouvard et Pécuchet* in a Russian translation, and exchanging banter with an Irish priest who thought he was a Communist. His ideal at that time, and again immediately after the war, was to live among a small group of friends who shared his passion for the history of thought in all its varieties—discussing, for example, Russian intellectuals before the Revolution, the French Enlightenment, the golden generation in Paris, Heine and Bellini, the errors of Russell and Carnap, Karl Marx and anti-Semitism.

He was the least academic of all the academics in the humanities that I have known. His love of the movement of ideas, and of their possible life in conversation, carried him over all dividing hedges and fences. This cross-country flying was precisely Virginia Woolf's definition of highbrow, and a gentle, benign, amazingly effortless, and modest highbrow he was. At the same time he venerated the true scholarship of his friends Meyer Schapiro, Arnaldo Momigliano, Ernst Gombrich, and Ronald Syme, just as he admired the extravagant sympathies and occasional polemics of his friends Edmund Wilson and Joseph Alsop—high spirits in a classical form.

He had a capacious memory for the particularities of persons, living and dead, their origins, friends, families, and habits, and he had a gift like Aubrey's for the odd anecdote, or the fragment of speech, that illuminates a person. He was notoriously profligate in giving his time to the great number of strangers, particularly foreign scholars, who consulted him. Both superficially and at a deep level, he understood and sympathized with the varieties of human mentalities and of styles of thought across the Continent. He turned aside to found Wolfson College and to preside over its innovations, and it remains a college that is delightfully unlike any other.

His essays show him as a master of praise and he had a talent for hero worship: among his characteristic heroes were David Hume, Diderot, Rossini, Verdi, Herder, Herzen, Chaim Weizmann, Turgenev (because he was so unheroic), Leonard Woolf.

One feature of his long life and of his personality now stands out in my mind before all others—his amazement in the face of the immense affection and admiration that he inspired in persons of very different kinds, both inside and outside universities. It is as if he had been for years talking in his usual helter-skelter manner among his ever-widening circle of friends—which included musicians, writers, artists, politicians, journalists, captains of industry, professors—and then he suddenly looked up and saw a great sea of faces, an audience that stretched away to Italy and to Poland and to countless people without public labels who responded to the spontaneity and heat of his speech.

He had never expected to be, or intended to be, an internationally famous leader of thought. He had never planned his publications. A meticulous editor, Henry Hardy, made marvelous books out of his scattered lectures and essays. He had simply gone forward, consumed with curiosity and with the intense pleasures of speculation, leaving much of his life to impulse and to chance. He was pleasure-loving, and he never thought particularly well of himself in any role. He was superbly unpretentious and unpretending.

Michael Ignatieff (essay date 1997)

SOURCE: "On Isaiah Berlin," in *The New York Review of Books*, Vol. XLIV, No. 20, December 18, 1997, p. 10.

[*In the following tribute, his biographer sketches a portrait of Berlin as an intellectual.*]

He was born in the twilight of imperial Russia and he was buried on a grey Friday morning at the end of the century in the Jewish section of Oxford's Wolvercote cemetery. At the age of seven, he watched the banners of the Russian Revolution waving below the balcony of his parent's apartment in Petrograd; he lived long enough to witness the collapse of Soviet tyranny. The Russian Revolution framed both his life and work: as an intellectual historian he uncovered its totalitarian impulses, and as a political theorist he defended the liberal civilization it sought to destroy.

He was the last representative of the passionate, comic, voluble, and morally serious intelligentsia of old Russia. When he and Anna Akhmatova talked through the night in her bare apartment in the Fontanny Dom in November 1945, sharing a dish of boiled potatoes, it was as if two Russian traditions—one exiled, the other persecuted—were meeting to pledge that they would endure and persevere. He lived long enough to see the pledge honored.

Exile in England never left him beset by nostalgia. In Englishness, he discovered a skeptical empiricism which became the central strand of his identity and which he combined with the Russian and Jewish elements of his character. All of these elements, the Russian, the Jewish, and the English, became relatives in his soul and they argued together and told jokes to each other throughout his life.

He had a Humian temperament—worldly, unsentimental, and serene—which managed to turn episodes of self-doubt into opportunities for self-transformation. Doubting that he could ever become a philosopher, historian, or political theorist of the first rank, he became by turns all three. The intellectual trajectory he followed was thus daringly original. No other major figure in twentieth-century Anglo-American letters made contributions across such a range of disciplines: in analytical philosophy, in the intellectual history of Marxism, the Enlightenment, and the Counter-Enlightenment, and in liberal political theory.

He seemed like the quintessential fox, but now that his journey is completed, it is possible to see that he was a hedgehog all along. The unity to his work grew from a sustained concentration on what he took to be the Enlightenment's central flaw: its belief that the truth was one and that the goods which men valued could not ultimately conflict. From Vico and Herder and from the German Romantics he distilled the idea that some human ends were actually incommensurable and incompatible. Justice and mercy, for example, or liberty and equality were in contradiction, and there was no science of human affairs capable of resolving the conflict. Knowledge, he memorably said, does not set us free from the dilemmas of human choice. "We are doomed to choose," he wrote, and "every choice may entail an irreparable loss." Utopia was not merely unrealizable, it was "conceptually incoherent," and the attempt to build heaven on earth could only end in tyranny.

"Ends, moral principles, are many," he once wrote. "But not infinitely many: they must be within the human horizon." He kept his intellectual gaze firmly upon that horizon, trying to understand what human beings could genuinely comprehend about one another. His work was a passionate defense of human empathy. The precondition of a liberal society was not consensus or shared values, he insisted, but our capacity to understand moral worlds different from our own.

He believed the state should try to create conditions of equality for its citizens, but he thought it was self-deceiving to suppose that equality could always be reconciled with liberty. Bishop Butler's remark—"Everything is what it is and not another thing"—was a talisman for him. The most astringent—and influential—sentence he ever wrote insisted that liberals must not fool themselves into believing that liberal society could be everything they wished: "Liberty is liberty, not equality or fairness or justice or culture, or human happiness or a quiet conscience."

"The concrete situation is almost everything," he wrote. "There is no escape: we must decide as we decide; moral risk cannot, at times, be avoided." The particular quality he admired in great men and women was their "sense of reality." His own was unfailingly acute and it was why his friends called him wise.

When I once asked him how he thought he would like to be remembered, he was characteristically brisk: "After I'm dead, I don't mind what is said or thought about me. This is the truth." It had always been a matter of wry amusement to him that his own reputation had been systematically overvalued in his lifetime. The possibility that he might be undervalued after his death was a matter of indifference. He wished he could live forever—wished there might be an afterlife—but saw no grounds to believe that such a place existed.

The wet earth falling on his plain casket in Wolvercote cemetery momentarily obliterates that other sound—the low, rapid rumble of his voice—which was music to those who loved him. It mingled Oxford, Petersburg, and Riga together in an intonation we will never hear again. But he left the moral quality of his voice behind him, in the long tumbling paragraphs and the clauses within clauses of his best essays, and it is to these that we can turn when we need to remind ourselves what intellectual life can be: joyful, free of illusion, and vitally alive.

Aileen Kelly (essay date 1997)

SOURCE: "On Isaiah Berlin," in *The New York Review of Books,* Vol. XLIV, No. 20, December 18, 1997, p. 13.

[*In the following homage, Kelly describes Berlin as a teacher and conversationalist.*]

Few teachers will ever be as much loved and mourned as Isaiah. As a graduate student at Wolfson College, Oxford, whose first president he became in the late 1960s, I was constantly made aware of my great luck: my choice of college within the University had brought me into the daily orbit of what we all sensed was the most fascinating, the most remarkable person we would ever encounter. Soon after I joined the College, he sent me a note asking me to come and discuss my research on the Russian intelligentsia. Out of nervousness I delayed replying until one day he descended on me at lunch, commanding me to come back with him to his office. I emerged nearly three hours later after a dazzling tour of the landscape of Russian thought combined with a passionate vindication of the subject of my research, which others had frequently urged me to change. In the Sixties Western liberal academics tended to regard the Russian intelligentsia mainly as fanatical precursors of communism. With a warmth that recreated them as persons, Isaiah defended them as worthy of admiration for their moral commitment to dispelling illusions about the world and our place in it.

Much of that afternoon we spent discussing Alexander Herzen, whom Isaiah described as his hero. Later that day I sought out his essays on Herzen and came upon a precise description of my own recent impressions:

> I was puzzled and overwhelmed, when I first came to know [him]—by this extraordinary mind which darted from one topic to another with unbelievable swiftness, with inexhaustible wit and brilliance; which could see in the turn of somebody's talk, in some simple incident, in some abstract idea, that vivid feature which gives expression and life. He had . . . a kind of prodigal opulence of intellect which astonished his audience. . . . [His talk] demanded of those who were with him not only intense concentration, but also perpetual alertness, because you had always to be prepared to respond instantly. On the other hand, nothing cheap or tawdry could stand even half an hour of contact with him. All pretentiousness, all pompousness, all pedantic self-importance, simply fled from him or melted like wax before a fire.

Isaiah was citing a contemporary's portrait of Herzen. His own resemblance to that extraordinary figure was striking (many of us would echo, with regard to Isaiah, Tolstoy's comment on Herzen—that he had never met anyone with "so rare a combination of scintillating brilliance and depth"), but his sense of affinity with Herzen was based above all on a shared moral outlook. They both combined a deep respect for honesty and purity of motivation with an unerring ability to detect artificiality and self-deception in intellectual endeavor and everyday behavior. Students sensed that with Isaiah they were not required to perform, amuse, or entertain, but simply to give their best, and this paradoxically put us at ease with him, the more so as we soon found out that straining to impress him was counterproductive. (Once, hoping to be congratulated on the originality of an essay I had given him for comment I was chagrined to find that he had read the footnotes just as closely as the text and had unearthed some errors of fact which I had overlooked in my haste to impress.)

Isaiah's personality and utterances were the subject of continual discussion by the students of his College. His Russian connections and his exotic past provided much food for inventive speculation: Had the unusual circular hole in his ancient felt hat been acquired during hostile action somewhere in the Baltic states? More than once he walked unexpectedly into a room where a passable imitation of his own unforgettable voice was in full flow.

I believe that his true voice can be found at its clearest in his essays on Herzen. More self-revealing than anything else he ever wrote, they shed light on the most enduring mystery about him: his combination of what many have seen as a tragic vision of the world with an inexhaustible curiosity and an irrepressible sense of fun.

Isaiah can be said to have rediscovered Herzen, who he believed had either been ignored or misrepresented for so long because he had revealed a truth too bleak for most people to bear: that faith in universally valid formulas and goals was an attempt to escape from the unpredictability of life into the false security of fantasy. His devotion to Herzen remained undiminished to the end of his life. Not long ago he wrote reproaching me for obscuring the uniqueness of Herzen's contribution by drawing parallels between him and thinkers such as Mikhail Bakhtin who had considered similar problems: "I can think of none, but perhaps I am too fanatical an admirer." He often cited Herzen's phrase "history has no libretto": all questions make sense and must be resolved not in terms of final goals but of the specific needs of actual persons at specific times and places. Herzen, he wrote, believed "that the day and the hour were ends in themselves, not a means to another day or another experience."

Here we have the key to one of the central paradoxes of Isaiah. Although his diary was always full and he was scrupulous about keeping appointments, he never gave the impression of being in a hurry, of being distracted from a person or an issue by anticipation of the next person or problem in line. Young academics were often astonished (as I was in my first encounter with him) that so important and busy a man was prepared to give them so much of his time. An American Slavist whom I met recently at a conference recalled having sent him her first book, not expecting a reply. His warm and detailed response, she told me, had her walking on air for weeks. On the evening after his death I remembered him with a Russian colleague whom he had encouraged in the same way in Oxford many years ago. A "*svetlaia lichnost*" (luminous personality), she said.

But we would diminish him if we did not appreciate that the instinctive goodness we loved was coupled with a carefully thought-through moral vision of whose validity he earnestly sought to persuade us. One of its distinctive characteristics, which he saw embodied in Herzen, was the total absence of a utilitarian approach to people and events, an "unquenchable delight in the variety of life and the comedy of human character." This was also one of Isaiah's most entrancing qualities. I remember him as the only one of us to emerge unexasperated from an interminable and contentious College meeting, happily quoting Kant's statement that "from the crooked timber of humanity no

straight thing can ever be made." He was convinced (again I quote him on Herzen) that there was value in the very irregularity of the structure of human beings, "which is violated by attempts to force it into patterns or straitjackets."

Like Herzen (and Schiller) he believed profoundly in the seriousness of the play of life and human creativity, and was easily drawn into all kinds of frivolity. One night after dinner at Wolfson he joined a conversation in which a student was explaining the board game Diplomacy, where each player represented one of the Great Powers of pre-1914 Europe. He invited us to his house the following Sunday morning to initiate him into the game; he then gave an impressive performance as the Ottoman Empire. I have another memory of him sitting on a bale of hay in his three-piece suit, complete with watch chain and hat, holding forth to a group of fascinated students at a bonfire party held in a damp field on the bank of the Isis, where the building of the new College was to start the next day. It was late evening; a more typical college president, having put in the obligatory early appearance, would have been long gone.

All those who knew him well were asked over the years to persuade him to write more and not to squander his gifts in conversation. Yet his profligacy has not prevented him from being recognized as one of the major liberal thinkers of the twentieth century, and he belongs to an even more select group who achieved harmony between their moral vision and their life. He showed us virtue in action, not as obedience to a set of rules but as a generous responsiveness to the creative possibilities of the present moment. One always came away from a few hours in his company with a sense of living more intensely, with all one's perceptions heightened, although the topics of conversation were often far from exalted. He much enjoyed exchanging news about the latest academic scandals in Oxford and Cambridge, and expected the exchange to be on equal terms: his view of humanity required that Cambridge should be as fertile a source of stories about human frailty as Oxford, and he was never disappointed. We had an unfinished debate lasting several years over the precise difference between a cad and a bounder; he could always find fresh examples of each to offer from among our mutual acquaintances.

He loved to gossip about the concerns and quarrels of nineteenth-century Russian thinkers as though they were our common friends, but there was a serious side to this entertainment. He had the greatest respect for these thinkers' commitment to acting out their beliefs in their daily lives, and fiercely championed them against what he perceived as misjudgments of their motives; our one painful difference was over the question of how Turgenev would have behaved under particular pressures.

Isaiah saw no contradiction between recognizing that moral ideals were not absolute and believing one's own ideals binding on oneself. Again, his model was Herzen, who, he tells us, for all his skepticism, had an unshakable belief in the sanctity of personal liberty and the noble instincts of the human soul, as well as a hatred of "conformism, cowardice, submission to the tyranny of brute force or pressure of opinion, arbitrary violence, and anxious submissiveness . . . the worship of power, blind reverence for the past, for institutions, for mysteries or myths; the humiliation of the weak by the strong, sectarianism, philistinism, the resentment and envy of majorities, the brutal arrogance of minorities." Here, albeit in the third person, is Isaiah's profession of faith, in his own cadences.

He admired Herzen more than Turgenev because while neither had any illusions about the permanence of human existence and human values, Turgenev had achieved a cool detachment from the struggles and triumphs of contingent life, while Herzen "cared far too violently"; his realism was therefore the more courageous. In his last years Isaiah confronted the tragic side of his own philosophy with the same unflinching directness as his hero. On arriving for dinner in Cambridge sixteen months ago, he told me that something "very terrible" concerning him had just appeared in the press. He would say no more about it and I assumed it was some adverse review. The next day I found the interview, reprinted in the London *Times,* in which he reflects on his own death, declaring that, much though he would like it to be otherwise, the idea that there was some world in which there would be perfect truth, love, justice, and happiness made no sense in any conceptual scheme he knew. It was just a comforting idea for people who could not face the possibility of total extinction. But, he adds, "I wouldn't mind living on and on. . . . I am filled with curiosity and long to know, what next?

Morton J. Frisch (essay date 1998)

SOURCE: "A Critical Appraisal of Isaiah Berlin's Philosophy of Pluralism," in *The Review of Politics,* Vol. 60, No. 3, Summer, 1998, pp. 421-33.

[*In the following essay, Frisch argues that despite his allegiance to the equal authority of several incomparable and incommensurate values, Berlin, in fact, had an implicit standard of values.*]

During the past year Isaiah Berlin died at the age of 88. He has undoubtedly been one of the leading British essayists in political philosophy in the twentieth century, covering a very wide range of topics in that discipline. One might justly say that he has written more extensively on human freedom than anyone since John Stuart Mill. Born in Latvia, Berlin attended Corpus Christi College, Oxford, from 1928-32 and seems there to have taken the first important steps toward the influential role in British and Western intellectual life which he came to hold. His academic career was interrupted by service, 1941-45, in the British Embassies in Washington and Moscow. He was a fellow at Oxford's All Souls College from 1932-38 and at

the university's New College from 1938-50. Later he was Chichelle Professor of Social and Political Theory at All Souls College, 1957-67, remaining afterward as a Fellow of that College while serving as President of Oxford's Wolfson College, 1966-75, and President of the British Academy, 1974-78.

Some of his most provocative essays are **"Political Ideas in the Twentieth Century," "Two Concepts of Liberty," "Does Political Theory Still Exist?"** in which he asserted that "no commanding work in political philosophy has appeared in the twentieth century," **"Historical Inevitability," "The Purpose of Philosophy,"** and **"The Hedgehog and the Fox."** Particularly revealing of the character of his work is a book entitled ***Conversations with Isaiah Berlin,***[1] published in 1991, where he is queried on such questions as "Do you consider your work a philosophical investigation or an historical one?" It also contains an unusually fascinating description of his evaluation of one of his well-known contemporaries in the same discipline entitled **"The Magic Eye of Leo Strauss."** Those published sets of his essays which have drawn much attention in the discipline are ***Four Essays on Liberty*** (1969), ***Concepts and Categories: Philosophical Essays*** (1978), and ***The Crooked Timber of Humanity: Chapters in the History of Ideas*** (1990).[2]

There are, as it seems to Isaiah Berlin, two distinct kinds of freedom, the negative freedom of non-interference and the positive freedom of self-realization. Negative freedom means "freedom from," a certain area of private freedom in which no one can interfere with my activity, compatible with the minimum demands of civil society, whereas positive freedom means "freedom to" or the power of the individual to be the instrument of his own acts of will. Each of these notions of freedom makes absolute claims which can come into sharp collision with the other, but which, according to Berlin, have an equal status insofar as absolute values are concerned.[3] They do not merely differ from each other, but contradict one another. Berlin maintains that a resolution of the conflicting claims of non-interference and self-realization must come from choosing between them and moderating them in order to accommodate the other claim. It appears that the choosing would give its value to freedom of choice as an end in itself, and would therewith be the hallmark of a free society.[4] The choosing is more important than the choice inasmuch as the choice is based on mere preference and therefore not a rational choice.[5] There are preferences but not principles in the strict sense of the word, since we cannot have any genuine knowledge concerning the ultimate principles of our choosing.

The theoretical posture which Berlin posits to accommodate this collision of values is moral pluralism or a plurality of values, equally genuine, equally ultimate, and therefore incapable of being judged in terms of some absolute standard. His brand of pluralism would allow for the freedom to choose without claiming ultimate validity for the choice itself, that is, it is neutral with regard to the choice.

It would recognize the fact that human values are many, and not all of them commensurable; they may even be in continuous conflict with each other.[6] Therefore, from that awareness, it would be understood that "values, principles must yield to each other, in varying degrees, in specific situations. . . . The best that can be done, as a general rule, is to maintain a precarious equilibrium that will prevent the occurrence of . . . desperate situations, of intolerable choices."[7] The doctrine of moral pluralism, meant as a way of accommodating variability in the absence of agreement on substantive ends, might conceivably be understood as an attempt at a resuscitation of present-day liberalism as a movement of political thought.

Berlin emphatically maintains that moral pluralism is not moral relativism, which would appear, at least from a surface, to separate itself from the loose relativism of the liberal perspective.[8] He confesses that while moral principles are many, they are not infinitely many, which implies that moral principles as they appear to him would have absolute limits as to their variability.[9] It becomes apparent that the positing of a limit beyond which no moral choices can move would require an absolute basis, but, according to Berlin, all absolutes have no basis in reality. It would seem to us therefore that his moral pluralism cannot exist *without* an absolute basis, a maximum level of opportunity for choice below which human activity ceases to be free, and cannot exist *with* an absolute basis because for him there are no absolute values.

It is worth remarking that Berlin, who is distrustful of absolutes in the full and strict sense of the word, cannot avoid speaking of contemptible human qualities—injustice, oppression, falsity in human relations, moral and spiritual blindness, egoism, cruelty, and so on.[10] He seems to admit by the very use of these terms that there are standards which enable us to distinguish justice from injustice, kindness from cruelty, right on through the whole range of virtues and vices. But these humanistic values, viewed from his perspective, have no status at all other than arbitrary preferences. For, as Berlin might have put it, the reasons we give for our preferences are not reasonable, hardly more than mere rationalizations. We nevertheless doubt whether one can ascribe to him the viewpoint of an all-out relativism. It therefore becomes incumbent on us to penetrate the obscurities of his position in order to determine precisely where he stands relative to the status of the humanistic values he holds so dear.

Berlin cannot explain what freedom is except by distinguishing between two conceptions of freedom, two divergent and irreconcilable attitudes toward the ends of human life. But are the claims between "freedom from" and "freedom to" as irreconcilable as he would have us believe? Berlin understands freedom essentially in the sense of opportunity to choose, but in the context of this assumption, freedom understood as noninterference and freedom understood as self-realization are not all that inconsistent on the level of thought. The fact that Berlin regards negative freedom to be higher than positive freedom does not make these contrasted notions of freedom any less compatible, but rather places them at different gradations on the same scale of values.

We are not surprised to learn that for Berlin the human condition is essentially a predicament characterized by the clash of irreconcilable values.[11] He asserts that we must understand values widely different from our own in their own terms, understand how these values came about, but without evaluating them.[12] It is not unduly difficult to see that Berlin wants to extract civility from the destabilizing divisiveness of the human condition and he suggests that the way to do this is to insist on a willingness to tolerate a wide spectrum of values. He maintains that toleration or a willingness to tolerate is possible and even necessary because the values we hold are mere preferences rather than principles which are rationally defensible. But we can see that Berlin has at least some notion of the limits of toleration. He apparently understands, even though he does not say so in so many words, that to tolerate other values is not to relativize all values by putting them on an equal plane, but simply to accommodate certain values other than our own. It would be hard to imagine that he would be willing to accommodate a value system which would exclude at least a minimum of freedom of choice in civil society, for that would constitute what he would regard as an illegitimate exercise of political power. We would venture the thought that illegitimacy for Berlin would reside in the complete absence of freedom of choice, and it is for this reason that tolerance is not pushed by him to the extreme.

It becomes all too clear on reflection that the limits on tolerance are built into the very definition of toleration itself. It seems reasonable to assume, as Berlin does, that without tolerance the conditions for rational discussion are destroyed, but we would add that tolerance of intolerance cannot be tolerated for the very same reason.[13] It therefore becomes apparent that it is practically impossible to leave it at the equality of all preferences or choices. It is rather remarkable that Berlin's humane desire for tolerance, which was intended to satisfy in the highest degree the desire for freedom of choice, transforms itself into a design for the measured limitation of freedom, although it is extremely unlikely that he would be willing to admit that.

We have suggested that Berlin's primary concern is the delineation of the closest possible approximation to the state of freedom for the individual in civil society. It is not at all surprising to find that he identifies completely with Benjamin Constant's view that "the real cause of oppression lay in the mere fact of the accumulation of power itself, . . . since [freedom is] endangered by the mere existence of authority as such."[14] It is therefore necessary to consider the possibility that it is not the allegedly insoluble conflict between negative and positive freedom which is fundamental for Berlin's thought, but rather the problematic character of the relation between freedom and authority. He evidently believes that there is a tendency in all governments to an augmentation of power or authority at the expense of freedom even though he certainly realizes that freedom may be endangered by the existence of freedom as well as by the abuses of authority. Berlin seems to assume that to be free, or to be oneself, is simply incompatible with the exercise of authority, and that would make him a libertarian in the older sense of the word. It comes as no surprise that there is no balance to be achieved between freedom and authority in his political thought inasmuch as authority for him invariably constitutes a threat to freedom both in its positive and negative forms.

The politically relevant character of freedom appears most clearly in Edmund Burke's remark that "the great contests for freedom" in England were in the past "chiefly upon the question of taxing." On this point, he explains that the ablest pens and most eloquent tongues "took infinite pains to inculcate, as a fundamental principle, that . . . the people must in effect themselves, mediately or immediately, possess the power of granting their own money, or no shadow of liberty could exist."[15] The motto of the American Revolution would come as no surprise to Burke for it was a restatement of a fundamental Lockean principle that private property under the protective right of taxation placed in the people or its representatives is the very foundation of political freedom. It should be obvious that this version of freedom with which Burke had no reason to disagree is distinctly Lockean, that is, that without control over the power of taxation, which can take away your property, there is no freedom in civil society. But Berlin seems to overlook the possibility that political freedom comes from making judgments about the kinds of taxes which are to be levied and acting on such judgments through representatives who have the power of the purse. He maintains rather that the essence of freedom is freedom to choose, the painful privilege of choosing, the necessity and agony of choice, but a choice based on no more than mere preference. He does not appear to recognize that freedom in the politically relevant sense of the term derives essentially from the discriminating activity of the mind which precedes choice, whether that choice be a choice of ends or of means to ends.

It becomes a question whether Berlin's distinction between moral pluralism and moral relativism can ultimately be sustained, especially in view of his explicit rejection of absolute values as having any rational foundation. We must not forget the fact that moral absolutes for Berlin are no more than mere preferences. What is decisive for him is the view that the claims of equally ultimate ends collide, which is worsened by the fact that these claims are irreconcilable. Berlin regards "the powerful privilege" to choose ends without claiming eternal validity for them as "the burden of freedom."[16] We would say that choosing ends that have no other support than one's arbitrary preferences is surely a burden of freedom, a burden created by this experience of a fundamental groundless choice, but it can hardly be called a privilege.

It is perhaps possible to say, what Berlin does not come right out and say, that the doctrine of moral pluralism would be irrelevant for the guidance of a liberal democratic community without marking the limits of tolerance. In other words, that doctrine must necessarily rule out extreme forms of intolerance in the interest of freedom of choice. It simply comes down to this, that freedom of choice must be limited by some other standard for the sake of freedom of choice, but Berlin does not abandon his fundamental orientation of freedom of choice as an end in itself, a freedom of choice which may not be preceded by deliberation at all. It would seem to us more correct to say that freedom of choice is simply insufficient without prior deliberation concerning the validity of the choice to be made, that is, without the supervention of deliberation. Berlin acknowledges that judgments (and presumably choices following those judgments) cannot be based on ignorance, but this apparently has no bearing on his faith in freedom of choice as an end in itself.[17] In studying a doctrine, we must take into consideration everything the author of that doctrine said or thought relevant to that doctrine, regardless of whether he seems to have considered it or not.

Berlin refers to "our imperfect understanding of individuals and societies," which implies that, by his understanding of what constitutes an imperfect understanding, he has some understanding of what constitutes a more perfect understanding.[18] It goes without saying that it is only possible to have an understanding of what constitutes a less than perfect understanding with a view as to what constitutes a more perfect understanding. Berlin appears to agree with the view that "indifference to freedom is not compatible with being human, or, at least, fully human." He also says that "those who have ever valued [freedom] for its own sake believed that to be free to choose, and not to be chosen for, is an inalienable ingredient in what makes human beings human."[19] We can take it as certain that Berlin is one of those who values freedom for its own sake. It would not be far-fetched to assume that he regards freedom in the sense of freedom to choose as consistent with the requirements of the excellence or perfection of humanness. He values this, in other words, not as a preference, but as a truism, as absolutely valid.

Berlin discusses modern political thinkers in his *Four Essays on Liberty,* especially from the perspective of the evolution of the idea of freedom, suggesting that the view of freedom as freedom to live as one likes, in its more developed state, is scarcely older than the Renaissance or Reformation.[20] He seems to think that there was hardly any discussion of individual freedom in the ancient world, but apparently does not regard Aristotle's remark as authoritative that the ideal of living as one likes as well as that of self-government were regarded as the defining principles of a democratic regime in Athens and elsewhere.[21] It should also be obvious from reading Thucydides's Periclean Funeral Oration that the notion of living as one likes did exist as a political ideal in the ancient world, although it was treated with disdain by the classical political philosophers. The classical political philosophers understood very well this notion of freedom and were unequivocally opposed to it.

Berlin states rather emphatically that there is no necessary connection between individual liberty and democratic rule, although he concedes that self-government has been more conducive to the preservation of individual liberties than other regimes.[22] It is easy to see why he would have said that inasmuch as he believed that the Greeks had no clear conception of individual liberty as a conscious political ideal, even though there was democratic political rule there.[23] It would certainly be wrong to believe that democratic rule has always fostered individual liberties, and much has been made of their absence in the ancient democracies. But it is difficult to see how democratic political rule can be separated from the democratic ideal of living as one likes on the level of thought, as Berlin maintains. It would be more accurate to say that constitutional guarantees for individual liberties had to wait for the formulations of the seventeenth-and eighteenth–century natural right theorists and the democratic regimes which emerged in the wake of their formulations.

Berlin learned from his Oxford teachers that political philosophy is a branch of moral philosophy, and this leads him to the conclusion that the central question of politics is that of the permissible limits of obedience and coercion in the interest of individual freedom.[24] The emphasis is on obedience and coercion as the fundamental political phenomenon, and by inference, by whom, and in what degree, and in the name of what, and for the sake of what, one should obey.[25] It is no accident that Berlin chooses obedience and coercion rather than persuasion and coercion to supply political life with its fundamental orientation, inasmuch as the real foundation for his political thought is a radical questioning of political authority as such referred to before. It would be hard to exaggerate the extent to which he regarded accumulations of power as antithetical to the human condition. He cannot seem to separate himself from the radical individualism by which his thought is so strongly influenced.[26]

Berlin cannot but admit, seemingly contrary to his principles, that it is sometimes necessary to discuss the relevance of absolute values, at least with reference to freedom of choice. It becomes apparent that he cannot defend freedom of choice as essential to the human condition other than in absolute terms. He may be said to have conceded, or at least implied, that freedom of choice is an absolute value, but what he understands by freedom of choice as the capacity for free commitment to choices governed by no overriding principle can simply be described as the free exercise of the will. It is in this necessity that the notion of the freedom of the will is at the bottom of the fact that Berlin chooses to focus on freedom of choice, a choice which has its own intrinsic value. Berlin apparently takes it for granted that the act of choosing in and of itself means more than the validity of the conviction determining the choice. We would venture to say therefore that the notion of the free exercise of the will, or the capacity for willing freely, although not explicitly formulated by him, is a significant if somewhat concealed theme in his political thought.

The problem of human freedom can be seen, from a Berlinian perspective, as the problem of freedom of choice, and freedom of choice is bound to advance into the focus of one of the deepest premises of late modern political philosophy, the freedom of the will. The free expression of the will is never altogether out of sight in his writings on freedom, conspicuously in his strictures against determinism. Berlin briefly but darkly suggests at the end of the introduction to his landmark work that he is "well aware of how much more needs to be done, especially on the issue of free will, the solution of which seems to me to require a set of new conceptual tools [which no one] has yet been able to provide."[27] Berlin emphasizes freedom of choice as a counterweight to authoritarianism in all its forms. The idealistic philosophy of freedom which he espouses endorses a movement toward ever more freedom for the individual, free in the sense of having an opportunity for making choices, with will rather than deliberation as the mechanism of that choice.

It would be hard for us to understand how freedom of choice unhinged to anything else can sustain itself as an absolute value for Berlin inasmuch as his moral variation presupposes an area where one's freedom of choice must not be unalterably in conflict with another's freedom of choice. There is clearly no choice without freedom, as indicated by the term "freedom of choice," but paradoxically freedom of choice must be curtailed in order to make room for the freedom of choice of others.[28] Berlin says outright that "there is no justification for compromise on . . . mindless killing," killing without a reason, thus marking the limits of freedom of choice in no uncertain terms.[29] He takes for granted the necessity and possibility of freedom of choice as an essential of the human condition, but obfuscates the standards necessary for making viable choices. He simply looks at limitations on freedom of choice as restraints rather than as reasonable standards scrutinizing its exercise.

Berlin asserts that absolute values are irreconcilable in principle, but suggests that conflicting values can be accommodated in practice through a willingness to tolerate moral variation. He seeks to extricate humanism from the clash of absolute values, a clash which he regards as a given of the human condition. He rules out the possibility of examining and evaluating the various and conflicting claims about freedom with a view to their reasonableness, accepting, as he does, the questionably insoluble clash of human values as a given. It is for this reason that his focus on freedom of choice, a freedom which does not regard any justifications we give for our choices as reasonable, is out of focus, at least insofar as resuscitating a viable liberalism is concerned. It is easy enough to understand Berlin's passionate attachment to freedom of choice, but nothing whatsoever can explain his failure to consider the quality of the choice which freedom makes possible.

Berlin, holding the view which he does of absolute values, speaks of creating agreement in the political arena between conflicting claims made in the name of freedom through compromise rather than persuasion. He apparently believes that compromises on matters of principle or agreements to disagree are the best that can be had in settling political controversies, thus obscuring the effect of reasoned persuasion in dealing with such matters, that is, the effort to persuade others that our reasons are better than theirs. Berlin's writings remain devoid of any serious reference to the rational dimension of the persuasive power, the reasonings by which we are led to making our choices. What is not possible for him to imagine is that politics, with all its irrationalities, points the way to its refinement through invigorating political disputation. It is precisely from this point of view that politics is the realm of persuasion, but Berlin's emphasis is almost entirely on freedom of choice rather than freedom of discussion or freedom of thought. Any serious work in political philosophy would require that one should take into account the rationality implicit in political life, that is, that politics finds its end and culmination, or achieves its full self consciousness, through the seriousness of political discourse, and the freedom of the mind on which all serious political discourse rests.

Berlin's counsel against perfectionism so characteristic of his thought is underscored in a statement of Immanuel Kant's that "out of the crooked timber of humanity no straight thing was ever made," which statement furnishes the title for his (*i.e.,* Berlin's) most recent collection of essays. The straight things he speaks of are perfect societies demanded by dogmatically believed-in theoretical convictions which in his view almost always lead to inhumanity, not to mention a substantial loss of freedom.[30] It is true that the sphere of practice is always endangered by false theoretical opinions, those theories which do not regard sufficiently the intricacies of that sphere, but contrary to what Berlin appears to suggest, practice would be altogether directionless in the absence of theoretical thought. The complicated relation between theory and practice needs more elaboration than Berlin's political thought is able to provide. The very least that can be said in this regard is that premodern political philosophy with all its perfectionism never claimed to have direct application to political practice.

CONCLUSION

One could conceivably understand Berlin's moral pluralism either as an alternative to the perverted liberalism which insists on the relative value of all beliefs or convictions, or simply as a protection for diversity in the interest of freedom. The politically problematic character of Berlin's thought reveals itself most clearly in his remark that human thoughts on freedom are in a state of disagreement, which thoughts do not merely differ, but contradict one another.[31] But there is no reason to assume that his brand of pluralism would provide an adequate solution to that problem, for even pluralism at its best was never intended as a way of accommodating irreconcilable values. Berlin recognizes that one cannot remain tolerant (the tolerance that his pluralism attempts to provide for) when faced with

absolute intolerance, and yet he cannot seem to see that to tolerate means to endure a deviation within limits from some fixed set standard of excellence. He asserts that there cannot be an absolute standard, but surreptitiously introduces such a standard in the form of "a minimum opportunity for choice . . . below which human activity ceases to be free in any meaningful sense."[32] Berlin even goes so far as to say that "genuine belief in the inviolability of a minimum extent of individual liberty entails some . . . absolute stand," frontiers of freedom which nobody should be permitted to cross.[33] It would seem reasonable therefore to assume that freedom in the sense of freedom to choose and opportunity to be left alone cannot be seen independent of a closedness to those who would place great restrictions on freedom. It is in accordance with this reasoning that a proper understanding of freedom in its political setting would require some absolute standards governing its exercise.

Berlin has made an effort to formulate a philosophy of freedom, but there is in his approach a refusal to take cognizance of the essentially rational character of freedom, that political freedom which justifies itself through thoughtful deliberation, through the discretion of wisdom. All other considerations aside, we might say that it is not freedom of choice, but the thought behind that choice, or freedom of the mind, which gives freedom its essential character. Berlin leaves us with the feeling that he would like to have something more solid than freedom of choice as an end in itself, but his perspective is clouded by an orientation which prevents him from considering the possibility of a principle which would allow him to place limitations on the exercise of freedom. Something of the character of his ambivalence can be seen in his failure to recognize that there is a higher principle than freedom operative in political life, but he nevertheless believes that there are frontiers, not artificially drawn, within which individuals should be inviolable in their rights.[34] If we were to reduce the whole of Berlin's thought to a single sentence, it would be his statement that "unlimited liberty [must be curtailed, but] no clear principles [limiting the extent of that liberty] can be enunciated."[35]

Notes

1. Isaiah Berlin and Ramin Jahanbegloo, *Conversations with Isaiah Berlin* (New York: Charles Scribner's Sons, 1991).

2. *Four Essays on Liberty* (London, New York: Oxford University Press, 1969); *Concepts and Categories: Philosophical Essays* (London: Hogarth Press, 1978); *The Crooked Timber of Humanity: Chapters in the History of Ideas* (London: John Murray, 1990).

3. *Four Essays on Liberty,* p. 168.

4. *Ibid.,* p. 169; *Conversations with Isaiah Berlin,* p. 43.

5. *Four Essays on Liberty,* p. li.

6. *Ibid.,* pp. 169, 171.

7. *The Crooked Timber of Humanity,* pp. 17-18.

8. *Ibid.,* p. 87.

9. *Ibid.,* p. 11.

10. *Ibid.,* pp. 2-3.

11. *Four Essays on Liberty,* p. li.

12. *The Crooked Timber of Humanity,* p. 9.

13. *Four Essays on Liberty,* p. 184.

14. *Ibid.,* p. 163.

15. Speech on Conciliation with America, *Works of Edmund Burke,* 7th ed.,12 vols. (Boston: Little, Brown, and Company, 1881), II: 121.

16. *Ibid.,* pp. 159, 172.

17. *Ibid.,* pp. 96-97.

18. *The Crooked Timber of Humanity,* p. 18.

19. *Four Essays on Liberty,* p. lx.

20. *Ibid.,* pp. xl, 129.

21. *Politics* 1317b

22. *Four Essays on Liberty,* p. 130.

23. *Ibid.,* pp. xl, 129.

24. *Ibid.,* pp. 120, 121.

25. *Ibid.,* p. 121.

26. *Ibid.,* p. lv.

27. *Ibid.,* p. lxiii.

28. *The Crooked Timber of Humanity,* pp. 11-12.

29. *Ibid.,* p. 18.

30. *Ibid.,* p. 19.

31. *Four Essays on Liberty,* pp. 169, 171.

32. *Ibid.,* p. lii.

33. *Ibid.,* pp. 165, 164.

34. *Ibid.,* p. 165.

35. *Conversations with Isaiah Berlin,* p. 41.

David McCabe (essay date 1998)

SOURCE: "Isaiah Berlin: Understanding, Not Mastery," in *Commonweal,* Vol. CXXXV, No. 14, August 14, 1998, p. 16.

[*In the following tribute, McCabe asserts that one of Berlin's outstanding qualities was his attempt to understand, rather than to master, his subject.*]

Isaiah Berlin's greatest contribution to the world of ideas may have been his exemplary commitment to the ideal of genuine understanding over mere intellectual mastery. More than most philosophers, he understood not only that mastery of a subject is not synonymous with deep understanding, but also that the pursuit of the first may imperil the second. The drive for intellectual mastery grows out of the assumption that the world is ultimately made for us and that the disciplined exercise of a properly trained mind can make all things clear: the deepest fabric of reality, the unvarying structures of human consciousness, the proper end of human activity. It is a comforting idol, but a false and distorting one. Whatever contemporary philosophers think on the question of whether the world was designed for our purposes, most recognize (partly as a result of Berlin's efforts) that our ways of conceptualizing, the very tools of organized thought, are shot through with contingency reflecting our particular time in history and our distinctive forms of life.

But for Berlin, this ideal of mastery and its underlying hubris about human reason were not only intellectually unsound, but potential sources of great cruelty as well. As he suggested in his famous essay **"Two Concepts of Liberty,"** the "one belief, more than any other, responsible for the slaughter of individuals on the altars of the great historical ideals" is the belief that somewhere there exists a single definitive answer to the question of how human beings should live. He was thinking of Hitler and Stalin: he was warning of Pol Pot and Milosevic.

For Berlin, then, there were both intellectual and moral reasons to replace the ideal of mastery with the more humane and demanding one of understanding. Humane, because it allows greater space for such things as feelings, sensitivities, and traditions; demanding, because anyone who is willing to open himself to the world's diversity, and who forgoes the urge to reduce it to the neatness of the philosopher's categories, must always be prepared to have his deepest beliefs undermined and to find that he knows less than he thought. The result of this sort of inquiry is likely to be not a single magisterial work setting forth a system, but instead, as in Berlin's case, a constantly startling body of essays on a dazzling array of issues and thinkers, rays of light illuminating areas that we either had not attended to carefully or had misunderstood by imposing our own sets of problems and expectations. If any one theme dominates Berlin's work, it is his commitment to the truth of pluralism—to the view that a fulfilling human life can take many forms, and that there is no single formula to guide the choices we make about which goods to pursue either individually or collectively. What this commitment implies is that the goal of understanding those who think and act differently from us must always be prior to that of jan idea of enormous impact in contemporary moral and political philosophy.

But though the ideal of mastery is ultimately ill-conceived, the qualities that dispose one for apparent success in it are, unfortunately, doled out more liberally than those conducive to deep understanding. The former include cleverness, an obsession with scoring points in argument, and a willingness to sacrifice humane engagement in the name of analytic rigor. What is needed for real understanding, for making the strange coherent and revealing the complexity in the familiar, is not only deep learning and an expansive intellect, but also qualities like charity, compassion, and humility. That Berlin could yoke these traits to a felicity of expression and analytic skills of the highest order ensures that his influence will be felt in humanistic studies for decades to come. For many of us who style ourselves intellectuals and seek better to understand the human world, he will remain a model we strive vainly, but happily, to emulate.

Ned O'Gorman (essay date 1998)

SOURCE: "My Dinners With Isaiah," in *Commonweal*, Vol. CXXXV, No. 14, August 14, 1998, pp. 15-6.

[*In the following reminiscence, O'Gorman writes of Berlin's love of music.*]

Isaiah Berlin (1907-97), my friend of only six years, was the happiest man I ever met. He simply knew all about it. He saw the shadows and the terrible light hidden in the shadows. He listened to the world as he listened to Schubert and Bach, as he read Akhmatova and Herzen, touching them with his wit and the speed of his manner. What he perceived in literature and art, in political epochs and in their recorders, in composers and musicians, in the fine differences between virtuoso pianists Alfred Brendel and Sviatoslav Richter and their interpretations of Schubert, was a prodigy of practical knowledge, grace, and almost transcendent intuition.

He told me at our first meeting in Oxford, in April 1991, that he was an old man and would soon die. Might I have lunch with him in Salzburg in August at Tomaselli's? It was a cafe I loved, and our conversation that April day was filled with wonderful correspondences. Who, he asked, were the pianists I most admired? I named five and was right on the money: Radu Lupu, Richter, Brendel, Murray Perahia, and Andras Schiff. I asked him, quite terrified that I would be taken for a fool, did he not think Horowitz was very bad? He did.

When Isaiah was twenty-one, he wrote music criticism for the Oxford Outlook under the pseudonym of Albert Alfred Apricott. Even then he knew who he was—a mixture, a plural man, part Ariel, Puck, and Falstaff, and part sage, each lovely human facet of him cohering and radiating complete delight and the most elegant and yet not unflamboyant manner. He made the balance endure with grace.

I think that Isaiah found the world a marvelously interesting place. He was caught up in it, in its curiosities, in its absolutes, in its queer turns and sudden precipices, and how one wanted to know all about it. We used to play a little game: we thought of an imaginary line. On one side was genius and a sort of dwelling place of the great, and there was the space leading to it. Who got close, who got over the line, and who didn't get anywhere near it? We deliberated long about the quartets of Shoshtakovich, five of which I had heard the previous night. We decided that no

matter how harrowing and tragic his quartets, somehow they are too exposed to the tempests of his feelings, too raw, too muddled to achieve the divine. But Isaiah could move with the agility of a tumbler to exclaim the next instant over what a "fine picture" Georg Frederich Kersting's Lesender bei Lamenlicht was. (He did not make it over the line.) It was the mix Isaiah understood so well. Pluralism is a mix, and in it one can discern, if one looks with a pure eye, the lineaments of truth.

I used to come to London or Salzburg, where we met over the years, armed with ideas, a new book, and once with the discovery that Andras Schiff played Bach quite as well as Glenn Gould, if not better, perhaps, being less rigid and less technical and closer to the soul of Bach. Isaiah loved Schiff's Bach. It was that mercury in Isaiah, that breakneck way he had of going from one thing to another as if he were composing a sonata: the melodies and sonorities of the mind and the imagination always in tune, at perfect pitch. During a chat about the Jewish mystics, especially about one Uriel Acosta who was a heretic and died a most gory death, a rich American lady, a friend of a certain great age, entered the restaurant and sat across from us. Isaiah said, "I cannot talk to her," and was out onto the sidewalk in a flash.

I think that the notion that the speed and the dance of the mind might soon stop made him so resent the idea of death. He was annoyed that he had to die, as if one had to expect that in the middle of a Schubert sonata or a Beethoven string quartet the music would stop and the players would sprint out for a game of cricket, leaving the beauty and the wonder abandoned to the void. There was still so much to do, to see. Once, at the Atheneum, one of his London clubs, he reflected that he had never written about the Romantic poets and wished to do exactly that soon. Isaiah was intent on it because I do not think poetry came easily to him. I once sent him a first edition of the American literary critic Richard Blackmur and wondered if he had a chance to look at it. I think they would have been great friends. And at that tea, in the midst of musings about death and the Romantics, we talked of Verdi's *Falstaff* and of his sublime aria in the second act when Falstaff recollects his life as a page in the Court of the Duke of Norfolk ("Quand ero paggio del Duca di Norfolk"). We sang it loud enough so that some eyes turned toward us. I pronounced some word incorrectly. Isaiah corrected me and looked at that moment at a beautiful young woman with a fall of the most luminous blond hair who was seated nearby.

In December 1995, I had gotten the notion that Isaiah and Mitsuko Uschida, the colossal Japanese pianist, should meet. I brought them together in a lowly basement bar in Picadilly. All the clubs were closed. It was a terrible day—sleet, rain, snow, strong winds. We drank champagne, and oh, what wonderful stories I heard. When we said farewell to Mitsuko, I walked Isaiah back to his flat in Albany. Along the way we began to hum the opening bars of Schubert's Sonata, in B Flat, D. 960. I remember how cold it was. Undaunted, he paced along. Isaiah wore neither scarf nor gloves; he pushed away the air, thc sleet, his voice piercing the winds. I got something wrong, the trills, I think, that crash up out of the abyss of Schubert's melancholy in the first movement. Isaiah set me right. Got me on pitch.

Once, over lunch at the Garrick, he told me that one of the first songs he ever learned was "A Bicycle Built for Two." As we sang it together "Daisy, Daisy, give me your answer true . . ."—we began to muse over just how Susanna's aria in the last act of *The Marriage of Figaro* went, going over bits of it to get it more or less right.

Music always, always its clarion call to the mystery, always at the center of everything Isaiah found true and beautiful in his radiant life, even in the storm of the early evening in Picadilly. I left him at the entrance to Albany, that grand and imposing set of flats tucked in behind the traffic where all who are anybody in the world of the mighty might choose to live, but Isaiah was beyond that, what with the Romantics in his mind and Schubert bringing order to the present little winter tempest.

Isaiah's soul is most clear to me in his essay on Verdi, **"The Naivete of Verdi."** His sensibility is captured there, all the themes of his intellect, of his spirit. He wrote, "He [Verdi] was the last master to paint with positive, clear primary colors, to give direct expression to the eternal, major human emotions: love and hate, jealousy and fear, indignation and passion; grief, fury, mockery, cruelty, irony, fanaticism, the passions that all men know."

Isaiah said to me the year before he died not his exact words (I never kept notes after my visits with him, thinking it a violation of some kind of trust) but true to the spirit of his thought "Ned, when I die, there will be a grand memorial and you must come to it and push through the crowds and say, 'I knew Sir Isaiah Berlin, he was my friend. I want to speak.'"

Of course, when I went to London for his memorial in the Hamstead Synagogue, I could not do that for, as he had said, it was a grand and grave event. The space was filled with his friends, titles and all of that, and it would have been a silly gesture and not tolerated. Alfred Brendel played the second movement of Schubert's B Flat Major Sonata, D. 960 with care, and a sense of loss in every note, with complete sorrow as if he played it just for his beloved friend, as if he were there before him. (Isaiah could not understand why Brendel could not bear Richter—Brendel turned off the radio once when a recording of Richter's was played.) Isaac Stern, with fragile reverence and some torment, played the Sarabande from the D. Minor Partita of Bach. All very solemn—adagio, andante, no vivace, allegro, presto, scherzo—no music to recall Albert Alfred Apricott.

The memorial held later in the month at the British Embassy in Washington, D.C., was just the sort Isaiah would have disapproved of with impatient but charitable annoy-

ance. Dull, loving remembrances and no music anywhere—no piano, violin, string quartet—just sweet reflections that went on far too long. "Daisy, Daisy, give me your answer true," now that would have added a decent zing and would have revealed an Isaiah someone other than I must have known.

No death but my own son's has left me so alone. On the trip back to New York I wept. London would be a strange place without him now, as if the recitative had been lifted out of Bach's B Minor Mass, as if the branches of a flowering tree had suddenly withered and left their blossoms on the ground. I shall always hope that he might just walk into a room and greet me. "Caro amico," he would say, and then, when we had settled down to some hot chocolate (his) and wine (mine), "Now Ned, what is your news?"

And about Isaiah's troubles with death and a final annihilation, I offer this last reflection. During Easter of 1996 when I saw Isaiah in London, I had just come from Rome where I had scattered my son's ashes beneath an umbrella pine on a terrace in the Vatican. My son had died of AIDS a month before. I told Isaiah how transcendent Rome had been, how filled with light and flowers and cool fountains' bright tumult in the sun, cascading through my grief. I told him it was the only city in the world I loved, and he said, "Yes, I too find it the best of cities." Ah, I thought, that is good to know because my son, through all his tribulations with his sickness, through his loss of faith, yet asked me to scatter his ashes there where we had spent many summers. I found it a sign that he knew the eternal when he saw it. I think Isaiah saw it there as well, as he of course discerned it in Schubert and in Falstaff and in Bach.

I trust Isaiah's quicker-than-light wit to smile at this notion. I think that that just slightly mad and music-stricken, romantic corner of paradise where Keats and Shelley, Wordsworth, Byron, and Coleridge dwell will greet Isaiah with delight. They will be a revelation to him. "I'm drawn to mad people," he told me when we were talking about Hamann. Though from time to time, to flee eternal encounters with his friends—Tolstoy, Shakespeare, Mozart, especially Schubert—he might drift away and look downward from the divine promontories toward earth, ardently and with rue, wishing to be part again of its enchanted spin through space.

Norman Podhoretz (essay date 1999)

SOURCE: "A Dissent on Isaiah Berlin," *Commentary*, Vol. 107, No. 2, February, 1999, pp. 25-37.

[*Staking his Neo-Conservatism claim against Berlin's Liberalism, Podhoretz argues, in the following essay, that Berlin has been over-esteemed as a thinker and as a personality.*]

By the time Sir Isaiah Berlin died in 1997 at the age of eighty-eight, a thick layer of piety and even reverence had long since come to surround his name, and accordingly the obituaries both here and in England took it more or less for granted that he had been, if not the leading political philosopher of the age, then at least a strong contender for that position. He was celebrated for the brilliance of his mind, for the profundity of his thought, for the depth and range of his learning and—not least—for his steadfast defense of liberal values against their rivals both on the Left and on the Right.

Now, there can be no question that in some ways Berlin was an admirable figure. But there are also grounds for believing that he was overrated as a thinker (whether one classifies him as a political philosopher or more precisely as a historian of ideas). In my judgment, too, he suffered as a person from a serious character flaw that robbed even what many conservatives would consider his best and most valuable ideas of any real force in practice. These ideas were thereby prevented from having the salutary influence they might have exerted at certain crucial and difficult moments.

In due course I will get to my reasons for not joining in the chorus of adulation for Berlin, and why arriving at a more temperate estimate of him seems to me important to our general intellectual health. But I want to dwell first on why, even so, I was hit by a sense of loss when he died and by a great feeling of regret at how few were the hours I got to spend in his company. Sharp as it was at the time, this feeling has now been reignited and exacerbated by a reading of Michael Ignatieff's new book, *Isaiah Berlin: A Life*.[1] This is an official biography in that it was authorized by Berlin, who cooperated in every way. He did not, however, ask for the right to approve the manuscript. On the contrary, he refused to read it and stipulated that the book be published only after his death.

Ignatieff is a very good and a very intelligent writer, and not the least of his literary virtues is that he has been able to digest ten years of taped conversations with a famously voluble subject, a nonstop talker of legendary proportions, and then to recast all this material which, when transcribed, must have run into thousands upon thousands of pages, into a book running to only a little over 300. In this mercifully brief space, Ignatieff manages to do an excellent, if understandably quite uncritical, job of covering both the thought and the life of Isaiah Berlin.

One problem faced by Ignatieff is that Berlin never produced a major work conveniently pulling together the various elements of his philosophy. Nevertheless, Ignatieff is able to extract a lucid and coherent account of it from the many scattered essays and lectures through which Berlin most naturally expressed himself. But there was also another kind of problem Ignatieff had to contend with in telling the story of Berlin's life—a life compounded, as Berlin himself once summed it up, of "three strands": Russian, English, and Jewish.

Being himself of Russian ancestry and a longtime resident of England, Ignatieff was well equipped to unravel the first two of these strands. But not being Jewish, he might have

been expected to run into a bit of trouble with the third. Yet he almost always gets things right in dealing with its nuances and complexities—a feat that not that many Jewish writers would have been able to pull off with comparable accuracy, particularly when we consider that the strand of Jewishness in Berlin was further complicated by being both familiar and unusual.

The familiar part is the journey of a Jewish boy of eleven from Riga, Latvia (then under czarist rule), where he was born in 1909 and lived until the age of six, and then Petrograd, where he spent the next five years, to the upper reaches of intellectual life in the new country to which his family had been forced to flee. Countless such journeys with similar outcomes were traversed—both earlier and later, and by both rich and poor—to America: young immigrants arriving with little or no English and themselves or their children becoming within an amazingly short time major figures in the culture as writers, painters, composers, scientists, philosophers, professors, journalists.

One tends to assume that there were fewer such instances in England, whose society, being both more stratified and more insular, was less permeable than America's to foreigners of any stripe, let alone Jews. Yet as the economist P.T. Bauer—himself a penniless teenage immigrant "of Jewish origin" from Hungary who, capping a distinguished academic career, wound up sitting in the House of Lords—has never tired of pointing out, England was far more welcoming to foreign-born talent than is often imagined. Which is to say that the career of Isaiah Berlin *qua* intellectual was by no means unique. The faculties of Oxford and Cambridge and the London School of Economics (LSE) had a fair share of immigrant Jews (especially in the physical and social sciences) even before their number was swollen by refugees fleeing from Nazi Germany.

Still—and here we come to the unusual part of Berlin's story—very few even of the foreign-born English Jews who were knighted, and/or made it to the House of Lords, ever ascended the most rarefied heights of English society to anything like the extent that Berlin eventually did. No doubt not all these people had the insatiable appetite for high society that was one of Berlin's ruling passions; some of them may positively have disdained dining with duchesses or becoming frequent guests at Buckingham Palace. But whether or not their ambitions ran in that direction, and whether or not, in one of Berlin's own formulations, they were great "diners-out," the fact of their Jewishness—however faintly they might have borne its stigmata or however distant they might have grown from the mores and practices of their ancestors—remained enough of a disqualification to keep them in their social place.

There may have been more exceptions to this rule than I am aware of, but the only one I happen personally to have encountered who scaled the same social battlements as Berlin was—and is—George Weidenfeld. A decade younger, a publisher rather than an academic, and a post-Hitler refugee from Vienna rather than from Bolshevik

Russia, Weidenfeld still had much in common with Berlin. The two men also had a professional association that turned out to be very important. As Ignatieff informs us:

> Weidenfeld had been shrewd enough to see the commercial potential locked up in an obscure essay, "Lev Tolstoy's Historical Skepticism," which Isaiah had published in *Oxford Slavonic Papers* in 1951. By retitling it "The Hedgehog and the Fox," and putting it out for a general readership with additions by Isaiah, Weidenfeld did more for Isaiah's public reputation than any other publisher.

Like many (most?) of their foreign-born English co-religionists, above all in the universities and the intellectual world outside them, both men became thoroughly assimilated into British culture and as Jews they were both frank nonbelievers. Being such, they were also nonobservant, though they might (Berlin much more regularly than Weidenfeld) attend a synagogue on the High Holy Days or a seder on Passover. In Berlin's case, as he himself quipped, "the Orthodox synagogue is the synagogue I am not attending"—except, that is, on the High Holy Days; and "wherever he was in the world on Yom Kippur," we learn from Ignatieff, "he made a point of fasting." Also, "As long as his mother was alive he celebrated the Passover every year in her house." But after her death, Berlin being Berlin, the seder naturally tended to turn into "a grand social occasion, with Lord Rothschild, Lord Goodman, the painter R.B. Kitaj and Murray Perahia, the pianist, in attendance."

Yet nonbelieving and nonobservant though they were, both Berlin and Weidenfeld were entirely open about and comfortable in the skin of their Jewishness, and both were lifelong and highly dedicated Zionists. One might have thought that this would have denied them access to the most fashionable circles. Which is what happened, for example, to Sir Lewis Namier (1888-1960), a Jew from Galicia and a Zionist activist whose great achievements as a historian of 18th-century England were enough to earn him a knighthood and other honors without also securing him entrée (except for purposes of research) into the aristocratic world whose acceptance he yearned for in vain and to whose past he devoted enormous scholarly labor. But no such barrier was erected against Weidenfeld and still less against Berlin.

To be sure, Namier was so acerbic and unpleasant that (as Berlin himself tells us in a touching essay about him) not only was he spurned by the "London clubmen (whom he often naively pursued)" but, even though everyone at Oxford acknowledged his greatness and originality as a historian, he was also even repeatedly passed over for the professorship he coveted there. In the sharpest possible contrast, Berlin and Weidenfeld were so charming and witty and such great raconteurs as to be irresistible companions, whether tête-à-tête or at a large gathering. In combination with these qualities, their Jewishness perhaps lent just the right dose—not too much, not too little—of an intriguing exoticism. Someone once said that if you were in low spirits, there was no one you would rather see walk through your door than Isaiah Berlin. I would say much the same thing about George Weidenfeld, as would many others.

Apart from everything else, Berlin and Weidenfeld had no peers in the realm of classy gossip. Both also specialized in that branch of snobbish Jewish genealogy known in Yiddish as *yiches,* or distinguished family connections. Once, for instance, when on a visit to London I was invited to tea by Berlin at (where else?) the Ritz, I asked him in the course of an inevitably wide-ranging conversation about a Harvard professor with a name that the professor pronounced very differently from the way it was spelled. "Well, you see," Berlin replied with a wicked little smile as he told me how the name actually should sound—a pronunciation that immediately gave away its East European origin—the professor did not really mind its being known that he was Jewish, but he most assuredly wanted it thought that his family was not from Minsk or Pinsk but from an aristocratic Sephardi clan "in Mantua or Nantua, as the case may be." And where Gentiles were concerned, if by chance there were a Jew hidden somewhere in an aristocratic woodpile, Berlin and Weidenfeld would be more certain to have dug him out than the editors of *Burke's Peerage.* The question of converted Jews and the children of converted Jews also fascinated them: one of the best things Berlin ever wrote was an essay entitled "Benjamin Disraeli, Karl Marx, and the Search for Identity."[2]

Speaking of *yiches,* Berlin had plenty of it, both in his own right and by marriage. Through his father he was related to the Schneersons, the family of the Lubavitch dynasty of hasidic *rebbes;* and through his wife Aline, the granddaughter of the banker Baron Guenzburg, he was also connected to one of the richest and most eminent Jewish philanthropists in Europe. (Aline's inherited fortune was multiplied by her former marriage to a very rich man.) As a Zionist, he had *yiches* as well: Yitzhak Sadeh, one of the founding fathers of Palmach, the elite striking force of the Haganah, out of which after statehood the Israeli army emerged, was simultaneously his uncle and his cousin.

There was a certain *yiches,* too, in the fact that Berlin's Russian childhood differed radically from that of the vast majority of Jews who emigrated from that part of the world in the late 19th and early 20th centuries. Most of them had lived in dire poverty and in the constricted physical conditions of the Pale of Settlement in Russia and the ghettoized *shtetlakh* of Poland, forbidden or unable to travel outside these areas or to practice certain occupations. But for a variety of historical reasons, the Jews of Riga were exempt from these rules. Berlin's father was a very well-to-do timber merchant, and his mother, while remaining a reasonably observant Jew, was far more highly cultivated than the typical Russian-Jewish woman of her generation. She read widely in secular literature in several languages, and Russian rather than Yiddish was spoken in the household. Berlin, an only child, even had a governess. Indeed, the family left Russia not because of czarist anti-Semitism but because of the Bolshevik assault on the bourgeoisie, the class to which they belonged. In this respect, the emigration of the Berlins resembled and anticipated the later flight of the prosperous Jews of Germany and Austria who succeeded in escaping from Hitler.

In any event, once the Berlins were settled in England, Isaiah was sent to the upscale St. Paul's school in London and then to Oxford, where he studied philosophy and would spend most of his professional life as a scholar and a teacher.

To my great good fortune, I have passed manyhours in the company of Lord Weidenfeld (as he has been for some years now), but I was not so lucky with Sir Isaiah Berlin (who was both knighted and then decorated with the Order or Merit, or OM, an even higher honor than the life peerage awarded to Weidenfeld). I did, however, see enough of him to get a strong taste of the delights that his company afforded (even one meeting would have sufficed for such a taste). I therefore have no difficulty in understanding why he was sought after as a dinner guest in England by Lady This and the Duchess of That. The same was true of their untitled counterparts in America, whom he first got to know during World War II as a junior official at the British embassy in Washington.

His job in Washington was to write weekly reports on the state of American opinion, to be sent out under the signature of the British ambassador, Lord Halifax. But it was obvious to everyone, including Prime Minister Winston Churchill, that Halifax himself could not possibly have produced such brilliant work, and it soon became widely known that the actual author was, as the Foreign Office reported in response to Churchill's inquiry, a "Mr. Berlin, of Baltic Jewish extraction, by profession a philosopher."

Incidentally, Churchill's discovery of the identity of the author of Halifax's dispatches led to a wonderful comic episode. "In early February 1944," as Ignatieff recounts it,

Clementine Churchill informed her husband that Irving Berlin was in London, and could he find time to thank him for his war work. On the contrary, the Prime Minister said, he must come to lunch. . . . The guests included Sir Alan Brooke, Commander of the Imperial General Staff, and the Duchess of Buccleuch. . . . At the head of the table, Churchill kept up a steady stream of talk about the war situation. At the end of lunch, . . . Churchill . . . asked Berlin when he thought the war would end. "Mr. Prime Minister, I shall tell my children and grandchildren that Winston Churchill asked *me* that question." By now thoroughly confused, Churchill asked what was the most important thing that Mr. Berlin had written. He replied, "White Christmas."

It was only after the lunch was over that Churchill's secretary "broke the case of mistaken identity to the Prime Minister," whose bewilderment of course gave way to great amusement. When the "Irving-Winston-Isaiah" story got around, it only served to enhance Isaiah's already rising status.

Being the genius of sociability he was, Berlin also (and, from the point of view of his professional duties, quite legitimately) used his job to make personal contacts. By the time he returned to England, he had gotten to know practically everyone who was anyone in Washington and New York. Enduring friendships were formed not only with upcoming young academics and diplomats of his own generation like Arthur Schlesinger, Jr., and George F. Kennan, but also with older public figures like Felix Frankfurter—as well, inevitably, as with great hostesses of the time like Alice Longworth (the notoriously wicked-tongued daughter of Theodore Roosevelt) and future ones like Katharine Graham (who would in due course become the publisher of the *Washington Post* and the American social equivalent of a duchess herself).

As I have already suggested, that this should have occurred is not in the least surprising. For, again with the exception of Weidenfeld—who would later travel in many of the same circles on both sides of the Atlantic—I have never in my life encountered a more effervescent conversationalist than Isaiah Berlin. He was not, as Ignatieff acknowledges, a great wit in the Oscar Wilde mode: he did not toss off epigrams that everyone would remember and quote. But there was wit in every other turn of phrase and in the way he framed the conceptions and descriptions with which he regaled everyone within earshot. Words poured out of him in such profusion and such a rush that his interlocutors sometimes had trouble understanding him, or else complained that they themselves could never get a word in when he was at the other end of a conversation. Yet in my own limited experience, I was always struck by how attentive a listener he could be—much more so than most of the great talkers I have known (and I have known my share). His mind was so quick that he could grasp a point one was making before it scarcely had a chance to get out of one's mouth; and he could give it back in a paraphrase that immediately cut to its intellectual quick.

That Berlin was so awesomely articulate perhaps proved a greater gift to others than to himself. So, at any rate, he seems to have felt. He often denigrated his own achievements, a trait that might be considered the intellectual's equivalent of the unseemly game of a rich person playing at being poor. Yet Ignatieff, who speaks often of this habit, mainly interprets it as "part of a carefully cultivated strategy . . . intended to deflect and disarm criticism." Probably it was. For despite his oft-professed indifference to the opinions others held of his work, or for what posterity might say about it, Berlin was very thin-skinned—as the following story I recently heard sadly illustrates.

On the occasion of his eightieth birthday, when tributes were pouring in from all over the world and the British press could hardly find enough space to report on the encomia coming his way, a lone voice—that of the conservative philosopher Roger Scruton—piped up in one paper with a tribute that was not wholly free of a few mildly critical remarks. The scandal this article created within the British intellectual establishment was so disproportionate—Berlin's friends being as thin-skinned on his behalf as he was on his own—that a man who had been close to Berlin for many years was puzzled: what, he was heard to wonder at a private dinner party, was so terrible about Scruton's piece? This question was immediately relayed by the drum-beaters in the London jungle to Berlin, who responded to it the very next day with an eighteen-page handwritten letter full of hurt feelings and accusations of betrayal. Berlin even compared Scruton to Goebbels, and refused to retract when challenged by his morally stunned correspondent.

I tell this story not in order to expose Berlin as a hypocrite for pretending not to care about his reputation, but rather as a suggestive piece of evidence for the genuineness of the self-doubt that afflicted him—an affliction that I would guess was caused by his inability ever to write anything that for dazzle and sweep could match his extemporaneous talk. This was a problem he tried to solve by dictating his essays, and his legion of admirers assured him and everyone else that he had succeeded. But Berlin himself, I suspect, knew better, which was why it was only after much persuasion from young disciples that he allowed those essays to be published—some for the first time—in a series of collections that were issued in his later years.

I gather from Ignatieff that Berlin was also tormented by his failure to write the big book, the great book, that was expected of him. When, in those same later years, he made a sustained effort to satisfy this expectation with a major study of Romanticism—a subject upon which he had touched in many of his essays—he spent much time reading and taking notes but, like a graduate student getting bogged down in a doctoral dissertation, he finally had to give it up.

Berlin, of course, was not the only great talker or lecturer whose written work never measured up to his spoken word. For example, anyone who reads Samuel Taylor Coleridge's *Biographia Literaria* is bound to wonder why he was held in such intellectual awe by his contemporaries in the early 19th century; and one might well have felt the same way about Samuel Johnson's reputation among his own contemporaries a century earlier if there were only his *Lives of the Poets* to go by and James Boswell had never come along to record his table talk.

Good as Ignatieff's biography is, he is no Boswell. He therefore cannot help illserving his subject, who could really have used a Boswell, all the more so in that Berlin's published writings, even at their best, are not in the same league as those of Coleridge or Johnson. Coming closer to home for another case in point, I would also cite the American art historian Meyer Schapiro, a Lithuanian-born Jew whose lectures and conversation were in their own style as exhilarating and scintillating and rich in texture and context as Berlin's, but who similarly had trouble capturing it all on paper and could equally have benefited from a Boswell of his own.

Interestingly, Berlin himself makes a very similar observation about the 19th-century Russian revolutionary Alexander Herzen, who was "a brilliant and irrepressible talker . . . always in an overwhelming flow of ideas and images; the waste, from the point of view of posterity . . . , is probably immense: he had no Boswell . . . to record his conversation." Yet there was compensation for posterity in Herzen's memoirs, *My Past and Thoughts,* which Berlin considered "a literary masterpiece worthy to be placed by the side of the novels of his contemporaries and countrymen, Tolstoy, Turgenev, Dostoevsky." Never having read this book, I cannot say for certain that Berlin's praise is more than a bit extravagant, though I strongly suspect that it is. Be that as it may, Berlin himself left behind nothing that even his most fervent admirers would think of placing on so high a plane.

Herzen was not Jewish, and neither of course were Coleridge and Johnson. Furthermore, neither Berlin nor Schapiro ever had a truly extensive Jewish education. Nevertheless I cannot help wondering whether there may not have been something deeply rooted in Jewish culture that produced the problem with writing experienced by them and a few other great Jewish talkers I could name. What I have in mind is the intimidating effect that talmudic pedagogy has sometimes had on those who have aspired to its deepest levels. Serious students of the Talmud have often been made to feel that they have no business saying anything at all until they have swallowed not only the vast "ocean" of the talmudic text itself but everything the commentators have said about it over the centuries, by which time they discover that anything they might have to add has been said already, and better, by some ancient forebear.

It is true that enough young people overcome the inhibitions this ethos creates to keep the enterprise alive and kicking; and there are those who are able to move with perfect authority into other areas as well. Being educated almost entirely at a Lithuanian yeshiva, for instance, did not prevent Harry Wolfson of Harvard from going on in later life to produce huge and definitive works on subjects as far afield from the Talmud as the early Fathers of the Church and the great medieval Isalmic theologians. Still, all exceptions and qualifications duly noted, rereading Berlin's essays, with their incessant and compulsive references to the thinkers of the past, I got the sense that something like the inhibition that has stymied many Jewish scholars—imbibed, I would suppose, by osmosis as a child—was operating in him and that he was sincerely bothered by the conviction that he himself had nothing original to add.

I would exempt from this generalization his essay on Machiavelli, which begins with a breathtakingly concise survey of just about every interpretation ever offered of that notorious writer, and only then ventures on a new one of his own. Yet even here, revealingly, Berlin feels constrained to apologize:

> Where more than twenty interpretations hold the field, the addition of one more cannot be deemed an impertinence. At worst it will be no more than yet another attempt to solve the problem, now more than four centuries old.

Whether or not there is any validity in my speculation,[3] rereading Berlin was a disappointment. Not that this came as a shock, since my very first introduction to him as a thinker about 45 years ago also resulted in disappointment. He was then (1953) teaching at Oxford, his home base for most of his academic life, and I was a student at "the other place" (that is, Cambridge), but the occasion was a lecture he gave at LSE. The lecture followed hard upon a series of six hour-long talks he had delivered in as many weeks on BBC radio on the general theme of "Freedom and its Betrayal." These talks had become famous not so much because they were difficult and devoted to relatively obscure thinkers like Helvetius and de Maistre as because they were done extemporaneously, from notes, without so much as a pause or a stammer. It was, as Ignatieff rightly says, a "prodigious feat of studied verbal improvisation," and it drew hundreds of thousands of listeners, turning Berlin, then about forty years old and not yet known outside academic circles, into a veritable national celebrity.

I never heard these lectures, but I did hear about them, and when I discovered that Berlin would shortly be speaking at LSE, I wangled an invitation through a friend who was studying there. The auditorium was packed, with the front rows occupied by all the great eminences of the LSE faculty (including Karl Popper, then at the height of his fame as the author of *The Open Society and Its Enemies*) and a large pack of highly distinguished academics who had come down from Oxford and Cambridge.

The excitement in the air was intensified by two titillating circumstances. One was that Berlin was to be introduced by Michael Oakeshott, the leading conservative thinker in England who, to the dismay and even horror of the socialists at LSE and elsewhere, had recently been chosen to succeed one of their main intellectual leaders and heroes, the late Harold Laski, as professor of politics. Obviously Oakeshott, the great critic of liberalism, would not wish to praise Isaiah Berlin, the great exponent of liberalism; but how would he get around the problem? And, since this was the first in a series of lectures that had been endowed to honor the memory of Auguste Comte—who a century earlier had, among other things abominable in Oakeshott's eyes, invented the idea of sociology as a science—Oakeshott would need to figure out how to avoid celebratory words about him as well.

A great hush, charged with suspense, thus descended upon the auditorium as Oakeshott approached the podium. Glancing around with what seemed a look of disapproval bordering on contempt at the size and composition of the

audience for this speaker on this subject, he welcomed us all to the first August Comte Memorial Lecture with the reminder that it had been a hundred years since Comte had burst upon the intellectual scene. At this point he paused and again swept the room with a disdainful glance before continuing: "And what a century it has been for *him*!"

Even Oakeshott's enemies, who far outnumbered his fans in this crowd, were forced to laugh appreciatively at so masterful a stroke, made even more telling by being left to stand alone with no further elaboration. But now it was Berlin's turn to get the Oakeshott treatment, and while it did not go down so well with this audience as his handling of Comte, it was also masterful. How fortunate we were, Oakeshott said, to have as our first Comte Memorial Lecturer the man who had so recently dazzled us all with the virtuosity of his performance on the BBC; so great was Mr. Berlin's virtuosity, indeed, that one might call him "a very Paganini of ideas."[4]

This was a very tough putdown to overcome, and Berlin did not do well. Although I was a liberal in those days, and on his side, I came away wondering why so much fuss was being made about him. The lecture was an attack on historical determinism, with which I entirely agreed but which seemed to me obvious, platitudinous, and—most unexpectedly—labored. Nor was I alone in my disappointment. Ignatieff:

> The fame he had acquired from "Freedom and Its Betrayal" guaranteed a full turnout; his nervousness was increased by Oakeshott's barbed encomium to his skills as a lecturer; and he had ludicrously overprepared. The text was much too long for delivery and he began abridging it as he went, wildly putting pages aside, struggling to keep the argumentative thread together, talking in an ever faster, high-pitched gabble. When he staggered to a conclusion, the reactions were perfunctory and polite and he came away, not for the last time, with the uneasy feeling that his peers were asking themselves whether his reputation was deserved.

Eventually, Berlin turned the lecture into along paper entitled **"Historical Inevitability,"** which Ignatieff characterizes as "an impressive statement of his most fundamental beliefs." That it is a statement of his most fundamental beliefs is certainly true; but "impressive"? Reading it today in a much fuller version than the one I heard in 1953, I was prepared to discover that I had been wrong about it back then. Instead, I was struck by how academic it is, how internal to the professional concerns of historians and other scholars, if somewhat less so than some of the other papers he wrote during this phase of his career demonstrating the fallacy of using the physical sciences as a model for history and philosophy—papers like **"The Concept of Scientific History"** and **"Does Political Theory Still Exist?"** (These can be found, along with much else that came later, in a recently published anthology of his essays.[5]) What struck me even more forcibly is how little—for all its many references to the world outside—it really touches upon the living impact of the main ideas with which it deals.

In making this judgment, I am saying exactly the opposite of what is always said by those who see Berlin as one of the major thinkers of the age. They praise him precisely for addressing himself (as one of them has put it) to "the general reader," for being "erudite but . . . not academic"; or (in the words of another) for the "everyday practicality" of his writings, and for bringing abstract ideas to life by confronting them through "the people who conceived them." Yet to borrow a phrase Berlin himself borrowed in another context from his friend and Oxford colleague, the philosopher A.J. Ayer, much that he wrote amounted to nothing more than "a dramatized tautology." At one point in **"Historical Inevitability,"** he remarks, "All this seems too self-evident to argue." I could not agree more. That is how it seemed to me in 1953 and how it seems to me today.

But just as I would maintain that his essay on Machiavelli represents a rare escape from the inhibitions that may have undermined him as a thinker, there are two essays I would exempt from the strictures I have directed at **"Historical Inevitability"** and the other pieces like it.

The first is the famous **"Two Concepts of Liberty."** Here Berlin begins as usual with brilliant summaries of what all the other commentators have said about his subject over the centuries. But this time the survey of past opinion serves directly to clarify a distinction—between negative liberty and positive liberty, the former consisting of freedom from external obstructions to one's will, the latter of the freedom to pursue a goal defined as the one and only true good—that is anything but academic, having instead the greatest bearing on how different societies have organized themselves politically.

It is also in this essay that he offers what may be the most effective and passionate defense he ever gave of his commitment to "pluralism." In Berlin's usage of the term, "pluralism" signifies that "human goals are many, not all of them commensurable, and in perpetual rivalry with one another." The human fate is to choose among these goals, without the comforting certainty that they have "eternal validity." But this, he insists, is at least better than the various species of "monism," according to each of which there is only one ideal we must aspire to and attain through reason or scientific method or relevation or some other means. "There is little need to stress the fact that monism, and faith in a single criterion," Berlin writes, "has always proved a deep source of satisfaction both to the intellect and to the emotions." But, he adds, it has also been used to justify "the a-priori barbarities of Procrustes—the vivisection of actual human socieites into some fixed pattern dictated by our fallible understanding of a largely imaginary past or a wholly imaginary future."

To put Berlin's point a little less abstractly, "monism," sometimes disguised as "positive liberty," often leads to totalitarianism, while "pluralism" is at the basis of political freedom and its strongest guarantee.

Then there is the even more famous essay, **"The Hedgehog and the Fox,"** to whose publishing history I have already alluded. Contrary to what is often assumed, Berlin did not invent this image: as he tells us in the very first sentence, it comes from the Greek poet Archilocus, among whose surviving fragments is the line: "The fox knows many things, but the hedgehog knows one big thing." Nor is this mainly another essay about the superiority of pluralism (here represented by the fox) over monism (the hedgehog). Berlin does of course take up that theme and elaborates upon it once again with formulations that he has used before, and will use again, along with some that are new. But as its subtitle informs us, and as we know from the title of the original paper that Weidenfeld persuaded him to elaborate, **"The Hedgehog and the Fox"** is actually "An Essay on Tolstoy's View of History."

This is an accurate description as far as it goes, but it is also too modest, since Berlin uses Tolstoy's view of history—set forth in those large sections of *War and Peace* that so many readers have found irritatingly boring interruptions of the book's narrative sections—as a point of entry into the mind and spirit of arguably the greatest novelist who ever lived. Describing the qualities and powers that made Tolstoy great brings out the best in Berlin (as writing with unfailing generosity in appreciation of the genius of others always did):

> No author who has ever lived has shown such powers of insight into the variety of life—the differences, the contrasts, the collisions of persons and things and situations, each apprehended in its absolute uniqueness and conveyed with a degree of directness and a precision of concrete images to be found in no other writer.

Going on in these breathless cadences, Berlin picks up even more speed:

> No one has ever excelled Tolstoy in expressing the specific flavor, the exact quality of a feeling—the degree of its "oscillation," the ebb and flow, the minute movements . . .—the inner and outer texture and "feel" of a look, a thought, a pang of sentiment, no less than of a specific situation, of an entire period, of the lives of individuals, families, communities, entire nations.

And finally:

> The celebrated lifelikeness of every object and every person in his world derives from this astonishing capacity of presenting every ingredient of it in its fullest individual essence, in all its many dimensions, as it were: never as a mere datum, however vivid, within some stream of consciousness, with blurred edges, in outline, a shadow, an impressionist representation; nor yet calling for, and dependent on, some process of reasoning in the mind of the reader; but always as a solid object, seen simultaneously from near and far, in natural, unaltering daylight, from all possible angles of vision, set in an absolutely specific context in time and space—an event fully present to the senses or the imagination in all its facets, with every nuance sharply and firmly articulated.

Having delivered himself of this spectacularly unerring account of Tolstoy as a novelist, Berlin then abruptly, and without even a sentence of transition to soften the shock, asserts that "what [Tolstoy] believed in was the opposite." In other words, it was not enough for Tolstoy to be perhaps the greatest "fox" since Shakespeare (a writer he came to despise and disparage); what he wanted was to be a "hedgehog." In consequence, he himself

> preached not variety but simplicity, not many levels of consciousness but reduction to some single level—. . . some simple, quasi-utilitarian criterion, whereby everything is interrelated directly, and all the items can be assessed in terms of one another by some simple measuring-rod.

I once joked after reading a biography of Tolstoy (the one by Henri Troyat) that he emerges from it looking like a character out of Dostoevsky. Berlin goes even farther—in my opinion, much too far: "Beside Tolstoy, Gogol and Dostoevsky, whose abnormality is so often contrasted with Tolstoy's 'sanity,' are well-integrated personalities, with a coherent outlook and a single vision." But this presupposes, among other things, that Dostoevsky actually was, as Berlin classifies him (on the basis, I suppose, of his religious beliefs), a hedgehog. I, however, would argue that all great novelists, no matter what convictions they may hold or how single-mindedly they hold them, must necessarily be foxes, and that anyone who lacks the qualities of the fox cannot possibly succeed as a novelist; conversely, very few other kinds of writers can match the foxiness of the novelist.

Which is why I think Berlin spoils this otherwise splendid essay by bringing in Joseph de Maistre as another example of a fox who wanted to be a hedgehog. He spoils it in two ways: first by dwelling at length on the question of whether Tolstoy was more influenced by this 18th-century French counterrevolutionary, often considered the intellectual father of the French Right and of French chauvinism, than he was by Stendhal's novel *The Charterhouse of Parma*. But unless something more is done with it than Berlin does here, the question of influence is one of those truly academic issues of no great interest to anyone but professional scholars, and it is a weariness to the "general reader" (this one included) to whom Berlin's work is supposedly addressed.

The other way in which de Maistre's presence damages "The Hedgehog and the Fox" is that he does not enjoy the stature that would entitle him to co-star with a giant like Tolstoy. Emboldened by having learned from Ignatieff that Berlin was capable of discoursing with an air of authority about books into which he had only dipped, I am willing to admit that my own acquaintance with de Maistre is strictly of the dipping kind—and that, moreover, it took place many years ago. But surely it cannot be wrong to assume that he belongs in a lesser and lower realm than Tolstoy, and that speaking of the two of them as though they existed on the same plane undermines the unsurpassed tribute Berlin pays to Tolstoy himself.

Berlin's essays, then, could be undeniably impressive, and scintillating to boot, even if they do not seem to me to merit the hymns almost universally sung to his work and

his ideas. He certainly deserves great credit for having liberated himself from the sterilities of the logical positivism on which he cut his intellectual teeth, turning his attention instead to the great moral and political questions that had been dismissed as meaningless by his friends and colleagues who belonged to that philosophical school. Coming when and where it did, this in itself was an intellectual achievement, and even a brave one, quite apart from the results it produced.

Possibly the most significant and consequential of those results was to have taught the educated English class, including the radically empiricist and even anti-intellectual historians and philosophers within it, that ideas are of supreme importance in human affairs. Berlin attributed his own appreciation of "the vast and sometimes sinister power of ideas" to his Russian origins, for "Russia is a country whose modern history is an object-lesson in the enormous power of abstract ideas" both for good and ill. It was a lesson the English, much more than the French or the Germans or the Americans, needed to be taught, and some of the adulation that came to Berlin in his adopted country probably originated in gratitude to him for having taught it. (The other side of the coin was that this same stubborn empiricist resistance to big abstract or metaphysical ideas, as Berlin saw it, made England the most civilized and the most politically admirable country in the world.)

He had other impressive qualities as well. No one could surpass him in the extremely difficult enterprise of summarizing and tracing the pedigree of an idea and in cutting to the core of another thinker's point of view. And he was especially good in dealing with thinkers like de Maistre whose opinions, though repugnant to him, he could invariably summon up the intellectual imagination to describe with sympathy and great insight. His portraits of major Jewish—or formerly Jewish—figures like Marx, Disraeli, Moses Hess, and Chaim Weizmann are also as delightful as they are illuminating.

But what, substantively, does it all add up to? The answer Berlin's admirers give is that, in an age when fascism and Communism were rampant and sometimes seemed destined to triumph, he developed a profound defense of liberal pluralism that escaped the great pitfall of relativism which (at least in its more extreme forms) he supposedly found just as (or anyway almost as) objectionable as the determinism of such monistic philosophies as Marxism. Yet for the life of me, I cannot perceive any solid logical or philosophical ground in his work for exonerating him from the charge of relativism. He recognizes that relativism, though it can be animated by a spirit of tolerance for and generosity toward other points of view and is thus an antibody to the dangerous disease of fanaticism, is nonetheless vulnerable to a disease of its own: namely, the spinelessness that can develop from the rejection of any absolutes and the correlative failure to develop rock-bottom convictions. But neither his writings nor his own behavior bear out the claim of muscularity that he and others made for his kind of liberalism as compared with some of the other schools of liberal thought emerging from the Enlightenment that he criticized and from which he dissociated himself.

In the last paragraph of **"Two Concepts of Liberty,"** Berlin approvingly quotes the 20th-century economist Joseph Schumpeter: "To realize the relative validity of one's convictions and yet stand for them unflinchingly is what distinguishes a civilized man from a barbarian." Or again, in praising one of his heroes, the great Zionist leader Chaim Weizmann, Berlin writes:

> Weizmann had all his life believed that when great public issues are joined one must above all take sides; whatever one did, one must not remain neutral or uncommitted, one must always—as an absolute duty—
> . . . take part in the world's affairs with all the risk and blame and misrepresentation and misunderstanding of one's motives and character which this almost inevitably entails.

Yet, time after time, it was precisely this "absolute duty" that Berlin failed to discharge. Thus, when the universities—the institution to which he had devoted the better part of his life and which, with all its faults, came closer than any other to embodying the values he so volubly professed—came under assault by the radicals of the Left in the mid-and late 60's, where was Berlin? To put it charitably, he was nowhere to be seen on the field when the fight was raging most intensely. So much for his willingness to stand, in accordance with Schumpeter's noble dictum, unflinchingly for his convictions. When push came to shove, it was the relativism that won out over the convictions.

But there is more. I read in Ignatieff that Berlin's "distaste for the fashionable intellectuals of the 1960's . . . deepened into something approaching intellectual despair when he surveyed the student revolutionaries themselves." Ignatieff also tells us that "The whole experience of the 1960's made him uneasily aware that he had not understood the nihilist consequences of the Romantic esteem for sincerity and authenticity." He expressed this and kindred sentiments privately in letters to friends (e.g., "I feel depressed by the rapid growth of barbarism . . . among our young men," whom he then proceeds to compare unfavorably with the "revolutionaries of his own day"), but I personally cannot recollect, and Ignatieff gives no examples of, any pronouncements of this nature by Berlin in public. Just the opposite: in those very years of his "despair," he became a regular contributor to the *New York Review of Books,* in which the radicalism and/or barbarism that so distressed him in private were regularly accorded the greatest respect and found their most sophisticated intellectual defense.

One evening during this period—just when, disillusioned with the radical Movement that I too had in recent years been defending, I felt constrained to break with it altogether—I attended, along with my wife, a small dinner party given for the visiting Berlins by my former teacher

Lionel Trilling and his wife Diana in New York; the only other guest was one of Berlin's oldest and closest friends, the British poet and critic Stephen Spender. To the delight of the Trillings, who had never approved of my association with the Left of the 60's and were pleased by my growing disaffection with it, I seized upon the occasion to ask Berlin why he was willing to collaborate so closely with the *New York Review.* Though Spender too was writing regularly for it, I did not address this question to him, because I knew that he, as Ignatieff puts it, prided himself on "communing with the young" (he had even had himself hoisted into one of the buildings occupied by the radicals at Columbia where, of course, Trilling was the great luminary of the faculty). Yet along with everyone else in the room, Spender joined in what turned out to be one of the best and most serious discussions I have ever participated in. Contentious issues and their many ramifications were explored with frankness on both sides, without any rancor, and with everyone trying to do justice to the position against which he was arguing instead of reducing it to an easily ridiculed caricature.[6]

My challenge to Berlin, however, did not focus only on the issue of student radicalism; it also concerned Israel. "You still consider yourself a Zionist, don't you?" I asked him. "Certainly," he replied. "Then," I pressed on, "why do you lend your prestige and support to a paper that regularly publishes enemies of Israel like Noam Chomsky and I.F. Stone?" This question seemed to take Berlin by surprise and for once in his life he did not have a ready riposte. But after a few seconds he responded, and with the friendliest possible smile: "I see. You are accusing me of being a fellow-traveler of a fellow-traveler."

He did not follow up this witticism with a defense either of the *New York Review* or of himself. There was, after all, no denying that Stone (in that period of his life) and especially Chomsky were bitter enemies of the Zionism to which Berlin had been committed all his life. This commitment even formed the basis of his understanding that nationalism was ineradicable (an understanding not common among liberals of his era, who mostly regarded it as the major cause of Nazism and lesser evils), and that utopian efforts to ignore or wipe it out in pursuit of the ideal of an internationalist brotherhood were doomed to fail. Such efforts, he warned, were even as likely to lead to mass murder as nationalism in its more aggressive phases could and did.

Instead, therefore, of trying to justify his connection with the *New York Review,* Berlin stood pat on his witty remark and sat for a while giving my question what looked like thoughtful consideration as we moved on to the general question of student radicalism. Yet as time went on, and as the attacks being mounted in those years by the Left against Israel became ever more ferocious, he remained as silent as he did about its assault on the universities and the liberal ethos embodied in them.

In Ignatieff's interpretation, Berlin comforted himself with the thought that as an exponent of "liberal moderation," he was following the example of his beloved Ivan Turgenev, the great 19th-century Russian novelist who in his own day had incurred the disfavor both of the Left and the Right. Turgenev, says Ignatieff,

> was accused throughout his career of ingratiating himself with the authorities and revolutionaries alike, and of securing the trust of neither side. Even Herzen, who respected his literary genius, thought Turgenev an equivocating old maid in politics.

Having supplied this softening and rosy context, Ignatieff gets to the most serious criticism that can be made of Berlin:

> Such, in crude terms, was the charge whispered behind Berlin's back throughout his steady ascent through the upper reaches of English life: . . . All of these failings amounted to the single indictment that he lacked the existential courage to stand and be counted.

Ignatieff makes a valiant, if unsuccessful, effort to show that Berlin was innocent of the whispered charge. But Berlin himself was honest enough to recognize how much truth there was in the indictment, for (as Ignatieff himself emphasizes) "the charge of cowardice bothered him all his life" and "caused him real anguish." As well it should have done, considering how fearful he was of taking public political stands that might jeopardize his ever-growing intellectual and social prestige, or that might—to throw his own words on Weizmann back at him again—expose him to "the risk of blame."

A particularly distasteful example of his aversion to such risks concerned the writer Goronwy Rees, who had been Berlin's dear friend for many years. Some time after Guy Burgess, a mutual friend of theirs, escaped to Moscow just as he was about to be arrested as a Soviet agent, Rees published a series of articles about his now notorious old companion in a sensationalist tabloid. There he gave details of Burgess's libertinism as an incorrigible drunk and a wildly promiscuous homosexual, and strongly intimated that other spies like him were still at large in the British establishment. (He meant the art historian Anthony Blunt, who had not yet been exposed.)

For turning on dear old Guy in this vulgarly anti-Communist way, Rees was excommunicated by virtually the whole intellectual establishment of the country, most of whom, though loyal Englishmen themselves, found a certain merit in the novelist E.M. Forster's declaration that, given the choice, he would rather betray his country than his friend. But even Berlin, a principled and passionate anti-Communist who, Ignatieff assures us, "never had any difficulty thinking of himself as a cold warrior, as a liberal defender of the capitalist world and its freedoms," joined in the anti-Rees orgy. More unlovely yet, when Berlin ran into the left-wing journalist Tom Driberg at the Indonesian embassy in Moscow and heard that Driberg would be seeing Burgess, he asked him to send the traitor "his warmest love" and to tell him that "none of us are speaking to Goronwy." This, despite the fact that Berlin's

stated reason for being angry with Rees in the first place was that he thought Rees had hintingly accused him of having once been in cahoots with Burgess.

The two men later had something of a reconciliation, and the day after Rees died, Berlin wrote in a letter of consolation to Daniel Rees that "Your father's death is a deep grief to me"—so deep that he would be unable to speak at the memorial service: "too much painful feeling." Later, however, when he was invited to speak anyway, he begged off on the ground that he did not know how to deal with Rees's own suspected involvement in espionage. More likely the truth was that he did not wish to make so public a gesture of identification with a man who had come to be regarded as a renegade by much of the world Berlin lived in.[7]

Zionism and the fruit it bore in the state of Israel might seem to have provided Berlin with the chance to show some bravery; and at two points, at least, they did. Being an outspoken Zionist did indeed require courage in the England of the 30's and then again during the period of fierce anti-Zionism of the Attlee-Bevin government that came into power right after the war and that was aggravated by the Jewish struggle to drive the British out of Palestine. This was especially true in the social circles in which the young Berlin aspired so passionately to move as a full-fledged member. But his loyalty to the Jewish people was so solid and unswerving that it overcame his social ambitions and anxieties.

As, however, the account I have just given about the evening at the Trillings demonstrates, the same loyalty—which I have not the slightest doubt Berlin continued to feel—was not enough to loosen his world-famously loose tongue when it took even greater courage to defend Israel, this time not only in high society but also in the universities and among intellectuals in general. Or rather, it loosened his tongue to the opposite effect. Here is how Ignatieff describes Berlin's decision to make a rare public pronouncement about Israel toward the end of his life:

> Like his hero Turgenev who, when dying of cancer, had dictated "A Fire at Sea" . . . to acquit himself of a charge of cowardice, Berlin dictated a public appeal for political compromise in Israel. On 16 October 1997, on no one's initiative but his own, he composed a statement imploring Israelis to accept a final partition of the land with the Palestinians. . . . The alternative, he warned, was an interminable cycle of terrorist chauvinism on both sides and savage war.

Incredibly, Berlin thought, and Ignatieff agrees, that this statement showed courage. Of course, the fact is that it merely put Berlin solidly in line with the opinion being voiced by practically everyone else in the world. I am not suggesting that these were not his true sentiments. After all, in what may well have been the only time in his life he ever did such a thing, he had once refused to shake the hand of Prime Minister Menachem Begin because, as head of the Irgun in the pre-state period, Begin had been responsible for the bombing of the King David hotel, which then served as the headquarters of the British mandatory forces. And if a rumor going the rounds can be believed (it seems plausible enough), Berlin declared after Benjamin Netanyahu became Prime Minister that he had never hated anyone so much in his life.

In making the case for Berlin's greatness as a philosopher of liberalism, Ignatieff argues that

> empathy was, for Berlin, the core liberal attitude—the capacity to be open, receptive, unafraid in the face of opinions, temperaments, passions alien to one's own. . . . The result was a moral psychology of liberal life which, while unsystematic, was as deep as anything within the liberal canon since Adam Smith's *Theory of Moral Sentiments.*

Well, while such empathy could be summoned forth by Berlin for the extreme rightist views of a Joseph de Maistre, it clearly ran smack up against its limits where the hawkishness of the Israeli Right was concerned.[8] Nor did his commitment to and capacity for toleration extend to serious religious belief:

> Happy are those who live under a discipline which they accept without question, who freely obey the orders of leaders, spiritual or temporal, whose word is fully accepted as unbreakable law; or those who have, by their own methods, arrived at clear and unshakeable convictions about what to do and what to be that brook no possible doubt. I can only say that those who rest on such comfortable beds of dogma are victims of self-induced myopia, blinkers that may make for contentment, but not for understanding of what it is to be human.

Admittedly, Berlin seems to have been thinking here more about the followers of fascist leaders than about Roman Catholics or hasidic Jews like his own Lubavitcher cousins. Nevertheless, in this statement, so violently discordant for an apostle of tolerance to let slip from his pen, he makes not the slightest effort to distinguish between the "spiritual" and the "temporal." All the more outlandish do I find this when I read in Ignatieff that

> For all his skepticism . . . he was repelled by the callow anti-clericalism of the Voltairian Enlightenment and had traced most of the evils of the 20th century to the idolatry of secular reason. "Stone-dry atheists," he once wrote, "don't understand what men live by."

Yet the very same person who could write and think such things was capable of denying to the truly religious an understanding of "what it is to be human" (!) and to lump them together with fascists and Communists.

An extaordinarily brilliant man, then, a conversationalist of genius, and the most amusing companion one could ever hope to have, but not the great thinker he is so often taken to be. Even less is Berlin the moral hero that his biographer tries to make of him in an effort to cover over the spinelessness that the relativistic core of liberalism,

even in its most sophisticated and civilized form, invariably brings out when determined challenges are posed to it, especially from the Left.

We see this once again today in the supine response of liberals to "multiculturalism," which can be understood as a diseased mutation of the pluralism that Isaiah Berlin never ceased extolling. Pluralism as Berlin expounded it had real force when fascism and Communism were riding high, and when, to its eternal honor, it formed one of the crucial elements making the case for bourgeois democracy as the superior alternative. But today, when "multiculturalism" is all the rage, in England as well as in America, it can be of no help and may even do harm in the struggle to prevent the balkanization of our common culture and the dissolution of its intellectual and academic standards.

This is a process that I cannot believe Berlin himself would have wished to encourage. For to give credit where credit is due, he knew very well that pluralism was vulnerable to such diseases. Yet because he also knew that he had never really found a philosophical way of immunizing it against the ravages of relativism, and because he could never bear to be unpopular or to overcome the need to ingratiate himself—a need of which he was entirely aware and that he sometimes thought stemmed from his Jewishness—he made no contribution to the fight against multiculturalism while he was alive, and ideas like his still bear a certain responsibility for its spread.

A few months ago, at a symposium in New York on his work, critical questions of a kind rarely heard before were raised by a number of political theorists, mostly of the Left. It is much more common, however, for liberal intellectuals—in trying desperately to resurrect a point of view grown moribund with softness—to seek inspiration in the apparent solidity and strength of Isaiah Berlin's conception of liberalism. But they are misleading us when they inflate the importance of this great equivocator, and they are kidding themselves when they look to his writings as the source of a new moral validation and the fount of a new intellectual vitality.

Notes

1. Metropolitan Books, 336 pp., $35.00.

2. The essay appeared originally in 1970 in *Transactions of the Jewish Historical Society of England,* and was then reprinted ten years later in *Against the Current: Essays in the History of Ideas,* edited by Henry Hardy and published in this country by Viking.

3. And I should make it clear that Berlin would have dismissed it as "absurd," just as he did, conversely, when his father (as Ignatieff writes) would "attribute his son's memory and scholary achievements to his rabbinical ancestors." The same is true of the subject of *yiches.* Fascinated though he was by it, in his view, as summarized by Ignatieff, to take pride in one's origins was "to surrender to the dubious determinism of the blood."

4. In Ignatieff's version, the phrase Oakeshott used was "Paganini of the platform," but I am pretty certain that my version is the correct one. I did not know, however, that (again according to Ignatieff) T.S. Eliot, another conservative, had earlier come up with a barbed compliment of his own in congratulating Berlin for the "torrential eloquence" of the BBC lectures. Good, but in this case I would award the palm to the political philosopher rather than the poet.

5. *The Proper Study of Mankind,* edited by Henry Hardy and Roger Hausneer. Farrar, Straus & Giroux, 667 pp., $35.00.

6. To my astonishment and, if truth be told, disgust, I later learned that in reporting back to their friends in England on this discussion, Berlin and Spender said that they had spent a whole evening being berated by the editor of Commentary (as I then was) merely because they wrote for a rival publication. No wonder Berlin was (so Ignatieff reveals) sometimes accused of being "feline" as a gossip.

7. Neither the story about the message Berlin sent to Burgess through Driberg nor the one about his refusal to speak at Rees's memorial service comes from Ignatieff (who skates hastily over Berlin's relations with Rees on the one side and Burgess on the other). I found them in Jenny Rees's fascinating book about her father, *Looking for Mr. Nobody: The Secret of Goronwy Rees,* which was published by Weidenfeld and Nicholson in England but has never found an outlet in America. Her sources were Driberg's autobiography, *Ruling Passions,* and the letters she found among her father's papers.

8. Namier once ranted (in Berlin's paraphrase) that "The Jews of England were victims of pathetic illusions—ostriches with their heads in some very inferior sands. . . ." For Namier, this was typically intemperate, but as always with him, there was something to it. Witness the fact that English Jews like Isaiah Berlin, who could write so movingly about Churchill, and even Churchill's own biographer Martin Gilbert, have been advocates of a "peace" policy toward the Arabs that in the European context they would not have hesitated for a second to denounce as appeasement or to predict could only lead to war.

FURTHER READING

Biography

Ignatieff, Michael, *Isaiah Berlin: A Life,* New York: Metropolitan Books/Henry Holt, 1998, 356 p.
Critical study of Berlin's life and work.

Criticism

Anderson, Perry. "Components of a National Culture," *New Left Review* 50 (July-August 1968): 3-57.
Condemns Berlin for ignoring conditions of economic exploitation in his analyses of liberty.

Galipeau, Claude J. *Isaiah Berlin's Liberalism.* Oxford: Clarendon Press, 1994, 196 p.
Explores the components of Berlin's liberalism and includes a comprehensive bibliography.

Gray, John. *Isaiah Berlin,* Princeton: Princeton University Press, 1996, 189 p.
A study of Berlin's political thought and its relevance to political history and human character.

Kocis, Robert. *A Critical Appraisal of Sir Isaiah Berlin's Political Philosophy.* Wales: Edwin Mellen Press, 1989, 278 p.
A thorough and scholarly study of Berlin's political theory; includes a comprehensive bibliography.

Additional coverage of Berlin's life and career is contained in the following source published by the Gale Group: *Contemporary Authors,* Vols. 85-88, 162.

Ivan Cankar
1876-1918

Slovene novelist, dramatist, poet, essayist, and short story writer.

INTRODUCTION

Cankar is numbered among the finest Slovene writers of the twentieth century. Associated with the *Slovenska Moderna*, a modernist movement in the Slovene arts, he is credited with transforming the aging formalism and staid realism of his nation's literature through his prose. Focusing on the dismal lives of the poor in Vienna where he spent much of his life, Cankar's works offer his poetic view of anguish and of the struggles of the artist as outcast. At once naturalistic and symbolic, his works—including the short novel *Hlapec Jernej in njegova pravica* (1907; *The Bailiff Yerney and His Rights*) and the drama *Lepa Vida* (1912)—depict the squalor of turn-of-the-century life among the underclass and explore universal themes of human suffering and hope.

BIOGRAPHICAL INFORMATION

Cankar was born in Vrhnika, Slovenia, one of eight surviving children in the impoverished family of an out-of-work tailor. A gifted student, he attended Vrhnika elementary school and was later sent to high school in Ljubljana, where the destitute Cankar was forced to live a straitened existence and survive on charity. By age fourteen he had begun to write poetry and soon became the chief member of his high school's literary club. In the fall of 1896, Cankar briefly studied engineering at Vienna University, but soon dropped out of the program, preferring to read literature and philosophy. That year he published a number of naturalistic short stories in the periodical *Slovenec*. Cankar remained in Vienna and there familiarized himself with the European literature of his day while writing articles for Ljubljana newspapers in order to support himself financially. With no money, Cankar returned to Vrhnika in 1897 and began preparing the manuscript for his poetry collection *Erotika* (1899). By late 1898 he was back in Vienna with hopes of completing his studies. Again penniless, he became a lodger in the home of Albina Löffler, a divorcée. Eventually he abandoned his formal schooling at Vienna University and attempted to make a living as a full-time writer. He published several collections of short stories and produced three plays at the turn of the century. He also began the novel *Na klancu* (1902), for which Cankar received his first substantial acclaim. In the ensuing years, Cankar continued to produce fiction and briefly sought to enter Slovenian politics as a Social Democrat, but was defeated in the election of 1907. That year also saw the publication of one of his most successful works, the short novel *Bailiff Yerney and His Rights*. Once again in Austria, Cankar continued to fictionalize the people and events associated with his Viennese surroundings in works of prose and drama. He was imprisoned for several months in 1914 after the outbreak of World War I for voicing his Serbian sympathies. Cankar was later drafted into the Austrian army but was quickly discharged for poor health. He spent the remaining war years in the town of Rožnik, until September of 1917 when he returned to Ljubljana. Cankar died of pneumonia on 11 December 1918.

MAJOR WORKS

Among Cankar's earliest works, *Erotika,* his first published book, contains a number of decadent and sensual poems, while *Vinjete* (1899) offers naturalistic prose sketches of life among the Viennese poor. Cankar continued his process of dramatizing the downtrodden in the stories of *Knjiga za lahkomiselne ljudi* (1901), in which he introduces a figure that was to become a stock type in many of his later writings, the insipid, obese, and corrupt bureaucrat. Among his dramatic works of the period, *Popotovanje Nikolaja Nikiča* (1900) details the brief life and death of a poet misunderstood by society. The satirical *Za narodov blagor* (1901) describes rampant corruption in Slovene politics. *Kralj na Betajnovi* (1902; *King of Betajnova*) draws its inspiration from the Nietzschean idea of the superman. Cankar's idealized mother is the subject of the novel *Na klancu*, which depicts the life of a poor yet morally unsullied woman. The theme of abused children is central to *Hiša Marije Pomočnice* (1904; *The Ward of Our Lady of Mercy*), a novel that combines both naturalistic and symbolist styles to relate the story of a terminally ill girl. *Martin Kačur: Življenjepis idealista* (1907) recounts the tragedy of a young, idealistic teacher living among the unenlightened inhabitants of an isolated village. Biblical allusions predominate in the short novel *Bailiff Yerney and His Rights*, in which the old laborer Yerney, recently displaced from his farm, fails to find justice among men. A departure from realism to the world of folklore and fantasy occurs in *Kurent: Starodavna pripovedka* (1909), in which a legendary character, the fiddler Kurent, leads the impoverished Slovene peasantry from captivity in Vienna. Among his later dramas, *Hlapci* (1910) presents a theme similar to that of *Martin Kačur*, detailing the lives of Slovene teachers under a conservative political regime. Set in an abandoned Ljubljana sugar factory used as a homeless shelter, the symbolic *Lepa Vida* (1912) dramatizes the suffering of the poor and the sanctity of art. Cankar's final works include a collection of stories entitled *Podobe iz sanj* (1917; *Dream Visions and Other Stories*), and the posthumously published stories of *Moje življenje* (1920; *My Life and Other Sketches*).

CRITICAL RECEPTION

During his life, critics found Cankar's early works *Erotika* and *Vinjete* to be confused if not outright scandalous. His novel *Na klancu,* in contrast, was highly regarded by his contemporaries, who lauded the realistic style and moral theme of the work. Upon its publication, *Bailiff Yerney and His Rights* was considered an outstanding work of Slovene fiction, and has since been translated into numerous languages. Still, early twentieth-century commentators were generally dismissive of Cankar's dramatic works, though some among the *Moderna* did recognize his brilliance in such works as *Lepa Vida,* which the contemporary poet Oton Zupančič called, "the high mass of the Slovene language." Additionally, critics viewed the visionary stories of *Podobe iz sanj* as among Cankar's greatest. Since his death, Cankar's plays have been frequently staged, and while criticism of his works in English is still slight, Cankar has been acknowledged as the principal figure among the Slovene modernists, and the precursor of 1930s social realist fiction.

PRINCIPAL WORKS

Erotika (poetry) 1899
Vinjete (short stories) 1899
Jakob Ruda: Drama v treh dejanjih (drama) 1900
Popotovanje Nikolaja Nikiča (novella) 1900
Knjiga za lahkomiselne ljudi (short stories) 1901
Tujci (novella) 1901
Za narodov blagor: Komedija v štirih dejanjih (drama) 1901
Kralj na Betajnovi: Drama v treh dejanjih [*King of Betajnova*] (drama) 1902
Na klancu (novel) 1902
Ob zori (short stories) 1903
Življenje in smrt Petra Novljana (novella) 1903
Hiša Marije Pomočnice [*The Ward of Our Lady of Mercy*] (novel) 1904
Križ na gori: Ljubezenska zgodba (novel) 1904
Potepuh Marko in Kralj Matjaž; V mesečini: Zgodba iz doline šentflorjanske (novella) 1905
Nina (novella) 1906
"*Aleš iz Razora*" (short story) 1907
Hlapec Jernej in njegova pravica [*The Bailiff Yerney and His Rights*] (novel) 1907
Krpanova kobila (essays and short stories) 1907
Martin Kačur: Življenjepis idealista (novel) 1907
"*Smrt in pogreb Jakoba Nesreče*" (short story) 1907
Novo življenje (novel) 1908

Pohujšanje v dolini šentflorjanski: Farsa v treh aktih (drama) 1908
Zgodbe iz doline šentflorjanske (short stories) 1908
Kurent: Starodavna pripovedka (novel) 1909
Sosed Luka: Kmečka novela (novel) 1909
Za križem (short stories) 1909
Bela krizantema: Mojim recenzentom (essay and short stories) 1910
Hlapci: Drama v petih aktih (drama) 1910
Volja in moč (novel) 1911
Lepa Vida (drama) 1912
Milan in Milena: Ljubezenska pravljica (novel) 1913
Podobe iz sanj [*Dream Visions and Other Stories*] (short stories) 1917
Moje življenje [*My Life and Other Sketches*] (autobiographical sketches) 1920
Grešnik Lenart: Življenjepis otroka (autobiographical sketches) 1921
Romantične duše: Dramatična slika v treh dejanjih (drama) 1922
Zbrani spisi. 20 vols. (poetry, dramas, novels, short stories, and essays) 1926-35
Pisma Ivana Cankarja. 3 vols. (letters) 1948
Izbrana dela. 10 vols. (poetry, dramas, novels, short stories, and essays) 1951-59
Zbrano delo. 30 vols. (poetry, dramas, novels, short stories, letters, and essays) 1967-76

CRITICISM

Bratko Kreft (essay date 1968)

SOURCE: A preface in *The Bailiff Yerney and His Rights,* translated by Sidonie Yeras and H. C. Sewell Grant, Dražvna Založba Slovenije, 1968, pp. v-xviii.

[*In the following essay, Kreft considers the artistic and political significance of* Bailiff Yerney and His Rights, *calling the work Cankar's masterpiece.*]

The artistic value of a literary creation or of any other work of art does not depend on its author's origin. It does not matter whether he belongs to a great, powerful nation or to a small, almost unknown one. History gives us many examples confirming that truth. One of them is certainly the work of Ivan Cankar (1876–1918). Ivan Cankar is a classical writer of modern Slovene literature, that being one of the prominent literatures of the Yugoslavs. Among Cankar's works, the most conspicuous is perhaps ***Bailiff Yerney and His Rights,*** not only by the ideas it brings out, by its contents and its form but also by its artistic value. It is an original and somewhat peculiar work. In it, we find the powerful spirit of revolutionary humanism and, at the same time, a strong indictment against social injustices in human society, against social systems rendering them possible and permitting them, where society is founded on the social exploitation of the many, the people, by the few. That centuries old situation and the struggle of the trodden down against the masters are embodied by Cankar in old Yerney.

For forty years, Yerney has worked on Sitar's farm. He has ploughed, sown, mowed, moistened the soil with his sweat till it has yielded rich crops. In the times of hard field work, Yerney has sometimes lain down on his straw-bed with painful bleeding blisters. For forty years he has worked faithfully, serving God and his master. The ground, the homestead have been his only aim and he ha been one and all with them. Now the farm stands firm on Yerney's hard labour. He never complained, he never shunned any work, he always lovingly did his duty according to God's laws and to his conscience. He never felt humbled to be a servant, for old Sitar never beheaved like a master. They worked in harmony, both servant and master, ministering to the needs of the soil, and the servant has always been the chief and faithful aid and co-operator of the master. The links that bind Sitar and Yerney might perhaps be, from a social point of view, compared with those to be found in a patriarchal or a co-operative village before the class differences in the rural atmosphere had taken harsher forms introduced by capitalism.

In his classical tale "Master and servant", L. N. Tolstoi has described such links as must have existed between old Si-tar and Yerney, but they are psychologised and individual-ised, and written in the style of a psychological and de-scriptive realism. Cankar's parable is sociologically typified as is all that follows. Of course this does not mean that typification of persons and conditions are, in Cankar's tale, without psychological reasons, for typification does not exclude psychological laws. The only exception is Yer-ney and not yet a complete one, for in him is embodied and typified the psychology of the popular, the plebeian crowd. Such a mass neither organised nor well informed has to go a long way round before it reaches the final knowledge. Considered individually, Yerney's long roam-ing from judge to judge and from man to God is a quixo-tism and rather a queer story for a psychologist. He may well wonder—looking at Yerney from an individual, psy-chological stand point why he has not, during his quest, come to the knowledge that in human society there is no justice for him nor ever can be according to the principles that same society stands on. But the long wandering Yer-ney goes through, personifies the long historical process from ignorance to knowledge and to revolution of which the fire that destroys Sitar's house is the allegory and the symbol.

When finally Yerney knows there in no justice for him ei-ther in human society or in God, then he realises he must reach that justice by himself. And, because his work is im-mured in Sitar's homestead, he goes and sets fire to Sitar's house to make his labour and his rights known to the world. At the same time he kindles the torch of rebellion in the name of all Yerneys of the world. Old Yerney him-self as the personification of the first rebels meets with his

death in the flames where he is thrown by those who stick to the old "justice" which is to him an injustice. His death in the roaring flames is the torch of general revolution which is to free not only all bailiffs Yerneys but he whole of mankind. That fire threatens, warns and summons; it is symbol.

". . . As to the fire at the end of the tale, it is only the symbol of general revolution. I know, by Cankar's own words how little he cared to describe the fire. He told me that he wrote on purpose only two short pages about the conflagration, for he did not wish our gapers on to feast on a spectacle, but to feel the idea and to bow their heads to the symbol.

That is how Cankar spoke to his friend, the well known Slovene historian of literature and aesthetician Dr. Ivan Prijatelj. That is why, later on, in his essay "Fatherland, behold the artist", Prijatelj wrote that Bailiff Yerney's was a short but very powerful poetisation of Marx's Commu-nist Manifesto. Cankar's masterpiece has not its real value in the servile roaming from the Mayor to the Emperor . . . but in its allegorical heights, in the harmony of spheres that sing to us about a period now so tangibly near . . ." For more clearness and exactitude, Prijatelj ought to have written that Cankar's tale was a very powerful poeti-sation of the idea of the Communist manifesto and not of the manifesto itself, though Yerney's long roaming symb-olises also the long historical process Marx and Engels de-scribe in their work. Prijatelj's classical label is stamped on Cankar's work as to ideas, and in a deeper meaning as to politics and even as to aesthetics when he calls the tale a "very powerful poetisation" and a "masterpiece". The well known German poet and dramatic writer inclining to-wards social revolution, Bert Brecht, wanted to give a po-etisation of the *Comunist Manifesto* and make it into a revolutionary poem as to ideas but artistic and poetical as to shape, such as Lucretious gave his philosophical *De re-rum naturae* a poetical and not merely a versified form. In writing **Bailiff Yerney,** Ivan Cankar whose art is a blend-ing of symbolism and realism, laid on himself perhaps his hardest literary and artistic task.

He realised he must write a book for the people, not in the spirit of primitive, didactic, moralising popular tales but possessing as well all the qualities required by art. The tale must be simple enough to be understood by the largest popular crowds; its artistic force and tendency must be able to conceal the mere tendency, because it will be and it must be more than a tendency, it must be an idea. If the author wishes to meet those ends, he must find for his tale a form that will suit the popular character and the formal artistic laws. Till now, Cankar had written for an intellec-tual public though his intentions were general; when writ-ing **Bailiff Yerney,** he had to keep in view he was writing for large popular crowds he wished to gain to his ideas. He said himself that at first he had meant to give out a mere political pamphlet on an electional campaign; as it was to him a new experience, both the tale and its form crystallized rather slowly and came too late to be effective in the electional campaign. In fact it was published several months after the election had taken place and it became therefore a work of permanent value as to ideas and to art, a work that was meant by Cankar to have, through elections, an influence on future.

Though we find in *Bailiff Yerney,* as to style and language all the best Cankar's previous works give us, yet in that tale, style and language have a new voice. We do not see here any trace of intellectualism or of "literature", even if both are represented in their most noble form in Cankar's works preceeding and following *Bailiff Yerney.* No more do we find in the tale the lyricism and meditativeness that are so often interwoven in many Cankar's short stories and tales. Cankar knew that, as far back as Primož Trubar (1508-1586)—the founder of Slovene literature and Slovene literary language—the most popular book has been the Bible written in a higher tone but simple enough to be understood by the people. That is why Cankar listened to its style and words. But in writing his tale, Cankar had also to lend an ear to the language and style of our sagas. Thus Cankar had two samples of writings for the people, and in the language, rhythm and style of *Bailiff Yerney,* he combines both without essentially imitating them. Cankar's tale might as well be told by an unknown patriarch belonging to the people, by an anonymous prophet who accuses and warns in the name of all bailiffs Yerney's when relating Yerney's quest for justice.

"I tell you this story as it really happened, with all its injustice and all its great sadness. You will find in it no well-turned periods, no fictions, no hypocrisy.

. . . . .

Stupefied, the folks of Betajnova bowed their heads in terror: for a mysterious shadow, like a black ghost, rose upon the hill and extended into the valley; its head was a dark cloud; its feet, the mighty poplars of the valley; while a bright scythe resting on its shoulder shone far away, as far as Ljublijana."

. . . . .

Because of its rhythm and horror, because of its wording, because of its symbols, its visions and its reality, that introduction to Cankar's tale is a warning like St. John's Apocalypse. The very name of Betajnova, already used by Cankar in a drama of social and moral crime under the symbolical title of *A King in Betajnova* has here still a more dreadful sound, that of an apocalyptical ballade. Because of its rhythm and its melody, because of the musicalness of words and style, the whole tale is like a powerful symphony with many phrases but only one leading motif. That motif is nevertheless varied by the author from stage to stage of Yerney's calvary, so that it fully harmonises in this architecturally perfect Cankar's masterpiece. Lyricism and epicism join the tragical, for, from, place to place, Yerney's quest becomes more sorrowful and comes to his summit in a shakespearian sense in the encounter with the priest, followed by the fire and Yerney's violent death, that is the more accusing because it is the more tragical.

The dramatic character of Cankar's tale is a strong call for dramatisation, for making it fit for the stage. (It has even provided a theme for two opera librettos.) The best dramatisation is that of Ferdo Delak, an avant-garde theatrical man who worked between First and Second World War. In his dramatisation, Ferdo Delak has found the right form, the right expression for Cankar's parable with its allegory and symbol. Thus, in Delak's dramatisation, Cankar's tale becomes a modern revolutionary miracle-play.

When, after his long wanderings Yerney retuns to the village where he has worked for forty years, he is tired, sick and bent. When in his strained talk with the priest who shows him the door as to an unbeliever and a blasphemer, Yerney comes to the final, the bitterest knowlege, something breaks in him; the old man is imbued with a new strength. "Slowly, Yerney turned on his heels and went out. He walked now with swift strides, no longer bent, no longer sick, without sorrow and without hope in his heart."

The last hope of finding justice has gone. Therefore, as the rascal in jail had told him, he goes and gets his rights by himself. He goes and turns his labour of forty years into a fire in which, like a threatening torch, he burns and dies, but as a symbol still glares and blazes.

Through those flames, we also hear the sound of the last hard striking words in Cankar's essay **"Slovene People and Slovene Culture"**. That writing comes from the same feelings and the same knowledge, burns with the same fire that inspired Cankar when—about at the same time—he wrote *Bailiff Yerney.* Those words are inseparable from Cankar's tale:

> The only way is the struggle of the people, a reckless struggle till the last barricade falls down, till the last aim is reached. A struggle for a complete social and political freedom, for without social and politic liberty, culture cannot be free. As long as the people are the slave of society, the slave of that anonymous nation, so long culture will be in servitude, so long it will be humbled and without any rights. The struggle for the liberation of the people is a cultural struggle, and he who calumniates it, he who imputes it unclean aims, he is an enemy of he people and an enemy of culture.

There is no other Slovene writer who can, like Cankar, unite all progressive forces of every sphere in culture and art as well as of politics in their deepest meaning in such harmony, notwhistanding some oppositions almost wiped out by a boundless humanism. Here, Cankar can compete with the best writers of his time. There is no opposition between Cankar's socialism and his humanism, no more than between his classical masterpiece *Bailiff Yerney* and his classical essay **"Slovene People and Slovene Culture";** they are complementary. They are one body, one idea, one masterpiece.

Heinrich von Kleist too has told in "Michael Kohlhass" the tale of a man who is in search of justice, but Kleist's tale is the tale of an individual case of a given psychological character that cannot be generalised. Bailiff Yerney is a social, historical and psychological generalisation. The charm of the story is, besides, in Yerney being at the same time a live individual and the personification of crowds of bailiffs Yerneys throughout the world. Kleist's tale is a realistic chronicle written lightly in the style and language of old chronicles. Cankar wrote his ***Bailiff Yerney*** as a Gospel parable and a book for the people whose Bible it might be. L. N. Tolstoi too tried to create in the same way his stories for the people. But, without denying Tolstoi his grandeur, we may say that in his ***Bailiff Yerney,*** Cankar surpasses him. When Ivan Prijatelj wrote that Cankar's story is a powerful artistic poetisation of the Communist manifesto, he probably did not know that Marx and Engels had at first meant to write their manifesto in a popular-biblic language. The end of the tale sounds like Beethoven's marche funèbre, like an accusing ballade-psalm that could easily be written in the rhythm of free verse:

> They seized him
> They dragged him
> They struck him
> burnt and bleeding . . .
>
> . . . . .
>
> They swung him, once, twice, thrice . . .
> Sparks whirled from the flames, high, still higher . . .
> When Yerney's executioners came out of the blaze
> Their hands and faces were black.
>
> . . . . .
>
> And that happened in Betajnova . . .
>
> . . . . .
>
> God have mercy upon Yerney
> Upon his judges
> and upon all sinners . . .

How heavy and hard are those sounds at the end of the first three lines and how far to the invisible and the unreachable the last lines send their echoes. The best representatives of modern free verse, from T. S. Eliot to Pablo Neruda could not write better.

Cankar wrote his story in 1907 when he was a candidate of the social-democrat party at parlamentary elections. Though he was not elected, he won more votes than any of the other candidates. The ideas he expresses in his political writings **"Slovene Culture"** and later on in **"Cleansing and Rejuvenating"** and in **"Slovene Culture, War and the Working Class"** are given a final, artistic form in ***Bailiff Yerney.*** Cankar was quite right when he said. "I wanted to write an electional pamphlet and it happened to be my best story."

In order to understand Cankar's socialism, it is very important to know his short story **"Christ's Procession"** published in a social-democratic paper "The red banner" for the First of May 1907. The tale, published in the atmosphere of an electional campaign is an artistic and political manifestation. It is a propagandistic writing and a declaration like ***Bailiff Yerney.*** In a way, the legend of the Nazarean carpenter coming once again among men to deliver all the humbled and outraged ones, is even a prologue to ***Bailiff Yerney.*** The legend of Christ's procession is for Cankar what the "Legend of the Grand Inquisitor" is for Dostoievsky. The only difference between them being that the first is socially ethical and the second philosophically ethical; both are heretic as regards Church dogma and the various sects of Christianity. Cankar's legend of a Christ as a social rebel is politically revolutionary in the spirit of utopian socialism. The French utopian socialist Etienne Cabet thoroughly explained the importance and the meaning of the Nazarean carpenter by seeing in Christ a communist. The first Christian communities as well saw in Christ not only the announcer of a new religion but also the herald of a new social order where there would be no slaves, for all men would have equal moral and social rights and duties. If in the legend of **"Christ's Procession"** Cankar still shows a faith—though heretic—in a higher Being whose messenger is the stranger in a red cloak, he does not spare Yerney the last deception when the priest does not answer the question: "Is there a God?" . . . And then Yerney goes and acts as the rascal in jail advised him: "Do you know what I'd do, friend if I listened to you, if your faith found its way to my heart? I'd go, first of all and I'd kill the judges and all those who help them in administering the law, as well as a few others, who, since the hour of my birth have been my enemies; then I'd set this house on fire and I'd say: "Look! God has sent His justice upon earth; I have heard His words; I have obeyed His commandments! . . . Strike, apostle, strike! . . ." The rascal is no more heard of in the story, but at Yerney's last doings we remember him and the meaning of his words.

When he knows there is no justice for him, not even with God, Yerney follows the rascal's advice though it means death! Such a death as Yerney's was the lot of many before him, from Spartacus to the rebelling peasants, from the Commune to the Russian revolution of 1905 that was not forgotten in 1907 when Cankar wrote his tale. It glowed under the ashes through first World War till the Revolution of 1917, when in the Russia of the Tsars many Yerneys rose up. If a number of them did fall, crowds remained alive with their rights they began to enjoy under Lenine's leadership in spite of the whole world. Then Cankar's tale revived and is still living in many translations into various languages. It does not live on merely because of its ideas; people are moved by its artistic form, its contents, by what it irradiates and still more by its simplicity and humanity, by its tragedy and its grandeur. That is the reason why it is not a mere poetisation of the revolutionary ideas of our times; it is an original creation, a literary masterpiece that in world's literature stands equal to the greatest works on social struggle and revolution, from the simple songs of the Egyptian corn bearers of the 16th century B. C. to Maxim Gorky's "Mother", to Alexander Blok's poem on the October revolution "Twelve", in which the poet glorifies the Nazarean carpenter in a symbol akin to Cankar's in his Legend of Christ's procession.

Marija A. I. Ožbalt (essay date 1981)

SOURCE: "The Theme of the Unwed Mother in Slovene Literature," in *Slovene Studies: Journal of the Society for Slovene Studies,* Vol. 3, No. 2, 1981, pp. 59-71.

[*In the following essay, Ožbalt studies the representation of unwed mothers in the fiction of Cankar, Francè Prešeren, and Prežihov Voranc.*]

Marriage laws and customs almost universally condemn births out of wedlock. The form and degree of this condemnation vary, however, from society to society, as well as from time to time and among different strata of the same society. Impulses, a confused mass of feelings surrounding the sexual relationship, as well as the feeling of mystery about procreation, interact with social forces embodied in institutions and in the religious or other beliefs acknowledged in a society. Historically, illegitimacy has been dealt with very harshly in many societies. The same medieval ignorance which caused women to be burned as witches, imposed various primitive measures on unmarried mothers, and their offspring suffered social as well as legal disadvantages.[1]

In the twentieth century some European countries, such as Sweden, Norway, and the USSR, have tried to eradicate legal and social distinctions between children born in or out of wedlock. In the US some more liberal measures in dealing with the problem have been undertaken through adoption, foster homes and assistance to unwed mothers. The increasing demand for adoptable infants has tended to lessen the censure of such mothers who perform the social function of providing childless couples with babies. However, the attitudes to unwed mothers still echo the prejudices of tradition,[2] and although in our times these women do not face absolute social ostracism and physical torture, they are still considered an undesirable element in society. Sociologists typecast them according to current trends in psychology and sociology as social misfits of varying sorts.[3]

Since the unwed motherhood is a universal social, economic and moral problem and since the fate of unwed mothers is full of drama, tragedy and horror, it is not surprising that it has offered material to artists and writers all over the world. The motif of the unwed mother has found its way also into Slovene literature. In the following we will examine three portraits of unwed mothers, each of them representing a different era in Slovene history and social consciousness. The first one is a romantic, faceless, softly carved cameo, created by Francè Prešeren in his poem "Nezakonska mati"; the second is a composite face of a frightened, semi-insane young woman, shown through an impressionist-symbolist haze in the stories of Ivan Cankar; the last is a larger-than-life sculpture of a healthy, brave woman—a portrait whose realistic features make a statement surpassing the immediacy of its geographic and historic limitations. It appears in the story "Samorastniki," published by the realist Prežihov Voranc just before World War II.

The first portrait of an unwed mother in Slovene literature, Prešeren's "Nezakonska mati,"[4] is painted as a romantic mother-and-child idyll. The girl-mother, serene, loving and sweet, represents more the universal idea of motherhood than a particular situation in which an unwed mother and her child found themselves in Slovene society in the first half of the nineteenth century. The facts given about this woman do not define her as an individual but as a type. These facts are: she is a very young girl; she comes from a conventional family headed by a strict father, a family in which a mother may cry over the misery of her child but does not dare to defend her; she has relatives, most likely brothers and sisters[5]; her personal tragedy follows the beaten track—her lover has disappeared, leaving her to her fate[6]; this fate is also meted out in an established pattern: physical punishment and ostracism.

The lines describing the reaction of the girl's lover and those reporting the reaction of the surroundings to her pregnancy are the most realistic parts of the poem. The verses expressing the young mother's love for her baby—not necessarily a son, as the translation offers—are the most idealistic, though the most moving. The girl's fatalistic hope that the same God who feeds the birds under the sky will also provide for her child is the dream of a loving mother. It gives no hint of what is in store either for her or for her illegitimate child in the harsh reality of the nineteenth-century Slovene society.

"Nezakonska mati," written in the 1840's, was not a provocative, direct accusation of Jansenist society and its hypocrisy. However, it was a brave deed in the days when only pious literature was distributed for general consumption in Slovenia, when Prešeren's magnificent love poems were considered corrupt and evil, and when sex in any form was never mentioned. According to the Slovene literary historian Anton Slodnjak, this poem defied "Jansenist narrow-mindedness and false bourgeois morality more courageously than did 'Nova pisarija'[7] or any other of Prešeren's poems."[8]

According to some literary historians, "Nezakonska mati" grew out of Prešeren's relationship with Ana Jelovšek. Prešeren met Ana, a working-class girl, when she was only fifteen. She was serving as a nursemaid in the house of Prešeren's employer, Dr. Crobath. It was in the year 1837 when Prešeren had finally realized that Julija Primic, the woman of his dreams, was definitely lost to him forever. In despair, and probably to irritate the high-class Julija, he began to court the beautiful servant girl, who used to be Julija's mother's protégée. The relationship developed further, and Ana bore Prešeren three illegitimate children. Many literary historians up to the present time have pitied Prešeren for his involvement with Ana; they have pointed out that he was caught in a situation from which he could not extricate himself because of his honesty. Ana was his burden. She has been described as young, ignorant, simple-minded; her desire to get married to Prešeren has been interpreted as nagging; even her search for understanding and peace of mind in the confessional has been shown as disrespect for Prešeren's beliefs. Ana has also been blamed for giving her children away to foster homes, while Prešeren has been excused from any wrongdoing on account of his spiritual superiority to Ana and his limited financial means. Most literary historians and critics seem to agree that Prešeren did not love Ana, that he stooped to her in despair. They see the proof of this in the fact that Prešeren did not dedicate any love poems to Ana. They do not consider the poem "Nezakonska mati" a portrait of Ana, but Prešeren's vision of an ideal unwed mother, such as he would have wished Ana to be. Ivan Prijatelj goes even further: he denies Ana even this kind of presence in Prešeren's art. He considers people who see any traces of Ana in "Nezakonska mati" naive.[9]

Half a century after Prešeren's time, the fate of the unwed mothers in Slovenia remained unchanged. Because of geographical limitations and the proximity of people in small villages, an unmarried woman had no opportunity to hide either her pregnancy or the birth of her baby. Neither homes for unmarried mothers nor adoption agencies existed in Slovenia. Until the end of World War II all such mothers went through the same kind of experience, although the harshness of their fate might vary slightly from village to village. As soon as a pregnant girl was caught in her "shame" she was at least beaten and sometimes tortured in elaborate ways, full of medieval cruelty. She would go through her pregnancy like a social outcast. After she had given birth, the baby was her sole responsibility. Only a few girls were determined enough to sue the child's father for support. Social ostracism and hatred were transferred also to the illegitimate children. Sometimes they were marked for life at the very start by priests who baptized them with strange Greek and Latin names.

Ivan Cankar, the champion of all the oppressed and downtrodden, was moved and enraged by the suffering of unmarried mothers and their children. A great number of poets, artists and vagabonds in his stories are illegitimate children, doomed at birth, misfits forever. In these stories the emphasis is on the fate of the child, therefore the mothers appear only briefly and remain nameless. Like Prešeren's, Cankar's unmarried mother is less an individual than a type. This type, however, is not a similing Madonna; she is a semi-insane, desperate woman, who often tries to kill her newborn baby, always hides him away and then tries to lead a normal life, but never succeeds.

One of Cankar's strongest protests against the fate of unwed mothers and their offspring is the story **"Polikarp."** This grotesque shows, in somber tones and with cruel probing into a guilty man's conscience, the fate of an illegitimate boy and the punishment of his sly, cowardly father. The unwed mother appears only on the edge of the events. She is a young, nameless woman, who has come to a certain village only to give birth. She has chosen this particular place not only to hide from her acquaintances but especially to confront the new, young village priest with his own baby. After the delivery, she lies motionless in the little hut in which she has found shelter; she stares at the ceiling, does not answer any questions, and she refuses food. The only time she speaks is when she asks the merciful midwife to take the baby to church and have him christened Francis. But the priest refuses to give the baby his own name and christens him Polikarp. When they bring the baby back to his mother and tell her what his name is, she stops fighting for her life and dies.

Another Cankar story which shows an unmarried mother tortured to the point of insanity is **"Smrt in pogreb Jakoba Nesreče."** Here too a young girl has given birth in a dismal shelter provided for such misfits by a cunning old woman. As soon as the baby is born, the mother tries to kill him by filling his feeding bottle with brandy. The old woman stops her, however. At night the young mother decides to take the hateful bundle up into the hills where her own mother lives. She hopes the boy might die there; if he lives, nobody will ever know about him. On the way over the swamps, the half-crazy girl decides to drop the bundle into a ditch. But the baby opens his eyes and whimpers. Over-whelmed by hatred and despair, the mother curses her child and wishes that he would pay with his life for her suffering of this night, the night when her torn body is aching all over and her soul is filled with misery to the brim. As soon as she delivers the boy to his grandmother, she disappears. Later she recovers and tries to forget her son. She even gets married and becomes a fine lady. Years later, when the foster mother brings little Jakob for a visit, she gets rid of them, and when Jakob—a grown man by then—once comes to ask if she really cursed him at birth, she screams and faints. Her guilt, however, does not die, and when Jakob dies a vagabond, she goes insane. She comes running to the cemetery, disrupting the burial service, her city finery torn and bedraggled, her eyes burning: "Have mercy on me, my fellow Christians, his brothers . . . I cursed him, the sin is all mine . . . my curse is lying in his grave . . . it is weighing heavily on him."[10] The peasants, however, jeer at her, and the bailiff arrests her. There is no salvation for an unmarried mother. Torn between her natural feelings and the fear of a cruel society, she can commit crimes, she can disown her own flesh and blood, she can curse and cry—but she is doomed.

In the story **"Aleš iz Razora"** we see an unwed mother through her son's memory. She is a young peasant woman who has come to the city to hide her pregnancy and give birth to her son. She then abandons her baby, but only after making sure that he is taken in by some good people. Then she disappears not to interfere with her son's destiny. The illegitimate boy in this story fights odds against him so valiantly that he even becomes a priest. He learns about his mother later from a merciful woman who tells him that the girl was seduced by a pious village hypocrite and that she became sick and died young. This story differs greatly from others about the fate of unwed mothers and their offspring. This time the pharisee father is punished by insanity, and the illegitimate child becomes an important member of society. However, even in this optimistic story the unmarried mother dies after having lived a life of poverty, obscurity and sickness.

A very brief glance at the same type of a loving unmarried mother is given in the short story **"Jure."** Jure's mother did not allow society to rob her of her son; she supported him as long as she could and was happy in spite of hardships. Yet, she had to be sacrificed, too. Incessant work and worry undermines her health, and she dies of tuberculosis, leaving her son to his fate. Jure is then shipped to the village poorhouse, where the rosary-rattling old women keep reminding him of his "illegitimate" place in the world by telling him constantly: "Pray for your sinful mother!"[11]

Cankar's unwed mothers are more defined than Prešeren's. Yet their features are still nebulous and to some extent distorted by generalizations and the exaggerations of their psychotic state.

A clearly defined, unique depiction of an unwed mother was made thirty years after Cankar's time by the self-educated writer from the Carinthian mountains, Lovro Kuhar, whose best work was produced under the pseudonym Prežihov Voranc. In his story "Samorastniki,"[12] which is considered the peak of his artistic achievement, he paints the portrait of an unwed mother with all the brutality of realistic detail, yet with such passionate involvement in the exposition of an outrageous social injustice that he gives it an aura of supernatural beauty and a universal meaning.

The peasant heroine, Meta, in opposition to the faceless Madonna of Prešeren's "Nezakonska mati" and to Cankar's nameless semi-insane women, is not only a clearly defined individual, but is also shown in her growth and development. When the seventeen-year-old beauty comes to the farm, Karnice, she is an innocent, naive, obedient girl. She does her penance and she prays. When she falls in love with Ožbej, the owner's son, she does not speculate about any kind of social climbing; therefore she cannot understand the wrath of Ožbej's father, Karničnik. When she realizes that Karničnik wants her to give up Ožbej, she cannot understand that, either. How can she give up the father of her child? But as she is tortured at Karnice, a change occurs within Meta: she realizes not only that her lover is a weakling but also that the family is inflicting a horrible injustice on her. Her naiveté gives way to courage and self-sufficiency. Voranc describes this transformation as follows:

> She was overcome by horror and disgust, yet she found enough strength to get up; she approached the bench with a firm step and calmly sat down to face her torture. Her mother's behavior as well as pity for Ožbej gave her courage of which she had not been aware before. Her sobbing ceased, and the tears which kept pouring from her eyes were not bitter tears of heartfelt misery any more; soon they dried up in the new strength growing inside her.[13]

The second step in the development of Meta's character comes during her torture at her trial. This time it is not the compassion for her mother and the pity for her lover which toughen her during the barbarous beating. It is her feeling of a horrible injustice and her disdain for her torturers that make her remove the wet sheet into which they had wrapped her broken body, get up and walk proudly through the town of Doberla ves. Meta then lives as a hardworking, honest woman, brave, independent, her pride growing with her suffering and physical deterioration. This new Meta is shown in a dramatic scene at the village cemetery, where she is attacked by Karničnik's maids and daughter. Meta, pregnant with Ožbej's fifth child and accompanied by his oldest two, refuses to fight with the hysterical women. Voranc describes the scene as follows:

> The whore did not bend her head, the harlot stood proudly erect in front of everybody, exuding an invincible charm of beauty, motherhood and strength . . . She was overcome by a feeling of which she had not been aware until that time, a feeling of self-importance, equality, and this feeling permeated her with cold, lofty disdain.[14]

Supporting her brood with hard work, toiling in the fields, spinning, knitting, weaving straw mats and carving wooden utensils, Meta reaches the final step in her development. Calm and serene she finally realizes that her suffering has not been an isolated case of bad luck but a product of the social system in which she lives. She knows now that she is no sinner and that society has perpetrated a gross injustice on her. Therefore, she does not hide her life story from her children; instead, she teaches them to defend their honor wherever they might be, instilling in them self-respect and hatred for hypocrisy and injustice.

The short story "Samorastniki" was first published in 1937. In 1940 it was chosen as the title story for a collection of Voranc's starkly realistic stories about the peasants in the Carinthian mountains. Since the war the book has been reprinted in several editions; the story "Samorastniki" was made into a film. It is interesting that in spite of legal reforms concerning unwed mothers and their children in post-war Slovenia, the critics have underplayed the character of Meta and overemphasized the revolutionary ideas of "Samorastniki." Thus, for example, in 1968, Slodnjak defines the story as "a tale about the economic fiasco of a mighty house of a Carinthian farmer, who was destroyed in the second half of the previous century by an economic crisis." Slodnjak also adds that "Kuhar . . . employed symbols and allegory in order to put across his message that poor peasants have the right to own their land and enjoy its products."[15] Slodnjak does not mention the central problem of the unwed mother at all. In 1969 L. Legiša classified "Samorastniki" as a story about forbidden love between a poor beauty and a rich farmer, disregarding the fact that Voranc does not describe a single love scene between Meta and Ožbej and that the point of the story is the character of an unwed mother and the fate of her offspring and not the trials and tribulations through which a romantic idyll had to pass.[16] In his study of Voranc's peasants, attached to the 1969 edition of Samorastniki, Marjan Kramberger analyses certain traits in Meta's character, but only from the point of view of "Meta, the peasant woman." He explains Meta's physical endurance and her ability to suffer as another manifestation of the iron will which all Voranc's peasants share, a will "which so obstinately negates any kind of limitation to this endurance that just because of this we can hardly envisage it."[17] Kramberger's point of observation, however, being strictly materialistic, cannot encompass Meta's personality as a whole. He says, for example, that neither Meta nor Voranc speak the truth when they say that Meta loved Ožbej for himself only; according to Kramberger Meta was primarily fighting for property and loved Ožbej only as the future master of Karnice, whether she was aware of her ambition or not. Kramberger often refers to an uneducated peasant as an uncivilized human being, incapable of emotions surpassing his immediate greed for property and his stubborn fight for and against the cruel earth. Thus, according to the critic, Meta, too, is incapable of any sublime erotic feelings; her relationship with Ožbej is based on her subconscious desire to climb the social and economic ladder. It is interesting that Kramberger, a Marxist and socialist, does not define Meta's position in a capitalist society as a defiant revolutionary stand. On the contrary: he seems to defend Karničnik's position and accuses the author of painting this character black and white.

Be that as it may, Voranc's Meta is the portrait of an unwed mother, clearly defined as an individual in space and time. In its monumental proportions it exposes the problem clearly, and defiantly demands from the reader an honest effort to sort out his attitudes and face his own prejudices.

Prešeren, Cankar and Voranc lived approximately fifty years apart. Their education and lifestyles were entirely different. Their literary output appeared in forms that had nothing in common. Yet all three chose, sometime during their literary careers, to deal with the theme of the unwed mother and the fate of her offspring. The common denominator to which the choice of this theme could be traced lies in their characters. Prešeren, Cankar and Voranc were men who disliked hypocrisy to such an extent that they were ready to expose it in whatever shape or form it raised its ugly head, regardless of the consequences for their personal comfort and security: Prešeren, a man of classical education, a spirit of Faustian dimension, a genius whose poetry measures up to the peaks of world literature, remained a poverty-stricken bachelor-lawyer until his death at forty-nine; Cankar, a man whose identification with the philosophy and art of the fin-de-siècle made him a citizen of the world, and whose masterpieces had no model and have had no heir in Slovene literature, remained a homeless wanderer, an annoying presence in petty Slovene society until he, too, died in his forties; Voranc, a man without formal education but with tremendous zest for learning, a writer whose peasant characters are, in Župančič's words, "kot da goram se iz bokov izvili so," spent his final year as an embittered loner.

Persecution of unmarried mothers and their helpless children was one of the outstanding injustices that all three writers witnessed in the society of their time. Prešeren was touched by it through personal tragedy; Cankar's keen eye for social evil born of ignorance, noticed it in the small town of Vrhnika as well as in the slums of Vienna; Voranc saw it among the sturdy peasants of the Carinthian mountains whose passion for life mingled with medieval attitudes and fears and made them victims of their own ignorance.

Prešeren was Cankar's first model and master, and Cankar, of course, knew "Nezakonska mati" just as he knew the drama of Prešeren's life. It is possible that Prešeren's poem focused Cankar's attention on the problem of motherhood out of wedlock. However, in Cankar's stories this problem is tightly interwoven with his attacks on religious hypocrites and sinful priests. Thus, while Prešeren's unwed mother plays the central part in his lovely poem, unwed mothers provide, more or less, only the background against which Cankar exposes a social evil. Voranc certainly knew both Prešeren's and Cankar's work. It does not seem likely, though, that he moulded Meta of "Samorastniki" according to literary models. Her portrait is one in the group of Carinthian peasants, a unique face, but belonging to the composite relief consisting of lumberjacks, sinewy well-diggers and laboring tillers of the skimpy soil on mountain slopes. It is neither a saintly, smiling face of a sad young maiden, nor a pale mask of a semi-insane woman. It is a face carved of rock, defiant and peaceful.

Prešeren, Cankar and Voranc are not the only writers who have dealt with the theme of the unwed mother in Slovene literature. Prešeren was the first to smash the tabu, expose the problem and bravely deal with it in a literary form. After him, the theme of the unwed mother has been exposed by many Slovene writers, great and humble, up to the most recent years. However, the above three interpretations of this social issue are the most vivid because of their masters' total involvement and their literary genius.

Notes

1. Among the Romans, the children born of concubines were entitled to support from their father but had no right of inheritance from him. Germanic law, which lasted throughout the early feudal period, recognized as legitimate only those whose parents were of the same social rank. The children regarded as bastards had no rights of inheritance. Under the Common Law of England the illegitimate child was regarded as "filius nullius" and until the sixteenth century he was supported by the parish in which he was born. An act of 1576, however, made it an offence to beget an illegitimate child and shifted the burden of support onto the mother. Frantic mothers, branded now not only as whores but also as criminals, often abandoned newborn infants. These were then taken to special "Foundling Hospitals." Nowadays, in twentieth-century England, the support of an illegitimate child is primarily the mother's duty. Affiliation proceedings are complicated and even if successful, the father's contribution to the support of the child is limited to a small sum weekly. The

United States followed English Common Law, and special institutions for out-of-wedlock children were established. Affiliation proceedings are quasi-criminal in nature.

2. As late as the 1960's some groups have tried to legalize compulsive sterilization in the US for females having more than one illicit pregnancy. Others have argued that illegitimate children should be excluded from financial benefits.

3. In the 1920's unwed mothers were generally considered immoral, mentally deficient charity types; in the 1930's they were supposed to come from broken or poor homes; in the 1940's and 1950's they were regarded as emotionally disturbed girls, who could also come from middle-class families.

4. For an English version of the poem, see *Poems* by Francè Prešeren (eds., W. K. Matthews and A. Slodnjak) (London: John Calder, 1969), 37.

5. The translation "my friends would blush and pass me by" is not accurate. The original says, "Moji se mene sram'vali so," which means "my close relatives were ashamed of me."

6. Again the translation ("And he who was my own true love, / Your father by the will above, / He wanders God knows how far from here, / shamed because of us, poor dear") gives a slightly slanted view of the relationship between the girl and her lover. In the original the verses are:

"On, ki je sam bil ljubi moj, On, ki je pravi oča tvoj, Šel je po sveti Bog ve kam, Tebe in mene ga je sram!"

7. A polemical poem about new styles and topics in Slovene poetry.

8. Anton Slodnjak, *Pregled slovenskega slovstva* (Ljubljana: Akademska založba, 1934), 82.

9. Ivan Prijatelj, *Izbrani eseji in razprave* (ed., A. Slodnjak) (Ljubljana: Slovenska Matica, 1952), 356.

10. Ivan Cankar, *Izbrana dela* (ed., Boris Merhar) (Ljubljana: Cankarjeva založba, 1951-59), Vol. 5, 322.

11. Ibid., Vol. 6, 25.

12. Prežihov Voranc, *Samorastniki* (ed., Marjan Kramberger) (Maribor: Založba Obzorja, 1969). The title could be translated "the selfsown."

13. Ibid., 77.

14. Ibid., 98.

15. Anton Slodnjak, *Slovensko slovstvo* (Ljubljana: Mladinska knjiga, 1968), 423.

16. Lino Legiša, *Zgodovina slovenskega slovstva* (Ljubljana: Slovenska Matica, 1957-71), Vol. VI, 396.

17. Voranc, op. cit., 266.

Irma M. Ozbalt (essay date 1982)

SOURCE: "Emigrants in Ivan Cankar's Fiction," in *Slov-* *ene Studies: Journal of the Society for Slovene Studies,* Vol. 4, No. 2, 1982, pp. 99-112.

[*In the following essay, Ozbalt presents an overview of Cankar's emigrant stories, summarizing their thematic and symbolic content.*]

Ivan Cankar wrote about emigrants with deep personal involvement. Not only was he a native of Slovenia, a tiny country that had been providing labor for the rich Western European countries and the USA, he was also born into a family from which laborers had often travelled to foreign lands in search of daily bread. His childhood friends as well as his own brothers were swallowed by the world beyond the boundaries of Slovenia. Therefore his reasoning about the emigrant is neither detached nor calmly speculative. His stories about emigrants read like ballads, their style sometimes transcending narrative or even lyrical prose and approaching biblical expression. Many of his stories open with an atmosphere-creating, meditative paragraph in the first person, which gives the narrative a strong frame of authenticity. Such an introduction also provides a bridge between the nucleus of the story, which is usually a realistic episode in an emigrant's life, and the symbolic extension and artistic interpretation of the event.

Cankar's emigrant stories were nearly all written the first decade of this century. In those years the writer was living in Ottakring, a working-class suburb of Vienna, as a boarder with a working-class family, the Löfflers. He had already given up the idea of obtaining a university degree at the Vienna University, and even of getting steady employment. His chosen occupation was writing. Through daily correspondence with literary friends and publishers in Ljubljana he was informed about the problems and upheavals in contemporary political, economic and cultural situation in Slovenia. At the same time, he was surrounded by the reality of a central European metropolis, with its cultural richness and cosmopolitan polish on one hand and its miseries and injustices on the other. Cankar's fiction of the Vienna period, therefore, reflects this dual aspect of his existence and loyalties. He writes about Slovene intellectuals, politicians, artists, peasants, and suffering children at the same time as he portrays miscellaneous misfits of Ottakring, alcoholics, prostitutes, sickly children and unemployed. His stories about emigrants form two distinct groups as well. One group represents the artistic interpretation of the fate of Slovene emigrants in the countries of Western Europe and the United States of America, while the other deals with Czech immigrants in Vienna. Regardless of which emigrants Cankar portrays, however, he always chooses only those who have found neither luck nor happiness in their new, chosen country. His emigrants to America fall into the midst of an economic crisis only to roam New York streets and flop-houses with other unemployed laborers—until they return home as failures. Those who had worked in West German mines and factories return home sick, exhausted and poor, only to die and be buried in their native soil. Czech immigrants in Vienna become Ottakring outcasts—unemployed, poor, sick, despised, their children prematurely grown, never assimilated.

1. SLOVENE EMIGRANTS.

By 1900, when Cankar was twenty-four years old, he had already become aware of the threatening problem that his native land was bleeding to death, and that the Slovenes were doomed to extinction if the emigration tide was not stopped. In his correspondence with friends he talks about this gloomy prospect with great apprehension:

> . . . it makes me feel very sad if I stop and think what kind of future our peasant nation will have. This nation is disappearing and dying. In the Dolenjsko region some villages practically have no male population any more; everybody is leaving to get lost forever. . . . If things continue this way, in two hundred years we won't exist any more.[1]

To another friend he writes:

> . . . I intend to write a drama about our peasants; this sad, general bankruptcy of our people, especially in Dolenjsko villages, is something tragic; it is taking place slowly and imperceptibly, and is, therefore, even more shocking . . . this terrible passivity is something enormous.[2]

The "bankruptcy" which Cankar writes about, was the economic crisis in which the Slovene peasants, who had until 1848 been serfs on the land they tilled, found themselves after the agrarian reform. Unable to pay for the land they "owned" and heavily taxed, they sank into debt, and one after another were forced to sell their land. In 1870's this crisis reached its peak, and mass emigration followed.

Cankar started planning two dramas: one a tragedy about the proletarization of the Slovene countryside, and the other dealing with emigration. The first plan he partially realized in his play *The King of Betajnova* in 1901; of the second plan, however, only four pages of a play were ever written, in spite of the fact that Cankar worked on it for eight years. The problem disturbed him deeply, and he was trying to convey the idea in a perfect form. That he was striving for perfection is shown in those four pages which are in themselves a masterpiece. The drama was to be called *Niobe*. The name and the motif from Greek mythology would symbolically represent three problems: firstly, the universal tragedy of an old mother whose children have left; secondly, the loneliness and sorrow of a Slovene peasant mother wasting away after all her children have emigrated; and thirdly, the decline of Slovenia, the motherland of a doomed people, a land dying of wounds from mass emigration. But the play never materialized. Cankar delayed writing it because he felt that he should leave Vienna and go to Slovenia to study the situation firsthand. But his perpetual poverty prohibited such trips.

Nevertheless, Cankar did not put the problem of emigration aside. Instead of writing one big piece about the problem, he portrayed the emigrants and expressed his ideas about emigration from Slovenia in shorter, less involved works, in short stories, as well as in some chapters of his longer prose works.

The earliest traces of the emigrant motif could be seen in Cankar's first novel *Strangers* and in the short story **"Rue des Nations."** There is no direct mention of emigrants in either, but in both the author expresses the feelings of homesickness and love for his homeland which he must have been experiencing in Vienna where he lived as a at least temporary immigrant. In *Strangers* he says:

> He remembered those beautiful places, those hills and valleys, those rustling woods; it seemed to him that down there the spring sun kept shining brightly, meadows melting in its light, wheat waving in caressing breezes, dewy happiness spilling all over. . . . Oh, how he would kneel down and kiss that soil, he, the wanderer.[3]

But no matter how deep Cankar's love for his homeland was, he could not overlook the fact that this beautiful country could not support all who were born into it. He realized that people were forced to leave in search of a better, dignified life. Thus, his emigrants soon displayed a new, tragic feature: they were people torn between their love for their homeland and their urge to live, to fight for a better life. By their very decision to emigrate they brought on themselves an existence of split loyalties, guilt complexes and sorrow.

The character of the emigrant developed step by step, with each step becoming less romantic, sentimental, and more and more magic.

One of the first emigrant characters appeared in the story **"The Cross on the Mountain,"** in 1905. The hero is not yet tragic;—maybe momentarily sad, but neither physically nor spiritually broken. The man is one of those lucky emigrants who have found bread and butter if not a fortune in America. He has come home to find himself a bride. He is fat, red-cheeked, showing off and strutting through his native village, smoking a cigar, flashing a golden ring and generally behaving like a rich "Amerikanec." Yet he falls in love with the wrong girl and has to return to America alone and crest-fallen. This first figure of Cankar's emigrants is a loser, but he is not a tragic character. He is not unhappy because he is an emigrant; he is unhappy because of unhappy love.

The next step in the development of the emigrant in Cankar's stories could be seen in the short story **"The Idiot Martinec,"** written in the same year as **"The Cross on the Mountain."** Here the emigrants are shown in a new light: although the decision to emigrate is supposed to be the act of strong, young people who refuse to be tied to their doomed home and die with it, it is nevertheless an act of despair. In **"The Idiot Martinec"** the young would-be emigrants pretend to be happy; on the eve of their departure they drink and dance themselves into a stupor. The village fool, Martinec, plays the accordion for them. He, too, has decided to emigrate. Next morning he follows the little procession of three strong young men and the village beauty Hana, with whom he is in love. Yet he cannot carry out his decision. He watches Hana's red silk scarf disappear beyond the hill, then he returns to the villages in the gully, to merge and die with the old folk. Sorrow and the feeling of doom envelop Martinec as well as the little procession of brave young emigrants.

A year after **"The Idiot Martinec"** Cankar wrote the story **"Vagabond Marko and King Matjaž."** Like Martinec, Marko is a musician, and he, too, wanders through empty, dying-out villages and across untilled fields overgrown with weeds. He encounters only half-dead old men and women; all the young people have disappeared. But here the story continues where **"The Idiot Martinec"** left off: we encounter the character of a forsaken mother, a Niobe. In the story, she is Marko's aunt Agata, an old woman living alone in a decaying house; she moves around wrapped in a grey shawl, pale and wrinkled. She laments:

> Five sons I had! five handsome young men, a pleasure to the eye. . . . Then, my oldest son became sick, very sick at heart. 'Mother, I can't live here any more, my home is strangling me, my heart is longing for far-away lands.' I cried and I begged, but he tore himself from my embrace and he left and I have never seen him since. A year later my second son became sick. . . .[4]

Agata lost all her sons, including her youngest, whom she had begged on her knees to stay. Although Marko remains with his aunt for a while, he cannot help her: he, too, is young and he, too, has been infected with the longing for the Eldorado somewhere beyond his native hills. While Martinec could not cut the ties which bound him to his beloved, doomed homeland, Marko has succeeded, as have his five cousins and other strong, brave young people. Yet all of them have taken with them their memories and homesickness, as well as the feeling of guilt because they left behind their mothers; Niobes to die a lonely death. Thus, the emigrant in Cankar's stories, is split within himself, a misfit even before he had tried his luck in a new, adopted country.

A year after **"The Vagabond Marko,"** in 1907, Cankar drew a symbolic portrait of the emigrant which was to remain unchanged in all his emigrant stories yet to follow. He outlined him in a lyrical parable entitled the **"Way of the Cross."** In the parable Christ leads a procession of the humiliated and the down-trodden out of their valley of tears across Golgotha into the glory of resurrection. Among the sufferers in Christ's procession are abused children, pauper-peasants, factory workers and—emigrants. While the American in **"The Cross on the Mountain"** was a successful man if not happy, while the three boys and the lovely girl in the **"Idiot Martinec"** at least pretended to be happy, and while Niobe's sons left because their youthful ambition overcame their love for their mother, the emigrants in Christ's procession pretend no more:

> They were carrying bundles of clothing and staring at the ground. They were bent at the waist, covered with

dust. Men and women, old people and children. The children, too, were silent and stared at the ground.

> 'Where to, my dear folks?' asked the stranger.

> 'To America, to the promised land, to find bread and soil and homeland.'

> They walked on and did not raise their heads; and they all started to sing a sad pilgrims' hymn.[5]

Thus, the profile of the emigrant acquired the feature of a tragic, even cynical weakling, who has sacrificed his homeland for a crust of bread and has in the process lost his identity, his very soul.

In the stories which followed this portrayal of the emigrant, that is, in the stories after 1907, Cankar tried to follow the emigrant's destiny in his new homeland. Cankar knew about the life of Slovene emigrants in America and Western Europe only from reports. He never travelled to these countries himself. And the reports were not good. A great number of Slovene emigrants in the years 1907-1908 was hit by the great economic depression in the USA. Unemployment struck hard. Many newcomers left America and returned home, usually poorer than when they had left. Cankar wrote about these unfortunate people from the point of view of an idealist, a patriotic observer. Since he never lived among Slovene emigrants himself, he could not write emigrant stories based on real people and real events. The stories are, thus, lyrical, poetic and symbolistic. Symbolism is clearly demonstrated already in the short sketch **"Welcome!,"** written in 1907, and it intensifies with years. It reaches its peak in the poetic tale **Kurent,** in 1909.

The lyrical sketch **"Welcome!"** is written in a solemn, biblical style. It opens with a rhetorical introductory paragraph, an accusation and reproach to America:

> "Oh, America, you land of yearning, the blessed Eldorado of immeasurable riches, the land where in the days of woe all the poor and oppressed found a haven—where are you, America, you promised land? It is no more. . . . The mines are empty, the factories closed, the steel wheels idle and rusting. As after a lost battle black battalions are running away, in silence, without hope. Each week, my dear folks, each week thirty thousands.[6]

Cankar then selects three men from this defeated swarm, and we hear their triple chant, colored with sorrow and feeling of guilt and shame when they approach the village in which the first one had left a bride, the second an old mother, and the third a large family. They are apprehensive about facing their folks, embarrassed about their defeat in the foreign land. But the relatives do not reproach them for anything; they embrace and welcome their guilt-ridden men.

In conclusion, Cankar sends a message of compassion to all emigrants who are returning home as failures:

You who fertilized foreign lands with the sweat of your brow, you who drenched it with your warm blood—welcome! Each of you is like a child who had run away because his mother could not provide his daily bread. But when he became sick, he returned home to his poor mother, and they greeted each other with tears.[7]

But forgiveness and compassion are not the lot of the emigrant in another story Cankar wrote in the same year as **"Welcome!"** The short story **"Oh My Homeland, You Are Like Health"**[8] was written for *Hrvatski dnevnik* in Sarajevo, therefore the hero is a Croatian, and Cankar's language in this narrative colored by Croatian words. But the fate of the emigrant is the same as of his Slovene counterpart: Gjuro had left for Germany fifteen years ago. And there, according to the author

. . . every time he returned from the factory, his body was weaker for three drops of blood: one drop had been swallowed by the powerful machines, the second dissipated in the black dust, and the third melted in brandy.[9]

Then, one day Gjuro fainted beside his machine, black blood streaming out of his mouth. He realized that his days were numbered. He tied his bag and returned to his homeland. As he stepped onto his native soil, he was moved to tears:

Fifteen years and more my poor eyes have not seen you, my mother . . . . Greetings to you, my wide, sweet-smelling fields. . . . Blessings and thanks to you, my land . . . you who had given me my life, you in whose embrace one can be reborn.[10]

But unlike the three men in the story **"Welcome!,"** Gjuro is not welcomed by the people in his native village. A new note is sounded in the evaluation of the emigrants: they are considered healthy, brave people no more. They are a cowardly minority who were unable to endure the hardships together with their fellow countrymen; after having given the best years of their lives to a foreign country they have no right to return home and reap where they did not sow. The villagers bring Gjuro a pile of straw and install him in a barn. Gjuro, a man who once had two homelands and now has none, cries bitterly; he kisses a lump of soil and dies.

The third variation on the theme of the defeated emigrant who returns home after an unsuccessful attempt to improve his lot appeared in the story **"A Tale of Two Young People,"** written in 1909. It is the story of Pavle and Mana, a poor couple, who cannot afford to marry. So they decide that Pavle would go to America for a while and earn some money, while Mana would stay at home and also work hard to save some money. Then they would go back to their native village and get married. Pavle is full of doubts and apprehension when he hears his fellow-passengers discuss the prospects of life in America. They are saying that:

Years ago it did happen that a man returned from America with a purse full of money and with a golden watch. But these days when a poor man steps onto one ship, his poverty steps onto another and sails right behind him.[11]

In America Pavle is faced with unemployment, starvation and temptation into crime. But since he is healthy and spiritually strong—he has not been drained yet by slaving in a foreign land—he decides to admit his mistake and return home. When he meets Mana, he discovers that she, too, had not managed to gather any dowry by working in the city. They decide, however, to return to the village, get married, and work their patch of land, having each other's love to sustain them.

This naively optimistic end of the story was Cankar's concession to the publisher Mohorjeva družba, which distributed books mainly among the peasant population, whom it tried to enlighten and elevate. The moral of the story is obvious: save your courage, your strength and your love for your homeland, and you will be repaid—not with riches, but with dignity and with the warm feeling of belonging.

This idea permeates and brings to its high-pitched conclusion Cankar's most symbolistic prose-work on the theme of the emigrant, *Kurent*. Written in the same year as **"A Tale of Two Young People,"** it proclaims the same idea, but in an entirely different form. *Kurent* is a magnificent rhythmic narrative, in which the fantastic is superimposed on the underlying gloomy reality. The symbol has replaced the character completely.

In *Kurent* Cankar used motifs from some of his previous stories: like the idiot Martinec and like the vagabond Marko. Kurent is a musician, playing his tunes to the sad, the doomed, all over Slovenia; he, too, catches only a passing glimpse of the beautiful girl in her red, shiny scarf. The types of the oppressed and downtrodden for whom Kurent plays his tunes are the same that have walked in Christ's procession. To these old motifs Cankar now added a new one, borrowed from folklore and literature: Kurent, a miserable boy sells his soul to the devil and obtains from him a magic flute, which makes people forget their miseries. Kurent's roamings end when he joins a procession of emigrants bound for the seaport.

Their faces were burnt from the sun, so that no one could say whether they were young or old; they were all dark and bitter, all to the last one. Thick dust covered their coats, their cheeks, their eyes.[12]

But all these people are determined to go—no matter where; even death is better than the life they are leaving behind. In the biblically powerful triple complaint we hear an old man, a young man, and a girl, saying their sorrowful good-bys. Kurent sees the plight of this sad procession. He takes his fiddle and plays a happy tune. But as soon as the emigrants have embarked on their ship and Kurent's song can be heard no more, they realize they have made a mistake. Staring at the shore, their eyes fill with tears as they beg:

Smile to us for the last time, oh homeland, you poor, dearly beloved! Smile to us, the dead. What is happiness, what youth, what life without you?[13]

This rhetorical question contains Cankar's final belief about emigration: no amount of money, no comforts in life can replace the loss of your homeland. Even if you succeed in a foreign land, you will never be happy. But most likely you will not succeed. Therefore, stay at home, suffer with your country, and love her—she is your one and only mother.

When the ship disappears with her load of emigrants, doomed in advance, Kurent, who has nothing except his magic fiddle, falls on his knees, hits the grey rock with his forehead, and cries out: "My land, my beloved, dear homeland, my mother! If you can't give me bread, give me stone. Even the stone will make me sing."[14]

2. Czech Immigrants In Vienna

In the same decade when Cankar wrote symbolic stories about Slovene emigrants he also created a number of realistic, even naturalistic portrayals of Czech immigrants in Vienna.

The Czechs who congregated in Ottakring were Cankar's neighbors and acquaintances. He was deeply touched by their predicament, especially by the suffering of their children. His landlady and intimate friend, Albina Löffler, was Moravian herself. Unlike the stories about Slovene emigrants, all the stories about the Czechs in Vienna are based on real people and events.

In the short story **"In the Springtime"** the author tells the story of a little girl from Moravia who is destroyed by poverty and homesickness. Mařenka lives in a gray house opposite the author's. She has been brought to Vienna by her father, who had been in jail and now wants to get lost in a big city, in a foreign country. He is a drunk, and Mařenka's mother is ill; nobody cares much for the six-year-old girl. She often stands all alone in the stony backyard, dressed in Slovak peasant clothes that were not made for her. She never speaks. But when she hears a music-box peddler play a song in her native language about green, unmown meadows, she bursts into a wild cry and decides to escape and go back "home." That night her mother dies, and in general commotion Mařenka leaves. She walks and walks, but when she finally reaches fields, she realizes that they are foreign fields, that there is no path leading home. As in a trance she returns to the city and gets trampled to death under a horse-drawn wagon.

Another story, **"Pavliček's Crown,"** also describes the fate of an underprivileged immigrant child, although it mainly concerns the child's father. Pavliček is an old, unemployed cabinet-maker. His wife has died of poverty; now he has to look after his invalid little son, Janjek,

alone. In the story, Pavliček is faced with an unsurmountable problem: he has promised Janjek a ball, a piece of cake and a penknife for his birthday, and now he desperately needs a crown. He goes begging—but his landlord, the grocer and the inn-keeper all chase him away. Finally, he steals the crown from the change bowl in the bakery. He gets arrested. The little cripple is left alone on his birthday, watching his "tatinek" being taken away by the police and insulted by the crowd.

The third story, **"Zdenko Petersilka,"** again deals with sick, unemployed Czech immigrant parents and a helpless child. Petersilka is a very nice, soft-hearted man, sick with tuberculosis, extremely poor and unemployed. He is also an alcoholic. But his wife loves him loyally, and together they often get drunk and provide circus entertainment for the whole street. Their seven-year-old son, Zdenko, a pale, intelligent boy, suffers enormously. One day he first attacks the children who are making fun of his parents, and then hits his father in the face. This sobers Petersilka for a while. But they cannot fight the odds against them. For a while they try to save some money and they work hard, sewing day and night; but it is too late. Jan's tuberculosis has progressed, and during one of his drunk "performances" in the street he drops dead, blood gushing from his mouth. The ten-year-old Zdenko, who had watched the children poking fun at his father, silently knocks down one of his attackers. Then he stands there, calmly waiting for his fate—a child who has grown up painfully and prematurely.

But the Czechs who failed in Vienna were not all sick or alcoholics or parents with sick children. Some of them were single, young, strong men—and yet they did not fare much better.

The story **"Homeless"** describes three factory workers, of whom two are practical men, employed and healthy, if not particularly happy. The third one, however, is a sensitive, frail man, without a job. One night, after a socialist meeting where somebody shouted into the crowd "Vaterloses Gesindel!," he decides to return to his green Moravia, to his sweetheart. His two friends, with whom he shares humble living quarters, try to talk him out of it, but he persists. However, he only gets drunk in the nearest tavern, and then hangs himself on a pear tree.

ll the good, softhearted Czechs who suffered poverty, illness, unemployment and homesickness, but especially their children, who became unwanted misfits in the society into which they were brought, kept haunting Cankar long after he had left Ottakring. Even in his last years at Rožnik, when past injustices had mostly lost their edge, the suffering of Czech immigrants in Vienna remained painfully vivid in his memory. In 1912 and 1913 he published two more stories from their life.[15]

The miserable hero of the first one, **"The Sun Is Setting,"** is another of Cankar's former neighbors in Ottakring. Konopa is a jobless tailor. He has tuberculosis. He is single. For years he has dreamt of returning to his native Tatras, but has never managed to scrape together enough money for the journey. When his landlord gives him some cloth to sew him a suit, Konopa, instead, goes and sells it, and is—of course—arrested. Ironically, he is deported to his native land, to the Tatras.

In the second story, **"A Bunch of Flowers,"** similar fates are narrated. Jan Vymetal has advanced tuberculosis, he is a jobless tailor, he has a loyal wife and one tiny, prematurely wise child, Jelenka. On the eve of their landlord's birthday the mother has an idea: let us send the landlord a bunch of flowers with our good wishes; he might realize that we are good people, although temporarily unable to pay the rent. The Vymetals spend their last few pennies on a few cheap white asters and send Jelenka, all dressed up, to deliver the message. The landlord throws the child out.

. . . . .

If we summarize Cankar's description of emigrants-immigrants as well as his beliefs about emigration in general, we come to the following conclusions:

1. For Cankar, an emigrant is a miserable, homeless wanderer, who has two homelands but does not belong to either. In the new land the immigrant encounters numerous difficulties: he does not understand the language, his clothes and habits differ from those of the natives, his own children are embarrassed and ashamed of him. But these troubles are minor, compared with those which destroy the majority of Cankar's emigrants: unemployment and poverty, leading to disease, alcoholism and crime. Many emigrants are too proud to return home. Some keep dreaming of returning home with a fortune. But they never do. Those who are forced to return because of illness, old age or unemployment are faced with a final disappointment: their former friends and neighbors consider them cowards who had run away when times were bad, but who shamelessly returned to be kept and fed by the strong ones who had remained at home and survived.

2. Cankar was neither interested in nor acquainted with the emigrants who had "made it," with those who had pushed their way into the pattern of the rich, money-making society of their adopted land. He never met or lived among well-to-do Slovenes in either America or Western Europe. Living in Ottakring and being poor himself, he paid no attention to the fact that many Czechs established their homes, businesses and careers in Austria quite successfully.

3. Cankar treated the emigrant with deep compassion, while at the same time he blamed his tragedy not only on the selfish society which exploited him but also on his native, overly sensitive disposition. Cankar was especially touched by the suffering of the immigrant children, who—robbed of their childhood—grew up prematurely wise, children denied not only toys, games and sweets, but also their daily bread and even the space in which to grow.

4. Cankar seems to have reached the conclusion that it is a mistake to leave your native land, no matter how poor it might be. It is easier to suffer poverty among your own people: you at least have a home in which you can live and die as a man who knows where his roots are, where he belongs. Of course, Cankar never knew any political refugees, and therefore he neither described nor pronounced any judgment on this type of emigrant.

Notes

1. *Pisma Ivana Cankarja,* 3 vols., ed. Izidor Cankar (Ljubljana: Državna založba Slovenije, 1948), 2:363. All translations are by myself.

2. Ivan Cankar, *Izbrana dela,* 10 vols., ed. Boris Merhar (Ljubljana: Cankarjeva založba, 1951-59), 3:523.

3. Ibid., 2:416.

4. Ibid., 4:429.

5. Ibid., 6:14.

6. Ivan Cankar, *Zbrani spisi,* 20 vols., ed. Izidor Cankar (Ljubljana: Nova založba, 1925-1935), 13:150.

7. Ibid., 13:154.

8. The title was taken from A. Mickiewicz's epos *Pan Tadeusz.*

9. *Izbrana dela,* 6:171.

10. Ibid., 6:172.

11. Ibid., 7:27.

12. Ibid., 6:347.

13. Ibid., 6:350.

14. Ibid.

15. Whether Cankar wrote these stories at the same time as the previous ones about the Czech immigrants in Vienna and only published them in 1912-13, or whether he wrote them at that time is an unanswered question. Their style—first person narration, long introductions dealing with the author's moods, similarity of types, and time references—would suggest their earlier genesis.

FURTHER READING

Criticism

Slodnjak, Anton. "Ivan Cankar in Slovene and World Literature." *The Slavonic and East European Review* 59, No. 2 (April 1981): 186–96.

Surveys Cankar's literary career, highlighting his major influences and themes.

Additional coverage of Cankar's life and career is contained in the following source published by the Gale Group: *Dictionary of Literary Biography,* **Vol. 147.**

J. M. McTaggart
1866-1925

(Full name John McTaggart Ellis McTaggart) English philosopher.

INTRODUCTION

McTaggart is known for his unique interpretation of Hegelian idealism, which held that ultimate reality is spiritual, consisting only of individual minds and not including time, space, and material objects, (none of which he believed had any place in reality). McTaggart's theories, particularly that of the unreality of time, continue to intrigue contemporary philosophers.

BIOGRAPHICAL INFORMATION

McTaggart was born in London in 1866 to Francis and Caroline Ellis. His father later changed the family name to McTaggart to satisfy a requirement for an inheritance. McTaggart attended Trinity College, Cambridge, graduating with honors in 1888. On a trip to New Zealand in 1892 to visit his widowed mother, he met Margaret Elizabeth Bird, whom he married in 1899. The couple moved back to Cambridge, where McTaggart taught until his retirement in 1923. He died suddenly in 1925.

MAJOR WORKS

McTaggart's first published work was *Studies in the Hegelian Dialectic* (1896), which focused on Hegel's methodology in developing his notion of idealism. He next published *Studies in Hegelian Cosmology* (1901), a collection of essays that covered such topics as the nature of sin, the moral criterion, and Christianity; it is in this volume McTaggart began to develop his own theory of the spiritual community being the essence of ultimate reality. In *Some Dogmas of Religion* (1906) McTaggart explained several metaphysical belief systems significant to Christianity and then questioned the existence of an omnipotent God, arguing instead for determinism and immortality based on his notion of the ultimate reality. In *Commentary on Hegel's Logic* (1910) McTaggart further expounded on Hegel's ideas, this time concentrating on his system of logic. The two-volume *Nature of Existence* (1921-1927) is McTaggart's magnum opus, containing his entire treatise on metaphysics as well as some of his most important theories, particularly his notion of the unreality of time, which depends on the categorization of temporal events into A-series (past-present-future) and B-series (earlier-later). McTaggart argued that change is essential to time,

but it is impossible for B-series characteristics to change an event because they are either earlier or later than another event. Events in the A-series must possess all of the characteristics of being past, present, and future at once, which is also impossible. Therefore, time cannot exist in reality. *Philosophical Studies* (1934) is a posthumously published volume of McTaggart's previously uncollected essays. McTaggart's most important metaphysical notion is that, although there is no God, the self develops toward the absolute, which he termed a "timeless and endless state of love" through a series of incarnations. This emphasis on the individual self, or personhood, and love eventually played an important role in the development of the Cambridge school of Humanism, the Apostles, and later, the Bloomsbury group.

CRITICAL RECEPTION

McTaggart produced philosophical theories that many critics have considered engaging and provocative, even if they have disagreed with them. Two of McTaggart's best-known students at Cambridge, Bertrand Russell and G. E. Moore, began as Idealists in the same mode as McTaggart but soon found empiricism more appealing. Others have pointed to flaws of incoherency in McTaggart's A-series; the Cambridge Realists, in particular, censured his notion of the unreality of time. Nonetheless, McTaggart retains a readership, and many critics have praised his originality.

PRINCIPAL WORKS

Studies in the Hegelian Dialectic (philosophy) 1896
Studies in Hegelian Cosmology (philosophy) 1901
Some Dogmas of Religion (philosophy) 1906
Commentary on Hegel's Logic (philosophy) 1910
The Nature of Existence 2 vols. (philosophy) 1921-1927
Philosophical Studies [edited by S. V. Keeling] (philosophy) 1934

CRITICISM

C. D. Broad (essay date 1921)

SOURCE: A review of *The Nature of Existence,* in *The Hibbert Journal,* Vol. XX, No. 1, October, 1921, pp. 172-75.

[In the following review of The Nature of Existence, *Broad praises the first volume of the treatise despite reservations about several of McTaggart's conclusions, particularly his tendency to take certain propositions to be self-evident.]*

For the last twenty years or so the labours of philosophers have been devoted rather to the investigation of the nature and certainty of alleged scientific knowledge than to the attempt to determine the nature of Reality as a whole by abstract reasoning. This limitation has been mainly the result of bitter experience of the futility of previous attempts at speculative metaphysics. A distrust of elaborate philosophical systems has always characterised England in general, and of late years has been specially characteristic of Cambridge in particular. To all these rules Dr M'Taggart is probably the most eminent living exception. He has always held that interesting and important facts can be proved of Reality as a whole by processes of deductive reasoning. Until lately he thought that this could be done by a method akin to the Hegelian dialectic. In the last work that he published before the present one [*The Nature of Existence*] his position was that the dialectic method is logically sound, and that it is applicable to the actual world, but that in the argument used by Hegel there are certain mistakes of detail, although the final result is substantially correct.

In the present work he has departed considerably further from Hegel. He still thinks that the dialectical method of reasoning, when properly understood, is logically sound. He still thinks, so far as I can gather from this volume, which is only the first of two, that Reality is of much the same nature as Hegel, on M'Taggart's interpretation of the Absolute Idea, asserted it to be. But he no longer thinks that Reality is such that the dialectical method applies to it. His present argument is a perfectly straight-forward deductive one. At various stages new premises are introduced, but these are supposed either to be *a priori* self-evident propositions, or to be empirical propositions which everyone will in fact grant. There are only two of the latter used in this book, viz. (i.) that something exists, and (ii.) what exists has parts. Even the latter can be dispensed with if a certain important proposition, which M'Taggart introduces later on, and which he holds to be self-evident, be granted. And, unless it be granted, the most exciting things in the book cannot be proved.

I think it must be admitted that no *general* objection can be taken to such a method, however sceptical we may personally feel as to whether anything really important can be proved about Reality as a whole in this way. Each transition must, of course, be scrutinised to see if it is logically sound; but this is equally necessary with any deductive argument on any subject. It may be said at once that M'Taggart is most unlikely to be caught in a purely logical fallacy. The other place where careful scrutiny is needed is at the introduction of each new premise. There are two great dangers about propositions that are alleged to be self-evident. One is that they may prove to be merely verbal. Another is that you may accept them simply because you can see no alternative; and your failure to see an alternative may arise, either through lack of the necessary experience or imagination, or through an unconscious desire *not* to see it.

M'Taggart is fully awake to the second danger. This first volume is mainly a general discussion of categories, but in the next its results are to be applied to concrete problems, like human survival. M'Taggart sees quite clearly that here one is liable to be biassed by one's wishes, and that, in any case, the fact that we can *think of* only one sort of thing that fulfils the conditions laid down for existents in general does not *prove* conclusively that Reality can only *consist of* existents of that kind.

The first danger, I think, hardly gets the attention that it deserves. It seems to me that in a long chain of reasoning a word is liable to have one meaning in the self-evident premise in which it is first introduced, and another in some of the remote consequences that are deduced from this premise. Probably, if you give it this second meaning, the premise will no longer seem self-evident. I should say that the word "part" in M'Taggart's reasoning is liable to this objection. It is certainly ambiguous, and it certainly plays an important rôle in the development of the system; yet its ambiguity is nowhere explicitly noticed.

A great deal of M'Taggart's argument turns on alleged infinite regresses. He has no objection to infinity, as such, but he holds that certain kinds of infinite regress are vicious. His argument at many places takes the form: Unless so-and-so be true of Reality there will be an infinite regress at this point, and it is of the vicious kind. He seems to have taken over, without question, from Russell's *Principles of Mathematics,* the doctrine that an infinite regress is vicious when and only when it concerns the "meaning" of some concept. In view of the extreme ambiguity of the word "meaning," and of the important part that infinite regresses play in the argument, it would have been wise to give an independent discussion of the whole subject.

These are the main general criticisms that can be made on M'Taggart's argument. To enter into detailed criticism of particular transitions would be out of place here. I will, therefore, confine myself to mentioning some of M'Taggart's main results, and some of the more important and doubtful of his premises.

He first tries to show that, in dealing with the existent, we are dealing with the whole of Reality. The actual argument seems to me to be in places very thin; but the discussion is valuable as containing some excellent remarks on the nature of judgment, truth, and falsehood. M'Taggart rejects propositions, in the sense of Meinong's Objectives, and holds that truth and falsehood can be adequately dealt with by assuming nothing but facts, acts of judgment, and an ultimate relation of correspondence between the two.

M'Taggart now passes on to the category of substance. He defines it, rightly, as it seems to me, in such a way that events, states of mind, and many other entities which would not usually count as substances, do so. He accepts as self-evident that no two substances agree with each other in *all* their attributes, although they might agree in all those attributes which do not involve relations. He then tries to prove from this that every substance has a description which (i.) applies to it alone, and (ii.) is entirely in terms of general characteristics. The proof is performed by threats of a vicious infinite regress. I am not at all clear that the regress is vicious, and the proposition itself appears to me to be highly doubtful. It seems to me that, whenever we try to give a sufficient description of any existent, we have to bring in a reference to some substance (even if it be only a certain moment of time) which is known bodily by acquaintance. Thus a description like "the worst woman in London" contains an *explicit* reference to the substance London, and only becomes exclusive through a further *implicit* reference to the date at which the speaker uses the phrase.

M'Taggart next tries to prove that, if we arbitrarily suppose any substance to be different from what it actually is in any characteristic, we have no right to assume that any other substance would remain the same in any respect. This he calls the *Principle of Extrinsic Determination,* and carefully distinguishes from the *Intrinsic Determination,* which holds between one attribute and another when the first implies the second. The former is universal and reciprocal; the latter—which is the essence of what we mean by causation—is not universal, and is not in general reciprocal. In connection with the last point, there is an admirable discussion of Causation and of Induction.

Probably the most important, and certainly the hardest part of the book, is that which starts by dealing with the notion of Groups of Substances. The best example that one can take of this conception is a spatial whole, such as England, and the various sets of parts into which it can be cut. Any set of divisions which exactly fit together, without overlapping, to make up the surface of England, is a Set of Parts of England; and such a set of parts is a Group. All the various sets of parts of England are said to have the same Content. The meanings of all these terms are quite clear for a substance, like England, which has extensive magnitude. M'Taggart applies them, however, to all kinds of substances, an extension which seems to me to call for a good deal of discussion.

This brings us to the crucial point of the whole system. It seems self-evident to M'Taggart that every substance has content, *i.e.* that it has sets of parts, and that every part in every set has sets of parts, and so on without end. Now, when this is combined with the proposition, which he claims to have proved earlier, that every substance must have an exclusive description in general terms, we are threatened with an infinite regress, which he holds to be vicious. The only way to avoid the regress is to suppose that every substance has a set of parts whose sufficient descriptions imply sufficient descriptions of their own and all subsequent sets of parts. This subject is treated under the title of Determining Correspondence. The matter is too

technical for discussion here, and the reader must be referred to M'Taggart's book. It is enough to say that the only example that M'Taggart can suggest of a substance which fulfils the required conditions is a society of percipient beings who perceive each other, themselves, and the parts of each other and themselves, and so on, and perceive nothing else. Certain other conditions have to be fulfilled by their perceptions, which render these beings, on the face of them, rather unlike ourselves. Thus at last, and by a very peculiar route, we reach a proof that a certain kind of Spiritual Pluralism is probably the only satisfactory description of Reality as a whole.

In the next volume the details of this view will no doubt be worked out, and an attempt will be made to reconcile it with the many *prima-facie* appearances to the contrary which the world, as we think we know it, presents. In the meanwhile, philosophers cannot do better than to study this most interesting volume carefully, so as to make themselves familiar with the general topography of the Celestial City, before it finally descends from the University Press.

W. R. Matthews (essay date 1925)

SOURCE: "Three Philosophers on Religion," in *The Church Quarterly Review,* Vol. 100, No. CXCIX, April, 1925, pp. 122-38.

[*In the following essay, Matthews includes three works by McTaggart in a discussion on religion and philosophy.*]

An ancient Indian legend describes the creation of woman. It is said that Brahma, thinking it not good for man to be alone, created woman. After a time, however, the man came to Brahma with the request that the woman might be removed as she appeared to be incurably loquacious. The petition was granted by the complacent deity; but it was not long before the man returned with the prayer that the woman might be restored to him, saying 'She is a strange creature, for it seems impossible to live either with or without her.' This story might perhaps serve as a parable of the relations between religion and philosophy. It is certain that philosophy is 'incurably loquacious,' and that any attempts made by religion to stop her mouth have had at the most a temporary success. Nor have the efforts which have frequently been made to ignore her remarks been any more propitious. Sooner or later they have broken down before the persistent iteration of awkward questions, and we may now accept the position that Religion and Philosophy are indissolubly linked together by a bond which is neither that of complete agreement nor of fundamental difference, but the more fruitful because it necessitates action and reaction. Religion, we may predict, will always present philosophy with its highest problem, and philosophy will always be heating the furnace in which the intuitions of religion are to be tested. Perhaps there is still, however, one outstanding question: who is to be the predominant partner in the inevitable alliance?

It would of course be very far from the truth to say that the situation suggested by our parable is even now accepted by all reasonable men. There are still Ritschlians who sternly abstain from dalliance with metaphysics; and, pending further news of the development of that agile intelligence, we must assume that Mr. Bertrand Russell is still engaged in the crusade to purge philosophy of all interest in values or in God. Still more inaccurate would it be to imagine that there had been from the beginning any settled opinion on this subject in the Christian Church. The story of the attitude of the dominant minds in the Christian society towards secular thought is one of curious vicissitudes, and leaves upon the mind an impression of opportunism. St. Paul has more than one remark which indicates no favourable view of the philosophy of this world, though he himself has been hailed by some as the originator of the philosophy of history. The early literature of Christianity discloses, however, a strong disposition to use the writings of pagan philosophers in the defence and the articulation of the Gospel. To the Apologists and to Clement of Alexandria, the religion of the heathen appeared to contain no good, and its worship to be inspired by devils and offered to them; but in the thinkers of paganism they seemed to catch gleams of the inspiration of the Logos, and indeed so great were the affinities which they discerned in Plato with the truths of Christianity that some were impelled to accept the astonishing belief that the *Republic* and the *Timaeus* were influenced by the writings of Moses. To turn from the pages of Clement or Justin Martyr to those of Tertullian is like passing from the tolerant optimism of the *Modern Churchman* to the exponents of a fiercer and less articulate creed. Philosophy is the enemy. It is the cause of sinful pride and the source of all heresies. The porch of Solomon has nothing to do with that other porch, the ςτοὰ ποιχιλή, where Zeno discoursed of God, the universe, and man's duty. These fierce denunciations did not avail to keep their author from falling into heresy or the Church from making use of the wisdom of the Greeks. In Augustine we find that Platonism has become a road by which the mind may approach the true conception of God and a means of expounding the mysteries of the faith. It is not, however, until we reach the Scholastic period that we come upon any clear and definite theory of the proper relation of philosophy and revealed religion. In St. Thomas' view the office of philosophy is precise. It furnishes the *preambula fidei* as well as providing the categories in which the truths of Revelation may be expressed. The unaided human reason can demonstrate the being and the unity of God; and the Roman Church has enforced by its anathemas the logic of the great Doctor. The fundamental truths which reason can thus attain have, it is true, been the subject of divine Revelation; but, so far as they are concerned, the effect of Revelation has only been to confirm and promulgate the general conclusions of Aristotle.

The *modus vivendi* thus established was not destined to be of long duration, and even before the Renaissance and the Reformation had changed the whole intellectual situation, the confidence that speculative reason could be relied upon as a constant ally of faith had waned. The modern period of thought, which begins with Bacon and Descartes, presents us with a different relation between religion and philosophy. In it speculation once more emancipates itself from tutelage and develops independently. The great thinkers of the pre-Kantian era however were very far from being hostile to religion. Though Bacon objects to the teleological interpretation of nature as inimical to the progress of science and wishes to be rid in that sphere of final causes, those 'barren virgins,' yet he believes that 'depth in philosophy' will bring us back to religion. Some have thought that Descartes' respectful attitude towards theology was inspired chiefly by a regard for his own safety, but with little reason. There is no real ground for thinking that he was dishonest, and his conviction seems to have been that, though speculation must proceed freely about its business, it will be found, when that business is completed, to have supported and clarified the dogmas of religion. This is even more clear in the case of Leibniz. That unquenchable optimist conceived that in his very original cosmology he had provided a means not only of justifying the ways of God to men but even of performing the more difficult task of justifying the ways of Christians to one another. The Monadology and the Theodicy, so he believed, offered both a rational basis for the doctrines of Christianity and a ground of reconciliation for divided Christendom.

The first hint of a new attitude comes with Spinoza. The theologians who called him 'the Atheist' have perhaps been unjustly blamed for their intolerance, for they were surely not wrong in seeing in him the strong man armed who might despoil them of their goods. In Spinoza we hear philosophy claiming to be the mistress in the house, not a servant nor even a coequal, claiming to be even the reality of which the religion of the theologian and the Church and the mass of pious men is the imperfect avatar. It is the reliance of religion on revelation which marks its inferiority. 'I am astonished that anyone should wish to subject reason, the greatest of gifts and a light from on high, to the dead letter which may have been corrupted by human malice; that it should be thought no crime to speak with contempt of mind, the true handwriting of God's word, while it is considered the greatest of crimes to say the same of the letter, which is merely the image and reflexion of God's word.' Theology and the doctrines of religion may have value for the ignorant, but in the long run they tell us no more than that we shall be blessed through simple obedience without understanding. Revealed religion is concerned with conduct and the direction of the unenlightened. But Spinoza has a more excellent way—the way of understanding. Let a man pursue the dialectic path which leads him to the Eternal and Infinite Substance, and he will be able to see himself and all life *sub specie aeterni,* and possess that intellectual love of God which is too rational to expect that God will love in return. Thus philosophy can provide the satisfactions which religion has offered, and can provide them in a higher way. The enlightened may possess all the values of religion, not precariously and in blindness, but securely and in the light of full understanding. Spinoza is really the figure of crucial importance in the history of modern thought on religion. He poses the fundamental problem with which the philosophy of religion must grapple. Is there any independent status to be vindicated for religion? Is it a necessary 'moment' in the life of Spirit? Or is religion only philosophy speaking in parables, mythological metaphysics, and faith merely a stop-gap for the true system of logic? From this point of view the philosophy of Kant appears as a kind of interlude. His attempt to find a sphere for religious faith in the practical reason, and to entrench it there over against the speculative intellect, was a return to the earlier view, though in a diminished form. But it was not successful. We may perhaps agree that he answered Hume, but did he answer Spinoza? At least it is certain that the delimitation of territory did not survive in the systems of Kant's successors. Modern idealism is the child of Spinoza in as great a measure as it is the child of Kant. It is true that Hegel maintained the position of religion as the antithesis in the supreme Traid of the life of the Spirit—art, religion, philosophy; but, as Croce has pointed out, the implication of this is that the truth of religion is contained in the synthesis—philosophy—and the genuine consequence that which Croce draws, that religion is absorbed into philosophy.

The last twelve months have taken a heavy toll of English thinkers. Bradley, Rashdall, McTaggart, Ward, von Hügel, have been taken from us, and have left the already thin ranks of those who are able to deal with great problems in a great way sadly depleted. There is something sadly impressive in the simultaneous disappearance of so many great figures, and their passing suggests that we are standing at the beginning of a new epoch in English thought. It may be instructive to illustrate the present position of the question of the relation of philosophy and religion by reference to the work of three men who have recently died.

When Macaulay published the *History of England* he looked anxiously for the opinions of foreign reviews, believing that the verdict of French and German scholars was the best indication of the probable opinion of posterity. If this criterion has any value we may safely conclude that of the eminent thinkers who have recently died in England F. H. Bradley has the greatest chance of a permanent place in the roll of philosophers of the first rank. The histories of contemporary thought which have appeared in considerable numbers in the last few years in German and Italian give several respectful pages to Bradley. Indeed he, along with T. H. Green, may be said to have done more than anyone else to remove the impression which used to prevail in Teutonic academies that English thought stopped with J. S. Mill and Herbert Spencer.

One reason for the influence of Bradley on foreign minds is his architectonic power. He has avoided the characteristic vice of English thought, desultoriness. His enemies were accustomed to say that he had also avoided the characteristic English virtue, common sense; but even if the charge were made out, it is not one which would weigh

greatly with those who are metaphysicians *sans phrase*. Bradley built up his system of thought from the foundations. Beginning with logic he laid, by an analysis of the judgment and of inference, the stones on which the whole of the building was to rest. The complete doctrine is really implicit in the contention that in every predication the true subject is Reality as a whole, for in that is implied the conception of truth as systematic unity and the task of philosophy as the search for the coherent whole. From these beginnings he passed on, with the thread in his hand, to tread the labyrinths of Ethics and Ontology.

The historians of philosophy to whom we have referred are fond of describing him as a 'Hegelian of the right.' There is doubtless truth in this phrase, since the dialectic process by which Bradley reaches the conception of the Absolute is closely akin to that of Hegel, and the great German Absolutist is one of the few thinkers to whom he refers in his writings with respect. The final result of Bradley's reflexion bears, however, at least as close a resemblance to the system of Spinoza, and this is specially the case with respect to his treatment of religion. We shall not attempt here to indicate even in outline the manner in which Bradley establishes the reality and the nature of the Absolute. It must be sufficient to say that he examines all those concepts which may claim to have reality, substance, thing, person, and convicts them all of inconsistency. The root of the defect which condemns them to the realm of appearance is that they all involve relations, and a 'relational way of thinking' is in the long run contradictory. Thus we are led to the great distinction between appearance and Reality. All that we commonly regard as most real and certain is to some extent illusory, doubtless a manifestation, but taken by itself a misleading manifestation, of the Absolute.

What then is the Absolute? The answer to this question brings out the analogy between Bradley and Spinoza. Like the eternal Substance of the latter thinker, the Absolute of Bradley is intended to be the most real being, the sum and truth of all concrete existence. But in fact the statements we can make about it are, like the statements we can make about Spinoza's Substance, almost wholly negative. It is experience, since nothing can be conceived to exist except experience of some kind. But it is an experience which cannot be characterized by any positive predicates. It is neither personal nor good. It is perfectly harmonious, in it all the contradictions of the appearances are resolved, and the incoherences of temporal existence are abolished in a timeless unity.

The contrast between Reality and appearances is at once the central thought and the standing difficulty of Bradley's philosophy. The perplexity has been succinctly put by Ruggiero, writing from the standpoint of the immanent idealism of Croce:

> 'Appearance is the appearance of something, which is not itself appearance, that is to say of an absolute; and lo! after having rejected "relation" Bradley is constrained to readmit it. But since by now he has burnt

his boats the readmission does not save the situation; it only leads to absurdities. The Absolute is motionless, yet movement is an appearance of the Absolute; the Absolute has no history, yet it contains in itself infinite histories; experience is imperfect, yet it is an appearance of the perfect. At times one almost feels as if Bradley were wilfully blind. He goes so far as to recognize that unless it "appeared" the Absolute would be nothing; but, as he has denied the concept of relation, he fails to see that the true Absolute is not this phantom of a reality in itself, motionless and perfect (for if it requires to appear it is not already perfect), but is appearance itself, in so far as it is the absolute process of appearing, the phenomenalization of the Absolute.'[1]

Ruggiero goes on to speak scornfully of the device, if the word may be used, by which Bradley seeks to re-unite the sundered realms of appearance and reality. This is the famous doctrine of degrees of truth and reality. Though the view may deserve Ruggiero's criticism it is certainly a vital element in Bradley's system. Not all appearance is equally remote from the truly real. There are grades among the appearances, the higher approaching indefinitely closer to the Absolute than the lowest, and consequently containing more of reality.

This brings us to the position of Bradley on the subject of religion. It is clear that the main question is the relation between God and the Absolute and consequently of the value of religious experience. We may say at once that for practical purposes Bradley has no quarrel with the belief in God and attaches a high significance to the religious sentiment. Even though it may not be true that God is ultimately real, yet He is vastly more real than our own selves, and the experience of communion with God is among the highest of those possible to man. But if we ask whether the religious conception of God is finally true it must be replied that it is not. The most refined and spiritual view of God must be, in the last resort, only a figurative representation of Reality, a symbol of the Absolute which falls short of Reality to a degree which we cannot estimate.

In what was probably his last writing on the subject Bradley sums up his position in terms which leave no possibility of mistake. Any conception of God which the religious consciousness can form must be one which is partly illusory.

> 'God for me has no meaning outside of the religious consciousness, and that essentially is practical. The Absolute for me cannot be God, because in the end the Absolute is related to nothing, and there cannot be a practical relation between it and the finite will. When you begin to worship the Absolute or the Universe and make it the object of religion, you in that moment have transformed it. It has become something forthwith which is less than the Universe.'[2]

This inherent defect in the idea of God is reflected in a 'fundamental inconsistency' in religion. Any high religion must think of God as perfect, as the 'complete satisfaction of all finite aspiration,' and yet at the same time must think of my will as different from the will of God. But if perfection is actually realized there can be no separate will. We are required by religion to assert two contradictory truths, 'our wills are ours to make them thine,' and the Good Will is already completely realized. Bradley will not allow that there is any way out of this dilemma by the way of a 'limited God.' It is an illusion to suppose that when we have admitted that God is less than the supreme Perfection and Reality we can place any bounds upon the imperfection which we have admitted.

> 'The assertor of an imperfect God is, whether he know it or not, face to face with a desperate task or a forlorn alternative. He must try to show (how I cannot tell) that the entire rest of the Universe outside his limited God is known to be still weaker and more limited. Or he must appeal to us to follow our Leader blindly and, for all we know, to a common and overwhelming defeat. In either case the prospect offers to the religious mind an unquestionable loss to religion.'[3]

The fact that religion by its very nature involves inconsistency is not, in Bradley's view, a condemnation, if only we remember that religion ought not to claim to be, in the full sense, true. It takes its place among the partial and imperfect truths which form the contents of our mind when we are engaged in the practical enterprise of living. Even the philosophical doctrine of the Absolute cannot be completely true, for to know the Absolute involves a relation of knower and known, and hence distorts the object in the process of knowing it. Nevertheless the philosophical doctrine of the Absolute is nearer to the Reality than the religious doctrine of God, and it is only in the light of metaphysics that we can perceive the nature and relative validity of religion. It might seem, perhaps, that a theory of this kind would naturally lead to the conclusion that, ideally, religion should be absorbed into philosophy and possibly the further corollary that, since all religions are infected with error, the precise form which religious belief may take is hardly worthy the attention of the philosopher. It does not seem, however, that Bradley drew either of these inferences. He does not contemplate the disappearance of religion, nor does he believe that metaphysics can be the foundation for a creed. The present form of religion is not adequate to the needs of the present day. 'We want a creed to recognise and justify in due proportion all human interests, and at the same time to supply the intellect with that to which it can hold with confidence. . . . All that, in my opinion, we can reasonably desire is on one side a general faith, and on the other side such a critical philosophy as would be able in some sense to justify and support this faith.'[4]

The reader who has followed the exposition so far will doubtless have become aware of a strange indeterminateness in Bradley's treatment of religion. There can be no doubt that he speaks with two voices. On the one hand, when he has in mind the dogmatic positivist or naturalist, he asserts stoutly the higher truth of religion, but on the other hand, when he has in mind the pretensions of religious belief to be true absolutely and of religious experience to be the experience of reality, he maintains no less definitely the supremacy of philosophy and tends to relegate religion to the level of mythology. We may well wonder whether theologians would be wise to accept the compliments which he pays to their subject. There is a sting in them. The Absolute who cannot be worshipped lurks waiting to swallow up their God. Nor need theologians be unduly terrified by the dialectic which Bradley confronts them with, for the Absolute itself is, as we have seen, scarcely more secure. Bradley's philosophy has been called with some reason a 'veiled scepticism,' and so in fact it is. If God cannot be ultimately real because He is worshipped, the Absolute of philosophy cannot be ultimately real because it is known. We can only determine the Absolute by treating it as an object of knowledge, and so falsifying it. All statements which we make about it, therefore, are infected with error. It is surely difficult to see why one 'relational way of thought'—worship—should be more a mark of error than that other relational way of thought—knowing.

Dr. McTaggart has left behind him no such rounded whole as that achieved by Bradley. Death interrupted the task of presenting a systematic view of the problems of reality when only the first volume of what was to have been his greatest work had been published. There is hope that the second volume may yet appear, as it is understood that it had been completed, though it had not received the author's final revision. The first volume of *The Nature of Reality* does not touch upon the problem of religion, and we are compelled, therefore, to fall back upon his two earlier works, *Studies in Hegelian Cosmology* and *Some Dogmas of Religion.* There is ground for believing that he had not greatly changed his opinions at the end of his life. McTaggart is far more definitely an Hegelian than any other English thinker of the present day. He appears before us as the devout exponent of the system of his master, though his version of Hegelianism is so original that it has some right to be considered an independent philosophy.

We are met by some difference in tone between the two books in which McTaggart dealt with the problem of religion. The work which he devoted explicitly to the question—*Some Dogmas of Religion*—has, as he himself confessed, an almost completely negative conclusion. Religion may be defined, he holds, as 'an emotion resting on a conviction of a harmony between ourselves and the universe at large.' But this conviction, which is the source of religious sentiment, must depend upon the truth of certain beliefs about the nature of existence; in other words, upon dogma. Dogma is necessary to religion. 'Dogma is not religion any more than the skeleton is the living body. But we can no more be religious without dogma than our bodies could live without their skeletons.'[5] The greater part of this book is occupied with a destructive criticism of the dogmas on which religion depends. Immortality, it is argued, cannot be reasonably maintained apart from pre-existence, but the eternity of finite selves is not impossible, though we cannot say that there is any positive evidence that it is true. The fundamental dogma of religion

is, however, in a far less favourable position. The concept of God leads us to contradictions. Whether we choose to define God as omnipotent or decide to admit that He is limited, we are equally confronted with insoluble problems. The traditional arguments are not valid, and even if they were they lead to conclusions which are incompatible with one another. Moreover, the existence of evil is a fatal objection to belief in a deity who is both good and omnipotent. All this is sufficiently familiar, though the difficulties of Theism have been stated by McTaggart with unequalled force and clarity.

The point which is of special importance to us here is his conception of the relation between philosophy and religion. This is peculiarly interesting. McTaggart does not argue that philosophy can supersede religion in the sense that it can provide in a higher way for the needs which religion met in an imperfect manner. Nevertheless he holds that religion is entirely dependent on metaphysics. The dogmas of religion can only be supported by metaphysical arguments, and if those fail we have no right to believe. Moreover, there can be no resort to authority or consensus in this matter, because there is no dogma of religion which is not questioned or denied by some competent students. 'It follows that a man is not entitled to believe a dogma except in so far as he has investigated it for himself. And since the investigation of dogma is a metaphysical process, and religion must be based on dogma, it follows further that no man is justified in a religious attitude except as a result of metaphysical study. The result is sufficiently serious, for most people, as the world stands at present, have not the disposition, the education and the leisure necessary for the study of metaphysics. And thus we are driven to the conclusion that, whether any religion is true or not, most people have no right to accept any religion as true.' It would surely be impossible to find anywhere a more astonishing combination of extreme intellectualism and extreme individualism than in this utterance. We are led to believe that man's emotional nature and his values should have no audience when we judge the nature of the universe. We are taught to regard ourselves as isolated intelligences on whom has been imposed the impossible task of finding something about the world which we can rationally believe. But when we turn to *Studies in Hegelian Cosmology* we are in a different atmosphere. It is true that the belief in God as understood by Theism is no less decisively rejected, but it is argued that an idealist philosophy leads us to the conviction that the differentiations of the Absolute into finite selves are eternal. The doctrine that the supreme reality is spirit carries with it the assurance that values are integral to the structure of the universe. In seeking to determine the Absolute still further 'we start from what may be called the religious standpoint. It assures us of an ultimate solution which shall only differ from our present highest ideals and aspirations by far surpassing them.' This 'ultimate solution' is found in the conception of the Absolute as love. Personality, knowledge and will all fail to satisfy the requirements of absolute reality. They are not able to stand as above all difference and the reconciliation of opposites. The absolute reality is the love which binds together the timeless selves in a completely harmonious unity.

The final results to which McTaggart is led are, as he himself confesses in the well-known concluding paragraph of the ***Hegelian Cosmology,*** of a mystical character. 'A mysticism which ignored the claims of the understanding would be doomed. None ever went about to break logic but in the end logic broke him. But there is a mysticism which starts from the standpoint of the understanding and only departs from it in so far as that standpoint shows itself not to be ultimate, but to postulate something beyond itself. To transcend the lower is not to ignore it, and it is only in this sense that I have ventured to indicate the possibility of finding, above all knowledge and volition, one all-embracing unity, which is only not true, only not good, because all truth and all goodness are but distorted shadows of its absolute perfection.'[6]

If we take McTaggart as represented by the ***Hegelian Cosmology*** and not by ***Some Dogmas of Religion*** we shall find little essential difference between his interpretation of religion and that of Bradley. It is true that the two philosophers diverge considerably in their conception of Reality, and the 'social' Absolute of the one would be anathema to the other. But the Absolute of McTaggart is not further removed from the God of Theism than is the Absolute of Bradley, and there seems no reason why the same theory about the relation of religion and philosophic truth should not be held by both. It is natural to suppose on McTaggart's view that the God of religion, and particularly the Christian Trinity, is an imaginative and distorted representation of the Absolute. It is obvious also that the same difficulties to which we have briefly referred occur with equal force in McTaggart's system. In particular his 'Platonizing' Hegelianism lays him peculiarly open to the charge of introducing a chasm into the universe and dividing existence into two unrelated spheres. It is at any rate far from easy to see how the timeless and perfect society is connected with the temporal and very imperfect world of experience. We may hope that some guidance on this subject will be found in his unpublished work, for in the writings which we have so far had there is little serious attempt to grapple with the question, and few readers, we may suspect, have been satisfied with the remark that it is a problem which must present itself to any idealist philosophy.

We have unfortunately little space to do justice to the third of our philosophers—Dr. Rashdall. It has always been one of the characteristics of orthodoxy to be unable to recognize its real friends, and the truth of this has never been more clearly illustrated than in the reception which Rashdall's writing had from the Church. Theologians were still convinced that they could found Christian doctrine on the Idealism of Green and Caird, while Bradley and McTaggart were demonstrating with abundant clarity the kind of conclusion to which those premises really led. Rashdall was essentially a Christian philosopher, and he saw that there could be no harmony between Christianity and pantheism. He was essentially Christian too in the manner of

his approach to the problems of metaphysics. For him the path to Reality lay through the moral consciousness, and the firm basis of a theory of the Universe could be found only in the moral values. Thus he was compelled to reject every form of absolute Idealism which made moral distinctions unreal and taught the timeless perfection of the whole. Rashdall was moreover in the true succession of orthodox theology in his staunch rationalism. He believed that Theism could be established by rational arguments, though they were not precisely the same as those of Aristotle or St. Thomas. By a line of thought closely analogous to that of Berkeley he thought we could prove the existence of an eternal Mind, and by the moral argument we could shew that this Mind is perfect righteousness.

The reputation for unorthodoxy which Rashdall acquired was due to the clearness with which he saw and stated the consequences of ethical Monotheism. If we are to gain any light upon the problem of evil, and if we are to take seriously the moral life and its conditions, we must hold that there is a real distinction between God and finite spirits. God cannot be all inclusive. And therefore in the strict sense we ought not to say that God is infinite. God is not the Absolute. It is indeed doubtful if the conception Absolute has any value, but if we mean by it the whole of Reality it consists of God and created spirits—not of God alone. 'Together they form a unity, but that unity is not the unity of self-consciousness; nor can it without serious danger of misunderstanding be thought of as even analogous to that personal unity which is characteristic of consciousness in the highest form in which we know it.'[7]

It must be confessed that Rashdall left us no more than the outline of a Theistic philosophy, and that there are many problems on which, alas! now we can have no further help from him. Consider, for example, the following sentence which occurs in the passage from which we have already quoted. 'The ultimate Being, we may say, is One—a single Power, if we like we may even say a single Being, who is manifested in a plurality of consciousnesses, one consciousness which is omniscient and eternal, and many consciousnesses which are of limited knowledge, which have a beginning and some of which, it is possible or probable, have an end.' It is obvious that here we have suggested a whole series of problems concerning the manner of the relation between the entities which are brought together in one sentence. On this point and on the relation between the temporal and the eternal we should need some definite view if the sketch of a Theistic philosophy is to be turned into a philosophy of Theism. Perhaps a defect in Rashdall's thought is due to his small personal sympathy with mysticism, and in consequence his tendency to represent religious experience as the acceptance of and loyal acting upon reasonable convictions about God and the world.

We cannot bring this hasty and imperfect review to an end without a word of admiration for the amount of solid and sincere thinking which the works of these three authors represent. The points of view which they advocated have already become antiquated in the rapid change of intellectual fashions. New Realists and New Idealists have reached, in their own opinion, more adequate though divergent standpoints. At least we may hope that their reasoning will be as rigorous and their contempt for easy phrases as profound as that of the distinguished minds of the generation which has just passed away. Whether in fact their assertion that philosophy has once more moved forwards to a clearer conception of its problems is justified 'belongs to another enquiry.'

Notes

1. Ruggiero, *Modern Philosophy,* E.T. p. 274.

2. *Essays on Truth and Reality,* p. 428.

3. *Op. cit.* p. 430.

4. *Op. cit.* p. 446.

5. *Some Dogmas of Religion,* p. 13.

6. *Hegelian Cosmology,* p. 292.

7. *Theory of Good and Evil,* vol. ii p. 240.

R. M. Blake (essay date 1928)

SOURCE: "On McTaggart's Criticism of Propositions," in *Mind,* Vol. XXXVI, No. 148, October, 1928, pp. 439-53.

[*In the following essay, Blake presents several arguments against McTaggart's theories on propositions.*]

The second chapter of **The Nature of Existence** contains an elaborate argument against the reality of something which McTaggart calls "propositions". In what follows I wish first to point out that despite his polemic McTaggart does explicitly admit that there are propositions, in a certain sense of the term; but that he nevertheless betrays a very strong reluctance to state his theory of truth and falsity in terms of this admission—a reluctance which can only be explained by the fear that if propositions are admitted at all, they will turn out to be of a sort the reality of which he wishes to deny. I shall then proceed to argue that this fear is by no means baseless—that in fact the admission of the reality of propositions in the sense in which McTaggart does explicitly admit them inevitably commits him, by virtue of his own further assumptions, to the admission of the reality of propositions of a sort which he apparently wishes particularly to avoid. And the implication will be that anyone who admits that there are propositions in McTaggart's sense at all, and who makes other assumptions similar to those which he makes, will inevitably be committed to a like conclusion. Finally, I shall observe that it *may be* that McTaggart was not *really* concerned to deny that there are propositions of the sort which he *apparently* wished particularly to avoid, but only to deny that there are propositions of still another sort. And with regard to this sort of propositions I shall argue that even if they were in fact the only sort of propositions that he really intended to deny, it is nevertheless clear that he has no right to make even this denial.

I.

The main aim of Chapter II. is to show "that there is no reason to hold that there is anything real which is non-existent" (Sec. 7). And it is in order to establish this conclusion that McTaggart thinks it necessary to argue against the reality of "propositions". But it is very plain that, as I have said, he does not really mean to deny that in *some* sense of the term there are such entities as propositions. For in Section 106 he describes implication as "an indefinable relation between propositions," and in Section 107 he speaks of "the proposition P asserted in the judgment M," etc. And again in Section 23 he states explicitly that he has no objection to admitting that there are propositions, provided "propositions are maintained to be real as constituents of beliefs, and not otherwise". For "such propositions would be existent, since it is impossible that a constituent of an existent thing should not itself exist" (Sec. 23). A "proposition" in the sense in which McTaggart admits that there are propositions must, I think, be identified with what he elsewhere terms an "assertion" which he refers to as something that "is believed" (Sec. 16), and with what he speaks of as "what is asserted in a belief" (Sec. 18).

Nevertheless it is fairly obvious that McTaggart is by no means in love with propositions even in this sense of the term; for he persistently ignores them whenever it is possible to do so, and at times indulges in the most extraordinary shifts and turns, apparently simply in order to avoid mentioning them. For example, he states his theory of the nature of true beliefs quite as though there were no propositions at all, and as though nothing entered into the situation, but, on the one hand, beliefs as mental occurrences, and, on the other, the facts to which these true beliefs "correspond" (Sec. 10). And he proceeds to argue explicitly against the view that anything further whatsoever in the way of "propositions" is involved (*cf.* Secs. 14, 16). Again, the nature of false beliefs is explained in similar terms, without reference to any sort of "propositions" (*cf.* Sec. 19). But most striking of all is the avoidance of any mention of propositions in the account of what it means for two beliefs to be beliefs "in the same thing" (*cf.* Sec. 18 and note; Sec. 21). For *prima facie* this would appear to mean simply that the two beliefs in question assert the same proposition. Now McTaggart does not, as we have seen, altogether deny that there are propositions, and he is not unaware of the possibility of this simple explanation (*cf.* Sec. 21). Yet he studiously avoids it, and offers instead an explanation couched in terms well calculated to create the impression that no propositions are involved at all.

What is the reason for this procedure? Why does McTaggart, despite the fact that he fully admits that there are propositions, in some sense of the term, so persistently ignore them? Why does he constantly state his views in terms which seem to imply that there are no propositions at all? Why is he so concerned to keep them in the background, and to hustle them out of sight as much as possible whenever they embarrassingly obtrude themselves?

The answer is, I think, clear. McTaggart is afraid that if he gives propositions an inch they will take an ell. He fears that if they are allowed any standing at all they will begin to put on airs, and instead of contenting themselves with being "real as constituents of beliefs and not otherwise" will before his very eyes take on some sort of independent status. And especially he fears that they will turn out to possess characteristics such that according to his view of the matter, they would, if real at all, have to be non-existent. And in point of fact we shall, I think, find that McTaggart's fears are well-grounded. We shall find that if he admits that there are propositions at all, in any sense of the term, he will inevitably be driven to the recognition that there are propositions of the sort that he particularly wishes to avoid.

II.

In the first place, if we take at their face value certain of McTaggart's statements concerning the sort of proposition that he desires not to recognise, it will be immediately evident that if anything at all be really asserted in any belief whatever, it will be in some sense precisely of this sort. He states the view that he wishes to defend as the view that there are no *non-existent* propositions—no propositions that "are real without existing" (Sec. 7). But what, more precisely, does this mean? In introducing the terms *reality* and *existence* (in Chapter I.) McTaggart lays it down that these terms, though distinct in meaning, are both equally indefinable. Nevertheless he holds (Sec. 5) that "we are able to say in what cases reality involves existence," and also in what cases it would involve non-existence. In particular, we are told, a proposition such as "'Socrates is wise' (as distinguished on the one hand from the man Socrates who is wise, and, on the other hand, from the psychical event of my knowledge that Socrates is wise) does not exist, even if it is real". Again we learn that by a proposition, in the sense in which it has been asserted that propositions are real without existing, "is meant such a reality as 'Socrates is wise,' or 'the multiplication table is green,' as distinguished on the one hand from anyone's belief that Socrates is wise or that the multiplication table is green (which belief would, of course, be existent), and on the other hand from any existent thing about which the proposition may be made—such as, in the case of our first example, the existent Socrates" (Sec. 7). And "existence belongs to real substances . . . but not . . . to propositions, should . . . propositions be real" (Sec. 5). Advocates of propositions argue that if truth is objective then "there is something true besides beliefs". This McTaggart disputes. According to him "nothing is true but mental states". And there is no necessity that a true belief "should depend for its truth on anything *true* other than itself" (Sec. 16).

But we have already found McTaggart himself admitting that there is involved in a belief, in addition to the mental state or act of believing, another factor in the situation—something which "is believed," something, moreover, which is called an "assertion," or even a "proposition".

And further, it is clearly stated, concerning this proposition, that *it* is true, if, and only if, *it* corresponds to a fact (Sec 16; *cf.* Sec. 18, 23). Now any factor in a total state of affairs is obviously other than any other factor in the same state of affairs; and, equally obviously, it is other than the total state of affairs within which it is a factor. And accordingly, the "assertion" involved in the case of a belief is something "other than" that belief itself—whether the term "belief" be interpreted as referring to the mental act of believing as distinguished from the assertion believed, or as referring rather to the total state of affairs as inclusive both of the believing and the assertion believed. But McTaggart admits that in the case of a true belief the assertion involved is true. Consequently there *is* in the case of a true belief (and an analogous conclusion must clearly hold for false beliefs) something "other than itself" which is nevertheless true.[1]

But what then becomes of McTaggart's contention that "nothing is true but mental states"? An act of believing a certain assertion is doubtless a mental state; but there is no reason whatever to suppose that *what is asserted* in any such mental act is *itself* either an act of believing, or a mental state of any kind, or even an occurrence at all. But then, if what is asserted in some beliefs is admitted to be true, and if there is no reason to suppose (as there clearly is not) that what is believed is a mental state at all, how can it be denied that there may be something true besides mental states?[2]

But further, the "proposition" which we have found McTaggart admitting as something asserted in a belief is not only other than the *belief,* but is clearly other also than the *fact* which makes it true, for it is said to "correspond" to the fact; and the relation of "correspondence" in the sense in which this relation is identified with "truth" surely implies the diversity of its terms. Moreover I think it is plain, although McTaggart does not explicitly say so, that this "assertion" must also be other than any existent thing about which the assertion may be made—such as, for example, in the case of the assertion "Socrates is wise," the existent Socrates (supposing that there were any existent Socrates). But if A is "other than" B, it is clearly also true that in a quite legitimate sense it may also be said to be "distinguished from" B. And therefore McTaggart appears to be committed to the conclusion that there are propositions in precisely the sense in which he tells us that he wishes to deny that there are propositions, *i.e.,* propositions that are distinguished both from belief on the one hand, and from fact, or from "any existent thing about which the proposition may be made" on the other. And since, as he assures us, "Whatever is, is real" (Sec. 2) these propositions, concerning which he has told us that they do not exist even if they are real (Sec. 5), must be, according to his own statements, both real and non-existent. Thus McTaggart appears to be committed precisely to the conclusion which he most wishes to avoid, *viz.,* that there are non-existent propositions.

III.

But perhaps we have been misinterpreting McTaggart's real position. Perhaps when he asserted that any proposition "distinguished from" belief on the one hand, and from fact on the other, would, if it were real at all, be non-existent, he did not intend the expression "distinguished from" to be taken in the sense in which we have hitherto been taking it. Perhaps by a proposition that is "distinguished from" a belief he meant a proposition which should be not merely "other than" a belief, but rather a proposition that should be *independent* of beliefs, in the sense that it is something which does not begin to be real when asserted by some belief, nor cease to be real when no belief is any longer asserting it; but, on the contrary, is, if real at all, real even though there have been times, or is now a time, or are going to be times, when no beliefs asserting it were, or are, or will be, occurring—a proposition, accordingly, the reality of which is, in this sense, not dependent upon the occurrence or non-occurrence of beliefs which should be beliefs in that proposition. Perhaps it is such "independent" propositions that McTaggart has in mind in allowing only such propositions "as are maintained to be real as constituents of beliefs, and not otherwise" (Sec. 23) and in insisting that "there is no truth independent of . . . beliefs" (Sec. 15);—*i.e.,* that there are no true propositions independent of beliefs. Perhaps it is with regard merely to such "independent" propositions that he intends to maintain (1) that if there were any such propositions at all they would be non-existent, and (2) that there is no reason to hold that there are any such propositions.

But can McTaggart really get on without admitting that there are such "independent" propositions? I shall argue that he cannot; and that this is indicated by the fact that he does not succeed in developing any tenable theory of true and false beliefs without introducing propositions of precisely this sort. The central difficulty is to account for timelessly true and timelessly false beliefs. McTaggart admits that, whether or no it be the case that all truths are timeless, it is nevertheless certain that at least *some* beliefs are, in *some* sense of the term, timelessly true. For there are, he tells us, beliefs that "assert something which is true or false without reference to the time at which it is asserted" (Sec. 18). But his position with regard to such timelessly true beliefs is that "It does not follow that, if there are beliefs which would be true whenever they are made, they must correspond to timeless propositions, or to anything timeless. . . . It does not require anything timeless to secure that" such beliefs "shall be true whenever they are made" (Sec. 18).[3]

But now in precisely what way does McTaggart propose to account for the reality of beliefs that are in some sense timelessly true, without admitting that their reality involves the reality of anything that is strictly speaking timeless at all? His theory is, I take it, that what would commonly be called a timeless truth is really always simply a true *belief,* which, although not strictly timeless at all

(inasmuch as a belief is a psychical occurrence limited to one particular mind at one particular time), may nevertheless be called "timeless" or "timelessly true" in the sense that it is a belief which would be true whenever it is made, or is true without reference to the time at which it is made (*cf.* Sec. 18).

But there is a difficulty here. Consider, for example, my present belief that green is more like yellow than it is like red.[4] This belief is both true and surely, if any belief is, "timelessly true". But in what sense is it timelessly true? It is indeed a belief which would be true whenever it is made; but this fact (inasmuch as no belief can ever occur, or be "made," but *once,* in a particular mind and at a particular time) in no way serves to distinguish it from true beliefs of the non-timeless sort, or indeed from true beliefs of any sort whatsoever. And it certainly is not true without reference to the time at which it is made; for it cannot be true (or possess any characteristic at all) except so long as it is real, and it is real only so long as it is actually occurring.

McTaggart is not unconscious of this difficulty. For although he speaks loosely of "beliefs which would be true whenever they are made" and of beliefs which "are true or false without reference to the time at which they are made," he nevertheless warns us that "we must not say . . . that such beliefs as these are always true since this would imply that the same belief can exist at different and separate times, which is not the case. A belief is a psychical fact in a man's mind, and my belief now cannot be the same as your belief now or as mine next year" (Sec. 18). And the trouble is, of course, that despite the fact that one and the same belief cannot exist at different and separate times, it is nevertheless certainly the case that different beliefs existing at different and separate times may yet in *some* sense be correctly described as the "same" belief. For example, if each of these different beliefs were a belief that green is more like yellow than it is like red, there is surely some sense in which these beliefs, different as they are, might none the less be correctly described as the "same" belief. What, according to McTaggart is this sense?

It is by no means easy to say; for although he very evidently feels the force of the problem, the language in which he presents his solution is full of ambiguity. Some of his statements concerning the matter seem plainly to recognise and to utilise "propositions," at least in the sense of "what is asserted" in a belief. It is suggested that a number of beliefs which, as psychical occurrences, are mutually diverse, may nevertheless be spoken of as the "same" timelessly true or false belief, in the sense that each of them asserts something which is "not sometimes true and sometimes false" but "something which is true or false without reference to the time at which it is asserted". "If a belief which makes an assertion X corresponds to a fact in such a way as to be true, then all beliefs which make the same assertion will be true, whenever they are made, unless the assertion contains a reference to past, present, or future" (Sec. 18).

But now the question arises whether the proposition thus involved must not after all be held to be something *timeless.* It seems to me that it must. McTaggart *wishes* to hold that this proposition, although true without reference to the time at which it is asserted, is nevertheless neither real nor true in independence of beliefs. But if so, it must come into being when it is asserted by some belief, and must cease to be when it is no longer asserted by any belief; and if this is the case it must be, like the beliefs upon which its reality is dependent, an occurrence, or an event. Now according to the present theory of timelessly true beliefs one and the same true proposition must in some cases be asserted by a number of different beliefs occurring at different and separate times. But then, on the view that a proposition comes into being when it is asserted and ceases to be when it ceases to be asserted, we should have on our hands one and the same *event* occurring at different and separate times. And this, as McTaggart himself admits (Sec. 18), cannot be. But the only alternative is that the proposition involved in a timelessly true belief should be something which is *not* an event—*i.e.,* something non-temporal or timeless. And we must therefore conclude that McTaggart has not made good his contention that "it does not require anything timeless to secure that" such beliefs "shall be true whenever they are made". Something timeless, and in fact a timelessly true *proposition, is* required. But, further, if this proposition is really something timeless, and not an event at all, then it can neither come into being nor cease to be, according as a belief asserting it now occurs and now fails to occur. And if so it will be independent of beliefs.

It seems to me that it must have been because of his sense of the immanence of these uncongenial conclusions that McTaggart was led to use other expressions which suggest another way of dealing with the matter of timelessly true and false beliefs which, by seeming to avoid altogether the assumption of any propositions at all, should not run the risk of having these propositions uncomfortably transform themselves into independent, and therefore, according to McTaggart, non-existent, propositions. According to this theory, a number of beliefs which, as psychical occurrences, are mutually diverse, may nevertheless be spoken of as the "same" timelessly true or false belief without assuming that each of them asserts one and the same proposition at all. "Two true beliefs are beliefs in the same thing when their truth consists in correspondence with the same fact." "Two false beliefs are beliefs in the same thing when it is the absence of the same fact which makes both of them false." Or, alternatively, "Two false beliefs are beliefs in the same thing when they both profess to be beliefs correspondent to the same fact" (Sec. 18, 21). A true belief, accordingly, will be "timelessly true" if all beliefs "in the same thing" are true whenever they are made; and a false belief will be "timelessly false" if all beliefs "in the same thing" are false whenever they are made.[5]

But even though it is thus possible for McTaggart to explain what is meant by timelessly true or false beliefs without for that purpose explicitly referring to any proposition asserted by the beliefs in question, it is *not* possible for him to hold that there *is* nothing "asserted" in these beliefs. To hold this would indeed be equivalent to holding that these are not beliefs at all; for to believe nothing is simply not to believe. And in fact McTaggart tells us distinctly, and quite generally, that "every belief professes to refer to some fact, and more specifically, to correspond to it" (Sec. 20), and that "the assertion of such a correspondence would be a quality of such beliefs" (Sec. 21).[6]

This means, I take it, that *every* belief, whether it be one of several beliefs "in the same thing" or not, asserts a certain proposition, *viz.,* the proposition that it corresponds to a certain fact. What McTaggart really wants to avoid, then, is not the view that beliefs, even though they be beliefs "in the same thing," must in any case each assert *some* proposition, but rather the view that two different beliefs "in the same thing" are two beliefs asserting *one and the same proposition.* And it is evidently to this end that he finds it useful to maintain that what every belief asserts is that it corresponds to some fact. For if this were the case it would seem that no two beliefs could ever assert one and the same proposition; inasmuch as the proposition asserted in each belief, even if both were beliefs "in the same thing," would be about that belief itself. To hold that every belief is thus reflexive is surely somewhat paradoxical; for *prima facie* there *seem* to be beliefs that do not make assertions about themselves. But we shall see that even if it were the case that every belief does assert something about itself McTaggart cannot really account for timelessly true and false beliefs without admitting the reality of timeless, and therefore "independent," propositions. For we must ask precisely what is meant by the view that every belief asserts that it corresponds to some fact.

(1) At first sight this would seem to mean that every belief (say A) asserts the proposition "This psychical state (A) corresponds to X" where X represents a certain supposed fact. But now a part of what is involved in believing such a proposition is the supposition that there is such a fact as X, and to suppose this is to believe a certain proposition which is not simply identical with (although it may be an element in) the proposition "This psychical state (A) corresponds to X". For example, if I believe that John is ill, and if this belief asserts "This belief of mine corresponds to the fact that John is ill," a part of what is here asserted is the proposition "John is ill," or "It is a fact that John is ill". And thus, even if it be true that every belief asserts that it corresponds to some fact, it will nevertheless be true also that every belief asserts as a part of this assertion, a proposition which is *not* in every case about itself. And there is nothing to assure us that *this* part of what is asserted might not be *one and the same* proposition for two *different* beliefs.

But is there anything to assure us that any such proposition ever *is* asserted in common by two different beliefs? It seems to me that there is. Two beliefs "in the same thing" both "*profess* to be beliefs correspondent to the same fact." Thus, for example, two beliefs that John is ill both profess to be beliefs correspondent to the fact that John is ill. A part of what each asserts is, accordingly, the proposition "John is ill," or "It is a fact that John is ill"; and this certainly *seems* to be one and the same proposition for both beliefs. But if this is not really the case—if this one form of words really expresses for each belief a *different* proposition, then in what, we must ask, do these propositions differ? Each appears to contain identically the same constituents. Can it be held that the constituents of the proposition asserted by the one belief are not literally identical with, but only exactly similar to, the corresponding constituents of the proposition asserted by the other belief? It is McTaggart's own theory that every proposition is composed wholly of characteristics. "An existential judgment, like all other judgments, asserts something. And what it asserts, as with all other judgments, is one or more characteristics. . . . But what is asserted is always characteristics" (Sec. 641; *cf.* Sec. 654 *sqq.*). Now if propositions were substances of which the constituent characteristics were characteristics, there might be *two* propositions possessing *identical* constituents. But propositions are clearly not substances. Again, if it be held that the characters of substances are themselves particular rather than universal, it might be suggested that while each of the characteristics involved in the one proposition is an instance of the same universal as the corresponding constituent of the other proposition, each of the constituents of the one proposition is nevertheless itself a particular characteristic characterising one substance, while the corresponding constituent of the other proposition is *another* particular characteristic characterising *another* substance. But (*a*) McTaggart himself holds that the characteristics of substances are universals—"qualities and relations . . . are universals, and not particular as substances are" (Sec. 5). And (*b*) even on the view that the characteristics of substances are themselves particular it is admitted that there are, in addition to particular characteristics characterising particular substances, universal characteristics of which these particular characteristics are instances. Now there are propositions the only constituents of which are precisely such universal characteristics—such propositions namely as assert simply relations between universal characteristics, *e.g.*, the proposition "green is more like yellow than it is like red". And there thus appears to be no way in which it could be maintained that the constituents of this part of what is asserted by one belief that "green is more like yellow than it is like red" differ, even numerically, from the constituents of the corresponding part of what is asserted by any other belief "in the same thing". Accordingly it cannot be denied that there is a proposition asserted in each of these beliefs which is simply one and the same for both of these beliefs. And if this is the case, then, by a course of reasoning now familiar, it will follow that a timeless and therefore independent proposition is here involved. But two beliefs "that green is more like yellow than it is like red" are precisely two timelessly true beliefs in the same thing. And it has thus proved impossible to give an adequate account of such beliefs without admitting something timeless, and in fact without admitting a timeless, and therefore independent, "proposition".

(2) We have hitherto proceeded upon the assumption that when McTaggart holds that every belief asserts that it corresponds to some fact what he means is that every belief asserts the proposition that itself as a psychical state corresponds to a certain fact. Even on this interpretation we have seen that he does not succeed in avoiding the admission of propositions of the sort that he is concerned to deny. But when he comes himself to state what he means by saying that every belief asserts that it corresponds to some fact he explains himself quite otherwise, as follows: "this only means that to believe anything means to believe it to be true". And this clearly implies that every belief asserts *not* that it, as a psychical state, is true; but rather that what it asserts, *i.e.,* the proposition asserted, is true. And if *this* interpretation is carried out in the case of two timelessly true beliefs "in the same thing" we shall clearly be led quite directly, by a course of reasoning now familiar, to the conclusion that there are not only timeless, and therefore independent propositions, but also that some of these propositions are themselves timelessly *true*.

IV.

It might, however, here be contended that the foregoing has misapprehended the true intention of McTaggart's polemic. In denying that there are propositions "independent" of belief he did not really intend, it might perhaps be said, to deny that there are propositions which neither begin to be when first asserted by some belief, nor cease to be when no longer asserted by any belief (although if he did *not* intend to deny this it is difficult to see why he should so strenuously object to "timeless" propositions), but only that there are propositions that never have been, are not now being, and are never going to be asserted in any belief whatsoever. It is only propositions that are in *this* sense independent of beliefs, it might be thought, that McTaggart was really concerned to deny. In support of this interpretation it might be pointed out that McTaggart, in denying the reality of propositions that are independent of beliefs, frequently puts his position in such terms as the following: "there is, I maintain, no reason to hold that the truth of beliefs involves their *correspondence* with true propositions" (Sec. 14); "It does not follow that, if there are beliefs which would be true whenever they are made, they must *correspond* to timeless propositions, or to anything timeless" (Sec. 18); "thus we can account for the falsity of false beliefs without basing it on their *correspondence* to false propositions" (Sec. 22; *cf.* also Sec. 23, italics mine throughout), etc. And it might be argued that McTaggart is here clearly not concerned to deny that there *are* true and false propositions, or even that there are timelessly true and false, and therefore, as we have seen, in a sense "independent," propositions; provided only it be allowed that every such proposition either has been, is now being, or is going to be asserted in some actual belief, so that all such propositions are "real as constituents of beliefs, and not otherwise". He merely wants to deny, it might be held, that there are, *in addition* to propositions of this sort, independent propositions of *another* sort which are such as never to get themselves *asserted in* any belief whatsoever, and to which, therefore, no belief can ever do more than "correspond". And in fact it seems to be against propositions of this sort that he is arguing in the section where he disputes the view "that many things are true which, in all probability, are never known or assumed" (Sec. 15).

There can be no doubt, I think, that McTaggart *was* concerned to deny that there are any propositions of this sort. But it seems to me very difficult to interpret his polemic as a whole on the assumption that this was *all* that he intended to deny. And even if this was, in fact, all that he really intended to deny, it seems to me quite clear that he has no right to make the denial. For (1) McTaggart has at any rate produced no positive ground whatever for denying that there are propositions of this sort; for the argument of the section in which he professes to give "a more positive ground for rejecting propositions—that there is no place left for them" (Sec. 37; *cf.* Sec. 38) will I think be seen to have been altogether undermined by considerations presented in the earlier sections of this paper. Moreover (2) it is very difficult to understand how McTaggart can have supposed, as he clearly did, that propositions that are independent of beliefs in *any* sense whatever, even in this most extreme sense, would if they were real at all, have to be non-existent; and should have felt constrained, on this ground, to reject them. For (*a*) it is by no means evident that the mere fact (if it were a fact) that some, or all, propositions are independent of beliefs would constitute any sufficient reason for declaring that such propositions must be non-existent. Indeed it would seem that in order to be non-existent propositions would have to be independent not merely of *beliefs* but of *any* existent thing whatsoever, "since it is impossible that a constituent of an existent thing should not itself exist" (Sec. 23). And from the mere fact that a proposition is real independently of beliefs it surely does not follow that it is independent of *every* existent thing whatsoever. Moreover (*b*) on McTaggart's own view propositions are composed of characteristics; and there are no non-existent characteristics (Sec. 31, 34). It follows that propositions, no matter how independent they might be from beliefs, could never in any case be non-existent. Again (*c*) McTaggart remarks (Sec. 5) that "even if it should be the case that qualities and relations were both existent, as qualities and relations of existent things, and non-existent, in their general aspects, I do not think that this would be an objection to our view. Qualities and relations are very different from substances, and the fact that a substance cannot be both existent and non-existent does not prove that qualities and relations—which are universal, and not particular as substances are—could not be existent in one aspect, and non-existent in another." But if so much latitude is to be allowed in the case of qualities and relations it is difficult to see why it should be denied in the case of propositions. For these always consist, as we have seen, of one or more characteristics; and these, too, must therefore be "very different from substances". And there thus seems to be no very obvious reason why they should not be allowed to be existent as constituents of beliefs, and non-existent in their

"independent" aspects; or existent in virtue of the fact that their constituent characteristics are existent as qualities and relations of existent things; and non-existent in virtue of the fact that their constituent characteristics are non-existent in their general aspects.

Finally (3) if propositions always consist simply of one or more characteristics, and if it be admitted that there are characteristics or combinations of characteristics which neither have been, or are now being, or are ever going to be asserted in any belief whatsoever (and I do not think that even McTaggart would be prepared to deny that this is the case), then it will seem to follow directly that there are propositions which are, in the fullest sense of the term, "independent" of beliefs.

Notes

1. It might perhaps here be objected that what McTaggart refers to as an "assertion," and which I have identified as a proposition asserted, may with equal propriety be referred to as a "belief," and that consequently McTaggart is not really, as I have insisted that he is, committed to the view that there is in the case of a true belief (*i.e.*, true "assertion") something "other than itself" (*i.e.*, other than this "assertion"), which is nevertheless true. But although I think that McTaggart's argument here and elsewhere profits by the ambiguity of the term *belief* to the extent of gaining an appearance of plausibility which it does not deserve, it seems to me quite clear that neither in the present passage nor elsewhere does he consciously intend to use the term *belief* in the sense in which it refers to *what is believed,* but rather, and only, in the sense in which it refers to the act of believing itself, or to the total situation within which the act of believing and the assertion believed are constituents. For all his formal statements regarding the status of beliefs invariably refer to them as psychical states, mental events, and the like. And at any rate in the present passage he clearly identifies his view that nothing is true but beliefs with the view that nothing is true but mental states.

2. We might inquire further whether the relation of correspondence to a fact which, according to McTaggart, constitutes the truth of a belief, is identical with the relation of correspondence to fact which constitutes the truth of its "assertion". If so, then so far is it from being the case that "nothing is true but mental states" or that there is no necessity that a true belief "should depend for its truth on anything *true* other than itself," that the truth of beliefs has no meaning whatever apart from that of propositions. If not, then we should be justified in turning against McTaggart a form of argument which he himself employs against those who believe that there are propositions (*cf.* Sec. 14). "If the proposition is true," we may say, "it will correspond to the fact. The belief which asserts it may also correspond to the fact, but in that case we shall have

two correspondences to the fact—one of the proposition to the fact, and another of the belief to the fact—and, consequently, two truths. But what reason is there to believe in this second correspondence at all? A sufficient meaning is given to the statement that the belief is "true" if we explain this as meaning that the proposition believed is true, in the sense that *it* corresponds to the fact. What further reason can be given why, in this same sense of correspondence, a *further* correspondence of the *belief* to the fact would be necessary?"

3. McTaggart must, of course, ultimately admit that *something* timeless *is* involved in the case of timelessly true or false beliefs, if there are any such beliefs at all; since he himself holds that everything whatsoever really is timeless, and that there simply are no events at all (*cf.* chap. xxxiii.). In the present chapter, however, he is arguing on the assumption that there *are* events. "My knowledge that Socrates is wise," for example, is referred to as a "psychical event"; and, moreover, "the squareness of the table is a fact, in distinction from the belief about it, which is an event in my mind" (Sec. 10). We must therefore suppose him to be here arguing that the occurrence of such mental events as timelessly true or false beliefs, supposing that there were really any such occurrences, would not *itself* presuppose the reality of anything timeless.

4. This is not McTaggart's own example of a "timelessly true" belief. He refers instead to the belief that the date of the battle of Waterloo is 1815. It seems to me doubtful, however, whether this belief, inasmuch as it appears to refer to an event, can really be held to be timelessly true at all. I therefore prefer to utilise as an example of a timelessly true belief one which certainly has to do not with events at all, but solely with characteristics. I do not think that McTaggart would deny that this *is* an example of a timelessly true belief.

5. It may be noted that McTaggart actually gives no definition at all of what, on this way of looking at the matter, it means *in general* for two beliefs to be beliefs "in the same thing". Yet that there *is* such a meaning is presupposed in his view that for a belief in X to be timelessly true or false means that all beliefs in the same X "will be true or false respectively whenever they are made". It is not difficult, however, to supply the missing definition, in full accordance with McTaggart's theory. Any one of the following would appear to serve: (1) Two beliefs are beliefs in the same thing when their truth would consist in their correspondence to the same fact; (2) two beliefs are beliefs in the same thing when it would be the absence of the same fact that would make both of them false; (3) two beliefs are beliefs in the same thing when *either* their truth consists in their correspondence to, *or* their falsity in the absence of, the same fact; (4) two beliefs are

beliefs in the same thing when both profess to be beliefs correspondent to the same fact.

6. The latter passage has explicit reference only to false beliefs "in the same thing," but I think there can be no doubt that McTaggart would say the same for true beliefs also.

D. W. Gotshalk (essay date 1930)

SOURCE: "McTaggart on Time," in *Mind,* Vol. XXXIX, No. 153, January, 1930, pp. 26-42.

[*In the following essay, Gotshalk attempts to refute McTaggart's notion against the reality of time as presented in his* The Nature of Existence.]

The topic of this article is McTaggart's argument against the reality of time. This important argument, first stated in this journal in 1908, and re-stated two years ago in ***The Nature of Existence,***[1] remains, so far as I know, unrefuted. And it is considered by many to be irrefutable. The aim of this article is to examine McTaggart's argument and to sketch out, as I think I can, a refutation.

McTaggart divides his argument into two parts. In the first part he endeavours to show that the distinctions of past, present, and future, are essential to time. Time, if real at all, must form an A series: that is to say, it must form a series of positions distinguished by the characteristics of past, present, and future. This is McTaggart's first contention. Then, McTaggart endeavours to show that the distinctions of past, present, and future, involve one in hopeless difficulty and in contradiction. An A series, he contends, is impossible and meaningless, and can have no place in a true view of the existent. From this McTaggart concludes that time is unreal. Time cannot exist unless it forms an A series. But an A series cannot be admitted to exist. Therefore time must be unreal.

McTaggart's argument, in the main, proceeds, as is obvious, on the assumption that whatever is impossible or contradictory for thought must be non-existent and unreal in fact. This assumption has been challenged, but for the purposes of this article I shall assume that it is true. And indeed I think that in a certain sense it is true, and that McTaggart in his argument keeps within this sense. But an adequate treatment of this topic would itself require an entire article.

I shall now summarise the two parts of McTaggart's argument. At appropriate points I shall add my critical comments.

I.

Part one, aiming to show, as I have said, that the A series is essential to time, may be stated as follows:

(1) Positions in time may be distinguished in two ways. First, each position is either Past, Present, or Future. Second, each position is Earlier than some and Later than some of the other positions. The series of positions running from the far past through the present to the far future, or conversely, may be called an A series. The series of positions running from earlier to later, or conversely, may be called a B series.

(2) Time involves change. There would be no time if nothing changed.

(3) But suppose there were no A series, only a B series, what then could change? There are two possibilities. Either the events that occupy the series might change, or the facts[2] concerning the events of the series might change. But if time were only a B series, neither of these two possibilities could be realised. First, the events occupying the series could not change. They could neither cease to be events, nor lose their identity by changing into other events—which are the possible ways they might conceivably change.

For if N, an event, is ever a member of a B series, and is ever earlier than another member O and later than a third member M, N will always be and has always been earlier than O and later than M. That is to say, N has always been and will always be a member of the B series. But the members of the B series are distinctive events. Therefore N has always been and never will cease to be an event, and has always been and will never cease to be the event in the B series which it is. This eliminates the first possibility. And the second possibility, that the facts concerning the events of the series might change, is equally out of the question. Take an event, the death of Queen Anne, for example. Conceived as a member merely of a B series, none of the facts concerning this event can change. "That it is a death, that it is the death of Anne Stuart, that it has such causes, that it has such effects—every characteristic of this sort never changes."[3] And the temporal facts concerning the event as a member of the B series, namely, the possession by it of the characteristics of 'being earlier than X,' and 'being later than Y'—these also do not change. Thus the death of Queen Anne is earlier than the death of Queen Victoria and later than the death of Queen Elizabeth. And in this respect it can never change.

(4) Change then is inexplicable, if time is a mere B series. There can be no change unless facts concerning an event change; events *qua* events can never change. But if time is merely a B series, no facts concerning an event can change. Change becomes impossible. On the other hand, if time is an A series, there can be change. Take the event, the death of Queen Anne. If this event is conceived as occupying an A series, then certain facts concerning it do change. "It was once an event in the far future. It became every moment an event in the nearer future. At last it was present. Then it became past, and will always remain past, though every moment it becomes further and further past." The event, in respect of its A-serial characteristics, thus exhib-

its constant change. "Such characteristics as these (moreover) are the only characteristics which can change. And therefore, if there is any change, it must be looked for in the A series, and in the A series alone."[4]

(5) Time is non-existent without change. Change is nonexistent without time as an A series. Therefore time, if it exists at all, must form an A series. Or, an A series is essential to time.

Such is the first half of McTaggart's argument. I will offer two critical comments on it. They are (1) the view of change on which this first part of the argument is based, is incorrect, but (2) the conclusion, that the A series is essential to time, is nevertheless correct.

(1) The view of change on which the argument above outlined rests, is that there is and can be no change unless the facts of an event change. Events, which are for McTaggart a species of substances, do not change. Only facts—the possession by events of qualities and relations—can change. And if the facts of an event do not change, then there is no change. This position, I venture to think, is incorrect. There is change, I venture to think, even if no fact of an event can change. Take the event M, which is—my fountain-pen, full at *t*, slowly loses its ink and becomes empty at *t'*. According to McTaggart, the only facts of this event that can change are A-serial facts—the possession by M of futurity, presentness, and pastness. That M is an event, that as an event M is a passage of my pen from a state of being full of ink at *t* to a state of being empty at *t'*, that M did not annoy the owner of the pen, that M might have been expected, and so on, are facts of the event which, as facts, it is said and may be admitted, neither do or can alter or change. But further, it is conceivable— perhaps it is more than conceivable—that a method could be devised by the aid of which one could say definitively, for any time, whether M is past, present, or future, and how much so—*i.e.*, it is conceivable that the A-serial facts of M, as well as all these other facts, could be fixed for all time, so that they too do not and cannot alter or change.[5]

In that case, according to McTaggart's view, there would be no change at all. No facts would change, so no change. I venture to think, however, that there would be change. And the facts, I venture further to think, bear this out. For, while every fact of M, as thus fixed for all time, might be as a consequence incapable of change, two root facts of M would still remain: (*a*) that M is an event, and (*b*) that M as an event is a passage of my pen P from an earlier state N to a later state O. But change, *at least in one valid sense,* is a passage from a state to a state, and such a passage of my pen P from an earlier state N to a later state O, is therefore truly a change. So, even if all the facts of M were fixed and could not change, it would still remain that there would be change. The change would be the passage of P from N to O. Moreover, since this change would be a fact, and the facts here would all be fixed, there would not only still be a change, but this would always be so.[6]

(2) Nevertheless, McTaggart's conclusion here, in the first half of his argument, must be admitted to be the truth. The

A series, with its distinctions of past, present, and future, is essential, as McTaggart contends, to our idea of change, and thus to our idea of time. If the A series were denied existence, change would have to be denied existence. And thus so would time. Take the event M, the above-mentioned change of my pen—if the distinctions of the A series could not be applied to it, if M could not, within the life of P, be distinguished by the characteristics of past, present, or future, then M as a change could not conceivably come off. The reason is this. The life of P is a passage including M as a stage which at one epoch lies ahead, at another epoch is reached, and at a third epoch is left behind. But if M were never future, it could never lie ahead, and if M were never present, it could never be reached, and if M were never past, it could never be left behind. Thus, if the distinction of past, present, and future, could not be possessed by M, M could not exist as part of the life of P. Indeed, the same would be true of any other part of the life of P, such as Y, so that, if M were not a member of an A series, not only could it not exist, but no other part of the life of P could exist. Or, the inclusive change which is the life of P could not itself come off.[7] We may therefore say that if the A series and its distinctions were denied existence, change must be denied existence. And since, if change is non-existent, there would be no time, we may consequently conclude that if there were no A series, there would be no time.[8]

McTaggart's general conclusion in regard to time in this first half of his argument, is therefore correct. The A series is essential to time. On the other hand, McTaggart's view of change, I am forced to think, is clearly incorrect, and hence his reason for holding that the A series is essential to time, being based on his view of change, is also erroneous.

II.

I pass now to the second half of McTaggart's argument. The aim of this half is to demonstrate that time, viewed as an A series, is unreal. This half has two stages, which I shall treat separately. The aim of the two stages is to show, by two different considerations, that time must be held to be unreal. Time involves an A series—this has been shown. But an A series referred to reality involves an impossibility and an absurdity, and cannot be granted within reason to exist there. This is now to be proved.

To summarise the first stage of this argument, which stage aims to show that the A series involves an impossibility.

(1) Past, present, and future, are relations, relations which we ascribe to events. If anything is rightly called past, present, or future, it must be because it has a relation—a relation to something else.

(2) And this something else must be outside the time series or the A series. For the relations of the A series, as we have already seen, are changing relations. Thus, in the case of the death of Queen Anne, this event was once fu-

ture, then present, then past. Its A-serial characteristics changed, it took on different relations. Relations exclusively between members of the time series, however, can never change. Two events, such as the death of Queen Anne and the death of Queen Victoria, are exactly in the same place in the time series one million years before they took place, while each is taking place, and years after each has taken place. Their relations to each other in the time series never change. Hence, if the relations of the A series change, and they do, it must be because the members of this series are in relation to something else besides other members of the time series. That is to say, it must be because the members of this series are in relation to something outside the temporal series itself.

(3) Let this something outside the time series be the entity X. Any series is then an A series when each of its terms has a relation to the entity X. This entity is itself not in time, yet it must be such that altering relations to it determine the other terms of these relations (the members of the A series are the other terms) as being past, present, or future. To find such an entity as X seems impossible, yet such an entity must exist, and must be found, if the A series is to be an established reality.

Such is the first stage of the argument here. The reality of the A series is shown to be contingent to the existence of a timeless entity X, and the discovery of such a timeless entity as X, it is suggested, is impossible. I shall make two critical comments on this stage of the argument. The centre of McTaggart's position here is obviously that the relations of the A series are changing relations. The timeless and impossible entity X is introduced because the members of the A series must be in relation to something outside it, and the members of the A series are said to be necessarily in relation to something outside the series because the relations of the A series are changing relations, whereas relations exclusively between members of the A series, never change. The proper question, accordingly, is this: Are the relations of the A series changing relations?

My first comment is that in a sense they are not. My second comment is that in the sense in which they are, their changing can be explained and satisfactorily understood without postulating the existence of a timeless entity such as X.

(1) In a sense the relations of the A series do not change. Thus, the death of Queen Victoria is *future* in respect to the death of Queen Anne, and the death of Queen Anne is *past* in respect to the death of Queen Victoria. And each is permanently so. The A-serial relations of these events here never do and never can change. Indeed, the A-serial relation of any one event, when the event is taken in relation to some other one event, *suitably chosen,* is fixed and permanent. The given event, in relation to the chosen event, is past, or present, or future, And it is permanently so. If this were the whole story concerning the relations of the A series, it would, according to McTaggart, be equivalent to giving up entirely the case for change, and thus for time.

It is not the whole story concerning the A-serial relations, but, even if it were, it would not be equivalent, I venture to think, to giving up the case for change or for time. That in McTaggart's view it would be so equivalent, is obvious. According to that view, only facts change, and the only facts of an event that can change are the possession by it of the temporal characteristics of past, present, and future. If an event does not change in respect of these, there is no other respect in which it can change. Where else can change come in? The answer to this question we have already stated in general form, and in the case of an event such as the death of Queen Anne, it is plain enough. Granting that the A-serial relations of this event in respect of any other one event taken separately, are fixed and never change, there is nevertheless change. The event *qua* event is a change. And any event with which it is related, such as the death of Queen Victoria, is a change. Each event here is *qua* event, at least a physico-chemical alteration in the organism of an English sovereign, and such an alteration in an organism is a passage from a state to a state, and so a change. And even if every characteristic of each event were fixed and could not change, this fact of change would remain a fact—a fact indeed as permanent as the existence of each event is.

(2) Still there is a sense in which the A-serial characteristics of an event may be said to change. Take an event, such as E, namely, the death of a mosquito biting my leg. This event is future for a certain specious present of my consciousness, it is present for a later specious present of my consciousness, and it is past (thank heaven!) for a third. That is to say, in relation successively to three different specious presents of my consciousness, the event is first future, then it is present, and then it is past. In this sense the A-serial characteristics of an event may be said to change, namely, when the event E is taken, not in relation *separately* to one other event suitably chosen, but in relation successively to three other suitably-chosen events—first, in relation to an event K, or an event preceding K, which is prior to E, then in relation to K^1, an event co-temporary with E, and finally in relation to K^2, or an event succeeding K^2, which is posterior to E. Under these conditions, and only under these conditions, can the A-serial characteristics of an event change. From this, however, it is clear that to understand the changing of the A-serial characteristics of an event, it is not necessary to postulate and discover an existing timeless X. This changing, such as it is, is explained, and exclusively explained, by the fact that the event in question is taken in relation to certain other events. The A-serial characteristics of E change because E is taken first in relation to K, then in relation to K^1, and then in relation to K^2. This was our point. The A-serial characteristics of an event can be understood as changing in the one sense in which they do change, wholly without introducing a timeless entity X. In order to understand whatever change in these relations an event may be said to have, it is only necessary that the event in question be understood as taken in relation to certain suitably successive events—more particularly in relation to the succeeding presents of a judging consciousness.[9]

Our conclusion then, at this stage, is that McTaggart's first argument against the reality of time does not hold. The reality of the A series is not contingent, as alleged, to the existence of a timeless, impossible X. This entity X was said to be necessitated because the relations of the A series were said to be changing relations. This latter position we have found to be in a sense false, and in the sense in which it is true, we have found that the changing of the temporal relations can be understood and wholly understood, without resort to a timeless X. X is not needed to make explicable how the relations of the A series can change as they change. This then disposes of the first objection to the reality of time. The reality of the A series and the operation of its distinctions of past, present, and future, are not contingent to the existence or the discovery of an impossible and timeless X.

III.

I pass now to the second and chief objection that McTaggart offers to the reality of the A series. This objection constitutes the other stage of McTaggart's argument against the reality of time. I will first state McTaggart's position.

(1) Past, present, and future, are incompatible determinations of events. Every event may be one *or* the other, but no event can be more than one. If I say an event is present, that implies that it is neither past nor future. If I say an event is past, that implies that it is neither present nor past. And so on. The characteristics past, present, and future, exclude each other. This exclusiveness, moreover, is essential to change, and therefore to time. For the only change we can get is from future to present, and from present to past. The temporal characteristics, as determinations of events, must therefore surely be exclusive, that is to say, they must be incompatible.

(2) Yet every event has all of them. If M is past, it has been present and future. If it is present, it will be past, and has been future. If it is future, it will be past and present. All three characteristics, past, present, and future therefore, in the end, belong to each event. The temporal characteristics, as determinations of events, must consequently be non-exclusive, or compatible.

(3) Hence a contradiction. The temporal characteristics, past, present, and future, are incompatible. Only for this reason is change and therefore time possible. Yet these characteristics must be compatible. For all events have all of them. The A-serial temporal characteristics, hence, are contradictory. But the contradictory is the false. Therefore these temporal distinctions are false, and the A series, which enshrines them, if affirmed of the existent, is also false.

Such is the second objection that McTaggart offers against the reality of time. The reply which, according to McTaggart, will be made to escape the contradiction asserted in the objection, is this: "It is never true, the answer will run, that M *is* present, past, and future. It *is* present, *will be* past, and *has been* future. Or it *is* past, and *has been* future and present, or again *is* future, and *will be* present and past. The characteristics are only incompatible when they are simultaneous, and there is no contradiction to this in the fact that each term has all of them successively."[10]

Stated more at length, the principle of this rejoinder, is as follows: Past, present, and future, are both compatible and incompatible determinations of events. But this is not contradictory. A contradiction occurs when two opposite characteristics, such as 'compatible' and 'incompatible,' are said to be true of the same thing (past, present, and future as event-determination) *under the same conditions.* But the condition under which past, present, and future, are incompatible determinations of events, is not the same as the condition under which they are compatible determinations. Past, present, and future are incompatible as simultaneous determinations of events. That is to say, they are incompatible under the condition of simultaneity. At a given moment an event is present, *or* it is past, *or* it is future. And it is only one of these then. On the other hand, the condition under which the temporal characteristics are compatible, is succession. An event, only successively, is future *and* present *and* past. At a given moment it is future, at some later succeeding moment it is present, at some still later succeeding moment it is past. It is under this condition of succession, but only then, that an event is future *and* present *and* past. But if this is true, the supposed contradiction vanishes. Past, present, and future, as event-determinations, are compatible and incompatible, but they are such under altogether different conditions. So there is no clash.

This position appears to be adequate to remove the difficulty with the A series which McTaggart presents here. It admits, as McTaggart claims, that the A-serial temporal characteristics are compatible and incompatible. But it states a condition under which these characteristics are compatible and a condition under which they are incompatible, and it shows that these conditions are different, and hence enables us to understand that the properties of the temporal characteristics will be different. They will vary with the circumstances. The alleged contradiction, thus, seems to have been escaped. And I think it has been escaped. McTaggart, however, is ready with a subtle objection to this alleged escape. This objection I will now state, and then I will add two critical comments upon it. These comments will endeavour to show that McTaggart's objection, thought through, does not hold.

As quoted above, the rejoinder to McTaggart's position had said: It is never true that M *is* present, past, and future. M *is* present, *will be* past, and *has been* future. Or it *is* past, and *has been* present and future. And so on. To this McTaggart replies: "But what is meant by 'has been' and 'will be'? And what is meant by 'is,' when, as here, it is used with a temporal meaning . . . ? When we say that X has been Y, we are asserting X to be Y at a moment of past time. When we say that X will be Y, we are asserting X to be Y at a moment of future time. When we say that

X is Y (in the temporal sense of 'is'), we are asserting X to be Y at a moment of present time. Thus our first statement about M—that it is present, will be past, and has been future—means that M is present at a moment of present time, past at some moment of future time, and future at some moment of past time. But every moment, like every event, is both past, present, and future. And so a similar difficulty arises. If M is present, there is no moment of past time at which it is past. But the moments of future time, in which it is past, are equally moments of past time, in which it cannot be past. Again, that M is future and will be present and past means that M is future at a moment of present time, and present and past at different moments of future time. In that case it cannot be present or past at any moments of past time. But all the moments of future time, in which M will be present or past, are equally moments of past time."[11]

Hence fresh contradictions, contradictions arising out of the nature of the temporal characteristics. When M is present, to take the first contradiction, there is no moment of past time at which it is past. Present and past are incompatible. Yet the moments of future time, in which M is past, are equally moments of past time. For future and past are compatible. Then, however, M is past, when it cannot be past. Thus a contradiction. More generally, the position is that "the moments at which M has any one of the three determinations of the A series are also moments at which it cannot have that determination".[12] The future moments at which M has the determination of past are also moments of past time, at which, however, M cannot have the determination of past. This contradiction, it is explained, is due to the fact that the temporal characteristics are compatible and incompatible for each moment no less than for each event. Thus our old difficulty, that contradiction is involved in the very nature of the A-serial characteristics, shows its head in the very attempt to explain it away. And it would re-appear in any successive attempt to explain it away. Such is McTaggart's conclusion.

Two questions may be asked at this point. First, are the contradictions alleged to be in the rejoinder genuinely in it or not? And second, if these contradictions are not in it, need the proof that they are *not* involve us in a fresh contradiction? I think that the contradictions alleged to be in the rejoinder are not in it, and that the proof that they are *not,* need not and does not start a fresh contradiction. In the above-quoted passage, there are two of these alleged contradictions. These, of course, are typical. The first begins, "If M is present," the second begins, "Again, that M is future". I will re-state each contradiction, and then endeavour to show, first, that neither contradiction is really in the rejoinder, and second, that no fresh contradiction is involved in the demonstration of this fact.

(1) "If M is present, there is no moment of past time at which it is past. But the moments of future time, in which it is past, are equally moments of past time, in which it cannot be past." The contradiction here is that the moments (future moments) at which M has one of the tempo-

ral characteristics (pastness) are also moments of a time (past time) at which, however, M cannot have that determination (the determination of pastness). This contradiction, I venture to think, can be explained away by a proper answer to the question: When are the moments of future time, in which M is past, also moments of past time? Under at least one condition, it is clear, these future moments are not at all moments of past time, namely, when M is present. When M is present, these moments are moments of future time, and they are exclusively moments of future time. They are not at all past then. When M is present, however, it cannot be past. So the moments of future time in which M is past, are not equally moments of past time, where M cannot be past. And the same result is obtained if we answer the above question, not negatively, but positively, and state the condition under which the future moments under consideration, can truly be moments of past time. These moments can be moments of past time only when M is dead past. Then and only then can they be past. But here, where these future moments are equally moments of past time, they are the very moments in which M can have and does have the determination of pastness. So once more the above contradictory proposition is false. When the future moments at which M has the determination of pastness, are equally past, they are not moments of a time when M cannot be past, but are moments of the very same time at which M is dead past.

The first contradiction, therefore, is specious. It disappears as soon as we state the condition under which the future moments, in which M is past, can alone be moments of past time, and the condition under which they cannot. When M is past, is the first condition. When M is present, is the second.[13] When M is present, these future moments are future and cannot be past. Only when M is past, can they be past. As a result, these future moments are not moments of past time, where M cannot be past, but indeed are, as past, moments solely of that past time where M is and can be past. Hence, the contradictory proposition—that the future moments in which M is past, are equally moments of a time in which M cannot be past—is a false account of the temporal properties of these future moments and, under examination, disappears.

Some one, however, may object: Do you not commit yourself to a fresh contradiction in this explanation of the falsity of the present contradictory proposition? For how can M, as you say, be past and be present? Is M past when it is present, or past when it is not present? And if the latter, and if it is possible, as your two conditions assume, for M to be present and past, are you not tacitly admitting that in respect of M the temporal characteristics are incompatible and compatible? That is to say, are you not, in explaining away the present contradiction, tacitly embracing the original contradiction?

To this I should reply: I think not, for I do not think there is an original contradiction. That M is present *and* past, present *or* past, I admit. How M can be present *and* past, present *or* past, and so on, is stated in the original rejoin-

der. And this statement, so we claim, is free of contradiction. This latter is the present point at issue. Is the rejoinder infested, as McTaggart claims, with contradictions? I have tried to show that, in regard to the first of the two contradictions, it is not. In doing this, I have not assumed that the rejoinder is true and used it as a standard—that would be to argue in a circle. I have merely assumed that the rejoinder is meaningful, and I have tried to state, consistently with its meaning, the nature of the pastness of the future moments in which M is past. That is to say, I have tried to state under what conditions, consistently with the rejoinder, these future moments are past and not past. When this is stated, the first contradiction alleged to be in the rejoinder, is seen not at all to be there. For when we are aware that, consistently with the rejoinder, these future moments cannot be past when M is present (or when M is future) and can be past only when M is past, we are aware that it is an error to say that these future moments are equally moments of past time, where M cannot be past. When these moments are equally past, M is past. When M cannot be past, these moments are future. So, consistently with the rejoinder, the first of the alleged contradictions is a false account of the temporal properties of the future moments in which M is past. Therefore, the rejoinder cannot be said to be infested with it.

(2) The second of the contradictions occurs in the following passage: "Again, that M is future and will be present and past means that M is future at a moment of present time, and present and past at different moments of future time. In that case it cannot be present or past at any moments of past time. But all the moments of future time, in which M will be present or past, are equally moments of past time." The contradiction here is that the moments (future moments) in which M will have one of the two temporal determinations (presentness or pastness), are equally moments of a time (past time) at which, however, M can have neither of the two determinations (pastness or presentness). This alleged contradiction, it is clear, has two parts: (*a*) the moments (future moments) in which M will be past, are equally moments of a time (past time), in which M cannot be past, and (*b*) the moments (future moments) in which M will be present, are equally moments of a time (past time), in which M cannot be present. Part (*a*) of this alleged contradiction, it will be noted, is identical with the first of the two contradictions. It has therefore been already treated and need not be treated here. As regards part (*b*), it can, as I think, be explained away by stating the condition under which alone the future moments in which M will be present, are equally and also past. It is clear, of course, that at any time at all they are not also past. For instance, they are not past when M is future or present. They are future or present then. And so far, namely where they are future or present, they are not equally moments of a time in which M cannot be present. They are indeed moments of a time in which M can be and is present, or can be and will be present. So far forth, hence, the above contradictory proposition does not hold. But if we answer our present question, not negatively, but positively, and state the condition under which these future

moments are truly also past, the same result is obtained. These future moments in which M will be present, are also past under one condition, namely, if M is past. If M is past, these moments are also past, and only then. But if M is past, it was present. So once more the contradictory proposition about these future moments, is false. These future moments in which M will be present, are, as truly past, not moments of a time in which M cannot be present. They are indeed, as past, moments of a time at which M was, and can alone be, present.

The second contradiction alleged to infest the rejoinder, therefore, is also specious. It disappears as soon as we state the condition under which the future moments, in which M will be present, can alone be moments of past time and the condition under which they cannot be. When M is past, is the first condition. When M is present or future, is the second condition. When M is present or future, these moments are present or future. Only when M is past, can they be past. But when M is past, it was present. So these future moments are not moments of past time, where M cannot be present, but indeed are, as past, moments solely of that time where M was and can alone be present. Hence the contradictory proposition—that the future moments in which M will be present, are equally moments of a time (past) in which M cannot be present—is a false account of the temporal properties of these future moments, and under critical examination, disappears.

Once more it may be asked: Do you not commit yourself to a fresh contradiction in this explanation of the falsity of the present contradictory proposition? For you say, in laying down the conditions governing the temporality of the future moments under consideration, 'when M is present or future,' and 'when M is past'. That is to say, you assume that M can be present *or* future, and that M can be present *and* be past, or, more generally, that the temporal characteristics are at once compatible and incompatible in respect of M. And this, is it not, is merely the original contradiction all over again?

Once more I should reply: In my opinion there is no original contradiction. The original rejoinder, as I think, states adequately the conditions (simultaneity, succession) under which M can be present *or* future, present *and* past, or, more generally, can have only one or all three of the determinations of the A series. It shows, and I think coherently, that there is no original contradiction. That it does this coherently, of course, is the present point at issue. Is the rejoinder infested, as McTaggart claims, with contradictions? In what I have just said, I have tried to show that the rejoinder is not infested with the second contradiction that McTaggart alleges, infests it. In doing this, I have not assumed that the rejoinder is true, and used it as a standard, but merely that the rejoinder has a meaning, and I have tried merely to state, consistently with this meaning, the nature of the pastness of the future moments in which M will be present. That is to say, I have tried to state under what conditions, consistent with the rejoinder, these future moments are truly past and truly not past. When these

conditions are laid down, the second contradiction alleged to be in the rejoinder is seen not to be there. Consistently with the rejoinder, these future moments, as past, are moments of a time in which M was present and can be present. So consistently with the rejoinder, it is impossible to say that these future moments are equally moments of a time (past) where M cannot be present. That is, it is impossible correctly to say that the rejoinder is genuinely infested with this contradiction.

The rejoinder therefore is a defensible solution of the problem arising out of the fact that the temporal characteristics are compatible and incompatible. It first defines a sense in which past, present, and future, are compatible determinations, and a sense in which they are incompatible. Because these senses are different, because the temporal characteristics are compatible under one condition and incompatible under an altogether different condition, it shows us that there is no original contradiction in the fact that the temporal characteristics are compatible and incompatible. Finally, it proves itself defensible against contradictions alleged to infest it. By an interpretation consistent with the rejoinder, these contradictions are shown to be specious and not to be in the rejoinder. The rejoinder therefore remains a coherent explanation of the A-serial characteristics as determinations of events.

IV.

This completes our examination of McTaggart's second and final argument for the unreality of time. The argument is invalid. It neither establishes that past, present, and future, as event-determinations, are contradictory, nor does it show that the explanation that they are not contradictory, is really infested with contradictions, or, finally, that the explanation of these contradictions is itself infested with contradiction.

Our general conclusion therefore is that the two objections offered by McTaggart against the reality of time, do not hold. Time, it is true, involves an A series. But the reality of the A series is not contingent to the discovery or existence of an impossible timeless X. Nor is the nature of the temporal characteristics of the A series torn with contradiction.

Many problems of course remain. Time, to be real, must not only be freed, as is I think the A series, both from impossibility and contradiction. It must also be squared with our idea of reality as a whole. Can time be a feature of reality as a whole? And if it cannot, is time therefore unreal? These questions, among others, must be satisfactorily answered before we may say unreservedly, if at all, that time is truly real. The present enquiry must pass them by. I have set myself herein merely the question: Is it true, as McTaggart claims, that time is unreal? These other questions, which remain unsolved, consture a different enquiry. Their solution therefore will not be attempted here.

Notes

1. Vol. ii., Bk. V., chap. xxxiii.

2. A fact is defined by McTaggart as "the possession by anything of a quality, or the connection of anything with anything by a relation" (*The Nature of Existence,* vol. i., p. 11). A quality or a relation McTaggart calls a 'characteristic'.

3. *Ibid.,* vol. ii., p. 13.

4. *The Nature of Existence,* vol. ii., p. 13.

5. By fixing the dates when M is past (nT—T^1), when M is present (T^1—T^2), when M is future (T^2—T^3n), the A serial facts of M would be fixed for all time, and unalterably so.

6. It may perhaps be said that the change here is after all a change of facts, though a change of facts of P, not of M. That change and change of facts of M are not equivalents, might be granted. That is, it might be granted that, even if all the facts of M were fixed, this would not eliminate, but indeed determine and perpetuate the fact that M as an event is a passage from N to O—*i.e.,* a change. But, it may be urged, facts of P, as time passes, change, and the event M is nothing but this change of certain of the facts of P. McTaggart's position in regard to change, if stated in the general form that only facts can change, it may be contended is therefore correct. This position, it is clear, cedes the point we urged above, namely, that there is change even if every fact of M is fixed and cannot change. Apart from this, however, I think it is incorrect. The chief facts of P here I submit are these: P is my pen at *t—t'*, P is in a state of being full at *t*, P is in a state of being empty at *t'*, P has passed, between *t* and *t'*, from a state of being full to a state of being empty, and so on. Further, I submit that these facts do not and cannot change. M, however, as a passage from N to O, is a change. So M, as real, cannot be a change of any of these facts of P, for they really do not change. Generally we may say, facts of a thing (*e.g.,* of P), properly documented and dated, do not and cannot change, but change nevertheless is a fact. At least this is clear here. The above facts of P and their like do not and cannot change, but one of the facts of P is that it has passed, between *t* and *t'*, from an earlier state to a later state. That is, one of the facts of P is change, since passage from such a state as N to such a state as O, is a change. For a fuller discussion of change than is possible here, the reader may consult an article by the author, entitled *The Nature of Change* and published in a forthcoming issue of *The Monist* (Chicago).

7. Our point here, of course, is not that change equals mere change of A-serial characteristics (McTaggart's view), but that change involves at least, the possession by an event of the various A-serial characteristics. Whether the event possesses these characteristics permanently or not, is a different point. It is enough for our present point to urge that if an event could not possess these characteristics at all, the change which is the event could not conceivably come off.

8. Dr. Broad has argued in *Scientific Thought,* chap. ii., that the future is just nothing. If this were true, our position here, I suppose, would need amendment. As amended it would state that, if the A series with its distinctions of past and present, were non-existent, change, and therefore time, would be non-existent. And our proof of this position would be similar to our proof of our previous position. McTaggart, however, has made an excellent and, as I think, a successful reply to Dr. Broad. See *Nature of Existence,* vol. ii., p. 23 ff. And see also R. M. Blake, *On Broad's Theory of Time,* Mind, N.S., 1925, vol. xxxiv., p. 418 ff.

9. The paradox embedded in our two comments here, namely, that the temporal characteristics of an event are permanent, yet change, is parallel to the paradox to be mentioned below, that the temporal characteristics are compatible, yet incompatible. This latter paradox can be resolved as we shall see. The present paradox is resolved, as I think, by observing that the condition under which the A-serial characteristics of an event change—namely, relationship to three suitable succeeding events, K, K^1, K^2—is wholly different from the condition under which the A-serial characteristics of an event do not change—namely, relationship to one suitable separate event, to K *or* K^1 *or* K^2. These conditions being totally different it is natural that the A-serial characteristics of an event under the conditions will have properties wholly different—namely, will have, in the one case, the property of changing, and will have, in the other case, the property of not changing. But see also Section III. below.

10. *Nature of Existence,* vol. ii., p. 21.

11. *Nature of Existence,* vol. ii., p. 21.

12. *Ibid.,* vol. ii., p. 21.

13. It is of course true that 'when M is future' is a condition under which these future moments are not past. For they are future then. But to introduce this condition into the argument would neither strengthen nor weaken it, so I have kept it out.

Hilda D. Oakeley (essay date 1930)

SOURCE: "Time and the Self in McTaggart's System," in *Mind,* Vol. XXXIX, No. 154, April, 1930, pp. 175-93.

[*In the following essay, Oakeley questions McTaggart's proposition in the second volume of* The Nature of Existence *that the self can exist in reality simultaneously with the unreality of time.*]

It is proposed in this article to examine the problem which confronts us throughout the second volume of ***The Nature of Existence***. Is it possible consistently to combine a doctrine of the reality of selves with rejection of the reality of time? It might be supposed that the history of philosophy had shown that these two positions can be consistently held together. There is the great example of Leibniz with whose treatment of time that of McTaggart has important affinities. I should, however, argue that Leibniz's pluralism of selves, in spite of the fact that his whole philosophy seems to be involved in the form he gives to this doctrine, cannot strictly be regarded as ultimate. The theory of the Monads as the infinite points of view of God underlies his epistemology, and the conception of the Monads as fulgurations of the Divine Monad, his metaphysic. Into the difficulties which would attend upon the consistent completion of Leibniz's system in this direction it is not necessary here to enter. Apart from the fact that his pluralism of selves is not ultimate in the sense in which this is true of McTaggart's pluralism, the most important distinction between their systems, in respect to the doctrine of selves, and one which leads to other far-reaching differences is that, whilst for McTaggart the selves in reality though not in temporal experience perceive each other directly, for Leibniz there is an absolute incommunicability between selves.

It is not necessary to my purpose to examine the logical foundations of the doctrine of substance laid down in the first volume of the ***Nature of Existence,*** from which it results (vol. ii.) that amongst the apparent existents of experience only what is spiritual can really be substance. The argument had proved in McTaggart's view that nothing can be substance unless it has "parts within parts without end determined by determining correspondence".[1] It is found that only spiritual existents can fulfil this condition, spirituality being "the quality of having content all of which is content of one or more selves".[2] And only perceptions can form an infinite series of the type required. This article is written from the point of view of agreement with the doctrine of the reality of selves, but not with that of the unreality of time. The reality of the self can, in my view, be based on other grounds than that of McTaggart's argument, and indeed this argument appears doubtful if only because it leads to the untenable conclusion that spirit can contain no parts except perceptions and groups of perceptions. It follows that judgments and assumptions have to be explained as kinds of perception, and volitions and emotions must be shown to be in truth cogitations. The problem to be primarily discussed, however, is the relation of certain aspects of the doctrine of the self, to the form taken by the interpretation of time.

1.

A question may be initially raised in regard to McTaggart's method in the combination of the *a priori* and the empirical arguments. The *a priori* argument gives mainly negative results concerning the nature of the existent. Thus, it can be shown "that certain characteristics . . . *cannot* be true of the existent . . . but it will not be possible to show that any of those characteristics which we consider here for the first time *must* be true of the existent".[3] The position then, that everything that exists (or even that any

existent) is spiritual remains only probable. It is difficult to say whether it has even a very high probability according to the argument, although this may be taken to be implied by the tenor of the whole treatise. For though it is possible to show by rigid demonstration that spirit is the only apparent form of substance, which conforms to the necessary conditions, it is impossible to be certain that all possible forms of substance have been suggested to us by our perception.[4] And the limitations of the information that perception can give us, are again and again indicated by McTaggart.[5] It seems then evident that McTaggart's admissions might lead to a greater scepticism as to our capacity for any positive theory of the nature of things than he contemplates. But the difficulty to which I would especially direct attention concerns the method of selection and rejection of data of experience which fulfil the conditions required by the *a priori* argument. There appears to be a kind of fallacy which occurs in the treatment of experience for this purpose by McTaggart—found also in other philosophies—for which the name of the *transformed empirical* may be suggested. A fact accepted from experience undergoes a certain alteration chiefly by omission of part of its nature for experience, before it can be included in the system which satisfies the logical conditions. It is then given a place, in which it appears almost to have attained the rank of a deduction from the *a priori.* Is not this due to the fact that there moves before the mind of the philosopher an *a priori* construction of the nature of things which does not only conform to the negative conditions required by his logic, but includes other positive principles determining his selection from experience? The suspicion of this fallacy is raised at various stages of the treatment of the nature of the self—as, for instance, when volition and emotion are admitted but only as forms of cogitation—and of the treatment of the fundamental misperception of time, *e.g.,* there must really be a series but not a temporal series. The problem whether the empirical fact in its transformation is merely a ghost of its former self or is the truth of which the other was, as it were, phantom and phenomenon, is of course a different problem in each case. One example in particular may be given here. It is argued that we know from self-knowledge the closeness of the union that exists where there is direct perception of a self. It is also postulated that in reality the self perceives other selves directly, and therefore the union between different selves has this peculiar intimacy. And this is the ground of love in reality. Now that love is the highest value is a fact of empirical knowledge. But in present experience we never do perceive other selves directly, whilst self-knowledge, of which, according to McTaggart, we do have experience, gives us no clue to the nature of love, since love must be for another, and self-love is therefore only a metaphor. It seems probable that the conception of self perceiving self directly, as also that of the closeness of the union, are deduced from the nature of love, when this fact of experience is abstracted from all conditions which cannot be reduced to the form of knowledge.

The position that a self can perceive himself directly, but cannot in present experience (which for McTaggart forms the "misperception" series) directly perceive other selves is one which primarily demands examination. The view that the self can be object to itself has of course been widely held, and is of fundamental importance, especially in McTaggart's system. Without it the whole system would have a different character, and, as will be suggested, the theory of the time-series and its status in reality would be profoundly affected. In the view which appears to me to be true, the self can be subject only and never directly its own object. This is a question in the first place of immediate experience, in the second of the conception which is implied of the nature of spirit. It is possible on this view to account for the fact that we do appear to make the self its own object, and thus to indicate "τὸ αἴτιον τοῦ ψεύδους". The subject experienced as self is not, as I should argue, identical with the object which I seem to perceive as myself, and think of as playing its part in life. I do not know the subject as I appear to know that object-self, since knowledge must have an object. Here Prof. Alexander's distinction between the experiences he terms respectively enjoyment and contemplation, is illuminating, though I by no means claim that he would agree with the present standpoint. For the notion of contemplation in his view cannot be applied to the subject's relation to himself. What then is the object-self which I can suppose myself to contemplate? It appears to consist partly of a projection from the subject, partly of content derived analogically from elements or qualities I perceive in other selves. On this view I do contemplate these others in the sense in which I contemplate other objects, though with a difference, in so far as I transfer to them something of that which I project as subject into my object-self. Amongst other grounds for questioning McTaggart's view that in present experience the only self of which the individual has direct perception is his own, may be mentioned the fact, which has a good deal of support and to me seems indubitable, that apparent self-knowledge does not in mental growth precede the apparent knowledge of other selves, but develops *pari passu* with this.[6] That there is a genuine experience, indicated by the term "self-knowledge", is not in question. The issue concerns the nature of this knowledge. In spite of the weight which must be attached to the opinions of those who affirm it to be knowledge by acquaintance, and in particular to McTaggart's conviction reaffirmed many years since it was first stated,[7] the object-self seems to be more truly described as known by construction. The self I appear to know as object is not, like the will of Schopenhauer, known through self-consciousness to be a thing in itself. If it were, familiar experiences such as the following would be inexplicable. An individual, prior to an expected event, believes himself to know infallibly how he will act on meeting it. And he finds that he has been deceived, for he acts quite otherwise when the occasion arises. Now for McTaggart the self as substance must be thing in itself. And although for him the series of events in time is a misperception series, this does not seem to make the type of error referred to less inexplicable, if the self, being real, is its own object. For if the error involved in perception of objects under the conditions of a temporal series, is to involve error in regard to

the form in which the real characteristics of the self appear in time, then to speak of direct knowledge of the self in present experience would be meaningless. The position that the object-self can only be known by construction does not imply that this knowledge may not in general be a good guide to understanding, and anticipation of the motives which will predominate in any particular situation, usually better in accuracy than our understanding of the motives of others, since each has more constant experience of himself than of any other selves. Hence, the justification of the Socratic practical precept γνῶθι σεαυτόν. I should then agree with Bradley that the self is construction, if this means a self which is object of knowledge, but with McTaggart that the self is real, if this can be taken to mean that it is, as subject, the principle which gives reality to our experience. The argument which convinced McTaggart that the self is known by acquaintance was that originally given, but later abandoned, by Mr. Bertrand Russell, and which McTaggart held to be valid.[8] Briefly, this is based on the position that in any assertion such as "I am aware of equality," I must know each constituent of the proposition, either by acquaintance or by description, and as I do not know "I" by description, I must know it by acquaintance. For I must know that the *I* which makes the assertion is the same as the *I* which has the awareness. The latter might be described as the person who has the awareness but not the former, as the same person. In the view taken in this article, the *I* which is a constituent of the proposition, being a construction, is known by description. But there is a unique quality in this type of knowledge by description, due to the fact that the object constructed is in part a projection of the subject. Hence this relation of subject and object is very close.

The doctrine that the self is known directly, by acquaintance, is the first step in McTaggart's argument for the existence of something of the nature of spirit. The quality of spirituality, being "the quality of having content, all of which is the content of one or more selves".[9] The second step is to show that there is not in the case of spirit, as there is in the case of matter and of sensa, reason to suppose that the apparent perception of it must be error or misperception. For spiritual substance fulfils the condition which McTaggart had laid down in the first volume as necessary to existence, *viz.*, the having parts within parts to infinity. It is this negative condition which most definitely determines and limits the conception of the nature of spirit. For the content of spirit is the content of selves, and we have to ask what it is in the nature of selves as we know them in experience which passes the test of admission to reality. It appears that it is only perception which can form an infinite series of the type required. It is in virtue of the nature of perception that spirituality satisfies the conditions essential to substance. Yet what I should term the unreality for metaphysics of a universe of perceivers, in which "B perceives himself and C, and the perceptions which he and C have of themselves and of one another, and the perceptions which they have of these perceptions, and so on to infinity,"[10] is only avoided by the admission of emotions and with them values, though emotions have no status except as kinds of cogitation. I think that the un-reality which seems to attach to this doctrine of substance is due to the fact that whilst the principle which is its centre cannot be given the full meaning which it has for experience, it does not, in sacrificing this, gain a profounder meaning in virtue of its place in the system of reality. The self which for experience is a principle of intelligence and will, becomes a principle of intelligence alone; for volition, as a form of cogitation, has to be reduced to acquiescence in what is. Like the deified thought of Aristotle, thinking upon itself, the personified perception of McTaggart seems in becoming eternal to lose the spiritual nature,[11] in virtue of which it could be accepted as the reality of realities. In the problem of metaphysical method with which we are here presented, *viz.,* whether the transformation of the empirical self suffices to give it the ontological nature required, the following maxim seems applicable. That principle which has been selected from experience must either carry with it its original meaning and value, or, if transformed, acquire through that change a meaning more in harmony with the doctrine of reality implied. There must be compensation for the loss of apparent value. Now when the principle of selfhood (or personality) is transformed into a principle of cogitation alone, the new meaning to which it points, and therefore the doctrine of reality implied, is that of the universal nature of thought, the ideal of which is sameness in all thinkers, the knowledge of which is only differentiated in so far as it is known from different points of view. The only significance remaining in the eternal distinctness of selves would then be due to the existence of that emotion which McTaggart describes in passages which are philosophical poems. But it seems doubtful whether the presence and perfection of human affection is fully intelligible when reduced to a form of cogitation in a timeless system. It may here, however, be observed, that the doctrine that the self is known by acquaintance, which is for McTaggart sufficient evidence for the *prima facie* existence of spirit, is not an indispensable proof on his view of the facts of experience. For the values which he admits as attributable to experience in reality, and pre-eminently those of love and self-reverence, are facts which, at least from his standpoint, are inconceivable without the existence of spiritual beings as substances.

2.

With a view to considering the relation of the doctrine of the unreality of time to the doctrine of the reality of selves in McTaggart's system, I would suggest a broad distinction of the philosophical grounds on which the reality of time has been rejected, according as they are formulated from the standpoint of the subject as experiencing, or of the world as object of knowledge. The logical doctrines of the unreality of time seem to derive mainly from the view of the world as an objective order made intelligible in a system of propositions whose relations to each other may be conceived as changeless. The appearance of change in time threatens to be an obstacle in the process of rationalising our experience, and the denial of it seems to forward the intellectual need. On the other hand the types of doc-trine which are motived by the subjective need for getting beyond the ceaseless flux of experience have their basis in the conception of the nature of mind which, as contemplating truth, cannot be, in reality, subject to such a flow of changing impressions. Now on this line of thought the conception of mind as unchanging and eternal seems necessarily to pass into a conception of mind unconfined by the limits of individual selfhood. The individual subject, endeavouring to pass beyond the process of change in which it seems to find itself and all its experiences involved, cannot overcome the illusion *qua* one amongst many subjects of experience; for continuous change seems to be involved in the interrelations of these subjects. It is a greater illusion which must be overcome, the illusion of separate selves; and the ultimate unreality of the self is thus the postulate required in order to validate, from this standpoint, the unreality of time. This result is perfectly illustrated in the philosophy of Spinoza. For the twin illusions (presuming them to be such) stand and fall together. In so far as the "mode" emphasises as it were its separate manifestation of substance *qua* limited at this point, and there is experience at the first stage of knowledge, time is needed as an "aid to the imagination". But with the advance to the third stage we pass out of the temporal into the eternal, and the mind becomes united with the whole. In the second stage the objective standpoint predominates. With the progress of scientific knowledge the systematisation of things is carried out with greater "tidiness" in proportion to our ability to omit the reference to time and to the self which insists on bringing its own measures. What seems unique in McTaggart's conception of the unreality of time, is that whilst his reason for this position is a logical doctrine of the contradiction which arises in our propositions about anything which is subject to change, his pluralism of real selves is determined by a spiritual doctrine of experience. I am here stating what appears to me to be the ultimate source of his position. It is not as an object amongst objects that the self cannot be under the condition of time. It is as the subject for which the highest values must be eternal. Yet, as I wish to maintain, McTaggart's conception of the experience of the self is in essence incompatible with the unreality of time.

His logical argument for treating the perception of the temporal as error, is based on the assumption that time is inseparable from change. I would suggest—in general agreement with M. Bergson, though from a somewhat different point of view—that it is impossible to separate the thought of existence from the condition of time as duration, and further, here of course differing from Bergson, that this would hold good even though the existent were devoid of change. Apart from this it might be objected to McTaggart's argument that although change involves contradiction if time be unreal, the contradiction is removed by the reality of time, and that thus the argument could be used in the opposite sense. Change involves what McTaggart calls the "A" series (past, present, future), and in this series every event has the incompatible determinations past, present, future.[12] This difficulty, as he shows, is only removed a step further back by the explanation that what is meant is, present at a moment of present time, past at some moment of future time, future at some moment of past time. But if time be real, since *now* is a different aspect of the universe from *then,* some determination may be possessed by an event *now,* consistently with its being denied of the same event *then.* Thus the contradiction only arises if time be unreal. A more general criticism of McTaggart's treatment of the problem of time by logical method might be founded on the position that the temporal series is necessary to logic. Unless either logical relations are conceived to be of the same type as mathematical, or logic be identified with metaphysics, neither of which positions appears to be held by McTaggart, it may be argued that they postulate a temporal experience. For there can be no progress from one position to another where all are eternally present together. I do not think that this involves a merely "epistemic" standpoint in logic, to use Mr. Johnson's expression. There would be no meaning in a statement that A is included in B unless behind the statement there lay the experience, actual or possible, of the occurrence of one after the other. How otherwise is the difference between the first and the second to be given its value, how otherwise is identity between the two to be avoided? The notion of inclusion is the one selected by McTaggart as the type of the real series, of which the temporal is phenomenal. When in our experience A precedes B in time, in the real order A is included in B. But how are we to conceive the relation of the included to the including unless we can think of the terms or events as *now* separated from each other and *then* coming together? Without the temporal form they become identical in inclusion and the series is no longer a series. What other form—schema, we may call it (though it is more indispensable in this sense to the logical movement than the Kantian schema to the category)—is adequate to supply the required difference? That a spatial distinction is at least not adequate to the significance of the inclusion series in McTaggart's conception of it, appears from his view that not all the elements of the pre-final are contained in the final stage of inclusion, not at least all the values of the pre-final. Is not the temporal transition necessary even to implication as a logical relation? Suppose it is asserted that A implies B. Unless my thought can rest upon A as in some sense really apart from B, as not already possessing B and still requiring a further step in order that the B which follows it by implication shall be revealed—unless the significance of A standing alone asserts itself as independent of our abstracting work, yet as something which cannot continue apart, but must summon B to follow it, is the complete significance of the implication given? It seems that no substitute for the temporal can supply this vital feature of the logical process. M. Emile Meyerson observes that it is not merely the language of every day but also that of philosophy which tends to establish a close connexion between the temporal and the logical relation in the notion of cause, and refers to the use of "le conséquent," and "la conséquence" and of the term "antériorité logique".[13] Again he points to "cette similitude des termes servant a caractériser la relation logique des phénomènes et leurs relations dans le temps".[14] This si-

militude, he considers, has not received as much attention from logicians as it seems to deserve. He quotes M. Goblot's explanation (*Traité de Logique*) that it is our discursive thought which finds itself obliged to admit the consequence *after* it has admitted the principle. "L'ordre intemporel de dépendance logique, préscrit a la pensée l'ordre temporel de ses assertions discursives," and observes that this explanation by reference to an external circumstance does not seem sufficient. "Once we are convinced that nature is entirely intelligible, is it not indifferent from what point we start in the discussion?" He considers a cognate question in connexion with the doctrine of the potential and development, pointing out that at times it is difficult to see which of the two conceptions we have in view—the temporal-historic or the rational-logical.[15] In the passages from which these references are taken M. Meyerson's general aim is to demonstrate that it is impossible for either philosophy or science (reason in his view being one in both) to avoid altogether the admission of the irrational factor in experience. In so far as the temporal series involves the irrational, I should accept this view.

For McTaggart, since time is unreal, the greatest, and at times it seems the all-sufficient source of error, is the fundamental misperception through which we perceive all things in a temporal series. This error he regards as universal and inescapable, the mystic's experience of the timeless is illusory.[16] There arises for him then in the most acute form the problem of the occurrence of misperception, since he also holds that the correctness of perception is self-evident. A subtle argument is directed to the solution of this enigma. The self-evident correctness is limited to a period in time measured from a point in time. Thus what I perceive as present must be within the specious present, but it may exist at the moment O and I perceive it at the moment P, both being within the specious present. I may thus be in error, although I perceive as present what is within the specious present.[17] This limitation has then to be translated into the terms of the real series, since time is unreal. Assuming (it is not certainly known) that error of perception may come in by means of the specious present character of our perception of a present experience containing distinct moments (any one of which we may take as our moment of experience whereas the experience may occur at another moment), McTaggart conceives this error as meaning an error in the inclusive or C series. Thus error in perception is not inconsistent with the self-evident correctness of perception. It appears that the prior and root error of perceiving a temporal series is to be rendered conceivable by this possible error which cannot be discovered by perception to occur. But the whole analysis depends on the preliminary assumption that there is a time series within which present and specious present have significance. For our belief that there is error in the C series depends on the supposition of error in the temporal series. The problem being how, since time is unreal, do we perceive events in time, perception being infallible, it is replied that under the conditions of time our perception is in a sense correct, and in a sense incorrect, on account of the specious present. Perception then may not be infallible. Although we are certain that every perception is correct at the time when it is made, "the time at which it is made is a misperception, the reality misperceived being the point in the C series at which it occurs".[18] But in order to prove this, or the possibility of this, have we not to assume that perception *is* infallible in regard to the fundamental perception of a time series, the very question at issue? The error has no meaning except on the assumption that there is a time series.It may further be asked in relation to this method of conceiving the problem of time, by what criterion are we enabled to determine the extent of the misperception? For the misperception is so profound as to introduce into our experience time with all its attendant illusions, illusions to which is due a transformation of reality such as to leave unaffected hardly a single important experience.[19] In McTaggart's view we have no reason for supposing that it extends to the point of perceiving as a series what is not in reality a series, but—for example—some type of whole of parts, which might be translated into a series by our misperception. "What appears as the temporal series is really a series though it only appears to be temporal."[20] We need not, it seems, entertain doubts concerning the appearance unless it contains a contradiction. There is then in reality a series though the temporal form is illusory. We may analyse what comes to us as a single and all embracing experience, and distinguish in it a part which is wholly illusory and a part which is veritable. The difficulty which McTaggart seems to experience in determining what type of real series it is of which the time-series is a misperception, may suggest doubts whether the notion of series is the true logical equivalent of the process of time. To some thinkers, the nature of time has appeared to be better indicated by the idea of a continuous passage which is discrete in its moments only in relation to our mode of conceiving it, stages in the passage being distinguished primarily on account of their importance whether in view of practice or in view of the systematic and intelligible conception of the world. This interpretation cannot be more than referred to since my purpose is not to discuss the alternatives to McTaggart's treatment of time, but the problem of the compatibility of the latter with his doctrine of the self. The employment of the notion of the inclusion series as being that type of which the order of time is phenomenal, enables him to present his highly original theory of the relation of appearance to reality in the most exact form possible, and so to satisfy himself in what respects its form, and in what respects its content, can be taken as reflexions of the truth. As regards the form, for instance, the transitive and asymmetrical characters of the relations in the order of time must have their source in the same characters of relations in the real (C) series. Perhaps the most remarkable peculiarity in McTaggart's doctrine of the relation of the apparent and the real series is the view of error in reality. The perceptions in the C series are not merely incomplete, they contain real error. "If they were not really misperceptions it would be impossible that the error for which we are trying to find a place, could be found in them." Thus the misperceptions of our experience do not only arise there, they have a real source.

What then is this cause of error which is beyond time? The doubt again arises whether this cause, or to be precise the order in which error really arises, the inclusive series, can be made intact so to speak or wholly pure from time. This doubt is strengthened when we come to the discussion of the relation of the prefinal to the final stages of experience and the idea of the "futurity of the whole".[21] That the terms of the inclusive series should appear to form an A series (past, present, future) and consequently a B series (earlier and later) is, as McTaggart observes, an ultimate fact. "We cannot explain why it should be so. But there is no reason why it should not be so."[22] But the reason why the inclusive series was selected was that it appeared to him to be amongst possible types that one of which the time-series could be reasonably regarded as the appearance. Now amongst the respects in which he recognises that the correspondence seems difficult to establish is one which belongs to the content. The content of the terms of the time-series, as we observe it, does not at all suggest that the terms do in reality stand in the relation of including and included. For the content does not appear to show any uniform change in either direction. "Everywhere we find persistence of content, recurrence of content, and oscillation of content." But all these features can be accounted for on the theory. "The oscillations, etc." which he examines, all belong to the cognitional experience in the strict sense in which (as I presume he would allow) we cannot speak of emotions and desires as cognitional: for instance, decrease or increase in clearness of perception. Let us grant that these can be explained on the theory, as in his demonstration.[23] But the explanation does not seem adequate if it does not include explanation of persistence, recurrence, oscillation in the quality of the content as value, in view of the place of value in his system. Since the problem of the relation of experience in time to the real order, concerns the whole of our experience, and McTaggart holds that the value qualities of our experience may in certain respects be attributed to reality, why "when enumerating the conditions which must be fulfilled by any theory of the C series, if that theory is to enable us to find in that series the explanation of error"[24] does he not consider it of the first importance to examine the oscillations and other irregularities of these qualities, whether as distinct from cognition, or as kinds of cognition? I would suggest that the ground or the chief ground of this omission is the failure to recognise that the whole meaning of the order of value in time depends on the nature or aspect of the temporal order as experience of the subject. The oscillations, persistences and recurrences of content he examines, all affect the nature of the object in its purely cognitional character.[25] Some reference, however, is made to oscillations of value in the concluding chapter.[26] Here the question as affecting nations or societies, *e.g.,* the question of moral progress in the general sense, is dismissed, since "nothing is intrinsically good or bad, as we have seen, except either selves, or parts of selves". And McTaggart's doctrine of pre-existence and post-existence involves that it is impossible for us to know whether that which is the reality of which the nation is appearance (the selves of the society) is the same in any sense from age to age. Progress or deterioration can only affect the individual. And here, though we might perceive it to last for a whole life, the insignificance of our field of observation compared with the greatness of the universe "reduces to insignificance, not only the importance of a single self, but the importance of all those groups which we are accustomed to regard with sympathy". For these reasons McTaggart rejects the whole testimony of experience on such questions as those of progress and retrogression, and prefers to decide the problem on "general considerations". His own view is optimistic, that is, of course, in what the theologians would call an eschatological rather than a humanitarian sense. But here we seem to meet what I have termed the fallacy of the transformed empirical, in a peculiarly insidious form. The theologian can rest his belief in the infinite importance of the individual on his theological doctrine. He usually assumes also the reality of time. But the philosopher without either theology or a positive principle to give him an *a priori* metaphysic would be expected to find in experience the basis for his view that the nature of the universe does secure the ultimate good of each self. The "general considerations" include considerable reference to empirical material, *e.g.,* in regard to the existence of selves and the nature of their experience in knowledge and emotion. Reflexion on experience also suggests that it "is so small in comparison with the whole that it is impossible to obtain any information about the whole by induction from what is observed". *A priori* reasoning demonstrates the unreality of time. Yet a meaning is to be retained for the positions that the self, in reality timeless, is to pass through an immense time and finally reach a very good state. What ground can there be for these conclusions excepting an *a priori* metaphysic of the self, from which the experiences of the self known in time may be deduced as *phenomena bene fundata?*

3.

By means of a very remarkable conception McTaggart seems to form a bridge between the temporal and the eternal, that is, by allowing a certain validity to a principle which can only have a place in experience occurring in a time-series, in so far as that principle has a permanent value. This conception is the conception of the "futurity of the whole". It is the form of the real or inclusion series which supplies to him the standpoint from which he arrives at the conception. This series "will contain at least one term which the misperception series does not include—for the inclusion series will have—as one of its terms—the term which is inclusive of all others and which is included by no other".[27] The whole must be a correct perception—it cannot therefore be a term in the misperception series. Now since a self misperceives any term in an inclusion series as being in time, he will perceive H (the term which is inclusive of all others) as a whole as being in time. But he will never perceive it as present. He could only perceive the whole as present if he were at the same stage as the whole. And only the self as a whole could be at the same stage, and as a whole he could not perceive anything in time.[28]

The whole is then "though not really future—future in the only way in which anything can be so—as appearing as future"—"*Sub specie temporis,* the whole *is* now future".[29] As McTaggart points out, this view is opposed to the view that the universe, taken as a whole, is at every moment of the time series manifested as present. The ground of the difference is that "what appears as the temporal series is really a series, though it only appears to be temporal. . . . Hence some eternal realities appear as being earlier in time, some as being later." But "the final term of the series which is also the whole, appears *sub specie temporis* only as future, and never as past or present". Whereas in the view McTaggart opposes "it is this term which is most emphatically asserted to exist as present". Now it happens that the results for ethics are much more satisfactory on McTaggart's than on the contrasted view. According to the rejected view we have to suppose that all the good which is in the universe as a whole is manifested in our present life. Either then there is less good than we demand, or some of our ideals are false. We may agree with McTaggart that the doctrine that the whole is completely manifested in the present has disastrous results for ethics. But are these really avoided in the doctrine of the futurity of the whole? Since the final term is all-inclusive, all the good that exists in the universe must be contained in it, and (though he does not seem to admit this) all the evil, since he does not regard it as that kind of whole in which the combination of the parts carries with it the possession of a new character or quality. There is not for McTaggart as there is for Bernard Bosanquet a transmutation by which either evil ceases to be evil in the whole, or we pass beyond both good and evil. McTaggart does not affirm that the whole is entirely good, but only that there is more good in it than evil. This position is certainly more in harmony with our moral experience than the neo-Hegelian position. Yet it may be questioned whether the degree and amount of error which he allows to affect our present moral judgments are not such as to create the kind of uncertainty about present estimates in this sphere which he supposes his doctrine to avoid. As an example may be taken the following observation. Having referred to his own view that an ungratified volition always means an erroneous perception, he asks whether his results will destroy the value of the emotional and moral life, and in relation to the latter concludes that "it is not certain that there is really any disapproval of crimes or any approval of, or acquiescence in, acts of virtue—but the fact that there are apparent approvals, disapprovals, and acquiescences, is sufficient for morality".[30] So far as the status of ethics is concerned, this result does not appear to give it more standing than Bosanquet's conception of morality as belonging to the stage of claims and counter-claims, a stage transcended in the Absolute, where separate individuality ceases to demand recognition. For McTaggart's ontology, however, separate individuality is fundamental.

But the greatest difficulty in connexion with the doctrine of the futurity of the whole is, I think, a logical one. The combination in a single conception of the meaning which can only belong to a fact of the temporal misperception series, and the meaning of that which is timeless, seems impossible. From the standpoint of the temporal experience, the whole is always future. From its own standpoint, since it is eternal, we can only apply temporal characterisations to it by metaphor, and presentness would be a better metaphor for the appearance of the whole at the last stage of the C series than pastness or futurity. What does this signify for the experience of the self? In so far as temporal conditions have meaning the whole is never reached, it is always future. In so far as the final stage is attained, the present with the past and future is really abolished. It appears to result that either we are having in time an experience of the highest value to look forward to, but never to attain, or we are with everything else in the universe eternally members of the whole. It is now as present as anything can be, and the neo-Hegelian paradox that all is already either good or neither good nor evil, is not escaped. Either we shall never attain the eternal or there is the eternal now. To McTaggart's position that "we shall in a finite time reach an endless state which is infinitely more good than bad,"[31] there seems to me to attach a difficulty which is the converse of that of the doctrine which Aristotle supposes himself to find in Plato's Timæus, that in an eternal world there is a beginning of time. Here in the course of a temporal experience we should enter upon eternity. I do not think that the difficulty is overcome by the distinction between the whole and the eternal. For the whole must *sub specie temporis* include the whole of the temporal series, it is the eternal which manifests itself in time.

The logical conception of the Inclusion series which is to form the transitional category between the temporal and the eternal, does not then seem capable of performing this function unless the temporal order really lies half concealed behind the relation of inclusion. When the final stage is reached we know that all the pre-final stages were or are permeated by misperception. As timeless, we perceive them in their true character, the final experience being as we are told similar to the experience of presentness. It seems impossible to hold that we are not eternally perceiving these stages without misperception, unless a status is allowed to the order of time in virtue of which it forces its distinctions of now and then, present and future into reality. Thus either we get the futurity of the whole which carries with it the pastness of the parts, and these distinctions must be carried over into reality, or our real experience is complete and perfect, and we dismiss the order of time as something that neither is, nor was.

If McTaggart, in spite of the logical power and exhaustive analysis of his method, has rendered himself liable to this criticism, I think the ultimate reason lies in the perhaps unconscious transition underlying the treatment of time, and affecting the treatment of the self, to which reference has been made; namely between the subjective and the objective methods of analysing the meaning of the temporal process. The doctrine of the timeless spiritual world has its birth in the objective view of the nature of things, from Plato's treatment (in his earlier period only) of the soul as an idea, to McTaggart's philosophy of the self as sub-

stance having qualities and relations. McTaggart does not obviously make use of the subjective method, but his philosophy seems to have need of it. The theory of the self would, however, have to be associated with acceptance of the reality of time, if the selves are to be independent beings. If time is unreal the selves in their true nature as subjects lose their distinctness which can only be maintained by creative activity, and the passage into the doctrine of universal mind takes place. This is obscured for McTaggart because his theory of the unreality of time is determined by logical argument in relation to the content of a world of substances, objectively regarded, although he believes that all substance must be spiritual. Amongst the results of this standpoint are the comparative lack of value attributed to memory, as to history, and the practical life. This is, of course, inevitable also on account of the rejection of the reality of change, and the view of volition as a kind of cognition, signifying in reality the feeling of acquiescence. But to discuss these points would be to go far beyond the limits of this article.

The difficulty which lies nearer to the heart of McTaggart's position is that of the assignment of grounds for the dissimilarity of selves. The greatest value depends upon the relations of selves; this relation is conceived as infinitely more perfect in the timeless than in the temporal experience. It would appear that unless these selves possess each a unique individuality, the value of the pluralistic universe would hardly exceed that of the monistic. This is, of course, no argument against its reality; but for McTaggart, obviously, only in a pluralistic universe can the highest value be attained. It may also be noted that McTaggart at times lays stress upon quantity rather than quality of value. A life of exceedingly small value would, if it went on long enough, become at some point better than a brief life of the highest value. The view that "quality is something which is inherently and immeasurably more important than quantity," he considers "neither self-evident, nor capable of demonstration".[32] It is very difficult to make this position consistent with his treatment of value in the final stage. For it would appear to lead to the result that no value is intrinsically better than another. A sufficient quantity of an inferior value would be superior to a small quantity of one greatly superior in itself. The quality of the selves experiencing value is then, from this standpoint, less important than their number, and in fact McTaggart conceives them as "qualitatively very much alike. Each of them perceives selves and the parts of selves, and has no other content but such perceptions" which are also states of emotion and acquiescence. As regards the way in which selves may be differentiated, it may be quantitative, or there may be "tone-differences" in the quality of their perceptions. It is very clear that McTaggart does not himself regard this similarity of selves as in any way diminishing the value of their experience. As his conclusion tells us[33], we are gradually approximating a final stage in which the good infinitely exceeds, not only any evil co-existent with it, but all the evil in the series by which it is attained. And he makes other impressive statements showing deep conviction of the certainty and greatness of the eternal value.

Yet on this point the Absolutist philosopher seems to recognise more truly what is involved in the rejection of time. He abandons the value of personality, and transforms the values of human relations into the principle that determines all which is finite and limited towards union in the whole. McTaggart conceiving reality from the subjective side as spiritual cannot sacrifice the uniqueness of selves since spirit is personal. The values of human relationship are therefore not totally transformed but either we must see them as weakened in certain respects essential to selfhood, or it must be allowed that his doctrine of the unlimited value of the final stage passes into a kind of mysticism. For there appears to be in his system no intelligible ground for the sense of intimate union between selves which is the basis of the highest value except in the nature of knowledge in which their experience essentially consists. Their whole content consists of perceptions, and the objects of these perceptions are selves having a content of perceptions, and the perceptions of these selves. In the attempt to conceive their nature clearly, we are inevitably led on to the thought of a perpetually increasing advance to unity which is never completed but indefinitely approached.

Notes

1. Vol. I., Bk. IV., Chap. XXIV.

2. Vol. II., Bk. V., Chap. XXXVI., "Spirit".

3. Vol. II., Bk. V., Chap. XXXII., p. 5.

4. Bk. V., Chap. XXXVIII., "Idealism".

5. See especially Bk. VI., Chap. XLIV., "Error," 516-517.

6. *Cf.* McTaggart's own observation, "The more vivid definite and extensive is our recognition of the other the more vivid and definite becomes our self-consciousness". *Some Dogmas of Religion,* Chap. VI., "God as Omnipotent".

7. Article on "Personality," *Encyclopædia of Religion and Ethics,* 1917.

8. Article in *Encyclopædia of Religion and Ethics,* and *The Nature of Existence,* Vol. II., Bk. V., Chap. XXXVI.

9. Vol. II., Bk. V., Chap. XXXVI., p. 62.

10. *The Nature of Existence,* Bk. V., XXXVII., "Cogitation," p. 89.

11. I think it must be agreed that the term "spirit" as used by McTaggart cannot be identified with "mind".

12. Vol. II., Bk. V., Chap. XXXIII., "Time".

13. *L'Explication dans les Sciences,* Chap. III., "La Déduction".

14. *Ibid.,* Chap. IV., "La Rationalité du Réel".

15. *Ibid.,* Bk. II., Chap. X., "L'Etat de Puissance".

16. *The Nature of Existence,* Vol. II., Bk. VI., Chap. XLV., "Error and the C series".

17. *Ibid.* See also Bk. VI., Chap. L., "Compliance with the Conditions".

18. *Ibid.,* Bk. VI., Chap. L., "Compliance with the Conditions".

19. See Bk. VI., Chap. XLIV., sections 516-517.

20. *Ibid.,* Bk. VI., Chap. XLV.

21. See Section 3.

22. Bk. VI., Chap. LIII., "Apparent Perceptions".

23. Bk. VI., Chap. L., "Compliance with the Conditions".

24. Bk. VI., Chap. XLVI.

25. Bk. VI., Chap. L.

26. Bk. VII., Chap. LXVIII., "Conclusion".

27. Bk. VI., Chap. XLIX., "The Three Series".

28. Bk. VI., Chap. XLIX.

29. *Ibid.,* Bk. VII., Chap. LXI.

30. Bk. VI., Chap. LVII., "Emotion and Volition".

31. Bk. VII., Chap. LXVIII., "Conclusion".

32. Bk. VII., Chap. LXVII.

33. Bk. VII., Chap. LXVIII.

C. D. Broad (essay date 1935)

SOURCE: A review of *Philosophical Studies,* in *Mind,* Vol. XLIV, No. 175, July, 1935, pp. 531-32.

[*In the following review, Broad praises the previously uncollected essays in the posthumously published* Philosophical Studies.]

Dr. Keeling has collected eleven papers of McTaggart's, which were either unpublished or scattered in back-numbers of Mind and other periodicals. He has prefaced them with an introduction and has provided them with notes referring the reader to relevant passages in McTaggart's published books.

The essays [in *Philosophical Studies*] cover a period of thirty years, from 1893, when McTaggart was twenty-seven years old, to 1923, two years before his death. As Dr. Keeling points out, there was no fundamental change during this period in McTaggart's views on the nature of metaphysics or in his metaphysical conclusions, but there was a profound change in his method of proof. Always a highly unorthodox Hegelian, he ended by proving conclusions which he thought to be more or less Hegelian by straight-forward deductive arguments from self-evident premises, instead of by the Hegelian method of thesis, antithesis, and synthesis.

The only one of these papers hitherto unpublished is the ninth. This is a syllabus of McTaggart's popular lectures on philosophy which he gave year after year to Cambridge undergraduates who were interested in the subject but were not reading it for their degree. It is an extremely clear and condensed synopsis of his general views on philosophy and his reasons for them. It should be compared with the eleventh essay, **'An Ontological Idealism,'** which is a most remarkable summary in twenty pages of McTaggart's final position as expounded in the two volumes of *The Nature of Existence.* The tenth paper, **'The Further Determination of the Absolute,'** is the one in which McTaggart first professed to prove an important proposition which the Fairy Queen in *Iolanthe* had already asserted:

> 'And in fact you will discover
> That we almost live on lover!'

This was privately printed when McTaggart was a young man. A considerable part of it was reproduced in his *Studies in Hegelian Cosmology,* but the complete essay has never before been available to the general public.

All the other articles have been published completely before; but some of them, *e.g.,* **'Dare to be Wise,'** **'Mysticism,'** and **'The Individualism of Value'** (Essays I, II, and IV), were very difficult to get hold of. **'The Individualism of Value'** would have been well worth reprinting at the present time if only for its concluding sentences: 'Compared with worship of the State, zoolatry is rational and dignified. A bull or a crocodile may not have great intrinsic value; but it has some, for it is a conscious being. The State has none. It would be as reasonable to worship a sewagepipe, which also possesses considerable value as a means.'

The two very important essays on time, **'The Unreality of Time'** and **'The Relation of Time to Eternity,'** have since been embodied in *The Nature of Existence.* The same is true of the third and seventh essays, **'Personality,'** and **'The Meaning of Causality.'** As they are intelligible by themselves, and highly important contributions to philosophy, it is very useful to have them reprinted. The one remaining essay, **'Propositions Applicable to Themselves,'** shows how well McTaggart could deal with purely logical questions when he chose to do so.

The philosophical public are under an obligation to Dr. Keeling, for the trouble that he has taken in collecting and annotating these papers, and to Messrs. Arnold for their enterprise in making the results of Dr. Keeling's labours available in a pleasant binding at a moderate price.

Robert Leet Patterson (essay date 1950)

SOURCE: "McTaggart's Conception of the Beatific Vision," in *The Review of Religion,* Vol. XV, Nos. 1-2, November, 1950, pp. 29-46.

[In the following essay, Patterson examines McTaggart's opinions regarding the notion of "man's last end," attempting to reconcile McTaggart's Hegelian cosmology with Christian orthodoxy.]

In the concluding paragraphs of the chapter on Hegelianism and Christianity in his *Studies in Hegelian Cosmology,* McTaggart makes the following pregnant observation:

> Christian apologists have not infrequently met the attacks of their opponents with Hegelian arguments. And as long as there are external enemies to meet, the results are all that they can desire. Against Scepticism, against Materialism, against Spinozistic Pantheism, against Deism or Arianism—nothing is easier than to prove by the aid of Hegel that wherever such creeds differ from orthodox Christianity, they are in the wrong. But this is not the end. The ally who has been called in proves to be an enemy in disguise—the least evident but the most dangerous. The doctrines which have been protected from external refutation are found to be transforming themselves till they are on the point of melting away, and orthodoxy finds it necessary to separate itself from so insidious an ally.
>
> This double relation of Hegelianism to Christian orthodoxy can be explained by the theory which I have propounded. If orthodox Christianity, while incompatible with Hegelianism, is nevertheless closer to it than any other religion, it is natural that Hegelianism should support Christianity against all attacks but its own, and should then reveal itself as an antagonist all the more deadly because it works not by denial but by completion. (Sec. 264).

It is not with the justice of this comment that I am now concerned. Perhaps most of us who have read McTaggart would feel inclined to agree with Dr. Broad's assertion that "if McTaggart's account of Hegelianism be taken as a whole and compared with Hegel's writings as a whole, the impression produced is one of profound unlikeness. 'Whatever Hegel may have meant,' the reader says to himself, 'it surely cannot have been this.' 'And,' he hastens to add, 'it was probably nothing nearly so sensible or plausible as this.'"[1] My present intention, however, is to raise the kindred question, To what extent can the claim which McTaggart makes for Hegel be plausibly advanced on behalf of his own philosophy? Needless to say, it is a question much easier to ask than to answer. Yet it is one well worth asking, if it be true, as Dr. Broad has affirmed, that "the system expounded in the *Nature of Existence* is equal in scope and originality to any of the great historical systems of European philosophy, whilst in clearness of statement and cogency of argument it far surpasses them all."[2]

To attempt a detailed examination both of Christian orthodoxy and of McTaggart's philosophy would obviously be an undertaking which would involve at least a volume. Accordingly, what I propose to do is to compare and contrast the conceptions of man's last end which they respectively proffer us. The advantage of so proceeding is that, in each instance, we thus place our finger upon the very pulse of the spiritual life. For religion is not merely a theoretical but also an intensely practical affair. Man is concerned, not only with knowing, but also with being and becoming. Moreover, it is in their agreement that there is a definite goal toward which we all may strive that the various historic religions are most at one. Although, if we contrast the mental outlook of an accomplished theologian—such as St. Thomas—with that of a Jain philosopher who has no theology at all, we might conclude that the two have nothing in common, yet, if we look more closely, we shall discover that the Jain, like St. Thomas, and like every other adherent of a faith that is intellectually mature, is endeavoring to orient himself with respect to his last end. Negatively conceived, such an end may be described as deliverance, emancipation, salvation; positively conceived, it may be described as attainment, fruition, blessedness.

Upon the reality of this last end all the great world-faiths are agreed. It is in their conceptions of it, and of its metaphysical setting, that they differ. When we survey these various differences, however, we find that they can all be subsumed under one or another of three clearly defined types.

In the first place there is the outlook of the theist for whom man's last end consists in communion with a living God, wholly other than, yet wholy united with, the illumined soul. In this direct, intuitive vision *facies ad faciem,* in this fellowship of mind with mind, in this ecstasy of love given and received, he sees the final goal of the religious quest, the supreme good in comparison with which all other goods are non-essential. It is significant that the burning devotion of the mystic has compelled the Christian theologian to identify heaven itself with the Beatific Vision. Thus, in Boehme's *Dialogue between a Scholar and his Master concerning the Super-Sensual Life,* the former asks with respect to the departing soul, "Doth it not enter into heaven or hell, as a man entereth into a house, or goeth through a door or passage into another place"? "No," replies the Master, "there is no such kind of entering; for heaven and hell are present everywhere, and it is but the turning of the will either into God's love or into his anger, that introduceth into them."[3]

In Sufism, it is worth observing, the same emphasis upon the supreme blessedness of mystical union is achieved by a different device. Heaven, far from being equated with the vision of God, is sharply distinguished from it; hence the desire for paradise is denounced as polytheism, inasmuch as it involves setting one's heart upon something other than God. This point of view is given forceful expression in the words of Abu'l Hasan Khurqānī: "I do not say that Paradise and Hell are non-existent, but I say that they are nothing to me, because God created them both, and there is no room for any created object in the place where I am."[4] The same thought is expressed less egotistically and more charmingly in Rābi'a's prayer, "O God! whatever share of this world Thou hast allotted to me, bestow it on Thine enemies; and whatever share of the next world Thou hast allotted to me, bestow it on Thy friends. Thou art enough for me."[5] And what is true of Christianity and Sufism is true of theism the world over. Everywhere we find present and active the same tendency to conceive of man's last end in terms of personal relationship to a personal God, of a fellowship productive of utter satisfaction.

In the second place, there is the pantheistic point of view, which either holds that personal relationships do not exist between man and God, or—if it admit them at all—denies their ultimacy. To the mystic in the flood tide of his enthusiasm, it seems that the deepest intimacy involves a passing beyond the realm of I and Thou to a state of absorption or identification. Even in Christian mysticism, we find this urge manifesting itself. Thus Ruysbroeck desires to penetrate beyond the Trinity into the Undifferentiated Godhead, that "dark silence where all lovers lose themselves."[6] But, for the most graphic, succinct, and passionate expressions of this yearning, we must turn, as we so often have to do, to the Sufis. In the following poem, strangely modern in spirit, yet withal thoroughly Sufi, Jalalu'd Din Rumi gives eloquent utterance to this type of piety.

> I died as mineral and became a plant,
> I died as plant and rose to animal,
> I died as animal and I was man.
> Why should I fear? When was I less by dying?
> Yet once more shall I die as man, to soar
> With angels blest; but even from angelhood
> I must pass on: all except God doth perish.
> When I have sacrificed my angel soul
> I shall become what no heart e'er conceived.
> Oh, let me not exist! for Non-existence
> Proclaims in organ tones, "To Him we shall return."[7]

And, in the third place, there is the outlook at once spiritualistic and atheistic, positing neither a personal God nor an all-devouring One, which we associate primarily with India, and which there appears in the Sāṁkhya and Mīmāṁsā philosophies and in Jainism. Each of these systems regards the soul or self as a permanent entity, involved during its sojourn in this world in error and evil, yet inherently capable of escaping from both. The self is the master of its own destiny. By spiritual training and self-discipline it can attain liberation, and so pass beyond birth and death. As to the nature of this liberated state there is, however, an important difference of opinion. The Sāṁkhya and Mīmāṁsā philosophies conceive of it negatively rather than positively. Deliverance, they teach, involves the dissociation of spirit and matter, and cessation on the part of the self from contact with physical objects. Since sorrow is, on this view, a more fundamental characteristic of experience than pleasure, it follows that elimination of the former carries with it elimination of the latter. Hence there is no ultimate bliss to be attained; there is only the termination of suffering. Jainism, on the other hand, regards the situation more optimistically. Positive bliss and boundless knowledge, it affirms, are the lot of the emancipated self. But, on either view, the self is an abiding and essential constituent of reality. It is neither created nor destroyed. Its end is the transcendence of all limitations and the full development of its highest capacities. And this end it attains, not, primarily, through the favor and by the aid of a superhuman self, nor yet through the loss of its own individuality, but by persistent obedience to the laws of the universe of which it is a part, whereby it is enabled to become the best that it has in it to be.

Now it would be very near the truth to assert that this third conception of man's last end has been introduced into western thought in the philosophy of McTaggart—near the truth, yet not quite the truth. It is, indeed, the case that McTaggart's view of man's last end does, in certain of its broad outlines, resemble that of the Hindu philosophies I have mentioned. His metaphysics, that is to say, is pluralistic and atheistic. Yet, if there be similarities, there are also profound differences, the nature of which will become apparent as we proceed.

There is, of course, no question of direct borrowing from Oriental sources on the part of McTaggart. He noted, indeed, with interest, the resemblances between his own conclusions and those of various eastern thinkers; yet his theory of man's destiny was developed out of his study of Hegel, and, in his later period after he had become convinced that it was necessary to abandon Hegel's dialectical method, was supported by arguments which, whatever else may be said of them, were certainly highly original.

Before we proceed further, however, it is essential that we should understand in what sense McTaggart was an atheist. As an ontological idealist he stands at the opposite pole from the materialist. And, in so far as religion can be identified with a concern for man's destiny both in this world and the next, his outlook is profoundly religious. No less than theism is his view utterly opposed to any philosophy which attempts to treat the individual self as an emergent or as a phenomenon, to derive it from that which is beneath it or to lose it in that which is above it. His attitude with respect to theism is, in fact, quite clear; yet it is perpetually liable to misrepresentation.

The word *God,* McTaggart points out, has been used both in popular phraseology and in theology to connote a being who is conceived of as personal. The history of religion fully bears out his assertion, not only with regard to the English word *God,* but also with regard to its equivalents in other languages. We all know what Osiris and Horus, Zeus and Apollo, Woden and Thor, or—to take a higher ground—what Ahura Mazda, Yahweh, and Allah, were supposed to be: namely, living conscious intelligences with whom it was possible to enter into personal relations. In philosophy, however, there is no corresponding unanimity. Thus various thinkers—Spinoza and Hegel among others—have used the word *God* to signify "all that truly exists, provided only that it possesses some sort of unity, and is not a mere aggregate, or a mere chaos."[8] This diversity of usage must be pronounced unfortunate, inasmuch as it is productive of a "dangerous ambiguity."[9] "It is impossible," McTaggart observes, "to keep philosophical terms for the use of philosophical students. Whenever the subject is one of general interest—and the existence of a God is certainly one of these—the opinions of great philosophers will be reported at second hand to the world at large."[10]

Since, therefore, a uniform usage is desirable, it is clearly the duty of philosophy to conform to that of religion and theology, and this for three reasons. In the first place, we cannot hope to change popular usage, inasmuch as this would involve altering the habitual phraseology of millions of people. In the second place, the average man has no substitute for the word *God,* whereas the philosopher can always talk about the Absolute. And, in the third place, the usage of philosophy is not itself uniform. Kant and Lotze, for instance, use the word *God* in the religious and theological sense.[11] Consequently, unless we believe in a God who is a Person, we ought to call ourselves atheists.[12]

To this conclusion Dr. Broad has advanced the objection that, if McTaggart's definition of God be taken strictly, "we should have to say that all Christians are atheists."[13] The point would have been put more accurately if he had written "that all Trinitarians are atheists," for not all Christians are Trinitarians. It is, of course, true that the Trinity cannot be a Person, since it is composed of three Persons.[14] But it does not at all follow that we should be forced to classify Trinitarians as atheists; on the contrary, we might more appropriately term them unconscious tritheists.

Those thinkers who use the word *God* in the sense in which Spinoza and Hegel used it are wont to say, consistently enough, that it is quite certain *that* God is, and that our sole task is to determine *what* he is. McTaggart's position is the direct antithesis of this. According to him, we know very well *what* God's nature is—that is to say, what we mean by the word *God;* the only question is, Does any existent entity actually possess this nature? McTaggart, then, would seem to be an atheist in the religious and theological, and—as he maintains—in the properly philosophical meaning of the word: namely, in the sense that he does not believe in a personal God. This is, indeed, the case; yet McTaggart does not completely close the door upon the theist, but leaves it slightly ajar. A few words of explanation will make my meaning clear.

In the first place, McTaggart is quite certain that God is not identical with the Absolute, for the Absolute includes all that exists, consequently it includes all selves. But, for McTaggart, it is an ultimate, synthetic, and self-evident proposition that one self cannot be included within another self.[15] Hence the Absolute cannot be a self, and so cannot be God. In the second place, the common view that God is at once omnipotent, creative, and good, is regarded by McTaggart as untenable. For there is evil in the universe, and this evil a good God would not tolerate, and an omnipotent God could prevent. In the third place, the hypothesis of a non-omnipotent creative God is rejected on the same ground, since a God who creates, even if non-omnipotent, is responsible for the nature of that which is created, inasmuch as it is an expression of his will. Moreover, the notion of creation is incompatible with McTaggart's doctrine of the unreality of time.

This leaves us with the hypothesis of a non-omnipotent, non-creative God, which McTaggart considers much more defensible. We cannot, indeed, assume that there is a non-omnipotent, non-creative Person who controls and governs the universe, for "it is only in time that the terms of a causal relation can be discriminated into a cause which is not an effect, and an effect which is not a cause, and so, since time is unreal, there can be no divine control."[16] Nevertheless, we must consider the possibility that there may be a self who *appears* to control the universe. "I see no reason," says McTaggart, "why there should not be such a person."[17] And, if there were, "the statement that there was a God would not be true, but it would have as close a relation to the truth as the statements that there are mountains in Switzerland, and that thunder follows lighting."[18] Such a being would be really a person, and really good. But he would not really be God, for his supreme power would not be real but apparent."[19]

There are two aspects of this conception which are of considerable interest. In the first place, it seems clear that McTaggart's apparent deity, like the gods of the Hindu philosophies to which I referred—who are themselves involved in the process of birth and death—is, *sub specie temporis,* himself in need of salvation rather than in a position to bestow it. And, in the second place, it is to be observed that, according to the view before us, when time fades into eternity God will cease to be God as men will cease to be men, and, on a basis of fully developed selfhood, they will one and all enjoy complete equality. We have here a remote analogy to the old Christian doctrine of deification, the equalitarianism being, of course, a characteristic peculiar to McTaggart's theory.

Would such a notion of God possess any religious value? McTaggart is doubtful whether it would have much. Napoleon would be said, in ordinary language, to have influenced the course of events in Europe to a vastly greater degree than did any one of his grenadiers. And it might be said of our apparent God, McTaggart observes, that

> if we regard him as supremely powerful in the same way in which we regard Napoleon as more powerful than the grenadier, we have got all that is practically wanted. But it may be doubted whether a religious emotion does not require to be based on something which is believed to be absolutely true. My feelings of fear and admiration towards Napoleon would probably not be diminished by my conclusion, based on philosophical arguments, that he was not powerful in absolute reality, but only appeared to be so, as there appear to be mountains in Switzerland. But then these emotions are not religious. And would the emotions with which I might regard a person whom I believed to be really God remain at all the same if I came to believe that he only appeared to be God?[20]

The question is one which does not greatly trouble McTaggart since, while he sees no impossibility in the existence of such a self, he sees not the faintest reason to believe that he actually does exist. Yet it is one which may concern us, inasmuch as we may conceivably find such a reason. I suggest, therefore, that the notion of such a self is capable of playing a greater rôle than McTaggart conceded it. For, even if it be true that time is unreal, and that con-

sequently, as McTaggart contended,[21] no causal relations can really hold between the self who appears to be God and other selves, still it would seem that there must be eternal relations which appear as causal relations, and which must be of great importance. In this connection, I wish to call attention to Dr. Broad's criticism of McTaggart's argument with respect to causal relations:

> I think that the argument is quite inconclusive, even if we accept McTaggart's analysis of causal propositions. According to this, the causal relation involves a relation of conveyance between certain characteristics. Now it is quite true that instances can be produced in which the relation of conveyance between two characteristics is reciprocal. E.g., being an equilateral triangle is conveyed by being an equiangular triangle. But it is also easy to produce instances in which the relation is not reciprocal. E.g., to take an example of McTaggart's, being now drunk conveys having drunk alcohol, but having drunk alcohol does not convey being now drunk. Or, to take a non-temporal example, being coloured conveys being spatial, but being spatial does not convey being coloured. Therefore there is no impossibility in there being a non-reciprocal relation of conveyance between certain timeless states of a certain self and certain other timeless states of all the rest of the selves in the universe.[22]

The criticism appears to be a just one. And the timeless relations between the self who appears as God—whom we may well call the *central* self—and the other selves must surely involve a peculiar intimacy which might well become the object of religious emotion.

It has seemed worth while thus briefly to review McTaggart's discussion of the problem of God for two reasons: first, to bring out the fact that his position is not utterly antagonistic to theism; and secondly—and this is of far greater importance—to show how completely divorced from the notion of God is his conception of man's last end. For, as we have seen, God is in no sense the bestower of salvation. In this respect McTaggart's outlook resembles that of the three Hindu philosophies which I have mentioned. On the other hand, his view differs from theirs in that he does not regard the attainment of salvation as dependent upon the free will of the individual, for, like the Calvinist, McTaggart is a strict determinist. Again, according to the Hindu thinkers, while the liberation of souls is perpetually going on, yet the temporal process will never come to an end, and since the number of souls is infinite, there will never be a time when all souls have been emancipated. For McTaggart, however, all selves, after undergoing an indefinite number of births and deaths, attain beatitude together at the end of the temporal process, as time fades into eternity. Salvation is thus identified with the transition from appearance to reality and from time to eternity. This notion of a heaven which is at once timeless and yet future bears, as McTaggart points out,[23] a distinct resemblance to the Christian conception. Furthermore, as salvation in his view is the ultimate destiny of all selves, McTaggart clasps hands with the Universalist.

Unlike the metaphysicians of the Sāṃkhya and Mīmāṃsā schools, with their emphasis upon the negative aspect of deliverance, McTaggart holds that the experience of the self, when freed from the illusion of time, will have a thoroughly positive content. He entirely concurs with the atheistic Jains, and with the pantheistic and theistic mystics, in maintaining that it will be an experience of bliss or beatitude. Moreover, he agrees with the theist that it will be an experience of love, of intense and soul-satisfying affection.

Sub specie temporis, love assumes various forms—the love of the sexes, the love of kinsfolk, the love of friends. It may arise in connection with physical desire, with blood-relationship, with habitual contact, with community of interests, or even for no apparent reason at all. But, whenever it does arise, it constitutes its own justification and presents itself as the supreme value. Moreover it brings with it a profound restlessness, a restlessness which springs from the desire to intuit directly the soul of the person loved. In this life the realization of that desire is impossible. We know others, even those dearest to us, only indirectly, through bodily manifestations. In eternity, however, it is otherwise. There the corresponding relation is one of direct perception by lover of beloved, there the accompanying emotion is far more intense than any which can be felt, or even imagined, here, and yet—because of the directness of the perception, and the completeness and intimacy of the union which this implies—the experience is one of utter satisfaction. Where there is neither change nor duration, there can be no sense of satiety; where the highest potentialities are brought to realization there can be no sense of inadequacy. This is the Beatific Vision, the enjoyment of which awaits us at the end of time. It is not a vision of God, but, in the case of each of us, it is a vision of those other selves who form the "differentiating group"[24] to which we belong. If there be any self who, *sub specie temporis,* appears as God, that self, *sub specie aeternitatis,* will be known and loved by the selves who perceive him precisely as other selves are known and loved.

From this consummation we are separated by that portion of the temporal series of events which stretches before us. Nevertheless, there are moments when, as McTaggart says, "it is curiously near us."[25] *Sub specie temporis,* the experience of love, however it arise and whatever form it take, constitutes, in McTaggart's words, "a strange dash into reality."[26] Though it lacks the intensity and intuitive directness which are present in the Absolute, it is still the very stuff of which eternity is made. Other values, indeed, are to be found there—knowledge, pleasure, virtue, and fulness of life. Yet none of these, nor any combination of these, can equal the value of love when it surpasses a certain degree of intensity,[27] and in the Absolute its intensity is at an extremely high level. The good and evil which characterize the various stages of the temporal series are, of course, preserved in the eternal. They qualify subordinate states included within it, but they do not qualify the Absolute as a whole; thus neither positive evil nor deficiency of good vitiates the unmixed good which characterizes it.

As we thus glance swiftly over the main outlines of his system, we may not inappropriately recall those lines of A. E.'s which might well have been written with McTaggart's philosophy in mind:

> I know when I come to my own immortal I will find there
> In a myriad instant all that the wandering soul found fair,
> Empires that never crumbled and thrones all glorious yet,
> And hearts ere they were broken and eyes ere they were wet.[28]

In this unavoidably brief and inadequate survey, I have sought to delineate the principal features of McTaggart's doctrine of eternal life, and of the Beatific Vision which is the content of that life. To deal in a short space with the complicated arguments advanced for its support would, needless to say, be impossible. The entire theory is, of course, based upon the doctrine of the unreality of time. The arguments whereby this basic doctrine is defended do not, indeed, depend upon conclusions previously reached in *The Nature of Existence,* and consequently can be examined without involving the rest of McTaggart's system; in the present connection, however, I can only say of them that they do not appear to me to have been satisfactorily refuted.[29] The positive characteristics of the theory in question, on the other hand, follow from the doctrine of determining correspondence; and it may be asserted that this last has been hopelessly ruined by the critique of Dr. Broad.[30] It is true that we cannot know what McTaggart might have said in reply to the points there made, and it is, perhaps, premature to conclude that the ruin is as irreparable as, at first glance, it appears to be. Nevertheless, even if we grant that the doctrine of determining correspondence is untenable, it does not follow that there is nothing left in McTaggart's theory of the Beatific Vision worthy of our consideration. After all, its main outlines are almost identical with those of the position elaborated in the *Studies in Hegelian Cosmology,* where very different arguments are employed to establish them. And, surely, the history of philosophy is full of instances where profound insight has outstripped logical demonstration.

Let me put the point in this way. If the naturalist or the emergent evolutionist be right, and what is higher has evolved—however mysteriously—from what is lower, a religious[31] view of the universe is rendered impossible. If, on the other hand, the universe be an intelligibly ordered system, and if values, as objective realities, be harmoniously included within that system, a religious attitude becomes inevitable. Now McTaggart has advanced a novel judgment as to the axiological primacy and metaphysical significance of love. Accordingly, anyone who believes that the universe is an intelligible system, whether because of McTaggart's arguments or for other reasons, is bound to consider whether the above judgment be true or false; and, if he accept it as true, he must also consider what the consequences will be for his general metaphysical outlook. I submit, therefore, that McTaggart has given the theist a great deal to think about, and that it behooves him to consider it with the utmost care.

Much of the non-theistic philosophy of our time has been written by men who are obviously strangers in the field of religious experience. All too frequently a shallow optimism betrays a woeful ignorance of values. In the present instance, however, it can scarcely fail to be recognized that McTaggart's doctrine of eternal life and of the Beatific Vision could have been elaborated only by a man of deep spirituality and a keen sense of values. What he has to say, therefore, is all the more worth listening to.

The contemporary theist is busy refuting the claims of an emergent-evolutionary naturalism, the general acceptance of which, he rightly believes, would prove disastrous to religion, to morality, and to civilization. From this point of view there is nothing to fear from McTaggart. His teaching provides the totalitarian with no material for propaganda. He is too difficult, too profound, too otherworldly. He is himself a religionist, and thus a fellow-citizen of the theist's. For the moment, then, he may be safely disregarded; but for the moment only. The present popularity of naturalism is largely due to three causes: (1) the reaction from an orthodoxy which seems no longer tenable; (2) the interest and excitement produced by various developments in physical science; and (3) the aspirations of a political radicalism which recognizes no moral standards. But this popularity will pass. The present intellectual and political turmoil will not endure forever. The inability of naturalism to provide a satisfactory foundation for civilization will become increasingly apparent, and, though it will doubtless long remain the favorite philosophy in certain circles, it is likely to be supplanted in popular estimation by a type of thinking of a more spiritual cast.

It is improbable, however, that its successor will be any form of orthodoxy; unless, indeed, general exhaustion cause the intellectual powers of mankind to undergo a complete eclipse. In liberal quarters the weaknesses of classical theism are widely acknowledged, and the effort is being made to rethink the whole problem. Such men as Professors Brightman, Dawes Hicks, and Hartshorne—to name no others—have already entered upon this task. And, as the undertaking progresses, the question is bound to arise, Can the theist answer McTaggart? Is his doctrine susceptible either of refutation or assimilation? And failure either to refute or to assimilate will mean that McTaggart has vanquished "not by denial but by completion."

Doubtless some will contend that McTaggart's philosophy, involving as it does, the unreality of time, is by that very fact ruled out of court. In reply to this objection, there are two things to be said. In the first place, the estimate of the value of love professes to be ultimate and self-evident, and consequently depends upon no prior assumptions. Hence, if true, it should be taken account of. And, in the second place, it is worth pointing out that it is difficult, if not impossible, to reconcile any conception—be it McTaggart's, the Christian, or any other—of a last end for man with an extreme temporalism.[32] Is final attainment conceivable so long as the permanent possibility of change remains; for, if such a possibility be real, must it not at some time pass into actuality? The philosophies of temporalism, however, have their own difficulties which, I should suggest, are not less formidable than those which confront McTaggart. Before adopting any one of them, therefore, the theist will do well to look before he leaps.

Obviously, it is not McTaggart's critique of theism that we have to examine so much as the implications of his positive teaching. The arguments which he brings against the theistic position are weighty, yet they are by no means wholy unfamiliar. The reality of evil, the relation of time to eternity—these are old problems with which theism has wrestled in the past, not always too successfully, and with which it will doubtless be ready to wrestle again. But, in his doctrine of the Beatific Vision, we have something which is new. And about it there is a spiritual magnificence to which the philosophy of religion cannot afford to be blind, even though it be to the conventional theist a stumbling block, and to the naturalist foolishness. We find, indeed, a hint of his teaching—as McTaggart himself has pointed out[33]—in the first epistle of St. John, and much of what he has written sounds like a commentary on the thirteenth chapter of First Corinthians. Yet these hallowed documents contain at most unconscious anticipations. In his explicit recognition of love *as such*—as distinct from altruism and benevolence[34]—as the supreme value, in his conception of it as involving a direct and eternal relation between selves, and in his estimate of its metaphysical importance, we have either a genuinely fresh insight or a fantastic dream.

It is easy to follow the example of Dr. Broad,[35] and to accuse McTaggart of sentimentality. But what do we mean by sentimentality? If we mean by it the affectation of emotion where none is felt, the charge is obviously unjust. McTaggart is transparently sincere and passionately in earnest. If we mean by sentimentality the undue exaltation of emotion, the exaggeration of it, or the wasting of it upon an undeserving object, then we beg the question with a word. McTaggart can be guilty of such things only if he be mistaken in his judgment that love of a certain depth and intensity is a greater good than any other value or possible combination of values, and it is precisely the soundness of this judgment which is now in question. Since it professes to be ultimate and self-evident, it cannot be argued about; it must be either simply accepted or rejected. If we accept it, we shall no doubt be called sentimentalists by those who reject it; yet we should not be very courageous if we permitted such a possibility to influence our decision in a matter in which truth should be our sole concern. The naturalist, of course, will reject it; he cannot do otherwise. Must the theist also reject it? McTaggart thinks that he must. Such is the obvious implication of the following statement in a letter of December 1898 to Mrs. McTaggart:

> It can't be nice to believe in God I should think. It would be horrible to think that there was anyone who

was closer to one than one's friends. I want to feel, and I do feel, that my love for them and the same love that other people have for their friends is the only real thing in the world. I have no room in my life for God, or rather my life is full of God already. I should say, as the Mahometan girl did in Kipling's story, "I bear witness that there is no God save thee, my beloved."[36]

What will the theist say to this? The Founder of Christianity taught that man should love God with all his heart and soul and mind and strength, and his neighbor as himself.[37] McTaggart holds that it is impossible for us to love ourselves,[38] but that is, perhaps, beside the point. It is evident that, for Jesus, God was the supreme object of love, and in this judgment classical theism has concurred. We are told to love the creatures, as it is said, "for God's sake," because he has created them and loves them. And it is frequently implied, and sometimes explicitly affirmed,[39] that we should love them with a love proportionate to their creatureliness, that too great a degree of love would amount to idolatry, to a giving to the creature of that which belongs to God alone.

McTaggart's position is, of course, the very opposite:

> Nothing but perfection could really deserve love. Hence, when it comes in this imperfect world, it only comes in cases in which one is able to disregard the other as he is now—that is, as he really is not—and to care for him as he really is—that is, as he will be.[40]

Thus the experience of love imparts a genuine, although a very inadequate, foretaste of the ultimate consummation. Concerning that consummation, writes McTaggart:

> We know that it is a timeless and endless state of love—love so direct, so intimate, and so powerful that even the deepest mystic rapture gives us but the slightest foretaste of its perfection. We know that then we shall know nothing but our beloved, and those they love, and ourselves as loving them, and that only in this shall we seek and find satisfaction.[41]

Plato, no doubt, would say that the love of persons is well enough in its way, yet that, after all, it is only a rung on the ladder whereby we ascend to the contemplation and love of the Good in itself. From this assertion McTaggart would vigorously dissent. He would say, I feel sure, that such an attitude would infect love with an element of infidelity utterly foreign to its nature. Love, he would insist, is itself our last end, wholly satisfying and all-sufficing. It is ultimate, and there is nothing beyond it.

This evaluation the traditional theist, who sees only in love directed toward God the supreme value, must and will reject. But many a liberal theist will, I believe, do so, if at all, only with a very bad grace. For, as a matter of fact, do not McTaggart's words ring true? Is it not the case that human love at its highest takes all there is of man or woman? Does not the entire personality offer itself with undivided and total devotion? And do we not account it the peculiar glory of our humanity that it is able so to do?

Can we find it in our hearts, for instance, to condemn Heloïse for refusing to pretend that she loved God more than she loved Abelard? Do we not really honor her? Must she not have seen in that very imperfect, all too weak and self-centered man, Abelard "as he will be," or as, perhaps, "he really is"; and did not her insight constitute in truth "a strange dash into reality"?

Contrast McTaggart's view with the traditional notion of a God who loves first and best only himself, who has created the world through no need of affection, but for his own glory and to diffuse his goodness, and who requires his creatures to love him more than they love one another. Is such a divine Narcissus a credible being? Can this doctrine escape the charge of inhuman coldness so often brought against otherworldly philosophies—a charge which emphatically fails to attaint McTaggart?

It is, in fact, McTaggart's profound humanity, his loyalty to the best in our nature, that constitutes the great charm of his thought. And for this very reason, I believe that in the long run he will prove a more potent enemy to traditional theism than the naturalist can ever be, precisely because he "works not by denial but by completion." He does not deny, that is to say, the claims and aspirations of personal affections and loyalties; on the contrary, he is concerned to establish their right to posit themselves as our last end. And it is by vindicating their ontological status as the very warp and woof of the Absolute that he seeks to complete the one-sided outlook of conventional otherworldliness through the conception of eternity, not as the negation, but as the consummation of the chief values manifested in time.

Is McTaggart's doctrine of the Beatific Vision capable of being assimilated as a whole or in part by a new theism? This is a question which only the future can answer definitely. The whole problem of theism is once more in the philosophic melting pot, and it is by no means clear as yet in what form it will come forth. I have already suggested that the notion of a non-omnipotent, non-creative God is capable of playing a greater part than McTaggart thought possible. Even if the central self can be looked upon as God only *sub specie temporis,* still his unique position in the universe, *sub specie aeternitatis,* would surely entitle him to be called *primus inter pares.* McTaggart thought the supposition "horrible" that God could be "closer to one than one's friends." Yet might not the central self also be a friend, to be loved as other friends are loved, with all there is of us, and can man give or God ask for more? Would it not be worth much to have such a friend ever present, never leaving or forsaking us? I shall not attempt to argue here in defense of this suggestion. But I am very sure that, unless the theist can accept McTaggart's evaluation of love and make good his case upon that basis, McTaggart will indeed have vanquished by "completion."

Notes

1. Introduction to the second edition of McTaggart's *Some Dogmas of Religion,* p. xxxi.

2. *Ibid.*, p. xliii.

3. See Watkin's reprint of the Bath edition of *The Way to Christ*, pp. 273 f.

4. R. A. Nicholson, *The Mystics of Islam*, p. 87.

5. *Ibid.*, p. 115.

6. See C. A. Wynschenk Dom's translation of *The Adornment of the Spiritual Marriage*, p. 178.

7. Nicholson, *op. cit.*, p. 168.

8. *The Nature of Existence*, vol. II, sec. 489.

9. *Loc. cit.*; cf. *Some Dogmas of Religion*, p. 188.

10. *Studies in Hegelian Cosmology*, p. 93.

11. *Some Dogmas of Religion, loc. cit.*

12. McTaggart's discussion of this subject is to be found in *Studies in Hegelian Cosmology*, sec. 96; in *Some Dogmas of Religion*, secs. 152-153; and in *The Nature of Existence*, vol. II. secs. 488-89.

13. *Examination of McTaggart's Philosophy*, II, II, 643.

14. Cf. Clement C. J. Webb's remark: "It is so often taken for granted that the Personality of God is a principal tenet of Christianity that it is not without surprise that we find this expression not only entirely absent from the historical creeds and confessions of the Christian Church, but even, until quite modern times, in the estimation of all but the minority of Christians who reject the doctrine of the Trinity, regarded as unorthodox." *God and Personality*, p. 61.

15. See *The Nature of Existence*, vol. II, secs. 401-4.

16. *Ibid.*, p. 182.

17. *Ibid.*, p. 183.

18. *Ibid.*

19. *Ibid.*

20. *Ibid.*

21. See above, p. 35.

22. *Examination of McTaggart's Philosophy*, II, II, 650.

23. *The Nature of Existence*, vol. II, secs. 738-39.

24. See *The Nature of Existence*, vol. II, ch. XXXIX.

25. *Studies in Hegelian Cosmology*, p. 253; *Philosophical Studies*, p. 213.

26. *Studies in Hegelian Cosmology*, p. 262; *Philosophical Studies*, p. 226.

27. *The Nature of Existence*, vol. II, sec. 851.

28. *Song and Its Fountains*, p. 48.

29. See my article entitled, "Dr. Broad's Refutation of McTaggart's Arguments for the Unreality of Time" in *The Philosophical Review* (Nov. 1941).

30. *Examination of McTaggart's Philosophy*, vol. I, bk. v.

31. We can, of course, apply the term *religion* to some ethical or political program, but then we are no longer talking about what has been meant historically by *religion*.

32. See my article, "This-wordliness and Otherworldliness, Time and Eternity," in *The Review of Religion* (Jan. 1944).

33. *Some Dogmas of Religion*, p. 121, n. 1.

34. *Studies in Hegelian Cosmology*, secs. 309-10; *Philosophical Studies*, pp. 267-69; *The Nature of Existence*, sec. 460.

35. *Examination of McTaggart's Philosophy*, II, 1, 123-24, 129-30.

36. See G. Lowes Dickinson's *McTaggart*, p. 87.

37. Mark, 12:29-31.

38. *The Nature of Existence*, vol. II, sec. 469.

39. See, for instance, Jonathan Edwards, *Dissertation on the Nature of True Virtue*, ch. II.

40. *Studies in Hegelian Cosmology*, p. 262; *Philosophical Studies*, pp. 225 f.

41. *The Nature of Existence*, II, 479.

Richard M. Gale (essay date 1966)

SOURCE: "McTaggart's Analysis of Time," in *American Philosophical Quarterly*, Vol. 3, No. 2, April, 1966, pp. 145-52.

[*In the following essay, Gale discusses McTaggart's theory of the unreality of time and examines the philosophical refutations of the theory, which fall into two separate and competing analyses.*]

McTaggart's famed argument for the unreality of time, first presented by him in 1908 in *Mind*, comprises both a positive and a negative thesis. The positive thesis, which is presented in the first part of the argument, contains an analysis of the concept of time, which McTaggart claims to be the only correct one. The negative thesis which is presented in the second part of the argument attempts to show that this analysis of the concept of time entails a contradiction. The assumption here is that any concept which is contradictory cannot be true of reality, and therefore time is unreal. It is vital to distinguish between these two theses, for, as we shall see, one group of analytic philosophers who answered his argument agreed with his positive thesis concerning the correct analysis of the concept of time, but they disagreed with his negative thesis that this analysis entails a contradiction. On the other hand, another group of analytic philosophers who refuted his argument disagreed with his positive thesis and claimed that time could be real even if his negative thesis is correct. Thus, while these two groups of philosophers are in agreement as to the unsoundness of McTaggart's argument, they adopt competing analyses of the concept of time in refuting this argument. The purpose of this paper will be to examine critically McTaggart's positive thesis and thereby bring into sharper focus the exact nature of the dispute between these two groups of analytic philosophers. But before doing this, a rough sketch will be given of McTaggart's argument as a whole.

In the first part of his argument McTaggart analyzes the concept of time in terms of two different types of temporal facts. First, there are facts about temporal relations of precedence and subsequence between events, and, second, there are facts about the pastness, presentness, and futurity of these same events. Corresponding to the first type of temporal facts is a series of events, called the "*B*-Series," which runs from earlier to later, its generating relation being *earlier (later) than;* while corresponding to the second type of temporal facts is a series of events, called the "*A*-Series," which runs from the past through the present and through the present to the future. While both of these series are essential for the reality of time, the *A*-Series is the more fundamental of the two, since the *B*-Series can be derived from it alone. The arguments advanced by McTaggart for the necessity and fundamentality of the *A*-Series will be examined shortly.

The second part of McTaggart's argument attempts to show that the *A*-Series, which has been shown in the first part to be essential for the reality of time, entails a contradiction and that therefore time is unreal. His main argument is as follows. Every event in the *A*-Series, assuming that there is no first or last event, has the mutually incompatible properties of being past, present, and future, which is a contradiction. The obvious reply to this seeming contradiction is to say that no event has two or more of these incompatible properties *at the same time,* but rather has them successively *at different moments of time.* But this reply will not do, since it involves either a vicious circle or a vicious infinite regress. What we have done is to explain away the contradiction of an event in the first-order time-series being past, present, and future by claiming that it has these determinations successively *at moments of time* in a second-order time-series. But since this second-order time-series is a time-series, the moments of time which are its members must have the properties of being past, present, and future. Therefore, we have explained away the contradiction inherent in the first-order *A*-Series, brought about by the fact that every event in it has all three mutually incompatible determinations of past, present, and future, by introducing a second-order *A*-Series. And this is to reason in a vicious circle, since we must presuppose an *A*-Series to rid the first *A*-Series of contradiction.

If we should try to remove the contradiction inherent in this second-order *A*-Series because all the moments of time in it are past, present, and future, by saying that these moments are *successively* future, present, and past at moments of time in some third-order *A*-Series, we are merely transferring this contradiction to this third-order *A*-Series. We are launched on a vicious infinite regress because at

any point in this regress at which we stop we are left with a contradictory *A*-Series. The curse of contradiction pursues us down this long infinite regress, being a sort of baton that each *A*-Series passes on to the *A*-Series which is one-order higher than itself.[1]

There are two different type of answers given to McTaggart's argument by analysts: (1) the *B*-Series alone is sufficient to account for time—the *A*-Series being reducible to the *B*-Series—and therefore the *A*-Series is not essential for the reality of time; and (2) the *A*-Series alone is sufficient to account for time—the *B*-Series being reducible to the *A*-Series—but the concept of the *A*-Series does not contain a contradiction. Answer (1), to be called the "*B*-Theory Answer," attacks McTaggart's positive thesis by denying that the *A*-Series is essential for time. It supports this contention by arguing that, contrary to what McTaggart said, the *A*-Series is reducible to the *B*-Series.[2] Answer (2), to be called the "*A*-Theory Answer," basically agrees with McTaggart's positive thesis that the *A*-Series is both necessary and fundamental, but denies his negative thesis that the concept of the *A*-Series is contradictory.[3] We shall now critically examine McTaggart's analysis of the *A*-Series to show that there is a crucial obscurity in the concept of the *A*-Series which has gone unnoticed by proponents of both the *A*- and *B*-Theory Answers. Once the concept of the *A*-Series is properly clarified, it will be seen that the *A*-Series, *properly understood,* is primitive, the *B*-Series being reducible to it. However, this thesis is not nearly as exciting as the one which the defenders of the *A*-Theory Answer thought they were espousing. While my clarification of the concept of the *A*-Series will tend to trivialize the *A*-Theory Answer's thesis of the primitiveness of the *A*-Series as opposed to the *B*-Series, what it will indicate about our concept of time is far from trivial, and, in fact, is of the highest importance.

Let us now scrutinize McTaggart's analysis of time. His analysis is phenomenological, being based on the way in which temporal position *appear* to us, but everything he says could be recast and for purposes of clarity needs to be recast, in linguistic idiom which describes the different way in which we *talk* about temporal positions. He begins by saying:

> Positions in time, as time appears to us *prima facie,* are distinguished in two ways. Each position is Earlier than some and Later than some of the other positions. . . . In the second place, each position is either Past, Present, or Future. The distinctions of the former class are permanent, while those of the latter are not.[4]

This can be rephrased linquistically as:

> There are two fundamentally different ways in which we make temporal determinations. First, we can say that one event *is*[5] earlier (later) than some other event; and, second, we can say that some event is now past (present, future). The sentences employed in making claims of the first sort make statements having the same truth-value every time they are uttered, while the sentences employed in the second sort of temporal deter-

mination may make statements having different truth-values if uttered at different times.

These two different ways of experiencing or talking about time are supposed to determine two different time-series.

> For the sake of brevity I shall give the name of the A-Series to that series of positions which runs from the far past through the near past to the present, and then from the present through the near future to the far future, or conversely. The series of positions which runs from earlier to later, or conversely, I shall call the B-series.[6]

McTaggart's concept of the B-Series is clear because we can see the connection between it and our use of the expression "earlier (later) than." This connection consists in the fact that *earlier (later) than* is the generating relation of the B-Series; that is, given any two non-simultaneous events, *x* and *y*, either *x is* earlier (later) than *y* or *y is* earlier (later) than *x*. The relation *earlier (later) than* is connected in the set of all non-simultaneous events.

Unfortunately, McTaggart's concept of the A-Series is not as clear, for while we can see the connection between the B-Series and talk about earlier or later than, we do not see the connection between the A-Series and our use of the predicates "is present," "is past" and "is future." Since the A-Series is a series, it must have a generating relation. But what could it be?[7] We know only that the generating relation of the A-Series, whatever it might be, must contain a temporal index since there is a different A-Series at any two different moments of time. The A-Series which McTaggart describes cannot be generated by the unqualified temporal indices "past," "present," and "future" since the A-Series involves not only that the events comprising it are past, present, and future but also that they are past and future by varying degrees. The necessity for the latter is contained in McTaggart's description of the A-Series as one "which runs from the *far* past through the *near* past. . . ." The use of the unqualified predicate "is now past" cannot distinguish between events in the far and in the near past: it determines a "blob past." Past, present, and future, rather than being the generating relation of the A-Series, merely indicate the kind of elements in the A-Series, just as +, - and o do not generate the series of integers but only indicate the kind of elements that belong to the series. Before attempting to answer the question as to what could be the generating relation of the A-Series, we shall consider McTaggart's arguments for the necessity and fundamentality of the A-Series.

McTaggart claimed that there could not be time without both a B-Series and an A-Series. His arguments in support of this are directed only to showing the necessity for the A-Series. Probably he thought that the necessity for the B-Series is so obvious as to require no further comment; for to conceive of a "time" which admitted of no distinctions between earlier and later times would be a conceptual absurdity.[8] While philosophers have rarely doubted the necessity for there to be a B-Series if there is to be time,

several of them, in particular those who defend the B-Theory Answer, have questioned the necessity of the A-Series. They have argued that although we always experience events as forming both a B- and an A-Series the determinations of events as past, present, and future are delusory or purely psychological, so that only the B-Series is objectively real. Against this line of reasoning McTaggart advances two arguments, the first showing tht change requires an A-Series and the second, which is also an argument for the fundamentality of the A-Series over the B-Series, showing that "earlier (later) than" can be defined in terms of "past," "present," and "future."

McTaggart's first argument for the necessity of the A-Series has as its basic premiss that there cannot be time without change, which would be granted by proponents of both the A- and B-Theory Answers to his argument. The purpose of this argument is to show that there could not be change (and therefore time) without the A-Series. The argument proceeds by examining every possible candidate for the title of "change" other than changes in the pastness, presentness, and futurity of events, and showing that none of them is logically possible. Thus, by a process of elimination, it is inferred that the only change possible is a change in an event's position in the A-Series. If time consisted only of a B-Series the following are the possible candidates for "change."

(i) It might be held that an event in the B-Series could change. Maybe the death of Queen Anne could somehow cease to be the death of Queen Anne. But this is absurd. Events can never cease to be just the sort of events they are.

> Take any event—the death of Queen Anne, for example—and consider what changes can take place in its characteristics. That it is a death, that it is the death of Anne Stuart, that it has such causes, that it has such effects—every characteristic of this sort never changes.[9]

Events remain just as sweet, young, and innocent as they always were for McTaggart. By the law of identity each event must forever remain itself.

(ii) It might be contended that two events in the B-Series could merge so as to form a new event. But such conjugal union between events is logically unthinkable for the reason given in (i): it would require that the two events which merge would cease to be themselves. If the death of Queen Anne and the death of Stalin were somehow to merge to form a new event consisting of the death of Queen Stalin then these events would no longer be the same events.

(iii) Events might be thought to have the ability to get in or out of a B-Series, and this could constitute the change we are seeking. But this sort of change also is logically impossible, for the B-Series is a sort of logically escape-proof prison. An event "can never get out of any time-series in which it once was." Nor can an event enter into a B-Series in which it is not a member, since positions in the B-Series are permanent.

(iv) Possibly change could arise from events shifting in their position in the *B*-Series? This also is logically impossible, for our concept of the generating relation of the *B*-Series—*earlier than*—is such that it is nonsensical to speak about events changing in their relations of precedence to other events or changing in the metrical features of these relations. "If *N* is ever earlier than *O* and later than *M,* it will always be, and has always been, earlier than *O* and later than *M,* since the relations of earlier and later are permanent." Events are not able to sneak up on each other.

From this McTaggart concludes that the *B*-Series cannot give us change, and therefore the *B*-Series, although necessary for the reality of time, is not sufficient. To get change and therefore time we must invoke the change in the position of an event in the *A*-Series. Such changes are the only logically possible ones. For there to be such change there must be an *A*-Series. Take away the *A*-Series and the *B*-Series ceases to be a temporal series.

A proponent of the *B*-Theory Answer would claim that McTaggart has overlooked one possible candidate for the title of "change," namely that it is things, rather than events, that change, and such change consists in a thing having a different quality at one phase of its history than it has at an earlier or later phase; e.g., a poker changes in that it is at one time hot and at a later time cool. Such qualitative changes *in* things can be analyzed solely in terms of the *B*-relations of subsequence or precedence between qualitatively different states which comprise the history of a single thing. Moreover, these qualitatively different states of a single thing can be described in a tenseless language, which makes no references to the *A*-determinations, i.e., pastness, presentness, or futurity, of these states; e.g., "The poker *is* hot on Monday" and "The poker *is* not hot at times other than Monday."[10] McTaggart raised the following objection to this analysis:

> This makes no change in the qualities of the poker. It is always a quality of that poker that it is one which is hot on that particular Monday. And it is always a quality of that poker that it is one which is not hot at any other time. Both these qualities are true of it at any time—the time when it is hot and the time when it is cold. And therefore it seems to be erroneous to say that there is any change in the poker.[11]

McTaggart's reply fails because of an equivocation on the word "always." He argues that because the tenseless statement "The poker *is* hot on Monday" is *always* true, i.e., true independently of time in the sense that the use of this sentence makes a true statement every time it is uttered, the state of affairs described by this statement must *always,* i.e., in the temporal sense of "always," be occurring or existent. Because statements describing events in a tenseless manner are *always* true it does not require that these events are sempiternal: to claim the opposite is an unwarranted addition of an eternalistic ontology to a tenseless (or token-reflexive free) logic.

McTaggart's other argument to show the dependency of the *B*-Series upon the *A*-Series fares no better than his first one. This argument, which is never stated explicitly, is that our understanding of the concept of earlier (later) than essentially involves reference to the concepts of past, present, and future. *Earlier than* is a temporal relation only because its relata have *A*-determinations. At one place he claimed that we could *define* "earlier than" in terms of the *A*-determinations of "past, present, and future."

> The term *P* is earlier than the term *Q,* if it is ever past while *Q* is present, or present while *Q* is future.[12]

If it is possible to define "earlier than" in terms of "past, present, and future" it will follow not only that there could be no *B*-Series without an *A*-Series, but also that the *B*-Series is reducible to the *A*-Series, since the generating relation of the *B*-Series is definable in terms of *A*-determinations.

McTaggart's attempt to define the *B*-relation "earlier than" in terms of the three *A*-determinations fails because of circularity. The *definiens* of the definition contains the statements, "*P is* past while *Q is* present" and "*P is* present while *Q is* future," which mean the same as, respectively, "*P is* past at *Q*" and "*Q is* future at *P*." The predicates ". . . *is* past at . . ." and ". . . *is* future at . . ." are synonyms for ". . . *is* earlier than . . . ," in that all three are tenseless two-place predicates which, when a non-indexical or non-token-reflexive event expressions are substituted for their blank spaces, express a timelessly true or false statement about a *B*-relation of precedence between two events.[13] "*Is* past (present, future) at some event or date," unlike "is now past (present, future)," does not contain a temporal index. But, as pointed out above, an *A*-determination must contain a temporal index, for two non-simultaneous uses of the *A*-determinations of "past," "present," and "future" will determine different *A*-Series of events. The event(s) which is present in one of them will not be in the other. Therefore, McTaggart is cheating by allowing "*is* past (future) at" to count as *A*-determinations. If the copulae of the statements in the *definiens* are taken to be tensed—"*P* is now past while *Q* is now present" and "*P* is now present while *Q* is now future"—then the *definiendum* is not logically equivalent to the *definiens;* for it might be the case that *P is* earlier than *Q,* but be false that *P* or *Q* is now present, in which case the *definiendum* is true and the *definiens* false.

If we take the *A*-Series to be determined by an unqualified past, present, and future, i.e., a past, present, and future that do not admit of degrees, then it can be shown that the *B*-Series cannot be reduced to the *A*-Series, this being due to the fact that the *B*-relation "earlier than" cannot be defined in terms of an unqualified "past, present, and future." In the first place, it is fallacious to argue that *earlier than* can be analyzed in terms of *A*-determinations because there are *A*-determinative statements which imply a tenseless *B*-relation statement but no tenseless *B*-relation statement that implies an *A*-determinative statement; e.g., "*P* is present and *Q* is future" entails, but is not entailed by, "*P* is earlier than *Q*."[14] For the fact that a statement containing a term *X* entails, but is not entailed by, a statement containing *Y* does not show that *Y* is analyzable in terms of *X*. For example, "All *animals* are mortal" entails, but is not entailed by, "All *men* are mortal," but this surely does not show that men are analyzable purely in terms of the concept of an animal. Thus, while it is true that there is an asymmetry in information content between a pure *B*-relation language and a pure *A*-determinative language, in that everything sayable in the former is sayable in the latter but not vice-versa, it does not establish that *B*-relations are reducible to *A*-determinations, and therefore that the *B*-Series is reducible to the *A*-Series.

Another attempt to reduce the *B*-Series to a *pure A*-Series, i.e., an *A*-Series determined by the use of an unqualified "past, present, and future," which is also unsuccessful, involves giving a "definition in use" of "earlier than" in terms of the three unqualified *A*-determinations, taken together. By a *definition in use* of a term is meant one which gives an analysis of a statement containing this term: a necessary, though possibly not sufficient, condition for a successful analysis is that the *analysandum* and the *analysans* are logically equivalent. Let us try to analyze a tenseless *B*-relation statement in terms of a logically equivalent disjunction of *A*-determinative statements:

> (I) *P is* earlier than *Q* ≡ *P* is past and *Q* is present *or P* is past and *Q* is future *or P* is present and *Q* is future

in which 'P' and 'Q' are expressions referring to an event or state of affairs. It is quite apparent that (I) is not a logical equivalence, for whereas it could not be the case that the disjunction of *A*-determinative statements in the *analysans* is true and the *B*-relation statement in the *analysandum* is false, it could be the case that the *analysandum* is true and the *analysans* is false. The reason for this, which has already been given in the above discussion of McTaggart's definition, is that if *P* and *Q* are either both past or both future, *P* being *more past* than *Q* or *Q* being *more future* than *P*, then each of the three disjuncts would be false. To give an adequate definition in use of a *B*-relation in terms of a disjunction of *A*-determinative statements we must enlarge our concept of an *A*-determination so as to include "more past" and "more future" as well as an unqualified "past," "present," and "future." With this expanded concept of an *A*-determination we can add two disjuncts to the *analysans* of (I):

> (II) *P is* earlier than *Q* ≡ *P* is past and *Q* is present *or P* is past and *Q* is future *or P* is present and *Q* is future *or P* is more past than *Q* or *Q* is more future than *P*.

What is to be concluded from this discussion is that the *B*-Series cannot be reduced to a *pure A*-Series, but that it can be reduced to an *impure A*-Series, i.e., an *A*-Series which is determined not only by an unqualified past, present, and future but also by more past and more future.[15] Thus the thesis of McTaggart and the *A*-Theory Answer that the *B*-Series is reducible to the *A*-Series is correct, provided that we are speaking of an *impure A*-Series. This qualification greatly trivializes their thesis. Not only

can the *B*-relation *earlier (later) than* be analyzed in terms of the *five A*-determinations, taken together, but the same is true for the relation *simultaneous with*. The latter can be classified as a *B*-relation for the following two reasons. First, the relation of *simultaneity* is needed to construct the *B*-Series. The *B*-Series includes the totality of events which make up the history of the world. The generating relation of this series—*is earlier than*—is not connected in this set of events, since some events are simultaneous with each other. *Is earlier than* related classes of simultaneous events. The relation of *simultaneity* is needed in determining the classes of events which are ordered by the relation of *earlier than* to form the *B*-Series. Therefore, the relation of *simultaneity* is needed in the construction of the *B*-Series. Second, ". . . *is* simultaneous with . . ." has the same logic as ". . . *is* earlier than . . ." in that both are tenseless two place predicates expressing a temporal relation which, when non-indexical event expressions are substituted for their blank spaces, make timelessly true or false statements. The following is a reduction of "*is* simultaneous with" to a disjunction of *A*-determinative statements:

> (III) *P is* simultaneous with *Q* ≡ (*P* is present and *Q* is present) *or* (*P* is past and *Q* is past and it is not the case that either *P* is more past than *Q* or *Q* is more past than *P*) *or* (*P* is future and *Q* is future and it is not the case that either *P* is more future than *Q* or *Q* is more future than *P*).

Once again, it was necessary to use "more past (future)" in carrying out the reduction.[16]

In summary, an impure, but not a pure, *A*-Series is also a *B*-Series, in that a statement describing the *A*-determinations of events entails a statement describing tenseless *B*-relations between these events. However, a *B*-Series is not also a specific *A*-Series, in that a statement describing *B*-relations between events does not entail a statement describing the specific *A*-determinations of these events, but only a disjunction of statements describing different possible combinations of the *A*-determinations of these events. Thus, an *A*-Series already is some specific *B*-Series, but a *B*-Series is not at the same time some specific *A*-Series. This conclusion helps us to see why McTaggart's attempt to derive the *B*-Series from a conjunction of the *A*-Series with a *C*-Series, i.e., a series whose generating relation is non-temporal, is either pointless or futile.

> We can now see that the *A*-Series, together with the *C*-Series is sufficient to give us time. . . . The *B*-Series . . . is not ultimate. For given a *C*-Series of permanent relations of terms, which is not in itself temporal, and therefore is not a *B*-Series, and given the further fact that the terms of this *C*-Series also form an *A*-Series, and it results that the terms of the *C*-Series become a *B*-Series, those which are placed first, in the direction from past to future, being earlier than those whose places are *further in the direction of the future*.[17]

If the *A*-Series referred to in this quotation is an impure *A*-Series, then it is already a *B*-Series; and therefore it is pointless, since unnecessary, to combine this *A*-Series with another series in order to derive the *B*-Series. But if the *A*-Series referred to by McTaggart is a pure *A*-Series then it can be shown that his attempt to derive the *B*-Series in the manner described is futile. Consider the problem of correlating the infinitely denumerable members of a pure *A*-Series with the members of a *C*-Series, such as the series of integers. There is no problem in correlating the present event(s) in the pure *A*-Series with the number o in the *C*-Series of integers. But it is impossible to correlate the past and future events of this *A*-Series respectively with the minus and plus integers because this *A*-Series contains a "blob" past and future, i.e., one which admits of no distinction between more past and less past. To make this correlation we must import a structural order into the past and future of the *A*-Series by introducing the concept of more past and more future, which, incidentally, is exactly what McTaggart does when he speaks of terms that are "*further* in the direction of the future." We must say something like "the more past (or future) an event is in the *A*-Series the smaller (or larger) the integer with which it is correlated."

Having clarified McTaggart's ambiguous concept of the *A*-Series and shown that only the impure *A*-Series is a series, we can now answer our original question concerning the generating relation of the (impure) *A*-Series. The answer is that its generating relation is *earlier than,* which is also the generating relation of the *B*-Series. Since a *B*-Series must also be an *A*-Series, though not any specific *A*-Series, it follows that the generating relation of the *B*-Series must also generate an *A*-Series, though not any one specific *A*-Series. There is another way of answering this question. The *A*-Series is formed from a conjunction of two different series having a common member, which serves as the *terminus ad quem* of one and the *terminus ab quo* of the other. There is a series whose generating relation is *more past than,* and there is another series whose generating relation is *more future than.* These two series can be conjoined to form an (impure) *A*-Series because the *terminus ad quem* of the series of past events is the present event(s) while the *terminus ab quo* of the series of future events is also the present event(s).

Regardless of which answer we give to the question concerning the generating relation of the *A*-Series we have to invoke the concepts of more past and more future. It might be objected, and not without plausibility, that these concepts involve a tenseless *B*-relation because a statement of the form, "*x* is now more past than *y*," must be *analyzed* into a conjunction of the *B*-relation statement, "*x is* earlier than *y*" and the *A*-determinative statement, "*y* is now past." And if this is so, then our reduction of *B*-relations to *A*-determinations by logical equivalence (II) is circular, since the final two disjuncts in the *analysans* (the ones using "more past" and "more future") contain *B*-relation statements. There are two ways of countering this objection. First, it could be argued that the statement, "*x* is more past than *y*," is an *A*-determinative or tensed statement because it employs a sentence which has the same temporal restrictions placed upon its use as are placed

upon the use of sentences, such as "*x* is now past," which unquestionably are used to make an *A*-determinative statement.[18] The utterance of "*x* is more past than *y*" at different times may make statements having different truth-values, which could not happen with different utterances of a sentence used in making a *B*-relation statement, such as "*x is* earlier than *y.*" This fact, however, is not decisive in showing that this statement cannot be analyzed into a conjunction of a *B*-relation statement and an *A*-determinative statement; for the conjunction of an *A*-determinative and *B*-relation statement will always make an *A*-determinative statement, just as, analogously, the conjunction of a contingent and a necessary statement will always make a contingent statement. A more effective way to meet this charge of circularity in our reduction of *B*-relations to *A*-determinations is to claim, as we do in (II), that "*x* is more past than *y*" *entails* "*x is* earlier than *y*" but deny that we must *analyze* "*x* is more past than *y*" into the conjunction of "*x is* earlier than *y*" and "*y* is now past." I know of no argument that can be given to show that we must accept this as an *analysis* of "*x* is more past than *y.*"

I am not very happy with this reply to the charge of circularity. It might be thought that this rather indecisive result could be avoided by offering a different reductive analysis of *B*-relations to *A*-determinations than that given in (II), e.g., instead of "more past than" we would have used "preceded," "was earlier than," or "occurred a longer time ago than," etc., but they are just as susceptible to the charge of circularity as is "more past than." We might try and recast McTaggart's question about the relation between the *B*- and the *A*-Series by using the *connectives* "before" and "while" instead of the *relations* "earlier than" (and "simultaneous with"). The former take sentences as their arguments, unlike the latter which take only event, or state of affairs, expressions as their arguments. The question then is whether we can analyze a statement containing the connective "before" and tenseless statements for its arguments into a logically equivalent disjunction of statements containing "before" and "while" and only *A*-determinative statements for their arguments. This can be accomplished as follows:

> (IV) *P is Q* before *R is S* ≡ (*P* was *Q* and *R is S*) *or* (*P* was *Q* and *R* will be *S*) *or* (*P is Q* and *R* will be *S*) *or* (*P* had been *Q* while *R* was *S*) *or* (*P* will have been *Q* while *R* will be *S*).[19]

Since (IV) is the analogue of (II) in connective discourse it should not surprise us to find that (IV) is haunted by the same specter of circularity as is (II). Once again the difficulty occurs in the final two disjuncts. Instead of the problem arising with "more past than," as it does with (II), it concerns the use of the compound tense "had (will have) been." One might claim that we must *analyze* "*P* had been *Q* while *R* was *S*" into the conjunction of the *A*-determinative statements, "*R* was *S*," with the tenseless *B*-relation statement, "*P is Q* before *R is S*," thus making the analysis circular. And once again the reply must be that there is no reason why we must accept this as an analysis. One thing is certain: by allowing, as we must, "more past (future) than" or a compound tense to count as an *A*-determination we trivialize the thesis of McTaggart and the *A*-Theory Answer that the *B*-Series is reducible to the *A*-Series. But what this indicates about our concept of time is far from trivial. It shows that our concept of time involves not only the three unanalyzable concepts of past, present, and future, but also the notion of a structural order, and it was because of the latter that we had to introduce the concepts of more past and more future.[20]

Notes

1. It is not the purpose of this paper to answer this argument. For a complete bibliography and summary of the answers given to this argument see L. Mink, "Time, McTaggart and Pickwickian Language," *The Philosophical Quarterly,* vol. 10 (1960), pp. 254-263.

2. The most illustrious defender of this thesis is Bertrand Russell, and among his followers are R. B. Braithwaite, A. J. Ayer, W. V. Quine, N. Goodman, D. Williams, and J. J. C. Smart.

3. C. D. Broad is the leading exponent of this answer, and among his followers are J. Wisdom, S. Stebbing, D. F. Pears, and W. Sellars.

4. J. M. E. McTaggart, *The Nature of Existence,* vol. II (Cambridge, 1927), pp. 9-10.

5. We will adopt the convention in this paper of italicizing tenseless verbs and copulae.

6. McTaggart, *op. cit.,* p. 10.

7. Surprisingly, none of McTaggart's commentators and critics have asked this basic question. The explanation for this strange oversight might be due to the ease with which we can *picture* the *A*-Series, and often this picture involves a correlation between the events of the *A*-Series and the marks on the edge of a ruler. Having such a picture of the *A*-Series we then think we understand it and forget to ask what is its generating relation. This is a good example of the danger of pictorial thinking.

8. H. Bergson's analysis of time, I believe, comes very close to committing this absurdity, for he denies that events are distinct from each other.

9. McTaggart, *op. cit.,* p. 13.

10. Russell's analysis of change as arising from the fact that there are propositional functions (e.g., "The poker is hot at *t,*" in which '*t*' is a free variable) which are true of some, but not all moments of time, is in *The Principles of Mathematics* (London, 1903), p. 472.

11. McTaggart, *op. cit.,* p. 15.

12. *Ibid.,* p. 271.

13. It is crucial to find a language-neutral criterion for distinguishing between an *A*-determinative, or tensed, statement and a *B*-relation, or tenseless, statement. The strategy in discovering this criterion is to begin with paradigm cases of *A*-determinative statements, such as "*S* is now (was, will be) *P,*" or "There now is a *P*ing of *S,*" and to extrapolate from these examples a set of rules of use for the sentences employed in making these statements. These rules of use are: a present tensed sentence can be used to make a true statement only if uttered simultaneously with the event described, and so on for the other tensed sentences. Thus, an *A*-determinative statement is one which is made by the use of a sentence which has temporal restrictions placed upon its use: its use at different times may make statements having different truth-values. A *B*-relation, or tenseless, statement is one which is made through the use of a sentence which has no temporal restrictions placed upon its use: the utterance of a tenseless sentence makes a statement having the same true-value whenever it is uttered. For a detailed account of the logic of tensed and tenseless statements see my articles: "Endorsing Predictions," *The Philosophical Review,* vol. 70 (1961), pp. 376-385; "Tensed Statements," *The Philosophical Quarterly,* vol. 12 (1962), pp. 53-59; "A Reply to Smart, Mayo, and Thalberg on 'Tensed Statements'," *The Philosophical Quarterly,* vol. 13 (1963), pp. 351-356; "Is It Now Now?" *Mind,* vol. 73 (1964), pp. 97-105; "The Egocentric Particular and Token-Reflexive Analyses of Tense," *The Philosophical Review,* vol. 73 (1964), pp. 213-228; and "Existence, Tense, and Presupposition," *The Monist,* vol. 50 (1966).

14. I committed this fallacy in my paper, "Tensed Statements," *op. cit.,* and am indebted to Professor J. J. C. Smart for pointing this out in his paper, "'Tensed Statements': A Comment," *The Philosophical Quarterly,* vol. 12 (1962), pp. 264-265.

15. It might be pointed out that the concept of more past (future) is not a metrical concept. Even if time has no intrinsic metric (due to there being no ultimately discrete events) and we have not laid down conventional co-ordinative definitions for the metricization of time, we can say that one temporal interval is more past (future) than another due to the fact that these intervals overlap, one of them containing the other as a part of itself. For an excellent discussion of this see A. Grünbaum, *Philosophical Problems of Space and Time* (New York, 1963), chap. I.

16. The thesis of the *B*-Theory Answer that the *A*-Series can be reduced to the *B*-Series obviously is false, since an *A*-determinative statement cannot be analyzed into a tenseless *B*-relation statement, or even a disjunction of such statements. "*P* is present and *Q* is future" certainly is not logically equivalent to "*P* is earlier than *Q,* or *P* is later than *Q,* or *P* is simultaneous with *Q,*" for the latter is a tautology, assuming that '*P*' and '*Q*' refer successfully, while

the former is contingent. And even if we make the latter non-tautological by dropping one of its three disjuncts it could still be true and the former tensed statement be false. "*P* is now present" can be analyzed into "*P is* simultaneous with this (or now)," in which "this" is a demonstrative referring either to some event experienced by the speaker when he makes his utterance or to the utterance-token itself, but the latter is a tensed or *A*-determinative statement according to the criterion given in n. 13 above.

17. McTaggart, "The Unreality of Time," *Mind,* vol. 17 (1908), p. 462. My italics. This article is reprinted in McTaggart, *Philosophical Studies* (London, 1934).

18. See n. 13 above.

19. "*S is P* while *R is T*" is logically equivalent to "*S is P* and *R is T or S* was *P* while *R* was *T or S* will be *P* while *R* will be *T.*" This is the analogue in connective discourse to reduction (III).

20. This paper was written while the author was engaged in research on "The Logic of Time Language" under a National Science Foundation grant. The author is indebted to Professor Edmund Gettier and Mr. Jay Rosenberg for their critical comments on a draft of the paper.

E. J. Lowe (essay date 1987)

SOURCE: "The Indexical Fallacy in McTaggart's Proof of the Unreality of Time," in *Mind,* Vol. 96, No. 381, January, 1987, pp. 62-70.

[*In the following essay, Lowe argues against McTaggart's theory in which he purports that time cannot be real because of contradictions in "A-series expressions."*]

Events, as McTaggart pointed out, may not only be described as being *earlier* and *later* than one another (and as such constituting the 'B series') but also as being *past, present* and *future* (and as such constituting the 'A series').[1] B-series sentences do not alter in truth value with time: if '*e*[1] is earlier than *e*[2]' is ever true, it is always true, whereas '*e* happened yesterday', if true today, will not be true tomorrow.[2] McTaggart holds that the reality of time demands the reality of the A series (the B series alone will not suffice) because, he considers, change is essential to time but can only be explained by reference to the A series. Suppose it is held (as Russell held) that my poker's changing from being hot to being cold consists merely in the fact that it is hot at one time and cold at a later time. According to McTaggart, this is inadequate, because although we may similarly say that my poker is hot at one end but cold at the other, this fact about it, which is formally analogous to the previous one, does not imply change.[3] There must in addition be something which distinguishes time from space in this regard, and only participation in the A

series seems to suffice. So, if the A series is unreal, so are the B series and time in general. (Hugh Mellor has argued recently that a further relevant difference is that objects like pokers are 'wholly' present at any time at which they exist, but not necessarily at any place at which they exist, because such objects have spatial but not temporal parts.[4] Although the merits of this suggestion are not something I mean to discuss here, my feeling is that while the doctrine about parts is correct, it does not constitute a relevant difference between time and space, i.e. one which explains why time, but not space, is the dimension of change.)

The structure of McTaggart's argument against the reality of time is, then, as follows:

(1) Time essentially involves change.

(2) Change can only be explained in terms of A-series expressions.

(3) A-series expressions involve contradiction and so cannot describe reality.

(4) Therefore, time is unreal.

Of course, not all philosophers accept (1), since some claim to be able to make sense of the notion of time in an unchanging world; but I shall not be questioning (1) here. Most philosophers who oppose McTaggart's conclusion would, I think, challenge either (2) or (3), or both—I have yet, of course, to examine McTaggart's reasons for holding (3), which I shall find wanting. An interesting position is held by Mellor, who accepts (3) but not (2). Mellor holds that McTaggart succeeds in demonstrating the unreality of *tense* (there are, for Mellor, no tensed facts), but not that of *time,* since he holds (as I have already remarked) that change can be explained without reference to the A series. Another interesting feature of Mellor's position is that, while rejecting the notion of tensed facts, he insists that the possession of tensed *beliefs* is indispensable for rational action, since without them agents cannot know *when* to act appropriately.[5] While admiring the ingenuity of Mellor's position, I have no sympathy for it, because instead of accepting (3) but not (2), I accept (2)—or at least find it very plausible—but not (3).

What exactly are McTaggart's reasons for holding (3), that the A series involves contradiction? McTaggart starts with the observation that *past, present,* and *future* are incompatible predicates. An event which is past, for example, is *ipso facto* neither present nor future. But, he says, change consists precisely in future events becoming present and present ones becoming past.[6] So, every event must, after all, be future *and* present *and* past, and so have incompatible predicates ascribable to it. (Even if there is a first event or a last event because time has a beginning or an end, such an event must still have *two* of the incompatible predicates ascribable to it; so let us ignore this complication.) Now, the obvious rejoinder to this, McTaggart realises, is to point out that we do not have to say that any event is *simultaneously* past, present, and future, which would indeed be contradictory. We can say instead that an event which *is* present *will be* past and *was* future. However, he argues, the same threat of contradiction then arises at this higher level of second-order tenses. For instance, to say that an event *was future* is to say that it is *future in the past* (where this last 'is' may be read as tenseless). But this same event is also *past in the past,* which is again inconsistent. To this the response might once more be made that such an event is not *simultaneously* past in the past and future in the past: rather, what *was* future in the past *will be* past in the past. However, repeated recourse to this manœuvre of resorting to higher-order tenses in order to evade the threatened contradiction can only serve to generate a (vicious) infinite regress, and so the manœuvre can by no means resolve the original difficulty arising with the first-order tenses.

Michael Dummett has perhaps expressed this crucial part of McTaggart's argument in the most succinct way to date.[7] He points out that there are nine second-order tenses, which may be represented as follows:

$$\left\{ \begin{array}{c} \text{past} \\ \text{present} \\ \text{future} \end{array} \right\} \text{ in the } \left\{ \begin{array}{c} \text{past} \\ \text{present} \\ \text{future} \end{array} \right\}$$

However, three of these, namely

$$\left\{ \begin{array}{c} \text{past} \\ \text{present} \\ \text{future} \end{array} \right\} \text{ in the present}$$

are, he says, just *equivalent* to the three first-order tenses, so that if there is a threat of contradiction on the first level it cannot be evaded merely by moving up a level.

Let us look at McTaggart's reasoning a little more closely. We attempt to avoid the initial threat of contradiction, it is said, by stating that an event that *is* present (i.e. is present in the present) *will be* past (i.e. is past in the future) and *was* future (i.e. is future in the past). (Of course, the parenthetical uses of 'is' in the previous sentence should again be seen as tenseless.) But is this move to second-order tenses the proper or only response to make, or does it just invite trouble? Does the notion of higher-order tenses, strictly speaking, even make sense at all? (The presence of pluperfect and future perfect constructions in European languages should not be seen as decisive on this point; nor should we be too deferential to the deliverances of so-called 'tense logic'.) Consider this: is it true to say of a future event that it *will be present* (is 'present in the future')? One might on first reflection be inclined to say yes, but in fact the answer is surely *no*. What *may* be correct is something significantly (though not unmistakably) different, namely, that if *e* is a future event, then there will be a time when the sentence '*e* is present' is true (expresses a true statement). Similarly, rather than saying of a past event *e* that it *was present* (or is 'present in the past'), we should at most say that the sentence '*e* is present', though now false, was true. I shall suggest that by emphasizing distinctions like these we may avoid the entanglements in which McTaggart tempts us to become ensnared.

At this point it is helpful to accentuate a feature of A-series expressions which McTaggart himself stressed less than do many modern philosophers of time, namely, their *indexicality* (or 'token-reflexiveness'). '*e* is present' means, of course, '*e* is happening *now*', and 'now' may usefully be compared with other indexical expressions like 'here' and 'I'. The truth conditions of utterances containing indexicals are context-dependent. Thus, the utterance of a token of the sentence '*e* is happening now' is true if and only if the token is uttered at a time *t* such that *e* is happening at *t* (where the last three occurrences of 'is' are to be read tenselessly, of course). Similarly, the utterance of a token of the sentence '*e* is happening here' is true if and only if the token is uttered at a place *s* such that *e* is happening at *s*. This is *not* to imply something undoubtedly false, that 'now' *means* 'the time of this utterance', or that 'here' *means* 'the place of this utterance', or, again, that 'I' *means* 'the utterer of this utterance'.

Now, does McTaggart's argument simply turn on a blunder in the logic of indexicals? Dummett, who endorses McTaggart's argument, thinks not. He at least *seems* to think that it is legitimate to say concerning a future event *e*, which is not happening now, that *e will be* happening now, or is happening now *in the future,* since he seems to think it equally legitimate to say that an event *e*, which is not happening *here,* but is happening over *there,* is happening *here over there.* Dummett writes.[8]

> Every place can be called both 'here' and 'there', both 'near' and 'far', and every person can be called both 'I' and 'you': yet 'here' and 'there', 'near' and 'far', 'I' and 'you' are incompatible. It would be no use for an objector to say that London is nearby far away, but far away nearby, or that it is 'here' there but 'there' here, since it can also be called 'nearby nearby' and '"here" here', and so on. Similarly, it would be no use an objector saying 'You are "you" to me, but "I" to you', because everyone can be called both '"you" to me' and '"I" to me'.

Note that Dummett is not contending that what the imagined objector says is *illegitimate* (certainly no more illegitimate than statements made with first-order indexicals), only that it is 'no use' for the purposes of removing the initial incompatibility. (One complication in Dummett's treatment is his frequent placing of indexical expressions in quotation marks, sometimes nested ones, in a not altogether consistent manner. It is because I am not quite clear as to the purpose behind this practice that I am somewhat tentative in attributing to him the opinions stated just before the quoted passage.) Dummett's overall position *vis-à-vis* McTaggart appears to be a *qualified* endorsement of each of claims (1) to (4) above; and the reason why he sees no danger of an extension of McTaggart's argument to the unreality of *space* or *personality* is simply that he accepts in their case nothing corresponding to claims (1) and (2), although he does accept something corresponding to claim (3). I speak only of a *qualified* endorsement because Dummett nevertheless questions what he takes to be McTaggart's implicit assumptions about the nature of 'reality'.

I cannot, however, concur with Dummett's defence of McTaggart on this point. I think that McTaggart *does* commit a simple, if understandable, blunder in the logic of indexicality. It is *not* legitimate to say that an event *e*, which is not happening *here*, but is happening over *there*, is happening *here over there*. All we can say really is that if *e* is happening there and not here, then an utterance *over there* of the sentence '*e* is happening here' is true. It does not follow that *e* is happening *here* over there—which is a blatant contradiction. Now, similarly, when I say that *e will happen*, I am not implying that *e* is happening now in the future, though I *am* implying that in the future it will be possible to make a true statement by saying '*e* is happening now'.

But how, exactly, does this bear on McTaggart's argument? Well, certainly, '*e* is present', '*e* is past', and '*e* is future', said simultaneously, express contradictory statements. But what about the claim that what is future will become present and then past (so that every event is past, present and future)? This is simply *false*, or, more strictly, *incoherent*. What should be said is that if *e* is a future event, i.e. if *e will* occur, then it *will* be possible to express a true statement by means of the sentence '*e* is present', or '*e* is happening now'. If it is asked whether *we* can *now* say something which expresses *now* what that sentence will then express, the answer is yes: for the statement that I now express by saying, for instance, '*e* will happen tomorrow' is the same as will be expressed tomorrow by saying '*e* is happening today'. By analogy, the statement that I express *here* by saying '*e* is happening over there' is the same as is expressed *over there* by saying '*e* is happening here': for speakers uttering these sentences in the respective locations will, clearly, be in agreement as to what is the case, and to this extent may be said to be expressing the same statement. (If 'statement' is not liked in this context, 'proposition' or any other suitable favoured term may be substituted; the terminology is unimportant so long as it enables us to refer to what is invariable as between two such speakers.)

Thus, I agree with McTaggart in so far as I accept claims (1) and (2), and disagree with him in rejecting claims (3) and (4): but, furthermore, I do not accept his elaboration of (2), that is, I do not accept that change is to be explained in terms of A-series expressions *in the way he suggests*, since I do not accept that change is to be explained in terms of *future events becoming present* and so on. Just what explanation I do want to adopt I shall discuss in a moment. But before doing so, I want to mention another rebuttal of McTaggart's argument that has been advanced recently, by Richard Sorabji.[9]

Sorabji's response to the initial threat of contradiction posed by McTaggart is to say that we can distinguish the times at which an event is past, present, and future by reference to *dates*, rather than, as McTaggart invites us, by resorting to (second-order) *tenses*. Rather than saying, of a present event *e*, that it is future in the past, past in the future, and present in the present, we may say, for instance, that it is present in 1986, future in 1985, and past in 1987,

and thus not past, present, and future at any one date. This response presupposes that dates can be identified independently of A-series determinations. I very much doubt whether this presupposition is warranted. However, Mellor (who is the more immediate object of Sorabji's attack) accepts it, for reasons which I shall not examine here, but which are connected with his belief that the earlier/later relation between events can at least sometimes be *observed*—when we observe movement, for instance—quite independently of whether the events in question are characterized by us as past, present, or future.[10] Nonetheless, Sorabji's response *is* inadequate, even waiving this issue, given that '*e* is present' means '*e* is happening now': because it simply is not, *timelessly*, true to say that *e* is happening now in 1986, where *e* is a present event—said in 1987 this is simply false. Said in 1987, '*e* is *present* or is happening *now* in 1986' would imply (just as it does now, in 1986) 'It is now 1986', and said in 1987 this last would, of course, be false. Moreover, for the same reasons, it never has been, is not, and never will be true that *e* is future in 1985 or past in 1987, where *e* is a present event (one that is happening now, in 1986).

Sorabji is making essentially the same indexical mistake that I have attributed to McTaggart, Mellor, and Dummett. If *e* is a present event (i.e. is happening now, in 1986), we should not say that it is a future event in 1985, but, at most, than in 1985 it was possible to express a true statement by means of the sentence '*e* will happen in 1986/next year'. The mistake consists in forgetting the *uneliminably* indexical nature of A-series expressions, at least while they are being *used* as opposed to being *mentioned*: philosophers writing on time are constrained to *use* these expressions in the same context-dependent way in which ordinary humanity is—they, too, cannot escape their own temporal perspective, however much they may be tempted to suppose that they can view things *sub specie aeternitatis*. They are thus tempted to think of events as being present *for* certain persons, past *for* others, and future *for* yet others. But when *I* use the expression 'present', or 'now', I can no more use it to refer to another temporal perspective than *I* can use 'I' to refer to another person. This is because what *I* can use such indexical expressions to refer to is not just up to me, but is constrained by my circumstances; the context of use of such an expression helps to determine its reference, my wishes notwithstanding. (This is not, of course, to deny that *I* can *now* refer to persons and times to which other persons at other times would refer by the expressions 'I' and 'now', only to insist that I must use appropriate indexical expressions to do so—the propriety being determined by *my* context of use.)

I return now to the problem of the nature of *change*. How are we to explain or describe it, given that we cannot say with McTaggart that change consists in future events becoming present and present ones 'receding' into the past? How can we capture the notion of the 'flow' of time without falling into paradox or absurdity? One's first thought, in an attempt to avoid the indexical fallacy I have identified in what McTaggart himself says, might be to propose that change simply consists in the existence of such facts as that what can now be truly stated by saying '*e* will happen tomorrow' will tomorrow only be truly stated by saying something different, namely, '*e* is happening today'. But nothing like this will do by itself, for such facts only reflect the indexical character of A-series expressions, and so fail to distinguish time from space as the dimension of change. Thus it is equally a fact that what can here be truly stated by saying '*e* is happening here' can yonder only be truly stated by saying '*e* is happening over there' or something equivalent: but this carries no implication of change.

However, one important difference between time and space in connection with the problem of change may be that, so to speak, we cannot choose *when* we are whereas we can—at least to some extent—choose *where* we are. Again, there is no temporal analogue to the sort of truth that can be stated by saying 'I have been here before'—'I am now elsewhere' is just absurd. The relevance of these facts to the problem of change (or, as I would prefer to call it, the problem of *flux* or *flow,* since my concern is with an intrinsic feature of time rather than with a feature of objects which they possess by virtue of inhabiting time) is that it is the *ineluctability* of time that chiefly motivates the simile of time as a river which 'like an ever-rolling stream, bears all its sons away'. It is not just that time has a direction, for space too might have been anisotropic. Rather, it is that each one of us has no choice but successively and unrepeatedly to adopt each of a fixed sequence of temporal perspectives, whereas there is no similar constraint on our spatial perspectives. The same spatial perspective may be adopted at many different times by the same person, and the temporal order in which spatial perspectives can be adopted by the same person is a matter open to that person's choice.

To this it may be objected that while it is true that the same temporal perspective may not be adopted analogously at many different places by the same person, none the less the spatial order in which temporal perspectives are adopted by the same person *is* analogously a matter open to that person's choice—so that what has been said so far does *not* capture the alleged 'ineluctability' of time. This objection is sound and shows that more care is needed in formulating the relevantly different facts about spatial and temporal perspectives. The idea we must try to articulate is that a person's route through space is open to choice in a way that his route through time is not. But, of course, every route is *at once* a route through space *and* a route through time: routes are just ordered sequences of space-time positions, of the form $<(s^1, t^1), (s^2, t^2), \ldots, (s^n, t^n)>$.[11] The relevant difference between space and time, then, comes down to this, that in all the possible space-time routes a person may take the order of temporal positions will be the same, while the order of spatial positions may vary (and, indeed, such routes may differ in respect of *all* of their spatial positions except, perhaps, the first—a fact that only partly reflects the isotropy and multidimensionality of space in contrast with the directedness and monodimensionality of time). Thus, if $<(s^1, t^1), (s^2, t^2), \ldots, (s^n, t^n)>$ is a possible route for a given person, any

other possible route for that person must be of the form $<(-, t^1), (-, t^2), \ldots, (-, t^n)>$ but it need not be of the form $<(s^1, -), (s^2, -), \ldots, (s^n, -)>$. (One crucial determinant of this result is the monodimensionality of time; but that is not all there is to the matter, since those routes are ruled out in which successive space-time positions contain the *same* temporal co-ordinate—time will not 'stand still'. Part of my suggestion is, therefore, that it is because we can make sense of the notion of 'staying at the same place' but not of 'staying at the same time' that we conceive of time rather than space as the dimension of change or flux.)

A problem arising from what has just been said is that if it succeeds in capturing what it is that makes time but not space the dimension of change or flux, it might appear to do so without invoking A-series expressions, inasmuch as 'routes' have been characterized in terms of space-time positions without any clear implication that these positions have to be referred to by means of A-series terminology. If this is so, McTaggart's claim (2) has been undermined, despite my earlier support of it. My answer is that I conceive of a 'route' not as something viewed *sub specie aeternitatis* but as a sequence of spatio-temporal *perspectives*. To think of what a route *is* therefore requires of us an effort of imaginative projection: we must conceive of what it would be like ('from the inside') to experience the world from perspectives other than here and now. In other words, we must understand what it would be to use the words 'now' and 'here' *correctly* at other times and places—times and places which I cannot now refer to other than by recourse to other indexical expressions. But, very arguably, such an understanding is essential to an understanding of the very *meaning* of words like 'now' and 'here' (how else could we communicate across time and space?), and so cannot be beyond us.

It might be thought that an alternative (or indeed additional) way of trying to capture the nature of change or flux consistent with the views that I have already expressed would be to build on the idea that, while time is real, the future (and perhaps also the past) is *not*. The suggestion might be that time—and more particularly change or flux, which is, we have claimed, essential to it—is real precisely *because* the future is not real, or, more precisely, because it is not *yet* real, but *will* be. This, of course, would allow us to distinguish time relevantly from space, inasmuch as we should not analogously wish to claim that only *here* is real, not *yonder.* While I have *some* sympathy with this line of thought,[12] it opens too many questions to be pursued here . . . examination of it must await another time and another place.

Notes

1. See J. M. E. McTaggart, *The Nature of Existence,* Cambridge, Cambridge University Press, 1927, Vol. II, Chap. 33. The advent of relativity theory has taught us to allow that there may be *more than one* B series, corresponding to different 'frames of reference' in motion with respect to one another. However, as others have pointed out, the important thing is that for each B series there is a unique A

series corresponding to it, and *vice versa;* and for our purposes we can assume that we are restricted to just one frame of reference. (McTaggart himself allowed the possibility of such plurality: see ibid., § 323.)

2. I should explain that expressions definable in terms of 'past', 'present', and 'future' are themselves to be accounted A-series expressions. Thus 'yesterday' qualifies, because it is definable as 'a day earlier than the present day'. This example should make it clear, incidentally, that the relations 'earlier' and 'later' (and relations definable in terms of them, such as 'a day earlier') do not exclusively appear in B-series sentences; rather, the special feature of the latter sentences is the absence from them of any A-series expressions. Events are ordered in the B series by the earlier/later relation without reference (however indirect) to *the present moment.*

3. This objection, though not explicitly expressed by McTaggart, may be extracted from what he says in op. cit., § 316.

4. See D. H. Mellor, *Real Time,* Cambridge, Cambridge University Press, 1981, p. 111.

5. Ibid., pp. 78 ff.

6. See McTaggart, op. cit., § 311.

7. See M. A. E. Dummett, 'A Defence of McTaggart's Proof of the Unreality of Time', reprinted in his *Truth and Other Enigmas,* London, Duckworth, 1978.

8. Ibid., p. 353.

9. See R. Sorabji, *Time, Creation and the Continuum,* London, Duckworth, 1983, p. 68.

10. See Mellor, op. cit., pp. 24 ff.

11. For simplicity, I ignore the fact (if it is a fact) that space and time are continuous rather than discrete.

12. It may be that our inclination to say that the past is not 'real' in the way that we conceive the present to be is connected with our sense of the 'irretrievability' of the past. Assuming that time is not circular, we cannot later return to an earlier time, in the way that we can by traversing space return to the same place. If we *did* conceive time to be circular, we would, I think, have less inclination to regard the past (and indeed the future) as 'unreal'. But if this is so, then it will not after all do to attempt to capture the notion that time is the

dimension of change or flux by emphasising the 'reality' of the present—for there would still be flux if time were circular.

FURTHER READING

Criticism

Broad, C. D. A review of *The Nature of Existence. Mind,* No. 119 (July 1921): 317- 32.
> Extensive review of the first volume of *The Nature of Existence,* which describes McTaggart's methodology in detail and praises the book highly.

———. *Examination of McTaggart's Philosophy.* 2 vols. New York: Cambridge at the University Press, 1933 and 1938, 460 p. and 796 p.
> Comprehensive exposition and criticism of *The Nature of Existence.*

Farmer, David J. *Being in Time: The Nature of Time in Light of McTaggart's Paradox.* Lanham, Md.: University Press of America, 1990, 221 p.
> Presents two differing theories of time and examines McTaggart's postulation and its inherent paradox.

Geach, P. T. *Truth, Love, and Immortality: An Introduction to McTaggart's Philosophy.* London: Hutchinson and Co., 1979, 182 p.
> Detailed examination of McTaggart's metaphysics and his conclusion that absolute reality is composed of individual selves united in love.

Mellor, D. H. "McTaggart, Fixity, and Coming True." In *Reduction, Time, and Reality: Studies in the Philosophy of the Natural Sciences,* pp. 79-97. Edited by Richard Healey. Cambridge, England: Cambridge University Press, 1981.
> Agrees with McTaggart's theory that "in reality nothing is either past, present, or future" but argues that this does not mean that time does not exist.

Wisdom, John. A review of *Examination of McTaggart's Philosophy* by C. D. Broad. *Mind* XLIII, No. 170 (April 1934): 204-24.
> Offers high praise for Broad's "sympathetic and very lucid exposition" and "trenchant criticism."

William Vaughn Moody
1869-1910

(Full name William Vaughn Stoy Moody) American poet and dramatist.

INTRODUCTION

Moody was a well-known American poet and dramatist at the beginning of the twentieth century whose reputation declined considerably as literary innovators turned away from the traditional forms in which he wrote. In his poetry Moody relied on such nineteenth-century conventions as strict metrics, classical symbolism, and inflated diction. Though derivative as a poet, Moody is seen as a transitional figure in American drama. In particular, his successful prose drama *A Sabine Woman* (1906; revised as *The Great Divide,* 1909) with its contemporary setting and colloquial speech, is seen to advance realistic drama in the United States and to point the way to such figures as Eugene O'Neill in the succeeding decades.

BIOGRAPHICAL INFORMATION

Moody was born in Spencer, Indiana, and grew up in New Albany, across the Ohio River from Louisville, Kentucky. His father, a native New Yorker, had been a steamboat captain and entrepreneur before taking a position in an iron works owned by his wife's family. In the mid-1880s Moody suffered the deaths of both his parents and an older sister; in the midst of these losses he graduated first in his high school class and began teaching school in rural Indiana to save money to attend college in the East. In 1897 he moved to Poughkeepsie, New York, where he served as a tutor to a wealthy family and attended a preparatory academy. He entered Harvard College in 1889. At Harvard, Moody associated with a group of writers that included Robert Morss Lovett, Hugh McCullough, and Philip Henry Savage, and came under the influence of prevailing intellects among the faculty including George Santayana and William James. He contributed poems to the *Harvard Advocate* and served on the editorial board of the *Harvard Monthly*. After completing his degree requirements in 1892, Moody spent a year abroad as a tutor. He was awarded a bachelor's degree in 1893 and completed a master's degree in 1894. After teaching at Harvard for a year, Moody became an English instructor at the University of Chicago in 1895. However, Moody did not find teaching an altogether congenial occupation and preferred to spend time on such pursuits as writing and editing. During the late 1890s he submitted poetry to periodicals including *Scribner's* and *Atlantic Monthly* and edited works by John Bunyan, Samuel Taylor Coleridge, Sir Walter Scott, John Milton, and Alexander Pope. His first book, the verse drama *The Masque of Judgment,* was published in 1900 with *Poems* following in 1901. The success of his *A History of English Literature* (1902), cowritten with Morss Lovett, allowed Moody a measure of financial security. After 1903 he stopped teaching but remained associated with the University of Chicago until 1908. In 1909 he married Harriet Brainard, whom he had met in 1901. Shortly after his marriage, Moody began to lose his sight and learned that he had a brain tumor. He died in Colorado Springs, Colorado, in October 1910.

MAJOR WORKS

Moody's career may be divided into two distinct phases, with the early part of his career devoted to poetry and the second part devoted to drama. Published in *Poems* and reissued as *Gloucester Moors, and Other Poems* (1909), Moody's verse is written largely in traditional European forms and employs mythical symbolism. Among the best known of his short works are "The Daguerreotype," an elegy inspired by a portrait of his mother at age 17 in which Moody contrasts her youthful expectations of life with the reality of her adulthood and death. "On a Soldier Dying in the Philippines" comprises a criticism of U.S. foreign policy as does "An Ode in Time of Hesitation," inspired by the monument on Boston Common to Colonel Robert Gould Shaw, the leader of the first African American regiment to fight in the American Civil War.

Moody was the author of five plays: a poetic trilogy that includes *The Fire-Bringer* (1904), *The Masque of Judgment,* and the unfinished *Death of Eve,* and the prose plays *The Great Divide* and *The Faith Healer* (1909). The earliest of his published dramas, *The Masque of Judgment,* depicts humanity in conflict with God and ends with the human spirit prevailing in the destruction of heaven. The second of Moody's verse dramas, *The Fire-Bringer,* presents a verse interpretation of the legend of Prometheus and advocates the necessity of human conflict with God. In the planned conclusion of the trilogy, *The Death of Eve,* the reconciliation of God and man would be achieved through Eve. While none of Moody's verse dramas has been produced on stage, the final two installments in particular retain critical interest and give evidence of Moody's aspirations for reviving the verse drama in contemporary theater.

In April 1906 Moody's prose drama *A Sabine Woman* premiered in Chicago; after the play was revised and retitled, it debuted to great success on Broadway as *The Great Di-*

vide six months later. The "divide" of the play's title refers to the cultural dichotomy in America between the Puritanical, subdued, cultured East and the carefree, democratic, unsophisticated West. The plot centers on an eastern woman who on a trip West is saved from sexual assault by a miner who pays off her attackers with a string of gold nuggets. Attracted to her benefactor, she agrees to marry him, but their union is clouded by the knowledge that she was purchased with gold. She earns the money to buy back the string of gold, gives it to her husband, and returns East. The final act of the play takes place in the East where the couple is reunited, and the wife voices her rejection of eastern society in favor of the West. Viewed as a departure from typical melodramas of the era, *The Great Divide* is valued for its realism, its simple prose, and its modern American setting.

Moody's final work, *The Faith Healer* (1909), treats the conflict between human physical and spiritual needs. Closed within a week of its New York debut in 1910, *The Faith Healer* features a miracle-working protagonist who faces opposition from both organized religion and scientific medicine.

CRITICAL RECEPTION

During his lifetime Moody was hailed as a poet and playwright of high literary ideals and achievement. Reviewing Moody's debut works in 1901, *Dial* commentator William Morton Payne noted that "no other new poet of the past score of years, either in America or in England, has displayed a finer promise upon the occasion of his first appearance, or has been deserving of more respectful consideration." During the first decade of the twentieth century, Moody gained prominence and influence with his series of poetic and prose dramas. According to a 1906 review of *The Great Divide* by critic John Corbin: "To say that it is the best product of the American drama thus far would doubtless be extravagant; yet the fact remains that it is inspired by precisely that fulness and wholesomeness of feeling, and is accomplished with precisely that technical firmness, the lack of which has thus far proved the cardinal defects of our most vivacious and amusing playwrights." However, with such advancements as the realistic dramas of Eugene O'Neill and the rise of experimentalism associated with the Modernist movement, Moody's reputation declined after the mid-1920s. In an overview of Moody's work published in 1931, F. O. Matthiessen defined Moody's lack of appeal to the younger generation of American writers: "No one could have been more earnest in his desire to be a poet . . . . But he never found quite an authentic voice of his own. He was so striving in his effort to create that it left a pale cast of heavy deliberateness over nearly all of his lines, so self-conscious in his determination to be a poet that it almost incapacitated him for writing poetry. In fact, his kind of eclectic reliance upon the past and absorption in its ways of expression became finally so oppressive that it was the very thing which caused the violent break of our contem-

porary poetry away from nineteenth-century literary tradition." Moody's reputation was never revived. To later observers he seemed the culminating figure of a formal tradition in poetry that proved insufficient to treat the emerging themes in twentieth-century literature, including the brutality of modern warfare and the alienation of the individual in modern society.

PRINCIPAL WORKS

The Masque of Judgment (drama) 1900
Poems (poetry) 1901; republished as *Gloucester Moors, and Other Poems,* 1909
A History of English Literature [with Robert Morss Lovett] (criticism) 1902
The Fire-Bringer (drama) 1904
A First View of English Literature (criticism) 1905
A Sabine Woman (drama) 1906; revised as *The Great Divide,* 1909
The Faith Healer (drama) 1909; revised edition, 1910
The Poems and Plays of William Vaughn Moody, 2 vols. (poetry and drama) 1912
Some Letters of William Vaughn Moody (letters) 1913
Selected Poems of William Vaughn Moody (poetry) 1931
Letters to Harriet (letters) 1935

CRITICISM

William Morton Payne (essay date 1901)

SOURCE: "The Poetry of Mr. Moody," in *The Dial,* Vol. XXX, No. 359, June 1, 1901, pp. 365-9.

[*In the following favorable review, Payne discusses style, form, theme, and mood in* The Masque of Judgment *and* Poems.]

Every two or three years, from some quarter of the critical horizon, there issue trumpetings of praise which herald the advent of a new singer of songs. A bright star has swum into the ken of some watcher upon the battlements, and the discovery is proclaimed to the world with much pomp of rhetorical eulogy. The number of new poets who have thus been discovered during the past quarter-century is considerable, but most of them have shared the fate of the *novæ* known to astronomers, and their magnitude has rapidly become dimmed. We have often envied the enthusiasm that could find so much to praise in these new interpreters of nature and human life, but have felt ourselves sorrowfully compelled to stand outside the chorus, and to mar its harmonies by the injection of certain discordant notes of caution and temperate restraint. A book of poetry must exhibit very great qualities indeed to constitute an event in literature, or to set its writer among the enduring poets of his age. In the memory of men now in their middle or advancing years there have been only two such events in English poetry—the appearance of Mr. Swinburne's *Poems and Ballads* in 1866 and of the *Poems* of Rossetti in 1870. Tested by these touchstones, *The Love Sonnets of Proteus* and *The City of Dreadful Night,* the books of Mr. Watson and Mr. Kipling and Mr. Phillips, have been phenomena of only secondary significance. Yet the writers of all these books, and other writers as well, have been hailed as new luminaries of the first rank, have been praised in terms that one would hesitate to apply to Arnold or Tennyson, and have been made, as far as indiscriminate eulogy could make them, the literary fashion of their respective hours. Praiseworthy they doubtless are, but not worthy of the sort of praise that has been injudiciously bestowed upon them to the confusion of all absolute values.

In making the following somewhat extended comment upon the poetical work of Mr. William Vaughn Moody, we are not going to say that he is a poet of the highest kind of accomplishment, or apply to him the language that must properly be reserved for poets whose work has stood the test of time and remained uncorroded by it. But we are going to say—and by our exhibits seek to prove—that no other new poet of the past score of years, either in America or in England, has displayed a finer promise upon the occasion of his first appearance, or has been deserving of more respectful consideration. There is no reason, for example, why his work should attract less attention than has been given of late to the work of Mr. Stephen Phillips, and we make not the slightest doubt that, had his work been the product of an Englishman, its author would have been accorded the resounding praise that has been accorded to the author of "Marpessa" and "Paolo and Francesca." We wish to say, furthermore, that we have not for many years been so strongly tempted to cast aside critical restraints and indulge in "the noble pleasure of praising," after the fashion, let us say, of the late Mr. Hutton when dealing with the poetry of Mr. William Watson. Nor do we hesitate to add that, with the possible exception of what has been done by Professor Woodberry, no such note of high and serious song has been sounded in our recent American poetry as is now sounded in *The Masque of Judgment* and the *Poems* of Mr. Moody.

The Masque of Judgment is a work that labors under extraordinary difficulties. The form itself is one that a writer must be greatly daring to attempt, and the substance is of a sort that heightens the difficulties of the form. Like the epics of Dante and Milton, it is concerned with no less a theme than the cosmogony; like *Faust,* it sets speech upon the lips of archangels; like the *Prometheus Unbound,* it personifies the creations of mythology. It might more fittingly be styled a Mystery than a Masque, but it cannot take an easy refuge in the *naivetés* of mediævalism, for it is no imitative exercise in archaism, but a poem conceived in the spirit of modern philosophy. So true is this that we are impelled to provide it with texts from the writings of the philosophers. Professor Royce says: "It is the fate of

life to be restless, capricious, and therefore tragic. Happiness comes, indeed, but by all sorts of accidents; and it flies as it comes. One thing only that is greater than this fate endures in us if we are wise of heart; and this one thing endures forever in the heart of the great World-Spirit of whose wisdom ours is but a fragmentary reflection. This one thing, as I hold, is the eternal resolution that if the world *will* be tragic, it *shall* still, in Satan's despite, be spiritual. And this resolution is, I think, the very essence of the Spirit's own eternal joy." And Professor James, writing in much the same spirit, says: "God himself, in short, may draw vital strength and increase of very being from our fidelity. For my own part, I do not know what the sweat and blood and tragedy of this life mean, if they mean anything short of this." On the lips of Mr. Moody's Raphael, the archangelic lover of mankind, this philosophy is given melodious utterance.

> Darkly, but oh, for good, for good,
> The spirit infinite
> Was throned upon the perishable blood;
> To moan and to be abject at the neap,
> To ride portentous on the shrieking scud
> Of the arousèd flood,
> And halcyon hours to preen and prate in the boon
> Tropical afternoon.
>
> Not in vain, not in vain,
> The spirit hath its sanguine stain,
> And from its senses five doth peer
> As a fawn from the green windows of a wood;
> Slave of the panic woodland fear,
> Boon-fellow in the game of blood and lust
> That fills with tragic mirth the woodland year;
> Searched with starry agonies
> Through the breast and through the reins,
> Maddened and led by lone moon-wandering cries.
> Dust unto dust complains;
> Dust laugheth out to dust,
> Sod unto sod moves fellowship,
> And the soul utters, as she must,
> Her meanings with a loose and carnal lip;
> But deep in her ambiguous eyes
> Forever shine and slip
> Quenchless expectancies,
> And in a far-off day she seems to put her trust.

Again, and in still clearer language, the archangel declares the glory of man's passionate self-contradictions:

> I have walked
> The rings of planets where strange-colored moons
> Hung thick as dew, in ocean orchards feared
> The glaucous tremble of the living boughs
> Whose fruit hath life and purpose; but nowhere
> Found any law but this: Passion is power,
> And, kindly tempered, saves. All things declare
> Struggle hath deeper peace than sleep can bring:
> The restlessness that put creation forth
> Impure and violent, held holier calm
> Than that Nirvana whence it wakened Him.

Thus the way is prepared for the Divine Tragedy. God, having created the race of men, and having sought to save man from himself by the mystery of the Incarnation, determines at last to destroy the impious brood.

> What if they rendered up their wills to His?
> Hushed and subdued their personality?
> Became as members of the living tree?

To Raphael, thus musing, the Angel of the Pale Horse makes reply:

> A whisper grows, various from tongue to tongue,
> That so He will attempt. Those who consent
> To render up their clamorous wills to Him,
> To merge their fretful being in His peace
> He will accept: the rest He will destroy.

In the fulness of time, the Day of Judgment dawns, and "God's vengeance is full wrought" upon the wicked. The following wonderful lyric is sung by the redeemed spirits on their upward flight:

> In the wilds of life astray,
> Held far from our delight,
> Following the cloud by day
> And the fire by night,
> Came we a desert way.
> O Lord, with apples feed us,
> With flagons stay!
> By Thy still waters lead us!
>
> As bird torn from the breast
> Of mother-cherishings,
> Far from the swaying nest
> Dies for the mother wings,
> So did the birth-hour wrest
> From Thy sweet will and word
> Our souls distressed.
> Open Thy breast, thou Bird!

Yet Raphael, who alone of the celestial hosts has understood the heart of man, and whose imagination has foreshadowed the consequences of his destruction, remains disconsolate.

> Never again! never again for me!
> Never again the lily souls that live
> Along the margin of the streams, shall grow
> More candid at my coming. Never more
> God's birds above the bearers of the Ark
> Shall make a wood of implicated wings,
> Swept by the wind of slow ecstatic song.
> Thy youths shall hold their summer cenacles;
> I am not of their fellowship, it seems.
> God's ancient peace shall feed them, as it feeds
> These yet uplifted hills. I would I knew
> Where bubbled that insistent spring. To drink
> Deep, and forget what I have seen to-day.

But the destruction of mankind is only the beginning of the Tragedy. When that awful fiat went forth, God likewise accomplished His own doom. To be dethroned and destroyed by the forces of His own creation is the fate that awaits Him, as it awaited the God of Scandinavian myth in the day of Ragnarök, as it awaited the God of Greek myth in Shelley's treatment of the tale of Prometheus. The instrument of His undoing is the Worm that Dieth not, His own monstrous miscreation, who, having swept mankind from the face of earth at the behest of his Creator, mounts upward to commit violent assault upon the hosts of Heaven.

> He mounts!
> He lays his length upward the visioned hills,
> The inviolable fundaments of Heaven!
> There where he climbs the kindled slopes grow pale,
> Ashen the amethystine dells, and dim
> The starry reaches.

The closing scene between the Spirits of the Lamps about the Throne, who have fled in terror from the terrific struggle, and the Archangels Raphael and Uriel, rises to a height of imaginative sublimity that leaves us fairly stricken with awe.

> URIEL. (approaching).
> The dream is done! Petal by petal falls
> The coronal of creatured bloom God wove
> To deck His brows at dawn.
> RAPHAEL.
>   No hope remains?
> URIEL.
> To save Him from Himself not cherubim
> Nor seraphim avail. Who loves not life
> Receiveth not life's gifts at any hand.
>
>   . . . . .
> RAPHAEL.
>   Would He had dared
> To nerve each member of His mighty frame—
> Man, beast, and tree, and all the shapes of will
> That dream their darling ends in clod and star—
> To everlasting conflict, wringing peace
> From struggle, and from struggle peace again,
> Higher and sweeter and more passionate
> With every danger passed! Would He had spared
> That dark Antagonist whose enmity
> Gave Him rejoicing sinews, for of Him
> His foe was flesh of flesh and bone of bone,
> With suicidal hand He smote him down,
> And now indeed His lethal pangs begin.
> FIRST LAMP. (to Uriel).
> Brother, what lies beyond this trouble? Death?
> URIEL.
> All live in Him, with Him shall all things die.
> SECOND LAMP.
> And the snake reign, coiled on the holy hill?
> URIEL.
> Sorrow dies with the heart it feeds upon.
> RAPHAEL.
> Look, where the red volcano of the fight
> Hath burst, and down the violated hills
> Pours ruin and repulse, a thousand streams
> Choked with the pomp and furniture of Heaven.
> In vain the Lion ramps against the tide,
> In vain from slope to slope the giant Wraths
> Rally but to be broken. Dwindling dim
> Across the blackened pampas of the wind
> The routed Horses flee with hoof and wing,
> Till their trine light is one, and now is quenched.

URIEL.
The spirits fugitive from Heaven's brink
Put off their substance of ethereal fire
And mourn phantasmal on the phantom Alps.
　　　　FOURTH LAMP.
Mourn, sisters! For our light is fading too.
Thou of the topaz heart, thou of the jade,
And thou sweet trembling opal—ye are grown
Grey things, and aged as God's sorrowing eyes.
　　　　FIRST LAMP.
My wick burns blue and dim.
　　　　SECOND LAMP.
　　　　　　My oil is spent.
　　　　RAPHAEL.
The moon smoulders; and naked from their seats
The stars arise with lifted hands, and wait.

We have endeavored to give, in the preceding analysis, some idea of the fashion in which Mr. Moody has dealt with his grandiose conception of the Creation, the Christian Mystery, and the Judgment. He has shown it possible to make in our own day a very noble poem, as Milton did, out of the Biblical Mythology, and as Shelley did, out of the most subtle spiritual symbolism. The poem is not without minor faults, and criticism of the microscopic sort might easily detect flaws here and there, words inaccurately used or inadequate as vehicles of their intention, forced imagery and moments of flagging imagination. We are content to leave to others this thankless task, feeling that the superb merits of the work make its occasional crudities quite insignificant. We have quoted many of its finest passages, but have reserved for the last the finest of them all—this glorious apostrophe to mankind:

O Dreamer! O Desirer! Goer down
Unto untravelled seas in untried ships!
O crusher of the unimagined grape
On unconceivèd lips!
O player upon a lordly instrument
No man or god hath had in mind to invent;
O cunning how to shape
Effulgent Heaven and scoop out bitter Hell
From the little shine and saltness of a tear;
Sieger and harrier,
Beyond the moon, of thine own builded town,
Each morning won, each eve impregnable,
Each noon evanished sheer!

We should not know where in recent poetry to look for the match to this melodious and sympathetic portrayal of "life's wild and various bloom" of passion and aspiration, of alternating defeat and victory, of the commingling of sense and spirit that makes of our existence so confused a web of self-contradictions, yet somehow suggests a harmony of design that must be apparent to the transcendental vision.

It is clear that the poet of *The Masque of Judgment* is no partisan of the ascetic ideal. His plea is for the richness of life, for the legitimate claims of sense no less than of spirit, for the working out of one's salvation by means that leave no human instinct athirst. Nor is his ideal one for the few favored by nature or circumstance; it is rather the all-embracing expression of a fine trust in the whole of human nature. This democratic outlook, which is somewhat obscured by the symbolism demanded for the dramatic work we have just had under discussion, is given a more definite expression in the volume of the *Poems,* to which we now turn. We find it in **"Gloucester Moors,"** with which the book opens, a striking poem which likens the earth to a ship bound with its freight of souls for some unknown port.

But thou, vast outbound ship of souls,
What harbor town for thee?
What shapes, when thy arriving tolls,
Shall crowd the banks to see?
Shall all the happy shipmates then
Stand singing brotherly?
Or shall a haggard ruthless few
Warp her over and bring her to,
While the many broken souls of men
Fester down in the slaver's pen,
And nothing to say or do?

It takes a robust optimism to bear up under the spectacle afforded by the darker aspects of human life, its physical failings and its spiritual agonies, and the mood of **"A Grey Day"** holds the poet under its obsession more than once.

I wonder how that merchant's crew
Have ever found the will!
I wonder what the fishers do
To keep them toiling still!
I wonder how the heart of man
Has patience to live out its span,
Or wait until its dreams come true.

But this mood is not lasting, nor does it insistently prevail in the writer's consciousness. Whatever the defeats life may bring, the strong spirit will not be cowed, nor will it seek a refuge in quietism. Some stanzas written **"At Assisi"** give us a clear statement of the poet's philosophy.

I turn away from the gray church pile;
I dare not enter, thus undone:
Here in the roadside grass awhile
I will lie and watch for the sun.
Too purged of earth's good glee and strife,
Too drained of the honied lusts of life,
Was the peace these old saints won!
　　　. . . . .
St. Francis sleeps upon his hill,
And a poppy flower laughs down his creed;
Triumphant light her petals spill,
His shrines are dim indeed.
Men build and build, but the soul of man,
Coming with haughty eyes to scan,
Feels richer, wilder need.
How long, old builder Time, wilt bide
Till at thy thrilling word
Life's crimson pride shall have to bride
The spirit's white accord,
Within that gate of good estate
Which thou must build us soon or late,
Hoar workman of the Lord?

There is not a poem among the score or more contained in Mr. Moody's volume that is commonplace or devoid of some arresting quality of imagery or emotion. Regretfully passing by the greater number of them we reserve our remaining space for the two pieces inspired by the dark page of recent American history. Our broken national faith, our lust of dominion, the subordination of morality to greed in our international dealings, and our desertion of the principles upon which our greatness as a people has hitherto been based,—these are things that have made the last two years a period of inexpressible sadness to Americans who have been taught to cherish the teachings of Washington and Jefferson, of Sumner and Lincoln. How we have longed for the indignant words of protest that our Whittier or our Emerson or our Lowell would have voiced had their lives reached down to this unhappy time! But in reading Mr. Moody's **"Ode in Time of Hesitation"** and his lines **"On a Soldier Fallen in the Philippines"** we are almost consoled for the silence of the prophet-voices that appealed so powerfully to the moral consciousness of the generation before our own. We seem to catch the very accent of Lowell's patriotic fervor in these lines suggested by the Shaw Memorial:

> Crouched in the sea-fog on the moaning sand
> All night he lay, speaking some simple word
> From hour to hour to the slow minds that heard,
> Holding each poor life gently in his hand
> And breathing on the base rejected clay
> Till each dark face shone mystical and grand
> Against the breaking day;
> And lo, the shard the potter cast away
> Was grown a fiery chalice crystal-fine
> Fulfilled of the divine
> Great wine of battle wrath by God's ring-finger stirred
> Then upward, where the shadowy bastion loomed
> Huge on the mountain in the wet sea light,
> Whence now, and now, infernal flowerage bloomed,
> Bloomed, burst, and scattered down its deadly seed,—
> They swept, and died like freemen on the height,
> Like freemen, and like men of noble breed.

Contrast this bright picture of heroic devotion to a great cause with the dark picture presented by the successors of these men now engaged in the bloody subjugation of an alien people who have done naught to offend us, and whose crime is that they love their country well enough to die by thousands for its sake.

> I will not and I dare not yet believe!
> Though furtively the sunlight seems to grieve,
> And the spring-laden breeze
> Out of the gladdening west is sinister
> With sounds of nameless battle over seas;
> Though when we turn and question in suspense
> If these things be indeed after these ways,
> And what things are to follow after these,
> Our fluent men of place and consequence
> Fumble and fill their mouths with hollow phrase,
> Or for the end-all of deep arguments
> Intone their dull commercial liturgies—
> I dare not yet believe! My ears are shut!
> I will not hear the thin satiric praise

> And muffled laughter of our enemies,
> Bidding us never sheathe our valiant sword
> Till we have changed our birthright for a gourd
> Of wild pulse stolen from a barbarian's hut
> Showing how wise it is to cast away
> The symbols of our spiritual sway,
> That so our hands with better ease
> May wield the driver's whip and grasp the jailer's
> keys.

By the memory of the fine altruistic impulse that stirred our national heart when the suffering Cubans besought us for aid, let it not be said of us that a mean motive underlay that frank outburst of active sympathy, that our protestations of unselfishness were the merest hypocrisy, and that our soldiers have given up their lives that their country might be dishonored.

> We charge you, ye who lead us,
> Breathe on their chivalry no hint of stain!
> Turn not their new-world victories to gain!
> One least leaf plucked for chaffer from the bays
> Of their dear praise,
> One jot of their pure conquest put to hire,
> The implacable republic will require.
>   . . . . .
> For save we let the island men go free,
> Those baffled and dislaurelled ghosts
> Will curse us from the lamentable coasts
> Where walk the frustrate dead.
> The cup of trembling shall be drainèd quite,
> Eaten the sour bread of astonishment,
> With ashes of the hearth shall be made white
> Our hair, and wailing shall be in the tent.

This impressive adjuration is supplemented by the lines suggested by the death of General Lawton.

> A flag for the soldier's bier
> Who dies that his land may live;
> O, banners, banners here,
> That we doubt not nor misgive!
> That he heed not from the tomb
> The evil days draw near
> When the nation, robed in gloom,
> With its faithless past shall strive.
> Let him never dream that his bullet's scream went
> wide of
>   its island mark,
> Home to the heart of his darling land where she
> stumbled
>   and sinned in the dark.

When our nation shall have won back its sanity, and once more learned to heed—although at what cost we tremble to think—the lessons of righteousness taught us by the Fathers of the Republic, these poems will seem as stars seen through the angry cloud-rifts of a tempestuous night, bearing shining witness to the fact that in our hour of darkness there were some souls that held the faith undaunted by all the powers of evil leagued against them. We are somehow reminded of an eloquent similitude employed by the late Frederic Myers. Speaking of the judgment of the men to come upon still another poet who, like Mr. Moody, would not despair of a seemingly hopeless cause, he said: "They will look back on him as Romans looked back on that unshaken Roman who purchased at its full price the field of Cannæ, on which at that hour victorious Hannibal lay encamped with his Carthaginian host."

Francis Thompson (essay date 1902)

SOURCE: "Promise," in *The Real Robert Louis Stevenson and Other Critical Essays by Francis Thompson,* edited by Rev. Terence L. Connolly, University Publishers Incorporated, 1959, pp. 187-9.

[*In the following essay, which was originally published in 1902, Thompson praises emotion and imagination in* Poems.]

[**Poems,** by William Vaughn Moody], is an American book; but whether "Vaughn" be an American spelling of our English name, or a specimen of the American printer at his own sweet will, this reviewer saith not. We love not modern American verse, which is for the most part very respectable magazine-stuff, and no more. There are exceptions, of course; and the present volume is very unexpectedly and pleasurably an exception. It comes to us, for a wonder, without any testimonials from this American paper or that American critic, certifying the author to be one of the most remarkable products of genius in the States. Perhaps that is why it proves to deserve honest, discriminating praise. It has more fundamental poetry in it than anything we have seen for some time. Mr. Moody's qualities make for strength rather than beauty; and like many young writers, in his lust for vivid and original expression he is given to violence and over-emphasis: there is a lack of repose, he can never be quiet and let a thing just say itself. This extends to, perhaps is conditioned by, the substance itself: he is turbulent and extreme in mood, and fond of seeking effect by rather glaring contrast and the like. But the root of the matter is in him. Moreover, he does not Whitmanise on the one hand, or follow the outworn Tennysonian convention on the other, as is the way of many of his countrymen: he does not seek barbaric vigour by any of the unliterary and vulgar methods which another class of American versifiers adopt. He has evidently studied the classic and earlier masters of English poetry, as few nowadays do, especially in America. And the result is poetry, whatever its shortcomings. He has imagination, the one quality which in poetry covers a multitude of sins, and which so very few "minor" poets nowadays possess. Sometimes, where he treats what we might call an external—as apart from a subjective—theme, he attains also much restraint and dignity; and then he is very good. A notable example of this is **"An Ode in Time of Hesitation."** It is a poem on the war in the Philippines, or rather a protest against the occupation of those islands. With its political views we are not concerned. But the great principles which he supposes, rightly or not, to be threatened by American action there are set forth with a fervour, a loftiness, an elevation of idea and diction which make it remarkable first work for a young poet—as we take Mr. Moody to be. It is written after seeing at Boston the statue of Robert Gould Shaw, who was killed at the head of the first enlisted negro regiment, while he was storming with them Fort Wagner in July, 1863. To this incident the following fine passage refers:—

> Then upward, where the shadowy bastion loomed
> . . . . .
> They swept, and died like freemen on the height,
> Like freemen, and like men of noble breed;
> And when the battle fell away at night
> By hasty and contemptuous hands were thrust
> Obscurely in a common grave with him
> The fair-haired keeper of their love and trust.
> Now limb doth mingle with dissolvèd limb
> In nature's busy old democracy
> To flush the mountain laurel when she blows
> Sweet by the southern sea,
> And heart with crumbled heart climbs in the rose.

But neither this poem nor **"The Quarry,"** on the kindred theme of the Chinese war, can be sampled by extracts. They are wholes, and must be read whole. One might quote from "Jetsam" such lines as—

> I whom the Spring had strained unto her breast,
> Whose lips had felt the wet vague lips of dawn.

Or again:—

> Once at a simple turning of the way
> I met God walking; and . . . the dawn
> Was large behind Him, and the morning stars
> Circled and sang about His face as birds
> About the fieldward morning cottager.

But Mr. Moody is no poet of extracts and fine "bits." He has a pulse of emotion and imagination, that is his strength; and though there is here little complete accomplishment, there is so much of promise that we shall look to his future work with a hope Transatlantic poets do not usually inspire in us.

John Corbin (essay date 1906)

SOURCE: "Moody's 'The Great Divide'," in *The American Theatre as Seen by Its Critics, 1752-1934,* edited by Montrose J. Moses and John Mason Brown, W. W. Norton & Company, Inc., 1934 pp. 176-8.

[*In the following essay, which was originally published in* The New York Sun *in 1906, Corbin offers a favorable assessment of* The Great Divide.]

Mr. William Vaughn Moody's new American drama, **The Great Divide,** which Henry Miller and Margaret Anglin presented last night at the Princess, is so bold and vital in theme, so subtly veracious and unaffectedly strong in the writing, that it is very hard in the few moments left by a tardy if excellent performance to speak of it in terms at once of justice and of moderation.

Yet it is abundantly clear that no play of the present season—a season unusually rich—has equalled it either in calibre or in execution, except only Pinero's *His House in Order.* And even this strikes less true and deep into the wells of human impulse and passion.

To say that it is the best product of the American drama thus far would doubtless be extravagant; yet the fact remains that it is inspired by precisely that fulness and wholesomeness of feeling, and is accomplished with precisely that technical firmness, the lack of which has thus far proved the cardinal defects of our most vivacious and amusing playwrights.

The fact is that Mr. Moody, who has already placed himself at the head of modern American poets, has not ceased to be a poet in essaying the stage—though his play is written in the simplest and most unaffected prose. And he has, furthermore, applied the finesse and precision essential in the true poetic craft to the no less rigid and requiring task of the dramatist. With the lesser order of writers it has been the lamentable custom to deal lightly in and insincerely with the theatre. Mr. Moody respects his new medium, copes with it courageously and with manful adherence to the simple truth of life, and masters it.

His theme is unusual—sensational, if you will. But it is unusual and sensational in the manner not of melodrama, but of true and original drama. The great divide of his title is the barrier which exists between the rigor and dry formality of old civilization and the larger and freer, if more brutal, impulses of the frontier.

An Eastern woman (Miss Anglin), left unprotected for a night on an Arizona ranch, is set upon by three drunken marauders, and to escape a worse fate promises to give herself in marriage to the least repulsive of them on condition that he will save her from the others. This Stephen Ghent (Mr. Miller) buys off one of his rivals, shoots up the other in equal combat and leads his Sabine Woman—that was Mr. Moody's original title for the piece—to the nearest Magistrate.

The second act shows how the shame of the transaction eats into the soul of the proud and puritanical woman, until she leaves her enforced husband to bring up their child in what to her is respectability. The final act, which takes place in New England, represents the triumph of the husband, whose sincere native honesty and strength have developed in contact with a refinement new to him. The great divide has ceased to exist and the Sabine Woman becomes a willing captive to primitive, wholesome passion.

A story which seems destined to melodrama and the false heroics of sentiment is treated with simplicity that verges always on bareness. There will be those no doubt who deprecate the boldness of the theme; but they will be the first to condemn the play as slow and dull.

The method throughout, in so far as a work of such simplicity can be said to have a method, is that of understatement. One sits up and takes notice because it all happens so much more naturally and subtly than it was possible to imagine. No phase in the conflict and development of the two souls is neglected, and no word rises above the utmost austerity of realism. Mr. Moody has the courage to be true, because he has the vision to see the truth in its deepest and most vital aspects.

The acting throughout was pitched in precisely the key the play demands. Miss Anglin has never been more precise in the portrayal of the finer shades of character, and though she has had showier and more sensational parts she has never been more poignantly emotional.

At the outset she denotes with consummate fineness the kindling of the Puritan maiden toward the freer and more vital life of the West. And even in her first horror of the deed of the half drunken and altogether reckless Ghent, she manages to denote her fascination before his rough manhood. It is in the second intermediate act that she rises to the fullest achievement, for here she has to display the opposing impulses blindly yet potently struggling within her for mastery. It was in *Zira* that she displayed the height of her powers. Here she develops their depth and subtlety.

Mr. Miller has never been more simple and sympathetically convincing. He spares no trait of the recklessness of the initial deed of violence, yet manages to win regard for its passional simplicity. And in the end, when shame and sorrow have transmuted his impulses into gold, the man he has become is still the child of the man he was. Under his touch dramatic character and dramatic emotion are one.

To Laura Hope Crews falls the part of a young married woman, the friend of the Sabine woman. It is full of amusing character and sprightly humor. At times it verges toward the function of a classical chorus. Polly Jordan is under suspicion of being the mouthpiece of Mr. Moody's thesis and his psychology. Yet the part is very naturally written, and as acted by Miss Crews takes on a high degree of lifelikeness and a humor which is as natural as it is effective in contrast with the prevailing sombreness of the play.

Robert Cummings was equally effective in the smaller part of a sensible and amusingly laconic miner in Ghent's employ, and Mrs. Thomas Whiffen portrayed a New England mother of the old school with her accustomed fidelity and accuracy in character.

Play and performance were applauded heartily and only too persistently. Both Mr. Moody and Mr. Miller were reluctantly forced to each make a brief speech. Beyond question the production is a popular success.

Nash O. Barr and Charles H. Caffin (essay date 1911)

SOURCE: "William Vaughn Moody: A Study," in *The Drama: A Quarterly Review of Dramatic Literature,* No. 2, May, 1911, pp. 177-211.

[In the following essay, Barr and Caffin examine Moody's dramatic poems.]

I. The Lyrist and Lyric Dramatist

William Vaughn Moody's journalistic eulogy has been intoned as a *De Profundis* from ocean to ocean, and echoes have reached the gulf, and doubtless the polar pack-ice affecting the barometric pressure and the boreal dawn. The product of our much derided Hoosierdom as to birth and early education, he received that academic baptism entitling him to serious poet-hood in New England's most sacred minster of the Muse, (A.B. '93; A.M. '94.) From Harvard as instructor in English, ('94-01), it was natural for him to migrate Westward to the metropolis of continental United States. There he performed the duties and wore the honors of an assistant professor ('01-'07) in what Chicago loves to denominate irreverently her "Midway School." Then it was that Moody's incipient career as playwright swirled him out into the full current of life, out of the side-eddies—the *sacrosanct* precincts where presideth the would-be goddess Erudition, unadmitted yet, alas, to the choir of the Muses nine or the naked Graces three! Let us quote in justification of our facetious attitude toward the higher institutions of learning, (being just foolish lovers of poetry), from James Russell Lowell: "The higher kinds of literature, the only kinds that live on, because they have life at the start, are not the fabric of scholarship, of criticism, diligently studying and as diligently copying the best models, but are much rather born of some *genetic principles in the character* of the people and the age that produces them."

Little indeed did Lanier, Hovey, McDowell, Woodberry and Moody have to gain from academic connections, whatever may be argued on the other side from Longfellow and Lowell. And the more's the pity for our higher institutions of learning, granted that we be right. They were founded to teach, to extend the limits of knowledge, but no wise, unluckily, to foster the creative spirit in art and letters. The technical scholar and laboratory worker may investigate and collate and experiment at leisure, irrespective of pedagogical brilliancy, (or dullness for the matter of that;) but the Promethean fire is contraband and to be fanned *sub rosa*. Evermore, it seems, poetry shall continue for us a by-product of the professional chair, of the editorial chair, or of the lecturer's ambulatory platform! May the day come of judicious sinecures! Nay, is it not already . . . faintly tinting the eastern sky?

But to return from our digression. Soon, alas too soon, after the emancipated Moody fronted the world alone, he was taken away in the plenitude of adult power, his poetic trilogy unfinished, (although we hear authoritatively that the third member had progressed far on towards satisfactory completion) and his sympathetic fellow-citizens uncertain whether they have lost in him a mere pathetic pretender to the poet's laurel, or a veritable scion of the lineage divine.

Miss Hildegarde Hawthorne (*New York Times Saturday Review,* October 29th, 1910) boldly asserts: "It is in his plays that Mr. Moody found fullest expression." An unsigned article on the other hand (*Harper's Weekly,* November 12th) concludes: "What we have chiefly to regret, is that there is but one volume of lyrics." Earlier in its clever course we read: "He began to write plays which were neither better nor worse than other machine-made plays. *The Great Divide* was popular but worthless from a literary point of view. *The Faith Healer* doubtless inspired by Bjornson's *Beyond Human Strength* (?) was neither popular nor a contribution to literature." To this anonymous writer we may retort from the previously quoted eulogy: "But in literary quality (*The Great Divide*) does not approach *The Fire Bringer,* still less *The Faith Healer*; thus evidently setting the last prose play far above the last published dramatic poem, (although "neither popular nor a contribution to literature," mark you) and which last published dramatic poem induced our *advocatus diaboli* to declare: "It was the cruellest irony that led William Vaughn Moody in search for success or fame or money to put behind him his gentle gift and try to make plays."

With such wide divergence of view among those in the seats of the mighty (though we trust not, of the scornful) any American may doubtless take a peep for himself from the vantage of his private ant-hill, (or aeroplane) at this bewildering land, still, alas for so many educated readers, one of Promise, t'other side the Jordan of their indifferent skepticism.

The present paper will confine itself (by conspiracy as will appear) to the dramatic poems of Moody, and attempt to prepare the way for an estimate of his positive achievement in the *genre*. His lyrical poems do not fall within our scope, except in so far as they may help us to appreciate and understand his type of imagination, the ethical standpoint of his temperament and culture, for the surer and saner interpretation of his more ambitious and difficult prophecy.

The Lyric Poems

Our singer, it would seem, has fallen on evil days. Nothing is ready to hand for his annointed spirit. The ancient idols are fallen, and for sale as antiquarian junk. Hierarchies terrestial and celestial are discredited, or at the least under suspicion. Old moralities are deprived of sanction, taking refuge in suburban Altenheims. One boon alone is his, that of "endless quest" (**"Road Hymn for the Start"**) which, for a being limited in energy and time, must ultimate in bitterest disappointment. No wonder we read in **"Jetsam"** of the foiled lover of beauty reaching his suicidal despair. Nor can he find in whole-hearted patriotic enthusiasm any balm for his spirit. His nation seems embarked on imperial adventure, disloyal to her holy call (**"Gloucester Moors," "An Ode in Time of Hesitation," "On a Soldier Fallen in the Philippines."**) But worse, there is in store for the poet a more intimate and awful disillusion. What if love were but a fateful deception, an adolescent dream leading unto death? **"The Golden Journey"** seems perhaps the most original and thrilling of

Moody's poems. The God Eros makes a lure of the ideal woman to bring his desired victim unto ritual suicide, a sacrifice at the feet of his godhead. The fair lurer, his priestess, is the innocent accomplice.

> She will not look or speak or stir,
> But with drowned lips and cheeks death white
> Will lie amid the pool of light
> Until, grown faint with thirst of her,
> He shall bow down his face and sink,
> Breathless beneath the eddying brink.

And the end will be—the "stare" of the "God's sweet cruel eyes!" Add to this poem a lyric for Ophelia, although not so entitled, (**"On The River"**) as the feminine side of the story, and we have read perhaps the most poetical indictment of romantic love in English. Not content with these two pieces Moody makes his charge more explicit, at least more applicable to later years (**"The Bracelet"**). We dispose of our hearts under conditions over which we have no control. They change, mock, undo us; and we can only regret with "ghostly pain," but get no healing for our mutual wounds.

The smug comfort, furnished by popular versions of evolutionary theory, Moody valiantly sets aside in a grim composition. The individual human being (not a particularly excellent specimen) confronts the race ideal in the rebuking eyes of the creatures which were set aside for him. **"The Menagerie"** is a poem to set by the side of Browning's "Mr. Sludge, the Medium," for a certain grotesque realism, but it would appear a far more disagreeable poem as assailing not one, but every sort of a man who betrays the ideal. Then whither turn for cleansing of life? Where bubbles the fountain of eternal youth?

Mr. Moody's strongest lyrical appeal to the ordinary reader will be perhaps his two poems, **"Sunflower and Poppy"** (that is, the first part of it, bearing the sub-title "In New York"), and **"The Brute."** To accept present ugliness for future beauty; to be glad of the privilege to herald the day (if such be his opportunity) and, therefore, necessarily a prisoner, though a willing prisoner, of our aesthetic night? Such might be the significance of the first-mentioned poem. **"The Brute,"** on the other hand, is an all but hallucinatory vision of machinery privately owned unto race deterioration, and some day to be socially controlled unto humane ends, saving then the race out of slum, and dive and morgue. This at least is a prophetic song that should go far to rank Moody among those effective seers who make their vision compelling through verse.

At this stage of our argument Mr. Moody sets before us in a most delicate spiritual study (**"Until the Troubling of the Waters"**) the possible revival of dynamic religion. A healer comes, claiming and exercising the miraculous gifts of apostolic days. And yet, does the soul desire divorce from its fate of accustomed anguish and weakness? If the doting mother be jealous of her child's healing because her child would not then be *her* same child, must not any virile soul much more resent external assistance which he

has not bought by adequate effort, so as to make the divine gift no human gift, but rather a bold taking of his own, a discovery of self in the depths? And if such earning of miraculous help may not come to pass, then must not the virile soul refrain, forego, remain poor, halt, blind, sinful?

For the strange poem **"Daguerreotype,"** in which Moody meditates at large on the theme which Rosetti dared but hint who

> . . . thought as his own mother kissed his eyes
> Of what her kiss was when his father wooed;
>
> **("House of Life; Inclusiveness")**

for this poem some will profess no partiality. It is a piteous resurrection we are given to behold of dear flesh in youth,—too dear perhaps,—for disillusioned filial eyes and heart. "Oh mother," he pleads at last:—

> Lay not on me these intolerable
> Looks of rejoicing love, of pride, of trust, . . .
> Strong eyes and brave
> Inexorable to save!

But though such they be, is theirs the quickening power?

Hearing regretfully of the poet's death I re-read his lyrics as a whole, and penciled on a fly-leaf a fresh impression obtained by excluding so far as possible all external knowledge, casting subjectively his horoscope, attempting a divination of his genius:—"A poet who has passed through evangelical, calvinistic theology, and has never been truly Hellenized. To him love is an illusion of youth, a delusion of later years. The best things in us are invisible, unreachable outflowerings, unheard overtones (**"Harmonics"**); yet is there an after life for their final garnering? Machinery and so called industrial civilization destroy the poet's golden dream. At home our imperialism is national treason to our original consecration. There is however, a beyond, glimpsed afar, of brotherhood and social hallowing,—for the yet unborn, if not for him and us. Let us then proceed and peer as best we may for consolation athwart the generations into the gray dawn."

FORERUNNERS OF THE DRAMATIC POEMS

We must no longer put off the evil hour. What of those two astonishing *tours-de-force*: *The Masque of Judgment* and *The Fire Bringer*? They have a pre-natal history which we shall attempt to sketch.

Goethe conceived and partly executed a "Prometheus" (1773) of which the final chorus to Act I puts into the mouth of the revolting divine man—

> Hast du nicht Alles selbst vollendet
> Heilig glühend Herz?

What man thought proceeded from external deities, came in truth from an imminent godhead? This was a bold word, transferring our quest of the divine essence from cosmology to psychology.

Shelley, dear Platonistic enthusiast, misled by 18th Century rationalism, passed nevertheless from "Queen Mab" and the "Revolt of Islam," from jubilant atheism, to a seeking of the power requisite unto social regeneration; and then "Prometheus Unbound" (1818-20) uttered forever in inspiring lyric form the cries:—

> Man, oh, not men! A chain of linked thought . . .
> Hope, till Hope creates
> From its own wreck the thing it contemplates."

In the mind, purified by suffering, the union with beauty, the vision of truth, the realization of goodness, shall man become at last his own god? From atheism to mysticism, from individualism to a transfigured socialism!

Elizabeth Barrett Browning made the tremendous Aeschylean poem of war between the gods—Prometheus, Man's champion, and Zeus, Man's oppressor,—a part forever of English poetry (1833). Excellent translations have since appeared (especially Plumptre's and Morsehead's) based upon a correcter text, that clarify obscure passages, but nevertheless Mrs. Browning's version will remain our very own for all time.

Now the pre-natal tale of Moody's dramatic poems shifts to this side of the Atlantic via Germany and England once more.

Faust, published complete in 1832, irresistibly challenges translation. Faust had with Goethe superseded Prometheus. The mediæval Teutonic personage was more suited than the Aeschylean Titan to his genius and his people, as vehicle of highest individual and social thought, destructive and reconstructive. Goethe's *Faust* had already in earlier form delighted Shelley and through Shelley inspired Byron's "Manfred" and "Cuin," and from Shelley (1821) we got morsels of exquisite translation. John Anster (I. 1835; II. 1864), Anna Swanwick ('49), Theodore Martin (I.'65; II.'70) Englished the entire world-poem in verse, with much inevitable failure but notwithstanding many an occasional felicity. The work clearly called for an easy, even virile, affluent, versifier, with almost the Italian improvisator's ingenuity and spontaneity, who should be at the same time a conscientious scholar. And there was an American traveler, lecturer and facile singer (all but improvisatore), who responded to the call, and out of deep love of the masterpiece set himself to indefatigable study. "I design nothing less," wrote he to a friend, "than to produce the English *Faust*; it can be done, I know, and pray Heaven that I may be the chosen man to do it." Hence there appeared (1871) that first American masterpiece of translation: Bayard Taylor's *Faust*; which while it never attained the freedom and tunefulness of Shelley's fragments surpassed on the whole everything before or since done.

Now, *Faust* itself in two parts, is a composite poem consisting of numerous independent compositions each in itself more or less complete. What is there not to be seen in that second *Divina Comedia*? A masque, a dramatic prelude, a poetic drama interrupted by a masque, a pageant, a classical tableau vivant set in motion to song, a festal procession, a dramatic idyl, a satirical interlude; indeed all hitherto known forms went to the fashioning of this monster—or miracle—as critics may choose to envisage it. Of course, only a genius like Dante or Goethe can triumph in a Ragnarök of conventional aesthetics, and woe be unto the man of lesser gift who flies into the white flame and scorches his filmy wings! The mere proposal of so complex a formal synthesis would alarm the most intrepid critics. The successful performance would be the Waterloo for all dogmas, and so its possibility must be stubbornly denied. Yet the reverent lover of poetry admires, rejoices, and gives thanks, and if need be quotes Ibsen *mutatis mutandis*: the work is poetry (dramatic poetry?); and if it is not yet, then it will become poetry! The prevailing conception of poetry will have to adjust itself to my work! And who shall dare to affirm the day will not soon roll up in the east (with our increasing theatrical facilities, and we hope our improving histrionic intelligence) for this *Kunstwerk der Zukunft* to be realized in festal splendor? With a Bayreuth in the past (and a Hippodrome in the present!) is this pious wish for the future a sure sign of dementia?

BAYARD TAYLOR'S POETIC DRAMAS

It is natural that one who had endeavored so successfully to English Goethe's *Faust*, should then gird up the loins of his talent for an independent undertaking: to erect a temple unto his own idea of Man and God; nothing less than an American "universal drama" divine and undivine! There followed soon, after a *Vorarbeit* for the same, a study of the Religious *primum mobile* in contemporary mysticism. Experience, illusory and real, produces the prophet; the prophet is obeyed, assisted and then unscrupulously exploited, even unto death, by the ecclesiastic; for this theme Taylor had the immediate story of Mormonism to furnish valuable hints. Better yet, he had his own Quaker instruction and rearing, and his personal religious experience. It is an effort at poetic drama without doubt structurally defective, naive in its psychology and incredibly conventional at times in theatrical procedure. But for all its shortcomings it remains a work worthy of careful study, and one surely not overlooked by Moody. Thence, rather than from Björnsen, would we derive the suggestion for the **Faith Healer**; unless indeed a similar psychological necessity and a similar opportunity (Christian Science offering Moody its history and practice as Mormonism lent itself to the elder poet) could together produce somewhat similar results. To us this seems by far the most likely account of the matter, although we would not for the world impugn Mr. Moody's wide acquaintance with American literature, even to that rare accomplishment: a first hand knowledge of the "Prophet!"

But before the "Prophet," Taylor had begun his Faust in the "Masque of the Gods" (1872) to be followed by "Prince Deukalion" ('75-'77). Its argument in brief: Elohim among the gods must pass away, and even Immanuel bow before The Greater God:—

If we look up
Beyond the shining form wherein Thy Love
Made holiest revelation, we must shade
Our eyes beneath the broadening wing of Doubt,
To save us from Thy splendor. All we learn . . .
But lifts Thee higher, seats Thee more august,
Till Thou art grown so vast and wonderful,
We dare not name Thee, scarce dare pray to Thee.
Yet what Thou art Thyself hast taught us: Thou
Didst plant the ladders which we seek to climb . . .
To grasp Thee. Chide us not: be patient: we
Are children still, we were mistaken oft,
Yet we believe that in some riper time
Thy perfect truth shall come.

With such a conclusion of heaven-questing faith (doubt but the veil to preserve our sight from blinding by too sudden a spiritual splendor) we are fully prepared for "Prince Deukalion," the argument of which runs as follows: Deukalion and Pyrrha are respectively the as yet unrealized but not, therefore, the less essential or dynamic ideals of man and woman. It is they, instructed by Epimetheus (the true understanding of the Past), and illumined by Prometheus (the true foresight of that Future destined to man if he will but rightly look and strive), who shall cast out Medusa (the Mediæval Church) and free the Muses (the arts and sciences), from her surviving sway; set Calchas, the high priest, aside; and with the aid of Agathon (the re-born spirit of humanism, casting out renunciations—be they Buddha's or a false Christ's) proceed to affirm, and together progress towards, a greater manhood and godhood. For Pandora, the beloved Prometheus, over-woman to the over-man, instructs:—

Till woman owns her equal half of life
And following some supernal instinct
Finds her half of godhead (p. 310)

they cannot strive, howsoever they may to

Make once more Life the noble thing it was
When gods were human, or the nobler thing
It shall be when The God becomes divine. (p. 276)
. . . . .
From the evangels of all races God
Begins to be. (p. 313)
. . . . .
Men grow,
But not beyond their hearts,—possess, enjoy,
Yet, being dependent, ever must believe;
So with thy knowledge rises HIM believed,
Shakes off as rags what once were holy names,
Treads underfoot as crackling potsherds all
The symbols of old races. (p. 308)
. . . . .
Though falling as ye fall
HE rises as ye rise! (p. 283)

The simple shepherd and shepherdess of the poem's opening, become illumined towards its close. Eos chants things unspeakable, and the lyric rush reaches, as nearly as Bayard Taylor can make it, Shelley's triumphant "intense inane."

It is easy to set aside such a poem (unread) as a *tour-de-force.* It is more difficult to consider it sympathetically, after conscientious scrutiny, and fail to regret that it does not perhaps altogether attain that required standard of power and transfiguring loveliness which would secure for it the rank of an abiding masterpiece. It is replete with beautiful description, and pregnant thought. To be sure it may seem romantically silly to some unco-wise in its plot, when it works up through adolescent yearnings down the ages to the climax of an osculatory hope deferred to the very verge of ecstatic agony! Still let no one damn the poem with quoted faint praise from Stedman, or the more supercilious irreverence of such as betray scarce a symptom of its flighty perusal! It may not be an ultimate achievement; but it is by all odds the most audacious undertaking in verse of any American up to its date, and far more original, masculine and tuneful at all events than the "Christus" of Longfellow, not to mention such British abominations as "Festus!"

MOORE AND HOVEY

Next after "Prince Deukalion" appeared Charles Leonard Moore's "Prometheus." One should distinguish between dialogue proceeding from imagined characters, and characters allowed to suggest themselves as best they can through a glass darkly, to account for dialogue-monologues employed with changing speakers that novel effects of description and lyric eloquence may be the more naturally introduced. It is on a far lower level than the work of Bayard Taylor in the respect of dramatic objectivity. But the conception of the story is singular and interesting, not to say suggestive for a consideration of Moody's ***Masque of Judgment.*** When Mr. Moore's poem opens, Prometheus is being visited by his Titan brethren, who are for their pedigree wondrously sentimental, not to say feminine. They pour forth wistful regrets and vain consolations, and are blissfully tortured by visions of the greater glory of Zeus, the new ruler who cruelly imposed ordered procedure on cosmic whim and fancy. Zeus, moved by "deep remorse" and by curiosity as to a certain vaunted secret, would if he might release his foe. He disarms himself, but vanquishes the rejoicing Titans through their childish sensuousness. Them he despises. Only Prometheus deserves his respect. He has suffered hell. But so long as there is a hell there can be no heaven, and Zeus has suffered heaven. He therefore delivers Prometheus, who then out of gratitude reveals his secret, to wit: that the universe depends really for its existence on his own continued suffering; should Prometheus cease to struggle, all would cease. Zeus repudiates such extravagant subjective idealism of the emotional sort. It is in his thought, and not in the passion of Prometheus, that the universe has its nourishing roots. Zeus offers Prometheus his throne, who then intones a long elegy on the world he loves. Too late would Zeus a second time impale his foe, who now cries out:

Joy! fierce lightnings leap into thy eyes,
And thy dilating stature terrible
Glowing with fire intense threatens the world
With newer tyrannies. Lift up thy bolts

And gather here together all thy gods,
Once more to overwhelm me, for my heart
Rushes unto my lips to hail the strife.
In battle, oh in battle, let it come
That word of mine that is to end the world!

Zeus already writhes in pain, and passes away. The Titans warble melodiously their cradle song and requiem in one, and then endeavor to rally some sort of primordial courage. All goes out into nothingness with the prayer of Prometheus, to the effect that, if again a world of order should appear, "some soul, fallen" like his on "evil days" may be inspired to—

Put half joys from him, and all wavering hopes,
And with undaunted heart again decree
Ruin and wreck that is the end of all!

It is a long step in dramatic feeling from Moore to Hovey. The years '98 and '99 respectively saw the appearance of two masques by Hovey, part of an extensive now well-known scheme of a poem to be done in nine "dramas." They have a particular human story in view and do not deal directly with our subject. But they illustrated to no small degree the possibilities of the versatile form which Moody was so soon to use, that is to say: the philosophical drama, the drama of ideas projected as mythical personages, who pass in a beautiful procession before our eyes, or settle in sculpturesque groups of loveliness, uttering all the while with polyphonic virtuosity their long-pondered, mistily yet irridescently visualized theme!

THE FIRE BRINGER

For ease of exposition we will defy chronology, and commence with a swift analysis of Moody's *Fire Bringer.* ('04):

Act I:—Prometheus has fetched fire, during an aeonian absence of Zeus, from his white acropolis among the cloud-crags of the sky. The bolt of the wrathful god on his return overtakes Prometheus, shattering to shards the precious jar he bore, and laming his right arm (pp. 23-26). The aged Deukalion fears the pride of his benefactor;

He will be plotting that whereby to climb
And lift us high above the peaks of God
One dizzy instant, ere we fall indeed
And he with us forever. (p. 16)
We cannot thank thee, though thy love be love.
Great is thy heart; we cannot praise thy deed. (p. 26)

He and Pyrrha endure life solely for the sake of their son Aeolus (p. 10) believing that abject humility can alone conciliate Heaven's wrath (p. 29). The stone men and clod women pray Prometheus for real life. He knows of a future glory (p. 28) to be snatched only with violence (p. 29). Pandora, the beloved of Prometheus, suggests the hollow fennel as the carrier of divine fire, (p. 34) so as to bring "hearth-cheer" to the world, and usher in the "new perfect race" (p. 9) which Pyrrha ponders as the only rational explanation of the deluge. Prometheus accepts Pandora's challenge to bring life out of death (p. 39).

Act II:—The Storm that accompanied the deluge is renewed with increased fury (p. 49).

Alas, the wind, the wind!
The trampling and the bellowing herds of rain
Loose on the mountain slopes! Bow down! bow down!

A propitiatory human sacrifice to Zeus is suggested by the despair of the survivers. Lykophon (shamed by his slave's superstitious oblation of his only son) offers his daughter Alcyone. Deukalion is asked for Aeolus. After a stout refusal, the storm bursts in greater rage, threatening utter ruin to the remnant. Deukalion yields Aeolus, his only begotten, and faints at the horror. (p. 50) The priest is distraught (p. 52). Where is the fire for the sacrifice? Pyrrha delays the act of immolation on the pretext of requiring Deukalion's conscious presence. Mutterings are rife. Will Prometheus come? Who is Prometheus? A god? or a halfman? (p. 55) Pandora, at least, seems to be an evil gift of Prometheus, showing the extreme malice of the gods by her revelation of the worth of life at the very moment they are minded to rob man utterly of it. Ere death however, they will praise Apollo (p. 57):—

Once more, once more, O sisters ere we die
I will lift up my cry
To Him who loved us though He puts us by.
For yonder singer with the golden mouth
Hath fallen upon us privily as falls
The still spring out of the south
On the shut passes and locked mountain walls;
And suddenly from out my frozen heart
Dark buds of sorrow start,
Freshets of thought through my faint being roll,
And dim remembrance gropes and travails in my soul.

Pandora draws nigh from above. Deukalion awakes to find sorrow has made him blind. Aeolus and Alcyone, the victims to be, mount the altar and behold with ravishment through a rift in the welkin the long extinguished stars. (pp. 61-63):—

The dark
Gathers and flees, and the wide roof of night
Leans in as it would break; the mountainous gloom
Unmoors, and streameth on us like a sea.
O Earth lift up thy gates! It is the stars!
It is the stars! It is the ancient stars!
It is the young and everlasting stars!

The heaven is cleared, and the universe at one again with man's earth now verily reborn from the flood. pandora sings the coming of the Spirit to the bride. A man sings: will; (p. 65) a woman: love; a Pyrrha: the new world. (pp. 66-69). Then breaks intolerable light upon them which only Deukalion, the blind, can behold and live (pp. 70-71). Is it a universal conflagration following the deluge?

Burning is laid unto the roots of the world;
The deep spouts conflagration from her springs;
And fire feeds on the air that feeds the stars.
Out of the sea has burst,—from rended deeps
Of the unthought-on rearward has leapt out—

> The appearance of the glory of the sun,
> Filling the one side of the roaring world
> With creatures and with branch-work of pale fire;
> And through the woods of fire the beasts of fire,
> The birds and serpents and the naked souls
> Flee, that their fleeting startles the slow dead.

Pandora sings the unity in trinity of Dionysos, Eros, and Apollo: the heightened sense of life, love, and inspired intelligence. Prometheus gives his once-more captured fire to the erstwhile victims, Aeolus and Alcyone, that they may kindle a truer sacrifice. (p. 76) And Pandora sings of the real union, super-carnal henceforward, of human bridegroom and bride-to-be.

Act III:—Deukalion has perished presumably of too great joy. Thanatos, Death, (p. 81) and Eros, Love, are kindred gods. Pyrrha is left with Aeolus to watch the dead until the dawn. The young men in chorus sing, as they recede down the steep, of Dionysos, the god of consciously heightened life, and ecstacy. (p. 84) A cloud appears! (p. 85) Is it the shadow of the eagle of celestial wrath? (p. 89) Pandora's cry of anguish is heard. (pp. 88-90) As Pyrrha paid the price of Deukalion's life for the world's redemption, must Pandora likewise lose Prometheus? Pandora kneels with Pyrra in common anguish, when Prometheus appears to comfort them (pp. 91-96):—He (Prometheus) is himself identical with Zeus (p. 92). Each spirit must fetch the divine fire *for* himself (pp. 92-93):—

> The sun whose rising and whose going down
> Are joy and grief and wonder in the heart;
> The moon whose tides are passion, thought, and will;
> The signs and portents of the spirit year,—
> For these, if you would keep them, you must strive
> Morning and night against the jealous gods
> With anger, and with laughter, and with love;
> And no man hath them till he brings them down
> With love, and rage, and laughter from the heavens,—
> Himself the heavens, himself the scornful gods,
> The sun, the sun-thief, and the flaming reed
> That kindles new the beauty of the world.

Each must rob the divine fire *from* himself, his own foe. For their human sakes is the world significant and lovely. (pp. 93-94):—

> For your sakes it was spoken of the soul
> That it shall be a sea whereon the moon
> Has might, and the four winds shall walk upon it,—
> Also it has great rivers in the midst,
> Unchartered islands that no sailor sees,
> And fathomless abysses where it breeds
> Mysterious life; yea, each its tiniest drop
> Flung from the fisher's oar-blade in the sun
> Has rivers, tempests, and eternal tides,
> Untouched-at isles, horizons never hailed,
> And fathomless abysses where it breeds
> Incredible life, without astonishment.

God calls them alone blessed who have dared Him, and He will cry to them some day for help. (pp. 95-97):

> Yea, He who is the Life of all this life,
> Death of this death and Riser from this death,

> Calleth us blessed in his heart of hearts;
> And once again, in the dim end of things,
> When the sun sickens, and the heaven of heavens
> Flames as a frosty leaf unto the fall,
> In swoon and anguish shall his stormed heart
> Cry unto us: His cry is ringing there
> In the sun's core! I heard it when I stood
> Where all things past and present and to come
> Ray out in fiery patterns, fading, unchanging,
> Forevermore unfaded and unchanged.

But the eagle is imminent. Pandora would share the fate of her beloved in the mortal encounter. He bids her tarry till the end, and blesses the stone-men and the clod-women. Then begins the fight of Prometheus with the eagle. (p. 100):—

> Look hither, look at last, for it is time.
> Up through the crud and substance of the cloud,
> Prometheus wrestles with the bird of God!

Pandora sings of the soul's identity with God, a unique lyric in seven stanzas beginning "I stood within the heart of God," (pp. 103-104) and the young men, hymning Apollo as spiritual vision, bring the poem to a close:—

> O thou alone art he
> Who settest the prisoned spirit free,
> And sometimes leadest the rapt soul on
> Where never mortal thought has gone;
> Till by the ultimate stream
> Of vision and of dream
> She stands
> With startled eyes and outstretched hands,
> Looking where other suns rise over other lands,
> And rends the lonely skies with her prophetic scream.

Throughout, the poet's descriptive work is always interesting and often eloquent and greatly imaginative. There is, however, in this dramatic poem little passion of the human sort, and no theatrical action. Taking into consideration the noble level of the whole, one is surprised at the absence of transfiguring magic. Moody seems always aware of his material, of his medium, of his method. He has less timidity than his forerunners in the field, but still he listens for the rhythm of his music that he may not miss the step. Never does a fine frenzy quite possess him as Shelley, and fling him on from felicity to felicity so that the reader shall likewise become possessed and whirled aloft willy-nilly in the prophet's chariot of fire! The poem, nevertheless, grows greatly in the reader's esteem upon a second or third reading. If it has not the easy fluency, the on-rush and spontaneity, the sense of intelligible contacts with common reality which Taylor's verse never lacks for long; on the other hand the diction of Moody and the phrasing, the metaphoric surprises, are often exquisite and thrillingly audacious, although not wholly shaken free from that reminiscent glory which is alas, quite recognizably their antenatal home.

The final conclusion, philosophically, of the poem rather hinted than spoken broadly, of the essential identity between Prometheus and Zeus reminds the reader of a like proposition set forth in the close of Iwan Gilkin's beautiful dramatic poem *Prométhée* (Paris, Librairie Fishbacher, 1899).

This essential identity is, however, revealed in the Belgian's poem as a euthanasia of Prometheus, the dying immortal, and it has therefore both poetically and philosophically a different complexion.

Now it is important to understand this conclusion, purely metaphysical as it may seem to some readers since it becomes in turn the major premise of the transcendental reasoning in the *Masque of Judgment* ('00). Prometheus is, really and subconsciously, Zeus. Zeus, therefore, aware of this profound identity, refrains himself, and refuses to challenge rebellion to the last internecine conflict. Yet he allots the rebel such wholesome punishment as is due, that he may thereby elicit in him the virtue of fortitude, and allot him martyrdom as supreme boon, thereby raising him to a divers divine equality with himself. In the resistance of Prometheus, Zeus tastes a treble bliss of being, corresponding to a threefold consciousness—as Zeus; as Prometheus; and as the over-Zeus, the atonement of the hostile twain. He as Zeus limits and punishes Prometheus; as Prometheus, he defies Zeus; and as Over-God, he rejoices in both and in his own free transcendant self. Prometheus in his function as Saviour of man comes to know vaguely of this deeper identity; ceases therefore from hate, and endures what is allotted him as the due of his glorious usurpation.

THE MASQUE OF JUDGMENT

Now, admitting for argument's sake the truth of this prophetic rhapsody, this apocalyptic vision, let us then go on to suppose that Zeus should some time lapse from his conscious Over-Godhead, and so forget that he is both Zeus and Prometheus; under the new name of Jehovah let him persecute Prometheus as foe to fiend, until he degrade him into the "Worm that dieth not." Then he would himself have become evil and therefore since Evil is essentially suicidal, give that Worm the power to destroy him. Thus we should arrive logically at the death of God (at least the apparent God, if not the Over-God), which constitutes the apocalyptic vision set forth poetically in the *Masque of Judgment.* Since Flaubert's "Temptation of St. Anthony" (1877), at length this year published in the English of Lafcadio Hearne's version, or Hugo's Epico-lyric *La Fin de Satan* ('57) and *Dieu* ('55), nothing so vertiginous, of such tremendously wide horizon has to our knowledge appeared.

An analysis also of this *Masque of Judgment* ('00), however inadequate, must here be attempted for the convenience of our reader.

Prelude:—Raphael loves the earth and man, and is rebuked for this partiality by Uriel, the archangel of the sun. They consider and deplore together some mysterious di-

vine distress issuing in creation and the evoluton of man (p. 10). Man, of course, involved woman. A girl's love song seems to intimate the reason for man's self-sufficient withdrawal from God. Bacchants destroy an inspired lad who sings of other possible lives and other adorable gods (pp. 13-20). The Pale Horse predicts God's deliverance by the destruction of his foes; that is, of all who yield not their wills to him (p. 19).

Act I:—Raphael sees the broken dragon and eagle. Uriel and he partly fathom the meaning of this mysterious heavenly war. The eagle and the lion, on and under the Tree of Knowledge, sleep and rehearse their futile war upon the Worm. The Tree declares that Man is the real foe, and reveals God's plan of postponing judgment by the incarnation.

Act II:—Awful storms in heaven are caused by God's absence from the central throne, absorbed in his own self dying upon the cross as man, to win back man unto himself as God.

Act III:—Raphael's pity of man. The vindication of God in making and marrying man. The crucifixion is perceived in the heavens of dawn, to involve the universe, and not alone man's earth. Michael rejoices in Puritan judgment, and justifies it by the joy of the courageous judged (p. 81):—

> Yonder where the fight
> Flung its main sea of blood and broken souls
> Into the nether dark, I saw a youth
> Cling for a moment to a jutting rock
> And gaze back at the angel shapes that rode
> The neck of the avalanche; between the wings
> Of the Pale Horse and the Red, his vision pierced
> (Between the ranks of spectred charioteers,
> Supernal arms and banners prone for speed)
> Up to the central menace of the Hand
> That launched that bulk of ruin; and I saw
> A light of mighty pleasure fill his eyes
> At all that harness and despatch of war
> Streaming aslope. He laughed defiance back
> Ere down cascades of blood and fire was flung
> His body indistinguishably damned.
> How should this puny valor rise in glee
> To greet the power that crushed it, and thy heart,
> Angelically dowered, stand listless by?

Raphael objects to pantheism as destroying man's sense of independent initiative. Better perish than not be one's self! Uriel sets forth his own doctrine of pantheism, preserving personal identity, so that to slay one's antagonist would mean suicide (p. 91). Judgment surely is an insufficient Finale for creation:—

> . . . as far as Uriel sees,
> Salvation lies annulled in yonder Vale,
> And prone are God's true helpers. (p. 88)
> This chiefly I would say: the restless joy
> Which called God from His sleep and bade His hand
> Depict much life and language on the dark,
> Had other aims and meanings than are writ

In yonder Valley for an epilogue.
Man's violence was earnest of his strength,
His sin a heady over-flow, dynamic
Unto all lovely uses, to be curbed,
And sweetened, never broken with a rod! (p. 89-90)

For struggle and consciousness are better than Nirvana:—

> Passion is power,
> And kindly tempered, saves. All things declare
> Struggle hath deeper peace than sleep can bring: . . .
> The Shining Wrestler, tired of strife, hath slain
> The dark Antagonist whose enmity
> Gave him rejoicing sinews; but of Him
> His foe was flesh of flesh and bone of bone;
> With suicidal hand He smote him down:
> Soon we shall feel His lethal pangs begin.

Act IV:—Michael tries to save Raphael from the certain doom which will overtake him, if he abandons himself to sympathy with man. The damned are allowed a respite of consciousness, a recovery from death, the better to realize their damnation. By the damned is sung the earth's beauty, in revolt against a pessimistic deity (p. 99); the independence of man; the war-spirit of man in response to a war god. Passion is sung, and natural lust; mysticism, all things but various moods of one god; and, lastly, the joy and pride of artistic creation against a hypocritical humility before the Creator. When the damned have thus superbly celebrated the glories of earth and man, Azaziel trumps the second death. Michael saves Raphael in spite of himself upon a high peak above the Valley of Decision which is now whelmed utterly by the Worm.

Act V:—Raphael recovers from his swoon only to see the Worm assail the battlements of Heaven. He would perish with the damned, but Michael retains him. At the sound of the last trump of celestial rally he flies toward the central throne, Raphael following, meets the fleeing wind-blown lamps of praise. The last stand is to be made. But Uriel explains that God is doomed already:—

> URIEL. To save him from Himself not cherubim, Nor seraphim avail. Who loves not life Receiveth not Life's gifts at any hand.
>
> RAPHAEL. And Life he loved not, though it sprang from Him?
>
> URIEL. He loved it not entirely, good and ill. (p. 124)
>
> RAPHAEL. Would He had spared, That dark Antagonist whose enmity Gave him rejoicing sinews. . . . (p. 125 cf. p. 91)
>
> 1ST LAMP. Brother, what lies beyond this trouble? Death?
>
> URIEL. All live in Him. With Him shall all things die.
>
> 2ND LAMP. And the snake reign, coiled on the holy hill?
>
> URIEL. Sorrow dies with the heart it feeds upon. . . . (p. 126)
>
> RAPHAEL. The moon smoulders; and naked from their seats The stars arise with lifted hands, and wait. (p. 127)

IMPLICATIONS AND CONCLUSION

Now it is clear we cannot justly estimate the significance of this apocalyptic rhapsody (to make use of Dr. Richard Green Moulton's term for such a prophetic poem) ere we have read the as yet unpublished and we fear imperfect third member of the trilogy. We must judge it provisionally, however, as it stands. The last act, if it be a logical sequence to the premises of **The Fire Bringer,** leads us however to suspect that the sublime is here very nigh neighbor to the ridiculous. To us the conclusion, in certain moods at least, would seem to over-vault itself, and land in squat absurdity. To be sure we knew already (speaking it of course with reverence), that God *could* go mad; but then it was only in a mad woman's hallucination in Act. II, Scene 8 of Krasinski's "Undivine Comedy" (1835). (Translation by Martha Walker Cook, Lippincott'75, p. 195). We knew also that the same awful thing might happen quite grotesquely in Aristophanic farce, with the aid of the rollicking genius of Henrik Ibsen. See the fourth act of *Peer Gynt* ('67). But a god dying, a supreme god, that is to say unincarnate, superhuman; and his elegy expectantly composed by trembling Archangels and Lamps . . . how shall we construe this as a latter day revelation? Of course, in dealing with theological imaginations one should, who knows, put a quietus on the sense of humor?

Nevertheless things may look worse than they are. When we attempt to speak of things transcendental, the threads of speech will snarl, and one should not be held too strictly accountable. Perhaps we have here only a belated onslaught on defunct Calvanistic theology? Or perhaps Moody intended to intimate that Monism may be stated, but cannot be thought out in terms of the will? That Dualists we must forever remain? The Christian, evangelical, monotheistic God knew not himself, nor his supreme need of being at one with himself in a perpetual strife? Which, translated into abstract language, might be merely equivalent to intimating that our popular god-conception is obsolete! For goodness consists not in being good, but in the choice rather of good; so that goodness must needs perish with the possibility of choice? Virtue is dynamic, resident in the will, and not static, inherent inorganic necessity? Besides, by way of apology for Moody, is suffering such to God? Is rest and peace an ideal only of us human beings, because with limited energy we readily tire? Are we not, when we speak of a god at perfect peace, applying our "values" (which depend on our restricted state and particular relations to one another and the universe), to the deity regardless of his infinity? Under divine conditions may not our "values" endure reversal, introversion? Yet undoubtedly, that way lies moral confusion! If God's psychology is to be drawn from man's (and must it not always be in a dramatic poem?), the **Masque of Judgment** has an ending which might be taken to argue something assuredly not overprudent in the moral sphere! Man also needs his own evil self for the maintenance of the good in him and lest he extirpate wholly his necessary Satan-self let his God-self proceed with due moderation in the moral struggle. Let him not use weapons of aggression that have developed ahead of defensive armour, lest inadvertent success in a war against sin should result in human extinction? Again, the comic sense should save us from so awful a heresy! Imagine it! existence imperiled from the perverse lack of sin!

These last few paragraphs, however, may intimate that, in our view at least, an apocalyptic poem ought to launch its readers upon more optimistic seas. Yet who knows but a triumphant conclusion is in store for us, with the promised publication of Moody's last poem? Will its reasoning run somewhat like this? The Over-God startled awake from his nightmare of death, the dead and the damned are restored to his side, that they may receive the culminating experience beholding in their own blessed resurrection from the second death Jehovah and the Worm perish together forever?

But let the metaphysical conclusion in store for us take care of itself. We bide our time. Meanwhile who shall deny the right of Moody or any other poet to take such cosmic and transcendental themes, if they can be made to open vast horizons and glorious vistas for the imagination, and above all cast the spell of poetry upon us? The Drama stages human life in the struggle of typical individuals under definite conditions. It can do much. But surely we need also to have spiritual race-ideals, eschatological dreams, concreted for the mind in shining figures and shadows awful, larger than life, and magnificent for the contemplation of the mind's eye. And must such a "dramatic poem" be necessarily considered a bastard form, because forsooth not intended for representation upon our stage as it is? The epic form certainly failed even a Hugo for such subjects. Flaubert furthermore, the novelist, fell into dialogue, or rather threw upon a vast screen, a spectacular phantasmagory, beyond the powers of the Hippodrome pressed into the service of Apollo! And the witness of Flaubert, the fastidious artist, to the inadequacy of epic form, prose or verse, for the treatment of such themes, should weigh with the considerate critic. To our mind at all events, the dramatic poem, in order to be legitimate (not bastard!), needs only so to be written as to project and body itself forth for the imagination on some *conceivable* stage. Wagner for instance did not bind himself to what the theater could do in his own day, and so he caused to appear for our edification a new scenic world. "Dass ich bei diesem Unternehmen nichts mehr mit unserem heutigen Theater zu thun habe." (Eine Mitheilung an Meine Freunde). "That I have in this undertaking of mine parted company forever with our theater of today." So, for the theater of tomorrow, ay and of yesterday (capable of revival as all but proved several times) the dramatic poet may legitimately create; but let him be sure it is for *a* theater, *some* stage, that his poem is so conceived and wrought that it would indeed gain by competent recitation, enaction with or without pantomime, tableaux vivants, dance, procession, light effects and all imaginable resources of an ideal dramatic art. Now actually, we fear that *The Masque of Judgment*'s staple is soliloquy and otiose dialogue; that is, a sequence of monologues directed

haphazard at one another rather than at their speakers. Description of the outer world alternates with description of the inner world. Epic moments lyrically interpreted are interrupted by metaphysical discussion in choice diction and rhythm. But then *The Masque of Judgment* seems far less to us a triumph of the dramatic poem, of the apocalyptic rhapsody re-created for our mental stage, than the *Fire Bringer*; or even, to be quite candid, than *Prince Deukalion.* Yet this argues progress for Moody when we remember the order of composition, and only raises our expectation higher to greet the appearance of the later-written concluding member of the trilogy, not merely for its poetical metaphysic moral and religious suggestions, but for a triumph, who knows, in spiritual drama on some sacred stage of a day that is not yet.

II. THE PLAYWRIGHT

The Great Divide possesses elements which procured it immediate popularity; *The Faith Healer,* so far as it has yet been tried upon the stage, has proved a failure. But neither the one reception nor the other is a true measure of the value of these respective dramas. It was the more obvious features of *The Great Divide* that were brought out in the stage presentation and, it is to be presumed, mainly attracted the vast audiences. The latter were interested in its melodramatic and sentimental aspects, and missed the spiritual motive which environed both. *The Faith Healer* lacks the garnish of incidental attractiveness, and still goes begging for an adequate interpretation of its spiritual motive, in the absence of which it is premature to pronounce it unsuitable to stage purposes. The truth is that both plays are ahead of their times. They demand a faculty of intellectual interpretation which is practically non-existent among our players, and of intellectual appreciation which is very sparsely represented in our audiences. Meanwhile, both dramas will remain among the most treasured companions of the library.

Both are realistic dramas in the true sense of the term, realism, as distinguished from naturalism. For while the naturalistic artist is satisfied to observe and record the facts of actual life, the true realist correlates the facts to the large issues of life, and views them in relation to the wide horizon of intellectual or spiritual significance. It is this larger vital significance that many a person, fascinated by the actualities of *The Great Divide,* has missed. It was missed in the acting; and can scarcely be appreciated to the full without reading and re-reading of the play. Then it is discovered that the idea involves a clarion appeal, so novel and stimulating that one may be disposed to regard it as the biggest and noblest voice of the New Democracy yet uttered.

For, back of the locality of this drama is a universal significance. It is not merely the conflict of the old East and the new West as represented in our own country; it is also and much more the world-wide dawning of a new thought that shall supersede the old. The wrappages of Puritan tradition and environment which encumber Ruth Jordan, are but symbols of the grave-clothes of intellectual and spiritual dead prejudices, out of which a new conception of Democracy is struggling to rise and live.

Truly one obstacle to a proper appreciation of Moody as a seer and prophet, (not of lamentation but of hope and constructive ideals) is the smug notion that the United States is the great exponent of the Democratic ideal. It offers the greatest opportunities of realising the ideal of a new Democracy, but at the same time a signal example of slowness in utilising them. As a nation, we are still intellectually, spiritually and artistically in bondage to the shackles that we originally brought over or are still importing from Europe. Indeed, in these respects, there are parts of Europe ahead of us in progress. They are facing the logic of Democracy, and shaping thereto their ideals and conduct, while we still, to a very large extent, are trying to solve Democracy by inherited or borrowed principles of Aristocracy.

Moody realised this. New England bred, he reached his maturity in the Middle West. It was the poignancy of the conflict in his own mind and soul between his bringing up and his acquired consciousness that formed the basis of **The Great Divide.** But the subjectivity of the motive expanded into an objective vision, which passed beyond the local and temporal to the universal and eternal. It was a vision of a new heaven and a new earth, of conduct founded not on dogmas, denunciations of sin and dread of retribution in a future life, but on the joy and strength of living in this life, so that this earth in the progress of time may become a heaven, and our conception of heaven may be realized out of the present facts of life.

The overwhelming fact of Ruth Jordan's life, as it is unfolded in the play, is that she has been foully trapped into a marriage with a man who thus outraged her instincts and traditions of womanhood. According to all the traditions of her race she should have died sooner than submit. But the call of life was loud in her blood. She chose the horror of living. Then the traditions of her race urged her to persist in regarding her life as a horror, even although she was not blind to the fact that the man who had wronged her was daily redeeming himself by straight conduct and devotion to herself. He had come under the spell of her spiritual ascendency and had grown to be a new man. Gradually, however, he compelled her to love him. "How was that?" he asks. "Oh! I don't wonder you ask," she replies. "Another woman would have gone straight to her goal. You might have found such an one, but instead you found me, a woman in whose ears rang night and day the cry of an angry heaven to us both: 'Cleanse yourselves!' And I went about it in the only way I knew [*pointing to the portraits of New England divines on the walls of her childhood home at Milford Corners, Mass.*], the only way my fathers knew—by wretchedness, by self-torture, by trying blindly to pierce your careless heart with pain. And all the while you—oh, as I lay there and listened to you, I realized it for the first time,—you had risen, in one hour, to a wholly new existence, which flooded the present and the

future with brightness, yes, and reached back into the past, and made of it—made of all of it—something to cherish."

And then follows the new message: that even in sin the virtue of life may have its roots. "You have taken the good of our life and grown strong. I have taken the evil and grown weak, weak unto death. Teach me to live as you do!"

This may have been the teaching of the great Socialist-democrat, Christ; but it has been overwhelmed by time, and it comes to-day as a new word; that out of sin may grow salvation. Meanwhile this is only part of the philosophy of the play. Its further message is that our salvation as individuals, as well as the collective salvation of society, must grow out of the actual facts of human nature, its weaknesses and its potentialities; and not out of an ideal, conceived as separate from and superior to our physical, mental and spiritual selves. It is out of the possibilites and limitations of our actual humanity that we can alone approximate to ideals of the divine.

A similar idea of humanity, as at once the basis of the ideal and the touchstone of conduct and aspiration, is involved in **The Faith Healer.** Michaelis, the visionary, with a faith in himself and in the Divine, which inspires faith in others with results such as are called miracles, is a latter-day Messiah in more than a strictly religious sense. He represents also the spiritual creator—call him artist or what you will—whose mission in life is the ideal: to uphold the realites of spirit alongside material actualities, to correlate one with the other, to lead humanity to a consciousness of its higher self. But Michaelis meets Rhoda, who personifies the color and warmth of life. In the heat of her physical allurement Michaelis' spirituality evaporates; his power goes from him. By degrees, however, he discovers the soul within the flesh of Rhoda. She has sinned and suffered and been weak, but has grown strong. The spirituality in him has lifted her up again onto a foundation of hope and happiness. Michaelis accepts the lesson. He has tried to live too purely the life of the spirit; thereby losing touch with the common facts of humanity, so that, confronted with the warmth and color of life, he became confused and also lost his grip upon the spiritual. It is only when he recognizes the cause of his failure and takes advantage of the strength of humanity in the person of Rhoda that his spiritual power returns to him. And in greater measure than before.

Thus in these two plays, Moody sets forth his philosophy of life, both in its social and spiritual aspects. He has searched Democracy not for what it is, but for what it may and will be: a larger opportunity of physical, mental and spiritual development. He bases it in philosophy, not on a theory of impossible perfection which contradicts the experiences of life, but on the imperfections of our actual existence. He is an idealist, not of the old kind but of the modern; that is to say, a realist in the true sense. For he accepts human nature as he finds it, and out of its very self would evolve the ideal. We were taught in our youth that "they were dangerous guides, the feelings;" but he would grasp the danger, and extract from it the possibilities of good. In a word, he would correlate the flesh and blood of life with its intellectual and spiritual aspirations, and maintain that so far from their being antagonistic, they are mutual reinforcements of the large and liberal conceptions of life which may be expected from the new conception of Democracy.

Harriet Monroe (essay date 1912)

SOURCE: "Moody's Poems," in *Poetry*, Vol. 1, No. 2, November, 1912, pp. 54-7.

[*In the following essay, Monroe sketches Moody's development as a poet, finding he had reached maturity at the time of his death.*]

The Poems and Plays of William Vaughn Moody will soon be published in two volumes by the Houghton-Mifflin Co. Our present interest is in the volume of poems, which are themselves an absorbing drama. Moody had a slowly maturing mind; the vague vastness of his young dreams yielded slowly to a man's more definite vision of the spiritual magnificence of life. When he died at two-score years, he was just beginning to think his problem through, to reconcile, after the manner of the great poets of the earth, the world with God. Apparently the unwritten poems cancelled by death would have rounded out, in art of an austere perfection, the record of that reconciliation, for nowhere do we feel this passion of high serenity so strongly as in the first act of an uncompleted drama, *The Death of Eve.*

Great-minded youth must dream, and modern dreams of the meaning of life lack the props and pillars of the old dogmatism. Vagueness, confusion and despair are a natural inference from the seeming chaos of evil and good, of pain and joy. Moody from the beginning took the whole scheme of things for his province, as a truly heroic poet should; there are always large spaces on his canvas. In his earlier poetry, both the symbolic *Masque of Judgment* and the shorter poems derived from present-day subjects, we find him picturing the confusion, stating the case, so to speak, against God. Somewhat in the terms of modern science is his statement—the universe plunging on toward its doom of darkness and lifelessness, divine fervor of creation lapsing, divine fervor of love doubting, despairing of the life it made, sweeping all away with a vast inscrutable gesture.

This seems to be the mood of the *Masque of Judgment,* a mood against which that very human archangel, Raphael, protests in most appealing lines. The poet broods over the earth—

> The earth, that has the blue and little flowers—

with all its passionate pageantry of life and love. Like his own angel he is

> a truant still
> While battle rages round the heart of God.

> The lamps are spent at the end of judgment day,

> and naked from their seats
> The stars arise with lifted hands, and wait.

This conflict between love and doubt is the motive also of **"Gloucester Moors," "The Daguerreotype, Old Pourquoi"**—those three noblest, perhaps, of the present-day poems—also of **"The Brute"** and **"The Menagerie,"** and of that fine poem manqué, the **"Ode in Time of Hesitation."** *The Fire-Bringer* is an effort at another theme—redemption, light after darkness. But it is not so spontaneous as the *Masque*; though simpler, clearer, more dramatic in form, it is more deliberate and intellectual, and not so star-lit with memorable lines. *The Fire-Bringer* is an expression of aspiration; the poet longs for light, demands it, will wrest it from God's right hand like Prometheus. But his triumph is still theory, not experience. The reader is hardly yet convinced.

If one feels a grander motive in such poems as the one-act *Death of Eve* and **"The Fountain,"** or the less perfectly achieved **"I Am the Woman,"** it is not because of the tales they tell but because of the spirit of faith that is in them—a spirit intangible, indefinable, but indomitable and triumphant. At last, we feel, this poet, already under the shadow of death, sees a terrible splendid sunrise, and offers us the glory of it in his art.

"The Fountain" is a truly magnificent expression of spiritual triumph in failure, and incidentally of the grandeur of Arizona, that tragic wonderland of ancient and future gods. Those Spanish wanderers, dying in the desert, in whose half-madness dreams and realities mingle, assume in those stark spaces the stature of universal humanity, contending to the last against relentless fate. In the two versions of *The Death of Eve,* both narrative and dramatic, one feels also this wild, fierce triumph, this faith in the glory of life. Especially in the dramatic fragment, by its sureness of touch and simple austerity of form, and by the majesty of its figure of the aged Eve, Moody's art reached its most heroic height. We have here the beginning of great things.

The spirit of this poet may be commended to those facile bards who lift up their voices between the feast and the cigars, whose muses dance to every vague emotion and strike their flimsy lutes for every light-o'-love. Here was one who went to his desk as to an altar, resolved that the fire he lit, the sacrifice he offered, should be perfect and complete. He would burn out his heart like a taper that the world might possess a living light. He would tell once more the grandeur of life; he would sing the immortal song.

That such devotion is easy of attainment in this clamorous age who can believe? Poetry like some of Moody's, poetry of a high structural simplicity, strict and bare in form, pure and austere in ornament, implies a grappling with giants and wrestling with angels; it is not to be achieved without deep living and high thinking, without intense persistent intellectual and spiritual struggle.

John M. Manly (essay date 1912)

SOURCE: An introduction in *The Poems and Plays of William Vaughn Moody*, Volume I, Houghton Mifflin Company, 1912, pp. vii-xlvi.

[*In the following essay, Manly offers a biographical and critical overview of Moody's career as a poet and dramatist.*]

Not merely because William Vaughn Moody was my colleague and my friend do I wish to speak of him, but because I feel that the poetry he left us is of unique and permanent value to us all, and believe that it was growing in depth, in sweetness, and in strength when the darkness descended so tragically upon him. The beauty of poetry as little needs the aid of argument as does that of a rose, and Moody's poetry is here to manifest its own loveliness and power; but the lover of beauty in a poem or in a rose may increase his delight by sharing it with another, and I, who have seen Moody's poetry growing into fuller and fuller kinship with that of the elder and most authentic poets of our tongue, while retaining its own unmistakable individuality, would gladly share my vision and delight.

Of the sanity and manifold charm of the man himself, no description, much less so brief an account as this must be, can give any adequate idea. A volume of his letters soon to be published under the care of one of his most intimate friends will make it possible for all to know something of his vigor, his grace, his humor, his courage, his large humanity, his daily passion for material and spiritual beauty; and these letters will give a fuller record of the notable incidents of his life than can be attempted here. But his work was so natural and inevitable a flowering of his whole being that something must be said of his character and his career.

Like so many men of unusual intellectual and emotional powers, Moody was one in whom different racial or temperamental strains met and blended. His father, Francis Burdette Moody, was of English and French descent; his mother, Henrietta Stoy, of English and German. To them were born three sons and four daughters. The third son and sixth child was William Vaughn, who was born at Spencer, Indiana, on July 8, 1869. That the father was a man of enterprise and of vigor is indicated not merely by his emigration from New York to the thriving State of Indiana, but also by the fact that he was for many years a steamboat captain, an occupation requiring no little resourcefulness, power of rapid decision, and ability to command men. To him his son pays a noble tribute in certain lines of **"The Daguerreotype."** But the mother doubtless had the larger share in the guidance and discipline of the growing boy, and the profound impression she left upon his mind and heart is recorded not only in **"The Daguerreotype"**—a poem so deep of thought, so full of poignant feeling and clairvoyant vision, so wrought of passionate beauty that I know not where to look for another tribute from any poet to his mother that equals it—and in the veiled but illuminating reference in **"Faded Pictures,"** but even more fully in that love and reverence for woman which became fundamental to his whole philosophy of life.

About 1871 the family moved to New Albany, on the Ohio River, and there the mother died in 1884 and the father in 1886. After his father's death the career of Moody was much like that of many another ambitious boy. He taught for a while in a country school near New Albany, and in the autumn of 1888 went to Riverside Academy, New York, where he helped with the teaching to put himself through school. From 1889 to 1893 he was technically an undergraduate at Harvard University, but, having completed the courses necessary for his degree, he went abroad in his senior year as tutor for a boy. The year was notable for a walking trip through the Black Forest and Switzerland with Robert Lovett and Norman Hapgood and L. H. Dow, for the winter which he spent in Florence, and for his first visit to Greece. In 1893-94 he was back at Harvard as a member of the Graduate School. What courses of study he took I do not know, but I remember hearing at the time from Professor Kittredge of his insatiable appetite for mediæval French romances. At the end of the year he took his master's degree and became a member of the staff of the department of English.

In the autumn of 1895 he came to the University of Chicago as instructor in English and continued to serve as instructor and assistant professor until 1903. His work as a teacher was relieved by various trips in this country and abroad. In June, 1896, he made a ten-day bicycle trip with Ferdinand Schevill through northern Illinois and southern Wisconsin. The spring and summer of 1897 he spent in Europe. His experiences there included a bicycle trip with Ferdinand Schevill from Rome to Lake Como, through the Alban Hills and over the Apennines. At Sorrento he saw the Eastertide procession that suggested his poem **"Good Friday Night."** During the bicycle trip mentioned he sketched the **"Road-Hymn for the Start."** The imagery of the poem recalls conditions and circumstances connected with Montefiascone and Lago di Bolsena. In June he was with his friends, the Lovetts, at Venice in the Casa Frollo on the Giudecca. Later he visited Asolo and tramped with Robert Lovett through the Dolomites. The same trip included an ascent of the Grosser Venediger. This was followed by a brief residence at Cortina, where he and Lovett found delight in climbing mountains and in ice-cold plunges into a pool fed by a neighboring glacier. He then returned to Ravenna and thence bicycled alone across Italy to Genoa. On account of the intense heat he was obliged to travel mostly by night, and an illness which had attacked him at Innsbruck returned at Genoa. In the summer of 1901 he made his first visit to Mackinac Island, and in

August went on a brief camping trip in Colorado with Hamlin Garland. In 1902 he was again abroad on a trip to Greece, notable for a lonely ride through the Peloponnesus; but he spent much of his time in Greece reading Greek tragedy, and upon his return remarked upon the deeper and clearer understanding of Greek art which came to one under Grecian skies. After giving up his work at the University he made several interesting and important trips, one in the spring of 1905 with Ferdinand Schevill to Arizona. They spent a week at Oraibi among the Hopi Indians, saw the Spring Dance at Walpi, and while there Moody definitely planned *The Great Divide,* which was rapidly written soon after his return. In the spring and early summer of 1907 he went with Ridgely Torrence to Tangier, Spain, Italy, and France.

These excursions are all significant of his tastes and of his fondness for physical activity. He was no mere bookish, indoor poet, but found his greatest delight in swimming, bicycling, golf, tennis, walking, mountain-climbing, and such athletic sports as are pursued for the love of the sport and not the applause of the public. Much as he loved literature and art and all the fruits of human culture, exquisite as was his sensitiveness to rhythm and melody and sonorous diction in verse, to interwoven and complex harmonies in music, to color and composition and tactile strain in painting, to imagination and truth in all the arts, his pleasure in the physical world of sense was no less exquisite or keen. Of slightly more than medium height, with a vigorous, well-knit body in which every organ of power and sensation was perfect, he not only theoretically but in fact felt that the perfection of life lies in the realization of all its resources of thought and emotion and bodily sensation. Not in less degree than a Greek of the age of Pericles was he an epicure of life, a voluptuary of the whole range of physical, mental, and spiritual perfections. To recognize this, one had only to look upon his body, sensitive to every delight and exuberant with vitality; to be suddenly fixed by his wonderful eyes, light, clear blue, and shining like large gems because of the sailor-like ruddiness that wind and sun had laid upon his cheek and brow; to hear his eager discourse upon art or life, both of which to him were one. But that his sensitiveness to all that is beautiful was due, not to weakness, but to vigor and health of mind and character, is shown by the unwavering determination with which he put aside softness and ease and lived hardly and barely in order to do his appointed work as poet.

After 1902 he ceased to teach in the University, though the authorities induced him to maintain for some years a nominal connection, in the hope that he might resume his work as a lecturer, even if only occasionally and for brief periods. But although courses were sometimes planned for him, they were always withdrawn before the time to give them arrived. Nothing is more characteristic of the man than the determination with which he pursued his own proper career. President Harper believed so thoroughly in his value to the University that he offered him the full salary of a professor if he would continue to lecture for a single quarter each year. Temptation of this sort and offers of financial assistance from friends he resolutely put aside, preferring to live hardly and poorly for the sake of living independently and doing the work to which he had long since determined to devote all his powers. Relief from the drudgery of teaching came with the publication of the *History of English Literature* which he wrote in collaboration with Robert M. Lovett. This book, like the others which he published to supplement his salary,—chief among them an edition of Bunyan's *Pilgrim's Progress* with introduction and notes, and a complete edition of the English and Latin poems of Milton,—was a brilliant and scholarly piece of work, the fruit of years of study and reflection.

There was never a more conscientious teacher than Moody, whether his task was lecturing on English literature or the monotonous grind of theme correction, and seldom a more brilliant and inspiring lecturer. Traditions of his teaching still linger about the University, but even from a child he had thought poetry was his proper function and he gave himself up entirely to his work as soon as it was possible to do so. Conscientious and successful as was his teaching, his heart was never in it. He looked forward eagerly to his vacations and counted the days till the summit of the quarter should be reached and the pleasant slope to the end should begin. In January, 1898, he wrote to a friend, "I started in to-day on another quarter's work at the shop— with vacation and restored consciousness three months away." This was partly because he felt, as all lovers of beauty feel, that the formal teaching of literature has in it something destructive and deadening. When, after his last visit to Greece, I was urging him to return to the University and lecture upon English poetry in the new light on Greek literature which had come to him, he steadily refused to do so, and finally said, "I cannot do it; I feel that at every lecture I slay a poet."

Moody's earlier work as a poet was, like that of Keats and, indeed, many other writers, purely experimental and detached from life. Some of these poems were never published; some were published in the *Harvard Monthly;* some he rewrote; but there were comparatively few which in later years he was willing to see reprinted. To this critical attitude is due, in part, the fact that, though he wrote with ease, the volume of short poems which he published in 1901, containing all he then wished made permanent, is small compared with the output of much less fertile and vigorous artists. The ease with which he wrote may be inferred from a remark he made to me in 1898. He had been reading a revised version of **"The Amber Witch,"** a poem inspired in his undergraduate years by Keats's "La Belle Dame Sans Merci," and then began to talk of a play he was planning to write in blank verse on a theme suggested by the meteoric glow and disappearance of Schlatter the Faith Healer. Upon my venturing the opinion that it was too late in the history of the world to write plays in anything but prose, he replied that for such a subject he thought blank verse more suitable and that it was easier to write blank verse than prose.

Like the experimental work of most young poets, Moody's was imitative, but he did not even then make himself "the sedulous ape" either of one writer or of many. Traces of Shakespeare, of Milton, of Keats, of Browning, of Rossetti, of William Morris, of Walt Whitman, one may find either in theme, or tone, or rhythm, or, though seldom, in phrasal echo. Of Tennyson there is perhaps not a trace, for he had long been rejected by the critical spirits of the English Club and the *Monthly*; and of Swinburne quite as little, for the Swinburne epidemic, once strong, had spent itself at Harvard the year that Moody entered as a freshman. Specimens, not of his earliest work, but of work which still recalls in some measure the manner of his favorite poets, are the song **"My Love Is Gone into the East," "The Ride to the Lady,"** now entitled **"The Ride Back," "How the Mead-Slave Was Set Free,"** and the sonnet **"Harmonics."**

But early as these poems are, it is singular to find in them so little of morbidity, so little of that aimless melancholy which marks the youthful work of most poets. Moreover, there is not one which does not contain some striking example of Moody's individuality and boldness of conception and phrasing. In **"The Ride Back,"** a purely ornamental, self-conscious bit of pre-Raphaelitism of the Morris type, occur such lines as:—

> About the dabbled reeds a breeze
> Went moaning broken words and dim,

and

> Lewd as the palsied lips of hags
> The petals in the moon did shake,

and

> And songs blown out like thistle seed;

and most wonderful of all is the whole of the fourth stanza from the end. Just as artificial and as literary in its inspiration is **"How the Mead-Slave was Set Free,"** but how characteristically and vividly conceived are the pictures of stanzas two and three and stanza eight, and how true and rare is the observation in the lines:—

> . . . thrill like happy things
> That flutter from the gray cocoons
> On hedgerows, in your gradual springs!

And who but Moody himself could speak, as he does in **"Harmonics,"** of

> . . . such a laddered music, rung on rung,
> As from the patriarch's pillow skyward sprung,
> Crowded with wide-flung wings and feet of fire?

In 1896 came the first poem suggested by his own experience. In May of that year, along with a copy of a poem called **"Wilding Flowers,"** he wrote to his friend Daniel G. Mason: "I send you a poem which I have just written about the Creature I once hinted to you of—a girl who haunted the Symphonies last winter. I hope you will like it, because it is almost the first thing I have done which

has been a direct impulse from real life, and you know I have theories about that." This poem, now entitled **"Heart's Wild-Flower,"** is in subject, diction, and melody not altogether without kinship to Rossetti, but the simple and exquisite phrasing, the subtle reticence of youthful adoration, reach a climax of sincerity and individuality in the last six lines. Again, in July of the same year, with a copy of **"Dawn Parley,"** a poem not in the present collection, he writes, "I inclose a reaction on a recent notable experience."

From this time on, much of his poetry was more or less directly suggested by real incidents or situations of his life; and the large body of it which still had an alien origin or inspiration is shot through with transformed emotional images of them. In some instances the later poems go back several years for the experiences they transcribe. Thus **"Old Pourquoi,"** written after 1901, recalls an incident of a walk from Caudebec to Yvetot in August, 1895. **"Good Friday Night,"** suggested by an Eastertide procession at Sorrento in April, 1897, was not completed till the end of the year. The **"Road-Hymn for the Start"** was sketched in May of the same year, but was not written until later. **"Song-Flower and Poppy,"** written in New York in the spring of 1899, is crowded with recollections of the Italian journeys of 1897. On the other hand, **"A Grey Day"** and **"Gloucester Moors"** were written among the scenes they transcribe; and the composition of **"The Daguerreotype,"** the **"Ode in Time of Hesitation," "On a Soldier Fallen in the Philippines," "The Quarry,"** and **"The Moon-Moth,"** followed close upon the incidents which gave them being.

But Moody's poetry, whether due to a direct impulse from life or suggested, like the **"Dialogue in Purgatory"** and **"The Fountain"** and **"Thammuz,"** by literature, is notable for its freedom from response to the obvious, the trivial, the merely pretty. This is, no doubt, one reason why, for all his rich and various melody, his wealth of fresh and vivid imagery, his modernity, his worship of beauty and love, his depth of spiritual emotion, he is not popular, is indeed hardly remembered by any except those to whom poetry is not an idle pastime, but a passion; for the idler wants art in all its forms to be obvious, and trivial, and pretty. Moody's themes are often the common themes of poetry: love, patriotism, human suffering, God, and the soul. But he sees them ever from some new angle, he finds in them new significance, he mingles them with unaccustomed but predestined associations. His vision and feeling are not simple, but interwoven with rich threads of reflection and transmuting emotion. Even the oldest theme or image becomes his own, because he has seen and felt it anew. What is there more common than a street song that seizes the heart of the listener and bears it far away? Wordsworth gives it perhaps as simple a rendering as it ever had in poetry. Moody's **"Song-Flower and Poppy"** shows no more effort at complexity than the **"Reverie of Poor Susan"**; it is richer in imagery and in meaning, more intense, more significant, just because the street song falls not on the ears of a housemaid but on those of a passionate lover of beauty and of life. All of us, in this day of human brotherhood and sympathy for the poor, have felt that we have, perhaps, more than our share of the good things of life; but who but Moody, watching the spring come up the land, has thought of his fellowmen and written:—

> To be out of the moiling street
> With its swelter and its sin!
> Who has given to me this sweet,
> And given my brother dust to eat?
> And when will his wage come in?

Ages ago old Omar wrote that

>   never blows so red
> The Rose as where some buried Cæsar bled;

and the

> e tumulo fortunataque favilla
> Nascentur violæ

of Persius has been echoed by Shakespeare and by Tennyson; but this pretty conceit, this sweet and pious prayer, found new and deeper significance when Moody wrote of the burial in a common grave of Robert Shaw and his faithful band of negroes:—

> Now limb doth mingle with dissolvèd limb
> In nature's busy old democracy,
> To flush the mountain laurel when she blows
> Sweet by the southern sea,
> And heart with crumbled heart climbs in the rose.

That Moody's poetry does not always reveal its meaning to the careless and casual reader is true; to such perhaps it never reveals itself entirely. This is due to several causes. For one thing, the only types of poetry that are easy to read are the narrative and what may be called the universal lyric. Moody rarely wrote narrative verse, and the little that he did write has, like most of his lyrics, dramatic quality also, and demands that the reader conceive a situation and follow it in all its changing phases. Even **"Good Friday Night"** and **"Second Coming,"** two of the simplest as well as the profoundest and most beautiful of his narrative poems, make large demands upon the imagination and the emotions; and even larger demands are made by *The Death of Eve* and **"The Moon-Moth."** Poems of other types are even more difficult. How many times have I not heard intelligent persons question what was intended by that marvelous personification of machinery, **"The Brute,"** that vision of the early roseate hopes for economic relief, the grimy present reality, and the final compelling of the Brute to bring the good time on! Insoluble, perhaps, without the hint given by the date, is **"The Quarry."** Yet even that becomes clear when one remembers that it was then that the beasts of prey gathered to dismember China, and that the attitude and intent of the Eagle were long doubtful.

Another cause of difficulty arises from the quality of Moody's imagination and his inexhaustible store of sensory images. He has few similes and his sense impressions are so specific that they make great demands upon both experience and memory. How many of us think of the fourth stanza of **"Gloucester Moors"** as anything but a fantastic image? And yet any one who will steadily watch the summer clouds as they sail overhead in a light wind will veritably feel the "velvet plunge and soft upreel" of the steadfast earth. Have you seen

> O'er the grey deep the dories crawl,
> Four-legged, with rowers twain?

Have you noted the "opal heart" of a summer afternoon, seen the "ashen lips" of the western storm, watched "the raindrops dot the sand," and "the shards of day sweept past"? Scarcely a page, certainly not a poem, however short, fails to yield some notable phrasing of a sight, a sound, an odor that gives us a more vivid realization of it than the object itself would give, and leaves us with a permanently greater capacity of enjoyment of such sensations.

Like his imagery, Moody's diction is rich, condensed, packed with meaning. Any one of the poems will furnish abundant instances. **"Good Friday Night"** is full of them: "twilight circles," "ancient square," "unspiritual," "throned in its hundred candles," "the doll-face, waxen white, flowered out a living dimness," "the odorous hill," "heart-stung." Often, as here, the words themselves are simple and separately not of special beauty, but partly from his native bent, and partly from his loving study of æschylus and Milton, Moody loved beautiful words for their own sakes, words sonorous, or melodious, or rich in suggestion. The second and third sections of the **"Ode in Time of Hesitation,"** for all their large meaning and their jeweled picturesqueness, are a veritable symphony of rich and melodious words. Of similar character are the speeches of Prometheus in the first act of *The Fire-Bringer.*

Moody has, too, especially in his lyrics, the gift of unaccountable magic—of simple phrases which stir the emotions or awaken a sense of significance far beyond the power of the words or the thought. His lyrics, especially the brief lyrics in the poetic dramas, are full of this, the songs of Pandora in *The Fire-Bringer* and those of the Spirits in *The Masque of Judgment*:

> Along the earth and up the sky
>   The Fowler spreads his net:
> O soul, what pinions wild and shy
>   Are on thy shoulders set?
> What wings of longing undeterred
> Are native to thee, spirit bird?

Or Raphael's song in *terza rima* of God's interest and pleasure in all his creatures great and small:—

> Down curved spaces He may warp
> With old planets, long and long;
> Where the snail doth tease and carp,
> Asking with its jellied prong,
> A whole summer he may bide,

Wondrous tiny lives among,
Curious, unsatisfied.

Or, most remarkable of all, the song of the Redeemed
Spirits, as they fly past:—

In the wilds of life astray,
Held far from our delight,
Following the cloud by day
And the fire by night,
Came we a desert way.
O Lord, with apples feed us,
With flagons stay!
By Thy still waters lead us!

What resides in those last three lines to make us accept
their poor offerings as heavenly food and drink and all the
joys that await the Redeemed? I cannot for the life of me
tell, any more than I know why an unfathomable fount of
sorrow lies in Wordsworth's

Perhaps the plaintive numbers flow
For old, unhappy, far-off things,
And battles long ago;

or why the whole riddle of the universe arises with Shakespeare's

We are such stuff as dreams are made on,
And our little life is rounded with a sleep.

That the words all have meanings and associations is true,
but the meanings and associations are inadequate to the
emotional effect. Is it the rhythm, the harmonic overtones?
Is it true that a single note of a violin will set a steel
bridge in vibration or shatter a stone building if only the
right tone be found?

In such lyrics as these, poetry perhaps makes its nearest
approach to pure music. Its effects are those of rhythm, of
melody of those wonderful interweavings of present tones
with past tones that still linger in the brain, if not in the
ear, and form harmonies. Such effects may be produced, as
we have seen, almost without reference to any thought or
associations conveyed by the words themselves; but they
are naturally most powerful and beautiful when joined
with beautiful thoughts and associations, as in many of the
stanzas of **"Song-Flower and Poppy,"** or in the Song of
the Stone Men and Earth Women in the last act of *The
Fire-Bringer,* or Pandora's songs in the second act, or the
song of the Girl in the Prelude to *The Masque of Judgment.*

Much of Moody's success in these lyrics, as elsewhere in
his poetry, comes from his fearless mastery of diction and
of movement. We have already seen, in part, the bold individuality of his sense impressions and of his imagery.
Only a master has the sincerity to see things freshly and
render fearlessly his vision of them. And in expression
Moody is as sincere and fearless as in vision. He gets his
idea and the phrase which renders it; and the movement,
the rhythm, takes care of itself. This is especially evident
in his handling of the long lines of the lyric portion of the
epic *Death of Eve* and of the song **"I am the Woman."**
Only a master of English verse could make lines of such
length move at all, while to make them run and dance and
sparkle with light is a triumphant achievement. The same
thing is true of the choral movements in *The Fire-Bringer.*
These rhythms may lack the elaborately varied structure of
Greek choral movements, but it would be difficult to find
in English any verse that more satisfactorily recalls the
Greek.

Thus far we have spoken mainly of the technical elements
of Moody's poetry. More interesting and more important
are his ideas. To say that they are new would be the same
as saying that they are unfit for poetry. Art never deals,
never can deal, with ideas that have not already been associated with powerful human emotions. But Moody's ideas,
though familiar and indeed in many cases ancient themes
of art, are made new and vital by subjection to his temperament and culture and by association with the elements
of his spiritual life. In later years his main themes were
social and economic injustice, patriotism, the heart of
woman, and the relations of God and the soul, the meaning of human life. To the reconception of all these large issues, he brought the richest intellectual and emotional endowment possessed by any American poet.

Hints have already been given of his classical culture, one
of the most important formative forces of his art. The influence of æschylus is evident in his diction, his music,
and his imagery, but most powerful and most evident is
the influence of the *Bacchæ* of Euripides. It appears not
only in the Prelude to *The Masque of Judgment* and the
songs and choruses of *The Fire-Bringer,* but probably
motived the choice of Thammuz as a subject, though the
subject be Biblical, and certainly aided the union of religious mysticism and joy in sensuous life which is the
dominant note of all Moody's later work. Indeed the *Bacchæ* seems to have meant even more to Moody than to
Shelley, and that is saying much. He was an excellent
classical scholar when he went up to Harvard. But for his
later and deeper interest in Greek literature he was largely
indebted to Trumbull Stickney, whose influence upon him
Moody rated high, and whose untimely death affected him
greatly. With Stickney he read or reread the whole body of
Greek Tragedy in 1902 at Paris.

Moody's knowledge of English literature of all periods
and of mediæval French romance has also been indicated.
He was equally at home in modern French and German
literature; and he had caught the very spirit and austere
manner of Dante, as his **"Dialogue in Purgatory"** witnesses. In the summer of 1894 he was reading Spanish
and sketching, as I learn from Mr. Mason. Whether he
pursued the study of Spanish literature further, I do not
know; but in 1903 he took up painting after an interval of
many years, and produced work so true and so well composed that several professional painters urged him to devote himself entirely to painting.

But his culture was not merely classical and artistic. The
theory of evolution with all its implications is implicit in

"The Menagerie," and, despite an antique cosmology retained for poetical purposes, runs through *The Fire-Bringer* and *The Masque of Judgment.* Modernity is, indeed, the note of all his thinking. His dream of the city beautiful as the final work of the Brute is the latest word of sociology; as his dream of leisure and intelligence and self-control and the enjoyment of nature as rights of all men has made "Gloucester Moors" a favorite poem with workers in the slums. His patriotism—passionate and beautiful—derives much of its passion and beauty from his sense of the opinion of mankind, his desire that in the eyes of the whole world his beloved land shall stand up clean and pure and beautiful, shall hold the Philippiness for no sordid motives, shall refrain from intervention in the dismemberment of China for no base fear.

Walter Pater has somewhere said that no great political poem can be written while men still care for the issues involved. This seems like a dictum uttered by the way to inclose some special case. Certainly Moody's political poetry—the "Ode in Time of Hesitation," "On a Soldier Fallen in the Philippines," and "The Quarry"—was written and set forth while the public mind was still divided; and however much men then differed as to the actions discussed, no one could deny the beauty, the power, or the lasting significance of the poems. We may all become reconciled to the holding of the islands and the partition of China as inevitable, but we shall never be able to minimize the large moral issues which at the moment were involved or to remain cold to Moody's clear and moving statement of them.

The largest literary plan of Moody's career and, though uncompleted, the fullest expression of his vision of life, is the trilogy which was to consist of *The Fire-Bringer, The Masque of Judgment,* and *The Death of Eve.* The sequence of these is subject to the logic of his solution of life, not to the chronology of action or of composition. To be judged fairly, they must be taken not as separate and complete wholes but as members of a trilogy, the final word of which was to be spoken at the end of the last. The trilogy, moreover, being Moody's vision of life as a whole, can hardly be understood without some further reference to his temperament and the influences of his childhood. He was, as we have seen, a pure pagan in his sensitiveness to beauty of all kinds, but he was also temperamentally a mystic, one who, without resort to ascetic austerities, though he may not have felt the divine warmth in his breast, heard the divine music, tasted the divine sweetness, or been surrounded by heavenly odors, at least saw, both in youth and in maturer age, with his physical eyes the habitants of heaven. Such a combination is strange enough, but in addition, Moody was born, as we must remember, in the United States of America about the middle of the nineteenth century. He was therefore born and brought up as a Puritan. Whether the ideals of his childhood came from north or from south, this is true. Much has been written about Puritan and Cavalier in the history of this country, but it is all fallacious; their ideals were, except superficially, the same; you had only to scratch a Cavalier ever so lightly to find below the surface a Puritan in full theological panoply. This early training, these early associations, left an indelible impress upon Moody. His task, as poet, was either to reject one or more of these elements or to unify them; but he could not reject any of them, and his whole nature called for the unification of them. He was not content—few of us are—to make his heart a battleground for his temperament and his training. So he fused his ancient cosmology and theology with his evolutionary theories, recharactered his God, as so many of us have done, and achieved a poetic solution of the universe.

This solution, with the problems which throw it into relief, he set forth in a trilogy of poetic dramas. These dramas contain much of his finest poetry, lyric, reflective, and—what is none too common in poetic drama—dramatic; and besides they exhibit a large and steady increase of strength and control, with no diminution of any of the poet's powers. That Moody was preoccupied with such questions as these dramas discuss, appears in a number of his shorter poems,—in the "Road-Hymn for the Start," in "Good Friday Night," in his patriotic poems, in the experimental and unsatisfactory "Until the Troubling of the Waters," in "Song-Flower and Poppy," and, if we accept "The Ride Back" as symbolic of the soul's return to God, in it also.

All three of the dramas are in large measure symbolic, and should be interpreted and judged as such. Strictly dramatic and subject to the laws of dramatic speech and action they were never intended to be, as was shown in the drama first written and published, *The Masque of Judgment,* by the presence of such *dramatis personæ* as the Spirits of the Throne-Lamps, the Lion and the Eagle of the Throne, and Spirits of the Saved and of the Lost; by the predominance of descriptive, expository, and lyric poetry, and by the very title of the drama. The critic may prefer dramatic action to broad oratorio-like movement; but the poet has the right to choose his form and medium and to be judged by his success in that. Strictly speaking, *The Masque of Judgment* is in structure and *personæ* more like a mediæval *mystère* than a masque, but Moody, who was familiar with these forms of drama, chose the term "masque" to indicate the symbolic character of his technique and to justify the large majesty of the action.

The order of the members of the trilogy is at first a little confusing: neither in date of composition nor in theme is chronology regarded. *The Masque of Judgment,* ranging in dramatic time from just before the Incarnation of Christ to the Evening of the Day of Judgment, and first in order of composition, is logically the second member of the trilogy. *The Fire-Bringer,* dealing with the myth of Prometheus and therefore hardly capable of adjustment to any time scheme of a Christian cosmogony, was second in time of composition, but is logically the first member of the trilogy. The third member of the trilogy, *The Death of Eve,* was unfortunately left fragmentary, only the first act having been completed. As these relations have occasioned difficulty to some readers, it may be well to give a brief statement of Moody's plan of the trilogy as a whole, premising that the precise development of the final theme had changed more than once in his conception and might conceivably have changed again.

The central or dominant thought of the trilogy is the inseparableness, and, in a certain sense, the unity of God and man. This thought is set forth in the first member, *The Fire-Bringer,* through the reaction on the human race of the effort of Prometheus to make man independent of God; in the second member, *The Masque of Judgment,* through a declaration of the consequences to God himself that would inevitably follow his decree for the destruction of mankind; in the third member, *The Death of Eve,* it was intended to set forth the impossibility of separation, the complete unity of the Creator and his creation.

Despite the fact that these poems were from the beginning known to be members of an organic plan, each of the two has been interpreted as if it were in itself a complete expression of Moody's thought, instead of a phase of its development. It is to be noted that, although Pandora is a prominent figure in *The Fire-Bringer,* and in many ways anticipates the feelings and attitudes finally expressed through Eve, Prometheus is the dominant figure, and the poem closes with a triumphant and somewhat insolent chorus of Young Men just awakened to power and sensual delight. Throughout the second drama, Raphael is the dominant figure. Despite his archangelic nature and his kinship with God as the first of his creatures, his long and watchful care of man has made him love and pardon even man's blindnesses and weaknesses; and torn as his heart is by his love for both God and man, he and Uriel and the Spirits of the Throne-Lamps join in expressing the desolation in Heaven as it becomes evident that the destruction of man involves the annihilation of God also.

The third member of the trilogy was to centre upon Eve, who, being the means of separation of man from God, is the appropriate and necessary means of reconciliation. She, having survived "ages of years," has undergone a new spiritual awakening, and with clearing vision sees that her sin need not have been the final, fatal thing it seemed; that God's creatures live by and within his being and cannot be estranged or divided from him. Seeing this dimly, she is under the compulsion of a great need to return to the place where her defiant thought had originated and there declare her new vision of life. She seeks among her kindred for one with understanding and courage, to accompany her; and being often refused, she accepts finally the companionship of the youngest of her descendants, Jubal,—a lad of spiritual insight, a poet and musician,— and with him sets out to find Cain and take him with her into the lost Paradise for the supreme reconciliation. The acceptance of her command by Cain and the expression by Jubal of the new-found joy of living close the first act in its present form. A concluding lyric, sung by Jubal as he leads the little maid Abdera up to the strong, mysterious city of Cain, was unfortunately never written. The other acts of this part of the trilogy, two in number, were to be diversified by many illuminating incidents, among them the instinctive wandering of the agestricken Adam back to the Garden, ostensibly following Eve, but really yearning forward to participate in the new and glorious solution of life. In the third act there was to be a song by Eve, the burden of which would be the inseparableness of God and man, during which, as she rises to a clearer and clearer view of the spiritual life, she gently passes from the vision of her beholders; while, delicately symbolizing the permanence and beauty of the earth, Jubal and Abdera draw together with broken words of tenderness.

The full vision of Eve, as has been said, never found lyric expression, but one may find anticipations of its thought, if not of its probably elaborate and jubilant form, in the wonderful song of Pandora, who in so many ways expresses the beauty and power of woman. The poem, beautifully simple in structure and in diction, indicates in its parallel phrasing the identity of the thoughts and desires of God and man.

> *Pandora* (sings)
> I stood within the heart of God;
> It seemed a place that I had known:
> (I was blood-sister to the clod,
> Blood-brother to the stone.)
>
> I found my love and labor there,
> My house, my raiment, meat and wine,
> My ancient rage, my old despair,—
> Yea, all things that were mine.
>
> I saw the spring and summer pass,
> The trees grow bare, and winter come;
> All was the same as once it was
> Upon my hills at home.
>
> Then suddenly in my own heart
> I felt God walk and gaze about;
> He spoke; His words seemed held apart
> With gladness and with doubt.
>
> "Here is my meat and wine," He said,
> "My love, my toil, my ancient care;
> Here is my cloak, my book, my bed,
> And here my old despair.
>
> "Here are my seasons: winter, spring,
> Summer the same, and autumn spills
> The fruits I look for; everything
> As on my heavenly hills."

Moody's conception of God was not, for all his insistence upon the inseparableness of God and man, pantheistic; indeed, it was not a formal philosophical conception, but a poetical vision incorporating the most diverse elements of culture. It must never be forgotten that in his sensitiveness to beauty and his sense of the eternal value of beauty he was a pagan; by nature also he was a mystic, with a feeling of the reality and nearness of God and of his own capacity for direct vision of Him and communication with Him. These elements of pagan "joy of living" and of mystic ecstasy were helped into union by the influence of Platonism and of the *Bacchæ* of Euripides. God figures ambiguously in his poetry: sometimes as the Puritan God, whom he does not love and in whom he does not believe; sometimes as the no less anthropomorphic God from whom he cannot keep his fellowship and love.

The tremendous part which woman plays in Moody's poetry and in his solution of the problem of life is worthy of special attention. In the first place, there is, as we have already seen, scarcely any hint in Moody's writings of sick and doubtful love, the weak sentimentality which is the main stock in trade of so many poets. This is due to the sanity of his mental and emotional natures, for he was a man of unusual sexual interest and sexual power, and he celebrated love as the universal Mother, the glorious and all-powerful being of whom Lucretius sang. Furthermore, woman, as idealized by him, is a far different creature from the bloodless angel who has been the subject of so many futile songs. Woman, as Moody conceived her, is glorious and wonderful, not because of the lack of human and even special weaknesses, but because of the possession of human and special powers. What he conceives her to be he has set forth in many a poem, but most conspicuously in the Girl's song in the Prelude to *The Masque of Judgment,* in the Girl's song on pages 57, 58, of *The Fire-Bringer,* in the epic vision of *The Death of Eve,* and, above all, in that marvelous outburst of varied melody, **"I Am the Woman."**

Only a word can be said of his work as a writer of prose plays. The impulse to write the two he wrote was imperative and irresistible. They embody important phases of his thought, and they show a power of humor and a capacity for dealing with the homely and familiar as well as the poetical which some critics were disposed to deny to him. They are now generally recognized as among the most encouraging signs of the possibility of an American drama that shall be at once popular, powerful, and worthily conceived and written. Some persons have supposed that Moody was seduced by the phenomenal success of *The Great Divide* into the hasty composition of another play. But, as I have said, he discussed the plan of *The Faith Healer* with me in the autumn of 1898, and even before that he had discussed it with Mr. Mason. That this play was not a popular success was due, I think, to Moody's refusal to use the sensational means of music and an excited crowd at the beginning of the first act necessary to establish the emotional atmosphere which alone could have prepared the audience to receive the theme sympathetically.

But even before this play was staged or even completed, he had definitely determined to return to poetry as his proper lifework. What he might have done had years of vigor been granted him we can in part infer from the increase in beauty and power shown in his latest work. He was growing in vigor and depth of thought, in breadth of vision, in sensitiveness to beauty, and in technical power up to the very time of his fatal attack, in the summer of 1909. Under the care of Harriet C. Brainerd,—for years a

constant source of strength and inspiration as his dearest friend, and for a few brief months his devoted partner in a marriage of ideal sweetness and unity of feeling,—he sought vainly for restoration to health and strength, but the end came at Colorado Springs on the seventeenth of October, 1910.

That a man so endowed in body, heart, mind, and soul should be taken away in the very flower of his manhood is a loss to the world; that so strong and sweet a soul is with us here no more is an irreparable loss to those who knew and loved him. But Moody, though he did not finish his work, had lived a life of singular richness and fullness. A strong, as well as a fine spirit, he had never compromised with circumstances or fate, and he could well say at the end, as he said long before in **"Song-Flower and Poppy"**—:

> Heart, we have chosen the better part!
> Save sacred love and sacred art,
> Nothing is good for long.

Charlton M. Lewis (essay date 1913)

SOURCE: "William Vaughn Moody," in *The Yale Review,* Vol. 2, No. 7, 1913, pp. 688-703.

[*In the following essay, Lewis identifies Moody with the Symbolist movement.*]

One of the great poets of our day died in 1910. He had created no public furor, but his power had been deeply felt by many; and to them his untimely death was a disaster. The recent publication of his collected works has reawakened their enthusiasm, for some of his best poetry is posthumous; and a wider appreciation of his genius is sure to come soon.

One's first impression of Moody is that he was a Symbolist—that his poetry marks the high-water level of the Symbolist movement. But Symbolism is in fact no longer a movement; it is partly a memory and partly an achievement. Even before Moody's day the tide had begun to recede; but it had first overflowed all the adjacent fields, and there the waters linger still, widespread and disconnected. The truth about Moody is rather this: that he, of all recent poets, best succeeded in absorbing what was essential and vital in Symbolism, while rejecting what was merely accessory and decadent.

Symbolism led a successful revolt against the material, the obvious, the commonplace; but it also sometimes parted company with the intelligible, the natural, the real. It explored many untrodden regions of poetic thought; but the search for new refinements of feeling involves some peril to the seeker's health. Moody escaped this peril, and effected a remarkable compromise between the claims of a delicate poetical temperament and the claims of a vigorous humanity. Perhaps he had not quite the genial otherworldliness of Mr. Yeats, nor the elusive subtlety of Paul Verlaine; perhaps he had no such astonishing robustness of heart as Browning, or even Henley; but for fineness and robustness together, in so equal a fusion as Moody exhibits, I do not know where to look among the moderns.

Symbolism at its best was capable of great things. It was at its best when it cleared itself of obscurity, of irrelevancy, and especially of that narrowness of poetic vision which is the penalty of too curious insight. It was at its best, for instance, in some of the lyries of Mr. Yeats, which with all their quintessential fineness are yet intelligible and natural; they utter a real human cry. But, even at its best, Symbolism was commonly not tonic. It played with virtuosity on many strings of the human heart, but it seldom touched with firmness the strings of resolution and courage. It avoided them, because they belonged to a foreign key. But the tonic quality is just what we do find in Moody. A specimen can hardly show him at his best, for Moody's best, more than that of most poets, is in the whole and not in the parts; but the specimen which I quote will show at least a high level of poetic attainment, and it will show especially how Moody made Symbolism the servant, not the master, of his own robust temperament. It is the second of Pandora's songs in *The Fire-Bringer.* The hero, Prometheus, has just failed in his first attempt to snatch fire from heven, and is ready to despair of further effort for mankind:

> Of wounds and sore defeat
> I made my battle stay;
> Wingèd sandals for my feet
> I wove of my delay; . . .
> From the shutting mist of death,
> From the failure of the breath,
> I made a battle-horn to blow
> Across the vales of overthrow.
> O hearken, love, the battle-horn!
> The triumph clear, the silver scorn!
> O hearken where the echoes bring,
> Down the grey disastrous morn,
> Laughter and rallying!

One of the Symbolists with whom Moody is in most obvious contrast is Francis Thompson—though Thompson was not, like Mr. Yeats, a Symbolist of the extreme left. Both Thompson and Moody were mystics, and both, though in different ways and degrees, found much of their inspiration in religious instinct. But Thompson went far in the revolt against the natural and the real, and, though an epicure in imagination, he was an ascetic by conviction. It is characteristic of him to express only revulsion at the wickedness of the world. Man is born

> To sweat, and make his brag, and rot,
> Crowned with all honor and all shamefulness; . . .
> Like fierce beasts that a common thirst makes brothers
> We draw together to one hid dark lake.

Characteristic, on the other hand, of Moody—and so notably characteristic that I wish to lay special stress upon it—is a passage which I will quote from *The Masque of*

Judgment. Two angels are discussing the waning of the joy of heaven, and one asks where lies the cause. The death-angel answers as Thompson might have done; but Raphael, who loves mankind, curiously turns the answer into the peculiar channel of Moody's own thought:

> *Angel of the Pale Horse.*
>   The cause is here, . . .
> Here in the wild and sinful heart of man,—
> Of all the fruits upon creation's vine
> The thirstiest one to drain the vital breast
> Of God, wherein it grows.
> *Raphael.*
>   Too fiery sweet
> Gushes the liquor from the vine He set,
> Man the broad leaf and maid the honeyed flower.

These last lines, I repeat, are especially characteristic of Moody. They reveal that peculiar conception of life which found expression in nearly all his writings. He was as much preoccupied as Thompson with the problems of evil, but he approached them from a widely divergent angle. Moody saw in evil not exactly the implacable foe of good, but rather its twin brother, bone of its bone and flesh of its flesh, since both good and evil are children of passion and will. Life is rich and wonderful because our spirits are charged with aspiration and liberty and love. If we are swayed also by jealousy and wrath, license and lust, these are but other manifestations of the same primal forces. The concords and the discords are sounded on the same strings, and are essential parts of one divine harmony.

This is not an opinion, it is merely a point of view; but in a point of view there may be much philosophy. And this point of view is seized so vigorously and held so persistently by Moody that it becomes, as a philosophy, almost the set thesis of his most important poems. This is true especially of his trilogy of verse-dramas, *The Fire-Bringer, The Masque of Judgment,* and *The Death of Eve.*

The first of these dramas is a retelling of the old myth of Prometheus, but Moody gives the story a new symbolic significance. Before the opening of the poem, Deukalion's flood has not only overwhelmed the earth with physical disaster, it has also extinguished the fire of passion and of will even in the most secret places of the human heart. The survivors of the flood are left abject and torpid, without choice or hope, incapable of either good or evil; and the first part of the poem, in scenes of extraordinary power, shows us what life must be under such conditions. In the second half of the drama, Prometheus brings the lost element. The flood recedes, starlight pierces the thick darkness, and the fire of life enters the souls of men, rekindling them to rapture and also to agony. Out of the mysterious dawn of the new light a man's voice is heard crying:

> My soul is among lions. God, my God,
> Thou see'st my quivering spirit what it is!
> O lay not life upon it! We not knew
> The thing we asked for.

But other voices give utterance to other emotions. A chorus of girls, awakened to the possibility of love, proclaim their sense of the love-god's presence:

> He came up out of the sun, yet he goeth not down
> therewith;
> For, ever warmer, closer, as the evening falleth pale,
> His arm is over our necks, and his breath
> Searches whispering under our hair; and his burning
> whisper saith
> A thing that maketh the heart to cease and the limbs
> to fail,
> And the hands to grope for they know not what;
> We would not find what he whispers of, and we die if
> we find it not!

The poem ends with a somewhat insolent chorus of youths just awakened to a sense of the triumphant destiny of manhood. I borrow the epithet "somewhat insolent" from Professor Manly's just and illuminating introduction to the collected edition, and I own that when I first read *The Fire-Bringer,* some ten years ago, I did not perceive that this chorus was meant to sound insolent. But Professor Manly is right. The insolence is there, and it is an essential feature of the poem. The first member of the trilogy ends appropriately with blended notes of enthusiasm and of ominous license. Good and evil have come into the world together.

Before *The Fire-Bringer* was written, Moody's friend Trumbull Stickney had published his "Prometheus Pyrphoros." Moody's indebtedness to Stickney is in one sense very great, for without his "Prometheus" it seems unlikely that *The Fire-Bringer* would have been thought of. But the indebtedness is for fertile suggestion rather than for direct contribution. Stickney tells of the darkness and the bringing of the fire; but the symbolism, which makes the later poem what it is, was not in the earlier. Some of the most striking passages in Moody's drama are the songs of hope sung by Pandora—rays of light that both relieve and intensify the gloom. The idea of interspersing these songs was borrowed from Stickney, but not their lyrical splendor. Occasionally a detail is directly transferred from one poem to the other, but always in such manner as to strengthen the impression of Moody's originality. Thus, after one of Pandora's songs, Stickney wishes to suggest its effect upon Deukalion and Pyrrha:

> *Deukalion.*
>   What a strange mournful voice is hers!
> *Pyrrha.*
> No, no! I feel a happiness bringing leaves
> Upon the branches, and the night is less
> Between now and tomorrow!

Moody seizes upon the idea, and realizes it with an ampler symbolism. We hear out of the darkness voices of men and women:

> *A Man's Voice.*
> Hearken! One sings upon the upper slopes.

> *Another Voice.*
> She opens many doors, which ere we look
> Are closed for everlasting, and their place
> Not to be guessed. . . .
> *A Woman's Voice.*
> Hush, hark the pouring music! Never yet
> The pools below the waterfalls, thy pools,
> Thy dark pools, O my heart—!
> *A Young Man's Voice.*
> Delirious breast!
> She jetteth as a sacred bird
> That o'er the springtime waves, at large of dawn,
> Off Delos to the wakening Cyclades
> Declares Apollo.

In the cry of the "woman's voice" we recognize the supreme touch of authentic Symbolism. This is, for once, the Symbolism of Mallarmé and Symons, the Symbolism which sought its subject matter in the inexpressible, the Symbolism which therefore aimed not to express but to suggest.

The fundamental idea of *The Fire-Bringer,* the idea of using the myth of flood and fire to explain the genesis of good and evil, was not in Stickney's poem; it was Moody's original creation. But here, too, I suspect an impulse from without. Giacomo Leopardi, in a curious philosophical romance called a "History of the Human Race," tells us that in the golden age men were bored to death because the world lacked variety. Deukalion's flood destroyed all but a few, and then Jove set about establishing life on a better basis. "He had learned by this time that human nature will not be satisfied with merely living, or with mere freedom from bodily pain. Whatever be its lot, the heart of man longs always for the unattainable; and it is afflicted most grievously with this vain desire when it is least beset with other ills. Accordingly Jove resolved upon new devices for the conservation of our wretched race, and his first device was this: to inject real evil into our lives. . . . And, to put an end to the torpor of the race, he sent among men . . . divers vain phantasms whose names were Justice, Power, Glory; and among them was also Love, who like the rest then came upon earth for the first time."

Had Moody read this? I think so. The parallels between his drama and Leopardi's romance are not many; my quotations almost exhaust them; but even so they are rather striking for mere coincidence. And Moody, who was a passionate lover of many literatures, among them the Italian, is unlikely to have passed by Leopardi. But he borrowed from him not the letter, and least of all the spirit—for Leopardi's was the gospel of irony and despair—but at most a hint for the process. As Stickney had anticipated Moody in dramatizing the myth of Deukalion, so had Leopardi in philosophizing it. Moody left Stickney far behind because his genius was riper; and he quickly parted company with Leopardi because his genius was more wholesome and sound.

The Masque of Judgment stands as the second member of the trilogy, though it was composed first. As *The Fire-Bringer* suggests that both good and evil are sprung from the seeds of divine fire and must stand together, so *The Masque of Judgment* suggests that they must fall together, if at all. The growing sin of the world is the growing anguish of God. But God knows that man is as necessary to him as he to man; and when, as the anguish becomes unbearable, he resolves upon the Judgment, he knows that he will be destroying the good with the evil, and that he himself must perish also. The Great Day is the end not only of the world, but of God's eternity.

The third member of the great trilogy was to have been *The Death of Eve,* but Moody did not live to complete it. We have only a lyrical sketch, contributed before Moody's death to a magazine, and one entire act of the projected drama, now first published. These, however, suffice to outline the plan of the whole, and to reveal at last the full meaning of the trilogy.

Moody seems to have found the germ of his last drama in "La Vision d'Eve" of Léon Dierx—the man who, at the age of sixty, succeeded Verlaine and Mallarmé as the poets' chosen "prince of poets." "La Vision d'Eve" is a poem of some thirty elegiac quatrains. It relates that once on a still morning, three years after the expulsion from Paradise, while Adam was hunting and the birds were singing, Eve sat by a spring watching her babes at play, and communing with the God whom she still adored. She praised him for his justice and mercy, and declared that her lot was happier now than before the Fall, for now it was made perfect with perfect human love. Just then the infant Cain was suddenly seized with wrath; his eye flashed savagely, and with clenched fist he struck Abel, who cried for help. Eve rushed to them, pale with a sudden horror, and fondled and soothed them both to sleep. Then came to Eve her "Vision" of the days to be. The death-angel, Azrael, showed her the crime of Cain, and Cain's long agony in his beleaguered city of Enoch. He showed her the after world, reeking with cruelty, wrath, and sorrow; and she comprehended that this was the real fruition of her love. She sat motionless beside her children, and from her eyes, which had been filled with infinite peace, fell streams of scalding tears.

I cannot doubt that Moody found here his first suggestion for *The Death of Eve.* He reproduces the death-angel, Azrael; and much of the first act pictures Cain's life of horror in the city of Enoch. There is, too, a reminiscence of the central incident of the French poem. Cain, in his extreme age, says to Eve:

> The first that I remember of my life
> Was such a place, such a still afternoon,
> I sitting thus, thy bright head in my knees,
> And such a bird above us as him yonder
> Who dips and hushes, lifts and takes his note.
> I know not what child's trespass I had done,
> Nor why it drove the girl out of thy face,
> Clutched at thy heart with panic, and in thine eyes
> Set shuddering love. . . .

But the main resemblance of one poem to the other is at the point of their most significant divergence. Dierx boldly made Eve justify the sin of Paradise *before* the crime of Cain, and the justification was love. Moody, still more boldly, designed to justify that sin after Cain's crime, and the justification was to be the whole of life, good and evil together. Eve in her old age resolved to seek Cain in his exile, and to go with him back to Paradise, there to confront the wrath of God. Her purpose was to declare to God her knowledge that she had done well, and that even the fruits of her disobedience were but the fiery fulfillment of His creative will. When she broke her enterprise to Cain he at first hung back, as others had done, fearing the wrath of the sky; but Eve said:

> I had a son
> Who questioned his own wrath, the skies thereof,
> His own heart's wrathful skies, what they were
>   prone to,
> And seeing where his will went, followed it.
> I came to find that son. And shall I find him
> But as the rest, whose marrow in their bones
> Curdles to hear Eve's whisper? Nay, thou Cain,
> Whose soul is as a torch blown back for speed,
> 'Tis thou shalt light me on that fearful way
> That I must go, and that I haste to go
> Ere darkness fall forever.

For this striking variation of the theme it is barely possible that Moody took a hint from a little poem of Baudelaire's. But the somewhat flashy blasphemy of Baudelaire was of course alien to Moody's thought—which is, indeed, but the culmination and consummation of the whole scheme of the trilogy.

It is plain that Moody's mind was eclectic and absorptive. Scholars of the next generation will find strange joy in tracing him to his sources. Professor Manly has pointed out his love of Euripides, and especially the influence of the "Bacchæ" upon many passages in his poetry. In one of these passages, to be sure, (the episode of the Prelude in the *Masque of Judgment*) Professor Manly will grant that the chief figure as the Orpheus of Apollodorus rather than the Pentheus of Euripides; but the general influence of the "Bacchæ" is indisputable and essential. Moody is Euripidean, sometimes, even in the ambiguity of his religious ideas! But indeed there are few of the great poets whom Moody may not here and there recall. He reminds us of Shelley in his lyrical ecstasy. He sometimes echoes the vague poignancy of the Pre-Raphaelites. His **"Good Friday Night"** and **"Second Coming"**—two companion pieces upon Christianity—are very suggestive in form (though not in spirit) of the two Obermann poems of Matthew Arnold. He recalls now and again the great odes of Coventry Patmore; and occasionally, it must be admitted, he even plays Patmore's trick of closing the gaps in his inspiration with a rubble-work of very clever rhetoric. But the gaps in Moody's inspiration are rare; and I trust I have sufficiently shown that, with all his echoings, he makes a final impression of distinct and powerful originality.

Moody wrote for the stage two prose plays, *The Great Divide* and *The Faith-Healer.* Both plays show true genius, and both breathe the same liberal philosophy as the trilogy in verse. Good may be wrung out of evil, and the highest aim of man is to wring out as much of it as possible. In each play this principle is wrought into a subtle and profound study of the workings of soul upon soul; and the fault of each play is that the theme is too subtly and profoundly treated for stage effectiveness. Seeing Moody's plays is something like reading the later novels of Mr. Henry James. In **The Great Divide,** however, the main theme was imbedded in a melodramatic action of crime, separation, and grief; and its melodramatic qualities made the play one of the brilliant popular successes of the last decade. People did not understand just why Ruth Jordan clung to her husband, or why she left him, or why she came back to him; but in her doing of these things there was so much passion and excitement that nobody cared much for her reasons. **The Faith-Healer,** on the other hand, was equally profound, equally clever in detail, and perhaps even superior in style; but it had no story that could be read from beyond the footlights. Instead of a gorge in the Rockies, the scene was the sick-room of an Ohio farmer's wife. Instead of the fury of a drunken cowboy, the main motive-force was the self-questioning spirit of a mystical revivalist. The play failed.

In view of Moody's early death, one must regret that some of his best vigor was put into these plays. I would much rather have now a finished **Death of Eve.** But if he had lived it would have become clear that there was no time wasted. Study of the stage was teaching Moody a needed lesson in consideration for his audience. A great poet cannot be too independent of his hearers, but he may easily be too forgetful of them; and this is what Moody too often was. **The Death of Eve,** however, shows a marked gain in clarity and orderliness—and this without loss of power. It is noteworthy, too, that the last drama is more dramatic than the others. It is not meant for the stage, to be sure; but even in the purely literary drama there is room for those effects which the stage cannot dispense with. The long dialogue between Eve and Cain is literary drama at its best. There is but one seriously exceptionable passage in it—a too salient reminiscence of the ghost of Banquo:

> Thou hag of hell,
> Glare not upon me with those caverned eyes!
> Whoever has done this, his life shall pay.

Such a defect would never have passed Moody's final revision—(**The Death of Eve** is obviously unrevised)—for he was a keen critic of his own work. Evidences of this are apparent in successive versions of the same poems. **"Old Pourquoi,"** for instance, appeared several years ago in a magazine, and now in the posthumous edition reappears much altered. Throughout the poem there is a strain of grotesque humor which weirdly enhances its imaginative power; but in the earlier version the strain was too insistent. Nearly all Moody's changes were softenings-down of this element of humor. Enough of the grotesque is retained to serve its artistic purpose, but it is not allowed to run riot. Moody knew the value of discords, but he also knew the limits of their usefulness. On this point one wishes that he might have given lessons to Browning, who

marred his stateliest edifices by scattering gargoyles too lavishly. Moody had the rare advantage of possessing a critical faculty which curbed his liberality without paralyzing it.

I have already hinted at Moody's most serious fault, which was obscurity. It is natural that obscurity should be the evil genius of Symbolism, for it is not easy to make the ultra-violet rays visible; but is not this difficult task a part of art's function? We all have rare emotions which we cannot express, and the business of the artist is to word them for us. When he leaves them in the dark, his art is only half achieved. Puzzles are not poetry. I have no right to say that any of Moody's puzzles are insoluble, but some of them baffle my most resolute efforts; and of others it may be said that they girp the reader's imagination mightily, but his intellect must be exercised to the point of fatigue before his imagination will come into play. In **"The Moon-Moth"** there are lines which show Moody's lyrical faculty at its highest, and other lines are models of poetic style:

> We cry with drowsy lips how life is strange,
> And shadowy hands pour for us while we speak
> Old bowls of slumber, that the stars may range
> And the gods walk unhowled-at;

but what does the poem mean as a whole? We shall doubtless be told, some day; but at present the uninitiated reader can hardly divine.

But the charge of obscurity is dangerous to make. It is always uncertain, and it often recoils upon the critic. Poetry is an experience which the reader must share with the writer, and there are kinds of experience of which some minds are incapable. I may fairly demand that everything be made clear; but suppose the poet asks, "Clear to whom?" And of course it must not be forgotten that a great deal of Moody's poetry is clear enough for anybody. Such poems as **"Gloucester Moors," "Song-Flower and Poppy,"** and **"Old Pourquoi"** demand no more effort than indolent readers may make unconsciously; and these are poems of a high quality.

Much of Moody's work, like that of the Symbolists, was intricate analysis of emotion. What men do was of less interest to him than what men feel. But the feeling that fills his poetry is commonly the great feeling that is stirred by great issues, not the sentimentality of mere temperament. True, he is alive to the beauty of delicate sensations:

> O heart of mine, with all thy powers of white beatitude,
> What are the dearest of God's dowers to the children of his blood?
> How blow the shy, shy wilding flowers in the hollows of his wood?

But he was a man of too much intellectual power, and also of too critical humor, ever to be mawkish or trivial in his imaginings. When, as in **"Gloucester Moors,"** he gives utterance to the cry of modern humanitarianism, it is with stern recognition of the inexorable difficulty of our problems. In **"The Daguerreotype,"** a poem upon a picture of his mother, there are many curious and remote strayings of fancy, but his vigorous originality secures a final effect of masculine directness. This poem, indeed, bears well the inevitable comparison with William Cowper's familiar "Lines" on the same subject. Those lines are touching and sincere; their very simplicity is a potent charm to all whose taste is unspoiled; and for my part I treasure them none the less affectionately for being locked up in the dear old general-housework couplets that our grandfathers loved. But Moody has attempted a higher flight and has sustained it. As a record of actual past experience his poem may seem not so inartificial as Cowper's, not so free from traces of conscious after-analysis; but as a passionate utterance of present emotion and present burning thought, it is a great achievement.

It is indeed one of the remarkable things about Moody that, with all his subtle emotions and subtle imaginings, he is almost free from over-elaboration and from frigid excess of heat. These are too common weaknesses in recent poetry—in the poetry, for instance, of Francis Thompson. Crowding of the emotions is, indeed, one of the defects of the qualities of Symbolism, though of course it has its analogues in the poetry of other schools. Honest Elizabethan rant, the vice of heroic drama, was not dissimilar. That, however, was but stage thunder, and it offends us because the noise is out of proportion to the accompanying illumination. The vice of Symbolism is more like heat lightning; all creation is transfigured by the lambent glow, and one only wonders that there is no shock. When we find these effects in the work of the Symbolists, we glance back with increased affection to the imperishable art of Cowper. But Moody's critical judgment and robust taste kept him out of danger; and consequently, when it is his work that we are reading, our prevailing impression is rather that Symbolism added a rich territory to the domain of modern poetry, and that Moody has taken this for his own by divine right.

If I have over-emphasized Moody's affiliations with the Symbolists, it would require another article to correct the error. It is his manner that recalls them more than his matter, for he was an interested student of much that they ignored. Indeed he promised, if he lived, to create for us just that satisfying poetic interpretation of the very complex life of to-day which the world is so eagerly looking for. The three great Victorians, while perhaps more strongly established than ever as classics, are becoming every year less contemporary; they are great poets, but they are not *our* poets. The social sense that is stirring in us finds little satisfaction in the dogmatic individualism of Browning; our scorn of intellectual compromise makes Tennyson no longer gospel; and even Arnold, in some respects the nearest to us of all, seems hardly to have realized that the world is alive and still young. What we most miss in these poets is just what Moody was beginning to give us; and he was not giving it in the spirit of ultra-modern naturalism,

for he was saturated with the old world's culture and he had the poetic vision.

I like to remember that among the first to recognize Moody's genius was Richard Watson Gilder. Moody was the subject of his stanzas entitled "A New Poet." I do not know whether this identification was ever publicly announced; but it cannot be impertinent to quote some of the verses here, and so link the memories of two fine and generous spirits. Gilder's praise was discerning and just; but his fear, alas, has been too tragically realized:

> Friends, beware!
> A sound of singing in the air!
> The love-song of a man who loves his fellow-men;
> Mother-love and country-love, and the love of sea and fen;
> Lovely thoughts and mighty thoughts and thoughts that linger long;
> There has come to the old world's singing the thrill of a brave new song.
>
> They said there were no more singers,
> But listen!—a master voice!
> A voice of the true joy-bringers!
> Now will ye heed and rejoice,
> Or pass on the other side,
> And wait till the singer has died,—
> Then weep o'er his voiceless clay?
> Friends, beware!
> A keen, new sound is in the air,—
> Know ye a poet's coming is the old world's judgment day!

Daniel Gregory Mason (essay date 1913)

SOURCE: An introduction in *Some Letters of William Vaughn Moody,* edited by Daniel Gregory Mason, Houghton Mifflin Company, 1913, pp. v-xxviii.

[*In the following essay, Mason discusses what Moody's letters reveal about his personality and development as an artist.*]

"He liberates the imagination with his prose," wrote one of Moody's friends when the project of collecting some of the letters was being discussed, "as effectively as he does with his poetry. And then besides there is the luminous personality which emerges from every folded sheet, looking out with large veiled eyes." The comment happily describes the double interest of these letters [in *Some Letters of William Vaughn Moody*]. They are, first of all, literature, and may be read, by those who know nothing of the personality of their author, for their purely literary charm, their power to "liberate the imagination." They carry, like his poetry, for such a reader, their own rich gifts of delight; they are as magnanimously conceived, as hauntingly phrased, as eloquently and ingeniously clothed in metaphor, even more mischievously touched with humor. Moody's poetry is destined, surely, to a high, if not to the supreme, place in the American poetry of his generation. His letters, it seems to me, are worthy to stand beside it; and there, so far as their purely literary quality is concerned, they may be left without further comment.

But like all good letters they are not only literature but self-revelation; and the clear vision of this more individual element may be helped not only by the large illumination shed upon them from the poetry, but by the countless casual side-lights that only personal acquaintance can note and interpret. The two or three essential qualities of Moody's mind were singularly persistent and ubiquitous, and like the few geologic strata that may underlie the most varied landscape, cropped out in his careless talk as unmistakably as in his poems or letters. His spiritual earnestness, for example, made him as indifferent to the merely conventional aspects of life as he was passionately curious about its essential structure. In his poetry he avoided superficial detail, to penetrate at once to essences. In his letters he often exasperatingly withheld the petty facts of which most correspondence consists, but was always frank and full in the revelation of mood. Similarly in everyday intercourse he combined intellectual candor and personal reserve in a way that many found bewildering. For his friends the paradox was symbolised in his eyes. In their liquidness and transparence, in their steadfastness and quietude, they seemed to open up quite fearlessly a way to his deepest thoughts. Beautiful serene eyes they were, telling all that mattered but ignoring the trivial and the irrelevant: it was as if he had both the honesty and the shyness of a child. This is perhaps what his friend means when he speaks of his personality "emerging from every folded sheet, with large veiled eyes."

Akin to the serenity of his gaze, and like it a little embarrassing on first acquaintance but endlessly refreshing to riper friendship, was his constitutional taciturnity. It used to be said of him in college that "It took Moody a pipeful to make a remark"—and the discerning added that it was worth while to wait. When I first met him, in the spring of 1894, during his instructorship in the English Department at Harvard, his manner was shy and somewhat self-consciously awkward, so that we undergraduates of a complacent local clique found it easy to dismiss him as "Western." An odd blend of floridity and negligence about him offended those whose ideal of manliness was a correct dandyism. And in his physical being there was indeed a sort of rough homeliness that made the epithet to a certain extent descriptive. But it did not take long to pass that stage, to find that he had also the freshness and magnanimity of the West, and that he saw things under wider horizons than those of the Cambridge tea-tables. Above all, one discovered the richness of his silences. He had a way of slightly knitting his brows, as if taking, from under half-closed lids, a bird's-eye view of the broadest possible stretch of his subject, while he communed with his pipe, frequently pressing down the tobacco with a forefinger long inured to that service, and finally producing a brief comment, usually metaphorical and often madly exaggerative, that liberated the mind more than floods of ordinary

talk. It was as if, instead of dissipating the thought supply as most talkers do, churning it up into a froth that gives only an illusion of increased substance, he was engaged in a quiet husbanding of truth, whereby it rose to higher levels in the reservoir. He gave one always a sense of increased insight, of renewed confidence, of a deeper and truer conspectus of things than that of everyday observation.

The liberating effect of his talk must have been due in no small degree to its vividly figurative quality. No matter to what extent one might have been led to expect this by the luxuriance of figure characteristic of his poetry, one could not but be struck afresh on each occasion, by the surprising variety, the ingenious complexity, and often the droll incongruity, of the metaphors that he would constantly strike out in the heat of conversation, mould with loving care for a moment, and then toss aside. The letters, too, it will be found, owe much of their individuality of flavor to a use of figure at once whimsical and persistently logical. Who but Moody would have thought of comparing himself to a bicycle in such elaborate detail as this: "Good fun, but rather hard on one's tire. I hasten to assure you that I am as yet unpunctured, though much worn at the rim, and rapidly losing resiliency by leakage. I relinquish the figure with reluctance." On another occasion, trying to solace a friend incapacitated for work, he lets himself be beguiled into some charming variations on the old theme, "The dark cellar ripens the wine." "And meanwhile," he says, "after one's eyes get used to the dirty light, and one's feet to the mildew, a cellar has its compensations. I have found beetles of the most interesting proclivities, mice altogether comradely and persuadable, and forgotten potatoes that sprouted toward the crack of sunshine with a wan maiden grace not seen above." But the most irresistible instance, in all the letters, of this peculiarly Moody-esque pursuit, with meticulous logic, of a more or less absurd metaphor, occurs in a letter to Mrs. Toy in which he hits off once for all that contrast between East and West which was always haunting him. "I am eager," he writes, "for the queer inimitable charm of Cambridge, for that atmosphere of mind at once so impersonal and so warm, for that neatness and decency of you children, who have been washed and dressed and sent to play on the front lawn of time by old auntie Ding-an-sich, while we hoodlums contend with the goat for tomato cans in the alley. I have a fair line of the same to lay before your eyes when I am admitted inside the aristocratic front gate: some of them will make a fine effect in a ring around your geranium bed."

Conceive this vigorous image-making faculty irresponsibly applied to the thousand and one subjects of casual talk; conceive it stimulated by the enthusiasm of youthful comradeships, and invited by the endless leisure of vagrant country walks in spring, or of long winter evenings spent toasting before an open-grate fire, in an atmosphere of tobacco smoke and hot rum toddy; conceive it returning upon itself at will, and constructing day by day a special cosmogony and vocabulary of its own. One such winter evening I shall never forget, when in the small hours the talk grew youthfully philosophic, and Moody, his ever ruddy face flushed with the excitement of improvisation, leaning out from swirls of smoke and emphasizing his points with outstretched pipe, drew a picture of man in the universe as a frog in a well, condemned always to darkness, destined never to know what was in the world above. I dare say it was only warmed-over Kantianism; certainly the toddy contributed much to its impressiveness; but when the rich cadences of his voice died away it was to a solemn silence, with the two youthful philosophers thoroughly awed at their own imaginings.

Something of the same solemnity that invests that image of the frog in the well hangs about certain other conceptions that acquired for us, chiefly from Moody's eloquence, a largely representative value. "It," for example, referred to in the letters, transcends the explanation it seems to require, because it both denotes something so indefinable, and connotes something so incommunicable. "It" is everything, taken together, that may be the object of a youthful idealist's devotion; it is the sum total of all that is beautiful and worthy of loyalty in the world; it is what it is happiness to remember, wretchedness to forget. A "diastole," also mentioned in the letters, is a mood in which, so to speak, the spiritual circulation is good (the figure is, of course, drawn from the physiology of the heart); it is a mood of vitality, of realization, of fulfilment. Such moods we made it a point of honor, as well as a privilege, to celebrate by communication. Systoles we may also have experienced, but usually we had the courage not to talk about them. The most curious term of all, naming a type of humanity rather than a general idea, was "Pritchard"—originally the name of a young working-man we met one evening during one of our long aimless walks. In some occult way he typified for us Philistinism—all the dull, prosaic world which was our enemy. In some still more occult way (though possibly cocktails had something to do with it) he mystically blossomed into one of the elect. From that time forth, "Pritchard" was for us the divinity in the average man.

Crudely youthful as were some of these notions and formulations, they played a genuine part in Moody's development, and reverberations of them may be caught by the attentive ear throughout his poems and letters. They were at any rate generous, and sprang from a fine idealistic enthusiasm. Moreover, they illustrate, in their persistent tendency to take on figurative form, what one comes finally to consider the fundamental quality of his mind. Metaphor was his natural mode of expression. It occurred to him as spontaneously for a capricious snap-shot at everyday life as for the more deliberate description in a letter or for the noble setting-forth of his poetic dramas. Its manifestations in casual talk had one element of charm peculiarly their own. One does not get, alas, in the poetry, or even in the letters, the comment of personal gesture and inflection on these crowding figments of his fancy: the gathering amusement in his eyes as he elaborated some conceit; the portentous seriousness with which he brought forth his exag-

gerations or absurdities; the final bursting shout of laughter, when the dam gave way, that shook his whole frame with its physical gusto.

The distinctive trait of his mind was thus, I have always thought, rather its imaginative power than its purely intellectual scope or subtlety: he was far more poet than philosopher. There is in his books, to be sure, even though it be obscured sometimes, especially in the prose plays, by touches of sentimentalism, a wisdom both noble and broad; in daily intercourse one loved the sweetness and sanity of his mind quite as much as one admired its bold constructiveness; and his imagination itself, however untrammeled, owed much of its vigor to a kind of tenacious consecutiveness akin to logic. Nevertheless must one insist that he characteristically saw the world not from the detached point of view of philosophy, and under its cold, even illumination, but rather as a glowing focus where the rays of passionate sympathetic interest for the moment converged, brilliantly relieved against semi-obscurity. He leaned always toward the extremes of statement in which such a vision, with its sharp chiaroscuro, naturally expresses itself. He was too eager in the vivid presentment of what he had felt intensely to linger over peddling accuracies of qualification. He seized upon his subject, isolated and magnified it. Many amusing instances of his exaggeration may be found in the letters. "There are three hundred and twenty-three hand-organs and ninety-seven pianos on our block," he writes from his New York lodgings in 1900, "and every hour thirty-five thousand drays loaded with sheet-iron pass the house. Irving Place, you know, is a quiet old-fashioned neighborhood, so we are justly proud of these slight evidences of animation." From Chicago he sends the plaint, during one of his periods of teaching: "I counted my vocabulary last night, and discovered it to consist of ninety-three words. You shall have them all, if you will promise not to be reckless with them." Such passages as these help us to understand the over-luxuriance of his youthful poetic style. If we consider, furthermore, that his native tendency to extravagance was fostered, almost from the first, by an acquired rhetorical virtuosity the exercise of which must have been highly exciting, we shall be able to account for the turgidity of much of his early verse.

But if both temperament and technical skill thus inclined him rather toward romantic luxuriance than toward classic chastity, only the more remarkable becomes the tireless discipline by which he trained himself to achieve the sobriety and distinction of such later pieces as, say, the lyrics in ***The Fire-Bringer.*** We are reminded of Verdi's progress from *Il Trovatore* to *Otello,* or Wagner's from *Rienzi* to *Die Meistersinger,* by a poet who begins with rococo effects like

> Yet her shy devious lambent soul
> With my slow soul should walk,

and ends with such noble simplicities as

> Of wounds and sore defeat
> I made my battle stay;

Wingèd sandals for my feet
I wove of my delay;
Of weariness and fear
I made my shouting spear;
Of loss, and doubt, and dread,
And swift oncoming doom,
I made a helmet for my head
And a floating plume."

No one not endowed by nature with a vivid imagination
and an eagerly sympathetic spirit could have written lines
like these; but furthermore, no one thus endowed could
have written them, had he not long schooled himself in the
subtle arts of moderation, just emphasis, and suggestion. I
hardly know which the more to admire in Moody as a
poet, the native richness of his mind, or the patient art by
which he learned to draw from it so pure a harmony.

The reader may perhaps welcome, for the insight they give
into both qualities, a few more examples of his early work
than he decided to include in the **Poems** of 1901. What he
rejected then, as not representative of his artistry at its
best, we may now find well worth study, as revealing
something of the processes by which it was attained, especially when we can examine the piece in the light of his
own comment, as in the case of **"Wilding Flower."**
"Heart's Wild-Flower," as he renamed the revised form
of it printed in the **Poems,** is one of his loveliest lyrics. It
succeeds in saying what he considered to be "a thing which
constitutes much of the poetry of a young man's life," and
in saying it not more eloquently than simply, with much of
exquisite music, and no jarring notes. With this version
well in mind, turn to the first draft, sent with the letter of
May 16, 1896, and examine it in some detail. First of all
may be noted so apparently trivial a matter as the way of
printing the stanza: six short verses in the earlier form,
three long ones in the later. The short verses break the free
sweep of the rhythm. In many places the difference may
be negligible, but at the end of the next to the last stanza,
for example, the wondrous charm of the rhythm is much
enhanced by printing all in one line

Awes, adorations, songs of ruth, hesitancies, and tears.

Secondly, the author has ruthlessly deleted stanzas II-VIII
of the original version—more than half of the entire poem.
So heroic an amputation was necessitated chiefly by the
obscurity of the suspended construction in stanzas IV-VI,
which he admitted only after considerable argument, and
reluctantly, as will be seen from the letter of June 23. Indeed, as in most revisions, there was here a loss as well as
a gain; for he was quite right in pointing out the effect of
"breathlessness and holding aloof" secured by the suspen-
sion, and in comparing its constructive value to that of an
organ point in music. The omission of stanza III also sacrifices the delicate preparation it made for the final stanza.
But sacrifices are not sacrifices unless they cost something, and skillful revision consists precisely in this wise
balancing of complex accounts. It was worth while at almost any price to get rid of the "flushed adventurous vio-
lins," "the tower noon-precipiced," and the "aching oboe

throat that twins Night's moonward melodist," which are
the youthful Moody at his worst.

In the third place, the substitutions made in the retained
stanzas are all noteworthy, most of them because they tend
toward simplicity. Such, for instance, are "spirit fire" for
"lilac fire," "crown of tears and flame" for "carcanet of
flame," "autumn woe" for "subtle woe," "a little gift" for
"a mystic gift," and the poignant "shy, shy wilding flowers" for the rather literary "lovesome wilding flowers."
Most interesting of all, however, are the alterations in the
third stanza of the present version, as not merely verbal
but affecting the conception itself, toning it down from the
extreme and acrid terms into which Moody's instinct for
potent expression had led him, into much juster, tenderer
ones.

Not such a sign as women wear
Who bow beneath the shame
Of marriage insolence, and bear
A housewife's faded name"—

which exaggerates the contrast and repels us by its harshness, becomes—

Not such a sign as women wear who make their fore-
heads
    tame
With life's long tolerance, and bear love's sweetest,
humblest
    name.

Here the rhetorical antithesis remains unimpaired, and
there is a marked gain in spiritual propriety, and consequently in artistic dignity.

Finally it is well to note, after we have made all possible
criticism of this first draft on the scores of obscurity of
construction, turgidity of thought, or intemperance of language, that these are after all the faults of excess rather
than of defect, and that in spite of them, and in some degree even because of them, the mind at work here shows
itself to be thoroughly alive. If it has the crudity, it has
also the teeming vitality of youth. Its exuberance is infinitely to be preferred to the pallid correctness of academi-
cism. Its mistakes are those of a generous, independent nature daring enough to attempt something new, and its
failures are of the inspiring kind that in all artistic paths
pave the way to future successes. One is glad to think that
even in his moments of discouragement he had the pioneer's sustaining sense of adventure and discovery, as
when he writes: "I think—pardon the egotism of the utterance (you would if you knew what tears of failure have
gone to water the obstreperous little plant)—I think you
are not tolerant enough of the instinct for conquest in language, the attempt to push out its boundaries, to win for it
continually some new swiftness, some rare compression,
to distil from it a more opaline drop. Is n't it possible, too,
to be pedantic in the demand for simplicity? It's a cry
which, if I notice aright, nature has a jaunty way of disregarding. Command a rose-bush in the stress of June to
purge itself; coerce a convolvulus out of the paths of cat-
achresis. Amen!"

In this endeavor, thus early put before himself as a conscious ideal, to win for language "some new swiftness, some rare compression," Moody found, as time went on, not only an unfailing interest, but an object worthy his most tireless devotion, his most unswerving loyalty: he had the passion of the old alchemists for the distillation of that "more opaline drop." Impatient as he might be of the drudgery of teaching or hack-writing, in his poetic work no labor could dismay him. He loved to take pains. I especially remember the trick he had, in his rough drafts, of making endless substitutions of words, choosing first one and then another, striking out each in turn and surmounting it with the next, until some of his lines looked like the pediments of ruined temples, with columns of words rising at irregular intervals to unequal heights. To find him in his studio on a working morning (if one had the temerity), in a cloud of tobacco smoke, threading a labyrinth of emendations, surrounded by the carnage of previous encounters—burnt matches, scattered ashes, and discarded sheets—was to conceive a new respect for an art which could so completely conceal itself. His production was necessarily slow. The *Masque of Judgment,* for example, was begun in the summer of 1897, written out in fragmentary shape a year later during the holiday in Italy, and elaborated in London in the spring of 1899 to twice its previous proportions. "There are," he mentions in December of that year, "counting rewriting and further development here and there, about five hundred lines to be added." It was finally completed in Boston early in 1900. *The Faith-Healer,* which was not finished until the last year of his life, 1910, was begun, as the letters show, fifteen years before, in December, 1895.

Some sense of the devotion and the deliberateness with which he wrote his poetry is necessary to an understanding of his loathing for what he calls in one of his early Chicago letters "the crowd of spiteful assiduous nothings that keep me from It." Although he recognized with his usual fair-mindedness that he must pay his way by teaching or some similar form of "useful" work, and punctilious as he was in the discharge of these duties, he could not but resent their intrusion on time that he needed for work of infinitely greater intrinsic value. And they not only absorbed his time—they dulled his mental edge, and when long continued robbed him of "the spirit of selection, the zest of appropriation" which is the life of an artist. Consequently no note is more recurrent in the first letters from Chicago than that of a discontent with his new surroundings which was doubtless only partly due to the specific quality of the place, and is chiefly to be attributed to the distastefulness of his pursuits there.

Indeed the comments on Chicago, though all interesting, are oddly contradictory, and suggest a ceaseless alternation of moods. The mere physical spaciousness of the Western landscape seems sometimes to have oppressed, sometimes to have excited him. "Cambridge, mellow and autumnal," he writes soon after his arrival, "begins already to loom symbolic, under the stress of this relentless prairie light and vast featureless horizon." Yet, a month later, "To be a poet," he cries, "is a much better thing than to write poetry—out here, at least, watched by these wide horizons, beckoned to by these swift streamers of victorious sunset." Both of these opposed moods are not only expressed but philosophically penetrated in the beautiful letter of February 16, 1896, about the Irish girl he met skating.

What he called the "Western heartiness and uniplexity" subjected him to similar fluctuations of feeling. "As for Chicago," he tells Mrs. Toy, "I find that it gives me days or at least hours of broad-gauge Whitmanesque enthusiasm, meagerly sprinkled over weeks of tedium." In the long run he seems to have felt the deprivations more than the advantages: "In the East . . . one had n't to go far before finding some refinement of feeling, some delicate arabesque of convention, to help make up for the lack of liberty. Out here there is even less liberty (because less thought) and there is nothing—or next to nothing—to compensate." He describes in a memorable sentence of the same letter the deadly effect of such monotony on his eagerly adventurous mind—"that awful hush settling down on everything, as if Tò Πᾶν had suddenly discovered himself to be stuffed with sawdust."

The truth is, Moody was not made to wear contentedly, anywhere, the academic harness and blinders: he was too full of the untamable wildness of the creative mind which he has expressed so incomparably in his **"Road-Hymn for the Start."**

> Dear shall be the banquet table where their
> singing spirits press;
> Dearer be our sacred hunger, and our pilgrim
> loneliness.

No one so insatiably curious about life as he was, so ardent to learn, could give himself with patience to teaching. How many times must he have felt that impulse he confesses to "trundle his little instructorial droning-gear into Lake Michigan, and step out west or south on the Open Road, a free man by the grace of God, and a tramp by Rachel's intercession"! How dead and buried must he have seemed to himself when he computed in January, 1898, "April is only eighty-eight lectures, forty committee meetings, and several thousand themes away"! And how archly, a little later, as the months nevertheless elapse, does he paraphrase Wordsworth: "My heart leaps up when I behold a calendar on the sly"! When the vacations do at last arrive, and he is free once more to take up his own work, it is exciting to read of his joy. "I can feel the holy influences that wait on him who loafs beginning to purge me and urge me, though I tremble to say so for fear of frightening back their shy inquiring tentacles." "The summer I am bound to have though the Heavens fall, or rather because they are not going to fall but remain as a fittingly modest framework for the spectacle of my felicity."

It is worth while to insist with some amplitude of detail on the disharmony between Moody's economic conditions and his spiritual needs, both because his resolution of the discord was accomplished with a tact and courage that reveal much of what is finest in his character, and more generally because this Apollo-Admetus problem is fundamental in the life of every artist, and Moody's example is therefore a widely inspiring one. His friends could never sufficiently admire the quiet self-respect with which he pursued a course midway between the extremes where so many gifted natures meet shipwreck. In the first place, he was both too honest and too shrewd to shirk his service to Admetus—that irreducible minimum of it which he had decided to be necessary. He could even, thanks to his imagination, take the point of view of the task-master, see what was reasonably to be expected of the servant, and understand the fatuity of evading it. He always fulfilled his obligations to the letter. When he was working on his *History of English Literature,* for instance, at Gloucester, in May, 1900,—a month when moors and sea are at their most seductive,—he may have found it necessary, as he whimsically states, to "put on blinders, stuff his ears with wax, and strap himself to the desk"; but at least the work done in that constricted position was solid and workmanlike, as any one may see for himself.

On the other hand, he never forgot for a moment that such work was but a means to an end; he never tolerated the sentimental fallacy that faithfulness in the treadmill exempts one from the higher responsibilities of a liberal leisure; he never gave Admetus one jot more than was nominated in the bond. Thus he refused the offer, from Chicago University, of the full salary of a professor for lectures during one quarter each year: a single quarter was too much. Of course the price of such devotion was poverty. His method was to labor at teaching or hack-writing until he had accumulated a little money, and then to live on it as simply as possible as long as it lasted, too happy in composition to mind small discomforts. That it lasted longer in Europe than at home was one reason of his frequent voyages. Fortunately he did not need a large income. Aside from a barbaric fondness for jewelry and fancy waistcoats his personal tastes were inexpensive; though fond of the society of cultivated people, he had not the least trace of snobbery; almost his only financial luxury was the help he often extended to relatives and friends less prosperous than himself. Even with these advantages, however, he showed, it seems to me, a clear-headedness in the discrimination between immediate and ultimate values, and a stanch courage in the refusal to let the nearer interfere with the greater, as difficult to attain, and as rare, as they are admirable and worthy of emulation.

The entire freedom of his work from the influences of commercialism, even in its most insidious and seductive forms, is due, I am sure, to this faculty he had of keeping money-earning and art as completely separated in his mind as they are in reality. It was placed in such striking relief by the circumstances, unprecedented in his hitherto obscure life, surrounding the production of *The Great Divide* in the autumn of 1906 (the single decisive worldly success of his short career) that I remember vividly what he told me of his affairs during a brief visit in the country soon after the opening night. He was then earning about five hundred dollars a week from the play, and was besieged by reporters, publishers, managers, and general social invitations. He was also quite unspoiled by it all, as simple in manner and cordial in talk as ever, and more enthusiastic over the beauties of the country than over the glories of Broadway. In the course of a long morning walk he told me that he hoped sometime to be able to buy a farm, where he could write undisturbed, and that now for the first time, among those New England hills, he realized how he had been tempted by large offers, received from four different publishers, for *The Great Divide* in novel form. Such sums had been mentioned as twenty-five, and even fifty, thousand dollars. But it had always seemed to him, he said, that the turning of a play into a novel, or *vice versa,* was a confounding of two essentially diverse types of art, and therefore a violation of a basic artistic principle; and he had refused all the offers.

Not that there was anything of the prig in him—his sympathies were far too broad for that. The notes in which he discusses with Mr. Gilder the suppression of his initials on the poem written in his honor reveal a characteristic mingling of modesty as to his own attainments with delight in the appreciation of others and tender concern for their feelings. He had, too, that rarest form of humor which enables a man to laugh at himself, and an artist to relish parodies of his own style. We see it in the letter of January 24, 1901, to Mr. Edwin Arlington Robinson, in which he plays with the notion of how his "florid vocabulary" may affect a brother poet of the opposed method, a devotee of under-statement. Even in college days, when some solemnity of egotism is almost the accepted attitude, he had already this self-immolating humor. A college mate, I remember, used to make fun of the "foolish little cricket thing" in the song, **"My Love Is Gone into the East,"** and to turn the third stanza into baldest prose by the simple device of changing "or late or soon" into "sooner or later." That Moody may have been a little nettled as well as amused is suggested by his request, when he sent me **"Dawn Parley"** a year or two later, that before reading it I abstract myself for twelve hours from the society of the jester; but all the same he thoroughly enjoyed the joke, and recurs to it with unction in his letter of December 1, 1895. When he was writing **"Gloucester Moors,"** at East Gloucester, in the spring of 1900, he asked a lady at the hotel, learned in wild-flowers, to tell him the names of all she knew, and used some of them in the second stanza—

> Jill o'er the ground is purple blue,
> Blue is the quaker-maid.

One item in the catalogue, baby blue-eye, brought from him a shout of laughter, and the suggestion that it ought to be incorporated in the line

> Baby blue is the baby blue-eye.

In the long run, and after all analysis, it is Moody's broad humanity that stands out as the most lovable trait of the man and the imperishable quality in the poet. He accepted human nature, and glorified it. He pitied its fallibility and admired its aspiration; and he identified himself with it, frankly recognizing in his own character the two conflicting elements. From one of his most serious letters, to a friend who does not wish it to be published entire, the following passage may be taken as a touching illustration:—

"Thanks for your word of cheer. It found me in a state of dejection compounded of grippe and unfaithfulness, and lifted me to the heights again—the only climate that suits my lungs these days, though the valleys with their lights and business are tempting when night sets in, and too often betray me downward. . . . I needed the good word you sent me more than a little, and am in your debt a trifle deeper than before—if a matter of a few thousands is worth counting in my hopeless insolvency. If my work, stumbling and delayed as it usually seems to me, gives you any help in the contemplation, consider what the candour and spiritual grace of your character have been and are to me, looking with eyes no less wistful after righteousness for being somewhat bleared and dazzled by sensuous strayings. These things are perhaps best left unsaid, but now and then one forgets that he is an Anglo-Saxon and remembers only that he is a man, with a man's eternal aims, and a man's chances of help and hindrance on the tragic road; for which former it is not unbecoming from time to time to give thanks somewhat soberly."

Such a passage as this evokes for us afresh, and with an even more intimate sense of personal presence, the generous nature that has expressed this religion of humanity with incomparable power in Raphael's hymn to man in Act III of the *Masque of Judgment.* Deeply spiritual, and as far as possible removed from the sensualism the thoughtless have found in it, is his paganism, as there set forth, his belief in the feelings, the passions, and the senses. He conceives them all as ministers of spirituality, and sees them transfigured in that ministration. He believes that through them alone is spirituality realized, or realizable.

> Not in vain, not in vain,

sings Raphael,—

> The spirit hath its sanguine stain,
> And from its senses five doth peer
> As a fawn from the green windows of a wood.

To his mind the only possible attitude was a hearty acceptance of life as a whole. He was an enemy of nothing that is positive, but only of the negative things: doubt, cowardice, indifference, all ascetic denials of life. The reader of the letters that follow will, it is hoped, come ever more clearly to recognize the warm-hearted, welcoming personality that speaks in them. He was one of the few who can use, in their fullest sense, the words he has put into the mouth of Raphael:—

> O struggler in the mesh
> Of spirit and of flesh
> Some subtle hand hath tied to make thee Man,

> . . . . .
> My bosom yearns above thee at the end,
> Thinking of all thy gladness, all thy woe;
>   Whoever is thy foe,
> I am thy friend, thy friend.

Joyce Kilmer (essay date 1916)

SOURCE: "William Vaughn Moody (1869-1910)," in *The Circus and Other Essays and Fugitive Pieces,* edited by Robert Cortes Holliday, George H. Doran Company, 1921, pp. 302-11.

[*In the following essay, which was originally published in 1916, Kilmer discusses technical strengths and weaknesses of Moody's poetry, key events in his life, and major influences on his development.*]

William Vaughn Moody was throughout his life regarded as the most promising of the younger American poets. And when he died in 1910 most critics mourned for the unwritten lyrics and poetic dramas of which American literature had thus been robbed; they mentioned the author as a gifted youth, whom fate had removed at the beginning of a splendid career.

To a certain extent this attitude was a tribute to the youthful spirit of William Vaughn Moody, to his vivacity, energy and cheerfulness. But it was chiefly a new illustration of the fact that nowadays poets flower late in the season. Moody was forty-one years old when he died—and there was a time when the poet of forty was considered well past the meridian of his genius. Most of the great poets established their fame before they were thirty years old—Keats and Shelley died at twenty-five and twenty-nine respectively. But nowadays the poet of forty-five is still called young and the poet of thirty our kind critics consider a precocious infant.

As a matter of stern fact, it is doubtful that American literature has really lost much by Moody's death. He wrote **"Gloucester Moors"** and the **"Ode in Time of Hesitation"** and *The Faith Healer.* The conscientious student of his work cannot escape the conviction that in these he gave the world all that he really had to give. Of course he would have written more—nature lyrics, poems on political and sociological questions, poetical dramas dealing with philosophical themes, prose plays of modern American life. But toward the end of his brief life his work was not gaining in force. Readers of *The Death of Eve* have little sorrow over the poet's failure to complete this play— the first two members of the trilogy which it was to conclude are nobly phrased, but they are so cloudy in thought and weak in dramatic construction that they do their author's fame little service. Prometheus, Pandora, Deucalion, Eve, Cain, Raphael, and Michael, angels and archangels, thrones, dominions and powers, were characters too mighty for the talent of this poet, who could handle adequately enough a problem of contemporary politics or draw quaint lessons from the caged beasts in a menagerie.

Perhaps the coldness which annoys some readers of Moody's poems, the sense of aloofness from the common experience of mankind, the artificiality which mars such expressions of sympathy for humanity as are intended in **"Gloucester Moors,"** are things for which it is unjust to blame the poet. His friend, John M. Manly, wrote in the preface to his *Poems and Plays*: "He was an epicure of life, a voluptuary of the whole range of physical, mental, and spiritual perfections." But in Moody's poetry we find more of the mind than of the heart; we feel that we are in the presence of a charming and cultured personality, but we have no feeling of intimacy with the writer.

"Of thine own tears thy song must tears beget," wrote Rossetti. "O singer, magic mirror hast thou none save thine own manifest heart." And a greater poet than Rossetti exclaimed, "Ah, must (Designer Infinite!) Thou char the wood ere thou canst limn with?" A similar thought was in Horace's mind when in the *Ars Poetica* he said, "if you wish me to weep you must first weep yourself."

Well, few tears are drawn by Moody's poems, nor did many tears go into their making. His wood was not charred. But he was a conscientious and accomplished artist, doing the best he could with the powers that were his. His work is thoughtful, imaginative, and well-wrought, his *Great Divide* is destined to periodic revivals, and the best of his lyrics are sure of a place in the anthologies.

William Vaughn Moody was born in Spencer, Indiana, on July 8th, 1869. He was the son of a prosperous retired steamboat captain. In 1871 the family moved to New Albany, on the Ohio River. The elder Moody died in 1886. William Vaughn Moody went to Riverside Academy and entered Harvard in 1889, being then twenty years old. In his senior year he went abroad with a wealthy family as tutor to their son. During the trip he made a walking tour of the Black Forest and Switzerland with a party of friends, including Norman Hapgood. He also spent some time in Greece and Italy.

He returned to Harvard to study for his master's degree and stayed on as an instructor in English. In the autumn of 1895 he went to the University of Chicago as instructor in English, reaching the rank of assistant professor before his departure eight years later. His life at the University of Chicago seems to have been rather leisurely. It was varied by journeys abroad and bicycle tours in Illinois and Wisconsin. Swimming, bicycling, golf, tennis, walking, and mountain-climbing are mentioned by Mr. Manly as Moody's favorite sports, and it is not to be wondered that he had little time for writing, however unexacting his academic duties may have been.

Although his connection with the University of Chicago did not cease until later, he taught no classes after 1902. He did, however, do a certain amount of work academic in character, editing some editions of the classics and collaborating with his friend Robert M. Lovett in a *History of English Literature.* He first became known to the general public by the successful presentation of his prose play, *The Great Divide.* He died in Colorado Springs on the seventeenth of October, 1910. A few months before his death he married Miss Harriet C. Brainerd.

It is interesting to trace the influences in Moody's work. He was very thoroughly a man of books, and some critics complain that there is more ink than blood in the veins of the people of whom he writes. Certainly it is possible to find traces of his reading on nearly every page that he wrote. The lovely fourth stanza of **"Gloucester Moors"** is Coleridge; **"Faded Pictures"** is Browning at his worst; and **"The Daguerreotype"** is a deliberate effort to imitate the irregular ode-form of Coventry Patmore. And of course **"Heart's Wildflower"** and **"A Dialogue in Purgatory,"** like the lyrics in *The Masque of Judgment,* are a Chicago version of Rossetti.

In his prose plays we find Moody writing with an energy which he seldom exhibited in his poetry. Not in Jerome K. Jerome's *The Passing of the Third Floor Back,* nor in Charles Rann Kennedy's *The Servant in the House,* is the idea of the beneficent effect of a powerful and virtuous nature more plausibly presented than in *The Faith Healer.* And Moody obtained his effect more honestly than did Jerome and Kennedy; his faith-healer is merely a faith-healer to the end of the play, there is no suggestion that he is more than human. In many respects *The Faith Healer* is Moody's most important work. There is more poetry in its prose than in all his poetic dramas put together. When Michaelis makes love to Rhoda and tells the story of his childhood home, when Beeler describes the picture of Pan and the Pilgrim, and when Uncle Abe chants his prophecies and visions, then there is real poetry—poetry not unlike some of the best passages in Synge's plays. The "strange mounting sing-song" of Uncle Abe's speech evidently was the inspiration of the best parts of Mr. Ridgley Torrence's *The Rider of Dreams.*

The Great Divide has been magnificently acted, but it is inferior in every respect to *The Faith Healer.* Its theme—the contrast between the Puritan spirit which Moody considered typical of the Eastern States, and the generous paganism which he thought characteristically Western,—might be, and probably will be, the basis of an important play. But there never was a New Englander remotely resembling Ruth Jordan, there never was a Westerner remotely resembling Stephen Ghent. Hero and heroine, or villain and villainess, or whatever they are supposed to be, have actuality, it is true—the actuality of figures seen in a nightmare. And the other characters in the play have no actuality whatsoever. And the author's total lack of humor never injured his work more than in this play. It is painful to see situations essentially humorous made banal and dull by the author's obtuseness. If only the idea had occurred to Bernard Shaw instead of to William Vaughn Moody!

Perhaps one reason why *The Great Divide,* convincing enough when well acted, is a lamentable thing on the printed page is because it is an attempt to prove a theory.

Moody was a Puritan, through and through, and like all modern literary Puritans he was desperately ashamed of his Puritanism. He glorified what he thought to be the pagan ideal, and in *The Great Divide* he wanted to show that the large acceptances of Ghent were nobler than the austere negations of Ruth. But paganism and Puritanism are nothing but terms, almost meaningless from much repetition, and *The Great Divide* is a play of terms, of symbols, of lay figures. And the only things that it proves are Moody's total inability to understand paganism and his reluctant but inevitable sympathy with Puritanism.

It was his Puritanism that made Moody try to stimulate the conscience of his land by means of **"An Ode in Time of Hesitation,"** his best sustained long poem, and his most passionate utterance. It was the Puritan who wrote **"On a Soldier Fallen in the Philippines."** It was the Puritan who wrote **"The Brute."** And I think that it was the Puritan who wrote **"Gloucester Moors."** A pagan, such as Moody desired to be, would not have worried about the "souls distraught in the hold," nor would he have worried over the fact that some of the crew had over-eaten. Also, a pagan would have enjoyed the loveliness of the wild geranium and the barberry without asking:

> Who has given to me this sweet,
> And given my brother dust to eat?
> And when will his wage come in?

These things are manifestations of that Puritan characteristic known as "the New England conscience"—the cause in recent years of many rather frantic efforts at social and economic and philosophical readjustment. Mr. John M. Manly says that **"Gloucester Moors"** is "a favorite poem with workers in the slums,"—a significant and startling observation.

Moody's Puritanism gives strength to many of his poems, but in others it produces strange inconsistencies and evasions. It helped him to write **"The Brute"**—a strong and sincere poem. But it caused him to fail ridiculously in **"A Dialogue in Purgatory,"** in **"Good-Friday Night,"** and in **"Song Flower and Poppy."** In the second half of the last-named poem we come upon the root of the matter—Moody's complete failure to understand any religious system, any philosophy of life, more warm and comprehensive than his own Puritanism. He rebelled against this Puritanism, yet he could not escape it. He sought vaguely after paganism, whereas he could no more have been a Bacchic reveller than he could have been a Druid. In spite of his reading of early French and Italian romances, he failed utterly to see the generous glories of the Middle Ages, when all that was noble and beautiful in paganism was made a part of the richest civilization the world has yet known. He thought of intellectual development and spiritual freedom as things beginning about 1517—and naturally this hampered him when he wrote about Michael, Raphael, Azaziel, Eve, Jubal, and Cain.

A longer residence in Italy might have given him a more liberal culture and a spiritual philosophy generous without being pagan, pure without being Puritanical. And therefore the critics who said that a poet of promise died in 1910 may have told the truth. A broader culture and more extensive human sympathies would have enabled this deft artist in words to give to the world a message of the kind it always welcomes—to express beautifully the beauty that is truth.

Martha Hale Shackford (essay date 1918)

SOURCE: "Moody's 'The Fire Bringer' For To-Day," in *The Sewanee Review*, Vol. 26, October, 1918, pp. 407-16.

[*In the following essay, Shackford considers the spiritual relevance of* The Fire Bringer *to audiences coping with the trauma of World War I.*]

In the midst of the catastrophe of the war we look to our poets for help in interpreting the mystery of human experience. We seek the guidance of their ideals, the inspiration to be won from the vision of those who see a meaning beyond the chaos and suffering and brutality of the present. But when we look about for an American poet able to divine our special needs we look almost in vain. Few of our poets have the power to sting us into thought and to lead our thoughts into regions where we shall be purified and enlightened in spirit to such a degree that we shall find courage and a well-justified hope. In the work of William Vaughn Moody there is just that challenge which we need so bitterly, and his drama *The Fire Bringer* is a most potent voice calling to us in tones that suit this very hour.

Moody's poetry, created and dominated by a personal passion for spiritual understanding, is wrought out with a beauty of form and a vigor of imagination which have not been surpassed in America. American most distinctively, despite strains of German, French, and Spanish blood, and despite his cosmopolitan education, Moody is the child of the Puritans. He inherited that grim, aspiring, relentless mood which would not be thwarted in its zeal for holiness. He had scant interest in local, temporal aspects of American life; he was concerned with America's soul, and he is the guide, the interpreter of our ideals, the prophet of the destiny towards which we stumble. Nothing but a profound tradition of religious passion could have produced his intense preoccupation with spiritual issues and his fierce rebellion against conventional faith. Possessing the energy which hews and builds, which endures all hardships for the sake of spiritual freedom, he is the pioneer who forces his way into the wilderness of truth, facing unknown dangers in his ceaseless search for knowledge of God. Pilgrim and martyr speak in this:—

> Truth is not soon made plain, nor in a breath
> Fluently solved while the chance listener waits,
> Nor by the elemental wrestling mind
> Wrung from the rock with sobs. Myself have held,
> Where in the sun's core light and thought are one,
> Æons of questions, and am darkling still.

One truth which Puritanism had not learned was clear to Moody,—the essential unity of body and spirit. It is the fusion, the reconciliation of these two aspects of life which gives his poetry so vital a significance. Most of us have failed to interpret life as a unit; we shift and evade in our effort to live, without meeting squarely the fundamental question of the duties of the body in servitude to the spirit. We divide existence into Sundays and weekdays. Moody knew no such distinctions; his whole purpose was to avoid a dualism of allegiance. Life must be a whole, not two parts:—

> How long, old builder Time, wilt bide
>   Till at thy thrilling word
> Life's crimson pride shall have to bride
>   The spirit's white accord,
> Within that gate of good estate
> Which thou must build us soon or late,
>   Hoar workman of the Lord?

The faithful survivor of one religious movement, he is the foreteller of another, for he voices the potent, inspiring truths to be won from the doctrine of evolution. No other idea in the nineteenth century so quickened idealism, aroused and directed high aspiration as did this doctrine interpreted by poets such as Browning and George Meredith. Moody, trained in these conceptions, accepted evolution with profound conviction, and saw all life illuminated by the faith that through ardent, unremitting struggle the individual can slowly progress toward spiritual perfection. There are still many persons to-day who repudiate with horror the doctrine of evolution, who still fail to perceive the transcendent beauty of the idea that man's will is superior to circumstance and can shape and form the plastic thing called self; that man may look forward with hope to a future whose perfection he must help create by his active aspiration, by his positive determination. There is scarcely a poem of Moody's which does not touch some aspect of evolution.

The ability to think profoundly and yet to express his thoughts in vivid concreteness of poetic image, distinguishes Moody from the mere versifier who turns out ethical and æsthetic commonplaces. Moody never succumbed to the desire to please the *Musa Meretrix,* and his greatness as a poet is due to his dogged tenacity and persistence in attempting to express a coherent, centred interpretation of man's spiritual destiny in a world of glowing beauty and appeal. His singleness of aim, his steadily increasing insight, his fastidious self-criticism kept him from rapid and vapid composition. Consequently we have not a large body of poetry from his pen, but what we do possess is most carefully wrought.

The note of studiousness and, too, of learning condemns him in the eyes of those who believe the poet must be a glorious, unattached apparition like a comet, but the very fact that he is profoundly familiar with the Bible, the Greek dramatists, Dante, Shakespeare, Milton, Keats, Browning, and Meredith, gives his work a value which is incontestable. He has the superior advantage of having assimilated their ideals and of being able to carry on the development of these ideals through his distinctly personal interpretation. Our faith in a poet's mission is greatly strengthened

if we know that he is no mere attenuated voice of the moment, but is, rather, the associate of older truths, of inherited ideas which he has pondered with all of a poet's kindling passion, and which he, in his era, seeks to understand and to transcend in a fuller, richer meaning, if possible; that intimate relationship to the slowly evolved continuity of human thought and feeling is essential for any poetic understanding of loyalty, constancy, or permanency and for any vision of the future. Fundamentally, Moody is original both in idea and in artistic method; his accents reveal individual potency of life and have a challenging sharpness of personality. The dominant traits of his poetry are uniquely, characteristically, Moody's own.

In the dramas, *The Fire Bringer* and *The Masque of Judgment,* he strove to express his essential conceptions of spiritual truth. His philosophy was by no means completely formulated, but was slowly being evolved as life and thought guided him to deeper insight. These dramas are the closely pondered utterances of a powerful human personality seeking to interpret man's relation to God, and to do this in the light of past theology and older literature as well as in the light of the present day. The casual reader may perceive chiefly the highly picturesque and mythological elements in the work, but closer study will reveal the fact that these poems represent an almost tragic struggle on the part of one devout by nature, skeptical through education and observation,—one who in an awful loneliness of mind endeavored to rend the veil from those mysteries which the spiritual man must know. By no means unquestionable masterpieces, with flaws in expression,—stiffness and frequent heaviness,—these dramas are nevertheless great poetic creations. The blank verse is often of an extraordinarily high order, as will be seen in the lines quoted. The choric odes, like the odes already mentioned, are skilfully adapted to give lyric relief to the drama.

Moody's theme was the immutable, eternal unity of God and man. Seeking to express this in poetic, concrete imagery, interpreting his spiritual conviction in terms comprehensible to all readers, he turned to the two chief religious traditions of the western world,—the pagan and the Christian. Although he availed himself of these associations he interpreted them with the greatest freedom, for he seemed to feel no need of complete verisimilitude. In pagan as well as in Christian setting he used freely whatever he chose of the essential teaching of evolution, of the developing philosophy of idealism, and the doctrines of complete freedom of the will, the individual's power of choice.

Although it was written later than *The Masque of Judgment,* Moody placed *The Fire Bringer* first in the trilogy which was to be completed by *The Death of Eve.* There is no inter-relationship in these works, except the reiteration of the essential theme, the inviolable unity of God and man. *The Fire Bringer* is Hellenic in background and in central imagery, but fused with traditions from the Greek are recollections of *Paradise Lost, Prometheus Unbound, Hyperion,* and also hints of Browning's influence. The drama is unquestionably the greatest of Moody's achievements, and reveals most completely the deep beauty and power of the poet's endowment. Here, in a myth of old Greece, is wonderful dramatic revelation of the meaning of evolution, the supremacy of spiritual over material forces. The story of Prometheus and his theft of fire from the gods is the dramatic medium by which Moody draws a realistic picture to embody his doctrine. The scene opens just after the flood has subsided, and Deucalion and Pyrrha, with a few other survivors, are revealed in the half-light, together with the men and women created, as in legend, from the stones which Deucalion and Pyrrha have thrown behind them. In a world dank, cold, desolate, crouch all these beings, fearful of what the gods may ordain next. Prometheus, failing in his first effort to gain the sacred fire, has come to add his dejection to the horror of those left—

> To rot and crumble with the crumbling world.

It is then that the most important figure in the drama appears,—Pandora, the mysterious being who represents, partly, woman, but still more the quality of spiritual energy, of aspiring vitality of will. Pandora, beloved of Prometheus, is the force that awakens him from his lethargy, and, giving him the stalk of fennel, inspires him to new vigor, so that he returns victorious, bringing back to listless humanity the fire, symbolic of material progress and of spiritual light and power. The scene of Prometheus' return shows Moody's remarkable skill in description of nature. The slow coming of dawn, as in *Prometheus Unbound* and in *Hyperion,* is eloquently pictured, but Moody is here no imitator. This is a Greek sunrise, such as he had often seen flood the Greek mountains.—

>   Paler grow
> The gulfs of shadowy air that brim the vales,
> As ocean bateth in her thousand firths,
> The grey and silver air draws down the land.
> The little trees that climb among the rocks
> As high as they can live, pierce with their spires
> The shoaling mist, swim softly into light,
> And stand apparent, shapely, every one
> A dream of divine life, a miracle.

As the glorious day brings them light and hope, the weak mortals quicken to new existence; joy, exaltation, love are wakened in the hearts of young and old, and a new era is begun.

The meaning of the drama may be interpreted without much involved symbolism. Man is dejected, sorrowful, inert, always looking backward toward a remembered or a fancied period of happiness. Lax, without purpose, without initiative, he is stirred to vigor of life by some force outside himself, by some mind keener, stronger, more daring than his own. Under the impetus of hope, brought by the gift of fire, even the clods are awakened and slowly—

> The unwrought shapes, the unmoulded attitudes,
> The tongues of earth, the stony craving eyes

begin to show marvelous signs of progress as the truth of the domination of mind over flesh is revealed to them. The scenes where the stone men and women are endowed with the gift of inner life, of life-direction, are impressively vivid. The reader is in the presence of primitive creation, watching mortality struggle away from shapelessness, sloth, dullness, into an ever-increasing power of controlled, significant life. All the persons in the drama reveal in some way the eternal awakening to higher, finer impulses. Not only in casting off physical torpor, but in ridding themselves of fear, superstition, and cruelty, the earth-dwellers reveal the far-reaching effects of spiritual illumination. Man's sharp dread of human experience is brought out in the realistic protest made against this unfolding of keener life. Humanity shrinks back, daunted, uneasy, loving the familiar, afraid of the mysteries to be revealed by existence. Even in the midst of spiritual revelation we cling to earth, hesitating, fearful of strange truths:—

>   God, my God,
> Thou see'st my quivering spirit what it is!
> O lay not life upon it. We know not
>   . . . . .
> The thing we asked for. We had all forgot
> How cruel was thy splendor in the house
> Of sense, how awful in the house of thought,
> How far unbearable in the wild house
> That thou hast cast and builded for the heart.

This is life for humanity, this mingled doubt, wonder, and splendor. And the leaders themselves, the spirits finer, more daring than the average have their sufferings also. The moments of exultation are swiftly passing; at his highest, man is subject to powers unknown; his visions and aspirations fluctuate and die away after a failure. The power of practical execution of an ideal seems hopelessly lost. It is then that a greater power comes to his aid, to spur him on. Invisible forces of spirit are the real source of fine action and achievement. Pandora is the symbol of quivering, ideal perception and an aspiration never quiescent, but always in motion, always seeking, finding truth. She is the soul of man, the tenacious faith, the boundless hope, and the love which is absence of the body in the presence of the spirit. Love quickens Prometheus, but not a selfish love; it is the revelation wrought by love that inspires him to victory. The song sung by Pandora as she gives him the fennel stalk is the consummate expression of human courage and hope. It is unquestionably the most perfect lyric ever written by Moody. The vividly imaginative use of figure, the yearning note of spiritual aspiration, give the poem ideal lyric beauty.—

> Of wounds and sore defeat
> I made my battle stay;
> Wingèd sandals for my feet
> I wove of my delay;
> Of weariness and fear,
> I made my shouting spear;
> Of loss, and doubt, and dread,
> And swift oncoming doom
> I made a helmet for my head,
> And a floating plume.
> From the shutting mist of death,
> From the failure of the breath,

I made a battle-horn to blow
Across the values of overthrow.
O hearken, love, the battle-horn!
The triumph clear, the silver scorn!
O hearken where the echoes bring,
Down the grey disastrous morn,
Laughter and rallying.

Even though the achievement of Prometheus brings hope and vigor to all, though latent power is released, he suffers for his magnanimity. Valor, virtue, generous action, are always achieved at great cost to the hero himself. Prometheus, actuated by the most noble motives, is, at the end, punished, made to atone for his audacity. And here is the crux of the human problem. Why is virtue so seldom rewarded? Why does the unselfish man suffer? Why is an heroic act so often a martyrdom? It is the spectacle of this which seems so fundamentally unjust that has darkened the faith of men, and has made life seem futile. But, as Moody would say, this verdict of ours is one more sign of our failure to have large conceptions. We judge meanly spiritual life and the opportunity for expression of high endeavor and aspiration. We flee from the truth that the fundamental law of the inner life is struggle. Virtue easily gained is valueless. Heroism amply rewarded is not heroism. The test of idealism, not Shelleyan vagueness but efficient idealism, is the courage to face the suffering that is the beneficent law of the universe. It is not passive reception of benefits that makes existence noble. God never intended man to sit in idle comfort, blandly receiving divine charity. It is a world of continued, desperate endeavor, of daring, of energy, of taking chances. It is the uncertainty, the knowledge that some price must be paid, the premonition of sacrifice that gives mankind spiritual strength and nobility. Insight, strength, idealism, are gained by effort, by perpetual striving.

What sort of God has, then, ordained a world of pain and struggle when he might so easily have created a world of pleasure? The definition of God is a most significant part of the drama, and we see God from various dramatic points of view as the characters of the drama discern him. To the lesser beings, there is a hierarchy of gods who must be propitiated, pleased, by bloody sacrifice; their conception of Deity is a conception of strength and cruelty. Deucalion and Pyrrha are wiser, but they, too, cower in dread of gods revengeful, indifferent, or teasing. Alert, on the defensive always, conscious of antagonism to the divine, Prometheus emphasizes man's power of achievement, and insists that it is illimitable, identical with the divine, although the conditions of life make it essential for man to take the initiative and wrest from the gods that which he would possess:—

For these, if you would keep them, you must strive
Morning and night against the jealous gods,
With anger, and with laughter, and with love;
But no man hath them till he brings them down
With love, and rage, and laughter from the heavens,—
Himself the heavens, himself the scornful gods,
The sun, the sun-thief, and the flaming reed
That kindles new the beauty of the world.

It is through the words of Pandora that we become aware of the true personality of the Ruler of the universe:—

I stood within the heart of God;
    It seemed a place that I had known;
(I was blood-sister to the clod,
    Blood-brother to the stone.)

I found my love and labor there,
    My house, my raiment, meat and wine,
My ancient rage, my old despair,—
    Yea, all things that were mine.

In these lines is the key to Moody's faith. The Divine Spirit is within us as well as without. He suffers with Prometheus. He is understanding, aspiration, and an eternal sympathizer in the life which He has created. Never more can the conception of a God of wrath and cruel vindictiveness be admitted by the minds of men. Most significantly, Moody makes the earth-men and women change their conception of God as they slowly develop higher ideas of life. Singing the might of Eros and of Iacchus, they gradually abandon their earthly ideas of the divine, and as their fleshly moods are refined away, as the splendor of existence is made clearer to them, they, through the mouths of the young men, acknowledge the supremacy of one God, a god of inner eternal light:—

For thou alone, O thou alone art he
Who settest the prisoned spirit free,
And sometimes leadest the rapt soul on
Where never mortal thought has gone.

He has shown that true religion is an outgrowth of the old; that evolution is always economy, pruning away the weak and useless and creating the new by saving and shaping every vestige of significance in the old. The greatness of **The Fire Bringer** is due to the large conception of the unity of a world organically related in time and in space; a world where every part must constantly adapt, adjust, discipline itself to contribute to the perfection of the whole. In showing that God has thus made man the arbiter of his own destiny, has thrown upon man the burden of perceiving and of developing the divine within himself, Moody has proved himself a poet of profoundest insight.

There has been no other poet since Browning who expresses as does Moody the deep questioning and spiritual endeavor of mankind. In a daring, unfettered effort to find truth, he was not afraid to follow where truth led, even into the utmost reaches of speculation. He did not avoid the logic of his thinking, nor bend his observations to prove his special theories. He had that impartial, intensely receptive attitude which animates the true student of things eternal. His cardinal belief, that man and God are inseparable, was to him a source of exhaustless hope, but he recognized the necessity laid upon man of constant, tireless, undaunted effort. Struggle is the law of life, and the persons who find life unendurable are the victims of their own negligence and inertia. The man who walks erect in the full light of his opportunities, gains a knowledge, an insight forever intensifying itself. Man, earth, God are co-partners in the eternal advance of spirit, subduing, transcending matter. Man must be purified until he knows the living truth and has by active effort gained his spiritual integrity. It is a doctrine of scant pleasure to those who yearn for peace at any price. The quiescence of the spiritually weak is a badge of their bondage to the flesh. Beauty, order, progress, nobility, idealism are all gained by struggle:—

> Darkly, but oh, for good, for good,
> The spirit infinite
> Was throned upon the perishable blood.

F. O. Matthiessen (essay date 1931)

SOURCE: A review of *Selected Poems of William Vaughn Moody,* in *The New England Quarterly,* Vol. 4, October, 1931, pp. 797-801.

[*In the following essay, Matthiessen discusses the scope of Moody's ideas and the manner of their presentation in* Selected Poems of William Vaughn Moody.]

William Vaughn Moody has been unusually fortunate in the tributes paid him by his friends. John M. Manly was the editor of his collected works; Daniel Gregory Mason brought out his letters; and now, after twenty years have elapsed since the poet's death, Robert Morss Lovett, a contemporary of Moody's both at Harvard and later on the teaching staff at Chicago, has added his long essay of reminiscence [in an introduction to *Selected Poems of William Vaughn Moody*]. Moody's personality made a strong impact on all of them. They unite in praising his vigor, his grace, his humor, his courage, his austere reserve as well as his abundance, the sweetness and sainty of his mind as much as its bold constructiveness, and, above all else, his broad humanity, the hearty acceptance of life as a whole which stood out as his most significant trait.

Mr. Lovett reiterates the scope of his importance. He reminds us that Moody was not only a lyric poet, but that he also had an impressive share in the revival of poetic drama, and that his prose plays, *The Great Divide* and *The Faith Healer,* were the one serious effort of his period to bring the American stage to the movement started by Ibsen, and make it a vehicle for actual criticism of life. But he values Moody most of all for having worked in the great tradition of the poetry of the world, and gets from his best lyrics the sense of exhilaration that only great poetry can give. This evaluation is very like that made by one of the most sensitive judges of poetry in Moody's time, the late Charlton Lewis of Yale. Writing in the *Yale Review,* in 1913, Professor Lewis took deep satisfaction in the mingled fineness and robustness of Moody's work, and particularly in its final effect of masculine directness, a quality that made him feel that it spoke to him of his own thoughts and aspirations in a way that the great Victorian poets of his youth were unable to do.

Such an evaluation is very difficult for a contemporary reader to respond to. The element that all Moody's critics agree in praising most highly, his rich gift of expression, is the very element that makes his poetry seem artificial. Affected partly by the Symbolists, working partly in a vein similar to that of Meredith, metaphor was his natural vehicle; he wanted his image to be the complete embodiment of his thought. But whether in the somewhat florid exuberance of his talk and letters, or in the even more studied figures of his poems, one feels that he has so strained and squeezed his image to make it yield every subtle implication that, as in the case of "the gallant, gallant ship" of **"Gloucester Moors,"** instead of giving the reader a more vivid realization of the idea, the image itself simply catches him in its meshes. Probably the chief reason why one feels this quality of over-abundance is that the diction, as well as the figures, seems too strenuously sought after. Moody thought himself as enthusiastic a pioneer in language as the Elizabethans. "You are not tolerant enough," he wrote to Mason, "of the instinct of conquest in language, the attempt to push out its boundaries, to win for it continually some new swiftness, some rare compression, to distill from it a more opaline drop." But that very passage, particularly its closing phrase, reveals the limitations of Moody's pioneering. Sometimes he brought a fresh word from the vernacular, as in the effective humorous line in **"The Menagerie"**: "a little man in trousers slightly jagged"; but more often he studded his language with the archaic and literary, "energic," "margent," or "blooth."

Both his manner of expression and his language would indicate Moody as an eclectic poet. He was seldom imitative in the narrower sense of being completely under the sway of any one writer, but the range of his debts was very wide: Browning, Keats, Shelley, Swinburne, and later Milton and the Greek drama, especially Euripides's *Bacchæ,* Francis Thompson, and Verlaine all contributed to his broad and diverse culture. The richness of that culture is known to every one who is familiar with his brilliant edition of Milton, a very mellow achievement; but for a poet such a large number of masters might seem to argue a lack of inner fibre of his own, an aloofness from life, an academic want of passion. Such a conclusion in the case of Moody, however, would be wholly false. Writing of his *Masque of Judgment,* he speaks of its most important theme being "the plea for passion as a means of salvation," and again and again his voice reverberates with the statement:

> Who loves not life
> Receiveth not life's gifts at any hand.

The fact is that the deeper one penetrates into Moody's work, the more one becomes interested in his ideas, and impressed by their solid quality and by the range and energy of his conceptions of life. He was indebted to America as well as to literature. His father was a steamboat captain on the rivers between Pittsburgh and New Orleans; his mother was a daughter of one of the earliest families to settle in southern Indiana; and through these parents Moody shared strongly in the pioneer heritage of devotion and patriotism. In his formative years he also came under the spell of Henry George and Hamlin Garland; so it was natural that his poems should cope directly with the issues of his day. Nowhere in our poetry is there a more fearless denunciation of blind and greedy imperialism than that in **"An Ode in Time of Hesitation"** or **"The Quarry,"** nor a nobler scorn of a base cause than that expressed in the lines **"On a Soldier Fallen in the Philippines."** In such poems as **"Road Hymn for the Start"** and **"I am the Woman,"** Moody is also strongly in the main tradition from Whitman, for, despite his antipathy to the form of *Leaves of Grass,* his vision of the potentialities of modern life, and, even more deeply, his mingled quality of being both pagan and mystic, have much in common, though given a more educated expression, with the nature of the elder poet.

The poems which Moody regarded most seriously, over which he brooded longest, and which contain the large bulk of his speculations on the meaning of life, are his poetic dramas, *The Fire-Bringer, The Masque of Judgment,* and the unfinished *Death of Eve.* Their scope and intention owe much to Milton; they are designed to do no less than to effect a reconciliation beyond that conceived of in the seventeenth century, to justify the ways of man to God. The first member of the trilogy is perhaps the least original in its treatment of the reaction on the human race of the effort of Prometheus to make man independent of God; *The Masque of Judgment* is much bolder imaginatively in the way it reveals how, through His destruction of mankind at the Judgment Day, God is Himself destroyed; *The Death of Eve* was intended to show the impossibility of separation between the Creator and His creation, the essential unity between them. These plays are philosophical poetry, and not an ordered scheme of philosophy, and are therefore inevitably more interesting in parts than as a whole. Moody never had a more generous conception of character than that of the broad humanism of Raphael in *The Masque of Judgment*; or a more thrilling poetic idea than that of portraying Eve in her old age, who, finding herself failed by every one else, seeks out Cain, her child of passion, and returns with him to the Garden to lay her life before God, not in fear or humiliation, but in the sense of having fulfilled through long years the deepest laws of the nature of woman.

Through exploring Moody's ideas one comes to have a high respect for him, and it is largely this approach which has produced the recent very favorable judgments of his work by the French and German critics, Regis Michaud and O. E. Lessing. Any final estimate of him must bear in mind that he was an exact contemporary of Edwin Arlington Robinson's, born in the same year, and that the two of them together were responsible for the re-birth of American poetry, which had sunk into decay after the death of Whitman. No one can examine Moody's work without feeling his excellent qualities: he is never trivial or sentimental; above all else he is calm, self-possessed, and of great dignity, but saved from pompousness by a salty humor. Yet even in the lines where one comes closest to his

spirit, in the poignant tribute to his mother in **"The Daguerreotype,"** in **"Jetsam"** where he tells how after long struggle he feels "strong now at last to give myself to beauty and be saved," in Pandora's stirring song of victory achieved through defeat, a great deal of the implied emotion is drowned in rhetorical virtuosity. He could not seem to escape the over-stuffed opulence of the late Victorian age, the defect of Pater, even of Meredith. But by far his worst limitation is his too elaborate assumption of the singing robes. As he grew older he became less studiously poetic in his expression, and, had he lived, he might have advanced even farther along this road, but just how far is doubtful in view of his early too complete insulation in literature. No one could have been more earnest in his desire to be a poet, no prayer could be more heartfelt than the lines in which he says:

> All my spirit hungers to repay
> The beauty that has drenched my soul with peace.

But he never found quite an authentic voice of his own. He was so striving in his effort to create that it left a pale cast of heavy deliberateness over nearly all of his lines, so self-conscious in his determination to be a poet that it almost incapacitated him for writing poetry. In fact, his kind of eclectic reliance upon the past and absorption in its ways of expression became finally so oppressive that it was the very thing which caused the violent break of our contemporary poetry away from nineteenth-century literary tradition.

Robert Morss Lovett (essay date 1931)

SOURCE: An introduction in *Selected Poems of William Vaughn Moody,* edited by Robert Morss Lovett, Houghton Mifflin Company, 1931, pp. ix-xcii.

[*In the following essay, Lovett ranges over such biographical subjects as Moody's family background, education, teaching career, and travel, and offers a critical overview of his poetry.*]

I

William Vaughn Moody was born at Spencer, Indiana, July 8, 1869. His father, Francis Burdette Moody, with two brothers, Norman and Gideon, had moved from Central New York about 1852. Norman, a lawyer, settled in Illinois. Gideon, also trained for the law, went to South Dakota, whence he was sent to the United States Senate. Francis Burdette settled in New Albany, Indiana, where he married Henrietta Emily Stoy, of mingled English, French, and Scotch descent, a daughter of one of the earliest pioneer families of southern Indiana. For years Francis Moody commanded a steamer, in which he owned a half-interest, one of the floating palaces of that picturesque era, plying between Pittsburgh and New Orleans. At the outbreak of the Civil War, his vessel was seized and held by Southern troops. After this financial loss he did not return to the river, but went into business in Spencer, Indiana. Returning to New Albany in 1871, he was, until his death, secretary of the Ohio Falls Iron Works in which he held a small interest. Thus it was at New Albany that the family chiefly lived—William Vaughn from about his second to his eighteenth year.

To Francis and Henrietta Moody were born three sons and four daughters, of whom William was next to the youngest. They lived in a pleasant, comfortable house of red brick with white porches, near the center of the town. Francis Moody was a handsome man, six feet two in height. He was not what the townsfolk called religious, but a great nature-lover, and a lover of books. His library was well supplied with the English classics, Scott, Dickens, Thackeray, and the English poets. The memory of Mrs. Moody's beauty and spiritual grace survives in the tenderly beautiful lines of **"The Daguerreotype."** It was perhaps due to her influence that the children were brought up to go to church and Sunday-School, though Francis Moody was a strict disciplinarian on this point. In every way he upheld the mother's wishes regarding the children. There were also in the family a number of old retainers, especially Jane, a quaint character who served the family for three generations. Next to her, in leaving an impression upon the imagination of the children, was an old Negro, Uncle Billy, who abounded in stories of the Civil War, in which the family had suffered. Religion and patriotism were thus two elements in Moody's early life.

In course of time the children went to grammar and high school, where William early showed ambition and promise. It was no effort for him to keep well ahead of his class. He had a remarkably strong and symmetrical body, and outdoor sports held decidedly more interest for him at times than his books. He was fond of music and played the guitar, an instrument in which he always took a shy pleasure. Drawing and painting interested him so deeply that after leaving high school he studied for a year at the local art academy, the Pritchett Institute of Design, at Louisville, Kentucky. To this pursuit he returned in after life, surprising his friends by his assured technique and sense of values. He was editor of two high-school papers and wrote poems which, with a self-criticism always characteristic of him, he usually tore up as soon as they were written. Among questions of the day he was particularly alive to those of faith and morals. Very early he showed a zest for experience of all kinds, religious, æsthetic, moral, and physical. It would seem that the only interest which Moody as boy and man failed to share was the acquisition and possession of material things.

In 1884, the happy, prosperous home was shattered by the death of Mrs. Moody. It throws a revealing light on the nature of Moody's father that he never recovered from the blow. He died two years later. After this the family was scattered. Two of Moody's sisters, Charlotte and Julia, went East to school under the guardianship of a cousin, Charles Rowley, of Poughkeepsie, New York. Henrietta, the youngest of the family, went to live with the eldest

brother, Francis Burdette, who was married and living at Lafayette, Indiana. William Vaughn, his delightful studies at the Pritchett Institute ended, found a place as teacher of a district school near New Albany, living with his cousin, Elizabeth Stoy. Charles Rowley, however, became interested in the lad, of whom his sisters spoke so often, and the next year brought him to the Riverview Academy, where he spent two years in preparation for college, at the same time tutoring Rowley's son for Yale.

Riverview was a military school, and the discipline was severe. The only reminiscence of his life there that I ever heard fall from Moody's lips was of marching around the drill field (with many others) a stated number of times as a penalty for smoking. He had other memories which he did not divulge. The head master was Harlan Page Amen, afterwards head master of Phillips Academy, Exeter, whom Moody loved and admired always. To Amen's fine ideals of scholarship and discipline Moody owed the rare intellectual training, especially in the classics, which fitted him for a distinguished university career. This, however, he renounced in favor of poetry.

In 1889, Moody entered Harvard, with the class of 1893. He had some money saved from school teaching, and his uncle Gideon Moody advanced a thousand dollars which his nephew repaid from his earnings by writing and tutoring during the summers. Although he worked his way through college in this manner, he suffered no real handicap. No student ever took fuller advantage of the opportunities of Harvard, which were then becoming magnificent. It was for such as he that Eliot carried through the elective system, and the use which Moody made of it must have delighted the President, who followed the careers of individual students more closely than most of them imagined. Moody chose his courses with fine economy, selecting subjects in which guidance counted most and avoiding those which he could master by himself. He took the classics and modern languages, and later, in a year of graduate study, modern philology. I do not remember him in any English literature or composition courses, and natural and social science I believe he ignored. He acted wisely in avoiding any academic influence upon his own reading and writing. To history and social theory he came later with a freshness and naïveté of mind that submitted the matter to the uses of the imagination, free from dulling memories of the classroom. He was, next to David S. Muzzey, now Professor of History at Columbia, the first student in his class, and held the largest scholarship, the Richard Augustin Gambrill, which yielded four hundred dollars.

My own recollection of Moody goes back to his freshman year. In Latin D, which was an advanced class for freshmen, we were reading the *Phormio,* when Professor C. L. Smith called, "Mr. Moody next," and for the first time I heard the clear, vibrant, musical voice which always expressed so perfectly the man and the poet. He sat directly behind me, and for many weeks he remained for me only a voice. Later in that year I read his first poem in the *Har-*

vard Monthly, **"A Chorus of Wagner,"** and as I was a candidate for the *Monthly* myself, the thought of having Moody for a colleague lent energy to my striving. I came to know him by sight, and I suppose he knew me likewise, but it was perhaps characteristic of Harvard in the nineties that we never spoke. The *Harvard Monthly* represented a high ambition in those days. The brilliancy of the first board of editors, Alanson Bigelow Houghton, George Santayana, George Rice Carpenter, and others, and of their immediate successors, George Pierce Baker and Bernhard Berenson, was a recent memory. It was the only undergraduate publication admitted to *Poole's Index.* Robert Herrick and Norman Hapgood divided the editorship-in-chief that year, and under their somewhat skeptical guidance Moody and I were admitted to the board.

During the next two years we were thrown much together by the *Monthly* and other interests. Moody was not an organization man. A figure of speech or a single flawless line of verse meant more to him than any institution. But as if he recognized this bias as a danger, he showed a heroic patience in performing any task that was laid upon him. You had only to say, "You ought to do that," and with dogged obedience he went about it.

It was always a keen pleasure to walk and talk with Moody. His joy in the purple shadows of the pines on the snow, in the smell of violets in fresh earth, was an experience which he gladly shared. Years later, walking around the Marmolada in the early morning, we came to a spot where the retreating snow-field met the green grass in a sharp edge, and Moody at once proposed that we should strip and take our morning bath by rolling down the slope to feel the stinging cold of the snow on our bodies, and the sudden release of the sun-warmed earth. Equal to his joy in nature was his joy in mind, in intellectual play. Norman Hapgood, who sometimes joined us, used to remark on Moody's faculty for setting a figure of speech in motion and following its implications in a sort of mock argument.

All this time Moody's verse was growing. Even in youth Moody felt himself dedicated to poetry, as Milton and Wordsworth had before him. He was not ashamed to learn from the masters. He was, perhaps unconsciously, preparing himself for a long career, and was content to begin at the beginning, with a thorough mastery of the great tradition in which he was to work. I remember once speaking in discouraged mood of the difficulty of achieving anything distinctive in a crowded world, to which he replied, with boyish solemnity, "No man can refuse to run at Olympia."

Most of Moody's verse of this time was destroyed, or is to be found only in the files of the *Harvard Monthly.* He was too critical of himself to preserve his juvenilia. One sonnet, however, is so characteristic in its inspiration, so perfect in its expression of what was in his soul at this time, that I hope to be forgiven any impiety in quoting it. A remark by Professor Tarbell in a Greek course, a journey to the Boston Art Museum, and the next evening he read to the *Monthly* Board, **"To the Niké of Paionios."**

I wonder did he dream of battle spears
Ahurtle on Greek hillsides in the sun;
Or of the moment when, the wild race won,
Some hyacinthine boy stands panting, hears
Like surfbeat on the sands, the shouts and cheers;
Or of such ecstasy the poet knows
When dazed and dumb he feeleth round his brows
The dusk-leaved ivy Dionysus wears;

Or haply did he look beyond the dawn
That paled above the purple eastern sea,
Beyond the things that seem to things that be,
And listen to the lips that trumpet on
From star-depth unto star-depth "Victory"!
Paionios—What time he fashioned thee?

If Moody ever thought of his vocation to poetry in such terms as Milton and Wordsworth, he must have recognized that in one respect his apprenticeship was happier than theirs. They found their English Cambridge a harsh and cold nurse; Moody found his altogether sympathetic and stimulating. Indeed, in these middle years of Eliot's presidency, Harvard offered to the undergraduate a life of extraordinary variety and freedom. The spirit of free election permeated all relations. The stiff aloofness between Harvard and what was then the Annex had broken down. There was the Comedy Club, a mixed group for acting plays, and the Browning Club which used to meet alternately in college rooms and Cambridge homes. The austere corridors of Hollis and Thayer without protest beheld ladies coming for an evening to read *Bishop Blougram's Apology.* There was no rule against it, and the absence of all bathing facilities in the dormitories obviated disconcerting encounters. Moody belonged to these groups, as well as to the regular college clubs—the Signet, the Delta Upsilon, and the O.K. In those days also, as a result of the elective system, there was free exchange between faculty and undergraduates, or such of the latter as cared to trade. The Hapgoods were great friends of William James, Charles Carroll Everett, and Crawford Howell Toy. I think it was Norman Hapgood who introduced Moody to the Toys, in whose home the boy, whose own home had long been only a sacred memory, found not only intellectual stimulation, but quiet happiness. There were a number of younger men, lately returned from Europe, bringing a new learning: George Santayana in philosophy, Edward Cummings in sociology, Arthur R. Marsh in comparative literature, and a little later, in English, Lewis E. Gates, who became Moody's close friend and critic.

Moody finished the courses required for his degree in three years, and spent his fourth abroad, in company with Ingersoll Bowditch, whom he prepared for college. That summer Norman Hapgood, Louis Henry Dow, and I were getting our first glimpse of Europe, and were met on the Rhine by Moody and his pupil. The five of us walked through the Black Forest and Switzerland. I remember particularly Moody's enthusiasm when after a night spent in a hut above Zermatt, and an early morning climb through mist and sleet on the Cima di Jazzi, we came out on the sunny slope above Domodossola, and gained our first view of Italy, a land which he was to love so much.

At Milan, Moody left us to go to England, but later in the year he came south again and made a long stay in Athens. Italy and Greece were two countries which, through landscape, history, literature, and contemporary peasant life, entered most deeply into Moody's consciousness. Both were associated in his mind with a solemn sense of humanity and the unseen powers which rule its fate: Italy with the medieval mysticism of Dante's theology, Greece with the classic feeling of joy in life restrained by measure and the decrees of the gods. One is the inspiration of *The Masque of Judgment,* the other of *The Fire-Bringer.*

During his absence Moody was elected Class Poet, and returned to deliver his poem on Class Day, 1893. In the summer he and I undertook a revision of Bulfinch's *Age of Fable,* and sought relaxation in cruising about Buzzard's Bay. For the next year he was a graduate student at Harvard, chiefly in medieval philology, and in the year following, he assisted Lewis E. Gates in reading manuscript for a sophomore course in composition, English 22. During these years he found new companions in Trumbull Stickney, who in the *Monthly* was giving promise of the career in poetry which was to be so untimely ended; in Josephine Preston Peabody, who made an enduring contribution to American poetry before her death; and in Daniel Gregory Mason, composer and writer on music. A special chapter should be written on Moody's friendships, and it should be written by a poet: His companionship was a precious thing, and though he had sometimes the reputation of being aloof and indifferent, he gave it generously to many. He could discern and delight in genuine human quality in very simple, humble forms. But he was at his best in association with the makers—those who like himself had seen the vision and not been disobedient to it.

Moody enjoyed the pleasant, civilized life of Cambridge, and renounced it with regret. Obligations to his family, however, made it necessary for him to add at once to his resources. Two positions were open: Mr. Amen asked him to teach at Exeter, and Robert Herrick and I urged him to join us in the Department of English at the University of Chicago. He chose the latter, fortunately, I think.

Before beginning as an instructor at Chicago, however, he spent three months in France with Daniel Gregory Mason. Professor Gates joined them for a short trip through Brussels, Ghent, Bruges, Lille, Amiens, and Beauvais. Of this trip Mr. Mason says, in *Some Letters of William Vaughn Moody*:

> Moody's delight in the beauty of the cathedrals, the picturesqueness of the landscapes, and the bits of talk with peasants, servants, and railway acquaintances which he never failed to snatch, was a constant pleasure. The easy transitions his mind made from poetic feeling and imagery to the broadest colloquial humor made him an incomparable companion. At Amiens, for example, he calls the delicate rose-window of the cathedral "God's spider-web"; at Comines, on the border of France, charmed with the pure French of the waitress, he asks the names of all the viands, and in return

communicates that the English name of raspberry jam is "Red-goo," and with a solemnity that convulses us watches her efforts to reproduce it, with much rolling of the R.

Of the short walking tour that followed Gates's departure, Mr. Mason says:

> At Caen, on a rainy afternoon, Moody made the first sketch of a poem which eventually, after much revision, became **"Jetsam."** At Tessy-sur-Vire we were awakened before dawn one morning by the bugles of a regiment passing up one of the narrow streets—a valorous music strangely impressive in that darkness and silence. Moody has commemorated it in the speech of the Third Youth in Act IV of *The Masque of Judgment*:

> > But always ere the dayspring took the sky,
> > Somewhere the silver trumpets were acry—
> > Sweet, high, oh, high and sweet!
> > What voice could summon so but the Soul's
> >   Paraclete?
> > Whom should such voices call but me, to dare and
> >   die?
> > O ye asleep here in the eyrie town,
> > Ye mothers, babes, and maids, and aged men,
> > The plain is full of foe-men! Turn again—
> > Sleep sound, or waken half
> > Only to hear our happy bugles laugh
> > Lovely defiance down,
> > As through the steep
> > Grey streets we sweep,
> > Each horse and man a ribbéd fan to scatter all
> >   that chaff!

The fundamental question concerning his decision to leave Cambridge for Chicago has to do with the effect of this translation on his own development as a poet. Moody had gone to Cambridge a youth from the Middle West, and had seized with genuine hunger upon the rich intellectual and civilizing influences which he found there. He was spiritually homesick at leaving them. The crudeness of the western scene as found in Chicago oppressed him sorely, and he resented still more at first the somewhat forced and pretentious quality of its nascent culture. In the end, however, it is impossible to doubt that the result was good, for it passed his own close criticism of himself as good. The experience brought him into contact with the stern necessities of living in a world which could only be described as realistic. The very bleakness of the environment forced him to take strong measures measures for defending his own inner life, of whose needs and responsibilities he became increasingly conscious. Even in the striving toward higher things by those whose efforts he was tempted to dismiss as vague and futile, he came to recognize a genuine and honest effort with which in the end he could not fail to sympathize. In the midst of much that was shallow and spurious, he had an unerring instinct for what was sound and true. He found others, like himself, conscious of a feeling of exile, and was closely drawn to them. His years in Chicago were years of growth as a human being, and humanity was the essence of his poetry.

This conclusion is borne out by his letters written at this time to friends of the Cambridge circle, collected by Mr. Mason in *Some Letters of William Vaughn Moody.* Here the theme of East and West is treated with all the gusto of personal experience. That Moody appreciated the momentous nature of his choice is shown in a letter to Josephine Preston Peabody, dated September 22, 1895—a few days after his arrival in the western city.

> I do not know what this place is going to do for me, but am sure of its potency—its alchemical power to change and transmute. It is appallingly ugly for one thing—so ugly that the double curtain of night and sleep does not screen the aching sense. For another thing it is absorbing—crude juice of life—intellectual and social protoplasm. Far aloft hovers phantom Poetry, no longer my delicate familiar. But I dream of another coming of hers, a new companionship more valorous and simple hearted. . . .

A later letter to the same correspondent reveals clearly his nostalgia for Cambridge, his sense of the abundant life about him, and a certain despair of breaking through the academic trammels and reaching down into it.

> The truth of the matter is, I suppose, that I am dissatisfied to the point of desperation with the kind of life that is possible out here. I used to have days in the east when a hedge of lilac over a Brattle Street fence or a strenuous young head caught against a windy sweep of sunset on Harvard Bridge, filled me with poignant perceptions of a freer life of sense and spirit—and I was frequently vaguely unhappy over it. But after all one hadn't far to go before finding some refinement of feeling, some delicate arabesque of convention, to help make up for the lack of liberty. Out here there is even less liberty (because less thought) and there is nothing—or next to nothing—to compensate. If my lines were cast in other places—even other places in this gigantic ink-blot of a town—I could make shift to enjoy my breath. I should make a very happy and efficient peanut-vender on Clark or Randolph Street, because the rush and noise of the blood in the city's pulse would continually solicit and engage me. The life of a motorman is not without exhilarating and even romantic features, and an imaginative boot-black is lord of unskirted realms. But out here, where there is no city life to gaze at, nothing to relieve the gaseous tedium of a mushroom intellectuality, no straining wickedness or valiant wrestling with hunger to break the spectacle of Gospel-peddling comfort—the imagination doth boggle at it! . . .

A very just perception of a weakness arising from the middle-western spirit of tolerance with which even the better part of Chicago regarded what it sadly termed its lack of standards, appears in a letter to Mrs. Mary L. Mason, dated January 11, 1896.

> The enervating thing about the place is its shallow kindness. People are so eager to give you credit for virtues that you do not possess that you feel ashamed to put forth those that are yours. Then when you do take heart of grace, and do or say or think a really good

thing, and win the facile applause, you have a bad taste in the mouth to think that any jigster's trick would have won you the same magnificent triumph. . . .

That he was, nevertheless, from the outset fitting his environment to his own needs, appears from letters written to Daniel Gregory Mason. In October, 1895, he says:

> I experience aching diastoles [a term, his editor explains, borrowed from physiology to denote moods of spiritual elation], however, and that is the great thing to my thinking. To be a poet is a much better thing than to write poetry—out here, at least, watched by these wide horizons, beckoned to by these swift streamers of victorious sunset.

That he, like Wordsworth, was coming to feel the value to the poet of a "wise passiveness," though in his case touched by stoicism, is clear from another letter to Mason:

> The hard bright sun of a western morning, with theme classes superimposed, reduces the golden tongue to phantom thinness of song and banishes the lute into the limbo of the ridiculous, but I plod on evening-wards with mole-like assiduity. I have come to realize the wonderful resources of passive enjoyment better than I ever did before—perhaps perversely, perhaps according to a mere instinct of self-preservation against the hurry and remorseless effectiveness of life out here. . . .

In another letter written to Mason the following year, he voices the conviction, which he shared with Browning, that it is better to live poetry than to write it:

> If you can only throttle your Dæmon, or make him forego his leonine admonition "Accomplish," and roar you as any sucking dove the sweet vocable, "Be,"—you ought to live. I have got mine trained to that pardee! and his voice grows not untunable. I pick up shreds of comfort out of this or that one of God's ash-barrels. Yesterday I was skating on a patch of ice in the park, under a poverty-stricken sky flying a pitiful rag of sunset. Some little muckers were guying a slim raw-boned Irish girl of fifteen, who circled and darted under their banter with complete unconcern. She was in the fledgling stage, all legs and arms, tall and adorably awkward, with a huge hat full of rusty feathers, thin skirts tucked up above spindling ankles, and a gay aplomb and swing in the body that was ravishing. We caught hands in midflight, and skated for an hour, almost alone and quite silent, while the rag of sunset rotted to pieces. . . . I came away mystically shaken and elate. . . . It is thus the angels converse. She was something absolutely authentic, new, and inexpressible, something which only nature could mix for the heart's intoxication, a compound of ragamuffin, pal, mistress, nun, sister, harlequin, outcast, and bird of God—with something else bafflingly suffused, something ridiculous and frail and savage and tender. With a world offering such rencontres, such aery strifes and adventures, who would not live a thousand years stone dumb?

A serious appraisal of his life at Chicago after a year appears in a letter to Mrs. Toy:

As for Chicago, I find that it gives me days or at least hours of broad-gauge Whitmanesque enthusiasm, meagrely sprinkled over weeks of tedium. The tedium is not of the acid-bath sort, however. Genuinely, I feel mellower, deeper-lunged, more of a lover of life, than I have ever felt before, and the reason is that I have had long somnolent spaces in which to feel the alchemy of rest.

One thing which Moody found from the beginning at the University of Chicago was an intellectual companionship and stimulus fully as valuable as that which Harvard had to offer. He possessed the instinct of humane scholarship, and went to the past not only with his mind but with his heart. It was the beauty perceived and uttered by poets that moved him, and as his vision of poetry widened, this tradition meant more and more to him. His colleagues at Chicago whose knowledge he laid most fruitfully under contribution were Paul Shorey in Greek, Ferdinand Schevill in the Italian Middle Age and Renaissance, and John Matthews Manly in English literature, all scholars of imagination and sympathetic understanding. At Harvard, Moody found plenty of critics who were abundantly useful to him, but I think, except perhaps for Professor Toy, he found no scholastic influence so directly contributing to his own creative life as at the University of Chicago.

Among other influences of his new environment must be set down his own teaching. Instead of acting as reader and consultant to a large course of sophomores, he had his own classes, limited to thirty, which involved close contact with a variety of human types. Close, but seldom intimate. One of his pupils writing in later years speaks of "the dreamy aloofness, the habit of slow, impersonal, vivid epigram which we associated with Mr. Moody." Moody never achieved such a degree of self-conquest as to suffer fools gladly, but he did suffer them patiently and courteously. Of the pupils in whom he took most genuine interest I recall two, Katharine Bates, who was afterwards instructor at Wellesley College, and Mrs. Katherine Gibbs, a woman who had come to college late in life, but fresh in mind and as ambitious as youth. I have always thought that his understanding of old age came to him largely through the woman whom he called, with real affection, Grandma Gibbs.

In all ways, Moody was an admirable teacher. Whether tutoring individual pupils or conducting classes, he gave his full mind to every exercise. His lectures were carefully thought out and delivered in perfect form. I have seen hundreds of students' themes, painfully corrected in red ink, with elaborate comment on the outside page written in his clear, beautiful hand. He was obliged to augment his salary by preparing texts for school use, among them an edition of Bunyan's *Pilgrim's Progress* for Houghton Mifflin Company's Riverside Literature Series, to which his introduction is a little masterpiece. His workmanlike instinct appeared in every task, and it may be said that, by virtue of an economy which consisted in putting his full strength into every undertaking, nothing that he did was without value to him.

In that first year in Chicago we had a coöperative household at 5488 East End Avenue, managed by my wife, with Moody and Ferdinand Schevill as members. We were all poor, but living was cheap in the days after the World's Fair. When the weekly budget was $8.38 for rent, service, and food, we felt entitled to a celebration in a private room at the Bismarck, where real Pschorrbräu made up for our exile from Jakey Wirth's ale in Boston. The youngest of the Hapgood brothers, William Powers, and his roommate Edward Kennard Rand, who had come to the University as tutor in Latin, regularly dined at our apartment, and joined in these parties. For some reason we used now and then to dress for these occasions, and I remember Moody in his tail coat, doing a dance to the tune of "Twinkle, Twinkle, Little Star," with a humorous solemnity that was most engaging. The guitar was often in play as accompaniment to his varied store of songs. Chicago's freer atmosphere brought to Moody, as to all of us, a certain expansion of mood after the decorum of Cambridge. I had never known him so natural, so easy, so blithe.

During his second year in Chicago, Moody lived in the family of Robert Herrick. These months are chiefly memorable for his work in editing Milton's poems, English and Latin, for Houghton Mifflin Company's Cambridge Poets Series. This he did with a thoroughness which lifted the task far above hack-work. The contract called for the conventional text, with introduction and notes, but Moody could not let it go at that. He scrutinized the text in the light of all the readings, and with a sure feeling for the atmosphere of the poems he returned to Milton's original spelling. He made a new translation of the Latin poems. Later, the accuracy of his rendering was in some cases challenged, but Professor Rand, who revised the work, informs me that in most cases of departure from the literal, he recognized Moody's sense of values in his adherence to poetic rather than grammatical accuracy. His essays introducing the several divisions of Milton's work are fine examples of exposition and appreciation, beautifully and eloquently written. All this was done for the fee originally agreed upon, which the publishers, however, voluntarily increased. But Moody's real compensation was far greater. Milton was not one of the poets for whom in his youth he greatly cared. He preferred the more lavish art of Shakespeare or Shelley. Moreover, Milton's theology was repulsive to him. But by dint of a conscientious effort to enter into the spirit of the Puritan poet, he learned to know his greatness. When Moody himself came to deal with the highest things, he had the example of Milton clearly before him, and his latest poetry shows this influence more than any other.

The result of Moody's emigration to Chicago is to be seen in his own poetry. Hitherto his inspiration had been literary and the result largely imitative. Now for the first time he drew on his own experience for subject-matter, and achieved a freer and more personal manner. A letter to Daniel Gregory Mason dated May 16, 1896, accompanied by the poem **"Wilding Flower,"** rewritten as **"Heart's Wild-Flower,"** contains the significant sentence, "I hope you will like it because it is almost the first thing I have done which has been a direct impulse from 'real life,' and you know I have theories about that."

This first continuous year and a half in Chicago was rewarded by the six months of freedom which followed, and which saw the beginning, not indeed of his life in poetry, but of his career as a poet. The force which had been expanding against the resistance of circumstances found sudden release. He sailed for Naples, and at Sorrento the experience befell him which he has recorded in **"Good Friday Night."** Joining Ferdinand Schevill on a bicycle trip northward, he found such joy and hope on a morning ride out of Orvieto as inspired the **"Road-Hymn for the Start."** In June he joined my family at Venice, at the Casa Frollo on the Giudecca. The Casa ran completely across the island, in two wings enclosing a garden. Moody's room was somewhere near the extremity of one of the wings, and though the insect life tormented him at night, still the nightingales sang in the garden. In our gondola, manned by one Luigi, we used to proceed to the Lido every morning, or took longer trips to Torcello and Murano, where Moody was endlessly enthralled by the skill of the glass-blowers. Craftsmanship in every form delighted him. One of our happiest memories is of his affection for my little son, about a year old, with whom he used to play for hours on the floor. In the evenings the singing on the Grand Canal charmed him, and I remember his full, clear baritone trolling out the chorus:

> Vieni sul mar;
> Vieni a vogar;
> Sentirai l'ebbrezza
> Del tu' marinar.

At Venice we went occasionally to an exhibition of modern art which included a triptych representing the Last Judgment: in the center, the Deity in his wrath, and on the sides the contorted bodies of the damned. I wondered at the fascination which that picture held for Moody. Later I realized that it was one of the sources of *The Masque of Judgment.*

From Venice, Moody and I bicycled to Asolo, where we found decent lodging, and foraged for food among the three little inns of the town. We had some thought of settling there for the summer, and engaged in long negotiations with Robert Barrett Browning who owned the only practicable villas, but Mr. Browning could not quite make up his mind which of them to rent. Miss Browning, the poet's sister, the *sindaco* of Asolo, and the postmaster, assisted at these conversations, and Moody often recalled the argument of the *sindaco* that it would be dangerous for a *bambino* to pass *subito* from Venice to the Dolomites, without breaking the journey in the hills. It grew hot in Asolo. At night we took our blankets to the hillside beneath the Rocca, and slept, to be wakened before dawn by the noise of men and women on their way to work, a confusion of forms vaguely moving in the twilight, with voices strangely subdued. My range of activity was limited by the fever I had brought from Rome, but Moody made bicycle trips to Bergamo and other places. It was difficult to induce him to take the road again, but at length our departure was fixed for an evening, when we were to ride to Feltre to take the diligence for San Martino di Castrozza next morning. At sunset, Moody had not appeared, and I finally set out alone. In the early morning at Feltre, I mounted the diligence ready to start, when far down the road I saw a little cloud of dust, out of which slowly emerged a man, pedaling for all he was worth. I assured the driver that it was another passenger. Five minutes later, Moody, covered with dust, came alongside, swung himself up and collapsed beside me, while his wheel was loaded on behind. For a long time he did not speak a word. Then he showed me two or three little notes in Italian—*sempre, sempre, ricordati di me*—signed Annunziata.

At San Martino we sent our bicycles ahead to Innsbruck and footed it across to Belluno. There we met my family and took carriage to Cortina, where we found rooms at the Bella Vista, with Cristallo and Tofana and Sorapis rising menacingly above the smiling valley. There was a *Schwimbed,* fed by icy streams from the glacier, in which we plunged daily. One evening we went to a Passion Play given in Italian by boys of the neighborhood.

Here Moody began to write *The Masque of Judgment,* the origins of which are clear. The picture at Venice gave the emotional shock, indignation that God could so treat his creation. The Dolomites furnished the setting. Milton supplied the intellectual background; in his capacity as attorney for the defense, justifying the ways of God to men, he challenged Moody to vigorous argument on the side of humanity, the plaintiff.

Moody wrote industriously through the mornings, complaining with some humor of the loquacity of Raphael, and wishing he would have done talking in order that we might start on our further tour of the Dolomites. At length the Archangel stayed his speech, and we set out afoot, going by way of Tre Croci, Lake Misurina and the Drei Zinnen. One morning we lay for an hour confronting a mass of tawny rock with huge red stains like congealed blood on its face, as if it had been gashed by a giant axe. Another glorious morning we walked around the Marmolada taking our bath in the snow. It was on this morning that I found in my mail the *Boston Transcript* with William James's oration on the dedication of the monument to Robert Gould Shaw, which gave the keynote to the **"Ode in Time of Hesitation."**

Our last exploit on this trip was an ascent of the Gross Venediger, from which we hoped to see Venice once more, but the mountain belied its name. We were shockingly unprepared for high altitudes. After we reached Innsbruck and I had started back to Cortina, leaving Moody alone, he was ill from exposure for some days. It was the first breach in his magnificent bodily health.

Moody rode back to Italy over the Brenner to Verona, and thence to Ravenna to see the mosaics, which perhaps also played their part in the imagery of *The Masque of Judg-*

ment. From Ravenna he crossed Italy, riding by night on account of the heat, to Viareggio. He made his way to Genoa, where he was again ill, lying half-conscious for days at an Italian inn, until one morning he realized that his steamer was due to sail on that day. Thereupon he got up, packed his bags, and made his way to the quay, to fall again unconscious in his berth.

In the succeeding years, Moody found conditions at Chicago more favorable to poetry. In 1898, John Matthews Manly became head of the Department of English, and Moody's close friend. Under his leadership the work of the department was reorganized, and Moody was relieved of much of the drudgery of composition courses. His special field was the early seventeenth century, whose poets and dramatists he came to know with the thoroughness which his conscientious preparation for teaching made necessary. He found also a group of writers in Chicago, Harriet Monroe, Hamlin Garland, Henry B. Fuller, William Morton Payne. With these he consorted at "The Little Room." He also found a welcome at 2970 Groveland Avenue, where Mrs. Harriet Brainerd was hostess to many young people of promise, such as William Penhallow Henderson, the painter; Alice Corbin (now Mrs. Henderson) the poet; Swinburne Hale and Milton Sills. For out-of-town excursions we discovered Saint Joseph, across the lake; and Lake Zurich, where there was a primitive country club.

Of his longer vacations one was spent on Cape Ann with Mason, another at Mackinac Island, where Mrs. Brainerd had a cottage, and a third on a horseback trip with Hamlin Garland, camping among the mountains of Colorado. His first extended stay in New York was from April to July of 1898. Here he worked on his edition of Milton, and finished the first draft of *The Masque of Judgment.* Here also he fell in with a group of rising young dramatists, as he wrote to Daniel Gregory Mason, "full of enthusiasm and practical expedient. The great thing about them is that they get their things played, and that sort of thing, begad, begins to appeal to me. Do not believe me quite recreant to ideals; Cambridge and her elegiac air seems still lovely and of good report. But these chaps here, though very moderately elegiac and of a dubious report, are splendidly American and contemporary; and I feel convinced that this is the place for young Americans who want to do something. (N.B. *I have not enlisted in the marines.*)" A different attitude toward his New York associates is suggested in a later letter to the same correspondent: "I am going in for people now, having made the discovery that the average man is among the most unexpected and absorbing of beings." For the rest of his teaching career, residence in Chicago was alternated with periods spent in Boston or New York.

The various influences of persons and places show clearly in his poetry. The Spanish War, fought in the summer of 1898, blended with memories of the Civil War in the **"Ode in Time of Hesitation,"** written in Boston, early in 1900. There was strong feeling in Chicago against the subjuga-tion by arms of the Philippines, which Moody expressed in his lines **"On a Soldier Fallen in the Philippines,"** published in the *Atlantic Monthly* for February, 1901—a very bold utterance which, in a university less tolerant than that of Chicago under President Harper, might have cost an instructor his position. Henry B. Fuller was an ardent anti-imperialist, and Hamlin Garland was a disciple of Henry George. The latter certainly was of influence in turning Moody's thought to social matters, of which **"Gloucester Moors,"** published in *Scribner's Magazine* for December, 1900, is unmistakable evidence. At the same time, Moody's powr of rendering actual experience was growing. Even a trivial event was for him hung about with mysterious intimations of high meaning. An example of this is found in **"Old Pourquoi,"** of which the germ incident had occurred on the walking trip in Northern France in 1895.

In July, 1900, Moody read the **"Anniversary Ode,"** at Cambridge, on the one hundred and twenty-fifth anniversary of Washington taking command of the American Army, published in the *Harvard Monthly* for October of that year. In the course of the same year appeared *The Masque of Judgment,* published by Small, Maynard and Company, and in 1901 his first collected *Poems.* In the fall of that year I joined him in Boston, where we worked through the winter on *A History of English Literature.* The *History* was a fortunate venture, for by it Moody became independent of teaching, which he forthwith renounced. President Harper made him a standing offer of a single quarter's service at the rate of a professor's salary, and Manly patiently arranged and announced courses for him, but they were always withdrawn. Aside from the necessity of saving himself for his true work, he felt that the formal teaching of literature involved a kind of sacrilege. He said to Manly, "I cannot do it. At every lecture I slay a poet."

In the spring of 1902, while Moody was visiting Mrs. Brainerd at Cape Henry, he spoke one evening of the Prometheus legend, as affording another expression of the problem of man's separation from God. This was the origin of *The Fire-Bringer.* The next morning he started for Greece. Here his most notable experience was traveling with a donkey through the Peloponnesus. Here also he felt, at Corinth, that sense of the power of human love to annihilate distance which is the subject of **"The Moon-Moth,"** and while in Crete he had for a second time a vision of the actual presence of Christ, recorded in **"Second Coming."** No one who knew Moody can doubt that these were real experiences—

> Closer to him than breathing, and nearer than
> hands and feet.

In July of that year, I found him in Paris in Trumbull Stickney's rooms on the rue d'Assas, where he was reading the entire body of Greek tragedy. Stickney, who was writing his thesis for his doctorate at the Sorbonne, in Greek literature, was an incomparable guide and stimulus.

He had himself written a lyric drama, *Prometheus Pyrfuros,* the influence of which is discernible in Moody's larger, full-bodied work.

In the autumn of 1902, Moody was in the Tyrol. After his return to America he made his headquarters in New York, at 50 West Tenth Street, later, at 107 Waverly Place, but he was a frequent visitor at Mrs. Brainerd's home in Chicago. In New York he had his intimate friend, Daniel Gregory Mason, and he was the center of a group of younger poets, especially Ridgely Torrence, Edwin Arlington Robinson, and Percy MacKaye. Mrs. C. P. Davidge was the hospitable friend of all this circle, and their intimate ways and sayings were constantly recalled in her vivid conversation. At this time Moody returned to his old love of painting, and found expression for his seeing eye and firm, sensitive fingers in pastel and oil.

Most of this time Moody was receiving a small income from the *History of English Literature,* but his livelihood, until the success of *The Great Divide,* was far from assured. There was a steady market for his verse in the *Atlantic Monthly,* the *Century,* and *Scribner's,* but he refused to exploit it. He was exceedingly scrupulous about giving his poetry to the world. He would rather go hungry than publish a poem which he thought unfinished, or beneath the best that he could do. He never starved, but he did meet hardship and denial like a good soldier in a cause which he would not betray, even by compromise.

The Fire-Bringer was published in 1904, and it is not too much to say that it was accepted by critics as placing Moody at the head of American poetry. Already William Morton Payne had written in *The Dial* (January 1, 1901): "No other new poet in the past score of years, either in America or in England, has displayed a finer promise upon the occasion of his first appearance, or has been deserving of more respectful consideration." Now Richard Watson Gilder welcomed him as a new poet in his stanzas published in the *Atlantic Monthly* of June, 1905:

> Friends, beware!
> A sound of singing in the air!
> The love-song of a man who loves his fellow men:
> Mother-love and country-love and the love of
>   sea and fen;
> Lovely thoughts and mighty thoughts that linger
>   long;
> There has come to the old world's singing the
>   thrill of a brave new song.
> They said there were no more singers,
> But listen!—a master's voice!
> A voice of the true joy-bringers!
> Now will ye heed and rejoice
> Or pass on the other side,
> And wait till the singer has died—
> Then weep o'er his voiceless clay?
> Friends, beware!
> A keen new sound is in the air—
> Know ye a poet's coming is the old world's
>   Judgment Day!

His work had been noted in England, where William Archer included the **"Ode in Time of Hesitation"** in an an-

thology of modern verse, and whence May Sinclair wrote for the *Atlantic Monthly* (September, 1906), an enthusiastic criticism hailing him as the first of a trio of American poets, the others being his friends, Edwin Arlington Robinson and Ridgely Torrence. It was, however, at this time that he chose to turn to prose drama, although from no temptation of "thieving ambition or paltering gain."

Moody was always fascinated by the dramatic form. It appealed to him as a vehicle for representing human experience, and it challenged his instinct of craftsmanship. As far back as 1896, he was taking a keen interest in the newspaper accounts of the work of a western faith healer named Schlatter, and speaking of him as a subject for a play. After *The Fire-Bringer* had appeared in 1904, and *A First View of English Literature* was finished, he went seriously to work on a prose play, which he at first called *The Sabine Woman,* subsequently *The Great Divide.*

It was generally thought that this play owed its inception to a trip to Arizona which he took in the spring of 1905 with Ferdinand Schevill, in the course of which they spent a week at Oraibi among the Hopi and saw the spring dance at Walpis. But this excursion gave confirmation rather than color to his background, for the play was already practically finished. It was based on a story from real life, related to him by Mrs. Brainerd. The first act keeps closely to the facts as they were told to him, but the rest of the play is Moody's development, through this situation, of a contrast which had always presented itself to him most forcibly: Puritan New England, as opposed to the pioneering West. It is obvious that he understood the latter far better, and was more fully in sympathy with it. It is noteworthy also that the difference in quality between the first, almost reportorial act, and those following, is perceptible even without a clue to its cause. The success of his first play does not cloud the fact that Moody was a poet rather than a dramatist; rather, it testifies to his superb endowment with those qualities which are common to both.

The Great Divide centers about the attack on a New England girl, alone in a cabin in Arizona, by a band of outlaws, one of whom, an American, buys her with gold from the others. She goes through with the bargain of marriage, but, though she comes to love her captor, she is possessed by a desperate necessity of earning and repaying the price for which she was bought. This accomplished, she parts from her husband, with pain on both sides, and returns to her New England home, where the reconciliation takes place. The play was shown to Miss Margaret Anglin, who was playing in Chicago in the spring of 1906, and she resolved to give it a trial at the close of her engagement. No one who was present on the opening night will forget the circumstances, almost as dramatic as the play itself. The curtain went down on the first act amid a whirlwind of applause. Then Miss Anglin's management summoned Moody from the audience and presented him with a contract to sign, threatening that otherwise they would not permit the play to continue. Moody hesitated. He had been warned by his friend Percy MacKaye of the danger of hasty engagements, illustrated so tragically in the case of the latter's father, Steele MacKaye. A lawyer was called from the body of the house, and while he scanned the document the audience waited in tension for the outcome of the drama which was being enacted during the intermission. At last an agreement was effected, and the curtain went up. The second act, which was mainly carried by the principals, went off fairly well. But the supporting company, inadequately rehearsed, had gone cold during the long wait. In the third act they forgot their lines and wandered vaguely about the stage, opening and shutting windows or reading newspapers. Toward midnight the play staggered to a lamentable conclusion. It was a harrowing experience for a man of Moody's sensitive temperament, but he was not blind to its humorous aspect.

In the summer he was resolutely at work revising the play, living at Cornish, New Hampshire, where I had an opportunity to see it grow anew under his hand. I had known Moody as a most conscientious and meticulous craftsman, but I had not known, nor ever have seen since, anything like his fierce power of concentration. There were many friends near by: the Herricks, the Hapgoods, the Churchills, Miss Ethel Barrymore. But Moody was not to be diverted for more than an occasional set at tennis, or a plunge in the swimming-pool. In the autumn the play was triumphantly produced in New York as *The Great Divide,* by Miss Anglin and Henry Miller, and has remained a landmark in the history of the American drama.

Moody had intended to complete his trilogy of poetic dramas by a third member. He had dealt with the Greek conception of the power behind the human scene in *The Fire-Bringer* and with the medieval in *The Masque of Judgment.* These have to do with the separation of Man from God. For the third member, dealing with reconciliation, he went directly to the Hebrew theme. *The Death of Eve* was the subject, not only of his poetic drama, but of an epic fragment published in the *Century Magazine* for December, 1906. That he never finished this drama was clearly a misfortune, and was felt by Moody as a kind of betrayal of his vocation.

The theme of *The Faith Healer* which had so long haunted him came to fruition in the play of that name, produced in St. Louis in the autumn of 1909, and in New York in December of that year, by Henry Miller, to whom Moody was indebted for genuine friendship and stimulating advice. This play cost Moody dearly in time and effort. It is, to a greater extent than is commonly supposed, a personal document. It embodies the question, always insistent in Moody's mind, to what extent a man who is dedicated to a great purpose may share the common lot. The fact that he threw the discussion into the life of a mystic, an itinerant healer, was owing to his early interest in the case of Schlatter, which seemed to Moody's imagination to offer precisely the example he needed of the opposition between the sense of a high calling and the joy of a human love. That the play was a discussion with himself is shown by the three versions extant, written at considerable intervals

of time. In the first, the healer gives up his love for the sake of his healing; in the second, he surrenders his healing for love; in the final version he realizes that his dedication to his work must also include the reaction of love upon that work.

Moody's health in early years was perfect. My first knowledge of any illness of his was after the ascent of the Gross Venediger, when he suffered from exposure, as later from continued exercise in the tropic heat of an Italian summer. The effects seemed to have passed away completely. He had, however, a severe fall while climbing Mount Parnassus on his trip to the Peloponnesus in 1902; some four years later, I met him in New York, walking quite unconcernedly to Dr. Bull's hospital to have a growth removed from his injured thigh. The operation proved more serious than was anticipated, but the surgeon assured him that, if there was no recurrence of the symptoms within a year, he might be pronounced cured. In the spring of 1907, he made an expedition to Spain, Italy, and France with Ridgely Torrence. While they were walking up the hill of Posilippo near Naples, Moody suddenly stopped and lay down. The pain in his thigh had come back. From that time on, Torrence saw a change in him—his usual even spirits yielded to deep depression. It must be remembered by those who noted a falling-off in Moody's work and an increasing withdrawal from human relations that from then on he walked in the shadow of doom. In 1908, he had a severe attack of typhoid fever. A cheering mark of recognition came to him that year in the degree of Doctor of Letters awarded him by Yale University. The summer was spent largely on the island of Monhegan off the Maine coast with Ridgely Torrence, whence he returned in better health and spirits. But the recurring growth proved to be malignant, and at last symptoms appeared in the brain. It was the same terrible malady from which Trumbull Stickney had died, and Moody must have had its horror clearly before him, but he bore himself always with stoical courage. My last meeting with him was in the winter of 1909, when he came out to Jackson Park for an afternoon of skating, a pastime he always greatly enjoyed. After twenty minutes he drew up at the bank, took off his skates, and we walked slowly away under the trees, which suddenly reminded him of the snowy woods on Arlington Heights above Cambridge, where we had spent many winter afternoons in his student days.

Later that winter, he went to California, where he painted with William Wendt, and seemed to regain strength and hope. He was married to Mrs. Harriet C. Brainerd in Quebec, May 7, 1909, and spent the summer in England. The devoted care of his wife and his sister Charlotte and the frequent companionship of Ferdinand Schevill were his last happiness. To the latter he confided his constant regret that he had given so much of his last precious time to prose, which he, like Milton, reckoned to be but "the work of his left hand." Once he said, "It is perhaps a judgment that this confusion has come upon me." He died at Colorado Springs on the seventeenth of October, 1910. The night before his death there came to him one of those visions which he had always held as the source of his highest poetry—as commands not to be disobeyed. This vision is touched upon in a stanza of the heart-felt threnody which Percy MacKaye wrote on his dead friend. (*North American Review,* October, 1911.)

> Darkling those constellations of his soul
> Glimmered, while racks of stellar lightnings shot
> The white, creative meteors of thought
> Through that last night, where—clad in cloudy stole—
> Beside his ebbing shoal
> Of life-blood, stood Saint Paul, blazing a theme
> Of living drama from a fiery scroll
> Across his stretchéd vision as in dream—
> When death, with blind dark, blotted out the whole.

II

It is difficult to think of a human being more perfectly endowed with strength and beauty of body and mind than William Vaughn Moody. Physically he was slightly above medium height, graceful and well proportioned, in young manhood with a strength beyond his stature, and with great endurance. In college he wore a mustache; later in life, a Van Dyke beard. His hands were unusually deft and sensitive. His voice was clear and resonant. Professor Manly speaks of his "wonderful eyes, light, clear blue, and shining like large gems because of the sailor-like ruddiness that wind and sun had laid upon his cheek and brow."

He was fond of all the grander phases of the physical world, the forest, the sea, the mountains, the desert. Whether his delight in nature or in the arts were the greater, there is no doubt that his senses, naturally keen, were schooled to a closer perception of values and a richer enjoyment by his æsthetic training in music, painting, and poetry. Moody respected his sensuous equipment as part of his endowment for his vocation. He was very fond of tobacco, but he declared once that if he thought smoking tended to dull the senses, he would never light his pipe again. In physical as in intellectual quality, he was a young Euphues, and he bore himself as if conscious of his distinction. When in college I first came on the portrait of Flavian in *Marius the Epicurean,* I instantly thought of Moody. In youth his habitual expression was one of calm self-possession, in the literal sense of the word. Certainly he did not wear his heart upon his sleeve and he abhorred sentimentality. Yet a guarded joy looked out from his eyes, with gleams of ironical amusement, and now and again his whole being would flame up in laughter. There was something of the faun in him, and occasionally his mood would verge toward the satyric when the flesh would threaten the control of the spirit. Later in life, his face took on the more somber, deeply inward expression shown in his portrait of himself.

He was always a good companion, walking, swimming, riding, at a concert or art gallery, spending the night smoking before the fire or under the stars. I think he was at his best with one other person, or at least a small group, for his rare personal quality came out mostly in the warmth of intimacy. Daniel Gregory Mason gives a delightful picture of him in conversation, "slightly knitting his brows, as if taking, from under half-closed lids, a bird's-eye view of the broadest possible stretch of his subject, while he communed with his pipe, frequently pressing down the tobacco with a forefinger long enured to that service, and finally producing a brief comment, usually metaphorical and often madly exaggerative, that liberated the mind more than floods of ordinary talk." In this personal intercourse, his faculty for making all communication a sort of fine art had full scope. Of such intimacy his play with words was a distinct promotion. About him there always grew up a special vocabulary which constituted a kind of secret language. Mason gives some examples: "'It' is everything, taken together, that may be the object of a youthful idealist's devotion; it is the sum total of all that is beautiful and worthy of loyalty in the world." "A 'diastole' is a mood in which, so to speak, the spiritual circulation is good: . . . it is a mood of vitality, of realization, of fulfillment." In large groups, or with people whom he did not know well, Moody was inclined to be self-conscious. Sometimes he played up with an effort; sometimes, especially when the company bored him, he fell utterly silent. His social sense, however, grew along with his capacity for life in other directions. I can quite believe that he found the group of literary men in New York, poets and playwrights, a most congenial company, and brought to them the larger conviviality which Percy MacKaye has noted in his poem "Uriel."

Places and human associations had a special significance for Moody, and as a true artist he did not mix his *genres.* His reticence in personal matters was extraordinary. At college I never heard him speak of his family or home, almost never of his school life. In Chicago he seldom talked of Cambridge, and the depth of his feeling for it revealed in his letters came to me as a surprise. Even with his intimate friends he was more given to impersonal talk than to that form of amusement which Mr. Howells says is described in Cambridge, not as gossip, but as "gathering material for formulating character." With his joy in life, with the extraordinary gusto which he brought to experience, with a sense of humor which did not fail to include himself, he had a personal reserve, an exact sense of values, and a fundamental seriousness, which set him apart from others, and which constituted an essential part of his character as poet.

Of Trumbull Stickney, Moody wrote in an article in the *North American Review* (November, 1906): "Though he had a richly varied and most human existence, with senses, affections, curiosities, all in vivid action, the truth indeed was that poetry was both the root and flower of his life, the point of repair for all his vital powers." So it was with Moody himself. His very being was poetry. He lived in the highest sense in his own, and he took the fullest pleasure in the poetry of others. When he read aloud, his voice was full of unforgettable emotion and reverence.

He grew up in the tradition of English poetry. It was natural that his first efforts should be imitative, and the fact that the imitation was so perfect has done some wrong to his later fame. In college he passed from one master to another, and the poets whom he was reading at the time found echoes in his verse—Wordsworth, Keats, Shelley, Tennyson, Browning, Rossetti, Swinburne. Later the robust manner of Kipling appealed to him, and his medieval fancy turned from Tennyson to William Morris. Professor Gates brought Francis Thompson to his attention, and during his first year in Chicago he read us "The Hound of Heaven," "Dream Tryst," and especially, "The Poppy" and "To Monica Thought Dying." Professor Sophie C. Hart, of Wellesley, who met Thompson a little later, remembers his asking her about Moody, "the man in America who writes like me." A fine passage would haunt his mind for years. I remember on our walk through the Black Forest his quoting quite suddenly the lines from Dante which stand as the text of **"A Dialogue in Purgatory,"** written much later. The great masters of poetry, those who exercised an enduring influence upon him, came to him sometimes as the result of circumstances. Dante he had never read until he reviewed, for the *Harvard Monthly,* Professor Charles Eliot Norton's translation of the *Inferno.* The occasion of his deep interest in Milton I have already indicated. Of Greek poetry, however, he was a student in his undergraduate time, and later the whole glorious body of Greek tragedy was vivified for him by his reading of it with Trumbull Stickney.

Such of Moody's early imitative verse as survived at all is to be found in the pages of the *Harvard Monthly* between 1889 and 1894. Throughout the poems published in the volume of collected verse will be found echoes of the Victorian poets, echoes which his friendly critic, Professor Gates, pointed out unsparingly in his review in *The Nation,* August 22, 1901. It was fortunate, however, that Moody did not suppress such poems as **"Harmonics,"** **"Heart's Wild-Flower," "The Bracelet of Grass," "A Grey Day," "The Brute,"** or **"The Menagerie,"** because of similarities in manner to older poets. These poems all deal with experiences and thoughts which were his own, and through them we can see coming into full authority a form and mode of utterance in which imitation has given way to genuine assimilation. Of this aspect of Moody's work, Professor Paul Shorey has given an illuminating discussion in a lecture at the University of Chicago, republished in the *University of Chicago Record,* July, 1927:

> At the most, we are haunted by a faintly familiar aroma, and say not, That is from Marlowe's *Faustus,* Shelley's *Prometheus,* or Keats's *Hyperion,* but, That is Moody writing as Marlowe, Shelley, or Keats might have written. . . . We cannot say what, if any, passage of Shakespeare or æschylus suggested the line:
>
> But yet conjecture clamors at thy heart.

We can only say that it is an æschylean or Shakespearean line. . . . We need not quote Marlowe in a footnote, but we think of Marlowe when we read:

Look where the giant wings rock down the slope,

or

Lo! where God's body hangs upon the cross,

Drooping from out you skyey Golgotha.

Still more distinct perhaps is the note of Shelley in:

All palpitant and doubtful on her head

A soft-winged splendour lit.

And faint echoes of Milton, whom Moody edited, are everywhere.

past the walls

Rhipean and the Arimaspian caves

I sought the far hyperborean day.

More explicit borrowings are rare.

As a fawn from the green windows of a wood,
Slave of the panic woodland fear,

recalls the fawn in Murray's translation of the *Bacchæ,* Moody's favorite Greek play. . . . It pleases me to believe that the explicit quotation of Pindar in **"The Moon-Moth,"**

as if Pindar heard
And loved again the sweet fruit of his breast,

preserves the memory of the afternoon when I called his attention to that phrase of Pindar.

It is Moody's strength and glory that he worked in the great tradition of the poetry of the world. He was a scholar. He made scholarship a high and living thing in its preservation of the noble and beautiful things of the past and its contribution to the wealth of those who would live nobly and beautifully in the present.

Possibly the most immediate and elementary quality to be noted in Moody's poetry is his sense of values in his medium, his craftsmanship in the use of his tools. He was always enamoured of words, both the noble and the base-born. An incident which occurred just after his arrival in Chicago affords a homely illustration of this trait. We had stepped into a bar, where an habitué accosted him with a familiarity from which Moody withdrew with some accentuation of the Cambridge manner, whereupon the stranger inquired, with resentment, why he was so "abrupt." Moody always enjoyed recalling the adjective in its new sense. Indeed, a great deal of the spice of our conversation in those days was his play with words. In his copies of Hardy's novels I find the fly-leaves containing lists of folk-words from that writer's vocabulary. Undoubtedly Moody's delight in Francis Thompson was in part due to that poet's power of fusing recalcitrant verbal material into poetic harmony. Miss Sinclair, in her appreciative criticism of

Moody's poetry in the *Atlantic Monthly* (September, 1906), comments on his use of archaic or unfamiliar terms: *bataillous, vesperine, energic, margent, blooth,* and *windelstræ.* Undoubtedly Moody laid himself open to criticism in this matter, but he had the spirit of the pioneer, he was willing to take chances. "I think," he wrote to Mason, "you are not tolerant enough of the instinct of conquest in language, the attempt to push out its boundaries, to win for it continually some new swiftness, some rare compression, to distil from it a more opaline drop. Isn't it possible, too, to be pedantic in the demand for simplicity? It's a cry which, if I notice aright, Nature has a jaunty way of disregarding."

Moody always dissented from Wordsworth's theory that there should be no difference between the diction of poetry and that of prose. For him the word with all its associations and imaginative suggestions was in itself an element of poetry and history, and he employed it with a reverent sense of its use by poets of the past and also by the mass of men and women to whom it had been part of life. At the same time he had a genuine feeling for present-day colloquial values. To those who knew him **"The Menagerie"** has a unique worth in preserving one phase of his personality. Even in his use of slang, Moody kept a certain fastidiousness. If he sacrificed something of what is called purity of diction to the demands of his theme, it was because he felt those demands truly. He strove for precision, *le mot juste,* and if the word he needed was unfamiliar or had to be reminted, he yielded to the necessity. This necessity was not merely one of thought, but also of mood and feeling. "A word was to him," wrote William Morton Payne in *The Dial* (December 16, 1912), "like a jewel reflecting manifold hues from its facets, or like the note of a violin with its gamut of attendant overtones which he made us overhear."

Akin to Moody's instinct for words was his pursuit of figures of speech to which they invited him. I have spoken of this also as characterizing his daily use and wont. Once coming back from a walk with Norman Hapgood, he said with satisfaction, "We chased a metaphor all the way across the Harvard Bridge and back again." This opulence of imagery was again a ground of criticism, particularly of his early work. Mr. Santayana once remarked that Moody's early verse reminded him of stained-glass windows. The critic in *The Nation* (February 6, 1913) declares that "The image has come in many cases to override the idea, until it is no longer a figure but a symbol. In this way there is something almost allegorical and even enigmatical about much of his verse, like **'The Quarry,' 'The Brute,'** or even **'The Moon-Moth.'**" This is an extreme statement of Moody's romantic tendency. On the other hand, we have Miss Sinclair praising him for the submission of this romantic strain to order: "His quality is opulence, a certain gorgeousness that is never barbaric, owing to his power of classic restraint. His sweetness is crystal, never luscious or impure."

In his use of meter, rhythm, and stanza-form, Moody was again an artist with a background of scholarship. He learned the practice of the English poets in these matters even before he knew the technical terms. Later, his study of primitive poetry, Old French and Old Norse, enriched his store of memories, and finally he found in Professor Shorey a guide to the more intricate effects of Greek tragic poetry and the ode. His genius was essentially lyrical; his greatest originality shows itself in his use of the simplest forms, to which he gave an accent peculiarly his own. For the dramas he drew on the great tradition of English blank verse, from Marlowe and Shakespeare to Milton, and thence to Keats and Swinburne. In movement, even more than in diction, we have echoes of these masters, giving a constant enrichment of tone. The ode, however, was his favorite form, with its effect of lyric freedom secured within the limits of precise measure and controlled variation. The **"Ode in Time of Hesitation"** marks the height of public poetry in America; it has an eloquence of form which is as native as its subject-matter. And it is impossible to close this brief technical consideration of Moody's poetry without calling attention to certain minor effects of phrasing and movement in which resides the poetic dispensation that Matthew Arnold called Natural Magic. There is the sense of sullen resistance in the consonants of the lines:

> As now, blind bulks of sheep, or hunger bitten
> To creep the stagnant bottom of the world;

and the fleetness of anapestic flight in

> Must she seek her lover, her king of kings
> Naked, stripped of her costly things?
> Must she have no garment but love?

Professor Shorey, with his sure sense of poetic values, recalls the lines from **"Old Pourquoi"**:

> Couched in the sweet, satirical,
> Impudent tongue of France,

"for sheer delight in the calculated effect of the division of the second epithet from the third by the verse-ending."

Alike in diction and in movement, Moody's poetry gives the impression of abundance and extraordinary variety, of a technical mastery quite complete. Among his lyrics the best known through anthologies and frequent quotation is **"Pandora's Song,"** "Of wounds and sore defeat." It may be noticed that the theme, victory in defeat, is one which has attracted many poets. Matthew Arnold has given utterance to it in a short lyric, "The Last Word," which may be quoted here for the sake of comparison.

> Creep into thy narrow bed,
> Creep, and let no more be said!
> Vain thy onset! all stands fast.
> Thou thyself must break at last.

> Let the long contention cease!
> Geese are swans, and swans are geese.
> Let them have it how they will!
> Thou art tired, best be still.

They out-talk'd thee, hissed thee, tore thee?
Better men fared thus before thee;
Fired their ringing shot and pass'd,
Hotly charged—and sank at last.

Charge once more, then, and be dumb!
Let the victors, when they come,
When the forts of folly fall,
Find thy body by the wall!

It is clear that Arnold's poem depends on the vividness of its picture, and the suggestion of its story. It is a direct statement of experience, and is full of the quality on which he based his famous definition of poetry as "criticism of life." Moody's lyric contains no story and no single picture, though it is full of appeal to the eye as to the ear. The theme is carried by the opposition of terms, those denoting defeat and others renewed combat: "wounds" and "sore defeat" surmounted by "battlestay"; "wingéd sandals" against "delay"; "weariness and fear" issuing in "shouting spear"; and "loss and doubt and dread," in "helmet and plume"; "the shutting mist of death," "the failure of the breath," becoming the

> battle horn to blow
> Across the vales of overthrow,

to which Pandora bids hearken

> Where its echoes bring,
> Down the gray disastrous morn,
> Laughter and rallying.

It was altogether like Moody to associate triumph with "silver scorn," and "laughter" with "rallying." His poem cannot be termed deficient in criticism of life; its popularity shows that it reaches many readers who enjoy poetry primarily for its meaning. But even to them the subtlety of suggestion by which that meaning is conveyed, through the connotation of words and the variation of movement, now retarded, then springing forward with triumphant acceleration, brings, perhaps unconsciously, an emotional reenforcement of the theme. Arnold encourages to life by exhortation; Moody, by exhilaration. In such poems as **"Pandora's Song"** we find an illustration of what Walter Pater declared that all fine art, and poetry most of all, was seeking: the approximation to pure feeling which is characteristic of music.

If the dominant effect of Moody's poetry is richness and abundance, it must be recognized that he escaped or conquered the temptation which comes to poets of lavish and facile art. He never allowed himself to be betrayed into excesses of publication. The great bulk of his writing up to the time of his death was experimental, and as such was destroyed. "It is certain," says Professor Shorey, "that unlike some other great poets—Shelley, Byron, Wordsworth, and even Keats, for instance—he gave to posterity no absolutely bad and silly verse, and very little if any that is plainly weak and commonplace."

As Moody progressed, his poetry took on a more austere and somber cast. In that written after *The Fire-Bringer* he achieved a freedom of utterance and a manner entirely his own, largely by a process of limitation and exclusion, setting the force within him to expand against the pressure of constant and severe restraint. This gives to such poems as **"I am the Woman"** and *The Death of Eve* a strain of sheer, concentrated energy which we find only in the greatest poets. The dialogue between Eve and Cain in the latter poem furnishes an excellent example, the force of which may be fully realized if we place beside it an older and more famous rendering of the same characters in Byron's "Cain." "For all the dramatic compression of Moody's lines," says Professor Manly, "they never cease to sing. Only a master of English verse could make lines of such length move at all, while to make them run and dance and sparkle with light is a triumphant achievement."

It is perhaps superfluous to point out that the two elements in Moody's poetic style, abundance and austerity, reflect two elements in his character and experience. He had, on the one hand, a great joy in nature and life, a natural paganism to which the visible and tangible world made instant and constant appeal; and on the other, a solemn sense of the mystery behind the external frame, which filled him with reverence and awe. At times he felt himself in immediate contact or communication with the spirits who on earth have freely and confidently touched the things beyond and unseen, especially with Him who said "The kingdom of Heaven is within you." It was Moody's task, as it was Keats's, to subdue the clamorous world of sense, to refine by meditation and discipline his mind and his art to the imperative demands of a vision and a music that came to him with an authority which he recognized as divine. But it was a transfiguration, not a renunciation. Moody was no ascetic. He would not have subscribed to Tennyson's "Higher Pantheism":

> The earth, these solid stars, this weight of body
>   and limb,
> Are they not sign and symbol of thy division from
>   Him?

Rather, he felt them the revelation of God; they wove "the garment thou seest Him by."

To Moody the separation of man from God was not of the senses, but of the intellect; to show the unity of the world with God was therefore the philosophical task to which he set himself in his trilogy of poetic dramas. The first, in his final order, deals with the striving of man in his great prototype, Prometheus, to rise in his own right from the elemental matter, to take part in the creative struggle. The second reveals the tragedy of a God who denies this element in his creation, and who through his annihilation of his world is himself involved in ruin. The third was to have set forth the search of mankind for reconciliation with God, through Eve who was the original means of the separation. It must not be forgotten that, though Moody in this trilogy is presenting a theme which was the center of his own thought, he is working through conceptions which, as myths or theologies, have expressed throughout history mankind's sense of its relation to God. This is explained admirably in the letters on **The Masque of Judgment,** quoted in the Notes, which remove a misconception too common among readers of the poetic dramas.

It would, therefore, be a mistake to judge Moody's poetic dramas as a cosmology. Far deeper than the definition of the philosophical inseparableness of man from God is the sense of a moral unity. And this is a pervading conception through all Moody's poetry. It was so recognized by his critics in the period between the appearance of **The Masque of Judgment** and that of the two-volume collection of his works in 1912. Professor Gates wrote on the first (*The Nation,* March 28, 1901):

> Doubtless **The Masque** is, on the whole, a plea for the rights of the "sanguine stain" and the "senses five." And yet, quite as surely, passion and richness of experience, as Mr. Moody conceives of them, have a spiritual cast and color, and the impression that the entire *Masque* leaves is that of a noble and lofty idealism.

Miss May Sinclair wrote in the *Atlantic Monthly* for September, 1906:

> He knows that the spirit does not maintain its purity by mere divorce from Nature. . . . It is the same divine thing which is housed in the flesh and shrined in the spirit of man, and the process of the world is the process of its unfolding.

Professor Charleton M. Lewis (*Yale Review,* July, 1913) puts the matter very justly:

> Moody saw in evil not exactly the implacable foe of good, but rather its twin brother, bone of its bone and flesh of its flesh, since both good and evil are children of passion and will. . . . Life is rich and wonderful because our spirits are charged with aspiration and liberty and love. If we are swayed also by jealousy and wrath, license and lust, these are but other manifestations of the same primal forces. The concords and discords are sounded on the same strings, and are essential parts of one divine harmony.

A final and exhaustive criticism on Moody's collected works by William Morton Payne may be quoted as summing up the impressions made by Moody upon one of the most catholic and fastidious of contemporary critics. (*The Dial,* December 16, 1912.)

> The main thing to be emphasized concerning Moody is that he was a poet by the grace of God, and such a poet as had not been raised up before him in America—or even in the English-speaking world— since the eclipse of the great line of the older singers. . . . He seems to be the one authentic "maker" that our young century has given to the world, achieving a height that none of his contemporary fellow craftsmen in the poetic art, either in England or America, could attain. . . .

> The stupendous task which Moody set himself in the trilogy is the highest which poetry has ever attempted.

> It is the task of æschylus and Dante and Milton, the task of Goethe in his *Faust* and of Shelley in his *Prometheus Unbound.* It is Milton's attempt to "justify the ways of God to man" coupled with the attempt of the later poets to justify the ways of man to God.

In the light of such sincere appreciation by the critics of his own decade, it is necessary to inquire why it is that during the twenty years succeeding, Moody's popularity has not been in any way commensurate with his achievement. It must be remembered that during the years after his death, poetry in England and America made a sudden turn into new fields and took on new forms of expression. In 1911, the group of poets who called themselves the Imagists was formed in London including Amy Lowell, Ezra Pound, Richard Aldington, and H.D. They felt, perhaps rightly, that the chief obstacle they had to encounter in conquering their public was its adherence to conventions of poetic form, traditional rhythms, limited meters, and rhyme. It was natural that they should adopt a certain militancy in their enterprise. I remember an occasion when Miss Lowell, inquiring about Moody, whom she had never met, murmured, as if to herself: "I wonder if he could have kept us back."

It is not to be inferred that the Imagists and poets of free verse made any organized attack upon their predecessors who worked within traditions which they considered hampering; but their success brought up a new generation of poets, critics, and readers, who were indifferent to older poetry and its masters. If Moody had lived, he would have held his own in the renaissance of poetry. It must be remembered that when he appeared, the public interest in poetry was at its ebb. In contrast to 1928, when fifty volumes were presented for the Pulitzer Prize, in 1900, publishers were reluctant to engage in what they assumed would be a losing venture, and Moody had his first volume of collected verse rejected by a leading house before Houghton Mifflin Company accepted it. In the decade which followed, the interest in contemporary poetry increased, partly in consequence of Moody's own powerful example; but a poetic reputation was still of slow growth, as in the past. Ten years did not afford time for Moody's poetry to secure a large number of readers, or for his reputation to become deeply rooted in the literature that comes to be historical. And close upon his death there came a revolution. To the tragedies of poets who died untimely, Chatterton, Shelley, Keats, Thomson, Brooke, Moody adds one of special poignancy.

Part of that poignancy lies in the fact that Moody had already shown himself in sympathy with much in the new program. The Imagists defined their æsthetic of poetry as: the presentation of a visual situation in the fewest possible concrete words, free from adjectives and conventional phrasing, unhampered by moralizing or speculation upon the philosophical significance of the visual idea—the form and rhythm developing out of the subject, not imposed upon it; the rhyme and meter determined by the judgment of the author. Some of these objectives Moody had already achieved; toward others he was clearly progressing. It is true that he would never have been satisfied with the visible world as a spectacle merely, with no curiosity as to its meaning; but the æsthetic principle that the form of poetry should grow out of the subject, rather than that the subject should be fitted to a given form, was entirely his own. His own practice tended constantly toward precision in diction and freedom in meter. For the latter reason he preferred the ode, and we find him, as early as 1898, writing of Milton's *Samson Agonistes,* "The idea might naturally have occurred to him of casting away the fixed line altogether as a useless fiction."

There are many other aspects of Moody's poetry in which he anticipates the most modern of his successors. The critic of *The Nation* (February 6, 1913) notes one which is akin to Expressionism:

> His significance lies rather in his manner of reproducing a complicated state of consciousness, even in the presence of plain and familiar objects.

And again,

> The clash of incongruous moods produces an effective sort of irony—a kind of grim cosmical humor—which is, after all, Moody's most original and powerful note.

With all his forward-looking qualities, Moody was, after all, distinctly a poet of his age. In looking back over his work, it is interesting to note how the forces of the time wrought themselves out in the form and substance of his verse. There is the eclecticism of the dying Victorian period, and its self-consciousness, its moral striving. There is something of the realism which reflected the influence of science, and the tendency of realism to extend itself into symbolism by the intimations which it carries of the world beyond that which we see and touch. Moody passed from the realm ruled by Tennyson and Browning, Rossetti and Swinburne, to that in which he was akin to Maeterlinck, Francis Thompson, Arthur Symons, and Ernest Dowson. Like the last, he confronted the eternal problem of the dualism of flesh and spirit and their inevitable union, although his solution was not the same. I feel sure that he wrote **"Good Friday Night"** and **"Second Coming"** before he knew Dowson's poetry, and in any case the impulse of these poems was entirely personal, but the kinship of the two poets is unmistakable. Like Dowson and Symons he was a lover of Verlaine and the early symbolists. In *The Masque* and *The Fire-Bringer* he shared in the revival of the poetic drama as a literary form, and his prose plays were the most distinctive contribution in the United States to the movement initiated by Ibsen to make the stage once more a vehicle for serious and significant criticism of life. Thus, historically, Moody has an important place in American literature—and, like Milton, he "has left something so written to after times as they should not willingly let it die."

David D. Henry (essay date 1934)

SOURCE: "The Poetic Drama," in *William Vaughn Moody: A Study,* Bruce Humphries, Inc., Publishers, 1934, pp. 111-40.

[*In the following essay, Henry discusses unifying subjects, themes, and techniques in Moody's trilogy of poetic dramas.*]

> Uriel, you that in the ageless sun
> Sit in the awful silences of light,
> Singing of vision hid from human sight,—
> Prometheus, beautiful rebellious one!
> And you, Deucalion,
> For whose blind seed was brought the illuming spark,
> Are you not gathered, now his day is done,
> Beside the brink of that relentless dark—
> The dark where your dear singer's ghost is gone?[1]

A purely objective estimate of Moody's trilogy of poetic dramas is scarcely to be obtained. Many different elements, such as the critic's personal appreciation for classical and cosmic themes, for traditional form, and for a subject sustained through three long narratives, must be considered. One's opinion is also influenced by observing the author's purpose and the symbolic meaning of his whole plan. Followers of Moody have always been divided in their opinions concerning the place of the trilogy in his work. An early sweeping judgment came from May Sinclair: "But the highest place must be given to his lyrical dramas, . . ."[2] After Moody's death, Professor Manly could endorse this opinion:

> The largest literary plan of Moody's career and, though uncompleted, the fullest expression of his vision of life, is the trilogy . . . These dramas contain much of his finest poetry, . . .[3]

With a still further perspective, Professor Percy Boynton places the trilogy as Moody's supreme accomplishment:

> Aside from these explicit poems of time and place, there is little of Moody's verse which may not be regarded as related and preliminary to the poetic dramas. The shorter poems contain the elemental ideas in the plays; they are harbingers which are confirmed and fulfilled by the event.[4]

On the other hand, the modernist has deplored that the author of the **Ode in Time of Hesitation** turned to obsolescent Miltonic and Aeschylean moods and legends.[5] Others have maintained that Moody's genius was essentially lyrical and that both his manner and message were ill adapted to dramatic expression.[6] Further, the complex symbolism displeased those who enjoyed only the direct and obvious representation of **"The Brute."**[7] Finally, it has been suggested that the trilogy does not reach the common reader.[8]

I

MATERIALS

Is a modern poet justified in handling ancient legends? Around this question has centered most of the controversy in the criticism of Moody's trilogy. The cry of American critics from the time of Irving has been for native subjects. Lowell, Whitman, Howells, to name but a few, in criticism stand typically for the insistence upon themes and topics from the world immediately about us. For this point of view, repetition built a tradition, until any other kind of theme became "taboo." There was the call for the great American poem as well as for the great American novel, and the great American drama. Emerson and Whitman had planted their seeds to bear fruit. The thesis of American literature since 1870 was the development of contemporary realism. Those who didn't fall in line were "parlor poets," "transition figures," "dreamy scholars."

As the single members of the trilogy appeared, their legendary themes were at once deplored. The following newspaper comment was the reaction of the average reader as well as of the journalist:

> . . . the difficulty at the beginning is the utter lack of human interest in it (*The Fire-Bringer*). The world is so busy nowadays, the needs of her children so importunate, that it seems a waste of time to spend it on purely imaginary scenes and beings, even though invited to do so through the medium of glowing and musical verses.[9]

Even the *Harvard Monthly* complained:

> **The Fire-Bringer** is all literary, not real, not suggestive of life, but seemingly another echo of books and books . . . and lonely thinking of a very impersonal sort.[10]

A little milder but just as representative is this statement from a Chicago paper:

> To the uneducated reader it will be as so much Greek, but to the few who can enjoy classic art it will be a thing of beauty. Yet I wish Mr. Moody had chosen to devote his powers to a theme closer to the heart of our own age.[11]

So intent upon looking for "a theme close to the heart" of the age, the critic could not see the implications underneath the classic theme—the eternal riddle of the universe and God's as well as Man's position in it.

It is difficult to understand how the reader of any part of the trilogy could fail to perceive that Moody was doing something more than reciting a story or recalling a legend, that the poet was presenting a vital problem of twentieth century civilization. In the discussion of the design of the trilogy in the following pages, the modern application of the themes will be clearly seen. It has already been explained that Moody's thinking as expressed through the shorter poems was in full accord with the science and philosophy of his age as well as in anticipation of many ideas of our own. So in the trilogy, Moody has kept the same point of view. For example, the *Promethean* problem of **The Fire-Bringer** deals with the importance of the emotional fire in Man's existence, a theme which needs discussion in a machine age. Then, there is the all-important modern philosophical query—can Man control God or can Man get along without God? **The Masque of Judgment,** likewise, as will be illustrated later, is a poetic foreshad-

owing of the modern impulses for richness of living, of the modern belief in the worth and joy of life, and of faith in individual good. Finally, the whole trilogy celebrates the spirit of rebellion against the restraints upon freedom; each major character, *Prometheus, Raphæl, Eve,* is a study in revolt, the spirit of the twentieth century youth. If we were to grant the justice of the adverse criticisms noted above, would we not by the same logic be compelled to say that *Faust,* that *King Arthur,* that *Hamlet* have nothing for the modern reader?

The detractors of the legends of the trilogy have ignored the author's fundamental attitude toward his text. He was not concerned primarily with theology or legend but with an underlying philosophical problem of the universe. The legend—Biblical or Greek—was the scaffolding which made possible the form or structure underneath. Moody has very clearly stated this idea in one of his letters:

> Your objection to the 'theology' of the Masque would be well taken if there were any theology in it. There isn't an ounce, or at least if there is it is there against my will. Of course I didn't intend my 'strangely unpleasant' God to be taken seriously. To me the whole meaning and value of the poem lies in the humanistic attitude and character of Raphael, the philosophic outlook of Uriel, and the plea for passion as a means of salvation everywhere latent. The rest of it is only mythological machinery for symbolizing the opposed doctrine—that of the denial of life. As Christianity (contrary of course to the wish and meaning of its founder) has historically linked itself with this doctrine, I included certain aspects of it in this mythological apparatus—always with a semi-satirical intention. I meant to write a poem, pure and simple; and my western friends, with the naiveté proper to them, seem to have accepted it as such; but Cambridge insists on treating it as a theological treatise. As such, they can but find it pretty foolish, I fear. . . .[12]

The great legends of the world have been worth telling in every age because every age has a new attitude toward and a new mood for the old story. It is true that too frequently we have bowed before the shrine of "Classics" for no reason better than the respect due to antiquity. Pedantic criticism has encouraged a false reverence for the literature of the past. This fact stimulated the two objections to the subject of the trilogy—one which held that a modern version of *Prometheus* was an irreverence, the other that such a poem was working with petrified materials unduly admired. But not all old stories are petrified; nor need they be romantically unreal. Legends, particularly, grow, find new life, power, elasticity as time lends new perspectives. The new perspectives of Moody's legends are considered in the following section of this chapter.

II

DESIGN

Moody's poetic dramas are subject to a variety of interpretations. In addition to the deliberate consideration of philosophical questions, there are latent meanings which even the author probably did not consciously intend to convey. For every reader each poem can have a very personal meaning, with ramifying applications. Nevertheless, it is wise to keep in mind the original design of the author if we wish to avoid distorting his message.

The unifying element in the trilogy is found in Moody's thesis: God and Man are inseparable. In *The Fire-Bringer, Prometheus* fails to make Man independent of God. The very potency of the stolen divine fire is fraught with danger. As the fire comes to the dark setting, confused voices cry out,

> Terrible wings!—
> Light awfuller than darkness on the sea![13]

A man's voice adds:

> We not knew
> The thing we asked for. We had all forgot
> How cruel was thy splendor in the house
> Of sense, how awful in the house of thought,
> How far unbearable in the wild house
> That thou hast cast and builded for the heart![14]

Through the theft, too, Man loses his benefactor *Prometheus.* On the other hand, God has been thwarted in his aim to destroy the human race and although he remains unreconciled his tyranny is at an end. In reply to *Pyrrha's* fear that the blessing will be removed after *Prometheus* goes, the *Titan* says:

> Be comforted; it is established sure.

As *The Fire-Bringer* shows that Man cannot be separated from God, conversely *The Masque of Judgment* portrays the consequences to God himself which would follow the destruction of men. *Raphaël* laments,

> Would he had spared
> That dark Antagonist whose enmity
> Gave Him rejoicing sinews, for of Him
> His foe was flesh of flesh and bone of bone,
> With suicidal hand He smote him down,
> And now indeed His lethal pangs begin.[15]

Finally, *The Death of Eve* proposes the eventual reconciliation of God and Man. Here we have a project of great proportions. It is to be regretted that the plan was not executed, for its completion would not only have yielded a very original poem but its ending would have made the other two members of the trilogy more intelligible. Moody's narrative is not found in *Genesis*; it is his own, a story, incidentally, which for the believers of the literal Biblical version of creation is a bit sacrilegious. Even *Seth,* mild and meek and patient, was horrified; at *Eve's* plan, his face became "with mortal fear disfigured."[16] *Eve's* sons thought her crazed. Just so wildly strange is the poet's suggestion. *Eve* is his answer to the riddle which *The Masque of Judgment* first raised. As the direct agent of the separation of Man and God, *Eve* will become, although God has forbidden her return to *Eden,* by her very rebellion the instrument of reconciliation.

Moody's trilogy, however, is more than a cosmology. Another element of unity ties together the three poems and makes the design of the whole clearer. This feature is the poet's belief that humanistic sympathy and an emotional or passionate response to life are fundamental in existence. Moody in writing about *The Masque of Judgment* refers to "The love of life and belief in its issues—which I meant to be the core of the matter."[17] Speaking of the same poem in another letter, he says,

> For me the kernel of the thing was Raphael's humanistic attitude and Uriel's philosophy, especially his 'confession of faith' in Act III, Scene II. The rest of it was only mythological machinery for exhibiting the opposed attitude and philosophy—that of the deniers of life. I hoped that the positive meaning might disengage itself as a kind of aroma or emotion from the whole, and that the poem would thus subserve just such a brave love of life and faith in its issues as you plead for.[18]

Seen narrowly, the annihilation of the heavenly along with the wicked, in the *Masque,* is depressing. Against this impression, as may be noted in his statement on page 114, Moody hoped the obvious idealism of his sympathies would prove an effective answer. The poet's view was humanistic and he saw good and evil as necessarily complementary in the scheme of things. Behind them is the fire of life. To repeat his phrase, the poem is a "plea for passion as a means of salvation everywhere latent."

The Fire-Bringer even more clearly is a poem in justification of "the wonder of the heart."[19] The conventional version of the *Prometheus* legend from Aeschylus to Shelley has made the gift of fire the source of art and science among men. In the *Prometheus Bound* are these lines:

> *Chor.* Do short-lived men the flaming fire possess?
> *Prom.* Yea, and full many an art they'll learn from it.[20]

Earlier in the play, *Prometheus* boasts:

> I snatched the hidden spring of stolen fire,
> Which is to men a teacher of all arts,
> Their chief resource.[21]

Similarly, in Shelley's *Prometheus Unbound, Asia's* lovely speech in Scene IV of Act II[22] recites the taming of fire as one of the *Promethean* gifts. She attributes to him, too, the gift of love but the two are not identical.[23] Moody, on the other hand, identifies the fire with the divine spark in human life—the zest for living, the passion of desire, the stimulation of the heart. It is significant that the final lines of *The Fire-Bringer* chant the praise of *Dionysus* and *Eros* as well as of *Apollo.*

> Eros, how sweet
> Is the cup of thy drunkenness!
> Dionysus, how our feet
> Hasten to the burning cup
> Thou liftest up!
> But O how sweetest and how most burning it is

To drink of the wine of thy lightsome chalices,
Apollo! Apollo![24]

Moody has been careful to place in the mouth of *Prometheus* the interpretation which he would have us accept. The *Titan* tells us he lurked in hiding in hope of finding *Dionysus* and wresting his pine-torch from him,

. . . or to snare
Some god-distracted dancing ægipan,
And from his garland crush a wine of fire
To light the passion of the world again
And fill man's veins with music; . . .[25]

Earlier, *Pyrrha* gives a similar view. She refers to the curse which withdrew—

The seed of divine fire,—yea, from our blood,
Yea, from the secret places of our frames
Sucked up the fire of passion and will,
And left us here by the desolate black ebb
To rot and crumble with the crumbling world.[26]

The fire becomes, then, not merely light for a gloomy world but warmth as well; it is the very essence of life, the wine of passion, the pulse of love. The song of the *Masque* in praise of "the windows five" here becomes a thesis with *Prometheus,* instead of a *Raphæl,* as the protagonist.

When we turn to **The Death of Eve** on this point, once again we find a main concern of the poet has been to celebrate the attributes of earthly beauty and the humanistic spirit. Mrs. Moody's exposition of the poet's plan for the completion of the fragment makes this conclusion very clear:

It might be worth while to consider the significance of Abdera and Jubal in the unfinished member of the trilogy, as they represent Will's ever-present consciousness of the beauty of the world in itself and in the logical order of human experience. The relationship of these two young creatures is an ever-present lightening of the somber background created by Eve and Cain, and a forward-looking influence for the conclusion of the drama. Will stressed the importance of this in talking of the play to me. He had it in mind especially to write two beautiful lyrics in which he intended to lay emphasis upon their significance. He had clearly conceived a lyric, sung as a duet by these two, as they followed Eve up a long stairway leading to the citadel of Cain. This lyric was never written, but it was a most exquisite love-song; and at the conclusion of the drama, if he had finished it, he intended to put a lyric murmur of pure human joy, based upon their consciousness of mutual life, into a duet between Abdera and Jubal, which was to give the feeling of renewal of the world after Eve's song of reconciliation. This lyric, as he explained it to me, would have given an unsurpassed assurance of happiness, truth, and beauty, as forever established on earth.[27]

With this comment of Mrs. Moody, Professor Manly has concurred. After epitomising the fragment as it now stands, he continues:

The other acts of this part of the trilogy, two in number, were to be diversified by many illuminating incidents, among them the instinctive wandering of the age-stricken Adam back to the Garden, ostensibly following Eve, but really yearning forward to participate in the new and glorious solution of life. In the third act there was to be a song by Eve, the burden of which would be the inseparableness of God and man, during which, as she rises to a clearer and clearer view of the spiritual life, she gently passes from the vision of her beholders; while, delicately symbolizing the permanence and beauty of the earth, Jubal and Abdera draw together with broken words of tenderness.[28]

From beginning to end, the two main strands of the poet's design stand out indelibly. That they came out of Moody's soul, out of his temperament and the influence of his career, is readily apparent. By nature Moody was wholehearted in his response to beauty and in the sensuous enjoyment of existence. With Whitman, he could exult in the worth of all things. At the same time, he was endowed with a profound religious sense. In his lyric poems, he tried to reconcile these seemingly contrasting issues. He finds his solution and unifies his impulses in his only creed: Life is good. This principle is the unifying force of the universe. God cannot destroy it, nor can Man; nor can either ignore it for faith in the wholesomeness of life is essential to the existence of each one.

For these ideas, the ancient myths seemed a natural vehicle. Even the early poems suggest some of the later cosmic concepts. In **"The Road Hymn for the Start"**, Moody speaks autobiographically:

We have felt the ancient swaying
Of the earth before the sun,
On the darkened marge of midnight heard sidereal rivers playing;
Rash it was to bathe our souls there, but we plunged and all was done.
That is lives and lives behind us—lo, our journey is begun!

The *Good Friday Night* protests to Christ "the thing they make of thee," and concludes with the plea for a world-wide friendship which Christ seemed to approve.

'Oh, by the light divine
My mother shares with thine,
'I beg that I may lay my head
Upon thy shoulder and be fed
With thoughts of brotherhood!'[29]

The vengeful God of the *Masque* is also in **"Troubling of the Waters"**:

A foolish fear: God could not punish so,
Yet until yesterday I thought He would.
My soul was always cowering at the blow
I saw suspended, ready to be dealt
The moment that I showed my fear too much.
Therefore I hid it from Him all I could,
And only stole a shaking glance at it

Sometimes in the dead minutes before dawn
When He forgets to watch.[30]

"Song-Flower and Poppy" in epitome anticipates the poet's thesis:

> St. Francis sleeps upon his hill,
> And a poppy flower laughs down his creed;
> Triumphant light her petals spill,
> His shrines are dim indeed.
> Men build and plan, but the soul of man,
> Coming with haughty eyes to scan,
> Feels richer, wilder need.[31]

Thus the design of the trilogy is the apogee of the evolution of Moody's thinking. Slowly but clearly he evolved that inspirational faith in Life which made arch-rebels of his three protagonists—*Prometheus, Raphæl,* and *Eve*—rebels who waged a single fight, for Man and Earth.

III

WORKMANSHIP

In spite of the fact that the chief merit of the lyrical dramas lies within their high attainment as poetry and not as dramas and in spite of some opinions to the contrary, it is reasonable to believe that Moody himself intended his trilogy for actual stage presentation. Professor Manly, apparently answering unfavorable criticism of the poems as plays, has implied that the author had in mind "closest drama" rather than good "theatre."

> All three of the dramas are in large measure symbolic, and should be interpreted and judged as such. Strictly dramatic and subject to the laws of dramatic speech and action they were never intended to be, as was shown in the drama first written and published, **The Masque of Judgment,** by the presence of such *dramatis personæ* as the Spirits of the Throne-Lamps, the Lion and the Eagle of the Throne, and Spirits of the Saved and of the Lost; by the predominance of descriptive, expository, and lyric poetry, and by the very title of the drama. The critic may prefer dramatic action to broad oratorio-like movement; but the poet has the right to choose his form and medium and to be judged by his success in that.[32]

That the plays have come to be regarded as closet dramas may not be disputed but whether Moody so intended them is another matter. It must be granted that he may not have been too certain about his purpose in regard to staging the **Masque.** He early called it "a rather hopelessly fantastic thing, . . . half-lyric, half-dramatic,"[33] but he said little more on the subject. We do know, however, that he very definitely planned to stage **The Fire-Bringer.** In 1906, at the time he was looking for a producer for **The Great Divide,** he wrote to Richard Watson Gilder:

> **The Fire-Bringer**—if all plans go through—is to be produced next winter in Chicago, in a new theatre which is being started there.[34]

Moreover, Moody's attitude toward the poetic drama in general throws some light upon his own purposes. From the beginning to the end of his creative career, he was quite decided in his opinions on this subject. An early letter (1904) to Percy Mac-Kaye is not at all indefinite:

> It is true, . . . that I am heart and soul dedicated to the conviction that modern life can be presented on the stage in the poetic mediums, and adequately presented only in that way.[35]

Even his success with prose plays did not lead him away from this conviction. In 1909, he wrote to Mrs. C. H. Toy:

> The thing I have most at heart just now is a poetic—I mean a *verse*—play . . . Also, I am torn between the ideal aspect of the theme and the stage necessities—the old, old problem. Perhaps in the end I will let the stage go to ballyhoo, and write the thing as I see it, . . . But this—after all—is an uncourageous compromise.[36]

The statement implies that in the past he has not yielded to the "uncourageous compromise;" in other words, that he has tried to be aware of the stage necessities even in his idealistic verse plays. It is not likely that Moody would have pretended his trilogy was drama if he had not so projected it. To analyze the plays too finely on the basis of stage composition would be an absurd violation of the obviously poetic mood and atmosphere. Yet we may criticise the poems, certainly, for any obvious neglect of the dramatic element.

At the outset, this feature is weakened by the author's apparent detachment from his audience. This fault he was able to avoid in his prose drama. But the earlier work is clearly marred by a steady ignoring of the needs and demands of the average auditor or reader. The author's design is not at once perceived and frequently the meaning cannot be fully comprehended. This blemish may be traced in part to the fact that the third member of the trilogy was left a fragment. The intelligibility of the whole is damaged by the incompletion of **The Death of Eve.** But a ready understanding of the single members, even, is precluded by lack of clarity of purpose and precision and definiteness of structure. The poems yield richly to study but the ordinary audience does not bring with it the student's attitude; even the critic resents *having* to study to understand the plays.

The ideas of the symbolism in themselves are of great beauty and tremendous power; at the same time, the persistently abstract meanings and the continuous allegorical action are too far removed from the world of the theatre public. Moreover, even though Moody was justified in using the materials he did, the legendary actors, the too-frequently unnecessary allusions rather diffusely scattered throughout, the rarefied atmosphere, limit the appeal to a small circle of readers. It is not to be intimated that Moody should have "stooped to the masses" for popular approval or that he should have compromised artistic idea or moral creed for the sake of winning an audience. On the other hand, every artist has the obligation to make himself intelligible to those for whom his work is intended. In the least measure, certainly, simplicity of presentation, sureness of touch, and complete co-ordination of parts may be expected. And although Moody's impatience with the commonplace and the trivial incites our admiration, an attempt to come in closer understanding and harmony with his reader or hearer would have made his accomplishment more effective and perhaps would have diminished the neglect which seems recently to have enveloped the *Promethean* story.

On the other hand, although the trilogy by its very nature was ordained not to be popular, and although for most people the characters are too rare or indistinct, being, in the words of the *Nation,* "gigantic and grandiose symbols of a semi-metaphysical speculation,"[37] it is not to be presumed that the great fundamental of all drama, human passion, is entirely lacking. Moody's tremendous humanitarianism is felt on every page and he frequently invests his legendary folk with a pathos and a humanness which startle and surprise.

One might quote at length from the dramas in support of this thesis, but a few brief references will suffice. *Raphaël* opens the **Masque** with an exquisitely human voice:

> Another night like this would change my blood
> To human: the soft tumult of the sea
> Under the moon, the panting of the stars,
> The notes of querulous love from pool and clod,
> In earth and air the dreamy under-hum
> Of hived hearts swarming—such another night
> Would quite unsphere me from my angelhood![38]

The *Youth* in Act IV voices a genuinely mortal love of life:

> Oh, for a voice
> Here in the doors of death
> To speak the praise of life, existence mere,
> The simple come and go of natural breath,
> And habitation of the body's house with its five
>   windows clear!
> O souls defeated, broken, and undone,
> Rejoice with me, rejoice
> That we have walked beneath the moon and sun
> Not churlishly, nor slanderous of the bliss;
> But rather leaving this
> To the many prophets strict and sedulous
> Of that sad-spoken god
> Who now hath conquered and is surely king,
> Have given our lips for life to closely kiss,
> Have heard the sweet persuasion of the sod
> And been heart-credulous
> To trust the signs and whispers of the spring.[39]

In **The Fire-Bringer,** *Pandora*'s love, *Prometheus*'s exultation, *Deukalion*'s tender care of and pleading for *Aeolus* are all typical instances of Moody's emotional intensity. Almost as full of sustained dramatic interest as one could wish is the scene before the altar, when *Deukalion,* consenting to the sacrifice of *Aelous,* falls and the dreaded deed is postponed only by the passionate motherly interference of *Pyrrha*:

> Hold off your hands, hold off! The king is fallen,
> And falling spake somewhat. But I, who drank
> Of his deep will, who ever was and am
> His heart's high furtherer, cry over him
> Ye shall not touch them yet! Not yet ye shall!
> Not till Prometheus comes or makes a sign![40]

Perhaps strongest of all is **The Death of Eve.** *Eve,* superbly conceived, has been subtly delineated. This is no abstraction speaking to *Cain* but humanity's mother to the prodigal of all ages:

> Thou wilt not hear me? Yea, but thou wilt hear!
> Thy ears be not thy ears. I moulded them.
> Thy life is not thy life. I gave it thee,
> And do require it back. Thy beating heart
> Beats not unto itself, but unto me,
> Whose voice did tell it when to beat and how.
> Thy deeds are not thy deeds. Ye conned them here,
> Under this breast, where lay great store of deeds
> Undone, for thee to choose from.

She uncovers the Sign on his forehead.

>   'Tis not thy head
> Weareth this Sign.'Tis my most cruel head,
> Whose cruel hand, whose swift and bloody hand
> Smote in its rage my own fair man-child down.
> Not thy hand, Cain, not thine; but my dark hand;
> And my dark forehead wears the sign thereof,
> And now I take it on me.

She kisses him on the Sign.[41]

Moody's poetic dramas cannot be seriously considered for practical presentation because of the confused elements of structure which remove the poems from that quick perception which is essential to a stage play. At the same time, they have a strong, dramatic element in the frequent human touches, in the profound and moving feeling, and in the elemental conflict of gods and men which they portray.

Considering the trilogy, then, as dramatic lyrics rather than lyrical dramas, it is appropriate to discuss at this point the workmanship of the poems singly.

The Masque of Judgment more than the other two members of the group shows the blemishes of the immature poet. Although careful in the editing and revision of his work, and practiced through previous experience, it was only natural that Moody's first long poem should lack the sustained accomplishment of the later ones. **The Masque of Judgment** is over-wrought. The conflict, mentioned in the discussion of his lyric poems, among various elements of his creative temperament—his intuitive artistic sense of simplicity, his native endowment of subtle comprehension which made him impatient of slowness of intellectual grasp in others, and his love of the luxuriant and highly colored—here finds obvious illustration. His tendency toward a "florid" vocabulary was a weakness which he half-humorously recognized, although there were times when he defended its value, and his attitude is admirably illustrated by the following excerpt from a letter to Edwin Arlington Robinson upon the occasion of the latter's praise of the *Masque*:

> You will not have thought it was indifference to your 'poor words of congratulation' about the *Masque* which has kept me from answering sooner. What you said gave me the deepest—joy, I was going to say; but remembering your distrust of exuberant language, I will say satisfaction. Still, it was joy, all the same—the feeling was exuberant enough to warrant, this once, my florid vocabulary. Your words were the more grateful because they came as a surprise. I thought in New York that you were bravely trying to be generous (you would have said 'just') toward a thing you rootedly deplored but suspected yourself of being by nature prejudiced against. . . .[42]

He came later to prune out the more objectionable usages, but in the *Masque* they are present in abundance. The *Bookman* critic, for example, resented the too frequently used unusual or obsolete words and listed *benedite, vair, strook, energic, lazuline,* and *margent.*[43] A random paging of the book will reveal a multitude of similar examples: *sibilance, eterne, scaur, refluent, purlieus, antinomy, nadir, chrysoprase, rimy, sward, divagant, chalcedony, pleached, galliard, ravin, taborists, idlesse, neap, adrad, rondure, vesperine, choregic, minatory, chrysalid, nacrous.*[44] Further, while the highly colored imagery makes possible the rich texture of the whole, at times its recklessness verges on the absurd. For example, not at all unrepresentative are: *delicious panting, honeyed swoon, clot of anxious clay, harsh blood, ripening suns, grey winds, amethystine dells, rejoicing sinews, woods of light, choiring orbs, drumming foam, shredded mist of song, beetling rosy crag, brows that wont to beacon, glow-worm ghost.*[45]

The form itself is suggestive of the fantastically romantic. The masque as a type has not found popular acceptance in America because of its use of materials too far removed from reasonableness. The new interest in this form at the close of the nineteenth century was short-lived,[46] and Moody had to face a definite prejudice against the form. To be sure, we must admire his daring although our admiration does not remove the obvious lack of convincingness. As a result, "soliloquy and otiose dialogue, . . . a sequence of monologues directed haphazard at one another rather than at their speakers," become the staple of the drama.[47] The very human touch of the mortal-loving *Raphaël* and the awe-struck shepherds of the Prelude seems to stand out in contrast to the remoteness of the remainder and shows by contrast the greatest defect of the whole poem. Professor Manly has justified the selection of the title believing that although "in structure and *personæ*" it is "more like a medieval *mystère* than a masque, . . . Moody, who was familiar with these forms of drama, chose the term 'masque' to indicate the symbolic character of his technique and to justify the large majesty of the action."[48] Such classification is appropriate. Nevertheless, the poet's selection of a mode for reasonable purpose does not excuse his falling prey to the recognized weakness of that vehicle. In Moody, who later showed an unusual capacity

for restraint, although his genius was susceptible to the luxuriant, it is even less excusable. For an example of the almost baroque manner of many parts, we may quote *Uriel*'s description of the troubling of the universe after the crucifixion:

> 'Neath pleachèd boughs and vines of ancient fire
> In the white centre of the sun I lay,
> And watched the armies of young seraphim
> Naked at play on the candescent plains,
> When suddenly the skies of flame were rent
> In sunder, and the plain became a sea
> Whereon the whirlwind walked through weltering lanes
> To the sun's core.[49]

The Spirit of the Lamps reports her discovery that *God*'s throne was empty:

> Intolerable lambence lit the air;
> The sea of glass whereon the nations stand
> At morn to carol, curdled red as blood,
> And rolled a moaning billow to the shore;
>
> . . . . .
> I found the shadowed fields about me, grey
> Each hearted amaranth and asphodel,
> The living forests with their veins of light
> Looped thickly, and the burning flowers between,
> The living waters, and the lily souls
> Along the waters—all a stricken grey![50]

Such passages as these are numerous; the bizarre descriptions, the decorative figures, the etherealism of archangel and seraphim, and the general atmosphere of the rococo, or at least, extravagant unreality, lead to the conclusion that in spite of the beauty of many parts of the poem, the coordination of these parts has not been perfectly effected. Forced figures, incongruities of imagery, and passages of flagging inspiration preclude any impression of sustained accomplishment.

On the other hand, if we disregard the rather complex form of the *Masque* and those blemishes of execution which very largely are directly due to the design, we find much that pleases the poetry lover. The chief delight of *The Masque of Judgment* lies within those passages which may be taken out from the text as isolated lyrics. The examples, obviously, are too numerous to quote in abundance and a listing would meet with no universal approval. Nevertheless, some of the more indisputably exquisite lines may be given. Perhaps the most sustained passage of the whole poem, and one which seems to have been the most popular single excerpt, is *Raphaël*'s Hymn to Man, which closes Act II. It begins:

> O dreamer! O desirer! Goer down
> Unto untraveled seas in untried ships!
> O crusher of the unimagined grape
> On unconceivèd lips!
> O player upon a lordly instrument
> No man or god hath had in mind to invent;
> O cunning how to shape
> Effulgent Heaven and scoop out bitter Hell

From the little shine and saltness of a tear;
Sieger and harrier,
Beyond the moon, of thine own builded town,
Each morning won, each eve impregnable,
Each noon evanished sheer!

　　　　. . . . .

O struggler in the mesh
Of spirit and of flesh
Some subtle hand hath tied to make thee Man,
That now is unto thee a wide domain
To laugh and love and dare in for a span,
And straightway is a prison-house of pain,
A den of loathing, and a violent place,
A hold for unclean wing and cruel face
That mock the seared heart and darkened brain,—
My bosom yearns above thee at the end,
Thinking of all thy gladness, all thy woe;

　　　　. . . . .

Not in vain, not in vain,
The spirit hath its sanguine stain,
And from its senses five doth peer
As a fawn from the green windows of a wood;

　　　　. . . . .

Dust unto dust complains,
Dust laugheth out to dust,
Sod unto sod moves fellowship,
And the soul utters, as she must,
Her meanings with a loose and carnal lip;
But deep in her ambiguous eyes
Forever shine and slip
Quenchless expectancies,
And in a far-off day she seems to put her trust.[51]

The songs of the **Masque of Judgment** form one of its
outstanding features. The delicate and lilting voice of *Pan-*
dora is missing here but the accomplishment in pure song
is noteworthy. When *Raphæl* wonders at the meaning of
the *Voices* which chant to him, at the opening of Scene II,
Act I, in "whispering witless words and prophecy," they
reply:

Where had his gadding spirit led?
Beside what peopled water-head
Stooped he, or on what sleeping face
Was he intent the dream to trace?
Had creature love upon him fawned
Or had he drunk of mortal mirth
That he knew not what a morning dawned
Over his darling earth?
Heard not the storm, heard not the cries,
Heard not the talk of the startled skies
Over the guilty earth?[52]

Later, *Raphæl*, the minstrel of *Heaven*, sings to the *Moon-*
Spirits to ask them to pause in their panic-stricken flight:

Shore-birds wet with deep-sea dew,
Fold your wings and stay your flight;
Stay, stay!
Long was the way,
Grieved with wind in your tender light,
Stay, till our love rekindle you.

Wood-birds that through lunar glens
Flood the noon of night with singing,

Hearken, Hearken!
Our minds undarken:
O'er your phosphor forests winging,
Say, what shadow scared you thence?[53]

To the ten songs written as such we may well add those
parts of the main text which are particularly invested with
a singing quality. These are well illustrated by the ominous conversation of the *Eagle, Lion, Angel of the White*
Horse, Angel of the Tree, and the *Angel of the Pale Horse*
at the close of Act I. The *Eagle* replies to the *Lion* about
the conflict with the *Worm*:

Drear are the depths, O brother,
Bitter the fight!
Vainly we stand by each other.
Thy might and my might
Are as straw, in the flame and the smother.[54]

The *Lion* tells how he "dared to venture down" to the conflict:

Ages and ages we gazed
Stricken at heart and amazed
Till the morning look
From his brow was strook,
Silver and vair
In the flame of his hair
And his lip with anguish crazed.

Then low I spoke to my mate,
My heart must unburden its hate.
I will walk through the pathless woods
Where the wild stars hatch their broods,
I will girdle the steppes
Where the meteor creeps
Like a slug on the rimy sward.
Perhaps at the trampled brink
Where the Bear goes down to drink,
Perhaps where on the purple leas
Dance the young Pleiades,
Somewhere at length
I shall laugh in my strength
Spying the Shape abhorred,
Somewhere at last
I shall break my fast
On the flesh of the Foe of the Lord![55]

Raphæl's long soliloquy comprising Scene I, Act III, already mentioned as a pæan to the restless, adventuresome,
grandly pathetic, earthly spirit of Man, belongs to this
classification of "dialogue-song." The rhymed complaints
of the lost souls in Act IV, some of which have been quoted
previously,[56] may serve as another illustration.

Then, for a final sampling of the **Masque,** we may turn to
the illustrations which form a balance for the forced or
overwrought imagery mentioned earlier as a blemish of
the poem. Sprinkled through all five acts are some of the
finest figures that Moody has created. As noted, his attempt to achieve sublime effect at times produced the over-
wrought; at other times, the results were brilliant. In example of the latter, we quote *Uriel's* complaint at the end
of Judgment:

The dream is done! Petal by petal falls
The coronal of creatured bloom God wove
To deck his brows at dawn.[57]

Earlier, *Uriel* described the earth:

Of all the bitter drops that dewed His brow
In his old agony, this earth-drop fell
Most bitter salt, and ever since hath been
Fuller of travailing than other worlds.[58]

Raphæl refers to humanity as,

. . . this lovely fruitage, this sweet vine
Of man the leaf and maid the honeyed flower
In mystic alternation, and when noon
Spread clamor in the pulses of the vine,
Was pined and plucked it up![59]

Uriel speaks of the creation of Man as follows:

At last! At last! O shaken Breast, nowhere
Couldst thou find quiet save in putting forth
This last imagination? Could no form
Of being stanch thee in thy groping thought
Save this of Man? Puny and terrible;
Apt to imagine powers beyond himself
In wind and lightning; cunning to evoke
From mould and flint-stone the surprising fire,
And carve the heavy hills to spiritual shapes
Of town and temple; nursing in his veins
More restlessness than called him from the void,
Perfidies, hungers, dreams, idolatries,
Pain, laughter, wonder, anger, sex, and song![60]

Opening the scene (I, Act III) which contains *Raphæl*'s famous soliloquy, we have this simple and pathetic picture:

        Raphael.
Alas, on this lone height my pinions fail,
And half my dreaming world unvisited!
As a sick woman, who, when morning glooms
Must leave for aye the house where she was wed,
Yearns to behold the thrice-familiar rooms,
And rises trembling, and with watch-lamp goes
From chamber unto chamber, stopping now
To muse upon her dead child's pictured brow,
And now to dream of little merriments
Enacted, and of trivial dear events,
Until her weakness grows
Upon her, and she sinks and cannot rise,—
So, since upon the sad and prescient skies
The darkness of this ultimate might was shed, . . .
My feet from haunted place to haunted place
Of my familiar earth have kept their pace.[61]

The Masque of Judgment was a daring experiment which popularly was only a half-success but which creatively was an unusual work. Far short of being a great poem by dint of its obscurity and vagueness, its too subtle representation and its blemishes of workmanship, at the same time from this, his first sustained work, Moody was led to the formation of his scheme for a trilogy. Moreover, in the midst of much that Poe would have called prose, there blossomed these flowers of the poet's genius, which we have meagerly illustrated.

The Fire-Bringer, like its predecessor, was received with both favorable and unfavorable criticism. Moody himself probably felt that his later work was the better for he allowed the publishers to advertise the book with a notice for reviewers stating that the critic would find an advance over the poet's former work. The adverse comments discouraged him, however, as he confessed to E. C. Stedman:

Your generous words concerning my ***Fire-Bringer*** have given me great joy. The poem got little praise, and that little mostly misdirected, so that I had come to think of it, as—so far as my hoped-for audience was concerned—a failure. But if you like it, it is no failure, and I can go on with a good heart.[62]

But it is a tribute to the workmanship of the poem that most of the fault-finding, as noted earlier, had to do with choice of theme, mode, and materials. These objections have already been weighed in sections I and II of this chapter. It is important to realize here, however, that the most antagonistic reviews directed no disparagement toward the purely poetic and structural features of the work.

The flaws in ***The Fire-Bringer*** are largely those of ***The Masque of Judgment,*** but with some of the most noticeable ones eliminated and the remainder modified. Here again, for example, the poet has not removed entirely the stale atmosphere of musty myth in academic attire. In a sense, this objection is rooted in the material itself; it is structural, however, in so far as the poet has not recreated the narrative element to appeal on its own account. The thrill of the episode wherein *Prometheus* is struck by *Heaven*'s thunder as he laughs defiantly at having stolen the vase of fire, is somewhat dulled by the maze of references to the classical, mythological geography and genealogy. In this passage of fifty-three lines there are five allusions to persons, four to places, and twelve to movements which by themselves, without the reader's familiarity with them, are scarcely comprehensible. Many other vivid scenes such as those at the proposed sacrifice of *Aeolus* and *Alcyone* are dramatically intense but have been somewhat obscured by the garb of the story.

Again, in spite of the lovely *Pandora,* the pathetic *Deukalion,* the patient *Pyrrha,* and the inspired *Prometheus,* there is a tinge of lifelessness about ***The Fire-Bringer*** which becomes a characteristic note, faint, but present. Several of the speeches in the opening pages are too obviously expository, lacking in naturalness, sounding forced. For example, in Act I, *Pyrrha* rehearses the whole story of the past action to *Deukalion* who knows it as well as she. The reader is informed, of course, but dramatic reality is lost. The same effect is produced in many of the long expository speeches throughout the poem. The story isn't always convincing nor is the allusion of conviction present.

Yet, the beauties outweigh these considerations and among them the greatest single delight of ***The Fire-Bringer*** is the varied loveliness of the verse. Closely knit, packed with thought and meaning the poet has retained the glow of deep feeling. Maintaining throughout a movement of stateliness and measured formality, he has injected a subtle use of plain speech which overflows with dramatic eloquence. *Deukalion*'s speech of self-sacrifice in Act II, beginning,

> I am king, hear ye, am I not king?
> Higher than I is none. Take me! Why him,
> Little of strength and wisdom?

and ending,

> What honor should the dread gods have on him?
> They shall have me, Deukalion—

is strong in its direct, vital appeal. At the same time the lines are melodious with a penetrating harmony and pregnant with suggestive phrase. "The chanting of the old religious trees," "the shutting mists of death," "the trampling and bellowing herds of rain," "the plunging prow of the world," "fierce and tedious prayer"—may be multiplied many times over, in long passage and short, as representatives of the poet's fertility.

Among isolated passages of unusual beauty, the songs of *Pandora* must be singled out for special mention. In them Moody the singer is heard at his best. Those who maintain that his genius was primarily lyrical here find almost indisputable evidence. Widely quoted, they stand out independently from the drama. Yet, structurally, they are not merely exercises for "atmosphere." They belong to the whole poem. Not one could be omitted without damage to the movement. Yet, they convey a second penetration into the reader's heart which brings to him a loveliness quite distinct from the narrative. There are eight of them and each one claims a place among Moody's most notable lyrics. The first place, if one may so rank poems, should go to *Pandora*'s song of encouragement to her lover:

> Of wounds and sore defeat
> I made my battle stay;
> Wingèd sandals for my feet
> I wove of my delay;
> Of weariness and fear,
> I made my shouting spear;
> Of loss, and doubt, and dread,
> And swift oncoming doom
> I made a helmet for my head,
>
> And a floating plume.
> From the shutting mist of death,
> From the failure of the breath,
> I made a battle-horn to blow
> Across the vales of overthrow.
> O hearken, love, the battle-horn!
> The triumph clear, the silver scorn!
> O hearken where the echoes bring,
> Down the grey disastrous morn,
> Laughter and rallying![63]

Another, which in imaginative suggestion and lyrical beauty shares honors with the one just quoted, is found in Act III:

> I stood within the heart of God;
> It seemed a place that I had known:

> (I was blood-sister to the clod,
> Blood-brother to the stone.)

> I found my love and labor there,
> My house, my raiment, meat and wine,
> My ancient rags, my old despair,—
> Yea, all things that were mine.

> I saw the spring and summer pass,
> The trees grow bare, and winter come;
> All was the same as once it was
> Upon my hills at home.

> Then suddenly in my own heart
> I felt God walk and gaze about;
> He spoke; his words seemed held apart
> With gladness and with doubt.

> 'Here is my meat and wine,' He said,
> 'My love, my toil, my ancient care;
> Here is my cloak, my book, my bed,
> And here my old despair.

> 'Here are my seasons: winter, spring,
> Summer the same, and autumn spills
> The fruits I look for; everything
> As on my heavenly hills.'[64]

Finally, we may turn to the totality of the poem's effect Although the unexpected page of exaltation is less frequent here than in *The Masque of Judgment,* there is quite evidently a gain in evenness of sustained power. The whole piece is much sharper in outline and clearer in dramatic progression. One gets the feeling in placing the two poems side by side that the later work is compressed, with loose ends tied into the whole pattern, and with irrelevancies and extravagances carefully pruned out. Each scene has its proper transition from the preceding one, with the gathering momentum of the theme carefully pointed to the burst of glory at the end, shadowed only by the prospective punishment of the benefactor, *Prometheus.* Every line from the gloomy forecast of the opening speeches through the soliloquies of *Prometheus* and the choral passages of obscure groups to the final hymn to *Apollo* is essential to the effectiveness of the poem. The *tone,* too, is characterized by a serenity which enhances the spiritual implications of the narrative. The poet has not lost the intensity of his story; he merely seems to have it more completely controlled. *The Fire-Bringer* quite obviously illustrates a step in the development of Moody's art; it is mid-way between the luxuriance of *The Masque* on the one hand and the austerity of *The Death of Eve* on the other.

It may well be said that *The Death of Eve* is the culmination of the trilogy in workmanship as well as in philosophical idea. Compared with the complete members, it shows a great gain not only in clarity and orderliness but in dramatic power. Whether the latter is due to Moody's having experimented with prose dramas or to an instinctive growth toward a more restrained art, we cannot tell. Certainly, whatever the cause, the directness and unobscured power of the poem are obvious. The great lyric heights are not reached, to be sure, but we must remember that the fragment was in tentative form. Even so, ***The Death of Eve*** has a "simple grandeur"[65] lacking in its companion pieces. For this reason, Harriet Monroe prefers ***The Death of Eve*** to Moody's other work—"because of the simplicity and plainness of the style, because it is not stiff with the gorgeous Miltonic brocade, the magnificent investiture, of the other two plays of the trilogy."[66] This simplicity and restraint have made for compression and concentration. Note, for example, the lines from the incident where *Eve* tells *Cain* that his father lives:

> Eve.
> —Why do you harshly thrust my hands away,
> And lift your clenched hands trembling to the sky
> With wild and smothered words?
> Cain.
> *Pushing her from him.*
> I know you not.
> Unclasp my knees.—I thought you were yourself
> Yours, therefore mine at last. It is not so.
> His, his, the same as when he cursed me forth
> And Eve stood stockish, never one plea made,
> One wail set up, one gesture of farewell,
> No more than from a stone![67]

Then, repenting of his harsh words and selfish anger when his mother swoons, *Cain* speaks:

> Pitiful God, not this!
> She could not come after the endless years,
> To go so soon.—Mother, thou wilt not deal
> Thus much unkindness to an unkind son,
> As leave him when harsh words were on his lips.
> Of old, when in our rage we thrust thee out,
> Thou wouldst return again, unreconciled
> To harshness and to wrath. O do it now,
> In pity![68]

These unadorned speeches penetrate with clean-cut thrusts.

With increase in dramatic power, a decrease in lyric fervor within the text of dialogue may be expected. Such transformation, as noted, lends greater effectiveness in a dramatic narrative; yet, the poem retains Moody's singing quality. The lines are free from the abstruse and unwieldy figure and in natural limpid flow, both rapid and smooth, the harmonies and rhythm of dialogue and soliloquy lend a music nearly as impressive as the previous poems possessed. *Eve*'s matriarchal command to *Cain*, already quoted, may be taken as an example. Another is *Eve*'s answer to *Cain*'s charge that she gave him no farewell, "No more than from a stone!"

> She was a stone;
> As afterwards, long years, a frozen stone.
> No seasons and no weather on the earth;
> Sun, moon, and stars dead in a field of death;
> And in her dead heart, nothing, nothing, nothing!
> After long years, she wakened, knew herself,
> Rose up to wring some profit from her days,
> Conceived again, and once again brought forth;
> Yea, saw the teeming race in circles kindle
> Roaring to God, a flame of generation.

> From out the tossing battle of that fire
> Flashed seldom and again wild news of thee,
> And one red instant, ere night drove between,
> Thy form would stand gigantic in the glare,
> Islanded huge among thine enemies,—
> As when the ice-bear rears upon the floe
> And swings her flailing paws against the pack,
> Or when the sea-volcano from his loins
> Shakes climbing cities.[69]

The purely lyrical passages planned for ***The Death of Eve,*** Moody did not finish. In *Act I* there is but one full song, the chorus of *Water-Bearers,* beginning,

> Till the coming up of day,
> Till the cool night flee away,
> Till the Hunter rises up to pursue,
> O my sisters, we will laugh, we will play!
> Though He wake and walk anear us,
> He is mused, He will not hear us;
> Though He wanders lone and late,
> He will never hear how mate whispereth to darkling mate.
> Yea, and though He hear, and though!
> Will He judge us, even so?
> He is mused, He walketh harmless. In the shadowy mountain hid
> We will lure our lovers to us, even as our mothers did!
> When He cometh forth at dawn, and His anger burns anew,
> As our hunted mothers did, even so we will do:
> Flee and crouch and feint and double, leap the snare or gnaw it
> through![70]

In connection with lyric expressions of the *Eve* subject, however, the earlier experiments may be considered. The song of *Eve* from the earliest poem is a notable lyric, excerpts from which have already been quoted.[71] *I Am the Woman*, also, is in itself a song.[72]

The Death of Eve was left a fragment but one can well say that, within the shortened scope of the poem, it remains in idea, form, and effectiveness, the climax of the trilogy.

Notes

1. Percy MacKaye, *Uriel,* Stanza I; *Uriel and other Poems,* p. 1.

2. *Atlantic Monthly,* September 1906.

3. Introduction, *Complete Works,* pp. xxxiii-v.

4. *American Poetry,* p. 692.

5. New York *Times,* September 17, 1904.

6. Richard Burton, *Book Buyer,* September 1901.

7. Philadelphia *Public Ledger,* May 8, 1904.

8. G. B. Rose, *Sewanee Review,* July 1901.

9. Los Angeles *Express,* April 16, 1904.

10. May, 1904.

11. E. L. Shuman, *Record-Herald*, April—, 1904.

12. *Some Letters of William Vaughn Moody*, pp. 133-4.

13. *Complete Works*, I, pp. 239-240.

14. *Complete Works*, I, pp. 239-240.

15. *Ibid.*, p. 391.

16. *Ibid.*, p. 404.

17. *Some Letters of William Vaughn Moody*, p. 133.

18. *Some Letters of William Vaughn Moody*, pp. 131-2.

19. Moody, *Complete Works*, I, p. 258.

20. Translation by E. H. Plumptre, ll. 260-261.

21. *Ibid.*, ll. 109-111.

22. ll. 34-109.

23. *Prometheus Unbound*, Act II, Sc. IV, ll. 63-65.

24. *Complete Works*, I, pp. 270-1.

25. *Ibid.*, p. 198.

26. *Ibid.*, p. 188.

27. Lovett, *Selected Poems of William Vaughn Moody*, Notes p. 238.

28. Manly, Introduction, *Complete Works of Moody*, I, xl.

29. Moody, *Complete Works*, I, p. 11.

30. *Ibid.*, p. 33.

31. *Ibid.*, pp. 89-90.

32. Introduction, *Complete Works*, p. xxxvi.

33. *Some Letters of William Vaughn Moody*, p. 87.

34. *Ibid.*, pp. 160-161.

35. *Ibid.*, p. 148.

36. *Some Letters of William Vaughn Moody*, p. 169.

37. February 6, 1913.

38. *Complete Works*, pp. 275-6.

39. *Ibid.*, pp. 366-7.

40. *Ibid.*, p. 224.

41. *Ibid.*, pp. 446-7.

42. *Some Letters of William Vaughn Moody*, pp. 136-7.

43. May, 1901.

44. *Complete works*, I, pp. 278, 281, 300, 302, 306, 309, 312, 313, 315, 317, 319, 325, 328, 331, 336, 342, 343, 344, 352, 363, 371, 373, 385 respectively.

45. *Ibid.*, pp. 280, 277, 278 282, 359, 383, 391, 290, 293, 303, 305, 309, 322 respectively.

46. An interesting parallel to the *Masque*, incidentally, at this time is Hardy's *The Dynasts*.

47. N. O. Barr, *The Drama*, May 1911.

48. Introduction, *Complete Works*, I. p. xxxvi-vii.

49. *Complete Works*, I, p. 325.

50. *Ibid.*, pp. 334-5.

51. *Complete Works*, I, pp. 339-343.

52. *Ibid.*, pp. 304-5.

53. *Ibid.*, p. 329.

54. *Ibid.*, pp. 313-315.

55. *Ibid.*, pp. 313-315.

56. See p. 124.

57. *Complete Works*, I, p. 389.

58. *Ibid.*, p. 279.

59. *Ibid.*, p. 353.

60. *Ibid.*, p. 283.

61. *Ibid.*, p. 337.

62. *Some Letters of William Vaughn Moody*, p. 150.

63. *Complete Works*, I, p. 208.

64. *Ibid.*, pp. 267-8.

65. Herman Hagedorn, *Independent*, February 6, 1913.

66. Shorey, University of Chicago *Record*, July 1927.

67. *Complete Works*, I, pp. 432-3.

68. *Ibid.*, p. 436.

69. *Ibid.*, p. 433.

70. *Ibid.*, p. 414.

71. See p. 91.

72. See p. 80.

Mark Van Doren (essay date 1935)

SOURCE: "A Dedicated Man," in *The Private Reader: Selected Articles & Reviews*, Kraus Reprint Co., 1968, pp. 225-28.

[*In the following essay, which was originally published in 1935, Van Doren discusses the relation of Moody's letters to his poetry, judging the letters superior.*]

As editor of these letters [**Letters to Harriet**] Mr. MacK-aye makes them tell a story which they were not written to tell, and which, in so far as they do tell it, is a less interesting story than Mr. MacKaye believes. It is the story of several persons who during the first decade of the present century set out self-consciously to produce an American poetic drama: to arrive at "Stratford and Weimar by route of Medicine Hat and Kalamazoo." They were in the habit of referring to themselves as "our little group," to their activity as a "crusade," and to their organization as a "phalanx." One of them wrote to Mr. MacKaye in 1905 begging him to "tell me of things dramatic and poetic, and what you are doing, and what I *ought* to be doing, and what hope—or fear—there is for all of us who are growing pale and thin watching for signs of American drama." And Moody himself wrote to Mr. MacKaye in 1904: "I am heart and soul dedicated to the conviction that modern life can be presented on the stage in the poetic mediums, and adequately presented only in that way." The failure of the story to be interesting now is not at all because we have ceased to consider the possibilities of poetic drama; indeed, such possibilities are the theme of a lively criticism at the moment, both in England and in America. Rather it is because these people worked in a hopelessly literary way, "dedicating" themselves in phrases and attitudes that could never have had anything to do with a living theater, and hating commercialism with the kind of holy air which results in the composition not of better plays but merely of different ones.

At any rate the story gets told in the voluminous introduction, conclusion, and notes to this book; and Mr. MacKaye does contrive to leave on record a good deal of information which historians will enjoy concerning the dramatic careers of Moody and himself, Edwin Arlington Robinson, Josephine Preston Peabody, and Ridgely Torrence. Nor is the story entirely irrelevant to one theme which Moody pursues throughout his letters to the woman, Mrs. Harriet Brainard, who became his wife a year before he died in 1910. This is the theme of his dedication to the poetic art. For he thought of himself first and last as a poetic artist, and his letters to his best friend are full of reports on the progress he is making, on the state of his mind and imagination at given moments, and on the processes which he discovers taking place inside his heart and soul. These reports, made by an intelligent and honest man, are nevertheless unconvincing. I fancy that if we had only them to go by we should know that Moody had not been a first-rate poet, as in fact he was not. His poems say so no less clearly than these introspective passages wherein he somehow never quite strikes a plausible balance between self-consciousness and its opposite. He knows both too little and too much about the mind of the poet; too little, or he could say more, and too much, or he would say less. He manages in the same breath to be modest and embarrassing, and to be tragic without realizing it. For it is surely tragic that intelligence, integrity, and a great personal decency should not be enough to make a poet out of a man who wants very badly to be one. God knows what is needed in addition, but whatever it is Moody did not have it.

In his poems, that is. He has it in these letters, which are not only his best work but among the best things of their kind. The truth comes out clearly enough in a comparison between the following lines of prose, written to Mrs. Brainard from Crete in 1902, and the poem called **"The Second Coming,"** written in New York two years later:

> The sailors were lying about asleep in the fierce sun— except one, who had heaved his boat on her side and was calking her. By him stood a man dressed in a long dark robe of coarse stuff, bareheaded, talking earnestly to the stooping sailor. I took him for a Greek priest, by reason of his long hair and spiritual profile. There was something in the spare frame of the man, the slight stoop of the shoulders, and the calm intensity of the attitude, which made my heart stop beating. Presently he turned to look at me, and it was indeed He. This has

happened to me twice now—once before at Sorrento seven years ago.

Moody seems not to have understood that this *was* the poem, and that the 120 lines which he lavished on the incident were doomed to mediocrity for the simple reason that the incident had been closed, both in his mind and in the words which already contained it. But no such comparison is needed to establish our point. The genius which is lacking in the poems is abundantly present in the letters, where a high seriousness lies down naturally with the most charming, the most unsubduable wit; where rhetoric is always correcting itself with warm-hearted humor and an eye to human detail; and where a sustained note of worship—literally worship—for Mrs. Brainard is never marred by failure to remember that she too is capable of comedy, that she is, indeed, "my gay and disquieting and ever incalculable companion, upon whose shifting moods I have learned to build from hour to hour my house of life." As a collection of letters the book is brilliant; as a love story it brings home to us one of the most honorable and amusing of American men.

George Arms (essay date 1980)

SOURCE: "The Poet as Theme Reader: William Vaughn Moody, a Student, and Louisa May Alcott," in *Toward a New American Literary History: Essays in Honor of Arlin Turner,* edited by Louis J. Budd, Edwin H. Cady, and Carl H. Anderson, Duke University Press, 1980, pp. 140-53.

[In the following essay, Arms examines Moody's comments on student papers he corrected while teaching English at Harvard.]

For English 22 at Radcliffe, William Vaughn Moody wrote this comment on a first fortnightly theme, a reminiscence by a student who had read *Little Women* and later met its author:

> A charming theme, both in spirit and treatment. It has the unmistakable note of sincerity, and has at times an imaginative and pathetic quality which touches and convinces the reader. On the other hand the phrasing is often weakly conventional, giving a note of false sentiment which is in sharp contrast with the pervading atmosphere. It could be shortened by the omission of unnecessary details and a more rigid economy in language. Your style is apt to degenerate into diffuseness. Your sentence structure is not always good, too much being crowded into one sentence, and the parts being strung together with loose connectives
>
> Rewrite.
>
> W. V. Moody.[1]

Before we turn to the theme itself, Moody's teaching of English 22 deserves a brief review.[2] Graduating from Harvard in 1893, he studied for his M.A. in the following year. In the year after that, he taught in the advanced composition course under the direction of Lewis E. Gates at Harvard and Radcliffe. This was the year that Frank Norris (whose themes were read mostly by Herbert V. Abbot, though some by Gates) and Gertrude Stein (whose themes were read mostly by Moody) were enrolled in English 22. Stein's extant essays have been printed, the fortnightly ones with Moody's comments and marginal entries.[3] The comments usually run the same length as that on the essay about Louisa May Alcott, though the marginal notations are less frequent, somewhere between seven and twelve as against the thirty in the Alcott theme. Rosalind S. Miller, the editor, thinks that Moody did less than full justice to Stein, largely because of his attachment to the genteel tradition. To a degree she is right, for Moody objects to treating "a morbid psychological state" or to "the cold-blooded methods of laboratory analysis" or to an "analysis of the girl's reaction" as "unpleasant." But more usually Moody concerns himself with style, point of view, structure, and mechanics. In comparing Stein's writing in English 22 with that of Norris, James D. Hart finds her "immature in ideas and techniques," apparently endorsing her course grade of C and Norris' B+ at midyear with a final A.[4]

Besides Stein's, the only other set of Moody-corrected themes that I have located are eight fortnightlies by Wilhelm Segerblom filed in the Harvard University Archives.[5] Segerblom was evidently not a man with literary interests, so that Moody's treatment of his work provides sharp contrast with that of Stein. Little marginal notation appears (an average of four entries an essay), suggesting that Moody regarded Segerblom as unlikely to improve his style. The general comments on the extant essays are, however, with one exception close to the hundred-word range that seems standard with Moody, though they strike me as harsher than Segerblom's workmanlike if unadorned prose deserves. On the first theme, an amusing report of a laboratory experiment that miscarried, Moody explodes, "This theme has not much literary value," but later concedes its "considerable merit of perfect clearness and directness of statement." When in "Theme No. 6" Segerblom attempts a story of a widow's change from squalor to salvation through the gift of a geranium, Moody leads off, "This would make a very good tract for a Flower mission, though to the unregenerate mind the effect seems hopelessly in excess of the cause." Ultimately the teacher and student come to guarded terms in the "connected work" of five sequential themes, of which happily we have the whole set—an argument for the Viking colonization of North America and its influence on the first voyage of Columbus. Mostly Moody regards the sequence with respect, allowing rather less solid documentation than I think a teacher would today. On the final essay of both the sequence and course he begins his comment, "You bring together a very considerable body of evidence and marshall it on the whole effectively." But he concludes his paragraph by advising Segerblom that he must learn to organize "if you expect to go on with work of an expository nature."

On the whole, then, though the evidence constitutes a small sampling, the general consensus that Moody read his

student's essays with care and perception is substantiated. That he did not detect genius in Stein or appreciate the interests of Segerblom are the lapses of distinguished critics as well as of teachers of writing. How many themes he usually corrected I have not been able to find out. As he wrote Robert M. Lovett on April 25, 1895, "You will forgive me for not sooner answering your kind letter, when you call to mind your early morning and midnight coping with the English 22 fortnightly."[6]

At this time Lovett and Robert Herrick were trying to persuade Moody to come to the University of Chicago, where indeed he became an instructor following his year at Harvard. About his early teaching there we have at least two accounts, a booklet by Grace N. Veeder, who took his English 4 in the fall of 1896, and a typescript by Charlotte Wilson, who took his course in the summer of 1898.[7] As one might expect from former students who were moved to write about him, both reminiscences are tributes to his effectiveness as a teacher. Mrs. Veeder has printed her class notes, which suggest that English 4, a "Course of Daily and Fortnightly Themes," was modeled closely on English 22. To the four kinds of writing in English 22— "Description, Narration, Exposition, and Argument"— Moody apparently added a fifth, "Persuasion." But as the surviving themes by Norris and Stein suggest, neither course adhered closely to these rhetorical genres. Perhaps more openly than at Harvard, Moody turned the direction of English 4 toward creative writing or literary criticism: the class notes report Moody's reading from submitted essays, but more frequently from novelists (as George Eliot, Meredith, and Thackeray) and poets (as Browning, Keats, and Tennyson). On one occasion Moody compared sonnets with daily themes and may have suggested that the students could write sonnets as an alternate for themes. As Veeder suggests, the course was "artistic" and not as systematic as English 3.

But it is time to turn to the author of the essay on Louisa May Alcott, the literary subject of which may partly have caused Moody to call it "charming." Her name was Florence Phillips, and except for what she says of herself in the reminiscence, I have not found out much about her. Since she was a Special Student, the Radcliffe College Archives have only a little information.[8] Born in 1864, she had attended Miss Annie Brown's School in New York City, and between 1892 and 1895 she took one or two courses each year at Radcliffe, receiving a grade of B in English 22 (about halfway between Stein's C and Norris' B+ / A) for the fall semester of 1894. The date of her death is still to be established: the alumnae directory lists her as deceased in 1926, but the preceding directory of 1922 gives her address as 245 West 76 Street.

In transcribing Miss Phillips' essay (her first fortnightly, October 10), I have used standard editorial symbols to show Moody's corrections, written in red ink: square brackets for comments (usually written in the margins but here placed after the matter to which they apply), pointed brackets for cancellations (by lining through, by parenthe-

ses, or by circling), vertical arrows for insertions, and italics for underlining. Phillips' manuscript, a model of neatness, has been transcribed exactly as she wrote it. In order
to avoid confusion with Moody's corrections, her relatively few cancellations and insertions (about a dozen)
have not been recorded. Mostly in the first paragraph Miss
Phillips makes some insertions (definitely in her own
handwriting), cancellations, and parenthetical markings in
pencil—also unrecorded. It seems likely that she pencilled
these changes in response to Moody's direction, "Rewrite";
and their appearance mostly in the first paragraph suggests
a conference with Moody before she made her revised
draft.

MY ROMANCE

The lowest drawer of my desk is seldom unlocked, and
it is never opened by any <other than> ↑one but[9]↓ myself. For there I keep my few cherished possessions,
the *"death in life" relics of my experience* [A trifle or-
nate]. Far back and quite at the bottom of my drawer
there is a little book. <.> ↑. T↓ the brown covers are
faded, and the gilt letters of the title are worn with age.
A few letters tied together with a string of white rib-
bon, and a blue silk marker with the words "Remember
me" in faded lettering, lie between the *tinged* [Ambigu-
ous] pages <of the volume.> On the <only remaining>
title page a verse is written in a child's cramped hand,
and over the headings of the chapters and on the margins of the leaves there are sentences like these,—"Jo
is a dear splendid tom-boy," "how good that Beth got
well," "what a good time they did have," "I love aunt
Jo better than anyone *almost.*"[10]

The *almost* was significant to me, *it symbolized my
mother* [Inexactly phrased]. Soon after she had made
me a gift of the book, ↑and↓ while I was still a very
little girl, my mother died. And my aunt, to whose care
I was left, did not give presents except on Christmas
and on birthdays. Two books a year will not make a library grow fast, and *if they would,* those *new books
were not always* [Not clear] the kind I liked. (And) my
gifts ↑moreover↓ no longer bore the dear inscription
"With mothers love." So my oldest friends remained
my dearest for two reasons, because they were associated with the memory of my Mother, and because I had
no others that I liked as well [Repetition of idea—
Condense the paragraph].[11]

I found refuge from all my little sorrows, (and I shared
all my little joys) [Disturbs the idiom.] in the companionship of *"Jo" and "Polly"* [Be more definite]. These
friends were as real to me as any in life. I pictured
them in other scenes than those in the stories, and when
I walked with my aunt on the avenue bright with shops
and busy life I often imagine*d myself one of my favor-
ites* [Not clear]. I tried to imitate their virtues. I learned
all that I could about Boston, where they lived; and
one day I learned something that troubled me. I heard a
lady say that the Boston people were cold, stiff in man-
ners, that all the women (there) wore eye glasses and
walked with a hop-skip-and-jump, that they aped the
English and were not at all like New-Yorkers. My governess was English <,> ↑.↓ I[12] tried to picture "Jo",
"Meg", "Rose", or even "aunt Jo" like <my governess>
↑her*darr;,[13] *with spectacles, and ejaculating* [Not quite

smooth] "fancy" every now-and-then <;> ↑.↓ I found it
impossible to walk with a hop-skip-and-jump. So finally I concluded that my friends were not that sort of
people, and thus healed the painful sense of separation
from them *caused by these peculiarities* [Inexact].
"Little Women" was once more my Bible, and the
brown house on the outskirts of Boston, the home of
the March family, was my Mecca, toward which I often looked from my window in an uptown street *in the
metropolitan city.* [Circumlocutory]

One day, with mingled feelings of regret and superior
wisdom, such as children feel when they learn that
Santa Claus is not Santa Claus <but that their parents is
Santa,> the thought came to me that "aunt Jo" was
Miss Alcott, that Miss Alcott created my people, and
that she didn't look like "Jo" or "Polly" but was grown
up and probably *quite* [?] serious. I pictured her a
sunny, motherly woman with soft brown hair and eyes
like my Mothers.[14] Evey bit of *news* [?] concerning her
that I could find <was> ↑I↓ treasured. One day an article written by <herself> ↑her↓ about her ↑own↓ early
life appeared in St. Nicholas, with a wood-cut portrait.[15] How I hovered over that article, and how *blith-
erly* [Best word?] I framed the wood-cut likeness of
my friend in a cardboard frame, the <corners tied to-
gether> with blue ribbons.

My affection for Miss Alcott did not lessen when I entered my teens, and my dearest hope and constant faith
was that I should see her some day,—some day when I
grew up and could do as I liked. At length I did *grow
up, for my* [Logical?] brother married. And then I knew
the time had come for me to see Miss Alcott. I felt that
if I could catch a glimpse of her as she passed her door
it would sooth my injured feelings for the loss of my
brother, and straighten the general crookedness of the
world. Permission to pass a month in *Boston* with a
friend once obtained it was not long before I found
myself riding out of the Grand Central Station toward
Boston, [Repetition][16] the city of my dreams [Diffuse].[17]

I knew that Miss Alcott's home was in Concord, and I
had pictured that village on a hill overlooking Boston;
a <sort of> ↑an↓ Arcadian place where many wise and
lovely beings lived together. It was, therefore, <rather>
disappointing to be obliged to take the train to reach it.
My friend and I went there one fair June morning. At
the Concord station a one armed man with a carry-all
was waiting for pilgrims, and *we were* at once *driven*
[Avoid passive constructions] to Miss Alcott's home.
Our <guide and> driver proved loquacious, and <he>
did not object to the questions showered upon him. We
soon learned, with a sense of relief, that Miss Alcott
was not in Concord; that she was a plain woman who
didn't "put on airs", and that she had a smile like a
sunbeam. He told us sundry other things about Mr. Alcott who was living, and Emerson and Thoreau who
were dead, but these accounts did not interest me very
much. I was absorbed in what I saw as we drove about
under the tall Elms: there was the beloved river where
<"> Jo <"> met Apollyon ↑,↓ there was the hill that
the "little pilgrims climbed", and there was "the square
brown house" where my beloved <"> March <"> family once had lived. I pictured <"> Jo <"> reading in the
friendly old apple tree which grew in the garden of
Miss Alcott's early home <;> ↑.↓ I fancied "Meg"

singing in the parlor of the old brown house to "Beths" accompaniment <;> ↑.↓ <and> "Mrs. March's" motherly face seemed to look out from one of an upper window, and I heard her cheery voice call "girls, girls have[18] you pocket handkerchiefs," and a gay, girlish laugh ring, as two little figures disappeared down the unpaved street *through the mists of long ago* [Sentimental and conventional]. I spent a long, blissful day roaming about the green, sweet-smelling village, full of *summer sights and sounds* [Quotation?], *till a shower blew up* [Destroys unity of sentence]. We were obliged to seek shelter from the big drops, and as we waited under a blooming chestnut tree, some one in a house nearby played the second movement of Chopin's "Funeral March"; the familiar, <beloved> melody mingled with my <half> dreamy thoughts, and made a fitting close to one of the happiest days of my life.

A few *days* after my eventful *day* in Concord, a lady waiting on the wharf at Nonquitt for the small steamtug which conveyed passengers from New Bedford, may have been annoyed by two eager faced girls trying to stare her out of countenance. Why I knew Miss Alcott at first sight I never felt quite sure, for she did not much resemble her photographs, that I had seen. [Remodel / Not well massed][19] <And> while we sailed across the bay, in the sunset, I had pictured Miss Alcott strolling on the beach, humming <"Three Fishers" or some other> ↑a↓ sea-song, for it was a romantic evening, *the air soft and* salt [Syntax], and the blue bay <quite> [Inexact use] tumbled with little waves. But the moment that I saw the plain, *almost English-governess-like looking* [Awkward] woman on the Nonquitt wharf II [*sic*] knew she was Louisa Alcott. The ↑?↓[20] tall figure, the fine head, the deep arch of the brows about the eyes, and the simple hat and gown <in those days of fuss and feathers,> marked her <with a distinction that was> unmistakabl <e> ↑y↓ [Diffuse]. Yet my disappointment at first was keen, for she did not look like the image I had cherished so fondly in my imagination. And when I was left alone in my room at the hotel, I threw myself in a disappointed heap on the bed moaning ↑,↓ "↑I↓ <i>s *that* my dear aunt Jo <."> ↑?"↓

Miss Alcott had a cottage at Nonquitt, near the sea, but she took her meals at the hotel, and by some happy chance we were placed at her table. How my heart beat when that first night at supper the *tall form "came down upon us"* [?]. I looked out of the opposite window steadily through that meal, and I left the table with my berries <quite> untasted. But I watched for her on the piazza, and when she passed out of the door, stopping to speak to an old lady, I felt a rush of sympathy and love. No, she was not the handsome woman I had pictured so fondly in the old days, glowing with health and life <, that> ↑. That↓ Miss Alcott belonged now to the cycle of departed fairy Kings and Queens. The real Miss Alcott was a dignified woman, past fifty, with a sad, careworn face and absent eyes. People said that she had faded since her Mother's death, ten years ago, and that she was suffering from the effects of overwork. But the beautiful head with its wealth of dark chestnut hair, and the strength and refinement in her expression and movements gave her a Queenly [No cap?] presence. Her smile was like sunshine, it transfigured her face; *and later I often caught glimpses of the droll, tender woman beloved by so many girls and boys* [Anticlimax—Also destroys the unity of your sentence].

One day, when I had been sitting opposite her at meals a full week, she spoke to me. And then one evening I found myself in her tiny parlor;—I was too excited by the event to sleep much that night! I haunted her steps at a respectful distance day <by> ↑after↓ day. A few times I met her on the cliffs, and one afternoon I sat by her side under a friendly tree which grew near her door. For her sake I braved the snakes, and ruined my clothes, in quest of water lilies, and <I> went alone into the tall wheat fields to gather crimson lilies. And how shy and glad I felt when she guessed my secret and said one morning, with a kind and penetrating glance, "are you the good fairy who leaves flowers on my doorstep"? I did not dream of telling her that I had come all the way from New York for the purpose of seeing her, but she guessed I wanted something, and one evening I had a long talk with her. She listened to my little tale of perplexities [Very charming][21] with sympathy, and something of amusement I think, her eyes turning often from my childish face *toward the summer sea*. That night when she kissed me I whispered "I shall never love anyone as I do you," and I never shall, <in the same way.> [This jars upon me as a false note of conventional sentiment. Find a fresher phrase][22]

The month soon passed and I was called home. I saw Miss Alcott twice the following winter; and at Christmas I sent her roses. One March night my brother gently broke the news to me that Miss Alcott was dead. I took my little book then, my mother's gift, the dear volume of "Little Women", from its nook on the bookshelf, and I put it away with a few letters in the bottom drawer of my desk. I felt that some warmth had gone forever from my life; I knew that a beautiful spirit had passed from this world, and that my little romance was ended.

I must apologize for making this theme longer than it should be, and shall try to keep within the limits in future.

We have already seen how Moody commented on the essay. Certainly he is justified in speaking of a touch of "false sentiment," especially in view of the writer's age when she wrote it—thirty years or well beyond that of the average undergraduate. And he is right too on the conventional phrasing, the diffuseness, and the loose connectives.[23] As for his asking the author to rewrite, his request is not unusual. Of the six Stein essays he read, he asked her to rewrite all or parts of three, though he gave her a choice of revising on one of these; and of the eight Segerblom themes he wanted rewriting of all or parts of three, but gave a choice of revising or rewriting three others, perhaps because he felt that rewriting would do no good.

But to return to his response to the Phillips essay on Alcott, one wonders whether Moody knew any of Alcott's books (he was born in the same year that the second part of *Little Women* appeared) and whether he had the ambivalent attitude toward it and its sequels generally held in the literary community. Finally, Moody might have entertained the possibility (as I have) that the meeting with Alcott was a fictional projection on Phillips' part—the coincidence of their being seated at the same hotel table perhaps going too far in this delightful fantasy!

Whatever Moody's knowledge of *Little Women,* Phillips knew the book well, as the most specific allusions—Jo meeting Apollyon on the river and others on the Concord visit—bear out. Though Polly appears in *An Old-Fashioned Girl* (1870), she is properly paired with Jo, since she has many of Jo's characteristics. Jo as an aunt does not emerge until *Little Men* (1871), third in the series, though she is technically an aunt (since her sister Meg has twins) in *Little Women* itself, and her persona merges with the author's increasingly, as the six miscellanies entitled *Aunt Jo's Scrap-Bag* (1872-1882) remind us. The girl Rose plays a part in *Eight Cousins* (1875), fourth in the series, and the main part in its sequel *Rose in Bloom* (1876). While some *Little Women* devotees may object to Phillips' notation "how good that Beth got well" in view of her dying in the second part of the novel, she does survive an attack of scarlet fever in the first part, when everyone has given up hope of her living.

As I suggested, I have speculated from time to time on the actuality of the meeting of Phillips and Alcott. It has seemed so fitly fortuitous that I am partly sorry to have verified it as a fact through the discovery of three letters from Alcott to a "Florence,"[24] who turns out definitely to be the writer of the essay. The three letters[25] deserve printing for their bearing on the Phillips-Alcott relationship and for the additional insight they provide of Louisa May Alcott in her final years.

Alcott almost certainly wrote the first letter of December 26 in 1885, acknowledging the Christmas gift of roses mentioned at the end of the Phillips essay. Main evidence for dating is the reference to *The Alcott Calendar for 1886,* which would have been marketed in the holiday season of late 1885 and which may have reproduced the Walton Ricketson bas-relief.[26] Though it is tempting to regard those roses as having been sent on Christmas, 1887 (the Christmas before Alcott's death on March 6, 1888), Phillips telescopes the time in her essay. As for the two winter visits of which she writes, one suspects that they came after the gift, perhaps in response to the letter of thanks, or again, with the fusion of time in the essay, that they may have been in separate years.

Dec. 26*th*

Dear Florence.

Many thanks for the roses & the Xmas wishes. Both were very sweet & pleasant to receive on that day, & I hope came from a happy, busy girl who begins to find her efforts & hopes blossom into contentment & peace of mind.

I have been poorly for some time, but keep about & am not quite a drone. We are in B. you know, & the boys & Mrs P.[27] enjoy it very much.

Lulu is losing her teeth & looks like a little granny, but is well & busy with school & play.

Have you had an Alcott Calender? If not let me send you one. They go very well & Fred is very fine with his first literary success.

The bas-relief is done, & people like it. Mr R. prefers softness to strength so has missed what I like best, but the old lady looks young & amiable, & as she was some ten or fifteen years ago. Are you going to have one?

I wish I had something *very* lovely to send you, but perhaps a very earnest wish for help & happiness is what you would like best, & much love

from your *friend* L. M. A.

Further support that the letter of December 26, 1885, is the first of the three comes from a less intimate tone than appears in the other letters, though this is the only one in which Alcott sends her love. The dating, especially in conjunction with the next letter, sets the latest possible year for Phillips' visit to Nonquitt as 1885. That year is also likely, since it seems more in keeping with the time that the young woman would not have traveled alone to Boston until she was twenty-one, which she had just become.[28] Under "May & June" the 1885 diary notes that Alcott settled in a little cottage with Lulu and her governess, most likely on June 20, with later entries indicating that she stayed until August 8. Though Lulu and the governess are not mentioned in the theme, it may be expected to focus on Louisa May Alcott alone. However, quite possibly the visit could have taken place anytime beginning in 1881, when Alcott first went to Nonquitt; and Lulu, the daughter of Alcott's sister May, who had died soon after her daughter's birth in 1879, would have been with her aunt since the first Nonquitt summer.[29]

The second letter follows on June 10, 1886, with the year established by Alcott's 1886 diary entry under "June" that shows her to be at Mt. Wachusett and to have just read Hedge's new book. The letter also points to the Nonquitt visit as in 1885, for if Phillips had met Alcott the previous June, quite probably she wrote the next year with the hope of seeing her again. Interestingly, it reverts to the "perplexities" for which Phillips had sought advice one evening at Nonquitt, and invites further correspondence.

Mt Wachuset.

June 10*th*

Dear Florence,

Your kind letter finds me on the hillside trying to get strength for home cares & duties after a winter of illness & idleness.

Dont despair, my dear, one gathers strength from falls, & experience is a grand teacher stern as she seems.

I am a very despondent old soul, & nothing but duty & an ever growing faith in the great Helper keeps me from despair when year after year goes by with no record but suffering.

Pain is *my* teacher, & my lesson to give up, to wait & be cheerful, [ca. 2 letters missing].[30] A serene soul can ma[ke] a feeble body <of> [un?] burden if it can only keep up high enough.

I am glad any words of mine help you, I wish I could set you a better example, but one's failures often serve others, & so have a use. I am not going to Nonquit this year but shall be here & at home.

No N.Y. nor any pleasure trips for me yet. I still hope but make no plans.

What are you reading? If you like German writers Hedge's new book "Hours with the German Classics" is good. I enjoyed it very much.

Write to me when you feel like it & tell me any troubles I can help. Keep hoping & trying, & be sure the strength & light will come, for no sincere effort is ever wasted.

With best wishes for a happy summer I am

    affectionately yrs [signature clipped out]

The letter of December 7 cannot be dated with the certainty of that of June 10, but very likely it belongs to 1886 too. Alcott probably did not move into the Dunreath Place sanatorium in Roxbury until January 1, 1887, and she had begun the fall of 1886 at 10 Louisburg Square, where she had been the winter before. Though she was ill "with my dyspepsia" throughout 1886, it does not appear from her diaries that she was nearly as ill as in 1887, a year in which her almost daily entries read like a medical casebook of a woman painfully dying. Yet at the end of 1887 she rallied and could conclude that year with the comment: "A hard year, but over now. Please God the next be happier for us all."[31]

Dec. 7*th.*

Dear Florence

I am always glad to hear from you, & to find that you are "creeping on," though I dare say I should think you were learning ↑to↓ walk fast if I saw you.

Being mortal we cannot expect to fly, & must content ourselves with a long slow climb, glad if each year we are one step higher than the last.

Watch, wait, *try* & leave the end to time sure that all will be well if we are patient, trusting & cheerful. It is hard for youn[g][32] people to believe th[at] *everything* has to wait, & in their hurry then are apt to help open the buds & so spoil them instead of letting them bloom as God pleases.

Find some poor people to help, even one girl to cheer up, or a child to clothe, & it will do you good. I'm very poorly with my dyspepsia & I cheer myself up by looking after a very destitute family, & giving them the food I cant eat. Try it.

We are in Boston where we were last winter, & Lulu is blooming and good with an excellent governess.

It *is* a comfort to know that out of my own experiences & trials I have extracted help or pleasure for others. I

suppose that was why they were sent me. Write when you feel like it. With much hope & all good wishes yr friend [signature clipped out]

The letter of December 7, 1886, if I have correctly surmised the date, is the most exhortational of the three; yet it still has the quality of moving, especially in view of the troubled life of the older woman at the time. Probably Florence Phillips continued to feel the "warmth," to use her term at the close of her essay, even though the moralizing seems to me to tend toward the expedient ethic that becomes increasingly prominent in the *Little Women* sequels—"Be nice to others because you'll feel nicer yourself," to put it rudely. Still, here is a girl who, like so many of her generation, found in Jo, that "dear splendid tom-boy," a real liberation; and as a young woman she found in Jo's creator much of Jo herself, a "beautiful spirit," whom we admire for her resilience and humanity.[33] But one regrets that the later fortnightly themes of Florence Phillips have disappeared along with Moody's comments. Whether under his sympathetic reading she achieved a less diluted "quality which touches and convinces the reader" we shall probably never know.

Notes

1. The comment and theme are owned by the author of this article. Moody's criticism and his later marginal commentary are printed with the kind permission of Frederick J. Fawcett, 2nd. Republication of all manuscript materials printed in this article requires the same permissions as are indicated here and elsewhere.

2. Moody's career at Harvard receives extended treatment in Maurice F. Brown, *Estranging Dawn: The Life and Works of William Vaughn Moody* (Carbondale, Ill., 1973). I am also indebted to Mr. Brown for help on many problems.

3. Rosalind S. Miller, *Gertrude Stein: Form and Intelligibility* (New York, 1949). Of the forty-seven themes printed, seven are fortnightlies with extended commentary, of which six are read by Moody. Of the remaining forty, two are rewritten fortnightlies and the rest are daily themes.

4. James D. Hart, ed., *A Novelist in the Making* (Cambridge, Mass., 1970), pp. 13 and 15. The forty-four extant themes by Norris are all dailies, all but seven relating to *Blix, McTeague,* and *Vandover and the Brute.* Mr. Hart's introduction includes an illuminating description of English 22.

5. William W. Whalen, of the University Archives, has generously searched the English 22 essay files for those corrected by Moody and has found only this set. Quotations are with the permission of Mr. Fawcett (see n. 1) and of the Harvard University Library. Segerblom (1872-1941) taught chemistry at Phillips Exeter Academy from 1899 to 1937; author of several books, he also published many articles and pamphlets.

6. Daniel G. Mason, ed., *Some Letters of William Vaughn Moody* (Boston, 1913), p. 23.

7. Grace N. Veeder, *Concerning William Vaughn Moody* (Waukesha, Wis., 1941), 19 pp.; Charlotte Wilson [Baker], "The Gift" (ca. 1913), 6 pp. Both works have been courteously supplied by Jane Colokathis, of the John Regenstein Library, University of Chicago. I have not tried to locate themes done at Chicago that were corrected by Moody.

8. Elizabeth Shenton, Assistant to the Director, the Arthur and Elizabeth Schlesinger Library, Radcliffe College, has kindly provided me with information on Florence Phillips in the archives. Inquiries in the usual places have not yielded further knowledge of her, and I would of course welcome a fuller biography from someone who knew her.

9. Moody wrote "except" before "but" and cancelled it.

10. The underlining of "almost" here and in the next paragraph is by Phillips.

11. Moody's vertical line from "remained" through "as well" applied these remarks to the whole passage.

12. Here, as usually elsewhere, in correcting run-on sentences Moody writes over the comma with an "x," which I have transcribed as a period. On this occasion he writes over the "I" of the essay with his own "I"—obviously the result of habit in capitalizing the first letter of a new sentence.

13. Phillips had deleted "her" with its uncertain antecedent and inserted "my governess," while Moody cancels "my governess" and restores "her." Students seldom win!

14. An apostrophe in "Mothers" appears probably in pencil, here omitted as a late correction. See also n. 23.

15. Not located. Phillips may have confused the *St. Nicholas* sketch with one in *The Youth's Companion*, but that has not been located either.

16. Moody has drawn a line between the first underlined "Boston" and the second.

17. A vertical line applies "Diffuse" to the whole sentence.

18. The underlining is by Phillips.

19. A vertical line probably applies the comment to the passage from "Why I knew" through "Nonquitt wharf."

20. An illegible word is inserted at this point in a somewhat darker ink than is usual in the essay and in handwriting probably not that of Phillips. Underlining of "that" at the end of the paragraph is by Phillips.

21. Moody's vertical line applies "Very charming" to the whole passage beginning with "sleep much that night!" toward the start of the paragraph.

22. Moody's comment may apply only to the cancelled phrase, but it begins where he underlines "toward the summer sea"—otherwise unexplained.

23. Like most theme readers, Moody does not catch everything. Most notably he is casual about missing apostrophes and irregular capitalization. Though he corrects most run-on sentences, they do not upset him as much as they still upset many.

24. The discovery owes to the careful search of the Alcott papers at the Houghton Library by Mrs. Richard B. Currier, of the Manuscript Department. She has also identified for me the Alcott diaries of 1885, 1886, and 1887. Though no references to Florence Phillips appear in them, they provide background for these later years. I am also indebted to John C. MacLean, of Orchard House, Concord, for carefully reading and describing the 1888 diary.

25. Printed here by the kind permission of the Louisa May Alcott Association and of the Houghton Library.

26. Raymond L. Kilgour, *Messrs. Roberts Brothers Publishers* (Ann Arbor, Mich., 1952), p. 227, describes the calendar as containing "Louisa's portrait and views of Concord homes." I have not been able to locate a copy. Though the Ricketson bas-relief was to appear as the frontispiece of *Jo's Boys*, published about October 9, 1886, the announcement that "The bas-relief is done" hardly suggests book publication, but appearance in the calendar seems possible.

27. Mrs. Anna Alcott Pratt and Louisa May Alcott's two nephews, John Sewall Pratt Alcott (whom his aunt adopted on July 10, 1887) and Frederick Alcott Pratt.

28. The essay speaks of Louisa May Alcott as "past fifty" (she was born in late 1832) and notes her mother's death (late 1877) as "ten years ago." This chronology, a bit inconsistent, still allows 1885 as reasonable.

29. Madeleine B. Stern, *Louisa May Alcott* (Norman, Okla., 1950, 1971), pp. 283-284 and 292-294. The book has provided most of my biographical information, and in addition Ms. Stern has helped grately by patiently providing further guidance.

30. These brackets and the two pairs following mark the clipping of the signature on the verso of the sheet. In this letter and the next, standard editorial symbols show Alcott's few corrections.

31. Printed here by the kind permission of the Louisa May Alcott Association and of the Houghton Library.

32. Again the brackets mark the clipping of the signature on the verso.

33. Martha Saxton, *Louisa May: A Modern Biography of Louisa May Alcott* (Boston, 1977), takes a different view of both *Little Women* and its author: "Jo's development is a sweetly sentimental version of the journey everyone has expected to make" (p. 4). "[Alcott] was divided between the impulsive,

outgoing, opinionated, large-spirited woman she was meant to be and the withdrawn, hostile introvert who kept that vital woman locked up" (p. 7).

FURTHER READING

Biography

Brown, Maurice F. *Estranging Dawn: The Life and Works of William Vaughn Moody.* Carbondale and Edwardsville: Southern Illinois University Press, 1973, 321 p.

> Describes Moody as "a talented and intelligent poet and dramatist, caught between the gestures of a dying nineteenth-century tradition and the emerging demands of twentieth-century experience" and assesses Moody's relevance to late twentieth-century readers.

Criticism

Bush, Douglas. "American Poets." In his *Mythology and the Romantic Tradition in English Poetry,* pp. 481-525. Cambridge, Mass.: Harvard University Press, 1969.

> Discusses the Promethean dramas of Harvard poets Moody, Trumbull Stickney, and George Cabot Lodge.

Flint, Allen. "Black Response to Colonel Shaw." *Phylon* XLV, No. 3 (1984): 210-19.

> Considers "An Ode in Time of Hesitation" in a discussion of works inspired by Colonel Robert Gould Shaw and the Massachusetts 54th Regiment, the first African American regiment to fight in the American Civil War.

Gregory, Horace, and Zaturenska, Marya. "William Vaughn Moody and His Circle." In their *A History of American Poetry, 1900-1940,* pp. 25-43. New York: Harcourt, Brace and Co., 1946.

> Introductory discussion of Moody, Stickney, and Lodge along with their contemporaries Ridgely Torrence and Josephine Preston Peabody.

Halpern, Martin. *William Vaughn Moody.* New York: Twayne, 1964, 208 p.

> Critical survey attempting to "describe, interpret, and evaluate the whole body of William Vaughn Moody's published work in poetry and the drama."

Loggins, Vernon. "William Vaughn Moody." In his *I Hear America . . . .: Literature in the United States since 1900,* pp. 45-51. New York: Thomas Y. Crowell Co., 1937.

> Biographical and critical sketch that judges Moody "one of the most gifted of American poets, and one of the most disappointing."

Review of *The Faith Healer,* by William Vaughn Moody. *The Nation* 88, No. 2,277 (18 February 1909): 175-76.

> Suggests that the play "would be stronger if it were clearer in meaning and purpose, more definite in argument and declaration," yet concludes that "Moody has written a thoughtful and suggestive work, which, whether it wins success upon the stage or not, will make a strong appeal to the imagination of all intelligent readers."

Payne, William Morton. "Two Poetic Dramas." *The Dial* XXXVI, No. 430 (16 May 1904): 319-23.

> Favorable review of *The Fire-Bringer.* According to Payne, Moody's work "shows us that even in this prosaic modern world of ours the poetic spirit may still achieve something of the accent and the utterance of the great voices of the past."

Perry, Bliss. "Thomas Wentworth Higginson, Julia Ward Howe, Francis Marion Crawford, William Vaughn Moody." In *Commemorative Tributes of the American Academy of Arts and Letters, 1905- 1941,* pp. 31-37. New York: American Academy of Arts and Letters, 1942.

> Obituary tribute concluding that in his literary works Moody "chose high and hard paths, but paths which were surely leading to serenity of vision, as they had already led him into the secret places of beauty and close to the passionate and troubled heart of the sons of Eve."

Willcox, Louise Collier. "Some Recent Poetry." *North American Review* 182, No. 5 (May 1906): 751-53.

> Appreciative review of *Poems* and *The Fire-Bringer.* Willcox comments: "There are two points that we look at in judging a new poet, imagery and diction, and in these two points only one poet of late years, Francis Thompson, and he already a classic, stands higher than Moody."

Additional coverage of Moody's life and career is contained in the following sources published by the Gale Group: *Contemporary Authors,* **Vol. 110; and** *Dictionary of Literary Biography,* **Vols. 7, 54.**

Dylan Thomas
1914-1953

(Full name Dylan Marlais Thomas) Welsh poet, short story writer, dramatist, screenplay writer, critic, and novelist.

The following entry presents criticism of Thomas's prose works. For further discussion of Thomas's life and works see *TCLC,* Volumes 1, 8, and 45.

INTRODUCTION

Remembered as a poet who pursued a bohemian lifestyle that included heavy alcohol drinking and womanizing, Thomas also created several respected works of short fiction. In the 1930s, when such poets as W. H. Auden and Stephen Spender established a trend of socially and politically conscious poetry, Thomas pursued more personal themes whose source was his own memory and imagination. The worlds of childhood, dream, and nature are pervasive throughout his poetry and prose, and are celebrated in a rich and often abstruse literary style.

BIOGRAPHICAL INFORMATION

Thomas was born and raised in Swansea, South Wales. His father was a grammar school English teacher. Thomas's first poems were printed in small literary journals and he published his first volume of poetry, *18 Poems* (1934), when he was nineteen. In 1939 Thomas moved to London to work for the BBC, writing and performing radio broadcasts. After World War II, financial need prompted him to devote more energy to his lucrative short stories and screenplays rather than to his poetry. Later Thomas gained public attention as a captivating reader of his own poetry and prose. At the height of his popularity in the early 1950s, Thomas agreed to a series of public poetry readings in America, bringing about a revival of the oral reading of poetry. Though Thomas was well-received on tour, his biographers report, he drank prodigiously and behaved outrageously. In late 1953, Thomas died of a brain hemorrhage.

MAJOR WORKS

Thomas's early work, *18 Poems,* belongs to his Swansea period of 1930-1934, when he drew upon his childhood and adolescent experiences for his poetry. Often described as incantatory, these poems record Thomas's experimentation with vibrant imagery and with sound as "verbal mu-

sic." A slightly later work, *The Map of Love* (1939), a collection of poetry and short stories, displays signs of his dabbling in surrealistic technique.

The physical and psychic havoc of World War II deeply affected Thomas, a conscientious objector, and shaped the major work of his middle period, which began with *Deaths and Entrances* (1946). In this volume Thomas's language and imagery became simpler, calmer, and more intelligible as he directs his vision and poetry toward the events and individuals around him. In his final volume of poems, *In Country Sleep* (1952), Thomas comes to terms with life while confronting the reality of his own death.

Thomas wrote mostly prose and screenplays during the last years of his life. Previous to this period, his most important prose pieces were his semiautobiographical short stories, *Portrait of the Artist as a Young Dog* (1940), which stylistically and thematically bear comparison to James Joyce's *Dubliners* and *Portrait of the Artist as a Young Man.* Both Joyce's and Thomas's works offer negative views of their respective backgrounds—Ireland and

Wales—each depicting what "for artists," as Kenneth Seib observed, "is a world of death, sterility, and spiritual debasement." The most popular prose piece to issue from Thomas's later period is his play for voices, *Under Milk Wood* (1954). Again critics noted the similarities between Thomas and James Joyce. In *Under Milk Wood* and Joyce's *Ulysses,* each author captures the life of a whole society as it is reflected in a single day; for Joyce it is the urban life in Dublin, while for Thomas it is the Welsh village of Llaregyub.

CRITICAL RECEPTION

From the outset of Thomas's career there has been much critical disagreement as to his stature as a poet and short story writer. Many commentators cite Thomas's work as being too narrow and unvarying; he essentially confines himself to the lyric expression of what Stephen Spender labeled "certain primary, dithyrambic occasions," chiefly birth, love, and death. Edith Sitwell spoke for many critics as she puzzled over the poet's distorted syntax and religious symbolism. The influence of the seventeenth-century metaphysical poets is often cited in connection with Thomas's unorthodox religious imagery; while the influence of the Romantic poets is seen in his recurrent vision of a pristine beauty in childhood and nature. Thomas's vivid imagery, involved word play, fractured syntax, and personal symbology did, however, change the course of modern poetry. Though a poet of undetermined rank, he set a new standard for many mid-twentieth-century poets. His prose work is often viewed by critics as financial enterprises, although it shares much thematically with his more respected poetry.

PRINCIPAL WORKS

18 Poems (poetry) 1934
Twenty-Five Poems (poetry) 1936
The Map of Love (poetry and short stories) 1939
The World I Breathe (poetry and sketches) 1939
Portrait of the Artist as a Young Dog (short stories) 1940
New Poems (poetry) 1943
Deaths and Entrances (poetry) 1946
Twenty-six Poems (poetry) 1950
Collected Poems, 1934-1952 (poetry) 1952
In Country Sleep (poetry) 1952
The Doctor and the Devils (drama) 1953
A Prospect of the Sea, and Other Stories and Prose (short stories and sketches) 1954
Quite Early One Morning (sketches and essays) 1954
Under Milk Wood (verse drama) 1954
Adventures in the Skin Trade, and Other Stories (unfinished novel and short stories) 1955
The Notebooks of Dylan Thomas (notebooks) 1967
Poet in the Making: The Notebooks of Dylan Thomas (poetry, short stories, and sketches) 1968

The Death of the King's Canary [with John Davenport] (novel) 1976
Collected Stories (short stories) 1980

CRITICISM

Jacob Korg (essay date 1965)

SOURCE: "Stories and Plays," in *Dylan Thomas,* Twayne Publishers, Inc., 1965, pp. 154-82.

[*In the following essay, Korg divides Thomas's nonpoetic works into two areas: fantasies and straightforward narratives.*]

I

Thomas was as prolific a writer of prose as of verse. He published the first of his short stories, **"After the Fair,"** in March, 1934, less than a year after his earliest poems had appeared; and he continued to write prose until his death. In addition to his numerous short stories, the uncompleted novel, *Adventures in the Skin Trade,* three prose dramas, the radio play, *Under Milk Wood,* and the two film scripts, *The Doctor and the Devils* and *The Beach at Falesá,* he wrote a number of book reviews, radio talks, and descriptive essays, many of them collected in the posthumous volume, *Quite Early One Morning.*[1]

Thomas' fiction may be divided sharply into two classifications: vigorous fantasies in poetic style, a genre he discontinued after 1939; and straightforward, objective narratives. Until 1939 he seems to have thought of the short prose narrative as an alternate poetic form—as a vehicle for recording the action of the imagination in reshaping objective reality according to private desire. Almost every story of this period (the exceptions being **"After the Fair"** and **"The Tree"**) perceives actuality through the screen of an irrational mind. The main characters are madmen, simpletons, fanatics, lechers, and poets in love: people enslaved by the dictates of feeling. Their stories are narrated in a heavily poetic prose reflecting the confusion of actual and imaginary experiences which constitutes their reality, so that the material and psychological intersect without a joint, forming a strange new area of being. For example, as Mr. Davies, the deluded rector of **"The Holy Six,"** is washing the feet of his six colleagues, believing that he is performing a holy deed, we are told that "light brought the inner world to pass," that his misconception was transformed into actuality. Some of the stories seem transitional in style, enabling the reader to witness these transformations as an outsider. In **"The Dress,"** the fleeing madman, who yearns for a chance to sleep, thinks of sleep as personified by another object of desire—a girl. When he breaks into the cottage where the young housewife is sitting, he follows the logic of his delusion, mistakes her for sleep, and puts his head in her lap.

The setting of most of these stories is the seaside Welsh town wickedly called Llareggub (to be read backwards), also the scene of *Under Milk Wood,* with its neighboring countryside, including a valley named after Jarvis, a lecherous nineteenth-century landlord, some farms, and a mountain called Cader Peak. Among the inhabitants of this region are young men obsessed by unfulfilled love, as in **"The Mouse and the Woman"** and **"The Orchards"**; clergymen crazed by lust, as in **"The Holy Six"** and **"The Burning Baby"**; wise men or women who teach some cabalistic magic art, as in **"The Tree," "The Map of Love," "The School for Witches,"** and **"The Lemon"**; and enigmatic girls who rise from the sea or the soil as in **"The Mouse and the Woman"** and **"A Prospect of the Sea."** The fancies of these people, narrated in a manner rendering them indistinguishable from objective reality, fill the town and the countryside with visions, supernatural forces, and fantastic episodes recalling the world of fairy tale and of folklore. People and objects are whisked into new shapes, small and intimate experiences are magnified until they embody fundamental realities—"creation screaming in the steam of the kettle"—and the order of nature is constantly subject to disruption. In this milieu the anomalous is the ordinary; at the end of **"Prologue to an Adventure,"** for example, the barroom where the two friends are standing runs down the drains of the town into the sea.

In one of his letters to Vernon Watkins, Thomas observes that the reader of verse needs an occasional rest but that the poet ought not to give it to him; this sustained intensity is more natural to poetry than to prose. In applying this principle to his stories, Thomas produced complex, involuted narratives with rich surfaces of language and imagery. At first impression they have no depths; but analysis shows that the order of imagination operating in them is the one which produced Thomas' poetry. His stories, unlike his earliest poems, deal with recognizable people and places; but they invest them with the same mythic atmosphere found in the poems. As we have already observed, there are numerous and detailed affinities between the poems and these early, fantastic stories. Common themes, the burning of a child, the "falling" of time, the unity of life, and the verbal capacities of nature provide subjects for both, and are also reflected in rhetorical details. But the most general resemblance is an awareness of the cosmic import of small events, a tendency to develop the significance of experiences by referring them to the absolute limits of the continuum of which they are a part. The lust of Rhys Rhys in **"The Burning Baby"** culminates in incest and in the murder of his child; the desire of the poet in **"The Mouse and the Woman"** raises a beautiful woman for him on the seashore; the vision of heaven the boy sees from the top of his ladder in **"A Prospect of the Sea"** is an endless Eden stretching to meet itself above and below.

II

In **"The Tree,"** which first appeared in the *Adelphi* in December, 1934, within a week of the publication of *18 Po-*

ems, the style typical of Thomas' fantastic stories is still at an early stage of its development, so that it is possible to distinguish actual events from the delusions going on in the minds of the characters. The story also provides a convenient dramatization of the creative process at work in these stories. The gardener transmits his obsession to the boy; the boy, at the end of the story, tries to transform it into actuality. In writing his fantastic stories, Thomas, the narrator, acted the part of the boy. Borrowing delusions from his characters, Thomas produced in the narrative itself a version of reality corresponding to the delusions.

The gardener in the story is a naïve religious who, by one of those primitive metaphorical associations familiar to us from Thomas' poems, takes all trees as counterparts of the "tree" of the cross. As he tells the boy the story of Jesus, the child fixes on the elder tree in the garden as the scene of the crucifixion. When he is let into the locked tower as a Christmas gift, the boy is bitterly disappointed to find it empty; but he associates the Jarvis hills, which are visible through the window, with Bethlehem; for they, like Bethlehem, are toward the east. The idiot standing under the tree in the garden, exposed to the wind and rain, has already had Christlike intimations of his destiny when the boy finds him in the morning. And when the boy learns that he has come from the eastern hills that he has mistaken for Bethlehem, he fits the tree, the hills, and the idiot into the pattern described by the gardener, and sets about making the story of Jesus a reality. As the story closes, he has put the idiot against the tree and is crucifying him on it. The ultimate point of the story is the idiot's acceptance of his suffering; in the final scene the ignorant piety of the gardener is being transformed, through the imagination of the child and the love and humility of the idiot, into a reality.

The narrative style blending actual and imagined worlds appears for the first time in **"The Visitor,"** whose main character, as he approaches death, perceives the continuity between the living and dead aspects of the cosmos. Because we know the actual world which is the background of his delusion, we can see that the first part of the narrative has a double structure; and we can easily separate Peter's delusions from external reality. His idea that the sheets are shrouds, that his heart is a clock ticking, and that he lacks feelings because he is dead are simply misinterpretations of sensory clues. Only occasionally does his mind drift into clear hallucination, as when he thinks he is looking down at his own dead face in the coffin. Otherwise his thoughts are perfectly intelligible; he recalls that his first wife died seven years earlier in childbirth, and the guilt he experiences is expressed in a remarkable metaphor: "He felt his body turn to vapour, and men who had been light as air walked, metal-hooved, through and beyond him."

In the second part of the story, however, we enter fully into Peter's dying delirium and the basis of fact offered by the external world fades away. In a region of pure fantasy, we are unable, like Peter himself, to distinguish the imaginary from the real or even to detect the moment of division between life and death. In his delirium, Callaghan, the visitor Peter has been expecting, comes and carries him away into a realm of essential being where the pulsations of alternate growth and destruction are perfectly visible in a stripped, transparent landscape. Here a new prose style, the one Thomas adopts as a means of objectifying mystical perception, presents itself. More descriptive than narrative, it is full of grotesque, clearly realized images. Sometimes rhapsodic, sometimes strangely matter of fact, it seeks to capture the disruption imposed upon nature by hallucinatory vision. As in the poems, metaphor ceases to compare, and equates instead, so that "the flowers shot out of the dead," and "the light of the moon . . . pulled the moles and badgers out of their winter."

The journey ends when Peter, suddenly returned to his sickbed again, feels restored to his body and speaks to his wife. But she does not hear him, and he does not realize he is dead until she pulls the sheet over his face. Just as he had the delusion, when he was living, that he was dead, so at the end Peter has the delusion, when he is dead, that he is alive. The division between the two states is slight, and disembodied vitality persists so powerfully that moving from the aspect of being we call life to the one we call death hardly matters to it. As one of the poems concludes, "The heart is sensual, though five eyes break."

In **"The Visitor,"** Peter experiences actual and imaginary realms at different times; the two meet only at the boundary between them, where their edges are not clear. But in the further development of his narrative style, Thomas presented situations where imagined and actual events are superimposed upon one another as single experiences. Two closely related short stories published in 1936, **"The Orchards"** and **"The Mouse and the Woman,"** illustrate this. Both have the same theme as **"The Hunchback in the Park"**: the creation of an imaginary woman by a mind obsessed by the need for love. And both are tragedies of delusion, for they show that the dreamer is pitifully exposed to the demands of the actual world.

The woman loved by Marlais, the poet of **"The Orchards,"** comes to him in a dream in the form of a scarecrow who stands, with her sister, in a landscape of burning orchards. When he wakes up, the memory of this dream persists and distracts him from his writing. Oppressed by the disparity between the passion of his dream thoughts and the dullness of the town outside his window, Marlais makes an effort of the imagination which leads him to mystic perception. What follows is perhaps Thomas' most complete description of mystic vision. The distinction between objective and subjective is canceled: "There was dust in his eyes; there were eyes in the grains of dust. . . ." Individual things seem part of greater wholes, saturated with absolute significance: "His hand before him was five-fingered life." Opposites are reconciled: "It is all one, the loud voice and the still voice striking a common silence. . . ." Intoxicated with the feeling that he commands both spiritual and actual realms, so that he is "man

among ghosts, and ghost in clover," Marlais now "moved for the last answer."

A second sleep shows him that the landscape of his dream and the woman he loves are still there; and when he wakes he goes out of the town to find it. The second half of the story, like that of **"The Visitor,"** is the journey of a mental traveler; but Marlais travels on the ground, not in the air, as Peter does. And his imagined world is spread over the real countryside, whose objective features emerge, like peaks rising out of the clouds of his thoughts. The Whippet valley, a part of the real countryside which has been destroyed by mining, is succeeded by a wood whose trees are said to spring from the legend of the Fall. As his walk continues, Marlais enters the realm of myth and becomes a myth himself; when he has penetrated into this imaginary world, he finds the orchards of his dream and the girl in it. An objective observer would probably say that Marlais had been invited to have a picnic tea with an ordinary girl; for the tablecloth, cups, and bread she produces are real enough. But, as Marlais views the scene, the conditions of his dream impose themselves upon this objective reality, and the scene is transformed to correspond with it. The orchards break into fire; the girl is changed into a scarecrow and calls up her sister, as in the dream; and Marlais has his desire.

But we have been warned at the beginning that Marlais' passion was "a story more terrible than the stories of the reverend madmen in the Black Book of Llareggub," and the conclusion tells us why. The fires of Marlais' dream are put out by "the real world's wind," and it becomes a fact, not a dream. The imaginative tide of his obsession recedes, leaving him stranded in actuality, kissing a scarecrow, and exposing his madness.

"The Mouse and the Woman" is a more elaborate treatment of the same theme: the betrayal of a poet by his obsession with love. In this story, as in **"The Orchards,"** the hero creates a dream woman, and he shuttles back and forth between a dream world and a waking world that seem equally real. But Thomas has added to the situation a moral aspect represented by the mouse. The story opens with a remarkable description of the madman in the lunatic asylum, and it then moves back in his memory to trace the steps of his alienation. As in **"The Orchards,"** the woman comes to him in a dream, and her memory persists when he is awake until he is caught between reality and delusion; he does not know whether to believe in her existence or not. He creates her by writing about her, ". . . it was upon the block of paper that she was made absolute," thus surrendering to imagination; he then goes out on the beach to find her and bring her to his cottage. This begins the part of the story where hallucination is perfectly superimposed upon actuality. The girl is, of course, pure imagination; but the mouse, which is associated with evil, and the mousehole the hero nails up to keep it away seem representative of objective actuality. Oddly, within this waking dream the hero has nocturnal dreams containing frightening enigmatic symbols. When he strips the girl and becomes her lover, two related events follow: the mouse emerges from its hole; and the notion of original sin enters the consciousness of the lovers as the man tells the girl the story of the Fall. She realizes that he has felt evil in their relationship.

The mouse and what it represents are the seed of destruction in his euphoric delusion; for the woman leaves him. Though he pursues her, she will not have him back. Her rejection of him is marvelously conveyed in the fairy tale episode where he lights upon her hand, like an insect, pleads with her, and is crushed as she closes her hand over him. Since he has created her by thought, he can kill her by thought. He writes "The woman died" on his writing pad, and we are told that "There was dignity in such a murder." He sees her dead body lying on the beach. But the knowledge that "he had failed . . . to hold his miracle" is too much for him, and he becomes the madman who appears at the beginning of the story.

The story goes a step further than **"The Orchards,"** for it explains why the certainty offered by delusion should disappear. The poet's sense of guilt, emerging from within his mind as the mouse emerges from the walls of the house, poisons his dream. His derangements are no longer orderly and joyful, but confused: "The secret of that alchemy that had turned a little revolution of the unsteady senses into a golden moment was lost as a key is lost in the undergrowth." He has regained some contact with the objective world, but he wants to kill the woman. And, in order to do this, he must return to the world of imagination where she exists. In killing her, he also kills the dream she dominates, on which his happiness depends. The mouse, now fully in possession of the kitchen, silently presides over the grief he feels at this self-destruction. Trapped between two systems of reality and unable to commit himself to either, the poet can only howl at life from behind the bars of the asylum.

In four stories published in 1937 and 1938, the hallucinatory technique advances so far that it is no longer possible—or desirable—to disentangle imagined from actual episodes. External reality responds flexibly to the thoughts and feelings of the characters, so that the narrative amounts to a psychological allegory. This genre, it will be recalled, is the one to which **"Ballad of the Long-Legged Bait"** belongs, and two of the four stories now under discussion are so closely related to this poem that they seem to be prose sketches for it. The member of this group closest to the earlier stories is **"A Prospect of the Sea."** It has the same elements as **"The Orchards"** and **"The Mouse and the Woman"**: a girl who is encountered at the seashore, and who disappears, and a delirious shuttling back and forth between different orders of reality.

In **"A Prospect of the Sea,"** the boy begins by enjoying the summer day and then makes up a story about a drowned princess; but this level of thought is intersected by another—the appearance of a country girl who confronts him in the actual landscape. This siren figure both tempts and terrifies him, for she has the power to make the world swell and shrink. His fantasies of death and disfigurement alternate with the actual events of her erotic advances. As evening comes, he yields himself to another daydream, a mystic's vision of power, piercing sight, and multiplied Edens. But the girl calls him into an actual world that is now strangely insubstantial: ". . . she could make a long crystal of each tree, and turn the house wood into gauze." She leads him on a race through a mystically disrupted realm; and then, in the morning, in spite of his agonized protests, she walks into the sea and disappears. As he turns to walk inland, he confronts the elements of the Noah story: an old man building a boat, the beginning of rainfall, and a stream of animals entering the door. Apparently, then, the episodes of the story belong to the corrupt time God had determined to end by means of the Flood.

But **"A Prospect of the Sea"** is an innocent pastoral in comparison with **"Prologue to an Adventure,"** a chronicle of town sin, a subject that offers a far richer opportunity for Thomas' grotesque metaphoric energies than the country scenes of the earlier stories. There is little action. The speaker wanders through the streets and, with an acquaintance named Daniel Dom (a variant of the name "Domdaniel" appearing in one of Thomas' unpublished poems),[2] visits two bars; then, as in **"A Prospect of the Sea,"** destructive water comes as the scene is immersed by waves.

The interest of this story lies in the remarkable play of scenes and imagery conveying the feverish atmosphere of a night on the town. "Now in the shape of a bald girl smiling, a wailing wanton with handcuffs for earrings, or the lean girls that live on pickings, now in ragged women with a muckrake curtseying in the slime, the tempter of angels whispered over my shoulder." As the speaker says, there is "more than man's meaning" in this torrent of fearsome, Hieronymus Boschlike visions, for holiness is caught up and debased in it. "I have the God of Israel in the image of a painted boy, and Lucifer, in a woman's shirt, pisses from a window in Damaroid Alley."

The two scenes in the bars are incoherent jumbles of fleeing images, glimpses of transcendental visions, and striking expressionistic effects. They look backward in technique and subject to the Circe scene of Joyce's *Ulysses* and forward to Thomas' *Doctor and the Devils* for their atmosphere of pinched debauchery. The speaker and his friend aspire for a moment to reach out of this welter of temptresses, oppressed children, and indifferent city streets to some heavenly goal, but they come instead to a new bar where, after joining the corrupt festivities, they turn to the window and witness the coming of the deluge. There are no alternate realms of reality in this story. It is all an inescapable mental reality, consisting entirely of representations of the desires, fears, suspicions, and other emotions of the narrator; for, as his visions tell him, "We are all metaphors of the sound of shape, of the shape of sound, break us we take another shape."

"In the Direction of the Beginning" and **"An Adventure from a Work in Progress"** are mythlike tales written in a hallucinatory style. The first, a short account of the creation, tells of the appearance of figures resembling Adam and Eve. Its enchanted, visionary prose presents a dizzying succession of images referring fleetingly to various seasons, ages, and episodes of history and legend. There is almost no physical action; the Fall is suggested as the man becomes entrapped by the woman's siren spell and as his obsession with her is projected through imagery showing that he feels her to be personified in every detail of the universe. The same obsession appears in **"An Adventure from a Work in Progress,"** an account of a man pursuing a shadowy woman through a strangely active archipelago where awesome cataclysms endanger him. At the climax of the story the woman merges with the mountain, just as the Eve in **"In the Direction of the Beginning"** merges with the soil. When the hero ultimately catches her, she undergoes a series of startling metamorphoses and shrinks to a tiny monster in the palm of his hand. After being thus betrayed by his obsession, like the lovers in **"The Orchards"** and **"The Mouse and the Woman,"** the hero returns from the imaginary world to the actual one, and sails away on "the common sea."

The "revolving islands and elastic hills" of this story show that it takes place in the realm that is more fully described in **"The Map of Love."** In the latter, the stages of sexual initiation are represented by a bewitched landscape; a curious animated map or model of this region exhibits its vital sexual properties, so that the children to whom it is being displayed blush at "the copulation in the second mud." The libido-charged land-scape represented by the map is the world as it presents itself to the heroes of the last two stories, who find the women they love embodied in cliffs, seas, and mountains. The children in **"The Map of Love"** are guided by Sam Rib, who is named for the origin of love, and are encouraged by the spirit of their lecherous Great-Uncle Jarvis, who speaks to them from the fields where he has lain with ten different mistresses. But they never succeed in swimming up the river to the island of the first beasts of love. Apparently, they are too shy, too lacking in lust; mere "synthetic prodigals" of Sam Rib's laboratory, they are unable to share the dangerous vitality of nature.

Four of the stories of this period form a separate subgroup; **"The Enemies," "The Holy Six," "The Burning Baby,"** and **"The School for Witches"** are all about the fictional town of Llareggub, and all are told in a narrative style that presents much objective material. Thomas has created a distinctive comic world in these stories, a world of lecherous, hypocritical clergymen and of submissive girls tumbling over an enchanted Welsh landscape into situations appropriate to myths and fairy tales. In **"The Enemies,"** Mr. Davies, the doddering rector of Llareggub, wanders onto the farm of Mr. and Mrs. Owen. The farmer and his wife are a strong pagan pair in tune with the fertility of the soil; and they feel pity for the poor rector who comes to them tired and bleeding, having been betrayed by the countryside where he has been lost. As they eat dinner in the pantheistic atmosphere of the Owen farm,

Mr. Davies is suddenly struck by the inadequacy of his own faith, and he falls to his knees to pray in fear. The story ends: "He stared and he prayed, like an old god beset by his enemies." Thomas is distinguishing between the religion he saw represented in the churches of Wales and the one he saw embodied in "the copulation in the tree . . . the living grease in the soil."

In **"The Holy Six,"** a sequel to **"The Enemies,"** Mr. Davies' adventure is turned into channels that are both comic and more deeply religious. Six of his colleagues receive a letter from Mrs. Owen informing them of Mr. Davies' plight. These six are confirmed lechers. "The holy life was a constant erection to these six gentlemen." Much of the story consists of uproarious descriptions of the visions their evil minds project upon actuality. (An allusion to Peter, the poet of **"The Visitor,"** who lives in the Jarvis valley where the Owen farm is, suggests that Thomas thought of all the Llareggub stories as interrelated, though he makes little effort to establish links among them.) When the Six arrive at the Jarvis valley, they find the countryside alien to them, just as Mr. Davies did; and the opposition between their hypocritical faith and that of the Owen couple is developed as Mrs. Owen sees the truth of things in her crystal ball.

Mr. Davies is brought forward, strangely transformed. He has apparently learned the lesson of the fertile soil, but his newly discovered passions have merged with his religious habits of mind to form a grotesque compound of lust and devotion: "his ghost who laboured . . . leapt out to marry Mary; all-sexed and nothing, intangible hermaphrodite riding the neuter dead, the minister of God in a grey image mounted dead Mary." He performs the service of washing the feet of his colleagues, while the thoughts of each are described, forming a series of remarkable surrealist fantasies. When he has finished this task, Mr. Davies cryptically claims the paternity of the child in Mrs. Owen's womb. Though Mr. Owen smiles at this, it is clear that Mr. Davies is right, for their "ghosts" have consummated a spiritual love in a realm different from that of the love of husband and wife.

Religious hypocrisy and repression are condemned in **"The Holy Six"** and in **"The Enemies"** mainly by comic means. But **"The Burning Baby"** treats this theme with a tragic force approaching grandeur. The spectacle of a child consumed by fire, as we know from his poems, impressed Thomas as the formulation of an ultimate question, for it involved the greatest imaginable suffering inflicted on the greatest imaginable innocence. Rhys Rhys, the vicar, who has been driven to seduce his daughter by an obsessive lust, burns the baby resulting from this union in an expurgatory ritual. The baby, like the devil, he considers "poor flesh," and he burns it to rid the earth of the fruit of the "foul womb" and of the evidence of his own sin. But Thomas, speaking in his own voice, corrects Rhys Rhys' view and insists upon the spiritual symmetry of nature: "The fruit of the flesh falls with the worm from the tree. Conceiving the worm, the bark crumbles. There lay the poor star of flesh that had dropped, like the bead of a woman's milk, through the nipples of a wormy tree." Though the child is dead, the flames awaken him to a shriek of protest which is significantly taken up by the landscape that witnesses his immolation.

"The Burning Baby" is probably the best-sustained and most carefully constructed of Thomas' early stories. Though it is about derangement, its style, with a few exceptions, is disciplined and objective. The moments when the emotions of the characters take over the story and shape the narration are clearly marked. For example, when Rhys Rhys is delivering his usual sermon, but thinking of his desire for his daughter, he thinks: ". . . the good flesh, the mean flesh, flesh of his daughter, flesh, flesh, the flesh of the voice of thunder howling before the death of man." At the moment of the incestuous union, the disruption of the normal order of feelings is reflected by a disruption of the normal conditions of external reality: "The lashes of her fingers lifted. He saw the ball under the nail." Minor events predict what is to come. Rhys Rhys' son, who he thinks is a changeling, brings in a dead rabbit, cradling it like a baby. The scene arouses Rhys Rhys' terrors, and he takes the dead rabbit away, thus appropriating death. But the changeling witnesses the seduction and the sacrifice of the baby, and he insanely re-enacts them after the others are dead.

"The School for Witches" is another story having a baby as the victim of worship, but this worship is not Christianity, but witchcraft. The cut accidentally inflicted on the black woman's baby at the moment of its birth is a warning that it is entering the "wicked world" of the school for witches where the black arts are taught. Most of the story is devoted to descriptions of the rituals, dances, and covens of the witches, the formalized evil that has risen from the cursed and bedeviled countryside. The doctor, the only lucid character, has bleak meditations as he and the midwife carry the baby back to his house: "What purpose there was in the shape of Cader Peak, in the bouldered breast of the hill and the craters poxing the green-black flesh, was no more than the wind's purpose that willy nilly blew from all corners the odd turfs and stones of an unmoulded world. The grassy rags and bones of the steep hill were . . . whirled together out of the bins of chaos by a winter wind." The baby's cry confirms this sadness, and rouses Mr. Griffiths, who thinks the sound is the scream of a mandrake being uprooted and goes out to investigate. When he finds the baby, it is dead, lying neglected at the door of the house where all the other characters in the story are whirling in the mad dance of the witches' coven.

The regional folklore exploited in "The School for Witches" appears in subtler forms in the other fantastic tales. The fairy lady, the changeling, the devil rolling in a ball on the ground (as the lecherous clergymen do in "The Holy Six"), and the spontaneous metamorphoses of scenes and people all belong to the atmosphere of Welsh mythology. The plot of "The Orchards" and of "The Mouse and the Woman," involving a man who meets and loses a

fairy woman, is common in these myths. "The Burning Baby" begins in the manner of a folktale, for the story is offered as a heuristic explanation of the sudden bursting into flame of dry bushes. The presence of these borrowings in the stories suggests that there is a similar element in the poems Thomas was writing at this period. The poems contain a few references to folklore, such as the beliefs concerning the vampire and the mandrake. Thomas' interest in this subject raises the possibility that the mythic awareness we have observed in the poems has its ultimate roots in the legends of Wales.

The poems, it will be recalled, encompass two conceptions of time: the unmoving time of mysticism and the conventional notion of time as a power that changes and destroys. Time is also an important theme in at least four of the imaginative stories, for mystic insights, or disruptions of the natural order, psychological or otherwise, are sometimes announced as disruptions of time. The derangement of the poet in "The Mouse and the Woman" takes the form of a decision that winter must be prevented from spoiling the beauty of the woman who has left him and maddened him with jealousy. He attacks "the old effigy" of time, flinging himself into a chaos of irrational images. There is a similar effect in "The Horse's Ha." When the undertaker drinks the magic brew intended to resurrect the dead, the movements of the sun and moon are disturbed, and the days pass with mysterious rapidity. One of the dreams of the boy in "A Prospect of the Sea" is a sweeping mystic vision in which he sees through time, relating remote things in a single historic unity. Finally, in "An Adventure from a Work in Progress," the man's capture of the first woman he sees on the islands is accompanied by a phenomenon Thomas calls the falling of time. This event is echoed in "Ballad of the Long-Legged Bait"; it involves a reversal of the development of living things; intense disturbances, including a windstorm, fires, earthquakes; and, in fact, all the elements of chaos. Clearly, the timelessness of the poems is inappropriate to the world of the stories. The reason may be that the stories, unlike the early poems, are about human beings living their earthly lives and that the standard of conventional time is indispensable to them. When mortals seek to evade time, as do the boys in "I see the boys of summer," in order to make love endure or to avoid death, chaos results.

III

Thomas was still working on the last of his fantastic narratives in 1938 when he began to write the realistic stories which were collected in *Portrait of the Artist as a Young Dog*. In March, 1938, he wrote to Watkins that the first of "a series of short, straightforward stories about Swansea" had already been published. This statement must refer to "A Visit to Grandpa's," which appeared in the *New English Weekly* on March 10, 1938. The change in narrative style between these two groups of stories is, of course, a radical one; moreover, it paralleled the much more subtle change in Thomas' poetic style that was going on at about the same time. Many of the casual details of these stories are drawn without change from Thomas' Swansea days, and some of the characters are based on actual people: the aunt in **"The Peaches"** is Ann Jones, and Dan Jenkyns in **"The Fight"** is Daniel Jones. In his **"Poetic Manifesto,"** Thomas declared that the title he assigned to the collection was a variant, not of Joyce's title, but of one often given by painters to self-portraits. He admitted that the general influence of *Dubliners* might be felt in his stories, but he added that this was an influence no good writer of short stories could avoid.[3]

The protagonist in all the stories is clearly Thomas himself, though the stories are narrated indifferently in first and third persons and though each presents him at a different age. They are about ordinary experiences: visits with relatives, excursions to the country, adventures with gangs of children, explorations of the town. In some of them the plot is so slight that the story approaches a reminiscence or cluster of impressions. Obviously written with only a loose unity in mind, they have no common theme; but taken as a group, they seem to trace the child's emergence from his domain of imagination and secret pleasures into an adult world where he observes suffering, pathos, and dignity.

Most of the stories are about an observer or witness, one whose experience consists of awakening to the experiences of others. The events are presented in sharp, well-selected impressions. When he is observing a general scene, such as a boy's room or a crowded street, Thomas proceeds by piling up a lively list of the quintessential details or characteristic people. Sometimes his attitude toward people, places, and episodes is affectionate or amused; sometimes he finds grotesque nightmare evocations in them. But he encounters his strongest emotions in moments of solitude when he can hug his general impressions of the external world to himself as personal possessions—while walking down a street late at night, wandering in moody isolation on a noisy beach, or enjoying the atmosphere of an expensive bar.

The first three stories—**"The Peaches," "A Visit to Grandpa's"** and **"Patricia, Edith and Arnold"**—set the idyllic existence of a child side by side with the trials of adults. As the grownups suffer, the child remains indifferent or cruel; yet it appears at the end that he has understood and sympathized more than he knew, thus anticipating the ultimate union of the childish and adult points of view. **"The Peaches"** may be said to have "separateness" as an identifiable theme. Mrs. Williams, who brings her son for a holiday at the farm, is too superior to stay a moment longer than necessary, and refuses the precious canned peaches that have been saved for her visit. Jim curses her snobbery, but he cannot keep himself from drinking up the profits of the farm and distressing his wife. Gwilym, the son, who closely resembles the religious gardener in **"The Tree,"** is occupied with a vision of himself as a preacher, and makes the barn a church for his pretended sermons. To these mutually uncommunicating attitudes toward life is added that of the boys who are

busy with their games of wild Indian and indifferent to the concerns of the adults. But even here a division occurs when Jack Williams betrays his playmate by telling his mother an incriminating mixture of truth and falsehood about his treatment at the farm, and is taken away. At the end of **"The Peaches,"** the boy waves his handkerchief at his departing betrayer, innocent that any wrong has been done to him, or to his aunt and uncle.

But in **"Patricia, Edith and Arnold,"** the child, at first cruelly indifferent to the pain felt by the two maidservants who have learned that the same young man has been walking out with both of them, gains some insight into adult sorrows. The story begins with a chaos of irreconcilable interests: the absorption of the girls in their love triangle, and the rambunctious joy of the child who is all-conquering in his imaginary play world. But as the painful comedy of Arnold's entrapment is played out, the boy, uncomfortably cold and wet, feels his own distress and unconsciously comes to sympathize with Patricia. Returning to the shelter to retrieve his cap, he sees Arnold reading the letters he has written to the other girl, but he mercifully spares Patricia this knowledge. And his own experience of pain, a minor counterpart of the adult pain Paticia has suffered, comes when he thaws his cold hands at the fire. Patricia's final remark, "Now we've all had a good cry today," formulates both the similarity of their trials and their capacity to endure them.

Cruel jokes, of the sort that life has played on Arnold, occur in some of the other stories. In **"Just Like Little Dogs,"** the brothers exchange partners with each other in the middle of an evening of casual love. As a result, when the women become pregnant, it is not clear which brother is the father of their respective children. The two forced but loveless marriages take place, and now the two fathers spend their evenings in the street, standing hopelessly in the cold night air. In **"Old Garbo,"** the neighbors take up a collection for Mrs. Prothero, whose daughter is supposed to have died in childbirth; after Mrs. Prothero has drunk up the money, it is learned that the daughter has survived. The mother, ashamed at having taken the money under false pretenses, jumps into the river.

It is significant that in each of these stories the anecdotal nucleus is subordinated to the vehicle which conveys it. The impressive element of **"Just Like Little Dogs"** is the spectacle of the young men sheltering aimlessly from the night under the railway arch; they have no place more interesting to go and nothing more interesting to do. **"Old Garbo"** is, in reality, a story of initiation; the young reporter, eager to share the knowledge and maturity of the older one, follows him into the haunts where Mrs. Prothero's comic tragedy occurs. In this way he exchanges the boyish pastimes of the cinema and the novelty shop in the first part of the story for the more serious experience in the slum pub. He is not a qualified observer, for he becomes drunk, sick, and helpless; and the older reporter tells him, in an odd conclusion, that the story which has just been narrated has certain confused details; but he is still naïvely determined to put all the things the older reporter has shown him into a story.

Some of the stories have a note of personal futility and inadequacy which conspires with their prevailing comic tone to produce penetrating irony. The inferior boy who is the hero of **"Extraordinary Little Cough"** is bullied and mocked. But he turns his shy habit of running away when girls appear into a feat; for, while the other boys are idling with the girls and yielding to romantic illusions, he runs the five miles of beach. As he falls to the ground exhausted at the end of the story, it is clear that he has risen nobly to a challenge while the others have ended in frustration and petty animosities. The two boys who go for a country hike in **"Who Do You Wish Was With Us?"** feel they are escaping their town lives in the freedom of the country and the beach. But Ray, whose life has been full of terrible family misfortunes, is overtaken by sorrow for his dead brother in the middle of his holiday. The sea turns cold and threatening, and both boys feel that they cannot really escape the life they have fled.

The most powerful story about escape, and the most impressive one in the volume is the last, **"One Warm Saturday."** Having rejected invitations to join his friends, the young man wanders despondently among the crowds on the beach, finding solace only in the face of a girl whom he flees shyly at first. Ultimately, he again meets the girl, Lou; and, as the two become involved in an oddly mixed group of drinkers, she promises him that his love for her will be fulfilled when they are alone. The party moves from the pub where it began to Lou's room in a huge ramshackle tenement. The young man's anxiety and Lou's demonstrations of affection are intensified, but the others show no signs of leaving. A grotesque frustration occurs when the young man goes out to the lavatory. He is unable to find his way back to Lou's room to claim the night of love she has promised him. Instead, he loses himself in the squalid maze of the tenement and stumbles into the rooms of other lodgers. Ultimately, he gives up and wanders out into the street, having made the "discovery" during his search that all the obscure people of the town share his experience of loss.

Thomas' uncompleted novel, *Adventures in the Skin Trade,* may be considered a continuation of the quasi-autobiography loosely sketched in *A Portrait of the Artist as a Young Dog,* though it is more broadly comic in style than any of the stories. It takes up the narrative of a life much like Thomas' at the point where the last of the stories ends, and its protagonist, Samuel Bennet, is not inconsistent with the wandering, imaginative youths found in the earlier book, though he is much better defined. Thomas seems to have begun *Adventures* in 1940; and, though the first section was published in *Folios of New Writing* in 1941 under the title **"A Fine Beginning"** and though he was encouraged to continue with it, it remained a fragment at the time of his death.

It may be described as a farce based on the fact that Samuel Bennet and his world are excruciatingly uncomfortable with each other. On the night before he leaves his home town for London, Samuel prepares a number of surprises for his family by breaking his mother's china, tearing up his sister's crochetwork, and scribbling on the lessons that his father, a teacher, is correcting. But he does all this in tears, as if it were a painful necessity; and he says an affectionate farewell the next morning. On the other hand, he is not eager to see London; unwilling to make any decisions or to take any actions, he lingers in the station café until a friend forces him to leave.

The London in which Samuel finds himself is a damp, angular, crowded, eccentric world; and it is both surprising and significant that he likes it as well as he does. The chaos he encounters is well represented by his first stop, a warehouse full of furniture piled up in unlikely heaps which nevertheless serves as living quarters for a number of people. The general technique of *Adventures* is suggested by the locked bathroom with its bird cages where a strange girl makes an attempt on Samuel's virtue in a tub full of used bathwater after drugging him with a drink of cologne. In the book, as in this scene, violent imaginative force explodes in a narrow enclosure filled with ordinary objects and people, toppling them into ludicrous attitudes and combinations. A mundane paraphernalia of Bass bottles, umbrellas, rubber ducks, bootpolish, Worcestershire sauce, and CocaCola is juggled into patterns of uproarious private meaning, sometimes by Samuel's imagination, sometimes by the author's. Realism swims in a whirlpool of uninhibited fancy.

If the atmosphere of *Adventure* is found anywhere else, it is in Brinnin's accounts of the social events Thomas attended, where the poet, guided by some motivation of wit or self-dramatization, cunningly introduced chaos. Mr. Allingham observes that the Bass bottle which has become wedged on Samuel's little finger is an enigma. Samuel, noticing that a barmaid looks like a duchess riding a horse, makes the irrelevant reply of "Tantivy" to some remark. But the curious thing is that Samuel, in spite of the hostility and defiance with which he confronts the world, is completely unready for the world's retaliation. As he is pushed and prodded from one place to another, drugged, undressed, bullied, and thrown out of a bar, he experiences terror and confusion. Samuel is too innocent to absorb what he sees. A stumbling, swooning, dreaming source of confusion, he is himself confused, and he seems destined to remain a timid and withdrawn picaro among the sharp and knowing characters who take possession of him. According to Robert Pocock, who discussed *Adventures* with Thomas, the novel was to end with Samuel stripped naked (except, no doubt, for the Bass bottle clinging enigmatically to his little finger), and arrested in Paddington Station.[4]

IV

The two film scripts Thomas completed during the period he was writing for the media of popular entertainment—*The Doctor and the Devils* and *The Beach at Falesá*—are entirely unlike his other work. Both were based on *don-*

nées, and they were translations of a given story from one medium to another. They made few demands on Thomas' original gifts, but they did demonstrate that he had unexpected capacities for adapting himself to new forms and for controlling an extended work.

Of the two, *The Doctor and the Devils* is by far the more interesting and successful. The idea for filming the story of the murderers, Burke and Hare, who supplied the early anatomist, Robert Knox, with corpses for dissection, was that of Donald Taylor. Taylor, after some research, wrote a narrative of these episodes; and he commissioned Thomas, then an employee of his Strand Film Company, to write the script. This was the beginning of an odd history. Thomas' script, completed and put into proof by 1947, was not published until 1953. In 1961 Callum Mill rewrote it as a stage play, produced it in this form at the Citizens' Theatre in Glasgow in 1961, and played the role of Dr. Rock. The play was performed a second time at the Edinburgh International Festival in 1962, where Mill staged it for performance "in the round" at the Assembly Hall. The film itself has never been produced.

The effectiveness of Thomas' script is due largely to its accounts of the low haunts of Edinburgh (which is, however, never identified by name), the curious characters found there, and their deeds of violence. The stage directions are cast in a considered prose of far greater finish and vigor than is strictly necessary. Some of them seem to call for inappropriate emphasis, but others display a creative and original approach to photographic possibilities. It is clear that Thomas found the cinematic idiom of concrete imagery entirely congenial. He is both resourceful and subtle in devising visual counterparts for ideas of his own and for the thoughts of his characters. The murder of Jennie Bailey is predicted by a shot showing Fallon, her murderer, unconsciously letting the drink from his bottle pour over her skirt during a carouse. While a student is drawing her corpse, her hand, opening in a death twitch, drops two pennies to the floor. The scenes in the pubs and the parties in the lodging house kept by Fallon and Broom, where they trap and murder old derelicts for Dr. Rock's dissecting table, present a great deal of this specific and telling detail.

The chief character, Dr. Rock, is a figure who resembles Faust or Paracelsus: he is an intellectual devoted to his discipline who is indifferent to ordinary human values. The actual Dr. Knox gave Thomas some of the rudiments of Dr. Rock's character; he was an effective orator and a dandy, and the figure in Thomas' script retains these qualities. Rock defends his practice of accepting bodies obtained by "Resurrectionists" on the ground that the legal limitation of using only bodies from the gallows for dissection is too restrictive. One of his weaknesses as a character is his universal and unfailing contempt; he despises his colleagues, the poor, the government that ignores their needs, and nearly everyone to whom he speaks. Yet he proclaims that he is in the service of mankind; and, when the murders are discovered, the other doctors, whom he has bitterly criticized, unite to defend him.

Rock is the center of the script's moral conflict. Believing not only that any means are justified in the pursuit of his science but that the lives of the poor and immoral people upon whom Fallon and Broom prey are not worth living, he accepts the bodies silently, even though he knows they have been murdered. When the truth becomes known, he is ostracized; and for a few sequences Rock has the odd aspect of an inverted Dr. Stockmann of *An Enemy of the People*: he stands alone against society in defense of his moral indifference. But he is brought to a realization of his crime at the end, when a child is frightened at hearing his name; he then learns that he has become a figure of horror.

In his review, James Agee called *The Doctor and the Devils* the hack work of a man of genius; but the fact that he found much to praise in it showed that he intended to characterize and not to condemn it with this description. He thought that Thomas had made good use of some of the movie devices, that the dialogue was "playable," and that the script showed that Thomas "could not work for money without also working with love."

This observation is not, unfortunately, supported by *The Beach at Falesá,* a script far inferior to *The Doctor and the Devils. The Beach* was written in 1948 for Gainsborough Pictures; like the earlier one it was never produced, and it was not published until 1959, when it appeared in *Harper's Bazaar.* A filming of a story by Robert Louis Stevenson, it has to do with an island in the South Seas dominated by a merchant who exploits the superstition of the natives to interfere with the business of a rival trader. It offers some interesting local color and some humor drawn from the life of white men in the tropics. There is a good scene in which the English hero sets up housekeeping with his native wife and tries to explain how his new household differs from his own home; but he finally surrenders to her naïveté, gives up the attempt, and contents himself with amusing her. In general, however, the script aims at melodrama, violent physical action in the form of fist fights, and spookiness. There are few signs that Thomas tried to make anything serious or original of the assignment.

Thomas' last completed work, *Under Milk Wood,* had a long gestation, for he first thought of writing something like it in 1945, as an expansion of the subject of **"Quite Early One Morning,"** a description of a Welsh village he had read on the radio during one of his programs. The original plan, according to Daniel Jones, was to have the town full of queer individualists defend its sanity at a trial; but, upon hearing a description of a sane town from the prosecutor, the inhabitants decide instead to shut themselves off from the outside world. After writing about half of the play, calling it *The Town Was Mad,* Thomas changed his mind about this structure. In the summer of 1951 he read some parts of the play—then called *Llareggub Hill*—to Brinnin; and in 1952 he published a selection closely resembling the first half of the final version in *Botteghe Oscure* as *Llareggub: A Piece for Radio Perhaps.*

When Brinnin suggested in September of 1952 that the play might serve as a program for the series of American readings they were planning, Thomas was encouraged to complete it. It was listed in the program of the Poetry Center for performance in May, 1953; Thomas wrote in March that he would not be able to complete it before leaving for America but that he would bring the manuscript with him. He continued work on it up to the very day he first read it as a solo performance at the Fogg Museum in Cambridge Massachusetts, on May 3, 1953. The reaction to this premiere was enthusiastic; according to Brinnin, it gave Thomas confidence in his ability to write drama. A first group reading was given at the Poetry Center on May 14; its effect was extraordinary, and there were fifteen curtain calls. Thomas continued to revise the play and to add to it through the ensuing performances, until the weeks just before his death. The play opened the Poetry Center's program in September, 1953, and was first performed in Britain as a broadcast on January 25, 1954.

In spite of its effectiveness, *Under Milk Wood,* like most of Thomas' writing about Wales, is essentially slight; its main assets are charm, exuberance, and mischievousness. Thomas took advantage of the radio-play form to give his work a reality that was as disembodied as possible; apart from the town itself and the well-marked progress of the day from morning to nightfall, there are few suggestions of time or place. There is no plot. The microphone simply makes a number of tours of the various inhabitants of the town at different hours of the day, guided on one occasion by the postman, to hear of their dreams, memories, and daily lives. There are no distinctions between the voices of characters and narrators, the speeches of the living and the dead; or among dreams, thought, and *viva voce* dialogue. In form—or, rather, in formlessness—its closest analogue is the Night-Town chapter of Joyce's *Ulysses;* but the nightmare violence and the horror of Joyce's chapter are supplanted by domestic comedy, cheerful lechery, and wistful memories of episodes of affection that are only incidentally sinful.

The comic vitality of *Under Milk Wood* suggests that Thomas, with his sense of humor, his eye for detail, and his love of humble people, might have done work reminiscent of Dickens. But the humor of *Under Milk Wood* is not an end in itself, but a means of emphasizing the theme, the sacredness of human attachments. Thomas advances a persuasive claim to respect for the sinful, eccentric, and even ludicrous loves that spring up in ordinary lives by investing them with comedy and pathos. This effect begins with the speeches of Captain Cat's drowned shipmates rehearsing the pleasures of their lives: ". . . we shared the same girl once. . . . come to a bad end, very enjoyable." This irresistible style of defense for whatever human beings may come to care for is continued with the dreams of Miss Price, the dressmaker, and Mog Edwards, the draper, whose love for each other never progresses beyond correspondence; with the love between the rowdy Cherry Owen and his wife; with Captain Cat's memories of Rosie Probert; with the Reverend Eli Jenkins' paean to the town and

Wales generally; and with Polly Garter's memory of Willy Wee, the one man among all her lovers for whom she cared the most. The more delusive and insubstantial these affections are, the more tenderly does Thomas treat them.

Under Milk Wood turns sharply away from anything resembling mysticism. It reflects the conclusion Thomas had reached in 1951 that "The joy and function of poetry is, and was, the celebration of man, which is also the celebration of God."[5] Thus, it can be seen as the last of Thomas' hymns of praise for the world of man's experience and its Creator. His early mystic poems had mingled the material world and its divine source in a dark, chaotic unity. In his later poems, the landscapes, animals, and people are treated as if they were taking part in a grave and radiant ceremonial; the sense of relation with divine energy has retreated, but its immanence is felt everywhere. In *Under Milk Wood,* with its loving depiction of people who would ordinarily be considered weak or foolish, Thomas continues to pursue this obscure joy.

V

Alfred Kazin has attributed the great popularity Thomas enjoyed in his lifetime to the fact that his resonant, passionate verse offered an alternative to the cool ironies of his contemporaries. Certainly the poets dominating the early 1930's, when *18 Poems* and *Twenty-Five Poems* were published—W. H. Auden, C. Day Lewis, Louis Mac-Neice, and Stephen Spender—differed from Thomas in two important respects. They were men who responded sensitively to social and historical conditions, and they were—with the exception of Spender—primarily poets of wit and intellect. They frequently dealt with themes related to the Depression, the Spanish Civil War, and the threat of World War II, and even their lyrics of personal disquiet are touched with an awareness of general conditions. As Auden wrote in his poem about the outbreak of the war, "September 1, 1939":

> Waves of anger and fear
> Circulate over the bright
> And darkened lands of earth,
> Obsessing our private lives. . . .

Even in their pessimism, these poets usually maintained a tone of civilized urbanity and a sense of decorum. Although they often took up the cause of the outsider or the proletarian, they expressed themselves in verse of an aristocratic, intellectual, and ironic temper.

However, there were dissidents among the young writers of the time who, like Thomas, favored a return to some of the values of Romanticism. By the mid-1930's, Auden, whose first book of verse had been published in 1930, was regarded by some as cold, brittle, and superficial; new sources of feeling for poetry were being sought in myth, religion, and the subconscious. Tendencies resembling those of Thomas' poetry and early stories were found in Surrealism, which began to attract the attention of English writers and artists at this period. David Gascoyne, the only

English poet fully committed to Surrealism, wrote *A Short Survey of Surrealism* in 1935, and in 1936 his book of Surrealist verse, *Man's Life Is This Meat,* was published by the Parton Bookshop, which had supported the publication of *18 Poems* two years earlier. Thomas attended the International Surrealist Exhibition held at the Burlington Gallery in 1936, and entered far enough into the spirit of it to carry a cup of tea made of boiled string which he offered to passers-by. Although he was critical of Surrealist theory in the "Manifesto" of 1951, the fantastic stories collected in *The World I Breathe* (which were written in the 1930's) certainly share the Surrealist spirit. Thomas' mythic qualities and Romantic egoism also harmonize with the aims of a later literary movement of the 1930's, the New Apocalypse.

Thomas' poetry may legitimately be considered a manifestation of the Neo-romantic stirrings of his time, but it has older and more illuminating affinities as well. Critics writing on Thomas have had much to say about influences and parallels, and it has been shown that he has something in common with nearly every good poet, even those as different from him as Shakespeare and Pope. Thomas' own casual statement on the subject was that he was open to the influence of any writers he might be reading, and his purposely indiscriminate list reads: "Sir Thomas Browne, de Quincey, Henry Newbolt, the Ballads, Blake, Baroness Orczy, Marlowe, Chums, the Imagists, the Bible, Poe, Keats, Lawrence, Anon, and Shakespeare."[6] The most significant name on this list, as Thomas implicitly acknowledges, and as his critics have often pointed out, is that of Blake. Thomas shared with Blake a hallucinatory commitment to the concreteness of what he imagined, and the sort of cosmic awareness that generates myth. Though Thomas' cosmos is far more fragmentary than the one found in Blake's Prophetic Books, it has some of the same energies, gigantic deities, and above all, the same "fearful symmetry" of balanced patterns formed by opposing forces.

Much has been said, also, about the religious or visionary aspect of Thomas' poetry, the quality he shares with Vaughan, Hopkins, and Yeats, as well as with Blake. In general, the critics have adopted one of two opposing points of view. One group thinks of Thomas as a religious poet who wrote, as he said in his introductory note to the *Collected Poems,* "for the love of man and in praise of God." T. H. Jones believes that the main poems of *Deaths and Entrances* clearly exhibit a Christianity that is disguised, but still detectable in the rhetoric of the earlier poems. G. S. Fraser finds in the "Altarwise . . ." sequence a "current of orthodox Christian feeling—feeling rather than thought" which became increasingly noticeable in Thomas' later work. W. S. Merwin's essay, "The Religious Poet" is probably the most cogent statement of this view. Merwin considers Thomas' work a "poetry of celebration," whose universe originates in love and remains suffused with it. It is natural, adds Merwin, that Thomas should have proceeded from lyric to dramatic modes, for the faith developed in the introspections of the earlier po-

ems is revealed, in the later ones, in the form of an increasingly inclusive sense of the orderliness of the external world.[7]

If Thomas said that he wrote "in praise of God," he also said, at another time, that he meant to write "poems in praise of God's world by a man who doesn't believe in God."[8] This statement, which seems more careful than the one in the introduction to *Collected Poems,* also seems intended to strike a note of qualified faith. Many, perhaps most of Thomas' critics, feel that his poetry, in spite of its Biblical allusions, its use of Christian myth and symbolism, and its ardent declarations of faith is not, in the final analysis, expressive of religious belief. "It would be ridiculous," wrote Francis Scarfe in one of the earliest analyses of the "Altarwise . . ." sequence, "to claim Thomas for any church."[9] And a recent critic, Ralph Maud, commenting on Thomas' allusions to God in "Over Sir John's hill" and the projected, but uncompleted "In Country Heaven," observes: "Thomas' God does nothing to alleviate the absurdity of the position of rational man in an irrational universe; Thomas' God does nothing to explain death in terms of higher values. As the eternal sympathetic spectator, He simply weeps, offering none of the usual consolations."[10]

The differences of opinion on this point among the critics are at least partly due to different notions of what is meant by "religion." Thomas is certainly concerned with such religious problems as the nature of the creator, the relation of man to his universe, and, particularly, the enigma of death. Also, his verse depends upon mystic perception, intuitions about the cosmos, and even upon such specifically Christian doctrines as atonement, immortality, and salvation. But his ideas about these things are personal, naïve, and, as we have said earlier, primitive. In spite of his use of conventional religious terms and symbols, Thomas' subject is really the primordial world view of the savage. It includes miracle, anthropomorphism, and pantheism, but offers no morality, no doctrine, no communal feeling. Thomas' religious symbolism, says Giorgio Melchiori, "is only a metaphorical means of expression of the poet's personal thought; it contributes to the creation of that personal myth which seems to be the real aim of his poetry."[11]

Thomas is a craftsman of language as well as a visionary. Though he explicitly denied that Joyce had influenced him, he is properly seen as one of the line of verbal experimenters of which Joyce is the most prominent member. We have already examined Thomas' imaginative use of words, and it is interesting to recall that he enjoyed reading old copies of the magazine *transition,* that museum of exploration in language. What Thomas has in common with Lewis Carroll, Hopkins, Joyce, and Cummings is the urge to probe the disparity between conventional language and the fruits of perception. Thomas, like the others, devised more or less systematic means of entering the virgin ground between language and experience. He followed Hopkins' example in discovering new reserves of expression in the sound of language, and in coining neologisms to convey the truths of private anguish and joy in nature. And, like Joyce, he practiced the art of doubling or trebling thicknesses of meaning, so that language becomes startlingly germane to its subject.

Thomas is a striking figure, however, not because of the debt he owed to other poets, but because of his undeniable originality. As we have seen, his ideas were not exceptional. He took his intuitions as they came to him, without trying to refine or reshape them, but he spent great effort on the elaboration of rhetorical resources. There are styles of primitive art that display this combination of the simple and the intricate. They offer no defenses against tribal fears and passions, but instead express them in the tangled pattern of a woven shield or the carved involutions of a witch doctor's mask. Thomas' verse strangely resembles objects of this kind. It embodies elemental, unformed feelings that usually lie below the threshold of consciousness in a technique so practiced and accomplished that it gives the illusion of issuing from long, secure traditions foreign to impatient modern craftsmanship. The result is a unique impression of double remoteness, a union of barbaric subject with an arcane, sophisticated style that is perhaps the distinctive quality of Thomas' art.

Notes

1. Thomas' book reviews and miscellaneous journalism are listed in *Dylan Thomas: A Bibliography* by J. Alexander Rolph (London and New York, 1956). His unpublished prose work, scripts written for film documentaries, and unpublished pieces read on broadcasts are listed in Maud, *Entrances to Dylan Thomas' Poetry,* Appendix I, "Chronology of Composition," pp. 121-48.

2. "Fifty," (July, 1933), in February, 1933, Notebook.

3. "Poetic Manifesto: A Manuscript," pp. 4-5.

4. Robert Pocock, *Adam International Review,* No. 238, 1953, pp. 30-31.

5. "Poetic Manifesto," p. 9.

6. "Poetic Manifesto," p. 3.

7. The passages referred to in this paragraph are: T. H. Jones, *Dylan Thomas* (Edinburgh and London, 1963), pp. 66-67; Fraser, *Vision and Rhetoric,* p. 224; and Merwin's essay in *Casebook,* p. 60 and p. 64.

8. Quoted by Brinnin in *Dylan Thomas in America,* p. 128.

9. Scarfe, *Auden and After,* 1942. Reprinted in *Casebook,* p. 29.

10. Maud, *Entrances to Dylan Thomas' Poetry,* p. 112.

11. Giorgio Melchiori, *The Tightrope Walkers* (London, 1956), p. 231.

Paul West (essay date 1967)

SOURCE: "Dylan Thomas: The Position in Calamity," in *The Southern Review,* Vol. 3, 1967, pp. 922-43.

[*In the following essay, West examines the stories contained in Thomas's collection,* Adventures in the Skin Trade.]

I

According to Wordsworth, "all men feel something of an honourable bigotry for the objects which have long continued to please them." *Something of*: it is what Englishmen say to maintain their reserve during enthusiasm and what most people say when they want to suggest reservations painlessly. Something of: the phrase comes naturally to the lips for Dylan Thomas, whom his detractors find only something of a charlatan, whom his admirers find only something of a genius. It is not easy to be absolute about him, yet half-measures don't seem appropriate—and this will show in what follows. So let him talk for himself while I, a bit fervently off-center about him and his works, muster something of a critical balance. Conceded, he is getting second word to Wordsworth's first; but his, almost certainly—beyond the perspectives of this essay and beyond the altercations of critics—will be the last laugh. To take him so seriously at all when in fact. . . . Why, man. . . .

"Regarded in England as a Welshman (and a waterer of England's milk, and in Wales as an Englishman)," he once told a society of Scottish writers (and foreigners, therefore), "I am too unnational to be here at all. I should be living in a small private leper house in Hereford or Shropshire, one foot in Wales and my vowels in England. Wearing red flannel trousers, a tall witch's hat, and a coracle tiepin, and speaking English so Englishly that I sound like a literate Airedale." See how the straddling provincial, to dissimulate some of the genuine pain of being in between, turns cosmopolite. A typical piece of the Thomas performance, it reveals not only the banterer and the self-deprecating prankster, but also—in that bravura dispersal of his identity—his profound disregard for names, regimens, fences; even for words. The main thing he wanted was the *feel* of life, which is not to say that he couldn't and didn't watch society with a keen, meticulous eye. He did. But he had always a knack of double vision by which the reporter fed the seer or (to use Karl Shapiro's terms) "the cultural fugitive or clown" the "joyous naturally religious mind."

Make no mistake about it, this man saw life whole even though—for sundry reasons—he often saw it unsteadily. Somehow he divined the sum without adding up the parts. He knew them all, and their relationship: the grave and the slight, the sober and the daft, the at-hand and the far-fetched, the noumenal and the empirical, the chemical-physical and the imagined, the inevitable and the avertable, the nonsense and the sense, the sublime and the suburban. He never found life homogeneous, decent or dignified, but he did—in the course of a literary career gambled on experimentally reconceiving it—learn to prize its texture: fingering it, so to speak, tinkering with it, isolating and recombining the constituents on a purely verbal level, as if working things' names against things and vice versa, and confident in his sportive way that these verbal assaults, while never changing the physical universe, intensified his sense of it. Ours too. The orderly exposition of things he left to experts in long division; his own exposition added incongruities to incongruities already built into life, the habit of his mind being jussive and meddlesome, never merely observant and receptive. He commanded experience to yield its maximum. He seized the human and the interstellar day and punished it; he gathered rosebuds and greedily transformed them, hardly knowing where to stop. It is clear that the division of the physical world into orthodox components had little meaning for him: one thing, no matter what, evoked another, became another, which then evoked. . . . It was a metamorphosis *ad infinitum.* Not that there is nothing of the finite in his writings; there is a great deal. But it has always a vulnerable, precarious look, as if at any moment Thomas the devout clown might reconsider it and place it where no rational man had ever found it before: drowning it in associations, dividing it up and preposterously marrying off the halves, re-naming them after nobody or nothing. *Unsex the skeleton this mountain minute, / And by this blow-clock witness of the sun / Suffer the heaven's children through my heart-beat.* Pretty much like that, and sometimes too much.

The process—like Rimbaud's systematic disorderings—has much to do with congruity: with what is fitting. Thomas finds the universe incongruous, but legal; he finds society almost as weird, but just as rich in laws. And, lusting after the maximum, the inconceivable sum, he makes both universe and society even weirder, never missing a chance to be surrealistic but, against his travesties and incongruous modifications, always working the congruity and finicking discipline of his art. On the religious plane we begin, decently enough, with the bread that once was oat; but then we find a Gabriel who is two-gunned. "O God, Thou art everywhere" rapidly becomes "O God, mun, you're like a bloody cat." Socially, there is the poignant matter-of-factness of the hunchback taunted in the park, "a solitary mister," but also an image of grandmother, her head appearing upside-down upon a cloud, and Samuel Bennet in *Adventures in the Skin Trade* with his finger stuck fast in a beer-bottle. "Up yours," Thomas seems to say, lewdly dismissing our conventional views. He just had to tamper, making field level with roof, defying time (the quiet gent whose beard wags in that Egyptian wind), and suspending gravity: the ball thrown up stays up. We have to stay with him as long as we can, trusting him with the same kind of trust as Byron wanted.

Thomas's two roles interpenetrate, and that is what saves him. The visionary learns from the clown the intrinsic steadiness of the *uni*verse (it is *one*) as well as the endless license accorded the mind. The clown learns therefore to respect his own daubs and freakish misalliances. Thomas, more than anyone, exposes the arbitrariness of things: birds eat worms, but birds might have been assigned to a diet of human knuckles and worms might have been pro-grammed to live and feed in between the toes of lions. Why things are as they are, and not otherwise, Thomas doesn't know. But he learns, and teaches us to respect, the stability of present arrangements at the same time as enriching our minds with a vision that evokes the eve of creation. And whatever he can manage through metaphor or joyous misconception (God as a fiddling warden; a baby burning; a lay preacher who thinks wars are begun only to boost the sales of newspapers) he uses to quicken our sense of man's mind and God's design. His piety is grounded in blasphemous interferences (like an urchin who draws horn-rimmed glasses round Christ's eyes) and his deep respect for human community, even the suburban, defines itself in the presence of miscellaneous misbehavior. His passion for experience involves him in a presumptuous, feckless summa to which nothing is irrelevant, within which nothing is impossible. He wants complete consciousness, a mind as big as the universe and more inventive than God's: in short, his own supreme "cut-and-come-again cardpack of references."

How vain it is, then, to blame him for not being clear, logical, mature, consistent or merely documentary. His very self (not so far from Edgar's Tom o' Bedlam in *King Lear*) precluded everyday lucidity, dispensed with logic, spurned maturity for the child's sense of wonder, disdained consistency as a Procrustean trap, and regarded documentary as a vaulting-board. To rebuke him for lewdness or salacity is as impertinent as to blame the pattern of the human physique or to complain to the water authorities about the primeval slime out of which life came slithering up before pipes. Thomas's writings add up to a sacred pantomime in which the words themselves are communion wafers. Because the joyous naturally religious man attends the pranks of the clown, what might otherwise have been dull blasphemy, obscure gimmickry or frivolous free-wheeling becomes a feat of mystical attentiveness, ramming the everyday back into the toolshed of Creation. We have only to read carefully his Note to *Collected Poems* and relate it to his other books as well. "These poems," he wrote, "with all their crudities, doubts, and confusions, are written for the love of Man and in praise of God, and I'd be a damn' fool if they weren't." See? He takes the risk of faith because faith is creative and prudent. And his exercises in serious triviality record nothing less than the awesome oddity of the universe itself, an oddity Thomas found both exhilarating and painful, both reassuring and unhinging. If, as some have found, his eccentric account of it starts nothing but bewilderment, mistrust and uncertainty (rather than reproducing the ascetic aplomb of Eliot, the well-upholstered diffidence of Wallace Stevens), there is only one answer: more than any other poet he returns us to the bewilderment of the first man initially waking on the lap of earth, to the mistrust and thrill felt by the first alchemists, to the uncertainty of men who didn't know the function of the sun, and in his own illicit way links up with the Palomar astronomers who in our own time study such radio-sources as 3C-9, receding from us at four-fifths the speed of light and something like nine billion light-years away—the most distant object we know of. He makes the cosmos local. Here, he says, (and watch your step) are "God's rough tumbling grounds," making us free within a "kingdom of neighbours," expressing always an almost Shakespearean love-hate fixation on chaos. If we are brave enough to want the experience, we must be willing to let it deprive us of our schemes and laws and codified defenses. Doubting Thomases he would make us all, but there is no doubting him: he is unverifiable. He goes from surrealism to applied surrealism, arriving eventually at the festive confabulations of **Under Milk Wood,** meditating his "long poem-to-be" (in which God mourns the self-destroyed Earth) and the libretto for Stravinsky about "the only man and woman alive on earth" after atomic catastrophe—a far cry from the young people who meet in the ordinary way in his projected play, **Two Streets.**

But, for all the grandiosity, the ultra-Miltonic audacity of three-quarters of his projects, he treasured his own sharp eye—much, I suppose, as a steeplejack might keep a lucky penny in his pocket. Take the affable earthiness of this comment, in a letter, on Persia (where the Anglo-Iranian Oil Company had incredibly sent him in 1951 to write a window-dressing film script):

> Beautiful Isfahan and Shiraz. Wicked, pompous, oily British. Nervous, cunning, corrupt and delightful Persian bloody bastards. Opium no good. Persian vodka, made of beetroot, like stimulating sock-juice, very enjoyable. Beer full of glycerine and pips.

I think no one who has read all of Thomas, who has absorbed the Fitzgibbon biography and such other records as the letters and the pictorial life by Read and McKenna, can help feeling that here was a man uniquely possessing two things which, fused (a fusion beyond his powers), go to make great literature. I mean vision and ordinary seeing: grand-mindedness and minor-mindedness, dynast and midget, druid and buffoon, Lear and Falstaff, demiurge and urchin. It is rare to find one man so gravely, so splendidly, reverential of the cosmic, the mysterious, the chthonic, and at the same time so eager for smut, trivia and banality. Blake has the one, Chaucer the other. Thomas has the two sides, but unfused. All the same, it is a great doubleness, and it seems to me to be implicit in his two versions of that pseudo-Welsh anagram, "Llareggub/ Llaregyb." Reading the first, we find "buggerall," which is standard British English slang for "nothing" and always uttered with nihilistic relish. Reading the second, we find what seems to be the "bigger-all," which is what Thomas always wanted: a state from which nothing is excluded. He stands, as Milk Wood does, between the everydayness of nothing and the everydayness of everything. **Under Milk Wood**—frothing, warbling, chiming, transforming clichés into bonds between beleaguered men—takes the doubleness very near to fusion: a heaven on earth, but not quite. Had Thomas survived, he would surely have arrived at an outlook repeating and extending what he himself called Wilfred Owen's "position-in-calamity . . . which, without intellectual choice, he chose to take" because he "believed there was no one true way . . . all ways are by-

tracked and rutted and pit-falled with ignorance and injustice and indifference. He was himself diffident and self-distrustful. He had to be wrong; clumsy; affected often; ambiguous; bewildered." It is as much Thomas on Thomas as Thomas on Owen, double-rich in levity and vision, double-dealing with the biggerall and the buggerall, double-crossed by the tragedy and comedy crowding into each day of every man he could imagine anywhere on the globe. Stern commentators find him no more than a casualty of relativism; others, less exigent and less rigid, prize that very sense of the interdependence of things.

II

Leaf through Fitzgibbon or *The Days of Dylan Thomas* and you find reams of homework lovingly done, but always pale beside Thomas's own prose (which is there in gratifyingly large amounts). See, for example, how he recalls the dame school, "so firm and kind and smelling of galoshes, with the sweet and fumbled music of the piano lessons drifting down from the upstairs to the lonely schoolroom." Almost on the brink of what Kingsley Amis called "sonorous whimsy"—Thomas appearing determined to find epithets that *sound*—the passage saves itself by settling into a lyrical decisiveness that seems less padded:

> Behind the school was a narrow lane where only the oldest and boldest threw pebbles at windows, scuffled and boasted, fibbed about their relations . . . and swapped gob-stoppers for slings, old knives for marbles, kite strings for foreign stamps. The lane was always the place to tell your secrets; if you did not have any, you invented them. . . . In the afternoons, when the children were good, they read aloud from Struwelpeter. And when they were bad, they sat alone in the empty classroom, hearing, from above them, the distant, terrible, sad music of the late piano lessons.

In that last sentence it is almost as if the whole world were being punished; and this almost hammy inclusiveness—Thomas's resolve to glean a near-apocalypse from any event or memory—characterizes his prose, giving even his mundane statements a force almost sibylline "that one refuses," as the dictionary says, "but is afterwards glad to get on worse terms." At other times he plays down the sibylline, doomy feeling by packing it with images—things, things, things—almost wrecking the syntax and suggesting landslide or flux. The following, an excerpt from a letter written at the other end of his life (June 1953), seems to me—for its vision, its realism and its lurching contrasts—prose of which any novelist might be proud.

> I missed you a lot my last days, and was Lizzed away to the plane alone. I almost liked the plane-ride, though; it was stormy and dangerous, and only my iron will kept the big bird up; lightning looked wonderful through the little eyeholes in its underbelly; the bar was open all the way from Newfoundland; and the woman next to me was stone-deaf so I spoke to her all the way, more wildly and more wildly as the plane lurched on through dark and lion-thunder and the fire-

water yelled through my blood like Sioux, and she un-heard all my delirium with a smile; and then the Red Indians scalped me; and then it was London, and my iron will brought the bird down, safely, with only one spine-cracking jar. And queasy, purple, maggoty, scalped, I weak-wormed through festoons, bunting, flags, great roses, sad spangles, paste and tinsel, the million cardboard simpers and ogrish plaster statuettes of the nincompoop queen, I crawled as early as sin in the chilly weeping morning through the city's hushed hangover and all those miles of cock-deep orange-peel, nibbled sandwiches, broken bottles, discarded vests, vomit and condoms, lollipops, senile fish, blood, lips, old towels, teeth, turds, soiled blowing newspapers by the unread mountain, all the spatter and bloody gravy and giant mouseness that go to show how a loyal and phlegmatic people—"London can break it!"—enjoyed themselves like hell the day before. And, my God, wouldn't I have enjoyed it too! In the house where I stay in London, a party was still going on, at half past seven in the wet, beige morning, that had started two nights before. Full of my news, of the latest American gossip from the intellectual underworld, of tall goings-on, of tiny victories and disasters, aching to gabble I found myself in a company of amiable, wrestling, maudlin, beetle-skulled men, semi-men, and many kinds of women, who did not know or care I had been so far and wildly away but seemed to think I had been in the party all the whooping time. Sober, airsick, pan-caked flat, I saw these intelligent old friends as a war-renful of blockish stinkers, and sulked all morning over my warm beer as they clamoured and hiccuped, rolled rogering down, fell gayly through windows, sang and splintered. And in the afternoon I stood—I was the only one who could—alone and disillusioned among the snorers and the dead. They grunted all around me, or went soughing and green to their Maker. As the little murdered moles in the Scotch poem, like sma' Assyr-ians they lay. I was close to crying there, in the chaotic middle of anti-climax.

It was the day after the coronation of Elizabeth II. Seldom has such a piously jubilant occasion released such a de-lirium of epitomes. True, he is making the most of his chance: Dylan the Iceman cometh indeed—he double-cometh; but it is impossible not to respond to the mix-up here of first-time freshness and hell *déjà-vu*. He is writing like a more exuberant Malcolm Lowry, with all of Low-ry's capacity to site himself at the center of a universe and to render miscellany into fluent vision.

Thomas's life was tough and, as everyone knows by now, he had an almost perverse fondness for making bad things worse. Such is the rhetoric of his life-style. And this ten-dency (seen above) to put life out of joint, to disarrange it and blur it, operated in his conduct—as if to live untidily, confusedly, were a surer way of getting at the heart of things: the sense of being human only, rather than of being specifically Dylan Thomas. It is not so much a reduction to absurdity as an elevation to community. E. F. Bozman, head of Dents, his English publishers, says Thomas "had no desire to understand" even his own poetry. "In fact he used to say that he couldn't be expected to do so. Hadn't he written it? Surely that was enough to ask of anyone."

This isn't just a matter of the vatic pose, although there is some of that in it. Rather, it is one of the facets of Tho-mas's improvident, accidental way of living. He tossed his fanatically patterned poems into the maelstrom of the world and left them to fend for themselves, almost as he tossed in his own identity. Like something sloughed off.

Romantic? Antic? Of course: every bit as much as Alex-ander Pope's flinging his manuscripts from a speeding car-riage instead of delivering them quietly in person. Tho-mas's poems, like the orthodoxies he garbled into metaphors—like the pieties he planted in his verbal clown-ing—had to take their chances. Intrinsically perfect (at least, as good as he could make them), they had been equipped with everything which, as poems, they could need. As commodities they didn't interest him, any more than the making of money or reputation did. It is not enough to say, as many have said, that he longed for the indulgences due to a child: he wanted, not childhood, or babyhood, but the raw, essential humanity that underlies the steady patterns, the solecisms, the nice appraisals and the reasoned amenities of judicious living. Not regression but the fanning of chaff from the grain. It may be, of course, that the chaff is essential to any account of man; and it may also be that the grain—man in the raw—isn't very interesting. But that is what, in his religious and cos-mic fervor, he preferred to attend to (and he did at least know and say exactly what the chaff is like). He had what I would call a processive view of things: something was always happening, somebody's blood running, somebody's blood stopping, the earth turning, always some kind of weather arriving, something being bought, broken or lost. And this sense of process was enough for him. Reductive, immature, uncivilized, simpleminded, unsophisticated, pseudobasic—call his attitude what we will—it helped him to feel more intensely where he had chosen not to try to understand. To him, "comprehend" is to take in, to in-clude, not to see the meaning of. No wonder he seems to mythologize his characters before he reveals what they are like: Ann Jones, mourned in "After the Funeral," is an oc-casion for words; in the poems on marriage, Caitlin Tho-mas is a mere figment in the churning rhetoric; and the personages of **Under Milk Wood** are only (as they were meant to be) voices. His final attitude, milky and maybe wooden, is "unjudging love," which is the human version of what he felt towards God, words and ideas.

Naturally, this makes him a problem to academic exegetes. What, after all, is the trained mind to make of a writer who feels at one with his own Mary Ann Sailor? Every morning she "shouts her age to the heavens; she believes the town is the chosen land, and the little river Dewi the River of Jordan; she is not at all mad; she merely believes in heaven on earth. And so with all of them . . . all, by their own rights, are ordinary and good." If such a view seems lumpish and undiscriminating, then we must lump it and not probe into it. Highest common factors and lowest common denominators go together in all his writings; and his poetic idiom—while subtle and finely wrought—itself is rich with clichés and slang deliberately flaunted against what Stephen Spender called (in words that Thomas thought "altogether true") "a correct idiom capable of refinements of beauty, but incapable of harsh effects, coarse texture and violent colours."

Oddly enough, Thomas's primitive view, exempting him from judging and mind reading, released him for cataloguing and description. He was ever alert to detail, to externals, to the absurdities of behavior. To him, these things were all part of the human circus; but, not feeling obliged to make sense of them, he often saw them with a sharper eye than any witch-hunting moralist or idea-mad missionary. The eye—the swift, focused, receptive organ of *Portrait of the Artist As A Young Dog,* of the nonsurrealistic stories, of the unfinished *Adventures in the Skin Trade,* of the Swansea-scapes, the Christmas reverie and the bubbling letters—is almost that of a satirist. Except that the satirist has correction and reform on the brain, whereas Thomas thinks of no such thing, practicing instead a documentary hedonism. He makes the most of every scene, permitting himself hyperbole and bits of dithyramb, but never losing the essentials of what confronts him. This side of him has never been given its due: Thomas the idiosyncratic reporter is every bit as important as Thomas the visionary music man. Perhaps he held to particulars to steady himself while scrambling the facts of life; perhaps it amused him to witness such multitudinously intricate surfaces and performances on the crust of a turning ball of rock dominated by a solar system anonymously created but, all the same, unerring in its detailed operation on every living, sentient or dead entity. I think so. Mostly on the side of the universe (the life-force or God or Nature), he was obliged, merely to preserve balance, to be on the side of man as well, but man seen one-souled, one-bodied, in a consanguinity beyond all formulas, regimes and policies, beyond etiquettes and names. It is, of course, the near-opinionlessness of the hierophant, and it explains his incredibly vague notions about communism, war and taxation. If this worries us, we can cheer up at once: there are scores of other writers, poets even, who understand these matters well, their minds never having been clouded by the myth of a man-shaped moon or their ears beguiled by a blind horse singing sweetly.

The authorized *Life* and the spate of memoirs—some of the latter hagiographical claptrap, some of them sly and biased, the best of them mercifully playing down the American tours—perform a useful service in bringing Thomas to earth, in revealing the matter-of-fact spectator who ranks with Chaucer and Byron. In fact the biographical materials do more for Thomas the spectator than some of the critical studies do for Thomas the poet. I am not sure, even, that the quality of the observation isn't consistently higher than the quality of the poems. Perhaps Thomas, given his handful of remarkable poems, might eventually emerge—once all his prose has been ferreted out and collected—as a minor poet who wrote major documentary. It doesn't matter yet; the main thing is to notice how precise, vivid and evocative his prose is (and there is a lot of it).

One of the fine things about Fitzgibbon's gracious, decent biography is the way he lets Thomas tell his own story. In prose, no matter how tired or off-color he was, Thomas never wrote dully, hardly ever failed to generate somewhere along the way an exuberance that rose to the occasion and sometimes engulfed it. Here, to plead the case, are some samples run together, giving the timbre and variety he made his own. He never, never—it is apparent—wrote prose for the sake of austerity:

> I liked the taste of beer, its live, white lather, its brass-bright depths, the sudden world through the wet-brown walls of the glass, the tilted rush to the lips and the slow swallowing down to the lapping belly, the salt on the tongue, the foam at the corners. . . . I think England is the very place for a fluent and fiery writer. The highest hymns of the sun are written in the dark. I like the grey country. . . . I'm not a country man; I stand for, if anything, the aspidistra, the provincial drive, the morning café, the evening pub; I'd like to believe in the wide open spaces as the wrapping around walls, the windy boredom between house and house, hotel and cinema, bookshop and tube-station; man made his house to keep the world and the weather out, making his own weathery world inside. . . . We have got to know lots of the young intellectuals of Florence, and a damp lot they are. They visit us on Sundays. To overcome the language, I have to stand on my head, fall in the pool, crack nuts with my teeth, and Tarzan in the cypresses. . . . What a sun-pissed pig I am not to dip a bristle in Chianti. . . . I went out of the house . . . to see if it was raining still, if the outhouse had been blown away, potatoes, shears, rat-killer, shrimpnets, and tins of rusty nails aloft on the wind, and if all the cliffs were left. . . . The rest of America may be all right, and perhaps I can understand it, but that is the last monument there is to the insane desire for power that shoots its buildings up to the stars and roars its engines louder and faster than they have ever been roared before and makes everything cost the earth and where the imminence of death is reflected in every last power stroke and grab of the great moron bosses, the big-shots, the multis one never sees. . . . I buried my head in the sands of America; flew over America like a damp, ranting bird; boomed and fiddled while home was burning. . . . I shall polish up my glass belly.

Sometimes he verged on incoherence, especially in letters; but there was not, I think, a tone or an attitude he did not command: from urchin pathos to the gusto of the roaring boy, from ironically staid self-definition to the BBC primness of a man with the Elgin marbles in his mouth, from the mock-agony of a shiverer in New York or Prague to arch hyperbole, from brokenhearted prolix amorousness to vaulting comminations, from self-astounding naïveté to the fatigue of a 100-year-old man of the world, from explosive profanity to quiet ribbing, from importunity to funereal tact. If I seem to be laboring this point, I am. It has to be said again and again that Thomas was a virtuoso of prose both descriptive and narrative. He was also a master of talk: the dialogue in *Adventures in the Skin Trade,* for example, has just the right sort of faltering stiltedness for what he is doing:

"I think my finger must have swollen, Mr. Allingham. The bottle's much tighter now."

"Let me have a look at you again." Mrs. Dacey put on a pair of spectacles with steel rims and a hanging chain. "He's only a baby."

"I'm twenty."

"Ikey Mo, the baby farmer." She walked carefully to the back of the shop and called, "Polly, come down here. Polly. Polly."

A girl's voice called back from high up in the house, "What for, Ma?"

"Come and get a gentleman's bottle off."

Surrealism is implicit, but it is the vernacular that carries the scene. Thomas's talk is usually of this kind, whereas that in Joyce becomes vernacular orchestrated far beyond the convention of written exchange. The essential difference between Thomas and Joyce (with whom, and always unfavorably, David Holbrook compares him in his articulate but niggling study) is that Thomas was not a pedant, had little learning, and was satisfied with the dictionary as he found it. Small wonder that Thomas in prose (and even in verse) appeals to readers of all kinds, both sophisticates and general readers, whereas Joyce, transmogrifying the idiom of simple people, gains in magic what he loses in readers. Joyce is a great writer, Thomas is not. But Thomas is a read writer, as available to greengrocer as to erudite don, and Joyce in comparison is not. Holbrook, setting out to chasten and subdue but managing only to distort and becloud, merits an answer or two—although this is merely to point out that it is no use blaming molasses for not being a disinfectant. But even hypocriticism must be answered; so here goes.

III

What is offensive in Holbrook's attack on Thomas is not his dissection of the obscurest poems (he does this with elegance, sense and occasional wit), nor his condemnation of babble, monotony, syntactical and punctuational sloppiness (all these are there in the poems), nor his lamenting Thomas's passion for drink (over-drinking he did kill himself). It is his presumption, made on the evidence of what he calls Thomas's infantilism, that Mrs. Thomas did not love her son. After quoting from Menninger's *Man Against Himself* he says, "In Dylan Thomas's life and in his poetry we witness the poignant quest of an adult to find the (mother) love he remains unconvinced of having had as a child." Thomas became what he became because, it seems, "The only way to integrated consciousness in the infant is through the gradual pains of disillusionment, at the hands of a mother who can enable the child to bear this by her continuing and loving presence." Mrs. Florence Hannah Thomas has a lot to answer for—at least if we credit this fancy bit of *a posteriori* snooping. It is enough to quote from Fitzgibbon's biography:

> Florence, his mother, was from all accounts a sweet, gentle, and rather childish woman, and she gave her

son the measureless and uncritical love that comes more easily from a simple heart. . . .

> She was a gay, garrulous woman. . . .

> And the placid, simple love and pride she felt for him still shines, cosy as a fire in a cottage kitchen, in what she said about him after his death when she had become, and signed her letters, "Dylan's Mam."

How sad it is when a critic with a half-baked theory self-righteously perverts the facts of a privacy. As Fitzgibbon says, when Dylan Thomas reached late adolescence, "he was to find his mother's ignorance and her conventional views irritating." He got over that and "Certainly he loved and looked after her in her old age." If he behaved like a baby (Holbrook gloatingly quotes Richard Eberhart's getting Thomas up in the morning "by plugging his mouth with a bottle of beer, this wonderful baby"), the reasons were complicated and obviously had little to do with his mother's early treatment of him. But Holbrook wants it all ways: whether she loved him or not, she unfitted him for life as an adult. And this determination to find a victim—to ram home what looks like a thesis or a diagnosis but actually is more like animus—shows too in Holbrook's discussion of the poems when he finally gets to them.

First, though, let's see what sort of a chap we have to deal with. There are glimpses. "Those qualities I find most satisfying in the poetry of the past," he begins, like a parsonical Blimp lamenting the lack of fiber in today's young men, "I seldom find in contemporary poetry." "Our language," he says a bit further on, although one doesn't know what he means or what evidence he has, "no longer seeks, as folk idiom sought, moral truths and attitudes to life as a natural habit." Discussing "Bit out the mandrake," he confides (in a footnote buried at the end of the book) that although the image is disgusting the genital kiss it evokes is not. So there: we're dealing with a real man; the damnation of Thomas is coming from no prude. But he does disapprove of Thomas's "frenetic sexual activity" (which Fitzgibbon says "was mostly talk") and, with spinsterly hauteur, observes that

> Thomas's deep fear of mature reality is a complement to his promiscuity, as is symbolized by his recurrent images of sexual potency being dissolved in alcohol or some other form of oblivion. (Kingsley Amis manifests the same symptoms. . . .)

I wonder what Amis thinks of that. In Holbrook's hands, literary criticism degenerates into moral objurgation. He doesn't like literature that displays what Arnold called "indifference to moral ideas." One gets the impression of a smug person who had a happy childhood, has no complexes, conducts his own life with immaculate sagacity, knows how everyone else ought to live and also what they should think about death. "Thomas," he incredulously says, "displays a neurotic fear of death." Well, poor all of us, to die prematurely on the altar of so vague a phrase. Holbrook sounds like a cosmic headmaster writing Little Thomas's school report (it is not surprising that Thomas had a neurotic fear of critics too).

Elsewhere, Holbrook chatters on about decent values, ancient virtues and lost roots (all that feudal saliva) about which he would be more convincing if he didn't sound like a censorious pedagogue who, simply because he isn't on Thomas's wave-length and dare not be, buries the poems in dogged analysis. I share his passion for things regional, for such rural idioms as "screwmatic" and "solintary," for poetry "enriched by contact with popular life." Yet when Thomas goes regional (which, as John Ackerman points out, is often)—imports some curious idiom or a bit of slang—Holbrook either ignores it or damns it on principle because the person who did it was Thomas. Let's face it: Thomas had the life he had; he was not a moralist, he was a sensation-stater sometimes beyond his own control; but, to any adult, and perhaps to some children, he speaks as honestly as he can, meriting not only sympathy but also (one shouldn't have to say it) fair play.

Take a few more samples. Holbrook quotes, as having "genuineness," the following lines: "No worse, there is none. Pitched past pitch of grief. . . ." and "No, Time, thou shalt not boast that I do change. . . ." I find an equal "genuineness" and memorableness in "Do not go gentle into that good night" and "It was my thirtieth year to heaven." If only Holbrook were as generous and discerning with Thomas as he is with *Sir Gawaine and the Grene Knight,* into which he plunges in much the same way as he claims Thomas does into a lost childhood.

See how he dogs the Welshman. At the lines, "she would lie dumb and deep / And need no druid of her broken body," he asks, "why not let her lie then?" Why write the poem? It is like asking why Keats didn't cut short his *Ode* to set up nest with the nightingale (which is presumably what he wanted to do all along). Again, when Holbrook complains of the "comic advertisement-copy language of some of his BBC talks," he is exaggerating the amount of poppycock in those talks and objecting because he doesn't appreciate comedy: for all his advocacy of the popular, he is disdainful of such things as "the cliché jest about freezing the testicles off a brass monkey." Thomas, of course, doted on such jests. Again, Holbrook contends "there is nothing in the prose writings of Dylan Thomas to assist our discriminating response to his poetry." Let him read that profound letter to Pamela Hansford Johnson on "earthiness" and John Donne, or the long letter which the egregious American student Richard Jones published as "Dylan Thomas's Poetic Manifesto," or the bizarre but revealing note to Charles Fisher: "Poetry, heavy in tare though nimble, should be as orgastic and organic as copulation, dividing and unifying, personal but not private, propagating the individual in the mass and the mass in the individual." How easily, too, he is taken in: "wherever he [Thomas] writes about his work he does so in a remarkably off-hand and even irresponsible manner." Naughty Thomas. Slap him on the knuckles with a ruler. It isn't true, of course; but it is true of, say, Byron and Faulkner, and their facetious *obiter dicta* misled nobody about their real intentions.

But Holbrook's obstinacy in what Dr. Johnson called "the habitual cultivation of the powers of dislike" shows most vividly when he picks three lines for paraphrase and comment. These are the lines:

> There was a saviour
> Rarer than radium,
> Commoner than water, crueller than truth.

This is the paraphrase:

> There was once a saviour *of mankind* who was at the same time *of a* rarer *quality* than radium, more common *than* water, and crueller than truth. (italics mine)

Funny: he understands the lines (this time not obscure enough—"the complications are not the felt complications in grappling with experience that we have in, say, the poetry of Hopkins") but, while holding that "the poem is an unsatisfactory way of putting something that is better said in prose," makes an even more unsatisfactory prose of his own. His comment goes thus: "Radium is something of which we have only intellectual knowledge, that water is common is a truism, and that truth is cruel is a platitude." To be more accurate: the conjunction of saviour with radium astonishes and suggests inexplicable, cosmic power (and radium needles, once used in treating birth marks on children's hands, are not intellectual—especially if you have seen some of the unfortunate results); the unfamiliar truism about water (not "muck") is there to steady us after the shock of the first two lines; and crueller than truth—a truism from everyday idiom—brings us back to things ordinary. It isn't one of Thomas's most remarkable poems, but one can make a case even for those first three lines as a revelation declining into the homespun mundane.

Holbrook fails to see that Thomas conceived his poems not *about* life, but *as* life, and expected his reader to respond in the same first-hand way—as if (I quote John Bayley) "we are being assaulted by something other than words." But words they are, shoved to memorable limits sometimes and more suasive than Holbrook, pedantically objecting at every turn, allows himself to see. Even when he manages to praise a few touches in **Under Milk Wood** he follows up with this: "**Under Milk Wood** is trivial. And, indeed, it is really dangerous, because it flatters and reinforces the resistance to those deeper insights we need. . . . **Under Milk Wood** reinforces untenderness. It is a cruel work, inviting our cruel laughter." Now who ever thought reading was a safe activity? Ah well. Holbrook further objects to the "sex, boozing, eccentricity, cruelty [again], dirty behaviour. . . ." Wouldn't we have a nice literature if there were only nice people to write about? **Under Milk Wood** isn't meant as a moral tract anyway. But Thomas must be allowed to get away with nothing: when he imports the phrase "dickybird watching" to give the texture some popular color, Holbrook calls it "a cliché of journalistic writing." And what Holbrook calls the play's "childish dirty jokes" express, as dirty jokes often do, an embarrassed reverence for life. He is willing to make a negative point: "We may remember how Joyce 'places'

Mrs. Bloom, by making her, in the shame of her adultery, want to shout out obscene words." But, being so negative, he perhaps doesn't know that many men and women in this climax of sexual bliss also shout out obscene words—in licentious gratitude and no doubt as a stimulus to further spontaneity. ***Under Milk Wood*** is a hymn to life, an apostrophe to an imagined heaven, and not (*pace* Holbrook's "no controlling irony") a short story by Henry James. But bawdy, nought-sticky, immoral, tough and whimsical by turns, down-to-earth, mocking, chattily stylish, racy, pungent, punitive? Yes. And schizoid, infantile, dangerous, ugly, sadistic, full of hate? No: only to someone too seraphic to stomach the daft vigors of average humanity.

John Ackerman's very different (although partly biographical) approach benefits from his knowledge of Wales. Take, for example, Evans the Death's dream in ***Under Milk Wood***: "he runs out into the field where his mother is making welshcakes in the snow, and steals a fistful of snowflakes and currants." This is not entirely fantasy, Ackerman says, because "it was the custom in Wales when making welshcakes to use snow in the mixture." Ackerman knows, as few of us do, his *Mabinogion* too, usefully indicating the geniality and "earthy, colloquial humour" that Thomas drew from it. He also makes fascinating mention of how Swansea responded to a performance of ***Under Milk Wood***. These four lines—

> We are not wholly bad or good
> Who live our lives under Milk Wood,
> And Thou, I know, wilt be the first
> To see our best side, not our worst

—London found amusing, as out of nervousness it finds almost anything. In Swansea, however, there were "murmurings of assent and approval." And he rightly observes that Thomas isn't satirical or mocking here.

His discussion of **"After the Funeral"** is—what Holbrook's is not—even tempered, attuned and intuitive: the poet, he comments, "is embittered by the facile and—to him—inadequate acquiescence of the bereaved, who find sufficient balm in the theology of their conventional Nonconformist beliefs." Although "inadequate" is at first misleading (he means "too ready" not "insufficient"), the comment is perceptive, as is this: "Thomas's way of life followed a working-class rather than middle-class pattern." As he points out, the social structure of Wales isn't that of England. This is the salt to be taken with Thomas's and his wife's protestations of being bourgeois, and with Holbrook's blithe assumption that ***Under Milk Wood*** is about the suburban bourgeoisie (it is much more esoteric than that).

We see from Ackerman's book how useful a critic can be who is not trying primarily to score off his author. He makes judicious use of the manuscripts, and his first two chapters, on the Welsh background, are essential reading. A less biographically inclined critic, William Moynihan, interests himself in Thomas's religiousness and his love of

sound. In the prefatory note to ***Collected Poems,*** he justly identifies "a religious impulse as old as the rites of Nemi, or as Genesis itself"—an impulse blatant in ***Under Milk Wood*** which he rescues from the irrelevant charge that it "shows no character change or development. Such a view is about as relevant as saying Captain Ahab had no sense of humor." Altogether less reassuring is his introduction into the argument of "Lupasco's new logic," of such language as "the potential-kinetic alternation of forces," and what he calls "affinitive patterns," by which he intends a semantics of alliteration—founded, with constructive piety, on Thomas's telling Pamela Hansford Johnson in 1934 that the word "drome" gave him a vision of the gates of heaven. It was, said Thomas, the long *m* that did it. And the long *o* suggested the movement of God. For my money, that long *m* suggests a cow in pensive, greeting mood, while the long *o* reminds me of the herald in Chaucer's *Knight's Tale*.

At his best when "placing" Thomas in relation to other writers, Moynihan points out how D. H. Lawrence "accepts death and looks forward to it as a release" whereas "there is neither rest nor peace in [Thomas's] vision of death; there is rather an alleluia of all the earth's potential energy." Later on he says that "Silence for Thomas was death, sound was life," and this explains not only death's being for Thomas a kind of cosmic boisterousness but also his developing—to extraordinary extremes—the principle of Welsh verse: that sound is as important as sense. Ackerman, says Moynihan, rather skimps the significance to Thomas of sound; but Ackerman does provide a local point that neatly fits into what Moynihan says: "As Thomas well knew, pub singing in Wales can move with complete ease from bawdy to a favourite hymn or folksong." In other words, as in Thomas's poems, routine divisions are forgotten in "the love of Man and in praise of God." It is Rilke's principle, quoted by Moynihan, of "*dennoch prisen*: praise still, praise in spite of everything." The praise is also a means of raging against the night, the not known. "Arguing simultaneously that man is incapable of ever knowing right from wrong and that man must believe, must have faith," Moynihan says, "was no paradox to Thomas." Confronted with "the determined amorality of existence" and "the need for faith," what could Thomas do but both praise and refuse the good night, the bad night, neither gently praising nor gently refusing.

After all the homages and allowances have been made, we still have to reckon with—and find our own adjustments to—what Thomas hoped would be a lucky naïveté, what Holbrook finds a tropic of whimper, and what in fact is the exploitation of language to allusive, rhythmic maxima in the quest for eternal "unaccommodated man." It is by now traditional to object that Thomas wrote for his own voice only (even to the extent of *his* performance of a poem being an essential part of the poem—Do not trespass on the alleluias) and to find incongruous majesty in steaksauce or Cinzano labels when chanted in the Thomas manner. The trouble is not the atavism or the dithyramb or the self-engrossed insufficiency; it is something else, unique to

Thomas, I think—an inscrutably complex mesh of gifts and vices that I would dub mystical Micawberism, whose inadequacies Thomas remedied with his own special brand of emergency panache. Something impulsive but lackadaisical too, something inspired but also forced, something too private to be naturally communicable, something too hammy to be honest—this something is what flaws the career.

But who, any more, wants to count the cost? Or ask why? The gains are there in his almost total disregard of what is rational in literature and life. Holbrook on Thomas sounds like Wyndham Lewis on Faulkner's "slipshod and redundant artistic machine," just as Thomas's defenders—or at least the stayers of his execution—sound like Richard Rovere arguing, in his preface to The Modern Library *Light in August,* the case for Faulkner's prose in a time that cherishes the concise, the functional, the tame. Let us not fence with this poet's bones or dump his indiscretions on his grave. Let us even try to numb our ears to the relentlessly dramatic din of his voice. Let us sift the words. If we can: for me, one image persists—not the Dunlop-rubber moon of a face, but the face of D. M. Thomas in the local newspaper, looking exhaustedly down after winning the mile race in the school sports. Whether he won or lost the race of his life I don't know or much care. He surely is not the competitor-type, but rather—and perhaps we shall increasingly come to see him like this—the spy, the watcher, the delver, the ponderer in his place, guessing at the infernal-divine machinery underlying his local patch: Cwmdonkin Drive, the pounded, curving spread of the tidal beach at the Boat House, the stark egg-white walls in the barnyard at Fern Hill. All he ever needed was that locality.

At the cremation of his father, Thomas remained outside only to be told by some ghoul how D. J. Thomas's skull had burst like a bomb in the heat of the furnace. The grisly image, by courtesy of Fitzgibbon, somehow epitomizes the son's subject matter. That a skull should do that, should have to do that or rot, is matter enough for anyone's lifetime of wondering. This mutability of the physical tormented Thomas into envisioning an ecological busyness no less thorough than Hamlet's. He wanted to know how the universe runs itself on earth, both before and beyond an ordinary life-span; he wanted, as I have said, a sense of the all, rather than everything making sense. It is the *how* rather than the *why* that nags at him; and that is why, after reading him, we are none the wiser, although we may be better informed.

Walford Davies (essay date 1968)

SOURCE: "Imitation and Invention: The Use of Borrowed Material in Dylan Thomas's Prose," in *Essays in Criticism,* Vol. XVIII, No. 3, July, 1968, p. 275-95.

[*In the following essay, Davies examines the influences of Thomas Hardy, the* Mabinogion, *Charles Dickens, Ambrose Bierce, and others on Thomas's stories and film scripts.*]

Brander Matthews once proposed a grading of the short story in terms of its compliance with a catalogue of qualities—something like a working list of litmus tests, of which the most notable were unity, compression, originality, ingenuity and fantasy (*Saturday Review,* July 1884). These features, or aspects of them, are certainly valid yardsticks, but Matthews's third requirement, 'originality', has to be defined and re-defined if it is to be a yardstick of any critical use. Influences which are assimilated into tone or theme in the ordinary run of prose fiction need not be closely defined; but when, on the other hand, whole plots, or segments of plot or descriptive narrative, are borrowed by an author from elsewhere, the test is to see in what way imitation becomes invention. Shakespeare survives because he is so much more resourceful than the plots he adopted, because poetry re-defines material radically. Even with prose, however, and even in the case of its less ambitious forms, the process is interesting and informative. With the short story, a genre which over the last half-century has moved further and further away from the formal requirements of plot in the strictest sense, increasing emphasis has been placed on the power to reveal rather than state. The insistence of E. M. Forster on aesthetic rather than structural compactness in *Aspects of the Novel* and of a commentator like I, Hendry on 'revealed' rather than stated meaning ('Joyce's Epiphanies', *Critiques and Essays on Modern Fiction,* 1952) has drawn attention more to vertical depth and less to horizontal plot in fiction. And so, where the horizontal apparatus of plot is in fact borrowed from elsewhere, the reader is now critically prepared to see the material function in new hands.

Dylan Thomas's prose works vary enormously and range from the intense and often moving early stories to the adept radio broadcasts; from the comic elegy of **Portrait of the Artist as a Young Dog** to the lyrical impressionism of **Under Milk Wood** and the melodramatic facility of the film scenarios. Nevertheless, a feature common to all his prose is the tendency to borrow material from his reading of other authors. The tendency ranges in quantity from the borrowing of a few words to the employment of total plots. As the range varies, so does the measure of success or failure, and often the habit is a good indication of the nature of Thomas's imagination. In the poetry the device sometimes provides successful drama by verbal allusion. In the late poem, **'In Country Sleep'**, for example, the young girl's growth to sexual self-determination is marked by an allusion to a striking clause in Hardy's 'A Broken Appointment'. The ominous arrival of Time and Maturity—'*he comes* designed . . . *He comes* to take . . . *He comes* to leave her . . . Naked and forsaken *to grieve he will not come*' catches the dramatic lament of Hardy's '*You did not come . . . Grieved I,* when, as the hope hour stroked its sum, *You did not come*'. The reference here (incidentally, it is a poem Thomas was once recorded reading) is part of the drama and is all the more fruitful for being recognised.

Similarly, the tendency in the prose works, where it functions more consistently, can be Eliotian in its ability to juxtapose old contexts with new. In this way it can point to the quality of satire in a work like the play for voices. When, for example, the narrator says, 'The music of the spheres is heard distinctly over Milk Wood. It is "The Rustle of Spring"', the response required, one invited by Thomas's own inverted commas, is to realise that the reference is to a salon piece called 'The Rustle of Spring' written by Sinding, a minor Danish imitator of Grieg, who was popular at the turn of the century. Immediately we are in touch with something like mock-heroics, comic because the nearest approximation to the music of the spheres can only be a piano cliché, redolent of suburbia with its aspidistra atmosphere. Or, again, when Eli Jenkins speaks of 'Llaregyb Hill, that mystic tumulus, the memorial of peoples that dwelt in the region of Llaregyb before the Celts left the Land of Summer and where the old wizards made themselves a wife out of flowers' (p. 82), the mock-romantic element is best savoured when we notice the direct source of the passage. Eli Jenkins's words are almost a verbatim rendering of some lines in Arthur Machen's *Autobiography* (1922), where the author recalls that 'as soon as I saw anything I saw Twyn Barlwm, that mystic tumulus, the memorial of the peoples that dwelt in that region before the Celts left the Land of Summer'. Thomas probably took the reference from Gwyn Jones's *A Prospect of Wales* (1948) where this exact section is quoted (p. 17). Mock-heroics at third hand seem particularly appropriate, and are further helped by the lifting of the idea of making 'a wife out of flowers' from Gwyn Jones's translation (with T. Jones) of *The Mabinogion* (1949, p. 65). The Eliotian idea of embarrassing present company by means of retrospective borrowings is here successful, and it deserves to be recognised.

A discussion of Thomas's borrowings in prose would, therefore, seem to be a suitable means of examining the nature of his work in this medium. But before looking at two examples of how Thomas's short stories are modelled on total plots from other sources, it may be profitable to point out further examples of this widespread tendency to borrow, thus establishing it as conscious effort rather than isolated accident. It is quite clear that in a work like **Under Milk Wood** the composition of something like paper-clippings from other authors is suitable to the pointilliste nature of the play for voices. The whole tone and manner of the narrating voices especially seems to benefit from the pattern of swift allusion. One example that is particularly successful is the description of Lord Cut Glass. This probably had Dickens's description of Mr. Sapsea in *Edwin Drood* as its direct original. The First Voice depicts Lord Cut Glass 'in his kitchen full of time', surrounded by untidy detail and especially by a fantastic collection of clocks. He is described as a man seeking to overcome Time by living in 'a house and a life at siege' afraid of that final time when 'the tribes and navies of the Last Black Day' will 'sear and pillage down Armageddon Hill' (p. 66). The same comic fortification had been attempted by Dickens's Mr. Sapsea who

> sits in his dull ground-floor sitting-room, giving first on his paved back yard; and then on his railed-off garden. Mr. Sapsea has a bottle of port wine on a table before

the fire . . . and is characteristically attended by his portrait, his eight-day clock, and his weather-glass. Characteristically, because he would uphold himself against mankind, his weather-glass against weather, and his clock against time (ch. IV).

The idea of a 'house and life at siege' had, then, a clear source in Dickens, for whom Mr. Sapsea's posture for combat was no doubt a more positive extension of that other house at siege, Wemmick's in *Great Expectations* (ch. XXV).

Dickens had been a source-author for Thomas from a very early period. No doubt the poet felt an affinity of comic attitude with the novelist: but the connection could also be made with the material of ordinary melodrama. In 1933, a short story called 'Jarley's' was published by Thomas in his school magazine. The nominal acknowledgement made in that title to the wax-works of the same name in Dickens's *The Old Curiosity Shop* is not the only connection; but a more interesting debt was contracted in a story which Thomas was to publish immediately afterwards. This was **'After the Fair'** which describes the flight of a young girl from the police to the safety of a fairground. The story suggests the sanctuary which Nell finds in Mrs. Jarley's wax-works in Dickens's novel and the parallel also centralises the specifically Dickensian pathos of Thomas's story, relieved as it is by the Dickensian figure of the Fat Man. Sporadic borrowings from Dickens are essentially of this nature, such as would consolidate convenient atmosphere and convenient comic touches. The debt can be traced through David Copperfield's initial fear of his own home (ch. II) to the small boy's fear of the house in the *Portrait* (p. 13); from Pip's fight with Herbert Pocket in *Great Expectations* (ch. XI) to the schoolboy fight of the *Portrait*'s 'The Fight'; and from Pip's Christmas meal with Wopsle, Hubble and Pumblechook (ch. IV) to Thomas's family evening meal in the *Portrait* (p. 90). The world of children as it is controlled and inhibited by grown-ups is a significant legacy from Dickens and to it Thomas brings his own considerable ear for dialogue, following Dickens in theme to the exclusion only of the novelist's insistence on human viciousness.

But even clearer is the presence of Dickens in Thomas's unfinished autobiographical novel, **Adventures in the Skin Trade.** Describing the novel at an early stage, Thomas wrote to Vernon Watkins that it was 'a mixture of Oliver Twist, Little Dorrit, Kafka, Beachcomber . . .' and the speed with which the novel was written was no doubt facilitated by this element of parody. Thus, when Samuel Bennet is ruining his teacher-father's exercise books, tearing up his mother's photographs, and breaking the family china the night before he leaves for London, his fear of detection is given imaginatively in terms of a Dickensian situation. He is afraid 'that the strangers upstairs he had known since he could remember would wake and come down with pokers and candles' (p. 19). Touched upon here is what Thomas must have considered an archetypal Dickensian situation—as, for example, described in Sikes's attempted burglary in *Oliver Twist* (ch. XXII) and illustrated in Cruikshank's drawing. The element of surface allusion may also function in the description of Bennet's sensations on regaining consciousness in Mrs. Dacey's house after drinking the daughter's eau-de-cologne. Shades of the bewildered Oliver Twist regaining consciousness in Mr. Brownlow's house (ch. XII) and again later in Mrs. Maylie's house (ch. XXVIII) seem to stand behind the description. The result is that some form of connotative irony comes into play, since the 'innocence' of Samuel Bennet is a ludicrous analogy to the real innocence of Oliver. Where the allusions come to the surface we have the direct confession of parody. For instance, when Bennet sees Mr. Allingham stealing the waitress's tip in the station restaurant in London, he thinks of the waitress with exaggerated sympathy as someone who would suffer unbearably through losing the money and who had a husband and two children to support. He first conceives the children's names to be Tristram and Eve, but changes the names quickly to Tom and Marge, as if correcting the nominal consistency of the Dickensian atmosphere. Immediately afterwards, he thinks of London's corrupting influence in a way which pushes the sources to the surface of the episode:

> I am not so innocent as I make out, he thought. I do not expect any old cobwebbed Fagin, reeking of character and stories, to shuffle out of a corner and lead me away into his grand, loud, filthy house; there will not be any Nancy to tickle my fancy in a kitchen full of handkerchiefs and beckoning, unmade beds . . . as I walked into London for the first time, rattling my fortune, fresh as Copperfield (pp. 44-5).

For the hero to recognise his experience as a literary permutation is, of course, part of the comedy.

But such suggestions are strengthened by more decisive borrowings. The best example occurs when Mr. Allingham takes Bennet back to his house immediately after his arrival in London. The first room they enter is seen to be full of furniture:

> Every inch of the room was covered with furniture. Chairs stood on couches that lay on tables; mirrors nearly the height of the door were propped, back to back, against the walls, reflecting and making endless the hills of desks and chairs with their legs in the air, sideboards, dressing tables, chests-of-drawers, more mirrors, empty bookcases, washbasins, clothes cupboards. There was a double bed, carefully made, with the ends of the sheets turned back, lying on top of a dining table on top of another table; there were electric lamps and lampshades, trays and vases, lavatory bowls and basins, heaped in the armchairs that stood on cupboards and tables and beds, touching the ceiling. The one window, looking out on the road, could just be seen through the curved legs of sideboards on their backs. The walls behind the standing mirrors were thick with pictures and picture frames (p. 53).

Grotesque emphasis is placed on the description of the overcrowded room and the second chapter is in fact called 'Plenty of Furniture'. Thomas clearly copied the comic potential of such a description from Dickens's *Dombey*

and Son. In that novel, Brogley the Broker's collection of secondhand furniture is described, and the source of Thomas's description becomes obvious, in detail as well as in comic intent:

> Dozens of chairs hooked on to washing stands, which with difficulty poised themselves on the shoulders of sideboards, which in their turn stood upon the wrong sides of dining-tables, gymnastic with their legs upward on the tops of other dining-tables, were among its most reasonable arrangements. A bouquet array of dish-covers, wine glasses, and decanters was generally to be seen, spread forth upon the bosom of a four-post bedstead, for the entertainment of such genial company as half-a-dozen pokers, and a hall lamp. A set of window curtains with no windows belonging to them, would be seen gracefully draping a barricade of chests of drawers, loaded with little jars from chemists' shops (ch. IX).

Such material had interested Dickens since his 'Brokers' and Marine-store Shops' in *Sketches By Boz*: for Thomas, the example was ready-made. But it is also clear that Thomas has here learnt something from Dickens's manner as well as from his material. There is in both cases a fidelity to the fact that shape dictates action or poise: chairs *stand* on couches which in turn *lie* on tables in Thomas's description, just as in Dickens washing-stands *poise* themselves on the *shoulders* of sideboards. The picture has the quiet animation of suggestions of human posture. Similarly, both pieces pinpoint chaos by referring to normality: the idea of a 'reasonable arrangement' and a 'bouquet array' of dish-covers suggest comically some method in madness, while in Thomas's attempt the mirrors seem somehow *designed* to duplicate the chaos and we get the perfect touch of the bed being 'Carefully made, with the ends of the sheets turned back' despite the fact that it stands on top of two tables. It is probably significant that Phillip Lindsay recalls seeing Thomas reading *Dombey and Son* with obvious enjoyment (*Adam International Review* XXI, 1953): it would appear that the source did not come without its accompanying lesson in comic description.

Yet, on the whole, this kind of borrowing remains fragmentary and is not ultimately justified by total transformation in new hands. Except where the borrowings function satirically, they remain for the most part surface, secondhand material and do not move satisfactorily from imitation to invention, being merely short-cuts to the kind of effects Thomas admired in other writers. In this connection it is, therefore, significant that some of Thomas's finest short stories still make use of borrowed material. The difference lies in the degree to which Thomas in his best work in prose is committed to the consistency of the work in progress over and above the skeleton of what is borrowed. In the two examples I shall examine in detail here it appears that the unifying factors are a convincing psychological interest, a penetrating human sympathy and something approaching obsession with poetic symbols. That the examples are some of the poet's most sombre stories may be significant: perhaps what allowed the dissipation of creative energy in mere surface borrowings was the comic mode itself—the comic mode in Thomas's prose works being too often and too conveniently second-hand Dickens.

It can be shown in the first instance that the poet took as his source-pattern for the early short story **'The Dress'** (1934), the American writer Ambrose Bierce's classic tale of the execution of a soldier in the American Civil War, 'An Occurrence at Owl Creek Bridge', which first appeared in *Tales of Soldiers and Civilians* (1891) and was reprinted in the English edition, *In the Midst of Life,* soon afterwards. It was conveniently reprinted in *The Eyes of the Panther* later, in 1928. Bierce's story describes the split-second fantasy which flashes through the soldier's mind at the point of death: he imagines that he thwarts the execution, falling into the river beneath the bridge from which he was to be hanged, and escaping to return home to his wife. After a difficult journey home, described in detail, he is about to embrace his wife when he feels a stunning blow on the back of his neck—and the reader is given a description of the soldier (Farquhar) hanging dead from the bridge. Bierce sought to give the human mind at the exact point of death the appearance and sensation of continuing life which to some degree turns the fact of death into elegy. No doubt Bierce employed the device largely for the sake of bizarre surprise, since the reader is not made aware until the end of the story that Farquhar is in fact dead. Narrative shock, or what A. J. A. Symons once called Bierce's 'dramatic elision' (*Ten Tales*, 1925, p. vii), is characteristic of the author, as a reading of 'Chickamauga' or 'One of the Missing' will show. Thomas, however, was interested in the life-death phenomenon more for the purpose of enlarging imaginative material than for surprise. His connection with Bierce's tale is two-fold: it was a classic use of a psychological phenomenon and also the source of the plot for his own story, **'The Dress',** which Richard Hughes has described as one of the most beautiful short stories in the language.

In suggesting that Thomas was interested in the actual psychological process on which Bierce's story is based, it can be said first of all that what we are dealing with here has very close affinities with the folk notion that a man's whole range of memorable experience comes before him in the event of death. Whatever its validity as psychological fact, it has certainly had wide use in literature. One thinks of *Richard III* (Clarence's dream, I, iv); Mrs. Gaskell's *North and South* (Mr. Hale compared to the Eastern king, ch. 3); Dickens's *Hard Times* (Stephen Blackpool's rescue from the Old Hell Shaft, ch. VI); and William Golding's *Pincher Martin* where it forms the total narrative metaphor of the work. Its function in the Russian film, *Ljetat Zhuravly* ('The Cranes Are Flying') is similar; and William Empson records a biographical fact in his poem 'Success': 'All losses haunt us. It was a reprieve made Dostoevsky talk out queer and clear'. The idea at its crudest and most naïve was used in one of Thomas's later film-scripts, ***The Beach of Falesá,*** where the Captain, waiting with Wiltshire for the arrival of Mr. Case's boat,

recalls that a sailor 'fell out of that boat one night and was drowned when he was drunk! That's a horrible death, drowned when you're drunk. Up comes all your past life in front of you and you're too boozed to see it' (p. 12). It has been touched upon in exactly this form in the ***Portrait*** story, **'Who Do You Wish Was With Us?'**: Ray stumbles down the cliff—'I thought I was done for . . . I could see all my past life in a flash'. But what I am concerned with here is the kind of use made of the idea in the early prose, where its imaginative potential is harnessed to the author's poetic view of experience; where it had not yet become a surface joke.

We first encounter the theme as early as 1931, when Thomas published a short story based on the phenomenon in his school magazine, called **'Brember'.** Here an old man enters a house in which he had lived many years before and walks through the room remembering. He discovers a dusty book which relates the history of his family. He 'turned over the pages, until he came to the last: George Henry Brember, last of the line, dies. . . . He looked down on his name, and then closed the book' (April 1931, p. 140). A few years later, another early uncollected story made use of similar material. In **'The End of the River',** Thomas described the last member of an aristocratic family seeking to bring the family line to a close. Though the material is dealt with here in a comic vein which contrasts markedly with the immature 'Gothic' atmosphere attempted in the earlier story, the narrative nevertheless makes sensitive use of extended sensation, seeing death in terms of a metaphor of continuing life. The last of the Quincey family reads the chronicles of his lineage. His own death is given in the metaphor of a journey to find a river's end. He meets a girl at the end of his quest: 'he saw her through his tears and heard her voice singing' (*New English Weekly,* Nov. 1934, p. 134). A later short story, significantly titled **'The True Story',** was to close on exactly the same phenomenon: an old woman lies dying and is nursed by a young girl; Helen kills the old woman and then 'She opened the window . . . and stepped out. "I am flying", she said. But she was not flying' (*Yellowjacket,* May 1939, p. 63).

This last example is doubly significant since **'The True Story'** sought to reproduce the main ingredients of a story which was, to date, Thomas's most comprehensive attempt to turn the phenomenon into total narrative metaphor. This was **'The Visitor'** in which a dying poet is being nursed by a girl called Rhianon. The 'visitor' is Callaghan who in the night takes the poet on a symbolic journey through the continuous mythical geography of the early prose works, the Jarvis valley and the Jarvis hills. The similarity of basic situation is added to in a similar fantasy of escape through flight, bridging sensibly the worlds of life and death. Peter, the poet in the earlier story, continues to 'live' in a world which, after his journey with Callaghan, no longer seems to be the world of literal life; when Rhianon enters his room in the morning, he asks why she is 'putting the sheet over [his] face' (***A Prospect of the Sea,*** p. 34).

Both the plot and the central psychological feature of **'The Visitor'** have sources and parallels in other Anglo-Welsh literature, which may help to explain why Bierce's story should have had such an attraction for Thomas. There is, for example, a close parallel in the story called 'Gone Fishing' by John Wright, where we find a night's stealthy expedition to the river to fish from the coracles to be an enactment of the death of Dad Elias. The situation is familiar: a man lies dying and is tended by his daughter; in the night he hears the voices of the fishermen calling him; he dresses and carries his coracle to the stream; the following morning, when the woman goes to call her father, she sees a smile on his face but cannot wake him: 'Dad Elias had gone fishing' (*Welsh Short Stories,* ed. G. E. Evans, 1959). The parallel is complete except that Thomas does not, like Wright and Bierce, seek to conceal the process of death for the sake of surprise—'Rhianon was attendant on a dead man' (p. 25). Yet the bridge from life to death through the excitement of metaphor is as clear in Wright's story—'The days meant little to him now and they passed with the light by the window. Tonight he would go with them he thought, if they called again' (p. 242)—as it is in Thomas's, where Callaghan 'left alone, leant over the bed and spread the soft ends of his fingers on Peter's eyes. "Now it is night", he said. "Where shall we go tonight?"' (p. 30).

Another exercise of the device, as well as of the attendant circumstances, could have been found by Thomas in the work of a Welshman he greatly admired. At the end of Caradoc Evans's *Nothing to Pay* (1930), Amos is dying and is tended by his wife, Sara. He follows her actions idly, and notices with the same heightened intensity as Peter's ordinary objects about the room. Amos, like Peter, is assured he will survive, and in the process of his death he experiences an intensification of consciousness. Similarly, in an earlier short story by Caradoc Evans, 'The Glory That Was Zion's', the main character is dying and is tended by his wife, Madlen. When he does die, Madlen prepares water to shave him—and the dead man is conscious of her actions. He hears the kettle hissing and gets up to sit by the fire, thinking that his wife is merely preparing tea. Immediately afterwards the situation is clarified by the author's 'From first to last Twm's years were five-and-forty' (*My People,* 1915, p. 65). The extraordinary happening complicates what would otherwise have been a stock situation of Anglo-Welsh fiction, death against a background of domestic ordinariness.

Such examples would no doubt have attracted Thomas and confirmed for him the imaginative potential of blurring life into death or imagination into fact. Such possibilities would perhaps account for his detailed interest in Bierce's story, to which we must now turn. There is no evidence that he had read 'An Occurrence at Owl Creek Bridge' before he wrote **'The Visitor,'** though there is evidence that he had read it before he published **'The Dress'**. Later in the year in which he published **'The Visitor,'** Thomas reviewed (in November, 1935) an anthology of horror stories edited by Denis Wheatley called *A Century of Horror.*

Along with stories by, for example, Poe, Wilkie Collins, Maupassant and Arthur Machen, Ambrose Bierce is here represented by his 'An Occurrence at Owl Creek Bridge'. Thomas published his review in the *Morning Post* some two months before the publication of **'The Dress,'** but his knowledge of the American story could easily have been gained long before this period.

'The Dress' concerns the escape of a man from an asylum. Closely pursued, he makes his way home to a woman who becomes for him the symbol of safety and welcome. 'He thought of the coals that might be hissing in the grate and of the young mother standing alone. He thought of her hair. Such a nest it would make for his hands' (*A Prospect of the Sea,* p. 78). The plan of the story and its narrative progress are immediately recognisable as those of Bierce's tale, and a number of direct parallels link the two. Both fugitives concentrate upon and try to interpret what their pursuers are doing—Farquhar being followed by soldiers and Thomas's fugitive by the asylum warders:

> Behind a tree on the ridge of the hills he had peeped down on to the fields where they hurried about like dogs, where they poked the hedges with their sticks and set up a faint howling as a mist came suddenly from the spring sky and hid them from his eyes (p. 78).

The man in Thomas's story uses the mist to quench his thirst (p. 78), just as Farquhar uses the cool air for the same purpose (*Eyes of the Panther,* p. 40); great emphasis is placed in both cases on the fugitive's flight through a dense forest—after which, in each case, the man unexpectedly finds a road leading in the right direction (Bierce, p. 39; Thomas, p. 78). The impetus which gives both men the power to outdistance their pursuers is the thought of the warmth and safety awaiting them in their respective homes where a beautiful woman waits patiently (Bierce, p. 39; Thomas, p. 79). Both writers emphasise the ominous appearance of the stars—Bierce describing the glimpse through the wood of stars set in strange constellations (p. 40), and Thomas, the appearance through the mist of the 'angles of the stars' (p. 78). The fugitives are both described making progress over distinctly spongy ground: Farquhar feels how 'softly the turf had carpeted the untravelled avenue—he could no longer feel the roadway beneath his feet' (p. 40); Thomas's fugitive walks towards the stars mumbling a tuneless song, 'hearing his feet suck in and out of the spongy earth' (p. 78). When they reach their destination, both men are described as standing at the gate to the house (Bierce, p. 40; Thomas, p. 80). Then the comfort of seeing the woman centres closely on a description of her dress. Farquhar sees 'a flutter of female garments; his wife, looking fresh and cool and sweet, steps down from the veranda to meet him' (p. 40). At this stage in Thomas's story, the title becomes symbolic, evoking the clean sanctuary that has awaited the fugitive's return:

> But the moving of her arm drew the neck of her dress apart, and he stared in wonder at her wide, white forehead, her frightened eyes and mouth, and down to the flowers on her dress. With the moving of her arm, her

dress danced in the light. She sat before him, covered in flowers. 'Sleep', said the madman. And, kneeling down, he put his bewildered head upon her lap (p. 81).

It would seem likely, therefore, that **'The Dress'** is a reworking of Bierce's plot, a fact which highlights the two authors' similar preoccupation with the sensibility-in-death idea. But, having exercised its possibilities in earlier stories, Thomas may have considered it superfluous to make the phenomenon itself too overt in **'The Dress'.** For one thing, it would evoke the source-story too completely. Yet vestiges of this feature may still reside in **'The Dress'.** The story certainly depends on an atmosphere of lyrical unreality, a hint of merely imagined happenings. Perhaps, in assuming that the reader would recognise the direct narrative source, Thomas was able to assume that the story's function as a brief examination of logic-in-sanity, innocence-in-guilt and freedom-in-captivity would be at least emotively apparent as an analogy to Bierce's treatment of the more obvious life-in-death. As a result, the explanation of the story as dream or projected desire lies outside the role of direct narrative statement. Certainly, after **'The Visitor,'** there was no need to be again so specific about the phenomenon.

Yet what makes the story essentially Thomas's own is the fact that in title and in theme it was a poetic consummation in prose of a hauntingly consistent image in his work. The author-story relationship cannot be fully appreciated in this instance until the image is 'placed'. The image is that of a girl's dress, confirmed as metaphor by its very consistency. The way in which it occurs again and again before and after the story which carries it in its title is symptomatic of the romantic oneness of the prose works, especially the early stories. A revealing example occurs in an early unpublished poem in the February, 1933 Notebook MS., where the poet imagines that he sees a boy and girl meeting outside a cemetery. By contrast with death, he sees their love as a transforming quality, turning empty kisses into meaning and the small island of their affection into a costly country. The radiant transience of the two is caught in the image of the girl's summer dress (Poem **'Thirteen'**). In **'After the Fair'** the baby found in the Astrologer's tent—later to be a child-Christ figure in a grotesque pantomime of the flight into Egypt, on the roundabout horses—is comforted on the bosom of the girl's dress (p. 23). In **'The Visitor'** the image was permanently fixed as a metaphor for freshness and comfort—'Rhianon passed in and out, her dress, he smelt as she bent over him, smelling of clover and milk' (p. 28). In his dejection, Peter,

> thinking of the island set somewhere in the south caverns, . . . thought of water and longed for water. Rhianon's dress, rustling about her, made the soft noise of water. He called her over to him and touched the bosom of her dress, feeling the water on his hands (p. 29).

In **'The Mouse and the Woman'**, the story opens in a lunatic asylum: the patients sit looking at the sun or the flowers and the quietness and comfort of the scene are ex-

tended into the narrator's suggestion that 'children in print dresses might be expected to play, not noisily, upon the lawns' (*A Prospect of the Sea,* p. 58). Later, the madman in the asylum remembers the inflections of his lover's voice and 'heard, again, her frock rustling'. When, as a man in the outside world, he had gone to seek her out in the cottage, he found that 'she was not sitting by the fire, as he had expected her to be, smiling upon the folds of her dress' (p. 70), a picture obviously re-worked from the end of **'The Dress'** itself. The image continued to function throughout Thomas's career. Hence, in *The Beach of Falesá,* Uma the native girl is described with her 'long black hair and her bright dress. . . . Shining wet from the sea or the streams' (p. 20). Similarly, there walks in the prim precincts of Milk Wood a girl like Gossamer Beynon, hardly aware of her visual suggestion of visionary purity—'The sun hums down through the cotton flowers of her dress' (p. 60). The image had long been trained for automatic suggestion, from its repeated use in **'A Prospect of the Sea'** (pp. 4, 5, 10) to the 'blossoming dresses' of **'Holiday Memory'** and the 'summery flowered dresses' of **'The English Festival of Spoken Poetry'** (*Quite Early One Morning,* pp. 30, 128). In writing **'The Dress'**, Thomas had at an early stage clarified the image, giving it something like an extended emotive gloss as a key image in his examination of the theme of tension and relief. Taking Bierce's basic plot, he contracted its narrative, isolating its main ingredients and enacting a fevered journey towards an ideal.

The second example of a borrowed scheme is one of the most successful parts of the *Portrait* autobiography. **'Who Do You Wish Was With Us?'** was the final story completed for the collection, finished in December, 1939. It was based fairly closely on James Joyce's 'An Encounter' in *Dubliners.* Thomas's general debt to Joyce was similar to that he owed to Dickens and just as fragmentary. Here he had almost as good a storehouse of childhood material as he found in Dickens and the debt was ostensibly acknowledged in his borrowing of Joyce's title, only partly changed as *Portrait of the Artist as a Young Dog.* Joyce's *Portrait,* like Thomas's, had sought to relate the growth of the artist's sensibility to the specific society which formed its background, though it showed a more mature grasp of the relevant religious, social and political factors involved. A major difference lay in the fact that Thomas's aim was more clearly to close the gap between experience and recollection by constantly remaining faithful to two psychologies at once: his *Portrait* is less obviously an objective document, the sounds and smells of young dog life remaining clearer than the adult perspective which brings them into focus. Yet much of the minor detail is common to both writers, suggesting that here again we have the copy and the copied. For example, the young Stephen Dedalus is frightened when the school messenger comes to announce that confessions are to be taken in chapel in a way which is converted to comedy when Thomas's hero is asked by his cousin to confess in the improvised barn-chapel of **'The Peaches'**. The moral prohibition of the Nonconformist pulpit suddenly fuses with the institution of the Catholic Church. Stephen would rather 'murmur out his shame' in seclusion, 'in some dark place' (p. 145), just as Thomas's school companions confess later in the privacy of their bedroom. Again, Stephen is accused (p. 240) of having eaten dried cowdung and Thomas's young dog recalls that he had once drunk a cup of his own water 'to see what it tasted like' (p. 33). The parallels continue: Stephen imagines that, if he sent some verses to the girl he met near Cork Hill, the 'suave priest, her uncle, seated in his armchair, would hold the page at arm's length, read it smiling and approve of the literary form' (p. 261); in Thomas's **'The Fight'** the young boy is asked by the Reverend Bevan to recite his latest poem and, after the recitation, is pompously told that 'The influence is obvious, of course. "Break, break, break, on thy cold grey stones, O sea"' (pp. 91-2). Youth laid embarrassingly bare in adult company is a mutual legacy from Dickens. Joyce was obviously fruitful copy: Stephen turns to the fly-leaf of his geography book and reads what he has written there—'himself, his name and where he was. Stephen Dedalus/ Class of Elements/Clongowes Wood College/Sallins/ County Kildare/Ireland/Europe/The World/The Universe' (pp. 11-12); in **'Old Garbo'** Thomas's young dog writes down his name and then, 'Reporters' Room, *Tawe News*, Tawe, South Wales, England, Europe, The Earth' (p. 192). But the cosmic address in both cases is merely the incidental comic cipher of a wider theme, part of the adult perspective, which places both heroes in touch with the paradox of romantic loneliness expanding into universal sympathy. Thus, for Joyce, Stephen

> was alone. He was unheeded, happy, and near to the wild heart of life. He was alone and young and wild-hearted, alone amid a waste of wild air and brackish waters and the seaharvest of shells and tangle and veiled grey sunlight and gay clad figures of children and girls and voices childish and girlish in the air. . . . So timeless seemed the grey warm air, so fluid and impersonal his own mood, that all ages were as one to him (pp. 198-9).

and Thomas's autobiography, less characteristically, evokes the same process:

> I was a lonely nightwalker and a steady stander-at-corners. . . . And I never felt more a part of the remote and overpressing world, or more full of love and arrogance and pity and humility, not for myself alone, but for the living earth I suffered on and for the unfeeling systems in the upper air (p. 122).

A final detail. On the wall of Stephen's room at Clongowes hangs an illuminated scroll, a 'certificate of his prefecture in the college of sodality of the Blessed Virgin Mary', while Thomas's Sunday school certificate hangs on the young hero's bedroom wall, an embarrassing trophy.

The list is endless and could be augmented with details from *Dubliners* as well. But the plan of the latter, with its break-up into short stories, offered a more total example. Thomas described it as 'a pioneering work in the world of the short story',[1] and in his **'Who Do You Wish Was**

With Us?' sought to reproduce something very near to the childhood adventure of Joyce's 'An Encounter'. Here Joyce had described a truant excursion into the countryside by two young schoolboys. An approximation to the idea of an excursion had already been attempted by Thomas in **'Extraordinary Little Cough'**, but the closer example of Joyce's story allowed him another and better attempt at its possibilities. In **'Who Do You Wish Was With Us?'**, the young hero is accompanied by a friend as in Joyce's story, and the journey of the adventurers out of town is similar in both instances with a mutual elegiac savouring of factual place-names. Similarly the destination in each case is part of the factual childhood scene; in Joyce, the 'Pigeon House' (Dublin's electric power station) and in Thomas, the 'Worm's Head' a well-known landmark on the Gower coast. Joyce's adventurers antagonise a crowd of ragged girls on their way, and a crowd of day-trippers is harassed by Thomas's young dogs in much the same way. Abuse is shouted after both pairs—'Swaddlers! Swaddlers!' in Joyce because the boys are taken to be Protestants, and 'Mutt and Jeff!' in Thomas's story because of the boys' comic difference in size. Out in the countryside, the young dogs are freed from the urban claustrophobia but in a way which heightens the example of hard reality they encounter. Joyce's pederast and Ray's inevitable submission to a morbid near-monologue on how his family had been wasted by tuberculosis complicate the freedom of the excursion: escape and no escape seems to be the pattern. This is particularly significant in Thomas since it was indeed the nearest approximation to tragic material in his autobiography, paralleled only by the theme of loneliness in the final story of the volume which shows distinct legacies from Joyce's 'The Dead'.

Both stories are a good example of how an ordinary event like a schoolboy adventure into the countryside is established as the semi-myth of heroic expedition in a manner similar to that noted in Proust by Maud Bodkin in *Archetypal Patterns in Poetry* (1934). As a remnant of myth it also has elementary suggestions of what E. B. Greenwood has recently described as a romantic concern with journey as quest for a neo-Adamic state (*Essays in Criticism* XVII 1 (1967)). The degree to which it was consciously intended by either Joyce or Thomas is a matter of conjecture. What is true, however, is that, in both, the journey undertaken has natural imaginative extensions. In Joyce it is largely the attraction of emigration, of visiting the places mentioned in school geography lessons but in Thomas it is given in several permutations. In **'Extraordinary Little Cough'** the suggestions is varied from the comic fusion of starting-point and destination in 'Thousands of miles. It's Rhossilli, U.S.A.' to the deeper, poignant description of the boys sitting in a circle, 'knowing always that the sea dashed on the rocks not far below us and rolled out into the world'. The theme is equally insistent in the later excursion story, where it ranges from the boys' imagining that the Worm's Head was moving out to sea ('Guide it to Ireland, Ray') to the description of the promontory, 'already covered with friends, with living and dead, racing against the darkness'. The liquid movement from the comic to the heroic suggestion narrows the gap between the child-hero and the adult-author's imagination.

It is the insistence on this theme which separates the artistic purpose of Thomas's story from that of Joyce's and justifies the borrowed plot. Thomas's story consolidates the image of separation from home and land as a statement of widening, though merely imagined, horizons. Ray's description of his family, ravaged by disease is given while he sits on the edge of the sea and so involves a tremendous juxtaposition. Waters at their priestlike task! The journey has ended in heroic gesture:

> This is a rock at the world's end. We're all alone. It all belongs to us, Ray. We can have anybody we like here and keep everybody else away. Who do you wish was with us?

And the story itself ends with a subtle suggestion of the separation become fact. On their journey, the boys passed some cyclists, and now:

> The sea was in. The slipping stepping-stones were gone. On the mainland in the dusk, some little figures beckoned to us. Seven clear figures, jumping and calling. I thought they were the cyclists.

As in the case of **'The Dress'**, the story suggests a concern with something like a poetic image, and the degree to which that image is consistent with other works is again remarkable here. The basic childhood concept of romantic voyages abounds in the unpublished poetry. One poem[2] uses as a narrative base the idea of children playing at sailing boats on a garden path, seeking to actualise the voyage by blurring their awareness of the garden setting. Another poem[3] of the same year includes the idea of imagined voyages in a discussion of religious faith and leadership. The collected poem, **'Grief thief of time'**, still retains part of a picture which, in the unpublished early version,[4] had been more elaborate:

> The old forget the cries,
> Lean time on tide and times the wind stood rough,
> Call back the castaways
> Riding the sea light on a sunken path.

The same picture is given in the short story **'The Tree'** where the child's vision re-enacts the voyage fantasy:

> The house changed to his moods, and a lawn was the sea or the shore or the sky or whatever he wished it. When a lawn was a sad mile of water, and he was sailing on a broken flower down the waves, the gardener would come out of his shed near the island of bushes. He too would take a stalk and sail (*A Prospect of the Sea*, p. 42).

Travelling on the lorry, the boys in **'Extraordinary Little Cough'** imagine that the vehicle is a raft and the green fields the open ocean. In this sense the young hero's shout to Ray in **'Who Do You Wish Was With Us?'** to guide the Worm's Head to Ireland is a repetition of the same image, and the comic surface of the imaginative motif which

is the story's ultimate significance. A deeper extension of the image itself would be the voyage of life in the later poems, **'Ballad of the Long-legged Bait'** and **'Poem on his birthday'**; and the visionary flood of the late **'Author's Prologue'**. Praise to our faring hearts!

Thomas, quite rightly, regarded his prose writings as essentially secondary to his poetry and no doubt the presence of much of the borrowed material discussed here is explained by that attitude. In his prose there was no literary reputation at stake. Yet it is clear that the nature of the borrowing varies and that, where governed by the poet's own imagination, it is transformed and justified. Casually lifted material smacks unmistakably of the copied article and remains valid only when it functions as parody. **'The Dress'** and **'Who Do You Wish Was With Us?'**, on the other hand, are valuable short stories over and above their inherited plots, and have the quality of fresh imagining which must be the touchstone of any critical attention the poet's prose may warrant. The last word can be left with the poet himself since he has conveniently stated the problem in the poem **'On no work of words'**. 'To take to give is all', but 'To lift to leave from the treasures of man is pleasing death'.

Notes

1. 'Poetic Manifesto', *Texas Quarterly* IV (1961) 49.

2. *Notebook 1930-1932,* Poem 'VII', dated 2nd January, 1931.

3. *Ibid,* Poem 'XXIII', dated 10th June, 1931.

4. *Notebook August 1933,* Poem 'Five', dated 26th August, 1933.

Richard Kelly (essay date 1969)

SOURCE: "The Lost Vision in Dylan Thomas' 'One Warm Saturday'", in *Studies in Short Fiction,* Vol. VI, No. 2, Winter, 1969, pp.

[*In the following essay, Kelly believes that the themes and structure of Thomas's short story "One Warm Saturday" are derived from James Joyce's* Portrait of the Artist as a Young Man.]

"One Warm Saturday," the last story in *Dylan Thomas: A Portrait of the Artist as a Young Dog,* shares with Joyce's *A Portrait of the Artist as a Young Man* the theme of a quest for perfection of the profane world. Thomas' flippant title, however, provides a significant clue to the outcome of his version of a youth's search for what Joyce calls "the unsubstantial image which his soul so constantly beheld."[1] Although Thomas' story may be read and enjoyed without any reference to Joyce, a critical reading of **"One Warm Saturday"** that takes Joyce into account will be illuminating. The purpose of this essay is to show that Thomas' autobiographical protagonist, like Joyce's Stephen Dedalus, undergoes a strikingly similar process of maturing with one important difference—whereas Joyce's wading girl provides Stephen with aesthetic and emotional autonomy, the girl in the anti-romantic **"One Warm Saturday"** fills the young man with anguish and frustration and returns him to an ugly, hostile world. Thomas' story, then, which the author constructed to a point like *A Portrait of the Artist as a Young Man,* takes a sudden turn that makes the tale thematically similar to "Araby."

Although Thomas denies that he got the title for his collection of tales from Joyce, he admits that Joyce had an influence upon his writing: "I cannot deny that the shaping of some of my **Portrait** stories might owe something to Joyce's stories in the volume, *Dubliners.*"² One cannot, of course, prove that Joyce's *Portrait* had a similar shaping influence upon **"One Warm Saturday,"** but the suggestive parallels between the two stories warrant critical comment for the insights they provide into the attempts of two very different artists to shape the mutability of their youthful experiences into enduring visions.

Like Stephen Dedalus, the youth in **"One Warm Saturday"** is estranged in a crowded, hostile world. In his wilderness he saw "the holiday Saturday set down before him, fake and pretty, as a flat picture under the vulgar sun . . ." (p. 136).³ His two-dimensional world is without meaning, and the crowded beach, a parched microcosm of humanity, is a mere collection of unrelated people and things: "outside all holiday, like a young man doomed forever to the company of his maggots, beyond the high and ordinary, sweating, sun-awakened power and stupidity of the summer flesh on a day and a world out . . ." (*ibid.*). The only other character who stands with him outside the absurd world is the hell-fire preacher Mr. Matthews, who talks to a "congregation of expressionless women" and casts down the scarlet town. Unlike Dedalus, Thomas' hero avoids the hell-fire sermon and strolls through Victoria Gardens, where he gains the vision that later damns him to a perpetual sense of loss.

Thomas describes his young dreamer: "He thought: Poets live and walk with their poems; a man with visions needs no other company" (p. 138). His reasoning, ironically, is flawed by his innocence, for as the narrator warns, "he was not a poet living and walking, he was a young man in a sea-town on a warm bank holiday." (*ibid.*)

The narrator objectively describes the youth's dream goddess: "She had chestnut hair arranged high on her head in an old-fashioned way, in loose coils and a bun, and a Woolworth's white rose grew out of it and dropped to touch her ear. She wore a white frock with a red paper flower pinned on the breast, and rings and bracelets that came from a fun-fair stall. Her eyes were small and quite green" (p. 139). The intensity of the romantic youth's vision, however, allows him to transform even the artificial flowers and cheap jewelry of the vulgar world of dime stores and fun fairs into symbols of love and purity. Instead of seeing the prostitute, he sees "her body bare and spotless . . . and she waited without guilt." (*ibid.*)

Like young Stephen, who chooses not to play with his schoolmates at Clongowes, Thomas' hero refuses the invitation of his friends to spend a night on the town. He, like Stephen, was "different from others" (Joyce, p. 64). So, too, his experience in Victoria Gardens parallels Stephen's encounter with "one whom magic had changed into the likeness of a strange and beautiful seabird," a girl also in white—"the white fringes of her drawers were like feathering of soft white down" (Joyce, p. 171). Both girls, apparently passive, innocent, and pure, appear to accept the worship of their young men: "and when she felt his presence and the worship of his eyes her eyes turned to him in quiet sufferance of his gaze, without shame or wantonness" (Joyce, p. 171); "She accepted his admiration. The girl in a million took his long look to herself, and cherished his stupid love" (Thomas, p. 140). Stephen can only exclaim "Heavenly God!" in an outburst of profane joy. His counterpart later describes his vision to the barman as "a piece of God helps us!" (p. 141). But whereas Stephen in fact discovers the incarnation of a joyous, liberating Heavenly God, the other youth faces the painful loss of his "piece of God helps us." In Carlyle's terms, the former is a transcendental, the latter a descendental experience.

The theme of mutability in **"One Warm Saturday"** establishes the counter-force to the youth's dream. In the bar scene he laments that "the holiday is drawing to an end . . . By-bye blackbird, the moment is lost . . ." (p. 142). In the midst of the boy's meditation, a drunk who has lost his bottom in an underground cave-in, stumbles towards him and asks the young dreamer to feel his vacant seat, thereby reinforcing the presence of decay and death. But the arrival of Lou, the dream-girl from Victoria Gardens, and two of her friends quickly displaces all thoughts of mortality in the young man. Despite the presence of Mr. O'Brien, Lou's "sugar daddy from old Ireland," the youth remains undaunted in his quest. Had Lou not appeared, the young man might have been able to sustain his dream, for in the Gardens he thought: "she does not know she is waiting and I can never tell her" (p. 139). Like the lover on Keats's Grecian urn, he then enjoyed the sweetness of timeless expectation; but now, with Lou's physical presence, he commits the great folly of attempting to realize his dream in the mutable world where the holiday is drawing to an irrevocable end.

Like the drunk, the barman also strengthens the theme of mutability with his announcement: "Time, gentlemen and others!" (p. 151). The three girls, Mr. O'Brien, the barman, the drunk, and the young man, in an attempt to prolong their evening fun, go to Lou's apartment. Lou expresses her wish that "this night could go on forever," and the young man exclaims, "Lou, don't you lose me" (*ibid.*), as the lights in the bar go out.

As a promise of ultimate union, Lou kisses the youth; but because they have brought the mutable world with them in the persons of O'Brien, the barman, and the three others, their moment alone together can never be enjoyed. The young man's final and unwitting transformation of Lou from a whore into a love goddess comes when he reads aloud from Tennyson's "Maud":

'I said to the lily, "There is but one
With whom she has heart to be gay.
When will the dancers leave her alone?
She is weary of dance and play."

. . . . .

'I said to the rose, "The brief night goes
In babble and revel and wine.
O young lord-lover, what sighs are those,
For one that will never be thine?
But mine, but mine," so I sware to the rose,
For ever and ever, mine." (p. 156)

The two main themes of the story combine at this point. The Woolworth's white rose and the red paper flower re-appear as romantic symbols of purity and passion. Here is the perfection of the profane world, but now the relentless passing of time threatens the dream with renewed intensity. The line "'The brief night goes / In babble and revel and wine'" reflects the futile attempts of Lou and her crowd to prolong the waning hours of the bank holiday by drinking and senseless banter. Nauseated from drinking, the young man leaves the room in search of the toilet on the lower floor of the apartment building. As he gropes blindly down halls and stairways, he imagines a voice calling to him: "Hurry! hurry! Every moment is being killed. Love, adored, dear, run back and whistle to me, open the door, shout my name, lay me down. Mr. O'Brien has his hands on my side" (p. 158). But in his drunken stupor the youth becomes lost and cannot relocate Lou's apartment to save her from defilement by O'Brien, who represents an infidel in the temple of romantic love. He knocks on wrong doors and the crude inmates of the apartment building drive him away. Lou's anguished voice continues in his head: "Hurry! hurry! I can't, I won't wait, the bridal night is being killed." (*ibid.*)

The victory of time over his dream of innocence, love, and purity leaves him with a sense of irreparable loss in a hellish world. Unlike the hero of "Maud," he has no Crimean War in which to bury his loss, and unlike Stephen Dedalus he has no symbolic wings to sustain his flight from a desecrated world of fact to one of sacred unity. His fate more closely resembles that of the boy in "Araby," who, after bearing his chalice through a throng of foes, discovers the crude, dark reality that lies under and corrupts the bright romantic façade of Araby. The hero of **"One Warm Saturday"** falls from his timeless, exotic dream of love to a decaying world of "the brickheaps and the broken wood and the dust that had been houses once" (p. 160). The loss of his goddess returns him to "the small and hardly known and never-to-be-forgotten people of the dirty town" who "had lived and loved and died and, always, lost." (*ibid.*)

"One Warm Saturday," then, uniquely explores the timeless theme of the loss of innocence and displays a hero whose fate is the tragedy of youth and the comedy of experience.

Notes

1. *A Portrait of the Artist as a Young Man* (New York, 1962), p. 65. Subsequent references to this work will be indicated in the text.

2. Quoted in Constantine Gibbon, *The Life of Dylan Thomas* (London, 1965), p. 370. There is some ambiguity surrounding the purpose and selection of the title: *A Portrait of the Artist as a Young Dog.* Gibbon states that Richard Hughes suggested the title to Thomas (p. 246). But Thomas claims that he chose it to poke fun at the painting title. And when Vernon Watkins suggested that Thomas drop the title and name the book after one of the stories, Thomas refused on the grounds that his publisher advised keeping it as a money-making device (*Dylan Thomas, Letters to Vernon Watkins,* Vernon Watkins, ed. (New York, 1957), p. 79. It is hard to believe that Thomas was innocent of a Joycean allusion.

3. Dylan Thomas, *Portrait of the Artist as a Young Dog* (New York, 1940). Subsequent references to this work will be indicated in the text.

Annis Pratt (essay date 1970)

SOURCE: "The Structure of Early Prose," in *Dylan Thomas' Early Prose: A Study in Creative Mythology,* University of Pittsburgh Press, 1970, pp. 30-51.

[*In the following essay, Pratt focuses on Thomas's early fiction, and applies Jungian psychology to determine the author's mental state when the stories were written.*]

I

Dylan Thomas never typed his own stories for submission to periodicals, but he would copy the finished version in careful handwriting into the Red Notebook, from which he would dictate to a friend. Reading aloud was as important for the prose as for the poetry, and many stories were tried out before a group of friends during the Wednesday lunch hour in Swansea. In the same manner **"The Enemies," "The Visitor," "The Orchards," "The Mouse and the Woman,"** and **"The Burning Baby"** were read aloud, mainly during 1934, to Pamela Hansford Johnson.[1]

Although from 1934 on many of the tales were published in Welsh and English periodicals, Thomas was as concerned with bringing them together into one volume as he was with publishing collections of his poems. By 1937 he had assembled the major early tales in *The Burning Baby* and had contracted with the Europa Press for publication. It was already advertised and the first edition subscribed when the printers balked on grounds of obscenity. A depressing back and forth of compromise and argument ensued, and, as the efforts of George Reavey of the Europa Press proved unavailing, Thomas began to toy with the idea of publishing the tales through Lawrence Durrell and

Henry Miller in Paris (several stories, including **"A Prospect of the Sea,"** were eventually translated in *l'Arche* by Francis Dufeu-L'Abeyrie). When the situation became hopeless Reavey turned the contract over to the Pearn, Pollinger, and Higham literary agency. Their good offices also proved useless, and although **"In the Direction of the Beginning"** found its way into a New Directions collection and several other stories were printed in *The Map of Love* and *The World I Breathe* (England and America, 1939), *The Burning Baby* never went to press.

The suppression of the early tales and the poor reception of the volumes that combined poetry and prose may have accounted in part for the abrupt change in prose style that occurred throughout 1938 and 1939. This was also, of course, a time of impending war when the outer world was pressing in upon Thomas as upon everyone else. The early prose tales were part of an inward universe that he constructed in his late teens and early twenties: the war not only disrupted this universe but afforded Thomas the opportunity of trying his hand at the more public genres of broadcasting and "straight" narrative fiction. The early prose tales are much more a unity with the poetry than the later, more simplistic *Portrait of the Artist as a Young Dog* (1940) and **"Adventures in the Skin Trade"** (1941), which Thomas himself tended to deprecate. Although the late Vernon Watkins disagreed with me entirely, thinking that "Dylan always did what he wanted to do, in spite of the success or failure of his work,"[2] I think that with his pressing financial needs at that time he could not afford to write in a prose genre that had been poorly received by both printers and public.

The early prose was not collected until after Thomas' death: the two posthumous volumes, *A Prospect of the Sea* (England) and *Adventures in the Skin Trade* (America), did not appear until 1955.[3] At that time they were often invidously compared to the later prose (*Portrait of the Artist as a Young Dog* and *Under Milk Wood*) which had become popular and even beloved. American critics reserved judgement on the "poetic" and "difficult" pieces following *Adventures in the Skin Trade*.[4] But Davies Aberpennar in Wales and Kingsley Amis in England had already found them irresponsibly irrational, full of "factitious surrealist artifice," and built upon "characters and situations . . . which people in full possession of their faculties would not find interesting or important."[5] Many admirers of the early poetry consigned the early prose to oblivion as juvenilia, or dismissed it as part of a macabre or dark phase which was as well forgotten. To G. S. Fraser they were the "pièces noires" of Thomas' later "celebration of innocence." Fraser insists that "in writing these pieces, Thomas was grappling with, and apparently succeeded in absorbing and overcoming, what Jungians call the shadow."[6]

Such an opinion overlooks Thomas' lifelong bout with a "shadow" which he never overcame. The life of the poet, wrote Jung in the June 1930 *transition,* "is, of necessity, full of conflicts, since two forces fight in him: the ordinary

man with his justified claim for happiness . . . , and the ruthless creative passion on the other which under certain conditions crushes all personal desires into the dust."[7] Throughout the forties Thomas was caught in the toils of just such a conflict, and he devoted neither his later poetry nor his later prose to gay reminiscence. Perhaps the critics of the fifties were looking for their own prewar innocence in suggesting that the stories of *Portrait of the Artist as a Young Dog,* the short novel *Adventures in the Skin Trade,* or the drama *Under Milk Wood* were visions of an unsullied, dirty-little-boy Eden. Like Blake's, Thomas' vision of innocence was through the eyes of experience.

Dylan Thomas was certainly not alone among twentieth-century writers in regarding madness, dream, and myth as a fertile source of imagery and narrative material. His tales are concerned with how the storyteller breaks from the bounds of consciousness into the unconscious world, what he experiences there, how he manages to return, and what happens if he does not return (Marlais takes something resembling a psychedelic "trip" in **"The Orchards,"** as does Peter in **"The Visitor"** and Nant in **"The Lemon"**). The inward journey of the poetic imagination, which is usually implicit in the poetry, is more explicit in the prose, where it is *the* adventure by which Thomas self-consciously defines his narrative mode.

Even though the symbolic forms of the unconscious provide both the goal of his heroes and the structure of his tales, he is careful that the unconscious world never usurps control of the narrative. As we shall see in Chapter 5, the only passages of "automatic writing" in the tales occur when Thomas wants to describe the abrogation of consciousness: he seems to have felt that the further inward the narrative penetrates, the stronger must be the role played by the intellect. "The more subjective a poem," he wrote, "the clearer the narrative line."[8] The intense and often hallucinatory subjectivity of the early tales required an unusual amount of conscious control, and it is probably for this reason that Thomas intruded so often as omniscient narrator. As Jacob Korg has noted, he shapes paranoia and hallucination into "an atmosphere where the mind rules the material world, exercising its powers of creation and distortion over it."[9]

II

The "progressive line, or theme, or movement" which Thomas insisted upon for every poem is also present in every tale, where it is defined by the progress of the hero from desire through quest to release and renewal. The plots are divided into three or four sections which succeed each other with the rhythm of ritual movements. The tales usually culminate in a sacrament or rite, an act of sexual release, or an archetypal vision. The release may take the form of the loosing of a flood (as in **"A Prospect of the Sea"** and **"The Map of Love"**) or of an apocalyptic event (**"The Holy Six," "An Adventure from a Work in Progress," "The Visitor"**). Often the beginning of a new epoch of search and birth is implicit in the cataclysmic denouement, giving a cyclical shape to the narrative.

William York Tindall includes "landscape and sea, enclosures such as garden, island, and cave, and in addition city and tower" under the category of archetype. He goes on to explain that "uniting the personal and the general and commonly ambivalent, these images, not necessarily symbolic in themselves, become symbolic by context, first in our sleeping minds and then in poems."[10] Thomas' landscapes embody the personal or sexual, the impersonal or mythical, and the poetic aspirations of his heroes. Images of the poetic quest seem to rise up as autonomous entities out of the countryside: words become incarnate in trees, in blood, and in the transforming sea. Often, at the denouement of a tale, they find their final expression in a "voice of thunder" which announces the hero's achievement.

Since Thomas' landscape is not only geographical but anatomical, personal or sexual imagery is latent in the countryside as well as in the bodies of hero and heroine. The hills and valleys of **"A Prospect of the Sea," "The Map of Love,"** the two fragments (**"In the Direction of the Beginning"** and **"An Adventure from a Work in Progress"**), and **"The Holy Six"** are metaphors of the feminine anatomy, the breasts, belly, and so forth, of the earth-mother herself. In **"The Map of Love"** the map which Sam Rib explicates is of sexual intercourse: the island "went in like the skin of lupus to his touch. . . . Here seed, up the tide, broke on the boiling coasts; the sand grains multiplied" (*AST*, p. 146). In the tales where the cyclical pattern is most pronounced the feminine landscape is itself circular, dominated by a woman who draws the hero into the "mothering middle of the earth." In **"In the Direction of the Beginning," "An Adventure from a Work in Progress," "The Enemies,"** and **"The Holy Six,"** the heroes walk from the rim of an island or valley through ancestral fields into intercourse. Each consummation is analogous to a mythological event, during which the island or circular valley participates in an orgy of division and regeneration. As Dr. Maud has aptly pointed out, Thomas' mingling of geographic and sexual imagery is a successful method of "distancing the intimate," a means of describing the act of love so that both its intimate and mythical qualities are dramatically embodied.[11]

Neither the aesthetic imagery, which expresses the poetic quest of the hero, nor the sexual imagery of a given tale predominates. In each case poetic and anatomical metaphors describe a narrative line which is essentially mythological, both in the inward sense ("the union of ritual and dream in the form of verbal communication") and in the outward or historical sense (the use of Welsh, Egyptian, and other folklore for background). The final synthesis is always personal: images describing the heroes' thrust towards sexual and poetic maturity are overlaid by thematic antitheses of unity and division, love and death. "Poetry in its social or archetypal aspect," notes Frye, "not only tries to illustrate the fulfillment of desire, but to define the obstacles to it. Ritual is not only a recurrent act, but an act expressive of a dialectic of desire and repugnance: desire for fertility or victory, repugnance to draught or to enemies."[12] We shall see how demonic vitality and senile re-

pression form the poles of **"The Enemies"** and **"The Holy Six"**; in **"The Mouse and the Woman"** and **"The Map of Love"** we shall find heroes suspended between fear of the flesh and sensual desire.

"If ritual is the cradle of language," declares Suzanne Langer, "metaphor is the law of its life."[13] Thomas' narratives depend upon the conflict, mergence, and progression of specific metaphors. Given the analogy of geography and anatomy which underlies most of the early tales, even his descriptive images bear a metaphorical burden. In **"The Burning Baby,"** for example, the relationship between images of gorse, flesh, and fire marks the progression of the plot towards its grim crescendo. At the outset, Thomas describes Rhys Rhys preaching a sermon on "The beauty of the harvest" and explains that in the preacher's mind "it was not the ripeness of God that glistened from the hill. It was the promise and the ripeness of the flesh, the good flesh, the mean flesh, flesh of his daughter, flesh, flesh, the flesh of the voice of thunder howling before the death of man" (*AST*, p. 91). The biblical metaphor of flesh to grass is the raw material of Rhys' perversion. It embodies both the sensual level ("the flesh of his daughter") and the poetic level ("the flesh of the voice of thunder") of the plot.

Further on in the tale a third element is added to the metaphor: the little brother "saw the high grass at [his sister's] thighs. And the blades of the upgrowing wind, out of the four windsmells of the manuring dead, might drive through the soles of her feet, up the veins of the legs and stomach, into her womb and her pulsing heart" (*AST*, p. 93). The grass has become an even more explicitly sexual metaphor, each blade being analogous to the father's phallus. The "upgrowing wind" surging through the grass is in turn analogous to the spirit, both as the biblical wind which "bloweth where it listeth" and as the impregnator of Mary. Coming into conjunction with flesh the fiery biblical wind ignites as the elements of gorse, flesh, wind, and fire merge in the burning baby. The denouement is organic, in the sense of propounding a natural, season-oriented or cyclical worldview. Rhys Rhys sets fire to the gorse to burn the incestuously begotten son as the tale concludes, its final scene a variation on Abraham's sacrifice of Isaac, God's sacrifice of Christ, and man's perennial sacrifice of himself.

"The Burning Baby" is a fairly early and straightforward tale from the Red Notebook in September, 1934. We shall see in Chapter 5 how, in **"The Mouse and the Woman," "The Lemon,"** and **"The Orchards,"** Thomas uses images from a series of related dreams to underline the narrative. In the tales where there is no dreaming he makes use of a similar mode of metaphorical progression. For each of the three key characters of **"The Enemies"** and **"The Holy Six,"** the world shapes itself into images appropriate to his perception of it. Mr. Owen is a kind of Great-Uncle Jarvis, a lover of the "vegetable world" that "roared under his feet." Endowing his garden with his own virility, he works upon the "brown body of the earth, the green skin of the grass, and the breasts of the Jarvis hills."

Mrs. Owen's feminine powers are embodied in her crystal ball, which contains the extremities of hot and cold, clarity and obscurity and is analogous both to her womb and to the round earth whirling outside of the house. Davies, withered with age and insubstantial with sterility, perceives the Jarvis valley as a place of demonic vitality, death, and nausea. Throughout the narrative, it remains a "great grey green earth" that "moved unsteadily beneath him."

Ghostliness, virility, and demonic lust are embodied in Davies' nausea, Owen's garden, and Mrs. Owen's crystal ball. As the narrative moves towards its consummation the action moves entirely indoors to concentrate upon the ball and Mrs. Owen's pregnant womb. The six clergymen are made to share in Davies' nausea, vomiting up their desires under the influence of "mustard and water." At the denouement the conflict centers upon a question of paternity: whose child is in Mrs. Owen's womb? Ghostliness triumphs as Davies is assured that he has not loved Amabel in vain. As Owen, like Callaghan, laughs that there should "be life in the ancient loins," Davies sees "the buried grass shoot through the new night and move on the hill wind." Mr. Owen is revealed as the midwife-gardener to Mrs. Owen and Davies, laboring to bring new life out of a woman who conceives only in the arms of death. The antithetical metaphors of virility and ghostliness are woven into a new synthesis by Mrs. Owen's paradoxical desires. The narrative as a whole is a symbolic representation of an apocalyptic union of spirit and flesh, the dead and the living.

So intensely does Thomas concentrate upon a metaphor to make it render its utmost significance that his figures nearly burst their usual function, no longer representing a similarity but a metamorphosis. It is as if he, like his heroes, could change real objects into their subjective equivalents, and elements of the outer world into his lyric image of them. Thus in **"A Prospect of the Sea"** the boy sees a tree turn into the countryside: "every leaf of the tree that shaded them grew to man-size then, the ribs of the bark were channels and rivers wide as a great ship; and the moss on the tree, and the sharp grass ring round the base, were all the velvet covering of a green country's meadows blown hedge to hedge" (*AST,* p. 127). By a process similar to hallucination the objects of the landscape become elements of a subjective vision, the tree on the hill becoming a symbolic expression of the boy's own transformation.

"The chief source of obscurity in these stories," remarks Jacob Korg, "is the fact that imagined things are expressed in the language of factual statement instead of the language of metaphor."[14] Thus when Thomas writes of the girl in **"A Prospect of the Sea"** that "the heart in her breast was a small red bell that rang in a wave," one cannot comprehend the metaphor until one accepts the previous statement that the waves not only resemble but *are* a "white-faced sea of people, the terrible mortal number of the waves, all the centuries' sea drenched in the hail before Christ" (*AST,* p. 131). The girl herself *is* a wave, her

heart a meeting place of men and mermen, land and sea. If the sea is a metaphor of the human race, it is what Tindall has termed a "metaphysical metaphor," symbolic in itself and an "element of a symbolic structure."[15]

Thomas' "metaphysical metaphors" are thematic symbols embodying the progression and antitheses upon which such a narrative depends. They are not literary tokens heightening realistic situations in the classic sense, nor are they incorporated into the tales from an external system. Within each story, they are distinguished from minor metaphors by the way that they juxtapose, blend, and contain the several dominant themes. The tree in **"The Tree," "A Prospect of the Sea,"** and **"The Orchards"**; the house in **"The Enemies," "The Holy Six"** and **"The Dress"**; and the tower in **"The Lemon"** and **"The School for Witches"** are such inclusive symbols. None of them is the only major symbol in its context, however. Tree, tower, and house form a symbolic triad in **"The Tree"**; orchard, scarecrow, and maiden are one among several such triads in **"The Orchards,"** while house, hill, and sea contain the thematic meaning of **"The Mouse and the Woman"** and **"A Prospect of the Sea."**

In each tale, objects contract and expand, merge and reshape themselves according to the pressure of the hero's mind. Like a magician, the poet-hero forces the image of a thing to become the thing itself. Although he draws upon the worlds of magic, folk belief, and madness for his material, Thomas exercises careful control over it, subordinating it to the expression of the hero's quest for meaning. Discontented with images and metaphors that are merely literary and decorative, the hero condemns the "dead word," story-princesses, and conventional metaphors, forcing himself into the dangerous world of the unconscious where symbols are live things which devour as they illuminate. Since the stories are about the search for a source of all story the symbolic visions which mark each denouement are ends in themselves.

III

It is a pity that there are no recordings of the early tales, which Thomas read aloud during the Wednesday lunch hours to his Swansea friends and, in London, to Pamela Hansford Johnson and her mother at 53 Battersea Rise. For all of its wordiness Thomas' prose style is extremely symmetrical, with orderly paragraphs progressing according to the dictates of balance and emphasis.

The texts alternate between lengthy descriptive passages, briefer paragraphs which sum up the descriptions or outline further action, and brief dialogues. Even in the longer descriptive sections there is a great deal of activity, the prose bristling with verbs of action and reaction describing the thematic conflict. Thomas often relies upon a series of clauses or phrases which he builds into a crescendo at the climax of a passage. In **"A Prospect of the Sea"** one paragraph begins with a brief and realistic statement: "It was hot that morning in the unexpected sunshine. A girl dressed in cotton put her mouth to his ear," and continues

Along the bright wrackline, from the horizon where the vast birds sailed like boats, from the four compass corners, bellying up through the weed-beds, melting from orient and tropic, surging through the ice hills and the whale grounds, through sunset and sunrise corridors, the salt gardens and the herring fields, whirlpool and rock pool, out of the trickle in the mountain, down the waterfalls, a white-faced sea of people. . . . (*AST,* pp. 130-31)

The participial series, "bellying," "melting," "surging," gives way to a series of adverbial phrases which finally find their subject at the middle of the paragraph. The prose catalogue suggests a sweeping up and down of the earth, a gathering of the "white-faced sea of people" from the north and south, the east and west.

Passages so rich and lengthy generally occur only near the climax of the tales. Thomas leads up to them with shorter paragraphs, composed of a simple sentence at the beginning and end and one or two more complex sentences in between. Brief statement, mounting descriptive rhythms, and brevity of concluding statement are the basic units not only of individual paragraphs but of each story as a whole. Each tale begins and ends with a simplicity which must take its significance from the complex material in between. In nearly every case the plot is rounded out with some such simple statement as

Hold my hand, he said. And then: Why are you putting the sheet over my face? (**"The Visitor"**)

or

Brother, he said. He saw that the child held silver nails in the palm of his hand. (**"The Tree"**)

or

Cool rain began to fall. (**"A Prospect of the Sea"**)

Thomas' dialogues are constructed along similar lines, occurring not as conventional conversations but as catechetical interchanges which usually precede or follow a complex and lengthy description. In **"The Visitor"** the paragraphs describing the arrival of Peter and Callaghan in the land of death are followed by this interchange:

What is this valley? said Peter's voice.

The Jarvis valley, said Callaghan. Callaghan, too, was dead. Not a bone or a hair stood up under the steadily falling frost.

This is no Jarvis valley.

This is the naked valley. (*AST,* p. 82-83)

From this dialogue, resembling that of God and Ezekiel in the valley of dry bones, the reader is flung on into the powerful description of the deluge of blood which causes even the "monstrous nostrils of the moon" to widen in horror. In **"The Tree,"** similarly, the description of the boy's view of the Jarvis valley is followed by his question and the gardener's answer:

Who are they, who are they?

They are the Jarvis hills, said the gardener, which have been from the beginning. (*AST,* p. 75)

A variation of the catechetical dialogue appears in the riddling interchanges that summarize the paradoxical themes of **"The Horse's Ha"** and **"In the Direction of the Beginning."** These bring the reader to a stop and make him, like the hero, puzzle over the significance of the adventure, giving him a pause for reflection before he is plunged into ever more complex prose. Thomas possibly derived this technique from the rhetoric of Welsh preachers.

No study of the metaphorical or rhetorical structure of Thomas' prose can explain its weirdly compelling lilt, indescribable except by reading the tales aloud. This lilt is more pronounced in the shorter paragraphs and depends upon delicate balance of sentence elements. It is not original to Thomas, who may have modeled his prose after the style of Caradoc Evans.[16] Take Thomas' description of Amabel Owen: "She was a tidy little body, with plump hands and feet, and a love-curl glistened on her forehead; dressed, like a Sunday, in cold and shining black, with a brooch of mother's ivory and a bone-white bangle, she saw the Holy Six reflected as six solid stumps . . ." (*AST,* p. 136), and compare it with a passage from Evans: "Silah Schoolen was a tidy bundle and she was dressed as if every day was a Sunday. She was not tall or short, fat or thin; her cheekbones were high and her lips were wide and her top teeth swelled from her mouth in a snowy white arch."[17] In Evans the lilt derives from the adaptation into English of the rhythms of spoken Welsh. Modified slightly by Thomas, it is present in combination with a terse descriptive economy in most of his early tales.

Although Evans' use of dialogue is more conventional and extensive than that of Thomas, Evans relies upon a similar combination of catechism and proverb:

"And who is the husband shall I say?"

"He was Shacki. O you heard of Shacki—Shacki stallion?"

"I have been in ships," said the man. "I have been with black heathens and whites Holy Sherusalem [sic]."

"The Sea is a stormy place. Have you rabbits to sell?"

Amos made this pronouncement: "There are no rabbits on tidy farms."[18]

Where Evans' prose is full of folk proverb, Thomas is more likely to invent proverbial statements from a combination of Welsh mythology, Christianity, and the sexual metaphors of a given story. Thus where one of Evans' heroes asserts that "Death is a great stiffener," Thomas asserts that "No drug of man works on the dead. The parson, at his pipe, sucked down a dead smoke." Evans' tales are terse and economical descriptions of the realistic tragedies of the country, Hardyesque in their reliance upon local dialogue and superstition. Usually curling into a bitter twist at the denouement, they are far more like Joyce's *Dubliners* than Thomas' early prose.

Although Evans is likely to start a story with a statement like "A tree of wisdom grew inside a certain farmer and sayings fell from it," he usually goes on to more realistic statements. Thomas is more likely to start out realistically and to become more and more fantastic. In this he certainly owes something to the influence of T. F. Powys. In *Mockery Gap,* for example, Powys endows the sea with much the same powers of love and regeneration as Thomas does in such tales as **"The Map of Love"** and **"A Prospect of the Sea"**: "Mr. Pattimore sat up. He heard the midnight sea, the wicked one, the beautiful, the inspirer of huge wickedness; he heard the sea. However much he had shut out from him all the gentle longings of his loving lady, the sound would come in. It came from the dark places of love, out of the bottom of the sea."[19] In *The Innocent Birds* the landscape suggests that of **"The Map of Love"**: the hero, "old Solly," overhearing two lovers on the "green summit" of the focal Madder Hill, associates them with the creative and destructive potentialities of the sea beneath them.

In Powys' *The Two Thieves* we find a macabre turn of events expressed in a style similar to that of Thomas' darker tales: "Grace crept into a corner of the room. She already felt the serpent growing in her womb. She tried to tear open her body with her nails: in three weeks she was measured for her coffin. The undertaker had expected her to be a little taller than she was. 'A beautiful corpse,' he said smilingly."[20] Powys' tales are structured upon the organic cyclical pattern beloved to Thomas: "Every Autumn God dies," he writes in *God,* "and in the spring He is given a new place in the lives of men, and is born again. It is the same with us; we die and go down to the pit, but until the worlds vanish, new life from our dust will arise and worship the sun."[21]

"The quality and organization of the language here," writes one commentator, "is poetic in its deep rhythms and its surface music."[22] Thomas once described his early prose as "this bastard thing, a prose-poetry."[23] Although his tales do not belong in the French genre of the *poème en prose* favored by Max Jacob and André Breton, in style and form they somewhat resemble such "prose-poems" as Rimbaud's *Illuminations* (compare "Après le Deluge" to **"The Map of Love,"** "Villes" to **"Prologue to an Adventure"** and Lautrémont's "Les Chants de Maldoror"). In England as in France the two separate genres of prose and poetry merged in the experimental novel of the twenties and thirties. While Anna Balakian notes in surrealist France "a fusion of poetry with prose,"[24] Professor Tindall has aptly pointed out that in England, at the same time, "the better novel became a poem" with its "narrative and subordinate details centered in image."[25]

Thomas' early tales, as we have seen, are "poetic" in their dependence upon a balance, progression, and contrast of thematic images and symbols. They differ from the work of Woolf, Lawrence, and Joyce, however, not only in their brevity but in their intense subjectivism. Where the other novelists create a number of distinct characters upon whose minds the outer world registers its impressions, Thomas' tales more often center upon one protagonist. Even when a consort, father-figure or antagonist is present he or she is absorbed, in the end, into an inward or personal vision. (The triad of Mrs. Owen, Mr. Owen, and Davies in **"The Enemies"** is a notable exception to this practice.) When a number of persons are involved, as in **"The Horse's Ha"** and **"The School for Witches,"** they all are absorbed into a demonic or ritual unity at the denouement. Thomas thus pays little heed to Stephen Daedalus' plea for dramatic distancing over lyric subjectivism, for the conflict within each tale is less between separate persons than between the hero's Blakean faculties of imagination, reason, and desire.

Thomas' tales are not as dependent upon conflicting and merging images as are his poems. Narrative is fundamental to their structures in which action and images are knit together with careful attention to plot coherence and rhetorical style. The result is a genre unique in contemporary fiction, which in its pattern of quest for a fabulous center is more like folktale or mythological legend than realistic fiction. In each story, the protagonist sways between moods of approach and withdrawal which shape the narrative into a strophic and antistrophic "dancing of an attitude."[26] In such stories as **"The Enemies," "The Holy Six," "The Orchards," "The Map of Love," "A Prospect of the Sea," "The Lemon,"** and **"The School for Witches,"** the protagonists move through a ritual series of trials and adventures towards the paradoxical goal of vision and destruction. In others, such as **"The Horse's Ha," "The Tree,"** and **"The Burning Baby,"** a similar ritual movement, sometimes circling, sometimes progressing, embodies a dance of death and renewal.

Each of Thomas' early tales contains elements of myth (pseudo-primitive folklore or inward ritual), theology (in the sense of a system of cosmic symbology, containing—but transcending—myth), the occult (heretical materials combining the primitive and organic with the transcendent) and, finally, surrealism (the contemporary practice of mingling unconscious, mythological and everyday images into a new, hallucinatory or super-real world view). In each story these elements are knit carefully into an artistic whole, and it might seem a violation of the artistic integrity of each piece to separate its various components, in the following chapters. Only the casual reader should be thrown off by this deliberate unravelling, however. The intent is to elucidate the various strands of Thomas' early prose style so that the reader, winding these strands back together in his perusal of the individual tales, will more fully grasp their richness.

Notes

1. Pamela Hansford Johnson, letter of July 4, 1963 to the author.

2. Vernon Watkins, letter of February 27, 1963 to the author.

3. *A Prospect of the Sea* was published by J. M. Dent & Sons in London (1955). The collection

Adventures in the Skin Trade and Other Stories was published by New Directions in New York (1955). Quotations in this study are taken from the New American Library Signet reprint of *Adventures* (New York, 1961), which will be referred to in the text as *AST*. (The tales discussed in this chapter can be found in both editions.)

4. See Reviews of *AST* in *Commonweal,* Vol. 62 (January 10, 1955), 262; the *New Yorker,* Vol. 31 (June 11, 1955), 158; the *Saturday Review of Literature,* Vol. 38 (July 2, 1955), 18.

5. Davies Aberpennar, review of "The Visitor" in *Wales,* Vol. II, No. 2 (1939-1940), 308; and Kingsley Amis, review of *A Prospect of the Sea* in *Spectator* (August 12, 1955), p. 227. See also the *London Times Literary Supplement,* Vol. 796 (September 30, 1955), 569.

6. G. S. Fraser, "Dylan Thomas," Chapter 15 in *Vision and Rhetoric* (London, 1959), pp. 224-25. See also Henry Treece, *Dylan Thomas, "Dog among the Fairies"* (London, 1949), p. 128.

7. C. G. Jung, "Psychology and Poetry," *transition* no. 19-20, (June 1930), p. 42. See Appendix C.

8. Dylan Thomas, "Replies to an Enquiry" in John Malcolm Brinnin, *A Casebook on Dylan Thomas* (New York: Thomas E. Crowell Co., 1960), p. 102.

9. Jacob Korg, "The Short Stories of Dylan Thomas," *Perspective,* Vol. 1 (Spring 1948), 184.

10. William York Tindall, *The Literary Symbol* (Bloomington, Ind., 1955), p. 130.

11. Ralph Maud, *Entrances to Dylan Thomas' Poetry* (Pittsburgh, 1963), pp. 81-103 (hereafter cited as *Entrances*).

12. Northrop Frye, *Anatomy of Criticism* (Princeton, 1957), p. 106.

13. Suzanne Langer, *Philosophy in a New Key* (Cambridge, Mass., 1952), p. 141.

14. Korg, "Short Stories," p. 184.

15. Tindall, *The Literary Symbol,* pp. 60-62.

16. T. H. Jones describes Evans' style as "based on the rhythms and idioms of Welsh nonconformity, a virile, exuberant, non-conforming prose that has influenced almost every Anglo-Welsh writer, and not least Dylan Thomas." T. H. Jones, *Dylan Thomas* (New York, 1963), p. 44. In a letter to the author of August 13, 1963, Glyn Jones affirms Evans' influence on Thomas.

17. Caradoc Evans, *The Earth Gives All and Takes All* (London, 1947), p. 1.

18. Caradoc Evans, *Nothing to Pay* (London, 1930), p. 27.

19. T. F. Powys, *Mockery Gap* (New York, 1925), p. 37.

20. T. F. Powys, *The Two Thieves* (New York, 1932), quoted in H. Coombes, *T. F. Powys* (London, 1960), p. 34.

21. T. F. Powys, *God* (New York, 1932), p. 41.

22. Coombes, *T. F. Powys,* p. 28.

23. Interview with Harvey Breit in the *New York Times Book Review* (February 17, 1952), p. 17.

24. Anna Balakian, *The Literary Origins of Surrealism* (New York, 1947), p. 1.

25. Tindall, *The Literary Symbol,* pp. 64, 91.

26. Kenneth Burke, *The Philosophy of Literary Form* (New York, 1957), p. 9.

Donald Tritschler (essay date 1971)

SOURCE: "The Stories in Dylan Thomas' *Red Notebook,*" in *Journal of Modern Literature,* Vol. 2, No. 1, September, 1971, pp. 33-56.

[*In the following essay, Tritshler examines Thomas's juvenilia, which is contained in his* Red Notebook.]

Dylan Thomas filled at least four copybooks with poetry and one, the Red Notebook,[1] with short stories by the time he was twenty. Though he had also written juvenilia that his mother carefully preserved,[2] these five notebooks contain early and late versions of most of his published poems and nine of his published short stories. Ralph Maud's publication of the four poetry copybooks,[3] which were nearly finished when Thomas began the Red Notebook, shows that he had already explored most of his major themes.

The ten Notebook stories likewise contain comparisons of divine, human and artistic creation and Thomas' obsessive paradox of creation as a destruction. They focus his sense of mankind's loss of innocence and love and the attendant ubiquity of evil and death in the world, and they present his criticism of the weak Christian religious practice that is unable to resolve the struggles of spirit and flesh. At least one of the stories was part of Thomas' first attempt to write a full-length novel. All of them seem to lie midway between the early poems and the later, more elaborate ones, perhaps because the time of composition was usually slightly later than most of the early poems, or because the short story form is roomier than the brief lyric and it obviously approaches the ideal of narrative that Thomas sought in his later poetry.

The Notebook itself is most interesting as a workbook. Several illuminating jottings, tables of contents and lists on the inside cover and on some of the final pages throw light on Thomas' publishing plans.[4] And because only one of the stories transcribed into it is unpublished, the differences between the Notebook and the published versions reveal much about Thomas' working methods and about the significance of the stories.

The first story, **"The Tree"** ("Finished December 28. '33"), is included in each of the five tables of contents that are listed on the inside cover and the seven end pages of the

Red Notebook. Its garden setting recalls the Creation—the gardener "knew every story from the beginning of the world"[5]—and the child's insistence on the specifics of the biblical stories leads him to recreate the Crucifixion. The boy's nature is imaginative and destructive, and his point of view, which can transform the lawn into a sea, the bushes into islands, birds into satanic omens, and the gardener into either a sinister figure or an "apostle," controls the structure of the story. The gardener himself views the biblical stories he tells the boy as examples of life and love in the earth. He is attuned to nature, a kind of minor deity of the microcosmic life in the garden, which is surrounded by the macrocosm of the Jarvis hills and the world they imply. He is aware of the fallen state of this world ("his god grew up like a tree from the apple-shaped earth"[6]), and he tells the boy, "God grows in strange trees" (p. 103). As a pantheist, he says, "Pray to a tree, *thinking of* Calvary and Eden" (p. 102—italics mine).

In this exchange, however, the boy insists the tree in their garden, that he sees as the one tree free of snow, is "the first tree," but the gardener politely overlooks his presumption by saying, "The elder is as good as another" (p. 103). The Red Notebook presented this as prudence: a star burned above the tree and the gardener would not confide in the stars of his god-infested world (p. 6a). In both versions the gardener attempts to repair the tines of the rake with a wire, and the boy suddenly sees him as sinister. Then he notices the gardener's pure white beard and sees him as an apostle telling of the stages of the cross. While the boy listens, he sees the noon shadows as blood staining the bark of the elder in their garden. The tree stands as the Tree of Life at the beginning of the story and becomes the Cross of Calvary at the end.

The transformations of this tree trace the growth of metaphor in the boy's mind. When the gardener compares the tree to the Tree in the Garden, the boy extends the analogy to include Satan's entrance into Eden by interpreting a blackbird in the tree as "a monstrous hawk perched on a bough or an eagle swinging in the wind."[7] After hearing of Bethlehem and confusing it with the Jarvis hills to the east, the boy falls into a cavernous sleep, in which he dreams of descending among the "shadows" of the house (corrected from the more explicit "shades," p. 4a). After this descent into an underworld, he dreams of stepping into his own deceptive garden and of seeing his tree illuminated by a star burning brightly over it. The tree resembles a woman with frozen "arms" that bend "as to his touch," and now he kneels on its "blackened twigs" to pray (p. 100); "then, trembling with love *and* cold" (101—italics mine), he returns to the house. The other aspect of "the illuminated tree" is evident when it appears leafless and black—deathly.

Into this ambiguous setting the idiot enters on Christmas day, after the boy sees the star above the tree. When the idiot begs for water, his goodness is so evident that the people give him milk. When he simply says he is from the east, they trust him (p. 101). The next montage shot of the idiot shows him looking into the "immaculate" Jarvis valley. He hungers for light, which he tastes in the green life of the grass (p. 103). He is a brother to all things of the world, and he restores light to it; he believes he is entering Bethlehem as he answers the call of the world's voices in the Jarvis valley. The final episode of Christmas morning compares the idiot to Christ in His passion, which was included in the garderner's stories. He prays in the garden. Then its shapes seem hostile. The wind threatens, "raising a Jewish voice out of the elder boughs," and a voice within the idiot asks why he was brought here, somewhat as Christ momentarily seemed to question God. When the boy finds him, he shows "divine patience" (p. 106), even as the boy wires his arms to the limbs of the tree and prepares to nail him to it. The use of the wire shows what the naïve boy has learned from his own sinister vision of the gardener repairing the rake; the child's insistence on the specifics of the gardener's stories has finally led him to the crucifixion of innocence and love. Though the parallels to the life of Christ are sketchy—the "birth" and crucifixion both occur on Christmas day—they provide a context in which the latent evil of an "apple-shaped earth" can work through a naïve boy to murder innocence. The justaposition of the "birth" and crucifixion points one more ironic comment at the excesses of man's religious zeal.

The revisions of the Red Notebook version for publication are mainly routine retouches. There is almost no rearrangement, but many incidental changes reduce wordiness, and especially remove irrelevance and vagueness. Verbs are often strengthened by modifiers or by substitution of more vivid words ("he bent" for "he went"). Thomas is usually more specific in the final version—"apples and serpents" (p. 98) replaces "the first sin" (p. 2b)—and he is thereby more expressive, as in the replacement of "a darkness" by the more womby "spinning cavern" (p. 99). Another type of revision is the temperance of extravagant words ("rushing" of the sap instead of "roaring"—p. 98) and the removal of many examples of pathetic fallacy. Nevertheless, though the tower no longer "gave a benediction" (p. 8a), nature is animated in order to stress the force of life in the world that creates and cuts down its innocent children of love (p. 98).

While **"The Tree"** contains oblique references to Christ, the next story in the Red Notebook, **"The True Story"** (January 22,'34), mentions various earthly visits to show its protagonist's naïveté: Martha is proud of her reading, and she vaguely recalls the stories of Zeus and Danaë, Satan's temptation of Eve, and Moses receiving God's commands from "a thing of fire" (p. 259). She thinks immediately of the dog she killed and buried under the manure at the end of the garden. That she wrote the epitaph and date backwards suggests "dog" is an inversion of *god*.[8] Surely her service to the old woman is mistaken. Like the biblical Martha, she selfishly makes it unthinking busywork, rather than service to her patient's being.[9] At the end of her reveries, in which she has plotted the old woman's death, she characteristically parodies the burial service with "in the midst of death. . . ." (p. 260).

During the exposition of the dull routine of service that Martha inherited from her mother, Martha associates the picking of currants with the money under the old woman's mattress. The next association is with the blood on her hands from chickens she has freshly killed. The first paragraph to focus on the present shows Martha's obsession with the fortune during this spring (which like Martha is "the undoer of winter,"—11a) of her twentieth year. In the manuscript Thomas emphasized "blood money," which stained in the same way the currants did (p. 10b). He may have removed this emphasis from the final version to avoid divulging the conclusion too quickly. Martha was surely more cold-blooded in the manuscript because her decision to murder was stated flatly and repeatedly. The published version startles the reader with her wish to fly in the window and suck the old woman's blood, her life's substance. The surprises that follow not only intensify the dreadful action, but the structure conveys the lack of values or feeling Martha's isolation fostered. The unfeeling combination of "One o'clock now, she said, and knocked the old woman's head against the wall"[10] renders her fatal naïveté exactly.

The plot of **"After the Fair"** (November 19. '33) is simpler than those of the first two Red Notebook stories, and while their motivation is amoral, this plot develops from human kindness. The prospective tables of contents and Thomas' collections of his works he jotted in the Notebook show he did not think this one of his most important stories. Nor does he seem to have labored over it as much as he did some of the other stories because the manuscript version contains only a few, superficial, textual changes. The Fat Man's idea that the baby in the Astrologer's tent comes from looking at the stars is both humorous and significant; the girl's selection of the Fat Man to help her care for the baby, the policeman looking for her, and their soothing of the baby by riding a merry-go-round may suggest a flight into Egypt, but little is done with the parallel. **"The Enemies"** (Feb. 11. '34), on the other hand, takes the reader to the strange heart of Thomas' mysterious Welsh valley.

The setting for Mr. and Mrs. Owen's cottage in the center of the Jarvis hills gives them a kind of proprietary interest—they came from their village to this isolated valley and fenced out the domestic cattle that grazed in it. Their valley has its special, hyperbolic identity: as Mr. Owen weeds, the descriptions of his garden and the surrounding hills suggest wars and oracles that are more human than vegetable. The grasses have heads and mouths (p. 90), and the green grass is flesh (p. 91). Mrs. Annis Pratt finds this valley in the heart of the fabulous Jarvis hills comparable to the immortal island of Welsh folklore, which she in turn relates to the personal mythology of initiation in **"The Map of Love"** and other stories.[11] In **"The Enemies,"** Reverend Davies is about to undergo an infernal initiation as he loses his way in this "wide world rocking from horizon to horizon" and comes upon a cottage that might have "been carried out of a village by a large bird and placed in the very middle of the tumultuous universe" (p. 92).

Such tumult fills the beginning of the story with images of separation—the bird from his mate and the valley by its stream (p. 89)—and it culminates in the dichotomy of flesh and spirit represented by Mr. and Mrs. Owen. Mr. Owen presides over the rise and fall of life in the garden (p. 90). He is a young, bearded Pan, lord of the concrete things of life, "of the worm in the earth, of the copulation in the tree, of the living grease in the soil" (p. 96). He cannot quite take Mrs. Owen's powers seriously, for they are intangible, dark powers from the other world. Her crystal ball gives up its dead like a grave; it is one of the abstractions, such as the sound of the wind and the shadow on the tablecloth, that indirectly reveal the nature of the world to her (p. 95). She resembles Mr. Owen only in that they both have superhuman powers and her strange, green eyes recall the green grass of his garden.

This dynamic, pagan world opposes Reverend Davies' pallid, Christian world. Mrs. Owen loves the dark that so frightens Mr. Davies. The old man loses his way in his own, dead world and enters their domain, where he senses both their conflicting forces as the hills seem to "storm" the sky and darkness gives him no comfort from the wind (p. 91). His black, clerical hat is replaced by a cloud as he moves out of Mrs. Owen's ball and into the fleshly valley of Mr. Owen, and while the rocks of the valley draw human blood from him, he becomes a shape among the stars in Mrs. Owen's crystal. In contrast to his powerful enemies, Mr. Davies is a white-haired phantom whose light is absorbed by Mrs. Owen's darkness—the world "had given under his feet" (p. 95).

Though the action is relatively static, the tense confrontation of enemies is a lyric poet's tableau of a world suffering the timeless clash of opposites. The clash of flesh and spirit in Mr. and Mrs. Owen, with all its related imagery mentioned briefly above, is complemented in another dimension: the clash of the Owens' pagan concentration on life and Mr. Davies' Christian preparation for death, as represented by dark and light imagery and other details. Mr. Davies reaches toward a blessed state in this clockless, roaring world, but his saintliness ambiguously emerges as a "ragged circle of light round his head" (p. 96). He is finally an insubstantial, ineffective "old god beset by his enemies" in the house of the proud flesh and the evil spirit.

Mrs. Owen's evil shows much more explicitly in **"The Holy Six,"** the sequel to **"The Enemies."** There she merges with *Miss* Myfanwy, as "Amabel Mary" (p. 203), and is pregnant with the fleshly child of Mr. Owen, though about to give virgin birth to the spiritual child of Mr. Davies. Apparently the child is the seventh and greatest sin, which is surrounded by the six sins that arrived at the Jarvis valley when Love's (Mr. Vole's) cart wrecked; their names are given as anagrams of lust, greed, envy, fear, cruelty and spite. In both stories the vitality of the world is too much for the ghostly Mr. Davies, and in the second one he takes his place among them. A weak god fails in this world, the house of sins.

Though **"The Holy Six"** unites the characters of **"The Enemies"** in a circle of sin, it is probably a different story from **"The Enemies United"** because both titles appear in two of the lists in the Red Notebook. (See note 4.) If **"The Enemies United"** was a third story about these characters, Thomas had written more of his short novel, **"A Doom on the Sun,"** than has been discovered. The phrase for this title first appeared in **"Find meat on bones,"** for which the Lockwood library has a manuscript including corrections, dated July 15'33 and January 1936. The earliest record of the projected novel was in a letter to Pamela Hansford Johnson on 2 May 1934: "My novel—I've done the first chapter—will be, when and if I finish it, no more than the hotch-potch of a strayed poet, or the linking together of several short story sequences. I shall scrap it in a few days." He had just received a telegram from *New Stories* accepting **"The Enemies"** for publication, but the news was a mixed pleasure because they paid nothing for it. He had also transcribed into the Red Notebook two other stories, **"The Tree"** and **"The Visitors,"** which are explicitly set in the Jarvis hills.

Nine days later he wrote to Miss Johnson, "My novel of the Jarvis valley is slower than ever. I have already scrapped two chapters of it. It is as ambitious as the Divine Comedy, with a chorus of deadly sins, anagrammatized as old gentlemen, with the incarnated figures of Love & Death, an Ulyssean page of thought from the minds of two anagrammatical spinsters, Miss P. & Miss R. Sion-Rees, an Immaculate Conception, a baldheaded girl, a celestial tramp, a mock Christ, & the Holy Ghost." The two chapters would seem to be **"The Tree"** and **"The Visitors [April '34],"** for the old gentlemen appear in **"The Holy Six."** Two days later Thomas was still struggling: "My novel, tentatively, very tentatively, titled *A Doom on the Sun* is progressing, three chapters of it already completed [**"The Enemies," "The Holy Six"** and, perhaps, **"The Enemies United"**?]. So far, it is rather terrible, a kind of warped fable in which lust, greed, cruelty, spite etc., appear all the time as old gentlemen in the background of the story. I wrote a little bit of it early this morning—a charming incident in which Mr. Stripe, Mr. Edger, Mr. Stull, Mr. Thade and Mr. Strich watch a dog dying of poison. I'm a nice little soul, and my book is going to be as nice as me." Apparently the novel was approaching the "lived happily ever after" stage when he scrapped it.[12]

The few revisions of **"The Enemies"** give it a story-teller's polish, but the infrequent revisions of **"The Dress"** (March,'34), the next story in the Red Notebook, are often to its key passages. The madman's pursuers sound like hounds baying after him, and he flees their bestial, adult world to recover an innocent relationship. The Red Notebook stressed a relationship with the mother: "As the moon rose, milkily it put a coat around his shoulders . . ." (p. 22b), and after the wish for shelter and food, "The mist was a mother, but he needed more than a mother's care. . . . He thought of the young woman bening [sic] over the pot. He thought of her hair." The relationship the madman desires with the world is larger than a mother's comfort, and the ending shows it is also more general than lust.

The innocence of the madman's wish is not certain at first, and this uncertainty is artfully controlled to develop the reader's anticipation. Though several references to blood on the madman were deleted from the published version, the kinship he feels with the deadly owl is ominous. At the same time, he pities the hare killed by the weasel. Next his isolation is stressed in the encounter with the old man, who flees when the madman says it no night for the son of woman. His violence with the butcher's knife is mentioned, but he has flung it into a tree (a "male" object), discarded it with his anger over his wife, who smiled at other men.

The farm wife he comes upon knows he has cut off his wife's lips. In the Red Notebook he felt guilt, for he cut his own throat after he did it (p. 24b), but the omission of this detail in the final version leaves the frightful possibility that he may do violence without any apparent motivation or qualms. The affinity of the madman for the young wife emerges when he thinks of sleep as a girl who will give him her dress to lie on with her; the earth itself is the place of love, for the twigs rustle like her dress as he flees. Shortly after this fantasy, the first glimpse of the farm wife shows her trying on the new flowered dress she has sewn (p. 249). The descriptions of her and her dress, which has a low-cut bodice and which she leaves unbuttoned at the neck, heighten her sexuality. In the Red Notebook this was emphasized by her holding the dress up and saying, "Naughty frock" (p. 24a), but the omission of this comment makes her more innocent in the final version.

Instead of the guns the madman expects as he enters the farm house, he sees a fearful girl, but then he is dazzled by the flowers of her dress. The Red Notebook was unnecessarily explicit in this lovely ending: "With the moving of her arm, her dress, *like a summer field,* danced in the light" (italics mine). The need for sleep was also over-stressed, and the Notebook stated "tired head," instead of the more significant "bewildered head." This story, which could be the banal account of a flight to innocence or simply the madman's search for sleep, becomes a delicate resolution of mad anger in gentle beauty.

"The Visitor" (April, '34) is more complex than **"The Dress,"** for its opposing images of life and death interpenetrate. The description of awakening day at the beginning is pervaded by images of death, a condition that reverses at the end. The movement of time displaces life: the heart of Peter the poet is replaced by a clock and his hands move as mechanically as those of a clock. All the places and events of his life converge in this dry day, and he imagines his only release from this dwindled life could be in the ghost of the boy he was when he walked the Jarvis hills (p. 109). Later he makes from words an olive tree, a symbol of long life, that grows under the lake, somewhat as he wishes to lurk beneath the water, but it is only "a tree of words." Then Peter thinks of Christ, whose body was taken from a tree and prepared for burial and resurrection, somewhat as his being is cared for by Rhianon.[13]

Peter's companions help him reach his destination. He watches Rhianon tidying the room around him and thinks the dead are surprised by the bloom under the skin of the living. He supposes this while she sweeps dust from the picture of Mary, the "lying likeness" (cf. **"Our Eunuch Dreams"**) of his dead wife (p. 110), but the facts that his hands feel like stones on the sea of shrouds covering him and that he has had a vision of his own corpse in a coffin show that he, in his near-dead state, is the one surprised by life. His travelling companion, Callaghan, brings an enemy into his room that threatens to destroy his world. But while death can destroy the webs of life, the poet still retains the walls of memory around Mary (p. 111).

The death Peter anticipates is exotic—he is an "island of rich and miraculous plants" (p. 112). He thinks of submersion in the watery sounds of Rhianon's dress. When he says, "Water," he has Rhianon hold a glass of water before his eyes, for he wishes to become "a green place under [the water], staring around a dizzy cavern" (p. 113). Though his self is more passive than the wild self in "How shall my animal," a poem about creativity, the image shows him descending to the deepest level of his being. When Callaghan carries him into the valley, the frost is falling. He sees apocalyptic horrors before all life on the earth dissipates and fresh life springs up (p. 117). This dwindling and renewing of life in the valley anticipates the structure of the spiritual journey in **"A Winter's Tale."** Peter cries out in joy at this renewal of life before it again recedes and he and Callaghan must race away, as all spirits must, before the cocks crow.

As the story of a writer for whom words are as tangible as things, it shows the loss of poetic powers.[14] At the beginning, Peter tastes the blood of Rhianon's and Callaghan's battling words, but toward the end the words he makes are no longer flesh—they seem empty of life. In another sense, the story is about the microcosm within the macrocosm it implies. Peter's room itself is a world within a world, and within even that lies his inner microcosm (p. 110). Peter perceives this world when he hears the blinded birds singing songs of the world within their eyes. (p. 115; cf. "Because the pleasure-bird whistles.") Though Peter in death is losing his senses as a poet—he can't hear Rhianon's singing any longer (p. 112)—and though he is surprised when she finds him dead, he has experienced a blissful world he created on his journey over the naked hills within him, which are represented by the Jarvis hills.

The double movements of **"The Visitor"**—into and out of both life and death, and out of the world and into the universe of the self—are conveyed symmetrically. The predicament at the beginning, in which Peter is haunted by thoughts of his death, reverses at the end, in which he is filled with life and surprised by the sheet being drawn over his face. Again, an image of day at the beginning—"A man with a brush had drawn a rib of colour under the sun and painted many circles around the circle of the sun. Death was a man with a scythe, but that summer day no living stalk was to be cut down" (p. 110)—is balanced by one of night at the end—"A man with a brush had drawn a red rib down the east. The ghost of a circle around the

circle of the moon spun through a cloud. . . . The cock cried again, and a bird whistled like a scythe through wheat" (pp. 118-119). By juxtaposing such organic and cosmic images as have been used elsewhere in the story, these passages emphasize the concentricity of the microcosm and the macrocosm. There are almost no significant revisions of the Red Notebook version for that in *Skin Trade,* but the *Criterion* deleted three passages, perhaps because an editor thought them too explicit, that were almost entirely restored when the story was collected by Thomas.[15]

Of those stories in the Red Notebook touching on derangement, **"The Vest"** (July 20. '34.) is most concerned with probing the sickness itself. The association of experiences that are logically unconnected, such as the boy in **"The Tree"** imposes and the madman in **"The Dress"** blissfully achieves, and amoral violence, such as Martha uses to escape her servitude, both occur in **"The Vest,"** but this story also investigates the immediate causes of sickness. The sight of a dog crushed by a car has bewildered the protagonist. The violence arouses pity in him, but also a glee upon touching the brain and blood, the inner being, of the animal. His mind then flickers between this violence and the violence he has done to his wife when he felt pain himself (p. 253). The confusion of the accident causes a fear in him that is represented by darkness, particularly by the large shadow in his house (p. 252). This shadow is a projection of the terrible self that he must release, and he does it blindly, insensitively, when he tears his wife's underclothes off. As he walks out of the house, he notices the shadow is broken into many pieces, in keeping with his character, which is represented by the many faces he sees in the mirror, each of which has "a section of his features" (p. 255).

He fears the mortality of the flesh, Women, particularly his wife, have betrayed him with their "blind, corrupted flesh" (p. 34a). When he learned of his mother-in-law's cancer, he felt it was his own face that was eaten by locusts. To avoid such corruption of the flesh, he imagined he lay by his wife's skeleton, but in the morning her flesh bloomed proudly with his love; he also made her skin blush when he beat her. The fantastic orgy of violence he imagines in the bar full of women confirms his perverted horror of the flesh. He seeks rational control of experience, as is suggested in the manuscript by his counting of steps and streetlamps and his measured ringing of the bell at the beginning of the story.

The published version deletes some of these opening details, which were presented in a more personal point of view than Thomas finally adopted. The final version is more consistent with the protagonist's cold formality: instead of "he smacked her face" (p. 34a), Thomas makes it "he struck her cheek." In the manuscript her name was Helen; in the final version, which is presented from his impersonal point of view, no name is mentioned. When he remembers her putting on her frock that morning, she is coldly described as an object, "thin in her nakedness, as a bag of skin and henna drifting out of the light" (p. 253). She has brought light into his life, and normally she would disperse the shadow in the house, she would comfort him, but any comforts he felt, such as heat from the dying fire, were removed from the manuscript.

The manuscript is more explicit about his feelings: thoughts of "poor dog" and his judgments of his own cruelty were removed, as were the graphic images of the slaughtered dog.[16] His reaction to the dog's accident there was "in the first darkness" (p. 34a). The manuscript also interpreted more explicitly the source of violence as his horror of human corruption. When the protagonist noticed the darkening room and tasted his sickness, he thought of man's fallen state, "all the pain of life, the pain of the damned, the pain of man . . ." (p. 34b).

In addition to removing many explicit statements, Thomas deleted unnecessary details. The removal of the names of bars, which began with the Duke of Wellington, went through the Rose, the Mason, the Men of Devon, and the Rising Sun, and ended significantly at the Waterloo, increases the anonymity of his lonely surroundings, as does the deletion of crowds seen near his destination. Large sections of the final orgy were transferred to that grotesquely humorous account of the fall of man as poet, **"Prologue to an Adventure"** (Summer, 1937). The man selling an almanac (a record of the temporal world), the girls dancing in sawdust (glass, in the Red Notebook) in that story's bar, the Seven Sins, and the Negress selling a pound of flesh (p. 212) are close to the passages in the Red Notebook (pp. 36b-37b).

The only unpublished story in the Red Notebook, **"Gaspar, Melchior, Balthasar"** (August 8. '34), is another story of nightmarish violence, but on the grander scale of an island setting, such as England, in a classconscious world. Since air raids and street fighting were dreadful possibilities in the economic struggles of the Thirties, **"Gaspar, Melchior, Balthasar"** is a *reductio ad absurdum* of the very real spiritual carnage in a sick society. The class war is a leveler of inequities—all die in the same gutters, all are hungry (p. 38b).

The conditions of this world seem the reverse of what they are supposed to be. The people starve "in the heart of plenty" (p. 38b—deletion by Thomas) because they lack love, the staff of life. The galvanic wheat, which death drove back into the bone, is bullets, "crow's food [that] sliced about them," and their sustenance, such as God gave to the chosen people, is the bombs they desire, "cupping their hands for the exploding manna. Two lovers, struck by the same shell, fell into bliss" in death, not in their love. The power elite, who slip gas masks onto faces that are used to wearing masks daily, who must even purchase sleep in this commercialized society, are surprised from their sybaritic preoccupations and their seedy occupations.[17] In their society life is denied (babies are starved), and money, leisure, and love are stolen. (These details were deleted.) In return, the workers to whom they give

guns turn them greedily against their former "slave masters," and "the keys of hate [are found in the blood of] the opened pulses" (p. 39a—all deleted by Thomas.). The new life born out of this strife is the ability to hate.

The story then shifts to the first person when two ghosts appear to search for something among the dead. All usual activity, such as commerce, travel, communication and ceremony, has halted in this barren world: "The ships were unloaded at the wharves, the engines cold in the stations, the printing presses silent, and the sentries before the island palace stiff, split like cabbages, in their boxes" (p. 39a—deletion by Thomas). The speaker feels out of place in this land that has only the appearance of life; he is "a ghost in a springing world, a solid man in a world that was all a ghost" (pp. 39a-b—deletion by Thomas.). Furthermore, this new world is only "the last of the first revolution" dying away as he enters "the first stages of the night" (p. 39b). The speaker draws nearer to the ghosts as they hunt the ruins and examine the corpses; he begins to take on the garb of a wise man—"I held my scarf to my face for the smell of the flowering dead" (p. 39b). Though these dead "flower," they are black plants, the ominous signs that "the hemlock & the upas sprouted for me from the gutter beds" (p. 39b).

Melodramatically, a minute before midnight, he sees a kind of "star of Bethlehem" at the end of the street. It is a lantern that first "was a red rose among the flowers that stank at my side"; this ironically Dantean image was changed to "It was bright & sweet among the flowers . . ." (p. 40a). The ghosts pass him and he follows them toward the lantern, "calling them by name," but revolutionists, "dark-eyed behind their lantern," stop him to ask, "Who are you, comrade?" When he says to let him pass because he is "of the wise men," they want to know where he is going. He knocks the lantern from their hands and runs past, pursued through a maze of alleys by shots from their revolvers.

When he reaches the ghosts in a moonlit square, "at their feet lay a dead woman, naked but for her shawl, with a bayonet wound in her breasts" (p. 40a). While he watches, "a miraculous life stirred in her belly, and the arms of the child in her womb broke, lifted, through the flesh" (p. 40b). The two ghosts bow down and offer gold and frankincense, and as the speaker kneels, his pursuers shoot him. Originally the ghosts were named Gaspar and Melchior and the speaker learned from them that his name was Balthasar when his ghost rose from him. But the names were deleted, "bitter as myrrh" was changed to "my blood streamed bitterly," and instead of anointing the mother's feet, his blood anoints "the emerging head." Such changes make the story less obvious but more maudlin. This quality and the over-intellectualized symbolism may have been among Thomas' reasons for abandoning the story, but still it is significant as one of many attempts to consider the Christian myth within a world such as ours, that reverses Christian values. Hate is born into this dark world. Though this bitter allegorical sketch of class warfare was clumsy,

Thomas used some of the same imagery years later, in his brilliant elegies for man in World War II. The bitterness is still there, but it becomes more powerful when barely controlled by such understatement as is used in **"A Refusal to Mourn."**

The child born in **"The Burning Baby"** (September. '34) is imagined by Rhys Rhys to be a Second Coming, but it is a child of the flesh, Vicar Rhy's supposed enemy. Like many Thomas characters in the Red Notebook and elsewhere, Rhys struggles with the flesh because of its mortal weaknesses, but he does not realize he has made it his god, somewhat as man has made God in his own fleshly image. Thomas treats this inverted relationship between God and man literally by suggesting sexuality is the "Word" of an anthropomorphic god when he has Rhys Rhys put the stem of his pipe in a "mouth" between his flybuttons (p. 130). He then casts down the Bible and reads in another book "of the old woman who had deceived the devil. [Since he thinks] the devil is poor flesh" (p. 131), he hopes to deceive it by producing a god from it, and he thereby deceives himself.

The woman who bore his daughter saw "the woman witch in his male eyes" and loved him passionately, but she died in child-birth. Then she stole the child of his second love and left a changeling in its place (p. 131), but this child is a shadow "cast by the grave sun," a pun that expresses an idea akin to what Thomas summarized in **"Twenty-four years"** as the meat-eating sun." When the story opens, only the changeling survives to wander over the fields like a personification of death, "with the motion of a man cutting wheat" (p. 128). Rhys Rhys has been obsessed with this cutting of ripeness. He said in his sermons that the world was "ripe for the second coming of the son of man" (p. 129), but the ripeness was of the flesh, his daughter's flesh. On the moming that the gorse burst into flames, almost as miraculously as when God spoke from the burning bush, and Rhys desired his daughter, the Red Notebook had him thinking, "She was the failure of the flesh, & the skinny field. Poor flesh, he said, and touched her arm. She trembled at the heat in his fingers. Only the poor are beautiful. The poor soil shudders under the sun, he said" (p. 41b). The purpose of the incest, Rhys seems to rationalize, is to achieve the second coming and redeem the poor flesh that is burned daily by the "grave sun."

But the changeling, that resulted from a death, haunts Rhys with his symbols of death, the skins and skulls that he covets. On the day of the incestuous conception, Rhys takes a rabbit carcass from him and keeps it in his pocket while he seduces his daughter. The section ends with the changeling's words, "I want the little skull," and though it recalls the carcass, it may also refer to the child of the union. During her pregnancy the changeling watches his sister in her daily dying and imagines her skull nailed above his bed. In both cases Rhys attempts to trick death of its due: by burying the dust of his daughter near him, in a "virginal" white coffin, and by burning the body of the baby. The Red Notebook emphasized the paganized import of the ritual by stating, "He stacked the torn heathers in the midst of the druid Bard's Circle where the stones still howled on the witches' sabbaths" (p. 46b). Though Rhys Rhys has enacted a ritual of man's triumph over death, the self-deception is clear when the flesh of the baby screams from the flames.

The final story is more obviously autobiographical than any other in the Red Notebook, and it is also one of the more complicated ones. Originally called **"Mr Tritas on the Roofs"** (October. '34), it became **"Anagram,"** a phantasy about the artist and thereby an anagram of what he does. The name Tritas is itself an anagram, but in the *Criterion* version he was renamed Peter—the name Thomas used for the poet in **"The Visitor"**—and for the *Map of Love* collection he became the more obviously autobiographical Marlais.[18] Another change was the setting of the story, which in the short **"Anagram"** version (five pages) was London, and in the expanded **"Orchards"** version was Swansea, Wales, and the world beyond. Thomas may have written **"Anagram"** in London, where as a freelance artist he began concentrating on fiction because of its greater commercial value; by publication time he had discovered how deep were his Welsh roots and turned to the notion of the artist as folk-hero adventuring through the land of his being. The additions to the beginning and end of the story (pp. 137-40 and 143-9) were the dream of the burning orchards and the artist's terrible journey through the dying world. Despite these changes, the story remains an anagram of the artist's struggle to unify his "three-cornered life" (pp. 49ab), the worlds of life, death and his own vision.

The burning apple orchards in his dream are his anagram of this life. The two scarecrows, "two fruit-trees out of a coal-hill" (p. 140), the sister trees in the vegetable garden, are the tree of knowledge, that is associated with light, and the tree of life (and death), that stands in a circular shadow with crows on her shoulders (p. 137). Marlais tries to write of his vision in which, "under the eyelids, where the inward night drove backwards, through the skull's base, into the wide, first world on the far-away eye, two love-trees smouldered like sisters" (p. 140). The artist looks inward at archetypal experience, from which comes "Marlais's death in life in the circular going down of the day" (p. 140; cf. **"Author's Prologue."**). When he steps onto the roofs (in a setting sometimes resembling Cwmdonkin Drive), he observes "below him, in a world of words, men on their errands moved to no purpose but the escape of time" (p. 141). As an artist standing halfway between the stars and the toy of the town below the roofs, on the one hand, and building images that touch both death and life,[19] on the other, he must involve himself by attempting to achieve a unity of awareness.

The unity is possible when, as a folk-hero or, in another part of this dream of man's fallen state, as an apple farmer, he adventures through eleven valleys. The first valley implies a unity of heaven and earth in its hills that are "unbroken walls, taller than the beanstalks that married a story on the roof of the world" (p. 146). Beyond these eleven valleys he realizes his own artistic vision when the orchards of time burst into flame at the edge of the sea. The three levels of the artist's awareness are represented, for example, in the three images of the moon: the shadow of the "mock moon" in the north, the real round moon shining on the earth, and "the half-moon of his thumb-nail rising and setting behind the leaden spire" (pp. 140-41). The struggle for unity of this awareness is stated directly in the final version—"It is all one, . . ." (p. 142)—and it was the revelation in the concluding lines of the manuscript:

> . . . he moved for the last answer (p. 142). And all was image and was image, but Mr Tritas on the roofs sought a cohesing image of the dead and the quick. So he came at last to a skylight by a chimney side, and leant over the leaded rim. There, in the attic, sitting upright in a dark coffin, a joyful gentleman smiled at the crowds of heaven and played on a violin.
>
> Death & life was one image & one anagram. Odd thief in the folds, cried Mr Tritas on the roofs.
>
> October. '34[20]

Thomas removed this ending and added a much more elaborate anagram for **"The Orchards."**

The artist's predicament is that he makes life—he has "five-fingered life" before him (p. 142), but he also kills with words, which are lifeless abstractions. They are words, not flesh, and life intrudes on the death he would put into his story of a woman wailing beside Russian seas in a cold wind from Antarctica (p. 139). What Thomas would later call "the meat-eating sun" defeats his struggles with words (p. 140). The artist's imagination can make people and angels of the chimneys on the roofs, but somewhat like Lot's wife, they turn to stone as he attempts to fix their reality with words (p. 138). Though the artist may scramble over the lives in the rooms below, while he watches the images of life and death in the stars (p. 48b), "the word is too much with us." This half humorous parody of *Words*worth keynotes a story that summarizes the predicament of the artist, who lives with insubstantial words, on the rooftops of the world.

The anagram that concludes the story shows the artist, "our virgin Marlais," as his rooftop creations call him, entering life, experiencing first-hand the vision of the burning orchards that he dreamed before. Until now he has been a coward, hesitant to embrace the "unholy" women of Llanasia, romantically willing to settle for his dream of "a life too beautiful to break" (p. 143), but he steps from the rooftops into the falling world. He sees the barren coal-tables that embrace Llanasia like a grave. All life is dominated by the sun that has shown since man fell from innocence, as Marlais is now falling. When he begins his rôle as a folk-hero, he passes through myths that summarize man's nature: the revolt in Heaven, the Fall from Paradise, the Homeric vision of the "wine-coloured sea," the notion of a single source of the sea, the destruction of

Sodom and Gomorrah, even Jack and the beanstalk. When he journeys to the last hour on the last hill down to the sea, he actually witnesses his dream image of burning life and finds the fair girl who possesses the being he has committed to life. At the end of the artist's life, which is all lives, Thomas says the story is more terrible than all those stories of the fictional Jarvis hills. The artist finally loves the world, but he is left with dead objects, in the embrace of a scarecrow, somewhat as the fisherman succumbs in "The furious ox-killing house of love" (**"Ballad of the Long-legged Bait,"** 1. 200). Art and life must both be insufficient at last to survive the dry twig of death. Thomas' obsession with death is as prominent in the Red Notebook as in most of his poetry: processes of time dominate the worlds of **"Martha," "The Visitor," "The Vest," "The Burning Baby"** and **"The Orchards."** Because the artist attempts to stop time in art[21] he must struggle against life's inevitable self-consummation, and he therefore feels the effects of process acutely. Peter in **"The Visitor"** and Marlais in **"The Orchards"** both attempt to preserve their worlds in the artifice of words, but they, like (or as) the dead, are continually surprised by the encroachments of actual life; whether it gives the lie to the abstractions of their medium or it pushes them relentlessly toward death, the process is the odd thief in the fold. (Cf. The Thief of **"In Country Sleep."**) Others, such as the protagonist of **"The Vest,"** attempt to escape time and decay in violence or, obversely, flee violence in an attempt to recover past innocence, as does the madman of **"The Dress."**

Death is often shown in the other stories as one of the results of man's fallen state. Thomas rarely depicts innocence, as represented by the idiot in **"The Tree"**; rather, those such as the boy in that story or Martha in **"A True Story"** commit outrageous acts in their amorality. In other words, they share in the fallen state of man by acting as naïve agents of evil when the free-flowing evil in the world fortuitously infests them. Others commit evil acts more pointedly. More knowing than the boy in **"The Tree,"** the vicar Rhys in **"The Burning Baby"** has perverted Christian values with the narrow nonconformism so traditional in Wales. Another foolish cleric is the Reverend Davies, who wanders into the Jarvis valley, the heart of life forces that the Owens control. Their pagan power is too much for the weak Christian values of Davies. An early theme of Thomas, this weakness is represented in the poetry as the Christian God's indifference—especially in **"Incarnate Devil"**—or man's perversion of Christian values. He treats the distortion lightly in "Shall gods be said to thump the clouds," seriously in "The spire cranes," and bitterly in the manuscript of "After the funeral,"[22] where the insincere mourners stand in contrast to the natural goodness of dead Ann.

The treatment in fiction of themes that Thomas used in his poetry is not surprising, nor are the occasional verbal echoes in his works. He quite naturally used motifs in one work that he planned for another. Mr. Tritas stood on the roof with the dust of the streets filling his eyes, and (p. 48a) Thomas finally deleted this passage showing supersensitivity, that had been used in a much different context of the preceding story, **"The Burning Baby"**: "It was not her eyes that saw him proud before her, nor the eyes in her thumbs. Her blood was fluttering as he moved. The lashes of her fingers lifted. He saw the ball under the nail."[23] Another passage of the **"Orchards"** manuscript may have been used for phrases and images of **"A grief ago"**:

> The sky is a strange land at night,
> where the seasons pass over in a drift of star & snow,
> and the dark, scythe-sided grasses in the lunar
> country drop at the dawn. (p. 48b)

The Red Notebook reveals much about Thomas' working habits and about his understanding of the artist's work. Though his first idea for a novel about the Jarvis hills and valley, *A Doom on the Sun,* was soon abandoned, it is not surprising that several of his stories, as well as his poems, use the Carmarthenshire setting around Fern Hill, the farm where he spent so much of his youth. **"The Dress," "The Burning Baby"** and **"Prospect of the Sea"** invoke a comparable setting. **"The Enemies," "The Tree," "The Visitor"** and **"The Holy Six"** name the Jarvis setting, and **"The Map of Love"** shows two children the love that remains of Jarvis himself and his baldheaded wife. His ambitious story **"The Orchards"** started from a sketch using an urban setting, but it was expanded to show the artist as folk-hero going out to a place even more dreadful than the magical Jarvis hills to encounter reality. Either of these strange places possesses life in its fullest sense and provides a counterpart to the conventionality of Llareggub, which is mentioned in some of these stories.

The heroism of the artist in **"The Orchards"** is his stepping out of a romanticized artistic world, one such as Thomas suspected in **"After the Funeral,"** into the tumult of life among the women of the street to seek the deepest resources of life and death in the last valley. The struggle to enter reality is a sustained theme in Thomas' works about the artist's creativity. The name of the artist in the *Criterion* version of **"The Orchards"** and in **"The Visitor"** evokes slang associations consistent with his advice to Charles Fisher (February, 1935): "Poetry . . . should be as orgiastic and organic as copulation, dividing and unifying . . . Men should be two tooled, and a poet's middle leg is his pencil. If his phallic pencil turns into an electric drill, breaking up the tar and the concrete of language worn thin by the tricycles tyres of nature poets and the heavy six wheels of the academic sirs, so much the better."[24] Thomas almost identifies creation and procreation, and as the letter implies, violence, or at least violent wrenching of symbols, such as many of the dream-like Red Notebook stories use, is necessary to reach "the first beasts' island" in his map of Love.

Notes

1. "The Red Notebook" is so catalogued by its owner, the Poetry Collection of the Lockwood Memorial Library, State University of New York at Buffalo. The previously unpublished material quoted here is Copyright © by the Trustees for the Copyrights of Dylan Thomas, 1971. Both the Trustees and the library have kindly granted me permission to quote from it.

   The Note book is a 7 ¾ × 6-inch copybook with a soft, deep-red cover that declares it "The ZENITH Exercise Book," and it advertises "Ruled Feint Lines" (twenty-two) and provides spaces for the student's name and school and the date (all unfilled). The back cover lists six "Danger Dont's & Safety First!" about playing near vehicles. If the schoolboy survived this first spelling lesson, he found on the inside back cover "Arithmetical Tables," tables of measures, and multiplication tables.

   The sheets of the Notebook, which are stapled at the center fold of the book, are numbered 2 through 53 (1 and 54 having been removed or lost) in the center of the headspace on the right-hand pages only. Most of the pages are numbered by Thomas in pencil, though almost all the writing in the book is in ink on both sides of the sheets. The first sheet apparently has been torn out by Thomas, for the second begins with "the clouds;" inked out, "in" overwritten with "In" as the beginning of the sentence, and "The Tree (Adelphi)." penciled beneath the page number.

2. The juvenilia and copious worksheets of some later works went to the University of Texas Humanities Research Center with the T. E. Hanley collection. The British Museum holds additional worksheets and typescripts of early poems; the Houghton Memorial Library at Harvard University holds the fourth major collection of manuscripts-copious worksheets of a few late poems. All four possess letters.

3. Ralph N. Maud, ed., *The Notebooks of Dylan Thomas* (New Directions, 1967).

4. The inside of the front cover provides a map of England. Its most striking entry is the words "The Birth," that Thomas penciled and framed with a rectangle between the Isle of Man and Northumberland. This may be a trial title, perhaps an alternative to "After the Fair," "The Visitor," or the unpublished "Gaspar, Melchior, Balthasar," where births of one sort or another occur. The stories in the Notebook and additional titles are listed in the North Sea. "The Witch," "Arecom [scratched] Genesis," "The Manor" and "The Knife" are inked in a column. These titles are probably the first jottings, because an additional title, "The Diarists," is penciled below that list. Thomas mentioned this last story, in a Christmas (1932?) letter to Trevor Hughes, as one *The London Mercury* accepted but did not publish (*Selected letters of Dylan Thomas,* ed. Constantine FigzGibbon [London: Dent, 1966] p. 8).

A table of contents directly west of this one is entirely in pencil and is almost the same as the order of stories in the Red Notebook:

+ The Tree

+ Martha

+ After The Fair

+ The Enemies

+ The Dress

The Visitors.

The Burning Baby

The Vest

Gaspar, Melchior, Balthazar

The two differences are that in the Notebook "The Burning Baby" follows "Gaspar, Melchior, Balthasar" and that the unlisted story, "Anagram," appears last in the Notebook and eventually constitutes the central section of "The Orchards."

The overleaf of sheet 53 also contains lists: three trials of a table of stories and a list headed by "Eighteen Poems." The next entry in this prospective list of "works" was originally "Ten Stories," the number in the Red Notebook, but the title of Thomas' next published book, "25 Poems" (Dent, 1936), has been inserted between these two. The insertion may date the lists in the Notebook. The rest of the list tries various titles: "Three Essays" (deleted), "Two Plays" (deleted), "Twenty Poems," "Six Stories" (deleted?), "Three Essays" (deleted), and "One Story" (deleted). The three versions of a table of contents for a collection of short stories on this overleaf not only show Thomas' uncertainty over what to include, but they indicate many other prose manuscripts were extant by this time.

The title of another elusive story, "An Uncommon Genesis," appears in most of these jotted tables. It was to be a short novel that Thomas began writing as early as 1932. He told Pamela Hansford Johnson it concerned "a man & a woman. And the woman, of course, is not human" (*Selected Letters,* p. 38; see also pp. 42 and 49). Mrs. Annis Vilas Pratt thinks the novelette probably became "The Mouse and the Woman," which does not appear in any of the lists of titles—"The Early Prose of Dylan Thomas," Unpublished Ph.D. dissertation, Columbia University, 1964, p. 16.)

Other titles that appear somewhere in the Red Notebook but are not among its stories are:

The End of the River

The Horse's Ha

The Map of Love

Selmer

The Tramp

The Holy Six

The Enemies United.

5. Dylan Thomas, *Adventures in the Skin Trade* (New Directions 1953), p. 98. Most future references to this volume will be noted parenthetically by page numbers in my text. References to the Red Notebook will likewise be noted, with the side of the leaf indicated by a or b.

6. *Skin Trade,* p. 98. His religious feeling was emphasized over the idea of the fall in the Red Notebook, where the phrase was "nave of the earth" (2b).

7. *Skin Trade,* p. 98. Cf. the "polar eagle" of "The Ballad of the Long-legged Bait."

8. Four months later (11 May 1934) he despaired to Pamela Hasford Johnson, "All sentences fall when the weight of the mind is distributed unevenly along the holy consonants and vowels. In the beginning was a word I can't spell, not a reversed Dog, or a physical light, . . ." (*Selected Letters,* p. 127.)

9. The Red Notebook shows Thomas considered dropping the name Martha, which was also the original title of the story. For some reason he scratched most appearances of "Martha" in the Notebook and penciled "Helen." In a letter to John Davenport (31 August 1938, according to *Selected Letters,* pp. 206-7). Thomas mentioned "'All Paul's Altar', the actual description of a murder committed by a naked woman (especially the phrase 'her head broke like an egg on the wall')," as one of the objectionable items for which puritannical standards had delayed publication of "The Burning Baby" volume. Eventually most of the selections proposed for that book were included in *The Map of Love.*

10. p. 261. The power of this understatement increased when Thomas removed "with a sudden movement" (p. 13a).

11. Annis Pratt, *Dylan Thomas' Early Prose: a Study in Creative Mythology* (University of Pittsburgh Press, 1970). Chapter II. She treats the Owens under her discussion of Thomas and the occult (Chapter IV).

12. *Selected Letters,* pp. 118, 126 and 130-31.

13. The name of the girl troubled Thomas. To Peter the poet it "meant nothing. It was a cool sound" (p. 113). In the fair copy of the Red Notebook it was to be "Millicent," but in two places he copied "Heather" and then changed it in pencil to "Hesther," apparently to support her characterization as like "a maiden out of the Old Testament." These were then corrected in ink to "Millicent," the name used in the version published by *Criterion,* XV (January 1935), 251-9, and not entirely removed from *Skin Trade* (p. 111). The final name, "Rhianon," Mrs. Pratt relates to the muse of poetry and learning by that name in *Y Barddas,* ed. William Ab Ithel (London, 1862)—*Dylan Thomas' Early Prose,* p. 93.

14. Thomas also used "Peter" as the name of the poet in the *Criterion* version of "The Orchards," and it became "Marlais" for publication in *The Map of Love*. Thomas might have drawn "Peter" from his part in H. F. Rubinstein's "Peter and Paul," that Miss Ethel Ross says he acted with the Swansea Little Theater in Mumbles during March, 1933—"Dylan Thomas and the Amateur Theater," *The Swan*, II (March 1958), 15-21. In the play Peter lost his poetic powers as he grew older and became involved in his happy family life. Such is the plight of the fisher-hero in "Ballad of the Long-legged Bait."

15. The passages deleted were:

    He was dead. Now he knew he was dead. (p. 116)

    He heard Callaghan's laughter like a rattle of thunder that the wind took up and doubled. [p. 118] Dead Peter, cried Callaghan, "I showed you death in the valley. And, Lord, you laughed (p. 32a—punctuation and corrections by Thomas.)

    There was the old rumour of Callaghan down his brain. From dawn to dark he had talked of death, had seen a moth caught in the candle, had heard the laughter that could not have been his ring in his ears (p. 199).

16. In the manuscript Thomas explicated the protagonist's sympathetic reaction to his mother-in-law's cancer: "He felt the locust of the cancer on his own face, in the mouth and the fluttering eyelid. He had knocked Helen over the mouth." (p. 34b—deletion by Thomas).

17. The Red Notebook reads, ". . . as they climbed out of a purchased sleep, puffed out of tenement offices, cupping their hands . . ." (p. 38b—deletion by Thomas.). It is difficult to ignore some of the many deletions in the manuscript. The description of the sky as a hangar was removed, apparently because it was confusing, and the explanatory "hangar of the shadow of death" may have been struck because it was stated too heavily. The trend of corrections on the first two pages removes much obvious sarcasm, but a guess about the corrections is risky because they are sometimes incomplete. The many inks and pencil used indicate Thomas tinkered with the story several times, even considered sending it to *Adelphi*, before he rejected it.

18. *Criterion*, XV (July 1936), 614-22. The *Skin Trade* version did not excise "Peter" entirely. (V. p. 147.)

19. A passage in the Red Notebook stated, "The housetops are a strange land where man might scramble over the easel and the typewriter. the mortal rooms, love and the winding-bed, (P. 48b—corrections by Thomas)

20. P. 50a. The last two lines and the change from "some" to "a," as well as the date, are in later pencil.

21. See my "The Metamorphic Stop of Time in 'A Winter's Tale,'" *PMLA*, LXXVIII (September 1963), 422-30.

22. Held by the Lockwood Library and dated "Feb 10.'33." See *The Notebooks of Dylan Thomas*, pp. 168 and 302.

23. P. 45b) The second sentence, which was not consistent with the changeling's point of view, was removed from the published version.

24. *Selected Letters,* p. 151. This association of the phallus with the poet's pen is very likely a reason for his early selection of the name "Peter" for his fictional poets. See also note 14.

Gerald L. Bruns (essay date 1973)

SOURCE: "Daedalus, Orpheus, and Dylan Thomas's *Portrait of the Artist,*" in *Renascence,* Vol. XXV, No. 3, Spring, 1973, pp. 147-56.

[*In the following essay, Bruns attempts to find the sources of inspiration for the stories contained in Thomas's* Portrait of the Artist as a Young Dog.]

One of the most fascinating themes in literary history concerns the poet's inquiry into the conditions which make his art possible. The origins of this theme are in Homer and, more explicitly, in Hesiod. It is the theme of Wordsworth's *Prelude* and Coleridge's "Dejection" ode. It was the inquiry into the possibility of poetry that moved Matthew Arnold to give up poetry in favor of prose discourses upon man's unpoetic cultural life, and which, by contrast, induced Paul Valéry to begin writing poetry again after twenty years of silence. It is the theme of Yeats's "Ego Dominus Tuus," Pound's "Mauberly, 1920," Auden's *The Sea and the Mirror,* and countless poems by Wallace Stevens. And it is the theme of two works of autobiographical fiction, Joyce's *A Portrait of the Artist as a Young Man,* and Dylan Thomas's *A Portrait of the Artist as a Young Dog.*

These last two works are of special interest, because they appear to be portraits of the artist grounded upon two radically different models: Daedalus and Orpheus. For Stephen Dedalus, the possibility of poetry is predicated upon a flight of the poet into transcendence. His imagination is dominated by the figure of "the hawklike man whose name he bore soaring out of his captivity on osierwoven wings," and in imitation of this mythic creature Stephen progressively dissociates himself from all that is tied to earth. But Dylan Thomas's young man is dominated by the earth and its people:

> In the safe centre of his own identity, the familiar world about him like another flesh, he sat sad and content in the plain room of the undistinguished hotel at the sea-end of the shabby, spreading town where everything was happening. He had no need of the dark interior

world when Tawe pressed in upon him and the eccentric ordinary people came bursting and crawling, with noise and colours, out of their houses, out of the graceless buildings, the factories and avenues, the shining shops and blaspheming chapels, the terminuses and the meeting halls, the falling alleys and the brick lanes, from the arches and shelters and holes behind the hoardings, out of the common, wild intelligences of the town.[1]

The artist here is incarnated in his world: it is "like another flesh," against which he feels nothing of Stephen's lust for transcendence. Withdrawal into a "dark interior world" defines exactly Stephen's typical mode of response to the shabbiness of Dublin. Thus we are told of Stephen's anger toward "the change of fortune which was reshaping the world about him into a vision of squalor and insincerity. Yet his anger lent nothing to the vision. He chronicled with patience what he saw, detaching himself from it and tasting its mortifying flavour in secret" (p. 67). But the shabbiness of Tawe induces no such need for detachment. The world of Thomas's artist is not a world of private experiences, the tasting of flavors in secret; on the contrary, it is a world of persons and objects that flood a broad and open field of experience, thus to induce a lyrical inventory: "the eccentric ordinary people came bursting and crawling . . . out of their houses, out of the graceless buildings"—out of factories, avenues, shops, chapels, terminuses, meeting halls, alleys, lanes, arches, shelters, "and holes behind the hoardings."

Such an inventory is typical of the way Thomas's prose seeks to gather to itself the furniture of his world. "I never felt more a part of the remote and over-pressing world," the speaker says in **"Just like Little Dogs,"** "or more full of love and arrogance and pity and humility, not for myself alone"—and at this point his language spins off into encyclopedic exuberance—

> but for the living earth I suffered on and for the unfeeling systems in the upper air, Mars and Venus and Brazell and Skully, men in China and St. Thomas, scorning girls and ready girls, soldiers and bullies and policemen and sharp, suspicious buyers of secondhand books, bad, ragged women who'd pretend against the museum wall for a cup of tea, and perfect, unapproachable women out of fashion magazines, seven feet high, sailing slowly in their flat, glazed creations through steel and glass and velvet (pp. 81-82).

This encyclopedic impulse to transpose a world of particulars into language contrasts sharply with Stephen's impulse to purge from his art those "elements which he deemed common and insignificant" (p. 70). This contrast corresponds roughly to the more extreme opposition between Mallarmé, whose work proceeded by climination and whose Beatrice was Destruction, and Whitman, whose "Song of Myself" breaks repeatedly into great inventories of the universe. it is an opposition between the Daedalian love for the purity of art and an Orphic love for the intensity of life.

"I felt all my young body like an excited animal surrounding me," says the speaker in **"Peaches,"** "the torn knees

bent, the sweat prickling in the hands, the tunnels down to the eardrums, the little balls of dirt between the toes, the eyes in the sockets, the tucked-up voice, the blood racing, the memory around and within flying, jumping, swimming and waiting to pounce" (p. 23). This intensity—the intensity of Whitman or Orpheus—exults in names, for by naming, as Heidegger says, the world is brought into being: "The poet names the gods and names all things in that which they are . . . when the poet speaks the essential word, the existent is by this naming nominated as what it is. So it becomes known *as* existent. Poetry is the establishing of being by means of the word."[2] The intensity of Stephen Dedalus, however, is of a different order and imposes upon the world a different fate: "His thinking was a dusk of doubt and self-mistrust, lit up at moments by the lightnings of intuition, but lightnings of so clear a splendour that in those moments the world perished about his feet as if it had been fire consumed: and thereafter his tongue grew heavy and he met the eyes of others with unanswering eyes for he felt that the spirit of beauty had folded him round like a mantle and that in reverie at least he had been acquainted with nobility" (p. 225). Here the poet's experience exceeds the power of speech, because it is an experience not of the world but of the transcendent spirit of beauty, whose light transfigures the poet and leaves the world in ashes about his feet.

The effect of the recurring inventories in Thomas's stories is to subordinate the poet to the world, for the inventories testify to the richness, not of the "dark interior world" of imagination, but of that "overpressing world" which breaks in upon imagination and illuminates it. This priority of reality over imagination is a theme especially to be marked in connection with **"One Warm Saturday,"** whose hero in the midst of his loneliness dreams the Daedalian dream of the transcendent poet: "Poets live and walk with their poems; a man with visions needs no other company; Saturday is a crude day; I must go home and sit in my bedroom by the boiler." At once, however, the narrator intervenes to subvert this myth by deflating the young man: "But he was not a poet living and walking, he was a young man in a sea-town on a warm bank holiday, with two pounds to spend; he had no visions, only two pounds and a small body with its feet on the littered sand . . ." (pp. 138-139).

Recall that in Part IV of Joyce's *Portrait,* when Stephen feels most deeply the mythic significance of his name, and so for the first time establishes his identity as an artist, he encounters the innocent young girl standing "in midstream, alone and still, gazing out to sea. She seemed like one whom magic had changed into the likeness of a strange seabird" (p. 171). By contrast, in **"One Warm Saturday,"** at precisely the moment when his identity as a poet is called into question by the narrator, the young man encounters Lou: "He marked, carefully and coldly in one glance, all the unusual details of her appearance; it was the calm, unstartled certainty of her bearing before his glance from head to foot, the innocent knowledge, in her smile and the set of her head, that she was defended by her gentleness and accessible strangeness against all rude encounters and picking looks, that made his fingers tremble" (p. 139). The coldness of the young man's glance is one point to mark here, and another is Lou's curious innocence, which is not innocence merely but, paradoxically, "innocent knowledge"—innocence joined with "calm, unstartled certainty of her bearing" and, most curious of all, her "accessible strangeness." The young man's coldness and Lou's innocence seem to be terms that measure an aesthetic rather than human distance. "How beautiful she is, he thought, with his mind on words and his eyes on her hair and red and white skin, how beautifully she waits for me, though she does not know she is waiting and I can never tell her." The role of words here is critical: the young man's eyes are on the girl, but his mind is on words that cohere to form an interior rhapsody—words, moreover, that evidently hold the magic by which Lou is transformed into a vision of innocence. For when the rhapsody ceases, the character of Lou unmistakably changes: "He had stopped and was staring. Like a confident girl before a camera, she . . . accepted his admiration" (pp. 139-140). Innocence splits off from knowledge, and the vision is dissipated, so that we can hardly fail to notice the radical difference between Lou and that birdlike creature who turned to Stephen Dedalus "in quiet sufferance of his gaze, without shame or wantonness . . . then quietly withdrew her eyes from his and bent them towards the stream" (p. 171). Lou, of course, is without shame, but not precisely without wantonness, as the young man at last perceives: "Midges [gnats] flew into his mouth. He hurried on shamefully. At the gates of the Gardens he turned to see her for the last time on earth. She had lost her calm with his abrupt and awkward going, and stared in confusion after him. One hand was raised as though to beckon him back. If he waited, she would call him"—and, just so, she evidently does call him, but with gnats in his mouth the young man flees to the security of the Victoria Saloon.

It is difficult not to regard this scene as a parody of Stephen's famous epiphany, particularly as it becomes clear that what the young man suffers is not so much the disillusionment of a failed visionary as it is a fate more typically human in character. For in the Victoria Saloon the young man encounters his image in a mirror, and the dialogue between self and image that follows renders explicitly the opposition between the visionary and the human:

> And what shall the terrified prig of a love-mad young man do next? he asked his reflection silently in the distoting mirror of the empty 'Victoria' saloon. His apelike, hanging face, with Bass across the forehead, gave back a cracked sneer.
>
> If Venus came in on a plate, said the two red, melon-sliced lips, I would ask for vinegar to put on her.
>
> She could drive my guilt out; she could smooth away my shame; why didn't I stop to talk to her? he asked.
>
> You saw a queer tart in a park, his reflection answered, she was a child of Nature, oh my! oh my! Did you see

the dew-drops in her hair? Stop talking to the mirror like a man in a magazine, I know you too well (p. 140).

The "apelike, hanging face" with "a cracked sneer" speaks with the voice of disillusionment—speaks, indeed, in the manner of Stephen Dedalus, who congenitally regarded with contempt and bitterness the reality that broke in upon imagination. Were Venus now to appear before him, so disabused is he, he would cover her with vinegar. But the young man's response to his experience is finally quite different from that of his distoted image: it is a complex response, one that moves him gradually to a sense of himself as a creature fitted into the world as a spirit into a body.

His first impulse is to think of himself as a ruined lover (a role, incidentally, which Stephen Dedalus, his imagination alive with the romances of Dumas, delighted to play): "he had found his own true happiness and lost her all in one bewildering half a minute . . . Older and wiser and no better, he would have looked in the mirror to see if his discovery and loss had marked themselves upon his face in the shadows under the eyes or lines about the mouth, were it not for the answer he knew he would receive from the distorted reflection" (p. 141). The key words in the young man's meditation are "discovery and loss." He will, we shall see, play out this drama of discovery and loss once more, but under different circumstances and with slightly different meaning. For the pose of the ruined lover is soon cast off: "he shook off the truthless, secret tragedy with a sneer and a blush, straightened his melancholy hat into a hard-brimmed trilby, dismissed the affected stranger" (p. 143). We come at this point to the passage quoted earlier: the young man settles into "the safe centre of his own identity, the familiar world about him like another flesh," and there discovers that "He had no need of the dark interior world." He is not the Daedalian poet, nor does he need to be: he need only open himself up to "the common, wild intelligence of the town"—open himself up, that is to say, to such a creature as Lou.

This, as it happens, is precisely what he does, for Lou enters the saloon, and, seeing her, the young man realizes that "only a sick boy with tossed blood would run from his proper love into a dream, lie down in a bedroom that was full of his shames, and sob against the feathery, fat breast and face of the damp pillow. He remembered his age and his poems, and would not move" (p. 144). The result is that, as he basks in the enchanting gaze of Lou, his next rhapsody is of an entirely different character from before: "Nothing can hurt me. Let the barman jeer. Giggle in your glass, our Em. I'm telling the world, I'm walking in clover, I'm staring at Lou like a fool, she's my girl, she's my lily. O love! O love! She's no lady, with her sing-song Tontine voice, she drinks like a deep-sea diver; but Lou, I'm yours and Lou, you're mine. He refused to meditate on her calmness now and twist her beauty into words" (p. 147). Whereas before the young man had disjoined mind and eye, word and thing, and so displaced the reality of

Lou with words that made her something other than she is, here he allows Lou to be herself ("She's no lady, with her sing-song Tontine voice"), and, what is more, he allows himself to be himself as well—not a poet with visions but a young man with two pounds to spend. For reality, whatever its squalor and however fallen its humanity, has a value peculiarly its own, which dreams of innocence and unearthly beauty can only destroy.

The difficulty is that the young man's imagination will not allow reality to be what it is. The Daedalian dreams which Stephen actively pursues appear in **"One Warm Saturday"** as forces over which the young man has yet to gain control. As he sits with Lou and her friends in the saloon, he begins to see "her as a wise, soft girl whom no hard company could spoil, for her soft self, bare to the heart, broke through every defence of her sensual falsifiers. As he thought this, phrasing her gentleness, faithlessly running to words away from the real room and his love in the middle, he woke with a start and saw her lively body six steps from him, no calm heart dressed in a sentence, but a pretty girl to be got and kept" (p. 148). We can see here the essential conflict of the story playing itself out—the war of words and world within whose ebb and flow Lou appears, disappears, and appears again, now an ideal figure of innocence "dressed in a sentence" by a young poet "faithlessly running to words," now "a pretty girl to be got and kept."

It is the young man's inability to keep faith with reality that drives the story to its melancholy conclusion. He is compelled to lift Lou out of the situation in which he finds her—compelled, that is, to abstract her from reality, thus to encounter her in the void of fantasy. It is in this context that we may read the following remarkable passage:

> I want Lou in my arms, the young man said to himself, watching Mr. O'Brien tap and smile and the barman draw Marjorie down deep. Mrs. Franklin's voice sang sweetly in the small bedroom where he and Lou should be lying in the white bed without any smiling company to see them drown. He and Lou could go down together, one cool body weighted with a boiling stone, on to the falling, blank white, entirely empty sea, and never rise. Sitting on their bridal bed, near enough to hear his breath, she was farther from him than before they met . . .
>
> He wished that the light would fail. In the darkness he and Lou could creep beneath the clothes and imitate the dead. Who would look for them there, if they were dead still and soundless? (pp. 154-155).

The company of revellers has adjourned to Lou's rooms, and it is against this company and their world that the young man directs the full energy of his imagination. He imagines that he and Lou have been cast together into the sea—"the falling, blank white, entirely empty sea," which is to say a universe whose undifferentiated character implies a kind of absolute freedom from reality. No wonder, as the young man sits with Lou on the bed—and not on the bed merely, but upon the "bridal bed" in full flush of

the fantasy of innocence—he feels that "she was farther from him than before they met." Indeed she is, for the Lou that he carries with him into the darkness, the darkness of his interior world where they can "imitate the dead," is a Lou utterly without substance, a creature impossible to get or keep.

Just so, the fantasy descends into painful irony. The young man imagines the revellers rummaging "in the silence about the narrow obstacled corridors" in search of the two lovers. In "the made-up dark" he hears the voice of Mr. O'Brien, his apparent rival, calling after the vanished Lou. Moments later, however, it is the young man who is rummaging in the corridors. Having left Lou in order to relieve himself, he finds his dream of darkness horribly realized: "He ran into a cavern. A draught blew out his matches . . . He made water at the dead end of the passage and hurried back towards Lou's room, finding himself at last on a silent porch of stairway at the top of the house; he put out his hand, but the rail was broken and nothing there prevented a long drop to the ground down a twisted shaft that would echo and double his cry . . ." (p. 158). This is an encounter with a real void, and in its real darkness it is the young man, not Mr. O'Brien, who calls out, "'Lou, where are you? . . . Answer! Answer!'" (p. 159). But Lou is not a creature of the void; it is not she but the young man who has vanished—quite as though Eurydice were not in the Underworld at all but on earth, and that Orpheus has lost her because of his inability to free himself from his "dark interior world." For the distortion which renders hopeless the young man's quest for Lou is but an extension of the more fundamental disorientation by which his imagination sought to displace reality.

The young man thus becomes a twice-damned hero, for Lou has twice been discovered and twice lost. This repetition or duplication of experience gives "One Warm Saturday" the character of a fable, one whose moral is twice invoked, so that it becomes the story of an unlearned lesson—or, perhaps, of a lesson not yet learned. But this duplication of the experience of loss suggests a further, perhaps more important point: it gives **"One Warm Saturday"** a circular structure—a structure of departures and returns. This is a point worth remarking, because the last sentence in the story both invokes an image of a circle and invites us to consider the story as part of a larger structure that is itself circular: "The light of the one weak lamp in a rusty circle fell across the brickheaps and the broken wood and the dust that had been houses once, where the small and hardly known and never-to-be-forgotten people of the dirty town had lived and loved and died and, always, lost" (p. 160). Within the "rusty circle" illuminated by the streetlamp lies the debris of a collective or communal experience, of which the young man's loss of his Eurydice forms a part, but an important part, because his experience closes the circle which the whole of Thomas's *Portrait* sought to describe.

For each of the stories in *A Portrait of the Artist as a Young Dog* plays a variation upon the theme of loss within a counterpoint formed by the opposition between an ideal or imagined existence and the claims of life in the world. In **"Peaches,"** for example, Gwilym's fantasy-life as a preacher shadowed by a sinister, feline divinity is one of the forces in a world of adult imagination that undercuts the earthly life of the young protagonist, whose imagination generates not fantasies but a growing self-consciousness: "There, playing Indians in the evening, I was aware of me myself in the exact middle of a living story, and my body was my adventure and my name" (p. 23). In **"Who Do You Wish Was with Us,"** the young man struggles against his friend's compulsion to reenact the trauma of a brother's lingering and melancholy death: "If he lost the world around him for a moment, if I left him alone, if he cast his eyes down, if his hand lost its grip on the hard, real fence or the hot bowl of his pipe, he would be back in ghastly bedrooms, carrying cloths and basins and listening for handbells" (p. 113). Or, again, in **"Where Tawe Flows,"** the opposition between the imagined and the real becomes the topic for a comic debate, in which Mr. Humphries proposes that "'The life of that mythical common denominator, the man-in-the-street, is dull as ditch-water,'" to which Mr. Evans triumphantly replies: "'. . . the everyday man's just as interesting a character study as the neurotic poets of Bloomsbury'" (p. 95). Just so, the stories in Thomas's **Portrait** are character studies, not of the poet, but of everyday men and women—quite as though they were the fulfillment of the vow taken by the young writer in **"Old Garbo"**: "'I'll put them all in a story by and by'" (p. 134).

The effect of these stories is to call into being an artist distinguished by his humanity—by his openness to man and his immersion in the trivial yet devastating experiences of man's earthly life—and not by any god-like or transcendent powers that he may be supposed to possess. Indeed, if a god of poetry hovers at all above the young *Künstler* in these stories, it is Orpheus, the poet of the earth, whose creativity derives not from the isolated, transcendent Word but from the unity of word and being—the word incarnate in the world, whose power it is to bring into being a universe in which the natural and the human are inextricably one. For the portrait of this artist, we need only look to Thomas's poetry:

> Especially when the October wind
> With frosty fingers punishes my hair,
> Caught by the crabbing sun I walk on fire
> And cast a shadow crab upon the land,
> By the sea's side, hearing the noise of birds,
> Hearing the raven cough in winter sticks,
> My busy heart who shudders as she talks
> Sheds the syllabic blood and drains her words.
>
> Shut, too, in a tower of words, I mark
> On the horizon walking likes the trees
> The wordy shapes of women, and the rows
> Of the star-gestured children in the park.
> Some let me make you of the vowelled beeches,
> Some of the oaken voices, from the roots
> Of many a thorny shire tell you notes,
> Some let me make you of the water's speeches.

> Behind a pot of ferns the wagging clock
> Tells me the hour's word, the neural meaning
> Flies on the shafted disk, declaims the morning
> And tells the windy weather in the cock.
> Some let me make you of the meadows signs;
> The signal grass that tells me all I know
> Breaks with the wormy winter through the eye.
> Some let me tell you of the raven's sins.
>
> Especially when the October wind
> (Some let me make you of autumal spells,
> The spider-tongued, and the loud hill of Wales)
> With fists of turnips punishes the land,
> Some let me make you of the heartless words.
> The heart is drained that, spelling in the scurry
> Of chemic blood, warned of the coming fury.
> By the sea's side hear the dark-vowelled birds.[3]

Here is Thomas's version of the transcendent poet, but notice that it confounds the gnostic vision of the Daedalus. The poet is, by turns, abroad in the world, casting "a shadow crab upon the land, / By the sea's side," and aloft in his "tower of words." But from his tower he commands a view of a landscape of "wordy shapes of women," "vowelled beeches," "oaken voices." "If we go to a spring or through the forest," writes Heidegger, "we are already passing through the word 'spring' and through the word 'forest,' even though we do not speak these words or think of anything linguistic."[4] For words are incarnate in the world, and it is upon the ground of this incarnation that the poet, in Thomas's view as well as Heidegger's, finds the possibility of his creation:

> Some let me make you of the vowelled beeches,
> Some of the oaken voices, from the roots
> Of many a thorny shire tell you notes,
> Some let me make you of the water's speeches.

For Thomas, the poet's creativity is not to be explained by recourse to a doctrine of imagination, but by recourse to the *Logos*—to the identity of language and the world of things. "Words are proximally present-at-hand," Heidegger writes in *Being and Time,* "that is to say, we come across them just as we come across Things; and this holds for any sequence of words, as that in which the *Logos* expresses itself."[5] Just so, in Thomas's view it is given to the poet to discover words present in the world, and by this discovery to become in his own right the medium by which the *Logos* expresses itself.

Notes

1. The quotation is from "One Warm Saturday," in *A Portrait of the Artist as a Young Dog* (New York, 1940), p. 23. For the Joyce quotation, see *A Portrait of the Artist as a Young Man* (New York, 1964), p. 225. It should be noticed that in context Stephen's attitude toward the god, Daedalus, is not unambiguous, nor, of course, is Joyce's.

I am grateful to Warren French for calling to my attention his fine essay, "Two Portraits of the Artist: James Joyce's *Young Man;* Dylan Thomas's *Young*

Dog," which appeared in *University Review,* 33 (1967), 261-266. The reader will find in this essay an excellent discussion of how the relationship between these two works is to be understood.

2. "Hölderlin and the Essence of Poetry," tr. Douglas Scott, in *Existence and Being* (Chicago: Gateway Edition, 1949), p. 281.

3. *The Collected Poems of Dylan Thomas* (New York, 1957), pp. 19-20.

4. *Holzwege* (Frankfurt, 1950), p. 286.

5. (New York and Evanston, Ill., 1962), p. 201.

Richard A. Davies (essay date 1977)

SOURCE: "Dylan Thomas's Image of the 'Young Dog' in the Portrait," in *The Anglo-Welsh Review,* Vol. 26, No. 58, Spring, 1977, pp. 68-72.

[*In the following essay, Davies examines canine allusions in Thomas's short stories, which he feels reveals the author's youthful bravado as well as his resolution that he is destined to lose his vitality.*]

The stance Dylan Thomas chose to emphasise in his ***Portrait*** stories, that of a "young dog", evokes an image of bravado, defiance and aggression in the face of life, a devil-may-care approach to existence that would seem to be well suited to Thomas's fertile comic fancy. I use the word "seem" because a reader would be insensitive to Thomas's vision of life if he failed to see the irony of the "young dog" pose. There is a pattern in Thomas's parade of youthful versions of himself but it is not the one that is generally emphasised.[1] The pattern is one of a gradual loss of courage and boldness, a consequent increase in fears and terrors, until the young dog is fully metamorphosed into a "terrified prig of a love-mad young man" (p. 104).[2]

The pattern starts to unfold itself in **'Patricia, Edith and Arnold'** and **'The Fight'** where we see Thomas as a bumptious young boy yet alarmed by his chance encounters with the human flesh and lovers. The surface impression of Thomas's emotional fright at seeing Patricia's leg close-up is one of comedy:

> The boy stood bewildered between them. Why was Patricia so angry and serious? Her face was flushed and her eyes shone. Her chest moved up and down. He saw the long black hairs on her leg through a tear in her stocking. Her leg is as big as my middle he thought. I'm cold; I want tea; I've got snow in my fly (p. 30-31).

The passage also registers the boy's emotional confusion at the sight of the hairy female leg. There is an uneasiness which doesn't go away. In **'The Fight'** which opens with the "young dog" at his exuberant best, Thomas writes of Mrs. Bevan:

> I tried to undress her, but my mind grew frightened when it came to her short flannel petticoat and navy bloomers to the knees. I couldn't even dare unbutton her tall boots to see how grey her legs were. She looked up from her plate and gave me a wicked smile. (p. 41)

If the fear wasn't recurrent we might pass by with a smile ourselves. Earlier in **'The Fight'** Thomas had walked past a young couple arm in arm commenting, "They would be tittering together now, with their horrid bodies close" (p. 37).

The strange thing is that what seems like an awkward stage in a young boy's growth in later stories germinates into a burden that Thomas finds very hard to carry. Indeed, as we shall see, in the later stories the "young dog" spirit masks a deep-seated anxiety that the world of sexual experience and female flesh is as Swift perceived is in scatological poems like 'The Lady's Dressing Room' (1731). We are not yet at the point where it is destroying him. The next story, **'Extraordinary Little Cough,'** is a subtle portrait of Thomas's own sexual development during adolescence. The story might seem unrelated to what I have just said because it dramatises Thomas's healthy yearnings for girls rather than revulsion from them. But this would be wrong. In **'Extraordinary Little Cough,'** the forces that are at war inside the young dog can be pin-pointed. First, Thomas prefigures in his imagination a day out at Rhossilli, meeting three girls and whisking them off their feet (pp. 47-48). However, when the encounter takes places, the girls prefer Brazell and Skully, two bullies, before Thomas, Dan, Sidney and George Hooping (extraordinary little cough). George Hooping, a boy who has no interest in the opposite sex, symbolises a world of innocence from which Thomas is trying to escape, but to which he is comically restricted:

> As I bent down, three lumps of sugar fell from my blazer pocket. "I've been feeding a horse", I said, and began to blush guiltily when all the girls laughed. (p. 51)

> We walked into Button's field, and I showed her inside the tents and gave her one of George Hooping's apples. "I'd like a cigarette", she said. (p. 52)

The gesture with the apple confines Thomas to the world of sexless but heroic exploit that Hooping inhabits by taking a dare made by the bullies seriously (to run across Rhossilli sands). Brazell and Skully, in contrast, represent a suavity with the opposite sex which Thomas recurrently wishes were his in later stories.[3] In dog terms, Brazell and Skully are mastiffs compared to the spaniel Thomas and the poodle Hooping. Brazell and Skully are part of the "remote and overpressing world", a central image in Thomas's repressed reveries in the next story, **'Just Like Little Dogs'** (p. 57). The phrase Thomas uses there to describe Brazell and Skully suggests both their distance from him and their burden upon him as a young man. They are as advanced toward manhood as George Hooping is set-back in his development.

'Extraordinary Little Cough' records the agonising stage between two states of development,

. . . they [Brazell and Skully] looked like a boy with two heads. And when I stared at George again he was lying on his back fast asleep in the deep grass and his hair was touching the flames. (p. 53)

Brazell and Skully are unreal and monster-like, George Hooping on the verge of immolation. This puts Thomas's own predicament and fears neatly. The very emphasis of the story which celebrates Hooping rather than Thomas deserves notice. Where is the "young dog" spirit? Where is the innocent heroic aggression that he showed against Dan in **'The Fight'**? The next story, **'Just Like Little Dogs,'** insists that a reader develop his inclination to see the "young dog" image as an ironic pose, carefully chosen to reveal its disappearance in the course of growing up. Jocular connotations of the "young dog" become replaced by more sinister ones.

'Just Like Little Dogs' portrays Thomas listening under a railway arch in pitch darkness to the story of Tom and Walter's sexual escapades with Doris and Norma. Thomas listens ". . . like a pimp in a bush at Tom's side . . . ," (p. 59) to an account of how Tom and Walter loved Doris and Norma and then changed partners, how paternity cases are brought against the young men and how Tom marries the girl he does not love. Thomas responds in a more serious manner than the 80 year old deaf magistrate Mr. Lewis who hears the paternity cases. Mr. Lewis chuckles philosophically to himself and mutters "Just like little dogs"! (p. 59). Thomas responds as he responded to Patricia's leg: "All at once I remembered how cold it was. I rubbed my numb hands together" (p. 59). The darkness of the arch adds to the sense of desolation consequent upon the encounter on the beach. The story is essentially a farcical account of how sex (without love)[4] is frightening. Thomas's reaction to what he hears is to pelt up the steep streets (presumably) for the warmth and comfort of home. Where is the "young dog" spirit now? As we shall see, he tries to use it to defend himself against the forces that press in towards him from the adult world. This can be seen in **'Who Do You Wish Was With Us'**.

There is a resurgence of the "young dog" spirit in **'Who Do You Wish Was With Us'**. Its opening is as juvenile as the opening of the first Rhossilli story, **'Extraordinary Little Cough'**, though Thomas is some years older. With his fellow gallant Ray, Thomas exudes typical bravado at the beginning of their day of escape from the town:

We went up Sketty Road at a great speed, our haver-sacks jumping on our backs. We rapped on every gate to give a terrific walkers' benediction to the people in the choking houses. Like a breath of fresh air we passed a man in office pin-stripes standing, with a dog-lead in his hand, whistling at a corner (p. 76).

Thomas tries to keep the exuberant mood going but fails in relation to Ray's depressive spirit which totally eclipses the fantasy of escape: "He [Ray] was stretched out like a dead man, his feet motionless in the sea, his mouth on the ruin of a rock pool, his hand clutched round my foot". (p.

84) The "young dog" spirit is powerless to resist such a depressive force. Thomas ironically evokes the memory of "mad Gwilym" of the very first story in the volume, **'The Peaches'** (p. 85). In **'The Peaches'** the boy Thomas was happy in his innocence unaware in emotional terms of the desolation of his landscape: ". . . the quiet untidy farm-yard, with its tumble-down, dirty-white cow-house and empty stables open" (p. 5). But as **'Who Do You Wish Was With Us'** symbolically concludes, the way back to such a state of mind is blocked: "The sea was in. The slip-ping stepping-stones were gone" (p. 86).

Instead, the "young dog" boldness becomes a mask of bra-vado, which characterises Thomas as he is led into the pub world of temptation by Mr. Farr in **'Old Garbo,'** the chain-smoking bitter-drinking, "round-faced and round-bellied" senior reporter in **'The Tawe News'**. In the world of **"The Three Lamps"**, after the initiations, comes "the threat of the clutched tankard" (p. 93) and a world of bewilderment and confusion.

Darkness and confusion engulf the young dog in **'One Warm Saturday'** and put him at one with the world around him. Hitherto, he has looked on the world wishing it to be purer, simpler and more congenial. Embodied as the "young dog" spirit, Thomas carries hope and vitality as far as he can to the point where they are destroyed and where the spirit aids in the destruction. Moving forward from his George Hooping world towards the complexity of adult experience, Thomas comes up against the rub of love in **'One Warm Saturday.'** The early sensations of a small boy and young adolescent in relation to the female body were the seeds of a failure and disillusionment more deep-seated. In **'One Warm Saturday'** Thomas is desperate (though drunk) to be left alone on the bridal bed of his fantasy with Lou, the girl he sees in Victoria Gardens and picks up at the pub. But Lou is not alone, in her entourage are Mrs. Franklin, Harold the barman, Marjorie, the drunk man with one buttock (a hint of *Candide* here), and the ri-val for Lou's hand, Mr. O'Brien.

The young man's desires are pure but sepulchral: "In the darkness he and Lou could creep beneath the clothes and imitate the dead" (p. 115). In the crowded tenement room Lou beckons to the young man from the bed, but the young dog has to obey the call of nature and search out the "House of Commons". As he exits looking for it, the black-ness and confusion of the world descend upon him. Blindly he gropes his way about the house trying to get back to Lou. He goes in and out of rooms but Lou has vanished. His romantic ideals come crashing down: "Love had grown up in an evening" (p. 117). We are left uncertain as to whether it has all been a dream or not, with ". . . only the approaching day to remember his discovery" (p. 119). The young man who walks out onto a waste space at the end of the *Portrait* does so with the knowledge that the life and vitality of the "young dog" has departed for ever. He becomes one with rubble of some houses ". . . where the small and hardly known and never-to-be-forgotten people of the dirty town had lived and loved and died and, always, lost" (p. 120). The disappearance of the spirited "young dog" and the emergence of another troubled animal is the point of the stories and the irony implicit in the "young dog" image from the very start.

Notes

1. Vernon Watkins has written: ". . . he [Thomas] released the spring of bubbling life and comic invention which his friends had always known, though he had, until then, kept it out of his work". ("Afterword", *Adventures In The Skin Trade,* Signet Classics, New York, 1960, p. 187).

2. All page references are to *Portrait Of The Artist As A Young Dog* (A New Directions Paperbacks, New York, Fourteenth Printing, 1968).

3. In 'Old Garbo': ". . . or to be called 'saucy' and 'a one' as I joked and ogled at the counter, making innocent, dirty love that could come to nothing among the spilt beer and piling glasses" (p. 94); in 'One Warm Saturday': "Oh boy! to be . . . telling the latest one to the girls. . . ." (p. 102).

4. Thomas goes in pursuit of that in 'One Warm Saturday'.

Valeria Tinkler (essay date 1981)

SOURCE: "Dylan Thomas as Poet and Story-Teller," in *Dutch Quarterly Review,* Vol. 11, No. 3, 1981, pp. 222-37.

[*In the following essay, Tinkler examines the differences between Thomas's poetry and prose.*]

The manuscript of ***Adventures in the Skin Trade,*** Dylan Thomas's first sustained piece of prose fiction, was returned to the author by the publishers with a note saying that it was not "the great and serious autobiographical work to which they had been looking forward". Vernon Watkins remembers that Thomas "was indignant and yet amused by the note. Why did publishers always want a writer to impress people, rather than entertain them? His serious work, he knew, was his poetry."[1] One wonders whether the last sentence really expresses what Thomas thought, in view of the fact that his later writing consists less and less of poetry, and more and more of a variety of forms in which entertainment plays a central part. Are we to take it that the broadcasts, the play for voices, the detective novel written with John Davenport, the operetta ***Me and My Bike,*** produced again by the BBC in the Christmas season 1978, and the opera planned with Igor Stravinsky were not, for Thomas, serious work? Since the gift for storytelling and entertainment, which are central in Thomas's later work, emerges and develops principally in the prose, it is more interesting, I believe, to try to assess the differences between what he achieves in his poetry and his prose than to attempt to read the one in terms of the other.

The early poetry and early prose are very close in the themes they explore and in the manner of their treatment, and consequently the early stories have been called poetic fantasies. Poetry, however, to Thomas seems to have always been a sign, a visible, audible, concrete form embodying and communicating a search of extreme significance. The poet is always an intermediator between man and God, or Christ, the victim redeeming the world, as in the **"Alterwise by Owl-light"** sonnet sequence, or later in the **"Ballad of the Long-legged Bait".** The prose, on the contrary, is less synthesized and lyrical, more verbal and descriptive. Accordingly, in the prose it is easy to identify, on the very surface, specific experience and ideas which had not yet been fully internalized and integrated and could not yet, therefore, be expressed in poetry. And, although the general themes are shared, still in the prose such themes are described and explored, while in the poetry they are lived through and there is no obvious, conscious struggle to express a theme within a symbolic tale. For example, in many of the stories Thomas is obviously trying to describe the struggles of adolescent frustrations, but in a poem like **"I See the Boys of Summer"** such a theme is perfectly integrated within the enacted experience. Again, the impact of surrealism or the search for verbal effectiveness are very obvious in the prose, which is often experimental. All this possibly explains why stories often seem roughdrafts of poems. Consider, for instance, the following from **"The Mouse and the Woman"** (first published in *Transition,* 25, Fall 1936):

> One winter morning, after the last crowing of the cock, in the walks of his garden, had died to nothing, she who for so long had dwelt with him appeared in all the wonder of her youth. She had cried to be set free, and to walk in his dreams no longer.[2]
>
> She moulded his images that evening. She lent light, and the lamp was dim beside her who had the oil of life glistening in every pore of her hand (67).
>
> The woman had shown him that it was wonderful to live. And how, when at last he knew how wonderful, and how pleasant the blood in the trees, and how deep the well of the clouds, he must close his eyes and die. He opened his eyes, and looked up at the stars. There were a million stars spelling the same word. And the word of the stars was written clearly upon the sky (76).
>
> In the eaves of the lunatic asylum the birds still whistled, and the madman, pressed close to the bars of the window near their nests, bayed up at the sun.
>
> Upon a bench some distance from the main path, the girl was beckoning to the birds . . . (77).

The theme of the story—woman as revelation, as both the inspiration of the poet and his poem, his creation—is the same as the theme of **"Love in the Asylum"** (*New Poems,* Norfolk, Connecticut, 1943):

> She has come possessed
> Who admits the delusive light through the bouncing wall,
> Possessed by the skies

She sleeps in the narrow trough yet she walks the dust
    Yet raves at her will
On the madhouse boards worn thin by my walking
tears.
And taken by light in her arms at long and dear last
    I may without fail
Suffer the first vision that set fire to the stars.[3]

A fairly long story structured around the alternation of past and present, madness and sanity, dream and reality is very different, both in the reading and actual resolution of the theme, from a short, very compressed poem. Interestingly, the poet who obviously succeeded in writing a poem has been able to "suffer" the vision; the protagonist of the story seems to have gone mad and he can only write prose.

Beyond this fundamental difference between the two mediums, however, the actual presentation of a theme is similar in the prose and in the poetry. "The force that through the green fuse drives the flower": this first line of the first poem published by Thomas has been quoted over and over as an example of what has been called "process poetry". Indeed, beyond the violent, explosive language, the words live and move; we actually see this force moving upwards through the stalk, pushing the flower open. It is a visual effect familiar to viewers of nature documentaries, where pictures of a blooming flower, taken at long intervals, are pieced together. In the same way both in the prose and in the poetry time quickens, a long process is packed, concentrated and shown in a flash:

> From their holes in the flanks of the hills came the rats and weasels, hairs white in the moon, breeding and struggling as they rushed downwards to set their teeth in the cattle's throat. . . . It was to Peter but a little time before the dead, picked to the bone, were huddled in under the soil by the wind . . . Now the worm and the death-beetle undid the fibres of the animal bones, worked at them brightly and minutely, and the weeds through the sockets and the flowers on the vanished breasts sprouted up with the colours of the dead life on their leaves. . . .
>
> Peter, in his ghost, cried out with joy. There was life in the naked valley, life in its nakedness (**"The Visitor"**, *A Prospect*, 32-3).

This reflects Thomas's concern, which was not with the moral choice as a result of a struggle, nor with learning from experience, but a re-enactment, a dramatic presentation of the struggle itself.

The short stories published after 1939 have been defined as straightforward, clear narratives as opposed to the poetic pieces of the past.[4] Certainly there could be nothing more startling than the difference between stories such as those quoted from above, and the later autobiographical narrative of *Portrait of the Artist as a Young Dog*.[5] A parallel, if dissimilar, change is evident in the poetry, where narrative becomes more important, and there is an identifiable pattern of human experience, or a character. Instead of the very general themes of birth, copulation and death, or the opposition of dream and reality, now specific ex-

amples are presented. The struggle is embodied in a particular case, and a personal theme is attributed to a particular individual. Titles such as **"Among those Killed in the Dawn Raid was a Man Aged a Hundred"**, or **"A Refusal to Mourn the Death, by Fire, of a Child in London"** show that the narrative seems necessary even in the title. These poems make it evident that the impact of war must have been a determining factor in opening the poet and prose-writer to human suffering and the question of the value of life. Nevertheless, some stories continue to anticipate, and be a first attempt at clarification of, a poem—for example the story **"The Burning Babe"** written in 1938, has close links with the second of the poems mentioned above—and the treatment of some themes, such as childhood, remains parallel.

In the early stories, the child was a figure of the poet. Both were potentially capable, through imagination, of creating a myth. In the stories of the *Portrait,* the vision of childhood changes. In the story **"The Peaches"** the protagonist, little Dylan, creates stories about himself when he is frightened, or wants to counteract reality; but he is unable to create for himself an alternative world. His imagination can transform a benevolent world into happiness and beauty, but when the world around him is malevolent, the child is helpless. This failure of the child corresponds to his ignorance of human suffering and his inability to understand and share experiences of grief and loss. The insult which his aunt Annie suffers when a rich lady refuses the peaches kept specially for her is not understood by the child. In **"The Peaches"** the child cannot be a figure of the poet, because he is lacking something. A similar separation between the innocence of childhood and the knowledge of human suffering by the poet is central to the poem **"The Hunchback in the Park"**. The world of this poem is very close to that of the stories of *Portrait,* and we know Thomas himself felt this from his inclusion of the poem in his broadcast entitled **"Reminiscences of Childhood"**. In the poem, the hunchback's experience is one of loss, of deprivation as he is shut out of the park every night. However, through deprivation he has learnt to create "a woman figure without fault" who remains in the park the whole night. The hunchback finds happiness and reward in a dream of his own creation; the cruel boys mock and torment him, and, "innocent as strawberries", they are like the park, the trees, the lake: part of the artist's inspiration and vision of beauty. Yet they cannot be the artist, because something is missing from their humanity.

Whether it is a man aged a hundred in a poem, or a child called Dylan in a story, Thomas the poet and storyteller is present in both mediums, and at this stage uses both as masks. He is not now recording a struggle in process, but recording a stage of understanding. In *Portrait*, each story is a stage of initiation into the universal human experience of loss; in the poetry, as in **"Ceremony after a Fire Raid"**, the poet says

Myselves
The grievers
Grieve.

It is the lament of an individual and of plurality at the same time; and the forced syntax stresses the ambiguity of "grievers" as possible subject, or object of "grieve". It is not a struggle, but an analysis of a state, of the human condition. From now on, the poetry becomes a formal celebration of life as it is. It involves an acceptance of and reconciliation with the reality of the human condition, but in the universe of the late poetry concrete reality is completely absent, and in this respect the difference between prose and poetry becomes remarkable.

The early stories, as poetic fantasies, are very close to the poems both in their themes and in their handling of the themes, as we have seen. One critic has remarked that "until 1939 [Dylan Thomas] seems to have thought of the short prose narrative as an alternative poet form—as a vehicle for recording the action of the imagination in reshaping objective reality according to private desire".[6] And indeed the interaction between objective reality and private desire are crucial to an understanding of both the prose and the poetry. In his early work reality seems nonexistent, while Nature is fantastic and undergoes innumerable metamorphoses under the eyes of the protagonist:

> He saw the many coloured county shrink like a coat in the wash. Then a new wind sprang from the pennyworth of water at the river-drop's end, blowing the hill field to its full size . . . (*A Prospect,* 5).

Reality and fantasy alternate until the boundaries between them are untraceable:

> "Come back! Come back!" the boy cried to the girl. She ran on unheeding over the sand and was lost among the sea. Now her face was a white drop of water in the horizontal rainfall, and her limbs were white as snow and lost in the white, walking tide. . . . He cried again, but she had mingled with the people moving in and out. Their tides were drawn by a grave moon that never lost an arc. Their long, sea gestures were deliberate, the flat hands beckoning, the heads uplifted, the eyes in the mask faces set in one direction (*A Prospect,* 11).

The boy does not answer the beckoning, but stays on the hard land—the landscape, therefore, hardly realistic even in its general description, is a visible form of an inner reality. The contrast between life and death, freedom and the limitations of conventional society, vital choice and paralysis presents itself in the opposing realities of land and water, and the discovery of the boundary between them. Here the boy refuses to join the "people moving in and out", yet what he should have done is left open to doubt. Who can blame him for keeping well clear of such "mask faces"? A proper choice seems impossible. In **"A Map of Love"** a boy and a girl are shown a map of fields and rivers and islands and the sea, and as they look the sea starts moving and the cherub-winds actually blow. They are urged to travel through this country, through the numbered fields and hills. Each feature of the landscape is a stage of sexual initiation. Their fear of this is presented as fear of the mixing of land and water:

> Beth Rib and Reuben marked the green sea around the island. It ran through the landcracks like a boy through his first caves. Under the sea they marked the channels, painted in skeleton, that linked the first beasts' island with the boggy lands. For shame of their half liquid plants sprouting from the bog, . . . the children blushed (*A Prospect,* 51).

A summary of the plot of this story would be extremely short: after a few attempts two children succeed in swimming up a river. Again here there are no real events, neither physical, nor mental. All events are purely symbolic: the discovery of the boundary between childhood innocence and knowledge, between life and death, or the acceptance or rejection of limits imposed from outside by fear or mental paralysis. In all the stories the action and the landscape are parallel manifestations of an attempt to control the process of life and death and to make an inner pattern out of the given physical reality. The protagonists of these universal human events—birth, copulation and death—are universalized characters: "the boy", "the madman", "the child", "the idiot". If a name is given, it is a symbolic name, such as Sam Rib. The early poems create a very similar kind of world in which universalized protagonists, such as "the boys of summer" or "I"—who is in turn baby being born, mother, young man—try to impose a poetic, verbal pattern on a given human reality such as birth or death.

Portrait of the Artist as a Young Dog is a complete reversal of the balance: it is not objective reality shaped by private desire, but objective reality is predominant while private desire here and there attempts, unsuccessfully, to bring a change or make sense of the world around. In this book the setting is a Welsh town, and the protagonist goes on an outing to such well known places as Worm's Head and Rhossilli sands. This protagonist is a child called Dylan, who grows in the course of the book into a young man and a poet. Events are trivial occurrences familiar to anyone, a visit to a grandfather, a holiday with an aunt, an outing with a friend, a child playing in the park. The seemingly different technique has, however, points of contact with the previous one, for now the growing child is a mask through which the writer can observe others. And beyond that, Dylan is a child whom both reader and writer can observe.

In a letter Thomas confided to a friend:

> I find I can't see a landscape, scenery is just scenery to me. . . . My own eyes, I know, squint inwards. When, and if, I look at the exterior world I see nothing, or me.[7]

The autobiographical mode serves Thomas perfectly because it identifies the two opposing worlds: external reality, and the self. Moreover, talking about himself Thomas is turning "the child" of the early stories into Dylan exposed to the common experiences of every child and young man, in a setting and in a world the writer knew and loved so well that he could let his skill and charm as a storyteller come into play. As he wrote in the second version of **"Reminiscencies of Childhood"**, "I like very much people telling me about their childhood, but they'll have to be quick or else I'll be telling them about mine".

But if reality takes over in the manner of the telling, and inner life appears subject to the external pattern of life as it is, the beauty of dream and the urge to try and control this outer pattern with an inner vision is even more central now. In **"A Visit to Grandpa"** the story is already told in the title, and it could be further summarized as the humorous and affectionate description of an old man whose mind is weakening. The climax of the story occurs on the last day of the boy's visit, when Grandpa disappears. He has left the town he lives in and is walking towards Llangadock, because it is there he wants to be buried:

> "But you aren't dead yet, Dai Thomas." For a moment grandpa reflected, then: "There's no sense in lying dead in Llanstephan," he said. "The ground is comfy in Llangadock, you can twitch your legs without putting them in the sea" (*Portrait,* 28).

Beyond the amusement of the character presentation the dignity and beauty of his attitude come through:

> But grandpa stood firm on the bridge, and clutched his bag to his side, and stared at the flowing river and the sky, like a prophet who has no doubt.

The thematic similarity with the early stories is obvious: the old man resists the given pattern of his death. He accepts the fact of death, but imposes on it his own imaginative idea which transforms the external reality into an eternal unity of man with earth and life. One cannot help noticing how well this figure of the old man, lost in a vision, standing on a bridge over the flowing Towy river fits in with the already observed pattern of the oscillating boundary between land and water. This old man is literally bridging the two realities, the inner and the external.

The inevitability of man's fate—whether his birth or death or frustration, or social set-backs—does not mean reject of life or disgust with it; neither does it mean resignation to it. Like grandpa in the story, the value that emerges throughout is the need and the ability to apply an imaginative creation to one's fate, to one's everyday life. It is the same approach that Thomas urges in his villanelle dedicated to his father: "Do not go gently into that good night; / Old rage should burn and rave at close of day; / Rage, rage against the dying of light". The night, however, is "good". The death to avoid is not the human fate, mortality, but a death to life, to friendship or love. Dylan grows into a young man who learns this lesson, and seems therefore to be moving in the right direction to fulfill his ambition of becoming a poet.

The unfinished novel **Adventures in the Skin Trade** seems to pick up and follow the thread of the story of **Portrait.** In the opening scenes—and scenes is the word to use to describe the visualized setting and dramatic presentation of character—we see Samuel, a young man with literary hopes who lives with his family in a small provincial town in Wales, systematically destroying and turning upside down his father, mother and sister's favourite or valuable objects, the evening before going to London. Samuel's literal attempt to destroy a suffocating pattern of life seems to invert the balance between inner and external reality as it was in the early stories. Here the inner life is silent, and the physical, literal destruction of things is a gesture of rebellion, not of creation, and in fact Samuel, in London, is extraordinarily passive. He simply rejects the old pattern, and waits for a new one to be imposed on him by people and events. Samuel deliberately avoids making plans: "I'm not going to choose anything" he says, and just sits and waits at the London station buffet. To Mr Allingham, a stranger who goes up and talks to him, and who irritably asks what on earth he expected would happen, and why he didn't do anything, Samuel answers: "Perhaps people would come and talk to me at the beginning. Women" (*AST,* 48).

If Samuel's arcadian expectations of his future life—no need to work, no contacts with home and the old world, love without complications—do not prove true, yet he finds that people do go up to him, and that the very trivial experiences and common people he meets lead him to a fantastic, Alice-in-Wonderland world where everyday reality proves to be beyond poetic vision. Samuel, half drunk on eau-de cologne, Mr Allingham and two friends enter a pub:

> "Here we are," Mr Allingham said, "four lost souls. What a place to put a man in."
>
> "The Antelope's charming," said George Ring. "There's some real hunting prints in the private bar (. . .)" "I mean the world. This is only a tiny bit of it. This is all right, it's got regular hours; you can draw the curtains, you know what to expect here. But look at the world. . . . What a place to drop a man in. In the middle of streets and houses and traffic and people" (93).

The world does prove to be a peculiar place—even the very house of such an apparently sane, normal man as Mr Allingham, who had previously said, "My name is Allingham, I live in Sewell street off Praed street, and I'm a furniture dealer. That's simple, isn't it?" When Samuel actually enters the house in Sewell street he finds it far from simple:

> "Hop in, boy." His voice came up from behind a high kitchen dresser hung with carpets; and, climbing over, Samuel looked down to see him seated on a chair on a couch, leaning back comfortably, his elbow on the shoulder of a statue (55).

> Two people came in, and climbed up the mattresses without a word. The first, a fat, short woman with black hair and a Spanish comb, who had painted her face as though it were a wall, took a sudden dive toward the corner behind Samuel and disappeared between two columns of chairs. She must have landed on cushions or a bed for she made no sound (57).

As these characters move through London, Samuel with his fingers stuck in the neck of a bottle, the story turns into a fairy tale. We ourselves are slowly led into this fantastic world which we accept as true and real. We have been buttonholed from the very beginning: Samuel's childish rebellion has carried the reader along a common plane of humanity and the straightforward humour, neither ironic nor sarcastic, has made us respond fully to its appeal to our involvement. More than any stylistic of technical trick, for example, many a teacher must have responded with embarassed anticipation of the father's horror the next morning on discovering obscene drawings all over his marked essays. We respond emotionally and relate the story to our own real world. Samuel's fear of discovery makes everything all the more true to experience:

> At first he peered uneasily into the known, flickering corners of the room, as though he feared that the family might have been sitting there in silence in the dark (26).

That the protagonist is not just a vandal, but is trying to break through a barrier and loves what he destroys, also captures the reader's sympathy and avoids cold or ironic detachment:

> "I should break the windows and stuff the cushions with the glass." He saw his round soft face in the mirror under the Mona Lisa. "But you won't," he said, turning away; "you're afraid of the noise." He turned back to his reflection. "It isn't that. You're afraid she'll cut her hands" (26).

The same pattern recurs in all the later stories: an amusing narrative, vividly told, of a trivial event leads the protagonist and the reader on to more than they had bargained for. In **"The Followers"** the two protagonists follow girls and peer at windows. They know that "it's kind of daft, it never takes you anywhere". For reality is so safe, repetitive, monotonous, and they are so passive. They end up by looking into a house where the mother of the girl they had followed, a "round, friendly, owlish woman in a pinafore", is cooking chips in a kitchen where everything is "good, dull and sufficient". After supper the two women sit and look at a photograph album—but some peculiar tension begins to build up:

> Then Hermione turned another page. And we knew, by their secret smiles, that this was what they had been waiting for.
>
> "My sister Katinka", Hetty said.
>
> "Auntie Katinka," Hermione said. They bent over the photograph. "Remember that day in Aberystwyth, Katinka?" Hetty said softly.(. . .)
>
> "I wore my new white dress," a new voice said.
>
> Leslie clutched at my hand.
>
> "And a straw hat with birds," said the new, clear voice . . .
>
> "Twenty-three come October, Katinka," Hetty said.

> "That's right, love," the voice said. "Scorpio I was. And we met Douglas Pugh on the Prom, and he said: 'You look like a queen to day, Katinka,' he said. (. . .) Why are those two boys looking in at the window?" (83).

The prose is clearly moving towards *Under Milk Wood*: this passage quoted, and in fact the whole story, could be a section of a play, and particularly a play for voices.

The later stories, like the play, are poetic fantasies, but their poetry lies in external reality itself, and can be seen and discovered there. There is no need to impose an inner vision on a bare, monotonous routine: everyday reality and common people are mysterious and fantastic. The protagonists of the stories do not know this initially. They are usually observers, or, as in **"The Followers"**, voyeurs who hope to find some kind of romantic adventure by living at one remove, and peering at life through a window, but reality proves to be beyond their wildest dreams.[8] The later prose—whether the stories, broadcasts, the detective story *Death of the King's Canary,* or *Under Milk Wood*—is full of all that is human, is full of the body, play, self-delusion, fallacy and meanness, stupidity and the foibles of men and women. The writings are not based on an inner struggle, but on an acceptance of the given in human life, and a discovery of the wonder and marvel of humanity. They offer a sympathetic, gay exposure of man as he is, revealing dignity and saintliness in his very weaknesses.

The poetry had also, as we have seen, moved to a celebration of life. But this celebration corresponds to the creation of a different dimension, a visionary universe detached from human reality, freed of any human presence. The landscape of **"Poem on His Birthday"**, or **"The Prologue"** is a natural world where no man appears. Man's youth and innocence become a fleeting recollection, assuming flesh and blood only as horses flashing by out of "whynnying green stables" in **"Fern Hill"**, or out of the foam of the sea in **"Poem on His Birthday"**. Men are helpless, unknowing sparrows and God, the judge, is a hawk, as in **"Over Sir John's Hill"**. The reader is sunk in a visionary universe where human presence and life must be read in the natural movements and colours, sounds and shades of light. The only human presence is the recollecting thought of the poet always accompanied by his symbolic bird, the heron, as in **"Poem on His Birthday"**. Then, the poet becomes one with the bird, and only the heron remains as spirit in the natural world of **"Poem in October"**.

Thomas's later achievement moves more and more in a direction where his gifts of storytelling, his delight in handling the existence of an audience can come into their own, and where the actual voice is heard shaping a narrative pattern, as in operas, broadcasts, and the play for voices. Even in his poetry Thomas intended to write a long composition, to be entitled **"In Country Heaven"**. It was to contain the only recollections the dead, in heaven, have of their life on earth, after this has destroyed itself:

It is black, petrified, wizened, poisoned, burnt . . . And, one by one, those heavenly hedgerow-men who once were of the earth call to one another, through the long night, Light and His tears falling, what they remember, what they sense in the submerged wilderness and on the exposed hair's breadth of the mind, what they feel trembling on the nerves of a nerve, what they know in their Edenic hearts, of that self-called place. They remember places, fears, loves, exultations, misery, animal joy, ignorance, and mysteries, all *we* know and do not know.[9]

This is the world and these are the voices of **Under Milk Wood,** where Polly Garter's words "Isn't life a terrible thing, thank God" express the vision that **"In Country Heaven"** would portray. But only three fragments of this poem were actually completed.

Maybe the earnestness and gravity that were part of Thomas's ideal of poetry turned into an obstacle to what he felt the urge to express, and the vision of life he was evolving in the prose was revealing itself more true. In the poetry, the poet is a druid. In the prose, the poet is one with the rest of humanity, someone who can be laughed at—not the laughter at the absurd irony of man's desires in contrast to the reality around him, but a smpathetic exposure of man as he is. In the verse, on very rare occasions, a touch of bitter sarcasm emerges, as in the poem **"Lament".** But in the prose writings humour is ever present, and even self-parody.

The protagonist of poems and stories had generally been a poet, trying to bridge the gap between the inner and external worlds, or growing to an understanding and sharing of suffering. But in a talk, published in 1950 with the title **"How to be a Poet",** the poet appears in a different role. After an amusing sketch of many possible poets—which has a possible connection with the first chapter of **Death of the King's Canary**—Thomas goes on:

> But let us look, very quickly, at some other methods of making poetry a going concern.
>
> The Provincial Rush, or the Up-Rimbaud-and-At-'Em approach. This is not wholeheartedly to be recommanded as certain qualifications are essential. Before you swoop and burst upon the centre of literary activity—which means, when you are very young, the right pubs, and later the right flats, and later still, the right club—you must have behind you a body (it need have no head) of ferocious and un-understandable verse. . . . And again, this poet must possess a thirst and a constitution like that of a salt-eating pony . . . and (. . .) a home to go *back* to in the provinces whenever he breaks down (**A Prospect,** 114-115).

Coming from the "Rimbaud of Cwmdonkin Drive" this is even more hilarious, but the last words strike a more serious and true note.

In **Adventures in the Skin Trade,** Samuel has almost completed his demolition job:

Even in the first moment of his guilt and shame, he remembered to put out his tongue and taste the track of tears. Still crying, he said, "It's salt. It's very salt. Just like in my poems" (26).

In the interest of entertainment one wishes an example was given of Samuel's poetry, based on this peculiar relationship between lived experience and literary cliches. Samuel's reliance on his poetic ideas—so far removed from the thing itself—is parodied and exposed throughout the novel. He comes to see that what he took to be a poet's vision is simple compared to the most plain events of everyday life. Life as it is is itself the richest and most complex imaginative creation. The general line of the story parodies pseudo-literary, artificial artistic approaches. The clearest parody is the whole bathroom scene, where Samuel's expectations of having an adventure with a girl are again foiled. He ends up stunned by eau de cologne, floating in a green bath in the pitch dark. Thomas was often accused of not growing up, and re-enacting a return to the womb. This scene is as much a parody of such a return as of the freudian labels at the disposal of some critics—the rubber duck really giving the finishing touch. The poet himself is here Samuel, a "lost soul", stunned by an unlikely drug, roaming through London with his finger stuck in the neck of a bottle, for everyone to see; not the druid intermediator between God and man, but an exposed, often ignored, patient man. The Reverend Eli Jenkins who "finds a rhyme and dips his pen in his cocoa" and goes "to visit the sick with jellies and poems" is another, and later, Samuel. This ability to show a fantastic, smiling exposure would seem to contradict the accusation that Thomas never grew up. More specifically, this detachment from one's own work, which by undercutting any gravity harmonizes the artistic creation with the life and story being narrated reveals a healthy avoidance of the pretentiousness which any poet or critic should hope to obtain. David Holbrook says of **Under Milk Wood** that "there is, as in the poetry, no controlling purpose to explore human reality".[10] In fact, all of Thomas's writing, particularly his prose fiction, is a continuous, controlled exploration of human reality, and his achievement flows directly into his play for voices. Now he is able to include, at last, his own reality as man and poet in the human reality he explores and narrates.

Notes

1. Vernon Watkins, "Foreword" to Dylan Thomas's *Adventures in the Skin Trade,* London, 1955; paperback edn, 1965, p. 99.

2. Dylan Thomas, *A Prospect of the Sea,* London, 1955; paperback edn, 1968, p. 61: all further page references in the text.

3. Dylan Thomas, *Collected Poems,* London 1967, p. 108. All further references in the text are to this edition.

4. T.H. Jones, *Dylan Thomas,* London, 1963; rpt. 1966, pp. 41-42.

5. Dylan Thomas, *Portrait of the Artist as a Young Dog,* London, 1940; paperback edn, 1965.

6. Jacob Korg, *Dylan Thomas,* New York, 1965, p. 154.

7. Dylan Thomas, *Selected Letters,* ed. Constantine Fitzgerald, London, 1965; paperback edn, 1968, p. 157.

8. Dylan Thomas, "The Followers" in *Miscellany One,* London, Aldine paperback, 1965, p. 79.

9. Dylan Thomas, "Three Poems" in *Quite Early One Morning,* London, 1954; paperback edn, 1967, p. 157.

10. David Holbrook, "'A Place of Love': *Under Milk Wood* in *Dylan Thomas, A Collection of Critical Essays,* ed. C.B. Cox, Englewood Cliffs, New Jersey, 1966, p. 109.

John Ackerman (essay date 1986)

SOURCE: "La Recherche du Temps Gallois: Dylan Thomas's Development as a Prose Writer," in *The Anglo-Welsh Review,* No. 83, 1986, pp. 86-95.

[*In the following essay, Ackerman defends Thomas's prose as equal in importance to his poetry.*]

I

Dylan Thomas's recognition as a major twentieth century writer, both in popularity and achievement, is now established, and the publication of his **Collected Stories** reminds us that his prose writing was in important ways as original and striking as his poetry. From the beginning Thomas wrote his prose alongside his poetry, initially more or less in the form of short stories that were strong in style and atmospheric and sensuous power but weak on narrative. These early stories are close to the universe of the early poems, being richly charged in their language, almost surreal in the worlds they create, and owing much to a fertile imagination and an adolescent's obsessional, introspective concerns with religion, sex, and death. Apart from four experimental prose pieces, including three stories-in-progress published in the Swansea Grammar School Magazine, Thomas's first actual story was the bizarre but compelling **'After The Fair'**, written soon after his nineteenth birthday, a strange fair-ground fiction that shows already his gift for dialogue. It also has an element of realism that was to take a lesser role in the early stories but anticipates his later comic, sharply focused prose style. Such stories as **'The Tree'** are rich in Biblical rhythms, while the satiric tone of **'The Burning Baby'**, a notable tale based on the episode of Dr. William Price's cremation of his son, in its grotesque portraiture of lecherous and hypocritical ministers, clearly shows the influence of Caradoc Evans, whom Dylan Thomas greatly admired. It is in this story, written in December 1934, that the anagram Llareggub first appears. Regrettably publishers were too squeamish to publish a collection of these stories in the thirties, and apart from the six included in **The Map of**

Love, I recall that when I first researched on Dylan Thomas in the fifties the others were available only in periodicals in such places as the British Library. Even as late as 1955 when Dents posthumously published **A Prospect of the Sea,** the phrase "the death from playing with yourself" was excluded from the title story of that name. Nowadays it would take a scholar to determine wherein these stories might have offended! Writing to his publishers in 1953 Dylan Thomas, contrasting these stories with his later broadcast reminiscences, aptly described them as "very young and violent and romantic . . . the death and blood group typified by **'The Burning Baby'**" a characteristically succinct and balanced judgement.

Perhaps the most charming and pleasing of these tales are the lyrical effusions such as **'A Prospect of the Sea'**, a beautiful evocation of high summer in Carmarthenshire countryside as experienced by a boy already a precocious pantheist. Is not this a picture of those green and golden summers of **'Fern Hill'**, albeit in prose but a powerfully sensuous and rhapsodic one?

> It was high summer and the boy was lying in the corn. He was happy because he had no work to do and the weather was hot. He heard the corn sway from side to side above him, and the noise of birds who whistled from the branches of the trees that hid the house. Lying flat on his back, he stared up into the unbrokenly blue sky falling over the edge of the corn. The wind, after the warm rain before noon, smelt of rabbits and cattle. . . . Now he was riding on the sea, swimming through the golden corn waves, gliding along the heavens like a bird. . . . This was the best summer since the first seasons of the world. He did not believe in God, but God had made this summer full of blue winds and heat and pigeons in the house wood.

A dream-like country girl, half princess, half temptress, appears and kisses him, exciting his desires and fears, but "if he cried aloud to his uncle in the hidden house, she would make new animals, beckon Carmarthen tigers out of the mile-away wood". And the afternoon moves to evening in a richly poetic prose, both precise and evocative in its effect, that demonstrates Thomas's early mastery of image and rhythm, particularly in the creation of an impressionist, yet holistic pastoralism:

> The afternoon was dying; lazily, namelessly, drifting westward through the insects in the shade, over hill and tree and river and corn and grass to the evening shaping in the sea; blowing away; being blown away from Wales in wind, in the slow, blue grains, like a wind full of dreams and medicines; down the tide of the sun on to the grey and chanting shore where the birds from Noah's ark glide by with bushes in their mouths, and tomorrow and tomorrow tower over the cracked sand castles.

Such writing anticipates the visionary and healing pantheism of the last poems. But now, racing the boy to the sea, Venus-like the girl disappears in the "flesh and bone water" and waves, "Come back! Come back!" cries the boy, his words chiming the theme that was to shape Thomas's development as a prose writer, an even more poignant search for 'temps perdu', and a quest later enriched by humorous and exact recollection. The story ends on a note of bucolic romanticism and mystery that is sustained by Biblical myth and language.

> On a hill to the horizon stood an old man building a boat. . . . And through the sky, out of the beds and gardens, down the white precipice built of feathers, the loud combes and mounds, from the caves in the hill, the cloudy shapes of birds and beasts and insects drifted into the hewn door. Cool rain began to fall.

Other stories like **'The Tree',** the second Thomas wrote, are more darkly, even savagely lyrical. Set in the Jarvis hills, even the natural world is more threatening than benign, and Bible-reading, as in Caradoc Evans, can be a rather sinister pastime. Even the child, a constant figure in Thomas's stories, is more malevolent than innocent as he listens to the gardener's story:

> 'In the beginning', he would say, 'there was a tree'.
>
> 'What kind of tree?'
>
> 'The tree where the blackbird's whistling'.
>
> 'A hawk, a hawk', cried the child . . .
>
> The gardener would look up at the tree, seeing a monstrous hawk perched on a bough or an eagle swinging in the wind.

We learn that "the gardener loved the Bible . . . reading of the first love and the legend of apples and serpents. But the death of Christ on the tree he loved most". While moving in primitive, Old Testament landscapes the inner lives of these figures follow pagan nature-worship and beliefs:

> His world moved and changed as spring moved along the branches, changing their nakedness; his God grew up like a tree from the apple-shaped earth, giving bud to His children and letting His children be blown from their places by the breezes of winter; winter and death moved in one wind.

Such lines recall the creative-destructive unity of man and nature perceived in such poems as **'The force that through the green fuse drives the flower'**, also written towards the end of 1933.

In the strange countryside of the Jarvis hills, with its primitive intensities and simplicities, a rural Carmarthenshire transformed by Biblical atmospherics clearly neighbours the stark world of Caradoc Evans's Cardiganshire, as in the idiot's entry to the tale:

> There was an idiot to the east of the country who walked the land like a beggar. Now at a farmhouse and now at a widow's cottage he begged for his bread. A person gave him a suit, and it lopped round his hungry ribs and shoulders and waved in the wind as he shambled over the fields.

But unlike Caradoc's suffering troglodytes, Dylan Thomas's idiot is nourished by his mysterious and lyrical bond with the natural world, an empathy Keatsian in its sensitivity and sensuousness but more metaphysical in its implications:

> He had known of the Jarvis Hills; their shapes rose over the slopes of the county to be seen for miles around, but no one had told him of the valley lying under the hills. Bethlehem, said the idiot to the valley, turning over the sounds of the word, and giving it all the glory of the Welsh morning. He brothered the world around him, sipped at the air, as a child newly born sips and brothers the light. The life of the Jarvis valley, steaming up from the body of the grass and the trees and the long hand of the stream, lent him a new blood. Night had emptied the idiot's veins, and dawn in the valley filled them again.
>
> 'Bethlehem', said the idiot to the valley.

On Christmas morning the child discovers the idiot, observes the Christ-like patience:

> So the child found him under the shelter of the tree, bearing the torture of the weather with a divine patience, letting his long hair blow where it would, with his mouth set in a sad smile.

As in his early poetry Dylan Thomas seems to be exploring the relationship between Biblical story and contemporary reality as the crucifixion in the garden proceeds swiftly, dramatically, yet with an ironically casual, almost homely touch:

> 'Stand up against the tree'.
>
> The idiot, still smiling, stood up with his back to the elder.
>
> 'Put out your arms like this'.
>
> The idiot put out his arms.
>
> The child ran as fast as he could to the gardener's shed, and, returning over the sodden lawns, saw that the idiot had not moved but stood, straight and smiling, with his back to the tree and his arms stretched out.
>
> 'Let me tie your hands'.
>
> The idiot felt the wire that had not mended the rake close round his wrists. It cut into the flesh, and the blood from the cuts fell shining onto the tree.
>
> 'Brother', he said. He saw that the child held silver nails in the palm of his hand.

Wittily, in this snowy Christmas setting, and thereby relating Biblical and present time, the reference to Bethlehem clearly echoes the Carmarthenshire village of that name, a hamlet near Llangadog. Evidently poet and prose writer run together in these early stories, and it is entirely harmoniously that **'The Map of Love'** contains prose and verse, so shared are themes and language, albeit a rare form of publication in a major poet.

Thus in **'The Enemies'** a clergyman lost in the Jarvis hills "is frightened of the worm in the earth, of the copulation in the tree, of the living grease in the soil". Threatened by dark, pantheistic forces he "felt desolation in his vein", a phrase used in the poem 'This bread I break' written six weeks earlier; and pagan and Christian conflicts are imaged and the story's end when he "stared and prayed, like an old god beset by his enemies". Likewise in **'The Visitor'** in dying Peter's vision where "the dead, picked to the symmetrical bones, were huddled under the soil of the wind . . . the worm and the death beetle undid the fibres of the animal bones . . . and the weeds through the sockets and the flowers on the vanished breasts sprouted up with the colours of the dead life fresh on their leaves" we are moving in the world of the poetry of this period. Such poems as 'The force that through the green fuse drives the flower' and 'And death shall have no dominion' are echoed in the imaging of death, a visitor like the thief in the later verse of **'In Country Sleep'** though at this stage more violent than benign:

> And the blood that had flowed flowed over the ground, strengthening the blades of the grass, fulfilling the wind-planted seeds in its course, into the mouth of the spring. Suddenly all the springs were red with blood, a score of winding veins. . . . He saw the streams and the beating water, how the flowers shot out of the dead.
> . . .

Notably, the somewhat morbid poetic fancy reaches an unusually arresting narrative climax to close the tale:

> Rhiannon, he said, hold my hand, Rhiannon.
>
> She did not hear him, but stood over his bed and fixed him with an unbreakable sorrow.
>
> Hold my hand, he said. And then: Why are you putting the sheet over my face?

Here Dylan Thomas's notion of the mysterious and inarticulate unity of man and nature in death is disturbingly and dramatically conveyed.

II

But of course it was *The Portrait of the Artist as a Young Dog* stories, written in Laugharne in the years immediately preceding the war, that mark Dylan Thomas's real emergence as a master of prose. Not only do they distinguish that humorous and passionate depiction of Welsh life that soon became a major feature of the Anglo-Welsh writing, both in their warm humanity and richness of observation, they also mark Dylan's discovery that his vein of comedy, already present in his letters and school magazine parodies and comic portraiture, could prove a new and significant means of expression. The composition early in 1938 of the first of these stories, 'A Visit to Grandpa's', a lively tale with its already sure and distinctive blend of pathos and comedy and its vivid Carmarthenshire settings seen through the innocent but acute observations of the child, was decisive in Thomas's growth as a prose writer. From

this point the jester and entertainer in the poet's personality, largely absent in the high seriousness of his best verse, had discovered a role in literature, a role where the poet's gift for comedy was enriched by a piercing nostalgia and that haunted perception of mutability and death that characterised his poetry. Elements of personal recollection heightened by Thomas's flair for dramatic presentation and precision of style no doubt directed the poet's newly acquired control of narrative:

> Mr. Griff raised his stunted barber's pole. 'And where do you think you are going', he said, 'with your old black bag?'
>
> Grandpa said: 'I am going to Llangadock to be buried'. And he watched the coracle shells slip into the water as bitterly as Mr. Price complained:
>
> 'But you aren't dead yet, Dai Thomas.'
>
> For a moment Grandpa reflected, then: 'There's no sense in lying dead in Llanstephan', he said. 'The ground is comfy in Llangadock; you can twitch your legs without putting them in the sea.'
>
> His neighbours moved close to him. They said: 'You aren't dead, Mr. Thomas.'
>
> 'How can you be buried, then? Nobody is going to bury you in Llanstephan.'
>
> 'Come on home, Mr. Thomas.'
>
> 'There's strong beer for tea!'
>
> 'And cake.'
>
> But Grandpa stood firmly on the bridge, and clutched his bag to his side, and stared at the flowing river and the sky, like a prophet who has no doubt.

This story was soon followed by **'The Peaches'** and **'One Warm Saturday'** in that same year, while 1939 saw the composition of the others in **'The Portrait',** as Thomas extended his impassioned and exact remembrance of childhood and adolescence to his Swansea days 'as a young dog' as well as the vignettes of visits to rural Carmarthenshire. Undoubtedly his experience working as a journalist on the South Wales Evening Post, albeit for little more than a year, had helped to turn his eye outward to the world around him, of the distinctive and varied life of Swansea and its neighbouring communities. It was a more profitable gaze for his development as a prose writer than the introspective stasis of his earlier, almost surreal fantasies, however rich and compelling the language. We may aptly recall the old reporter's comments in Thomas's carefully observed, though fictionally presented, comedy of his drinking tours of the Swansea pubs, and the poet's confident reply:

> When I showed this story a long time later to Mr. Farr, he said: 'You got it all wrong. You got the people mixed. The boy with a handkerchief danced in a 'Jersey'. Fred Jones was singing in the 'Fishguard'. Never mind. Come and have one tonight in the 'Nelson'. There's a girl down there who'll show you where the sailor bit her . . .'

'I'll put them all in a story by and by', I said.

During the thirties Dylan Thomas was of course becoming a connoisseur of pub life, both in Swansea, Laugharne, and the London bohemia of the Chelsea and Soho pubs, and no doubt collecting those anecdotes and snippets of heard and overheard conversation that were always to salt his prose comedy. In this loose-tongued, beery atmosphere it was his habit to jot down and phrase any vivid incident on cigarette packets or any handy and easily pocketed fragment of paper he might quickly scribble on—useful to his in any case retentive and exact memory of human behaviour and comment. By the early forties and the war years he was of course often the fount of entertainment with his talk and comic stories, famous now among the bars as Richard Burton recalled later. Such talk of course is as ephemeral as his beery conviviality that fostered it, though I think we may find echoes and instances of these arias of comedy not only in his later stories and dramatic narratives but also in such occasional prose pieces as his letters. Here, excuses for failures to turn up, whether at Vernon Watkin's wedding, or for a B.M.A. dinner in Swansea, or indeed to produce work on time—such as his letter to Madam Caetani on the composition of *Under Milk Wood,* incidentally the best critical introduction to the play, are, each in their way, entertaining, vivid, and wholly original apologies.

During the war, too, two other important factors determined his later development as a prose writer. The first was Dylan Thomas's employment to write film scripts, both documentaries for the Ministry of Information and also features such as *The Doctor And The Devils.* Clearly this work extended his control of narrative, dialogue and his sustaining of atmosphere and character in areas other than the short story. Perhaps more important was his work for radio, not only as a writer and broadcaster but as an actor and poetry reader. It made him even more sensitive and attuned to the possibilities of the spoken word; so that such broadcast talks as his **'Reminiscences of Childhood', 'Memories of Christmas'** and **'Holiday Memory'** and later works like **'A Visit to America'** and the now celebrated **'A Story',** which he first read in 1953 on television, belong to his most original, personal contribution to English prose style. They represented the creating of a medium of expression that used the full potential of language to evoke aurally and visually place, person, time, and atmosphere. It was the alchemy of the word and spell of the speaking voice that were returned to the dramatic preeminence they held on Shakespeare's bare and open stage, when the poet's language prompted "our imaginary forces". It was Thomas's genius in writing for radio that he realised and was able to exploit the possibilities of sound broadcasting. And his genius in this literary medium achieved of course its full expression in the 'play for voices' *Under Milk Wood,* undoubtedly one of the most popular and often performed plays of this century. While it seems likely that Dylan Thomas was the most accomplished actor and reader among the major English poets, it is well to remember that his favourite prose writer was

Dickens, whom he delighted to read aloud, and who was also of course, a popular performer of his own work, both men achieving particular fame and success on their American tours. Likewise both fashioned a prose style that was especially compelling when read aloud, and theatrically entertaining, even in its darker perceptions of the human condition. In saying this I particularly recall that *Under Milk Wood* opens with the voices of the drowned dead remembering the sweetness of life, the chains of mortality sounding like the seas' sounds through the play. Likewise the sad comedy and pathos of human life is encapsulated in such haunting episodes as Captain Cat and the dead Rosie Probert recalling their long gone sexual and prose life. It is the '*recherche du temps perdu* that gives Thomas's prose the profound, darkling seriousness that underlies and underpins the joyous and genial comedy. Relatedly, Thomas's finest celebration of Swansea life is in **'Return Journey',** the broadcast talk whose moving lamentation for loss and mutability, masked though it is by the hilarious comedy of the pub conversation and schoolboy and adolescent bravura and braggadocio, had its inspiration in the poet's heart-broken walk through that town on the morning after it was devastated by bombing, Dylan Thomas in tears as he surveyed the wounds of war. It is interesting that Dylan Thomas was in his poetry as uncompromisingly difficult and as full of stylistic hauteur as the other two great poets of the first half of the twentieth century, Yeats and Eliot. Yet in his prose he had the common touch and an easily turned key to the joy and comedy and never-far-off sadness of everyday life. This accounts, I think, for the fact that his recollections of Christmas, childhood, holidays, and whole sections of *Under Milk Wood,* are already part of our popular consciousness and commonly shared literary currency, so succinctly memorable was his expression and so richly and idiosyncratically human was his response to the world he breathed. Perhaps another reason for his popularity was his enduring perception of the first innocence of man. Discussing publication of his broadcast reminiscences Thomas, again his own best critic, epitomized them as "all fairly riotously innocent".

There has been some speculation on why Thomas never finished his projected novel *Adventures In The Skin Trade,* for we are left with only the first three sections of these comic and picaresque exploits of a young man who leaves his provincial home for a London paved with pleasure and adventure, if not gold. Entertaining though they are, I think the adventures remained incomplete because, like his own contributions to *The Death of the King's Canary,* they represented an amusing but light craft unanchored to that piercing nostalgia and perception of the death-touched transcience of man's joy and sadness which inspired his finest prose style. Cartoon-like in their comedy the zany encounters of Samuel Bennett among rooms full of furniture and in louche clubs tell of lost souls in a style that, *after* the gripping opening episode of Swansea home-leaving in **'A Fine Beginning'** lacks the passion and verbal spell-binding so characteristic of the poet. 'Come back, Come back!' was the cry that gave resonance and that grail-like quest to his best writing.

Of course from the beginning Dylan Thomas wrote prose fluently, though never loosely, prodigally and with amazing imagination. And not only did he quickly note and structure fantasies of human behaviour, he also had in his person the gift of comedy as abundantly as the gift of imagination. We see this in the way in which in his letters, which often begin to moods of everyday despair or self-denigrating apology, his feelings take wing on language of comic narration and fantasy, so that he himself is as revived as the reader.

Bearing in mind his last completed work, *Under Milk Wood,* his proposed collaboration with Stravinski for a libretto recalling the beauty and mystery of Earth following atomic misadventure (could there have been a more apt commission for Dylan Thomas?), clearly his death at thirty-nine was as tragic a loss of now notable prose writer as poet. Certainly, too, *Under Milk Wood* marked as much a new threshold as culmination of his powers. Importantly, despite the very apparent despairs and difficulties of his own life, and his openness to the world around—including war-time destruction and the new atomic threat, Dylan Thomas never succumbed to the nihilism and negative stridency of some twentieth century writers in English. Protected by the common touch, Thomas was still celebrating in poetry and prose the worth of man and the beauty of what he called "his apparently hell-bent earth". It was a vision which both faced and encompassed their shared vulnerability and mutability.

Richard F. Peterson (essay date 1986)

SOURCE: A review of *Dylan Thomas: The Collected Stories,* in *Studies in Short Fiction,* Vol. 23, No. 2, Spring, 1986, pp. 206-8.

[*In the following review of Thomas's* Collected Stories, *Peterson believes Thomas could not sustain longer works of fiction.*]

In **"Where Tawe Flows,"** one of twenty early stories in the first group in *The Collected Stories* of Dylan Thomas, a young Mr. Thomas and three friends are collaborating on a novel of provincial life. While the others concentrate on getting the "realism straight" for their characters, Mr. Thomas pleads for the fantastic. Rather than working on his contribution to the novel, he has spent the week writing the story of a cat that turned a children's governess into a vampire by jumping over the governess at the moment of her death.

The first twenty stories in *Collected Stories* are also a plea for the fantastic or at least the poetic in short-story writing. While Dylan Thomas went through several phases as a storyteller, he initially approached the short story with

the same extravagant attitude that produced his dense and provocative verse. Haunted by themes of loneliness, perversity, madness, and death, his early stories are often plagued by an expressionistic riot of shifting perspective and imagery. Even the most successful of these stories, those collected for *Map of Love* (1939), are interesting mostly because of their insight into the nature of the poetic imagination. Both published in *The Criterion,* **"The Visitor"** and **"The Orchards"** are contrasting reflections of the mad hallucinations of a dying poet and the artist's final triumph in his vision of reality. Perhaps the best story from his early fiction, **"The Mouse and the Woman,"** which first appeared in *transition,* is a stunning parable, enclosed within the images of the lunatic asylum, of the birth of the creative fires and the artist's failure to live up to the forged image of his imagination. With these few exceptions, however, Thomas's early stories read like the dark side of his poetic vision of womb and tomb in which innocence is seduced by its own imagination into a fantastical narrative encounter with madness and the grave.

In the ten stories from *Portrait of the Artist as a Young Dog* (1940), which make up the second major group in *Collected Stories,* Dylan Thomas apparently abandoned the fantastic for a more realistic and ironic narrative and format similar to James Joyce's in *Dubliners.* Thomas's autobiographical hero first appears as a wildly imaginative young boy in **"The Peaches,"** gradually turns into the awkward adolescent of the fifth story, **"Extraordinary Little Cough,"** and finally emerges as the young artist encountering a series of misadventures that finally end in **"One Warm Saturday"** with the poet drunkenly and hopelessly pursuing his muse through a maze of alleys in a disreputable part of town. While Joyce exposes the paralysis of his Dubliners in the mirror of scrupulous meanness, Thomas selects a theme and technique for his portrait of the artist, more reflective of his own poetic vision and more in recognition of, if not in keeping with, the narratives of his earlier fiction. His young poet sees the world through an exaggerated prose style, appropriate to the poetic sensibility but inadequate in the face of experiences too painful for the innocent eye. This tension between youthful imagination and real emotions makes the narratives in *Portrait of the Artist as a Young Dog* generally more interesting and comprehensive than those of Thomas's early fiction, but no one story has the beauty and energy of **"The Mouse and the Woman."** While *Portrait of the Artist as a Young Dog,* as a collection, achieves a clarity and air of realism lacking in the early stories, it also fails to yield stories that have the richness and symbolic power of Thomas's earlier portraits of the artist.

The rest of *Collected Stories* is a potpourri of three long stories that were first published together posthumously in 1953 under the title, *Adventures in the Skin Trade;* seven pieces from his later period, six of which were prepared for BBC broadcasts; and an appendix of four apprenticeship stories dating back to Thomas's *Swansea Grammar School Magazine* days. The apprenticeship fiction is an innocuous precursor of the first twenty stories, though its placement in an appendix rather than at the beginning of *Collected Stories* is never explained in the otherwise informative foreword written by Leslie Norris. *Adventures in the Skin Trade,* its stories published separately from 1941 to 1953, actually represents Thomas's failed effort to write a picaresque novel rather than signifying another phase or development in his career as a short-story writer. The broadcast narratives, on the other hand, are Thomas's most popular short prose pieces and include the memorable **"A Child's Christmas in Wales."**

Taken together, Thomas's early fantasies, his autobiographical stories, his abortive novel, his nostalgic tales of childhood are the testaments of a poet who could write short bursts of imaginative prose at times visionary in the revelation of the nature of poetic inspiration or the poet's life, especially his lost youth. While the stories in *Portrait of the Artist as a Young Dog* represent Thomas's most sustained effort to write a modern short story, his success as a fiction writer comes early or late, either in the story of the young poet quivering in the face of his own creation or the older poet, weary of the struggle of womb and tomb, creating in prose the magical world of childhood seen through the eyes of the child.

James A. Davies (essay date 1986)

SOURCE: A review of *The Collected Letters of Dylan Thomas,* in *The Anglo-Welsh Review,* No. 83, 1986, pp. 96-105.

[*In the following review of* The Collected Letters of Dylan Thomas, *Davies praises editor (and Thomas biographer) Paul Ferris for correcting errors in previous publications of Thomas's correspondence.*]

The publication of Dylan Thomas's **Collected Letters** is a major literary event. It makes a substantial addition to the works of a twentieth-century poet of central importance who is also a superb writer of prose. In 1977, when he published what has become the standard biography of Thomas, Paul Ferris had access to between 500 and 600 letters, of which about 300 had already been published (mainly in **Letters to Vernon Watkins** (1957) and **Selected Letters,** ed. Constantine Fitzgibbon (1966). This new volume adds over 400, to bring the total into four figures. Almost certainly others remain extant and it is to be hoped that this edition, like most such important and well-publicized ventures, will bring them to light.

This is not a full, scholarly edition to be compared with, say, the Pilgrim's edition of Dickens's letters, or Cecil Price's letters of Sheridan, in which the social and intellectual content and context of each letter are meticulously recreated. Rather, this is an edition, it seems, as much for the general reader as for the literary scholar: Paul Ferris, in providing lightly-annotated texts, provides as clean a page as possible. The notes usually do no more than iden-

tify people and works; occasionally they supply brief background material. Paul Ferris has a shrewd sense of the minimum necessary for intelligible reading but there is no doubt that the decision to forgo a full scholarly apparatus reduces any reader's understanding of Thomas's milieu and so of Thomas himself. Three examples make the point. In an early letter to Bert Trick Thomas recalls "'something attempted obscenely, something dung'" (p. 184); his inverted commas are not explained, though it is surely useful to know that he is parodying, of all things, a line from Longfellow's 'The Village Blacksmith'. Again, to Desmond Hawkins he writes of his constant need for money: 'night and day in my little room high above the traffic's boom I think of it' (p. 236) and many will not now recognise the allusions to Cole Porter's 'Night and Day'. Thirdly in a letter to Ted Kavanah Thomas refers to 'the haggisy stone-snaffling Scotch' (p. 790), a joke about a long-forgotten incident, the theft by Scottish Nationalists, two months before this letter, of the Stone of Scone from the coronation chair in Westminster Abbey. The letters are full of such buried life; Thomas was not only a rapt, book-soaked bard but also a young man alive to popular culture. The lack of extensive annotation is to be regretted but, of course, had it been provided the price of this volume would have escalated and publication much delayed. As it is, we have the letters and, in these times of ours, 982 pages in hard-back for £20 is good value.

Two further criticisms: it is a pity that Paul Ferris considers his readers to have boredom thresholds no higher than limbo-sticks and so relegates 70 short notes to an Appendix because they are 'of no great importance' (p. 919). 'Importance' is too often in the mind of the beholder and these notes seem to me to add to our sense of Thomas: no. 27, for example, shows his kindness to an unknown writer; no. 35 is a crucial document for understanding his relationship with Margaret Taylor; there is much general information about Thomas's earnings. All 70 should have been part of the main chronological sequence. Secondly, the index is very accurate and thoughtfully arranged but lacks comprehensiveness. For instance, its treatment of place-names is incomplete and inconsistent: 'Majorca' gets an entry but not 'Cardiff' (p. 145). 'Ischia' (p. 894), 'Porthcawl' (p. 902), or others.

That said, Paul Ferris has carried out triumphantly the editor's most important task: for the first time here are accurate texts, superbly proof-read and attractively presented. He exposes the general inaccuracy of **Selected Letters** and Fitzgibbon's many silent omissions, as well as Vernon Watkin's occasional ones. In particular, he convincingly reorganizes the crucial letters to Pamela Hansford Johnson that (we now see) Fitzgibbon jumbled hopelessly. One important by-product of this is the establishing of a full and accurate text of the early satirical poem, **'A Letter to My Aunt'**, which Fitzgibbon had confused and Daniel Jones printed only in part.

Very occasionally we are reminded that this edition is a few years too early for all texts to be complete. One or two names, one or two comments, have had to be omitted—we can only speculate on what Thomas said about Daniel Jones (pp. 192, 426)—but these rare omissions are scrupulously indicated. Indeed, there can be only one reservation about Paul Ferris's treatment of texts and this can be illustrated by an example: the letter to Vernon Watkin of 19 March 1940 (p. 445) has a footnote explaining a reference to Thomas's poem, **'The Countryman's Return'**, a copy of which he had sent with his letter. But on the reverse of this letter itself is an earlier, much-altered draft of part of the poem. Paul Ferris's note refers to the accompanying copy but not to the draft. Nor does he print the latter, even though it is part of the document. Thus, as far as Thomas's letters to Vernon Watkins are concerned, the reader can never be sure that there is no additional material. Put another way, *The Collected Letters* has not wholly superseded the long-out-of-print *Letters to Vernon Watkins.*

The new material includes much that is important, revealing and often entertaining. For the first time we have Thomas's letters to Caitlin, fascinating sets to John Davenport and Desmond Hawkins, numerous new letters to eminent literary figures, including T.S. Eliot, Stephen Spender and Edith Sitwell, fresh letters to his parents, to Princess Caetani, and to many others. These can now be read in proper sequence with the previously-published but only now fully-restored material. To Daniel Jones he is the brilliant punster: '"just a song at twilight"', he wrote, '"when the lights Marlowe and the Flecker Beddoes Bailey Donne and Poe"' (p. 196). In a letter to Desmond Hawkins he makes comedy out of desperation: 'I'm trying hard to think of respected gentry to get testimonials from', he wrote as he sought to avoid military service, 'I know one defrocked bard' (p. 421). To Clement Davenport his language is alive, sharp, but never quite humorous as it suggests the genuineness of his pacifism:

> . . . I think that unless I'm careful and lucky the boys of the Government will get me making munitions. I wish I could get a real job and avoid that. Clocking in, turning a screw, winding a wheel, doing something to a cog, lunching in the canteen, every cartridge case means one less Jerry, bless all the sergeants the short and the tall bless em all blast em all, evenings in the factory rest centre, snooker and cocoa, then bugs in digs and then clocking in and turning and winding and hammering to help to kill another stranger, deary me I'd rather be a poet anyday and live on guile and beer.

> (p. 478)

'I hear John Arlott's voice every weekend, describing cricket matches', he wrote nostalgically from Italy, 'He sounds like Uncle Tom Cobleigh reading Neville Cardus to the Indians' (p. 651).

Any review of such a volume risks being no more than a long list of beguiling quotations. But the letters are also full of new insights into Thomas's work. An intriguing draft letter to Hamish Miles claims some knowledge of 'Welsh rhythms' (p. 117), despite the much later and much-quoted disclaimer to Stephen Spender (p. 855): writing to

A.J. Hoppé, then a director of Dent's, returning proofs of *Deaths and Entrances,* Thomas's insistence on the late inclusion of **'Fern Hill'** because of its effect on the collection 'as a whole' (p. 569), has rewarding critical implications; and even when engaged on lesser work, such as the film-script of *The Beach of Falesá,* he is never less than the conscientious craftsman (p. 687).

As for the life, there are many interesting insights, such as his love of serious music—including Monteverdi (p. 153) and Samuel Barber (p. 745)—but two main impressions of Thomas dominate. The first is Thomas-the-sponger, the writer of begging letters. He is not, of course, a hitherto unknown figure: Paul Ferris's biography has seen to that and quoted Alec Waugh's remark that Thomas should be advised 'to write more stories and fewer letters' (*Dylan Thomas,* Penguin edn. (1978), p. 182), here quoted by an irritated Thomas in a letter to John Davenport (p. 476). But until *The Collected Letters* few could have realised the extent to which he was forced—or chose—to devote himself to the activity of financing his life or, which, for Thomas, was not quite the same thing, to the activity of writing begging letters. Few could have realised the expense of energy and the pains he took.

In 1951, with his finance in chaos and his life in its usual mess, he wrote to Princess Caetani, the generous owner of *Botteghe Oscure,* a letter that opens:

> I have been ill with almost everything from gastric influenza to ingrowing misery. And only now my wife Caitlin has given me a letter that Davenport had forwarded from you nearly six weeks ago: She didn't know who the letter came from, and had half-mislaid and half-forgotten it in the general hell of sickness, children, excruciating worry, the eternal yellow-grey drizzle outside and her own slowly accumulated loathing for the place in which we live.

> (pp. 790-1)

The first sentence opens directly and forcefully before modulating into a play on words that suggests brave humour amidst despair. It is followed by an excuse: Caitlin is to blame. But Caitlin herself must be excused because of the dreadful physical psychological pressures of her life. That life is also Dylan's, as the sentence insists through the quiet change of person from third singular to the collusive 'we'. The pressures, now on Dylan, are impressed vividly upon the reader through the general energy of the language and through considered rhetorical effects that include a stress on 'excruciating worry' and the extended emphasis of 'her own slowly accumulated loathing'. The 'worry' in the second sentence, which includes worry about his writing—he was then completing 'Lament'—becomes the 'nervous hag that rides me, biting and scratching into insomnia, nightmare and the long anxious daylight', and then domestic handwork, a tangible object, as it were, at which he is compelled to work 'day & night with a hundred crochet hooks'. But Thomas, typically and slyly, shifts from worrying about himself to seemingly selfless apologies for worrying his patron: and the crochetwork of 'worry' becomes, in a play on words, 'his crotchety poem' on which he is, nonetheless, working 'very hard'.

'I wish I knew what to do', he begins the final paragraph. 'I wish I cd get a job. I wish I wish I wish. And I wish you a happy Easter, with all my heart. The sun came out this morning, took one look at wet Wales, and shot back.' Emphasised concern for himself shifts, again, to what he wishes for the Princess, so that the letter ends by once again suggesting a selfless Thomas and with a defiant humour that makes him attractive to his patron—and so worth supporting—but which also ensures that a rich woman in sunny Italy will not forget a sad life in rainy Laugharne.

Thomas's letters cannot be like his poems; that is, they cannot be formally perfect structures but must seem to be spontaneous responses to specific situations and correspondents. His great achievement, in so many of these fund-raising performances—they were usually successful—is to seem artless whilst manipulating reader-response. Even to his agent, David Higham, to whom he writes brisk and competent business letters, he is anything but unconsidered. Thus, in 1953:

> I don't know how my account stands with you, but you should have received, from the BBC over £100 for four Personal Anthologies I recorded . . . on the Welsh Region, week by week. Also, I recorded a Childhood Reminiscences sketch for the Welsh Region, from Swansea, last week, for £20 (twenty pounds) and this coming Friday . . . I need £50 for various small bills here which simply *must* be paid this week. I have no money at all.
>
> (pp. 876-7)

The hint of financial innocence is followed by precise and detailed awareness of how things were. The lapidary finality of the last sentence, with its sequence of heavy stresses, seems far from accidental.

About the same time Thomas drafted a letter to Margaret Howard-Stepney, the wealthy Welsh eccentric who, briefly, became one of his benefactors. This begins with a rhythmic prose that is then rearranged as the opening of a poem:

> You told me, once, to call on you
>
> When I was beaten down . . .
>
> (p. 836)

This, in turn, is abandoned for three stanzas of vigorous light-verse appealing for money. Some months later he drafted a further letter to Princess Caetani that opened:

> What can I say?
>
> Why do I bind myself always into these imbecile grief-knots, blindfold my eyes with lies, wind my brass music around me, sew myself in a sack, weight it with guilt and pig-iron, then pitch me squealing to sea, so that time and time again I must wrestle out and unravel

in a panic, like a seaslugged windy Houdini, and ooze and eel up wheezily, babbling and blowing black bubbles, from all the claws and bars and breats of the mantrapping seabed?

(p. 915)

The 'Houdini' motif, linked to the notion of drowning, is then developed fantastically and forcibly through the letter.

Almost certainly neither letter was sent but this fact, in itself, suggests that the ostensible purpose of these drafts, like that of the *posted* cries for material help, had become secondary to the composing of their prose, the vigour and fresh experimentation of which contrast sharply with the apparent desolation of the life out of which they were written.

The second Thomas, revealed in detail for the first time, is Caitlin's husband and lover. With the publication of his letters to his wife and—an inspired insertion—a harrowing one from Caitlin to close friends, we can begin to understand their passionate and tormented relationship. One key to such understanding is in a letter written before 1943 from Dylan in London to Caitlin in Cardiganshire:

> God, Catly, if only I could see you now. I want to touch you, to see you, you are beautiful, I love you . . . tell me if you want me to come down . . . I want to see you terribly terribly soon . . . Please . . . tell me that you want me to come down . . . tell me when I can . . . I want to come as soon, as soon as I can . . . I could come to you now . . .
>
> (p. 499)

Repetition dramatises not only desperation but also fear and a sense of dependence that, as Paul Ferris notes in his short, stimulating introduction, can be 'slightly chilling' (p. xi). Where he seems mistaken, however, is in suggesting that the care Thomas took over his letters—to Caitlin as well as to potential benefactors—is evidence of insincerity.

Certainly the letters to Caitlin demonstrate his towering gifts as a writer, as we see in one written shortly after his first arrival in the U.S.A.. It opens frantically:

> *Caitlin my own own* own dearest love whom God and *my* love and *your* love for me protect, my sweet wife, my dear one, my Irish heart, my wonderful wonderful girl who is with me invisibly every second of these dreadful days, awake or sleepless, who is forever and forever with me and is my own true beloved amen—I love you, I need you, I want, want you, we have never been apart as long as this, never, never, and we will never be again.
>
> (p. 751)

Yet what can—and doubtless did, to the waiting wife—seem a passionate, uncontrolled outpouring is carefully constructed for maximum effect. The long and complex sentence is beautifully taut and balanced. The use of repetition, the accumulation of compliments and responses, the balancing of phrases ('*my* love and *your* love'; the inspired 'awake or sleepless''), the selective removal of punctuation to hurry the lines along, the ripples of alliteration, the conscious stress on key words ('I love you, I need you, I want, want you'; 'never, never, and we will never be again'), all contribute to the sentence's driving rhythm, to the fierce energy of the language.

The whole letter is too long to quote in full. As it proceeds it shifts abruptly from the language of love to the chatty and the newsy and so emphasises, for the later objective reader, the carefully 'composed' nature of the former, in which rhetorical effects continue to abound. They do so, also, in other letters from America: the very next one, written by Dylan from Brinnin's home in Connecticut, opens with a sentence ('You're mine for always as for always I am yours' (p. 753)) that immediately involves the reader in its rhythmic poignancy. A letter from San Francisco ends less successfully: 'I will come back alive & as deep in love with you as a cormorant dives, as an anemone grows, as Neptune breathes, as the sea is deep' (p. 755). Thomas, too obviously poetic, lapses into cliché.

He wrote differently to other women, even to his last mistress, Elizabeth Reitell:

> Liz love,
>
> I miss you terribly much.
>
> The plane rode high and rocky, and over Newfoundland it swung into lightning and billiard-ball hail, and the old deaf woman next to me, on her way to Algiers via Manchester, got sick in a bag of biscuits, and the bar—a real, tiny bar—stayed open all the bourbon way. London was still glassy from Coronation Day, and for all the custom-men cared I could have packed my bags with cocaine and bits of chopped women.
>
> (p. 891)

This is hardly a love-letter: Thomas is pre-occupied with recreating in prose his own separate experiences. To Caitlin he tries desperately—often with brilliant success—to capture and convey in prose his deep feelings for her. 'Sincerity' is always a slippery concept; the letters to Caitlin move us precisely because Thomas deploys literary skills. That he did so with such care and intensity in the midst of a crowded and hectic life in which, of course, he was often unfaithful, should make us believe that he took trouble *because* he loved her and desperately needed the relationship to continue.

We might also wish to say with equal certainty, what can be said of the begging-letters: despite all that has been said and written of Thomas's death-wish consequent upon his recognition that his creative powers were failing, in these letters we see a continuing obsession with words, with prose experiments, with capturing experience in patterns of language.

To adapt Charles Lamb's words: Thomas's life was a catastrophe that was not without a kind of tragic interest. Though his own fecklessness, or dishonesty, or naivity, or

hopeless but admirable poetic integrity, may have begun his slide to disaster, once the slipping began the circumstances of his life—the financial chaos, the stormy relationship with Caitlin, the difficulties of writing, his affairs, his suicidal drinking—forced him into uncontrolled careering. As he fell he remained cruelly self-aware: 'After all sorts of upheavals, evasions, promises, procrastinations, I write, very fondly, and fawning slightly, a short inaccurate summary of those events which caused my never writing a word before this' (p. 878), he wrote to Brinnin, with careful honesty, in 1953.

Caitlin Thomas put matters at their bleakest in her letter to Oscar Williams and wife in February 1953: 'The trouble is our lives are permanently in need of being saved, and I doubt, very forcibly, that they are worth it' (p. 865). But all who read these letters have, for Dylan at least, evidence to the contrary. Three extracts from later letters begin to make the point. The first is to Margaret Taylor, thanking her for money: 'I'm writing this in the heaven of my hut. Wild day, big seas for Laugharne & the boats of the Williamses lurching exactly like Williamses' (p. 716). 'Things are appalling here', he wrote from Laugharne to John Davenport,

> . . . temporary insolvency goes the glad rounds as swift as a miscarriage. . . . Yesterday I broke a tooth on a minto. . . . There are rats in the lavatory, tittering while you shit . . . the biggest prig in Wales, is coming to see me Saturday . . . looking about him, prig-brows lifted, in my fuggy room like an unloved woman sniffing at the maid's linen on the maid's day out. . . . If you see anyone likely, pinch his boots for me. . . . I'm sorry to write you such mournings. See you at the barracudas'
>
> (pp. 722-23)

Third is from another letter to Margaret Taylor, sent from the Boathouse in late 1951:

> Lizzie came into the Pelican yesterday afternoon, raving drunk, and gave my father a heart attack. Today, he is still shaking. Caitlin's black eye has just faded; a boy fell from a tree where he was picking conkers, quite near your Grist house, and his shoulderblade broke & pierced his lung, and at the postmortem in Carmarthen Infirmary they found he had been eating stamps; a white owl breathes on a branch right outside Phil the Cross's bedroom window, like a hundred people making love, and inflamed Phil so much he ran, for the first time in years, to his wife's bed and set about her so fiercely he nearly died of a fit of silicotic coughing and couldn't go to work next day; a printed form has just come that tells me that I shall be prosecuted herewith unless I send in my National Insurance book fully stamped for 1950; Ivy's teeth fell out one evening while she was playing skittles, and yesterday she told me she had been blind in one eye for twenty years; Colm's scalded chest is better, but he still has nightmares; there is little other news.
>
> (p. 816)

Common to all three, and to numerous similar passages, is an ever-fresh delight in the sound and movement of words and in the minutiae—comic moments, miniature dramas—of day-to-day living in small houses in small places by a Welsh sea. Such delight persisted to the end: 'My arm's fine now', he told Stravinsky, 'and quite as weak as the other one' (p. 917); in the very last item in this volume, a telegram from New York to Ellen Stevenson in Chicago, he agreed to perform *Under Milk Wood* 'With Or Without Cast But Not Without Cash' (p. 918).

The simple fact that Thomas, to quote Berowne, was always able 'to move wild laughter in the throat of death' makes him a figure who is never less than attractive and ensures that tragic interest. The reference to *Under Milk Wood* returns us to this articles's concern with Thomas's use of prose. For the comic play draws on the same kind of material as the letters; its small town is that celebrated in this volume's many moments of wild epistolary laughter; its prose-effects are those of these letters, those, indeed, of a poet working his desperate way from poetry to new areas of literature. The late letter-draft to Princess Caetani, already quoted in part, remains a key document:

> Deep dark down there, where I chuck the sad sack of myself . . . time and time again I cry to myself as I kick clear of the cling of my stuntman's sacking, 'Oh, one time the last time will come and I'll never struggle, I'll sway down here forever handcuffed and blindfold, sliding my woundaround music, my sack trailed in the slime, with all the rest of the self-destroyed escaplogists in their cages, drowned in the sorrows they drown and in my piercing own, alone and one with the coarse and cosy damned seahorsey dead, weeping my tons.'
>
> (p. 915)

Here are deeper notes, darker tones, more strangely compelling psychological explorations, than are dreamt of in Captain Cat's Llaregyb. It is useless to speculate where such writing might have led; all that can be done is to register and cherish the quality and potential of such prose. Though Thomas's life may well have been a 'wilderness', to the end it was redeemed by being a 'wordy' (p. 82) one. This marvellous volume insists that his death in New York, whether from 'winking needle' (p. 892) or whiskyed suicide, was hardly that of a written-out bard.

FURTHER READING

Bibliographies

Gaston, George. *Dylan Thomas: A Reference Guide*. Boston: G. K. Hall, 1987, 213 p.
  Comprehensive listing of secondary sources.

Maud, Ralph. *Dylan Thomas in Print: A Bibliographical History*. Pittsburgh: University of Pittsburgh Press, 1970, 261 p.
  Presents a thorough listing of primary and secondary sources.

Rolf, J. Alexander. *Dylan Thomas: A Bibliography*. London: J. M. Dent & Sons, 1956, 108 p.
  First full-length bibliography of works by and about Thomas; includes a foreword by Edith Sitwell.

Biographies

Ackerman, John. *Dylan Thomas: His Life and Work*. London: Oxford University Press, 1964, 201 p.
  Critical biography highlighting the influence of Thomas's Welsh background on his works.

Brinnin, John Malcolm. *Dylan Thomas in America: An Intimate Journal*. 1955. Reprint. London: Arlington Books, 1988, 313 p.
  Chronicles Thomas's four reading tours in America from 1950 to 1953.

Davies, Walford. *Dylan Thomas*. Rev. ed. New York: St. Martin's Press, 1990, 68 p.
  Biographical study emphasizing the importance of Welsh landscape and culture in Thomas's works.

Ferris, Paul. *Dylan Thomas*. London: Hodder and Stoughton, 1977, 309 p.
  Comprehensive biography incorporating previously unused or unpublished archive material as well as interviews with numerous friends and acquaintances of Thomas.

FitzGibbon, Constantine. *The Life of Dylan Thomas*. Boston: Little, Brown and Co., 1965, 370 p.
  Authorized critical biography.

Criticism

Bold, Alan, ed. *Dylan Thomas: Craft or Sullen Art*. London: Vision Press, 1990, 181 p.
  Contains essay by Margaret Moan Rowe on Thomas's *Portrait of the Artist as a Young Dog*.

Brinnin, John Malcolm, ed. *A Casebook on Dylan Thomas*. New York: Thomas Y. Crowell Co., 1960, 322 p.
  Collects reviews, essays, and appreciations by such noted critics and contemporaries of Thomas as Elder Olson, Henry Treece, and Geoffrey Grigson, as well as a selection of Thomas's most noted poems.

Cox, C. B., ed. *Dylan Thomas: A Collection of Critical Essays*. Englewood Cliffs, N.J.: Prentice-Hall, 1966, 186 p.
  Includes essays written in the decade following Thomas's death by David Daiches, Ralph Maud, Elder Olsen, and others.

Davies, Walford. *Dylan Thomas: New Critical Essays*. London: J. M. Dent & Sons, 1972, 282 p.
  Includes contributions by such critics as John Wain.

Gaston, Georg. *Critical Essays on Dylan Thomas*. Boston: G. K. Hall, 1989, 197 p.

Contains essays written since Thomas's death that focus on Thomas's craft, religion, and his influential reputation.

Peach, Linden. *The Prose Writing of Dylan Thomas*. London: MacMillan Press, 1988, 144 p.

Concludes by announcing Welsh poet R. S. Thomas as Thomas's poetic successor.

Additional coverage of Thomas's life and career is contained in the following sources published by the Gale Group: *Contemporary Authors,* **Vols. 104, 120;** *Contemporary Authors New Revision Series,* **Vol. 65;** *Concise Dictionary of British Literary Biography, 1945-1960;* *Dictionary of Literary Biography,* **Vols. 13, 20, 139;***DISCovering Authors; DISCovering Authors: British; DISCovering Authors: Canadian; DIS-Covering Authors Modules: Dramatists, Most-Studied Authors,* **and** *Poets; Major Twentieth-Century Writers; Poetry Criticism,* **Vol. 2;** *Short Story Criticism,* **Vol. 3;***Something About the Author,* **Vol. 60; and** *World Literature Criticism.*

How to Use This Index

The main references

> **Calvino, Italo**
> 1923-1985 .... CLC **5, 8, 11, 22, 33, 39,**
> **73; SSC 3**

list all author entries in the following Gale Literary Criticism series:

BLC = *Black Literature Criticism*
CLC = *Contemporary Literary Criticism*
CLR = *Children's Literature Review*
CMLC = *Classical and Medieval Literature Criticism*
DA = *DISCovering Authors*
DAB = *DISCovering Authors: British*
DAC = *DISCovering Authors: Canadian*
DAM = *DISCovering Authors: Modules*
      DRAM: *Dramatists Module;* *MST:* *Most-Studied Authors Module;*
      MULT: *Multicultural Authors Module;* *NOV:* *Novelists Module;*
      POET: *Poets Module;* *POP:* *Popular Fiction and Genre Authors Module*
DC = *Drama Criticism*
HLC = *Hispanic Literature Criticism*
LC = *Literature Criticism from 1400 to 1800*
NCLC = *Nineteenth-Century Literature Criticism*
NNAL = *Native North American Literature*
PC = *Poetry Criticism*
SSC = *Short Story Criticism*
TCLC = *Twentieth-Century Literary Criticism*
WLC = *World Literature Criticism, 1500 to the Present*

The cross-references

> See also CANR 23; CA 85-88;
> obituary CA116

list all author entries in the following Gale biographical and literary sources:

AAYA = *Authors & Artists for Young Adults*
AITN = *Authors in the News*
BEST = *Bestsellers*
BW = *Black Writers*
CA = *Contemporary Authors*
CAAS = *Contemporary Authors Autobiography Series*
CABS = *Contemporary Authors Bibliographical Series*
CANR = *Contemporary Authors New Revision Series*
CAP = *Contemporary Authors Permanent Series*
CDALB = *Concise Dictionary of American Literary Biography*
CDBLB = *Concise Dictionary of British Literary Biography*
DLB = *Dictionary of Literary Biography*
DLBD = *Dictionary of Literary Biography Documentary Series*
DLBY = *Dictionary of Literary Biography Yearbook*
HW = *Hispanic Writers*
JRDA = *Junior DISCovering Authors*
MAICYA = *Major Authors and Illustrators for Children and Young Adults*
MTCW = *Major 20th-Century Writers*
SAAS = *Something about the Author Autobiography Series*
SATA = *Something about the Author*
YABC = *Yesterday's Authors of Books for Children*

Literary Criticism Series
Cumulative Author Index

Anderson, C. Farley
See Mencken, H(enry) L(ouis); Nathan, George Jean

Anderson, Jessica (Margaret) Queale 1916- .... **CLC 37**
See also CA 9-12R; CANR 4, 62

Anderson, Jon (Victor) 1940- . **CLC 9; DAM POET**
See also CA 25-28R; CANR 20

Anderson, Lindsay (Gordon) 1923-1994 .... **CLC 20**
See also CA 125; 128; 146; CANR 77

Anderson, Maxwell 1888-1959 ...... **TCLC 2; DAM DRAM**
See also CA 105; 152; DLB 7, 228; MTCW 2

Anderson, Poul (William) 1926- ..... **CLC 15**
See also AAYA 5, 34; CA 1-4R, 181; CAAE 181; CAAS 2; CANR 2, 15, 34, 64; CLR 58; DLB 8; INT CANR-15; MTCW 1, 2; SATA 90; SATA-Brief 39; SATA-Essay 106

Anderson, Robert (Woodruff) 1917- .... **CLC 23; DAM DRAM**
See also AITN 1; CA 21-24R; CANR 32; DLB 7

Anderson, Sherwood 1876-1941 .... **TCLC 1, 10, 24; DA; DAB; DAC; DAM MST, NOV; SSC 1; WLC**
See also AAYA 30; CA 104; 121; CANR 61; CDALB 1917-1929; DA3; DLB 4, 9, 86; DLBD 1; MTCW 1, 2

Andier, Pierre
See Desnos, Robert

Andouard
See Giraudoux, (Hippolyte) Jean

Andrade, Carlos Drummond de ..... **CLC 18**
See also Drummond de Andrade, Carlos

Andrade, Mario de 1893-1945 ...... **TCLC 43**

Andreae, Johann V(alentin) 1586-1654 .... **LC 32**
See also DLB 164

Andreas-Salome, Lou 1861-1937 .. **TCLC 56**
See also CA 178; DLB 66

Andress, Lesley
See Sanders, Lawrence

Andrewes, Lancelot 1555-1626 .... **LC 5**
See also DLB 151, 172

Andrews, Cicily Fairfield
See West, Rebecca

Andrews, Elton V.
See Pohl, Frederik

Andreyev, Leonid (Nikolaevich) 1871-1919 .... **TCLC 3**
See also CA 104; 185

Andric, Ivo 1892-1975 .... **CLC 8; SSC 36**
See also CA 81-84; 57-60; CANR 43, 60; DLB 147; MTCW 1

Androvar
See Prado (Calvo), Pedro

Angelique, Pierre
See Bataille, Georges

Angell, Roger 1920- .... **CLC 26**
See also CA 57-60; CANR 13, 44, 70; DLB 171, 185

Angelou, Maya 1928- ... **CLC 12, 35, 64, 77; BLC 1; DA; DAB; DAC; DAM MST, MULT, POET, POP; PC 32; WLCS**
See also AAYA 7, 20; BW 2, 3; CA 65-68; CANR 19, 42, 65; CDALBS; CLR 53; DA3; DLB 38; MTCW 1, 2; SATA 49

Anna Comnena 1083-1153 .... **CMLC 25**

Annensky, Innokenty (Fyodorovich) 1856-1909 .... **TCLC 14**
See also CA 110; 155

Annunzio, Gabriele d'
See D'Annunzio, Gabriele

Anodos
See Coleridge, Mary E(lizabeth)

Anon, Charles Robert
See Pessoa, Fernando (Antonio Nogueira)

Anouilh, Jean (Marie Lucien Pierre) 1910-1987 .... **CLC 1, 3, 8, 13, 40, 50; DAM DRAM; DC 8**
See also CA 17-20R; 123; CANR 32; MTCW 1, 2

Anthony, Florence
See Ai

Anthony, John
See Ciardi, John (Anthony)

Anthony, Peter
See Shaffer, Anthony (Joshua); Shaffer, Peter (Levin)

Anthony, Piers 1934- ... **CLC 35; DAM POP**
See also AAYA 11; CA 21-24R; CANR 28, 56, 73; DLB 8; MTCW 1, 2; SAAS 22; SATA 84

Anthony, Susan B(rownell) 1916-1991 .... **TCLC 84**
See also CA 89-92; 134

Antoine, Marc
See Proust, (Valentin-Louis-George-Eugene-) Marcel

Antoninus, Brother
See Everson, William (Oliver)

Antonioni, Michelangelo 1912- .... **CLC 20**
See also CA 73-76; CANR 45, 77

Antschel, Paul 1920-1970
See Celan, Paul
See also CA 85-88; CANR 33, 61; MTCW 1

Anwar, Chairil 1922-1949 .... **TCLC 22**
See also CA 121

Anzaldua, Gloria (Evanjelina) 1942-
See also CA 175; DLB 122; HLCS 1

Apess, William 1798-1839(?) .... **NCLC 73; DAM MULT**
See also DLB 175; NNAL

Apollinaire, Guillaume 1880-1918 . **TCLC 3, 8, 51; DAM POET; PC 7**
See also CA 152; MTCW 1

Appelfeld, Aharon 1932- .. **CLC 23, 47; SSC 42**
See also CA 112; 133; CANR 86

Apple, Max (Isaac) 1941- .... **CLC 9, 33**
See also CA 81-84; CANR 19, 54; DLB 130

Appleman, Philip (Dean) 1926- .... **CLC 51**
See also CA 13-16R; CAAS 18; CANR 6, 29, 56

Appleton, Lawrence
See Lovecraft, H(oward) P(hillips)

Apteryx
See Eliot, T(homas) S(tearns)

Apuleius, (Lucius Madaurensis) 125(?)-175(?) .... **CMLC 1**
See also DLB 211

Aquin, Hubert 1929-1977 .... **CLC 15**
See also CA 105; DLB 53

Aquinas, Thomas 1224(?)-1274 ... **CMLC 33**
See also DLB 115

Aragon, Louis 1897-1982 . **CLC 3, 22; DAM NOV, POET**
See also CA 69-72; 108; CANR 28, 71; DLB 72; MTCW 1, 2

Arany, Janos 1817-1882 .... **NCLC 34**

Aranyos, Kakay
See Mikszath, Kalman

Arbuthnot, John 1667-1735 .... **LC 1**
See also DLB 101

Archer, Herbert Winslow
See Mencken, H(enry) L(ouis)

Archer, Jeffrey (Howard) 1940- ..... **CLC 28; DAM POP**
See also AAYA 16; BEST 89:3; CA 77-80; CANR 22, 52; DA3; INT CANR-22

Archer, Jules 1915- .... **CLC 12**

See also CA 9-12R; CANR 6, 69; SAAS 5; SATA 4, 85

Archer, Lee
See Ellison, Harlan (Jay)

Archilochus c. 7th cent. B.C.- ...... **CMLC 44**
See also DLB 176

Arden, John 1930- ..... **CLC 6, 13, 15; DAM DRAM**
See also CA 13-16R; CAAS 4; CANR 31, 65, 67; DLB 13; MTCW 1

Arenas, Reinaldo 1943-1990 . **CLC 41; DAM MULT; HLC 1**
See also CA 124; 128; 133; CANR 73; DLB 145; HW 1; MTCW 1

Arendt, Hannah 1906-1975 .... **CLC 66, 98**
See also CA 17-20R; 61-64; CANR 26, 60; MTCW 1, 2

Aretino, Pietro 1492-1556 .... **LC 12**

Arghezi, Tudor 1880-1967 .... **CLC 80**
See also Theodorescu, Ion N.
See also CA 167; DLB 220

Arguedas, Jose Maria 1911-1969 ... **CLC 10, 18; HLCS 1**
See also CA 89-92; CANR 73; DLB 113; HW 1

Argueta, Manlio 1936- .... **CLC 31**
See also CA 131; CANR 73; DLB 145; HW 1

Arias, Ron(ald Francis) 1941-
See also CA 131; CANR 81; DAM MULT; DLB 82; HLC 1; HW 1, 2; MTCW 2

Ariosto, Ludovico 1474-1533 .... **LC 6**

Aristides
See Epstein, Joseph

Aristophanes 450B.C.-385B.C. ..... **CMLC 4; DA; DAB; DAC; DAM DRAM, MST; DC 2; WLCS**
See also DA3; DLB 176

Aristotle 384B.C.-322B.C. ... **CMLC 31; DA; DAB; DAC; DAM MST; WLCS**
See also DA3; DLB 176

Arlt, Roberto (Godofredo Christophersen) 1900-1942 ..... **TCLC 29; DAM MULT; HLC 1**
See also CA 123; 131; CANR 67; HW 1, 2

Armah, Ayi Kwei 1939- ..... **CLC 5, 33, 136; BLC 1; DAM MULT, POET**
See also BW 1; CA 61-64; CANR 21, 64; DLB 117; MTCW 1

Armatrading, Joan 1950- .... **CLC 17**
See also CA 114; 186

Arnette, Robert
See Silverberg, Robert

Arnim, Achim von (Ludwig Joachim von Arnim) 1781-1831 .... **NCLC 5; SSC 29**
See also DLB 90

Arnim, Bettina von 1785-1859 ..... **NCLC 38**
See also DLB 90

Arnold, Matthew 1822-1888 .... **NCLC 6, 29, 89; DA; DAB; DAC; DAM MST, POET; PC 5; WLC**
See also CDBLB 1832-1890; DLB 32, 57

Arnold, Thomas 1795-1842 .... **NCLC 18**
See also DLB 55

Arnow, Harriette (Louisa) Simpson 1908-1986 .... **CLC 2, 7, 18**
See also CA 9-12R; 118; CANR 14; DLB 6; MTCW 1, 2; SATA 42; SATA-Obit 47

Arouet, Francois-Marie
See Voltaire

Arp, Hans
See Arp, Jean

Arp, Jean 1887-1966 .... **CLC 5**
See also CA 81-84; 25-28R; CANR 42, 77

Arrabal
See Arrabal, Fernando

Arrabal, Fernando 1932- .. **CLC 2, 9, 18, 58**
See also CA 9-12R; CANR 15

See also CA 164

Benn, Gottfried 1886-1956 .... **TCLC 3**
See also CA 106; 153; DLB 56

Bennett, Alan 1934- .... **CLC 45, 77; DAB; DAM MST**
See also CA 103; CANR 35, 55; MTCW 1, 2

Bennett, (Enoch) Arnold 1867-1931
.... **TCLC 5, 20**
See also CA 106; 155; CDBLB 1890-1914; DLB 10, 34, 98, 135; MTCW 2

Bennett, Elizabeth
See Mitchell, Margaret (Munnerlyn)

Bennett, George Harold 1930-
See Bennett, Hal
See also BW 1; CA 97-100; CANR 87

Bennett, Hal .... **CLC 5**
See also Bennett, George Harold
See also DLB 33

Bennett, Jay 1912- .... **CLC 35**
See also AAYA 10; CA 69-72; CANR 11, 42, 79; JRDA; SAAS 4; SATA 41, 87; SATA-Brief 27

Bennett, Louise (Simone) 1919- ..... **CLC 28; BLC 1; DAM MULT**
See also BW 2, 3; CA 151; DLB 117

Benson, E(dward) F(rederic) 1867-1940
.... **TCLC 27**
See also CA 114; 157; DLB 135, 153

Benson, Jackson J. 1930- .... **CLC 34**
See also CA 25-28R; DLB 111

Benson, Sally 1900-1972 .... **CLC 17**
See also CA 19-20; 37-40R; CAP 1; SATA 1, 35; SATA-Obit 27

Benson, Stella 1892-1933 .... **TCLC 17**
See also CA 117; 155; DLB 36, 162

Bentham, Jeremy 1748-1832 .... **NCLC 38**
See also DLB 107, 158

Bentley, E(dmund) C(lerihew) 1875-1956
.... **TCLC 12**
See also CA 108; DLB 70

Bentley, Eric (Russell) 1916- .... **CLC 24**
See also CA 5-8R; CANR 6, 67; INT CANR-6

Beranger, Pierre Jean de 1780-1857
.... **NCLC 34**

Berdyaev, Nicolas
See Berdyaev, Nikolai (Aleksandrovich)

Berdyaev, Nikolai (Aleksandrovich)
1874-1948 .... **TCLC 67**
See also CA 120; 157

Berdyayev, Nikolai (Aleksandrovich)
See Berdyaev, Nikolai (Aleksandrovich)

Berendt, John (Lawrence) 1939- .... **CLC 86**
See also CA 146; CANR 75, 93; DA3; MTCW 1

Beresford, J(ohn) D(avys) 1873-1947
.... **TCLC 81**
See also CA 112; 155; DLB 162, 178, 197

Bergelson, David 1884-1952 .... **TCLC 81**

Berger, Colonel
See Malraux, (Georges-)Andre

Berger, John (Peter) 1926- .... **CLC 2, 19**
See also CA 81-84; CANR 51, 78; DLB 14, 207

Berger, Melvin H. 1927- .... **CLC 12**
See also CA 5-8R; CANR 4; CLR 32; SAAS 2; SATA 5, 88

Berger, Thomas (Louis) 1924- . **CLC 3, 5, 8, 11, 18, 38; DAM NOV**
See also CA 1-4R; CANR 5, 28, 51; DLB 2; DLBY 80; INT CANR-28; MTCW 1, 2

Bergman, (Ernst) Ingmar 1918- .... **CLC 16, 72**
See also CA 81-84; CANR 33, 70; MTCW 2

Bergson, Henri(-Louis) 1859-1941 . **TCLC 32**
See also CA 164

Bergstein, Eleanor 1938- .... **CLC 4**
See also CA 53-56; CANR 5

Berkoff, Steven 1937- .... **CLC 56**
See also CA 104; CANR 72

Berlin, Isaiah 1909-1997 .... **TCLC 105**
See also CA 85-88; 162

Bermant, Chaim (Icyk) 1929- .... **CLC 40**
See also CA 57-60; CANR 6, 31, 57

Bern, Victoria
See Fisher, M(ary) F(rances) K(ennedy)

Bernanos, (Paul Louis) Georges 1888-1948
.... **TCLC 3**
See also CA 104; 130; CANR 94; DLB 72

Bernard, April 1956- .... **CLC 59**
See also CA 131

Berne, Victoria
See Fisher, M(ary) F(rances) K(ennedy)

Bernhard, Thomas 1931-1989 .... **CLC 3, 32, 61; DC 14**
See also CA 85-88; 127; CANR 32, 57; DLB 85, 124; MTCW 1

Bernhardt, Sarah (Henriette Rosine)
1844-1923 .... **TCLC 75**
See also CA 157

Berriault, Gina 1926-1999 ...... **CLC 54, 109; SSC 30**
See also CA 116; 129; 185; CANR 66; DLB 130

Berrigan, Daniel 1921- .... **CLC 4**
See also CA 33-36R; CAAE 187; CAAS 1; CANR 11, 43, 78; DLB 5

Berrigan, Edmund Joseph Michael, Jr.
1934-1983
See Berrigan, Ted
See also CA 61-64; 110; CANR 14

Berrigan, Ted .... **CLC 37**
See also Berrigan, Edmund Joseph Michael, Jr.
See also DLB 5, 169

Berry, Charles Edward Anderson 1931-
See Berry, Chuck
See also CA 115

Berry, Chuck .... **CLC 17**
See also Berry, Charles Edward Anderson

Berry, Jonas
See Ashbery, John (Lawrence)

Berry, Wendell (Erdman) 1934- .. **CLC 4, 6, 8, 27, 46; DAM POET; PC 28**
See also AITN 1; CA 73-76; CANR 50, 73; DLB 5, 6, 234; MTCW 1

Berryman, John 1914-1972 . **CLC 1, 2, 3, 4, 6, 8, 10, 13, 25, 62**
See also CA 13-16; 33-36R; CABS 2; CANR 35; CAP 1; CDALB 1941-1968; DLB 48; MTCW 1, 2

Bertolucci, Bernardo 1940- .... **CLC 16**
See also CA 106

Berton, Pierre (Francis Demarigny) 1920-
.... **CLC 104**
See also CA 1-4R; CANR 2, 56; DLB 68; SATA 99

Bertrand, Aloysius 1807-1841 .... **NCLC 31**

Bertran de Born c. 1140-1215 .... **CMLC 5**

Besant, Annie (Wood) 1847-1933 ... **TCLC 9**
See also CA 105; 185

Bessie, Alvah 1904-1985 .... **CLC 23**
See also CA 5-8R; 116; CANR 2, 80; DLB 26

Bethlen, T. D.
See Silverberg, Robert

Beti, Mongo . **CLC 27; BLC 1; DAM MULT**
See also Biyidi, Alexandre
See also CANR 79

Betjeman, John 1906-1984 ..... **CLC 2, 6, 10, 34, 43; DAB; DAM MST, POET**
See also CA 9-12R; 112; CANR 33, 56; CDBLB 1945-1960; DA3; DLB 20; DLBY 84; MTCW 1, 2

Bettelheim, Bruno 1903-1990 .... **CLC 79**

See also CA 81-84; 131; CANR 23, 61; DA3; MTCW 1, 2

Betti, Ugo 1892-1953 .... **TCLC 5**
See also CA 104; 155

Betts, Doris (Waugh) 1932- ..... **CLC 3, 6, 28**
See also CA 13-16R; CANR 9, 66, 77; DLBY 82; INT CANR-9

Bevan, Alistair
See Roberts, Keith (John Kingston)

Bey, Pilaff
See Douglas, (George) Norman

Bialik, Chaim Nachman 1873-1934
.... **TCLC 25**
See also CA 170

Bickerstaff, Isaac
See Swift, Jonathan

Bidart, Frank 1939- .... **CLC 33**
See also CA 140

Bienek, Horst 1930- .... **CLC 7, 11**
See also CA 73-76; DLB 75

Bierce, Ambrose (Gwinett) 1842-1914(?)
.... **TCLC 1, 7, 44; DA; DAC; DAM MST; SSC 9; WLC**
See also CA 104; 139; CANR 78; CDALB 1865-1917; DA3; DLB 11, 12, 23, 71, 74, 186

Biggers, Earl Derr 1884-1933 .... **TCLC 65**
See also CA 108; 153

Billings, Josh
See Shaw, Henry Wheeler

Billington, (Lady) Rachel (Mary) 1942-
.... **CLC 43**
See also AITN 2; CA 33-36R; CANR 44

Binyon, T(imothy) J(ohn) 1936- ..... **CLC 34**
See also CA 111; CANR 28

Bion 335B.C.-245B.C. .... **CMLC 39**

Bioy Casares, Adolfo 1914-1999 .. **CLC 4, 8, 13, 88; DAM MULT; HLC 1; SSC 17**
See also CA 29-32R; 177; CANR 19, 43, 66; DLB 113; HW 1, 2; MTCW 1, 2

Bird, Cordwainer
See Ellison, Harlan (Jay)

Bird, Robert Montgomery 1806-1854
.... **NCLC 1**
See also DLB 202

Birkerts, Sven 1951- .... **CLC 116**
See also CA 128; 133; 176; CAAE 176; CAAS 29; INT 133

Birney, (Alfred) Earle 1904-1995 . **CLC 1, 4, 6, 11; DAC; DAM MST, POET**
See also CA 1-4R; CANR 5, 20; DLB 88; MTCW 1

Biruni, al 973-1048(?) .... **CMLC 28**

Bishop, Elizabeth 1911-1979 .... **CLC 1, 4, 9, 13, 15, 32; DA; DAC; DAM MST, POET; PC 3**
See also CA 5-8R; 89-92; CABS 2; CANR 26, 61; CDALB 1968-1988; DA3; DLB 5, 169; MTCW 1, 2; SATA-Obit 24

Bishop, John 1935- .... **CLC 10**
See also CA 105

Bishop, John Peale 1892-1944 .... **TCLC 103**
See also CA 107; 155; DLB 4, 9, 45

Bissett, Bill 1939- .... **CLC 18; PC 14**
See also CA 69-72; CAAS 19; CANR 15; DLB 53; MTCW 1

Bissoondath, Neil (Devindra) 1955-
.... **CLC 120; DAC**
See also CA 136

Bitov, Andrei (Georgievich) 1937- .. **CLC 57**
See also CA 142

Biyidi, Alexandre 1932-
See Beti, Mongo
See also BW 1, 3; CA 114; 124; CANR 81; DA3; MTCW 1, 2

Bjarme, Brynjolf
See Ibsen, Henrik (Johan)

Bulgya, Alexander Alexandrovich 1901-1956
.... **TCLC 53**
See also Fadeyev, Alexander
See also CA 117; 181

Bullins, Ed 1935- .... **CLC 1, 5, 7; BLC 1; DAM DRAM, MULT; DC 6**
See also BW 2, 3; CA 49-52; CAAS 16; CANR 24, 46, 73; DLB 7, 38; MTCW 1, 2

Bulwer-Lytton, Edward (George Earle Lytton) 1803-1873 .... **NCLC 1, 45**
See also DLB 21

Bunin, Ivan Alexeyevich 1870-1953
.... **TCLC 6; SSC 5**
See also CA 104

Bunting, Basil 1900-1985 ... **CLC 10, 39, 47; DAM POET**
See also CA 53-56; 115; CANR 7; DLB 20

Bunuel, Luis 1900-1983 . **CLC 16, 80; DAM MULT; HLC 1**
See also CA 101; 110; CANR 32, 77; HW 1

Bunyan, John 1628-1688 .. **LC 4; DA; DAB; DAC; DAM MST; WLC**
See also CDBLB 1660-1789; DLB 39

Burckhardt, Jacob (Christoph) 1818-1897
.... **NCLC 49**

Burford, Eleanor
See Hibbert, Eleanor Alice Burford

Burgess, Anthony -1993 ... **CLC 1, 2, 4, 5, 8, 10, 13, 15, 22, 40, 62, 81, 94; DAB**
See also Wilson, John (Anthony) Burgess
See also AAYA 25; AITN 1; CDBLB 1960 to Present; DLB 14, 194; DLBY 98; MTCW 1

Burke, Edmund 1729(?)-1797 .... **LC 7, 36; DA; DAB; DAC; DAM MST; WLC**
See also DA3; DLB 104

Burke, Kenneth (Duva) 1897-1993 .. **CLC 2, 24**
See also CA 5-8R; 143; CANR 39, 74; DLB 45, 63; MTCW 1, 2

Burke, Leda
See Garnett, David

Burke, Ralph
See Silverberg, Robert

Burke, Thomas 1886-1945 .... **TCLC 63**
See also CA 113; 155; DLB 197

Burney, Fanny 1752-1840 .... **NCLC 12, 54**
See also DLB 39

Burns, Robert 1759-1796 . **LC 3, 29, 40; DA; DAB; DAC; DAM MST, POET; PC 6; WLC**
See also CDBLB 1789-1832; DA3; DLB 109

Burns, Tex
See L'Amour, Louis (Dearborn)

Burnshaw, Stanley 1906- .... **CLC 3, 13, 44**
See also CA 9-12R; DLB 48; DLBY 97

Burr, Anne 1937- .... **CLC 6**
See also CA 25-28R

Burroughs, Edgar Rice 1875-1950 . **TCLC 2, 32; DAM NOV**
See also AAYA 11; CA 104; 132; DA3; DLB 8; MTCW 1, 2; SATA 41

Burroughs, William S(eward) 1914-1997
... **CLC 1, 2, 5, 15, 22, 42, 75, 109; DA; DAB; DAC; DAM MST, NOV, POP; WLC**
See also AITN 2; CA 9-12R; 160; CANR 20, 52; DA3; DLB 2, 8, 16, 152; DLBY 81, 97; MTCW 1, 2

Burton, Sir Richard F(rancis) 1821-1890
.... **NCLC 42**
See also DLB 55, 166, 184

Busch, Frederick 1941- ... **CLC 7, 10, 18, 47**
See also CA 33-36R; CAAS 1; CANR 45, 73, 92; DLB 6

Bush, Ronald 1946- .... **CLC 34**

See also CA 136

Bustos, F(rancisco)
See Borges, Jorge Luis

Bustos Domecq, H(onorio)
See Bioy Casares, Adolfo; Borges, Jorge Luis

Butler, Octavia E(stelle) 1947- .... **CLC 38, 121; BLCS; DAM MULT, POP**
See also AAYA 18; BW 2, 3; CA 73-76; CANR 12, 24, 38, 73; CLR 65; DA3; DLB 33; MTCW 1, 2; SATA 84

Butler, Robert Olen (Jr.) 1945- ...... **CLC 81; DAM POP**
See also CA 112; CANR 66; DLB 173; INT 112; MTCW 1

Butler, Samuel 1612-1680 .... **LC 16, 43**
See also DLB 101, 126

Butler, Samuel 1835-1902 . **TCLC 1, 33; DA; DAB; DAC; DAM MST, NOV; WLC**
See also CA 143; CDBLB 1890-1914; DA3; DLB 18, 57, 174

Butler, Walter C.
See Faust, Frederick (Schiller)

Butor, Michel (Marie Francois) 1926-
.... **CLC 1, 3, 8, 11, 15**
See also CA 9-12R; CANR 33, 66; DLB 83; MTCW 1, 2

Butts, Mary 1892(?)-1937 .... **TCLC 77**
See also CA 148

Buzo, Alexander (John) 1944- .... **CLC 61**
See also CA 97-100; CANR 17, 39, 69

Buzzati, Dino 1906-1972 .... **CLC 36**
See also CA 160; 33-36R; DLB 177

Byars, Betsy (Cromer) 1928- .... **CLC 35**
See also AAYA 19; CA 33-36R, 183; CAAE 183; CANR 18, 36, 57; CLR 1, 16; DLB 52; INT CANR-18; JRDA; MAICYA; MTCW 1; SAAS 1; SATA 4, 46, 80; SATA-Essay 108

Byatt, A(ntonia) S(usan Drabble) 1936-
...... **CLC 19, 65, 136; DAM NOV, POP**
See also CA 13-16R; CANR 13, 33, 50, 75; DA3; DLB 14, 194; MTCW 1, 2

Byrne, David 1952- .... **CLC 26**
See also CA 127

Byrne, John Keyes 1926-
See Leonard, Hugh
See also CA 102; CANR 78; INT 102

Byron, George Gordon (Noel) 1788-1824
.. **NCLC 2, 12; DA; DAB; DAC; DAM MST, POET; PC 16; WLC**
See also CDBLB 1789-1832; DA3; DLB 96, 110

Byron, Robert 1905-1941 .... **TCLC 67**
See also CA 160; DLB 195

C. 3. 3.
See Wilde, Oscar (Fingal O'Flahertie Wills)

Caballero, Fernan 1796-1877 .... **NCLC 10**

Cabell, Branch
See Cabell, James Branch

Cabell, James Branch 1879-1958 ... **TCLC 6**
See also CA 105; 152; DLB 9, 78; MTCW 1

Cabeza de Vaca, Alvar Nunez 1490-1557(?)
.... **LC 61**

Cable, George Washington 1844-1925
.... **TCLC 4; SSC 4**
See also CA 104; 155; DLB 12, 74; DLBD 13

Cabral de Melo Neto, Joao 1920- . **CLC 76; DAM MULT**
See also CA 151

Cabrera Infante, G(uillermo) 1929- . **CLC 5, 25, 45, 120; DAM MULT; HLC 1; SSC 39**
See also CA 85-88; CANR 29, 65; DA3; DLB 113; HW 1, 2; MTCW 1, 2

Cade, Toni
See Bambara, Toni Cade

Cadmus and Harmonia
See Buchan, John

Caedmon fl. 658-680 .... **CMLC 7**
See also DLB 146

Caeiro, Alberto
See Pessoa, Fernando (Antonio Nogueira)

Cage, John (Milton, Jr.) 1912-1992 . **CLC 41**
See also CA 13-16R; 169; CANR 9, 78; DLB 193; INT CANR-9

Cahan, Abraham 1860-1951 .... **TCLC 71**
See also CA 108; 154; DLB 9, 25, 28

Cain, G.
See Cabrera Infante, G(uillermo)

Cain, Guillermo
See Cabrera Infante, G(uillermo)

Cain, James M(allahan) 1892-1977 . **CLC 3, 11, 28**
See also AITN 1; CA 17-20R; 73-76; CANR 8, 34, 61; DLB 226; MTCW 1

Caine, Hall 1853-1931 .... **TCLC 97**

Caine, Mark
See Raphael, Frederic (Michael)

Calasso, Roberto 1941- .... **CLC 81**
See also CA 143; CANR 89

Calderon de la Barca, Pedro 1600-1681
.... **LC 23; DC 3; HLCS 1**

Caldwell, Erskine (Preston) 1903-1987
. **CLC 1, 8, 14, 50, 60; DAM NOV; SSC 19**
See also AITN 1; CA 1-4R; 121; CAAS 1; CANR 2, 33; DA3; DLB 9, 86; MTCW 1, 2

Caldwell, (Janet Miriam) Taylor (Holland) 1900-1985 . **CLC 2, 28, 39; DAM NOV, POP**
See also CA 5-8R; 116; CANR 5; DA3; DLBD 17

Calhoun, John Caldwell 1782-1850
.... **NCLC 15**
See also DLB 3

Calisher, Hortense 1911- .... **CLC 2, 4, 8, 38, 134; DAM NOV; SSC 15**
See also CA 1-4R; CANR 1, 22, 67; DA3; DLB 2; INT CANR-22; MTCW 1, 2

Callaghan, Morley Edward 1903-1990
.. **CLC 3, 14, 41, 65; DAC; DAM MST**
See also CA 9-12R; 132; CANR 33, 73; DLB 68; MTCW 1, 2

Callimachus c. 305B.C.-c. 240B.C.
.... **CMLC 18**
See also DLB 176

Calvin, John 1509-1564 .... **LC 37**

Calvino, Italo 1923-1985 .. **CLC 5, 8, 11, 22, 33, 39, 73; DAM NOV; SSC 3**
See also CA 85-88; 116; CANR 23, 61; DLB 196; MTCW 1, 2

Cameron, Carey 1952- .... **CLC 59**
See also CA 135

Cameron, Peter 1959- .... **CLC 44**
See also CA 125; CANR 50; DLB 234

Camoens, Luis Vaz de 1524(?)-1580
See also HLCS 1

Camoes, Luis de 1524(?)-1580 .... **LC 62; HLCS 1; PC 31**

Campana, Dino 1885-1932 .... **TCLC 20**
See also CA 117; DLB 114

Campanella, Tommaso 1568-1639 ..... **LC 32**

Campbell, John W(ood, Jr.) 1910-1971
.... **CLC 32**
See also CA 21-22; 29-32R; CANR 34; CAP 2; DLB 8; MTCW 1

Campbell, Joseph 1904-1987 .... **CLC 69**
See also AAYA 3; BEST 89:2; CA 1-4R; 124; CANR 3, 28, 61; DA3; MTCW 1, 2

Campbell, Maria 1940- .... **CLC 85; DAC**
See also CA 102; CANR 54; NNAL

Campbell, (John) Ramsey 1946- ... **CLC 42; SSC 19**

Coe, Tucker
See Westlake, Donald E(dwin)

Coen, Ethan 1958- .... **CLC 108**
See also CA 126; CANR 85

Coen, Joel 1955- .... **CLC 108**
See also CA 126

The Coen Brothers
See Coen, Ethan; Coen, Joel

Coetzee, J(ohn) M(ichael) 1940- .... **CLC 23, 33, 66, 117; DAM NOV**
See also AAYA 37; CA 77-80; CANR 41, 54, 74; DA3; DLB 225; MTCW 1, 2

Coffey, Brian
See Koontz, Dean R(ay)

Coffin, Robert P(eter) Tristram 1892-1955
.... **TCLC 95**
See also CA 123; 169; DLB 45

Cohan, George M(ichael) 1878-1942
.... **TCLC 60**
See also CA 157

Cohen, Arthur A(llen) 1928-1986 .... **CLC 7, 31**
See also CA 1-4R; 120; CANR 1, 17, 42; DLB 28

Cohen, Leonard (Norman) 1934- .... **CLC 3, 38; DAC; DAM MST**
See also CA 21-24R; CANR 14, 69; DLB 53; MTCW 1

Cohen, Matt(hew) 1942-1999 .... **CLC 19; DAC**
See also CA 61-64; 187; CAAS 18; CANR 40; DLB 53

Cohen-Solal, Annie 19(?)- .... **CLC 50**

Colegate, Isabel 1931- .... **CLC 36**
See also CA 17-20R; CANR 8, 22, 74; DLB 14, 231; INT CANR-22; MTCW 1

Coleman, Emmett
See Reed, Ishmael

Coleridge, Hartley 1796-1849 .... **NCLC 90**
See also DLB 96

Coleridge, M. E.
See Coleridge, Mary E(lizabeth)

Coleridge, Mary E(lizabeth) 1861-1907
.... **TCLC 73**
See also CA 116; 166; DLB 19, 98

Coleridge, Samuel Taylor 1772-1834
.. **NCLC 9, 54; DA; DAB; DAC; DAM MST, POET; PC 11; WLC**
See also CDBLB 1789-1832; DA3; DLB 93, 107

Coleridge, Sara 1802-1852 .... **NCLC 31**
See also DLB 199

Coles, Don 1928- .... **CLC 46**
See also CA 115; CANR 38

Coles, Robert (Martin) 1929- .... **CLC 108**
See also CA 45-48; CANR 3, 32, 66, 70; INT CANR-32; SATA 23

Colette, (Sidonie-Gabrielle) 1873-1954
.... **TCLC 1, 5, 16; DAM NOV; SSC 10**
See also CA 104; 131; DA3; DLB 65; MTCW 1, 2

Collett, (Jacobine) Camilla (Wergeland)
1813-1895 .... **NCLC 22**

Collier, Christopher 1930- .... **CLC 30**
See also AAYA 13; CA 33-36R; CANR 13, 33; JRDA; MAICYA; SATA 16, 70

Collier, James L(incoln) 1928- .... **CLC 30; DAM POP**
See also AAYA 13; CA 9-12R; CANR 4, 33, 60; CLR 3; JRDA; MAICYA; SAAS 21; SATA 8, 70

Collier, Jeremy 1650-1726 .... **LC 6**

Collier, John 1901-1980 .... **SSC 19**
See also CA 65-68; 97-100; CANR 10; DLB 77

Collingwood, R(obin) G(eorge) 1889(?)-1943
.... **TCLC 67**
See also CA 117; 155

Collins, Hunt
See Hunter, Evan

Collins, Linda 1931- .... **CLC 44**
See also CA 125

Collins, (William) Wilkie 1824-1889
.... **NCLC 1, 18, 93**
See also CDBLB 1832-1890; DLB 18, 70, 159

Collins, William 1721-1759 . **LC 4, 40; DAM POET**
See also DLB 109

Collodi, Carlo 1826-1890 .... **NCLC 54**
See also Lorenzini, Carlo
See also CLR 5

Colman, George 1732-1794
See Glassco, John

Colt, Winchester Remington
See Hubbard, L(afayette) Ron(ald)

Colter, Cyrus 1910- .... **CLC 58**
See also BW 1; CA 65-68; CANR 10, 66; DLB 33

Colton, James
See Hansen, Joseph

Colum, Padraic 1881-1972 .... **CLC 28**
See also CA 73-76; 33-36R; CANR 35; CLR 36; MAICYA; MTCW 1; SATA 15

Colvin, James
See Moorcock, Michael (John)

Colwin, Laurie (E.) 1944-1992 ... **CLC 5, 13, 23, 84**
See also CA 89-92; 139; CANR 20, 46; DLBY 80; MTCW 1

Comfort, Alex(ander) 1920- .. **CLC 7; DAM POP**
See also CA 1-4R; CANR 1, 45; MTCW 1

Comfort, Montgomery
See Campbell, (John) Ramsey

Compton-Burnett, I(vy) 1884(?)-1969
.... **CLC 1, 3, 10, 15, 34; DAM NOV**
See also CA 1-4R; 25-28R; CANR 4; DLB 36; MTCW 1

Comstock, Anthony 1844-1915 ..... **TCLC 13**
See also CA 110; 169

Comte, Auguste 1798-1857 .... **NCLC 54**

Conan Doyle, Arthur
See Doyle, Arthur Conan

Conde (Abellan), Carmen 1901-
See also CA 177; DLB 108; HLCS 1; HW 2

Conde, Maryse 1937- ... **CLC 52, 92; BLCS; DAM MULT**
See also BW 2, 3; CA 110; CANR 30, 53, 76; MTCW 1

Condillac, Etienne Bonnot de 1714-1780
.... **LC 26**

Condon, Richard (Thomas) 1915-1996
... **CLC 4, 6, 8, 10, 45, 100; DAM NOV**
See also BEST 90:3; CA 1-4R; 151; CAAS 1; CANR 2, 23; INT CANR-23; MTCW 1, 2

Confucius 551B.C.-479B.C. .. **CMLC 19; DA; DAB; DAC; DAM MST; WLCS**
See also DA3

Congreve, William 1670-1729 .... **LC 5, 21; DA; DAB; DAC; DAM DRAM, MST, POET; DC 2; WLC**
See also CDBLB 1660-1789; DLB 39, 84

Connell, Evan S(helby), Jr. 1924- .... **CLC 4, 6, 45; DAM NOV**
See also AAYA 7; CA 1-4R; CAAS 2; CANR 2, 39, 76; DLB 2; DLBY 81; MTCW 1, 2

Connelly, Marc(us Cook) 1890-1980 . **CLC 7**
See also CA 85-88; 102; CANR 30; DLB 7; DLBY 80; SATA-Obit 25

Connor, Ralph .... **TCLC 31**
See also Gordon, Charles William
See also DLB 92

Conrad, Joseph 1857-1924 .. **TCLC 1, 6, 13, 25, 43, 57; DA; DAB; DAC; DAM MST, NOV; SSC 9; WLC**
See also AAYA 26; CA 104; 131; CANR 60; CDBLB 1890-1914; DA3; DLB 10, 34, 98, 156; MTCW 1, 2; SATA 27

Conrad, Robert Arnold
See Hart, Moss

Conroy, Pat
See Conroy, (Donald) Pat(rick)
See also MTCW 2

Conroy, (Donald) Pat(rick) 1945- .. **CLC 30, 74; DAM NOV, POP**
See also Conroy, Pat
See also AAYA 8; AITN 1; CA 85-88; CANR 24, 53; DA3; DLB 6; MTCW 1

Constant (de Rebecque), (Henri) Benjamin
1767-1830 .... **NCLC 6**
See also DLB 119

Conybeare, Charles Augustus
See Eliot, T(homas) S(tearns)

Cook, Michael 1933- .... **CLC 58**
See also CA 93-96; CANR 68; DLB 53

Cook, Robin 1940- ...... **CLC 14; DAM POP**
See also AAYA 32; BEST 90:2; CA 108; 111; CANR 41, 90; DA3; INT 111

Cook, Roy
See Silverberg, Robert

Cooke, Elizabeth 1948- .... **CLC 55**
See also CA 129

Cooke, John Esten 1830-1886 .... **NCLC 5**
See also DLB 3

Cooke, John Estes
See Baum, L(yman) Frank

Cooke, M. E.
See Creasey, John

Cooke, Margaret
See Creasey, John

Cook-Lynn, Elizabeth 1930- . **CLC 93; DAM MULT**
See also CA 133; DLB 175; NNAL

Cooney, Ray .... **CLC 62**

Cooper, Douglas 1960- .... **CLC 86**

Cooper, Henry St. John
See Creasey, John

Cooper, J(oan) California (?)- .... **CLC 56; DAM MULT**
See also AAYA 12; BW 1; CA 125; CANR 55; DLB 212

Cooper, James Fenimore 1789-1851
.... **NCLC 1, 27, 54**
See also AAYA 22; CDALB 1640-1865; DA3; DLB 3; SATA 19

Coover, Robert (Lowell) 1932- .... **CLC 3, 7, 15, 32, 46, 87; DAM NOV; SSC 15**
See also CA 45-48; CANR 3, 37, 58; DLB 2, 227; DLBY 81; MTCW 1, 2

Copeland, Stewart (Armstrong) 1952-
.... **CLC 26**

Copernicus, Nicolaus 1473-1543 .... **LC 45**

Coppard, A(lfred) E(dgar) 1878-1957
.... **TCLC 5; SSC 21**
See also CA 114; 167; DLB 162; YABC 1

Coppee, Francois 1842-1908 .... **TCLC 25**
See also CA 170

Coppola, Francis Ford 1939- .. **CLC 16, 126**
See also CA 77-80; CANR 40, 78; DLB 44

Corbiere, Tristan 1845-1875 .... **NCLC 43**

Corcoran, Barbara 1911- .... **CLC 17**
See also AAYA 14; CA 21-24R; CAAS 2; CANR 11, 28, 48; CLR 50; DLB 52; JRDA; SAAS 20; SATA 3, 77

Cordelier, Maurice
See Giraudoux, (Hippolyte) Jean

Corelli, Marie .... **TCLC 51**
See also Mackay, Mary
See also DLB 34, 156

Corman, Cid 1924- .... **CLC 9**
See also Corman, Sidney

Dickens, Charles (John Huffam) 1812-1870
...... NCLC **3, 8, 18, 26, 37, 50, 86; DA; DAB; DAC; DAM MST, NOV; SSC 17; WLC**
See also AAYA 23; CDBLB 1832-1890; DA3; DLB 21, 55, 70, 159, 166; JRDA; MAICYA; SATA 15

Dickey, James (Lafayette) 1923-1997
.. CLC **1, 2, 4, 7, 10, 15, 47, 109; DAM NOV, POET, POP**
See also AITN 1, 2; CA 9-12R; 156; CABS 2; CANR 10, 48, 61; CDALB 1968-1988; DA3; DLB 5, 193; DLBD 7; DLBY 82, 93, 96, 97, 98; INT CANR-10; MTCW 1, 2

Dickey, William 1928-1994 .... CLC **3, 28**
See also CA 9-12R; 145; CANR 24, 79; DLB 5

Dickinson, Charles 1951- .... CLC **49**
See also CA 128

Dickinson, Emily (Elizabeth) 1830-1886
. NCLC **21, 77; DA; DAB; DAC; DAM MST, POET; PC 1; WLC**
See also AAYA 22; CDALB 1865-1917; DA3; DLB 1; SATA 29

Dickinson, Peter (Malcolm) 1927- . CLC **12, 35**
See also AAYA 9; CA 41-44R; CANR 31, 58, 88; CLR 29; DLB 87, 161; JRDA; MAICYA; SATA 5, 62, 95

Dickson, Carr
See Carr, John Dickson

Dickson, Carter
See Carr, John Dickson

Diderot, Denis 1713-1784 .... LC **26**

Didion, Joan 1934- . CLC **1, 3, 8, 14, 32, 129; DAM NOV**
See also AITN 1; CA 5-8R; CANR 14, 52, 76; CDALB 1968-1988; DA3; DLB 2, 173, 185; DLBY 81, 86; MTCW 1, 2

Dietrich, Robert
See Hunt, E(verette) Howard, (Jr.)

Difusa, Pati
See Almodovar, Pedro

Dillard, Annie 1945- . CLC **9, 60, 115; DAM NOV**
See also AAYA 6; CA 49-52; CANR 3, 43, 62, 90; DA3; DLBY 80; MTCW 1, 2; SATA 10

Dillard, R(ichard) H(enry) W(ilde) 1937-
.... CLC **5**
See also CA 21-24R; CAAS 7; CANR 10; DLB 5

Dillon, Eilis 1920-1994 .... CLC **17**
See also CA 9-12R, 182; 147; CAAE 182; CAAS 3; CANR 4, 38, 78; CLR 26; MAICYA; SATA 2, 74; SATA-Essay 105; SATA-Obit 83

Dimont, Penelope
See Mortimer, Penelope (Ruth)

Dinesen, Isak -1962 . CLC **10, 29, 95; SSC 7**
See also Blixen, Karen (Christentze Dinesen)
See also MTCW 1

Ding Ling .... CLC **68**
See also Chiang, Pin-chin

Diphusa, Patty
See Almodovar, Pedro

Disch, Thomas M(ichael) 1940- .. CLC **7, 36**
See also AAYA 17; CA 21-24R; CAAS 4; CANR 17, 36, 54, 89; CLR 18; DA3; DLB 8; MAICYA; MTCW 1, 2; SAAS 15; SATA 92

Disch, Tom
See Disch, Thomas M(ichael)

d'Isly, Georges
See Simenon, Georges (Jacques Christian)

Disraeli, Benjamin 1804-1881 . NCLC **2, 39, 79**

See also DLB 21, 55

Ditcum, Steve
See Crumb, R(obert)

Dixon, Paige
See Corcoran, Barbara

Dixon, Stephen 1936- .... CLC **52; SSC 16**
See also CA 89-92; CANR 17, 40, 54, 91; DLB 130

Doak, Annie
See Dillard, Annie

Dobell, Sydney Thompson 1824-1874
.... NCLC **43**
See also DLB 32

Doblin, Alfred .... TCLC **13**
See also Doeblin, Alfred

Dobrolyubov, Nikolai Alexandrovich
1836-1861 .... NCLC **5**

Dobson, Austin 1840-1921 .... TCLC **79**
See also DLB 35; 144

Dobyns, Stephen 1941- .... CLC **37**
See also CA 45-48; CANR 2, 18

Doctorow, E(dgar) L(aurence) 1931-
.... CLC **6, 11, 15, 18, 37, 44, 65, 113; DAM NOV, POP**
See also AAYA 22; AITN 2; BEST 89:3; CA 45-48; CANR 2, 33, 51, 76; CDALB 1968-1988; DA3; DLB 2, 28, 173; DLBY 80; MTCW 1, 2

Dodgson, Charles Lutwidge 1832-1898
See Carroll, Lewis
See also CLR 2; DA; DAB; DAC; DAM MST, NOV, POET; DA3; MAICYA; SATA 100; YABC 2

Dodson, Owen (Vincent) 1914-1983
.... CLC **79; BLC 1; DAM MULT**
See also BW 1; CA 65-68; 110; CANR 24; DLB 76

Doeblin, Alfred 1878-1957 .... TCLC **13**
See also Doblin, Alfred
See also CA 110; 141; DLB 66

Doerr, Harriet 1910- .... CLC **34**
See also CA 117; 122; CANR 47; INT 122

Domecq, H(onorio Bustos)
See Bioy Casares, Adolfo

Domecq, H(onorio) Bustos
See Bioy Casares, Adolfo; Borges, Jorge Luis

Domini, Rey
See Lorde, Audre (Geraldine)

Dominique
See Proust, (Valentin-Louis-George-Eugene-) Marcel

Don, A
See Stephen, Sir Leslie

Donaldson, Stephen R. 1947- . CLC **46, 138; DAM POP**
See also AAYA 36; CA 89-92; CANR 13, 55; INT CANR-13; SATA 121

Donleavy, J(ames) P(atrick) 1926- ... CLC **1, 4, 6, 10, 45**
See also AITN 2; CA 9-12R; CANR 24, 49, 62, 80; DLB 6, 173; INT CANR-24; MTCW 1, 2

Donne, John 1572-1631 .... LC **10, 24; DA; DAB; DAC; DAM MST, POET; PC 1; WLC**
See also CDBLB Before 1660; DLB 121, 151

Donnell, David 1939(?)- .... CLC **34**

Donoghue, P. S.
See Hunt, E(verette) Howard, (Jr.)

Donoso (Yanez), Jose 1924-1996 .. CLC **4, 8, 11, 32, 99; DAM MULT; HLC 1; SSC 34**
See also CA 81-84; 155; CANR 32, 73; DLB 113; HW 1, 2; MTCW 1, 2

Donovan, John 1928-1992 .... CLC **35**
See also AAYA 20; CA 97-100; 137; CLR 3; MAICYA; SATA 72; SATA-Brief 29

Don Roberto
See Cunninghame Graham, Robert (Gallnigad) Bontine

Doolittle, Hilda 1886-1961 ...... CLC **3, 8, 14, 31, 34, 73; DA; DAC; DAM MST, POET; PC 5; WLC**
See also H. D.
See also CA 97-100; CANR 35; DLB 4, 45; MTCW 1, 2

Dorfman, Ariel 1942- ..... CLC **48, 77; DAM MULT; HLC 1**
See also CA 124; 130; CANR 67, 70; HW 1, 2; INT 130

Dorn, Edward (Merton) 1929-1999 . CLC **10, 18**
See also CA 93-96; 187; CANR 42, 79; DLB 5; INT 93-96

Dorris, Michael (Anthony) 1945-1997
.... CLC **109; DAM MULT, NOV**
See also AAYA 20; BEST 90:1; CA 102; 157; CANR 19, 46, 75; CLR 58; DA3; DLB 175; MTCW 2; NNAL; SATA 75; SATA-Obit 94

Dorris, Michael A.
See Dorris, Michael (Anthony)

Dorsan, Luc
See Simenon, Georges (Jacques Christian)

Dorsange, Jean
See Simenon, Georges (Jacques Christian)

Dos Passos, John (Roderigo) 1896-1970
..... CLC **1, 4, 8, 11, 15, 25, 34, 82; DA; DAB; DAC; DAM MST, NOV; WLC**
See also CA 1-4R; 29-32R; CANR 3; CDALB 1929-1941; DA3; DLB 4, 9; DLBD 1, 15; DLBY 96; MTCW 1, 2

Dossage, Jean
See Simenon, Georges (Jacques Christian)

Dostoevsky, Fedor Mikhailovich 1821-1881
.... NCLC **2, 7, 21, 33, 43; DA; DAB; DAC; DAM MST, NOV; SSC 2, 33; WLC**
See also DA3

Doughty, Charles M(ontagu) 1843-1926
.... TCLC **27**
See also CA 115; 178; DLB 19, 57, 174

Douglas, Ellen .... CLC **73**
See also Haxton, Josephine Ayres; Williamson, Ellen Douglas

Douglas, Gavin 1475(?)-1522 .... LC **20**
See also DLB 132

Douglas, George
See Brown, George Douglas

Douglas, Keith (Castellain) 1920-1944
.... TCLC **40**
See also CA 160; DLB 27

Douglas, Leonard
See Bradbury, Ray (Douglas)

Douglas, Michael
See Crichton, (John) Michael

Douglas, (George) Norman 1868-1952
.... TCLC **68**
See also CA 119; 157; DLB 34, 195

Douglas, William
See Brown, George Douglas

Douglass, Frederick 1817(?)-1895 . NCLC **7, 55; BLC 1; DA; DAC; DAM MST, MULT; WLC**
See also CDALB 1640-1865; DA3; DLB 1, 43, 50, 79; SATA 29

Dourado, (Waldomiro Freitas) Autran 1926-
.... CLC **23, 60**
See also CA 25-28R; 179; CANR 34, 81; DLB 145; HW 2

Dourado, Waldomiro Autran 1926-
See Dourado, (Waldomiro Freitas) Autran
See also CA 179

Dove, Rita (Frances) 1952- ...... CLC **50, 81; BLCS; DAM MULT, POET; PC 6**

See also CA 97-100; CANR 39; DLB 130

Dye, Richard
　　See De Voto, Bernard (Augustine)

Dylan, Bob 1941- .... **CLC 3, 4, 6, 12, 77**
　　See also CA 41-44R; DLB 16

E. V. L.
　　See Lucas, E(dward) V(errall)

Eagleton, Terence (Francis) 1943- . **CLC 63, 132**
　　See also CA 57-60; CANR 7, 23, 68; MTCW 1, 2

Eagleton, Terry
　　See Eagleton, Terence (Francis)

Early, Jack
　　See Scoppettone, Sandra

East, Michael
　　See West, Morris L(anglo)

Eastaway, Edward
　　See Thomas, (Philip) Edward

Eastlake, William (Derry) 1917-1997 . **CLC 8**
　　See also CA 5-8R; 158; CAAS 1; CANR 5, 63; DLB 6, 206; INT CANR-5

Eastman, Charles A(lexander) 1858-1939
　　.................... **TCLC 55; DAM MULT**
　　See also CA 179; CANR 91; DLB 175; NNAL; YABC 1

Eberhart, Richard (Ghormley) 1904-
　　.......... **CLC 3, 11, 19, 56; DAM POET**
　　See also CA 1-4R; CANR 2; CDALB 1941-1968; DLB 48; MTCW 1

Eberstadt, Fernanda 1960- .... **CLC 39**
　　See also CA 136; CANR 69

Echegaray (y Eizaguirre), Jose (Maria Waldo) 1832-1916 ... **TCLC 4; HLCS 1**
　　See also CA 104; CANR 32; HW 1; MTCW 1

Echeverria, (Jose) Esteban (Antonino) 1805-1851 .... **NCLC 18**

Echo
　　See Proust, (Valentin-Louis-George-Eugene-) Marcel

Eckert, Allan W. 1931- .... **CLC 17**
　　See also AAYA 18; CA 13-16R; CANR 14, 45; INT CANR-14; SAAS 21; SATA 29, 91; SATA-Brief 27

Eckhart, Meister 1260(?)-1328(?) .. **CMLC 9**
　　See also DLB 115

Eckmar, F. R.
　　See de Hartog, Jan

Eco, Umberto 1932- .... **CLC 28, 60; DAM NOV, POP**
　　See also BEST 90:1; CA 77-80; CANR 12, 33, 55; DA3; DLB 196; MTCW 1, 2

Eddison, E(ric) R(ucker) 1882-1945
　　................................. **TCLC 15**
　　See also CA 109; 156

Eddy, Mary (Ann Morse) Baker 1821-1910
　　................................. **TCLC 71**
　　See also CA 113; 174

Edel, (Joseph) Leon 1907-1997 . **CLC 29, 34**
　　See also CA 1-4R; 161; CANR 1, 22; DLB 103; INT CANR-22

Eden, Emily 1797-1869 .... **NCLC 10**

Edgar, David 1948- . **CLC 42; DAM DRAM**
　　See also CA 57-60; CANR 12, 61; DLB 13, 233; MTCW 1

Edgerton, Clyde (Carlyle) 1944- ..... **CLC 39**
　　See also AAYA 17; CA 118; 134; CANR 64; INT 134

Edgeworth, Maria 1768-1849 ... **NCLC 1, 51**
　　See also DLB 116, 159, 163; SATA 21

Edmonds, Paul
　　See Kuttner, Henry

Edmonds, Walter D(umaux) 1903-1998
　　................................. **CLC 35**
　　See also CA 5-8R; CANR 2; DLB 9; MAICYA; SAAS 4; SATA 1, 27; SATA-Obit 99

Edmondson, Wallace
　　See Ellison, Harlan (Jay)

Edson, Russell .... **CLC 13**
　　See also CA 33-36R

Edwards, Bronwen Elizabeth
　　See Rose, Wendy

Edwards, G(erald) B(asil) 1899-1976
　　................................. **CLC 25**
　　See also CA 110

Edwards, Gus 1939- .... **CLC 43**
　　See also CA 108; INT 108

Edwards, Jonathan 1703-1758 ..... **LC 7, 54; DA; DAC; DAM MST**
　　See also DLB 24

Efron, Marina Ivanovna Tsvetaeva
　　See Tsvetaeva (Efron), Marina (Ivanovna)

Ehle, John (Marsden, Jr.) 1925- ..... **CLC 27**
　　See also CA 9-12R

Ehrenbourg, Ilya (Grigoryevich)
　　See Ehrenburg, Ilya (Grigoryevich)

Ehrenburg, Ilya (Grigoryevich) 1891-1967
　　.................... **CLC 18, 34, 62**
　　See also CA 102; 25-28R

Ehrenburg, Ilyo (Grigoryevich)
　　See Ehrenburg, Ilya (Grigoryevich)

Ehrenreich, Barbara 1941- .... **CLC 110**
　　See also BEST 90:4; CA 73-76; CANR 16, 37, 62; MTCW 1, 2

Eich, Guenter 1907-1972 .... **CLC 15**
　　See also CA 111; 93-96; DLB 69, 124

Eichendorff, Joseph Freiherr von 1788-1857
　　................................. **NCLC 8**
　　See also DLB 90

Eigner, Larry .... **CLC 9**
　　See also Eigner, Laurence (Joel)
　　See also CAAS 23; DLB 5

Eigner, Laurence (Joel) 1927-1996
　　See Eigner, Larry
　　See also CA 9-12R; 151; CANR 6, 84; DLB 193

Einstein, Albert 1879-1955 .... **TCLC 65**
　　See also CA 121; 133; MTCW 1, 2

Eiseley, Loren Corey 1907-1977 .... **TCLC 7**
　　See also AAYA 5; CA 1-4R; 73-76; CANR 6; DLBD 17

Eisenstadt, Jill 1963- .... **CLC 50**
　　See also CA 140

Eisenstein, Sergei (Mikhailovich) 1898-1948
　　................................. **TCLC 57**
　　See also CA 114; 149

Eisner, Simon
　　See Kornbluth, C(yril) M.

Ekeloef, (Bengt) Gunnar 1907-1968
　　.............. **CLC 27; DAM POET; PC 23**
　　See also CA 123; 25-28R

Ekelof, (Bengt) Gunnar
　　See Ekeloef, (Bengt) Gunnar

Ekelund, Vilhelm 1880-1949 .... **TCLC 75**

Ekwensi, C. O. D.
　　See Ekwensi, Cyprian (Odiatu Duaka)

Ekwensi, Cyprian (Odiatu Duaka) 1921-
　　.............. **CLC 4; BLC 1; DAM MULT**
　　See also BW 2, 3; CA 29-32R; CANR 18, 42, 74; DLB 117; MTCW 1, 2; SATA 66

Elaine .... **TCLC 18**
　　See also Leverson, Ada

El Crummo
　　See Crumb, R(obert)

Elder, Lonne III 1931-1996 .... **DC 8**
　　See also BLC 1; BW 1, 3; CA 81-84; 152; CANR 25; DAM MULT; DLB 7, 38, 44

Eleanor of Aquitaine 1122-1204 .. **CMLC 39**

Elia
　　See Lamb, Charles

Eliade, Mircea 1907-1986 .... **CLC 19**
　　See also CA 65-68; 119; CANR 30, 62; DLB 220; MTCW 1

Eliot, A. D.
　　See Jewett, (Theodora) Sarah Orne

Eliot, Alice
　　See Jewett, (Theodora) Sarah Orne

Eliot, Dan
　　See Silverberg, Robert

Eliot, George 1819- . **NCLC 4, 13, 23, 41, 49, 89; DA; DAB; DAC; DAM MST, NOV; PC 20; WLC**
　　See also CDBLB 1832-1890; DA3; DLB 21, 35, 55

Eliot, John 1604-1690 .... **LC 5**
　　See also DLB 24

Eliot, T(homas) S(tearns) 1888-1965 . **CLC 1, 2, 3, 6, 9, 10, 13, 15, 24, 34, 41, 55, 57, 113; DA; DAB; DAC; DAM DRAM, MST, POET; PC 5, 31; WLC**
　　See also AAYA 28; CA 5-8R; 25-28R; CANR 41; CDALB 1929-1941; DA3; DLB 7, 10, 45, 63; DLBY 88; MTCW 1, 2

Elizabeth 1866-1941 .... **TCLC 41**

Elkin, Stanley L(awrence) 1930-1995
　　........ **CLC 4, 6, 9, 14, 27, 51, 91; DAM NOV, POP; SSC 12**
　　See also CA 9-12R; 148; CANR 8, 46; DLB 2, 28; DLBY 80; INT CANR-8; MTCW 1, 2

Elledge, Scott .... **CLC 34**

Elliot, Don
　　See Silverberg, Robert

Elliott, Don
　　See Silverberg, Robert

Elliott, George P(aul) 1918-1980 .... **CLC 2**
　　See also CA 1-4R; 97-100; CANR 2

Elliott, Janice 1931-1995 .... **CLC 47**
　　See also CA 13-16R; CANR 8, 29, 84; DLB 14; SATA 119

Elliott, Sumner Locke 1917-1991 ... **CLC 38**
　　See also CA 5-8R; 134; CANR 2, 21

Elliott, William
　　See Bradbury, Ray (Douglas)

Ellis, A. E. .... **CLC 7**

Ellis, Alice Thomas .... **CLC 40**
　　See also Haycraft, Anna (Margaret)
　　See also DLB 194; MTCW 1

Ellis, Bret Easton 1964- ... **CLC 39, 71, 117; DAM POP**
　　See also AAYA 2; CA 118; 123; CANR 51, 74; DA3; INT 123; MTCW 1

Ellis, (Henry) Havelock 1859-1939
　　................................. **TCLC 14**
　　See also CA 109; 169; DLB 190

Ellis, Landon
　　See Ellison, Harlan (Jay)

Ellis, Trey 1962- .... **CLC 55**
　　See also CA 146; CANR 92

Ellison, Harlan (Jay) 1934- .. **CLC 1, 13, 42, 139; DAM POP; SSC 14**
　　See also AAYA 29; CA 5-8R; CANR 5, 46; DLB 8; INT CANR-5; MTCW 1, 2

Ellison, Ralph (Waldo) 1914-1994 ... **CLC 1, 3, 11, 54, 86, 114; BLC 1; DA; DAB; DAC; DAM MST, MULT, NOV; SSC 26; WLC**
　　See also AAYA 19; BW 1, 3; CA 9-12R; 145; CANR 24, 53; CDALB 1941-1968; DA3; DLB 2, 76, 227; DLBY 94; MTCW 1, 2

Ellmann, Lucy (Elizabeth) 1956- .... **CLC 61**
　　See also CA 128

Ellmann, Richard (David) 1918-1987
　　................................. **CLC 50**
　　See also BEST 89:2; CA 1-4R; 122; CANR 2, 28, 61; DLB 103; DLBY 87; MTCW 1, 2

Elman, Richard (Martin) 1934-1997
　　................................. **CLC 19**

19, 62, 66; DA; DAB; DAC; DAM MST, NOV; SSC 11; WLC
See also DA3; DLB 119

Flecker, Herman Elroy
See Flecker, (Herman) James Elroy

Flecker, (Herman) James Elroy 1884-1915
.... **TCLC 43**
See also CA 109; 150; DLB 10, 19

Fleming, Ian (Lancaster) 1908-1964 . **CLC 3, 30; DAM POP**
See also AAYA 26; CA 5-8R; CANR 59; CDBLB 1945-1960; DA3; DLB 87, 201; MTCW 1, 2; SATA 9

Fleming, Thomas (James) 1927- ..... **CLC 37**
See also CA 5-8R; CANR 10; INT CANR-10; SATA 8

Fletcher, John 1579-1625 .... **LC 33; DC 6**
See also CDBLB Before 1660; DLB 58

Fletcher, John Gould 1886-1950 .. **TCLC 35**
See also CA 107; 167; DLB 4, 45

Fleur, Paul
See Pohl, Frederik

Flooglebuckle, Al
See Spiegelman, Art

Flora, Fletcher 1914-1969
See Queen, Ellery
See also CA 1-4R; CANR 3, 85

Flying Officer X
See Bates, H(erbert) E(rnest)

Fo, Dario 1926- .... **CLC 32, 109; DAM DRAM; DC 10**
See also CA 116; 128; CANR 68; DA3; DLBY 97; MTCW 1, 2

Fogarty, Jonathan Titulescu Esq.
See Farrell, James T(homas)

Follett, Ken(neth Martin) 1949- .... **CLC 18; DAM NOV, POP**
See also AAYA 6; BEST 89:4; CA 81-84; CANR 13, 33, 54; DA3; DLB 87; DLBY 81; INT CANR-33; MTCW 1

Fontane, Theodor 1819-1898 .... **NCLC 26**
See also DLB 129

Foote, Horton 1916- .... **CLC 51, 91; DAM DRAM**
See also CA 73-76; CANR 34, 51; DA3; DLB 26; INT CANR-34

Foote, Shelby 1916- ... **CLC 75; DAM NOV, POP**
See also CA 5-8R; CANR 3, 45, 74; DA3; DLB 2, 17; MTCW 2

Forbes, Esther 1891-1967 .... **CLC 12**
See also AAYA 17; CA 13-14; 25-28R; CAP 1; CLR 27; DLB 22; JRDA; MAICYA; SATA 2, 100

Forche, Carolyn (Louise) 1950- ..... **CLC 25, 83, 86; DAM POET; PC 10**
See also CA 109; 117; CANR 50, 74; DA3; DLB 5, 193; INT 117; MTCW 1

Ford, Elbur
See Hibbert, Eleanor Alice Burford

Ford, Ford Madox 1873-1939 . **TCLC 1, 15, 39, 57; DAM NOV**
See also Chaucer, Daniel
See also CA 104; 132; CANR 74; CDBLB 1914-1945; DA3; DLB 162; MTCW 1, 2

Ford, Henry 1863-1947 .... **TCLC 73**
See also CA 115; 148

Ford, John 1586-(?) .... **DC 8**
See also CDBLB Before 1660; DAM DRAM; DA3; DLB 58

Ford, John 1895-1973 .... **CLC 16**
See also CA 187; 45-48

Ford, Richard 1944- .... **CLC 46, 99**
See also CA 69-72; CANR 11, 47, 86; DLB 227; MTCW 1

Ford, Webster
See Masters, Edgar Lee

Foreman, Richard 1937- .... **CLC 50**
See also CA 65-68; CANR 32, 63

Forester, C(ecil) S(cott) 1899-1966 . **CLC 35**
See also CA 73-76; 25-28R; CANR 83; DLB 191; SATA 13

Forez
See Mauriac, Francois (Charles)

Forman, James Douglas 1932- .... **CLC 21**
See also AAYA 17; CA 9-12R; CANR 4, 19, 42; JRDA; MAICYA; SATA 8, 70

Fornes, Maria Irene 1930- . **CLC 39, 61; DC 10; HLCS 1**
See also CA 25-28R; CANR 28, 81; DLB 7; HW 1, 2; INT CANR-28; MTCW 1

Forrest, Leon (Richard) 1937-1997 . **CLC 4; BLCS**
See also BW 2; CA 89-92; 162; CAAS 7; CANR 25, 52, 87; DLB 33

Forster, E(dward) M(organ) 1879-1970
..... **CLC 1, 2, 3, 4, 9, 10, 13, 15, 22, 45, 77; DA; DAB; DAC; DAM MST, NOV; SSC 27; WLC**
See also AAYA 2, 37; CA 13-14; 25-28R; CANR 45; CAP 1; CDBLB 1914-1945; DA3; DLB 34, 98, 162, 178, 195; DLBD 10; MTCW 1, 2; SATA 57

Forster, John 1812-1876 .... **NCLC 11**

Forsyth, Frederick 1938- .... **CLC 2, 5, 36; DAM NOV, POP**
See also BEST 89:4; CA 85-88; CANR 38, 62; DLB 87; MTCW 1, 2

Forten, Charlotte L. .... **TCLC 16; BLC 2**
See also Grimke, Charlotte L(ottie) Forten
See also DLB 50

Foscolo, Ugo 1778-1827 .... **NCLC 8**

Fosse, Bob .... **CLC 20**
See also Fosse, Robert Louis

Fosse, Robert Louis 1927-1987
See Fosse, Bob
See also CA 110; 123

Foster, Stephen Collins 1826-1864 . **NCLC 26**

Foucault, Michel 1926-1984 . **CLC 31, 34, 69**
See also CA 105; 113; CANR 34; MTCW 1, 2

Fouque, Friedrich (Heinrich Karl) de la Motte 1777-1843 .... **NCLC 2**
See also DLB 90

Fourier, Charles 1772-1837 .... **NCLC 51**

Fournier, Pierre 1916- .... **CLC 11**
See also Gascar, Pierre
See also CA 89-92; CANR 16, 40

Fowles, John (Philip) 1926- . **CLC 1, 2, 3, 4, 6, 9, 10, 15, 33, 87; DAB; DAC; DAM MST; SSC 33**
See also CA 5-8R; CANR 25, 71; CDBLB 1960 to Present; DA3; DLB 14, 139, 207; MTCW 1, 2; SATA 22

Fox, Paula 1923- .... **CLC 2, 8, 121**
See also AAYA 3, 37; CA 73-76; CANR 20, 36, 62; CLR 1, 44; DLB 52; JRDA; MAICYA; MTCW 1; SATA 17, 60, 120

Fox, William Price (Jr.) 1926- .... **CLC 22**
See also CA 17-20R; CAAS 19; CANR 11; DLB 2; DLBY 81

Foxe, John 1516(?)-1587 .... **LC 14**
See also DLB 132

Frame, Janet 1924- . **CLC 2, 3, 6, 22, 66, 96; SSC 29**
See also Clutha, Janet Paterson Frame

France, Anatole .... **TCLC 9**
See also Thibault, Jacques Anatole Francois
See also DLB 123; MTCW 1

Francis, Claude 19(?)- .... **CLC 50**

Francis, Dick 1920- ...... **CLC 2, 22, 42, 102; DAM POP**
See also AAYA 5, 21; BEST 89:3; CA 5-8R; CANR 9, 42, 68; CDBLB 1960 to Present; DA3; DLB 87; INT CANR-9; MTCW 1, 2

Francis, Robert (Churchill) 1901-1987
.... **CLC 15**
See also CA 1-4R; 123; CANR 1

Frank, Anne(lies Marie) 1929-1945
.... **TCLC 17; DA; DAB; DAC; DAM MST; WLC**
See also AAYA 12; CA 113; 133; CANR 68; DA3; MTCW 1, 2; SATA 87; SATA-Brief 42

Frank, Bruno 1887-1945 .... **TCLC 81**
See also DLB 118

Frank, Elizabeth 1945- .... **CLC 39**
See also CA 121; 126; CANR 78; INT 126

Frankl, Viktor E(mil) 1905-1997 .... **CLC 93**
See also CA 65-68; 161

Franklin, Benjamin
See Hasek, Jaroslav (Matej Frantisek)

Franklin, Benjamin 1706-1790 . **LC 25; DA; DAB; DAC; DAM MST; WLCS**
See also CDALB 1640-1865; DA3; DLB 24, 43, 73

Franklin, (Stella Maria Sarah) Miles (Lampe) 1879-1954 .... **TCLC 7**
See also CA 104; 164; DLB 230; MTCW 2

Fraser, (Lady) Antonia (Pakenham) 1932-
.... **CLC 32, 107**
See also CA 85-88; CANR 44, 65; MTCW 1, 2; SATA-Brief 32

Fraser, George MacDonald 1925- ..... **CLC 7**
See also CA 45-48; 180; CAAE 180; CANR 2, 48, 74; MTCW 1

Fraser, Sylvia 1935- .... **CLC 64**
See also CA 45-48; CANR 1, 16, 60

Frayn, Michael 1933- .... **CLC 3, 7, 31, 47; DAM DRAM, NOV**
See also CA 5-8R; CANR 30, 69; DLB 13, 14, 194; MTCW 1, 2

Fraze, Candida (Merrill) 1945- .... **CLC 50**
See also CA 126

Frazer, J(ames) G(eorge) 1854-1941
.... **TCLC 32**
See also CA 118

Frazer, Robert Caine
See Creasey, John

Frazer, Sir James George
See Frazer, J(ames) G(eorge)

Frazier, Charles 1950- .... **CLC 109**
See also AAYA 34; CA 161

Frazier, Ian 1951- .... **CLC 46**
See also CA 130; CANR 54, 93

Frederic, Harold 1856-1898 .... **NCLC 10**
See also DLB 12, 23; DLBD 13

Frederick, John
See Faust, Frederick (Schiller)

Frederick the Great 1712-1786 .... **LC 14**

Fredro, Aleksander 1793-1876 .... **NCLC 8**

Freeling, Nicolas 1927- .... **CLC 38**
See also CA 49-52; CAAS 12; CANR 1, 17, 50, 84; DLB 87

Freeman, Douglas Southall 1886-1953
.... **TCLC 11**
See also CA 109; DLB 17; DLBD 17

Freeman, Judith 1946- .... **CLC 55**
See also CA 148

Freeman, Mary E(leanor) Wilkins 1852-1930
.... **TCLC 9; SSC 1**
See also CA 106; 177; DLB 12, 78, 221

Freeman, R(ichard) Austin 1862-1943
.... **TCLC 21**
See also CA 113; CANR 84; DLB 70

French, Albert 1943- .... **CLC 86**
See also BW 3; CA 167

French, Marilyn 1929- .... **CLC 10, 18, 60; DAM DRAM, NOV, POP**
See also CA 69-72; CANR 3, 31; INT CANR-31; MTCW 1, 2

Grunge
See Crumb, R(obert)

Grunwald, Lisa 1959- .... **CLC 44**
See also CA 120

Guare, John 1938- . **CLC 8, 14, 29, 67; DAM DRAM**
See also CA 73-76; CANR 21, 69; DLB 7; MTCW 1, 2

Gudjonsson, Halldor Kiljan 1902-1998
See Laxness, Halldor
See also CA 103; 164

Guenter, Erich
See Eich, Guenter

Guest, Barbara 1920- .... **CLC 34**
See also CA 25-28R; CANR 11, 44, 84; DLB 5, 193

Guest, Edgar A(lbert) 1881-1959 . **TCLC 95**
See also CA 112; 168

Guest, Judith (Ann) 1936- .... **CLC 8, 30; DAM NOV, POP**
See also AAYA 7; CA 77-80; CANR 15, 75; DA3; INT CANR-15; MTCW 1, 2

Guevara, Che .... **CLC 87; HLC 1**
See also Guevara (Serna), Ernesto

Guevara (Serna), Ernesto 1928-1967
.... **CLC 87; DAM MULT; HLC 1**
See also Guevara, Che
See also CA 127; 111; CANR 56; HW 1

Guicciardini, Francesco 1483-1540 ... **LC 49**

Guild, Nicholas M. 1944- .... **CLC 33**
See also CA 93-96

Guillemin, Jacques
See Sartre, Jean-Paul

Guillen, Jorge 1893-1984 ..... **CLC 11; DAM MULT, POET; HLCS 1**
See also CA 89-92; 112; DLB 108; HW 1

Guillen, Nicolas (Cristobal) 1902-1989
.... **CLC 48, 79; BLC 2; DAM MST, MULT, POET; HLC 1; PC 23**
See also BW 2; CA 116; 125; 129; CANR 84; HW 1

Guillevic, (Eugene) 1907- .... **CLC 33**
See also CA 93-96

Guillois
See Desnos, Robert

Guillois, Valentin
See Desnos, Robert

Guimaraes Rosa, Joao 1908-1967
See also CA 175; HLCS 2

Guiney, Louise Imogen 1861-1920 . **TCLC 41**
See also CA 160; DLB 54

Guiraldes, Ricardo (Guillermo) 1886-1927
.... **TCLC 39**
See also CA 131; HW 1; MTCW 1

Gumilev, Nikolai (Stepanovich) 1886-1921
.... **TCLC 60**
See also CA 165

Gunesekera, Romesh 1954- .... **CLC 91**
See also CA 159

Gunn, Bill .... **CLC 5**
See also Gunn, William Harrison
See also DLB 38

Gunn, Thom(son William) 1929- . **CLC 3, 6, 18, 32, 81; DAM POET; PC 26**
See also CA 17-20R; CANR 9, 33; CDBLB 1960 to Present; DLB 27; INT CANR-33; MTCW 1

Gunn, William Harrison 1934(?)-1989
See Gunn, Bill
See also AITN 1; BW 1, 3; CA 13-16R; 128; CANR 12, 25, 76

Gunnars, Kristjana 1948- .... **CLC 69**
See also CA 113; DLB 60

Gurdjieff, G(eorgei) I(vanovich) 1877(?)-1949 .... **TCLC 71**
See also CA 157

Gurganus, Allan 1947- . **CLC 70; DAM POP**
See also BEST 90:1; CA 135

Gurney, A(lbert) R(amsdell), Jr. 1930-
.... **CLC 32, 50, 54; DAM DRAM**
See also CA 77-80; CANR 32, 64

Gurney, Ivor (Bertie) 1890-1937 .. **TCLC 33**
See also CA 167

Gurney, Peter
See Gurney, A(lbert) R(amsdell), Jr.

Guro, Elena 1877-1913 .... **TCLC 56**

Gustafson, James M(oody) 1925- . **CLC 100**
See also CA 25-28R; CANR 37

Gustafson, Ralph (Barker) 1909- ... **CLC 36**
See also CA 21-24R; CANR 8, 45, 84; DLB 88

Gut, Gom
See Simenon, Georges (Jacques Christian)

Guterson, David 1956- .... **CLC 91**
See also CA 132; CANR 73; MTCW 2

Guthrie, A(lfred) B(ertram), Jr. 1901-1991
.... **CLC 23**
See also CA 57-60; 134; CANR 24; DLB 212; SATA 62; SATA-Obit 67

Guthrie, Isobel
See Grieve, C(hristopher) M(urray)

Guthrie, Woodrow Wilson 1912-1967
See Guthrie, Woody
See also CA 113; 93-96

Guthrie, Woody .... **CLC 35**
See also Guthrie, Woodrow Wilson

Gutierrez Najera, Manuel 1859-1895
See also HLCS 2

Guy, Rosa (Cuthbert) 1928- .... **CLC 26**
See also AAYA 4, 37; BW 2; CA 17-20R; CANR 14, 34, 83; CLR 13; DLB 33; JRDA; MAICYA; SATA 14, 62

Gwendolyn
See Bennett, (Enoch) Arnold

H. D. .... **CLC 3, 8, 14, 31, 34, 73; PC 5**
See also Doolittle, Hilda

H. de V.
See Buchan, John

Haavikko, Paavo Juhani 1931- . **CLC 18, 34**
See also CA 106

Habbema, Koos
See Heijermans, Herman

Habermas, Juergen 1929- .... **CLC 104**
See also CA 109; CANR 85

Habermas, Jurgen
See Habermas, Juergen

Hacker, Marilyn 1942- ..... **CLC 5, 9, 23, 72, 91; DAM POET**
See also CA 77-80; CANR 68; DLB 120

Haeckel, Ernst Heinrich (Philipp August) 1834-1919 .... **TCLC 83**
See also CA 157

Hafiz c. 1326-1389 .... **CMLC 34**

Hafiz c. 1326-1389(?) .... **CMLC 34**

Haggard, H(enry) Rider 1856-1925
.... **TCLC 11**
See also CA 108; 148; DLB 70, 156, 174, 178; MTCW 2; SATA 16

Hagiosy, L.
See Larbaud, Valery (Nicolas)

Hagiwara Sakutaro 1886-1942 .... **TCLC 60; PC 18**

Haig, Fenil
See Ford, Ford Madox

Haig-Brown, Roderick (Langmere) 1908-1976 .... **CLC 21**
See also CA 5-8R; 69-72; CANR 4, 38, 83; CLR 31; DLB 88; MAICYA; SATA 12

Hailey, Arthur 1920- .... **CLC 5; DAM NOV, POP**
See also AITN 2; BEST 90:3; CA 1-4R; CANR 2, 36, 75; DLB 88; DLBY 82; MTCW 1, 2

Hailey, Elizabeth Forsythe 1938- .... **CLC 40**
See also CA 93-96; CAAS 1; CANR 15, 48; INT CANR-15

Haines, John (Meade) 1924- .... **CLC 58**
See also CA 17-20R; CANR 13, 34; DLB 212

Hakluyt, Richard 1552-1616 .... **LC 31**

Haldeman, Joe (William) 1943- ...... **CLC 61**
See also Graham, Robert
See also CA 53-56, 179; CAAE 179; CAAS 25; CANR 6, 70, 72; DLB 8; INT CANR-6

Hale, Sarah Josepha (Buell) 1788-1879
.... **NCLC 75**
See also DLB 1, 42, 73

Halévy, Elie 1870-1937 .... **TCLC 104**

Haley, Alex(ander Murray Palmer) 1921-1992 . **CLC 8, 12, 76; BLC 2; DA; DAB; DAC; DAM MST, MULT, POP**
See also AAYA 26; BW 2, 3; CA 77-80; 136; CANR 61; CDALBS; DA3; DLB 38; MTCW 1, 2

Haliburton, Thomas Chandler 1796-1865
.... **NCLC 15**
See also DLB 11, 99

Hall, Donald (Andrew, Jr.) 1928- .... **CLC 1, 13, 37, 59; DAM POET**
See also CA 5-8R; CAAS 7; CANR 2, 44, 64; DLB 5; MTCW 1; SATA 23, 97

Hall, Frederic Sauser
See Sauser-Hall, Frederic

Hall, James
See Kuttner, Henry

Hall, James Norman 1887-1951 ... **TCLC 23**
See also CA 123; 173; SATA 21

Hall, Radclyffe -1943
See Hall, (Marguerite) Radclyffe
See also MTCW 2

Hall, (Marguerite) Radclyffe 1886-1943
.... **TCLC 12**
See also CA 110; 150; CANR 83; DLB 191

Hall, Rodney 1935- .... **CLC 51**
See also CA 109; CANR 69

Halleck, Fitz-Greene 1790-1867 ... **NCLC 47**
See also DLB 3

Halliday, Michael
See Creasey, John

Halpern, Daniel 1945- .... **CLC 14**
See also CA 33-36R; CANR 93

Hamburger, Michael (Peter Leopold) 1924-
.... **CLC 5, 14**
See also CA 5-8R; CAAS 4; CANR 2, 47; DLB 27

Hamill, Pete 1935- .... **CLC 10**
See also CA 25-28R; CANR 18, 71

Hamilton, Alexander 1755(?)-1804
.... **NCLC 49**
See also DLB 37

Hamilton, Clive
See Lewis, C(live) S(taples)

Hamilton, Edmond 1904-1977 .... **CLC 1**
See also CA 1-4R; CANR 3, 84; DLB 8; SATA 118

Hamilton, Eugene (Jacob) Lee
See Lee-Hamilton, Eugene (Jacob)

Hamilton, Franklin
See Silverberg, Robert

Hamilton, Gail
See Corcoran, Barbara

Hamilton, Mollie
See Kaye, M(ary) M(argaret)

Hamilton, (Anthony Walter) Patrick 1904-1962 .... **CLC 51**
See also CA 176; 113; DLB 191

Hamilton, Virginia 1936- ..... **CLC 26; DAM MULT**
See also AAYA 2, 21; BW 2, 3; CA 25-28R; CANR 20, 37, 73; CLR 1, 11, 40; DLB 33, 52; INT CANR-20; JRDA; MAICYA; MTCW 1, 2; SATA 4, 56, 79

Hammett, (Samuel) Dashiell 1894-1961
.... **CLC 3, 5, 10, 19, 47; SSC 17**

See also AITN 1; CA 81-84; CANR 42;
CDALB 1929-1941; DA3; DLB 226;
DLBD 6; DLBY 96; MTCW 1, 2

Hammon, Jupiter 1711(?)-1800(?) . **NCLC 5;
BLC 2; DAM MULT, POET; PC 16**
See also DLB 31, 50

Hammond, Keith
See Kuttner, Henry

Hamner, Earl (Henry), Jr. 1923- .... **CLC 12**
See also AITN 2; CA 73-76; DLB 6

Hampton, Christopher (James) 1946-
.... **CLC 4**
See also CA 25-28R; DLB 13; MTCW 1

Hamsun, Knut .... **TCLC 2, 14, 49**
See also Pedersen, Knut

Handke, Peter 1942- .. **CLC 5, 8, 10, 15, 38,
134; DAM DRAM, NOV**
See also CA 77-80; CANR 33, 75; DLB 85,
124; MTCW 1, 2

Handy, W(illiam) C(hristopher) 1873-1958
.... **TCLC 97**
See also BW 3; CA 121; 167

Hanley, James 1901-1985 .... **CLC 3, 5, 8, 13**
See also CA 73-76; 117; CANR 36; DLB
191; MTCW 1

Hannah, Barry 1942- .... **CLC 23, 38, 90**
See also CA 108; 110; CANR 43, 68; DLB
6, 234; INT 110; MTCW 1

Hannon, Ezra
See Hunter, Evan

Hansberry, Lorraine (Vivian) 1930-1965
. **CLC 17, 62; BLC 2; DA; DAB; DAC;
DAM DRAM, MST, MULT; DC 2**
See also AAYA 25; BW 1, 3; CA 109; 25-
28R; CABS 3; CANR 58; CDALB 1941-
1968; DA3; DLB 7, 38; MTCW 1, 2

Hansen, Joseph 1923- .... **CLC 38**
See also CA 29-32R; CAAS 17; CANR 16,
44, 66; DLB 226; INT CANR-16

Hansen, Martin A(lfred) 1909-1955
.... **TCLC 32**
See also CA 167; DLB 214

Hanson, Kenneth O(stlin) 1922- ..... **CLC 13**
See also CA 53-56; CANR 7

Hardwick, Elizabeth (Bruce) 1916-
.... **CLC 13; DAM NOV**
See also CA 5-8R; CANR 3, 32, 70; DA3;
DLB 6; MTCW 1, 2

Hardy, Thomas 1840-1928 . **TCLC 4, 10, 18,
32, 48, 53, 72; DA; DAB; DAC; DAM
MST, NOV, POET; PC 8; SSC 2; WLC**
See also CA 104; 123; CDBLB 1890-1914;
DA3; DLB 18, 19, 135; MTCW 1, 2

Hare, David 1947- .... **CLC 29, 58, 136**
See also CA 97-100; CANR 39, 91; DLB
13; MTCW 1

Harewood, John
See Van Druten, John (William)

Harford, Henry
See Hudson, W(illiam) H(enry)

Hargrave, Leonie
See Disch, Thomas M(ichael)

Harjo, Joy 1951- ..... **CLC 83; DAM MULT;
PC 27**
See also CA 114; CANR 35, 67, 91; DLB
120, 175; MTCW 2; NNAL

Harlan, Louis R(udolph) 1922- .... **CLC 34**
See also CA 21-24R; CANR 25, 55, 80

Harling, Robert 1951(?)- .... **CLC 53**
See also CA 147

Harmon, William (Ruth) 1938- .... **CLC 38**
See also CA 33-36R; CANR 14, 32, 35;
SATA 65

Harper, F. E. W.
See Harper, Frances Ellen Watkins

Harper, Frances E. W.
See Harper, Frances Ellen Watkins

Harper, Frances E. Watkins
See Harper, Frances Ellen Watkins

Harper, Frances Ellen
See Harper, Frances Ellen Watkins

Harper, Frances Ellen Watkins 1825-1911
.... **TCLC 14; BLC 2; DAM MULT,
POET; PC 21**
See also BW 1, 3; CA 111; 125; CANR 79;
DLB 50, 221

Harper, Michael S(teven) 1938- .. **CLC 7, 22**
See also BW 1; CA 33-36R; CANR 24;
DLB 41

Harper, Mrs. F. E. W.
See Harper, Frances Ellen Watkins

Harris, Christie (Lucy) Irwin 1907- . **CLC 12**
See also CA 5-8R; CANR 6, 83; CLR 47;
DLB 88; JRDA; MAICYA; SAAS 10;
SATA 6, 74; SATA-Essay 116

Harris, Frank 1856-1931 .... **TCLC 24**
See also CA 109; 150; CANR 80; DLB 156,
197

Harris, George Washington 1814-1869
.... **NCLC 23**
See also DLB 3, 11

Harris, Joel Chandler 1848-1908 .. **TCLC 2;
SSC 19**
See also CA 104; 137; CANR 80; CLR 49;
DLB 11, 23, 42, 78, 91; MAICYA; SATA
100; YABC 1

**Harris, John (Wyndham Parkes Lucas)
Beynon** 1903-1969
See Wyndham, John
See also CA 102; 89-92; CANR 84; SATA
118

Harris, MacDonald .... **CLC 9**
See also Heiney, Donald (William)

Harris, Mark 1922- .... **CLC 19**
See also CA 5-8R; CAAS 3; CANR 2, 55,
83; DLB 2; DLBY 80

Harris, (Theodore) Wilson 1921- .... **CLC 25**
See also BW 2, 3; CA 65-68; CAAS 16;
CANR 11, 27, 69; DLB 117; MTCW 1

Harrison, Elizabeth Cavanna 1909-
See Cavanna, Betty
See also CA 9-12R; CANR 6, 27, 85

Harrison, Harry (Max) 1925- .... **CLC 42**
See also CA 1-4R; CANR 5, 21, 84; DLB
8; SATA 4

Harrison, James (Thomas) 1937- .... **CLC 6,
14, 33, 66; SSC 19**
See also CA 13-16R; CANR 8, 51, 79;
DLBY 82; INT CANR-8

Harrison, Jim
See Harrison, James (Thomas)

Harrison, Kathryn 1961- .... **CLC 70**
See also CA 144; CANR 68

Harrison, Tony 1937- .... **CLC 43, 129**
See also CA 65-68; CANR 44; DLB 40;
MTCW 1

Harriss, Will(ard Irvin) 1922- .... **CLC 34**
See also CA 111

Harson, Sley
See Ellison, Harlan (Jay)

Hart, Ellis
See Ellison, Harlan (Jay)

Hart, Josephine 1942(?)- ...... **CLC 70; DAM
POP**
See also CA 138; CANR 70

Hart, Moss 1904-1961 .... **CLC 66; DAM
DRAM**
See also CA 109; 89-92; CANR 84; DLB 7

Harte, (Francis) Bret(t) 1836(?)-1902
... **TCLC 1, 25; DA; DAC; DAM MST;
SSC 8; WLC**
See also CA 104; 140; CANR 80; CDALB
1865-1917; DA3; DLB 12, 64, 74, 79,
186; SATA 26

Hartley, L(eslie) P(oles) 1895-1972 .. **CLC 2,
22**
See also CA 45-48; 37-40R; CANR 33;
DLB 15, 139; MTCW 1, 2

Hartman, Geoffrey H. 1929- .... **CLC 27**
See also CA 117; 125; CANR 79; DLB 67

Hartmann, Sadakichi 1867-1944 .. **TCLC 73**
See also CA 157; DLB 54

Hartmann von Aue c. 1160-c. 1205
.... **CMLC 15**
See also DLB 138

Hartmann von Aue 1170-1210 ..... **CMLC 15**

Haruf, Kent 1943- .... **CLC 34**
See also CA 149; CANR 91

Harwood, Ronald 1934- .... **CLC 32; DAM
DRAM, MST**
See also CA 1-4R; CANR 4, 55; DLB 13

Hasegawa Tatsunosuke
See Futabatei, Shimei

Hasek, Jaroslav (Matej Frantisek)
1883-1923 .... **TCLC 4**
See also CA 104; 129; MTCW 1, 2

Hass, Robert 1941- . **CLC 18, 39, 99; PC 16**
See also CA 111; CANR 30, 50, 71; DLB
105, 206; SATA 94

Hastings, Hudson
See Kuttner, Henry

Hastings, Selina .... **CLC 44**

Hathorne, John 1641-1717 .... **LC 38**

Hatteras, Amelia
See Mencken, H(enry) L(ouis)

Hatteras, Owen .... **TCLC 18**
See also Mencken, H(enry) L(ouis); Nathan,
George Jean

Hauptmann, Gerhart (Johann Robert)
1862-1946 ...... **TCLC 4; DAM DRAM;
SSC 37**
See also CA 104; 153; DLB 66, 118

Havel, Vaclav 1936- ... **CLC 25, 58, 65, 123;
DAM DRAM; DC 6**
See also CA 104; CANR 36, 63; DA3; DLB
232; MTCW 1, 2

Haviaras, Stratis .... **CLC 33**
See also Chaviaras, Strates

Hawes, Stephen 1475(?)-1523(?) .... **LC 17**
See also DLB 132

Hawkes, John (Clendennin Burne, Jr.)
1925-1998 . **CLC 1, 2, 3, 4, 7, 9, 14, 15,
27, 49**
See also CA 1-4R; 167; CANR 2, 47, 64;
DLB 2, 7, 227; DLBY 80, 98; MTCW 1,
2

Hawking, S. W.
See Hawking, Stephen W(illiam)

Hawking, Stephen W(illiam) 1942- . **CLC 63,
105**
See also AAYA 13; BEST 89:1; CA 126;
129; CANR 48; DA3; MTCW 2

Hawkins, Anthony Hope
See Hope, Anthony

Hawthorne, Julian 1846-1934 .... **TCLC 25**
See also CA 165

Hawthorne, Nathaniel 1804-1864 .. **NCLC 2,
10, 17, 23, 39, 79, 95; DA; DAB; DAC;
DAM MST, NOV; SSC 3, 29, 39; WLC**
See also AAYA 18; CDALB 1640-1865;
DA3; DLB 1, 74, 223; YABC 2

Haxton, Josephine Ayres 1921-
See Douglas, Ellen
See also CA 115; CANR 41, 83

Hayaseca y Eizaguirre, Jorge
See Echegaray (y Eizaguirre), Jose (Maria
Waldo)

Hayashi, Fumiko 1904-1951 .... **TCLC 27**
See also CA 161; DLB 180

Haycraft, Anna (Margaret) 1932-
See Ellis, Alice Thomas
See also CA 122; CANR 85, 90; MTCW 2

Hayden, Robert E(arl) 1913-1980 .... **CLC 5,
9, 14, 37; BLC 2; DA; DAC; DAM
MST, MULT, POET; PC 6**

Hume, David 1711-1776 .... **LC 7, 56**
See also DLB 104

Humphrey, William 1924-1997 .... **CLC 45**
See also CA 77-80; 160; CANR 68; DLB 212

Humphreys, Emyr Owen 1919- ...... **CLC 47**
See also CA 5-8R; CANR 3, 24; DLB 15

Humphreys, Josephine 1945- .... **CLC 34, 57**
See also CA 121; 127; INT 127

Huneker, James Gibbons 1857-1921
.... **TCLC 65**
See also DLB 71

Hungerford, Pixie
See Brinsmead, H(esba) F(ay)

Hunt, E(verette) Howard, (Jr.) 1918- . **CLC 3**
See also AITN 1; CA 45-48; CANR 2, 47

Hunt, Francesca
See Holland, Isabelle

Hunt, Howard
See Hunt, E(verette) Howard, (Jr.)

Hunt, Kyle
See Creasey, John

Hunt, (James Henry) Leigh 1784-1859
.... **NCLC 1, 70; DAM POET**
See also DLB 96, 110, 144

Hunt, Marsha 1946- .... **CLC 70**
See also BW 2, 3; CA 143; CANR 79

Hunt, Violet 1866(?)-1942 .... **TCLC 53**
See also CA 184; DLB 162, 197

Hunter, E. Waldo
See Sturgeon, Theodore (Hamilton)

Hunter, Evan 1926- . **CLC 11, 31; DAM POP**
See also CA 5-8R; CANR 5, 38, 62; DLBY 82; INT CANR-5; MTCW 1; SATA 25

Hunter, Kristin (Eggleston) 1931- .. **CLC 35**
See also AITN 1; BW 1; CA 13-16R; CANR 13; CLR 3; DLB 33; INT CANR-13; MAICYA; SAAS 10; SATA 12

Hunter, Mary
See Austin, Mary (Hunter)

Hunter, Mollie 1922- .... **CLC 21**
See also McIlwraith, Maureen Mollie Hunter
See also AAYA 13; CANR 37, 78; CLR 25; DLB 161; JRDA; MAICYA; SAAS 7; SATA 54, 106

Hunter, Robert (?)-1734 .... **LC 7**

Hurston, Zora Neale 1891-1960 . **CLC 7, 30, 61; BLC 2; DA; DAC; DAM MST, MULT, NOV; DC 12; SSC 4; WLCS**
See also AAYA 15; BW 1, 3; CA 85-88; CANR 61; CDALBS; DA3; DLB 51, 86; MTCW 1, 2

Husserl, E. G.
See Husserl, Edmund (Gustav Albrecht)

Husserl, Edmund (Gustav Albrecht) 1859-1938 .... **TCLC 100**
See also CA 116; 133

Huston, John (Marcellus) 1906-1987
.... **CLC 20**
See also CA 73-76; 123; CANR 34; DLB 26

Hustvedt, Siri 1955- .... **CLC 76**
See also CA 137

Hutten, Ulrich von 1488-1523 .... **LC 16**
See also DLB 179

Huxley, Aldous (Leonard) 1894-1963
... **CLC 1, 3, 4, 5, 8, 11, 18, 35, 79; DA; DAB; DAC; DAM MST, NOV; SSC 39; WLC**
See also AAYA 11; CA 85-88; CANR 44; CDBLB 1914-1945; DA3; DLB 36, 100, 162, 195; MTCW 1, 2; SATA 63

Huxley, T(homas) H(enry) 1825-1895
.... **NCLC 67**
See also DLB 57

Huysmans, Joris-Karl 1848-1907 .. **TCLC 7, 69**
See also CA 104; 165; DLB 123

Hwang, David Henry 1957- . **CLC 55; DAM DRAM; DC 4**
See also CA 127; 132; CANR 76; DA3; DLB 212; INT 132; MTCW 2

Hyde, Anthony 1946- .... **CLC 42**
See also CA 136

Hyde, Margaret O(ldroyd) 1917- ..... **CLC 21**
See also CA 1-4R; CANR 1, 36; CLR 23; JRDA; MAICYA; SAAS 8; SATA 1, 42, 76

Hynes, James 1956(?)- .... **CLC 65**
See also CA 164

Hypatia c. 370-415 .... **CMLC 35**

Ian, Janis 1951- .... **CLC 21**
See also CA 105; 187

Ibanez, Vicente Blasco
See Blasco Ibanez, Vicente

Ibarbourou, Juana de 1895-1979
See also HLCS 2; HW 1

Ibarguengoitia, Jorge 1928-1983 ..... **CLC 37**
See also CA 124; 113; HW 1

Ibsen, Henrik (Johan) 1828-1906 .. **TCLC 2, 8, 16, 37, 52; DA; DAB; DAC; DAM DRAM, MST; DC 2; WLC**
See also CA 104; 141; DA3

Ibuse, Masuji 1898-1993 .... **CLC 22**
See also CA 127; 141; DLB 180

Ichikawa, Kon 1915- .... **CLC 20**
See also CA 121

Ichiyo, Higuchi 1872-1896 .... **NCLC 49**

Idle, Eric 1943- .... **CLC 21**
See also Monty Python
See also CA 116; CANR 35, 91

Ignatow, David 1914-1997 . **CLC 4, 7, 14, 40**
See also CA 9-12R; 162; CAAS 3; CANR 31, 57; DLB 5

Ignotus
See Strachey, (Giles) Lytton

Ihimaera, Witi 1944- .... **CLC 46**
See also CA 77-80

Ilf, Ilya .... **TCLC 21**
See also Fainzilberg, Ilya Arnoldovich

Illyes, Gyula 1902-1983 .... **PC 16**
See also CA 114; 109

Immermann, Karl (Lebrecht) 1796-1840
.... **NCLC 4, 49**
See also DLB 133

Ince, Thomas H. 1882-1924 .... **TCLC 89**

Inchbald, Elizabeth 1753-1821 ..... **NCLC 62**
See also DLB 39, 89

Inclan, Ramon (Maria) del Valle
See Valle-Inclan, Ramon (Maria) del

Infante, G(uillermo) Cabrera
See Cabrera Infante, G(uillermo)

Ingalls, Rachel (Holmes) 1940- .... **CLC 42**
See also CA 123; 127

Ingamells, Reginald Charles
See Ingamells, Rex

Ingamells, Rex 1913-1955 .... **TCLC 35**
See also CA 167

Inge, William (Motter) 1913-1973 ... **CLC 1, 8, 19; DAM DRAM**
See also CA 9-12R; CDALB 1941-1968; DA3; DLB 7; MTCW 1, 2

Ingelow, Jean 1820-1897 .... **NCLC 39**
See also DLB 35, 163; SATA 33

Ingram, Willis J.
See Harris, Mark

Innaurato, Albert (F.) 1948(?)- . **CLC 21, 60**
See also CA 115; 122; CANR 78; INT 122

Innes, Michael
See Stewart, J(ohn) I(nnes) M(ackintosh)

Innis, Harold Adams 1894-1952 ... **TCLC 77**
See also CA 181; DLB 88

Ionesco, Eugene 1909-1994 .. **CLC 1, 4, 6, 9, 11, 15, 41, 86; DA; DAB; DAC; DAM DRAM, MST; DC 12; WLC**

See also CA 9-12R; 144; CANR 55; DA3; MTCW 1, 2; SATA 7; SATA-Obit 79

Iqbal, Muhammad 1873-1938 .... **TCLC 28**

Ireland, Patrick
See O'Doherty, Brian

Irenaeus St. 130- .... **CMLC 42**

Iron, Ralph
See Schreiner, Olive (Emilie Albertina)

Irving, John (Winslow) 1942- .. **CLC 13, 23, 38, 112; DAM NOV, POP**
See also AAYA 8; BEST 89:3; CA 25-28R; CANR 28, 73; DA3; DLB 6; DLBY 82; MTCW 1, 2

Irving, Washington 1783-1859 . **NCLC 2, 19, 95; DA; DAB; DAC; DAM MST; SSC 2, 37; WLC**
See also CDALB 1640-1865; DA3; DLB 3, 11, 30, 59, 73, 74, 186; YABC 2

Irwin, P. K.
See Page, P(atricia) K(athleen)

Isaacs, Jorge Ricardo 1837-1895 . **NCLC 70**

Isaacs, Susan 1943- ..... **CLC 32; DAM POP**
See also BEST 89:1; CA 89-92; CANR 20, 41, 65; DA3; INT CANR-20; MTCW 1, 2

Isherwood, Christopher (William Bradshaw) 1904-1986 . **CLC 1, 9, 11, 14, 44; DAM DRAM, NOV**
See also CA 13-16R; 117; CANR 35; DA3; DLB 15, 195; DLBY 86; MTCW 1, 2

Ishiguro, Kazuo 1954- . **CLC 27, 56, 59, 110; DAM NOV**
See also BEST 90:2; CA 120; CANR 49; DA3; DLB 194; MTCW 1, 2

Ishikawa, Hakuhin
See Ishikawa, Takuboku

Ishikawa, Takuboku 1886(?)-1912
.... **TCLC 15; DAM POET; PC 10**
See also CA 113; 153

Iskander, Fazil 1929- .... **CLC 47**
See also CA 102

Isler, Alan (David) 1934- .... **CLC 91**
See also CA 156

Ivan IV 1530-1584 .... **LC 17**

Ivanov, Vyacheslav Ivanovich 1866-1949
.... **TCLC 33**
See also CA 122

Ivask, Ivar Vidrik 1927-1992 .... **CLC 14**
See also CA 37-40R; 139; CANR 24

Ives, Morgan
See Bradley, Marion Zimmer

Izumi Shikibu c. 973-c. 1034 .... **CMLC 33**

J. R. S.
See Gogarty, Oliver St. John

Jabran, Kahlil
See Gibran, Kahlil

Jabran, Khalil
See Gibran, Kahlil

Jackson, Daniel
See Wingrove, David (John)

Jackson, Helen Hunt 1830-1885 ... **NCLC 90**
See also DLB 42, 47, 186, 189

Jackson, Jesse 1908-1983 .... **CLC 12**
See also BW 1; CA 25-28R; 109; CANR 27; CLR 28; MAICYA; SATA 2, 29; SATA-Obit 48

Jackson, Laura (Riding) 1901-1991
See Riding, Laura
See also CA 65-68; 135; CANR 28, 89; DLB 48

Jackson, Sam
See Trumbo, Dalton

Jackson, Sara
See Wingrove, David (John)

Jackson, Shirley 1919-1965 ...... **CLC 11, 60, 87; DA; DAC; DAM MST; SSC 9, 39; WLC**

See also AAYA 9; CA 1-4R; 25-28R; CANR 4, 52; CDALB 1941-1968; DA3; DLB 6, 234; MTCW 2; SATA 2

Jacob, (Cyprien-)Max 1876-1944 ... **TCLC 6**
See also CA 104

Jacobs, Harriet A(nn) 1813(?)-1897
.... **NCLC 67**

Jacobs, Jim 1942- .... **CLC 12**
See also CA 97-100; INT 97-100

Jacobs, W(illiam) W(ymark) 1863-1943
.... **TCLC 22**
See also CA 121; 167; DLB 135

Jacobsen, Jens Peter 1847-1885 ... **NCLC 34**

Jacobsen, Josephine 1908- .... **CLC 48, 102**
See also CA 33-36R; CAAS 18; CANR 23, 48

Jacobson, Dan 1929- .... **CLC 4, 14**
See also CA 1-4R; CANR 2, 25, 66; DLB 14, 207, 225; MTCW 1

Jacqueline
See Carpentier (y Valmont), Alejo

Jagger, Mick 1944- .... **CLC 17**

Jahiz, al- c. 780-c. 869 .... **CMLC 25**

Jakes, John (William) 1932- . **CLC 29; DAM NOV, POP**
See also AAYA 32; BEST 89:4; CA 57-60; CANR 10, 43, 66; DA3; DLBY 83; INT CANR-10; MTCW 1, 2; SATA 62

James, Andrew
See Kirkup, James

James, C(yril) L(ionel) R(obert) 1901-1989
.... **CLC 33; BLCS**
See also BW 2; CA 117; 125; 128; CANR 62; DLB 125; MTCW 1

James, Daniel (Lewis) 1911-1988
See Santiago, Danny
See also CA 174; 125

James, Dynely
See Mayne, William (James Carter)

James, Henry Sr. 1811-1882 .... **NCLC 53**

James, Henry 1843-1916 .... **TCLC 2, 11, 24, 40, 47, 64; DA; DAB; DAC; DAM MST, NOV; SSC 8, 32; WLC**
See also CA 104; 132; CDALB 1865-1917; DA3; DLB 12, 71, 74, 189; DLBD 13; MTCW 1, 2

James, M. R.
See James, Montague (Rhodes)
See also DLB 156

James, Montague (Rhodes) 1862-1936
.... **TCLC 6; SSC 16**
See also CA 104; DLB 201

James, P. D. 1920- .... **CLC 18, 46, 122**
See also White, Phyllis Dorothy James
See also BEST 90:2; CDBLB 1960 to Present; DLB 87; DLBD 17

James, Philip
See Moorcock, Michael (John)

James, William 1842-1910 ...... **TCLC 15, 32**
See also CA 109

James I 1394-1437 .... **LC 20**

Jameson, Anna 1794-1860 .... **NCLC 43**
See also DLB 99, 166

Jami, Nur al-Din 'Abd al-Rahman 1414-1492 .... **LC 9**

Jammes, Francis 1868-1938 .... **TCLC 75**

Jandl, Ernst 1925- .... **CLC 34**

Janowitz, Tama 1957- . **CLC 43; DAM POP**
See also CA 106; CANR 52, 89

Japrisot, Sebastien 1931- .... **CLC 90**

Jarrell, Randall 1914-1965 .. **CLC 1, 2, 6, 9, 13, 49; DAM POET**
See also CA 5-8R; 25-28R; CABS 2; CANR 6, 34; CDALB 1941-1968; CLR 6; DLB 48, 52; MAICYA; MTCW 1, 2; SATA 7

Jarry, Alfred 1873-1907 . **TCLC 2, 14; DAM DRAM; SSC 20**
See also CA 104; 153; DA3; DLB 192

Jawien, Andrzej
See John Paul II, Pope

Jaynes, Roderick
See Coen, Ethan

Jeake, Samuel, Jr.
See Aiken, Conrad (Potter)

Jean Paul 1763-1825 .... **NCLC 7**

Jefferies, (John) Richard 1848-1887
.... **NCLC 47**
See also DLB 98, 141; SATA 16

Jeffers, (John) Robinson 1887-1962 . **CLC 2, 3, 11, 15, 54; DA; DAC; DAM MST, POET; PC 17; WLC**
See also CA 85-88; CANR 35; CDALB 1917-1929; DLB 45, 212; MTCW 1, 2

Jefferson, Janet
See Mencken, H(enry) L(ouis)

Jefferson, Thomas 1743-1826 .... **NCLC 11**
See also CDALB 1640-1865; DA3; DLB 31

Jeffrey, Francis 1773-1850 .... **NCLC 33**
See also DLB 107

Jelakowitch, Ivan
See Heijermans, Herman

Jellicoe, (Patricia) Ann 1927- .... **CLC 27**
See also CA 85-88; DLB 13, 233

Jemyma
See Holley, Marietta

Jen, Gish .... **CLC 70**
See also Jen, Lillian

Jen, Lillian 1956(?)-
See Jen, Gish
See also CA 135; CANR 89

Jenkins, (John) Robin 1912- .... **CLC 52**
See also CA 1-4R; CANR 1; DLB 14

Jennings, Elizabeth (Joan) 1926- ..... **CLC 5, 14, 131**
See also CA 61-64; CAAS 5; CANR 8, 39, 66; DLB 27; MTCW 1; SATA 66

Jennings, Waylon 1937- .... **CLC 21**

Jensen, Johannes V. 1873-1950 ..... **TCLC 41**
See also CA 170; DLB 214

Jensen, Laura (Linnea) 1948- .... **CLC 37**
See also CA 103

Jerome, Jerome K(lapka) 1859-1927
.... **TCLC 23**
See also CA 119; 177; DLB 10, 34, 135

Jerrold, Douglas William 1803-1857
.... **NCLC 2**
See also DLB 158, 159

Jewett, (Theodora) Sarah Orne 1849-1909
.... **TCLC 1, 22; SSC 6**
See also CA 108; 127; CANR 71; DLB 12, 74, 221; SATA 15

Jewsbury, Geraldine (Endsor) 1812-1880
.... **NCLC 22**
See also DLB 21

Jhabvala, Ruth Prawer 1927- . **CLC 4, 8, 29, 94, 138; DAB; DAM NOV**
See also CA 1-4R; CANR 2, 29, 51, 74, 91; DLB 139, 194; INT CANR-29; MTCW 1, 2

Jibran, Kahlil
See Gibran, Kahlil

Jibran, Khalil
See Gibran, Kahlil

Jiles, Paulette 1943- .... **CLC 13, 58**
See also CA 101; CANR 70

Jimenez (Mantecon), Juan Ramon 1881-1958 .... **TCLC 4; DAM MULT, POET; HLC 1; PC 7**
See also CA 104; 131; CANR 74; DLB 134; HW 1; MTCW 1, 2

Jimenez, Ramon
See Jimenez (Mantecon), Juan Ramon

Jimenez Mantecon, Juan
See Jimenez (Mantecon), Juan Ramon

Jin, Ha
See Jin, Xuefei

Jin, Xuefei 1956- .... **CLC 109**
See also CA 152; CANR 91

Joel, Billy .... **CLC 26**
See also Joel, William Martin

Joel, William Martin 1949-
See Joel, Billy
See also CA 108

John, Saint 7th cent. - .... **CMLC 27**

John of the Cross, St. 1542-1591 .... **LC 18**

John Paul II, Pope 1920- .... **CLC 128**
See also CA 106; 133

Johnson, B(ryan) S(tanley William) 1933-1973 .... **CLC 6, 9**
See also CA 9-12R; 53-56; CANR 9; DLB 14, 40

Johnson, Benj. F. of Boo
See Riley, James Whitcomb

Johnson, Benjamin F. of Boo
See Riley, James Whitcomb

Johnson, Charles (Richard) 1948- ... **CLC 7, 51, 65; BLC 2; DAM MULT**
See also BW 2, 3; CA 116; CAAS 18; CANR 42, 66, 82; DLB 33; MTCW 2

Johnson, Denis 1949- .... **CLC 52**
See also CA 117; 121; CANR 71; DLB 120

Johnson, Diane 1934- .... **CLC 5, 13, 48**
See also CA 41-44R; CANR 17, 40, 62; DLBY 80; INT CANR-17; MTCW 1

Johnson, Eyvind (Olof Verner) 1900-1976
.... **CLC 14**
See also CA 73-76; 69-72; CANR 34

Johnson, J. R.
See James, C(yril) L(ionel) R(obert)

Johnson, James Weldon 1871-1938
...... **TCLC 3, 19; BLC 2; DAM MULT, POET; PC 24**
See also BW 1, 3; CA 104; 125; CANR 82; CDALB 1917-1929; CLR 32; DA3; DLB 51; MTCW 1, 2; SATA 31

Johnson, Joyce 1935- .... **CLC 58**
See also CA 125; 129

Johnson, Judith (Emlyn) 1936- .. **CLC 7, 15**
See also Sherwin, Judith Johnson
See also CA 25-28R; 153; CANR 34

Johnson, Lionel (Pigot) 1867-1902
.... **TCLC 19**
See also CA 117; DLB 19

Johnson, Marguerite (Annie)
See Angelou, Maya

Johnson, Mel
See Malzberg, Barry N(athaniel)

Johnson, Pamela Hansford 1912-1981
.... **CLC 1, 7, 27**
See also CA 1-4R; 104; CANR 2, 28; DLB 15; MTCW 1, 2

Johnson, Robert 1911(?)-1938 ...... **TCLC 69**
See also BW 3; CA 174

Johnson, Samuel 1709-1784 . **LC 15, 52; DA; DAB; DAC; DAM MST; WLC**
See also CDBLB 1660-1789; DLB 39, 95, 104, 142

Johnson, Uwe 1934-1984 . **CLC 5, 10, 15, 40**
See also CA 1-4R; 112; CANR 1, 39; DLB 75; MTCW 1

Johnston, George (Benson) 1913- ... **CLC 51**
See also CA 1-4R; CANR 5, 20; DLB 88

Johnston, Jennifer (Prudence) 1930- . **CLC 7**
See also CA 85-88; CANR 92; DLB 14

Joinville, Jean de 1224(?)-1317 ... **CMLC 38**

Jolley, (Monica) Elizabeth 1923- ... **CLC 46; SSC 19**
See also CA 127; CAAS 13; CANR 59

Jones, Arthur Llewellyn 1863-1947
See Machen, Arthur
See also CA 104; 179

Jones, D(ouglas) G(ordon) 1929- .... **CLC 10**

See also CA 89-92; CANR 24, 60; MTCW
1, 2; SATA 62

Kaye, Mollie
See Kaye, M(ary) M(argaret)

Kaye-Smith, Sheila 1887-1956 ...... **TCLC 20**
See also CA 118; DLB 36

Kaymor, Patrice Maguilene
See Senghor, Leopold Sedar

Kazakov, Yuri Pavlovich 1927-1982 . **SSC 43**
See also CA 5-8R; CANR 36; MTCW 1

Kazan, Elia 1909- .... **CLC 6, 16, 63**
See also CA 21-24R; CANR 32, 78

Kazantzakis, Nikos 1883(?)-1957 .. **TCLC 2,
5, 33**
See also CA 105; 132; DA3; MTCW 1, 2

Kazin, Alfred 1915-1998 .... **CLC 34, 38, 119**
See also CA 1-4R; CAAS 7; CANR 1, 45,
79; DLB 67

Keane, Mary Nesta (Skrine) 1904-1996
See Keane, Molly
See also CA 108; 114; 151

Keane, Molly .... **CLC 31**
See Keane, Mary Nesta (Skrine)
See also INT 114

Keates, Jonathan 1946(?)- .... **CLC 34**
See also CA 163

Keaton, Buster 1895-1966 .... **CLC 20**

Keats, John 1795-1821 .... **NCLC 8, 73; DA;
DAB; DAC; DAM MST, POET; PC 1;
WLC**
See also CDBLB 1789-1832; DA3; DLB
96, 110

Keble, John 1792-1866 .... **NCLC 87**
See also DLB 32, 55

Keene, Donald 1922- .... **CLC 34**
See also CA 1-4R; CANR 5

Keillor, Garrison .... **CLC 40, 115**
See also Keillor, Gary (Edward)
See also AAYA 2; BEST 89:3; DLBY 87;
SATA 58

Keillor, Gary (Edward) 1942-
See Keillor, Garrison
See also CA 111; 117; CANR 36, 59; DAM
POP; DA3; MTCW 1, 2

Keith, Michael
See Hubbard, L(afayette) Ron(ald)

Keller, Gottfried 1819-1890 .. **NCLC 2; SSC
26**
See also DLB 129

Keller, Nora Okja 1965- .... **CLC 109**
See also CA 187

Kellerman, Jonathan 1949- . **CLC 44; DAM
POP**
See also AAYA 35; BEST 90:1; CA 106;
CANR 29, 51; DA3; INT CANR-29

Kelley, William Melvin 1937- .... **CLC 22**
See also BW 1; CA 77-80; CANR 27, 83;
DLB 33

Kellogg, Marjorie 1922- .... **CLC 2**
See also CA 81-84

Kellow, Kathleen
See Hibbert, Eleanor Alice Burford

Kelly, M(ilton) T(errence) 1947- ..... **CLC 55**
See also CA 97-100; CAAS 22; CANR 19,
43, 84

Kelman, James 1946- .... **CLC 58, 86**
See also CA 148; CANR 85; DLB 194

Kemal, Yashar 1923- .... **CLC 14, 29**
See also CA 89-92; CANR 44

Kemble, Fanny 1809-1893 .... **NCLC 18**
See also DLB 32

Kemelman, Harry 1908-1996 .... **CLC 2**
See also AITN 1; CA 9-12R; 155; CANR 6,
71; DLB 28

Kempe, Margery 1373(?)-1440(?) .. **LC 6, 56**
See also DLB 146

Kempis, Thomas a 1380-1471 .... **LC 11**

Kendall, Henry 1839-1882 .... **NCLC 12**

See also DLB 230

Keneally, Thomas (Michael) 1935- .. **CLC 5,
8, 10, 14, 19, 27, 43, 117; DAM NOV**
See also CA 85-88; CANR 10, 50, 74; DA3;
MTCW 1, 2

Kennedy, Adrienne (Lita) 1931- .... **CLC 66;
BLC 2; DAM MULT; DC 5**
See also BW 2, 3; CA 103; CAAS 20;
CABS 3; CANR 26, 53, 82; DLB 38

Kennedy, John Pendleton 1795-1870
.... **NCLC 2**
See also DLB 3

Kennedy, Joseph Charles 1929-
See Kennedy, X. J.
See also CA 1-4R; CANR 4, 30, 40; SATA
14, 86

Kennedy, William 1928- . **CLC 6, 28, 34, 53;
DAM NOV**
See also AAYA 1; CA 85-88; CANR 14,
31, 76; DA3; DLB 143; DLBY 85; INT
CANR-31; MTCW 1, 2; SATA 57

Kennedy, X. J. .... **CLC 8, 42**
See also Kennedy, Joseph Charles
See also CAAS 9; CLR 27; DLB 5; SAAS
22

Kenny, Maurice (Francis) 1929- .... **CLC 87;
DAM MULT**
See also CA 144; CAAS 22; DLB 175;
NNAL

Kent, Kelvin
See Kuttner, Henry

Kenton, Maxwell
See Southern, Terry

Kenyon, Robert O.
See Kuttner, Henry

Kepler, Johannes 1571-1630 .... **LC 45**

Kerouac, Jack ..... **CLC 1, 2, 3, 5, 14, 29, 61**
See also Kerouac, Jean-Louis Lebris de
See also AAYA 25; CDALB 1941-1968;
DLB 2, 16; DLBD 3; DLBY 95; MTCW
2

Kerouac, Jean-Louis Lebris de 1922-1969
See Kerouac, Jack
See also AITN 1; CA 5-8R; 25-28R; CANR
26, 54; DA; DAB; DAC; DAM MST,
NOV, POET, POP; DA3; MTCW 1, 2;
WLC

Kerr, Jean 1923- .... **CLC 22**
See also CA 5-8R; CANR 7; INT CANR-7

Kerr, M. E. .... **CLC 12, 35**
See also Meaker, Marijane (Agnes)
See also AAYA 2, 23; CLR 29; SAAS 1

Kerr, Robert .... **CLC 55**

Kerrigan, (Thomas) Anthony 1918- . **CLC 4,
6**
See also CA 49-52; CAAS 11; CANR 4

Kerry, Lois
See Duncan, Lois

Kesey, Ken (Elton) 1935- ... **CLC 1, 3, 6, 11,
46, 64; DA; DAB; DAC; DAM MST,
NOV, POP; WLC**
See also AAYA 25; CA 1-4R; CANR 22,
38, 66; CDALB 1968-1988; DA3; DLB
2, 16, 206; MTCW 1, 2; SATA 66

Kesselring, Joseph (Otto) 1902-1967
.... **CLC 45; DAM DRAM, MST**
See also CA 150

Kessler, Jascha (Frederick) 1929- ..... **CLC 4**
See also CA 17-20R; CANR 8, 48

Kettelkamp, Larry (Dale) 1933- ..... **CLC 12**
See also CA 29-32R; CANR 16; SAAS 3;
SATA 2

Key, Ellen (Karolina Sofia) 1849-1926
.... **TCLC 65**

Keyber, Conny
See Fielding, Henry

Keyes, Daniel 1927- ..... **CLC 80; DA; DAC;
DAM MST, NOV**

See also AAYA 23; CA 17-20R, 181; CAAE
181; CANR 10, 26, 54, 74; DA3; MTCW
2; SATA 37

Keynes, John Maynard 1883-1946
.... **TCLC 64**
See also CA 114; 162, 163; DLBD 10;
MTCW 2

Khanshendel, Chiron
See Rose, Wendy

Khayyam, Omar 1048-1131 .... **CMLC 11;
DAM POET; PC 8**
See also DA3

Kherdian, David 1931- .... **CLC 6, 9**
See also CA 21-24R; CAAS 2; CANR 39,
78; CLR 24; JRDA; MAICYA; SATA 16,
74

Khlebnikov, Velimir .... **TCLC 20**
See also Khlebnikov, Viktor Vladimirovich

Khlebnikov, Viktor Vladimirovich 1885-1922
See Khlebnikov, Velimir
See also CA 117

Khodasevich, Vladislav (Felitsianovich)
1886-1939 .... **TCLC 15**
See also CA 115

Kielland, Alexander Lange 1849-1906
.... **TCLC 5**
See also CA 104

Kiely, Benedict 1919- .... **CLC 23, 43**
See also CA 1-4R; CANR 2, 84; DLB 15

Kienzle, William X(avier) 1928- .... **CLC 25;
DAM POP**
See also CA 93-96; CAAS 1; CANR 9, 31,
59; DA3; INT CANR-31; MTCW 1, 2

Kierkegaard, Soren 1813-1855 .... **NCLC 34,
78**

Kieslowski, Krzysztof 1941-1996 .. **CLC 120**
See also CA 147; 151

Killens, John Oliver 1916-1987 .... **CLC 10**
See also BW 2; CA 77-80; 123; CAAS 2;
CANR 26; DLB 33

Killigrew, Anne 1660-1685 .... **LC 4**
See also DLB 131

Killigrew, Thomas 1612-1683 .... **LC 57**
See also DLB 58

Kim
See Simenon, Georges (Jacques Christian)

Kincaid, Jamaica 1949- .... **CLC 43, 68, 137;
BLC 2; DAM MULT, NOV**
See also AAYA 13; BW 2, 3; CA 125;
CANR 47, 59; CDALBS; CLR 63; DA3;
DLB 157, 227; MTCW 2

King, Francis (Henry) 1923- ...... **CLC 8, 53;
DAM NOV**
See also CA 1-4R; CANR 1, 33, 86; DLB
15, 139; MTCW 1

King, Kennedy
See Brown, George Douglas

King, Martin Luther, Jr. 1929-1968
...... **CLC 83; BLC 2; DA; DAB; DAC;
DAM MST, MULT; WLCS**
See also BW 2, 3; CA 25-28; CANR 27,
44; CAP 2; DA3; MTCW 1, 2; SATA 14

King, Stephen (Edwin) 1947- ... **CLC 12, 26,
37, 61, 113; DAM NOV, POP; SSC 17**
See also AAYA 1, 17; BEST 90:1; CA 61-
64; CANR 1, 30, 52, 76; DA3; DLB 143;
DLBY 80; JRDA; MTCW 1, 2; SATA 9,
55

King, Steve
See King, Stephen (Edwin)

King, Thomas 1943- .. **CLC 89; DAC; DAM
MULT**
See also CA 144; DLB 175; NNAL; SATA
96

Kingman, Lee .... **CLC 17**
See also Natti, (Mary) Lee
See also SAAS 3; SATA 1, 67

Kingsley, Charles 1819-1875 .... **NCLC 35**
See also DLB 21, 32, 163, 190; YABC 2

Kingsley, Sidney 1906-1995 .... **CLC 44**
See also CA 85-88; 147; DLB 7

Kingsolver, Barbara 1955- .... **CLC 55, 81, 130; DAM POP**
See also AAYA 15; CA 129; 134; CANR 60; CDALBS; DA3; DLB 206; INT 134; MTCW 2

Kingston, Maxine (Ting Ting) Hong 1940- ...... **CLC 12, 19, 58, 121; DAM MULT, NOV; WLCS**
See also AAYA 8; CA 69-72; CANR 13, 38, 74, 87; CDALBS; DA3; DLB 173, 212; DLBY 80; INT CANR-13; MTCW 1, 2; SATA 53

Kinnell, Galway 1927- ... **CLC 1, 2, 3, 5, 13, 29, 129; PC 26**
See also CA 9-12R; CANR 10, 34, 66; DLB 5; DLBY 87; INT CANR-34; MTCW 1, 2

Kinsella, Thomas 1928- .... **CLC 4, 19, 138**
See also CA 17-20R; CANR 15; DLB 27; MTCW 1, 2

Kinsella, W(illiam) P(atrick) 1935- . **CLC 27, 43; DAC; DAM NOV, POP**
See also AAYA 7; CA 97-100; CAAS 7; CANR 21, 35, 66, 75; INT CANR-21; MTCW 1, 2

Kinsey, Alfred C(harles) 1894-1956
.... **TCLC 91**
See also CA 115; 170; MTCW 2

Kipling, (Joseph) Rudyard 1865-1936
... **TCLC 8, 17; DA; DAB; DAC; DAM MST, POET; PC 3; SSC 5; WLC**
See also AAYA 32; CA 105; 120; CANR 33; CDBLB 1890-1914; CLR 39, 65; DA3; DLB 19, 34, 141, 156; MAICYA; MTCW 1, 2; SATA 100; YABC 2

Kirkland, Caroline M. 1801-1864 . **NCLC 85**
See also DLB 3, 73, 74; DLBD 13

Kirkup, James 1918- .... **CLC 1**
See also CA 1-4R; CAAS 4; CANR 2; DLB 27; SATA 12

Kirkwood, James 1930(?)-1989 .... **CLC 9**
See also AITN 2; CA 1-4R; 128; CANR 6, 40

Kirshner, Sidney
See Kingsley, Sidney

Kis, Danilo 1935-1989 .... **CLC 57**
See also CA 109; 118; 129; CANR 61; DLB 181; MTCW 1

Kissinger, Henry A(lfred) 1923- .... **CLC 137**
See also CA 1-4R; CANR 2, 33, 66; MTCW 1

Kivi, Aleksis 1834-1872 .... **NCLC 30**

Kizer, Carolyn (Ashley) 1925- . **CLC 15, 39, 80; DAM POET**
See also CA 65-68; CAAS 5; CANR 24, 70; DLB 5, 169; MTCW 2

Klabund 1890-1928 .... **TCLC 44**
See also CA 162; DLB 66

Klappert, Peter 1942- .... **CLC 57**
See also CA 33-36R; DLB 5

Klein, A(braham) M(oses) 1909-1972
.... **CLC 19; DAB; DAC; DAM MST**
See also CA 101; 37-40R; DLB 68

Klein, Norma 1938-1989 .... **CLC 30**
See also AAYA 2, 35; CA 41-44R; 128; CANR 15, 37; CLR 2, 19; INT CANR-15; JRDA; MAICYA; SAAS 1; SATA 7, 57

Klein, T(heodore) E(ibon) D(onald) 1947-
.... **CLC 34**
See also CA 119; CANR 44, 75

Kleist, Heinrich von 1777-1811 ..... **NCLC 2, 37; DAM DRAM; SSC 22**
See also DLB 90

Klima, Ivan 1931- .... **CLC 56; DAM NOV**
See also CA 25-28R; CANR 17, 50, 91; DLB 232

Klimentov, Andrei Platonovich 1899-1951
.... **TCLC 14; SSC 42**
See also CA 108

Klinger, Friedrich Maximilian von 1752-1831 .... **NCLC 1**
See also DLB 94

Klingsor the Magician
See Hartmann, Sadakichi

Klopstock, Friedrich Gottlieb 1724-1803
.... **NCLC 11**
See also DLB 97

Knapp, Caroline 1959- .... **CLC 99**
See also CA 154

Knebel, Fletcher 1911-1993 .... **CLC 14**
See also AITN 1; CA 1-4R; 140; CAAS 3; CANR 1, 36; SATA 36; SATA-Obit 75

Knickerbocker, Diedrich
See Irving, Washington

Knight, Etheridge 1931-1991 . **CLC 40; BLC 2; DAM POET; PC 14**
See also BW 1, 3; CA 21-24R; 133; CANR 23, 82; DLB 41; MTCW 2

Knight, Sarah Kemble 1666-1727 .... **LC 7**
See also DLB 24, 200

Knister, Raymond 1899-1932 .... **TCLC 56**
See also CA 186; DLB 68

Knowles, John 1926- . **CLC 1, 4, 10, 26; DA; DAC; DAM MST, NOV**
See also AAYA 10; CA 17-20R; CANR 40, 74, 76; CDALB 1968-1988; DLB 6; MTCW 1, 2; SATA 8, 89

Knox, Calvin M.
See Silverberg, Robert

Knox, John c. 1505-1572 .... **LC 37**
See also DLB 132

Knye, Cassandra
See Disch, Thomas M(ichael)

Koch, C(hristopher) J(ohn) 1932- .. **CLC 42**
See also CA 127; CANR 84

Koch, Christopher
See Koch, C(hristopher) J(ohn)

Koch, Kenneth 1925- ... **CLC 5, 8, 44; DAM POET**
See also CA 1-4R; CANR 6, 36, 57; DLB 5; INT CANR-36; MTCW 2; SATA 65

Kochanowski, Jan 1530-1584 .... **LC 10**

Kock, Charles Paul de 1794-1871 . **NCLC 16**

Koda Rohan 1867-
See Koda Shigeyuki

Koda Shigeyuki 1867-1947 .... **TCLC 22**
See also CA 121; 183; DLB 180

Koestler, Arthur 1905-1983 . **CLC 1, 3, 6, 8, 15, 33**
See also CA 1-4R; 109; CANR 1, 33; CDBLB 1945-1960; DLBY 83; MTCW 1, 2

Kogawa, Joy Nozomi 1935- ... **CLC 78, 129; DAC; DAM MST, MULT**
See also CA 101; CANR 19, 62; MTCW 2; SATA 99

Kohout, Pavel 1928- .... **CLC 13**
See also CA 45-48; CANR 3

Koizumi, Yakumo
See Hearn, (Patricio) Lafcadio (Tessima Carlos)

Kolmar, Gertrud 1894-1943 .... **TCLC 40**
See also CA 167

Komunyakaa, Yusef 1947- .... **CLC 86, 94; BLCS**
See also CA 147; CANR 83; DLB 120

Konrad, George
See Konrad, Gyorgy

Konrad, Gyorgy 1933- .... **CLC 4, 10, 73**
See also CA 85-88; DLB 232

Konwicki, Tadeusz 1926- ...... **CLC 8, 28, 54, 117**
See also CA 101; CAAS 9; CANR 39, 59; DLB 232; MTCW 1

Koontz, Dean R(ay) 1945- ... **CLC 78; DAM NOV, POP**
See also AAYA 9, 31; BEST 89:3, 90:2; CA 108; CANR 19, 36, 52; DA3; MTCW 1; SATA 92

Kopernik, Mikolaj
See Copernicus, Nicolaus

Kopit, Arthur (Lee) 1937- ... **CLC 1, 18, 33; DAM DRAM**
See also AITN 1; CA 81-84; CABS 3; DLB 7; MTCW 1

Kops, Bernard 1926- .... **CLC 4**
See also CA 5-8R; CANR 84; DLB 13

Kornbluth, C(yril) M. 1923-1958 ... **TCLC 8**
See also CA 105; 160; DLB 8

Korolenko, V. G.
See Korolenko, Vladimir Galaktionovich

Korolenko, Vladimir
See Korolenko, Vladimir Galaktionovich

Korolenko, Vladimir G.
See Korolenko, Vladimir Galaktionovich

Korolenko, Vladimir Galaktionovich 1853-1921 .... **TCLC 22**
See also CA 121

Korzybski, Alfred (Habdank Skarbek) 1879-1950 .... **TCLC 61**
See also CA 123; 160

Kosinski, Jerzy (Nikodem) 1933-1991
.... **CLC 1, 2, 3, 6, 10, 15, 53, 70; DAM NOV**
See also CA 17-20R; 134; CANR 9, 46; DA3; DLB 2; DLBY 82; MTCW 1, 2

Kostelanetz, Richard (Cory) 1940- . **CLC 28**
See also CA 13-16R; CAAS 8; CANR 38, 77

Kotlowitz, Robert 1924- .... **CLC 4**
See also CA 33-36R; CANR 36

Kotzebue, August (Friedrich Ferdinand) von 1761-1819 .... **NCLC 25**
See also DLB 94

Kotzwinkle, William 1938- .... **CLC 5, 14, 35**
See also CA 45-48; CANR 3, 44, 84; CLR 6; DLB 173; MAICYA; SATA 24, 70

Kowna, Stancy
See Szymborska, Wislawa

Kozol, Jonathan 1936- .... **CLC 17**
See also CA 61-64; CANR 16, 45

Kozoll, Michael 1940(?)- .... **CLC 35**

Kramer, Kathryn 19(?)- .... **CLC 34**

Kramer, Larry 1935- . **CLC 42; DAM POP; DC 8**
See also CA 124; 126; CANR 60

Krasicki, Ignacy 1735-1801 .... **NCLC 8**

Krasinski, Zygmunt 1812-1859 ...... **NCLC 4**

Kraus, Karl 1874-1936 .... **TCLC 5**
See also CA 104; DLB 118

Kreve (Mickevicius), Vincas 1882-1954
.... **TCLC 27**
See also CA 170; DLB 220

Kristeva, Julia 1941- .... **CLC 77, 140**
See also CA 154

Kristofferson, Kris 1936- .... **CLC 26**
See also CA 104

Krizanc, John 1956- .... **CLC 57**
See also CA 187

Krleza, Miroslav 1893-1981 ...... **CLC 8, 114**
See also CA 97-100; 105; CANR 50; DLB 147

Kroetsch, Robert 1927- . **CLC 5, 23, 57, 132; DAC; DAM POET**
See also CA 17-20R; CANR 8, 38; DLB 53; MTCW 1

Kroetz, Franz
See Kroetz, Franz Xaver

Kroetz, Franz Xaver 1946- .... **CLC 41**
See also CA 130

Kroker, Arthur (W.) 1945- .... **CLC 77**
See also CA 161

See also BW 1, 3; CA 125; 111; CANR 82; DA; DAB; DAC; DAM MST, MULT; DA3; MTCW 1, 2

Littlewit, Humphrey Gent.
See Lovecraft, H(oward) P(hillips)

Litwos
See Sienkiewicz, Henryk (Adam Alexander Pius)

Liu, E 1857-1909 .... **TCLC 15**
See also CA 115

Lively, Penelope (Margaret) 1933- . **CLC 32, 50; DAM NOV**
See also CA 41-44R; CANR 29, 67, 79; CLR 7; DLB 14, 161, 207; JRDA; MAICYA; MTCW 1, 2; SATA 7, 60, 101

Livesay, Dorothy (Kathleen) 1909- .. **CLC 4, 15, 79; DAC; DAM MST, POET**
See also AITN 2; CA 25-28R; CAAS 8; CANR 36, 67; DLB 68; MTCW 1

Livy c. 59B.C.-c. 17 .... **CMLC 11**
See also DLB 211

Lizardi, Jose Joaquin Fernandez de 1776-1827 .... **NCLC 30**

Llewellyn, Richard
See Llewellyn Lloyd, Richard Dafydd Vivian
See also DLB 15

Llewellyn Lloyd, Richard Dafydd Vivian 1906-1983 .... **CLC 7, 80**
See Llewellyn, Richard
See also CA 53-56; 111; CANR 7, 71; SATA 11; SATA-Obit 37

Llosa, (Jorge) Mario (Pedro) Vargas
See Vargas Llosa, (Jorge) Mario (Pedro)

Lloyd, Manda
See Mander, (Mary) Jane

Lloyd Webber, Andrew 1948-
See Webber, Andrew Lloyd
See also AAYA 1; CA 116; 149; DAM DRAM; SATA 56

Llull, Ramon c. 1235-c. 1316 .... **CMLC 12**

Lobb, Ebenezer
See Upward, Allen

Locke, Alain (Le Roy) 1886-1954 . **TCLC 43; BLCS**
See also BW 1, 3; CA 106; 124; CANR 79; DLB 51

Locke, John 1632-1704 .... **LC 7, 35**
See also DLB 101

Locke-Elliott, Sumner
See Elliott, Sumner Locke

Lockhart, John Gibson 1794-1854 . **NCLC 6**
See also DLB 110, 116, 144

Lodge, David (John) 1935- .. **CLC 36; DAM POP**
See also BEST 90:1; CA 17-20R; CANR 19, 53, 92; DLB 14, 194; INT CANR-19; MTCW 1, 2

Lodge, Thomas 1558-1625 .... **LC 41**
Lodge, Thomas 1558-1625 .... **LC 41**
See also DLB 172

Loennbohm, Armas Eino Leopold 1878-1926
See Leino, Eino
See also CA 123

Loewinsohn, Ron(ald William) 1937-
.... **CLC 52**
See also CA 25-28R; CANR 71

Logan, Jake
See Smith, Martin Cruz

Logan, John (Burton) 1923-1987 ...... **CLC 5**
See also CA 77-80; 124; CANR 45; DLB 5

Lo Kuan-chung 1330(?)-1400(?) .... **LC 12**

Lombard, Nap
See Johnson, Pamela Hansford

London, Jack .... **TCLC 9, 15, 39; SSC 4; WLC**
See also London, John Griffith
See also AAYA 13; AITN 2; CDALB 1865-1917; DLB 8, 12, 78, 212; SATA 18

London, John Griffith 1876-1916
See London, Jack
See also CA 110; 119; CANR 73; DA; DAB; DAC; DAM MST, NOV; DA3; JRDA; MAICYA; MTCW 1, 2

Long, Emmett
See Leonard, Elmore (John, Jr.)

Longbaugh, Harry
See Goldman, William (W.)

Longfellow, Henry Wadsworth 1807-1882 .. **NCLC 2, 45; DA; DAB; DAC; DAM MST, POET; PC 30; WLCS**
See also CDALB 1640-1865; DA3; DLB 1, 59, 235; SATA 19

Longinus c. 1st cent. - .... **CMLC 27**
See also DLB 176

Longley, Michael 1939- .... **CLC 29**
See also CA 102; DLB 40

Longus fl. c. 2nd cent. - .... **CMLC 7**

Longway, A. Hugh
See Lang, Andrew

Lonnrot, Elias 1802-1884 .... **NCLC 53**

Lopate, Phillip 1943- .... **CLC 29**
See also CA 97-100; CANR 88; DLBY 80; INT 97-100

Lopez Portillo (y Pacheco), Jose 1920-
.... **CLC 46**
See also CA 129; HW 1

Lopez y Fuentes, Gregorio 1897(?)-1966
.... **CLC 32**
See also CA 131; HW 1

Lorca, Federico Garcia
See Garcia Lorca, Federico

Lord, Bette Bao 1938- .... **CLC 23**
See also BEST 90:3; CA 107; CANR 41, 79; INT 107; SATA 58

Lord Auch
See Bataille, Georges

Lord Byron
See Byron, George Gordon (Noel)

Lorde, Audre (Geraldine) 1934-1992
...... **CLC 18, 71; BLC 2; DAM MULT, POET; PC 12**
See also BW 1, 3; CA 25-28R; 142; CANR 16, 26, 46, 82; DA3; DLB 41; MTCW 1, 2

Lord Houghton
See Milnes, Richard Monckton

Lord Jeffrey
See Jeffrey, Francis

Lorenzini, Carlo 1826-1890
See Collodi, Carlo
See also MAICYA; SATA 29, 100

Lorenzo, Heberto Padilla
See Padilla (Lorenzo), Heberto

Loris
See Hofmannsthal, Hugo von

Loti, Pierre .... **TCLC 11**
See also Viaud, (Louis Marie) Julien
See also DLB 123

Lou, Henri
See Andreas-Salome, Lou

Louie, David Wong 1954- .... **CLC 70**
See also CA 139

Louis, Father M.
See Merton, Thomas

Lovecraft, H(oward) P(hillips) 1890-1937
.... **TCLC 4, 22; DAM POP; SSC 3**
See also AAYA 14; CA 104; 133; DA3; MTCW 1, 2

Lovelace, Earl 1935- .... **CLC 51**
See also BW 2; CA 77-80; CANR 41, 72; DLB 125; MTCW 1

Lovelace, Richard 1618-1657 .... **LC 24**
See also DLB 131

Lowell, Amy 1874-1925 ... **TCLC 1, 8; DAM POET; PC 13**

See also CA 104; 151; DLB 54, 140; MTCW 2

Lowell, James Russell 1819-1891 .. **NCLC 2, 90**
See also CDALB 1640-1865; DLB 1, 11, 64, 79, 189, 235

Lowell, Robert (Traill Spence, Jr.) 1917-1977 ... **CLC 1, 2, 3, 4, 5, 8, 9, 11, 15, 37, 124; DA; DAB; DAC; DAM MST, NOV; PC 3; WLC**
See also CA 9-12R; 73-76; CABS 2; CANR 26, 60; CDALBS; DA3; DLB 5, 169; MTCW 1, 2

Lowenthal, Michael (Francis) 1969-
.... **CLC 119**
See also CA 150

Lowndes, Marie Adelaide (Belloc) 1868-1947
.... **TCLC 12**
See also CA 107; DLB 70

Lowry, (Clarence) Malcolm 1909-1957
.... **TCLC 6, 40; SSC 31**
See also CA 105; 131; CANR 62; CDBLB 1945-1960; DLB 15; MTCW 1, 2

Lowry, Mina Gertrude 1882-1966
See Loy, Mina
See also CA 113

Loxsmith, John
See Brunner, John (Kilian Houston)

Loy, Mina ..... **CLC 28; DAM POET; PC 16**
See also Lowry, Mina Gertrude
See also DLB 4, 54

Loyson-Bridet
See Schwob, Marcel (Mayer Andre)

Lucan 39-65 .... **CMLC 33**
See also DLB 211

Lucas, Craig 1951- .... **CLC 64**
See also CA 137; CANR 71

Lucas, E(dward) V(errall) 1868-1938
.... **TCLC 73**
See also CA 176; DLB 98, 149, 153; SATA 20

Lucas, George 1944- .... **CLC 16**
See also AAYA 1, 23; CA 77-80; CANR 30; SATA 56

Lucas, Hans
See Godard, Jean-Luc

Lucas, Victoria
See Plath, Sylvia

Lucian c. 120-c. 180 .... **CMLC 32**
See also DLB 176

Ludlam, Charles 1943-1987 ...... **CLC 46, 50**
See also CA 85-88; 122; CANR 72, 86

Ludlum, Robert 1927-2001 ...... **CLC 22, 43; DAM NOV, POP**
See also AAYA 10; BEST 89:1, 90:3; CA 33-36R; CANR 25, 41, 68; DA3; DLBY 82; MTCW 1, 2

Ludwig, Ken .... **CLC 60**

Ludwig, Otto 1813-1865 .... **NCLC 4**
See also DLB 129

Lugones, Leopoldo 1874-1938 ..... **TCLC 15; HLCS 2**
See also CA 116; 131; HW 1

Lu Hsun 1881-1936 .... **TCLC 3; SSC 20**
See also Shu-Jen, Chou

Lukacs, George .... **CLC 24**
See also Lukacs, Gyorgy (Szegeny von)

Lukacs, Gyorgy (Szegeny von) 1885-1971
See Lukacs, George
See also CA 101; 29-32R; CANR 62; MTCW 2

Luke, Peter (Ambrose Cyprian) 1919-1995
.... **CLC 38**
See also CA 81-84; 147; CANR 72; DLB 13

Lunar, Dennis
See Mungo, Raymond

Lurie, Alison 1926- .... **CLC 4, 5, 18, 39**

See also DLB 21, 55, 159, 163, 166, 190;
YABC 2

Martines, Julia
See O'Faolain, Julia

Martinez, Enrique Gonzalez
See Gonzalez Martinez, Enrique

Martinez, Jacinto Benavente y
See Benavente (y Martinez), Jacinto

Martinez Ruiz, Jose 1873-1967
See Azorin; Ruiz, Jose Martinez
See also CA 93-96; HW 1

Martinez Sierra, Gregorio 1881-1947
.... **TCLC 6**
See also CA 115

Martinez Sierra, Maria (de la O'LeJarraga)
1874-1974 .... **TCLC 6**
See also CA 115

Martinsen, Martin
See Follett, Ken(neth Martin)

Martinson, Harry (Edmund) 1904-1978
.... **CLC 14**
See also CA 77-80; CANR 34

Marut, Ret
See Traven, B.

Marut, Robert
See Traven, B.

Marvell, Andrew 1621-1678 . **LC 4, 43; DA;
DAB; DAC; DAM MST, POET; PC 10;
WLC**
See also CDBLB 1660-1789; DLB 131

Marx, Karl (Heinrich) 1818-1883 . **NCLC 17**
See also DLB 129

Masaoka Shiki .... **TCLC 18**
See also Masaoka Tsunenori

Masaoka Tsunenori 1867-1902
See Masaoka Shiki
See also CA 117

Masefield, John (Edward) 1878-1967
.... **CLC 11, 47; DAM POET**
See also CA 19-20; 25-28R; CANR 33;
CAP 2; CDBLB 1890-1914; DLB 10, 19,
153, 160; MTCW 1, 2; SATA 19

Maso, Carole 19(?)- .... **CLC 44**
See also CA 170

Mason, Bobbie Ann 1940- . **CLC 28, 43, 82;
SSC 4**
See also AAYA 5; CA 53-56; CANR 11, 31,
58, 83; CDALBS; DA3; DLB 173; DLBY
87; INT CANR-31; MTCW 1, 2

Mason, Ernst
See Pohl, Frederik

Mason, Lee W.
See Malzberg, Barry N(athaniel)

Mason, Nick 1945- .... **CLC 35**

Mason, Tally
See Derleth, August (William)

Mass, William
See Gibson, William

Master Lao
See Lao Tzu

Masters, Edgar Lee 1868-1950 ...... **TCLC 2,
25; DA; DAC; DAM MST, POET; PC
1; WLCS**
See also CA 104; 133; CDALB 1865-1917;
DLB 54; MTCW 1, 2

Masters, Hilary 1928- .... **CLC 48**
See also CA 25-28R; CANR 13, 47

Mastrosimone, William 19(?)- .... **CLC 36**
See also CA 186

Mathe, Albert
See Camus, Albert

Mather, Cotton 1663-1728 .... **LC 38**
See also CDALB 1640-1865; DLB 24, 30,
140

Mather, Increase 1639-1723 .... **LC 38**
See also DLB 24

Matheson, Richard Burton 1926- ... **CLC 37**

See also AAYA 31; CA 97-100; CANR 88;
DLB 8, 44; INT 97-100

Mathews, Harry 1930- .... **CLC 6, 52**
See also CA 21-24R; CAAS 6; CANR 18,
40

Mathews, John Joseph 1894-1979 . **CLC 84;
DAM MULT**
See also CA 19-20; 142; CANR 45; CAP 2;
DLB 175; NNAL

Mathias, Roland (Glyn) 1915- .... **CLC 45**
See also CA 97-100; CANR 19, 41; DLB
27

Matsuo Basho 1644-1694 .... **LC 62; DAM
POET; PC 3**

Mattheson, Rodney
See Creasey, John

Matthews, (James) Brander 1852-1929
.... **TCLC 95**
See also DLB 71, 78; DLBD 13

Matthews, Greg 1949- .... **CLC 45**
See also CA 135

Matthews, William (Procter, III) 1942-1997
.... **CLC 40**
See also CA 29-32R; 162; CAAS 18; CANR
12, 57; DLB 5

Matthias, John (Edward) 1941- .... **CLC 9**
See also CA 33-36R; CANR 56

Matthiessen, F(rancis) O(tto) 1902-1950
.... **TCLC 100**
See also CA 185; DLB 63

Matthiessen, Peter 1927- .. **CLC 5, 7, 11, 32,
64; DAM NOV**
See also AAYA 6; BEST 90:4; CA 9-12R;
CANR 21, 50, 73; DA3; DLB 6, 173;
MTCW 1, 2; SATA 27

Maturin, Charles Robert 1780(?)-1824
.... **NCLC 6**
See also DLB 178

Matute (Ausejo), Ana Maria 1925- . **CLC 11**
See also CA 89-92; MTCW 1

Maugham, W. S.
See Maugham, W(illiam) Somerset

Maugham, W(illiam) Somerset 1874-1965
.... **CLC 1, 11, 15, 67, 93; DA; DAB;
DAC; DAM DRAM, MST, NOV; SSC
8; WLC**
See also CA 5-8R; 25-28R; CANR 40; CD-
BLB 1914-1945; DA3; DLB 10, 36, 77,
100, 162, 195; MTCW 1, 2; SATA 54

Maugham, William Somerset
See Maugham, W(illiam) Somerset

Maupassant, (Henri Rene Albert) Guy de
1850-1893 . **NCLC 1, 42, 83; DA; DAB;
DAC; DAM MST; SSC 1; WLC**
See also DA3; DLB 123

Maupin, Armistead 1944- .... **CLC 95; DAM
POP**
See also CA 125; 130; CANR 58; DA3;
INT 130; MTCW 2

Maurhut, Richard
See Traven, B.

Mauriac, Claude 1914-1996 .... **CLC 9**
See also CA 89-92; 152; DLB 83

Mauriac, Francois (Charles) 1885-1970
.... **CLC 4, 9, 56; SSC 24**
See also CA 25-28; CAP 2; DLB 65;
MTCW 1, 2

Mavor, Osborne Henry 1888-1951
See Bridie, James
See also CA 104

Maxwell, William (Keepers, Jr.) 1908-2000
.... **CLC 19**
See also CA 93-96; CANR 54; DLBY 80;
INT 93-96

May, Elaine 1932- .... **CLC 16**
See also CA 124; 142; DLB 44

Mayakovski, Vladimir (Vladimirovich)
1893-1930 .... **TCLC 4, 18**
See also CA 104; 158; MTCW 2

Mayhew, Henry 1812-1887 .... **NCLC 31**
See also DLB 18, 55, 190

Mayle, Peter 1939(?)- .... **CLC 89**
See also CA 139; CANR 64

Maynard, Joyce 1953- .... **CLC 23**
See also CA 111; 129; CANR 64

Mayne, William (James Carter) 1928-
.... **CLC 12**
See also AAYA 20; CA 9-12R; CANR 37,
80; CLR 25; JRDA; MAICYA; SAAS 11;
SATA 6, 68

Mayo, Jim
See L'Amour, Louis (Dearborn)

Maysles, Albert 1926- .... **CLC 16**
See also CA 29-32R

Maysles, David 1932- .... **CLC 16**

Mazer, Norma Fox 1931- .... **CLC 26**
See also AAYA 5, 36; CA 69-72; CANR
12, 32, 66; CLR 23; JRDA; MAICYA;
SAAS 1; SATA 24, 67, 105

Mazzini, Guiseppe 1805-1872 .... **NCLC 34**

McAlmon, Robert (Menzies) 1895-1956
.... **TCLC 97**
See also CA 107; 168; DLB 4, 45; DLBD
15

McAuley, James Phillip 1917-1976 . **CLC 45**
See also CA 97-100

McBain, Ed
See Hunter, Evan

McBrien, William (Augustine) 1930-
.... **CLC 44**
See also CA 107; CANR 90

McCabe, Patrick 1955- .... **CLC 133**
See also CA 130; CANR 50, 90; DLB 194

McCaffrey, Anne (Inez) 1926- .... **CLC 17;
DAM NOV, POP**
See also AAYA 6, 34; AITN 2; BEST 89:2;
CA 25-28R; CANR 15, 35, 55; CLR 49;
DA3; DLB 8; JRDA; MAICYA; MTCW
1, 2; SAAS 11; SATA 8, 70, 116

McCall, Nathan 1955(?)- .... **CLC 86**
See also BW 3; CA 146; CANR 88

McCann, Arthur
See Campbell, John W(ood, Jr.)

McCann, Edson
See Pohl, Frederik

McCarthy, Charles, Jr. 1933-
See McCarthy, Cormac
See also CANR 42, 69; DAM POP; DA3;
MTCW 2

McCarthy, Cormac 1933- .... **CLC 4, 57, 59,
101**
See also McCarthy, Charles, Jr.
See also DLB 6, 143; MTCW 2

McCarthy, Mary (Therese) 1912-1989
..... **CLC 1, 3, 5, 14, 24, 39, 59; SSC 24**
See also CA 5-8R; 129; CANR 16, 50, 64;
DA3; DLB 2; DLBY 81; INT CANR-16;
MTCW 1, 2

McCartney, (James) Paul 1942- ..... **CLC 12,
35**
See also CA 146

McCauley, Stephen (D.) 1955- .... **CLC 50**
See also CA 141

McClure, Michael (Thomas) 1932- .. **CLC 6,
10**
See also CA 21-24R; CANR 17, 46, 77;
DLB 16

McCorkle, Jill (Collins) 1958- .... **CLC 51**
See also CA 121; DLB 234; DLBY 87

McCourt, Frank 1930- .... **CLC 109**
See also CA 157

McCourt, James 1941- .... **CLC 5**
See also CA 57-60

McCourt, Malachy 1932- .... **CLC 119**

McCoy, Horace (Stanley) 1897-1955
.... **TCLC 28**
See also CA 108; 155; DLB 9

Meyer, June
See Jordan, June
Meyer, Lynn
See Slavitt, David R(ytman)
Meyer-Meyrink, Gustav 1868-1932
See Meyrink, Gustav
See also CA 117
Meyers, Jeffrey 1939- .... **CLC 39**
See also CA 73-76; CAAE 186; CANR 54;
DLB 111
Meynell, Alice (Christina Gertrude
Thompson) 1847-1922 .... **TCLC 6**
See also CA 104; 177; DLB 19, 98
Meyrink, Gustav .... **TCLC 21**
See also Meyer-Meyrink, Gustav
See also DLB 81
Michaels, Leonard 1933- ... **CLC 6, 25; SSC**
16
See also CA 61-64; CANR 21, 62; DLB
130; MTCW 1
Michaux, Henri 1899-1984 .... **CLC 8, 19**
See also CA 85-88; 114
Micheaux, Oscar (Devereaux) 1884-1951
.... **TCLC 76**
See also BW 3; CA 174; DLB 50
Michelangelo 1475-1564 .... **LC 12**
Michelet, Jules 1798-1874 .... **NCLC 31**
Michels, Robert 1876-1936 .... **TCLC 88**
Michener, James A(lbert) 1907(?)-1997
. **CLC 1, 5, 11, 29, 60, 109; DAM NOV,**
POP
See also AAYA 27; AITN 1; BEST 90:1;
CA 5-8R; 161; CANR 21, 45, 68; DA3;
DLB 6; MTCW 1, 2
Mickiewicz, Adam 1798-1855 .... **NCLC 3**
Middleton, Christopher 1926- .... **CLC 13**
See also CA 13-16R; CANR 29, 54; DLB
40
Middleton, Richard (Barham) 1882-1911
.... **TCLC 56**
See also CA 187; DLB 156
Middleton, Stanley 1919- .... **CLC 7, 38**
See also CA 25-28R; CAAS 23; CANR 21,
46, 81; DLB 14
Middleton, Thomas 1580-1627 .... **LC 33;**
DAM DRAM, MST; DC 5
See also DLB 58
Migueis, Jose Rodrigues 1901- .... **CLC 10**
Mikszath, Kalman 1847-1910 .... **TCLC 31**
See also CA 170
Miles, Jack .... **CLC 100**
Miles, Josephine (Louise) 1911-1985 . **CLC 1,**
2, 14, 34, 39; DAM POET
See also CA 1-4R; 116; CANR 2, 55; DLB
48
Militant
See Sandburg, Carl (August)
Mill, John Stuart 1806-1873 ... **NCLC 11, 58**
See also CDBLB 1832-1890; DLB 55, 190
Millar, Kenneth 1915-1983 .. **CLC 14; DAM**
POP
See also Macdonald, Ross
See also CA 9-12R; 110; CANR 16, 63;
DA3; DLB 2, 226; DLBD 6; DLBY 83;
MTCW 1, 2
Millay, E. Vincent
See Millay, Edna St. Vincent
Millay, Edna St. Vincent 1892-1950
... **TCLC 4, 49; DA; DAB; DAC; DAM**
MST, POET; PC 6; WLCS
See also CA 104; 130; CDALB 1917-1929;
DA3; DLB 45; MTCW 1, 2
Miller, Arthur 1915- ..... **CLC 1, 2, 6, 10, 15,**
26, 47, 78; DA; DAB; DAC; DAM
DRAM, MST; DC 1; WLC
See also AAYA 15; AITN 1; CA 1-4R;
CABS 3; CANR 2, 30, 54, 76; CDALB
1941-1968; DA3; DLB 7; MTCW 1, 2
Miller, Henry (Valentine) 1891-1980 . **CLC 1,**
2, 4, 9, 14, 43, 84; DA; DAB; DAC;
DAM MST, NOV; WLC
See also CA 9-12R; 97-100; CANR 33, 64;
CDALB 1929-1941; DA3; DLB 4, 9;
DLBY 80; MTCW 1, 2
Miller, Jason 1939(?)- .... **CLC 2**
See also AITN 1; CA 73-76; DLB 7
Miller, Sue 1943- .... **CLC 44; DAM POP**
See also BEST 90:3; CA 139; CANR 59,
91; DA3; DLB 143
Miller, Walter M(ichael, Jr.) 1923- .. **CLC 4,**
30
See also CA 85-88; DLB 8
Millett, Kate 1934- .... **CLC 67**
See also AITN 1; CA 73-76; CANR 32, 53,
76; DA3; MTCW 1, 2
Millhauser, Steven (Lewis) 1943- ... **CLC 21,**
54, 109
See also CA 110; 111; CANR 63; DA3;
DLB 2; INT 111; MTCW 2
Millin, Sarah Gertrude 1889-1968 . **CLC 49**
See also CA 102; 93-96; DLB 225
Milne, A(lan) A(lexander) 1882-1956
. **TCLC 6, 88; DAB; DAC; DAM MST**
See also CA 104; 133; CLR 1, 26; DA3;
DLB 10, 77, 100, 160; MAICYA; MTCW
1, 2; SATA 100; YABC 1
Milner, Ron(ald) 1938- ..... **CLC 56; BLC 3;**
DAM MULT
See also AITN 1; BW 1; CA 73-76; CANR
24, 81; DLB 38; MTCW 1
Milnes, Richard Monckton 1809-1885
.... **NCLC 61**
See also DLB 32, 184
Milosz, Czeslaw 1911- .... **CLC 5, 11, 22, 31,**
56, 82; DAM MST, POET; PC 8; WLCS
See also CA 81-84; CANR 23, 51, 91; DA3;
MTCW 1, 2
Milton, John 1608-1674 .... **LC 9, 43; DA;**
DAB; DAC; DAM MST, POET; PC 19,
29; WLC
See also CDBLB 1660-1789; DA3; DLB
131, 151
Min, Anchee 1957- .... **CLC 86**
See also CA 146; CANR 94
Minehaha, Cornelius
See Wedekind, (Benjamin) Frank(lin)
Miner, Valerie 1947- .... **CLC 40**
See also CA 97-100; CANR 59
Minimo, Duca
See D'Annunzio, Gabriele
Minot, Susan 1956- .... **CLC 44**
See also CA 134
Minus, Ed 1938- .... **CLC 39**
See also CA 185
Miranda, Javier
See Bioy Casares, Adolfo
Miranda, Javier
See Bioy Casares, Adolfo
Mirbeau, Octave 1848-1917 .... **TCLC 55**
See also DLB 123, 192
Miro (Ferrer), Gabriel (Francisco Victor)
1879-1930 .... **TCLC 5**
See also CA 104; 185
Mishima, Yukio 1925-1970 .. **CLC 2, 4, 6, 9,**
27; DC 1; SSC 4
See also Hiraoka, Kimitake
See also DLB 182; MTCW 2
Mistral, Frederic 1830-1914 .... **TCLC 51**
See also CA 122
Mistral, Gabriela
See Godoy Alcayaga, Lucila
Mistry, Rohinton 1952- .... **CLC 71; DAC**
See also CA 141; CANR 86
Mitchell, Clyde
See Ellison, Harlan (Jay); Silverberg, Robert

Mitchell, James Leslie 1901-1935
See Gibbon, Lewis Grassic
See also CA 104; DLB 15
Mitchell, Joni 1943- .... **CLC 12**
See also CA 112
Mitchell, Joseph (Quincy) 1908-1996
.... **CLC 98**
See also CA 77-80; 152; CANR 69; DLB
185; DLBY 96
Mitchell, Margaret (Munnerlyn) 1900-1949
.... **TCLC 11; DAM NOV, POP**
See also AAYA 23; CA 109; 125; CANR
55, 94; CDALBS; DA3; DLB 9; MTCW
1, 2
Mitchell, Peggy
See Mitchell, Margaret (Munnerlyn)
Mitchell, S(ilas) Weir 1829-1914 .. **TCLC 36**
See also CA 165; DLB 202
Mitchell, W(illiam) O(rmond) 1914-1998
.... **CLC 25; DAC; DAM MST**
See also CA 77-80; 165; CANR 15, 43;
DLB 88
Mitchell, William 1879-1936 .... **TCLC 81**
Mitford, Mary Russell 1787-1855 .. **NCLC 4**
See also DLB 110, 116
Mitford, Nancy 1904-1973 .... **CLC 44**
See also CA 9-12R; DLB 191
Miyamoto, (Chujo) Yuriko 1899-1951
.... **TCLC 37**
See also CA 170, 174; DLB 180
Miyazawa, Kenji 1896-1933 .... **TCLC 76**
See also CA 157
Mizoguchi, Kenji 1898-1956 .... **TCLC 72**
See also CA 167
Mo, Timothy (Peter) 1950(?)- . **CLC 46, 134**
See also CA 117; DLB 194; MTCW 1
Modarressi, Taghi (M.) 1931- .... **CLC 44**
See also CA 121; 134; INT 134
Modiano, Patrick (Jean) 1945- .... **CLC 18**
See also CA 85-88; CANR 17, 40; DLB 83
Moerck, Paal
See Roelvaag, O(le) E(dvart)
Mofolo, Thomas (Mokopu) 1875(?)-1948
.... **TCLC 22; BLC 3; DAM MULT**
See also CA 121; 153; CANR 83; DLB 225;
MTCW 2
Mohr, Nicholasa 1938- .... **CLC 12; DAM**
MULT; HLC 2
See also AAYA 8; CA 49-52; CANR 1, 32,
64; CLR 22; DLB 145; HW 1, 2; JRDA;
SAAS 8; SATA 8, 97; SATA-Essay 113
Mojtabai, A(nn) G(race) 1938- .... **CLC 5, 9,**
15, 29
See also CA 85-88; CANR 88
Moliére 1622-1673 .... **LC 10, 28, 64; DA;**
DAB; DAC; DAM DRAM, MST; DC
13; WLC
See also DA3
Molin, Charles
See Mayne, William (James Carter)
Molnar, Ferenc 1878-1952 . **TCLC 20; DAM**
DRAM
See also CA 109; 153; CANR 83
Momaday, N(avarre) Scott 1934- .... **CLC 2,**
19, 85, 95; DA; DAB; DAC; DAM MST,
MULT, NOV, POP; PC 25; WLCS
See also AAYA 11; CA 25-28R; CANR 14,
34, 68; CDALBS; DA3; DLB 143, 175;
INT CANR-14; MTCW 1, 2; NNAL;
SATA 48; SATA-Brief 30
Monette, Paul 1945-1995 .... **CLC 82**
See also CA 139; 147
Monroe, Harriet 1860-1936 .... **TCLC 12**
See also CA 109; DLB 54, 91
Monroe, Lyle
See Heinlein, Robert A(nson)
Montagu, Elizabeth 1720-1800 .... **NCLC 7**
Montagu, Mary (Pierrepont) Wortley
1689-1762 .... **LC 9, 57; PC 16**

Mphahlele, Es'kia
See Mphahlele, Ezekiel
See also DLB 125, 225

Mphahlele, Ezekiel 1919- .... **CLC 25, 133; BLC 3; DAM MULT**
See also Mphahlele, Es'kia
See also BW 2, 3; CA 81-84; CANR 26, 76; DA3; DLB 225; MTCW 2; SATA 119

Mqhayi, S(amuel) E(dward) K(rune Loliwe) 1875-1945 ..... **TCLC 25; BLC 3; DAM MULT**
See also CA 153; CANR 87

Mrozek, Slawomir 1930- .... **CLC 3, 13**
See also CA 13-16R; CAAS 10; CANR 29; DLB 232; MTCW 1

Mrs. Belloc-Lowndes
See Lowndes, Marie Adelaide (Belloc)

M'Taggart, John M'Taggart Ellis
See McTaggart, John McTaggart Ellis

Mtwa, Percy (?)- .... **CLC 47**

Mueller, Lisel 1924- ...... **CLC 13, 51; PC 33**
See also CA 93-96; DLB 105

Muir, Edwin 1887-1959 .... **TCLC 2, 87**
See also CA 104; DLB 20, 100, 191

Muir, John 1838-1914 .... **TCLC 28**
See also CA 165; DLB 186

Mujica Lainez, Manuel 1910-1984 . **CLC 31**
See also Lainez, Manuel Mujica
See also CA 81-84; 112; CANR 32; HW 1

Mukherjee, Bharati 1940- ...... **CLC 53, 115; DAM NOV; SSC 38**
See also BEST 89:2; CA 107; CANR 45, 72; DLB 60; MTCW 1, 2

Muldoon, Paul 1951- ...... **CLC 32, 72; DAM POET**
See also CA 113; 129; CANR 52, 91; DLB 40; INT 129

Mulisch, Harry 1927- .... **CLC 42**
See also CA 9-12R; CANR 6, 26, 56

Mull, Martin 1943- .... **CLC 17**
See also CA 105

Muller, Wilhelm .... **NCLC 73**

Mulock, Dinah Maria
See Craik, Dinah Maria (Mulock)

Munford, Robert 1737(?)-1783 .... **LC 5**
See also DLB 31

Mungo, Raymond 1946- .... **CLC 72**
See also CA 49-52; CANR 2

Munro, Alice 1931- .. **CLC 6, 10, 19, 50, 95; DAC; DAM MST, NOV; SSC 3; WLCS**
See also AITN 2; CA 33-36R; CANR 33, 53, 75; DA3; DLB 53; MTCW 1, 2; SATA 29

Munro, H(ector) H(ugh) 1870-1916
See Saki
See also CA 104; 130; CDBLB 1890-1914; DA; DAB; DAC; DAM MST, NOV; DA3; DLB 34, 162; MTCW 1, 2; WLC

Murdoch, (Jean) Iris 1919-1999 .. **CLC 1, 2, 3, 4, 6, 8, 11, 15, 22, 31, 51; DAB; DAC; DAM MST, NOV**
See also CA 13-16R; 179; CANR 8, 43, 68; CDBLB 1960 to Present; DA3; DLB 14, 194, 233; INT CANR-8; MTCW 1, 2

Murfree, Mary Noailles 1850-1922 .. **SSC 22**
See also CA 122; 176; DLB 12, 74

Murnau, Friedrich Wilhelm
See Plumpe, Friedrich Wilhelm

Murphy, Richard 1927- .... **CLC 41**
See also CA 29-32R; DLB 40

Murphy, Sylvia 1937- .... **CLC 34**
See also CA 121

Murphy, Thomas (Bernard) 1935- . **CLC 51**
See also CA 101

Murray, Albert L. 1916- .... **CLC 73**
See also BW 2; CA 49-52; CANR 26, 52, 78; DLB 38

Murray, Judith Sargent 1751-1820
.... **NCLC 63**

See also DLB 37, 200

Murray, Les(lie) A(llan) 1938- .... **CLC 40; DAM POET**
See also CA 21-24R; CANR 11, 27, 56

Murry, J. Middleton
See Murry, John Middleton

Murry, John Middleton 1889-1957
.... **TCLC 16**
See also CA 118; DLB 149

Musgrave, Susan 1951- .... **CLC 13, 54**
See also CA 69-72; CANR 45, 84

Musil, Robert (Edler von) 1880-1942
.... **TCLC 12, 68; SSC 18**
See also CA 109; CANR 55, 84; DLB 81, 124; MTCW 2

Muske, Carol 1945- .... **CLC 90**
See also Muske-Dukes, Carol (Anne)

Muske-Dukes, Carol (Anne) 1945-
See Muske, Carol
See also CA 65-68; CANR 32, 70

Musset, (Louis Charles) Alfred de 1810-1857
.... **NCLC 7**
See also DLB 192

Mussolini, Benito (Amilcare Andrea) 1883-1945 .... **TCLC 96**
See also CA 116

My Brother's Brother
See Chekhov, Anton (Pavlovich)

Myers, L(eopold) H(amilton) 1881-1944
.... **TCLC 59**
See also CA 157; DLB 15

Myers, Walter Dean 1937- .... **CLC 35; BLC 3; DAM MULT, NOV**
See also AAYA 4, 23; BW 2; CA 33-36R; CANR 20, 42, 67; CLR 4, 16, 35; DLB 33; INT CANR-20; JRDA; MAICYA; MTCW 2; SAAS 2; SATA 41, 71, 109; SATA-Brief 27

Myers, Walter M.
See Myers, Walter Dean

Myles, Symon
See Follett, Ken(neth Martin)

Nabokov, Vladimir (Vladimirovich) 1899-1977 ..... **CLC 1, 2, 3, 6, 8, 11, 15, 23, 44, 46, 64; DA; DAB; DAC; DAM MST, NOV; SSC 11; WLC**
See also CA 5-8R; 69-72; CANR 20; CDALB 1941-1968; DA3; DLB 2; DLBD 3; DLBY 80, 91; MTCW 1, 2

Naevius c. 265B.C.-201B.C. .... **CMLC 37**
See also DLB 211

Nagai, Kafu 1879-1959 .... **TCLC 51**
See also Nagai, Sokichi
See also DLB 180

Nagai, Sokichi 1879-1959
See Nagai, Kafu
See also CA 117

Nagy, Laszlo 1925-1978 .... **CLC 7**
See also CA 129; 112

Naidu, Sarojini 1879-1943 .... **TCLC 80**

Naipaul, Shiva(dhar Srinivasa) 1945-1985
.... **CLC 32, 39; DAM NOV**
See also CA 110; 112; 116; CANR 33; DA3; DLB 157; DLBY 85; MTCW 1, 2

Naipaul, V(idiadhar) S(urajprasad) 1932-
...... **CLC 4, 7, 9, 13, 18, 37, 105; DAB; DAC; DAM MST, NOV; SSC 38**
See also CA 1-4R; CANR 1, 33, 51, 91; CDBLB 1960 to Present; DA3; DLB 125, 204, 206; DLBY 85; MTCW 1, 2

Nakos, Lilika 1899(?)- .... **CLC 29**

Narayan, R(asipuram) K(rishnaswami) 1906- . **CLC 7, 28, 47, 121; DAM NOV; SSC 25**
See also CA 81-84; CANR 33, 61; DA3; MTCW 1, 2; SATA 62

Nash, (Frediric) Ogden 1902-1971 . **CLC 23; DAM POET; PC 21**

See also CA 13-14; 29-32R; CANR 34, 61; CAP 1; DLB 11; MAICYA; MTCW 1, 2; SATA 2, 46

Nashe, Thomas 1567-1601(?) .... **LC 41**
See also DLB 167

Nashe, Thomas 1567-1601 .... **LC 41**

Nathan, Daniel
See Dannay, Frederic

Nathan, George Jean 1882-1958 .. **TCLC 18**
See also Hatteras, Owen
See also CA 114; 169; DLB 137

Natsume, Kinnosuke 1867-1916
See Natsume, Soseki
See also CA 104

Natsume, Soseki 1867-1916 ...... **TCLC 2, 10**
See also Natsume, Kinnosuke
See also DLB 180

Natti, (Mary) Lee 1919-
See Kingman, Lee
See also CA 5-8R; CANR 2

Naylor, Gloria 1950- ... **CLC 28, 52; BLC 3; DA; DAC; DAM MST, MULT, NOV, POP; WLCS**
See also AAYA 6; BW 2, 3; CA 107; CANR 27, 51, 74; DA3; DLB 173; MTCW 1, 2

Neihardt, John Gneisenau 1881-1973
.... **CLC 32**
See also CA 13-14; CANR 65; CAP 1; DLB 9, 54

Nekrasov, Nikolai Alekseevich 1821-1878
.... **NCLC 11**

Nelligan, Emile 1879-1941 .... **TCLC 14**
See also CA 114; DLB 92

Nelson, Willie 1933- .... **CLC 17**
See also CA 107

Nemerov, Howard (Stanley) 1920-1991
.. **CLC 2, 6, 9, 36; DAM POET; PC 24**
See also CA 1-4R; 134; CABS 2; CANR 1, 27, 53; DLB 5, 6; DLBY 83; INT CANR-27; MTCW 1, 2

Neruda, Pablo 1904-1973 . **CLC 1, 2, 5, 7, 9, 28, 62; DA; DAB; DAC; DAM MST, MULT, POET; HLC 2; PC 4; WLC**
See also CA 19-20; 45-48; CAP 2; DA3; HW 1; MTCW 1, 2

Nerval, Gerard de 1808-1855 . **NCLC 1, 67; PC 13; SSC 18**

Nervo, (Jose) Amado (Ruiz de) 1870-1919
.... **TCLC 11; HLCS 2**
See also CA 109; 131; HW 1

Nessi, Pio Baroja y
See Baroja (y Nessi), Pio

Nestroy, Johann 1801-1862 .... **NCLC 42**
See also DLB 133

Netterville, Luke
See O'Grady, Standish (James)

Neufeld, John (Arthur) 1938- .... **CLC 17**
See also AAYA 11; CA 25-28R; CANR 11, 37, 56; CLR 52; MAICYA; SAAS 3; SATA 6, 81

Neumann, Alfred 1895-1952 .... **TCLC 100**
See also CA 183; DLB 56

Neville, Emily Cheney 1919- .... **CLC 12**
See also CA 5-8R; CANR 3, 37, 85; JRDA; MAICYA; SAAS 2; SATA 1

Newbound, Bernard Slade 1930-
See Slade, Bernard
See also CA 81-84; CANR 49; DAM DRAM

Newby, P(ercy) H(oward) 1918-1997
.... **CLC 2, 13; DAM NOV**
See also CA 5-8R; 161; CANR 32, 67; DLB 15; MTCW 1

Newlove, Donald 1928- .... **CLC 6**
See also CA 29-32R; CANR 25

Newlove, John (Herbert) 1938- .... **CLC 14**
See also CA 21-24R; CANR 9, 25

Newman, Charles 1938- .... **CLC 2, 8**
See also CA 21-24R; CANR 84

O'Doherty, Brian 1934- .... **CLC 76**
　　See also CA 105
O'Donnell, K. M.
　　See Malzberg, Barry N(athaniel)
O'Donnell, Lawrence
　　See Kuttner, Henry
O'Donovan, Michael John 1903-1966
　　... **CLC 14**
　　See also O'Connor, Frank
　　See also CA 93-96; CANR 84
Oe, Kenzaburo 1935- .... **CLC 10, 36, 86;**
　　DAM NOV; SSC 20
　　See also CA 97-100; CANR 36, 50, 74;
　　DA3; DLB 182; DLBY 94; MTCW 1, 2
O'Faolain, Julia 1932- ... **CLC 6, 19, 47, 108**
　　See also CA 81-84; CAAS 2; CANR 12,
　　61; DLB 14, 231; MTCW 1
O'Faolain, Sean 1900-1991 .... **CLC 1, 7, 14,**
　　32, 70; SSC 13
　　See also CA 61-64; 134; CANR 12, 66;
　　DLB 15, 162; MTCW 1, 2
O'Flaherty, Liam 1896-1984 ...... **CLC 5, 34;**
　　SSC 6
　　See also CA 101; 113; CANR 35; DLB 36,
　　162; DLBY 84; MTCW 1, 2
Ogilvy, Gavin
　　See Barrie, J(ames) M(atthew)
O'Grady, Standish (James) 1846-1928
　　... **TCLC 5**
　　See also CA 104; 157
O'Grady, Timothy 1951- .... **CLC 59**
　　See also CA 138
O'Hara, Frank 1926-1966 ...... **CLC 2, 5, 13,**
　　78; DAM POET
　　See also CA 9-12R; 25-28R; CANR 33;
　　DA3; DLB 5, 16, 193; MTCW 1, 2
O'Hara, John (Henry) 1905-1970 .... **CLC 1,**
　　2, 3, 6, 11, 42; DAM NOV; SSC 15
　　See also CA 5-8R; 25-28R; CANR 31, 60;
　　CDALB 1929-1941; DLB 9, 86; DLBD
　　2; MTCW 1, 2
O Hehir, Diana 1922- .... **CLC 41**
　　See also CA 93-96
Ohiyesa
　　See Eastman, Charles A(lexander)
Okigbo, Christopher (Ifenayichukwu)
　　1932-1967 . **CLC 25, 84; BLC 3; DAM**
　　MULT, POET; PC 7
　　See also BW 1, 3; CA 77-80; CANR 74;
　　DLB 125; MTCW 1, 2
Okri, Ben 1959- .... **CLC 87**
　　See also BW 2, 3; CA 130; 138; CANR 65;
　　DLB 157, 231; INT 138; MTCW 2
Olds, Sharon 1942- .. **CLC 32, 39, 85; DAM**
　　POET; PC 22
　　See also CA 101; CANR 18, 41, 66; DLB
　　120; MTCW 2
Oldstyle, Jonathan
　　See Irving, Washington
Olesha, Yuri (Karlovich) 1899-1960 . **CLC 8**
　　See also CA 85-88
Oliphant, Laurence 1829(?)-1888 . **NCLC 47**
　　See also DLB 18, 166
Oliphant, Margaret (Oliphant Wilson)
　　1828-1897 .... **NCLC 11, 61; SSC 25**
　　See also DLB 18, 159, 190
Oliver, Mary 1935- .... **CLC 19, 34, 98**
　　See also CA 21-24R; CANR 9, 43, 84, 92;
　　DLB 5, 193
Olivier, Laurence (Kerr) 1907-1989 . **CLC 20**
　　See also CA 111; 150; 129
Olsen, Tillie 1912- .... **CLC 4, 13, 114; DA;**
　　DAB; DAC; DAM MST; SSC 11
　　See also CA 1-4R; CANR 1, 43, 74;
　　CDALBS; DA3; DLB 28, 206; DLBY 80;
　　MTCW 1, 2
Olson, Charles (John) 1910-1970 . **CLC 1, 2,**
　　5, 6, 9, 11, 29; DAM POET; PC 19

See also CA 13-16; 25-28R; CABS 2;
　　CANR 35, 61; CAP 1; DLB 5, 16, 193;
　　MTCW 1, 2
Olson, Toby 1937- .... **CLC 28**
　　See also CA 65-68; CANR 9, 31, 84
Olyesha, Yuri
　　See Olesha, Yuri (Karlovich)
Ondaatje, (Philip) Michael 1943- .. **CLC 14,**
　　29, 51, 76; DAB; DAC; DAM MST; PC
　　28
　　See also CA 77-80; CANR 42, 74; DA3;
　　DLB 60; MTCW 2
Oneal, Elizabeth 1934-
　　See Oneal, Zibby
　　See also CA 106; CANR 28, 84; MAICYA;
　　SATA 30, 82
Oneal, Zibby .... **CLC 30**
　　See also Oneal, Elizabeth
　　See also AAYA 5; CLR 13; JRDA
O'Neill, Eugene (Gladstone) 1888-1953
　　... **TCLC 1, 6, 27, 49; DA; DAB; DAC;**
　　DAM DRAM, MST; WLC
　　See also AITN 1; CA 110; 132; CDALB
　　1929-1941; DA3; DLB 7; MTCW 1, 2
Onetti, Juan Carlos 1909-1994 .. **CLC 7, 10;**
　　DAM MULT, NOV; HLCS 2; SSC 23
　　See also CA 85-88; 145; CANR 32, 63;
　　DLB 113; HW 1, 2; MTCW 1, 2
O Nuallain, Brian 1911-1966
　　See O'Brien, Flann
　　See also CA 21-22; 25-28R; CAP 2; DLB
　　231
Ophuls, Max 1902-1957 .... **TCLC 79**
　　See also CA 113
Opie, Amelia 1769-1853 .... **NCLC 65**
　　See also DLB 116, 159
Oppen, George 1908-1984 ..... **CLC 7, 13, 34**
　　See also CA 13-16R; 113; CANR 8, 82;
　　DLB 5, 165
Oppenheim, E(dward) Phillips 1866-1946
　　... **TCLC 45**
　　See also CA 111; DLB 70
Opuls, Max
　　See Ophuls, Max
Origen c. 185-c. 254 .... **CMLC 19**
Orlovitz, Gil 1918-1973 .... **CLC 22**
　　See also CA 77-80; 45-48; DLB 2, 5
Orris
　　See Ingelow, Jean
Ortega y Gasset, Jose 1883-1955 .. **TCLC 9;**
　　DAM MULT; HLC 2
　　See also CA 106; 130; HW 1, 2; MTCW 1,
　　2
Ortese, Anna Maria 1914- .... **CLC 89**
　　See also DLB 177
Ortiz, Simon J(oseph) 1941- . **CLC 45; DAM**
　　MULT, POET; PC 17
　　See also CA 134; CANR 69; DLB 120, 175;
　　NNAL
Orton, Joe .... **CLC 4, 13, 43; DC 3**
　　See also Orton, John Kingsley
　　See also CDBLB 1960 to Present; DLB 13;
　　MTCW 2
Orton, John Kingsley 1933-1967
　　See Orton, Joe
　　See also CA 85-88; CANR 35, 66; DAM
　　DRAM; MTCW 1, 2
Orwell, George -1950 ..... **TCLC 2, 6, 15, 31,**
　　51; DAB; WLC
　　See also Blair, Eric (Arthur)
　　See also CDBLB 1945-1960; CLR 68; DLB
　　15, 98, 195
Osborne, David
　　See Silverberg, Robert
Osborne, George
　　See Silverberg, Robert
Osborne, John (James) 1929-1994 ... **CLC 1,**
　　2, 5, 11, 45; DA; DAB; DAC; DAM
　　DRAM, MST; WLC

See also CA 13-16R; 147; CANR 21, 56;
　　CDBLB 1945-1960; DLB 13; MTCW 1,
　　2
Osborne, Lawrence 1958- .... **CLC 50**
Osbourne, Lloyd 1868-1947 .... **TCLC 93**
Oshima, Nagisa 1932- .... **CLC 20**
　　See also CA 116; 121; CANR 78
Oskison, John Milton 1874-1947 . **TCLC 35;**
　　DAM MULT
　　See also CA 144; CANR 84; DLB 175;
　　NNAL
Ossian c. 3rd cent. - .... **CMLC 28**
　　See also Macpherson, James
Ossoli, Sarah Margaret (Fuller marchesa d')
　　1810-1850 .... **NCLC 5, 50**
　　See also Fuller, Margaret; Fuller, Sarah
　　Margaret
　　See also CDALB 1640-1865; DLB 1, 59,
　　73, 183, 223; SATA 25
Ostriker, Alicia (Suskin) 1937- ...... **CLC 132**
　　See also CA 25-28R; CAAS 24; CANR 10,
　　30, 62; DLB 120
Ostrovsky, Alexander 1823-1886 . **NCLC 30,**
　　57
Otero, Blas de 1916-1979 .... **CLC 11**
　　See also CA 89-92; DLB 134
Otto, Rudolf 1869-1937 .... **TCLC 85**
Otto, Whitney 1955- .... **CLC 70**
　　See also CA 140
Ouida .... **TCLC 43**
　　See also De La Ramee, (Marie) Louise
　　See also DLB 18, 156
Ousmane, Sembene 1923- .. **CLC 66; BLC 3**
　　See also BW 1, 3; CA 117; 125; CANR 81;
　　MTCW 1
Ovid 43B.C.-17 . **CMLC 7; DAM POET; PC**
　　2
　　See also DA3; DLB 211
Owen, Hugh
　　See Faust, Frederick (Schiller)
Owen, Wilfred (Edward Salter) 1893-1918
　　... **TCLC 5, 27; DA; DAB; DAC; DAM**
　　MST, POET; PC 19; WLC
　　See also CA 104; 141; CDBLB 1914-1945;
　　DLB 20; MTCW 2
Owens, Rochelle 1936- .... **CLC 8**
　　See also CA 17-20R; CAAS 2; CANR 39
Oz, Amos 1939- .... **CLC 5, 8, 11, 27, 33, 54;**
　　DAM NOV
　　See also CA 53-56; CANR 27, 47, 65;
　　MTCW 1, 2
Ozick, Cynthia 1928- .... **CLC 3, 7, 28, 62;**
　　DAM NOV, POP; SSC 15
　　See also BEST 90:1; CA 17-20R; CANR
　　23, 58; DA3; DLB 28, 152; DLBY 82;
　　INT CANR-23; MTCW 1, 2
Ozu, Yasujiro 1903-1963 .... **CLC 16**
　　See also CA 112
Pacheco, C.
　　See Pessoa, Fernando (Antonio Nogueira)
Pacheco, Jose Emilio 1939-
　　See also CA 111; 131; CANR 65; DAM
　　MULT; HLC 2; HW 1, 2
Pa Chin .... **CLC 18**
　　See also Li Fei-kan
Pack, Robert 1929- .... **CLC 13**
　　See also CA 1-4R; CANR 3, 44, 82; DLB
　　5; SATA 118
Padgett, Lewis
　　See Kuttner, Henry
Padilla (Lorenzo), Heberto 1932- ... **CLC 38**
　　See also AITN 1; CA 123; 131; HW 1
Page, Jimmy 1944- .... **CLC 12**
Page, Louise 1955- .... **CLC 40**
　　See also CA 140; CANR 76; DLB 233
Page, P(atricia) K(athleen) 1916- .... **CLC 7,**
　　18; DAC; DAM MST; PC 12

See also CA 53-56; CANR 4, 22, 65; DLB 68; MTCW 1

Page, Stanton
See Fuller, Henry Blake

Page, Stanton
See Fuller, Henry Blake

Page, Thomas Nelson 1853-1922 ...... **SSC 23**
See also CA 118; 177; DLB 12, 78; DLBD 13

Pagels, Elaine Hiesey 1943- .... **CLC 104**
See also CA 45-48; CANR 2, 24, 51

Paget, Violet 1856-1935
See Lee, Vernon
See also CA 104; 166

Paget-Lowe, Henry
See Lovecraft, H(oward) P(hillips)

Paglia, Camille (Anna) 1947- .... **CLC 68**
See also CA 140; CANR 72; MTCW 2

Paige, Richard
See Koontz, Dean R(ay)

Paine, Thomas 1737-1809 .... **NCLC 62**
See also CDALB 1640-1865; DLB 31, 43, 73, 158

Pakenham, Antonia
See Fraser, (Lady) Antonia (Pakenham)

Palamas, Kostes 1859-1943 .... **TCLC 5**
See also CA 105

Palazzeschi, Aldo 1885-1974 .... **CLC 11**
See also CA 89-92; 53-56; DLB 114

Pales Matos, Luis 1898-1959
See also HLCS 2; HW 1

Paley, Grace 1922- . **CLC 4, 6, 37, 140; DAM POP; SSC 8**
See also CA 25-28R; CANR 13, 46, 74; DA3; DLB 28; INT CANR-13; MTCW 1, 2

Palin, Michael (Edward) 1943- .... **CLC 21**
See also Monty Python
See also CA 107; CANR 35; SATA 67

Palliser, Charles 1947- .... **CLC 65**
See also CA 136; CANR 76

Palma, Ricardo 1833-1919 .... **TCLC 29**
See also CA 168

Pancake, Breece Dexter 1952-1979
See Pancake, Breece D'J
See also CA 123; 109

Pancake, Breece D'J .... **CLC 29**
See also Pancake, Breece Dexter
See also DLB 130

Pankhurst, Emmeline (Goulden) 1858-1928
.... **TCLC 100**
See also CA 116

Panko, Rudy
See Gogol, Nikolai (Vasilyevich)

Papadiamantis, Alexandros 1851-1911
.... **TCLC 29**
See also CA 168

Papadiamantopoulos, Johannes 1856-1910
See Moreas, Jean
See also CA 117

Papini, Giovanni 1881-1956 .... **TCLC 22**
See also CA 121; 180

Paracelsus 1493-1541 .... **LC 14**
See also DLB 179

Parasol, Peter
See Stevens, Wallace

Pardo Bazan, Emilia 1851-1921 .... **SSC 30**

Pareto, Vilfredo 1848-1923 .... **TCLC 69**
See also CA 175

Paretsky, Sara 1947- . **CLC 135; DAM POP**
See also AAYA 30; BEST 90:3; CA 125; 129; CANR 59; DA3; INT 129

Parfenie, Maria
See Codrescu, Andrei

Parini, Jay (Lee) 1948- .... **CLC 54, 133**
See also CA 97-100; CAAS 16; CANR 32, 87

Park, Jordan
See Kornbluth, C(yril) M.; Pohl, Frederik

Park, Robert E(zra) 1864-1944 .... **TCLC 73**
See also CA 122; 165

Parker, Bert
See Ellison, Harlan (Jay)

Parker, Dorothy (Rothschild) 1893-1967
. **CLC 15, 68; DAM POET; PC 28; SSC 2**
See also CA 19-20; 25-28R; CAP 2; DA3; DLB 11, 45, 86; MTCW 1, 2

Parker, Robert B(rown) 1932- .... **CLC 27; DAM NOV, POP**
See also AAYA 28; BEST 89:4; CA 49-52; CANR 1, 26, 52, 89; INT CANR-26; MTCW 1

Parkin, Frank 1940- .... **CLC 43**
See also CA 147

Parkman, Francis Jr., Jr. 1823-1893
.... **NCLC 12**
See also DLB 1, 30, 186, 235

Parks, Gordon (Alexander Buchanan) 1912-
.... **CLC 1, 16; BLC 3; DAM MULT**
See also AAYA 36; AITN 2; BW 2, 3; CA 41-44R; CANR 26, 66; DA3; DLB 33; MTCW 2; SATA 8, 108

Parmenides c. 515B.C.-c. 450B.C. . **CMLC 22**
See also DLB 176

Parnell, Thomas 1679-1718 .... **LC 3**
See also DLB 94

Parra, Nicanor 1914- ..... **CLC 2, 102; DAM MULT; HLC 2**
See also CA 85-88; CANR 32; HW 1; MTCW 1

Parra Sanojo, Ana Teresa de la 1890-1936
See also HLCS 2

Parrish, Mary Frances
See Fisher, M(ary) F(rances) K(ennedy)

Parson
See Coleridge, Samuel Taylor

Parson Lot
See Kingsley, Charles

Parton, Sara Payson Willis 1811-1872
.... **NCLC 86**
See also DLB 43, 74

Partridge, Anthony
See Oppenheim, E(dward) Phillips

Pascal, Blaise 1623-1662 .... **LC 35**

Pascoli, Giovanni 1855-1912 .... **TCLC 45**
See also CA 170

Pasolini, Pier Paolo 1922-1975 . **CLC 20, 37, 106; PC 17**
See also CA 93-96; 61-64; CANR 63; DLB 128, 177; MTCW 1

Pasquini
See Silone, Ignazio

Pastan, Linda (Olenik) 1932- .... **CLC 27; DAM POET**
See also CA 61-64; CANR 18, 40, 61; DLB 5

Pasternak, Boris (Leonidovich) 1890-1960
.... **CLC 7, 10, 18, 63; DA; DAB; DAC; DAM MST, NOV, POET; PC 6; SSC 31; WLC**
See also CA 127; 116; DA3; MTCW 1, 2

Patchen, Kenneth 1911-1972 . **CLC 1, 2, 18; DAM POET**
See also CA 1-4R; 33-36R; CANR 3, 35; DLB 16, 48; MTCW 1

Pater, Walter (Horatio) 1839-1894 . **NCLC 7, 90**
See also CDBLB 1832-1890; DLB 57, 156

Paterson, A(ndrew) B(arton) 1864-1941
.... **TCLC 32**
See also CA 155; DLB 230; SATA 97

Paterson, Katherine (Womeldorf) 1932-
.... **CLC 12, 30**

See also AAYA 1, 31; CA 21-24R; CANR 28, 59; CLR 7, 50; DLB 52; JRDA; MAI-CYA; MTCW 1; SATA 13, 53, 92

Patmore, Coventry Kersey Dighton 1823-1896 .... **NCLC 9**
See also DLB 35, 98

Paton, Alan (Stewart) 1903-1988 ..... **CLC 4, 10, 25, 55, 106; DA; DAB; DAC; DAM MST, NOV; WLC**
See also AAYA 26; CA 13-16; 125; CANR 22; CAP 1; DA3; DLB 225; DLBD 17; MTCW 1, 2; SATA 11; SATA-Obit 56

Paton Walsh, Gillian 1937- .... **CLC 35**
See also Walsh, Jill Paton
See also AAYA 11; CANR 38, 83; CLR 2, 65; DLB 161; JRDA; MAICYA; SAAS 3; SATA 4, 72, 109

Paton Walsh, Jill
See Paton Walsh, Gillian

Patton, George S. 1885-1945 .... **TCLC 79**

Paulding, James Kirke 1778-1860 . **NCLC 2**
See also DLB 3, 59, 74

Paulin, Thomas Neilson 1949-
See Paulin, Tom
See also CA 123; 128

Paulin, Tom .... **CLC 37**
See also Paulin, Thomas Neilson
See also DLB 40

Pausanias c. 1st cent. - .... **CMLC 36**

Paustovsky, Konstantin (Georgievich) 1892-1968 .... **CLC 40**
See also CA 93-96; 25-28R

Pavese, Cesare 1908-1950 . **TCLC 3; PC 13; SSC 19**
See also CA 104; 169; DLB 128, 177

Pavic, Milorad 1929- .... **CLC 60**
See also CA 136; DLB 181

Pavlov, Ivan Petrovich 1849-1936 . **TCLC 91**
See also CA 118; 180

Payne, Alan
See Jakes, John (William)

Paz, Gil
See Lugones, Leopoldo

Paz, Octavio 1914-1998 . **CLC 3, 4, 6, 10, 19, 51, 65, 119; DA; DAB; DAC; DAM MST, MULT, POET; HLC 2; PC 1; WLC**
See also CA 73-76; 165; CANR 32, 65; DA3; DLBY 90, 98; HW 1, 2; MTCW 1, 2

p'Bitek, Okot 1931-1982 ... **CLC 96; BLC 3; DAM MULT**
See also BW 2, 3; CA 124; 107; CANR 82; DLB 125; MTCW 1, 2

Peacock, Molly 1947- .... **CLC 60**
See also CA 103; CAAS 21; CANR 52, 84; DLB 120

Peacock, Thomas Love 1785-1866 . **NCLC 22**
See also DLB 96, 116

Peake, Mervyn 1911-1968 .... **CLC 7, 54**
See also CA 5-8R; 25-28R; CANR 3; DLB 15, 160; MTCW 1; SATA 23

Pearce, Philippa .... **CLC 21**
See also Christie, (Ann) Philippa
See also CLR 9; DLB 161; MAICYA; SATA 1, 67

Pearl, Eric
See Elman, Richard (Martin)

Pearson, T(homas) R(eid) 1956- ..... **CLC 39**
See also CA 120; 130; INT 130

Peck, Dale 1967- .... **CLC 81**
See also CA 146; CANR 72

Peck, John 1941- .... **CLC 3**
See also CA 49-52; CANR 3

Peck, Richard (Wayne) 1934- .... **CLC 21**
See also AAYA 1, 24; CA 85-88; CANR 19, 38; CLR 15; INT CANR-19; JRDA; MAICYA; SAAS 2; SATA 18, 55, 97; SATA-Essay 110

Peck, Robert Newton 1928- ... **CLC 17; DA; DAC; DAM MST**
See also AAYA 3; CA 81-84, 182; CAAE 182; CANR 31, 63; CLR 45; JRDA; MAICYA; SAAS 1; SATA 21, 62, 111; SATA-Essay 108

Peckinpah, (David) Sam(uel) 1925-1984
.... **CLC 20**
See also CA 109; 114; CANR 82

Pedersen, Knut 1859-1952
See Hamsun, Knut
See also CA 104; 119; CANR 63; MTCW 1, 2

Peeslake, Gaffer
See Durrell, Lawrence (George)

Peguy, Charles Pierre 1873-1914 . **TCLC 10**
See also CA 107

Peirce, Charles Sanders 1839-1914
.... **TCLC 81**

Pellicer, Carlos 1900(?)-1977
See also CA 153; 69-72; HLCS 2; HW 1

Pena, Ramon del Valle y
See Valle-Inclan, Ramon (Maria) del

Pendennis, Arthur Esquir
See Thackeray, William Makepeace

Penn, William 1644-1718 .... **LC 25**
See also DLB 24

PEPECE
See Prado (Calvo), Pedro

Pepys, Samuel 1633-1703 .... **LC 11, 58; DA; DAB; DAC; DAM MST; WLC**
See also CDBLB 1660-1789; DA3; DLB 101

Percy, Thomas 1729-1811 .... **NCLC 95**
See also DLB 104

Percy, Walker 1916-1990 ..... **CLC 2, 3, 6, 8, 14, 18, 47, 65; DAM NOV, POP**
See also CA 1-4R; 131; CANR 1, 23, 64; DA3; DLB 2; DLBY 80, 90; MTCW 1, 2

Percy, William Alexander 1885-1942
.... **TCLC 84**
See also CA 163; MTCW 2

Perec, Georges 1936-1982 .... **CLC 56, 116**
See also CA 141; DLB 83

Pereda (y Sanchez de Porrua), Jose Maria de 1833-1906 .... **TCLC 16**
See also CA 117

Pereda y Porrua, Jose Maria de
See Pereda (y Sanchez de Porrua), Jose Maria de

Peregoy, George Weems
See Mencken, H(enry) L(ouis)

Perelman, S(idney) J(oseph) 1904-1979
.... **CLC 3, 5, 9, 15, 23, 44, 49; DAM DRAM; SSC 32**
See also AITN 1, 2; CA 73-76; 89-92; CANR 18; DLB 11, 44; MTCW 1, 2

Peret, Benjamin 1899-1959 ... **TCLC 20; PC 33**
See also CA 117; 186

Peretz, Isaac Loeb 1851(?)-1915 . **TCLC 16; SSC 26**
See also CA 109

Peretz, Yitzhok Leibush
See Peretz, Isaac Loeb

Perez Galdos, Benito 1843-1920 . **TCLC 27; HLCS 2**
See also CA 125; 153; HW 1

Peri Rossi, Cristina 1941-
See also CA 131; CANR 59, 81; DLB 145; HLCS 2; HW 1, 2

Perlata
See Peret, Benjamin

Perloff, Marjorie G(abrielle) 1931-
.... **CLC 137**
See also CA 57-60; CANR 7, 22, 49

Perrault, Charles 1628-1703 .. **LC 3, 52; DC 12**
See also MAICYA; SATA 25

Perry, Anne 1938- .... **CLC 126**
See also CA 101; CANR 22, 50, 84

Perry, Brighton
See Sherwood, Robert E(mmet)

Perse, St.-John
See Leger, (Marie-Rene Auguste) Alexis Saint-Leger

Perutz, Leo(pold) 1882-1957 .... **TCLC 60**
See also CA 147; DLB 81

Peseenz, Tulio F.
See Lopez y Fuentes, Gregorio

Pesetsky, Bette 1932- .... **CLC 28**
See also CA 133; DLB 130

Peshkov, Alexei Maximovich 1868-1936
See Gorky, Maxim
See also CA 105; 141; CANR 83; DA; DAC; DAM DRAM, MST, NOV; MTCW 2

Pessoa, Fernando (Antonio Nogueira) 1888-1935 .... **TCLC 27; DAM MULT; HLC 2; PC 20**
See also CA 125; 183

Peterkin, Julia Mood 1880-1961 ..... **CLC 31**
See also CA 102; DLB 9

Peters, Joan K(aren) 1945- .... **CLC 39**
See also CA 158

Peters, Robert L(ouis) 1924- .... **CLC 7**
See also CA 13-16R; CAAS 8; DLB 105

Petofi, Sandor 1823-1849 .... **NCLC 21**

Petrakis, Harry Mark 1923- .... **CLC 3**
See also CA 9-12R; CANR 4, 30, 85

Petrarch 1304-1374 .... **CMLC 20; DAM POET; PC 8**
See also DA3

Petronius c. 20-66 .... **CMLC 34**
See also DLB 211

Petrov, Evgeny .... **TCLC 21**
See also Kataev, Evgeny Petrovich

Petry, Ann (Lane) 1908-1997 .. **CLC 1, 7, 18**
See also BW 1, 3; CA 5-8R; 157; CAAS 6; CANR 4, 46; CLR 12; DLB 76; JRDA; MAICYA; MTCW 1; SATA 5; SATA-Obit 94

Petursson, Halligrimur 1614-1674 .... **LC 8**

Peychinovich
See Vazov, Ivan (Minchov)

Phaedrus c. 18B.C.-c. 50 .... **CMLC 25**
See also DLB 211

Philips, Katherine 1632-1664 .... **LC 30**
See also DLB 131

Philipson, Morris H. 1926- .... **CLC 53**
See also CA 1-4R; CANR 4

Phillips, Caryl 1958- . **CLC 96; BLCS; DAM MULT**
See also BW 2; CA 141; CANR 63; DA3; DLB 157; MTCW 2

Phillips, David Graham 1867-1911
.... **TCLC 44**
See also CA 108; 176; DLB 9, 12

Phillips, Jack
See Sandburg, Carl (August)

Phillips, Jayne Anne 1952- .... **CLC 15, 33, 139; SSC 16**
See also CA 101; CANR 24, 50; DLBY 80; INT CANR-24; MTCW 1, 2

Phillips, Richard
See Dick, Philip K(indred)

Phillips, Robert (Schaeffer) 1938- ... **CLC 28**
See also CA 17-20R; CAAS 13; CANR 8; DLB 105

Phillips, Ward
See Lovecraft, H(oward) P(hillips)

Piccolo, Lucio 1901-1969 .... **CLC 13**
See also CA 97-100; DLB 114

Pickthall, Marjorie L(owry) C(hristie) 1883-1922 .... **TCLC 21**
See also CA 107; DLB 92

Pico della Mirandola, Giovanni 1463-1494
.... **LC 15**

Piercy, Marge 1936- ... **CLC 3, 6, 14, 18, 27, 62, 128; PC 29**
See also CA 21-24R; CAAE 187; CAAS 1; CANR 13, 43, 66; DLB 120, 227; MTCW 1, 2

Piers, Robert
See Anthony, Piers

Pieyre de Mandiargues, Andre 1909-1991
See Mandiargues, Andre Pieyre de
See also CA 103; 136; CANR 22, 82

Pilnyak, Boris .... **TCLC 23**
See also Vogau, Boris Andreyevich

Pincherle, Alberto 1907-1990 ... **CLC 11, 18; DAM NOV**
See also Moravia, Alberto
See also CA 25-28R; 132; CANR 33, 63; MTCW 1

Pinckney, Darryl 1953- .... **CLC 76**
See also BW 2, 3; CA 143; CANR 79

Pindar 518B.C.-446B.C. .. **CMLC 12; PC 19**
See also DLB 176

Pineda, Cecile 1942- .... **CLC 39**
See also CA 118

Pinero, Arthur Wing 1855-1934 .. **TCLC 32; DAM DRAM**
See also CA 110; 153; DLB 10

Pinero, Miguel (Antonio Gomez) 1946-1988
.... **CLC 4, 55**
See also CA 61-64; 125; CANR 29, 90; HW 1

Pinget, Robert 1919-1997 ...... **CLC 7, 13, 37**
See also CA 85-88; 160; DLB 83

Pink Floyd
See Barrett, (Roger) Syd; Gilmour, David; Mason, Nick; Waters, Roger; Wright, Rick

Pinkney, Edward 1802-1828 .... **NCLC 31**

Pinkwater, Daniel Manus 1941- ...... **CLC 35**
See also Pinkwater, Manus
See also AAYA 1; CA 29-32R; CANR 12, 38, 89; CLR 4; JRDA; MAICYA; SAAS 3; SATA 46, 76, 114

Pinkwater, Manus
See Pinkwater, Daniel Manus
See also SATA 8

Pinsky, Robert 1940- ...... **CLC 9, 19, 38, 94, 121; DAM POET; PC 27**
See also CA 29-32R; CAAS 4; CANR 58; DA3; DLBY 82, 98; MTCW 2

Pinta, Harold
See Pinter, Harold

Pinter, Harold 1930- . **CLC 1, 3, 6, 9, 11, 15, 27, 58, 73; DA; DAB; DAC; DAM DRAM, MST; WLC**
See also CA 5-8R; CANR 33, 65; CDBLB 1960 to Present; DA3; DLB 13; MTCW 1, 2

Piozzi, Hester Lynch (Thrale) 1741-1821
.... **NCLC 57**
See also DLB 104, 142

Pirandello, Luigi 1867-1936 .... **TCLC 4, 29; DA; DAB; DAC; DAM DRAM, MST; DC 5; SSC 22; WLC**
See also CA 104; 153; DA3; MTCW 2

Pirsig, Robert M(aynard) 1928- .. **CLC 4, 6, 73; DAM POP**
See also CA 53-56; CANR 42, 74; DA3; MTCW 1, 2; SATA 39

Pisarev, Dmitry Ivanovich 1840-1868
.... **NCLC 25**

Pix, Mary (Griffith) 1666-1709 .... **LC 8**
See also DLB 80

Pixerecourt, (Rene Charles) Guilbert de 1773-1844 .... **NCLC 39**
See also DLB 192

Plaatje, Sol(omon) T(shekisho) 1876-1932
.... **TCLC 73; BLCS**

See also BW 2, 3; CA 141; CANR 79; DLB 225

Plaidy, Jean
See Hibbert, Eleanor Alice Burford

Planche, James Robinson 1796-1880
.... **NCLC 42**

Plant, Robert 1948- .... **CLC 12**

Plante, David (Robert) 1940- ..... **CLC 7, 23, 38; DAM NOV**
See also CA 37-40R; CANR 12, 36, 58, 82; DLBY 83; INT CANR-12; MTCW 1

Plath, Sylvia 1932-1963 .... **CLC 1, 2, 3, 5, 9, 11, 14, 17, 50, 51, 62, 111; DA; DAB; DAC; DAM MST, POET; PC 1; WLC**
See also AAYA 13; CA 19-20; CANR 34; CAP 2; CDALB 1941-1968; DA3; DLB 5, 6, 152; MTCW 1, 2; SATA 96

Plato 428(?)B.C.-348(?)B.C. .. **CMLC 8; DA; DAB; DAC; DAM MST; WLCS**
See also DA3; DLB 176

Platonov, Andrei
See Klimentov, Andrei Platonovich

Platt, Kin 1911- .... **CLC 26**
See also AAYA 11; CA 17-20R; CANR 11; JRDA; SAAS 17; SATA 21, 86

Plautus c. 251B.C.-184B.C. .. **CMLC 24; DC 6**
See also DLB 211

Plick et Plock
See Simenon, Georges (Jacques Christian)

Plieksans, Janis 1865-1929
See Rainis, Janis
See also CA 170; DLB 220

Plimpton, George (Ames) 1927- ...... **CLC 36**
See also AITN 1; CA 21-24R; CANR 32, 70; DLB 185; MTCW 1, 2; SATA 10

Pliny the Elder c. 23-79 .... **CMLC 23**
See also DLB 211

Plomer, William Charles Franklin 1903-1973
.... **CLC 4, 8**
See also CA 21-22; CANR 34; CAP 2; DLB 20, 162, 191, 225; MTCW 1; SATA 24

Plowman, Piers
See Kavanagh, Patrick (Joseph)

Plum, J.
See Wodehouse, P(elham) G(renville)

Plumly, Stanley (Ross) 1939- .... **CLC 33**
See also CA 108; 110; DLB 5, 193; INT 110

Plumpe, Friedrich Wilhelm 1888-1931
.... **TCLC 53**
See also CA 112

Po Chu-i 772-846 .... **CMLC 24**

Poe, Edgar Allan 1809-1849 .... **NCLC 1, 16, 55, 78, 94; DA; DAB; DAC; DAM MST, POET; PC 1; SSC 1, 22, 34, 35; WLC**
See also AAYA 14; CDALB 1640-1865; DA3; DLB 3, 59, 73, 74; SATA 23

Poet of Titchfield Street, The
See Pound, Ezra (Weston Loomis)

Pohl, Frederick 1919- .... **CLC 18; SSC 25**
See also AAYA 24; CA 61-64; CAAS 1; CANR 11, 37, 81; DLB 8; INT CANR-11; MTCW 1, 2; SATA 24

Poirier, Louis 1910-
See Gracq, Julien
See also CA 122; 126

Poitier, Sidney 1927- .... **CLC 26**
See also BW 1; CA 117; CANR 94

Polanski, Roman 1933- .... **CLC 16**
See also CA 77-80

Poliakoff, Stephen 1952- .... **CLC 38**
See also CA 106; DLB 13

Police, The
See Copeland, Stewart (Armstrong); Summers, Andrew James; Sumner, Gordon Matthew

Polidori, John William 1795-1821 . **NCLC 51**
See also DLB 116

Pollitt, Katha 1949- .... **CLC 28, 122**
See also CA 120; 122; CANR 66; MTCW 1, 2

Pollock, (Mary) Sharon 1936- .... **CLC 50; DAC; DAM DRAM, MST**
See also CA 141; DLB 60

Polo, Marco 1254-1324 .... **CMLC 15**

Polonsky, Abraham (Lincoln) 1910-1999
.... **CLC 92**
See also CA 104; 187; DLB 26; INT 104

Polybius c. 200B.C.-c. 118B.C. ..... **CMLC 17**
See also DLB 176

Pomerance, Bernard 1940- .. **CLC 13; DAM DRAM**
See also CA 101; CANR 49

Ponge, Francis 1899-1988 . **CLC 6, 18; DAM POET**
See also CA 85-88; 126; CANR 40, 86

Poniatowska, Elena 1933- .. **CLC 140; DAM MULT; HLC 2**
See also CA 101; CANR 32, 66; DLB 113; HW 1, 2

Pontoppidan, Henrik 1857-1943 ... **TCLC 29**
See also CA 170

Poole, Josephine .... **CLC 17**
See also Helyar, Jane Penelope Josephine
See also SAAS 2; SATA 5

Popa, Vasko 1922-1991 .... **CLC 19**
See also CA 112; 148; DLB 181

Pope, Alexander 1688-1744 ..... **LC 3, 58, 60, 64; DA; DAB; DAC; DAM MST, POET; PC 26; WLC**
See also CDBLB 1660-1789; DA3; DLB 95, 101

Porter, Connie (Rose) 1959(?)- .... **CLC 70**
See also BW 2, 3; CA 142; CANR 90; SATA 81

Porter, Gene(va Grace) Stratton
1863(?)-1924 .... **TCLC 21**
See also Stratton-Porter, Gene(va Grace)
See also CA 112

Porter, Katherine Anne 1890-1980 .. **CLC 1, 3, 7, 10, 13, 15, 27, 101; DA; DAB; DAC; DAM MST, NOV; SSC 4, 31, 43**
See also AITN 2; CA 1-4R; 101; CANR 1, 65; CDALBS; DA3; DLB 4, 9, 102; DLBD 12; DLBY 80; MTCW 1, 2; SATA 39; SATA-Obit 23

Porter, Peter (Neville Frederick) 1929-
.... **CLC 5, 13, 33**
See also CA 85-88; DLB 40

Porter, William Sydney 1862-1910
See Henry, O.
See also CA 104; 131; CDALB 1865-1917; DA; DAB; DAC; DAM MST; DA3; DLB 12, 78, 79; MTCW 1, 2; YABC 2

Portillo (y Pacheco), Jose Lopez
See Lopez Portillo (y Pacheco), Jose

Portillo Trambley, Estela 1927-1998
See also CANR 32; DAM MULT; DLB 209; HLC 2; HW 1

Post, Melville Davisson 1869-1930 . **TCLC 39**
See also CA 110

Potok, Chaim 1929- . **CLC 2, 7, 14, 26, 112; DAM NOV**
See also AAYA 15; AITN 1, 2; CA 17-20R; CANR 19, 35, 64; DA3; DLB 28, 152; INT CANR-19; MTCW 1, 2; SATA 33, 106

Potter, Dennis (Christopher George)
1935-1994 .... **CLC 58, 86, 123**
See also CA 107; 145; CANR 33, 61; DLB 233; MTCW 1

Pound, Ezra (Weston Loomis) 1885-1972
. **CLC 1, 2, 3, 4, 5, 7, 10, 13, 18, 34, 48, 50, 112; DA; DAB; DAC; DAM MST, POET; PC 4; WLC**

See also CA 5-8R; 37-40R; CANR 40; CDALB 1917-1929; DA3; DLB 4, 45, 63; DLBD 15; MTCW 1, 2

Povod, Reinaldo 1959-1994 .... **CLC 44**
See also CA 136; 146; CANR 83

Powell, Adam Clayton, Jr. 1908-1972
.... **CLC 89; BLC 3; DAM MULT**
See also BW 1, 3; CA 102; 33-36R; CANR 86

Powell, Anthony (Dymoke) 1905- . **CLC 1, 3, 7, 9, 10, 31**
See also CA 1-4R; CANR 1, 32, 62; CD-BLB 1945-1960; DLB 15; MTCW 1, 2

Powell, Dawn 1897-1965 .... **CLC 66**
See also CA 5-8R; DLBY 97

Powell, Padgett 1952- .... **CLC 34**
See also CA 126; CANR 63; DLB 234

Powell, Talmage 1920-
See Queen, Ellery
See also CA 5-8R; CANR 2, 80

Power, Susan 1961- .... **CLC 91**
See also CA 160

Powers, J(ames) F(arl) 1917-1999 ... **CLC 1, 4, 8, 57; SSC 4**
See also CA 1-4R; 181; CANR 2, 61; DLB 130; MTCW 1

Powers, John J(ames) 1945-
See Powers, John R.
See also CA 69-72

Powers, John R. .... **CLC 66**
See also Powers, John J(ames)

Powers, Richard (S.) 1957- .... **CLC 93**
See also CA 148; CANR 80

Pownall, David 1938- .... **CLC 10**
See also CA 89-92; 180; CAAS 18; CANR 49; DLB 14

Powys, John Cowper 1872-1963 .. **CLC 7, 9, 15, 46, 125**
See also CA 85-88; DLB 15; MTCW 1, 2

Powys, T(heodore) F(rancis) 1875-1953
.... **TCLC 9**
See also CA 106; DLB 36, 162

Prado (Calvo), Pedro 1886-1952 .. **TCLC 75**
See also CA 131; HW 1

Prager, Emily 1952- .... **CLC 56**

Pratt, E(dwin) J(ohn) 1883(?)-1964
.... **CLC 19; DAC; DAM POET**
See also CA 141; 93-96; CANR 77; DLB 92

Premchand .... **TCLC 21**
See also Srivastava, Dhanpat Rai

Preussler, Otfried 1923- .... **CLC 17**
See also CA 77-80; SATA 24

Prevert, Jacques (Henri Marie) 1900-1977
.... **CLC 15**
See also CA 77-80; 69-72; CANR 29, 61; MTCW 1; SATA-Obit 30

Prevost, Abbe (Antoine Francois) 1697-1763
.... **LC 1**

Price, (Edward) Reynolds 1933- .. **CLC 3, 6, 13, 43, 50, 63; DAM NOV; SSC 22**
See also CA 1-4R; CANR 1, 37, 57, 87; DLB 2; INT CANR-37

Price, Richard 1949- .... **CLC 6, 12**
See also CA 49-52; CANR 3; DLBY 81

Prichard, Katharine Susannah 1883-1969
.... **CLC 46**
See also CA 11-12; CANR 33; CAP 1; MTCW 1; SATA 66

Priestley, J(ohn) B(oynton) 1894-1984
... **CLC 2, 5, 9, 34; DAM DRAM, NOV**
See also CA 9-12R; 113; CANR 33; CD-BLB 1914-1945; DA3; DLB 10, 34, 77, 100, 139; DLBY 84; MTCW 1, 2

Prince 1958(?)- .... **CLC 35**

Prince, F(rank) T(empleton) 1912- . **CLC 22**
See also CA 101; CANR 43, 79; DLB 20

Prince Kropotkin
    See Kropotkin, Peter (Aleksieevich)
Prior, Matthew 1664-1721 .... **LC 4**
    See also DLB 95
Prishvin, Mikhail 1873-1954 .... **TCLC 75**
Pritchard, William H(arrison) 1932-
    .... **CLC 34**
    See also CA 65-68; CANR 23; DLB 111
Pritchett, V(ictor) S(awdon) 1900-1997
    .... **CLC 5, 13, 15, 41; DAM NOV; SSC
    14**
    See also CA 61-64; 157; CANR 31, 63;
    DA3; DLB 15, 139; MTCW 1, 2
Private 19022
    See Manning, Frederic
Probst, Mark 1925- .... **CLC 59**
    See also CA 130
Prokosch, Frederic 1908-1989 ..... **CLC 4, 48**
    See also CA 73-76; 128; CANR 82; DLB
    48; MTCW 2
Propertius, Sextus c. 50B.C.-c. 16B.C.
    .... **CMLC 32**
    See also DLB 211
Prophet, The
    See Dreiser, Theodore (Herman Albert)
Prose, Francine 1947- .... **CLC 45**
    See also CA 109; 112; CANR 46; DLB 234;
    SATA 101
Proudhon
    See Cunha, Euclides (Rodrigues Pimenta)
    da
Proulx, Annie
    See Proulx, E(dna) Annie
Proulx, E(dna) Annie 1935- . **CLC 81; DAM
    POP**
    See also CA 145; CANR 65; DA3; MTCW
    2
**Proust, (Valentin-Louis-George-Eugene-)
    Marcel** 1871-1922 ...... **TCLC 7, 13, 33;
    DA; DAB; DAC; DAM MST, NOV;
    WLC**
    See also CA 104; 120; DA3; DLB 65;
    MTCW 1, 2
Prowler, Harley
    See Masters, Edgar Lee
Prus, Boleslaw 1845-1912 .... **TCLC 48**
Pryor, Richard (Franklin Lenox Thomas)
    1940- .... **CLC 26**
    See also CA 122; 152
Przybyszewski, Stanislaw 1868-1927
    .... **TCLC 36**
    See also CA 160; DLB 66
Pteleon
    See Grieve, C(hristopher) M(urray)
    See also DAM POET
Puckett, Lute
    See Masters, Edgar Lee
Puig, Manuel 1932-1990 ... **CLC 3, 5, 10, 28,
    65, 133; DAM MULT; HLC 2**
    See also CA 45-48; CANR 2, 32, 63; DA3;
    DLB 113; HW 1, 2; MTCW 1, 2
Pulitzer, Joseph 1847-1911 .... **TCLC 76**
    See also CA 114; DLB 23
Purdy, A(lfred) W(ellington) 1918- .. **CLC 3,
    6, 14, 50; DAC; DAM MST, POET**
    See also CA 81-84; CAAS 17; CANR 42,
    66; DLB 88
Purdy, James (Amos) 1923- ... **CLC 2, 4, 10,
    28, 52**
    See also CA 33-36R; CAAS 1; CANR 19,
    51; DLB 2; INT CANR-19; MTCW 1
Pure, Simon
    See Swinnerton, Frank Arthur
Pushkin, Alexander (Sergeyevich) 1799-1837
    .... **NCLC 3, 27, 83; DA; DAB; DAC;
    DAM DRAM, MST, POET; PC 10; SSC
    27; WLC**
    See also DA3; DLB 205; SATA 61
P'u Sung-ling 1640-1715 ...... **LC 49; SSC 31**

Putnam, Arthur Lee
    See Alger, Horatio Jr., Jr.
Puzo, Mario 1920-1999 ...... **CLC 1, 2, 6, 36,
    107; DAM NOV, POP**
    See also CA 65-68; 185; CANR 4, 42, 65;
    DA3; DLB 6; MTCW 1, 2
Pygge, Edward
    See Barnes, Julian (Patrick)
Pyle, Ernest Taylor 1900-1945
    See Pyle, Ernie
    See also CA 115; 160
Pyle, Ernie 1900-1945 .... **TCLC 75**
    See also Pyle, Ernest Taylor
    See also DLB 29; MTCW 2
Pyle, Howard 1853-1911 .... **TCLC 81**
    See also CA 109; 137; CLR 22; DLB 42,
    188; DLBD 13; MAICYA; SATA 16, 100
Pym, Barbara (Mary Crampton) 1913-1980
    .... **CLC 13, 19, 37, 111**
    See also CA 13-14; 97-100; CANR 13, 34;
    CAP 1; DLB 14, 207; DLBY 87; MTCW
    1, 2
Pynchon, Thomas (Ruggles, Jr.) 1937-
    . **CLC 2, 3, 6, 9, 11, 18, 33, 62, 72, 123;
    DA; DAB; DAC; DAM MST, NOV,
    POP; SSC 14; WLC**
    See also BEST 90:2; CA 17-20R; CANR
    22, 46, 73; DA3; DLB 2, 173; MTCW 1,
    2
Pythagoras c. 570B.C.-c. 500B.C. . **CMLC 22**
    See also DLB 176
Q
    See Quiller-Couch, SirArthur (Thomas)
Qian Zhongshu
    See Ch'ien Chung-shu
Qroll
    See Dagerman, Stig (Halvard)
Quarrington, Paul (Lewis) 1953- .... **CLC 65**
    See also CA 129; CANR 62
Quasimodo, Salvatore 1901-1968 .... **CLC 10**
    See also CA 13-16; 25-28R; CAP 1; DLB
    114; MTCW 1
Quay, Stephen 1947- .... **CLC 95**
Quay, Timothy 1947- .... **CLC 95**
Queen, Ellery .... **CLC 3, 11**
    See also Deming, Richard; Dannay, Fre-
    deric; Davidson, Avram (James); Fairman,
    Paul W.; Flora, Fletcher; Hoch, Edward
    D(entinger); Kane, Henry; Lee, Manfred
    B(ennington); Marlowe, Stephen; Powell,
    Talmage; Sheldon, Walter J.; Sturgeon,
    Theodore (Hamilton); Tracy, Don(ald
    Fiske); Vance, John Holbrook
Queen, Ellery, Jr.
    See Dannay, Frederic; Lee, Manfred
    B(ennington)
Queneau, Raymond 1903-1976 .... **CLC 2, 5,
    10, 42**
    See also CA 77-80; 69-72; CANR 32; DLB
    72; MTCW 1, 2
Quevedo, Francisco de 1580-1645 ..... **LC 23**
Quiller-Couch, SirArthur (Thomas)
    1863-1944 .... **TCLC 53**
    See also CA 118; 166; DLB 135, 153, 190
Quin, Ann (Marie) 1936-1973 .... **CLC 6**
    See also CA 9-12R; 45-48; DLB 14, 231
Quinn, Martin
    See Smith, Martin Cruz
Quinn, Peter 1947- .... **CLC 91**
Quinn, Simon
    See Smith, Martin Cruz
Quintana, Leroy V. 1944-
    See also CA 131; CANR 65; DAM MULT;
    DLB 82; HLC 2; HW 1, 2
Quiroga, Horacio (Sylvestre) 1878-1937
    .... **TCLC 20; DAM MULT; HLC 2**
    See also CA 117; 131; HW 1; MTCW 1
Quoirez, Francoise 1935- .... **CLC 9**
    See also Sagan, Francoise

    See also CA 49-52; CANR 6, 39, 73;
    MTCW 1, 2
Raabe, Wilhelm (Karl) 1831-1910 . **TCLC 45**
    See also CA 167; DLB 129
Rabe, David (William) 1940- . **CLC 4, 8, 33;
    DAM DRAM**
    See also CA 85-88; CABS 3; CANR 59;
    DLB 7, 228
Rabelais, Francois 1483-1553 .... **LC 5, 60;
    DA; DAB; DAC; DAM MST; WLC**
Rabinovitch, Sholem 1859-1916
    See Aleichem, Sholom
    See also CA 104
Rabinyan, Dorit 1972- .... **CLC 119**
    See also CA 170
Rachilde
    See Vallette, Marguerite Eymery
Racine, Jean 1639-1699 . **LC 28; DAB; DAM
    MST**
    See also DA3
Radcliffe, Ann (Ward) 1764-1823 . **NCLC 6,
    55**
    See also DLB 39, 178
Radiguet, Raymond 1903-1923 ..... **TCLC 29**
    See also CA 162; DLB 65
Radnoti, Miklos 1909-1944 .... **TCLC 16**
    See also CA 118
Rado, James 1939- .... **CLC 17**
    See also CA 105
Radvanyi, Netty 1900-1983
    See Seghers, Anna
    See also CA 85-88; 110; CANR 82
Rae, Ben
    See Griffiths, Trevor
Raeburn, John (Hay) 1941- .... **CLC 34**
    See also CA 57-60
Ragni, Gerome 1942-1991 .... **CLC 17**
    See also CA 105; 134
Rahv, Philip 1908-1973 .... **CLC 24**
    See also Greenberg, Ivan
    See also DLB 137
Raimund, Ferdinand Jakob 1790-1836
    .... **NCLC 69**
    See also DLB 90
Raine, Craig 1944- .... **CLC 32, 103**
    See also CA 108; CANR 29, 51; DLB 40
Raine, Kathleen (Jessie) 1908- .... **CLC 7, 45**
    See also CA 85-88; CANR 46; DLB 20;
    MTCW 1
Rainis, Janis 1865-1929 .... **TCLC 29**
    See also Plieksans, Janis
    See also CA 170; DLB 220
Rakosi, Carl 1903- .... **CLC 47**
    See also Rawley, Callman
    See also CAAS 5; DLB 193
Ralegh, SirWalter 1554(?)-1618
    See Raleigh, SirWalter
Raleigh, Richard
    See Lovecraft, H(oward) P(hillips)
Raleigh, SirWalter 1554(?)-1618 . **LC 31, 39;
    PC 31**
    See also CDBLB Before 1660; DLB 172
Rallentando, H. P.
    See Sayers, Dorothy L(eigh)
Ramal, Walter
    See de la Mare, Walter (John)
Ramana Maharshi 1879-1950 .... **TCLC 84**
Ramoacn y Cajal, Santiago 1852-1934
    .... **TCLC 93**
Ramon, Juan
    See Jimenez (Mantecon), Juan Ramon
Ramos, Graciliano 1892-1953 .... **TCLC 32**
    See also CA 167; HW 2
Rampersad, Arnold 1941- .... **CLC 44**
    See also BW 2, 3; CA 127; 133; CANR 81;
    DLB 111; INT 133

See also AAYA 2; CA 17-20R; CANR 13,
47; CLR 2; JRDA; MAICYA; SAAS 2;
SATA 3, 68; SATA-Essay 110

Sachs, Nelly 1891-1970 .... **CLC 14, 98**
See also CA 17-18; 25-28R; CANR 87;
CAP 2; MTCW 2

Sackler, Howard (Oliver) 1929-1982
.... **CLC 14**
See also CA 61-64; 108; CANR 30; DLB 7

Sacks, Oliver (Wolf) 1933- .... **CLC 67**
See also CA 53-56; CANR 28, 50, 76; DA3;
INT CANR-28; MTCW 1, 2

Sadakichi
See Hartmann, Sadakichi

**Sade, Donatien Alphonse Francois, Comte
de** 1740-1814 .... **NCLC 3, 47**

Sadoff, Ira 1945- .... **CLC 9**
See also CA 53-56; CANR 5, 21; DLB 120

Saetone
See Camus, Albert

Safire, William 1929- .... **CLC 10**
See also CA 17-20R; CANR 31, 54, 91

Sagan, Carl (Edward) 1934-1996 .. **CLC 30,
112**
See also AAYA 2; CA 25-28R; 155; CANR
11, 36, 74; DA3; MTCW 1, 2; SATA 58;
SATA-Obit 94

Sagan, Francoise .... **CLC 3, 6, 9, 17, 36**
See also Quoirez, Francoise
See also DLB 83; MTCW 2

Sahgal, Nayantara (Pandit) 1927- .. **CLC 41**
See also CA 9-12R; CANR 11, 88

Said, Edward W. 1935- .... **CLC 123**
See also CA 21-24R; CANR 45, 74; DLB
67; MTCW 2

Saint, H(arry) F. 1941- .... **CLC 50**
See also CA 127

St. Aubin de Teran, Lisa 1953-
See Teran, Lisa St. Aubin de
See also CA 118; 126; INT 126

Saint Birgitta of Sweden c. 1303-1373
.... **CMLC 24**

Sainte-Beuve, Charles Augustin 1804-1869
.... **NCLC 5**

**Saint-Exupery, Antoine (Jean Baptiste
Marie Roger) de** 1900-1944 .. **TCLC 2,
56; DAM NOV; WLC**
See also CA 108; 132; CLR 10; DA3; DLB
72; MAICYA; MTCW 1, 2; SATA 20

St. John, David
See Hunt, E(verette) Howard, (Jr.)

Saint-John Perse
See Leger, (Marie-Rene Auguste) Alexis
Saint-Leger

Saintsbury, George (Edward Bateman)
1845-1933 .... **TCLC 31**
See also CA 160; DLB 57, 149

Sait Faik .... **TCLC 23**
See also Abasiyanik, Sait Faik

Saki .... **TCLC 3; SSC 12**
See also Munro, H(ector) H(ugh)
See also MTCW 2

Sala, George Augustus .... **NCLC 46**

Saladin 1138-1193 .... **CMLC 38**

Salama, Hannu 1936- .... **CLC 18**

Salamanca, J(ack) R(ichard) 1922- . **CLC 4,
15**
See also CA 25-28R

Salas, Floyd Francis 1931-
See also CA 119; CAAS 27; CANR 44, 75;
93; DAM MULT; DLB 82; HLC 2; HW
1, 2; MTCW 2

Sale, J. Kirkpatrick
See Sale, Kirkpatrick

Sale, Kirkpatrick 1937- .... **CLC 68**
See also CA 13-16R; CANR 10

Salinas, Luis Omar 1937- .... **CLC 90; DAM
MULT; HLC 2**

See also CA 131; CANR 81; DLB 82; HW
1, 2

Salinas (y Serrano), Pedro 1891(?)-1951
.... **TCLC 17**
See also CA 117; DLB 134

Salinger, J(erome) D(avid) 1919- . **CLC 1, 3,
8, 12, 55, 56, 138; DA; DAB; DAC;
DAM MST, NOV, POP; SSC 2, 28;
WLC**
See also AAYA 2, 36; CA 5-8R; CANR 39;
CDALB 1941-1968; CLR 18; DA3; DLB
2, 102, 173; MAICYA; MTCW 1, 2;
SATA 67

Salisbury, John
See Caute, (John) David

Salter, James 1925- .... **CLC 7, 52, 59**
See also CA 73-76; DLB 130

Saltus, Edgar (Everton) 1855-1921 . **TCLC 8**
See also CA 105; DLB 202

Saltykov, Mikhail Evgrafovich 1826-1889
.... **NCLC 16**

Samarakis, Antonis 1919- .... **CLC 5**
See also CA 25-28R; CAAS 16; CANR 36

Sanchez, Florencio 1875-1910 .... **TCLC 37**
See also CA 153; HW 1

Sanchez, Luis Rafael 1936- .... **CLC 23**
See also CA 128; DLB 145; HW 1

Sanchez, Sonia 1934- .. **CLC 5, 116; BLC 3;
DAM MULT; PC 9**
See also BW 2, 3; CA 33-36R; CANR 24,
49, 74; CLR 18; DA3; DLB 41; DLBD 8;
MAICYA; MTCW 1, 2; SATA 22

Sand, George 1804-1876 ... **NCLC 2, 42, 57;
DA; DAB; DAC; DAM MST, NOV;
WLC**
See also DA3; DLB 119, 192

Sandburg, Carl (August) 1878-1967 . **CLC 1,
4, 10, 15, 35; DA; DAB; DAC; DAM
MST, POET; PC 2; WLC**
See also AAYA 24; CA 5-8R; 25-28R;
CANR 35; CDALB 1865-1917; CLR 67;
DA3; DLB 17, 54; MAICYA; MTCW 1,
2; SATA 8

Sandburg, Charles
See Sandburg, Carl (August)

Sandburg, Charles A.
See Sandburg, Carl (August)

Sanders, (James) Ed(ward) 1939- . **CLC 53;
DAM POET**
See also CA 13-16R; CAAS 21; CANR 13,
44, 78; DLB 16

Sanders, Lawrence 1920-1998 .... **CLC 41;
DAM POP**
See also BEST 89:4; CA 81-84; 165; CANR
33, 62; DA3; MTCW 1

Sanders, Noah
See Blount, Roy (Alton), Jr.

Sanders, Winston P.
See Anderson, Poul (William)

Sandoz, Mari(e Susette) 1896-1966 . **CLC 28**
See also CA 1-4R; 25-28R; CANR 17, 64;
DLB 9, 212; MTCW 1, 2; SATA 5

Saner, Reg(inald Anthony) 1931- ...... **CLC 9**
See also CA 65-68

Sankara 788-820 .... **CMLC 32**

Sannazaro, Jacopo 1456(?)-1530 .... **LC 8**

Sansom, William 1912-1976 .... **CLC 2, 6;
DAM NOV; SSC 21**
See also CA 5-8R; 65-68; CANR 42; DLB
139; MTCW 1

Santayana, George 1863-1952 ...... **TCLC 40**
See also CA 115; DLB 54, 71; DLBD 13

Santiago, Danny .... **CLC 33**
See also James, Daniel (Lewis)
See also DLB 122

Santmyer, Helen Hoover 1895-1986 . **CLC 33**
See also CA 1-4R; 118; CANR 15, 33;
DLBY 84; MTCW 1

Santoka, Taneda 1882-1940 .... **TCLC 72**

Santos, Bienvenido N(uqui) 1911-1996
.... **CLC 22; DAM MULT**
See also CA 101; 151; CANR 19, 46

Sapper .... **TCLC 44**
See also McNeile, Herman Cyril

Sapphire
See Sapphire, Brenda

Sapphire, Brenda 1950- .... **CLC 99**

Sappho fl. 6th cent. B.C.- .... **CMLC 3; DAM
POET; PC 5**
See also DA3; DLB 176

Saramago, Jose 1922- .... **CLC 119; HLCS 1**
See also CA 153

Sarduy, Severo 1937-1993 .... **CLC 6, 97;
HLCS 1**
See also CA 89-92; 142; CANR 58, 81;
DLB 113; HW 1, 2

Sargeson, Frank 1903-1982 .... **CLC 31**
See also CA 25-28R; 106; CANR 38, 79

Sarmiento, Domingo Faustino 1811-1888
See also HLCS 2

Sarmiento, Felix Ruben Garcia
See Dario, Ruben

Saro-Wiwa, Ken(ule Beeson) 1941-1995
.... **CLC 114**
See also BW 2; CA 142; 150; CANR 60;
DLB 157

Saroyan, William 1908-1981 .. **CLC 1, 8, 10,
29, 34, 56; DA; DAB; DAC; DAM
DRAM, MST, NOV; SSC 21; WLC**
See also CA 5-8R; 103; CANR 30;
CDALBS; DA3; DLB 7, 9, 86; DLBY 81;
MTCW 1, 2; SATA 23; SATA-Obit 24

Sarraute, Nathalie 1900-1999 .. **CLC 1, 2, 4,
8, 10, 31, 80**
See also CA 9-12R; 187; CANR 23, 66;
DLB 83; MTCW 1, 2

Sarton, (Eleanor) May 1912-1995 .... **CLC 4,
14, 49, 91; DAM POET**
See also CA 1-4R; 149; CANR 1, 34, 55;
DLB 48; DLBY 81; INT CANR-34;
MTCW 1, 2; SATA 36; SATA-Obit 86

Sartre, Jean-Paul 1905-1980 .... **CLC 1, 4, 7,
9, 13, 18, 24, 44, 50, 52; DA; DAB;
DAC; DAM DRAM, MST, NOV; DC 3;
SSC 32; WLC**
See also CA 9-12R; 97-100; CANR 21;
DA3; DLB 72; MTCW 1, 2

Sassoon, Siegfried (Lorraine) 1886-1967
. **CLC 36, 130; DAB; DAM MST, NOV,
POET; PC 12**
See also CA 104; 25-28R; CANR 36; DLB
20, 191; DLBD 18; MTCW 1, 2

Satterfield, Charles
See Pohl, Frederik

Satyremont
See Peret, Benjamin

Saul, John (W. III) 1942- ..... **CLC 46; DAM
NOV, POP**
See also AAYA 10; BEST 90:4; CA 81-84;
CANR 16, 40, 81; SATA 98

Saunders, Caleb
See Heinlein, Robert A(nson)

Saura (Atares), Carlos 1932- .... **CLC 20**
See also CA 114; 131; CANR 79; HW 1

Sauser-Hall, Frederic 1887-1961 ..... **CLC 18**
See also Cendrars, Blaise
See also CA 102; 93-96; CANR 36, 62;
MTCW 1

Saussure, Ferdinand de 1857-1913
.... **TCLC 49**

Savage, Catharine
See Brosman, Catharine Savage

Savage, Thomas 1915- .... **CLC 40**
See also CA 126; 132; CAAS 15; INT 132

Savan, Glenn 19(?)- .... **CLC 50**

Sayers, Dorothy L(eigh) 1893-1957
.... **TCLC 2, 15; DAM POP**

130; BLC 3; DAM MULT, POET; PC 25
See also BW 2; CA 116; 125; CANR 47, 74; MTCW 1, 2

Senna, Danzy 1970- .... **CLC 119**
See also CA 169

Serling, (Edward) Rod(man) 1924-1975
.... **CLC 30**
See also AAYA 14; AITN 1; CA 162; 57-60; DLB 26

Serna, Ramon Gomez de la
See Gomez de la Serna, Ramon

Serpieres
See Guillevic, (Eugene)

Service, Robert
See Service, Robert W(illiam)
See also DAB; DLB 92

Service, Robert W(illiam) 1874(?)-1958
.... **TCLC 15; DA; DAC; DAM MST, POET; WLC**
See also Service, Robert
See also CA 115; 140; CANR 84; SATA 20

Seth, Vikram 1952- .... **CLC 43, 90; DAM MULT**
See also CA 121; 127; CANR 50, 74; DA3; DLB 120; INT 127; MTCW 2

Seton, Cynthia Propper 1926-1982 . **CLC 27**
See also CA 5-8R; 108; CANR 7

Seton, Ernest (Evan) Thompson 1860-1946
.... **TCLC 31**
See also CA 109; CLR 59; DLB 92; DLBD 13; JRDA; SATA 18

Seton-Thompson, Ernest
See Seton, Ernest (Evan) Thompson

Settle, Mary Lee 1918- .... **CLC 19, 61**
See also CA 89-92; CAAS 1; CANR 44, 87; DLB 6; INT 89-92

Seuphor, Michel
See Arp, Jean

Sevigne, Marie (de Rabutin-Chantal)
Marquise de 1626-1696 .... **LC 11**

Sewall, Samuel 1652-1730 .... **LC 38**
See also DLB 24

Sexton, Anne (Harvey) 1928-1974 ... **CLC 2, 4, 6, 8, 10, 15, 53, 123; DA; DAB; DAC; DAM MST, POET; PC 2; WLC**
See also CA 1-4R; 53-56; CABS 2; CANR 3, 36; CDALB 1941-1968; DA3; DLB 5, 169; MTCW 1, 2; SATA 10

Shaara, Jeff 1952- .... **CLC 119**
See also CA 163

Shaara, Michael (Joseph, Jr.) 1929-1988
.... **CLC 15; DAM POP**
See also AITN 1; CA 102; 125; CANR 52, 85; DLBY 83

Shackleton, C. C.
See Aldiss, Brian W(ilson)

Shacochis, Bob .... **CLC 39**
See also Shacochis, Robert G.

Shacochis, Robert G. 1951-
See Shacochis, Bob
See also CA 119; 124; INT 124

Shaffer, Anthony (Joshua) 1926- ... **CLC 19; DAM DRAM**
See also CA 110; 116; DLB 13

Shaffer, Peter (Levin) 1926- . **CLC 5, 14, 18, 37, 60; DAB; DAM DRAM, MST; DC 7**
See also CA 25-28R; CANR 25, 47, 74; CDBLB 1960 to Present; DA3; DLB 13, 233; MTCW 1, 2

Shakey, Bernard
See Young, Neil

Shalamov, Varlam (Tikhonovich)
1907(?)-1982 .... **CLC 18**
See also CA 129; 105

Shamlu, Ahmad 1925- .... **CLC 10**

Shammas, Anton 1951- .... **CLC 55**

Shandling, Arline
See Berriault, Gina

Shange, Ntozake 1948- ... **CLC 8, 25, 38, 74, 126; BLC 3; DAM DRAM, MULT; DC 3**
See also AAYA 9; BW 2; CA 85-88; CABS 3; CANR 27, 48, 74; DA3; DLB 38; MTCW 1, 2

Shanley, John Patrick 1950- .... **CLC 75**
See also CA 128; 133; CANR 83

Shapcott, Thomas W(illiam) 1935- . **CLC 38**
See also CA 69-72; CANR 49, 83

Shapiro, Jane .... **CLC 76**

Shapiro, Karl (Jay) 1913- . **CLC 4, 8, 15, 53; PC 25**
See also CA 1-4R; CAAS 6; CANR 1, 36, 66; DLB 48; MTCW 1, 2

Sharp, William 1855-1905 .... **TCLC 39**
See also CA 160; DLB 156

Sharpe, Thomas Ridley 1928-
See Sharpe, Tom
See also CA 114; 122; CANR 85; DLB 231; INT 122

Sharpe, Tom .... **CLC 36**
See also Sharpe, Thomas Ridley
See also DLB 14

Shaw, Bernard
See Shaw, George Bernard
See also BW 1; MTCW 2

Shaw, G. Bernard
See Shaw, George Bernard

Shaw, George Bernard 1856-1950 . **TCLC 3, 9, 21, 45; DA; DAB; DAC; DAM DRAM, MST; WLC**
See also Shaw, Bernard
See also CA 104; 128; CDBLB 1914-1945; DA3; DLB 10, 57, 190; MTCW 1, 2

Shaw, Henry Wheeler 1818-1885 . **NCLC 15**
See also DLB 11

Shaw, Irwin 1913-1984 .... **CLC 7, 23, 34; DAM DRAM, POP**
See also AITN 1; CA 13-16R; 112; CANR 21; CDALB 1941-1968; DLB 6, 102; DLBY 84; MTCW 1, 21

Shaw, Robert 1927-1978 .... **CLC 5**
See also AITN 1; CA 1-4R; 81-84; CANR 4; DLB 13, 14

Shaw, T. E.
See Lawrence, T(homas) E(dward)

Shawn, Wallace 1943- .... **CLC 41**
See also CA 112

Shea, Lisa 1953- .... **CLC 86**
See also CA 147

Sheed, Wilfrid (John Joseph) 1930- . **CLC 2, 4, 10, 53**
See also CA 65-68; CANR 30, 66; DLB 6; MTCW 1, 2

Sheldon, Alice Hastings Bradley
1915(?)-1987
See Tiptree, James, Jr.
See also CA 108; 122; CANR 34; INT 108; MTCW 1

Sheldon, John
See Bloch, Robert (Albert)

Sheldon, Walter J. 1917-
See Queen, Ellery
See also AITN 1; CA 25-28R; CANR 10

Shelley, Mary Wollstonecraft (Godwin)
1797-1851 .... **NCLC 14, 59; DA; DAB; DAC; DAM MST, NOV; WLC**
See also AAYA 20; CDBLB 1789-1832; DA3; DLB 110, 116, 159, 178; SATA 29

Shelley, Percy Bysshe 1792-1822 . **NCLC 18, 93; DA; DAB; DAC; DAM MST, POET; PC 14; WLC**
See also CDBLB 1789-1832; DA3; DLB 96, 110, 158

Shepard, Jim 1956- .... **CLC 36**
See also CA 137; CANR 59; SATA 90

Shepard, Lucius 1947- .... **CLC 34**
See also CA 128; 141; CANR 81

Shepard, Sam 1943- ... **CLC 4, 6, 17, 34, 41, 44; DAM DRAM; DC 5**
See also AAYA 1; CA 69-72; CABS 3; CANR 22; DA3; DLB 7, 212; MTCW 1, 2

Shepherd, Michael
See Ludlum, Robert

Sherburne, Zoa (Lillian Morin) 1912-1995
.... **CLC 30**
See also AAYA 13; CA 1-4R; 176; CANR 3, 37; MAICYA; SAAS 18; SATA 3

Sheridan, Frances 1724-1766 .... **LC 7**
See also DLB 39, 84

Sheridan, Richard Brinsley 1751-1816
.. **NCLC 5, 91; DA; DAB; DAC; DAM DRAM, MST; DC 1; WLC**
See also CDBLB 1660-1789; DLB 89

Sherman, Jonathan Marc .... **CLC 55**

Sherman, Martin 1941(?)- .... **CLC 19**
See also CA 116; 123; CANR 86

Sherwin, Judith Johnson 1936-
See Johnson, Judith (Emlyn)
See also CANR 85

Sherwood, Frances 1940- .... **CLC 81**
See also CA 146

Sherwood, Robert E(mmet) 1896-1955
.... **TCLC 3; DAM DRAM**
See also CA 104; 153; CANR 86; DLB 7, 26

Shestov, Lev 1866-1938 .... **TCLC 56**

Shevchenko, Taras 1814-1861 .... **NCLC 54**

Shiel, M(atthew) P(hipps) 1865-1947
.... **TCLC 8**
See also Holmes, Gordon
See also CA 106; 160; DLB 153; MTCW 2

Shields, Carol 1935- ...... **CLC 91, 113; DAC**
See also CA 81-84; CANR 51, 74; DA3; MTCW 2

Shields, David 1956- .... **CLC 97**
See also CA 124; CANR 48

Shiga, Naoya 1883-1971 .... **CLC 33; SSC 23**
See also CA 101; 33-36R; DLB 180

Shikibu, Murasaki c. 978-c. 1014 . **CMLC 1**

Shilts, Randy 1951-1994 .... **CLC 85**
See also AAYA 19; CA 115; 127; 144; CANR 45; DA3; INT 127; MTCW 2

Shimazaki, Haruki 1872-1943
See Shimazaki Toson
See also CA 105; 134; CANR 84

Shimazaki Toson 1872-1943 .... **TCLC 5**
See also Shimazaki, Haruki
See also DLB 180

Sholokhov, Mikhail (Aleksandrovich)
1905-1984 .... **CLC 7, 15**
See also CA 101; 112; MTCW 1, 2; SATA-Obit 36

Shone, Patric
See Hanley, James

Shreve, Susan Richards 1939- .... **CLC 23**
See also CA 49-52; CAAS 5; CANR 5, 38, 69; MAICYA; SATA 46, 95; SATA-Brief 41

Shue, Larry 1946-1985 .... **CLC 52; DAM DRAM**
See also CA 145; 117

Shu-Jen, Chou 1881-1936
See Lu Hsun
See also CA 104

Shulman, Alix Kates 1932- .... **CLC 2, 10**
See also CA 29-32R; CANR 43; SATA 7

Shuster, Joe 1914- .... **CLC 21**

Shute, Nevil .... **CLC 30**
See also Norway, Nevil Shute
See also MTCW 2

Shuttle, Penelope (Diane) 1947- .... **CLC 7**

See also CA 93-96; CANR 39, 84, 92; DLB 14, 40

Sidney, Mary 1561-1621 .... **LC 19, 39**

Sidney, SirPhilip 1554-1586 . **LC 19, 39; DA; DAB; DAC; DAM MST, POET; PC 32**
See also CDBLB Before 1660; DA3; DLB 167

Siegel, Jerome 1914-1996 .... **CLC 21**
See also CA 116; 169; 151

Siegel, Jerry
See Siegel, Jerome

Sienkiewicz, Henryk (Adam Alexander Pius)
1846-1916 .... **TCLC 3**
See also CA 104; 134; CANR 84

Sierra, Gregorio Martinez
See Martinez Sierra, Gregorio

Sierra, Maria (de la O'LeJarraga) Martinez
See Martinez Sierra, Maria (de la O'LeJarraga)

Sigal, Clancy 1926- .... **CLC 7**
See also CA 1-4R; CANR 85

Sigourney, Lydia Howard (Huntley)
1791-1865 .... **NCLC 21, 87**
See also DLB 1, 42, 73

Siguenza y Gongora, Carlos de 1645-1700
.... **LC 8; HLCS 2**

Sigurjonsson, Johann 1880-1919 .. **TCLC 27**
See also CA 170

Sikelianos, Angelos 1884-1951 ..... **TCLC 39; PC 29**

Silkin, Jon 1930- .... **CLC 2, 6, 43**
See also CA 5-8R; CAAS 5; CANR 89; DLB 27

Silko, Leslie (Marmon) 1948- .. **CLC 23, 74, 114; DA; DAC; DAM MST, MULT, POP; SSC 37; WLCS**
See also AAYA 14; CA 115; 122; CANR 45, 65; DA3; DLB 143, 175; MTCW 2; NNAL

Sillanpaa, Frans Eemil 1888-1964 .. **CLC 19**
See also CA 129; 93-96; MTCW 1

Sillitoe, Alan 1928- .. **CLC 1, 3, 6, 10, 19, 57**
See also AITN 1; CA 9-12R; CAAS 2; CANR 8, 26, 55; CDBLB 1960 to Present; DLB 14, 139; MTCW 1, 2; SATA 61

Silone, Ignazio 1900-1978 .... **CLC 4**
See also CA 25-28; 81-84; CANR 34; CAP 2; MTCW 1

Silver, Joan Micklin 1935- .... **CLC 20**
See also CA 114; 121; INT 121

Silver, Nicholas
See Faust, Frederick (Schiller)

Silverberg, Robert 1935- . **CLC 7, 140; DAM POP**
See also AAYA 24; CA 1-4R, 186; CAAE 186; CAAS 3; CANR 1, 20, 36, 85; CLR 59; DLB 8; INT CANR-20; MAICYA; MTCW 1, 2; SATA 13, 91; SATA-Essay 104

Silverstein, Alvin 1933- .... **CLC 17**
See also CA 49-52; CANR 2; CLR 25; JRDA; MAICYA; SATA 8, 69

Silverstein, Virginia B(arbara Opshelor)
1937- .... **CLC 17**
See also CA 49-52; CANR 2; CLR 25; JRDA; MAICYA; SATA 8, 69

Sim, Georges
See Simenon, Georges (Jacques Christian)

Simak, Clifford D(onald) 1904-1988 . **CLC 1, 55**
See also CA 1-4R; 125; CANR 1, 35; DLB 8; MTCW 1; SATA-Obit 56

Simenon, Georges (Jacques Christian)
1903-1989 .... **CLC 1, 2, 3, 8, 18, 47; DAM POP**
See also CA 85-88; 129; CANR 35; DA3; DLB 72; DLBY 89; MTCW 1, 2

Simic, Charles 1938- .. **CLC 6, 9, 22, 49, 68, 130; DAM POET**

See also CA 29-32R; CAAS 4; CANR 12, 33, 52, 61; DA3; DLB 105; MTCW 2

Simmel, Georg 1858-1918 .... **TCLC 64**
See also CA 157

Simmons, Charles (Paul) 1924- .... **CLC 57**
See also CA 89-92; INT 89-92

Simmons, Dan 1948- ... **CLC 44; DAM POP**
See also AAYA 16; CA 138; CANR 53, 81

Simmons, James (Stewart Alexander) 1933-
.... **CLC 43**
See also CA 105; CAAS 21; DLB 40

Simms, William Gilmore 1806-1870
.... **NCLC 3**
See also DLB 3, 30, 59, 73

Simon, Carly 1945- .... **CLC 26**
See also CA 105

Simon, Claude 1913- .... **CLC 4, 9, 15, 39; DAM NOV**
See also CA 89-92; CANR 33; DLB 83; MTCW 1

Simon, (Marvin) Neil 1927- . **CLC 6, 11, 31, 39, 70; DAM DRAM; DC 14**
See also AAYA 32; AITN 1; CA 21-24R; CANR 26, 54, 87; DA3; DLB 7; MTCW 1, 2

Simon, Paul (Frederick) 1941(?)- ... **CLC 17**
See also CA 116; 153

Simonon, Paul 1956(?)- .... **CLC 30**

Simpson, Harriette
See Arnow, Harriette (Louisa) Simpson

Simpson, Louis (Aston Marantz) 1923-
.... **CLC 4, 7, 9, 32; DAM POET**
See also CA 1-4R; CAAS 4; CANR 1, 61; DLB 5; MTCW 1, 2

Simpson, Mona (Elizabeth) 1957- ... **CLC 44**
See also CA 122; 135; CANR 68

Simpson, N(orman) F(rederick) 1919-
.... **CLC 29**
See also CA 13-16R; DLB 13

Sinclair, Andrew (Annandale) 1935- . **CLC 2, 14**
See also CA 9-12R; CAAS 5; CANR 14, 38, 91; DLB 14; MTCW 1

Sinclair, Emil
See Hesse, Hermann

Sinclair, Iain 1943- .... **CLC 76**
See also CA 132; CANR 81

Sinclair, Iain MacGregor
See Sinclair, Iain

Sinclair, Irene
See Griffith, D(avid Lewelyn) W(ark)

Sinclair, Mary Amelia St. Clair 1865(?)-1946
See Sinclair, May
See also CA 104

Sinclair, May 1863-1946 .... **TCLC 3, 11**
See also Sinclair, Mary Amelia St. Clair
See also CA 166; DLB 36, 135

Sinclair, Roy
See Griffith, D(avid Lewelyn) W(ark)

Sinclair, Upton (Beall) 1878-1968 .... **CLC 1, 11, 15, 63; DA; DAB; DAC; DAM MST, NOV; WLC**
See also CA 5-8R; 25-28R; CANR 7; CDALB 1929-1941; DA3; DLB 9; INT CANR-7; MTCW 1, 2; SATA 9

Singer, Isaac
See Singer, Isaac Bashevis

Singer, Isaac Bashevis 1904-1991 . **CLC 1, 3, 6, 9, 11, 15, 23, 38, 69, 111; DA; DAB; DAC; DAM MST, NOV; SSC 3; WLC**
See also AAYA 32; AITN 1, 2; CA 1-4R; 134; CANR 1, 39; CDALB 1941-1968; CLR 1; DA3; DLB 6, 28, 52; DLBY 91; JRDA; MAICYA; MTCW 1, 2; SATA 3, 27; SATA-Obit 68

Singer, Israel Joshua 1893-1944 ... **TCLC 33**
See also CA 169

Singh, Khushwant 1915- .... **CLC 11**
See also CA 9-12R; CAAS 9; CANR 6, 84

Singleton, Ann
See Benedict, Ruth (Fulton)

Sinjohn, John
See Galsworthy, John

Sinyavsky, Andrei (Donatevich) 1925-1997
.... **CLC 8**
See also CA 85-88; 159

Sirin, V.
See Nabokov, Vladimir (Vladimirovich)

Sissman, L(ouis) E(dward) 1928-1976
.... **CLC 9, 18**
See also CA 21-24R; 65-68; CANR 13; DLB 5

Sisson, C(harles) H(ubert) 1914- ...... **CLC 8**
See also CA 1-4R; CAAS 3; CANR 3, 48, 84; DLB 27

Sitwell, Dame Edith 1887-1964 .... **CLC 2, 9, 67; DAM POET; PC 3**
See also CA 9-12R; CANR 35; CDBLB 1945-1960; DLB 20; MTCW 1, 2

Siwaarmill, H. P.
See Sharp, William

Sjoewall, Maj 1935- .... **CLC 7**
See also Sjowall, Maj
See also CA 65-68; CANR 73

Sjowall, Maj
See Sjoewall, Maj

Skelton, John 1463-1529 .... **PC 25**

Skelton, Robin 1925-1997 .... **CLC 13**
See also AITN 2; CA 5-8R; 160; CAAS 5; CANR 28, 89; DLB 27, 53

Skolimowski, Jerzy 1938- .... **CLC 20**
See also CA 128

Skram, Amalie (Bertha) 1847-1905
.... **TCLC 25**
See also CA 165

Skvorecky, Josef (Vaclav) 1924- ..... **CLC 15, 39, 69; DAC; DAM NOV**
See also CA 61-64; CAAS 1; CANR 10, 34, 63; DA3; DLB 232; MTCW 1, 2

Slade, Bernard .... **CLC 11, 46**
See also Newbound, Bernard Slade
See also CAAS 9; DLB 53

Slaughter, Carolyn 1946- .... **CLC 56**
See also CA 85-88; CANR 85

Slaughter, Frank G(ill) 1908- .... **CLC 29**
See also AITN 2; CA 5-8R; CANR 5, 85; INT CANR-5

Slavitt, David R(ytman) 1935- .... **CLC 5, 14**
See also CA 21-24R; CAAS 3; CANR 41, 83; DLB 5, 6

Slesinger, Tess 1905-1945 .... **TCLC 10**
See also CA 107; DLB 102

Slessor, Kenneth 1901-1971 .... **CLC 14**
See also CA 102; 89-92

Slowacki, Juliusz 1809-1849 .... **NCLC 15**

Smart, Christopher 1722-1771 . **LC 3; DAM POET; PC 13**
See also DLB 109

Smart, Elizabeth 1913-1986 .... **CLC 54**
See also CA 81-84; 118; DLB 88

Smiley, Jane (Graves) 1949- .... **CLC 53, 76; DAM POP**
See also CA 104; CANR 30, 50, 74; DA3; DLB 227, 234; INT CANR-30

Smith, A(rthur) J(ames) M(arshall)
1902-1980 .... **CLC 15; DAC**
See also CA 1-4R; 102; CANR 4; DLB 88

Smith, Adam 1723-1790 .... **LC 36**
See also DLB 104

Smith, Alexander 1829-1867 .... **NCLC 59**
See also DLB 32, 55

Smith, Anna Deavere 1950- .... **CLC 86**
See also CA 133

Smith, Betty (Wehner) 1896-1972 ... **CLC 19**
See also CA 5-8R; 33-36R; DLBY 82; SATA 6

Smith, Charlotte (Turner) 1749-1806
.... **NCLC 23**
See also DLB 39, 109

Smith, Clark Ashton 1893-1961 ...... **CLC 43**
See also CA 143; CANR 81; MTCW 2

Smith, Dave .... **CLC 22, 42**
See also Smith, David (Jeddie)
See also CAAS 7; DLB 5

Smith, David (Jeddie) 1942-
See Smith, Dave
See also CA 49-52; CANR 1, 59; DAM
POET

Smith, Florence Margaret 1902-1971
See Smith, Stevie
See also CA 17-18; 29-32R; CANR 35;
CAP 2; DAM POET; MTCW 1, 2

Smith, Iain Crichton 1928-1998 ...... **CLC 64**
See also CA 21-24R; 171; DLB 40, 139

Smith, John 1580(?)-1631 .... **LC 9**
See also DLB 24, 30

Smith, Johnston
See Crane, Stephen (Townley)

Smith, Joseph, Jr. 1805-1844 .... **NCLC 53**

Smith, Lee 1944- .... **CLC 25, 73**
See also CA 114; 119; CANR 46; DLB 143;
DLBY 83; INT 119

Smith, Martin
See Smith, Martin Cruz

Smith, Martin Cruz 1942- ... **CLC 25; DAM
MULT, POP**
See also BEST 89:4; CA 85-88; CANR 6,
23, 43, 65; INT CANR-23; MTCW 2;
NNAL

Smith, Mary-Ann Tirone 1944- ...... **CLC 39**
See also CA 118; 136

Smith, Patti 1946- .... **CLC 12**
See also CA 93-96; CANR 63

Smith, Pauline (Urmson) 1882-1959
.... **TCLC 25**
See also DLB 225

Smith, Rosamond
See Oates, Joyce Carol

Smith, Sheila Kaye
See Kaye-Smith, Sheila

Smith, Stevie .... **CLC 3, 8, 25, 44; PC 12**
See also Smith, Florence Margaret
See also DLB 20; MTCW 2

Smith, Wilbur (Addison) 1933- .... **CLC 33**
See also CA 13-16R; CANR 7, 46, 66;
MTCW 1, 2

Smith, William Jay 1918- .... **CLC 6**
See also CA 5-8R; CANR 44; DLB 5; MAI-
CYA; SAAS 22; SATA 2, 68

Smith, Woodrow Wilson
See Kuttner, Henry

Smolenskin, Peretz 1842-1885 ...... **NCLC 30**

Smollett, Tobias (George) 1721-1771 .. **LC 2,
46**
See also CDBLB 1660-1789; DLB 39, 104

Snodgrass, W(illiam) D(e Witt) 1926-
.... **CLC 2, 6, 10, 18, 68; DAM POET**
See also CA 1-4R; CANR 6, 36, 65, 85;
DLB 5; MTCW 1, 2

Snow, C(harles) P(ercy) 1905-1980 .. **CLC 1,
4, 6, 9, 13, 19; DAM NOV**
See also CA 5-8R; 101; CANR 28; CDBLB
1945-1960; DLB 15, 77; DLBD 17;
MTCW 1, 2

Snow, Frances Compton
See Adams, Henry (Brooks)

Snyder, Gary (Sherman) 1930- .... **CLC 1, 2,
5, 9, 32, 120; DAM POET; PC 21**
See also CA 17-20R; CANR 30, 60; DA3;
DLB 5, 16, 165, 212; MTCW 2

Snyder, Zilpha Keatley 1927- .... **CLC 17**
See also AAYA 15; CA 9-12R; CANR 38;
CLR 31; JRDA; MAICYA; SAAS 2;
SATA 1, 28, 75, 110; SATA-Essay 112

Soares, Bernardo
See Pessoa, Fernando (Antonio Nogueira)

Sobh, A.
See Shamlu, Ahmad

Sobol, Joshua .... **CLC 60**

Socrates 469B.C.-399B.C. .... **CMLC 27**

Soderberg, Hjalmar 1869-1941 .... **TCLC 39**

Sodergran, Edith (Irene)
See Soedergran, Edith (Irene)

Soedergran, Edith (Irene) 1892-1923
.... **TCLC 31**

Softly, Edgar
See Lovecraft, H(oward) P(hillips)

Softly, Edward
See Lovecraft, H(oward) P(hillips)

Sokolov, Raymond 1941- .... **CLC 7**
See also CA 85-88

Solo, Jay
See Ellison, Harlan (Jay)

Sologub, Fyodor .... **TCLC 9**
See also Teternikov, Fyodor Kuzmich

Solomons, Ikey Esquir
See Thackeray, William Makepeace

Solomos, Dionysios 1798-1857 ...... **NCLC 15**

Solwoska, Mara
See French, Marilyn

Solzhenitsyn, Aleksandr I(sayevich) 1918-
..... **CLC 1, 2, 4, 7, 9, 10, 18, 26, 34, 78,
134; DA; DAB; DAC; DAM MST, NOV;
SSC 32; WLC**
See also AITN 1; CA 69-72; CANR 40, 65;
DA3; MTCW 1, 2

Somers, Jane
See Lessing, Doris (May)

Somerville, Edith 1858-1949 .... **TCLC 51**
See also DLB 135

Somerville & Ross
See Martin, Violet Florence; Somerville,
Edith

Sommer, Scott 1951- .... **CLC 25**
See also CA 106

Sondheim, Stephen (Joshua) 1930- . **CLC 30,
39; DAM DRAM**
See also AAYA 11; CA 103; CANR 47, 67

Song, Cathy 1955- .... **PC 21**
See also CA 154; DLB 169

Sontag, Susan 1933- ... **CLC 1, 2, 10, 13, 31,
105; DAM POP**
See also CA 17-20R; CANR 25, 51, 74;
DA3; DLB 2, 67; MTCW 1, 2

Sophocles 496(?)B.C.-406(?)B.C. .. **CMLC 2;
DA; DAB; DAC; DAM DRAM, MST;
DC 1; WLCS**
See also DA3; DLB 176

Sordello 1189-1269 .... **CMLC 15**

Sorel, Georges 1847-1922 .... **TCLC 91**
See also CA 118

Sorel, Julia
See Drexler, Rosalyn

Sorrentino, Gilbert 1929- . **CLC 3, 7, 14, 22,
40**
See also CA 77-80; CANR 14, 33; DLB 5,
173; DLBY 80; INT CANR-14

Soto, Gary 1952- .. **CLC 32, 80; DAM MULT;
HLC 2; PC 28**
See also AAYA 10, 37; CA 119; 125; CANR
50, 74; CLR 38; DLB 82; HW 1, 2; INT
125; JRDA; MTCW 2; SATA 80, 120

Soupault, Philippe 1897-1990 .... **CLC 68**
See also CA 116; 147; 131

Souster, (Holmes) Raymond 1921- .. **CLC 5,
14; DAC; DAM POET**
See also CA 13-16R; CAAS 14; CANR 13,
29, 53; DLB 88; SATA 63

Southern, Terry 1924(?)-1995 .... **CLC 7**
See also CA 1-4R; 150; CANR 1, 55; DLB
2

Southey, Robert 1774-1843 .... **NCLC 8**

See also DLB 93, 107, 142; SATA 54

Southworth, Emma Dorothy Eliza Nevitte
1819-1899 .... **NCLC 26**

Souza, Ernest
See Scott, Evelyn

Soyinka, Wole 1934- .. **CLC 3, 5, 14, 36, 44;
BLC 3; DA; DAB; DAC; DAM DRAM,
MST, MULT; DC 2; WLC**
See also BW 2, 3; CA 13-16R; CANR 27,
39, 82; DA3; DLB 125; MTCW 1, 2

Spackman, W(illiam) M(ode) 1905-1990
.... **CLC 46**
See also CA 81-84; 132

Spacks, Barry (Bernard) 1931- .... **CLC 14**
See also CA 154; CANR 33; DLB 105

Spanidou, Irini 1946- .... **CLC 44**
See also CA 185

Spark, Muriel (Sarah) 1918- ... **CLC 2, 3, 5,
8, 13, 18, 40, 94; DAB; DAC; DAM
MST, NOV; SSC 10**
See also CA 5-8R; CANR 12, 36, 76, 89;
CDBLB 1945-1960; DA3; DLB 15, 139;
INT CANR-12; MTCW 1, 2

Spaulding, Douglas
See Bradbury, Ray (Douglas)

Spaulding, Leonard
See Bradbury, Ray (Douglas)

Spence, J. A. D.
See Eliot, T(homas) S(tearns)

Spencer, Elizabeth 1921- .... **CLC 22**
See also CA 13-16R; CANR 32, 65, 87;
DLB 6; MTCW 1; SATA 14

Spencer, Leonard G.
See Silverberg, Robert

Spencer, Scott 1945- .... **CLC 30**
See also CA 113; CANR 51; DLBY 86

Spender, Stephen (Harold) 1909-1995
... **CLC 1, 2, 5, 10, 41, 91; DAM POET**
See also CA 9-12R; 149; CANR 31, 54;
CDBLB 1945-1960; DA3; DLB 20;
MTCW 1, 2

Spengler, Oswald (Arnold Gottfried)
1880-1936 .... **TCLC 25**
See also CA 118

Spenser, Edmund 1552(?)-1599 .. **LC 5, 39;
DA; DAB; DAC; DAM MST, POET;
PC 8; WLC**
See also CDBLB Before 1660; DA3; DLB
167

Spicer, Jack 1925-1965 .... **CLC 8, 18, 72;
DAM POET**
See also CA 85-88; DLB 5, 16, 193

Spiegelman, Art 1948- .... **CLC 76**
See also AAYA 10; CA 125; CANR 41, 55,
74; MTCW 2; SATA 109

Spielberg, Peter 1929- .... **CLC 6**
See also CA 5-8R; CANR 4, 48; DLBY 81

Spielberg, Steven 1947- .... **CLC 20**
See also AAYA 8, 24; CA 77-80; CANR
32; SATA 32

Spillane, Frank Morrison 1918-
See Spillane, Mickey
See also CA 25-28R; CANR 28, 63; DA3;
DLB 226; MTCW 1, 2; SATA 66

Spillane, Mickey .... **CLC 3, 13**
See also Spillane, Frank Morrison
See also DLB 226; MTCW 2

Spinoza, Benedictus de 1632-1677 . **LC 9, 58**

Spinrad, Norman (Richard) 1940- . **CLC 46**
See also CA 37-40R; CAAS 19; CANR 20,
91; DLB 8; INT CANR-20

Spitteler, Carl (Friedrich Georg) 1845-1924
.... **TCLC 12**
See also CA 109; DLB 129

Spivack, Kathleen (Romola Drucker) 1938-
.... **CLC 6**
See also CA 49-52

Spoto, Donald 1941- .... **CLC 39**
See also CA 65-68; CANR 11, 57, 93

See also DLB 129

Storni, Alfonsina 1892-1938 . **TCLC 5; DAM MULT; HLC 2; PC 33**
See also CA 104; 131; HW 1

Stoughton, William 1631-1701 .... **LC 38**
See also DLB 24

Stout, Rex (Todhunter) 1886-1975 .... **CLC 3**
See also AITN 2; CA 61-64; CANR 71

Stow, (Julian) Randolph 1935- .... **CLC 23, 48**
See also CA 13-16R; CANR 33; MTCW 1

Stowe, Harriet (Elizabeth) Beecher
1811-1896 ...... **NCLC 3, 50; DA; DAB; DAC; DAM MST, NOV; WLC**
See also CDALB 1865-1917; DA3; DLB 1, 12, 42, 74, 189; JRDA; MAICYA; YABC 1

Strabo c. 64B.C.-c. 25 .... **CMLC 37**
See also DLB 176

Strachey, (Giles) Lytton 1880-1932
.... **TCLC 12**
See also CA 110; 178; DLB 149; DLBD 10; MTCW 2

Strand, Mark 1934- .... **CLC 6, 18, 41, 71; DAM POET**
See also CA 21-24R; CANR 40, 65; DLB 5; SATA 41

Straub, Peter (Francis) 1943- . **CLC 28, 107; DAM POP**
See also BEST 89:1; CA 85-88; CANR 28, 65; DLBY 84; MTCW 1, 2

Strauss, Botho 1944- .... **CLC 22**
See also CA 157; DLB 124

Streatfeild, (Mary) Noel 1895(?)-1986
.... **CLC 21**
See also CA 81-84; 120; CANR 31; CLR 17; DLB 160; MAICYA; SATA 20; SATA-Obit 48

Stribling, T(homas) S(igismund) 1881-1965
.... **CLC 23**
See also CA 107; DLB 9

Strindberg, (Johan) August 1849-1912
... **TCLC 1, 8, 21, 47; DA; DAB; DAC; DAM DRAM, MST; WLC**
See also CA 104; 135; DA3; MTCW 2

Stringer, Arthur 1874-1950 .... **TCLC 37**
See also CA 161; DLB 92

Stringer, David
See Roberts, Keith (John Kingston)

Stroheim, Erich von 1885-1957 .... **TCLC 71**

Strugatskii, Arkadii (Natanovich) 1925-1991
.... **CLC 27**
See also CA 106; 135

Strugatskii, Boris (Natanovich) 1933-
.... **CLC 27**
See also CA 106

Strummer, Joe 1953(?)- .... **CLC 30**

Strunk, William, Jr. 1869-1946 .... **TCLC 92**
See also CA 118; 164

Stryk, Lucien 1924- .... **PC 27**
See also CA 13-16R; CANR 10, 28, 55

Stuart, Don A.
See Campbell, John W(ood, Jr.)

Stuart, Ian
See MacLean, Alistair (Stuart)

Stuart, Jesse (Hilton) 1906-1984 .. **CLC 1, 8, 11, 14, 34; SSC 31**
See also CA 5-8R; 112; CANR 31; DLB 9, 48, 102; DLBY 84; SATA 2; SATA-Obit 36

Sturgeon, Theodore (Hamilton) 1918-1985
.... **CLC 22, 39**
See also Queen, Ellery
See also CA 81-84; 116; CANR 32; DLB 8; DLBY 85; MTCW 1, 2

Sturges, Preston 1898-1959 .... **TCLC 48**
See also CA 114; 149; DLB 26

Styron, William 1925- .. **CLC 1, 3, 5, 11, 15, 60; DAM NOV, POP; SSC 25**

See also BEST 90:4; CA 5-8R; CANR 6, 33, 74; CDALB 1968-1988; DA3; DLB 2, 143; DLBY 80; INT CANR-6; MTCW 1, 2

Su, Chien 1884-1918
See Su Man-shu
See also CA 123

Suarez Lynch, B.
See Bioy Casares, Adolfo; Borges, Jorge Luis

Suassuna, Ariano Vilar 1927-
See also CA 178; HLCS 1; HW 2

Suckling, John 1609-1641 .... **PC 30**
See also DAM POET; DLB 58, 126

Suckow, Ruth 1892-1960 .... **SSC 18**
See also CA 113; DLB 9, 102

Sudermann, Hermann 1857-1928 . **TCLC 15**
See also CA 107; DLB 118

Sue, Eugene 1804-1857 .... **NCLC 1**
See also DLB 119

Sueskind, Patrick 1949- .... **CLC 44**
See also Suskind, Patrick

Sukenick, Ronald 1932- ...... **CLC 3, 4, 6, 48**
See also CA 25-28R; CAAS 8; CANR 32, 89; DLB 173; DLBY 81

Suknaski, Andrew 1942- .... **CLC 19**
See also CA 101; DLB 53

Sullivan, Vernon
See Vian, Boris

Sully Prudhomme 1839-1907 .... **TCLC 31**

Su Man-shu .... **TCLC 24**
See also Su, Chien

Summerforest, Ivy B.
See Kirkup, James

Summers, Andrew James 1942- ...... **CLC 26**

Summers, Andy
See Summers, Andrew James

Summers, Hollis (Spurgeon, Jr.) 1916-
.... **CLC 10**
See also CA 5-8R; CANR 3; DLB 6

Summers, (Alphonsus Joseph-Mary Augustus) Montague 1880-1948
.... **TCLC 16**
See also CA 118; 163

Sumner, Gordon Matthew .... **CLC 26**
See also Sting

Surtees, Robert Smith 1803-1864 . **NCLC 14**
See also DLB 21

Susann, Jacqueline 1921-1974 .... **CLC 3**
See also AITN 1; CA 65-68; 53-56; MTCW 1, 2

Su Shih 1036-1101 .... **CMLC 15**

Suskind, Patrick
See Sueskind, Patrick
See also CA 145

Sutcliff, Rosemary 1920-1992 .... **CLC 26; DAB; DAC; DAM MST, POP**
See also AAYA 10; CA 5-8R; 139; CANR 37; CLR 1, 37; JRDA; MAICYA; SATA 6, 44, 78; SATA-Obit 73

Sutro, Alfred 1863-1933 .... **TCLC 6**
See also CA 105; 185; DLB 10

Sutton, Henry
See Slavitt, David R(ytman)

Svevo, Italo 1861-1928 .... **TCLC 2, 35; SSC 25**
See also Schmitz, Aron Hector

Swados, Elizabeth (A.) 1951- .... **CLC 12**
See also CA 97-100; CANR 49; INT 97-100

Swados, Harvey 1920-1972 .... **CLC 5**
See also CA 5-8R; 37-40R; CANR 6; DLB 2

Swan, Gladys 1934- .... **CLC 69**
See also CA 101; CANR 17, 39

Swanson, Logan
See Matheson, Richard Burton

Swarthout, Glendon (Fred) 1918-1992
.... **CLC 35**
See also CA 1-4R; 139; CANR 1, 47; SATA 26

Sweet, Sarah C.
See Jewett, (Theodora) Sarah Orne

Swenson, May 1919-1989 ..... **CLC 4, 14, 61, 106; DA; DAB; DAC; DAM MST, POET; PC 14**
See also CA 5-8R; 130; CANR 36, 61; DLB 5; MTCW 1, 2; SATA 15

Swift, Augustus
See Lovecraft, H(oward) P(hillips)

Swift, Graham (Colin) 1949- .... **CLC 41, 88**
See also CA 117; 122; CANR 46, 71; DLB 194; MTCW 2

Swift, Jonathan 1667-1745 ... **LC 1, 42; DA; DAB; DAC; DAM MST, NOV, POET; PC 9; WLC**
See also CDBLB 1660-1789; CLR 53; DA3; DLB 39, 95, 101; SATA 19

Swinburne, Algernon Charles 1837-1909
... **TCLC 8, 36; DA; DAB; DAC; DAM MST, POET; PC 24; WLC**
See also CA 105; 140; CDBLB 1832-1890; DA3; DLB 35, 57

Swinfen, Ann .... **CLC 34**

Swinnerton, Frank Arthur 1884-1982
.... **CLC 31**
See also CA 108; DLB 34

Swithen, John
See King, Stephen (Edwin)

Sylvia
See Ashton-Warner, Sylvia (Constance)

Symmes, Robert Edward
See Duncan, Robert (Edward)

Symonds, John Addington 1840-1893
.... **NCLC 34**
See also DLB 57, 144

Symons, Arthur 1865-1945 .... **TCLC 11**
See also CA 107; DLB 19, 57, 149

Symons, Julian (Gustave) 1912-1994
.... **CLC 2, 14, 32**
See also CA 49-52; 147; CAAS 3; CANR 3, 33, 59; DLB 87, 155; DLBY 92; MTCW 1

Synge, (Edmund) J(ohn) M(illington)
1871-1909 . **TCLC 6, 37; DAM DRAM; DC 2**
See also CA 104; 141; CDBLB 1890-1914; DLB 10, 19

Syruc, J.
See Milosz, Czeslaw

Szirtes, George 1948- .... **CLC 46**
See also CA 109; CANR 27, 61

Szymborska, Wislawa 1923- .... **CLC 99**
See also CA 154; CANR 91; DA3; DLB 232; DLBY 96; MTCW 2

T. O., Nik
See Annensky, Innokenty (Fyodorovich)

Tabori, George 1914- .... **CLC 19**
See also CA 49-52; CANR 4, 69

Tagore, Rabindranath 1861-1941 .. **TCLC 3, 53; DAM DRAM, POET; PC 8**
See also CA 104; 120; DA3; MTCW 1, 2

Taine, Hippolyte Adolphe 1828-1893
.... **NCLC 15**

Talese, Gay 1932- .... **CLC 37**
See also AITN 1; CA 1-4R; CANR 9, 58; DLB 185; INT CANR-9; MTCW 1, 2

Tallent, Elizabeth (Ann) 1954- .... **CLC 45**
See also CA 117; CANR 72; DLB 130

Tally, Ted 1952- .... **CLC 42**
See also CA 120; 124; INT 124

Talvik, Heiti 1904-1947 .... **TCLC 87**

Tamayo y Baus, Manuel 1829-1898 . **NCLC 1**

Tammsaare, A(nton) H(ansen) 1878-1940
.... **TCLC 27**
See also CA 164; DLB 220

Tam'si, Tchicaya U
See Tchicaya, Gerald Felix
Tan, Amy (Ruth) 1952- . **CLC 59, 120; DAM MULT, NOV, POP**
See also AAYA 9; BEST 89:3; CA 136; CANR 54; CDALBS; DA3; DLB 173; MTCW 2; SATA 75
Tandem, Felix
See Spitteler, Carl (Friedrich Georg)
Tanizaki, Jun'ichiro 1886-1965 .. **CLC 8, 14, 28; SSC 21**
See also CA 93-96; 25-28R; DLB 180; MTCW 2
Tanner, William
See Amis, Kingsley (William)
Tao Lao
See Storni, Alfonsina
Tarantino, Quentin (Jerome) 1963-
.... **CLC 125**
See also CA 171
Tarassoff, Lev
See Troyat, Henri
Tarbell, Ida M(inerva) 1857-1944 . **TCLC 40**
See also CA 122; 181; DLB 47
Tarkington, (Newton) Booth 1869-1946
.... **TCLC 9**
See also CA 110; 143; DLB 9, 102; MTCW 2; SATA 17
Tarkovsky, Andrei (Arsenyevich) 1932-1986
.... **CLC 75**
See also CA 127
Tartt, Donna 1964(?)- .... **CLC 76**
See also CA 142
Tasso, Torquato 1544-1595 .... **LC 5**
Tate, (John Orley) Allen 1899-1979 . **CLC 2, 4, 6, 9, 11, 14, 24**
See also CA 5-8R; 85-88; CANR 32; DLB 4, 45, 63; DLBD 17; MTCW 1, 2
Tate, Ellalice
See Hibbert, Eleanor Alice Burford
Tate, James (Vincent) 1943- .... **CLC 2, 6, 25**
See also CA 21-24R; CANR 29, 57; DLB 5, 169
Tauler, Johannes c. 1300-1361 ..... **CMLC 37**
See also DLB 179
Tavel, Ronald 1940- .... **CLC 6**
See also CA 21-24R; CANR 33
Taylor, Bayard 1825-1878 .... **NCLC 89**
See also DLB 3, 189
Taylor, C(ecil) P(hilip) 1929-1981 ... **CLC 27**
See also CA 25-28R; 105; CANR 47
Taylor, Edward 1642(?)-1729 .... **LC 11; DA; DAB; DAC; DAM MST, POET**
See also DLB 24
Taylor, Eleanor Ross 1920- .... **CLC 5**
See also CA 81-84; CANR 70
Taylor, Elizabeth 1912-1975 .... **CLC 2, 4, 29**
See also CA 13-16R; CANR 9, 70; DLB 139; MTCW 1; SATA 13
Taylor, Frederick Winslow 1856-1915
.... **TCLC 76**
Taylor, Henry (Splawn) 1942- .... **CLC 44**
See also CA 33-36R; CAAS 7; CANR 31; DLB 5
Taylor, Kamala (Purnaiya) 1924-
See Markandaya, Kamala
See also CA 77-80
Taylor, Mildred D. .... **CLC 21**
See also AAYA 10; BW 1; CA 85-88; CANR 25; CLR 9, 59; DLB 52; JRDA; MAICYA; SAAS 5; SATA 15, 70
Taylor, Peter (Hillsman) 1917-1994 . **CLC 1, 4, 18, 37, 44, 50, 71; SSC 10**
See also CA 13-16R; 147; CANR 9, 50; DLBY 81, 94; INT CANR-9; MTCW 1, 2
Taylor, Robert Lewis 1912-1998 . **CLC 14**
See also CA 1-4R; 170; CANR 3, 64; SATA 10

Tchekhov, Anton
See Chekhov, Anton (Pavlovich)
Tchicaya, Gerald Felix 1931-1988 . **CLC 101**
See also CA 129; 125; CANR 81
Tchicaya U Tam'si
See Tchicaya, Gerald Felix
Teasdale, Sara 1884-1933 ... **TCLC 4; PC 31**
See also CA 104; 163; DLB 45; SATA 32
Tegner, Esaias 1782-1846 .... **NCLC 2**
Teilhard de Chardin, (Marie Joseph) Pierre 1881-1955 .... **TCLC 9**
See also CA 105
Temple, Ann
See Mortimer, Penelope (Ruth)
Tennant, Emma (Christina) 1937- . **CLC 13, 52**
See also CA 65-68; CAAS 9; CANR 10, 38, 59, 88; DLB 14
Tenneshaw, S. M.
See Silverberg, Robert
Tennyson, Alfred 1809-1892 .. **NCLC 30, 65; DA; DAB; DAC; DAM MST, POET; PC 6; WLC**
See also CDBLB 1832-1890; DA3; DLB 32
Teran, Lisa St. Aubin de .... **CLC 36**
See also St. Aubin de Teran, Lisa
Terence c. 184B.C.-c. 159B.C. .... **CMLC 14; DC 7**
See also DLB 211
Teresa de Jesus, St. 1515-1582 .... **LC 18**
Terkel, Louis 1912-
See Terkel, Studs
See also CA 57-60; CANR 18, 45, 67; DA3; MTCW 1, 2
Terkel, Studs .... **CLC 38**
See also Terkel, Louis
See also AAYA 32; AITN 1; MTCW 2
Terry, C. V.
See Slaughter, Frank G(ill)
Terry, Megan 1932- .... **CLC 19; DC 13**
See also CA 77-80; CABS 3; CANR 43; DLB 7
Tertullian c. 155-c. 245 .... **CMLC 29**
Tertz, Abram
See Sinyavsky, Andrei (Donatevich)
Tesich, Steve 1943(?)-1996 .... **CLC 40, 69**
See also CA 105; 152; DLBY 83
Tesla, Nikola 1856-1943 .... **TCLC 88**
Teternikov, Fyodor Kuzmich 1863-1927
See Sologub, Fyodor
See also CA 104
Tevis, Walter 1928-1984 .... **CLC 42**
See also CA 113
Tey, Josephine .... **TCLC 14**
See also Mackintosh, Elizabeth
See also DLB 77
Thackeray, William Makepeace 1811-1863 . **NCLC 5, 14, 22, 43; DA; DAB; DAC; DAM MST, NOV; WLC**
See also CDBLB 1832-1890; DA3; DLB 21, 55, 159, 163; SATA 23
Thakura, Ravindranatha
See Tagore, Rabindranath
Tharoor, Shashi 1956- .... **CLC 70**
See also CA 141; CANR 91
Thelwell, Michael Miles 1939- .... **CLC 22**
See also BW 2; CA 101
Theobald, Lewis, Jr.
See Lovecraft, H(oward) P(hillips)
Theodorescu, Ion N. 1880-1967
See Arghezi, Tudor
See also CA 116; DLB 220
Theriault, Yves 1915-1983 ... **CLC 79; DAC; DAM MST**
See also CA 102; DLB 88
Theroux, Alexander (Louis) 1939- ... **CLC 2, 25**

See also CA 85-88; CANR 20, 63
Theroux, Paul (Edward) 1941- .... **CLC 5, 8, 11, 15, 28, 46; DAM POP**
See also AAYA 28; BEST 89:4; CA 33-36R; CANR 20, 45, 74; CDALBS; DA3; DLB 2; MTCW 1, 2; SATA 44, 109
Thesen, Sharon 1946- .... **CLC 56**
See also CA 163
Thevenin, Denis
See Duhamel, Georges
Thibault, Jacques Anatole Francois 1844-1924
See France, Anatole
See also CA 106; 127; DAM NOV; DA3; MTCW 1, 2
Thiele, Colin (Milton) 1920- .... **CLC 17**
See also CA 29-32R; CANR 12, 28, 53; CLR 27; MAICYA; SAAS 2; SATA 14, 72
Thomas, Audrey (Callahan) 1935- .. **CLC 7, 13, 37, 107; SSC 20**
See also AITN 2; CA 21-24R; CAAS 19; CANR 36, 58; DLB 60; MTCW 1
Thomas, Augustus 1857-1934 .... **TCLC 97**
Thomas, D(onald) M(ichael) 1935- . **CLC 13, 22, 31, 132**
See also CA 61-64; CAAS 11; CANR 17, 45, 75; CDBLB 1960 to Present; DA3; DLB 40, 207; INT CANR-17; MTCW 1, 2
Thomas, Dylan (Marlais) 1914-1953 . **TCLC 1, 8, 45, 105; DA; DAB; DAC; DAM DRAM, MST, POET; PC 2; SSC 3; WLC**
See also CA 104; 120; CANR 65; CDBLB 1945-1960; DA3; DLB 13, 20, 139; MTCW 1, 2; SATA 60
Thomas, (Philip) Edward 1878-1917
.... **TCLC 10; DAM POET**
See also CA 106; 153; DLB 98
Thomas, Joyce Carol 1938- .... **CLC 35**
See also AAYA 12; BW 2, 3; CA 113; 116; CANR 48; CLR 19; DLB 33; INT 116; JRDA; MAICYA; MTCW 1, 2; SAAS 7; SATA 40, 78
Thomas, Lewis 1913-1993 .... **CLC 35**
See also CA 85-88; 143; CANR 38, 60; MTCW 1, 2
Thomas, M. Carey 1857-1935 ...... **TCLC 89**
Thomas, Paul
See Mann, (Paul) Thomas
Thomas, Piri 1928- .... **CLC 17; HLCS 2**
See also CA 73-76; HW 1
Thomas, R(onald) S(tuart) 1913- ..... **CLC 6, 13, 48; DAB; DAM POET**
See also CA 89-92; CAAS 4; CANR 30; CDBLB 1960 to Present; DLB 27; MTCW 1
Thomas, Ross (Elmore) 1926-1995 . **CLC 39**
See also CA 33-36R; 150; CANR 22, 63
Thompson, Francis Clegg
See Mencken, H(enry) L(ouis)
Thompson, Francis Joseph 1859-1907
.... **TCLC 4**
See also CA 104; CDBLB 1890-1914; DLB 19
Thompson, Hunter S(tockton) 1939-
.... **CLC 9, 17, 40, 104; DAM POP**
See also BEST 89:1; CA 17-20R; CANR 23, 46, 74, 77; DA3; DLB 185; MTCW 1, 2
Thompson, James Myers
See Thompson, Jim (Myers)
Thompson, Jim (Myers) 1906-1977(?)
.... **CLC 69**
See also CA 140; DLB 226
Thompson, Judith .... **CLC 39**
Thomson, James 1700-1748 .. **LC 16, 29, 40; DAM POET**

See also DLB 95

Thomson, James 1834-1882 .... **NCLC 18; DAM POET**
See also DLB 35

Thoreau, Henry David 1817-1862 . **NCLC 7, 21, 61; DA; DAB; DAC; DAM MST; PC 30; WLC**
See also CDALB 1640-1865; DA3; DLB 1, 223

Thornton, Hall
See Silverberg, Robert

Thucydides c. 455B.C.-399B.C. ... **CMLC 17**
See also DLB 176

Thumboo, Edwin 1933- .... **PC 30**

Thurber, James (Grover) 1894-1961 . **CLC 5, 11, 25, 125; DA; DAB; DAC; DAM DRAM, MST, NOV; SSC 1**
See also CA 73-76; CANR 17, 39; CDALB 1929-1941; DA3; DLB 4, 11, 22, 102; MAICYA; MTCW 1, 2; SATA 13

Thurman, Wallace (Henry) 1902-1934
.... **TCLC 6; BLC 3; DAM MULT**
See also BW 1, 3; CA 104; 124; CANR 81; DLB 51

Tibullus, Albius c. 54B.C.-c. 19B.C.
.... **CMLC 36**
See also DLB 211

Ticheburn, Cheviot
See Ainsworth, William Harrison

Tieck, (Johann) Ludwig 1773-1853
.... **NCLC 5, 46; SSC 31**
See also DLB 90

Tiger, Derry
See Ellison, Harlan (Jay)

Tilghman, Christopher 1948(?)- ...... **CLC 65**
See also CA 159

Tillich, Paul (Johannes) 1886-1965
.... **CLC 131**
See also CA 5-8R; 25-28R; CANR 33; MTCW 1, 2

Tillinghast, Richard (Williford) 1940-
.... **CLC 29**
See also CA 29-32R; CAAS 23; CANR 26, 51

Timrod, Henry 1828-1867 .... **NCLC 25**
See also DLB 3

Tindall, Gillian (Elizabeth) 1938- ..... **CLC 7**
See also CA 21-24R; CANR 11, 65

Tiptree, James, Jr. .... **CLC 48, 50**
See Sheldon, Alice Hastings Bradley
See also DLB 8

Titmarsh, Michael Angelo
See Thackeray, William Makepeace

Tocqueville, Alexis (Charles Henri Maurice Clerel, Comte) de 1805-1859 . **NCLC 7, 63**

Tolkien, J(ohn) R(onald) R(euel) 1892-1973
.... **CLC 1, 2, 3, 8, 12, 38; DA; DAB; DAC; DAM MST, NOV, POP; WLC**
See also AAYA 10; AITN 1; CA 17-18; 45-48; CANR 36; CAP 2; CDBLB 1914-1945; CLR 56; DA3; DLB 15, 160; JRDA; MAICYA; MTCW 1, 2; SATA 2, 32, 100; SATA-Obit 24

Toller, Ernst 1893-1939 .... **TCLC 10**
See also CA 107; 186; DLB 124

Tolson, M. B.
See Tolson, Melvin B(eaunorus)

Tolson, Melvin B(eaunorus) 1898(?)-1966
.... **CLC 36, 105; BLC 3; DAM MULT, POET**
See also BW 1, 3; CA 124; 89-92; CANR 80; DLB 48, 76

Tolstoi, Aleksei Nikolaevich
See Tolstoy, Alexey Nikolaevich

Tolstoy, Alexey Nikolaevich 1882-1945
.... **TCLC 18**
See also CA 107; 158

Tolstoy, Count Leo
See Tolstoy, Leo (Nikolaevich)

Tolstoy, Leo (Nikolaevich) 1828-1910
. **TCLC 4, 11, 17, 28, 44, 79; DA; DAB; DAC; DAM MST, NOV; SSC 9, 30; WLC**
See also CA 104; 123; DA3; SATA 26

Tomasi di Lampedusa, Giuseppe 1896-1957
See Lampedusa, Giuseppe (Tomasi) di
See also CA 111

Tomlin, Lily .... **CLC 17**
See also Tomlin, Mary Jean

Tomlin, Mary Jean 1939(?)-
See Tomlin, Lily
See also CA 117

Tomlinson, (Alfred) Charles 1927- .. **CLC 2, 4, 6, 13, 45; DAM POET; PC 17**
See also CA 5-8R; CANR 33; DLB 40

Tomlinson, H(enry) M(ajor) 1873-1958
.... **TCLC 71**
See also CA 118; 161; DLB 36, 100, 195

Tonson, Jacob
See Bennett, (Enoch) Arnold

Toole, John Kennedy 1937-1969 .... **CLC 19, 64**
See also CA 104; DLBY 81; MTCW 2

Toomer, Jean 1894-1967 .. **CLC 1, 4, 13, 22; BLC 3; DAM MULT; PC 7; SSC 1; WLCS**
See also Pinchback, Eugene; Toomer, Eugene; Toomer, Eugene Pinchback; Toomer, Nathan Jean; Toomer, Nathan Pinchback
See also BW 1; CA 85-88; CDALB 1917-1929; DA3; DLB 45, 51; MTCW 1, 2

Torley, Luke
See Blish, James (Benjamin)

Tornimparte, Alessandra
See Ginzburg, Natalia

Torre, Raoul della
See Mencken, H(enry) L(ouis)

Torrence, Ridgely 1874-1950 .... **TCLC 97**
See also DLB 54

Torrey, E(dwin) Fuller 1937- .... **CLC 34**
See also CA 119; CANR 71

Torsvan, Ben Traven
See Traven, B.

Torsvan, Benno Traven
See Traven, B.

Torsvan, Berick Traven
See Traven, B.

Torsvan, Berwick Traven
See Traven, B.

Torsvan, Bruno Traven
See Traven, B.

Torsvan, Traven
See Traven, B.

Tournier, Michel (Edouard) 1924- ... **CLC 6, 23, 36, 95**
See also CA 49-52; CANR 3, 36, 74; DLB 83; MTCW 1, 2; SATA 23

Tournimparte, Alessandra
See Ginzburg, Natalia

Towers, Ivar
See Kornbluth, C(yril) M.

Towne, Robert (Burton) 1936(?)- .... **CLC 87**
See also CA 108; DLB 44

Townsend, Sue .... **CLC 61**
See also Townsend, Susan Elaine
See also AAYA 28; SATA 55, 93; SATA-Brief 48

Townsend, Susan Elaine 1946-
See Townsend, Sue

Townshend, Peter (Dennis Blandford) 1945-
.... **CLC 17, 42**
See also CA 107

Tozzi, Federigo 1883-1920 .... **TCLC 31**
See also CA 160

Tracy, Don(ald Fiske) 1905-1976(?)
See Queen, Ellery
See also CA 1-4R; 176; CANR 2

Traill, Catharine Parr 1802-1899 . **NCLC 31**
See also DLB 99

Trakl, Georg 1887-1914 ..... **TCLC 5; PC 20**
See also CA 104; 165; MTCW 2

Transtroemer, Tomas (Goesta) 1931-
.... **CLC 52, 65; DAM POET**
See also CA 117; 129; CAAS 17

Transtromer, Tomas Gosta
See Transtroemer, Tomas (Goesta)

Traven, B. (?)-1969 .... **CLC 8, 11**
See also CA 19-20; 25-28R; CAP 2; DLB 9, 56; MTCW 1

Treitel, Jonathan 1959- .... **CLC 70**

Trelawny, Edward John 1792-1881
.... **NCLC 85**
See also DLB 110, 116, 144

Tremain, Rose 1943- .... **CLC 42**
See also CA 97-100; CANR 44; DLB 14

Tremblay, Michel 1942- .... **CLC 29, 102; DAC; DAM MST**
See also CA 116; 128; DLB 60; MTCW 1, 2

Trevanian .... **CLC 29**
See also Whitaker, Rod(ney)

Trevor, Glen
See Hilton, James

Trevor, William 1928- . **CLC 7, 9, 14, 25, 71, 116; SSC 21**
See also Cox, William Trevor
See also DLB 14, 139; MTCW 2

Trifonov, Yuri (Valentinovich) 1925-1981
.... **CLC 45**
See also CA 126; 103; MTCW 1

Trilling, Diana (Rubin) 1905-1996 . **CLC 129**
See also CA 5-8R; 154; CANR 10, 46; INT CANR-10; MTCW 1, 2

Trilling, Lionel 1905-1975 ..... **CLC 9, 11, 24**
See also CA 9-12R; 61-64; CANR 10; DLB 28, 63; INT CANR-10; MTCW 1, 2

Trimball, W. H.
See Mencken, H(enry) L(ouis)

Tristan
See Gomez de la Serna, Ramon

Tristram
See Housman, A(lfred) E(dward)

Trogdon, William (Lewis) 1939-
See Heat-Moon, William Least
See also CA 115; 119; CANR 47, 89; INT 119

Trollope, Anthony 1815-1882 .. **NCLC 6, 33; DA; DAB; DAC; DAM MST, NOV; SSC 28; WLC**
See also CDBLB 1832-1890; DA3; DLB 21, 57, 159; SATA 22

Trollope, Frances 1779-1863 .... **NCLC 30**
See also DLB 21, 166

Trotsky, Leon 1879-1940 .... **TCLC 22**
See also CA 118; 167

Trotter (Cockburn), Catharine 1679-1749
.... **LC 8**
See also DLB 84

Trotter, Wilfred 1872-1939 .... **TCLC 97**

Trout, Kilgore
See Farmer, Philip Jose

Trow, George W. S. 1943- .... **CLC 52**
See also CA 126; CANR 91

Troyat, Henri 1911- .... **CLC 23**
See also CA 45-48; CANR 2, 33, 67; MTCW 1

Trudeau, G(arretson) B(eekman) 1948-
See Trudeau, Garry B.
See also CA 81-84; CANR 31; SATA 35

Trudeau, Garry B. .... **CLC 12**
See also Trudeau, G(arretson) B(eekman)
See also AAYA 10; AITN 2

See also CA 45-48; CAAS 2; CANR 1, 48; DLB 7

van Ostaijen, Paul 1896-1928 .... **TCLC 33**
See also CA 163

Van Peebles, Melvin 1932- .... **CLC 2, 20; DAM MULT**
See also BW 2, 3; CA 85-88; CANR 27, 67, 82

Vansittart, Peter 1920- .... **CLC 42**
See also CA 1-4R; CANR 3, 49, 90

Van Vechten, Carl 1880-1964 .... **CLC 33**
See also CA 183; 89-92; DLB 4, 9, 51

Van Vogt, A(lfred) E(lton) 1912-2000 . **CLC 1**
See also CA 21-24R; CANR 28; DLB 8; SATA 14

Varda, Agnes 1928- .... **CLC 16**
See also CA 116; 122

Vargas Llosa, (Jorge) Mario (Pedro) 1936-
..... **CLC 3, 6, 9, 10, 15, 31, 42, 85; DA; DAB; DAC; DAM MST, MULT, NOV; HLC 2**
See also CA 73-76; CANR 18, 32, 42, 67; DA3; DLB 145; HW 1, 2; MTCW 1, 2

Vasiliu, Gheorghe 1881-1957
See Bacovia, George
See also CA 123; DLB 220

Vassa, Gustavus
See Equiano, Olaudah

Vassilikos, Vassilis 1933- .... **CLC 4, 8**
See also CA 81-84; CANR 75

Vaughan, Henry 1621-1695 .... **LC 27**
See also DLB 131

Vaughn, Stephanie .... **CLC 62**

Vazov, Ivan (Minchov) 1850-1921 . **TCLC 25**
See also CA 121; 167; DLB 147

Veblen, Thorstein B(unde) 1857-1929
.... **TCLC 31**
See also CA 115; 165

Vega, Lope de 1562-1635 ... **LC 23; HLCS 2**

Vendler, Helen (Hennessy) 1933- .. **CLC 138**
See also CA 41-44R; CANR 25, 72; MTCW 1, 2

Venison, Alfred
See Pound, Ezra (Weston Loomis)

Verdi, Marie de
See Mencken, H(enry) L(ouis)

Verdu, Matilde
See Cela, Camilo Jose

Verga, Giovanni (Carmelo) 1840-1922
.... **TCLC 3; SSC 21**
See also CA 104; 123

Vergil 70B.C.-19B.C. .... **CMLC 9, 40; DA; DAB; DAC; DAM MST, POET; PC 12; WLCS**
See also Virgil
See also DA3; DLB 211

Verhaeren, Emile (Adolphe Gustave)
1855-1916 .... **TCLC 12**
See also CA 109

Verlaine, Paul (Marie) 1844-1896 . **NCLC 2, 51; DAM POET; PC 2, 32**

Verne, Jules (Gabriel) 1828-1905 .. **TCLC 6, 52**
See also AAYA 16; CA 110; 131; DA3; DLB 123; JRDA; MAICYA; SATA 21

Very, Jones 1813-1880 .... **NCLC 9**
See also DLB 1

Vesaas, Tarjei 1897-1970 .... **CLC 48**
See also CA 29-32R

Vialis, Gaston
See Simenon, Georges (Jacques Christian)

Vian, Boris 1920-1959 .... **TCLC 9**
See also CA 106; 164; DLB 72; MTCW 2

Viaud, (Louis Marie) Julien 1850-1923
See Loti, Pierre
See also CA 107

Vicar, Henry
See Felsen, Henry Gregor

Vicker, Angus
See Felsen, Henry Gregor

Vidal, Gore 1925- ..... **CLC 2, 4, 6, 8, 10, 22, 33, 72; DAM NOV, POP**
See also AITN 1; BEST 90:2; CA 5-8R; CANR 13, 45, 65; CDALBS; DA3; DLB 6, 152; INT CANR-13; MTCW 1, 2

Viereck, Peter (Robert Edwin) 1916-
.... **CLC 4; PC 27**
See also CA 1-4R; CANR 1, 47; DLB 5

Vigny, Alfred (Victor) de 1797-1863
.... **NCLC 7; DAM POET; PC 26**
See also DLB 119, 192

Vilakazi, Benedict Wallet 1906-1947
.... **TCLC 37**
See also CA 168

Villa, Jose Garcia 1904-1997 .... **PC 22**
See also CA 25-28R; CANR 12

Villarreal, Jose Antonio 1924-
See also CA 133; CANR 93; DAM MULT; DLB 82; HLC 2; HW 1

Villaurrutia, Xavier 1903-1950 ..... **TCLC 80**
See also HW 1

Villehardouin 1150(?)-1218(?) ...... **CMLC 38**

Villiers de l'Isle Adam, Jean Marie Mathias Philippe Auguste, Comte de 1838-1889
.... **NCLC 3; SSC 14**
See also DLB 123

Villon, Francois 1431-1463(?) ..... **LC 62; PC 13**
See also DLB 208

Vine, Barbara .... **CLC 50**
See also Rendell, Ruth (Barbara)
See also BEST 90:4

Vinge, Joan (Carol) D(ennison) 1948-
.... **CLC 30; SSC 24**
See also AAYA 32; CA 93-96; CANR 72; SATA 36, 113

Violis, G.
See Simenon, Georges (Jacques Christian)

Viramontes, Helena Maria 1954-
See also CA 159; DLB 122; HLCS 2; HW 2

Virgil 70B.C.-19B.C.
See Vergil

Visconti, Luchino 1906-1976 .... **CLC 16**
See also CA 81-84; 65-68; CANR 39

Vittorini, Elio 1908-1966 .... **CLC 6, 9, 14**
See also CA 133; 25-28R

Vivekananda, Swami 1863-1902 ... **TCLC 88**

Vizenor, Gerald Robert 1934- ...... **CLC 103; DAM MULT**
See also CA 13-16R; CAAS 22; CANR 5, 21, 44, 67; DLB 175, 227; MTCW 2; NNAL

Vizinczey, Stephen 1933- .... **CLC 40**
See also CA 128; INT 128

Vliet, R(ussell) G(ordon) 1929-1984 . **CLC 22**
See also CA 37-40R; 112; CANR 18

Vogau, Boris Andreyevich 1894-1937(?)
See Pilnyak, Boris
See also CA 123

Vogel, Paula A(nne) 1951- .... **CLC 76**
See also CA 108

Voigt, Cynthia 1942- .... **CLC 30**
See also AAYA 3, 30; CA 106; CANR 18, 37, 40, 94; CLR 13, 48; INT CANR-18; JRDA; MAICYA; SATA 48, 79, 116; SATA-Brief 33

Voigt, Ellen Bryant 1943- .... **CLC 54**
See also CA 69-72; CANR 11, 29, 55; DLB 120

Voinovich, Vladimir (Nikolaevich) 1932-
.... **CLC 10, 49**
See also CA 81-84; CAAS 12; CANR 33, 67; MTCW 1

Vollmann, William T. 1959- . **CLC 89; DAM NOV, POP**

See also CA 134; CANR 67; DA3; MTCW 2

Voloshinov, V. N.
See Bakhtin, Mikhail Mikhailovich

Voltaire 1694-1778 .... **LC 14; DA; DAB; DAC; DAM DRAM, MST; SSC 12; WLC**
See also DA3

von Aschendrof, BaronIgnatz
See Ford, Ford Madox

von Daeniken, Erich 1935- .... **CLC 30**
See also AITN 1; CA 37-40R; CANR 17, 44

von Daniken, Erich
See von Daeniken, Erich

von Hartmann, Eduard 1842-1906
.... **TCLC 96**

von Heidenstam, (Carl Gustaf) Verner
See Heidenstam, (Carl Gustaf) Verner von

von Heyse, Paul (Johann Ludwig)
See Heyse, Paul (Johann Ludwig von)

von Hofmannsthal, Hugo
See Hofmannsthal, Hugo von

von Horvath, Odon
See Horvath, Oedoen von

von Horvath, Oedoen -1938
See Horvath, Oedoen von
See also CA 184

von Liliencron, (Friedrich Adolf Axel) Detlev
See Liliencron, (Friedrich Adolf Axel) Detlev von

Vonnegut, Kurt, Jr. 1922- . **CLC 1, 2, 3, 4, 5, 8, 12, 22, 40, 60, 111; DA; DAB; DAC; DAM MST, NOV, POP; SSC 8; WLC**
See also AAYA 6; AITN 1; BEST 90:4; CA 1-4R; CANR 1, 25, 49, 75, 92; CDALB 1968-1988; DA3; DLB 2, 8, 152; DLBD 3; DLBY 80; MTCW 1, 2

Von Rachen, Kurt
See Hubbard, L(afayette) Ron(ald)

von Rezzori (d'Arezzo), Gregor
See Rezzori (d'Arezzo), Gregor von

von Sternberg, Josef
See Sternberg, Josef von

Vorster, Gordon 1924- .... **CLC 34**
See also CA 133

Vosce, Trudie
See Ozick, Cynthia

Voznesensky, Andrei (Andreievich) 1933-
.... **CLC 1, 15, 57; DAM POET**
See also CA 89-92; CANR 37; MTCW 1

Waddington, Miriam 1917- .... **CLC 28**
See also CA 21-24R; CANR 12, 30; DLB 68

Wagman, Fredrica 1937- .... **CLC 7**
See also CA 97-100; INT 97-100

Wagner, Linda W.
See Wagner-Martin, Linda (C.)

Wagner, Linda Welshimer
See Wagner-Martin, Linda (C.)

Wagner, Richard 1813-1883 .... **NCLC 9**
See also DLB 129

Wagner-Martin, Linda (C.) 1936- .. **CLC 50**
See also CA 159

Wagoner, David (Russell) 1926- .. **CLC 3, 5, 15; PC 33**
See also CA 1-4R; CAAS 3; CANR 2, 71; DLB 5; SATA 14

Wah, Fred(erick James) 1939- .... **CLC 44**
See also CA 107; 141; DLB 60

Wahloo, Per 1926- .... **CLC 7**
See also CA 61-64; CANR 73

Wahloo, Peter
See Wahloo, Per

Wain, John (Barrington) 1925-1994 . **CLC 2, 11, 15, 46**

Webster, John 1579(?)-1634(?) . **LC 33; DA; DAB; DAC; DAM DRAM, MST; DC 2; WLC**
See also CDBLB Before 1660; DLB 58

Webster, Noah 1758-1843 .... **NCLC 30**
See also DLB 1, 37, 42, 43, 73

Wedekind, (Benjamin) Frank(lin) 1864-1918 .... **TCLC 7; DAM DRAM**
See also CA 104; 153; DLB 118

Weidman, Jerome 1913-1998 .... **CLC 7**
See also AITN 2; CA 1-4R; 171; CANR 1; DLB 28

Weil, Simone (Adolphine) 1909-1943 .... **TCLC 23**
See also CA 117; 159; MTCW 2

Weininger, Otto 1880-1903 .... **TCLC 84**

Weinstein, Nathan
See West, Nathanael

Weinstein, Nathan von Wallenstein
See West, Nathanael

Weir, Peter (Lindsay) 1944- .... **CLC 20**
See also CA 113; 123

Weiss, Peter (Ulrich) 1916-1982 . **CLC 3, 15, 51; DAM DRAM**
See also CA 45-48; 106; CANR 3; DLB 69, 124

Weiss, Theodore (Russell) 1916- .. **CLC 3, 8, 14**
See also CA 9-12R; CAAS 2; CANR 46, 94; DLB 5

Welch, (Maurice) Denton 1915-1948 .... **TCLC 22**
See also CA 121; 148

Welch, James 1940- ... **CLC 6, 14, 52; DAM MULT, POP**
See also CA 85-88; CANR 42, 66; DLB 175; NNAL

Weldon, Fay 1931- . **CLC 6, 9, 11, 19, 36, 59, 122; DAM POP**
See also CA 21-24R; CANR 16, 46, 63; CDBLB 1960 to Present; DLB 14, 194; INT CANR-16; MTCW 1, 2

Wellek, Rene 1903-1995 .... **CLC 28**
See also CA 5-8R; 150; CAAS 7; CANR 8; DLB 63; INT CANR-8

Weller, Michael 1942- .... **CLC 10, 53**
See also CA 85-88

Weller, Paul 1958- .... **CLC 26**

Wellershoff, Dieter 1925- .... **CLC 46**
See also CA 89-92; CANR 16, 37

Welles, (George) Orson 1915-1985 . **CLC 20, 80**
See also CA 93-96; 117

Wellman, John McDowell 1945-
See Wellman, Mac
See also CA 166

Wellman, Mac 1945- .... **CLC 65**
See also Wellman, John McDowell; Wellman, John McDowell

Wellman, Manly Wade 1903-1986 .. **CLC 49**
See also CA 1-4R; 118; CANR 6, 16, 44; SATA 6; SATA-Obit 47

Wells, Carolyn 1869(?)-1942 .... **TCLC 35**
See also CA 113; 185; DLB 11

Wells, H(erbert) G(eorge) 1866-1946 .... **TCLC 6, 12, 19; DA; DAB; DAC; DAM MST, NOV; SSC 6; WLC**
See also AAYA 18; CA 110; 121; CDBLB 1914-1945; CLR 64; DA3; DLB 34, 70, 156, 178; MTCW 1, 2; SATA 20

Wells, Rosemary 1943- .... **CLC 12**
See also AAYA 13; CA 85-88; CANR 48; CLR 16, 69; MAICYA; SAAS 1; SATA 18, 69, 114

Welty, Eudora 1909- .... **CLC 1, 2, 5, 14, 22, 33, 105; DA; DAB; DAC; DAM MST, NOV; SSC 1, 27; WLC**

See also CA 9-12R; CABS 1; CANR 32, 65; CDALB 1941-1968; DA3; DLB 2, 102, 143; DLBD 12; DLBY 87; MTCW 1, 2

Wen I-to 1899-1946 .... **TCLC 28**

Wentworth, Robert
See Hamilton, Edmond

Werfel, Franz (Viktor) 1890-1945 .. **TCLC 8**
See also CA 104; 161; DLB 81, 124

Wergeland, Henrik Arnold 1808-1845 .... **NCLC 5**

Wersba, Barbara 1932- .... **CLC 30**
See also AAYA 2, 30; CA 29-32R, 182; CAAE 182; CANR 16, 38; CLR 3; DLB 52; JRDA; MAICYA; SAAS 2; SATA 1, 58; SATA-Essay 103

Wertmueller, Lina 1928- .... **CLC 16**
See also CA 97-100; CANR 39, 78

Wescott, Glenway 1901-1987 . **CLC 13; SSC 35**
See also CA 13-16R; 121; CANR 23, 70; DLB 4, 9, 102

Wesker, Arnold 1932- .. **CLC 3, 5, 42; DAB; DAM DRAM**
See also CA 1-4R; CAAS 7; CANR 1, 33; CDBLB 1960 to Present; DLB 13; MTCW 1

Wesley, Richard (Errol) 1945- .... **CLC 7**
See also BW 1; CA 57-60; CANR 27; DLB 38

Wessel, Johan Herman 1742-1785 .... **LC 7**

West, Anthony (Panther) 1914-1987 .... **CLC 50**
See also CA 45-48; 124; CANR 3, 19; DLB 15

West, C. P.
See Wodehouse, P(elham) G(renville)

West, Cornel (Ronald) 1953- .... **CLC 134; BLCS**
See also CA 144; CANR 91

West, (Mary) Jessamyn 1902-1984 .. **CLC 7, 17**
See also CA 9-12R; 112; CANR 27; DLB 6; DLBY 84; MTCW 1, 2; SATA-Obit 37

West, Morris L(anglo) 1916-1999 .... **CLC 6, 33**
See also CA 5-8R; 187; CANR 24, 49, 64; MTCW 1, 2

West, Nathanael 1903-1940 ..... **TCLC 1, 14, 44; SSC 16**
See also CA 104; 125; CDALB 1929-1941; DA3; DLB 4, 9, 28; MTCW 1, 2

West, Owen
See Koontz, Dean R(ay)

West, Paul 1930- .... **CLC 7, 14, 96**
See also CA 13-16R; CAAS 7; CANR 22, 53, 76, 89; DLB 14; INT CANR-22; MTCW 2

West, Rebecca 1892-1983 .. **CLC 7, 9, 31, 50**
See also CA 5-8R; 109; CANR 19; DLB 36; DLBY 83; MTCW 1, 2

Westall, Robert (Atkinson) 1929-1993 .... **CLC 17**
See also AAYA 12; CA 69-72; 141; CANR 18, 68; CLR 13; JRDA; MAICYA; SAAS 2; SATA 23, 69; SATA-Obit 75

Westermarck, Edward 1862-1939 . **TCLC 87**

Westlake, Donald E(dwin) 1933- ..... **CLC 7, 33; DAM POP**
See also CA 17-20R; CAAS 13; CANR 16, 44, 65, 94; INT CANR-16; MTCW 2

Westmacott, Mary
See Christie, Agatha (Mary Clarissa)

Weston, Allen
See Norton, Andre

Wetcheek, J. L.
See Feuchtwanger, Lion

Wetering, Janwillem van de
See van de Wetering, Janwillem

Wetherald, Agnes Ethelwyn 1857-1940 .... **TCLC 81**
See also DLB 99

Wetherell, Elizabeth
See Warner, Susan (Bogert)

Whale, James 1889-1957 .... **TCLC 63**

Whalen, Philip 1923- .... **CLC 6, 29**
See also CA 9-12R; CANR 5, 39; DLB 16

Wharton, Edith (Newbold Jones) 1862-1937 ... **TCLC 3, 9, 27, 53; DA; DAB; DAC; DAM MST, NOV; SSC 6; WLC**
See also AAYA 25; CA 104; 132; CDALB 1865-1917; DA3; DLB 4, 9, 12, 78, 189; DLBD 13; MTCW 1, 2

Wharton, James
See Mencken, H(enry) L(ouis)

Wharton, William (a pseudonym) . **CLC 18, 37**
See also CA 93-96; DLBY 80; INT 93-96

Wheatley (Peters), Phillis 1754(?)-1784 ..... **LC 3, 50; BLC 3; DA; DAC; DAM MST, MULT, POET; PC 3; WLC**
See also CDALB 1640-1865; DA3; DLB 31, 50

Wheelock, John Hall 1886-1978 ..... **CLC 14**
See also CA 13-16R; 77-80; CANR 14; DLB 45

White, E(lwyn) B(rooks) 1899-1985 .... **CLC 10, 34, 39; DAM POP**
See also AITN 2; CA 13-16R; 116; CANR 16, 37; CDALBS; CLR 1, 21; DA3; DLB 11, 22; MAICYA; MTCW 1, 2; SATA 2, 29, 100; SATA-Obit 44

White, Edmund (Valentine III) 1940- .... **CLC 27, 110; DAM POP**
See also AAYA 7; CA 45-48; CANR 3, 19, 36, 62; DA3; DLB 227; MTCW 1, 2

White, Patrick (Victor Martindale) 1912-1990 ..... **CLC 3, 4, 5, 7, 9, 18, 65, 69; SSC 39**
See also CA 81-84; 132; CANR 43; MTCW 1, 2

White, Phyllis Dorothy James 1920-
See James, P. D.
See also CA 21-24R; CANR 17, 43, 65; DAM POP; DA3; MTCW 1, 2

White, T(erence) H(anbury) 1906-1964 .... **CLC 30**
See also AAYA 22; CA 73-76; CANR 37; DLB 160; JRDA; MAICYA; SATA 12

White, Terence de Vere 1912-1994 . **CLC 49**
See also CA 49-52; 145; CANR 3

White, Walter
See White, Walter F(rancis)
See also BLC; DAM MULT

White, Walter F(rancis) 1893-1955 .... **TCLC 15**
See also White, Walter
See also BW 1; CA 115; 124; DLB 51

White, William Hale 1831-1913
See Rutherford, Mark
See also CA 121

Whitehead, Alfred North 1861-1947 .... **TCLC 97**
See also CA 117; 165; DLB 100

Whitehead, E(dward) A(nthony) 1933- .... **CLC 5**
See also CA 65-68; CANR 58

Whitemore, Hugh (John) 1936- ...... **CLC 37**
See also CA 132; CANR 77; INT 132

Whitman, Sarah Helen (Power) 1803-1878 .... **NCLC 19**
See also DLB 1

Whitman, Walt(er) 1819-1892 . **NCLC 4, 31, 81; DA; DAB; DAC; DAM MST, POET; PC 3; WLC**
See also CDALB 1640-1865; DA3; DLB 3, 64, 224; SATA 20

Literary Criticism Series
Cumulative Topic Index

This index lists all topic entries in Gale's *Classical and Medieval Literature Criticism, Contemporary Literary Criticism, Literature Criticism from 1400 to 1800, Nineteenth-Century Literature Criticism,* and *Twentieth-Century Literary Criticism.*

TCLC Cumulative Nationality Index

AMERICAN

Adams, Andy **56**
Adams, Brooks **80**
Adams, Henry (Brooks) **4, 52**
Addams, Jane **76**
Agee, James (Rufus) **1, 19**
Allen, Fred **87**
Anderson, Maxwell **2**
Anderson, Sherwood **1, 10, 24**
Anthony, Susan B(rownell) **84**
Atherton, Gertrude (Franklin Horn) **2**
Austin, Mary (Hunter) **25**
Baker, Ray Stannard **47**
Barry, Philip **11**
Baum, L(yman) Frank **7**
Beard, Charles A(ustin) **15**
Becker, Carl (Lotus) **63**
Belasco, David **3**
Bell, James Madison **43**
Benchley, Robert (Charles) **1, 55**
Benedict, Ruth (Fulton) **60**
Benet, Stephen Vincent **7**
Benet, William Rose **28**
Bierce, Ambrose (Gwinett) **1, 7, 44**
Biggers, Earl Derr **65**
Bishop, John Peale **103**
Black Elk **33**
Boas, Franz **56**
Bodenheim, Maxwell **44**
Bok, Edward W. **101**
Bourne, Randolph S(illiman) **16**
Bradford, Gamaliel **36**
Brennan, Christopher (John) **17**
Bromfield, Louis (Brucker) **11**
Broun, Heywood **104**
Bryan, William Jennings **99**
Burroughs, Edgar Rice **2, 32**
Cabell, James Branch **6**
Cable, George Washington **4**
Cahan, Abraham **71**
Cardozo, Benjamin N(athan) **65**
Carnegie, Dale **53**
Cather, Willa Sibert **1, 11, 31, 99**
Chambers, Robert W(illiam) **41**
Chandler, Raymond (Thornton) **1, 7**
Chapman, John Jay **7**
Chesnutt, Charles W(addell) **5, 39**
Chopin, Kate **5, 14**
Cobb, Irvin S(hrewsbury) **77**
Coffin, Robert P(eter) Tristram **95**
Cohan, George M(ichael) **60**
Comstock, Anthony **13**
Cotter, Joseph Seamon Sr. **28**
Cram, Ralph Adams **45**
Crane, (Harold) Hart **2, 5, 80**
Crane, Stephen (Townley) **11, 17, 32**
Crawford, F(rancis) Marion **10**
Crothers, Rachel **19**
Cullen, Countee **4, 37**
Darrow, Clarence (Seward) **81**
Davis, Rebecca (Blaine) Harding **6**
Davis, Richard Harding **24**

Day, Clarence (Shepard Jr.) **25**
Dent, Lester **72**
De Voto, Bernard (Augustine) **29**
Dewey, John **95**
Dreiser, Theodore (Herman Albert) **10, 18, 35, 83**
Dulles, John Foster **72**
Dunbar, Paul Laurence **2, 12**
Duncan, Isadora **68**
Dunne, Finley Peter **28**
Eastman, Charles A(lexander) **55**
Eddy, Mary (Ann Morse) Baker **71**
Einstein, Albert **65**
Erskine, John **84**
Faust, Frederick (Schiller) **49**
Fenollosa, Ernest (Francisco) **91**
Fields, W. C. **80**
Fisher, Dorothy (Frances) Canfield **87**
Fisher, Rudolph **11**
Fitzgerald, F(rancis) Scott (Key) **1, 6, 14, 28, 55**
Fitzgerald, Zelda (Sayre) **52**
Flecker, (Herman) James Elroy **43**
Fletcher, John Gould **35**
Ford, Henry **73**
Forten, Charlotte L. **16**
Freeman, Douglas Southall **11**
Freeman, Mary E(leanor) Wilkins **9**
Fuller, Henry Blake **103**
Futrelle, Jacques **19**
Gale, Zona **7**
Garland, (Hannibal) Hamlin **3**
Gilman, Charlotte (Anna) Perkins (Stetson) **9, 37**
Glasgow, Ellen (Anderson Gholson) **2, 7**
Glaspell, Susan **55**
Goldman, Emma **13**
Green, Anna Katharine **63**
Grey, Zane **6**
Griffith, D(avid Lewelyn) W(ark) **68**
Griggs, Sutton (Elbert) **77**
Guest, Edgar A(lbert) **95**
Guiney, Louise Imogen **41**
Hall, James Norman **23**
Handy, W(illiam) C(hristopher) **97**
Harper, Frances Ellen Watkins **14**
Harris, Joel Chandler **2**
Harte, (Francis) Bret(t) **1, 25**
Hartmann, Sadakichi **73**
Hatteras, Owen **18**
Hawthorne, Julian **25**
Hearn, (Patricio) Lafcadio (Tessima Carlos) **9**
Hecht, Ben **101**
Henry, O. **1, 19**
Hergesheimer, Joseph **11**
Higginson, Thomas Wentworth **36**
Holley, Marietta **99**
Holly, Buddy **65**
Holmes, Oliver Wendell Jr. **77**
Hopkins, Pauline Elizabeth **28**
Horney, Karen (Clementine Theodore Danielsen) **71**

Howard, Robert E(rvin) **8**
Howe, Julia Ward **21**
Howells, William Dean **7, 17, 41**
Huneker, James Gibbons **65**
Ince, Thomas H. **89**
James, Henry **2, 11, 24, 40, 47, 64**
James, William **15, 32**
Jewett, (Theodora) Sarah Orne **1, 22**
Johnson, James Weldon **3, 19**
Johnson, Robert **69**
Kinsey, Alfred C(harles) **91**
Kornbluth, C(yril) M. **8**
Korzybski, Alfred (Habdank Skarbek) **61**
Kuttner, Henry **10**
Lardner, Ring(gold) W(ilmer) **2, 14**
Lewis, (Harry) Sinclair **4, 13, 23, 39**
Lewisohn, Ludwig **19**
Lewton, Val **76**
Lindsay, (Nicholas) Vachel **17**
Locke, Alain (Le Roy) **43**
London, Jack **9, 15, 39**
Lovecraft, H(oward) P(hillips) **4, 22**
Lowell, Amy **1, 8**
Mankiewicz, Herman (Jacob) **85**
March, William **96**
Markham, Edwin **47**
Marquis, Don(ald Robert Perry) **7**
Masters, Edgar Lee **2, 25**
Matthews, (James) Brander **95**
Matthiessen, F(rancis) O(tto) **100**
McAlmon, Robert (Menzies) **97**
McCoy, Horace (Stanley) **28**
McKay, Claude **7, 41**
Mead, George Herbert **89**
Mencken, H(enry) L(ouis) **13**
Micheaux, Oscar (Devereaux) **76**
Millay, Edna St. Vincent **4, 49**
Mitchell, Margaret (Munnerlyn) **11**
Mitchell, S(ilas) Weir **36**
Mitchell, William **81**
Monroe, Harriet **12**
Moody, William Vaughan **105**
Morley, Christopher (Darlington) **87**
Muir, John **28**
Nathan, George Jean **18**
Neumann, Alfred **100**
Nordhoff, Charles (Bernard) **23**
Norris, (Benjamin) Frank(lin Jr.) **24**
O'Neill, Eugene (Gladstone) **1, 6, 27, 49**
Osbourne, Lloyd **93**
Oskison, John Milton **35**
Park, Robert E(zra) **73**
Patton, George S. **79**
Peirce, Charles Sanders **81**
Percy, William Alexander **84**
Phillips, David Graham **44**
Porter, Gene(va Grace) Stratton **21**
Post, Melville Davisson **39**
Pulitzer, Joseph **76**
Pyle, Ernie **75**
Pyle, Howard **81**
Rawlings, Marjorie Kinnan **4**
Reed, John (Silas) **9**

447

Nationality Index

Khlebnikov, Velimir **20**
Khodasevich, Vladislav (Felitsianovich) **15**
Klimentov, Andrei Platonovich **14**
Korolenko, Vladimir Galaktionovich **22**
Kropotkin, Peter (Aleksieevich) **36**
Kuprin, Aleksander Ivanovich **5**
Kuzmin, Mikhail **40**
Lenin, V. I. **67**
Mandelstam, Osip (Emilievich) **2, 6**
Mayakovski, Vladimir (Vladimirovich) **4, 18**
Merezhkovsky, Dmitry Sergeyevich **29**
Pavlov, Ivan Petrovich **91**
Petrov, Evgeny **21**
Pilnyak, Boris **23**
Prishvin, Mikhail **75**
Remizov, Aleksei (Mikhailovich) **27**
Rozanov, Vassili **104**
Shestov, Lev **56**
Sologub, Fyodor **9**
Stalin, Joseph **92**
Tolstoy, Alexey Nikolaevich **18**
Tolstoy, Leo (Nikolaevich) **4, 11, 17, 28, 44, 79**
Trotsky, Leon **22**
Tsvetaeva (Efron), Marina (Ivanovna) **7, 35**
Zabolotsky, Nikolai Alekseevich **52**
Zamyatin, Evgeny Ivanovich **8, 37**
Zhdanov, Andrei Alexandrovich **18**
Zoshchenko, Mikhail (Mikhailovich) **15**

SCOTTISH

Barrie, J(ames) M(atthew) **2**
Bridie, James **3**
Brown, George Douglas **28**
Buchan, John **41**
Cunninghame Graham, Robert (Gallnigad) Bontine **19**
Davidson, John **24**
Frazer, J(ames) G(eorge) **32**
Gibbon, Lewis Grassic **4**
Lang, Andrew **16**

MacDonald, George **9**
Muir, Edwin **2, 87**
Sharp, William **39**
Tey, Josephine **14**

SLOVENIAN

Cankar, Ivan **105**

SOUTH AFRICAN

Bosman, Herman Charles **49**
Campbell, (Ignatius) Roy (Dunnachie) **5**
Mqhayi, S(amuel) E(dward) K(rune Loliwe) **25**
Plaatje, Sol(omon) T(shekisho) **73**
Schreiner, Olive (Emilie Albertina) **9**
Smith, Pauline (Urmson) **25**
Vilakazi, Benedict Wallet **37**

SPANISH

Alas (y Urena), Leopoldo (Enrique Garcia) **29**
Barea, Arturo **14**
Baroja (y Nessi), Pio **8**
Benavente (y Martinez), Jacinto **3**
Blasco Ibanez, Vicente **12**
Echegaray (y Eizaguirre), Jose (Maria Waldo) **4**
Garcia Lorca, Federico **1, 7, 49**
Jimenez (Mantecon), Juan Ramon **4**
Machado (y Ruiz), Antonio **3**
Martinez Sierra, Gregorio **6**
Martinez Sierra, Maria (de la O'LeJarraga) **6**
Miro (Ferrer), Gabriel (Francisco Victor) **5**
Ortega y Gasset, Jose **9**
Pereda (y Sanchez de Porrua), Jose Maria de **16**
Perez Galdos, Benito **27**
Ramoacn y Cajal, Santiago **93**
Salinas (y Serrano), Pedro **17**
Unamuno (y Jugo), Miguel de **2, 9**

Valera y Alcala-Galiano, Juan **10**
Valle-Inclan, Ramon (Maria) del **5**

SWEDISH

Bengtsson, Frans (Gunnar) **48**
Dagerman, Stig (Halvard) **17**
Ekelund, Vilhelm **75**
Heidenstam, (Carl Gustaf) Verner von **5**
Key, Ellen (Karolina Sofia) **65**
Lagerloef, Selma (Ottiliana Lovisa) **4, 36**
Soderberg, Hjalmar **39**
Strindberg, (Johan) August **1, 8, 21, 47**

SWISS

Ramuz, Charles-Ferdinand **33**
Rod, Edouard **52**
Saussure, Ferdinand de **49**
Spitteler, Carl (Friedrich Georg) **12**
Walser, Robert **18**

SYRIAN

Gibran, Kahlil **1, 9**

TURKISH

Sait Faik **23**

UKRAINIAN

Aleichem, Sholom **1, 35**
Bialik, Chaim Nachman **25**

URUGUAYAN

Quiroga, Horacio (Sylvestre) **20**
Sanchez, Florencio **37**

WELSH

Davies, William Henry **5**
Evans, Caradoc **85**
Lewis, Alun **3**
Machen, Arthur **4**
Thomas, Dylan (Marlais) **1, 8, 45, 105**

Nationality Index

TCLC-105 Title Index

ISBN 0-7876-4565-6

90000